The Sunday Telegraph

GOLF COURSE GUIDE

—— TO ——

BRITAIN & IRELAND

The Sunday Telegraph

GOLF COURSE GUIDE
—— TO ——
BRITAIN & IRELAND

14th Edition

CollinsWillow

An Imprint of HarperCollins*Publishers*

*The publishers would like to acknowledge the help of the following
in the compilation of the 14th edition of this book:*

Text updating and revision
Jack Carroll
Val Coxon
Michelle Hakim
Jenni Patterson
Shanna Tavoussi

Research co-ordination
Richard Weekes
Tricia Gibson

Technical and text organisation
Richard Weekes
Howard Scott

Map compilation and artwork
Katie Murray
Richard Weekes

Cover photographs
Celtic Manor

This edition published 2000 by
CollinsWillow
an imprint of HarperCollins*Publishers*
London

First published 1968
Fourteenth revised edition 2000

© The Sunday Telegraph 2000
1 3 5 7 9 8 6 4 2

A CIP catalogue record for this book
is available from the British Library

ISBN 0 00 218954 2

This edition produced by
Richard Weekes Publishing, London N8

Printed and bound in Great Britain by Scotprint

CONTENTS

INTRODUCTION
by Derek Lawrenson

In the final years of the 20th century something went terribly wrong in the field of golf course architecture. The blueprints laid down by Harry Colt, Donald Ross, Alister Mackenzie, and James Braid were suddenly neglected and allowed to gather dust. In their place we had grandiose designs that might have looked good on the drawing board and when explained to owners but in practice caused great sadness to anyone who actually pitched up to play.

All these courses cost many millions to build and almost all of them were high folly. They tried to tell us that this was golf in the 21st century: a long, landscaped entrance leading to a multi-level clubhouse with locker rooms so big you could drive the ball from one end to the other; lunch menus that would not look out of place at the Savoy; par threes over water that the average player could only reach with a driver; par fours where the same golfer needed two woods simply to leave himself a pitch to the green; par fives with more lakes to carry before reaching the sanctuary of the putting surface.

Is this how we want to play our golf in the new millenium? I don't think so. It is not just a coincidence that so many have run into financial difficulty, that so few ever make anyone's list of the great golf courses of the British Isles.

Instead the venues that dominate such lists continue to be those that were built in the 19th century, not the twentieth, and similarly hidden gems like Cruden Bay in Aberdeenshire or Silloth in Cumbria.

To be fair to the modern golf course designer, it is not all his fault. Many of the owners they work for let their egos run away with them. Build me a golf course that will test Tiger Woods, they cry, something that will give Colin Montgomerie food for thought. Construct me a venue that will attract the best tournaments. So in go the lakes, the par fives that go on forever, the greens with more tiers than a wedding cake.

As the 1990s wore on, things got only worse. Part of the problem was that the standard of golf at the highest level kept rising at an amazing rate, fuelled not just by the players' desire but the sadly lackadaisacal attitude of the game's ruling body, the Royal and Ancient Golf Club of St Andrews, to improvements in golf equipment.

At Augusta seven years ago I was collared by a member of the R&A's inner sanctum over an article I had written saying that if something was not done it would be too late. "You don't know what you're talking about," he argued. "Players hardly hit the ball any further now than they did 20 years ago. Look at the statistics."

But only the foolhardy cling to statistics for conclusive evidence. Most people could see with their own eyes the difference that equipment was making. I remember my first trip to Augusta in 1985, watching from the first tee as players wondered how to tackle the deep fairway bunker that guards the right-hand side of the fairway. Ten years on, they were just blowing the ball straight over the top of it.

Golf course designers could see what was happening. So they built their championship courses ever longer, to protect their precious creations from the Woods and the Montgomeries.

The only trouble was what they built was not worthy of the great architects who came before them. They never learned from Mackenzie, or Colt, or Ross, who designed courses so that they could be played by all. Instead they built faceless creations that were only playable by that exclusive band of players who possessed low, single-figure handicaps or better.

Of the golf courses built in Great Britain and Ireland in the last 15 years of the 20th century, no more than a handful would cause me to drive any great distance to play.

One wonderful exception is Loch Lomond, where my favourite modern designers, Tom Weiskopf and Jay Morrish, built a course worthy of its wondrous setting. The only trouble with Loch Lomond is that it is too exclusive for its own good.

Another -- and I can hardly believe I am writing this -- is The Belfry, which did nothing for me for the first 14 years of its creation. If ever there was a four-hole golf course, this was it. But Dave Thomas has done a remarkable job in redesigning some of the more boring holes, like the third, the fourth and the 12th. The Belfry returns to the tournament roster in 2000 and I predict some rave reviews.

But perhaps the best example of all is the European, situated an hour's drive south of Dublin and illustrative of what is still possible in these times. Its owner is the architect and journalist Pat Ruddy, who toured the coastal land of Ireland looking for a suitable site to build a links course in the final years of the century that would be talked about in the same breath as those that came long before.

Ruddy ploughed all his savings into the project; he got a grant from the European Union – hence the name. He manned the tractors himself to plough the land; other members of his family played their part as well.

When it opened, the European represented most people's idea of what makes golf the finest of games to play. The clubhouse is modest, like all the great clubhouses, like Porthcawl and Brancaster, but crucially a convivial place to drink with friends.

The course is not dissimilar to those two great links venues either, full of charm and personality, a sublime place on a grand summer's day, and all but impossible to negotiate when the wind tears at your outer layers.

This, I believe, is how most people want to play golf in the 21st century; in other words, how they played it over the course of the 20th century.

My new millenium message to owners and architects, therefore, would be to dust down the blueprints of Ross, Braid, Mackenzie, and Colt. Learn from the past, not ignore it. And build courses today that will provoke verses of admiration, not rebuke, from the golf correspondent of *The Sunday Telegraph* 100 years from now.

www.rbs.co.uk

For over 40 years our banking service has been a feature of the Open Championship…

Our rain capes prove popular at Royal Birkdale

Tom Lehman on his way to victory at Royal Lytham

...no matter what the weather!

Barry Lane inaugurates Britain's first mobile ATM at Turnberry

HOW TO USE THE GUIDE
by Colin Gibson

The 14th edition of the *Sunday Telegraph Golf Course Guide* continues a sporting tradition that started way back in the 1960s when clubs were made of wood and when the sport was seen as a haven for the elite.

But these are now boom times for golf and it is now a sport that not only encompasses all the latest technical developments of science but also every stratum of life. Golf has never been more popular or more accessible. This trend is superbly captured within the pages of the country's leading guide to where and when to play the game and how much it is likely to cost.

It would be impossible to put together such a comprehensive guide without the help and understanding of golf club secretaries, managers and professionals up and down the country. Many have taken the time to field enquiries from a team of researchers that has led to this definitive work.

It means that within the guide's easy-to-access information, with new quick reference symbols, every golfer can find a course to suit both taste and pocket throughout the country. And that is the most important role of the book.

So many golfers, in small groups or bigger societies, are now using the guide as the focal point for weekend breaks or longer golfing holiday excursions.

The Sunday Telegraph hopes that within the biggest ever *Golf Course Guide to Britain and Ireland* the enthusiastic golfer can be directed not only to some of the great courses in these islands but also to some of the hidden gems.

To that end Derek Lawrenson, acknowledged as one of the leading golf writers in the world, has produced a series of introductions to the regions that allow the discerning golfer to plan with great satisfaction his next trips.

The majors are not forgotten either. There are guides to both St Andrews Old Course, the home of the Millennium Open Golf Championship, and also Royal Lytham, which will follow in 2001.

For many of the golf fans who will flock to these two famous courses it will be just as important to find out not only when they can follow in the footsteps of the greats and play these venues but also where to play a round of golf while visiting the championships themselves.

So there are also a few pointers to which courses should be experienced both on the Fife and Lancashire coasts. A word of warning though – the Open Championship is a very popular time for playing golf and checking availability of the courses mentioned is always crucial.

This edition also includes a special feature on Celtic Manor, the course in South Wales that has attracted so much favourable comment in recent years. It was the host of the recent Solheim Cup and has the support of Ian Woosnam, the 1991 Masters champion.

Celtic Manor follows courses like the London, the Roxburghe and the magnificent Loch Lomond, which is now a regular venue on the European tour, as one of the venues featured on the cover of the guide during the last decade.

This edition of the guide also coincides with the creation of The Sunday Telegraph Golf Course of the Year Award. If you would like to nominate your favourite course in the British Isles, please turn to page 381 for details of the competition and information on how to nominate a course.

How to use the book: The country is divided into regions. There are some strange anomalies which are caused primarily by some courses belonging to golf unions that do not necessarily correspond to local government boundaries.

There is a comprehensive directory in the back of the book which will direct any user to the chapter and number of each course. Each club has a phone number, postal address and relevant travel directions plus a brief description of the type of course.

We have tried to indicate to golfers when they will be welcome at each course and whether individuals or societies are allowed. There is also a short description of the catering facilities each club provides.

It is, of course, a common courtesy to telephone any club you plan to visit to check both the availability of the date you plan to play and also any restrictions which may be placed on visitors.

In the main it is recommended to make a tee-off time reservation, thus preventing any frustrating delays at the courses. Always remember to leave plenty of time to get to the course – it will improve your enjoyment and almost certainly your play!

Most clubs provide catering facilities for societies and many make a point of offering special packages that include both refreshments, food and golf. Again it is vital to ring in advance to check prices and the times that kitchens are open as well as the range of services on offer.

Prices. This is the main bone of contention with every golfer. While every care has been taken to list accurate prices for a round or a day ticket it is quite usual for the green fees to change from season to season and often from day to day. Some clubs offer special twilight fees, while others habitually charge more at weekends and on Bank Holidays.

Again it is vital that golfers check the prices, which can sometimes rise quite dramatically, before they step into the car or before they plan a trip. Often clubs are open to negotiating special deals but this is more likely to be achieved before rather than after arriving at the course.

All the information on green fees, club policy on visitors, societies, catering, etc has been gleaned from the secretaries, managers and professionals and *The Sunday Telegraph* thanks them for their time.

Comments. *The Sunday Telegraph* welcomes feedback on the book and comments on courses that readers visit. We would be also keen to hear of alterations, errors or extensions regarding any of the courses.

Comments should be addressed to The Publisher, Telegraph Books, The Sunday Telegraph, 1 Canada Square, Canary Wharf, London E14 5DT or sent by email to emma.wagstaff@telegraph.co.uk

KEY TO COURSE DETAILS

☎ .... Telephone

▭ .... Website

⌨ .... Email

🕴 .... Visitors

⛳ .... Green Fees

📋 .... Societies

🍽 .... Catering

🛏 .... Hotels

COURSE NOTES

18-hole courses over 5,800 yards beginning with a par 3

Aboyne
Accrington
Addington
Anglesey
Ashburnham
Ballards Gore
Berkshire (Blue)
Churston
City of Derry
Cochrane Castle
Colville Park
Crow Wood
Dartford
Davenport
Davyhulme Park
Deer Park
Easingwold
Eastham Lodge
Falkirk Tryst
Hayling
Hollingbury Park
Horam Park
Houldsworth
Huntercombe
Kettering
Kingsknowe
Knole Park
Largs
La Moye
Liphook
Llandudno (Maesdu)
Llanymynech
Longcliffe
Macroom
Manor of Groves
Meyrick Park
Monkstown
Pebbles
Pontypridd
Preston
Purley Downs
Royal Lytham and St Annes
Royal Mid-Surrey
Royal Norwich
Southport and Ainsdale
South Moor
Thetford
Upton by Chester
Wearside
Wellow
West Bowling
West Cornwall
Whitchurch (Cardiff)
Withington
Yelverton

18-hole courses over 5,800 yards ending with a par 3

Aberystwyth
Airdrie
Alloa
Arkley
Ashford (Kent)
Bandon
Barnard Castle
Beadlow Manor
Berkshire (Red)
Boyce Hill
Breightmet
Bremhill Park
Bright Castle
Brinkworth
Brora
Carlyon Bay
Cawder (Cawder)
Chapel-en-le-Frith
Chelmsford
Cold Ashby
Courtown
Darenth Valley
Deeside
Dewsbury
Dorset Heights
Douglaston
Downes Crediton
Dunstable Downs
Dunwood Manor
East Herts
Ellesmere
Erewash Valley
Fairlop Waters
Forest of Arden
Fortrose and Rosemarkie
Glamorganshire (Penarth)
Goodwood
Great Barr
Hayston
Hoebridge
Howley Hall
Ilfracombe
Kennilworth
Killarney (Mahony's Point)
Kilsyth Lennox
Kirkcaldy
Lancaster
Langley Park
Leasowe
Leeds
Lindrick
Lochwinnoch
Louth
Milford Haven
Moor Park (High)
Mount Oswald
Northcliffe
Nottingham City
Old Padeswood
Old Ranfurly
Padeswood and Buckley
Parkstone
Penwortham
Piltdown
Prestwick St Nicholas
Rhos on Sea
Rolls of Monmouth
Royal Eastbourne
Royal Guernsey
Royal St David's
Ryton
Saffron Walden
St Pierre
Saltburn-by-the-Sea
Sandy Lodge
Shanklin and Sandown
Sickleholme
Stocksfield
Stoke by Nayland (both)
Stone
Tredegar Park
Vale of Llangollen
Wallsend
Welwyn Garden City
West Linton
Wetherby
Whitburn
Woodbury (Oaks)
Woodhall Hills (both)
Worksop

18-hole courses beginning and ending with a par 3

Aboyne
Aldwark Manor
Bala
Bearsted
Deane
Didsbury
Eltham Warren
Harpenden Common
Hawick
Peacehaven
Southwold
Upminster

18-hole courses over 5,800 yards with two consecutive par 3s

Ashford Manor
Ballybunion (Old)
Balmoral
Bandon
Barnard Castle
Bawburgh
Birr
Bishop Auckland
Brancepeth Castle
Bristol & Clifton
Brough
Burntisland
Chester-le-Street
Clonmel
Consett and District
Cruden Bay
Elgin
Erewash Valley
Harburn
Hartsbourne

Hayston
Holywood
Ganstead Park
Glamorganshire
  (Penarth)
Haywards Heath
Ilkley
Kidderminster
Killymoon
Knott End
Lee-on-the-Solent
Leyland
Linlithgow
Loudoun (twice)
Lurgan
Machrihanish
The Manor, Laceby
Market Rasen
Millport
North Oxford
Potters Bar
Roehampton
Royal Eastbourne
Royal Jersey
Rushmere
Sandy Lodge
Shipley
Stoneham
Tain
Thurlestone
Tredegar Park
Waterlooville
West Linton
West Monmouthshire
West Sussex
Willesley Park

**18-hole courses over
6,000 yards with fewer
than three par 3s**
St Andrews (Old) – 2
Golf House Club,
  Elie – 2

**18-hole courses over
5,900 yards with more
than five par 3s**
Barnard Castle – 6
Berkshire (Red) – 6
Bigbury – 6
Darlington – 6
Downes Crediton – 6
Killymore – 6
Richmond – 6

Sandy Lodge – 6
Shipley — 6
Tredegar Park – 6

**Courses with holes
over 600 yards**
Aldenham G & CC
  (13th, 636 yards)
Belton Woods
  (Wellington)
  (18th, 613 yards)
Bright Castle
  (16th, 735 yards)
East Dorset
  (6th, 604 yards)
Gedney Hill
  (2nd, 671 yards)
Manor of Groves
  (18th, 614 yards)
Overstone Park
  (11th, 601 yards)
Portal
  (6th, 603 yards)
Welwyn Garden City
  (17th, 601 yards)

**Courses over 7,000
yards**
Austin Lodge
  (7,118 yards)
Ballards Gore
  (7,062 yards)
Barkway Park
  (7,000 yards)
Bidford Grange
  (7,233 yards)
The Belfry
  (Brabazon)
  (7,177 yards)
Belton Woods
  (Lancaster)
  (7,021 yards)
Bowood
  (7,317 yards)
Bright Castle
  (7,143 yards)
Carnoustie
  (7,272 yards)
Chart Hills
  (7,086 yards)
Dartmouth
  (7,012 yards)
East Dorset
  (7,027 yards)

East Sussex
  (West)
  (7,154 yards)
Forest of Arden (Arden)
  (7,102 yards)
Gleneagles
  (The Monarch's
  Course)
  (7,081 yards)
Hanbury Manor
  (7,011 yards)
Killarney (Killeen)
  (7,079 yards)
Loch Lomond
  (7,053 yards)
The London Club
  (Heritage) (7,208 yards)
  (International)
  (7,005 yards)
Millbrook
  (7,100 yards)
Moatlands
  (7,060 yards)
Mount Juliet
  (7,100 yards)
The Oxfordshire
  (7,143 yards)
Notts (Hollinwell)
  (7,020 yards)
Perton Park
  (7,007 yards)
Portal (7,145 yards)
Royal Liverpool
  (7,100 yards)
Slaley Hall
  (7,038 yards)
Stocks Hotel
  (7,016 yards)
Thorpe Wood
  (7,086 yards)
Waterville
  (7,184 yards)
West Berkshire
  (7,059 yards)
Loch Lomond
  (7,053 yards)

**18-hole courses with
holes under 100 yards**
Bridport and West
  Dorset
  (2nd, 81 yards)
Dun Laoghaire
  (7th, 95 yards)

Erewash Valley
  (4th, 89 yards)
Ilfracombe
  (4th, 81 yards)
Tilsworth
  (13th, 97 yards)

**Courses with par 3s
numbered all odds or
all evens**
Addington
Auchterarder
Cape Cornwall
Cirencester
Chipping Sodbury
County Armagh
County Louth
Hoebridge
Liphook
Oake Manor
Scunthorpe
Stockwood Park
Sundridge Park
  (West)
West Cornwall
Uttoxeter

**18-hole courses with
notable differences
between the lengths of
their two nines**
Chapel-en-le-Frith
  (821 yards)
Davids Heath
  (786 yards)
Flackwell Heath
  (786 yards)
Goodwood Park
  (712 yards)
Kings Lynn
  (584 yards)
Kirkhill
  (648 yards)
Old Ranfurly
  (507 yards)
Reddish Vale
  (534 yards)
Thurlestone
  (821 yards)
Woodhall Hills
  (754 yards)
Worcestershire
  (655 yards)

Half price golf
at top rate courses

when you join the
Telegraph Golf Network

The **Telegraph Golf Network** is a club for readers of the *Daily* and *Sunday Telegraph*, the principal benefit of membership being **two green fees for the price of one** at nearly **400 courses** in the UK and abroad. Members also benefit from a range of golf-related offers and promotions, from **equipment and tickets** to golfing holidays and EGU membership, all of which are detailed in a **regular newsletter.**

Look out for the **TGN symbol** within this guide, indicating courses that currently participate in the Telegraph Golf Network **two-for-one scheme**. Membership costs **£35 for the first year** and **£30 per year after that.**

For more information or to join the Telegraph Golf Network, call **0541 557 200***
between **9am and 5pm** Monday to Fridays, quoting reference ST14. Alternatively, you can email your name and postal address to tgn@telegraph.co uk

The 1st hole at St Andrews

Since it started we haven't missed one.

The Royal Bank of Scotland is proud to be the exclusive supplier of banking services to The Open Championship.

 **The Royal Bank of Scotland**

The Royal Bank of Scotland plc. Registered Office: 36 St. Andrew Square, Edinburgh EH2 2YB. Registered in Scotland No. 90312.

KEY TO THE MAPS

1

LONDON AND THE
HOME COUNTIES

The West and East Courses at Wentworth have long been considered among the finest inland venues, prime examples of the work of the designer Harry Colt. But in recent years they have been further improved, and the intelligent work undertaken by the club has illustrated the way forward for anyone wondering how past classics can evolve so that they retain their status.

Naturally it helps to have such a talented course superintendent as Chris Kennedy, and the budget to carry out the necessary improvements. But any professional will tell you that the West Course now is a better course than it was 10 years ago, and equally any amateur will enjoy the East in 2000 more than in 1990.

The West, of course, has been home each October for the past 36 years to the World Matchplay and looks wonderful in its autumn colours. From the humblest amateur to the best professional, only those who are on their mettle can hope to prosper, but few will walk away unimpressed by the experience.

The East is a gentler test but one that many will perhaps enjoy even more. Here you will find five par threes of intriguing variety; from the short 12th, with its viciously sloping green, to the long 17th, which has tarnished many a card.

Colt was responsible for many of the best layouts in the Home Counties, including St George's Hill and the glorious Old Course at Sunningdale. Perhaps it is to be expected that the price to pay these venues is exorbitantly high, if one can get on at all.

Thankfully, however, this is not exclusively the case. Just a taxi ride from the centre of London is a relatively undiscovered Colt gem, Hendon Golf Club. Built in 1903, it was an early example of the genius that would follow.

Moving further north from the capital lie South Herts and Hadley Wood, two courses somewhat tucked away but well worth discovering. The former has earned some repute for having had Harry Vardon and Dai Rees among its past professionals but deserves fame for its course as well. Hadley, designed by Alister Mackenzie, with its beautiful tree-lined fairways, represents excellent inland golf.

South of London lies James Braid's finest work, the gorgeous Walton Heath, resplendent in the spring; if Walton Heath proves difficult to arrange or too expensive to play, investigate the neighbouring Kingswood, designed by the same man and well worth a game.

Naturally, visitors to Kent tend to spend their days on its bounteous links courses, and with Littlestone, Prince's, Royal Cinque Ports, and, best of all, Royal St George's from which to choose, little wonder. It is said that St George's is not the most favoured Open venue of the American players, because of its crumpled fairways that are occasionally hidden from view. That is their loss. This remains one of those courses that every player should visit at least once in a lifetime. — **DL**

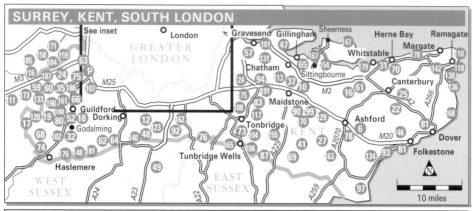

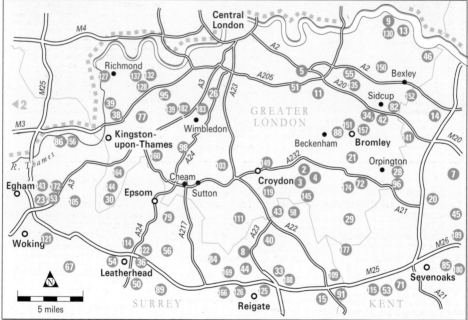

1A 1 Abbey Moor
Green Lane, Addlestone, Surrey
KT15 2XU
☎ (01932) 570741, Pro 570765,
Bar/Rest 570293.
Leave M25 at Junction 11 and
proceed on St Peter's Way towards
Weybridge; take right turn at large
roundabout towards Addlestone on
A318, then over railway bridge; take
2nd turning right at small roundabout
into Green Lane; course 0.5 mile on
right.
Public parkland course.
Pro Paul Tigwell; Founded 1991.

Designed by David Taylor.
9 holes, 5104 yards, S.S.S. 66
† Welcome WD and WE; advisable
to book early.
� WD £8.00; WE £9.00.
⌖ WD only; terms on application.
🍽 Full bar and restaurant facilities.
↪ White Lodge.

1A 2 The Addington
205 Shirley Church Rd, Croydon,
Surrey CR0 5AB
☎ (020) 8777 1055, Sec 8777 6057
Through Addington village, 2.5 miles

from East Croydon station.
Heather, bracken, silver birch and
pine parkland.
Founded 1913
Designed by J.F. Abercromby
18 holes, 6242 yards, S.S.S. 71
† WD only.
� WD £35;
⌖ WD only; terms on application.
🍽 Restaurant and bar.

1A 3 Addington Court
Featherbed Lane, Croydon, Surrey
CR0 9AA

KEY							
		39 Coombe Wood	78 Homelands B'golf Centre	117 Poult Wood	155 Staplehurst Park
1 Abbey Moor	40 Coulsdon Manor	79 Horton Park CC	118 Prince's	156 Sunbury
2 The Addington	41 Cranbrook	80 Hurtmore	119 Purley Downs	157 Sundridge Park
3 Addington Court	42 Cray Valley	81 Hythe Imperial	120 Puttenham	158 Sunningdale
4 Addington Palace	43 Croham Hurst	82 Jack Nicklaus GC	121 Pyrford	159 Sunningdale Ladies
5 Aquarius	44 Cuddington	83 Kings Hill	122 RAC Country Club	160 Surbiton
6 Ashford (Kent)	45 Darenth Valley	84 Kingswood Golf & CC	123 Redhill & Reigate	161 Sutton Green
7 Austin Lodge	46 Dartford	85 Knole Park	124 Redlibbets	162 Tandridge
8 Banstead Downs	47 Deangate Ridge	86 Laleham	125 Reigate Heath	163 Tenterden
9 Barnehurst	48 Dorking	87 Lamberhurst	126 Reigate Hill	164 Thames Ditton & Esher
10 Bearsted	49 The Drift	88 Langley Park	127 Richmond	165 Tunbridge Wells
11 Beckenham Place Park	50 Duke's Dene	89 Leatherhead	128 Richmond Park	166 Tyrrells Wood
12 Betchworth Park	51 Dulwich & Sydenham Hill	90 Leeds Castle	129 The Ridge	167 Upchurch River Valley
13 Bexleyheath	52 Dunsfold Aerodrome	91 Limpsfield Chart	130 Riverside	168 Walmer & Kingsdown
14 Birchwood Park	53 Edenbridge G&CC	92 Lingfield Park	131 Rochester & Cobham Pk	169 Walton Heath
15 Bletchingley	54 Effingham	93 Littlestone	132 Roehampton	170 Weald of Kent
16 Boughton	55 Eltham Warren	94 The London	133 Roker Park	171 Wentworth
17 Bowenhurst	56 Epsom	95 London Scottish	134 Romney Warren	172 West Byfleet
18 Bramley	57 Falcon Valley	96 Lullingstone Park	135 Royal Blackheath	173 West Hill
19 Broadwater Park	58 Farleigh Court	97 Lydd	136 Royal Cinque Ports	174 West Kent
20 Broke Hill	59 Farnham	98 Malden	137 Royal Mid-Surrey	175 West Malling
21 Bromley	60 Farnham Park	99 Marriott Tudor Pk CC	138 Royal St George's	176 West Surrey
22 Broome Park CC	61 Faversham	100 Merrist Wood	139 Royal Wimbledon	177 Westerham
23 Burhill	62 Fernfell G & CC	101 Mid-Kent	140 Rusper	178 Westgate & Birchington
24 Camberley Heath	63 Foxhills	102 Milford	141 Ruxley	179 Whitstable & Seasalter
25 Canterbury	64 Gatton Manor	103 Mitcham	142 St Augustine's	180 Wildernesse
26 Central London GC	65 Gillingham	104 Moatlands	143 St George's Hill	181 Wildwood
27 Chart Hills	66 Goal Farm Par 3	105 Moore Place	144 Sandown Golf Centre	182 Wimbledon Common
28 Chelsfield Lakes	67 Guildford	106 Nevill	145 Selsdon Pk Hotel & GC	183 Wimbledon Park
29 Cherry Lodge	68 Hankley Common	107 New Zealand Golf Club	146 Sene Valley	184 Windlemere
30 Chessington	69 Hawkhurst	108 Nizels	147 Sheerness	185 Windlesham
31 Chestfield	70 Herne Bay	109 North Downs	148 Shillinglee Park	186 The Wisley
32 Chiddingfold	71 Hever	110 North Foreland	149 Shirley Park	187 Woking
33 Chipstead	72 High Elms	111 Oak Park	150 Shooters Hill	188 Woodcote Park
34 Chislehurst	73 Hilden	112 Oaks Sports Centre	151 Shortlands	189 Woodlands Manor
35 Chobham	74 Hindhead	113 Oastpark	152 Sidcup	190 Worplesdon
36 Clandon Regis	75 Hoebridge Golf Centre	114 Pachesham Golf Centre	153 Silvermere	191 Wrotham Heath
37 Cobtree Manor Park	76 Holtye	115 Park Wood	154 Sittingbourne & Milton	
38 Coombe Hill	77 Horne Park	116 Pine Ridge Golf Centre	Regis	

☎ (020) 8657 0281, Fax 8651 0282, Sec 8651 0282
2 miles E of Croydon off the B281 in Addington village.
Undulating parkland.
Pro Adam Aram/John Dempster; Founded 1931
Designed by F. Hawtree Snr
18 holes, 5577 yards, S.S.S. 67
� WD £14; WE £17.
† Welcome.
⌖ Welcome by prior arrangement; catering packages available; terms on application.
▥ Full catering facilities.
(Falconwood Academy Course: 18 holes, 5360 yards. � WD £12; WE £15)
⌐ Selsdon Park.

1A 4 Addington Palace
Gravel Hill, Addington Park, Croydon, Surrey CR0 5BB
☎ (020) 8654 3061, Fax 8655 3632, Pro 8654 1786, Bar/Rest 8655 1290
2 miles E of Croydon on the A212.
Undulating parkland.
Pro Roger Williams; Founded 1927
Designed by J H Taylor
18 holes, 6304 yards, S.S.S. 71
† Welcome if acompanied by a member.
� WD £30; WE £15.
⌖ Welcome Tues, Wed, Fri; details on application; £57.
▥ Bar and catering facilities.

1A 5 Aquarius
Marmora Rd, Honor Oak, London SE22 0RY
☎ (020) 8693 1626
SE of London, just off the A2.
Set around a reservoir.
Pro Frod Private, Founded 1912
9 holes, 5422 yards, S.S.S. 65
† Welcome with members only.
� WD £10; WE £10.
⌖ Terms on request.
▥ Terms on request.
⌐ Selsdon Park.

1A 6 Ashford (Kent)
Sandyhurst Lane, Ashford, Kent TN25 4NT
☎ (01233) 620180, Fax 622655, Pro 629644, Sec 622655
Course is 1.5 miles from Junction 9 on the M20.
Parkland course.
Pro Hugh Sherman; Founded 1903.
Designed by C.K. Cotton.
18 holes, 6263 yards, S.S.S. 70
† Welcome with handicap certs.
� WD £24; WE £40.
⌖ Tues, Thurs; packages available; £25-£45.
▥ Bar and restaurant.

1A 7 Austin Lodge
Upper Austin Lodge Road, Eynsford, Kent DA4 0HU
☎ (01322) 863000, Fax 862406
A225 to Eynsford station; course is in road behind station.
Rolling parkland course.
Pro Paul Edwards; Founded 1991.
Designed by Peter Bevan & Mike Walsh.
18 holes, 7118 yards, S.S.S. 73
† Welcome.
� WD Mon-Wed £18; Thurs, Fri £20; WE £25.
⌖ Mon-Friday; WE after 2pm.
▥ Meals and bar.
⌐ Castle, Eynsford.

1A 8 **Banstead Downs**
Burdon Lane, Belmont, Sutton,
Surrey SM2 7DD
☎(020) 8642 2284, Fax 8642
5252, Pro 8642 6884, Bar/Rest
8643 9286
On A217 from M25 Junction 8.
Downland course.
Pro Robert Dickman; Founded 1890
Designed by J H Taylor/ J Braid
18 holes, 6194 yards, S.S.S. 69
† Welcome WD; WE with member
only.
⌐ WD £30; WE £30.
◡ Welcome, Thurs preferred; full
day's golf and catering £51.
◉ Full clubhouse facilities.

1A 9 **Barnehurst**
Mayplace Rd East, Bexleyheath, Kent
DA7 6JU
☎(01322) 551205, Fax 528483,
.Sec 523746, Bar/Rest 552952
N of Crayford town centre.
Mature inland course.
Founded 1904
Designed by James Braid
9 holes, 5474 yards, S.S.S. 68
† Welcome.
⌐ WD £8.25; WE £11.25.
◡ Welcome; terms available on
application.
◉ Full facilities and function room.
◡ Swallow, Bexleyheath.

1A 10 **Bearsted**
Ware St, Bearsted, Kent ME14 4PQ
☎(01622) 738389, Fax 738198, Pro
738024, Sec 738198
M20 to Junction 7 and follow
Bearsted Green signs.
Parkland course.
Pro Tim Simpson; Founded 1895
Designed by Golf Landscapes
18 holes, 6486 yards, S.S.S. 71
† Welcome with handicap certs.
⌐ WD £28; WE £28.
◡ Tues-Fri; 36 holes of golf, coffee,
lunch and dinner; £54.50.
◉ Full facilities.
◡ Stakis Country Court, Tudor Park,
Great Danes.

1A 11 **Beckenham Place Park**
Beckenham Hill Rd, Beckenham,
Kent BR3 2BP
☎(020) 8650 2292, Fax 8663 1201
1 mile from Catford towards Bromley,
right at Homebase.
Parkland course.
Founded 1932
18 holes, 5722 yards, S.S.S. 68

† Welcome.
◡ Terms on application.
◉ Meals and snacks.
◡ Bromley Court.

1A 12 **Betchworth Park**
Reigate Rd, Dorking, Surrey RH4
1NZ
☎(01306) 882052, Fax 877 462
Course is 1 mile E of Dorking on A25,
entrance is opposite horticultural
gardens.
Parkland course.
Pro A Tocher; Founded 1913
Designed by H. Colt
18 holes, 6266 yards, S.S.S. 70
† Welcome except Tues am, Sat
and Sun am.
⌐ WD £34; WE £45.
◡ Mon and Thurs; packages
including meals available; terms on
application.
◉ Lunch and tea facilities available.
◡ White Horse.

1A 13 **Bexleyheath**
Mount Rd, Bexleyheath, Kent DA6
8JS
☎(020) 8303 6951
1 mile from Bexleyheath station off
Upton road.
Undulating course.
Founded 1907
9 holes, 5239 yards, S.S.S. 66
† Welcome WD.
⌐ WD £20.
◡ Welcome WD by appointment.
◉ Full bar and catering facilities,
except Monday.
◡ Swallow.

1A 14 **Birchwood Park**　♗
Birchwood Rd, Wilmington, Dartford,
Kent DA2 7HJ
☎(01322) 660554, Fax 667 283
Off A20 or M25 at Swanley turn-off.
Meadowland course.
Pro Gary Orr; Founded 1990
Designed by Howard Swan
18 holes, 6364 yards, S.S.S. 71
† Welcome.
⌐ WD £15; WE £19.
◡ Welcome WD; WE limited to pm,
contact Sec; terms on application.
◉ Full facilities.
Practice range, 38 bays; floodlit.
◡ Stakis.

1A 15 **Bletchingley**　♗
Church Lane, Bletchingley, Surrey
RH1 4LP

☎(01883) 744666, Fax 744284, Pro
744848
From M25 Junction 6 take A25;
course 3 miles.
Parkland course.
Pro Alisdair Dyer; Founded 1993
18 holes, 6531 yards, S.S.S. 71
† Welcome
⌐ WD £20; WE £28.
◡ Welcome by appointment; terms
on application.
◉ Bar and restaurant.
◡ Priory, Redhill.

1A 16 **Boughton**
Brickfield Lane, Boughton, Nr
Faversham, Kent ME13 9AJ
☎(01227) 752277, Fax 752 361
At intersection of the A2/M2 follow
signs for Boughton and Dunkirk.
Upland course.
Pro Trevor Dungate; Founded 1993
Designed by P Sparks
18 holes, 6452 yards, S.S.S. 71
† Welcome.
⌐ WD £16; WE £22.
◡ Welcome; terms available on
application.
◉ Bar and restaurant.

1A 17 **Bowenhurst**
Mill Lane, Crondall, Nr Farnham,
Surrey GU10 5RP
☎(01252) 851695, Fax 851695, Pro
851344
M3 Junction 5, 4 miles on A287 to
Farnham.
Parkland course.
Pro Sean Harrison, Paul Young;
Founded 1994
Designed by N Finn/G Baker
9 holes, 4014 yards, S.S.S. 60
† Welcome
⌐ WD £11; WE £14.
◡ Welcome by arrangement with
Sec.
◉ Function facilities.
Practice range, 20 bays; floodlit.

1A 18 **Bramley**
Bramley, Nr Guildford, Surrey GU5
0AL
☎(01483) 893042, Fax 894673, Pro
893685, Sec 892696, Bar/Rest
898313
3 miles S of Guildford on A281.
Parkland course.
Pro Gary Peddie; Founded 1914
Designed by Charles Mayo,
Redesigned by James Braid
18 holes, 5990 yards, S.S.S. 69
† Welcome with member.

⌐ WD £27; WE £27.
↻ Contact Sec; full bar and catering with driving range and practice area; £43-£54.
🍽 Full catering with grill menu.
↴ Harrow, Compton; Parrot, Shalford.

1A 19 Broadwater Park
Guildford Rd, Farncombe, Nr Godalming, Surrey GU7 3BU
☎(01483) 429955, Fax 429955
On A3100 between Godalming and Guildford.
Par 3 parkland course.
Pro K Milton; Founded 1989
Designed by K.D. Milton
9 holes, 1301 yards
† Welcome.
⌐ WD £4.35; WE £4.90.
↻ Not available.
🍽 Bar and snacks.
Practice range, 16 bays; floodlit.

1A 20 Broke Hill
Sevenoaks Road, Halstead, Kent TN14 7HR
☎(01959) 533225, Fax 532880, Pro 533810
Close to M25 Junction 4 opposite Knockholt station.
Parkland course/downland.
Pro Chris West; Founded 1993
Designed by D Williams
18 holes, 6374 yards, S.S.S. 71
† Welcome WD.
⌐ WD £35.
↻ Welcome Tues, Thurs (pm), Fri; packages available; from £34.
🍽 Full clubhouse facilities.
↴ Post House, Borough Green; Bromley Court Hotel; Brands Hatch Thistle.

1A 21 Bromley
Magpie Hall Lane, Bromley, Kent BR2 8JF
☎(020) 8462 7014
A21 2 miles S of Bromley.
Public parkland course.
Pro Danny Williams
9 holes, 5490 yards, S.S.S. 67
† Welcome; no restrictions.
⌐ WD £5.15; WE £6.75.
↻ Welcome by appointment; terms on application.
🍽 Snacks available.

1A 22 Broome Park CC
Broome Park Estate, Barham, Canterbury, Kent CT4 6QX

☎(01227) 831701, Fax 821973
Just off A2 E of Canterbury.
Parkland course.
Founded 1982
Designed by Donald Steel
18 holes, 6610 yards, S.S.S. 72
† Welcome.
⌐ WD £28; WE £32.
↻ Welcome by prior arrangement; terms on application.
🍽 Clubhouse facilities.
Practice range, 13 bays.

1A 23 Burhill   ℭ
Walton-on-Thames, Surrey KT12 4BL
☎(01932) 227345, Fax 267159, Pro 221729
M25 Junction 10; off A3 London-bound towards Byfleet on the A245.
Parkland course.
Founded 1907
Designed by Willie Park
18 holes, 6179 yards, S.S.S. 71
† Welcome weekdays only.
⌐ £57 per day; £37 per round.
↻ By prior arrangement only; terms on application.
🍽 Full facilities.
Driving range, practice bunkers and short-game area; full irrigation system. (New course opening Spring 2001: Parkland course with 3 feature lakes; 18 holes, 6940 yards, par 72; USGA greens and tees; designed by Simon Gidman; † welcome weekdays only; ↻ welcome Mon-Fri, terms on application)
↴ Oatlands Park Hotel, Weybridge.

1A 24 Camberley Heath
Golf Drive, Camberley, Surrey GU15 1JG
☎(01276) 23258, Fax 692505
Off A325 Portsmouth road between Bagshot and Frimley.
Pine and heather.
Pro Glenn Ralph; Founded 1913
Designed by H. S. Colt
18 holes, 6637 yards, S.S.S. 70
† Welcome WD only.
⌐ WD £36.
↻ Welcome weekdays by appointment; terms available on application.
🍽 Full facilities.
↴ Frimley Hall Hotel.

1A 25 Canterbury
Scotland Hills, Canterbury, Kent CT1 1TW
☎(01227) 453532, Fax 784277, Pro 462865, Bar/Rest 781871

1 mile from Town Centre on A257 road to Sandwich.
Parkland course.
Pro Paul Everard; Founded 1927
Designed by H.S. Colt
18 holes, 6249 yards, S.S.S. 70
† Welcome if carrying handicap certs.
⌐ WD £27; WE £36.
↻ Welcome Tues and Thurs; minimum 15; package of coffee, 36 holes, light lunch, 3-course evening meal, £46.50.
🍽 Full facilities and bar.
↴ Many in Canterbury.

1A 26 Central London GC
Burntwood Lane, Wandsworth, London SW17 0AT
☎(020) 88712468, Fax 8874 7447
Take Garratt Lane from A3 in Wandsworth. Burntwood Lane is off Garratt Lane after Earlsfield.
Parkland course.
Pro Jeremy Robson; Founded 1992
Designed by Patrick Tallack
9 holes, 4468 yards, S.S.S. 62
† Welcome anytime.
⌐ WD £7.50; WE £9.50.
↻ By arrangement.
↴ In Wimbledon.

1A 27 Chart Hills
Weeks Lane, Biddenden, Kent TN27 8JX
☎(01580) 292222, Fax 292233
M20 to Junction 8; follow signs to Leeds Castle before turning on to A274 through Sutton Valence; 7 miles turn into Weeks Lane.
Parkland course; European HQ of David Leadbetter Academy.
Pro Danny French; Founded 1993
Designed by Nick Faldo
18 holes, 7086 yards, S.S.S. 72
† Welcome any day other than Saturday.
⌐ WD £65; WE £75.
↻ Restricted; full facilities including lunch and coffee; £75-£105.
🍽 Full facilities.
↴ Great Danes; Forstal B&B.

1A 28 Chelsfield Lakes
Court Rd, Orpington, Kent BR6 9BX
☎(01689) 896266, Fax 824577
From M25 Junction 4 follow signs to Orpington; course 300 yds from 2nd roundabout.
Parkland course.
Pro Nigel Lee; Founded 1993
Designed by MRM Leisure

18 holes, 6077 yards, S.S.S. 69
Warren course: 9 holes, par 3
Welcome.
WD £15; WE £18.
Welcome by prior application; minimum 8; golf and catering packages available; terms on application.
Full clubhouse facilities.

1A 29 **Cherry Lodge**
Jail Lane, Biggin Hill, Kent TN16 3AX
(01959) 572250, Fax 540672, Pro 572989
3 miles N of Westerham off A233.
Parkland course.
Pro Nigel Child; Founded 1970
Designed by John Day
18 holes, 6652 yards, S.S.S. 73
WD by prior arrangement; with a member only at WE.
WD £20; WE £20.
Welcome by arrangement; £35.
Full bar and restaurant facilities available.
Kings Arms, Westerham.

1A 30 **Chessington**
Garrison Lane, Chessington, Surrey KT9 2LW
(020) 8391 0948
Opposite Chessington South station, very near Chessington Zoo.
Parkland course.
Pro Sean Smith; Founded 1983
Designed by Patrick Tallack
9 holes, 1856 yards, S.S.S. 29
Welcome.
WD £6; WE £7.
Welcome; terms available on application.
Full facilities.
Practice range, 18 bays; floodlit.
Seven Hills; Oatlands Park.

1A 31 **Chestfield**
103 Chestfield Rd, Whitstable, Kent CT5 3LU
(01227) 794411, Fax 794454, Pro 793563, Bar/Rest 792243
0.5 mile S of A299 at Chestfield station.
Parkland course, with sea views.
Pro John Brotherton; Founded 1924
18 holes, 6200 yards, S.S.S. 70
WDs only.
WD £15.
Welcome WD except Thurs; packages available; terms on application.
Facilities available.
Marine, Tankerton.

1A 32 **Chiddingfold**
Petworth Rd, Chiddingfold, Surrey GU8 4SL
(01428) 685888
Take A283 off A3 and course is 10 minutes away, 50 yards S of Chiddingfold.
Downland course.
Pro Paul Creamer; Founded 1994
Designed by J Gaunt & P Alliss
18 holes, 5482 yards, S.S.S. 67
Welcome.
WD £15, WE £20.
Welcome; packages available; terms on application.
Full facilities; conference suite.
Practice range, 4 bays.
Lythe Hill.

1A 33 **Chipstead**
How Lane, Coulsden, Surrey CR33PR
(01737) 555781
Follow signs to Chipstead from the A217.
Undulating parkland course.
Pro Gary Torbett; Founded 1906
18 holes, 5491 yards, S.S.S. 67
Welcome WD.
WD £20.
Welcome WD by appointment; terms on application.
Lunch served; booking required. Bar snacks.
Reigate Manor.

1A 34 **Chislehurst**
Camden Place, Camden Park Rd, Chislehurst, Kent BR7 5HJ
(020) 8467 3055, Fax 8295 0874, Pro 8467 6798, Sec 8467 2782, Bar/Rest 8467 2888
Off A20/A222 from Junction 3 of M25. 0.5 miles from Chislehurst station.
Parkland course.
Pro Mark Lawrence; Founded 1894
18 holes, 5106 yards, S.S.S. 65
Welcome WD; with a member at WE.
WD £25; WE £25
Welcome Mon-Fri; 36 holes available Thurs; £33.
Full facilities.

1A 35 **Chobham**
Chobham Rd, Knaphill, Woking, Surrey GU21 2TZ
(01276) 855584, Fax 855663, Pro 855748
Take the A322 from the M3 Junction 3 towards Guildford; at the first roundabout take the A319 to Chobham, course is 2 miles on right towards Knaphill.
Wooded parkland with lakes.
Pro Tim Coombes; Founded 1994
Designed by Clive Clark & Peter Alliss
18 holes, 5959 yards, S.S.S. 69
Members' guests welcome only in midweek.
WD £16.50 before 2pm.
Welcome by appointment; terms on application.
Restaurant, bar and function rooms.

1A 36 **Clandon Regis**
Epsom Road, West Clandon, Nr Guildford, Surrey GU4 7TT
(01483) 224888, Fax 211781, Pro 223922
Course is four miles E of Guildford on the A246.
Parkland course.
Pro Steve Lloyd; Founded 1994
Designed by D Williams
18 holes, 6412 yards, S.S.S. 71
Welcome by prior arrangement.
WD £25; WE £35
Welcome by prior arrangement; terms on application.
Full bar and restaurant.

1A 37 **Cobtree Manor Park**
Chatham Rd, Maidstone, Kent ME14 3AZ
(01622) 753276
Take A229 from M20.
Municipal parkland course.
Pro Paul Foston; Founded 1984
Designed by F. Hawtree
18 holes, 5586 yards, S.S.S. 67
Welcome.
WD £14; WE £18.
Terms on application.
Available.

1A 38 **Coombe Hill**
Golf Club Drive, Kingston, Surrey KT2 7DF
(020) 8942 2284, Fax 8949 5815, Pro 8949 3713, Bar/Rest 8942 2284
1 mile W of New Malden on A238.
Undulating, tree-lined.
Pro Craig Defoy; Founded 1911
Designed by J.F. Abercromby
18 holes, 6293 yards, S.S.S. 71
WD by prior arrangement.
WD £65.
Welcome by prior arrangement with Sec; terms on application.
Restaurant and bar.
Kingston Lodge.

1A 39 Coombe Wood
George Rd, Kingston Hill, Kingston-on-Thames, Surrey KT2 7NS
☎(020) 8942 0388, Fax 8942 0388, Pro 8942 6764, Bar/Rest 8942 3828
From the A3 take the A308 (E) or the A238 (W).
Mature parkland.
Pro David Butler; Founded 1904
Designed by T. Williamson
18 holes, 5299 yards, S.S.S. 66
⚑ Welcome WD; with a member only at WE.
⌊ WD £23; WE £23.
⤵Welcome Wed, Thurs, Fri; packages available; from £22.50.
⦿ Full bar and restaurant facilities available.
⌁ Kingston Lodge.

1A 40 Coulsdon Manor
Coulsdon Rd, Coulsdon, Surrey CR5 2LL
☎(020) 8668 0414, Pro 8660 6083
Just off A23, 2 miles S of Croydon, 2 miles N of M25 and M23.
Parkland course.
Pro David Copsey; Founded 1926
Designed by H.S. Buck
18 holes, 6037 yards, S.S.S. 68
⚑ Welcome.
⌊ WD £13.90; WE £17.25.
⤵Welcome by prior arrangement; terms on application.
⦿ Full facilities.
⌁ Coulsdon Manor.

1A 41 Cranbrook
Golford Rd, Cranbrook, Kent TN17 4AL
☎(01580) 712833, Fax 714274, Bar/Rest 715771
Off A262 at Sissinghurst; turn right at Bull towards Benenden; 1 mile on left.
Tree-lined parkland.
Founded 1969
Designed by John D. Harris
18 holes, 6295 yards, S.S.S. 70
⚑ Welcome except Mon.
⌊ WD £25; WE £30.
⤵Welcome Tues-Fri; packages available; from £19.50.
⦿ Full clubhouse facilities.
⌁ Kennel Holt; The George.

1A 42 Cray Valley
Sandy Lane, St Paul's Cray, Orpington, Kent BR5 3HY
☎(01689) 839677, Fax 891428, Pro 837909

Leave the A20 off Ruxley roundabout; course is on Sandy Lane, 0.5 miles on left.
Parkland course.
Pro Gary Stuart; Founded 1972
Designed by Golf Centres Ltd
18 holes, 5669 yards, S.S.S. 67
⚑ Pay and play.
⌊ WD £15; WE £20.
⤵Bookings requested 7 days in advance.
⦿ Bar and restaurant.

1A 43 Croham Hurst
Croham Rd, South Croydon, Surrey CR2 7HJ
☎(020) 8657 5581, Pro 8657 7705, Sec 8657 5581
1 mile from S Croydon; from M25 exit 6 N on to A22, take B270 to Warlingham at roundabout, then B269 to Selsdon; at traffic lights turn left into Farley Road, clubhouse is 1.75 miles on left.
Parkland course.
Pro Eric Stillwell; Founded 1911
Designed by Hawtree & Sons
18 holes, 6290 yards, S.S.S. 70
⚑ Welcome, handicap certs required; with member only at WE.
⌊ WD £36; WE £45.
⤵Welcome Wed, Thurs, Fri by arrangement; terms available on application.
⦿ Full facilities every day 10am-6pm; banqueting.
⌁ Selsdon Park.

1A 44 Cuddington
Banstead Rd, Banstead, Surrey SM7 1RD
☎(020) 8393 7097, Fax 8786 7025, Pro 8393 5850, Sec 8393 0952, Bar/Rest 393 0951
200 yards from Banstead station.
Parkland course.
Pro Mark Warner; Founded 1929
Designed by H.S. Colt
18 holes, 6394 yards, S.S.S. 70
⚑ Welcome if carrying handicap certs.
⌊ WD £35; WE £35.
⤵Welcome Thurs; full day's golf and meals, including dinner; £60.
⦿ Full catering service.
⌁ Heathside; Driftbridge.

1A 45 Darenth Valley
Station Rd, Shoreham, Kent TN14 7SA
☎(01959) 522944, Fax 525089, Pro 522922

Along A225 Sevenoaks-Dartford road, 4 miles N of Sevenoaks.
Parkland course.
Pro Scott Fotheringham; Founded 1973
18 holes, 6394 yards, S.S.S. 71
⚑ Welcome; bookings daily.
⌊ WD £15; WE £20.
⤵Welcome by prior arrangement with manager; terms available on application.
⦿ Bar meals, society catering, functions (up to 100 persons).

1A 46 Dartford
Dartford Heath, Dartford, Kent DA1 2TN
☎(01322) 223616, Pro 226409, Sec 226455
0.5 miles from A2 Dartford-Crayford turn-off.
Park/heathland course.
Pro John Gregory; Founded 1897
Designed by James Braid
18 holes, 5914 yards, S.S.S. 69
⚑ WDs with handicap certs; with member only at WE.
⌊ WD £30; WE £12.50.
⤵Mon and Fri by prior arrangement; full day's package of golf and catering, including evening meal; £49.
⦿ Full clubhouse facilities.
⌁ Swallow, Bexleyheath; The Stakis, Dartford Bridge.

1A 47 Deangate Ridge
Hoo, Rochester, Kent ME3 8RZ
☎(01634) 251180, Fax 255370
A228 from Rochester to Isle of Grain, then road signposted to Deangate.
Municipal parkland course.
Pro Richard Fox; Founded 1972
Designed by Hawtree & Sons
18 holes, 6300 yards, S.S.S. 70
⚑ Welcome anytime; bookings essential at WE.
⌊ WD £10.89; WE £14.20.
⤵Welcome; terms available on application.
⦿ Lunch and dinner served.
Practice range, 11 bays; floodlit.

1A 48 Dorking
Chart Park, Dorking, Surrey RH5 4BX
☎(01306) 886917, Bar 885914
1 mile S of Dorking on A24.
Parkland course.
Pro Paul Napier; Founded 1887
Designed by James Braid
9 holes, 5163 yards, S.S.S. 65
⚑ Welcome WD only.
⌊ WD £12.

Welcome by prior arrangement.
Restaurant and bar.
Burford Bridge, Boxhill.

1A 49 The Drift
The Drift, East Horsley KT24 5HD
(01483) 284641, Fax 284642, Pro 284772, Bar/Rest 282432
On B2039 East Horsley road off A3.
Woodland course.
Pro Liam Greasley; Founded 1975
Designed by H. Cotton/R Sandow
18 holes, 6425 yards, S.S.S. 72
WD only unless member's guest.
Terms on application.
Mon-Fri by appointment; club cleaning service, coffee, lunch, dinner; £37-£58.
Full restaurant and bar.
Jarvis Thatcher Hotel, E Horsley; Hauthoy, Ockham.

1A 50 Duke's Dene
Slines New Rd, Woldingham, Surrey CR3 7HA
(01883) 653501, Pro 653541
From M25 Junction 6 towards Caterham; at roundabout take Woldingham exit.
Valley course.
Pro Nick Bradley; Founded 1996
18 holes, 6393 yards, S.S.S. 70
Welcome except after 12 at WE.
WD £25; WE £35.
Welcome WD.
Bar and brasserie.
Practice range.

1A 51 Dulwich & Sydenham Hill
Grange Lane, College Rd, London SE21 7LH
(020) 8693 3961, Fax 8693 2481, Pro 8693 8491
Off S Circular road at Dulwich College and College Rd.
Parkland course.
Pro David Baillie; Founded 1894
18 holes, 6008 yards, S.S.S. 69
Welcome WD with handicap certs.
WD £25; WE £25.
Welcome WD by prior arrangement; terms available on application.
Lunch daily, dinner by appointment.

1A 52 Dunsfold Aerodrome
British Aerospace, Dunsfold Aerodrome, Nr Godalming, Surrey GU8 4BS

(01483) 265403
12 miles S of Guildford on A281.
Parkland course.
Founded 1965
Designed by John Sharkey
9 holes, 6099 yards, S.S.S. 69
With member only.
Member's responsibility.
Welcome from British Aerospace.
Bar and snacks.

1A 53 Edenbridge G & CC
Crouch House Rd, Edenbridge, Kent TN8 5LQ
(01732) 865097, Fax 867029
Travelling N through Edenbridge High Street, turn left into Stangrove Road (30 yds before railway station), at end of the road turn right, course is on the left.
Undulating meadowland.
Founded 1975
Old: 18 holes, 6577 yards, S.S.S. 72
New (Skaeynes Course): 18 holes, 5605 yards, S.S.S. 67
9 hole beginners (Blue) course: 1546 yards
Welcome, except WE mornings on Old course.
Old – WD £20; WE £27.50; Skaeynes – WD £12; WE £16; Blue – £4.
Welcome WD by appointment; packages available; terms on application.
Clubhouse bar and catering facilities available.
Practice range, 14 bays; floodlit.
Langley Arms, Tonbridge.

1A 54 Effingham
Guildford Rd, Effingham, Surrey KT24 5PZ
(01372) 452203, Fax 459959, Pro 452606
On A246 8 miles E of Guildford.
Downland course.
Pro Stephen Hoatson; Founded 1927
Designed by H.S. Colt
18 holes, 6524 yards, S.S.S. 71
WD only by arrangement; handicap certs required.
WD £35.
Welcome Wed, Thurs and Fri; terms on application.
Lunch, tea, evening meal, snacks, etc.
Thatchers (East Horsley); Preston Cross (Great Bookham).

1A 55 Eltham Warren
Bexley Rd, Eltham, London SE9 2PE

(020) 8850 1166, Pro 8859 7909, Sec 8850 4477
0.5 miles from Eltham Station on A210.
Parkland course.
Pro Gary Brett; Founded 1890
9 holes, 5840 yards, S.S.S. 68
Welcome on WD.
WD £25.
Thurs only; green fees, morning coffee, ploughman's lunch, evening meal; £42.
Full bar and catering.
Swallow, Bexleyheath.

1A 56 Epsom
Longdown Lane South, Epsom, Surrey KT17 4JR
(01372) 721666, Fax 817183, Pro 741867, Bar/Rest 723363
Course is 0.5 miles south of Epsom Downs Station on the road to Epsom College.
Downland course.
Pro Ron Goudie; Founded 1889
18 holes, 5658 yards, S.S.S. 68
Welcome except before noon on Tues, Sat and Sun.
WD £24; WE £26.
Welcome WD except Tues, and WE pm; min 12, max 40; packages available; terms available on application.
Full clubhouse facilities.
Heathside hotel.

1A 57 Falcon Valley (formerly Corinthian GC)
Gay Dawn Farm, Fawkham, Longfield, Kent DA3 8LY
(01474) 707144, Fax 707911
Take A20 off Junction 3 of M25 towards Brands Hatch and turn left towards Fawkham/Longfield.
Wooded parkland.
Pro Cameron McKillop; Founded 1986
Designed by Greg Turner
9 holes, 6800 yards, S.S.S. 70
Welcome WD, after 1pm at WE.
WD £12; WE £18.
Welcome midweek; packages available; terms available on application.
Bar and restaurant.
Brands Hatch Hotel; Brands Hatch Thistle.

1A 58 Farleigh Court
Old Farleigh Rd, Farleigh, Surrey CR6 9PX
(01883) 627711, Pro 627733

Ten minutes from Croydon town centre.
Parkland course.
Designed by John Jacobs; Founded 1997
Members' course: 18 holes, 6409 yards, S.S.S. 71. Visitors' course: 9 holes, 3255 yards
† Welcome 7 days.
⌇ Terms available on application.
⌁Welcome WD.
◉ Restaurant, bar and function rooms.
Golf academy, full practice facilities.

1A 59 **Farnham**

The Sands, Farnham, Surrey GU10 1PX
☎(01252) 783163, Fax 781185, Pro 782198, Sec 782109
On A31 from Runfold.
Heathland, pines, parkland.
Pro Grahame Cowlishaw; Founded 1896
18 holes, 6325 yards, S.S.S. 70
† Welcome WDs.
⌇ WD £37.50.
⌁Wed, Thurs, Fri only; 2 rounds of golf, coffee and roll on arrival, snack lunch and evening meal; golf clinics available; £58.50.
◉ Bar and restaurant facilities available.
⌐ Hogs Back Hotel.

1A 60 **Farnham Park**

Folly Hill, Farnham, Surrey GU9 0AV
☎(01252) 715216, Fax 718246
On A287 next to Farnham Castle.
Parkland course.
Pro P Chapman; Founded 1966
Designed by Henry Cotton
9 holes, 2326 yards, S.S.S. 54
† Public pay and play.
⌇ WD £4.25; WE £4.75.
⌁By prior arrangement.

1A 61 **Faversham**

Belmont Park, Faversham, Kent ME13 0HB
☎(01795) 890561, Fax 890760, Pro 890275
Leave M2 at Junction 6, A251 to Faversham, then A2 to Sittingbourne for 0.5 mile, turn left at Brogdale Rd, and then follow signs.
Parkland course.
Pro Stuart Rokes; Founded 1902
18 holes, 6030 yards, S.S.S. 69
† WD; only with member WE and Bank Holidays.
⌇ WD £30; WE £30.

⌁By arrangement; terms on application.
◉ By arrangement with Steward.
⌐ Granary; Porch House.

1A 62 **Fernfell G & CC**

Barhatch Lane, Cranleigh, Surrey GU6 7NG
☎(01483) 268855, Pro 277188
Take A281 out of Guildford, 1 mile through Cranleigh take Ewhurst road, then turn into Barhatch Road and Barhatch Lane.
Parkland course.
Pro Trevor Longmuir; Founded 1985
18 holes, 5648 yards, S.S.S. 68
† Welcome WD; restrictions WE.
⌇ WD £23; WE £25.
⌁Welcome WD; terms on application.
◉ Bar, restaurant, snacks, banquets.

1A 63 **Foxhills**

Stonehill Rd, Ottershaw, Surrey KT16 0EL
☎(01932) 872050, Fax 874762, Pro 873961
From the M25 Junction 11 follow the signs for Woking; at the 2nd roundabout take the 3rd exit into Foxhills Road.
Treelined course.
Pro A Good; Founded 1972
Designed by F Hawtree
Bernard Hunt: 18 holes, 6883 yards, S.S.S. 73
Longcross: 18 holes, 6743 yds, S.S.S. 72
† Welcome WD if carrying handicap certs.
⌇ WD £55.
⌁WD only; packages available; driving range facilities; £75-£125.
◉ Full clubhouse facilities.
⌐ Accommodation on site.

1A 64 **Gatton Manor**

Ockley, Dorking, Surrey RH5 5PQ
☎(01306) 627555, Fax 627713, Pro 627557
Course is 1.5 miles SW of Ockley on the A29.
Parkland course.
Pro Rae Sergeant; Founded 1969
Designed by D.B. & D.G. Heath
18 holes, 6653 yards, S.S.S. 72
† Welcome except Sunday until 10.15am
⌇ WD £21; WE £28.
⌁Welcome WD; coffee, lunch, dinner, 36 holes of golf; conference

facilities, tennis with gym and health suite; £29-£55.
◉ Bar and restaurant.
⌐ Gatton Manor.

1A 65 **Gillingham**

Woodlands Rd, Gillingham, Kent ME7 2AP
☎(01634) 853017, Fax 574749, Pro 855862, Bar/Rest 850999
On A2 at Gillingham, about 2 miles from M2 turn off to Gillingham.
Parkland/meadowland course.
Pro Barry Coomber; Founded 1908
Designed by James Braid
18 holes, 5514 yards, S.S.S. 67
† Welcome WD with handicap certs; with member only at WE.
⌇ WD £18; WE £18.
⌁Welcome WD except Thurs; terms on application.
◉ Wed-Sun lunch and evening meals available.
⌐ The Crest.

1A 66 **Goal Farm Par 3**

Gole Rd, Pirbright, Surrey GU24 0PZ
☎(01483) 473183
1 mile from Brookwood station off A322 towards Pirbright.
Parkland course.
Founded 1977
9 holes, 1128 yards, S.S.S. 48
† Welcome except Thurs am or Sat am.
⌇ WD £4; WE £4.25.
⌁Welcome.
◉ Bar and bar snacks.
⌐ Lakeside.

1A 67 **Guildford**

High Path Rd, Merrow, Guildford, Surrey GU1 2HL
☎(01483) 563941, Fax 453228, Pro 566765, Bar/Rest 531842
Course is 2 miles E of Guildford on the A246.
Downland course.
Pro P G Hollington; Founded 1886
Designed by James Braid
18 holes, 6090 yards, S.S.S. 70
† Welcome WD; members' guests only at WE.
⌇ WD £28; WE £28.
⌁Welcome by prior arrangement; packages including practice areas and indoor practice rooms and snooker; terms available on application.
◉ Full bar and catering facilities available.
⌐ White Horse; Angel.

1A 68 Hankley Common
Tilford Rd, Tilford, Farnham, Surrey GU10 2DD
☎(01252) 792493, Fax 795699, Pro 793761, Bar/Rest 793145
Off M3 or A3 to Farnham, along A31 Farnham by-pass to lights; left to Tilford.
Heathland course.
Pro P Stow; Founded 1897
Designed by James Braid
18 holes, 6438 yards, S.S.S. 71
⚑ Welcome only with telephone booking and handicap certs.
⚐ WD £42; WE £55.
⌣Tues, Wed; packages available; £77.
🍽 Full catering and bar.
↪ Bush, Farnham; Frensham Ponds, Pride of Valley, Churt.

1A 69 Hawkhurst
High St, Hawkhurst, Cranbrook, Kent TN18 4JS
☎(01580) 752396, Fax 754074, Pro 753600
On A268 3 miles from A21 at Flimwell, 0.5 mile from junction with A229.
Undulating parkland course.
Pro Tony Collins; Founded 1968

Designed by Rex Baldock
9 holes, 5751 yards, S.S.S. 68
⚑ Welcome weekdays; only with member at weekends.
⚐ WD £15; WE £10.
⌣Welcome by prior arrangement; mostly Fri; £18.
🍽 By arrangement.
↪ Royal Oak; Tudor Court; Queens.

1A 70 Herne Bay
Eddington, Herne Bay, Kent CT6 7PG
☎(01227) 373964, Pro 374727, Bar/Rest 374097
Off A299 Thanet road at Herne Bay-Canterbury junction.
Parkland course/links.
Pro S Dormoy; Founded 1895
18 holes, 5567 yards, S.S.S. 66
⚑ Welcome WD, and afternoons at WE.
⚐ WD £18; WE £28.
⌣By prior arrangement; terms on application.
🍽 Full facilities.

1A 71 Hever
Hever, Edenbridge, Kent TN8 7NP
☎(01732) 700771, Fax 700775, Bar/Rest 700016

Course is off the A21 between Sevenoaks and Edenbridge adjacent to Hever Castle.
Parkland course, with water hazards.
Pro Richard Tinworth; Founded 1992
Designed by Dr Peter Nicholson
18 holes, 7002 yards, S.S.S. 72
⚑ Welcome.
⚐ WD £34; WE £54.
⌣By prior appointment; coffee, golf, dinner; use of gymnasium included.
Also on site: sauna, spa, snooker, tennis; £38-£68.
🍽 Restaurant and bar.
↪ Hotel on site.

1A 72 High Elms
High Elms Rd, Downe, Kent BR6 7SL
☎(01689) 858175, Pro 853232
5 miles out of Bromley off the A21 to Sevenoaks.
Public parkland course.
Pro Peter Remy; Founded 1969
Designed by Fred Hawtree
18 holes, 6209 yards, S.S.S. 70
⚑ Welcome.
⚐ WD £10.80; WE £14.
⌣Welcome WD only; terms on application.
🍽 Full meals and snacks.
↪ Bromley Court.

1A 73 **Hilden**

Rings Hill, Hildenborough, Kent TN11 8LX
☎(01732) 833607
Course is off the A21 towards Tunbridge Wells adjacent to Hildenborough station.
Parkland course.
Pro Nicky Way; Founded 1994
9 holes, 1558 yards, S.S.S. 54
† Welcome.
▯ WD £5.95; WE £7.50.
⌁ Welcome; terms on application.
◉ Full facilities.
Practice range, 36 bays; floodlit.

1A 74 **Hindhead**

Churt Rd, Hindhead, Surrey GU26 6HX
☎(01428) 604614, Fax 608508, Pro 604458
1.5 miles N of Hindhead on the A287. Heathland course.
Pro Neil Ogilvy; Founded 1904
18 holes, 6373 yards, S.S.S. 70
† Welcome WD; by appt WE.
▯ WD £47; WE £57.
⌁ Wed, Thurs only; 36 holes of golf, coffee, snack lunch, evening meal; £65.
◉ Full catering and bar.
⌐ Mariners, Farnham; Devils Punch Bowl, Hindhead; Frensham Pond.

1A 75 **Hoebridge Golf Centre**

Old Woking Rd, Old Woking, Surrey GU22 8JH
☎(01483) 722611, Fax 740369
On B382 between Old Woking and West Byfleet.
Public parkland, one par 3 course; one 18-hole course; one 9-hole course.
Pro Tim Powell; Founded 1982
Designed by John Jacobs
† Welcome 7 days per week.
Hoebridge: 18 holes, 6536 yards, S.S.S. 71
▯ WD £16.50; WE £19.50.
Sheycopse: 9 holes, 2294 yards, S.S.S. 31; ▯ WD £8.50; WE £9.20.
Maybury: 18 holes par 3, 2230 yards, S.S.S. 54; ▯ WD £7; WE £7.50.
⌁ WD by prior arrangement; snooker room; terms on application.
◉ Restaurant and bar facilities.
Practice range, 36 floodlit bays.
⌐ Travel inns nearby.

1A 76 **Holtye**

Holtye Common, Cowden, Kent TN8 7ED
☎(01342) 850635, Fax 850576, Pro 850957, Sec 850576
On the A264 1 mile S of Cowden. Forest/heathland with 10-acre practice ground.
Pro K Hinton; Founded 1893
9 holes, 5325 yards, S.S.S. 66
† Welcome Mon, Tues, Fri; Restrictions other days.
▯ WD £16; WE £18.
⌁ By prior arrangement; terms on application.
◉ Catering and bar facilities available.
⌐ White Horse Inn (next door).

1A 77 **Home Park**

Hampton Wick, Kingston-upon-Thames KT1 4AD
☎(020) 8977 2423, Fax 8977 4414, Pro 8977 2658, Bar/Rest 8977 6645
Entrance to Home Park is through Kingston Gate at Hampton Wick roundabout.
Parkland course/links.
Pro Len Roberts; Founded 1895
18 holes, 6611 yards, S.S.S. 71
† Welcome.
▯ WD £22; WE £27.50.
⌁ Welcome with prior appointment; packages available; terms on application.

1A 78 **Homelands Bettergolf Centre**

Ashford Rd, Kingsnorth, Kent TN26 1NJ
☎(01233) 661620, Fax 720553
M20 Junction 10 following signs for International station until 2nd roundabout where course is signposted.
Parkland course.
Pro Mark Belsham; Founded 1995
Designed by D Steel
9 holes, 4410 yards, S.S.S. 64
† Public pay as you play.
▯ WD £7; WE £14.
⌁ Welcome; bar snacks, driving range, academy pitch and putt; terms on application.
◉ Bar with drinks and snacks; BBQs can be arranged.
Practice range, 14 bays; floodlit.
⌐ Eastwell Manor.

1A 79 **Horton Park Country Club**

Hook Road, Epsom, Surrey KT19 8QG
☎(020) 8393 8400, Fax 8394 1369
M25 Junction 9; follow signs to Chessington, turning right at Malden Rushett lights. 2 miles, then left into Horton Lane.
Parkland course.
Pro H Omidiran/J September; Founded 1987
Designed by P Tallack
18 holes, 6293 yards, S.S.S 70
† Bookings WD; WE.
▯ WD £14; WE £16.
9 holes, 1637 yards; ▯ WD £6; WE £7.50.
⌁ Welcome; packages include golf and lunch/dinner.
◉ Restaurant, bar, private suites.
Practice range, 26 bays; floodlit.
⌐ Chalk Lane Hotel, Epsom.

1A 80 **Hurtmore**

Hurtmore Rd, Hurtmore, Godalming, Surrey GU7 2RN
☎(01483) 426492, Fax 426121, Sec 424440
4 miles S of Guildford on A3 at Hurtmore exit.
Parkland course.
Pro Maxine Burton; Founded 1990
Designed by Peter Alliss & Clive Clark
18 holes. 5514 yards, S.S.S. 67
† Public pay and play.
▯ WD £10; WE £15.
⌁ Welcome by appointment; from £12.75.
◉ Full facilities available.
⌐ Squirrel.

1A 81 **Hythe Imperial**

Princes Parade, Hythe, Kent CT21 6AE
☎(01303) 267554, Pro 267441
Turn off M20 to Hythe, to E end of seafront.
Seaside course.
Pro Gordon Ritchie; Founded 1950
9 holes, 5560 yards, S.S.S. 68
† Welcome; must be member of a club, handicap certs required.
▯ WD £10; WE £15.
⌁ Welcome by prior appointment; terms on application.
◉ Hotel/club bar.
⌐ Hythe Imperial.

1A 82 **Jack Nicklaus Golf Centre**

Sidcup By-pass, Chislehurst, Kent BR7 6RP
☎(020) 8309 0181, Fax 8308 1691
Course is on the main A20, London road.
Parkland course.

Pro David Bailey; Founded 1995
Designed by M Gillett
9 holes, 1055 yards
† Welcome only if accompanied by
a member.
⌑ WD £3.50; WE £3.50.
⌇ Welcome; terms on application.
⍟ Full facilities.
Practice range, 54 bays, floodlit.

1A 83 **Kings Hill**

Kings Hill, West Malling, Kent ME19
4AF
☎ (01732) 875040, Fax 875019, Pro
842121
From M20 Junction 4 take A228
towards Tonbridge.
Parkland course.
Pro David Hudspith; Founded 1996
Designed by David Williams
18 holes, 6622 yards, S.S.S. 72
† Welcome WD; WE with member.
⌑ WD £30
⌇ Welcome by appointment; £37-53.
⍟ Full bar and catering.
Practice range, 12 bays.

1A 84 **Kingswood Golf & CC**

Sandy Lane, Tadworth, Surrey KT20
6DP
☎ (01737) 832188, Fax 833920, Pro
832334, Bar/Rest 832316
From A217 take Bonsor Drive
(A2032) to Kingswood Arms. Club
0.25 miles down Sandy Lane.
Parkland course.
Pro James Dodds; Founded 1928
Designed by James Braid
18 holes, 6904 yards, S.S.S. 73
† Welcome but WE restrictions.
⌑ WD £36; WE £50.
⌇ Welcome; terms on application.
⍟ Bar and restaurant.
⌁ Club will provide list.

1A 85 **Knole Park**

Seal Hollow Rd, Sevenoaks, Kent
TN15 0HJ
☎ (01732) 452709, Fax 463159, Pro
452150, Sec 452150, Bar/Rest
740221
0.5 miles from Sevenoaks town
centre.
Parkland course.
Pro Phil Sykes; Founded 1924
Designed by J.A. Abercromby
18 holes, 6266 yards, S.S.S. 70
† Welcome after 9am WD.
⌑ WD £35
⌇ Tues, Thurs, Fri by appt. £65.
⍟ Full facilities.
⌁ Royal Oak, Sevenoaks.

1A 86 **Laleham**

Laleham Reach, Chertsey, Surrey
KT16 8RP
☎ (01932) 564211, Fax 564448, Pro
562877, Bar/Rest 502188
From M25 Junction 11 take A320 to
Thorpe Park roundabout then to
Penton Marina and signposted.
Parkland course.
Pro Hogan Scott; Founded 1908
18 holes, 6211 yards, S.S.S. 70
† Welcome with handicap certs.
⌑ WD £20
⌇ Mon, Tues, Wed; catering
facilities; £21-£48.50.
⍟ Full facilities.

1A 87 **Lamberhurst**

Church Rd, Lamberhurst, Kent TN3
0DT
☎ (01892) 890241, Fax 891140, Pro
890552, Sec 890591
6 miles S of Tunbridge Wells on A21;
turning on to B2162 at Lamberhurst.
Parkland course.
Pro Brian Impett; Founded 1890/1920
Designed by Frank Pennink
18 holes, 6345 yards, S.S.S. 70
† Welcome WD, and pm at WE.
⌑ WD £22; WE £36.
⌇ Welcome Tues, Wed and Thurs,
April to October; 36 holes, coffee,
lunch and 3-course dinner; min 16,
max 36; £49.
⍟ Full clubhouse facilities.
⌁ Pembury Resort, Pembury;
George & Dragon, Lamberhurst.

1A 88 **Langley Park**

Barnfield Wood Rd, Beckenham, Kent
BR3 6SZ
☎ (020) Pro 8650 1663, Sec 8658
6849, Bar/Rest 8650 2090
1 mile from Bromley South station.
Parkland course.
Pro Colin Staff; Founded 1910
Designed by J.H. Taylor
18 holes, 6488 yards, S.S.S. 71
† Welcome WD by arrangement
with Pro shop. WE only with member.
⌑ WD £35; WE £15
⌇ Wed and Thurs only; maximum 24
Thurs; 36 holes of golf, lunch and
dinner; £52.
⍟ Full bar and restaurant.
⌁ Bromley Court Hotel.

1A 89 **Leatherhead**   ℭ

Kingston Rd, Leatherhead, Surrey
KT22 0EE
☎ (01372) 843966, Fax 842241, Pro
843956

From M25 Junction 9 take A243
towards London, course entrance 500
yards.
Parkland course.
Pro Simon Norman; Founded 1903
18 holes, 6203 yards, S.S.S. 70
† Welcome by appointment; WE not
before 12 am.
⌑ WD £35; WE £45.
⌇ Welcome; terms available on
application.
⍟ Restaurant, brasserie, bar.
⌁ Woodlands Park (Oxshott).

1A 90 **Leeds Castle**

Leeds Castle, Maidstone, Kent ME17
1PL
☎ (01622) 880467, Fax 735616
M20 Junction 8 and follow signs to
Leeds Castle on A20.
Parkland course.
Pro Steve Purvis; Founded 1933
Designed by Neil Coles
9 holes, 2416 yards, S.S.S 33
† Can book 6 days ahead; no jeans
please.
⌑ WD £11; WE £12.
⌇ WD only; terms available on
application.
⌁ Tudor Park, Maidstone.

1A 91 **Limpsfield Chart**

Limpsfield, Oxted, Surrey RH8 0SL
☎ (01883) Sec 723405, Bar/Rest
722106
Course is on the A25 between Oxted
and Westerham, over the traffic lights
300 yards on right, east of Oxted.
Heathland course.
Founded 1889
9 holes, 5718 yards, S.S.S. 69
† WD welcome; WE by prior
arrangement or with member.
⌑ WD £18; WE £20.
⌇ Can be arranged; terms on
application.
⍟ Meals served.
⌁ Kings Arms (Westerham).

1A 92 **Lingfield Park**   ℭ

Racecourse Road, Lingfield, Surrey
RH7 6PQ
☎ (01342) 834602, Fax 836077, Pro
832659
From A22 at E Grinstead take the B
2028 to Lingfield.
Parkland course.
Pro Chris Morely Founded 1987
18 holes, 6487 yards, S.S.S. 72
† Welcome WD, WE by appt.
⌑ WD £32; WE £45.
⌇ Welcome by prior arrangement;

Merrist Wood Golf Club

Merrist Wood GOLF/CLUB

A beautiful but challenging golf course laid out over 240 acres of Surrey

Coombe Lane,
Worplesdon,
Guildford,
GU3 3PE

Driving range, 2 short game practice areas and a putting green to hone your game before you take up the challenge.
Full bar/restaurant facilities will take care of you both before and after your round. Tel: 01483 884045 or e-mail:mwgc@merristwood-golfclub.co.uk

packages include golf and catering; from £35.
🏮 Facilities available.
🛏 Felbridge; Copthorne.

1A 93 Littlestone
St Andrews Rd, Littlestone, New Romney, Kent TN28 8RB
☎ (01797) 363355, Fax 362740, Pro 362231, Bar/Rest 362310
In New Romney on A259 between Brenzett and Hythe; 15 miles S of Ashford.
Links course.
Pro Stephen Watkins; Founded 1888
Designed by Laidlaw Purves
18 holes 6486 yards S.S.S 72
Blue Course: 18 holes, 6676 yards, S.S.S. 73
🏌 Welcome by prior arrangement at WD and WE.
▯ WD £35; WE £45.
🛒 Welcome WD; golf and catering packages; from £36.
🏮 Full facilities.
Practice ground; chipping green with bunker, putting green.
🛏 Romney Bay House; Broadacre; Rose and Crown; White House B&B.

1A 94 The London
South Ash Manor Estate, Ash, Nr Sevenoaks, Kent TN15 7EN
☎ (01474) 879899, Fax 879912
Off A20 near Brands Hatch at W Kingsdown.
Parkland course.
Pro K Morgan/Paul Way is touring pro; Founded 1993
Designed by Jack Nicklaus
Heritage: 18 holes, 7208 yards, S.S.S. 72
International: 18 holes, 7005 yards, S.S.S. 74
🏌 Welcome only if accompanied by a member.
▯ Heritage: WD £50; WE £60.
International: WD £40; WE £45.
🛒 Corporate days arranged.
🏮 Restaurant, bar, function rooms and coffee shop.
🛏 Brands Hatch Thistle; Brands Hatch Place.

1A 95 London Scottish
Windmill Enclosure, Wimbledon Common, London SW19 5NQ
☎ (020) 8788 0135, Fax 8789 7517, Pro 8789 1207
1 mile from Putney station.
Parkland course.
Pro Steve Barr; Founded 1865
18 holes, 5458 yards, S.S.S. 66
🏌 Welcome WD, except BH; must wear red upper garment.
▯ WD £15
🛒 Welcome except WE, Mon; terms on application.
🏮 Lunch served, dinner if ordered.
🛏 Wayfarer.

1A 96 Lullingstone Park
Park Gate, Chelsfield, Orpington, Kent BR6 7PX
☎ (01959) 533793, Bar/Rest 532928
Signposted from M25 Junction 4.
Municipal parkland course.
Pro Mark Watt; Founded 1923
Designed by Fred Hawtree
18 holes, 6779 yards, S.S.S. 72
9 hole, 2432 yards
🏌 Welcome.
▯ WD £10.50; WE £13.
🛒 Welcome by prior arrangement; terms on application.
🏮 Bar, snacks; meals ordered.
Practice range, 32 bays; floodlit.
🛏 Thistle (Brands Hatch).

1A 97 Lydd ☎
Romney Road, Lydd, Romney Marsh, Kent TN29 9LS
☎ (01797) 320808, Pro 321201
Take Ashford exit off M20 and follow A2070 signs to Lydd Airport. At Brenzett turn left and take B2075, club is on left.
Links type course.
Pro Andrew Jones; Founded 1993
Designed by M Smith
18 holes, 6517 yards, S.S.S. 71
🏌 Welcome.
▯ WD £17; WE £23.
🛒 Welcome only by prior appointment; terms available on application.
🏮 Bar and restaurant.
Practice range, 25 bays; floodlit.

1A 98 Malden
Traps Lane, New Malden, Surrey KT3 4RS
☎ (020) 8942 0654, Fax 8336 2219, Pro 8942 6009, Bar/Rest 8942 3266
0.5 miles from New Malden station, close to the A3 between Wimbledon and Kingston.
Parkland course.
Pro Robert Hunter; Founded 1926
18 holes, 6295 yards, S.S.S. 70
🏌 Welcome WD; WE restrictions.
▯ WD £27.50; WE £50.
🛒 Wed, Thurs, Fri only.
🏮 Full clubhouse facilities.
🛏 Kingston Lodge.

1A 99 Marriott Tudor ☎
Park Hotel & CC
☎ (01622) 734334
Ashford Rd, Bearsted, Maidstone, Kent ME14 4NQ
Follow A20 Ashford road; 3 miles from Maidstone centre.
Parkland course.
Pro Nick McNally, Founded 1988
Designed by Donald Steel
18 holes, 6041 yards, S.S.S. 69
🏌 Welcome with handicap certs.
▯ WD £25; WE £35.
🛒 Welcome WD by appointment.
🏮 Hotel bar and restaurant.
🛏 Marriott Tudor Park.

1A 100 Merrist Wood ☎
Coombe Lane, Worplesdon, Guildford, Surrey GU3 3PE
☎ (01483) 884045, Pro 884050, Bar/Rest 884048
Off A323 at Worplesdon.
Parkland/woodland course.
Pro Andrew Kirk; Founded 1997
Designed by David Williams
18 holes, 6909 yards, S.S.S. 73
🏌 Welcome WDs.
▯ WD £35.
🛒 Welcome by appointment.
🏮 Bar and restaurant facilities.
🛏 Worplesdon Place.

1A 101 Mid-Kent
Singlewell Rd, Gravesend, Kent DA11 7RB

☎(01474) 568035, Fax 564218, Pro 332810, Bar/Rest 352387
On A227 after leaving A2 signposted Gravesend.
Parkland course.
Pro Mark Foreman; Founded 1909
Designed by Frank Pennink
18 holes, 6218 yards, S.S.S. 70
† Welcome WDs if members of a club with handicap certs; WE with member only.
Ⅼ WD £20; WE £12
⌁ Terms on application.
🍽 Full facilities.
⌐ Manor, Tolgate.

1A 102 **Milford**
Milford, Nr Guildford, Surrey GU8 5HS
☎(01483) 419200, Fax 419199, Pro 416291
From A3 take Milford exit and head for station.
Parkland course.
Pro Nick English; Founded 1993
Designed by Peter Alliss, Clive Clark
18 holes, 5960 yards, S.S.S. 69
† Welcome.
Ⅼ WD £20; WE £35.
⌁ Welcome; from £35.
🍽 Full clubhouse facilities.
⌐ Inn on the Lake.

1A 103 **Mitcham**
Carshalton Rd, Mitcham Junction, Surrey CR4 4HN
☎(020) 8648 1508, Pro 8640 4280, Sec 8648 4197
A237 off A23, by Mitcham Junction station.
Meadowland course.
Pro Jeff Godfrey; Founded 1886
18 holes, 5935 yards, S.S.S. 68
† Welcome by appointment WD; pm only at WE.
Ⅼ WD £14; WE £14.
⌁ Terms on application.
🍽 Full facilities.
⌐ Hilton.

1A 104 **Moatlands** ♺
Watermans Lane, Brenchley, Kent TN12 6ND
☎(01892) 724400, Fax 723300, Pro 724252
From A21 take B2160 to Paddock Wood travelling through Matfield.
Parkland course.
Pro Simon Wood; Founded 1993
Designed by K. Saito/Taiyo International
18 holes, 7060 yards, S.S.S. 74

† Welcome WD; pm at WE.
Ⅼ WD £29; WE £39.
⌁ Welcome Mon, Tues, Thurs; terms on application.
🍽 Clubhouse bar and restaurant.
⌐ Jarvis Pembury Resort.

1A 105 **Moore Place**
Portsmouth Rd, Esher, Surrey KT10 9LN
☎(01372) 463533, Fax 460274
On A3 Portsmouth road, 0.5 mile from centre of Easher towards Cobham.
Public undulating parkland course.
Pro David Allen; Founded 1926
Designed by David Allen
9 holes, 2148 yards, S.S.S. 30
† Welcome.
Ⅼ WD £5.80; WE £7.70
⌁ Welcome WD; terms on application.
🍽 Full facilities.
⌐ Haven.

1A 106 **Nevill**
Benhall Mill Rd, Tunbridge Wells, Kent TN2 5JW
☎(01892) 525818, Fax 517861, Pro 532941, Bar/Rest 517860
S of Tunbridge Wells on A21.
Parkland course.
Pro Paul Huggett; Founded 1914
Designed by C.K. Cotton
18 holes, 6349 yards, S.S.S. 70
† Welcome with handicap certs.
Ⅼ WD £25; WE £32.50.
⌁ Welcome Wed, Thurs; terms on application.
🍽 Full facilities.
⌐ Spa Hotel, Tunbridge Wells.

1A 107 **New Zealand GC**
Woodham Lane, Addlestone, Surrey KT15 3QD
☎(01932) 345049, Fax 342891, Pro 349619
On A245 from W Byfleet to Woking.
Wooded heathland course.
Pro V Evelvidge; Founded 1895
Designed by Muir-Ferguson/Simpson
18 holes, 6012 yards, S.S.S. 69
† Welcome by appointment.
Ⅼ Terms on application.
⌁ Welcome by appointment; terms on application.
🍽 Full facilities.

1A 108 **Nizels**
Nizels Lane, Hildenborough, Nr Tonbridge, Kent TN11 8NU

☎(01732) 833138, Fax 833764, Pro 838926
Take the A21 southbound from M24 Junction 5; then take the B245 towards Tonbridge. At roundabout head for Hildenborough and the first right is Nizels Lane.
Parkland course.
Pro Brendan Wynne; Founded 1992
Designed by Lennan/Purnell
18 holes, 6297 yards, S.S.S. 71
† Welcome except am WE.
Ⅼ WD £40; WE £45.
⌁ Welcome by prior arrangement; minimum 12.
🍽 Full facilities and bar.
⌐ Rose & Crown, Tonbridge; Philpots Manor, Hildenborough.

1A 109 **North Downs**
Northdown Rd, Woldingham, Surrey CR3 7AA
☎(01883) 652057, Fax 652832, Pro 652004, Sec 652298, Bar/Rest 652027
Travel 2 miles north of the M25 Junction 6 to the roundabout, take the 5th exit to Woldingham (2miles); the clubhouse is 0.5 mile through village on left.
Downland course.
Pro Mike Homewood; Founded 1899
Designed by J.J. Pennink
18 holes, 5843 yards, S.S.S. 68
† Welcome WD with handicap certs or prior enquiry to manager.
Ⅼ WD £20; WE £12 (with member).
⌁ WD, half or full day (half-day only Thurs); terms available on application.
🍽 Restaurant, snacks.
⌐ Lodge Road Chef (M25).

1A 110 **North Foreland**
Convent Rd, Broadstairs, Kent CT10 3PU
☎(01843) 862140, Fax 862663, Pro 604471
A28 from Canterbury, or A2/M2/A299 from London to Kingsgate to Broadstairs; course 1.5 miles from Broadstairs station.
Seaside/clifftop course.
Pro Neil Hansen; Founded 1903
Designed by Fowler and Simpson
18 holes, 6430 yards, S.S.S. 71
Short course: 18 holes, 1752 yards, par 3
† Prior booking, not Sun, Mon, Tues am; handicap certs required; short course unrestricted.
Ⅼ WD £27.50; WE £37.50; Short course: WD £6; WE £7.

⌖ Welcome by appointment; terms on application.
🍽 Full clubhouse facilities.
⌐ Castle Keep.

1A 111 **Oak Park**
Heath Lane, Crondall, Nr Farnham, Surrey GU10 5PB
☎ (01252) 850850, Fax 850851, Pro 850066
Course is 1.25 miles off the A287 Farnham-Odiham road; and 5 miles from M3 Junction 5.
Woodland course; also 9-hole Village parkland course.
Pro Gary Murton; Founded 1984
Designed by Patrick Dawson
18 holes, 6318 yards, S.S.S. 70
⚑ Welcome.
⌐ WD £20; WE £28; 9-hole course: WD £10; WE £12.
⌖ Welcome by appointment.
🍽 Conservatory bar, restaurant with cocktail bar.
⌐ Bishops Table; Bush, both Farnham.

1A 112 **Oaks Sports Centre**
Woodmansterne Rd, Carshalton, Surrey SM5 4AN
☎ (020) 8643 8363, Fax 8770 7303, Sec 8642 7103
Couse is on the B2032 past Carshalton Beeches station, the Oaks Sports Centre signposted N of the A2022, halfway between the A217 and the A237.
Public meadowland course.
Pro Craig Mitchell/Michael Pilkington; Founded 1972
Designed by Alphagreen
18 holes, 6033 yards, S.S.S. 69
⚑ Welcome.
⌐ WD £13.50; WE £16.
⌖ Welcome by appointment; terms on application.
🍽 Restaurant and bar.

1A 113 **Oastpark**
Malling Rd, Snodland, Kent ME6 5LG
☎ (01634) 242818, Fax 240744, Pro 242661, Bar/Rest 242659
On A228 close to M20 Junction 4 and M2 Junction 2.
Parkland course.
Pro David Porthouse; Founded 1992
Designed by Terry Cullen
18 holes, 5220 yards, S.S.S. 66
⚑ Welcome.
⌐ WD £10; WE £14.
⌖ Welcome WD and after 11am at WE; minimum 8; from £15.

🍽 Full clubhouse facilities.
⌐ Swan; Larkfield Priory; Forte Crest.

1A 114 **Pachesham Golf Centre**
Oaklawn Road, Leatherhead, Surrey KT22 0BT
☎ (01372) 843453, Fax 844076
M25 Junction 9; A244 towards Esher.
Parkland course.
Pro Phil Taylor; Founded 1992
Designed by Phil Taylor
9 holes, 5608 yards, S.S.S. 67
⚑ Welcome; book 48 hours ahead.
⌐ WD £9; WE £10.50.
⌖ Welcome by appointment; terms on application.
🍽 Full facilities.
⌐ Woodlands Park.

1A 115 **Park Wood**
Chestnut Avenue, Westerham, Kent TN16 2EG
☎ (01959) 577744, Fax 572702
From the centre of Westerham take Oxted Road then turn right into Croydon Road, go under M25 to small crossroads; course is right and immediate right.
Parkland and lakes course.
Pro Nick Terry; Founded 1993
Designed by L Smith & R Goldsmith
18 holes, 6835 yards, S.S.S. 72
⚑ Welcome.
⌐ WD £20; WE £30.
⌖ Welcome Mon-Fri.
🍽 120-seat restaurant, Full bar.
⌐ Kings Arms (Westerham).

1A 116 **Pine Ridge Golf Centre**
Old Bisley Rd, Frimley, Camberley, Surrey GU16 5NX
☎ (01276) 675444
5 mins from M3 Junction 3; location map available on request.
Public pine-forested course.
Pro Peter Sefdon; Founded 1992
Designed by Clive D. Smith
18 holes, 6012 yards, S.S.S. 71
⚑ Welcome.
⌐ WD £19; WE £24.
⌖ Welcome WD, min 12; terms on application.
🍽 Bar and restaurant, all day.
⌐ Lakeside; Frimley Hall.

1A 117 **Poult Wood**
Higham Lane, Tonbridge, Kent TN11 9QR

☎ (01732) 364039, Bar/Rest 366180
Course is 1 mile N of Tonbridge off the A227.
Municipal wooded course.
Pro Chris Miller; Founded 1972
Designed by Fred Hawtree
18 holes, 5569 yards, S.S.S. 67
⚑ Welcome; booking required.
⌐ WD £11.30; WE £16.50.
9 holes, 1281 yards; ⌐ WD £4.90; WE £6.40.
⌖ Welcome WD by appointment; terms on application.
🍽 Restaurant and bar.
⌐ Langley; Rose & Crown.

1A 118 **Prince's**
Sandwich Bay, Sandwich, Kent CT13 9QB
☎ (01304) 611118, Fax 612000, Pro 613797
M2, A2 to A256 then follow signs for Sandwich; course signposted.
3 loops of 9 holes; links course.
Pro Derek Barber, Founded 1904
Designed by Sir Guy Campbell & John Morrison
18 holes, 6690 yards, S.S.S. 72
⚑ Welcome.
⌐ WD £38; WE £44.50.
⌖ Welcome by appointment.
🍽 Spike bar; restaurant (shirt and tie required).
⌐ The Bell; The Blazing Donkey, Ham; Royal, Deal.

1A 119 **Purley Downs**
106 Purley Downs Road, South Croydon, Surrey CR2 0RB
☎ (020) 8657 1231, Fax 8651 5044, Pro 8651 0819, Sec 8657 8347
3 miles S of Croydon on A235.
Downland course.
Pro Graham Wilson; Founded 1894
18 holes, 6275 yards, S.S.S. 70
⚑ Welcome WD. WE with members.
⌐ WD £24; WE £15.
⌖ Welcome Mon, Thurs; terms on application.
🍽 19th hole bar, lounge bar and restaurant.
⌐ Selsdon Park; Trust House Forte; Croydon Hilton.

1A 120 **Puttenham**
Heath Rd, Puttenham, Guildford, Surrey GU31A L
☎ (01483) 810609, Fax 810988, Pro 810277, Sec 810498, Bar/Rest 811087
Off A31 Hogs Back at Puttenham sign (B3000).

Prince's

There can be few more blessed areas for golf than Sandwich Bay. Royal St George's, with all its splendour, was the first course outside Scotland to host the Open Championship.

To this day Royal St George's remains on the Open rota and suffers only because of the drain on the corporate pound around the time of Ryder Cups.

There is also Royal Cinque Port at nearby Deal which is a superb natural links course and another that hosted two early Open Championships and the wonderful Rye, which hosts the President's Putter each winter, just down the coast.

So Prince's sits in some pretty exalted company. To be special when surrounded by so many courses of great beauty is not an easy task.

So how does Prince's achieve it? On the face of it Prince's does not have the same stature as the other courses but there are some memorable features.

It is not surprisingly flat. The links course was originally designed by Sir H Mallaby-Deeley and P M Lucas and was first played early in the last century.

When it opened it was dominated by a massive range of sand dunes which ran across the centre of the course. With no great originality but a degree of realism they were called the Himalayas.

But after the Second World War, when Kent and its coast was heavily bombed, there was an urgent need to reconstruct the course and it did not re-emerge in its present form until 1948.

Then JSF Morrison and Sir Guy Campbell laid out 27 holes, as a result of which the course was no longer dominated by the giant sand dunes, but rather by wide flat fairways.

So the danger had passed? Well, not entirely. Now the flatness of the course was the golfer's concern. With a lack of visible landmarks and fast-running fairways and greens, judgment as well as accuracy is everything.

Kent, and in particular the Sandwich Bay area, offers a magnificent golfing break for those seeking a slice of history heavily laced with challenge. — **CG**

Tight heathland course.
Pro Gary Simmons; Founded 1894
18 holes, 6214 yards, S.S.S. 69
⚑ Welcome WD by prior
arrangement; with a member only at
WE.
▯ WD £23; WE £23.
⚲ Welcome Wed, Thurs, Fri; terms
on application.
🍽 Full catering and bar.
⌐ Hogs Back Hotel.

1A 121 **Pyrford**
Warren Lane, Pyrford, Woking,
Surrey GU22 8XR
☎ (01483) 723555, Fax 729777, Pro
750170
From A3 take Ripley/Wisley exit
(B2215) through Ripley, follow signs
for Pyrford.
Parkland course.
Pro Nick Sharratt; Founded 1993
Designed by Peter Alliss & Clive
Clark
18 holes, 6230 yards, S.S.S. 70
⚑ Welcome.
▯ WD £36; WE £52.
⚲ Welcome; from £45.
🍽 Full bar and catering.
⌐ Cobham Hilton.

1A 122 **RAC Country Club**
Woodcote Park, Epsom, Surrey KT18
7EW
☎ (01372) 276311
On the A24 1.75 miles from Epsom
Parkland courses.
Pro Ian Howieson Founded 1913
Coronation course: 18 holes, 6223
yds, S.S.S. 70
Old course: 18 holes, 6709 yds,
S.S.S. 72
⚑ with a member only.
▯ £23 Old Course; £19 Coronation
Course
⚲ WD only, terms available on
application.
🍽 Full facilities.

1A 123 **Redhill & Reigate**
Clarence Lodge, Pendleton Rd,
Redhill, Surrey RH1 6LB
☎ (01737) 240777, Fax 240777, Pro
244433, Bar/Rest 244626
1 mile S of Redhill between A23 and
A25.
Wooded parkland course.
Pro Warren Pike; Founded 1887
Designed by James Braid
18 holes, 5272 yards, S.S.S. 68
⚑ Welcome WD and after 11am at
WE.

▯ WD £12; WE £18.
⚲ Welcome by prior arrangement;
packages available; from £37.50.
🍽 Full facilities.
⌐ Reigate Manor.

1A 124 **Redlibbets**
Manor Lane, West Yoke, Ash,
Sevenoaks, Kent TN15 7HT
☎ (01474) 872278, Fax 879290,
Sec 879190
Take the A20 exit from the M25
towards Brands Hatch, course is on
Paddock side next to Fawkham
Manor Hospital, 8 miles from
Sevenoaks.
Parkland course.
Pro Ross Taylor; Founded 1996
Designed by J Gaunt
18 holes, 6639 yards, S.S.S. 72
⚑ Welcome with a member.
▯ WD £28.50 (without a member),
WD £15; WE £25.
⚲ Tues, Thurs; terms available on
application.
🍽 Full facilities.
⌐ Brands Hatch Place.

1A 125 **Reigate Heath**
Reigate Heath, Reigate, Surrey RH2
8QR
☎ (01737) 242610, Fax 226793, Pro
243077, Sec 226793, Bar/Rest
226793
1.5 miles W of Reigate on Flanchford
Road off A25.
Heathland course.
Pro Barry Davies; Founded 1895
9 holes, 5658 yards, S.S.S. 67
⚑ Welcome in midweek.
▯ WD £18; WE n/a.
⚲ Wed, Thurs; max 30; terms on
application.
🍽 Full facilities.
⌐ Cranleigh Hotel, Reigate.

1A 126 **Reigate Hill**
Gatton Bottom, Reigate, Surrey RH2
0TU
☎ (01737) Fax 642650, Sec 645577,
Pro 646070
Course is 1 mile from Junction 8 of
the M25.
Parkland course.
Pro Martin Platts; Founded 1995
Designed by D Williams
18 holes, 6175 yards, S.S.S. 70
⚑ WD, WE after 12pm.
▯ WD £25; WE £35.
⚲ Welcome by appointment; terms
on application.
🍽 Full facilities.

⌐ Bridge House, Reigate Hill; The
Priory, Nutfield.

1A 127 **Richmond**
Sudbrook Park, Richmond, Surrey
TW10 7AS
☎ (020) 8940 1463, Pro 8940 7792,
Sec 8940 4351
On A307 1 mile S of Richmond, look
for Sudbrook Lane on left.
Parkland course.
Pro Nick Job; Founded 1891
Designed by Tom Dunn
18 holes, 5785 yards, S.S.S. 69
⚑ WD by appointment. WE with
members.
▯ WD £27; WE £25.
⚲ Tues, Thurs, Fri by appointment;
terms on application.
🍽 Bar snacks, lunches every day.
⌐ Petersham; Richmond Gate.

1A 128 **Richmond Park**
Roehampton Gate, Richmond Park,
London SW15 5JR
☎ (020) 8876 3205, Fax 8878 1354,
Pro 8876 1795
Inside Richmond Park; enter through
Roehampton Gate off Priory Road.
Parkland courses.
Pro David Bown; Founded 1923
Designed by Hawtree & Sons
Dukes's: 18 holes, 6036 yards, S.S.S.
68
Prince's: 18 holes, 5868 yards, S.S.S.
67
⚑ Pay and play course.
▯ WD £14; WE £17.50.
⚲ Welcome.
🍽 None.
⌐ Richmond Gate Hotel.

1A 129 **The Ridge**
Chartway St, East Sutton, Maidstone,
Kent ME17 3DL
☎ (01622) 844382, Fax 844168, Pro
844243
From M20 Junction 8 take B2163 to
Sutton Valence.
Old apple orchards.
Pro Matthew Rackham; Founded
1993
Designed by Tryton Design Ltd
18 holes, 6254 yards, S.S.S. 70
⚑ Handicap certs required; midweek
only.
▯ WD £30; WE £18 (pm, with
members only).
⚲ Tues, Thurs, welcome by prior
appointment; golf and catering; £35-
£57.
🍽 Full catering facilities.

1A 130 **Riverside**
Summerton Way, Thamesmead SE28 8PP
☎(020) 8310 7975
Course is off te A2, 10 mins from Blackheath, 15 mins from Bexleyheath; near Woolwich.
Pay-as-you-play course on reclaimed marshland.
Pro Mark Nicholls; Founded 1991
Designed by Heffernan & Heffernan
9 holes, 5482 yards
† Welcome subject to reasonable standard of golf.
▯ WD £6.50; WE £8.50.
⌁Welcome by appointment WD, only small societies WE; terms on application.
▮❙ 2 bars, à la carte.
Practice range, 30 bays floodlit.
↝ Black Prince (Bexleyheath); Swallow.

1A 131 **Rochester & Cobham Park**
Park Pale by Rochester, Kent ME2 3UL
☎(01474) 823411, Fax 824446, Pro 823658, Bar/Rest 823412
3 miles E of Gravesend east exit off A2.
Parkland course.
Pro Iain Higgins
Founded 1891/1997
Designed by Donald Steel
18 holes, 6596 yards, S.S.S. 71
† WD with handicap certs; WE with member only.
▯ WD £30; WE £30.
⌁Tues and Thurs; packages available; £39-£60.
▮❙ Full catering facilities.
↝ Inn on the Lake, A2; Tolgate Motel, Gravesend.

1A 132 **Roehampton**
Roehampton Lane, London, SW15 5LR
☎(020) 8480 4200 Fax 8392 2386, Pro 8876 3858, Sec 8876 5505, Bar/Rest 8876 2037
Just off the South Circular road between Sheen and Putney.
Private members parkland course.
Pro Alan Scott; Founded 1901
18 holes, 6011 yards, S.S.S. 69
† Members' guests only.
▯ WD £20; WE £26.
⌁Welcome by members' introduction only; terms available on application.
▮❙ Restaurant, buttery, bar and 3 function rooms.

1A 133 **Roker Park**
Holly Lane, Aldershot Rd, Guildford, Surrey GU3 3PB
☎(01483) 236677, Fax 232324, Sec 232324, Bar/Rest 237700
2 miles W of Guildford on A323.
Parkland course.
Pro Kevin Warn; Founded 1992
Designed by W.V. Roker
9 holes, 6074 yards, S.S.S. 72
† Public pay and play course.
▯ WD £7.50; WE £9.
⌁WD preferable; minimum 12; WD £12; WE £15.
▮❙ Facilities available.

1A 134 **Romney Warren**
St Andrews Rd, Littlestone, New Romney, Kent TN28 8RB
☎(01797) Pro 362231, Bar/Rest 366613
Take A259 to New Romney, turn right into Littlestone Road and after 0.5 miles into St Andrews Road.
Links course.
Pro Stephen Watkins; Founded 1993
Designed by J.D. Lewis, B.M. Evans
18 holes, 5126 yards, S.S.S. 65
† Welcome with booking.
▯ WD £13; WE £18.
⌁Apply at Pro shop; from £13.

1A 135 **Royal Blackheath**
Court Rd, Eltham, London SE9 0LR
☎(020) 8850 1795, Fax 8859 0150, Pro 8850 1763, Bar/Rest 8850 1042
Junction 3 M25-A20 to London; 2nd lights turn rt; club is 600 yards on right.
Parkland course; oldest known golf club in the world.
Pro Ian McGregor; Founded 1608
Designed by James Braid
18 holes, 6219 yards, S.S.S. 70
† Welcome midweek by arrangement/ handicap cert; WE only with member.
▯ WD £35; WE nominal fee.
⌁Welcome Wed-Fri by appointment; from £65.
▮❙ Full catering and bar facilities.
↝ Bromley Court, Bromley; Clarendon, Blackheath.

1A 136 **Royal Cinque Ports**
Golf Rd, Deal, Kent CT14 6RF
☎(01304) 374007, Fax 379530 Pro 374170, Sec 367856
Follow coast road through Deal to end and turn left on to Goldwyn Rd, at the end turn right on to Golf Rd.
Seaside links.

Pro Andrew Reynolds; Founded 1892
Designed by Tom Dunn, Guy Campbell
18 holes, 6754 yards, S.S.S. 72
† Welcome WD; WE by appointment; handicap certs required.
▯ WD £60; WE £70.
⌁Welcome WD by prior appointment; terms available on application.
▮❙ Full facilities, dress code required.
↝ Royal; Kings Head, both Deal; Bell, Sandwich.

1A 137 **Royal Mid-Surrey**
Old Deer Park, Richmond, Surrey TW9 2SB
☎(020) 8940 1894, Fax 8332 2957, Pro 8940 0459
On A316 300 yards before the Richmond roundabout heading to London.
Parkland courses.
Pro Phillip Talbot; Founded 1892
Designed by J.H. Taylor
Inner: 18 holes, 5544 yards, S.S.S. 68
Outer: 18 holes, 6385 yards, S.S.S. 68
† WDs with handicap cert; WE only with a member.
▯ WD £63; WE (for member's guests only) £22.
⌁Contact Sec; terms available on application.
▮❙ Lunches served every day except Mon; bar and snacks available.
↝ Richmond Hill; Richmond Gate.

1A 138 **Royal St George's**
Sandwich, Kent CT13 9PB
☎(01304) 613090 Fax 611245, Pro 615236
2 miles E of Sandwich on road to Sandwich Bay.
Open Championship course 1993; Links course.
Pro Andrew Brooks; Founded 1887
Designed by Dr Laidlaw Purves
18 holes, 6610 yards, S.S.S. 72
† Welcome midweek but with maximum 18 handicap; certificate required.
▯ WD £65-£90 per day.
⌁Mon, Tues, Wed, but not mid-July to end of August; £115.
▮❙ Full facilities.

1A 139 **Royal Wimbledon**
29 Camp Rd, Wimbledon SW19 4UW
☎(020) 8946 2125

0.75 mile of War Memorial in Wimbledon village.
Parkland course.
Pro Hugh Boyle; Founded 1865
18 holes, 6362 yards, S.S.S. 70
⚑ Members only.
⚐ Wed, Thurs only; terms on application.
🍽 Full facilities.
⌂ Wayfarer Hotel.

1A 140 **Rusper**
Rusper Rd, Newdigate, Surrey RH5 5BX
☎ (01293) 871871
M25 exit 9 and A24 towards Dorking, follow signs to Newdigate and Rusper.
Parkland course.
Pro Janice Arnold; Founded 1992
Designed by S. Hood
18 holes, 6218 yards, S.S.S. 69
⚑ Welcome.
⚐ WD £11.50; WE £15.50
🍽 Bar and snacks
⌂ Ghyll Manor, Rusper.

1A 141 **Ruxley**
Sandy Lane, St Paul's Cray, Orpington, Kent BR5 3HY
☎ (01689) 839677, Fax 891428, Pro 871490, Bar/Rest 871490
M20 exit 1, follow signs to St Pauls Cray and then signs to course.
Parkland course.
Pro Paul Deeprose; Founded 1973
Designed by Gilbert Lloyd
18 holes, 5712 yards, S.S.S. 68
⚑ Public pay and play.
⚐ WD £15; WE £20.
⚐ Welcome; terms available on application.
🍽 Facilities available.

1A 142 **St Augustine's**
Cottington Rd, Cliffsend, Ramsgate, Kent CT12 5JN
☎ (01843) 590333, Fax 590444, Pro 590222
On B2048 off Ramsgate to Sandwich road.
Parkland course.
Pro Derek Scott; Founded 1907
Designed by Tom Vardon
18 holes, 5282 yards, S.S.S. 66
⚑ Welcome with handicap certs.
⚐ WD £21.50; WE £23.50.
⚐ Welcome by appointment; from £25-£40.
🍽 Clubhouse facilities.
⌂ Jarvis Marine, Ramsgate; Blazing Donkey, Ham.

1A 143 **St George's Hill**
St George's Hill, Weybridge, Surrey KT13 0NL
☎ (01932) 847758, Fax 821564, Pro 843523
B374 towards Cobham, 0.5 miles from station.
Wooded heathland courses.
Pro A C Rattue; Founded 1913
Designed by H.S. Colt
18 holes, 6569 yards, S.S.S. 71
⚑ Welcme Wed, Thurs, Fri by prior appointment.
⚐ WD £65.
⚐ Wed, Thurs, Fri only; £100-£110.
🍽 Full facilities available.
⌂ Oatlands Park Hotel; Hilton, Cobham.

1A 144 **Sandown Golf Centre**
More Lane, Esher, Surrey KT10 8AN
☎ (01372) 461234
In centre of Sandown Park racecourse.
Parkland course.
Pro Cronfield Golf Academy; Founded 1967
Designed by John Jacobs
9 holes, 5656 yards, S.S.S. 67
⚑ Welcome.
⚐ WD £6.25; WE £8.
⚐ Welcome.
🍽 Facilities available.
⌂ Haven Hotel, Sandown.

1A 145 **Selsdon Park Hotel & GC** ♛
Addington Road, Sanderstead, South Croydon, Surrey CR2 8YA
☎ (020) 8657 8811 x 659, Fax 8657 3401, Pro 8657 8811 x 694, Sec 8657 8811, Bar/Rest 8657 8811
Take A2022 towards Selsdon. Hotel entrance is 0.5 miles opposite junction with Upper Selsdon Road.
Parkland/downland course.
Pro Malcolm Churchill; Founded 1929
Designed by J.H. Taylor
18 holes, 6473 yards, S.S.S. 71
⚑ Welcome by prior arrangement.
⚐ WD £27.50; WE £32.50.
⚐ Welcome by prior arrangement; terms on application.
🍽 Catering in hotel.
⌂ Selsdon Park.

1A 146 **Sene Valley**
Sene, Folkestone, Kent CT18 8BL
☎ (01303) 268513, Fax 237513, Pro 268514
M20 Junction 12, take A 20 towards Ashford and left at 1st roundabout.

Downland course.
Pro Nick Watson; Founded 1888
Designed by Henry Cotton
18 holes, 6196 yards, S.S.S. 69
⚑ Welcome with handicap certs.
⚐ WD £20; WE £25.
⚐ Wed,Thurs, Fri only; £45.
🍽 Catering and bar facilities.
⌂ Sunny Bank House.

1A 147 **Sheerness**
Power Station Rd, Sheerness, Kent ME12 3AE
☎ (01795) 662585, Fax 666840, Pro 666840
M2/M20 to A249 to Sheerness
Seaside course.
Pro Dayne Hawkins; Founded 1906
18 holes, 6460 yards, S.S.S. 71
⚑ WD welcome; WE with a member.
⚐ WD £18; WE £18.
⚐ Welcome WD by prior arrangement; from £34.
🍽 Clubhouse bar and catering facilities available.
⌂ Kingsferry GH, Isle of Sheppey.

1A 148 **Shillinglee Park** ♛
Chiddingfold, Godalming, Surrey GU8 4TA
☎ (01428) 653237, Fax 644391
Leave A3 at Milford, S on A283 to Chiddingfold; at top end of green turn left along local road, then after 2 miles turn right signposted Shillinglee; entrance to course on left after 0.5 mile.
Public undulating parkland course.
Pro David Parkinson; Founded 1980
Designed by Roger Mace
9 holes, 2516 yards, S.S.S. 64
⚑ Welcome, book in advance.
⚐ WD £8.50; WE £9.50.
⚐ Welcome; terms on application.
🍽 Bar and restaurant 8.30am-6pm (3pm Sun); evening meals and parties by arrangement.
⌂ Lythe Hill.

1A 149 **Shirley Park**
194 Addiscombe Rd, Croydon, Surrey CR0 7LB
☎ (020) 8654 1143, Fax 8654 6733, Pro 8654 8767
On A232 1 mile E of E Croydon station.
Parkland course.
Pro Raith Grant; Founded 1914
18 holes, 6210 yards, S.S.S. 70
⚑ Welcome WD; with a member only at WE.
⚐ WD £30; WE £16.

WD except Wed; £51.50.
Full catering and bar.

1A 150 Shooters Hill
Lowood, Eaglesfield Rd, London
SE18 3DA
(020) 8854 6368, Fax 8854 0469,
Pro 8854 0073
Just past water tower on A207
Shooters Hill.
Hilly parkland/woodland course.
Pro Dave Brotherton; Founded 1903
18 holes, 5721 yards, S.S.S. 68
Welcome WD with handicap cert.
WD £22.
Tues, Thurs only; terms on
application.
Full clubhouse facilities.
Clarendon, Blackheath.

1A 151 Shortlands
Meadow Road, Shortlands, Kent BR2
0PB
(020) 8460 2471, Pro 8464 6182
2 miles S of Bromley.
Parkland course.
Pro John Murray; Founded 1894
9 holes, 5261 yards, S.S.S. 66
With member only and handicap
cert.
£10.
By arrangement; terms on
application.
Bar and catering.

1A 152 Sidcup
7 Hurst Rd, Sidcup, Kent DA15 9AE
(020) Pro 8309 0679, Sec 8300
2150
A222 off A2, 400 yards N of station.
Parkland course.
Pro Nigel Willis; Founded 1891
Designed by James Braid And H.
Myrtle
9 holes, 5722 yards, S.S.S. 68
Welcome; WE with member only;
handicap certs required, smart casual
dress.
WD £18.
Welcome; terms on application.
Bar, restaurant, except Mon.
Bickley Arms; Swallow.

1A 153 Silvermere
Redhill Rd, Cobham, Surrey KT11
1EF
(01932) 867275, Fax 868259, Pro
866894
At Junction 10 of M25 and A3 take
A245 to Byfleet; Silvermere is 0.5
mile.

Parkland course.
Pro Doug McClelland; Founded 1976
18 holes, 6377 yards, S.S.S. 71
Welcome WD; WE by appointment
from Apr-Oct.
WD £20; WE £30.
Welcome WD; terms on
application.
Bar, restaurant.
Bickley Arms; Swallow.

1A 154 Sittingbourne & Milton Regis
Wormdale, Newington, Sittingbourne,
Kent ME9 7PX
(01795) 842261
1 mile N of exit 5 off M2 on A249.
Undulating course.
Pro John Hearn; Founded 1929
Designed by Harry Hunter
18 holes, 6279 yards, S.S.S. 70
Welcome WD if carrying handicap
certs.
WD £22.
Welcome Tues and Thurs; terms
on application.
Facilities available.
Coniston, Sittingbourne;
Newington Manor.

1A 155 Staplehurst Park
Craddock Lane, Staplehurst, Kent
TN12 0DR
(01580) 893362
Course lies 9 miles south of
Maidstone on the A229 Hastings
Road, turning on to Headcorn Road
at Staplehurst and then right into
Craddock Lane.
Parkland course.
Founded 1993
Designed by John Sayner
12 holes, 5417 yards, S.S.S. 67
Welcome.
WD £11; WE £13.
Welcome except Sun; terms on
application.
Bar and snacks.
Bell Inn.

1A 156 Sunbury
Charlton Lane, Shepperton,
Middlesex TW17 8QA
(01932) 770298, Pro 772898
2 miles from M3 Junction 1.
Public parkland course.
Pro Alistair Hardaway
27 holes, 5103 yards, S.S.S. 65
Welcome; no restrictions.
WD £14; WE £20.
Welcome by appointment; terms
on application.

Bar and restaurant facilities in
16th century clubhouse.
Warren Lodge Hotel, Moat
House.

1A 157 Sundridge Park
Garden Rd, Bromley, Kent BR1 3NE
(020) 8460 0278, Fax 8289
3050, Pro 8460 5540, Bar/Rest
8460 3060
N of Bromley on A2212.
Parkland courses.
Pro Bob Cameron; Founded 1901
Designed by Willie Park
East: 18 holes, 6538 yards, S.S.S. 71
West: 18 holes, 6016 yards, S.S.S.
69
Welcome WD; WE only with a
member.
WD £40; WE £40.
Welcome WD by prior
appointment; terms available on
application.
Full catering and bar.

1A 158 Sunningdale
Ridgemount Rd, Sunningdale, Surrey
SL5 9RR
(01344) 621681, Fax 624154, Pro
620128
From M3 Junction 3 or M 25 Junction
13; take A30.
Heathland courses.
Pro Keith Maxwell; Founded 1900
Designed by H S Colt
New: 18 holes, 6083 yards, S.S.S. 70
Old: 18 holes, 6094 yards, S.S.S. 69
Mon-Thurs only; with max 18
handicap and letter of introduction.
WD £75 (New); £105 (Old); £130
(both).
Tues, Wed, Thurs only; min 20
players, max 20 handicap; £175.
Full catering and bar.

1A 159 Sunningdale Ladies
Cross Rd, Sunningdale, Surrey SL5
9RX
(01344) 620507
S of A30 600 yards W of Sunningdale
level crossing.
Heathland course.
Founded 1902
Designed by Edward Villiers/H S Colt
18 holes, 3616 yards, S.S.S. 60
Welcome with handicap certs but
not before 11am at WE.
WD £18 (men £20); WE £22 (men
£27).
Ladies societies only; terms on
application.
Full facilities, not Sundays.

1A 160 **Surbiton**
Woodstock Lane, Chessington,
Surrey KT9 1UG
☎(020) 8398 3101, Fax 8339 0992
From the A3 westbound, take the
Esher/Chessington turn-off, turn left
to Claygate, and the club is 400 yards
on right.
Parkland course.
Pro Paul Milton; Founded 1896
18 holes, 6055 yards, S.S.S. 69
† Welcome WD only; handicap certs
required; members' guests only at
WE.
⌙ WD £30; WE £17.
⌀Welcome by prior arrangement;
terms on application.
🍴 Full facilities.
⌐ Haven, Esher; Travelodge.

1A 161 **Sutton Green** ⓣ
New Lane, Sutton Green, Nr
Guildford, Surrey GU4 7QF
☎(01483) 747898, Fax 750289, Pro
766849
Midway between Guildford and
Woking on A320.
Parkland course with water features.
Pro Tim Dawson; Founded 1994
Designed by Laura Davies and D
Walker
18 holes, 6400 yards, S.S.S. 70
† WD; after 1pm at WE.
⌙ WD £30; WE £40.
⌀Welcome WD; packages
available; from £29.50.
🍴 Full catering and bar.
Practice range; grass covered driving
range.
⌐ Forte Post House, Guildford;
Cobham Hilton; Worplesdon Place.

1A 162 **Tandridge**
Oxted, Surrey RH8 9NQ
☎(01883) 712274, Fax 730537, Pro
713701, Bar/Rest 712273
From M25 Junction 6, take A22 and
then A25.
Parkland course.
Pro Chris Evans; Founded 1924
Designed by H.S. Colt
18 holes, 6250 yards, S.S.S. 70
† Welcome Mon, Wed, Thurs.
⌙ WD £49.
⌀Welcome Mon, Wed, Thurs;
£72.50.
🍴 Full clubhouse facilities.

1A 163 **Tenterden**
Woodchurch Rd, Tenterden, Kent
TN30 7DR
☎(01580) 763987, Fax 763987

Take A28 to Tenterden and at St
Michaels take B2067.
Woodland course.
Pro Kyle Kerlsall; Founded 1905
18 holes, 6152 yards, S.S.S. 69
† Welcome by appointment. with
member at WE.
⌙ WD £22; WE £15.
⌀Contact Sec J M Wilson; terms on
application.
🍴 Catering facilities and bar.
⌐ White Lion; Little Silver.

1A 164 **Thames Ditton & Esher**
Scilly Isles, Portsmouth Rd, Esher,
Surrey KT10 9AL
☎(020) Pro 8398 1551
Off A3 by Scilly Isles roundabout
(0.25 mile from Sandown Park Race
Course).
Parkland course.
Pro Mark Rodbard; Founded 1892
9 holes, 2537 yards, S.S.S. 33
† Welcome Mon-Sat and Sun pm.
⌙ WD £12; WE £14
⌀Max 28 booked in advance with
Sec; terms on application.
🍴 Bar and snacks available.

1A 165 **Tunbridge Wells**
Langton Rd, Tunbridge Wells, Kent
TN4 8XH
☎(01892) Pro 541386, Sec 536918,
Bar/Rest 523034
Behind Marchants Garage next to
Spa Hotel.
Undulating parkland course.
Pro Mike Barton; Founded 1889
9 holes, 4728 yards, S.S.S. 62
† Welcome.
⌙ WD £15; WE £25.
⌀Contact Sec; terms on application.
🍴 By arrangement.
⌐ Spa; Periquito; Royal Wells.

1A 166 **Tyrrells Wood**
The Drive, Tyrrells Wood,
Leatherhead, Surrey KT22 8QP
☎(01372) 376025, Fax 360836, Pro
375200, Bar/Rest 360702
2 miles SE of Leatherhead off the
A24; M25 Junction 9 1 mile.
Undulating parkland.
Pro Max Tayler; Founded 1924
Designed by James Braid
18 holes, 6063 yards, S.S.S. 70
† Welcome WD.
⌙ WD £34.
⌀Welcome by appointment; from
£37.
🍴 Full clubhouse facilities.

1A 167 **Upchurch River Valley**
Oak Lane, Upchurch, Sittingbourne,
Kent ME9 7AY
☎(01634) 360626, Fax 387784, Pro
379592
From M2 Junction 4 take A278
Gillingham road; then A2 for 2.5 miles
towards Rainham.
Moorland/seaside courses.
Pro Roger Cornwell; Founded 1991
Designed by David Smart
18 holes, 6237 yards, S.S.S. 70
9 holes, 3192 yards, par 60
† Welcome; book 2 days in
advance.
⌙ WD £10.95; WE £13.95.
⌀Welcome WD; min of 12 in party;
terms on application.
🍴 Restaurant and bar facilities
available.
⌐ Newington Manor; Rank Motor
Lodge.

1A 168 **Walmer & Kingsdown** ⓣ
The Leas, Kingsdown, Deal, Kent
CT14 8EP
☎(01304) 373256, Fax 363017, Pro
363017, Bar/Rest 374832
Off A258 Dover to Deal road; follow
signs to Kingsdown from Ringwould,
signposted thereon.
Downland course with panoramic
views of English Channel.
Pro M Paget; Founded 1909
Designed by James Braid
18 holes, 6444 yards, S.S.S. 71
† Welcome by appointment with
Pro.
⌙ WD £25; WE £30.
⌀Welcome by appointment; terms
on application.
🍴 Full catering and bar.

1A 169 **Walton Heath**
Off Deans Lane, Walton-on-the-Hill,
Tadworth, Surrey KT20 7TP
☎(01737) 812380, Fax 814225, Pro
812152, Bar/Rest 813777
From the M25 exit at Junction 8 and
take the A217, London bound. After
the 2nd roundabout turn left into Mill
Road and at the next junction left into
Dorking Road. Deans Lane is 1.5
miles on right.
Heathland course.
Pro Ken MacPherson; Founded 1903
Designed by Herbert Fowler/James
Braid
Old: 18 holes, 6817 yards, S.S.S. 73
New: 18 holes 6609 yards S.S.S 72
† By appointment only.

Walton Heath

There are certain courses around Britain that just seep history. There is no doubt that the Old Course at Surrey's Walton Heath is just one of those clubs that will charm anyone fortunate enough to play this heathland course. The experience of the Herbert Fowler-designed course will never disappoint.

It was one of a number of outstanding courses that sprung up in the area just south of London at the turn of the 19th century. In many ways it resembles a seaside course in terms of lay-out, with its deep bunkers and big greens that always rate very highly with its American visitors.

It was never more welcoming to the Americans than in 1981, when Dave Marr's team completed one of the most comprehensive victories in the Ryder Cup on the course. The $18\frac{1}{2}$ to $9\frac{1}{2}$ victory was a margin that has never looked likely to be repeated since.

But there is no questioning the quality of that American side who strode imperiously around Walton Heath that weekend. Many argue that it was the finest side ever to be fielded in the Ryder Cup and when you consider the names and their form at the time it is very hard to disagree.

Marr had the luxury of putting out such giants of the game as Lee Trevino, who was to win all his matches, including two crushing victories over Sam Torrance, who was partnering the young Nick Faldo in the fourballs, and then again beating the Scotsman in the singles.

Faldo at least managed a singles victory, one of only three by the European team, against Johnny Miller. Fittingly for such a historic course it was to provide the showcase for Jack Nicklaus's last Ryder Cup as a player. He finished, as you would expect, in some style.

But his final 5 and 3 victory over Eamonn Darcy meant that he didn't get to play the punishing but distinctive finishing holes of the Walton Heath course. It is the 16th, 17th and 18th holes that give the Old Course at Walton Heath its true status. The 16th, which measures almost exactly 500 yards in the 6801-yard course, demands length and a fair degree of courage.

It is important that the drive is long and accurate to open up the green from a fairway that is guarded by tough heather and then, to the right, a series of bunkers. Add to that the fact that the green slopes left to right and also has a giant bunker, and it makes this a hole to test the most competent player.

It is followed by the short 17th which also has a huge bunker and then the 18th, where the green is defended by another huge bunker about 50 yards from the pin. Long at 412 yards, it can punish anything other than two long accurate shots.

The New Course, which is slightly shorter at 6700 yards, is also a more than adequate test and is also credited to Fowler's design. His original nine holes were transformed to create the New Course. — **CG**

Wentworth

Imposing on and off the golf course. That is how many see the home of the Volvo PGA and the end-of-season World Matchplay event, sponsored in the last couple of years by Cisco.

The long drive to the car park cuts in front of the first tee of the West Course and takes you past the clubhouse that looks like a mock castle. It is an area that exudes exclusivity and quality. Situated 21 miles south-west of London in Virginia Water in Surrey, Wentworth is more than just one classic course.

The championship course that graces the television screens every year is the West. It is no coincidence that the tournaments are held in the spring and autumn because that is undoubtedly when this tree-lined course is at its most colourful and most magnificent.

Many of the holes are familiar not only to the television viewers but also to the large number of corporate guests who pack into the hospitality lounges around the course each year. For many ordinary golfers, or at least the lucky few who manage to get to play that course at Wentworth, it is the opening holes that set the agenda. And a tough agenda it is.

Sandwiching a par three are two tough and long par fours which require accuracy and length. But those are the two key words for Wentworth. It is a course that never allows the golfer a moment's relaxation in terms of concentration and the West Course's finish is as testing as anything in golf with two par-five dog-legs.

The 17th is by far the toughest. Playing out right allows only those of Tiger Woods proportions the chance to strike the green in two while the 18th does offer more realistic birdie chances. But in terms of championship golf the finish is almost unique.

But while the West gathers the television audiences, there are those who prefer the 6176-yard East Course, designed by Harry Colt and opened in the 1920s. The West was to follow a year or two later. It has a delightful lay-out and like the West demands the greatest of skill and application.

In the early 1990s a third course, the Edinburgh, was added to the Wentworth stable but this does not have either the history or the appeal of the East and West. It is slightly longer but length without tradition does not bring it close to the other two courses as far as the golfers are concerned. — **CG**

⌐ WD £72 (before 11:30am), £60 (after 11.30am); WE £72
⌐ By prior arrangement only; terms on application.
⍾ Full facilities in clubhouse.
⌐ Club can provide list.

1A 170 Weald of Kent
Maidstone Rd, Headcorn, Kent TN27 9PT
☎ (01622) 890866, Fax 891793
7 miles from Maidstone on A274.
Parkland course.
Founded 1991
Designed by John Millen
18 holes, 6169 yards, S.S.S. 70
⚑ Public pay and play course.
⌐ WD £16; WE £20.
⌐ Welcome; from £15.
⍾ Catering and bar facilities.
⌐ Chilston Park; Great Danes; Shant.

1A 171 Wentworth
Wentworth Drive, Virginia Water, Surrey GU25 4LS
☎ (01344) 842201, Fax 842804, Pro 846306, Bar/Rest 846300
21 miles SW of London on A30/A329 junction.
Heathland courses.
Pro D Rennie; Founded 1924
Designed by H.S. Colt (East and West); J.R.M. Jacobs (Edinburgh)
East: 18 holes, 6198 yards, S.S.S. 70; West: 18 holes, 6957 yards, S.S.S. 74; Edinburgh: 18 holes, 6979 yards, S.S.S. 73
⚑ Welcome WD by appointment.
⌐ WD £175.
⌐ Welcome by appointment Mon-Thurs; min 20; from £115.
Driving range, caddies, buggies and golf clinics.
⍾ Top-class catering facilities available.
⌐ 16 rooms available at course.

1A 172 West Byfleet
Sheerwater Rd, West Byfleet, Surrey KT14 6AA
☎ (01932) 345230, Fax 340667, Pro 346584, Sec 343433
On A245 in West Byfleet.
Woodland course.
Pro David Regan; Founded 1906
Designed by Cuthbert Butchart
18 holes, 6211 yards, S.S.S. 70
⚑ Welcome by appointment. not WE.
⌐ WD £32.
⌐ Welcome Mon, Tues, Wed; £62
⍾ Full clubhouse facilities.

1A 173 West Hill
Bagshot Rd, Brookwood, Surrey GU24 0BH
☎ (01483) 474365, Fax 474252, Pro 473172, Bar/Rest 472110
5 miles W of Woking on A322.
Heathland course.
Pro John Clements; Founded 1909
Designed by Willie Park/ Jack White
18 holes, 6368 yards, S.S.S. 70
⚑ Welcome WD with handicap certs; WE only with member
⌐ WD £42.50.
⌐ WD except Wed, by prior arrangement; packages available.
⍾ Full facilities and bar; jacket and tie required in dining room.
⌐ Worplesdon Place, Perry Hill.

1A 174 West Kent
West Hill, Downe, Orpington, Kent BR6 7JJ
☎ (01689) 851323, Pro 856863
A21 to Orpington, head for Downe village; leave on Luxted Lane for 300 yards then right into West Hill.
Parkland/downland course.
Pro Roger Fidler; Founded 1916
18 holes, 6399 yards, S.S.S. 70
⚑ Welcome WD with letter from Sec or handicap cert; must phone in advance.
⌐ WD £28.
⌐ Welcome by appointment; terms on application.
⍾ Full facilities.
⌐ Bromley Continental.

1A 175 West Malling
London Rd, Addington, Maidstone, Kent ME19 5AR
☎ (01732) 844785, Fax 844795, Pro 844022
Course is off the A20 8 miles NW of Maidstone.
Parkland courses.
Pro Duncan Lambert; Founded 1974
Hurricane: 18 holes, 6256 yards, S.S.S. 70
Spitfire: 18 holes, 6142 yards, S.S.S. 70
⚑ Welcome WD; WE after noon.
⌐ WD £25; WE £35.
⌐ Welcome by appointment; terms on application.
⍾ Full facilities.
⌐ Larkfield.

1A 176 West Surrey
Enton Green, Godalming, Surrey GU8 5AF
☎ (01483) 421275, Fax 415419

0.5 miles SE of Milford Station.
Wooded parkland course.
Pro A Tawse; Founded 1910
Designed by Herbert Fowler
18 holes, 6259 yards, S.S.S. 70
⚑ By appointment with Sec.
⌐ WD £27; WE £36.
⌐ Welcome Wed, Thurs, Fri by appointment; £58.
⍾ Full catering facilities.
⌐ Inn on the Lake.

1A 177 Westerham
Valence Park, Brasted Rd, Westerham, Kent TN16 1LJ
☎ (01959) 563700, Fax 563787
On A25 between Brasted and Westerham.
Woodland course.
Pro Ewan Campbell; Founded 1997
Designed by David Williams
18 holes, 6272 yards, S.S.S. 70
⚑ Welcome WD.
⌐ WD £27.
⌐ Welcome WD by appointment with Sec; from £27.
⍾ Restaurant, bar and function room.
⌐ Jarvis Fellbridge.

1A 178 Westgate & Birchington
176 Canterbury Rd, Westgate-on-Sea, Kent CT8 8LT
☎ (01843) 831115
0.25 miles from Westgate station off A27.
Seaside links.
Pro Roger Game; Founded 1892
18 holes, 4926 yards, S.S.S. 64
⚑ Welcome after 10am Mon-Sat; after 11am Sun.
⌐ WD £13.50; WE £15.50.
⌐ Welcome by appointment; Thurs preferred; terms on application.
⍾ Clubhouse facilities.
⌐ Ivyside.

1A 179 Whitstable & Seasalter
Collingwood Rd, Whitstable, Kent CT5 1EB
☎ (01227) 272020, Fax 272020
On A290 to Whitstable.
Seaside links.
Founded 1910
9 holes, 5357 yards, S.S.S. 63
⚑ By arrangement.
⌐ WD £15; WE £15.
⌐ Not welcome.
⍾ Full catering facilities.
⌐ Marine Hotel, Tankerton.

1A 180 Wildernesse
Seal, Sevenoaks, Kent TN15 0JE
☎(01732) 761526, Pro 761527, Sec
761199
Off A25 in Seal village.
Rolling parkland course.
Pro Craig Walker; Founded 1890
Designed by W Park
18 holes, 6448 yards, S.S.S. 72
� Letter of introduction is required;
not WE.
⌐ WD £32.
⌐Apply to Sec; terms on
application.
🍴 Bar and restaurant.

1A 181 Wildwood
Horsham Rd, Alfold, Cranleigh,
Surrey GU6 8JE
☎(01403) 753255, Fax 752005
On A281 Guildford to Horsham road
10 miles from Guildford.
Parkland course.
Pro Nick Parfrement; Founded 1992
Designed by Martin Hawtree
18 holes, 6655 yards, S.S.S. 72
♦ Welcome.
⌐ WD £20; WE £30.
⌐Welcome WD; packages
available; from £26.
🍴 Full catering and bar.
Large practice area.
↪ Random Hall, Slinfold.

1A 182 Wimbledon Common
Camp Rd, Wimbledon Common,
London SW19 4UW
☎(020) 8946 0294, Fax 8947 8697,
Sec 8946 7571
1 mile NW of War Memorial past Fox
and Grapes.
Links type wooded course.
Pro J S Jukes; Founded 1865
Designed by Tom and Willie Dunn
18 holes, 5438 yards, S.S.S. 66
♦ Welcome WD.
⌐ WD £15 (Mon £10)
⌐Welcome Tues-Fri by
appointment; terms on application.
🍴 Full facilities.

1A 183 Wimbledon Park
Home Park Rd, Wimbledon, London
SW19 7HR
☎(020) 8946 1002, Fax 8944 8688,
Pro 8946 4053, Sec 8946 1250
Near Wimbledon Park District Line
tube.
Parkland course.
Pro Dean Wingrove; Founded 1898
Designed by Willie Park Jnr
18 holes, 5492 yards, S.S.S. 66

♦ Welcome WD with handicap certs.
⌐ WD £40.
⌐Welcome Tues, Thurs by
appointment; terms available on
application.
🍴 Full facilities available except
Mon.
↪ Canizaro House.

1A 184 Windlemere
Windlesham Rd, West End, Woking,
Surrey GU24 9QL
☎(01276) 858727
Take A322 from Bagshot towards
Guildford; turn left on A319 towards
Chobham, course is on left opposite
Gordon Boys School.
Gently undulating public parkland
course.
Pro David Thomas; Founded 1978.
Designed by Clive D. Smith
9 holes, 2673 yards, S.S.S. 34
♦ Open to public on payment of
green fees.
⌐ WD £9; WE £10.50.
⌐By appointment with Pro; terms on
application.
🍴 Bar snacks always available.

1A 185 Windlesham   ☏
Grove End, Bagshot, Surrey GU19
5HY
☎(01276) 452220, Fax 452290
At Junction of A30 and A322.
Parkland course.
Pro Lee Mucklow; Founded 1994
Designed by Tommy Horton
18 holes, 6650 yards, S.S.S. 72
♦ Welcome except before noon at
WE; handicap certs required.
⌐ WD £25; WE £35.
⌐Welcome Mon-Fri by prior
appointment; terms available on
application.
🍴 Bar and restaurant.
Practice range, 3 covered bays, 10
outdoor.
↪ Berrystead.

1A 186 The Wisley
Mill Lane, Ripley, Nr Woking, Surrey
GU23 6QU
☎(01483) 211022, Fax 211622
Exit A3 at Ockham, Send and Ripley,
3rd exit from the roundabout and first
left into Mill Lane.
Parkland course; 3 x 9 holes.
Pro Hugh Marr Founded 1991
Designed by Robert Trent Jones, Jr.
27 holes, 6858 yards, S.S.S. 73
♦ Private members' club.
⌐None.

🍴 Full clubhouse catering and bar
facilities.
Large practice ground.

1A 187 Woking
Pond Rd, Hook Heath, Woking,
Surrey GU22 0JZ
☎(01483) 760053, Fax 772441, Pro
769582
Off A322 after West Hill GC.
Oldest heathland course in Surrey.
Pro Carl Bianco; Founded 1893
Designed by Tom Dunn
18 holes, 6340 yards, S.S.S. 70
♦ WD with a handicap cert; WE only
with member.
⌐ WD £78.
⌐By appointment with 12 months'
notice; £78.
🍴 Full facilities.
↪ Glen Court, Woking; Worplesdon
Place, Worplesdon.

1A 188 Woodcote Park
Meadow Hill, Bridleway, Coulsden,
Surrey CR5 2QQ
☎(020) 8668 2788, Fax 8668
2788, Pro 8668 1843, Bar/Rest
8660 0176
2 miles N of Purley on Coulsdon-
Wallington road.
Parkland course.
Pro Ian Golding; Founded 1912
18 holes, 6669 yards, S.S.S. 72
♦ Welcome by appointment and with
handicap certs, not WE.
⌐ WD £30.
⌐Welcome by appointment; £57.50.
🍴 Catering and bar facilities.

1A 189 Woodlands Manor
Tinkerpot Lane, Sevenoaks, Kent
TN15 6AB
☎(01959) 523805, Pro 524161, Sec
523806
Off A225, 4 miles NE of Sevenoaks,
5 miles S of M25 Junction 3.
Undulating parkland course in AONB.
Pro Phil Womack; Founded 1928
Designed by N. Coles, J. Lyons
18 holes, 6037 yards, S.S.S. 68
♦ Welcome WD; not WE.
⌐ WD £21.
⌐Welcome Mon-Fri by appointment;
terms on application.
🍴 Meals served.
↪ Thistle (Brands Hatch).

1A 190 Worplesdon
Heath House Rd, Woking, Surrey
GU22 0RA

☎(01483) Fax 473303, Pro 473287, Sec 472277
Leave Guildford on A322 to Bagshot, 6 miles turn rt into Heath House Rd.
Heathland course.
Pro Jim Christine; Founded 1908
Designed by J.F. Abercromby
18 holes, 6440 yards, S.S.S. 71
♦ Welcome WD only with intro from Club Sec.
◻ WD £45 (Nov-Feb £30)
☺Welcome WD by prior appointment (except Tues); terms on application.
🍽 Bar every day, lunch every day except Tues.
✎ Worplesdon Place.

1A 191 **Wrotham Heath**
Seven Mile Lane, Borough Green, Sevenoaks, Kent TN15 8QZ
☎(01732) 884800, Fax 887370
Off A20 near junction with A25.
Woodland/heathland course.
Pro Harry Dearden; Founded 1906
Designed by Donald Steel
18 holes, 5954 yards, S.S.S. 69
♦ Welcome WD with handicap certs, not WE or BH without member.
◻ WD £25.
☺Welcome Fri only; terms on application.
🍽 Full catering by arrangement with Steward, except Mon.
✎ Post House.

1B 1 **Abbey View**
Holywell Hill, Westminster Lodge, St Albans, Herts AL1 2DL
☎(01727) 868227
In centre of St Albans.
Public parkland course.
Pro Roddy Watkins; Founded 1990
Designed by Jimmy Thomson
9 holes, 1383 yards
♦ Open to public at all times.
◻ WD £5.20; WE £5.20.
☺Welcome; terms on application.
🍽 Tea/coffee on site; café in main centre.

1B 2 **Abridge G & CC**
Epping Lane, Stapleford Tawney, Essex RM4 1ST
☎(01708) 688396, Fax 688550, Pro 688333
M11 from London exit 5 via Abridge; from the N, M11 exit 7 via Epping.
Parkland course.
Pro Stuart Layton; Founded 1964
Designed by Henry Cotton
18 holes, 6686 yards, S.S.S. 72

♦ Welcome WD only; handicap certs required.
◻ WD £30.
☺Mon, Wed and Fri; terms on application.
🍽 Available every day.
✎ Post House, Epping.

1B 3 **Airlinks**
Southall Lane, Hounslow, Essex TW5 9PE
☎(020) 8561 1418
M4 Junction 3 on to A312 and A4020; part of David Lloyd Tennis Centre.
Public meadowland/parkland course.
Pro Tony Martin; Founded 1984
Designed by P. Alliss
18 holes, 5813 yards, S.S.S. 68
♦ Welcome; some restrictions at weekends.
◻ WD £10; WE £16.
☺Welcome Mon-Fri; fees negotiable.
🍽 Bar, snacks, hot and cold meals available.
Practice range 24 bays; floodlit.
✎ London Airport hotels nearby.

1B 4 **Aldenham G & CC** ☏
Church Lane, Aldenham, Nr Watford, Herts WD2 8AL
☎(01923) 853929, Fax 858472
M1 Junction 5 on to A41, left at roundabout to A462 and then into Church Rd.
Parkland course.
Pro Tim Dunstan; Founded 1975
18 holes, 6480 yards, S.S.S. 71
9 holes, 2350 yards
♦ Welcome WD but afternoon only at WE.
◻ WD £24; WE £33.
☺Welcome WD and WE afternoons; Full catering packages and 36 holes of golf; from £52.
🍽 Full facilities.
✎ Watford Hilton National; Jarvis International.

1B 5 **Aldwickbury Park**
Piggottshill Lane, Harpenden, Herts AL5 1A B
☎(01582) 760112, Fax 760113, Sec 765112, Bar/Rest 766463
10 mins from M1 Junction 9 on road between Harpenden and Wheathampstead.
Parkland course.
Pro Simon Plumb; Founded 1995
Designed by K Brown / M Gillett
18 holes, 6352 yards, S.S.S. 70
♦ Welcome WD; after 1pm WE.

◻ WD £21; WE £25.
☺Welcome WD: 36 holes, coffee and biscuits, lunch, 3-course dinner; other packages available; £49.
🍽 Full catering and bar.
✎ Harpenden House.

1B 6 **Arkley**
Rowley Green Rd, Barnet, Herts EN5 3HL
☎(020) 8449 0555, Fax 8440 5214, Pro 8440 8473, Sec 8449 0394, Bar/Rest 8449 0394
Off A1 at Arkley.
Parkland course.
Pro Martin Porter; Founded 1909
Designed by James Braid
18 holes, 6117 yards, S.S.S 69
♦ Welcome WD but with members only at WE.
◻ WD £20.
☺Welcome Wed and Fri; terms on application.
🍽 Full catering facilities.

1B 7 **Ashford Manor**
Fordbridge Rd, Ashford, Middx TW15 3RT
☎(01784) 257687, Fax 420355, Pro 255940, Bar/Rest 252049/ 258410
Off A308 between Staines and Sunbury. 0.5 miles from Fordbridge roundabout.
Wooded parkland course.
Pro Mike Finney; Founded 1898
18 holes, 6352 yards, S.S.S. 70
♦ Welcome WD with handicap certs.
◻ WD £25.
☺Welcome WD by prior arrangement; golf, morning coffee, lunch, afternoon tea, dinner; £40-60.
🍽 Full catering facilities.
✎ Shepperton Moathouse; The Ship, Shepperton.

1B 8 **Ashridge**
Little Gaddesden, Berkhamsted, Herts HP4 1LY
☎(01442) 842244, Fax 843770, Pro 842307, Bar/Rest 842379
4 miles N of Berkhamsted on B4506.
Parkland course.
Pro Andrew Ainsworth; Founded 1932
Designed by Sir Guy Campbell, Colonel Hotchkin and Cecil Hutch
18 holes, 6547 yards, S.S.S. 71
♦ Welcome WD only.
◻ WD £30.
☺WD only; terms on application.
🍽 Full facilities.

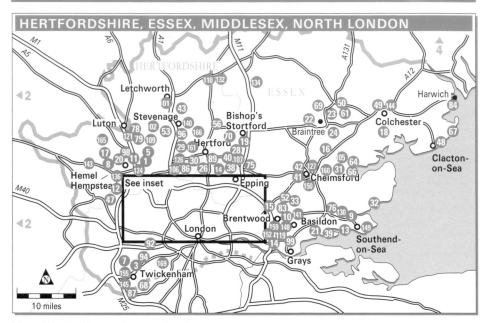

HERTFORDSHIRE, ESSEX, MIDDLESEX, NORTH LONDON

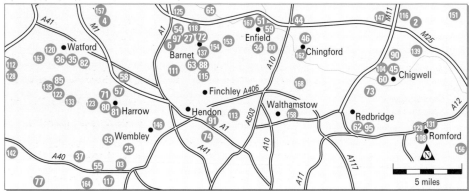

1B 9 Ballards Gore

Gore Rd, Canewdon, Essex SS4 2DA
☎ (01702) 258917, Pro 258924
From London via A127 to Southend
Airport, then through Rochford on to
Great Stambridge road; course 1.5
miles from Rochford centre.
Parkland course.
Pro Richard Emery; Founded 1980
Designed by D. and J.J. Caton
18 holes, 6845 yards, S.S.S. 73
† Welcome WD; guest of member
only at WE, Sun after 2 pm.
� WD £20.
⌐ WD by arrangement with Sec,
subject to availability; terms on
application.

🍽 Bar and restaurant; private
functions.
↵ Renouf.

1B 10 Basildon

Clay Hill Lane, Basildon, Essex SS16
5JP
☎ (01268) 533297, Fax 533849, Pro
533352
On A176 S of Basildon via either
A127 or A13.
Undulating wooded parkland.
Pro Mike Oliver; Founded 1967
Designed by A H Cotton
18 holes, 6236 yards, S.S.S. 70
† Welcome.

⌐ WD £9; WE £15.
⌐ Welcome, packages by prior
arrangement; terms on application.
🍽 Restaurant and bar.
↵ Haywain; Campanile, Basildon.

1B 11 Batchwood Hall

Batchwood Tennis and Golf Centre,
St Albans, Herts AL3 5XA
☎ (01727) 833349, Fax 850586, Pro
844250
NW corner of St Albans; 5 miles S of
M1 Junction 9.
Parkland course.
Pro Mark Flitton; Founded 1935
Designed by J.H. Taylor

KEY

1	Abbey View	34	Bush Hill Park	68	Fulwell	102	Little Hay Golf Complex
2	Abridge G & CC	35	Bushey G & CC	69	Gosfield Lake	103	London Golf Centre
3	Airlinks	36	Bushey Hall	70	Great Hadham	104	Loughton
4	Aldenham G & CC	37	C & L Golf & CC	71	Grim's Dyke	105	Maldon
5	Aldwickbury Park	38	Canons Brook	72	Hadley Wood	106	Malton
6	Arkley	39	Castle Point	73	Hainault Forest	107	Manor of Groves G & CC
7	Ashford Manor	40	Chadwell Springs	74	Hampstead	107	Maylands Golf & CC
8	Ashridge	41	Channels	75	Hanbury Manor G& CC	109	Mid-Herts
9	Ballards Gore	42	Chelmsford	76	Hanover	110	Mill Green
10	Basildon	43	Chesfield Downs	77	Harefield Place	111	Mill Hill
11	Batchwood Hall	44	Cheshunt	78	Harpenden	112	Moor Park
12	Batchworth Park	45	Chigwell	79	Harpenden Common	113	Muswell Hill
13	Belfairs Park	46	Chingford	80	Harrow Hill	114	The Nazeing
14	Belhus Park (Thurrock)	47	Chorleywood	81	Harrow School	115	North Middlesex
15	Bentley	48	Clacton-on-Sea	82	Hartsbourne G & CC	116	North Weald Golf Club
16	Benton Hall	49	Colchester	83	Harwood	117	Northwood
17	Berkhamsted	50	Colne Valley (Essex)	84	Harwich & Dovercourt	118	Old Fold Manor
18	Birch Grove	51	Crews Hill	85	Haste Hill	119	Orsett
19	Bishop's Stortford	52	Crondon Park	86	Hatfield London CC	120	Oxhey Park
20	Boxmoor	53	Danesbury Park	87	Hazelwood	121	Panshanger
21	Boyce Hill	54	Dyrham Park	88	Hendon	122	Perivale Park
22	Braintree	55	Ealing	89	The Hertfordshire	123	Pinner Hill
23	Braintree Towerlands	56	East Herts	90	High Beech	124	Porters Park
24	Braxted Park	57	Edgewarebury	91	Highgate	125	Potters Bar
25	Brent Valley	58	Elstree	92	Hillingdon	126	Redbourn
26	Brickendon Grange	59	Enfield	93	Horsenden Hill	127	Regiment Way
27	Bridgedown	60	Epping Forest Golf & CC	94	Hounslow Heath	128	Rickmansworth
28	Briggens House Hotel	61	Essex Golf & CC	95	Ilford	129	Risebridge (Havering)
29	Brocket Hall	62	Fairlop Waters	96	Knebworth	130	Rochford Hundred
30	Brookmans Park	63	Finchley	97	Laing Sports Club	131	Romford
31	Bunsay Downs	64	Five Lakes Hotel	98	Lamerwood	132	Royston
32	Burnham-on-Crouch	65	Forest Hills	99	Langdon Hills	133	Ruislip
33	The Burstead	66	Forrester Park	100	Lee Valley	134	Saffron Walden
		67	Frinton	101	Letchworth	135	Sandy Lodge

136	Shendish Manor
137	South Herts
138	Stanmore
139	Stapleford Abbotts
140	Stevenage
141	Stock Brook Manor
142	Stockley Park
143	Stocks Hotel & CC
144	Stoke-by-Nayland
145	Strawberry Hill
146	Sudbury
147	Theydon Bois
148	Thorndon Park
149	Thorpe Hall
150	Three Rivers Golf & CC
151	Toothill
152	Top Meadow
153	Trent Park
154	Tudor Park Sports Gd
155	Twickenham Park
156	Upminster
157	Verulam
158	Wanstead
159	Warley Park
160	Warren
161	Welwyn Garden City
162	West Essex
163	West Herts
164	West Middlesex
165	Whipsnade Park
166	Whitehill
167	Whitewebbs
168	Woodford
169	Wyke Green

---

18 holes, 6509 yards, S.S.S. 71
† Welcome.
⌴ WD £10; WE £13.
⤳ Welcome by prior arrangement; packages available; tennis courts; 2 squash courts; fitness gym; dance studio.
🍽 Bar and restaurant.
18-hole putting green.
⌁ Aubrey Park.

1B 12 Batchworth Park

London Rd, Rickmansworth, Herts WD3 1JS
☎ (01923) 711400
From M25 Junction 17 towards Rickmansworth to the Batchworth roundabout; course 400 yards.
Parkland course.
Pro Steven Proudfoot, Founded 1996
Designed by Dave Thomas
18 holes, 6723 yards, S.S.S. 72
† Private; members and guests only.
⌴ Not available.
🍽 Bar and restaurant.
Practice range for members and guests.

1B 13 Belfairs Park (Southend-on-Sea)

Starter's Hut, Eastwood Rd North, Leigh-on-Sea, Essex SS9 4LR
☎ (01702) 525345, Pro 520202
4.5 miles from Southend centre;
Eastwood Rd links A127 and A13
Set in Belfairs Park;
parkland/woodland course.
Pro Martin Foreman; Founded 1926
Designed by H.S. Colt
18 holes, 5840 yards, S.S.S. 68
† unrestricted; bookings every day, week in advance on day.
⌴ WD £10; WE £15.80.
⤳ Welcome; terms available on application.
🍽 Public restaurant.
⌁ Westcliff Hotel.

1B 14 Belhus Park (Thurrock)

Belhus Park, South Ockendon, Essex RM15 4QR
☎ (01708) 854260
A13 to Avely.
Public parkland course.
Pro Gary Lunn; Founded 1972
Designed by Frank Pennink
18 holes, 5589 yards, S.S.S. 69
† Bookings can be made at course WD; in advance by phone WE (booking card required).
⌴ WD £9.50; WE £14.
⤳ Welcome; terms available on application.
🍽 Bar and restaurant.

Practice range 12 bays; floodlit.
⌁ Thurrock Hotel.

1B 15 Bentley

Ongar Rd, Brentwood, Essex CM15 9SS
☎ (01277) 373179, Fax 375097, Pro 372933
On A128 between Brentwood and Ongar.
Parkland course with water hazards.
Pro Nick Garrett; Founded 1972
Designed by Alec Swan
18 holes, 6709 yards, S.S.S. 72
† Welcome WD.
⌴ WD £21.
⤳ Welcome WD; terms on application.
🍽 Full catering facilities.

1B 16 Benton Hall

Wickham Hill, Witham, Essex CM8 3LH
☎ (01376) 502454, Fax 521050
Off A12 at Witham; course is well signposted.
Woodland course.
Pro J Hudson/C Fairweather;
Founded 1993
Designed by Alan Walker and Charlie Cox
18 holes, 6495 yards, S.S.S. 72

† Welcome by prior arrangement.
ℂ WD £25; WE £30.
☞ Welcome WD by prior arrangement; packages available; from £37.50.
|◉| Clubhouse facilities.

1B 17 **Berkhamstead**
The Common, Berkhamstead, Herts HP4 2QB
☎ (01442) 865832, Fax 863730, Pro 865851, Bar/Rest 862648
1 mile N of Berkhamstead.
Heathland course.
Pro Basil Proudfoot; Founded 1890
Designed by G.H. Gowring (1890-92 Founder), 1912 C.J. Gilbert with advice from Harry Colt)
18 holes, 6605 yards, S.S.S. 72
† Welcome with handicap of 24 or better.
ℂ WD £25; WE £35.
☞ Welcome Wed and Fri; maximum 50; £60.
|◉| Meals and bar facilities.
☜ Hemel Hempstead Post House.

1B 18 **Birch Grove**
Layer Rd, Colchester, Essex CO2 0HS
☎ (01206) 734276, Sec 734103
On B1026 3 miles S of Colchester.
Parkland course.
Founded 1970
Designed by course owners
9 holes, 4038 yards, S.S.S. 60
† Welcome.
ℂ WD £10; WE £10.
☞ Welcome by arrangement; golf and 4-course dinner, bar, dining area; £15-21.
|◉| Full facilities.

1B 19 **Bishop's Stortford**
Dunmow Rd, Bishop's Stortford, Herts CM23 5HP
☎ (01279) 654715, Fax 655215, Pro 651324, Bar/Rest 461779
From M11 Junction 8 follow signs to Bishop's Stortford; course is 1.5 miles on left.
Well-established, undulating, parkland course; a true test of golf
Pro Vince Duncan; Founded 1910
Designed by James Braid
18 holes, 6404 yards, S.S.S. 71
† Welcome with handicap certs; not at WE.
ℂ WD £27 (round), £35 (day); WE guest of members only.
☞ Welcome by prior arrangement; varied packages available (minimum

12); Tues (Ladies' day) exc; special winter deals; from £35-65.
|◉| Full restaurant and bar bistro.
☜ Stansted Airport; Downhall, Hatfield Heath.

1B 20 **Boxmoor**
18 Box Lane, Hemel Hempstead, Herts HP3 0DJ
☎ (01442) 242434
On A41 0.75 miles from Hemel Hempstead station.
Undulating parkland.
Founded 1890
9 holes, 4812 yards, S.S.S. 64
† Welcome except Sun.
ℂ WD £10; WE £15.
☞ Welcome with month's notice.
|◉| Limited service; meals available by prior arrangement.
☜ Boxmoor Lodge.

1B 21 **Boyce Hill**
Vicarage Hill, South Benfleet, Essex SS7 1PD
☎ (01268) 793625, Fax 750497, Pro 752565
7 miles W of Southend-on-Sea; A127 to Rayleigh Weir (3 miles from course); A13 to Victoria House Corner (1 mile from course).
Undulating parkland course.
Pro Graham Burroughs; Founded 1922
Designed by James Braid
18 holes, 6000 yards, S.S.S. 68
† Welcome WD; WE with member; handicap certs required and 24 hours notice.
ℂ WD £25.
☞ Thurs only; terms available on application.
|◉| Service 7.30am-8pm.
☜ Crest Maisonwyck.

1B 22 **Braintree**   ♆
Kings Lane, Stisted, Braintree, Essex CM7 8DA
☎ (01376) 324117
A120 eastbound after Braintree by-pass, 1st left, 1 mile to course signposted.
Parkland course.
Pro Tony Parcell; Founded 1891
Designed by Hawtree and Son
18 holes, 6191 yards, S.S.S. 69
† Welcome; handicap certs required Sat and Sun pm.
ℂ WD £20; WE £40.
☞ By arrangement Mon, Wed and Thurs (Tues Ladies Day); terms on application.

|◉| Meals served.
☜ White Hart.

1B 23 **Braintree Towerlands**
Panfield Rd, Braintree, Essex CM7 5BJ
☎ (01376) 326802, Fax 552487, Pro 347951, Sec 552794
Course is 1 mile NW of Braintree on the B1053.
Picturesque parkland course.
Founded 1985
Designed by G.R. Shiels/Golf Landscapes
9 holes, 5559 yards, S.S.S. 68
† Welcome.
ℂ WD £10; WE £12.
☞ Welcome by appointment; contact C W Hunnable or J C Sillett; terms on application.
|◉| Clubhouse facilities.
Practice range.
☜ Old House; Old Court; Hare and Hounds.

1B 24 **Braxted Park**
Braxted Park, Witham, Essex CM8 3EN
☎ (01376) 572372, Fax (01621) 892840
1.5 miles off A12 near Kelvedon.
Parkland course.
Pro Tony Parcell; Founded 1953
Designed by Sir Allen Clark
9 holes, 5704 yards, S.S.S. 68
† Public pay as you play WD; members only WE.
ℂ WD £12.
☞ Welcome WD; pool, tennis, sauna, snooker; terms on application..
|◉| Restaurant, bar.
☜ Braxted Park; Rivenhall.

1B 25 **Brent Valley**
Church Rd, Hanwell, London W7 3BE
☎ (020) 8567 4230, Pro 8567 1287
A4020 Uxbridge Rd, Hanwell, on to Greenford Ave then on to Church Rd.
Public meadowland course.
Pro Peter Bryant; Founded 1938
Designed by P. Alliss and D. Thomas
18 holes, 5446 yards, S.S.S. 66
† Welcome.
ℂ WD £10; WE £14.95
☞ Organised via the Pro; terms on application.
|◉| Restaurant from 8am.

1B 26 **Brickendon Grange**
Brickendon, Nr Hertford, Herts SG13 8PD

☎(01992) 511258, Fax 511411, Pro
511218, Bar/Rest 511228
3 miles S of Hertford near Bayford
BR station.
Undulating parkland course.
Pro G Tippett; Founded 1968
Designed by C.K. Cotton
18 holes, 6394 yards, S.S.S. 70
♦ Welcome WD; handicap certs
required.
⌐ WD £35.
◡ WDs except Wed; terms on
application.
☜ Bar lunches.
↙ White Horse.

1B 27 Bridgedown
St Albans Rd, Barnet, Herts EN5 4RE
☎(020) 8441 7649, Pro 8440 4009
1.5 miles from M25 Junction 23 at
South Mimms exit.
Parkland course.
Pro David Beal; Founded 1994
18 holes, 6626 yards, S.S.S. 72
♦ Welcome.
⌐ WD £15; WE £17.
◡ Welcome by prior arrangement;
terms on application.
☜ Bar and catering facilities
available.
Practice range, 12 bays.

1B 28 Briggens House Hotel
Stanstead Road, Stanstead Abbots
Ware, Herts SG12 8LD
☎(01279) 829955, Fax 793685, Pro
793742, Sec 793742, Bar/Rest
793742
Situated on A414.
Parkland course.
Pro Alan Battle; Founded 1988
9 holes, 5582 yards, S.S.S. 69
♦ Welcome at all times.
⌐ WD £13; WE £16.
◡ Terms on application.
☜ Facilities available.
↙ On site.

1B 29 Brocket Hall
Brocket Hall, Welwyn Garden City,
Herts AL8 7XG
☎(01707) 390055, Fax 390052, Pro
390063
On B653 to Wheathampstead off A1
(M) Junction 4.
Parkland course.
Pro Keith Wood; Founded 1992
Designed by Peter Alliss / Clive Clark
18 holes, 6616 yards, S.S.S. 72
♦ Members' guests only.
◡ Corporate days can be arranged;
terms on application.

☜ Clubhouse restaurant and bar
facilities.
Comprehensive golf academy.

1B 30 Brookmans Park
Golf Club Rd, Hatfield, Herts AL9 7AT
☎(01707) 652459, Fax 661851, Pro
652468, Sec 652487.
10 min from M25 through Potters Bar.
Parkland course.
Pro Ian Jelley; Founded 1930
Designed by Hawtree & Taylor
18 holes, 6460 yards, S.S.S. 71
♦ Welcome by prior arrangement,
not WE
⌐ WD £30.
◡ Welcome WD, terms on
application.
☜ Full facilities, bar and catering.
↙ Brookmans Park Hotel.

1B 31 Bunsay Downs
Little Baddow Rd, Woodham Walter,
Nr Maldon, Essex CM9 6RW
☎(01245) 222648, Sec 223258
Leave A414 at Danbury towards
Woodham Water; course 0.5 W of
village.
Gently undulating meadowland.
Pro Mickey Walker; Founded 1982
9 holes, 5864 yards, S.S.S. 68
Also Badgers course: 9 holes, 1319
yards, par 27.
♦ Welcome.
⌐ WD £10; WE £12.50.
◡ Welcome WD except BH;
packages available.
☜ Full facilities all week.
Practice facilities.

1B 32 Burnham-on-Crouch ☏
Ferry Rd, Creeksea, Burnham-on-
Crouch, Essex CM0 8PQ
☎(01621) 782282, Fax 782282, Pro
786280, Bar/Rest 785508
1 mile before entering Burnham on
B1010.
Undulating parkland.
Pro K Smith/S Cardy; Founded 1923
Designed by Howard Swan (2nd 9)
18 holes, 6056 yards, S.S.S. 69
♦ Welcome WD.
⌐ WD £22.
◡ Welcome WD except Thurs; Full
catering facilities; from £30.
☜ Full bar and restaurant facilities.

1B 33 The Burstead
The Common Rd, Little Burstead,
Billericay, Essex CM12 9SS
☎(01277) 631171, Fax 632766

Leave A127 at Research
Centre/Laindon exit; 1st exit at
roundabout and then right into
DuntonRoad; left into Rectory Road.
Parkland course.
Pro Keith Bridges; assisted by D
Bullock; Founded 1993
Designed by Patrick Tallack
18 holes, 6275 yards, S.S.S. 70
♦ Welcome WD if carrying handicap
certs.
⌐ WD £19.
◡ Welcome WD by prior
arrangement; packages available;
from £19.
☜ Clubhouse bar and restaurant
facilities.
Practice range; practice area.
↙ Trust House Forte and
Camponile, both A127; Hill House,
Horndon on the Hill.

1B 34 Bush Hill Park
Bush Hill, Winchmore Hill, London
N21 2BU
☎(020) 8360 5738
0.5 mile S of Enfield town.
Parkland course.
Pro Adrian Andrews; Founded 1895
18 holes, 5828 yards, S.S.S. 68
♦ Welcome WD except Wed am.
⌐ WD £25.
◡ On application. except Wed; terms
on application.
☜ Bar snacks, restaurant service.
↙ West Lodge.

1B 35 Bushey Golf & CC
High St, Bushey, Herts WD2 1BJ
☎(020) 8950 2283, Pro 8950 2215
On A411, 1.5 miles from M1/A411
junction.
Parkland course.
Pro Mike Lovegrove; Founded 1980
Designed by Donald Steel
9 holes, 6400 yards, S.S.S. 69
♦ Welcome WD except Wed, Thurs
mornings; WE and Bank Holidays
after 0.00pm.
⌐ WD £9; WE £11.
◡ Maximum 50 by arrangement; not
available Wed or Thurs mornings;
terms on application.
☜ Meals served.
Practice range 30 bays; floodlit.
↙ The Hilton.

1B 36 Bushey Hall ☏
Bushey Hall Drive, Bushey, Herts
WD2 2EP
☎(01923) 222253, Fax 229759, Pro
225802, Sec 222253

1 mile SE of Watford.
Undulating parkland course.
Pro Ken Wickham; Founded 1886
Designed by Robert Stewart Clouston
18 holes, 6099 yards, S.S.S. 69
♦ Welcome; must book with Pro
shop.
Ⅼ WD £18; WE £25.
⌒ Welcome WD; terms on
application.
🍽️ Full facilities.

1B 37 C & L Golf & Country Club

West End Road, Northolt, Middlesex
UB5 6RD
☎ (020) 8845 5662, Fax 8841 5515
Junction of West End Rd and A40,
travelling from London; opposite
Northolt Airport.
Parkland course.
Pro Richard Kelly; Founded 1991
Designed by Patrick Tallack
9 holes, 2251 yards
♦ Welcome; no jeans or T-shirts;
golf shoes only.
Ⅼ WD £6.50; WE £7.50.
⌒ Welcome WD; terms on
application.
🍽️ Bar, restaurant, banqueting hall
available.
⌐ Master Brewer.

1B 38 Canons Brook

Elizabeth Way, Harlow, Essex CM19
5BE
☎ (01279) 421482, Fax 626393, Pro
418357, Bar/Rest 421542
1 mile W of Harlow Town station.
Parkland course.
Pro A McGinn; Founded 1963
Designed by Sir Henry Cotton
18 holes, 6763 yards, S.S.S. 73
♦ Welcome WD.
Ⅼ WD £27
⌒ Welcome Mon, Wed, Fri; golf and
catering; £45.

🍽️ Full catering facilities.
⌐ Churchgate Hotel; Moat House.

1B 39 Castle Point

Somnes Avenue, Canvey Island,
Essex SS8 9FG
☎ (01268) Pro 510830
A13 to Southend, right on A130 to
Canvey Island at Saddler's Farm
roundabout, over Waterside Farm
roundabout to Somnes Ave, course
on left.
Public seaside links course.
Pro Michael Otteridge; Founded 1988
Designed by Golf Landscapes
18 holes, 6096 yards, S.S.S. 69
♦ No restrictions; booking required
at WE; smart attire.
Ⅼ WD £9.50; WE £13.50.
⌒ On request; telephone in advance;
terms on application.
🍽️ Bar and restaurant facilities
available.
⌐ Crest, Basildon; Oyster Fleet.

1B 40 Chadwell Springs

Hertford Rd, Ware, Herts SG12 9LE
☎ (01920) 461447, Pro 462075
On A119 halfway between Hertford
and Ware.
Parkland course.
Pro Mark Wall; Founded 1975
Designed by J.H. Taylor
9 holes, 3209 yards, S.S.S. 71
♦ Welcome WD; WE by
arrangement.
Ⅼ WD £10 WE £15
⌒ Welcome Mon and Wed; terms on
application.
🍽️ Full facilities.
⌐ Salisbury, Hertford; Moat House,
Ware.

1B 41 Channels

Belsteads Farm Lane, Little Waltham,
Chelmsford, Essex CM3 3PT

☎ (01245) 440005, Fax 442032, Pro
441056
Course is two miles NE of
Chelmsford off the A130.
Undulating parkland course.
Pro Ian Sinclair; Founded 1974
Designed by Henry Cotton
Belsteads: 9 holes, 4779 yards,
S.S.S. 63; Channels: 18 holes, 6376
yards, S.S.S. 71
♦ Welcome anytime.
Ⅼ Belsteads course: WD £18, WE
£20; Channels course: WD £25.
⌒ Welcome WD; packages involve
playing both Channels and Belsteads
courses; £26-60.
🍽️ Full catering facilities.
⌐ County Hotel, Chelmsford.

1B 42 Chelmsford

Widford Rd, Chelmsford, Essex CM2
9AP
☎ (01245) 256483, Fax 256483, Pro
257079, Bar/Rest 268581
Off A1016 Chelmsford road.
Parkland course.
Pro Mark Welch; Founded 1893
Designed by Harry Colt (1924)
18 holes, 5981 yards, S.S.S. 69
♦ Welcome WD only.
Ⅼ WD £27
⌒ Welcome Wed and Thurs only;
terms on application..
🍽️ Full facilities.
⌐ South Lodge, Chelmsford.

1B 43 Chesfield Downs

Jack's Hill, Graveley, Herts SG4 7EQ
☎ (01462) 482929, Fax 482390
From A1M follow signs on B197 to
Graveley.
Parkland course.
Pro Jane Fernley/Henry Arnott;
Founded 1991
Designed by Jonathan Gaunt
18 holes, 6646 yards, S.S.S. 71
♦ Welcome.

WD £16; WE £24.
🕗 Welcome; various packages available; terms on application.
🍽 Full facilities.
🛏 Blackmore Hotel, Little Wymondley.

1B 44 Cheshunt
Park Lane, Cheshunt, Herts EN7 6QD
☎ (01992) 624009
From M25 Junction 25 towards Hertford, at 2nd lights turn left to mini-roundabout, turn right then signposted.
Municipal parkland course.
Pro Andy Trainer; Founded 1976
18 holes, 6613 yards, S.S.S. 71
♦ Welcome WD and by arrangement at WE.
WD £11 (pm £7.50); WE £15.
🕗 By arrangement; terms on application.
🍽 Café service all day.
🛏 Marriott.

1B 45 Chigwell
High Rd, Chigwell, Essex IG7 5BH
☎ (020) 8500 2059, Fax 8501 3410, Pro 8500 0384
On A113, 13.5 miles NE of London
Undulating parkland course.
Pro Ray Beard; Founded 1925
18 holes, 6279 yards, S.S.S. 70
♦ Welcome Mon-Thurs with handicap certs; only with member at WE.
WD £35.
🕗 Welcome Mon, Wed and Thurs by prior arrangement; terms on application.
🍽 Bar and catering facilities.
🛏 Prince Regent; Roebuck.

1B 46 Chingford
Bury Rd, Chingford London E4 7QJ
☎ (020) Pro 8529 5708, Sec 8529 2107
Off Station Road, 300 yards S of Chingford station.
Public parkland course.
Pro John Francis; Founded 1888
Designed by James Braid
18 holes, 6342 yards, S.S.S. 69
♦ Welcome; red outer garment must be worn.
WD £10.40; WE £14.25.
🕗 Welcome by appointment; terms on application.
🍽 Snacks, no bar; café available next to club.
🛏 Ridgeway (Chingford).

1B 47 Chorleywood
Common Rd, Chorleywood, Herts WD3 5LN
☎ (01923) 282009
0.5 mile from Chorleywood station near Sportsman Hotel.
Wooded heathland course on common land.
Founded 1890
9 holes, 5712 yards, S.S.S. 67
♦ Welcome WD except Tues am. WE restrictions apply.
WD £16; WE £20.
🕗 Small societies; terms on application.
🍽 Bar and catering.

1B 48 Clacton-on-Sea
West Rd, Clacton-on-Sea, Essex CO15 1A J
☎ (01255) 421919, Fax 424602, Pro 426804, Sec 421919 Bar/Rest 424793
On the seafront at Clacton.
Parkland course.
Pro Stuart Levermore; Founded 1892
Designed by Jack White
18 holes, 6532 yards, S.S.S. 71
♦ Welcome WD; WE restrictions apply.
WD £20; WE £25.
🕗 Welcome WD; full day of golf plus lunch and dinner; £45.
🍽 Full facilities and bar.
🛏 Kingcliff; Plaza; Chudleigh.

1B 49 Colchester
Braiswick, Colchester, Essex CO4 5AV
☎ (01206) 852946, Fax 852698, Pro 853920, Sec 853396
0.75 miles NW of Colchester North station on the B1508.
Parkland course.
Pro Mark Angel; Founded 1907
Designed by James Braid
18 holes, 6307 yards, S.S.S. 70
♦ Welcome with handicap certs.
WD £20; WE £30.
🕗 Welcome by arrangement, terms on application.
🍽 Full facilities.
🛏 George Hotel; Rose & Crown; both Colchester.

1B 50 Colne Valley (Essex) ♔
Station Road, Earls Colne, Essex CO6 2LT
☎ (01787) 224343, Fax 224126, Pro 224233, Bar/Rest 224233
10 miles W from A12/A604 junction.
Parkland course.

Pro James Tayloy; Founded 1991
Designed by Howard Swan
18 holes, 6301 yards, S.S.S. 70
♦ Welcome midweek and after 10.30am at WE with prior arrangement.
WD £18; WE £23.
🕗 Welcome; in-house catering, corporate days for up to 200; pool and snooker; terms available on application.
🍽 Restaurant and bar.
🛏 Bull Hotel; Forte Posthouse; Marks Tey Hotel.

1B 51 Crews Hill
Cattlegate Rd, Crews Hill, Enfield, Middx EN2 8AZ
☎ (020) 8363 6674
Off A1005 Enfield to Potters Bar road into East Lodge Lane, turn right into Cattlegate Rd.
Parkland course.
Pro Neil Wichelow; Founded 1921
Designed by H. Colt
18 holes, 6244 yards, S.S.S. 70
♦ Must be members of a recognised golf club; WE and BH only with a member.
WD £22.
🕗 Welcome with advance booking; terms on application.
🍽 Full facilities, except Mon.
🛏 Royal Chase.

1B 52 Crondon Park
Stock Road, Stock, Essex CM4 9DP
☎ (01277) 841115, Fax 841356, Pro 841887
Off the B1007 outside the village of Stock.
Parkland course.
Pro Paul Barham/Freddy Sunderland; Founded 1984
Designed by M Gillett
18 holes, 6585 yards, S.S.S. 71
♦ Welcome.
WD £15; WE £20.
🕗 WDs only, full clubhouse facilities; from £23.50.
🍽 Full bar and restaurant.
🛏 South Lodge; County Hotel; Miami Hotel, all Chelmsford.

1B 53 Danesbury Park
Codictoe Rd, Welwyn Garden City, Herts
☎ (01438) 840100, Fax 846109
0.5 miles from A1M Junction 6 on B656 to Hitchin.
Parkland course.
9 holes, 4150 yards, S.S.S. 60

ENFIELD GOLF CLUB
Old Park Road South, Enfield, Middlesex EN2 7DA Tel: 020-8363 3970
A warm welcome awaits you at Enfield. Course designed by James Braid.
Casual green fees (with Handicap Certificate) and Society Days welcome.
Call Secretary for details.

1893

☦ Restrictions at weekends; by prior arrangement only.
⌇ WD £12.
✎ By arrangement only.
🍽 Facilities; meals by prior arrangement.

1B 54 **Dyrham Park**
Galley Lane, Barnet, Herts EN5 4RA
☎ (0181) Pro 4403904, Sec 4403361
2 miles outside Barnet near Arkley, off A1 and M25.
Parkland course.
Pro Bill Large; Founded 1963
Designed by C.K. Cotton
18 holes, 6428 yards, S.S.S. 71
☦ Only as guest of member or member of golf society.
⌇ Golf society rate: WD £25; WE £35.
✎ Wed only; two rounds golf, light lunch and dinner or lunch and afternoon tea; terms available on application.
🍽 Full restaurant facilities.
⌁ Post House.

1B 55 **Ealing**
Perivale Lane, Greenford, Middx UB6 8SS
☎ (020) 8997 0937, Fax 8998 0756, Pro 8997 3959
Off A40 W opposite Hoover building.
Parkland course.
Pro Ian Parsons; Founded 1898
Designed by H. Colt
18 holes, 6216 yards, S.S.S. 70
☦ Welcome WD only, phone for advance booking.
⌇ WD £30
✎ Mon, Wed and Thurs only; terms on application.
🍽 Full facilities.
⌁ The Bridge (Greenford).

1B 56 **East Herts**
Hamels Park, Buntingford, Herts SG9 9NA
☎ (01920) 821923, Fax 823700, Pro 821922, Sec 821978, Bar/Rest 821922
On A10 N of Puckeridge.
Parkland course.

Pro Stephen Bryan; Founded 1899
18 holes, 6456 yards, S.S.S. 71
☦ WDs with handicap certs; WE with member only.
⌇ WD £26
✎ Terms available on application; 18 holes of golf, bar, catering; £54.50.
🍽 Full facilities.

1B 57 **Edgewarebury**
Edgeware Way, Edgeware, Middlesex AL4 0BR
☎ (020) 8958 3571, Sec 8905 3393
On A41 between Edgeware and Elstree.
Pitch and putt course.
Founded 1946
9 holes, 2090 yards, S.S.S. 27
☦ Welcome 9am until dusk; no booking necessary.
⌇ WD £4; WE £4.50
✎ Welcome; terms on application.
🍽 No facilities.
⌁ Edgewarebury Hotel.

1B 58 **Elstree**
Watling St, Elstree, Herts WD6 3AA
☎ (020) 8953 6115, Fax 8207 6390
On A5183 between Elstree and Radlett.
Parkland course.
Pro Marc Warwick; Founded 1984
18 holes, 6556 yards, S.S.S. 72
☦ Welcome WD and after midday at WE.
⌇ WD £20; WE £25.
✎ Welcome WD except Wed, by prior arrangement; minimum 8 players in party; golf and catering packages available; Ingolf Simulator room; from £15.
🍽 Full catering and bar.
Practice range, 60 bays, floodlit.
⌁ Edgewarebury Hotel, Elstree; Oaklands, Boreham Wood; North Medburn Farm B&B.

1B 59 **Enfield**
Old Park Rd South, Enfield, Middx EN2 7DA
☎ (020) Fax 8342 0381, Pro 8366 4492, Sec 8363 3970, Bar/Rest 8363 3970

Leave the M25 at Junction 24; take the A1005 to Enfield, turn right at the roundabout in Slades Hill, then the first left into Old Park View, at the end of the road turn right into Old Park Road South.
Parkland course.
Pro Lee Fickling; Founded 1893
Designed by James Braid
18 holes, 6154 yards, S.S.S. 70
☦ WD, except Tuesday.
⌇ WD £25.
✎ WD only with references; full clubhouse facilities; from £50.
🍽 Full catering facilities.
⌁ West Lodge Park, Cockfosters; Royal Chase, Enfield.

1B 60 **Epping Forest G & CC**
Woolston Manor, Abridge Rd, Chigwell, Essex IG7 6BX
☎ (020) 8500 2549, Fax 8501 5452, Pro 8559 8272
From M11 Junction 5 take the A113; course is 1 mile on between Abridge and Chigwell.
Parkland course.
Pro Craig Stephenson; Founded 1994
Designed by Neil Coles
18 holes, 6408 yards, S.S.S. 71
Visitors:Welcome.
⌇ WD £18; WE £38 after 2pm.
✎ WD welcome by prior arrangement; terms on application.
🍽 Full catering and bar facilities.
⌁ Swallow Hotel, Waltham Abbey.

1B 61 **Essex Golf & CC** ☎
Earls Colne, Nr Colchester, Essex CO6 2NS
☎ (01787) 224466, Fax 224410
On B1024 2 miles N of A120 at Coggeshall.
Parkland course.
Pro Mark Spooner; Founded 1990
Designed by Reg Plumbridge
18 holes, 6982 yards, S.S.S. 73
Also 9-hole academy course, par 34
☦ Welcome by prior arrangement.
⌇ WD £16; WE £20.
✎ Welcome WD by prior arrangement; packages available; health and beauty facilities; terms on application.

🍽 Restaurant and bar.
Practice range, 20 bays, floodlit.
🛏 The Lodge.

1B 62 **Fairlop Waters**

Forest Rd, Barkingside, Ilford, Essex
IG6 3HN
☎ (020) 8500 9911, Pro 8501 1881
Signposted from the M11 and along
the A12; near Fairlop station (Central
Line).
Public heathland course.
Pro Bradley Preston; Founded 1988
Designed by John Jacobs
18 holes, 6281 yards, S.S.S. 69
🏌 Welcome; tidy dress required.
⏷ WD £10.50; WE £15.
✏ Welcome WD by prior
arrangement; sailing, children's play
area, country park; terms available on
application.
🍽 Bar, Daltons American Diner, 2
banqueting suites.
Practice range 36 bays; floodlit.
🛏 Granada Travel Inn (Redbridge).

1B 63 **Finchley**

Nether Court, Frith Lane, Mill Hill,
London NW7 1PU
☎ (020) 8346 2436, Fax 8343 4205,
Pro 8346 5086, Bar/Rest 8349 2314
2 miles from M1 Junction 2.
Parkland course.
Pro David Brown; Founded 1929
Designed by James Braid
18 holes, 6411 yards, S.S.S. 71
🏌 By prior arrangement only.
⏷ WD £24; WE £30.
✏ Terms on application.
🍽 Full facilities.

1B 64 **Five Lakes Hotel**   ♛
Golf & CC

Colchester Rd, Tolleshunt Knight,
Maldon, Essex CM9 8HX
☎ (01621) 862326, Fax 862320,
Bar/Rest 868888
Off A12 at Kelvedon, take B1023 to
Tiptree following tourist signs.
Links style course.
Pro Gary Carter; Founded 1991
Designed by N Coles
Lakes course: 18 holes, 6767 yards,
S.S.S. 70; Links course: 18 holes,
6250 yards, S.S.S. 70
🏌 Welcome by prior arrangement.
✏ Welcome by prior arrangement;
corporate days organised; minimum
of 8; terms on application.
🍽 Clubhouse and hotel facilities
available.
🛏 Five Lakes.

1B 65 **Forest Hills**

Newgate St Village, Herts SG13 8EW
☎ (01707) 876825
5 mins from M25 Junction 25 at
Cuffley.
Hilly parkland course.
9 holes, 6440 yards, S.S.S. 71
🏌 Welcome.
⏷ WD £15; WE £20.
✏ By arrangement packages
available.
🍽 Chinese restaurant available in
clubhouse.

1B 66 **Forrester Park**

Beckingham Rd, Great Totham, Nr
Maldon, Essex CM9 8EA
☎ (01621) 891406, Fax 891406, Pro
893456
Off A12 at Rivenhall End, follow signs
to Great Braxted until B1022. Turn
right to Maldon, course is 1.8 miles
on left.
Parkland course.
Pro Gary Pike; Founded 1968
Designed by D.A.H. Everett & T.R.
Forrester-Muir
18 holes, 6073 yards, S.S.S. 69
🏌 Welcome by arrangement.
⏷ WD £18; WE £20; twilight rates
available £12.
✏ WD, after midday at WE.
🍽 Facilities available.
🛏 Rivenhall Motor Inn, Rivenhall;
Blue Boar, Maldon.

1B 67 **Frinton**

1 The Esplanade, Frinton-on-Sea,
Essex CO13 9EP
☎ (01255) 674618, Fax 674618, Pro
671618, Bar/Rest 650405
On B1033 in Frinton.
Seaside course, not traditional links.
Pro Peter Taggart; Founded 1895
Designed by Tom Dunn (1895)/ Willie
Park Jnr (1904)
18 holes, 6265 yards, S.S.S. 70
🏌 Welcome by prior arrangement
with Sec.
⏷ WD £25, WE £26.
✏ Welcome Wed, Thurs and some
Fri by arrangement with Sec; catering
by arrangement; £25-45.
🍽 Facilities available.
🛏 Maplin Hotel; Rock Hotel; Glenco
Hotel.

1B 68 **Fulwell**

Wellington Rd, Hampton Hill, Middx
TW12 1JY
☎ (020) Pro 8977 3844, Sec 8977
2733

2 miles S of Twickenham on A311,
opposite Fulwell bus station.
Meadowland course.
Pro Nigel Turner; Founded 1904
Designed by D. Morrison
18 holes, 6544 yards, S.S.S. 71
🏌 Welcome WD; book through Pro
shop.
⏷ WD £30.
✏ Welcome by prior arrangement;
terms on application.
🍽 By arrangement.
🛏 The Winning Post.

1B 69 **Gosfield Lake**

The Manor House, Hall Drive,
Gosfield
Halstead, Essex CO9 1SE
☎ (01787) 474747, Fax 476044, Pro
474488, Bar/Rest 474400
7 miles N of Braintree on A1017; 1
mile W of Gosfield village.
Parkland course.
Pro Richard Wheeler; Founded 1988
Designed by Sir Henry Cotton,
Howard Swan
Lakes: 18 holes, 6756 yards, S.S.S.
72
Also Meadows course: 9 holes, 4180
yards
🏌 Welcome.
⏷ WD £25; WE £30.
✏ Welcome; 36 holes, lunch,
carvery; from £42.
🍽 Full catering facilities.
🛏 Bull, Halstead.

1B 70 **Great Hadham**   ♛

Great Hadham Rd, Much Hadham,
Herts SG10 6JE
5 mins on the B1004 off the A120
and M11 at Junction 8.
18-hole meadowland course.
Pro Kevin Lunt; Founded 1993
18 holes, 6854 yards, S.S.S. 73
🏌 Welcome every day except before
noon at WE.
⏷ WD £18; WE £25.
✏ Welcome WD except Wed;
packages available from £19.
🍽 Two bars, fully licensed dining
area.
All-weather driving range, 15 bays, 3
practice holes, practice bunker.
Hadham Health Club; Kevin Lunt Golf
College.
🛏 Down Hall, Hatfield Heath; Hilton
International.

1B 71 **Grim's Dyke**

Oxhey Lane, Hatch End, Pinner,
Middx HA5 4AL

☎(020) 8428 4539, Fax 8421
5494, Pro 8428 7484, Bar/Rest
8428 4093
On the A4008 between Hatch End
and Watford.
Gently undulating parkland.
Pro J Rule; Founded 1910
Designed by James Braid
18 holes, 5590 yards, S.S.S. 67
† Welcome WD.
⌊ WD £25.
⌁Welcome Tues-Fri; 36 holes, 2
meals; £50.
🍴 Full catering facilities.

1B 72 **Hadley Wood**
Beech Hill, Barnet, Herts EN4 0JJ
☎(020) 8449 4328, Fax 8364 8633,
Pro 8449 3285, Bar/Rest 8441 8023
Off A111 Cockfosters road, a mile
from M25 Junction 24.
Parkland course.
Pro Peter Jones; Founded 1922
Designed by A MacKenzie
18 holes, 6457 yards, S.S.S. 71
† Welcome WD if carrying handicap
certs.
⌊ WD £36.
⌁Welcome Mon, Thurs and Fri;
terms on application.
🍴 Full catering and bar facilities
available.
⌐ West Lodge Park, Cockfosters.

1B 73 **Hainault Forest**
Chigwell Row, Hainault, Essex IG7
4QW
☎(020) 8500 0385, Pro 8500 2131,
Sec 8500 0385
On A12 12 miles central London.
Parkland course.
Pro Chris Hope; Founded 1912
Lower: 18 holes, 6618 yards, S.S.S.
72
Upper: 18 holes, 5893 yards, S.S.S.
68
† Welcome, pay and play course.
⌊ WD £12.50; WE £15.50.
⌁ Welcome by prior arrangement;
packages available.
🍴 Meals and bar service.

1B 74 **Hampstead**
Winnington Rd, Hampstead, London
N2 0TU
☎(020) 8455 0203, Fax 8731 6194,
Pro 8455 7089
400 yards down Winnington Road
near Kenwood House.
Undulating parkland course with
mature trees.
Pro Peter Brown; Founded 1893

Designed by Tom Dunn
9 holes, 5822 yards, S.S.S. 68
† Welcome with handicap certs or
letter of introduction; restrictions Tues
and WE.
⌊ WD £30; WE £35.
⌁Not available.
🍴 Not available.

1B 75 **Hanbury Manor Golf & CC**
Ware, Herts SG12 0SD
☎(01920) 487722, Fax 487692
Junction 25 off M25 and take A10 N
for 12 miles.
Parkland course.
Pro Peter Blaze; Founded 1990
Designed by Jack Nicklaus II
18 holes, 7016 yards, S.S.S. 74
† Welcome if hotel resident or
member's guest.
⌊ Hotel residents: WD/WE £75.
⌁Welcome by prior arrangement
with the golf co-ordinator; terms on
application.
🍴 Hotel and clubhouse facilities.
⌐ Marriott Hanbury Manor.

1B 76 **Hanover**
Hullbridge Rd, Rayleigh, Essex SS6
9QS
☎(01702) 232377
Undulating course.
Pro Tony Blackburn; Founded 1991
Designed by Reg Plumbridge
Georgian course: 18 holes, 6696
yards, S.S.S. 72
Regency course: 18 holes, 3700
yards, par 61
† Members' guests only.
⌁Affiliated society enquiries only;
terms on application.
🍴 Full clubhouse service.
⌐ The Watermill.

1B 77 **Harefield Place**
The Drive, Harefield Place, Uxbridge,
Middx UB10 8AQ
☎(01895) 272457, Fax 810262, Pro
237287
B467 towards Ruislip off A40. 1st left
down The Drive.
Undulating parkland.
Pro Jeff Chartlon
18 holes, 5677 yards, S.S.S. 68
† Welcome.
⌊ WD £12.50; WE £17-£50.
⌁Welcome midweek; afternoons at
WE; terms on application.
🍴 Full catering facilities, including
carvery, and bar.
⌐ Master Brewer, Hillingdon.

1B 78 **Harpenden**
Hammonds End, Redbourn Lane,
Harpenden, Herts AL5 2AX
☎(01582) 712580, Fax 712725, Pro
767124, Bar/Rest 462014
On A487 Redbourn road.
Parkland course.
Founded 1894/1931
Designed by Hawtree & Taylor
18 holes, 6381 yards, S.S.S. 70
† Welcome WD except Thurs; with a
member at WE.
⌊ WD £25
⌁Welcome WD except Thurs; £52-
£58.
🍴 Full facilities.
⌐ Gleneagles, Harpenden;
Harpenden House Hotel.

1B 79 **Harpenden Common**
Cravells Rd, East Common,
Harpenden, Herts AL5 1BL
☎(01582) 712856, Fax 715959, Pro
460655, Sec 715959
Course is 4 miles north of St Albans
on the A1081.
Parkland course.
Pro D Fitzsimmons; Founded
1894/1931/
1995
Designed by Ken Brown (1995)
18 holes, 6214 yards, S.S.S. 67
† Welcome WD.
⌊ WD £25
⌁Welcome on Thurs and Fri; £48.
🍴 Full facilities.
⌐ Gleneagles, Harpenden.

1B 80 **Harrow Hill**
Kenton Road, Harrow Middlesex HA1
2BW
☎(020) 8864 3754
Off main Harrow by-pass near
Northwick Park roundabout.
Park beginners course.
Pro Simon Bishop; Founded 1982
Designed by S. Teahan
9 holes, 850 yards
† Public beginners par 3.
⌊ WD £3.80; WE £4.20.
🍴 Cold soft drinks and sweets
available.

1B 81 **Harrow School**
Harrow School, 5 High St, Harrow-on-
the-Hill, Middlesex HA1 3JE
☎(020) 8872 8000, Green Keeper
(0956) 312290, Golf Club info (020)
8422 5174
Parkland course.
Founded 1979
Designed by Donald Steel

9 holes, 3690 yards, S.S.S. 57
† No visitors.

1B 82 **Hartsbourne G & CC**
Hartsbourne Ave, Bushey Heath,
Herts WD2 1JW
☎ (020) 8950 1133, Pro 8950 2836
Turn off A411 at entrance to Bushey
Heath village; 5 miles SE of Watford.
Parkland course.
Pro Alistair Cardwell; Founded 1946
Designed by Hawtree and Taylor
18 holes, 6385 yards, S.S.S. 70
Also 9 holes, 5773 yards, par 70
† Members guests' only.
⌴ WD £20; WE £30.
⌁ Welcome WD only; catering
packages available.
⦿ Full catering and bar facilities.
⌁ Hilton National.

1B 83 **Hartswood**
King George's Playing Fields,
Ingrave Road, Brentwood, Essex
CM14 5AE
☎ (01277) 214830, Pro 218714, Sec
2188501 mile from Brentwood town
centre on A128 Ingrave road.
Parkland course.
Pro Steve Cole; Founded 1965
18 holes, 6192 yards, S.S.S. 69
† Municipal course.
⌴ WD £9; WE £11.50.
⌁ Welcome WD, minimum 20; meals
and 18 or 36 holes, coffee on arrival;
£25-£35.
⦿ Facilities available.

1B 84 **Harwich & Dovercourt**
Station Rd, Parkeston, Harwich,
Essex CO12 4NZ
☎ (01255) 503616, Fax 503616
Turn left off the A120 roundabout for
Harwich International port; course is
100 yards.
Parkland course.
Founded 1907
9 holes, 5900 yards, S.S.S. 69
† WD welcome if carrying handicap
certs; WE welcome only if guests of a
member.
⌴ WD £17.
⌁ Welcome by prior arrangement;
catering by prior arrangement; from
£14.
⦿ Clubhouse facilities.
⌁ Tower; Cliff, both at Dovercourt.

1B 85 **Haste Hill**
The Drive, Northwood, Middx HA6
1HN

☎ (01923) 829808, Pro 822877,
Sec M Grooves 825224, Bar/Rest
739484
On A404 at Northwood
Tree-lined parkland.
Pro Cameron Smilie; Founded 1933
10 holes, 5797 yards, S.S.S. 68
† Welcome; book in advance.
⌴ WD £12.50; WE £18.50.
⌁ Welcome; terms on application.
⦿ Facilities available.
⌁ Tudor Lodge, Eastcote.

1B 86 **Hatfield London CC**
Bedwell Park, Essendon, Hatfield,
Herts AL9 6JA
☎ (01707) 642624
A1000 from Potters Bar, B158
towards Essendon.
Undulating parkland course.
Pro Norman Greer; Founded 1976
Designed by Fred Hawtree
18 holes, 6385 yards, S.S.S. 70
† Welcome by advance booking
only.
⌴ WD £17; WE £27.
⌁ Welcome; terms on application.
⦿ Full facilities.

1B 87 **Hazelwood**
Croysdale Ave, Sunbury-on-Thames,
Middlesex TW16 6QU
☎ (01932) 770981, Fax 770933, Pro
770932, Bar/Rest 783496
1 mile from M3 Junction 1.
Parkland course.
Pro Francis Sheridan; Founded 1993
Designed by Jonathan Gaunt
9 holes, 5660 yards, S.S.S. 68
† Welcome.
Grren Fee WD £10.50 WE £13.75
⌁ Welcome; terms available on
application.
⦿ Full facilities
Practice range 36 bays.
⌁ Thames Lodge, Staines;
Runnymede Hotel, Egham; Moat
House, Shepperton.

1B 88 **Hendon**
Ashley Walk, Devonshire Road, Mill
Hill, London NW7 1DG
☎ (020) 8346 6023, Fax 8343 1974,
Pro 8346 8990
From Hendon Central take Queens
Rd through Brent St, continue to
roundabout, take 1st exit on left, club
0.5 mile on left in Devonshire Rd.
Parkland course.
Pro Stuart Murray; Founded 1903
Designed by H.S. Colt
18 holes, 6266 yards, S.S.S. 70

† Welcome Tues-Fri, limited Mon,
not Sat/Sun morning.
⌴ WD £28; WE £35.
⌁ Welcome Tues-Fri by
arrangement; terms on application.
⦿ Snacks only Mon; other days
lunch, snacks, high tea to 6pm.
⌁ Holiday Inn (Brent Cross);
Hendon Hall.

1B 89 **The Hertfordshire**
Broxbournebury Mansion, White St,
Broxbourne, Herts EN10 7PY
☎ (01992) 466666, Fax 470326
M25 Junction 25, take A10 towards
Cambridge. Take A10 exit for
Turnford and then A1170 to Bell
Lane. Turn left, Bell Lane becomes
White Stubbs Lane. Course is on the
right.
Parkland course.
Pro Nicola Stroud; Founded 1995
Designed by Jack Nicklaus (his first
pay and play course in Europe)
18 holes, 6388 yards, S.S.S. 70
† Welcome.
⌴ WD £22; WE £26.
⌁ Welcome; corporate days
available; health club, tennis club,
golf academy with chipping green;
terms on application.
⦿ Restaurant and bar.
Practice range 30 bays, floodlit.
⌁ The Cheshunt Marriott.

1B 90 **High Beech**
Wellington Hill, Loughton, Essex IG10
4AH
☎ (020) 8508 7323
5 mins from M25 Junction 26 at
Waltham Abbey.
Parkland course.
Pro Clark Baker, Founded 1963
9 holes, 1477 yards
† Public pay and play.
⌴ WD £3.25; WE £4.25.
⌁ Welcome.
⦿ No facilities.

1B 91 **Highgate**
Denewood Rd, London N6 4AH
☎ (020) 8340 1906, Pro 8340 5467,
Sec 8340 3745
Off Hampstead Lane near Kenwood
House, turn into Sheldon Ave then
1st left into Denewood Rd.
Parkland course.
Pro Robin Turner / Mark Tompkins /
Darren Turner; Founded 1904
18 holes, 5985 yards, S.S.S. 69
† Welcome WD (after noon on
Wed); no visitors at WE.

⌐ WD £30.
⌐ Welcome Tues, Thurs, Fri; terms on application.
⌐ Full facilities 12am-8pm.

1B 92 Hillingdon
18 Dorset Way, Hillingdon, Middx
UB10 0JR
☎ (01895) 233956, Pro 460035
Turn off A40 to Uxbridge past RAF station, up Hillingdon Hill to turn left at Vine Public House into Vine Lane.
Undulating parkland.
Pro Phil Smith; Founded 1892
Designed by Harry Woods & Chas E. Stevens.
9 holes, 5490 yards, S.S.S. 68
⌐ Welcome WD except Thurs pm; WE with a member only after 12.30pm.
⌐ WD £15.
⌐ Welcome Mon by prior arrangement; special golf and catering packages available; from £25.
⌐ Bar and catering facilities available.
⌐ Master Brewer; Old Cottage.

1B 93 Horsenden Hill
Woodland Rise, Greenford, Middx
UB6 0RD
☎ (020) Pro 8902 4555
Signposted off Whitton Ave East, at the rear of Sudbury Golf club.
Public undulating parkland course.
Pro Simon Hoffman; Founded 1935
9 holes, 1632 yards, S.S.S 28
⌐ Welcome, no restrictions.
⌐ WD £4.25; WE £6.20.
⌐ Welcome any time by prior arrangement.
⌐ Bar and restaurant.

1B 94 Hounslow Heath
Staines Rd, Hounslow, Middx TW4 5DS
☎ (020) 8570 5271
A315 main road between Hounslow and Bedfont, on left hand side.
Heathland course.
Founded 1979
Designed by Fraser Middleton
18 holes, 5901 yards, S.S.S. 68
⌐ Welcome.
⌐ WD £8; WE £11.50.
⌐ Welcome by arrangement; terms on application.
⌐ No bar; snacks and soft drinks available.
⌐ Several available in Hounslow or Heathrow.

1B 95 Ilford
291 Wanstead Park Rd, Ilford, Essex
IG1 3TR
☎ (020) Pro 8554 0094, Sec 8554 2930
0.5 mile from Ilford railway station.
Parkland course.
Pro Stuart Dowsett; Founded 1906
18 holes, 5297 yards, S.S.S. 66
⌐ Welcome with advance booking; restricted Tues and Thurs; Sat 10.30am-12.30pm, Sun 12.30pm-1.30pm.
⌐ WD £15; WE £19.
⌐ Welcome WD by prior arrangement with Sec; terms available on application.
⌐ Restaurant available most days.
⌐ Woodford Moat House.

1B 96 Knebworth
Deards End Lane, Knebworth, Herts
SG3 6NL
☎ (01438) 812752, Fax 815216, Pro 812757
1 mile S of Stevenage on B197, leave A1M at Junction 7.
Undulating parkland.
Pro Garry Parker; Founded 1908
Designed by Willie Park
18 holes, 6492 yards, S.S.S. 71
⌐ Welcome WD.
⌐ WD £30
⌐ Welcome Mon, Tues and Thurs only; terms on application.
⌐ Full catering and bar.

1B 97 Laing Sports Club
Rowley Lane, Arkley, Barnet, Herts
EN5 3HW
☎ (020) 8441 6051
Off A1 S at Borehamwood.
Parkland course.
Designed by employees of John Laing and members.
9 holes, 4178 yards, S.S.S. 60
⌐ Welcome only as the guest of a member.
⌐ Limited.
⌐ Limited.

1B 98 Lamerwood
Codicote Rd, Wheathampsted, Herts
Al4 8RH
☎ (01582) 833013, Fax 641831
5 miles W of A1 junction 4 on B653.
Woodland/parkland course.
18 holes, 6588 yards, S.S.S. 72
⌐ Welcome by prior arrangement; weekend restrictions.
⌐ WD £17; WE £30.
⌐ Packages available.

⌐ Bar and English and Japanese restaurant.

1B 99 Langdon Hills   ℧
Lower Dunton Road, Bulphan, Essex
RM14 3TY
☎ (01268) 548444, Fax 490084, Pro 544300
Course is 8 miles from M25 Junction 30; take the A13 E towards Tilbury, after approx 7 miles turn off on the B1007 towards Horndon on the Hill; after approx 1 mile turn left into Lower Dunton Rd.
Parkland course.
Pro Terry Moncur; Founded 1991
Designed by MRM Sandow
27 holes, 9558 yards, S.S.S. 71
Play three courses in certain combinations; Langdon course: 3132 yards; Bulphan course: 3372 yards; Horndon course: 3054 yards
⌐ Welcome WD; not before 10.30am WE.
⌐ WD £14.85; WE £19.75.
⌐ Welcome WD by prior arrangement; European School of golf; special packages; function suite; terms on application.
⌐ Bar and restaurant.
Practice range 22 bays; floodlit.
⌐ Langdon Hills.

1B 100 Lee Valley
Lee Valley Leisure Golf Course, Edmonton, London N9 0AS
☎ (020) 8803 3611
1 mile N of North Circular road, Junction with Montagu Rd.
Public parkland course with large lake and river.
Pro Richard Gerken; Founded 1974
18 holes, 4902 yards, S.S.S. 64
⌐ Open to public every day, no restrictions.
⌐ WD £11.30; WE £13.90.
⌐ Welcome WD only; max 30 persons; sporting facilities at leisure centre; terms on application.
⌐ Breakfast until midday, bar and bar snacks daily.
Practice range 20 bays; floodlit.
⌐ Holt Whites Hotel, Enfield.

1B 101 Letchworth
Letchworth Lane, Letchworth, Herts
SG6 3NQ
☎ (01462) 683203, Fax 484567, Pro 682713
1 mile S of Letchworth off A505.
Parkland course.
Pro Steve Allen; Founded 1905

Designed by Harry Vardon
18 holes, 6181 yards, S.S.S. 69
↑ Welcome WD; restrictions Tues.
⌣ WD £25.
⌣ Welcome Wed, Thurs and Fri; 36
holes of golf, snack lunch and dinner;
£52.
⍟ Full clubhouse facilities.
⌐ Ambassador, Letchworth;
Letchworth Hall.

1B 102 Little Hay Golf Complex
Box Lane, Bovingdon, Hemel
Hempstead, Herts HP3 0DQ
☎ (01442) 833798
Just off A41, turn left at first traffic
lights, past Hemel Hempstead
station, turn right up hill at lights; 1.5
miles up hill, complex on right.
Public parkland pay and play course.
Pro Morris Campbell
Designed by Hawtree & Son
18 holes, 6311 yards, S.S.S. 70
↑ Welcome.
⌣ WD £11.40; WE £15.55.
⌣ Welcome by prior arrangement;
bookings accepted on the day after
8.30am by phone; golf and catering
packages available on request; terms
on application.
⍟ Full meals.
Practice range 22 bays; floodlit.
⌐ Bobsleigh.

1B 103 London Golf Centre
Ruislip Rd, Northolt, Middx UB5 6QZ
☎ (020) 8845 3180, Fax 8845 0542,
Sec 8842 0442
0.5 miles S of Polish War Memorial
on A4180.
Parkland course.
Pro Neil MacDonald; Founded 1982
9 holes, 5836 yards, S.S.S. 69
↑ Welcome.
⌣ WD £11; WE £14.50.
⌣ Welcome WD; unlimited golf, 2-
course lunch; from £20.
⍟ Bar and catering facilities.

1B 104 Loughton
Clay's Lane, Debden Green,
Loughton, Essex IG10 2RZ
☎ (020) 8502 2923
From M25 Junction 26 take A121
towards Loughton; 3rd exit at
roundabout; first turning on left.
Hilly parkland course.
Pro Richard Layton; Founded 1982
9 holes, 4652 yards, S.S.S. 63
↑ Welcome; book after Thurs for
WE.

⌣ WD £8.50; WF £10
⌣ Terms available on application.
⍟ Facilities available but limited.

1B 105 Maldon
Beeleigh, Langford, Maldon, Essex
CM9 6LL
☎ (01621) 853212
2 miles NW of Maldon on B1019.
Turn off at Essex Waterworks.
Parkland course.
Founded 1891
9 holes, 6253 yards, S.S.S. 70
↑ Welcome WD; with a member only
at WE.
⌣ WD £15
⌣ Welcome; maximum of 32;
packages; terms available on
application.
⍟ Clubhouse catering and bar.
⌐ Blue Boar, Maldon.

1B 106 Malton
Malton Lane, Meldreth, Royston,
Herts
☎ (01763) 262200, Fax 262209
A10 towards Cambridge, turn at
Melbourne towards Meldreth, 4 miles.
Parkland course.
Founded 1994
18 holes, 6708 yards, S.S.S. 72
↑ Welcome.
⌣ WD £10; WE £14.
⌣ Welcome; packages available;
from £12.
⍟ Bar and bar snacks.
Driving range, 10 bays.
⌐ Cambridge Motel.

1B 107 Manor of Groves Golf & CC ☎
High Wych, Sawbridgeworth, Herts
CM21 0LA
☎ (01279) 722333, Fax 726972, Pro
721486
On A1184 to High Wych; leave M11
at Junction 7 on A414.
Parkland course.
Pro Craig Laurence; Founded 1991
Designed by S. Sharer
18 holes, 6280 yards, S.S.S. 70
↑ Welcome WD; pm at WE.
⌣ WD £15; WE £20.
⌣ Welcome WD; packages arranged
for parties; from £26.
⍟ Full hotel facilities.
⌐ Manor of Groves Hotel.

1B 108 Maylands Golf & CC
Colchester Rd, Harold Park, Romford,
Essex RM3 0AZ

☎ (01708) 342055, Fax 373080, Pro
346466, Sec 373080, Bar/Rest
346273
1 mile W of M25 Junction 28.
Parkland course.
Pro J S Hopkin/R Cole Touring Pro;
Founded 1936
Designed by Colt, Alison and
Morrison
18 holes, 6361 yards, S.S.S. 70
↑ WD Welcome with prior
arrangement and handicap certs.
⌣ WD £20
⌣ Mon, Wed and Fri; packages
available; terms on application.
⍟ Full catering facilities.
⌐ Brentwood Post House; Mary
Green Manor.

1B 109 Mid-Herts ☎
Gustard Wood, Wheathampstead, St
Albans, Herts AL4 8RS
☎ (01582) 832242, Fax 832260, Pro
832788
6 miles N of St Albans on B651.
Parkland course.
Founded 1892
18 holes, 6060 yards, S.S.S. 69
↑ Welcome except Tues morning
and Wed afternoon.
⌣ WD £24
⌣ Welcome Thurs and Fri; terms on
application.
⍟ Catering and bar facilities.
⌐ Hatfield Lodge Hotel.

1B 110 Mill Green
Gypsy Lane, Welwyn Garden City,
Herts AL7 4TY
☎ (01707) 276900, Fax 276898, Pro
270542
Off A100 Welwyn Garden City past
Bush Hall, at lights turn left, 2nd rt
and then into Gypsy Lane.
Parkland course.
Pro Alan Hall; Founded 1994
Designed by Peter Alliss & Clive
Clark
18 holes, 6615 yards, S.S.S. 72
Also Romany par 3 course.
↑ Welcome.
⌣ WD £19(Mon £15); WE £25.
⌣ Welcome by prior arrangement;
packages available; par 3 course;
terms on application.
⍟ Full catering and bar.
Practice range, grass.
⌐ Jarvis Comet, Hatfield.

1B 111 Mill Hill ☎
100 Barnet Way, Mill Hill, London
NW7 3AL

☎ (020) 8959 2282, Fax 8906 0731, Pro 8959 7261, Sec 8959 2339
From Junction of A1/A41, going N, immediately filter right and cross into Marsh Lane, after 0.5 mile turn left into Hankins Lane, leading to clubhouse; going S, 1 mile from Stirling Corner.
Parkland course.
Pro David Beal; Founded 1925
Designed by J.F. Abercromby (1931 remodelled by H.S. Colt)
18 holes, 6247 yards, S.S.S. 70
† Welcome WD; WE reservations only.
⌐ WD £25; WE £30.
⌁ Welcome Mon, Wed, Fri (except BH); terms on application.
🍽 Facilities daily.
⌐╕ Jarvis; Hilton National.

1B 112 Moor Park
Rickmansworth, Herts WD3 1QN
☎ (01923) 773146, Fax 777109, Pro 774113
1 mile SE of Rickmansworth off Batchworth roundabout on A4145.
Parkland course.
Pro L Farmer; Founded 1923
Designed by H.S. Colt
High: 18 holes, 6713 yards, S.S.S. 72
West: 18 holes, 5815 yards, S.S.S. 68
† WDs only with handicap certs.
⌐ WD West £35; High £45
⌁ Welcome WD only; packages available; terms on application.
🍽 Full restaurant facilities.

1B 113 Muswell Hill
Rhodes Ave, Wood Green London N22 4UT
☎ (020) 8888 1764, Fax 8889 9380, Pro 8888 8046
1 mile from Bounds Green tube station, 1.5 miles from N Circular Rd.
Undulating course.
Pro David Wilton; Founded 1893
18 holes, 6432 yards, S.S.S. 70
† WD, not Tues am; WE and BH limited bookings through Pro.
⌐ WD £23.
⌁ Welcome WD by arrangement; packages available; terms on application.
🍽 Meals and snacks, bar.
⌐╕ Raglan Hall.

1B 114 The Nazeing
Middle St, Nazeing, Essex EN9 2LW
☎ (01992) 893915, Fax 893882, Pro 893798, Sec 893798

On B194 in Nazeing.
Parkland course.
Pro Robert Green, Founded 1992
Designed by Martin Gillett
18 holes, 6598 yards, S.S.S. 71
† Welcome after 8.30am WD and 12 at WE.
⌐ WD £20; WE £28.
⌁ Welcome WD with a minimum of 12 players; packages involving breakfast, lunch and dinner and 18, 27 or 36 holes can be arranged; terms on application.
🍽 Full catering and bar.
⌐╕ Swallow Hotel, Waltham Abbey.

1B 115 North Middlesex
The Manor House, Friern Barnet Lane, Whetstone, London N20 0NL
☎ (020) 8445 1732, Fax 8445 5023, Pro 8445 3060, Sec 8445 1604, Bar/Rest 8343 7275
Course is 5 miles south of M25 Junction 23 between Barnet and Finchley.
Parkland course.
Pro Steve Roberts; Founded 1905
Designed by Willie Park Jnr
18 holes, 5625 yards, S.S.S. 67
† Welcome by prior arrangement. WE after pm.
⌐ WD £22; WE £27.50.
⌁ Welcome WD by prior arrangement with Sec; discounts available for groups of 15+; from £27.50.
🍽 Full clubhouse facilities available.

1B 116 North Weald GC
Rayley Lane, North Weald, Essex CM16 6AR
☎ (01992) 522118, Fax 522881, Pro 524725
On A414 Chelmsford road from M11 Junction 7.
Parkland course.
Pro M Janes; Founded 1996
Designed by D Williams
18 holes, 6311 yards, S.S.S. 70
† Welcome; book with Pro.
⌐ WD £20; WE £27.50.
⌁ Welcome with prior arrangement with Sec; bar and restaurant facilities; driving range; from £20.
🍽 Bar and restaurant.

1B 117 Northwood
Rickmansworth Rd, Northwood, Middx HA6 2QW
☎ (01923) 821384, Fax 840150, Pro 820112, Bar/Rest 825329
0.25 miles S of Northwood on A404.

Parkland course.
Pro C Holdsworth; Founded 1891
Designed by James Braid
18 holes, 6553 yards, S.S.S. 71
† Welcome WD.
⌐ WD £26
⌁ Welcome Mon and Thurs; packages available; terms on application.
🍽 Full catering facilities.
⌐╕ Tudor Lodge, Eastcote.

1B 118 Old Fold Manor
Old Ford Lane, Hadley Green, Barnet, Herts EN5 4QN
☎ (020) 8449 1650, Fax 8441 4863, Pro 8440 7488, Sec 8440 9185, Bar/Rest 8440 2266
On A1000 1 mile N of Barnet close to M25 Junction 23
Heathland course.
Pro Gary Potter; Founded 1910
18 holes, 6260 yards, S.S.S. 71
† Welcome with handicap certs.
⌐ WD £20; WE £20.
⌁ Welcome Thurs and Fri; packages for golf and catering available; £51.50.
🍽 Full clubhouse facilities.
⌐╕ Hadley Hotel; West Lodge Park.

1B 119 Orsett
Brentwood Rd, Orsett, Essex RM16 3DS
☎ (01375) 891226, Fax 892471, Pro 891797, Sec 891352, Bar/Rest 891352
4 miles NE of Grays on the A128.
Heathland/parkland course.
Pro Paul Joiner; Founded 1899
Designed by James Braid
18 holes, 6614 yards, S.S.S. 72
† Welcome if accompanied by a member.
⌐ WD £22.50, day ticket £32.50.
⌁ Welcome Mon, Tues and in afternoon on Wed; packages include all meals; £40-50.
🍽 Full catering and bar facilities.
⌐╕ Orsett Hall; Stifford Moat House, near Grays.

1B 120 Oxhey Park
Prestwick Rd, South Oxhey, Watford Herts WD1 6DT
☎ (01923) 248312
2 miles SW of Watford.
9 holes, 1637 yards, S.S.S. 58
† Welcome.
⌐ £10.
Driving range.

1B 121 Panshanger
Old Herns Lane, Welwyn Garden City, Herts AL7 2ED
☎(01707) Pro 333350, Sec 332837
Off B1000 close to A1, 1 mile NE of town.
Municipal undulating parkland course.
Pro Mick Corlass/Bryan Lewis;
Founded 1976
18 holes, 6347 yards, S.S.S. 70
♦ Welcome; no restrictions.
◻ WD £11.75; WE £16.20
☞ Welcome by prior arrangement; terms on application.
🍽 Lunch every day.
↙ Homestead Court.

1B 122 Perivale Park
Stockdove Way, Argyle Road, Greenford, Middx UB6 8EN
☎(020) Pro 8575 7116
On Ruislip Rd East between Greenford and Perivale, entrance from Argyle Rd.
Public parkland course.
Pro Peter Bryant; Founded 1932
9 holes, 2733 yards, S.S.S. 67
♦ Welcome
◻ WD £5; WE £7.85.
☞ No societies.
🍽 Café serving meals, tea, coffee etc; no bar.
↙ Kenton, Hanger Hill.

1B 123 Pinner Hill
South View Rd, Pinner Hill, Middx HA5 3YA
☎(020) 8866 0963, Fax 8868 4817, Pro 8866 2109, Sec 8866 0963
1 mile W of Pinner Green.
Parkland course.
Pro Mark Grieve; Founded 1928/47
Designed by J.H. Taylor/ Hawtree
18 holes, 6330 yards, S.S.S. 70
♦ Welcome WD, particularly Wed and Thurs.
◻ WD £25, Wed & Thurs; £12
☞ Welcome WD for groups of 12-40 players; package of Full meals and Full day's golf, £40-£42.
🍽 Full facilities.
↙ Barn House, Eastcote; Harrow Hotel; Frithwood GH, Northwood.

1B 124 Porters Park
Shenley Hill, Radlett, Herts WD7 7AZ
☎(01923) 854127, Fax 855475, Pro 854366
From M25 Junction 22 to Radlett via A5183, turn at railway station, 0.5 mile to top of Shenley Hill.
Undulating parkland course.

Pro David Gleeson; Founded 1899
18 holes, 6313 yards, S.S.S. 70
♦ Welcome WD; handicap certs required, phone 24 hours in advance; member guest only at WE.
◻ WD £30.
☞ Wed, Thurs only; min 20, max 50; £68 inc.
🍽 Full catering available for societies, breakfast (pre-ordered), bar menu.
↙ Red Lion.

1B 125 Potters Bar
Darkes Lane, Potters Bar, Herts EN6 1DE
☎(01707) 652020, Fax 655051, Pro 652987
1 mile N of M25 Junction 24 close to Potters Bar station.
Parkland course.
Pro G A'ris; Founded 1924
Designed by James Braid
18 holes, 6291 yards, S.S.S. 70
♦ Welcome WD with handicap certs.
◻ WD £25.
☞ Welcome WD except Wed; full lunch and dinner with 36 holes of golf; £55.
🍽 Full clubhouse facilities.

1B 126 Redbourn
Kinsbourne Green Lane, Redbourn, Herts AL3 7QA
☎(01582) 793493, Fax 794362, Sec 794888, Bar/Rest 793363
Off A5183, turn into Luton Lane and club is 0.5 miles.
Parkland course.
Pro Stephen Hunter; Founded 1971
Designed by H. Stovin
18 holes, 6506 yards, S.S.S. 71
♦ Welcome with prior bookings, accepted 3 days in advance.
◻ WD £20; WE £25.
☞ Welcome WD; full golfing day either on 18-hole course and 9-hole par 3 Kinsbourne or at Aldwickbury Park; golf clinics, golf ranger, buggies, £21-49.
🍽 Full restaurant and bar facilities available.
Practice range, 20 bay target range.

1B 127 Regiment Way
Pratts Farm Lane, Little Waltham, Chelmsford, Essex CM3 3PR
☎(01245) 361100
On A130 off the A12 at Boreham.
Parkland course.
Pro D March; Founded 1995
9 holes, 4887 yards, S.S.S. 64

♦ Welcome; pay and play.
◻ WD £11; WE £12.
☞ Welcome by arrangement.
🍽 Snack facilities.
Practice range, 16 bays floodlit.

1B 128 Rickmansworth
Moor Lane, Rickmansworth, Herts WD3 1QL
☎(01923) 775278, Pro 773163
0.5 miles S of Rickmansworth on A4145.
Undulating parkland.
Pro Alan Dobbins; Founded 1944
Designed by H S Colt
18 holes, 4493 yards, S.S.S. 62
♦ Welcome.
◻ WD £9.60; WE £13.80.
☞ Welcome with prior appointment; terms on application.
🍽 Available in the Fairway Inn.
↙ Long Island Hotel.

1B 129 Risebridge (Havering)
Risebridge Chase, off Lower Bedfords Road, Romford, Essex RM1 4DG
☎(01708) 727376, Pro 741429
From A12 Gallows Corner, left and then left again.
Parkland course.
Pro Paul Jennings; Founded 1972
Designed by F W Hawtree
18 holes, 6271 yards, S.S.S. 70
♦ Welcome except between 8am and 10am at WE.
◻ WD £10.50; WE £13.50.
☞ Welcome by prior arrangement with Pro; packages available; terms on application.
🍽 Full clubhouse catering.
Driving range, 15 bays; 9 hole pitch and putt.
↙ Forte Lodge, Brentwood.

1B 130 Rochford Hundred
Rochford Hall, Hall Rd, Rochford, Essex SS4 1NW
☎(01702) 544302, Fax 541343, Pro 548968
On B1013 off the A127.
Parkland course.
Pro Graham Hill; Founded 1893
Designed by James Braid
18 holes, 6302 yards, S.S.S. 70
♦ Welcome with handicap certs except Sun.
◻ WD £25; WE £30.
☞ Welcome; packages available include 36 holes of golf and meals; £48.
🍽 Full clubhouse facilities.

1B 131 **Romford**

Heath Drive, Gidea Park, Romford,
Essex RM2 5QB
☎(01708) 740986, Pro 749393
1.5 miles Romford centre, off A12.
Parkland course.
Pro Harry Flatman; Founded 1894
Designed by MacKintosh (redesigned
By H.S.Colt 1921)
18 holes, 6185 yards, S.S.S. 69
🏌 WD with handicap certs and by
arrangement with Pro; with member
only at WE.
⌣ WD £25.
⌣ Welcome by prior arrangement;
packages available; terms on
application.
🍽 Facilities available.
⌐ Coach House.

1B 132 **Royston**   ☊

Baldock Rd, Royston, Herts SG8
5BG
☎(01763) Sec 242696, Fax 242696,
Pro 243476
On A505 on outskirts of town to W,
course on Therfield Heath.
Undulating heathland course.
Pro Sean Clark; Founded 1892
18 holes, 6080 yards, S.S.S. 69
🏌 Welcome WD; WE with member
only.
⌣ WD £25.
⌣ By prior arrangement with Sec;
packages available; terms on
application.
🍽 Full clubhouse dining facilities
available.
⌐ Old Bull Inn; The Banyers.

1B 133 **Ruislip**

Ickenham Rd, Ruislip, Middx HA4
7DQ
☎(01895) Pro 638835, Fax 635780
Course is opposite West Ruislip Tube
station.
Parkland course.
Pro Paul Glozier/Paul Hendrick;
Founded 1936
Designed by Sandy Herd
18 holes, 5571 yards, S.S.S. 67
🏌 Public pay and play.
⌣ WD £12.50; WE £17.50.
⌣ Terms on application: contact
(01923) 825224.
🍽 Facilities available.
⌐ Barn, Ruislip.

1B 134 **Saffron Walden**

Windmill Hill, Saffron Walden, Essex
CB10 1BX
☎(01799) Pro 527728, Sec 522786

Take the B184 from Stumps Cross
roundabout on the M11 (exit at
Junction 9), course entrance is just
before entering town.
Parkland course.
Pro Philip Davis; Founded 1919
18 holes, 6606 yards, S.S.S. 72
🏌 Welcome WD with handicap certs;
with member WE and BH.
⌣ WD £30.
⌣ Welcome Mon, Wed, Thurs; terms
on application.
🍽 Lunch available WD; evening
meals for societies.
Practice range 6 bays.
⌐ Saffron.

1B 135 **Sandy Lodge**

Sandy Lodge Lane, Northwood,
Middx HA6 2JD
☎(01923) 825429, Fax 824319, Pro
825321
Off A404 adjacent to Moor Park
underground station.
Inland links.
Pro J Pinsent; Founded 1910
Designed by Harry Vardon
18 holes, 6347 yards, S.S.S. 71
🏌 Welcome WD by prior
arrangement.
⌣ WD £25 till April; May-October
£31
⌣ Welcome Mon and Thurs; full
catering and bar facilities available;
£28-£40.
🍽 Full clubhouse facilities.
Practice range, 20 bays.
⌐ Hilton National, Watford; Bedford
Arms, Rickmansworth.

1B 136 **Shendish Manor**

Shendish House, Apsley
Hemel Hempstead, Herts HP3 0AA
☎(01442) 251806, Fax 217446,
Bar/Rest 232220
3 miles from M25 Junction 20 on
A4251. M1 Junction 8 is 5 miles
away.
Parkland course.
Pro Murray White; Founded 1984/96
Designed by Henry Cotton, Extension
by Donald Steel
18 holes, 5660 yards, S.S.S. 67
🏌 Welcome by prior arrangement.
⌣ WD £15; WE £20.
⌣ Welcome WD and by special
arrangement at WE; packages
available include 18-hole course,
health club, 9-hole pitch and putt,
conference and banqueting rooms.
Lessons also available; from £21.
🍽 Full clubhouse facilities with
private function rooms.

1B 137 **South Herts**

Links Drive, Totteridge London N20
8QU
☎(020) 8445 0117, Fax 8445 7569,
Pro 8445 4633, Sec 8445 2035,
Bar/Rest 8446 3951
On Totteridge Lane 2.5 miles E of
A1M at Mill Hill.
Parkland course.
Pro R Mitchell; Founded 1899
Designed by Harry Vardon
18 holes, 6432 yards, S.S.S. 71
🏌 Welcome with handicap of 24 or
less.
⌣ WD £30; WE £30.
⌣ Welcome Wed, Thurs and Fri;
terms on application.
🍽 Full clubhouse catering and bar
facilities.
⌐ Queens Moat House, Boreham
Wood; South Mimms Post House.

1B 138 **Stanmore**

Gordon Ave, Stanmore, Middx HA7
2RL
☎(020) 8954 2599, Pro 8954 2646,
Bar/Rest 8954 4661
Between Stanmore and Belmont off
Old Church Lane.
Parkland course.
Pro V R Law; Founded 1893
18 holes, 5860 yards, S.S.S. 68
🏌 Welcome WD - reduced rates on
Mon and Fri.
⌣ WD £26.
⌣ Welcome Wed and Thurs;
packages available include breakfast,
lunch, dinner; 3-balls favoured; £32-
£49.50.
🍽 Full catering service and bar.

1B 139 **Stapleford Abbotts**

Horseman's Side, Tysea Hill,
Stapleford Abbotts, Essex RM4 1JU
☎(01708) 381108 (Abbots), Pro
373344 (Priors)
Course is 3 miles from M25 Junction
28 off the B175 Romford to Ongar
road; left at Stapleford Abbots up
Tysea Hill.
Parkland course.
Pro John Stanion; Founded 1972
Designed by Howard Swan
18 holes, 6501 yards, S.S.S. 71
🏌 Welcome.
⌣ Terms on application.
⌣ Welcome by prior arrangement;
packages available; sauna; function
room; also Friars course: 2280 yards,
par 3; Priors course: 5720 yards.
🍽 Full bar and restaurant facilities
available.
⌐ Post House, Harlow.

1B 140 Stevenage
Aston Lane, Aston, Stevenage, Herts
SG2 7EL
☎(01438) 880424, Fax 880040 Sec.
880322, Bar/Rest 880223
Leave A1(M) Stevenage South, then
on A602 to Hertford, course
signposted about 1.5 miles.
Public parkland/meadowland course.
Pro Steve Barker, Founded 1980
Designed by John Jacobs
18 holes, 6341 yards, S.S.S. 71
♦ Welcome every day; book in
advance.
⌴ WD £10.90; WE £14.40.
⏃Welcome WD; packages
available; terms available on
application.
⭗ Full meals and bar snacks.
Practice range 24 bays; floodlit.
⌁ Roebuck.

1B 141 Stock Brook Manor Golf & CC
Queens Park Avenue, Stock,
Billericay, Essex CM12 0SP
☎(01277) 653616, Fax 633063
M25 Junction 28 then A12 to
Gallywood/Stock exit following the
B1007 to Stock.
Parkland course.
Pro Kevin Merry; Founded 1992
Designed by Martin Gillett
27 holes, 6728 yards, S.S.S. 72
3 9-hole courses: Stock/Manor: 6481
yards, par 71; Brook/Manor: 6241
yards, par 71.
♦ Welcome.
⌴ WD £25; WE £30.
⏃Welcome by prior arrangement;
country club facilities; bowls; tennis;
croquet.
⭗ Full clubhouse facilities.
⌁ Trust House, Basildon.

1B 142 Stockley Park
Uxbridge, Middx UB11 1A Q
☎(020) 8813 5700, Fax 8813 5655,
Sec 8561 6339, Bar/Rest 8813 570
Course is 5 mins from Heathrow
airport, and 2 mins from the M4
Junction 4 towards Uxbridge.
Hilly parkland championship course.
Pro Alex Knox; Founded 1993
Designed by Robert Trent Jones Snr
18 holes, 6539 yards, S.S.S. 71
♦ Welcome, pay as you play, correct
dress, no denims, golf shoes
required.
⌴ WD £23; WE £33.
⏃Welcome WD, booked in advance;
packages available; terms on
application.

⭗ Bar and restaurant.
⌁ Novotel.

1B 143 Stocks Hotel Golf & Country Club
Stocks Rd, Aldbury, Nr Tring, Herts
HP23 5RX
☎(01442) 851341, Fax 851253, Pro
851491
From either Junction 20 of M25 or
Junction 11 of M1, follow signs to
Tring. Then follow signs to Aldbury.
Parkland course.
Pro Peter Lane; Founded 1993
Designed by Mike Billcliff
18 holes, 7016 yards, S.S.S. 74
♦ Welcome WD any time, WE after
12 noon; handicap certs required.
⌴ WD £25; WE £40.
⏃WD by prior arrangement; terms
on application.
⭗ Full club and hotel facilities
available.
⌁ Stocks Hotel Golf & Country
Club.

1B 144 Stoke-by-Nayland
Keepers Lane, Leavenheath,
Colchester, Essex CO6 4PZ
☎(01206) 262836, Fax 263356, Pro
262769
Off A134 on B1068 between
Colchester and Sudbury.
Parkland with lake features.
Pro Kevin Lovelock; Founded 1972
Designed by W Peake
Constable course: 18 holes, 6544
yards, S.S.S. 71
Gainsborough course: 18 holes, 6498
yards, S.S.S. 71
♦ Welcome at all times with
handicap certs.
⌴ WD £22; WE £27.50.
⏃Welcome WD; 36 holes of golf on
2 courses, plus driving range and full
facilities; from £30.
⭗ Full clubhouse facilities available.
Practice range 20 bays.
⌁ Stoke by Nayland Club Hotel

1B 145 Strawberry Hill
Wellesley Rd, Strawberry Hill,
Twickenham, Middx TW2 5SD
☎(020) 8894 0165, Pro 8898 2082,
Bar/Rest 8894 1264
Near Strawberry Hill BR station.
Parkland course.
Pro Peter Buchan; Founded 1900
Designed by J.H. Taylor
9 holes, 4762 yards, S.S.S. 62
♦ Welcome WD only.
⌴ WD £16

⏃Fri only; maximum 25; terms on
application.
⭗ Bar and catering facilities
available.

1B 146 Sudbury
Bridgewater Rd, Wembley, Middx
HA0 1A L
☎(020) Fax 8903 2966, Pro 8902
7910, Sec 8902 3713
At Junction of Bridgewater Rd
(A4005) and Whitton Ave East
(A4090).
Undulating parkland course.
Pro Neil Jordan; Founded 1920
Designed by H. Colt
18 holes, 6277 yards, S.S.S. 70
♦ Welcome WD with handicap certs;
Mon open day (no handicap certs
required); WE as a guest of member
only.
⌴ WD £30.
⏃Welcome Tues pm, Wed, Thurs,
Fri by appointment; terms on
application.
⭗ Full catering service, bar.
⌁ The Cumberland, Harrow.

1B 147 Theydon Bois
Theydon Rd, Epping, Essex CM16
4EH
☎(01992) 812279, Pro 812460, Sec
813054, Bar/Rest 812260
1 mile S of Epping on B1721.
Woodland course; no par 5s.
Pro Richard Hall; Founded 1897
Designed by James Braid
18 holes, 5487 yards, S.S.S. 68
♦ Welcome with handicap certs.
⌴ WD £25; WE £25.
⏃Welcome Mon, Tues, Fri; £35.
⭗ Full clubhouse facilities available.
⌁ The Bell, Theydon Bois.

1B 148 Thorndon Park
Ingrave, Brentwood, Essex CM13
3RH
☎(01277) 811666, Pro 810736, Sec
810345
Course is 2 miles SE of Brentwood
on the A128.
Parkland course.
Pro Brian White; Founded 1920
Designed by H. Colt
18 holes, 6492 yards, S.S.S. 71
♦ Welcome WD and with member
WE; handicap certs required.
⌴ WD £35
⏃Welcome Mon, Tues and Fri;
terms on application.
⭗ Meals served WD.
⌁ Post House.

1B 149 **Thorpe Hall**

Thorpe Hall Ave, Thorpe Bay, Essex SS1 3AT
☎ (01702) 585331, Fax 582205, Pro 588195, Sec 582205
4 miles E of Southend on Sea on seafront at Thorpe Bay.
Parkland/meadowland course.
Pro Bill McColl; Founded 1907
18 holes, 6286 yards, S.S.S. 71
🏌 Welcome on WD by prior arrangement.
⚑ WD £30
🏌 Fri only; maximum party of 40; catering by arrangement; terms available on application.
🍽 Full catering facilities available.
🛏 Rosylin Hotel.

1B 150 **Three Rivers Golf & Country Club**

Stow Rd, Cold Norton, Purleigh, Nr Chelmsford, Essex CM3 6RR
☎ (01621) 828631, Fax 828060, Pro 829781
From the M25 Junction 29 take the A127 and then the A132 to South Woodham Ferrers. Then follow the signs for Cold Norton. Course is 4 miles.
Parkland; new heathland course.
Pro Scott Clark Founded 1973
Designed by Fred Hawtree
18 holes, 6500 yards
Jubilee course:18 4500 yards, par 65
🏌 Welcome.
⚑ WD £20; WE £30.
🏌 Welcome by prior arangement; combination of 18, 27, 36 holes, driving range, video analysis, clubhouse and private rooms; squash and tennis; from £20.
🍽 Full facilities.
🛏 Three Rivers.

1B 151 **Toothill**

School Road, Toot Hill, Ongar, Essex CM5 9PU
☎ (01277) 365523, Fax 364509, Pro 365747
2 miles off A414 between N Weald and Ongar.
Parkland course.
Pro Mark Bishop; Founded 1991
Designed by Martin Gillett
18 holes, 6053 yards, S.S.S. 69
🏌 Welcome, WE after 2.30pm.
⚑ WD £25; after 2.30pm WE £25.
🏌 Welcome Tues and Thurs; packages include lunch and/or dinner; from £34.
🍽 Full catering facilities.
🛏 Post House, Epping.

1B 152 **Top Meadow**

Fen Lane, North Ockendon, Essex RM14 3PR
☎ (01708) Pro 859545, Sec 852239
Off B186 in North Ockendon.
Parkland course.
Pro Paul King/Kevin Smith; Founded 1986
18 holes, 6227 yards, S.S.S. 72
🏌 Welcome WD; only with member at WE.
⚑ WD £12 inc breakfast.
🏌 Welcome WD by advance booking; terms on application.
🍽 Bar and restaurant.
Practice range.
🛏 Top Meadow Guest House.

1B 153 **Trent Park**

Bramley Rd, Oakwood London N14 4UT
☎ (020) 8367 4653, Fax 8366 3823
200 yards from Oakwood underground station between Barnet and Enfield on A110.
Parkland course.
Pro Ray Stocker; Founded 1973
18 holes, 6176 yards, S.S.S. 69
🏌 Public course (booking available).
⚑ WD £12; WE £15.25.
🏌 Welcome; restaurant and bar facilities; driving range, buggies, video analysis; terms on application.
🍽 Facilities available.
Practice range; video teaching bay and range heaters.

1B 154 **Tudor Park Sports Ground**

Clifford Rd, New Barnet, Herts EN5
☎ (020) 8449 0282
Off Potters Rd.
Public parkland course.
9 holes, 3772 yards, S.S.S. 58
🏌 Welcome.
⚑ WD £5.30; WE £6.80.
🏌 Apply for details.
🍽 Clubhouse for members only.

1B 155 **Twickenham Park**

Staines Rd, Twickenham, Middx TW2 5JD
☎ (020) Fax 8941 9134, Pro 8783 1698
On A305 near Hope and Anchor roundabout
Municipal parkland course.
Pro Suzy Watt; Founded 1977
Designed by Charles Lawrie
9 holes, 6076 yards, S.S.S. 69
🏌 Welcome.
⚑ WD £6.50; WE £7.

🏌 Welcome by arrangement; catering packages available; terms on application.
🍽 Full licensed bar, snacks, function room.
Practice range 24 bays; floodlit.
🛏 Richmond Gate.

1B 156 **Upminster**

114 Hall Lane, Upminster, Essex RM14 1A U
☎ (01708) 222788, Pro 220000, Bar/Rest 220249
On A127 towards Southend from M25 Junction 29.
Parkland course.
Pro Neil Carr; Founded 1927
Designed by H.A. Colt
18 holes, 6013 yards, S.S.S. 69
🏌 Welcome WD by arrangement, with handicap certs.
⚑ WD £25.
🏌 Welcome Wed- Fri by arrangement; some small societies possible Mon and Tues.
🍽 Full clubhouse facilities.
🛏 Post House, Brentwood.

1B 157 **Verulam** ♛

228 London Rd, St Albans, Herts AL1 1JG
☎ (01727) 853327, Fax 812201, Pro 861401, Bar/Rest 839016
Turn off London Road A1081 at railway bridge.
Parkland course.
Pro Nick Burch; Founded 1905
Designed by James Braid/upgrade by D Steel
18 holes, 6448 yards, S.S.S. 71
🏌 Welcome WD; with member at WE.
⚑ WD £25 (Mon £15)
🏌 Tues and Thurs only by arrangement with Sec; Full day golf and catering packages available; from £55.
🍽 Full facilities.
🛏 Apple Hotel; Sopwell House.

1B 158 **Wanstead** ♛

Overton Drive, Wanstead, London E11 2LW
☎ (020) 8989 3938, Fax 8532 9138, Pro 8989 9876, Bar/Rest 8989 0604
Close to Wanstead Tube station.
Parkland/heathland course.
Pro David Hawkins; Founded 1893
Designed by James Braid
18 holes, 6262 yards, S.S.S. 69
🏌 Welcome Mon, Tues and Fri.
⚑ WD £28.

⌕ Welcome Mon, Tues and Fri; facilities include 36 holes of golf, lunch and dinner; £48.
⍝ Full clubhouse facilities.

1B 159 Warley Park
Magpie Lane, Little Warley, Brentwood, Essex CM13 3DX
☎ (01277) 224891, Fax 200679, Pro 200441, Bar/Rest 231352
Off B186.
Parkland with 3 x 9 holes.
Pro Jason Groat; Founded 1975
Designed by R. Plumbridge
27 holes, 6232 yards, S.S.S. 69
⚑ Welcome WD only.
⌕ WD £25
⍝ Welcome WD; packages available; terms available on application.
⍝ Restaurant, bar and spike bar.
⌐ Forte Post House; New World Inn; Marygreen Manor.

1B 160 Warren
Woodham Walter, Maldon, Essex CM9 6RW
☎ (01245) 223258, Fax 223989, Pro 224662
A414 6 miles E of Chelmsford towards Maldon.
Undulating parkland course.
Pro Mickey Walker OBE; Founded 1934
18 holes, 6263 yards, S.S.S. 70
⚑ Welcome WD and WE after 2pm; booking essential.
⌕ WD £30; WE £35.
⍝ Mon, Tues, Thurs, Fri; packages available; terms available on application.
⍝ Full facilities 7 days.
⌐ Pontlands Park; Blue Boar.

1B 161 Welwyn Garden City
Mannicotts, High Oaks Rd, Welwyn Garden City, Herts AL8 7BP
☎ (01707) 322722, Fax 303213, Pro 325525, Sec 325243
1 mile north of Hatfield from A1M Junction 4.
Parkland course.
Pro Richard May; Founded 1922
Designed by Hawtree & Son
18 holes, 6074 yards, S.S.S. 69
⚑ Welcome by arrangement.
⌕ WD £25; WE £35.
⍝ Welcome Wed and Thurs; 36 holes, coffee, lunch and dinner; £52.
⍝ Full clubhouse bar and catering.
⌐ Homestead Court, Welwyn; Bush Hall Hotel, Hatfield.

1B 162 West Essex ☂
Bury Rd, Sewardstonebury, Chingford, Essex E4 7QL
☎ (020) 8529 7558, Fax 8524 7870, Pro 8529 4367, Bar/Rest 8529 1029
1.5 miles N of Chingford station.
Parkland course.
Pro Robert Joyce; Founded 1900
Designed by James Braid
18 holes, 6289 yards, S.S.S. 70
⚑ Welcome WD except Tues am and Thurs pm.
⌕ WD £28.
⍝ Welcome Mon, Wed and Fri; package includes coffee, lunch, dinner and 36 holes of golf, plus driving range; £50.
⍝ Bar and catering facilities.
⌐ Swallow Hotel, Waltham Abbey.

1B 163 West Herts
Cassiobury Park, Watford, Herts WD1 7SL
☎ (01923) 236484, Fax 222300, Pro 220352, Bar/Rest 224264
Off A412 between Watford and Rickmansworth.
Parkland course.
Pro Charles Gough, Founded 1890
Designed by Tom Morris & Harry Vardon
18 holes, 6528 yards, S.S.S. 71
⚑ Welcome.
⌕ WD £20; WE £30.
⍝ Welcome Wed, Fri; Full facilities; £50.
⍝ Full facilities.

1B 164 West Middlesex
Greenford Rd, Southall, Middx UB1 3EE
☎ (020) 8574 3450, Pro 8574 1800, Bar/Rest 8574 0166
At Junction of Greenford and Uxbridge road.
Parkland course.
Pro I P Harris; Founded 1891
Designed by James Braid
18 holes, 6119 yards, S.S.S. 69
⚑ Welcome.
⌕ WD £15.50 (Mon £10 Wed £12)
⍝ Welcome; minimum 20; coffee, lunch, evening meal, 2 rounds of golf; £44.
⍝ Full catering and bar.

1B 165 Whipsnade Park
Studham Lane, Dagnall, Herts HP4 1RH
☎ (01442) 842330, Fax 842090, Pro 842310, Bar/Rest 842331

Between villages of Studham and Dagnall.
Parkland course.
Pro Matthew Green; Founded 1974
18 holes, 6704 yards, S.S.S. 72
⚑ Welcome WD; WE with member.
⌕ WD £24
⍝ Welcome Tues, Wed, Thurs, Fri; coffee, 2 rounds of golf with lunch and 4-course dinner; £52.
⍝ Full catering facilities.
⌐ Post House, Hemel Hempstead.

1B 166 Whitehill
Dane End, Ware, Herts SG12 0JS
☎ (01920) 438702, Fax 438891, Pro 438326, Sec 438495, Bar/Rest 438495
4 miles N of Ware just off A10.
Parkland course.
Pro D Ling/M Belsham; Founded 1990
Designed by Golf Landscapes
18 holes, 6681 yards, S.S.S. 72
⚑ Welcome with handicap certs.
⌕ WD £19.50; WE £22.50.
⍝ Welcome WD; maximum 16 at WE; golf and catering packages available; £20-40.
⍝ Full facilities.
⌐ County, Ware; Vintage Corner, Puckeridge.

1B 167 Whitewebbs
Beggars Hollow, Clay Hill, Enfield, Middx EN2 9JN
☎ (020) Pro 8363 4454
1 mile N of Enfield town.
Public parkland course.
Pro Peter Garlick; Founded 1932
18 holes, 5866 yards, S.S.S. 68
⚑ Welcome; book 6 days in advance.
⌕ WD £12; WE £15.
⍝ Welcome by arrangement; café on site; nature trails and horseriding; various packages avalable on application.
⍝ Public café on site.
⌐ Royal Chase.

1B 168 Woodford ☂
2 Sunset Ave, Woodford Green, Essex IG8 0ST
☎ (020) 8504 0553, Fax 8504 3330, Pro 8504 4254, Sec 8504 3330
11 miles northeast of London; 2 miles N of North Circular Road on A11.
Forest course.
Pro Ashley Johns Founded 1890
Designed by Tom Dunn
9 holes, 5867 yards, S.S.S. 68

† Welcome except Tues am; Sat, or Sun am; red clothing must always be worn.

WD £15; WE £15 (£8 twilight).

Welcome by prior arrangement with Sec; packages including meals can be arranged; terms on application.

Dining facilities, bar.

Packfords, Woodford Green.

1B 169 **Wyke Green**
Syon Lane, Isleworth, Middx TW7 5PT
☎ (020) 8560 8777 Fax 8569 8392, Pro 8847 0685, Bar/Rest 8847 1956
0.5 miles north of A4 near Gillettes corner.
Flat parkland course.
Pro Neil Smith; Founded 1928
Designed by W.H. Tate

18 holes, 6211 yards, S.S.S. 70

† Members' guests only, or with handicap cert.

WD £28; WE £25 after 4pm.

Welcome Tues and Thurs; 3 different packages available; minimum 12 players; £32-42.

Full catering and bar.

Master Robert; Osterley Four Pillars.

2

THE SOUTH

The education of any links golfer remains incomplete without a visit to Rye, where the game proceeds in this new century pretty much as it did for most of the last one. It says everything about its timeless virtues that there continues to be a full complement of players who turn up in the first week of January each year to play in the President's Putter. If Rye can attract such a gathering at that inclement time in the golfing season, it can attract them anytime.

Ashdown Forest and Crowborough are two more of Sussex's established venues, both crisscrossing the famous Downs, the former gaining further repute for not possessing a single bunker. A personal favourite is West Sussex at Pulborough, with its five par threes offering the chance of a good score. For those players in the county wishing to brush up on their embryonic skills, Chichester Golf Centre has much to commend it.

On to Hampshire where Liphook, North Hants and Blackmoor have long been regarded as outstanding examples of inland golf, all embracing the rich seam of heather, gorse and silver birch which begins with Sunningdale and Wentworth and continues down through Swinley Forest and Camberley Heath. Mention must also be made of Hayling Island, a links course that is once said to have measured 7,480 yards but now thankfully a more manageable 6,500.

The Isle of Wight has two 18-hole courses and five with nine holes.

Shanklin and Sandown, co-designed by James Braid, is the best known, while of the nine-holers Osborne is beautifully scenic.

One of the perks of being a golf writer is turning up each November for a match at The Berkshire, where the Red and Blue courses are both magnificent. The 18 holes on the Red comprise six par threes, six par fours, and six par fives, an unusual combination but no less delightful for that. Then there is the clubhouse lunch – suffice to say that those on a diet should stay well clear.

Across the road lies Swinley Forest, beloved of royalty and no wonder, for this is another Harry Colt gem. One of the county's newer courses is Mill Ride, where the *Sunday Telegraph* has certainly left its mark. For starters it was designed by Donald Steel, the paper's first golf correspondent; for another, his successor, a lucky so-and-so, had a hole-in-one there and won a Lamborghini. Finally, in this county laden with riches, there is the Duke's Course at Woburn.

The best course in Buckinghamshire is Stoke Poges, which Colt also designed, and which has been restored to its former lustre in recent years. The Buckinghamshire, designed by John Jacobs, is considered one of the best courses to open in recent times.

The Oxfordshire has become well-known for its staging of the Benson and Hedges International but Frilford Heath's three courses remain the essential place to visit in the county. — **DL**

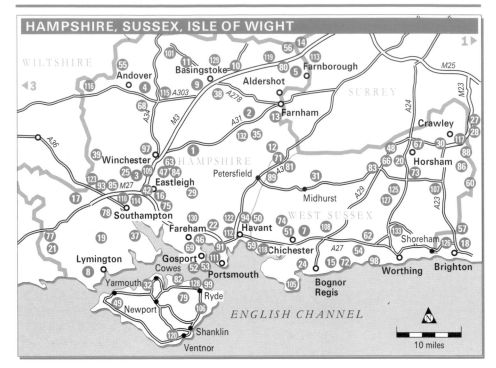

HAMPSHIRE, SUSSEX, ISLE OF WIGHT

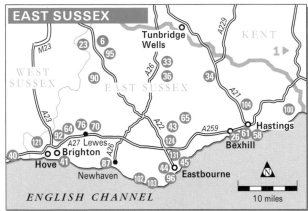

EAST SUSSEX

2A 1 **Alresford**
Cheriton Rd, Tichborne Down,
Alresford, Hants, SO24 0PN
☎(01962) 733746, Fax 736040, Pro
733998, Bar/Rest 733067
One mile S of Alresford on B3046.
Downland course.
Pro Malcolm Scott; Founded 1890
Designed by Scott Webb Young
18 holes, 5622 yards, S.S.S. 68
† Members only.
⌐ Not applicable.
↷Welcome by prior arrangement
with Sec; terms on application.
¶⊙¶ Full facilities.
↪ The Swan, Alresford.

2A 2 **Alton**
Old Odiham Rd, Alton, Hants, GU34
4BU
☎(01420) 82042, Pro 86518
On B3349 Alton to Odiham road; turn
off at Golden Pot.
Parkland course.
Pro Paul Brown; Founded 1908
Designed by James Braid
9 holes, 5744 yards, S.S.S. 68
† Welcome; restrictions on Sun.
⌐ WD £15; WE £18.
↷Welcome by prior arrangement;
bar, catering, PGA professional,

practice area; terms on application.
¶⊙¶ Full facilities.
↪ Wheatsheaf Inn; Alton House;
Grange Hotel.

2A 3 **Ampfield Par 3 G & CC**
Winchester Rd, Ampfield, Romsey,
Hants, SO51 9BQ
☎(01794) 368480, Pro 368750
A31 Winchester/Romsey road,
opposite Keats restaurant, next to

White Horse public house.
Parkland course.
Pro Richard Benfield; Founded 1965
Designed by Henry Cotton
18 holes, 2478 yards, S.S.S. 53
† Welcome but advisable to
telephone first.
⌐ WD £9; WE £15.50.
↷Welcome by arrangement;
function room; terms on application.
¶⊙¶ Bar and catering by arrangement.
↪ Potters Heron, Ampfield.

KEY	28 Copthorne Effingham	55 Hampshire	82 Osborne	109 South Winchester
1 Alresford	Park	56 Hartley Wintney GC	83 Osiers Farm	110 Southampton
2 Alton	29 Corhampton	57 Hassocks Golf Club	84 Otterbourne GC	111 Southsea
3 Ampfield Par 3 G & CC	30 Cottesmore	58 Hastings	85 Paultons Golf Centre	112 Southwick Park
4 Andover	31 Cowdray Park	59 Hayling Golf Club	86 Paxhill Park	113 Southwood
5 Army Golf Club	32 Cowes	60 Haywards Heath GC	87 Peacehaven	114 Stoneham
6 Ashdown Forest Hotel	33 Crowborough Beacon	61 Highwoods	88 Pease Pottage GC	115 Test Valley
7 Avisford Park	34 Dale Hill Hotel	62 Hill Barn	& Driving Range	116 Tidworth Garrison
8 Barton-on-Sea	35 Dean Farm (Kingsley)	63 Hockley	89 Petersfield	117 Tilgate Forest Golf
9 Basingstoke	36 Dewlands Manor GC	64 Hollingbury Park	90 Pilldown	Centre
10 Basingstoke Golf Centre	37 Dibden	65 Horam Park	91 Portsmouth	118 Tournerbury
11 Bishopswood	38 Dummer	66 Horsham Golf Park	92 Pyecombe	119 Tylney Park
12 Blackmoor	39 Dunwood Manor GC	67 Ifield G & Country Club	93 Romsey	120 Ventnor
13 Blacknest	40 The Dyke Golf Club	68 Lockford & Longstock	94 Rowlands Castle	121 Waterhall
14 Blackwater Valley	41 East Brighton	69 Lee-on-the-Solent	95 Royal Ashdown Forest	122 Waterlooville
15 Bognor Regis	42 East Horton Golf Centre	70 Lewes	96 Royal Eastbourne	123 Wellow
16 Botley Park Hotel	43 East Sussex	71 Liphook	97 Royal Winchester	124 Wellshurst Golf &
& Country Club	44 Eastbourne Downs	72 Littlehampton	98 Rustington Golf Centre	Country Club
17 Bramshaw	45 Eastbourne Golfing Park	73 Mannings Heath	99 Ryde	125 West Chiltington
18 Brighton & Hove	46 Fleetlands	74 Marriott Goodwood Park	100 Rye	126 West Hove
19 Brockenhurst Manor	47 Fleming Park	Golf & Country Club	101 Sandford Springs	127 West Sussex
20 Brookfield	48 Foxbridge	75 Meon Valley Hotel	102 Seaford	128 Westride
21 Burley	49 Freshwater Bay	Golf & Country Club	103 Seaford Head	129 Weybrook Park
22 Cams Hall Estates Golf	50 Furzeley	76 Mid-Sussex	104 Sedlescombe	130 Wickham Park
23 Chartham Park	51 Goodwood	77 Moors Valley Golf Centre	(Aldershaw)	131 Willingdon
24 Chichester Golf Centre	52 Gosport & Stokes Bay	78 New Forest	105 Selsey	132 Worldham Park
25 Chilworth Golf Centre	Golf Club	79 Newport	106 Shanklin & Sandown	133 Worthing
26 Cooden Beach	53 Great Salterns GC	80 North Hants	107 Singing Hills Golf Course	
27 Copthorne	54 Ham Manor Golf Club	81 Old Thorns	108 Slinfold Park G & CC	

2A 4 **Andover**

51 Winchester Rd, Andover, Hants, SP10 2EF
☎(01264) 358040 Fax 358040, Pro 324151, Bar/Rest 323890
Turn off A303 at Wherwell/ Stockbridge turning; take Andover direction, golf course 0.5 mile.
Parkland course.
Pro Derrick Lawrence; Founded 1907
Designed by J.H. Taylor
9 holes, 5873 yards, S.S.S. 68
♦ Welcome.
[Terms on application.
☞ Welcome.
▥ Full facilities.
⌐ White Hart Hotel, Andover.

2A 5 **Army Golf Club**

Laffans Rd, Aldershot, Hants, GU11 2HF
☎(01252) 336776, Fax 337562, Pro 336722, Sec 337272
Access from Eelmoor Bridge off A323 Aldershot-Fleet road.
Heathland course.
Pro Graham Cowley; Founded 1883
18 holes, 6550 yards, S.S.S. 71
♦ Welcome on WD by prior arrangement. WE Members and their guests only
[WD £24.
☞ Welcome by prior arrangement.
▥ Facilities available.
⌐ Trust House Forte, Farnborough; Potters International Hotel, Farnborough.

2A 6 **Ashdown Forest Hotel** ℭ

Chapel Lane, Forest Row, E Sussex, RH18 5BB
☎(01342) 824866, Fax 824869
3 miles S of East Grinstead on A22 in village of Forest Row, E on B2110; Chapel Lane 4th on right.
Heathland/woodland course.
Pro Martyn Landsborough; Founded 1985
Designed by Horace Hutchinson (1930s); Henry Luff (1965)
18 holes, 5606 yards, S.S.S. 67
♦ Welcome but advisable to phone first, particularly at WE.
[WD £16; WE £21.
☞ Welcome by prior arrangement; full facilities; terms on application.
▥ Full restaurant service and bar snacks; banqueting facilities for up to 100.
⌐ Ashdown Forest.

2A 7 **Avisford Park**

Avisford Park, Yapton Lane, Walberton, Arundel, BN18 0LS
☎(01243) 554611, Fax 555580, Pro 55461
On A27 4 miles W of Arundel, 6 miles E of Chichester.
Parkland course.
Pro Richard Beach
18 holes, 5669 yards, S.S.S. 68
♦ Welcome; pay as you play.
[WD £12; WE £15.
☞ Welcome by arrangement; terms on application.

▥ Bar and catering.
⌐ Stakis Arundel.

2A 8 **Barton-on Sea**

Milford Road, New Milton, Hants, BH25 5PP
☎(01425) 615308, Fax 621457, Pro 611210
From New Milton take B3058 towards Milford-on-Sea; club is signposted about 0.75 mile on right.
Clifftop links course.
Pro Peter Rodgers; Founded 1897
Designed by J Hamilton Stutt
27 holes 6296 yards, S.S.S. 70
♦ Welcome with handicap certs by prior arrangement.
[WD £30; WE £35.
☞ Welcome by arrangement.
▥ Snacks and teas available, other catering by arrangement.
⌐ Chewton Glen; Westover Hall.

2A 9 **Basingstoke**

Kempshott Park, Basingstoke, Hants, RG23 7LL
☎(01256) 465990, Fax 331793, Pro 351332
3 miles W of Basingstoke on A30; M3 Junction 7.
Parkland course.
Pro guy shoesmith; Founded 1928
Designed by James Braid
18 holes, 6334 yards, S.S.S. 70
♦ Welcome WD; WE with a member.
[WD £26

✑ Welcome Wed and Thurs; packages available.
🍽 Full clubhouse bar and restaurant facilities.
⌐ Wheatsheaf, N Waltham.

2A 10 **Basingstoke Golf Centre**
Worting Rd, West Ham, Basingstoke, Hants, RG23 0TY
☎ (01256) 350054
M3 Junction 7; 0.5 mile from Basingstoke town centre.
Public parkland course.
9 holes, 908 yards
† Welcome.
⌐ WD £2.70; WE £3.20
Practice range 24 bays; floodlit.
🍽 Confectionery machine.

2A 11 **Bishopswood**
Bishopswood Lane, Tadley, Basingstoke, Hants, RG26 4AT
☎ (0118) 981 5213
6 miles N of Basingstoke, off A340.
Public parkland course.
Pro Stephen Ward; Founded 1976
Designed by Blake and Phillips
9 holes, 6474 yards, S.S.S. 71
† Welcome WD.
⌐ WD £10 (9 holes).
✑ Welcome WD by arrangement; full facilities.
🍽 Bar snacks and restaurant.
Practice range, 12 bays floodlit.
⌐ Romans.

2A 12 **Blackmoor**
Firgrove Road, Whitehill, Bordon, Hants, GU35 9EH
☎ (01420) 472775, Fax 487666, Pro 472345
Located on A325 between Petersfield and Farnham; at Whitehill crossroads turn left into Firgrove Road; Blackmoor is 1000 yards on right.
Parkland/heathland course.
Pro Steve Clay; Founded 1913
Designed by H.S. Colt
18 holes, 6232 yards, S.S.S. 68/69/72
† Welcome WD; guest of member only at WE.
⌐ WD £33.
✑ Welcome Mon/Wed/Thurs/Fri by arrangement; packages available.
🍽 Full facilities.

2A 13 **Blacknest**
Binstead Rd, Binstead, Alton, Hants, GU34 4QL

☎ (01420) 22888
Take A31 to Bentley, then the Bordon road, course is immediately on right.
Parkland/heathland course.
Pro Ian Benson; Founded 1994
Designed by P Nicholson
18 holes, 6038 yards, S.S.S. 69
† Welcome; no jeans.
⌐ WD £15; WE £17.
✑ Welcome by arrangement; full facilities.
🍽 Bar and restaurant.
Practice range, 13 bays, gym.
⌐ Alton House; The Bush; The Farnham Park.

2A 14 **Blackwater Valley**
Chandlers Lane, Basingstoke, Hants, GU46 7SZ
☎ (01252) 874725
5 miles from Camberley on the Reading road.
Parkland course with lakes.
Pro James Rodger; Founded 1994
9 holes, 2372 yards, S.S.S. 66
† Welcome.
⌐ WD £7; WE £8.
✑ Welcome by arrangement; full facilities.
🍽 Full facilities.
Practice range, 36 bays floodlit.

2A 15 **Bognor Regis**
Downview Rd, Felpham, Bognor Regis, PO22 8JD
☎ (01243) 821929, Fax 860719, Pro 865209
A259 Bognor-Littlehampton road; at Felpham traffic lights turn left into Downview Road.
Parkland course.
Pro Stephen Bassil; Founded 1892
Designed by James Braid
18 holes, 6238 yards, S.S.S. 70
† Welcome with handicap certs WD; with member at WE during summer.
⌐ WD £25; WE £30.
✑ Welcome by arrangement, tee-off times allocated; full facilities available; £45 package.
🍽 Restaurant and bar.
⌐ The Beachcroft, Felpham.

2A 16 **Botley Park Hotel & CC**
Winchester Road, Boorley Green, Botley, Hants, SO32 2UA
☎ (01489) 780888, Fax 789242, Pro 789771
NW of Botley on B3354 Winchester road, within easy reach of M27 Junction 7, or M3/A33.

Parkland course.
Pro Tim Barter; Founded 1990
Designed by Charles Potterton
18 holes, 6341 yards, S.S.S. 70
† Welcome by arrangement; handicap certs or letter of intro required.
⌐ WD £30; WE £30.
✑ Welcome Mon, Weds and Thurs by arrangement; full facilities.
🍽 Full facilities; banqueting service
Practice range, 10 bays;
⌐ hotel in complex.

2A 17 **Bramshaw**
Brook, Lyndhurst, Hants, SO43 7HE
☎ (0203) 8081 3433, Fax 8081 3958, Pro 8081 3434, Bar/Rest 8081 4628
10 miles SW of Southampton, 1 mile from Junction 1 M27.
Open New Forest course.
Pro Clive Bonner; Founded 1880
Forest: 18 holes, 5774 yards, S.S.S. 69; Manor: 18 holes, 6517 yards, S.S.S. 71
† Welcome WD; members' guests only WE.
⌐ Terms on application.
✑ Welcome Mon to Fri; Packages available.
🍽 Catering and bar facilities.
⌐ Bell Inn, Brook.

2A 18 **Brighton & Hove**   ℗
Devil's Dyke Rd, Brighton, BN1 8YJ
☎ (01273) 556482, Fax 554427, Pro 540560, Bar/Rest 507861
A23 / A27 NW Brighton.
Downland course - oldest golf club in Sussex.
Pro P Bonsall; Founded 1887
Designed by James Braid
9 holes, 5710 yards, S.S.S. 68
† Welcome with some restrictions.
⌐ WD £15; WE £25 (18 holes)
✑ Welcome by arrangement; restaurant facilities.
🍽 Full facilities available.

2A 19 **Brockenhurst Manor**
Sway Rd, Brockenhurst, Hants, SO42 7SG
☎ (01590) 623332, Fax 624140, Pro 623092
A337 to Brockenhurst then B3055 S from village centre, club 1 mile on right.
Undulating forest/parkland course.
Pro Bruce Parker; Founded 1919
Designed by H.S. Colt, Alterations by J. Hamilton

Ashdown Forest

Deep in the forests of East Sussex there is a magnificent example of the merging of a modern approach and a traditional golf course that has pushed Royal Ashdown Forest into the top 50 in the country.

So often modern hotel complexes ruin the ambience of their courses but at Ashdown Forest there has been a constant updating of the facilities without destroying the character of the club.

Designed in the 1930s by Horace Hutchinson, the course was the venue for the 1932 British Ladies Championships and was temptingly close to London by rail en route to the south coast.

It went through several changes. Henry Luff was responsible for the design work again in 1965 and the West course was added to the club's repetoire in 1985.

But it is the Royal Ashdown Forest club which is the real attraction for so many golfers these days as it picks its way through the beautiful forest. Protection orders ensure that there are few changes to the Royal course over the years since it was laid down rather than designed in the 1930s.

The distinctive feature of the course is that it has no bunkers. There were no natural sand traps of course and preservation orders meant that none could be built.

Many, however, rate it as one of the most beautiful courses in the Home Counties and it is well worth the green fee if you are lucky enough to organise a tee-off time.

The most challenging part of the round comes after the turn where the water comes into play at the 13th and leads the golfer to the most difficult – as befits the stroke index one hole – 14th. At 435 yards its length is the first of its hurdles but with the stream cutting across the fairway there is the real threat of ending up in the water.

For many a driver off the tee is going to spell trouble so with a three-wood the next worry is to reach the green with the second shot or to elect to lay up. Few manage to negotiate the hole for the first time without finding trouble.

Another unusual feature of the course is that it possesses just one par five – the 17th – but it is not sheer distance that will provide the ultimate test.

In recent years more than £1 million has been spent on restoring and renovating the Edwardian house which doubles as a luxury hotel and the club house. Because of the hotel facilities, and the conference rooms and other sporting facilities such as the tennis courts it has been a popular venue with many overseas visitors.

As Gatwick Airport is so convenient there have been a constant and ever-growing stream of Scandinavian golfers in recent years taking full advantage of the club's outstanding course. — **CG**

18 holes, 6222 yards, S.S.S. 70
♦ Welcome by arrangement; must have handicap certs.
▯ WD £32; WE £58.
⌁Welcome on Thurs by prior arrangement; also small parties welcome Mon, Wed and Fri by prior arrangement; full facilities.
⬤⬤⬤ Full facilities.

2A 20 **Brookfield**
Winterpit Lane, Lower Reading, Horsham, W Sussex, RH13 6LY
☎(01403) 891191, Fax 891499
From the M23 take A279 to Handcross, through village, then second right and first left; from Horsham take the A281 towards Brighton, at Mannings Heath Dun Horse pub turn left, over crossroads into Winterpit Lane.
Public parkland course.
Founded 1991
Designed by P. Webster
9 holes, 4000 yards
♦ Welcome at all times.
▯ WD £10; WE £10.
⌁Welcome; also corporate days available; full facilities.
⬤⬤⬤ 2 bars, lounge, restaurants.
Practice range.
⌁ Brookfield Farm.

2A 21 **Burley**
Cott Lane, Burley, Ringwood, Hants, BH24 4BB
☎(01425) 402431, Fax 402431, Bar/Rest 403737
From A31 through Burley towards New Milton/Brockenhurst; turn immediately after cricket pitch.
Open heathland course.
Founded 1905
9 holes, 6149 yards, S.S.S. 69
♦ Welcome with handicap certs preferred. Dress code applies to all visitors.
▯ WD £14; WE £20.
⌁Groups up to 14 Welcome but phone in advance
⬤⬤⬤ Bar and limited food available.
⌁ Burley Manor; Moorhill; White Buck.

2A 22 **Cams Hall Estates Golf**
Cams Hall, Fareham, Hants, PO16 8UP
☎(01329) 827222, Fax 827111, Pro 827732
Close to M27, Junction 11.
18-hole links course, 9-hole parkland course.

Pro Jason Neue; Founded 1993
Designed by Peter Alliss & Clive Clark
18 holes, 6244 yards, S.S.S. 70
♦ Welcome.
▯ WD £20; WE £27.50.
⌁Welcome, subject to availability; full facilities; £21-£47 for range of packages.
⬤⬤⬤ Full facilities available.
Practice range; £2 bucket of balls.
⌁ Marriott Hotel, Cosham; Trust House Forte, Fareham; Solent Hotel, Whiteley.

2A 23 **Chartham Park**
Felcourt Rd, Felcourt, E Grinstead, RH19 2JT
☎(01342) 870340, Fax 870719
1 mile out of E Grinstead town centre on the Lingfield road.
Mature parkland course.
Pro David Hobbs; Founded 1992
Designed by N Coles
18 holes, 6680 yards, S.S.S. 72
♦ Welcome but not before 12 noon at WE.
▯ WD £27; WE £40.
⌁Welcome WD; full facilities.
⬤⬤⬤ Full facilities.
⌁ Felbridge.

2A 24 **Chichester Golf Centre** ♌
Hoe Farm, Hunston, Chichester, PO20 6AX
☎(01243) 533833, Fax 539922, Sec 536666
3 miles S of Chichester (A27) on B2145 to Selsey, on left after Hunston.
Public Floriday-style course with membership.
Pro John Slinger/Emma Fields; Founded 1990
Designed by Philip Sanders
Cathedral: 18 holes, 6461 yards, S.S.S. 71; Tower: 18 holes, 6175 yards, S.S.S. 69
♦ Welcome; tee reservations required; handicap certs required for Cathedral.
▯ Cathedral WD £20, WE £28; Tower WD £15; WE £20.
⌁Welcome by prior arrangement; society clubroom available; terms on application.
⬤⬤⬤ Full catering/refreshments.
Practice range; 27 bays; floodlit; academy hole; par 3 course.
⌁ Millstream (Bosham); Hunston Mill B&B (Hunston); Post House (Hayling Island).

2A 25 **Chilworth Golf Centre**
Main Rd, Chilworth, Southampton, Hants, SO16 7JP
☎(023) 8074 0544, Fax 8073 3166
On A27 between Romsey and Southampton.
Parkland course.
Pro C Aby; Founded 1989
18 holes, 5740 yards, S.S.S. 69
♦ Welcome.
▯ WD £12; WE £15.
⌁Welcome by prior arrangement; terms on application.
⬤⬤⬤ Catering facilities available.

2A 26 **Cooden Beach** ♌
Cooden Sea Rd, Nr Bexhill-on-Sea, TN39 4TR
☎(01424) 842040, Fax 842040, Pro 843938, Bar/Rest 843936
From the A259 Eastbourne-Hastings road; follow Cooden Beach sign at Little Common roundabout; course is 1 mile further on.
Seaside course.
Pro Jeffrey Sim; Founded 1912
Designed by Herbert Fowler
18 holes, 6450 yards, S.S.S. 71
♦ Welcome with handicap certs, telephone first.
▯ WD £29; WE £35.
⌁Welcome by arrangement; full facilities; £49 package.
⬤⬤⬤ Full facilities available.
⌁ Jarvis Cooden Resort; Brickwall Hotel, Lansdowne Hotel; Netherfield Place.

2A 27 **Copthorne**
Borers Arms Rd, Copthorne, Crawley, RH10 3LL
☎(01342) 712033, Fax 717682, Pro 712405, Bar/Rest 712508
M23 Junction 10; follow A264 to East Grinstead; course 3 miles on left.
Heathland course.
Pro Joe Burrell; Founded 1892
Designed by James Braid
18 holes, 6221 yards, S.S.S. 71
♦ Welcome with handicap certs. WE only after 1pm.
▯ WD £30-40; WE £32.
⌁Mon-Fri by arrangement with Sec; full facilities available; £45-£60 packages.
⬤⬤⬤ facilities available.
⌁ Copthorne; Effingham Park.

2A 28 **Copthorne Effingham Park**
West Park Rd, Copthorne, W Sussex, RH10 3EU

☎ (01342) 716528, Fax 716039
From M23 Junction 10 on to A264.
Parkland course.
Pro Mark Root; Founded 1980
Designed by Francisco Escario
9 holes, 3630 yards, S.S.S. 57
† Welcome with prior booking.
Ⓛ WD £9; WE £10.
☺ Welcome by prior arrangement;
terms on application.
Ⓞ Two restaurants and bar facilities
available.
⤳ Copthorne Effingham Park;
Copthorne Gatwick.

2A 29 **Corhampton**
Sheeps Pond Lane, Droxford,
Southampton, Hants, SO32 1LP
☎ (01489) 877279, Pro 877638
Right off A32 at Corhampton on
B3135 for 1 mile.
Downland course.
Pro Ian Roper; Founded 1891
18 holes, 6444 yards, S.S.S. 71
† Welcome WD; with member at
WE.
Ⓛ WD £24; WE £24.
☺ Welcome by arrangement Mon
and Thurs; full facilities; terms on
application.
Ⓞ Lunch, teas and dinners
available.
⤳ The Uplands Hotel; Little Uplands
Country Guest House.

2A 30 **Cottesmore**
Buchan Hill, Pease Pottage, Crawley,
Sussex, RH11 9AT
☎ (01293) 528256, Fax 522819, Pro
535399
Take M23 Junction 11 and follow
signs for Pease Pottage Services; go
past services and take 3rd exit;
course 1.5 miles on right.
Undulating meadowland course; start
and finish par 5.
Pro Calum Callam; Founded 1975
Designed by M.D. Rogerson
Griffin: 18 holes, 6248 yards, S.S.S.
70; Phoenix: 18 holes, 5514 yards,
S.S.S. 67
† Welcome WD, WE and Bank
Holidays.
Ⓛ Griffin WD £19.50, WE £25;
Phoenix WD £15, WE £20.
☺ Welcome; packages to suit all
needs; health club and tennis
facilities; conference and function
facilities.
Ⓞ Full restaurant, coffee shop and
bar, including spike bar, facilities.
⤳ Country club has 12 bedrooms on
site.

2A 31 **Cowdray Park**
Midhurst, W Sussex, GU29 0BB
☎ (01730) 813599, Fax 815900, Pro
812091
About 1 mile E of Midhurst on A272.
Parkland course.
Pro Richard Gough; Founded 1920
18 holes, 6212 yards, S.S.S. 70
† Welcome but handicap certs
essential.
Ⓛ WD £26; WE £36.
☺ Welcome by arrangement; full
facilities; terms on application.
Ⓞ Bar snacks daily, evening meals
by arrangement.
⤳ Angel; Spread Eagle.

2A 32 **Cowes**
Crossfield Ave, Cowes, Isle of Wight,
PO31 8HN
☎ (01983) 280135; Sec 292303
Next to Cowes High School.
Parkland course.
Founded 1908
9 holes, 5923 yards, S.S.S. 68
† Welcome.
Ⓛ WD £15; WE £18.
☺ Welcome; packages available;
from £12.
Ⓞ Full clubhouse facilities.
⤳ New Holmwood; Fountain.

2A 33 **Crowborough Beacon**
Beacon Rd, Crowborough, E Sussex,
TN6 1UJ
☎ (01892) 661511, Fax 667339, Pro
653877
8 miles S of Tunbridge Wells on A26.
Heathland course.
Pro Dennis Newnham; Founded 1895
18 holes, 6256 yards, S.S.S. 70
† Welcome WD; handicap certs or
letter of introduction required.
Ⓛ WD £25; WE £30.
☺ Welcome WD by arrangement; not
Thurs; terms on application.
Ⓞ For up to 60; breakfast available
by prior arrangement.
⤳ Winston Manor.

2A 34 **Dale Hill Hotel**   ℂ
Ticehurst, Wadhurst, TN5 7DQ
☎ (01580) 200112, Fax 201249, Pro
201090
On A21 from Tunbridge Wells.
Parkland course with lake features.
Founded 1974
Old: 18 holes, 5856 yards, S.S.S. 69;
Woosnam: 18 holes, 6512 yards,
S.S.S. 69
† Welcome by arrangement.
Ⓛ Old: WD £20, WE £30; Woosnam:

WD £45, WE £55.
☺ Welcome by prior arrangement;
restaurant, golf clinics, pool and
leisure facilities; terms on application.
Ⓞ Restaurant and full facilities.
⤳ Dale Hill.

2A 35 **Dean Farm (Kingsley)**
Main Rd, Kingsley, Bordon, Hants,
GU35 9NG
☎ (01420) 489478, Sec 472313
On B3004 between Alton and Bordon
on W side of Kingsley.
Parkland course.
Founded 1984
9 holes, 1600 yards
† Public pay and play.
Ⓛ WD £4; WE £4.
☺ Not available.

2A 36 **Dewlands Manor Golf**
Course
Cottage Hill, Rotherfield, E Sussex,
TN6 3JN
☎ (01892) 852266, Fax 853015
Sec, 853015
0.5 mile S of village of Rotherfield
just off B2101 to Five Ashes, 10 miles
from Tunbridge Wells.
Parkland/woodland course with water
hazards.
Pro Nick Godin; Founded 1991
Designed by R.M. And Nick Goding
9 holes, 3186 yards, S.S.S. 70
† Welcome all year; 15 minute tee
intervals.
Ⓛ WD £13.50; WE £15.50.
Concessions apply
☺ Small business groups Welcome,
maximum 20 persons; full facilities;
terms on application. Corporate days
also available
Ⓞ Bar, light snacks at all times,
special orders by arrangement.
⤳ Spa; Royal Wells (Tunbridge
Wells); Winston Manor
(Crowborough).

2A 37 **Dibden**
Main Rd, Dibden, Southampton,
Hants, SO45 5TB
☎ (023) 8020 7508, Pro 8084 5596,
Bar/Rest 8084 5060
Turn off A326 at Dibden roundabout,
course situated 0.5 mile on right.
Public parkland course.
Pro John Slade; Founded 1974
Designed by J. Hamilton Stutt
18 holes, 5965 yards, S.S.S. 69
† Welcome; no restrictions.
Ⓛ WD £10.75; WE £12.75.
☺ Welcome by arrangement with

Pro; full facilities; terms on application.
🔘 Full facilities
Practice range, 20 bays; floodlit (also 9-hole par 3 course).
🔄 Four Seasons; Pilgrim; Fountain Court.

2A 38 **Dummer**   ♗

Dummer, Nr Basingstoke, Hants, RG25 2AR
☎ (01256) 397888, Fax 397889, Pro 397950
Website: www.dummergc.co.uk
E mail: golf@dummergc.co.uk
M3 exit 7.
Parkland course.
Pro A Fannon/ Anthony Weir; Founded 1992
Designed by Peter Alliss and Clive Clark
18 holes, 6427 yards, S.S.S. 71
🏌 Welcome.
🌣 WD £27; WE £30.
🌣 Welcome by arrangement; full facilities; terms on application.
🔘 Full facilities.
🔄 Audley's Wood; Hilton National (Basingstoke).

2A 39 **Dunwood Manor Golf Club**

Danes Road, Awbridge, Romsey, Hants, SO51 0GF
☎ (01794) 340112, Fax 341215, Pro 340663 Sec 340549, Bar/Rest 340549
Off A27 Romsey to Salisbury road; after 2 miles turn right at Shootash crossroads into Danes Road; club is 800 yards on left.
Undulating parkland course.
Founded 1972
18 holes, 5474 yards, S.S.S. 68
🏌 Welcome WD by prior arrangement.
🌣 WD £22.
🌣 Welcome Mon/Tues/Thurs/ Fri all day and Wed pm; packages available.
🔘 Facilities available.
🔄 Luxury farmhouse accommodation available; details on request. Abbey Hotel; Bell Inn.

2A 40 **The Dyke Golf Club**

Devil's Dyke, Devil's Dyke Rd, Brighton, BN1 8YJ
☎ (01273) 857296, Fax 857078, Pro 857260, Bar/Rest 857230
A27 Brighton by-pass; follow directions for Devil's Dyke; course 2.5

miles west of by-pass.
Downland course.
Founded 1906
Designed by Fred Hawtree
18 holes, 6611 yards, S.S.S. 72
🏌 Welcome by prior arrangement; Sundays not before 12 noon.
🌣 WD £28; WE £40.
🌣 Welcome by arrangement; full facilities available; £48 package.
🔘 Full facilities.
🔄 Tottington Manor, nr Henfield.

2A 41 **East Brighton**

Roedean Rd, Brighton, BN2 5RA
☎ (01273) 604838, Fax 680277, Pro 603989, Bar 621461
1.5 miles east of Palace Pier, just off A259 behind Brighton Marina.
Undulating downland course.
Pro Mark Stewart-Willian; Founded 1894
Designed by James Braid
18 holes, 6020 yards, S.S.S. 69
🏌 Welcome WD except Tues am; WE and Bank Holidays after 11am.
🌣 WD from £20; WE from £24.
🌣 Welcome Mon-Fri, except for Tues am, by arrangement.
🔘 Facilities available.
🔄 Old Ship; Grand; Metropole.

2A 42 **East Horton Golfing Centre**

Mortimers Lane, Fair Oak, Hants, SO50 7EA
☎ (023) 8060 2111
From M27 Junction 7 follow signs for Fair Oak.
Parkland course.
Pro Trevor Pearce; Founded 1993
Greenwood: 18 holes, 5920 yards, S.S.S. 70; Parkland: 18 holes, 5097 yards, S.S.S. 70
🏌 Welcome; 7 day advance booking system.
🌣 WD £11; WE £14.
🌣 Welcome everyday by prior arrangement.
🔘 Bar and restaurant facilities.
Practice range, 15 bays; floodlit.
🔄 Marwell Lodge; Botley Grange.

2A 43 **East Sussex National**

Little Horsted, Uckfield, E Sussex, TN22 5ES
☎ (01825) 880088, Fax 880066, Pro 880256, Sec, 880233 Bar/Rest 880224
Situated on the A22 between East Grinstead and Eastbourne just outside Uckfield

American style layout in English countryside
Pro Iain Naylor; Founded 1989
Designed by Bob Cupp
East: 18 holes, 7138 yards, S.S.S. 74; West: 18 holes, 7154 yards, S.S.S. 74
🏌 Welcome.
🌣 Terms on application.
🌣 Welcome with handicap certs;
🔘 Full catering and entertaining as well as bar facilities, sauna and steam rooms.
🔄 Club will provide comprehensive list of hotels and B&B.

2A 44 **Eastbourne Downs**

East Dean Rd, Eastbourne, E Sussex, BN20 8ES
☎ (01323) 720827, Fax 412506, Pro 732264, Bar/Rest 730809
0.5 miles W of Eastbourne on the A259
Downland course.
Pro Terry Marshall; Founded 1908
Designed by J.H. Taylor
18 holes, 6601 yards, S.S.S. 72
🏌 Welcome.
🌣 Terms on application.
🌣 Welcome WD; some WE by arrangement; packages available.
🔘 Full clubhouse facilities.
Practice range.
🔄 Landsdown.

2A 45 **Eastbourne Golfing Park**

Lottbridge Drove, Eastbourne, BN23 6QJ
☎ (01323) 520400, Fax 520400, Bar/Rest 504134
East side of Eastbourne.
Parkland course.
Pro Barrie Finch; Founded 1993
Designed by David Ashton
9 holes, 5046 yards
🏌 Welcome.
🌣 WD £8-£15; WE £8-£15.
🌣 Welcome by arrangement; full facilities; terms on application.
🔘 Full facilities.
Practice range, 24 bays, floodlit all-weather driving range; £2 for 50 balls, £5 for 250 balls.
🔄 Wish Tower Hotel.

2A 46 **Fleetlands**

N.A.R.O. Fleetlands Division, Gosport, Hants, PO13 0AA
☎ (023) 9254 4384
Off A32 2 miles S of Fareham..
Parkland course.

Founded 1963
9 holes, 4852 yards, S.S.S. 64
† Welcome with a member.
⌴ WD £5; WE £7.
⌁ None.
🍽 Bar.

2A 47 Fleming Park
Magpie Lane, Eastleigh, Hants, SO50 9LM
☎ (023) 8064 3671
A27/M27, turn off at Eastleigh sign, 1 mile to course.
Parkland course.
Pro Chris Strickett; Founded 1973
Designed by Charles Lawrie
18 holes, 4378 yards, S.S.S. 61
† Welcome.
⌴ Terms on application.
⌁ Terms on application to Sec; full facilities; packages available; terms on application.
🍽 Bar snacks and meals.
⌁ Crest Hotel; Gateway.

2A 48 Foxbridge
Foxbridge Lane, Plaistow, W Sussex, RH14 0LB
☎ (01403) 753303, Fax 753433
Take B2133 from Billingshurst to Lockswood; then take Plaistow road and course is signposted.
Parkland course.
Pro Steven Hall/ Janice Arnold; Founded 1991
Designed by P Clark
9 holes, 6236 yards, S.S.S. 70
† Welcome.
⌴ WD £14; WE £18.
⌁ Welcome WD by arrangement; full facilities; terms on application.
🍽 Full facilities and bar available.

2A 49 Freshwater Bay
Afton Down, Freshwater Bay, Isle of Wight, PO40 9TZ
☎ (01983) 752955
3 miles from Yarmouth on A3055 overlooking Freshwater Bay.
Seaside downland course.
Founded 1893
18 holes, 5725 yards, S.S.S. 68
† Welcome after 9.30am on WD and 10am on Sun.
⌴ WD £20; WE £24.
⌁ Welcome by arrangement; after 9.30am on WD and 10am on Sun; full facilities; terms on application.
🍽 Full catering facilities; licensed bar.
⌁ Albion, Country Garden, Farringford.

2A 50 Furzeley
Furzeley Road, Denmead, Hants, PO7 6TX
☎ (023) 9223 1180, Fax 9223 0921
2 miles NW of Waterlooville.
Parkland course.
Pro Derek Brown; Founded 1993
Designed by M Sale
18 holes, 4363 yards, S.S.S. 61
† Welcome, bookings taken 2 days in advance.
⌴ WD £10; WE £11.50.
⌁ Welcome; packages available; terms on application.
🍽 Available.

2A 51 Goodwood
Kennell Hill, Goodwood, Chichester, West Sussex, PO18 0PN
☎ (01243) 785012, Fax 781741, Pro 774994, Sec 774968, Bar/Rest 774504
3 miles NE of Chichester on road to racecourse.
Downland course.
Pro Keith Macdonald; Founded 1892
Designed by James Braid
18 holes, 6000 yards, S.S.S. 69
† Welcome with handicap certs.
⌴ WD £32; WE £42 (£21 with member).
⌁ Welcome Wed/Thurs only; minimum 16; full facilities.
🍽 Full facilities by arrangement.

2A 52 Gosport & Stokes Bay
Fort Rd, Gosport, Hants, PO12 2AT
☎ (023) 9258 1625, Fax 9252 7941, Pro 9258 2220, Sec 9252 7941,Bar/Rest 9258 0226
M27 to Fareham; A32 Gosport; Haslar Bridge to Haslar Road to Fort Road.
Links course.
Founded 1885
9 holes, 5999 yards, S.S.S. 69
† Welcome.
⌴ Terms on application.
⌁ Welcome by arrangement; full facilities.
🍽 Full facilities.
⌁ The Old Lodge; The Alverbank; The Anglesey (all in Alverstoke).

2A 53 Great Salterns
Burrfields Road, Portsmouth, Hampshire, PO3 5HH
☎ (023) 9266 4549, Fax 9265 0525, Pro 9266 4549
From M27 Junction A2030 towards Southsea; turn right at 3rd set of lights.

Parkland course.
Pro Terry Healy; Founded 1914
18 holes, 5737 yards, S.S.S. 68
† Welcome, municipal course.
⌴ WD £10.30; WE £12.30.
⌁ Welcome.
🍽 At public house adjacent to course.
Practice range; £2.50 for 50 balls.
⌁ Inn Lodge; Hilton Hotel.

2A 54 Ham Manor Golf Club
Angmering, BN16 4JE
☎ (01903) 783288, Fax 850886, Pro 783732, Bar 775653
Off A259 between Littlehampton and Worthing.
Parkland course.
Pro Simon Buckley; Founded 1936
Designed by H.S. Colt
18 holes, 6092 yards, S.S.S. 70
† Welcome with handicap certs.
⌴ WD £26; WE £40.
⌁ Welcome Wed/Thurs/Fri by arrangement; full facilities; packages available.
🍽 Full facilities.
⌁ Arundel Hotel; Lamb Inn, Angmering.

2A 55 Hampshire   ☎
Winchester Road, Goodworth Clatford, Nr Andover, Hants, SP11 7TB
☎ (01264) 357555, Fax 356606
From Andover take the Stockbridge road on the A3057, course is 0.5 mile S of Andover.
Downland course.
Pro John Slade/Paul Smith; Founded 1993
Designed by T Fiducia & A Mitchell
18 holes, 6376 yards, S.S.S. 70
† Welcome.
⌴ WD £15; WE £25.
⌁ Welcome by arrangement; full facilities; packages available; terms on application.
🍽 Full facilities.
Practice range, covered bays.
⌁ White Hart (Andover).

2A 56 Hartley Wintney
London Rd, Hartley Wintney, Hants, RG27 8PT
☎ (01252) 842214, Pro 843779, Sec 844211
A30 between Camberley (5 miles) and Basingstoke (12 miles).
Parkland course.
Pro Martin Smith; Founded 1891
9 holes, 6096 yards, S.S.S. 69

♦ Welcome, WE/Bank Holiday only with member.
ⓘ WD £20.
⌁ Tues/Thurs only by arrangement with Sec; full facilities.
🍴 comprehensive menu availale.
⌁ Lismoyne Hotel, Fleet.

2A 57 **Hassocks**
London Road, Hassocks, Sussex, BN6 9NA
☎ (01273) 846630, Fax 846070, Pro 846990, Bar/Rest 846949
Take A273 towards Hassocks from Brighton; club is between Hassocks and Burgess Hill.
Parkland course.
Pro Charles Ledger; Founded 1995
Designed by P Wright
18 holes, 5439 yards, S.S.S. 68
♦ Welcome anytime; tee time booking recommended.
ⓘ WD £14.25; WE £17.50.
⌁ Welcome by arrangement with Sec; full facilities.
🍴 Full facilities.
⌁ The Birch Hotel, Haywards Heath; Hickstead Hotel, Bolney.

2A 58 **Hastings**
Battle Rd, St Leonards-on-Sea, E Sussex, TH38 0TA
☎ (01424) 852981, Fax 852981, Sec 852977
A2100 from Battle to Hastings, 3 miles NW of Hastings.
Municipal undulating parkland course.
Pro Charles Giddings/Sean Creasy; Founded 1973
Designed by Frank Pennink
18 holes, 6248 yards, S.S.S. 70
♦ Welcome; no restrictions WD; booking system in use at WE 7am-10.30am.
ⓘ WD £11; WE £14.
⌁ Welcome Mon-Fri; full facilities; terms on application.
🍴 Full facilities.
Practice range, 14 bays; floodlit.
⌁ Beauport Park.

2A 59 **Hayling Golf Club**
Links Lane, Hayling Island, Hants, PO11 0BX
☎ (023) 9246 4446, Fax 9246 4446, Pro 9246 4491, Bar/Rest 9246 3712
From Havant junction on A27 take A3023 to SW corner of Hayling Island.
Links course.
Founded 1883
Designed by J H Taylor/Tom Simpson

18 holes, 6521 yards, S.S.S. 71
♦ Welcome with handicap certs.
ⓘ WD £26; WE £35.
⌁ Welcome Tues/Wed by prior arrangement; full facilities.
🍴 Full facilities.
Practice range; putting green; 2 covered driving nets.
⌁ Newton House Hotel; Broad Oak Country Hotel.

2A 60 **Haywards Heath**
High Beech Lane, Haywards Heath, Sussex, RH16 1SL
☎ (01444) 414310, Fax 458319, Pro 414866, Sec 414457
1.5 miles north of Haywards Heath on the Ardingly road.
Parkland course.
Pro Michael Henning; Founded 1922
18 holes, 6204 yards, S.S.S. 70
♦ Welcome with handicap certs.
ⓘ WD £26; WE £36.
⌁ Welcome by prior arrangement with the Secretary; packages from £27.
🍴 Full facilities.

2A 61 **Highwoods**
Ellerslie Lane, Bexhill-on-Sea, E Sussex, TN39 4LJ
☎ (01424) 212625, Pro 212770, Bar/Rest 21262
Off A259 from Eastbourne or Hastings; 2 miles from Bexhill; from Battle, A269 via Ninfield, turn right in Sidley.
Parkland course.
Pro Mike Andrews; Founded 1925
Designed by J.H. Taylor
18 holes, 6218 yards, S.S.S. 70
♦ Welcome with handicap certs; no visitors Sun before 12 noon unless with member.
ⓘ WD £25; WE £30.
⌁ Welcome by prior arrangement; full facilities; terms on application.
🍴 Full facilities.
⌁ Cooden Resort; Granville.

2A 62 **Hill Barn**
Hill Barn Lane, Worthing, Sussex, BN14 9QE
☎ (01903) 237301
N of Worthing off London & Edinburgh Building Society roundabout on A27, take last exit before the Brighton exit; course is signposted.
Municipal downland course.
Founded 1935
Designed by Hawtree & Son

18 holes, 6224 yards, S.S.S. 70
♦ Welcome.
ⓘ WD £13.50; WE £14.50.
⌁ Welcome WD only; minimum 12; terms on application.
🍴 Breakfasts, snacks, hot meals available all day.
⌁ Beach; Ardington & Chatsworth.

2A 63 **Hockley**
Twyford, Winchester, Hants, SO21 1PL
☎ (01962) 713165, Fax 713612, Pro 713678, Bar/Rest 714572
Leave M3 at Junction 11 and follow signs for Twyford.
Downland course.
Pro Mr T Lane; Founded 1914
Designed by James Braid
18 holes, 6296 yards, S.S.S. 70
♦ Welcome anytime.
ⓘ WD £30; WE £40.
⌁ Welcome Wed/Fri by prior arrangement; full facilities.
🍴 Full facilities every day except Mondays.
Practice range for members only.
⌁ Winchester Royal Hotel; Harestock Lodge; Potters Heron.

2A 64 **Hollingbury Park**
Ditchling Rd, Brighton, Sussex, BN1 7HS
☎ (01273) 552010, Pro 500086
1 mile from Brighton, astride the Downs between A23 London Rd and A27 Lewes Rd.
Public undulating downland course.
Pro Graeme Crompton; Founded 1908
Designed by J. Braid and J.H. Taylor
18 holes, 6400 yards, S.S.S. 71
♦ Welcome anytime.
ⓘ WD £12; WE £16.
⌁ Welcome WD; full facilities; terms on application.
🍴 Full restaurant facilities.
⌁ Old Ship; Preston Resort.

2A 65 **Horam Park**
Chiddingly Rd, Horam, East Sussex, TN21 0JJ
☎ (01435) 813477, Fax 813677
Off M25 at Junction 6; A22 to Eastbourne; A267 to Heathfield; before reaching Horam, take Chiddingly road, 200 yards on right.
Parkland course with lakes.
Pro Giles Velvick; Founded 1985
Designed by Glen Johnson
9 holes, 5968 yards, S.S.S. 68
♦ Welcome.

WD £9-£15; WE £9-£15.
Welcome by arrangement.
Full facilities.
Practice range, bucket of balls £2,
members £1.
The Boship Hotel, Hailsham.

2A 66 Horsham Golf Park
Worthing Rd, Horsham, RH13 7AX
(01403) 271525, Fax 274528
A24 between Horsham and
Southwater; off Hop-Oast
roundabout.
Parkland course.
Pro Guy Hovil; Founded 1993
9 holes 4122 yards, S.S.S. 60
Welcome at all times except
before 11 am Sat.
WD £7; WE £8.
Welcome by arrangement except
before 11am Sat; full facilities.
Full facilities.
Practice range; £2.50 bucket of balls.

2A 67 Ifield Golf & Country Club
Rusper Rd, Ifield, Crawley, RH11 0LN
(01293) 520222, Fax 612973, Pro
523088
M23 Junction on the outskirts of
Crawley near Gossops Green.
Parkland course.
Pro Jon Earl; Founded 1927
Designed by Bernard Darwin.
18 holes, 6330 yards, S.S.S. 70
Welcome WD but should phone in
advance.
WD £22 per day.
Society bookings taken for 16
people or more; coffee, buffet lunch,
3-course dinner in carvery and 36
holes of golf; £55.
Full facilities.
Ifeld Court Hotel.

2A 68 Leckford and Longstock
Leckford, Stockbridge, Hants, SO20
6JF
(01204) 810320
2.5 miles N of Stockbridge on
Andover road.
Parkland course.
Pro Tony Ashton
9 holes, 6394 yards, S.S.S. 72; also
New course: 9 holes, 4562 yards, par
66
Employees of John Lewis
Partnership and guests only.
WD £10; WE £14.
Welcome with prior arrangement
None.

2A 69 Lee-on-the-Solent
Brune Lane, Lee-on-the-Solent,
Hants, PO13 9PB
(023) 9255 0207, Pro 551181, Sec
551170
3 miles S of M27 Junction 11.
Heathland course.
Pro John Richardson; Founded 1905
18 holes, 5933 yards, S.S.S. 69
Welcome WD.
WD £25.
Welcome Thurs by prior
arrangement.
Full clubhouse facilities.
Practice range.
Delle Vue.

2A 70 Lewes
Chapel Hill, Lewes, E Sussex, BN7
2BB
(01273) 483474, Fax 483474, Pro
473245, Bar/Rest 473245
E of town centre on the A27.
Downland course.
Founded 1896
18 holes, 6213 yards, S.S.S. 70
Welcome WD and after 2pm at
WE.
WD £19; WE £30.
Welcome; terms on application.
Full bar and restaurant facilities.
White Hart Hotel, Lewes.

2A 71 Liphook
Wheatsheaf Enclosure, Liphook,
Hants, GU30 7EH
(01428) 723785, Fax 724853
1 mile S of Liphook on B2070 (old
A3).
Heath and heather course.
Pro Geoffrey Lee; Founded 1922
Designed by Arthur Croome
18 holes, 6167 yards, S.S.S. 69
Welcome with handicap certs but
not on Tues and only pm at WE.
WD £30; WE £50.
Welcome Wed, Thurs, Fri; min 16,
max 36; terms on application.
Bar, bar snacks and restaurant
facilities.

2A 72 Littlehampton
170 Rope Walk, Riverside West,
Littlehampton, W Sussex, BN17 5DL
(01903) 717170, Fax 726629, Pro
716369
From Littlehampton take A259
Bognor Regis road; take 1st left after
new river bridge, signs to golf club.
Seaside links course.
Pro Guy McQuitty; Founded 1898
18 holes, 6258 yards, S.S.S. 70

Welcome any time; after 12 noon
on Sun.
WD £28; WE £35.
Welcome WD; full facilities; terms
on application.
Full facilities.
Bailiff's Court; Norfolk Arms.

2A 73 Mannings Heath
Fullers, Hammerpond Rd, Mannings
Heath, Horsham, W Sussex, RH13
6PG
(01403) 210228, Fax 270974
2 miles S of Horsham on A281 from
Junction 11 on the M23; 4 miles
along Grouse Road; turn right at T
junction.
Undulating wooded course.
Pro Clive Tucker; Founded 1905
Kingfisher Course designed by D
Williams
Kingfisher: 18 holes, 6217 yards,
S.S.S. 70; Waterfall: 18 holes, 6378
yards, S.S.S. 70
Welcome.
WD £36; WE £40.
Welcome; full catering available,
tennis, steam rooms and practice
facilities; £57.50-£69.50.
Full facilities.
South Lodge.

2A 74 Marriott Goodwood Park Golf & CC
Goodwood, Nr Chichester, W Sussex,
PO18 0QB
(01243) 775537, Fax 520120
3 miles N of Chichester.
Parkland course.
Pro Adrian Wratting; Founded 1989
Designed by Donald Steel
18 holes, 6530 yards, S.S.S. 71
Welcome with handicap certs.
WD £28; WE £35.
Welcome; packages available for
golf, catering and hotel; aerobic
studio, swimming pool, tennis, gym,
driving range; from £55.
Full facilities, restaurant and
sports cafe bar.
Marriott Goodwood Park.

2A 75 Meon Valley Hotel Golf & Country Club
Sandy Lane, Shedfield, Hampshire,
SO32 2HQ
(01329) 833455, Fax 834411, Pro
832184
Off M27 at Junction 7, take Botley
exit A334 towards Wickham; course
is on Sandy Lane.
Wooded parkland course.

Pro Jason O'Malley; Founded 1978
Designed by J. Hamilton Stutt
18 holes, 6519 yards, S.S.S. 71; also
Valley course: 9 holes.
⚑ Book in advance.
💰 WD £34; WE £40.
📋 Welcome; parties catered for;
terms on application.
🍽 Full facilities.
Full driving range.
🛏 Meon Valley Country Club.

2A 76 **Mid-Sussex**   ℭ
Spatham Lane, Ditchling, East
Sussex, BN6 8XJ
☎ (01273) 846567, Fax 845767
1 mile E of Ditchling on Lewes road.
Parkland course.
Pro Christopher Connell; Founded
1995
Designed by D Williams Partnership
18 holes, 6446 yards, S.S.S. 71
⚑ Welcome WD and afternoons at
WE.
💰 WD £22; WE £22.
📋 Welcome on WD; restaurant and
practice facilities; from £28.
🍽 Full facilities.
Practice range, grass tees available.
🛏 Many in Brighton area.

2A 77 **Moors Valley Golf Centre**
Horton Road, Ashley Heath, Nr
Ringwood, Hants, BH24 2ET
☎ (01425) 480448, Fax 472057, Pro
479776
A 31 through Ringwood, right at
roundabout to Ashley Heath, course 2
miles on right.
Parkland/heathland course; par 3
course planned.
Pro Michael Torrens; Founded 1988
Designed by Martin Hawtree
18 holes, 6270 yards, S.S.S. 70
⚑ Municipal.
💰 WD £11; WE £13.
📋 Welcome in advance.
🍽 Full bar and catering facilities.
🛏 Struan, St Leonards.

2A 78 **New Forest**
Southampton Rd, Lyndhurst, Hants,
SO43 7BU
☎ (023) 8028 2752
On the A35 between Ashurst and
Lyndhurst.
Forest heathland course.
Founded 1888
Designed by Peter Swann
18 holes, 5772 yards, S.S.S. 68
⚑ Welcome.

💰 WD £10; WE £12.
📋 Welcome but must book in
advance; bar and lounge facilities.
🍽 Full facilities.

2A 79 **Newport**
Near Shide, Newport, Isle of Wight,
PO30 3BA
☎ (01983) 525076
On A3056 Newport-Sandown road
0.5 miles from Newport.
Downland course.
Founded 1896
Designed by Guy Hunt
9 holes, 5660 yards, S.S.S. 68
⚑ Welcome with handicap certs.
💰 Terms on application.
📋 Welcome by arrangement;
catering packages available by
special arrangement with caterer;
from £12.
🍽 Bar and catering facilities.

2A 80 **North Hants**
Minley Rd, Fleet, Hants, GU13 8RE
☎ (01252) 616443, Fax 811627, Pro
616655
0.5 mile N of Fleet Station on B3013,
Junction 4A, M3.
Heathland course.
Pro Steve Porter; Founded 1904
Designed by James Braid
18 holes, 6257 yards, S.S.S. 70
⚑ Welcome by prior arrangement
with Sec; letter of introduction and
handicap certs required.
💰 WD £30; WE £35.
📋 Welcome Mon-Fri by arrangement
with Sec; full facilities; packages
available; terms on application.
🍽 Lunch, tea, dinner; pre-booking
required.
🛏 Various in Fleet, Camberley and
Farnborough.

2A 81 **Old Thorns**   ℭ
Old Thorns, Longmoor Rd, Griggs,
Liphook, Hants, GU30 7PE
☎ (01428) 724555, Fax 725063
Signposted from A3 at Griggs Green.
Parkland course.
Founded 1982
Pro P Loxley/ A Bott
Designed by Commander John
Harris; adapted by Peter Alliss and
Dave Thomas
18 holes, 6533 yards, S.S.S. 71
⚑ Welcome.
💰 WD £35; WE £40.
📋 Welcome any day; corporate and
society days can be arranged;
packages available; function rooms.

🍽 European and Japanese
restaurants.
🛏 Old Thorns.

2A 82 **Osborne**
Osborne House Estates, East Cowes,
Isle of Wight, PO32 6JX
☎ (01983) 295421
1 miles from Red Funnel Terminal in
grounds of Osborne House.
Parkland course.
Founded 1903
2 holes opened for Royal household
in 1892 : extended to 9 by Osborne
House Governor in 1904.
9 holes, 6418 yards, S.S.S. 70
⚑ Welcome by prior arrangement
except Tues, Sat and Sunday am.
💰 Terms on application.
📋 Welcome by arrangement but a
maximum of 24; bar and restaurant
facilities; terms on application.
🍽 Facilities available.
🛏 Memories, East Cowes;
Wheatsheaf, Newport.

2A 83 **Osiers Farm**
London Road, Petworth, W Sussex,
GU28 9LX
☎ (01798) 344097
1.5 miles N of Petworth on A283.
Parkland course over farmland.
Pro Mr Little; Founded 1991
Designed by Chris Duncton
18 holes, 6191 yards, S.S.S. 69
⚑ Welcome.
💰 WD £10; WE £10.
📋 Welcome; new clubhouse opened
1999 with full facilities; terms on
application.
🍽 Full facilities in new clubhouse.
🛏 B & B on course; Stonemasons
Arms, Petworth.

2A 84 **Otterbourne GC**
Poles Lane, Otterbourne, Nr
Winchester, SO21 1DZ
☎ (01962) 775225
On A31 between Hursley and
Otterbourne villages.
Parkland course.
Founded 1995
9 holes, 1939 yards, Par 30
⚑ Public pay and play.
💰 WD £4; WE £5.
📋 None.
🍽 None.

2A 85 **Paultons Golf Centre**
Old Salisbury Rd, Ower, Nr Romsey,
Hants, SO51 6AN

☎ (023) 8081 3345
Exit 2 off M27 in direction of Ower, left at 1st roundabout, then right at Heathlands Hotel, then signposted.
Parkland course.
Pro Rod Park; Founded 1993
18 holes, 6238 yards, S.S.S. 70
† All Welcome at all times.
⌾ available on request
✑ Welcome by arrangement; full facilities; terms on application.
🍽 Bars and restaurant
Practice range 24 bays; floodlit.
↵ Heathlands (500 yards).

2A 86 **Paxhill Park**
East Mascalls Lane, Lindfield, W Sussex, RH16 2QN
☎ (01444) 484467, Fax 482709, Pro 484000
2 miles outside Haywards Heath on Lindfield road.
Parkland course.
Pro P Lyons; Founded 1990
Designed by Patrick Tallack
18 holes, 6117 yards, S.S.S. 69
† Welcome WD and after 12 noon at WE.
⌾ WD £15; WE £20.
✑ Welcome Mon-Fri; full facilities but no food on Mon evenings; from £45.
🍽 Full facilities except Mon evenings.
↵ Birch Hotel, Haywards Heath.

2A 87 **Peacehaven**
Brighton Rd, Newhaven, E Sussex, BN9 9UH
☎ (01273) 514049, Pro 512602
On A259 1 mile W of Newhaven.
Undulating downland course.
Pro Ian Pearson; Founded 1895
Designed by James Braid
9 holes, 5488 yards, S.S.S. 67
† Welcome WD; after 11.30am WE and Bank Holidays.
⌾ WD £10; WE £15.
✑ Welcome WD; full facilities; terms on application.
🍽 Available WE; by prior arrangement WD.

2A 88 **Pease Pottage GC**
& Driving Range
Horsham Rd, Pease Pottage, Crawley, RH11 9AP
☎ (01293) 521706
Leave M23 at Junction 11, then course is signposted from large roundabout.
Public parkland course.
Pro David Blair; Founded 1986

Designed by Adam Lazar
9 holes, 3511 yards, S.S.S. 60
† Welcome.
⌾ WD £8.50; WE £11.
✑ Welcome by arrangement; full facilities; terms on application.
🍽 Full bar and restaurant facilities.
Practice range, 26 bays; floodlit.
↵ Cottismore Hotel.

2A 89 **Petersfield**
Tankerdale Lane, Liss, Petersfield, Hants, GU33 7QY
☎ (01730) 895324, Fax 894713, Pro 895216, Sec 895165
Off A3 between Petersfield/Midhurst & Liss exit.
Parkland course.
Pro Greg Hughes; Founded 1892; Now course founded 1997
New course designed by Martin Hawtree
18 holes, 6387 yards, S.S.S. 71
† Welcome with handicap certificates.
⌾ WD £25; WE £30.
✑ Welcome Mon, Wed and Fri; modern new clubhouse facilities; terms on application.
🍽 Full facilities.
↵ Concord Hotel.

2A 90 **Piltdown**
Piltdown, Uckfield, E Sussex, TN22 3XB
☎ (01825) 722033, Fax 724192, Pro 722389
1 mile W of Maresfield on the A272.
Heathland course.
Pro J Amos/ J Partridge; Founded 1904
Designed by J. Rowe, G.M. Dodd, Frank Pennink
18 holes, 6070 yards, S.S.S. 69
† Welcome by arrangement.
⌾ WD £27.50; WE £27.50 (WD and WE £20 after 2pm).
✑ Welcome Mon, Wed and Fri; packages available; terms on application.
🍽 Full facilities.

2A 91 **Portsmouth**
Crookhorn Lane, Purbrook, Portsmouth, Hants, PO7 5QL
☎ (023) 9220 1827, Fax 9220 0766, Pro 9237 2210, Sec 9220 1827
1.5 miles from A3(M), junction of Purbrook/Leigh Park.
Parkland course.
Pro Jason Banting; Founded 1972
Designed by Hawtree

18 holes, 5760 yards, S.S.S. 70
† Welcome with prior booking.
⌾ WD £10.50; WE £12.50.
✑ Welcome at any time by prior arrangement; packages available
🍽 Bar and restaurant facilities available.
↵ Innlodge Hotel

2A 92 **Pyecombe**
Clayton Hill, Pyecombe, Sussex, BN45 7FF
☎ (01273) 844176, Fax 843338, Pro 845398, Sec 845372
Off A23 at Hassocks and Pyecombe. Turn left on to A273 and course is 300 yds on right
Downland course.
Founded 1894
18 holes, 6278 yards, S.S.S. 70
† Welcome.
⌾ WD £18; WE £25.
✑ Welcome by prior arrangement; terms on application.
🍽 Full facilities.
↵ Club can advise.

2A 93 **Romsey**
Romsey Rd, Nursling, Southampton, Hants, SO16 0XW
☎ (023) 8073 4637, Fax 8074 1036, Pro 8073 6673
2 miles SE of Romsey on A3057 Southampton road, near M27/M271 Junction 3.
Wooded parkland course.
Pro Mark Desmond; Founded 1900
Designed by Charles Lawrie
18 holes, 5856 yards, S.S.S. 68
† Welcome WD.
⌾ WD £23.
✑ Welcome by arrangement Mon, Tues and Thurs; full facilities; terms on application.
🍽 Full facilities.
↵ White Horse (Romsey); Travel Inn (Nursling); Novotel (Southampton).

2A 94 **Rowlands Castle**   ℭ
31 Links Lane, Rowlands Castle, Hants, PO9 6AE
☎ (023) 9241 2784, Fax 9241 3649, Pro 9241 2785, Bar/Rest 9241 2216
3 miles on the B2149 off Junction 2 of the A3M.
Parkland course.
Pro P Klepacz; Founded 1902
18 holes, 6612 yards, S.S.S. 72
† Welcome except for Sat.
⌾ WD £25; WE £30.
✑ Welcome Tues and Thurs by prior

SANDFORD SPRINGS GOLF CLUB
(A339 halfway between Basingstoke and Newbury).

This **27 HOLE COURSE** is ideal for your **LARGE EVENT**

CORPORATE AND SOCIETY DAYS OUR SPECIALITY
Up to 120 comfortably catered for both on and off the course.
Contact us now to discuss your requirements:
Sandford Springs, Wolverton, Tadley, Hants RG26 5RT.
Tel: 01635 296800 Fax: 01635 296801

arrangement; packages include 36 holes plus lunch and dinner; £41-£45.
🍽 Full facilities.

2A 95 **Royal Ashdown Forest**
Chapel Lane, Forest Row, E Sussex, RH18 5LR
☎ (01342) 822018, Fax 825211, Pro 822247
A22 East Grinstead-Eastbourne road, 4.5 miles S of East Grinstead turn left in Forest Row opposite church on to B2110, after 0.5 mile turn right into Chapel Lane, top of hill turn left, over heath to clubhouse.
Undulating moorland course with views over forest.
Pro Martyn Landsborough; Founded 1888
18 holes, 6477 yards, S.S.S. 70
† Welcome by arrangement only; restrictions at WE and Bank Holidays.
↳ WD £40; WE £50.
↻ Welcome by prior arrangement; catering; full facilities, except Mon.
🍽 Lunch, tea; casual visitors requested to book in advance or before teeing off.
↴ Ashdown Forest; Brambletye (E Grinstead); Chequers.

2A 96 **Royal Eastbourne** ℭ
Paradise Drive, Eastbourne, Sussex, BN20 8BP
☎ (01323) 729738, Fax 729738, Pro 736986, Bar/Rest 730412
0.5 miles from Town Hall.
Downland course.
Pro Richard Wooller; Founded 1887
18 holes, 6118 yards, S.S.S. 69
† Welcome but handicap certs needed on the Devonshire course.
↳ WD £20; WE £25.
↻ Welcome on WD only; golf, lunch and 3-course dinner; £30-£40.
🍽 Full facilities.
9-hole course, 4294 yards, S.S.S. 61
↴ Grand; Lansdowne; Chatsworth, all in Eastbourne.

2A 97 **Royal Winchester** ℭ
Sarum Rd, Off Romsey Rd, Winchester, Hants, SO22 5QE
☎ (01962) 852462, Fax 865048, Pro 862473, Sec 852462, Bar/Rest 851694
Take M3 to Junction 11 and at Pitt roundabout follow sign to Winchester; left into Kilham Lane and then right into Sarum Road.
Downland course.
Founded 1888
Designed by H.S. Colt And A.P. Taylor
Pro: Steve Hunter
18 holes, 6212 yards, S.S.S. 70
† Welcome WD; with a member only at WE.
↳ WD £30.
↻ Mon, Tues and Wed only by prior arrangement; £55.
🍽 Full facilities.

2A 98 **Rustington Golf** ℭ **Centre**
Golfers Lane, Rustington, W Sussex, BN16 4NB
☎ (01903) 850790, Fax 850982
A259 at Rushington, between Worthing and Chichester.
Public parkland course.
Pro David Phillips/Gerry Newham/Daniel Moxham/Andy Henderson; Founded 1995
Designed by David Williams P'ship
9 holes, 5735 yards, S.S.S. 68
† Welcome 8:30am to 9pm 7 days a week; bookings taken.
↳ WD £9.50; WE £11.50.
↻ Welcome by arrangement; full facilities; terms on application.
🍽 Coffee shop serving hot and cold lunches; licensed bar.
Practice range, 30 covered bays, 6 outdoor bays.

2A 99 **Ryde**
Binstead Rd, Ryde, Isle of Wight, PO33 3NF
☎ (01983) 614809, Pro 562088
Main Ryde-Newport road.
Parkland course.
Pro Peter Hammond; Founded 1895
9 holes, 5287 yards, S.S.S. 66
† Welcome; not Wed pm or Sun am.
↳ WD £15; WE £20.
↻ Welcome WD except Wed;

contact Sec; facilities and packages by arrangement; terms on application.
🍽 By arrangement.
↴ Newlands.

2A 100 **Rye**
New Lydd Road, Camber, Rye, E Sussex, TN31 7QS
☎ (01797) 225241, Fax 225460, Pro 225218
From Rye take the A259 to New Romney; 2 miles out of town turn right towards Camber; course is 1.5 miles on right.
Links course.
Founded 1894
Designed by H.S. Colt
27 holes, 6308 yards, S.S.S. 71
† Welcome, but only with a member.
↳ Not available.
↻ None.
🍽 Full facilities.
↴ Hope; Anchor; Mermaid, all in Rye.

2A 101 **Sandford Springs** ℭ
Wolverton, Tadley, Hants, RG26 5RT
☎ (01635) 296800, Fax 296801, Pro 296808
Off the A339 at Kingsclere between Basingstoke and Newbury.
Picturesque varied course overlooking 5 counties.
Pro Gary Edmunds; Founded 1988
Designed by Hawtree & Son
27 holes, 3 courses (Parks, Woods & Lakes)
Parks & Woods, 6143 yards, S.S.S. 69; Woods & Lakes, 6222 yards, S.S.S. 70; Lakes & Parks, 6005 yards, S.S.S. 69
† Welcome WD, booking system in operation; WE subject to availability.
↳ WD £23.
↻ Society and Company days welcome by prior arrangement.
🍽 Full bar and restaurant facilities.
↴ Hilton National, Basingstoke & Newbury.

2A 102 **Seaford**
Firle Road, East Blatchington, Seaford, E Sussex, BN25 2JD

Rye

They say that the hardest shot at beautiful Rye is the second on the short par threes. It is that sort of place amid the sand dunes of Camber Bay.

Rye sits in a rich golfing area. Just down the coast in Sandwich Bay is the Open Championship course of Royal St George's and the equally impressive Prince's.

But across the golfing border into Sussex is Rye. Unique Rye. Wonderful Rye. Difficult Rye. Treacherous Rye. Beautiful, historic Rye.

The simple script tells you that Rye is a links course, which of course it is. But that doesn't tell you the full story of the course which hosts the President's Putter each year.

Its unique aspect is that the course is either played along or across sand dunes and if there is a hole that offers the best insight into the course it is the seventh.

At 159 yards it is a short par three but little other than sand separates the tee box from the saucer-like green which is full of bumps and borrows.

Putting may be difficult enough but it is nothing like the trouble that is to be found if the player misses the green. It is surrounded not only by bunkers but difficult burrows as well.

The seventh may be as awkward as the par threes come but there are several other very difficult par fours as well, including the fourth and the 13th.

The fourth is a long dog-leg through the sand dunes while the 13th involves driving into the neck of the fairway between dunes and then finding the green over the dunes with only the two marker posts for assistance. If that doesn't sound difficult enough then just factor in the cross winds that pound the coast through long periods of the year.

But if the course is magnificent the clubhouse holds even more delights with the President's Putter, or putters, hanging from the wall with the golf balls of all the winners of the event that has been held in the dead of winter since 1920.

The first putter, according to the legend under the three hickory clubs, was given to the Society by its President John Low and blues from Oxford and Cambridge have played for it ever since.

The putter originally belonged to Hugh Kirkaldy, at one time professional to Oxford University Golf Club, who played with it when he won the Open Championship at St Andrews in 1891. Low then used it in the final of the Amateur at St Andrews 10 years later and it was his putting which took Harold Hilton to the last hole.

After that every winner's golf ball was hung in a silver band from the club until in 1956 a second club was required and this was provided by Laurie Auchterlonie of St Andrews. The club had belonged to W T Lindskill, one of the founders of the University match in 1898.

By 1987 the second putter was full and the present club was one of two given to the Society by Eustace Storey in 1969. They were made by Willie Park of Musselburgh, father and son both winning the Open Championship. — **CG**

☎(01323) 892442, Fax 894113, Pro 894160
1 miles N of Seaford on A259.
Downland course.
Pro D Mills; Founded 1887
Designed by J.H. Taylor
18 holes, 6551 yards, S.S.S. 71
† Welcome by arrangement.
⌊ WD £25; WE £25.
⌁By arrangement; terms on request.
⏺ Full facilities available.
⌐ Dormy House available.

2A 103 **Seaford Head**
Southdown Rd, Seaford, E Sussex, BN25 4JS
☎(01323) 894843, Pro 890139
S of A259, 12 miles from Brighton.
Public seaside course.
Pro Tony Lowles; Founded 1887
18 holes, 5848 yards, S.S.S. 68
† Welcome at all times.
⌊ WD £13; WE £15.50.
⌁Welcome; full facilities; terms on application.
⏺ Light snacks.
⌐ Traslyn.

2A 104 **Sedlescombe (Aldershaw)**
Sedlescombe, E Sussex, TN33 0SD
☎(01424) 870898
On main A21 near Sedlescombe.
Parkland course.
Pro James Andrews; Founded 1991
18 holes, 6321 yards, S.S.S. 70
† Welcome.
⌊ WD £16; WE £20.
⌁Full facilities; terms on application.
⏺ Bar and snacks.
Practice range, 25 bays; floodlit.
⌐ Brickwall.

2A 105 **Selsey**
Golf Links Lane, Selsey, Chichester, W Sussex, PO20 9DR
☎(01243) 607101
On B2145 7 miles S of Chichester.
Seaside course.
Pro Peter Grindley; Founded 1909
9 holes, 5848 yards, S.S.S. 68
† Welcome.
⌊ WD £12; WE £15.
⌁Small societies welcome; full facilities; terms on application.
⏺ Lunch and snacks.
⌐ Chichester Ship (Bedford).

2A 106 **Shanklin & Sandown**
The Fairway, Lake, Sandown, Isle of Wight, PO36 9PR

☎(01983) 403217, Fax 403217, Pro 404424, Bar/Rest 403170
Off main Sandown & Shanklin road at Lake (A3055).
Sandy parkland course with some steep slopes.
Pro Peter Hammond; Founded 1900
Designed by Dr. J. Cowper, James Braid
18 holes, 6083 yards, S.S.S. 69
† Welcome with handicap certs; restrictions at WE before lunch.
⌊ WD £25; WE £30.
⌁Welcome on WD except Tues by prior arrangement; packages available; terms on application.
⏺ Full facilities available.

2A 107 **Singing Hills Golf Centre**
Albourne, E Sussex, W Sussex, BN6 9EB
☎(01273) 835353, Fax 835444
On the B2117 off the A23.
Parkland course with 3 x 9 holes (River, Valley & Lake).
Pro Wallace Street; Founded 1992
Designed by Richard Hurd (Sandow)
27 holes, 6079 yards, S.S.S. 71
† Welcome.
⌊ WD £18; WE £16.(18 holes)
⌁Welcome for groups of more than 12; prices and packages vary each day.
⏺ Restaurant and bar facilities available.
Practice range, 15 bays.
⌐ Hickstead Hotel, Bolney; Birch Hotel, Haywards Heath.

2A 108 **Slinfold Park Golf ℧ & Country Club**
Stane Street, Slinfold, Horsham, W Sussex, RH13 7RE
☎(01403) 791154, Fax 791465, Pro 791555
On A29 S of junction with A281.
Parkland course.
Pro: Tony Clingan; Founded 1992
Designed by John Fortune
27 holes, 6418 yards, S.S.S. 71
† Welcome.
⌊ WD £25; WE £25.
⌁Welcome Mon-Fri although some restrictions on Tues; full facilities; from £25.
⏺ Full facilities.
Practice range, 19 bays floodlit.
⌐ Ramson Hall, Slinford.

2A 109 **South Winchester**
Pitt, Winchester, Hants, SO22 5QW

☎(01962) 877800, Fax 877900, Pro 840469
S of Winchester on Romsey road.
Championship style links course.
Pro Richard Adams; Founded 1993
Designed by Dave Thomas, Peter Alliss, Clive Clark
18 holes, 6729 yards, S.S.S. 73
† Guests of members only.
⌊ Not available.
⌁Welcome; terms on application.
⏺ Full bar and dining facilities.
Practice range for teaching and members only.
⌐ Lainstone Hotel; Royal Hotel; Hotel du Vin.

2A 110 **Southampton**
Golf Course Rd, Bassett, Southampton, Hants, SO16 7AY
☎(023) 8076 0546, Pro 8076 8407, Bar/Rest 8076 7996
N end of city, off Bassett Ave, halfway between Chilworth roundabout and Winchester Rd roundabout.
Municipal parkland course.
Pro Jon Waring; Founded 1935
18 holes, 6213 yards, S.S.S. 70
† Welcome.
⌊ WD £8.20; WE £11.30.
⌁Welcome by arrangement; full facilities; terms on application.
⏺ Breakfast, lunch, bar snacks.
Also a 9-hole course.
⌐ Hilton (Chilworth).

2A 111 **Southsea**
Portsmouth Golf Centre, Great Salterns GC, Burfields Rd, Portsmouth, PO3 5HH
☎(023) 9266 4549, Fax 9265 0525
2 miles off M27/A27/A3 on E road into Portsmouth.
Municipal meadowland course
Pro Terry Healy; Founded 1935
18 holes, 5575 yards, S.S.S. 67
† Welcome.
⌊ WD £10.30; WE £12.30.
⌁Welcome by arrangement; catering available in adjacent farmhouse pub; terms on application.
⏺ Available in adjacent farmhouse pub.
Practice range, 24 bays; floodlit.

2A 112 **Southwick Park**
Pinsley Drive, Southwick, Fareham, Hants, PO17 6EL
☎(023) 9237 0683, Fax 9221 0289, Pro 9238 0442, Sec 9238 0131
B2177 to Southwick village.
Parkland course.

Pro J Green; Founded 1977
Designed by Charles Lawrie
18 holes, 5992 yards, S.S.S. 69
† Strictly by prior arrangement.
⌊ Not available.
⌁Welcome by prior arrangement; 36
holes with coffee, lunch and dinner;
£20-£35.
⦿ Full bar and dining facilities

2A 113 Southwood
Ively Rd, Cove, Farnborough, Hants,
GU14 0LJ
☎(01252) 548700, Fax 515855,
Bar/Rest 515139
0.25 miles W of Farnborough.
Parkland course.
Pro Bob Hammond; Founded 1977
Designed by Hawtree & Son
18 holes, 5738 yards, S.S.S. 68
† Welcome.
⌊ Terms on application.
⌁Welcome on WD; full facilities
available; terms on application.
⦿ Full facilities.
⌐ Potters International.

2A 114 Stoneham
Monks Wood Close, Off Bassett
Green Rd, Southampton, Hants,
SO16 3TT
☎(023) 8076 8151, Fax 8076 6320,
Pro 8076 8397, Sec 8076 9272
Close to M3 and M27.
Undulating parkland course with
heather.
Founded 1908
Designed by Willie Park
Pro: Ian Young
18 holes, 6310 yards, S.S.S. 70
† Welcome by prior arrangement.
⌊ Terms on application.
⌁Welcome Mon, Thurs and Fri; 36
holes, coffee, lunch and dinner; golf
clinic, video analysis; from £49.
⦿ Full facilities.
⌐ Hilton, Southampton.

2A 115 Test Valley
Micheldever Rd, Overton, Nr
Basingstoke, Hants, RG25 3DS
☎(01256) 771737, Bar/Rest 771153
2 miles S of Overton village junction
with B3400 or1.5 miles N of A303
from Overton turn-off.
Inland links course.
Pro Alastair Briggs; Founded 1992
Designed by D. Wright (E. Darcy)
18 holes, 6883 yards, S.S.S. 72
† Welcome WD and WE; advisable
to phone first.
⌊ WD £16; WE £22.

⌁Welcome 7 days; full facilities
⦿ Full bar and dining facilities;
dining room for up to 100.

2A 116 Tidworth Garrison
Bulford Rd, Tidworth, Wiltshire SP9
7AF
☎(01080) 842301, Fax 842301, Pro
842393, Bar/Rest 842321
A338 Salisbury to Marlborough into
Bulford road.
Treelined downland course.
Pro Terry Gosden; Founded 1908
Recent upgrade by Donald Steel
18 holes, 6101 yards, S.S.S. 69
† Welcome.
⌊ WD £24; WE £24.
⌁Welcome Tues and Thurs; full
facilities and packages on application.
⦿ Full catering facilities.

2A 117 Tilgate Forest Golf Centre
Titmus Drive, Tilgate, Crawley, W
Sussex, RH10 5EU
☎(01293) 530103, Fax 523478
M23 Junction 11 for Pease Pottage,
follow main road to Crawley, at 1st
roundabout turn right, follow signs.
Public parkland course.
Pro Shaun Trussll; Founded 1983
Designed by Huggett And Coles
18 holes, 6359 yards, S.S.S. 70
† Welcome.
⌊ WD £12.70; WE £17.50.
⌁Welcome Mon-Thurs; full facilities;
terms on application.
⦿ Restaurant and bar all day.
Practice range, 36 bays. Also a 9
hole course
⌐ Holiday Inn (Crawley).

2A 118 Tournerbury
Tournerbury Lane, Hayling Island,
Hants, PO11 9DL
☎(023) 9246 2266
Off A27 on Hayling Island.
Seaside course.
Pro Robert Brown; Founded 1994
9 holes, 5912 yards, S.S.S. 66
† Welcome; pay and play.
⌊ WD £8.30; WE £12.50.
⌁Welcome by arrangement.
⦿ None; local pub.
Practice range, 16 bays; floodlit.
⌐ Forte Post House.

2A 119 Tylney Park
Rotherwick, Hook, Hants, RG27 9AY
☎(01256) 762079, Fax 763079
Take M3 to Junction 5 and then 2

miles to Rotherwick via Hook or
Newnham.
Take M4 Junction 11 and then A33
and B3349 to Rotherwick.
Mature parkland course; fine
specimen trees; practice areas
Pro Chris de Bruin; Founded 1974
Designed by W. Wiltshire
18 holes, 6200 yards, S.S.S. 69
† Welcome on WD; must be with
member or have handicap certs. WE
telephone for availability.
⌊ WD £22; WE £30.
⌁Welcome Mon to Thurs inc; 36
holes of golf plus coffee, lunch and
dinner max £47; alternative packages
available throughout golfing year.
⦿ Full facilities.
⌐ Tylney Hall; AA hotels in Hook.

2A 120 Ventnor
Steephill Down Rd, Ventnor, Isle of
Wight, PO38 1BP
☎(01983) 853326
On A3055 to Ventnor.
Undulating downland course.
Founded 1892
12 holes 5767 yards, S.S.S. 68
† Welcome; not before 1pm Sunday.
Tees closed until 12PM Monday
⌊ WD £15; WE £17.
⌁Welcome by arrangement.
⦿ Bar and bar snacks.
⌐ Eversly; Bonchurch Manor;
Mayfair, Shanklin.

2A 121 Waterhall
Waterhall Road, Brighton, E Sussex,
BN1 8YR
☎(01273) 508658
3 miles N of Brighton off A27.
Hilly downland course.
Pro Paul Charman; Founded 1923
18 holes, 5713 yards, S.S.S. 68
† Welcome.
⌊ WD £12; WE £16.
⌁Welcome; full catering facilities
and packages on request; terms on
application.
⦿ Restaurant and bar.

2A 122 Waterlooville
Cherry-Tree Ave, Cowplain,
Waterlooville, Hants, PO8 8AP
☎(023) 9226 3388, Fax 9234 7513,
Pro 9225 6911
A3 (M) Junction 3 take B2150 to
Waterlooville; at 1st roundabout take
exit for Hurstwood.
Parkland course.
Pro John Hay; Founded 1907
Designed by Henry Cotton

18 holes, 6602 yards, S.S.S. 72
♦ Welcome WD.
[WD £25.
⌁ Welcome Thurs with prior arrangement with secretary; 36 holes of golf; coffee on arrival, light lunch and evening meal; other packages also available; £46.
🍽 Full catering and bar facilities.
⌐ Hilton National.

2A 123 **Wellow**
Ryedown Lane, East Wellow, Romsey, Hants, SO51 6BD
☎ (01794) 322872, Pro 323833
Take M27 to Junction 2 then A36 for 2 miles to Whinwhistle road then 1.5 .miles to Ryedown Road.
Parkland course; 27 holes, three 9s: Ryedown, Embley, Blackwater.
Pro Neil Bratley; Founded 1991
Designed by W. Wiltshire
27 holes, 5966 yards
♦ Welcome.
[WD £16; WE £19.
⌁ Welcome on WD; 27 holes, full catering; terms on application.
🍽 Full catering available.
⌐ Vine Hotel, Ower Romsey; Bramble Hill, Bramshaw.

2A 124 **Wellhurst Golf &**
Country Club
North St, Hellingly, E Sussex, BN27 4EE
☎ (01435) 813636, Fax 812444, Pro 813456
Take A267 Heathfield and Wellshurst road.
Parkland course.
Pro M Jarvis; Founded 1992
Designed by Golf Corporation
18 holes, 5771 yards, S.S.S. 68
♦ Public pay and play.
[WD £15; WE £20.
⌁ Welcome; packages available.
🍽 Available.
Practice range, 8 bays and 2 bunker bays.
⌐ Boship Farm Hotel, Hailsham.

2A 125 **West Chiltington**
Broadford Bridge Road, West Chiltington, RH20 2YA
☎ (01798) 813574, Fax 812631, Pro 812115
On A29 proceed south and turn left at Advesane.
Undulating parkland course.
Pro Barry Aram; Founded 1988
Designed by Brian Barnes and Max Faulkner

18 holes, 5877 yards, S.S.S. 69
♦ Welcome.
[WD £15; WE £17.50.
⌁ Welcome by arrangement; terms on application.
🍽 Full facilities.
⌐ Roundabout Hotel, W Chiltington; Chequers Hotel, Pulborough.

2A 126 **West Hove**
Church Farm, Hangleton, Hove, E Sussex, BN3 8AN
☎ (01273) 419738, Fax 439988, Pro 413494, Bar/Rest 413411
On A27 Brighton by-pass at the Hangleton Interchange.
Downland course relocated in 1990.
Pro Darren Cook; Founded 1910/1991
Designed by Hawtree
18 holes, 6255 yards, S.S.S. 70
♦ Welcome.
[WD £20; WE £25.
⌁ Welcome; packages available for groups; terms on application.
🍽 Full bar and catering.
Practice range, 15 bays.

2A 127 **West Sussex**
Pulborough, W Sussex, RH20 2EN
☎ (01798) 872563, Fax 872033, Pro 872426
1.5 miles E of Pulborough on A283.
Heathland course.
Pro Tim Packham; Founded 1931
Designed by Sir Guy Campbell, Major C.K. Hutchison
18 holes, 6221 yards, S.S.S. 70
♦ Welcome WD only.
[WD £42.50.
⌁ Welcome Wed and Thurs; full facilities; terms available on application.
🍽 Lunch and tea.
Practice range, 12 bays
⌐ Amberley Castle; Roundabout.

2A 128 **Westridge**
Brading Rd, Ryde, Isle of Wight, PO33 1QS
☎ (01983) 613131, Fax 567017
A3054 Ryde to Sandown road 2 miles S of Ryde.
Flat parkland course.
Pro Mark Wright; Founded 1992
9 holes, 3228 yards, S.S.S. 55
♦ Welcome.
[WD £8,50; WE £9.50 (9 holes)
⌁ Welcome by arrangement; terms on application.
🍽 Bar and food available.
Practice range, 19 bays floodlit.

2A 129 **Weybrook Park**
Aldermarston Rd, Basingstoke, Hants, RG24 9NT
☎ (01256) 320347, Fax 812973, Pro 333232, Bar/Rest 331159
2 miles NW of town centre between A339 and A340.
Parkland course.
Pro Anthony Dillon; Founded 1971
18 holes, 6468 yards, S.S.S. 70
♦ Welcome by arrangement.
[WD £17.50; WE £22.50.
⌁ Welcome by prior arrangement.
🍽 Available.
Practice range, grass.

2A 130 **Wickham Park**
Titchfield Lane, Wickham, Nr Fareham, Hants, PO17 5PJ
☎ (01329) 833342, Fax 834798
2 miles N of Fareham off M27 junc 10.
Parkland course.
Pro Robynn Gordon; Founded 1995
Designed by J Payne
18 holes, 6022 yards, S.S.S. 69
♦ Public pay and play.
[WD £11; WE £14
⌁ Welcome by prior arrangement WD; packages available; society room
🍽 Clubhouse facilities.

2A 131 **Willingdon**
Southdown Rd, Eastbourne, E Sussex, BN20 9AA
☎ (01323) 410981, Fax 411510, Pro 410984, Bar/Rest 410983
2 miles N of Eastbourne off A22
Downland course.
Pro: Troy Moore; Founded 1898
Designed by J.H. Taylor; modernised by Dr MacKenzie 1925
18 holes, 6044 yards, S.S.S. 69
♦ Welcome WD.
[WD £25 .
⌁ By prior arrangement WD except Tues; packages available; terms on application.
🍽 By arrangement.
⌐ Grand; Queens; Lansdown.

2A 132 **Worldham Park**
Caker Lane, E Worldham, Nr Alton, Hants, GU34 3AG
☎ (01420) 543151, Sec 544606
Take A31, then A3004 to Bordon; course 100 yards on right.
Parkland course.
Pro Jon Le Roux; Founded 1994
Designed by F Whidborne
18 holes, 5864 yards, S.S.S. 68

BERKSHIRE, BUCKINGHAMSHIRE, OXFORDSHIRE

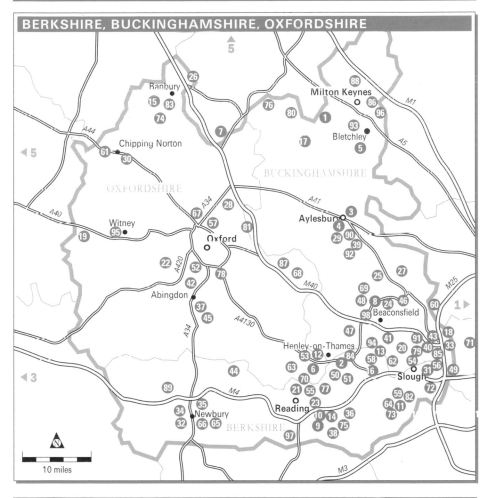

KEY

1	Abbey Hill	19	Burford	39	Ellesborough	59	Lavender Park Golf Centre
2	Aspect Park	20	Burnham Beeches	40	Farnham Park (Bucks)		
3	Aylesbury	21	Calcot Park	41	Flackwell Heath	60	Little Chalfont
4	Aylesbury Park	22	Carswell Golf & CC	42	Frilford Heath	61	Lyneham
5	Aylesbury Vale	23	Castle Royle	43	Gerrards Cross	62	Maidenhead Golf Club
6	Badgemore Park	24	Chalfont Park	44	Goring & Streatley	63	Mapledurham
7	Danbury	25	Chartridge Park	45	Hadden Hill	64	Mill Ride
8	Beaconsfield	26	Cherwell Edge	46	Harewood Downs	65	Newbury & Crookham
9	Bearwood	27	Chesham & Ley Hill	47	Harleyford Golf	66	Newbury Golf Centre
10	Bearwood Lakes	28	Chesterton	48	Hazlemere Golf & Country Club	67	North Oxford
11	The Berkshire	29	Chiltern Forest			68	The Oxfordshire
12	Billingbear Park	30	Chipping Norton	49	Heathpark GC	69	Princes Risborough
13	Bird Hills (Hawthorn Hill)	31	Datchet	50	Henley Golf Club	70	Reading
		32	Deanwood Park	51	Hennerton	71	Rectory Park
14	Blue Mountain Golf Centre	33	Denham	52	Hinksey Heights	72	Richings Park
		34	Donnington Grove CC	53	Huntercombe	73	Royal Ascot
15	Brailes	35	Donnington Valley Hotel	54	Huntswood	74	Rye Hill
16	Braywick			55	Hurst	75	Sandmartins
17	Buckingham	36	Downshire	56	Iver	76	Silverstone
18	The Buckinghamshire	37	Drayton Park	57	Kirtlington	77	Sonning
		38	East Berkshire	58	Lambourne	78	Southfield
79	Stoke Poges Golf Club						
80	Stowe						
81	Studley Wood						
82	Swinley Forest						
83	Tadmarton Heath						
84	Temple						
85	Thorney Park						
86	Three Locks						
87	Waterstock						
88	Wavendon Golf Centre						
89	West Berks						
90	Weston Turville						
91	Wexham Park						
92	Whiteleaf						
93	Windmill Hill						
94	Winter Hill						
95	Witney Lakes						
96	Woburn						
97	Wokefield Park						
98	Wycombe Heights Golf Centre						

10 miles

BADGEMORE PARK GOLF CLUB

Badgemore, Henley-on-Thames, Oxon RG9 4NR.
Telephone: Henley (STD Code 01491) Professional: 574175, Clubhouse: 573667, Fax: 576899.
Badgemore Park is renowned in the area and prides itself on the friendly welcome all visitors receive.
The beautiful but challenging parkland course, founded in 1972, was formerly the McAlpine country estate.
A Wide variety of Society days are available. Golfers may also make up specific days to suit their
requirements; this can include overnight accommodation.

---

† Pay and play.
▯ WD £11; WE £13.
⟳ Welcome Mon to Fri; terms on
application
🍽 Full bar and catering.
⌐ Alton Hotel; Swan Hotel.

2A 133 **Worthing**
Links Rd, Worthing, W Sussex, BN14
9QZ
☎(01903) 260801, Fax 694664, Pro
260718
On A27 near junction with A24.
Downland course.
Pro Stephen Rolley; Founded 1905
Designed by H Vardon
Lower: 18 holes, 6530 yards, S.S.S.
72; Upper: 18 holes, 5243 yards,
S.S.S. 66
† Welcome except at WE April-Oct.
▯ WD £36; WE £40.
⟳ Welcome by arrangement; full
day's golf and catering arrangements;
from £55.
🍽 Full facilities.
⌐ Windsor House; Rosedale GH;
Ardington Hotel.

2B 1 **Abbey Hill**   ℭ
Monks Way, Two Mile Ash, Stony
Stratford, MK8 8AA
☎(01908) 562566, Fax 569538, Pro
563845
2 miles S of Stony Stratford.
Parkland course.
Pro K Bond/M Booth; Founded 1982
18 holes, 6122 yards, S.S.S. 69
† Public pay and play.
▯ Available on application.
⟳ Welcome WD; golf and catering
packages; £19-£25.
🍽 Available.
Practice range, 21 bays floodlit.
⌐ Friendly Hotel, Milton Keynes.

2B 2 **Aspect Park**
Remenham Hill, Henley-on-Thames,
Oxon, RG9 3EH
☎(01491) 578306, Fax 578306, Pro
577562
On A4130 Henley-Maidenhead road
0.75 miles from Henley.
Historic parkland course.

Pro Terry Notley; Founded 1988
Designed by Tim Winsland
18 holes, 6559 yards, S.S.S. 71
† Welcome WD; limited WE.
▯ WD £20; WE £25.
⟳ Welcome WD; terms on
application.
🍽 Facilities available.
Practice range, grass.
⌐ Red Lion.

2B 3 **Aylesbury**
Hulcott Lane, Bierton, Aylesbury,
Bucks, HP22 5GA
☎(01296) 393644
1 mile N of Aylesbury on the A418
Leighton Buzzard road.
Parkland course.
Pro Mitch Kierstenson; Founded 1992
Designed by T S Benwell
18 holes, 5965 yards, S.S.S. 69
† Welcome.
▯ WD £10; WE £12.
⟳ Welcome at all times; terms on
application.
🍽 Facilities available.
Practice range, 30 floodlit bays.
⌐ Forte Crest; Holiday Inn.

2B 4 **Aylesbury Park**
Oxford Road, Aylesbury, Bucks,
HP17 8QQ
☎(01296) 399196, Fax 336830
Parkland course.Founded 1996
Designed by Hawtree & Son
18 holes, 6150 yards, S.S.S. 69
† Welcome at all times.
▯ WD £12; WE £18.
⟳ Welcome at all times; terms on
application.
🍽 Bar.
⌐ Forte Post House; Hartwell
House.

2B 5 **Aylesbury Vale**   ℭ
Stewkley Rd, Wing, Leighton
Buzzard, Beds, LU7 0UJ
☎(01525) 240196, Fax 240848, Pro
240197
Course lies three miles west of
Leighton Buzzard between Wing and
Stewkley.
Parkland course.

Pro Colin Burden/ C Skeet; Founded
1990
Designed by D Wright/ Mick Robinson
18 holes, 6612 yards, S.S.S. 72
† Welcome with prior booking.
▯ WD £12; WE £21.
⟳ Welcome midweek;
🍽 Meals and bar facilities.

2B 6 **Badgemore Park**
Badgemore Park, Henley-on-Thames,
Oxon, RG9 4NR
☎(01491) 573667, Fax 576899, Pro
574175, Sec 572206
1 mile from centre of Henley.
Parkland course.
Pro J Dunn; Founded 1972
Designed by Bob Sandow
18 holes, 6112 yards, S.S.S. 69
† Welcome WD and afternoons at
WE.
▯ Terms on application.
⟳ Welcome WD; full catering
facilities for lunch and dinner; £30-
£47.
🍽 Full facilities.
⌐ Red Lion.

2B 7 **Banbury**   ℭ
Aynho Road, Adderbury, Banbury,
Oxon, OX17 3NT
☎(01295) 810419, Fax 810056
5 miles S of Banbury on the B4100;
10 mins from M40 Junction 10.
Parkland course.
Pro Sarah Jarrett; Founded 1994
27 holes, 2872/3066/5938 yards,
S.S.S. 71
† Welcome.
▯ WD £12; WE £15 (18 holes).
⟳ Welcome by prior arrangement;
terms on application.
🍽 Clubhouse facilities.

2B 8 **Beaconsfield**
Seer Green, Beaconsfield, Bucks,
HP9 2UR
☎(01494) 676545, Fax 681148, Pro
676616
Off M40 on to A355 Amersham road
adjacent to Seer Green/Jordans
railway station.
Parkland course.

Pro Michael Brothers; Founded 1914
Designed by H.S. Colt
18 holes, 6493 yards, S.S.S. 71
† Welcome WD with handicap certs.
⌐ WD £30.
⌐ Welcome Tues and Wed.
⌐ Full facilities.
Practice range, 6 bays.
⌐ Bellhouse.

2B 9 Bearwood

Mole Rd, Sindlesham, Berks, RG11
5DB
☎(0118) 9761330, Pro 9760156,
Sec 9760060
On B3030 1.5 miles N of Arborfield
Cross.
Parkland course.
Founded 1986
Designed by B Tustin
9 holes, 5600 yards, S.S.S. 68
† Welcome WD; with member at
WE.
⌐ WD £18; WE £22 (18 holes).
⌐ Small societies welcome by prior
arrangement.
⌐ Facilities and special packages
available.
10-bay covered driving range, 2
chipping greens and practice bunkers
⌐ Reading Moat House.

2B 10 Bearwood Lakes

Bearwood Rd, Sindlesham, Berks
RG41 4SJ
☎(0118) 9797900, Fax 9792911
Half mile S of M4 Junction 10 for
Wokingham & Sindlesham.
Parkland course.
18 holes, 6800 yards, S.S.S. 72
† Members and guests only.
⌐ Not applicable.
⌐ Not allowed.
⌐ Full facilities for members and
guests.

2B 11 The Berkshire

Swinley Rd, Ascot, Berks, SL5 8AY
☎(01344) 621495
On A332 between Ascot and
Bagshot.
Heathland course.
Pro Paul Anderson; Founded 1928
Designed by Herbert Fowler
Red course: 18 holes, 6379 yards,
S.S.S. 71; Blue course: 18 holes,
6260 yards, S.S.S. 71
† Welcome WD by prior
arrangement with the secretary.
⌐ WD £60.
⌐ Welcome by prior arrangement;
packages available.

⌐ Full clubhouse facilities.
Golf lessons by arrangement with Pro
⌐ Berystede; Cricketers; Royal
Foresters.

2B 12 Billingbear Park

The Straight Mile, Wokingham,
Berkshire, RG40 5SJ
☎(01344) 869259
From M4 Junction 10 take A329M to
Binfield; after Coppid Beech
roundabout, left at Travelodge lights;
then into Foxley Lane; left at T
junction to mini roundabout then right
for 1 mile.
Parkland course; second 9-hole
course planned.
Pro Martin Blainey; Founded 1994
9 holes, 5750 yards, S.S.S. 68
† Pay and play; advance booking
available.
⌐ Terms on application.
⌐ Welcome by arrangement.
⌐ None; clubhouse planned.
⌐ Coppid Beech.

2B 13 Bird Hills (Hawthorn Hill)

Drift Rd, Hawthorn Hill, Nr
Maidenhead, Berks, SL6 3ST
☎(01628) 771030, Fax 631023
M4 Junction 8/9; take A330 towards
Bracknell for 2.5 miles; course on
right at crossroads.
Parkland course.
Pro Nick Slimming; Founded 1984
Designed by Clive D. Smith
18 holes, 6176 yards, S.S.S. 69
† Welcome subject to club
competitions; pay as you play.
⌐ WD £7.50; WE £12.
⌐ Welcome WD; packages
available; terms on application.
⌐ Extensive facilities including
baronial function room.
Practice range, 36 floodlit bays.
⌐ Holiday Inn, Maidenhead;
Frederick's, Maidenhead; Thames
Riviera, Maidenhead.

2B 14 Blue Mountain Golf Centre

Wood Lane, Binfield, Berks, RG42
4EX
☎(01344) 300200, Fax 360960
At Binfield on the A322 off the A329.
Parkland course with lake features.
Founded 1992
18 holes, 6097 yards, S.S.S. 70
† Welcome any day.
⌐ WD £16; WE £22.
⌐ Welcome.

⌐ Full restaurant and hospitality
facilities.
Practice range, 33 bays; floodlit with
video and tuition.

2B 15 Brailes   ✆

Sutton Lane, Lower Brailes, Banbury,
Oxon, OX15 5BB
☎(01608) 685336, Pro 685633,
Bar/Rest 685611
On B4035 4 miles from Shipston on
Stour towards Banbury.
Parkland/meadowland course.
Founded 1992
Designed by Brian A. Hull
18 holes, 6270 yards, S.S.S 70
† Welcome.
⌐ WD £18; WE £26.
⌐ Welcome Mon, Tues, Fri and
afternoons on Wed and Thurs; lunch
and dinner available; from £30.
⌐ Full facilities and bar.

2B 16 Braywick

Braywick Road, Maidenhead, Berks,
SL6 1DH
☎(01628) 676910
On A308 Maidenhead-Windsor road.
Parkland course.
Pro Mike Upcott; Founded 1992
Designed by Mike Upcott
9 holes, 2514 yards, S.S.S. 55
† With member only.
⌐ WD £7.50; WE £7.50.
⌐ By arrangement.
Practice and driving range.
⌐ Oakley Court.

2B 17 Buckingham

Tingewick Rd, Buckingham, Bucks,
MK18 4AE
☎(01280) 815566, Fax 821812, Pro
815210, Bar/Rest 813282
2 miles SW of Buckingham on A421.
Parkland course.
Pro Tom Gates; Founded 1914
18 holes, 6068 yards, S.S.S. 69
† Welcome WD.
⌐ WD £28 (day ticket).
⌐ Welcome Tues and Thurs; bar,
restaurant, conference facilities, full
day's golf.
⌐ Full facilities.
⌐ Four Pillars; Villiers.

2B 18 The Buckinghamshire

Denham Court, Denham Court Drive,
Denham, Bucks, UB9 5BG
☎(01895) 835777, Fax 835210
Follow signs to Denham Country Park
from M40 Junction 1.

Gently undulating parkland course.
Pro John O'Leary; Founded 1992
Designed by John Jacobs
18 holes, 6880 yards, S.S.S. 73
♦ Members' guests only.
⌁ WD £45; WE £55.
⌁by prior arrangement only; full
catering and bar facilities; lunch and
dinner; £90-£130.
⦿ Catering and clubhouse bar.
⌐ Bull Hotel; Bellhouse both
Gerrards Cross.

2B 19 **Burford**
Burford, Oxon, OX18 4JG
☎(01993) 822583, Fax 822801, Pro
822344, Catering 822149
19 miles W of Oxford at junction of
A40 and A361 at Burford roundabout.
Parkland course.
Pro Michael Ridge; Founded 1936
18 holes, 6414 yards, S.S.S. 71
♦ By arrangement, Mon-Fri only.
⌁ Apply for details.
⌁By arrangement.
⦿ Full facilities.

2B 20 **Burnham Beeches**
Green Lane, Burnham, Bucks SL1
8EG
☎(01628) 661448, Fax 668968, Pro
661661
M40 exit Beaconsfield, follow signs to
Slough, turn right and follow Burnham
signs (not Burnham Beeches) to
Green Lane.
Parkland course.
Pro Ronnie Bolton; Founded 1891
18 holes, 6449 yards, S.S.S. 71
♦ Welcome WD; at WE only with
member.
⌁ WD £32.
⌁ Welcome Wed, Thurs, Fri; full
catering facilities; from £62.
⦿ Full facilities except Mon.

2B 21 **Calcot Park**
Bath Rd, Calcot, Reading, RG31 7RN
☎(0118) 9427124, Fax 9453373,
Pro 9427797, Bar/Rest 9414952
1.5 miles from M4 Junction 12 on A4.
Parkland course.
Pro I J Campbell; Founded 1930
Designed by H.S. Colt
18 holes, 6283 yards, S.S.S. 70
♦ Welcome WD.
⌁ WD £36.
⌁ Welcome WD; minimum of 15
with £100 deposit; coffee, lunch,
dinner, 36 holes, trolley hire, course
planners and refreshment hut; £60.
⦿ Full facilities.

2B 22 **Carswell Golf & Country Club**
Carswell, Nr. Faringdon, Oxon SN7
8PU
☎(01367) 870422
Off A420 near Faringdon.
Parkland course.
Pro Geoff Robbins; Founded 1993
Designed by Ely Brothers
18 holes, 6183 yards, S.S.S. 70
♦ Welcome at all times.
⌁ WD £18; WE £22.
⌁ Welcome WD only; full facilities;
terms on application.
⦿ Facilities available.
Practice range, 19 bays covered
floodlit.
⌐ Sudbury House.

2B 23 **Castle Royle**
Knowl Hill, Reading, Berks, RG10
9XA
☎(01628) 829252, Fax 829299
▤ www.clubhouse.com
From M4 Junction 8/9 follow A4 signs
to Reading and course is 2.5 miles.
Inland links course; Founded 1992
Designed by Neil Coles
18 holes, 6828 yards, S.S.S. 73
♦ Members and their guests only.
⌁ Not applicable.
⦿ Facilities available.
Function room available for hire, golf
tuition for non members, 24000sq ft
health and fitness cub, driving range.
⌐ Bird in Hand; Holiday Inn,
Maidenhead.

2B 24 **Chalfont Park**
Bowles Farm, Three House Holds,
Chalfont St Giles, Bucks, HP8 4LW
☎01494) 876293, Fax 874692
Beaconsfield junction off M40; course
is off A413 Amersham road.
Parkland course.
Pro Alistair Thatcher; Founded 1994
Designed by J Gaunt
18 holes, 5208 yards, S.S.S. 66
♦ Welcome WD.
⌁ WD £20.·
⌁Welcome WD; terms on
application.
⦿ Facilities available.
Driving range.

2B 25 **Chartridge Park** ☎
Chartridge, Chesham, Bucks, HP5
2TF
☎(01494) 791772, Fax 786462
From M25 Junction 19 take A41 W to
Aylesbury until Chesham sign.
Parkland course.

Pro Peter Gibbins; Founded 1990
Designed by John Jacobs
18 holes, 5580 yards, S.S.S. 67
♦ Welcome with booking.
⌁ WD £20; WE £25.
⌁ Welcome by arrangement;
unlimited golf and catering.
⦿ Full catering facilities.
⌐ Club can recommend.

2B 26 **Cherwell Edge**
Chacombe, Banbury, Oxon, OX17
2FN
☎(01295) 711591, Fax 712404
3 miles E of Banbury, A442 to
Northampton; 1.5 miles E of M40
Junction 11.
Parkland course.
Pro Joe Kingston; Founded 1983
Designed by Richard Davies
18 holes, 5947 yards, S.S.S. 68
♦ Welcome any time.
⌁ WD £12; WE £16.
⌁ Welcome by arrangement; full
facilities; £33 full day.
⦿ Lunches, bar snacks, evening
meals.
Practice range, 18 bays; floodlit.
⌐ Whatley Arms.

2B 27 **Chesham & Ley Hill**
Ley Hill, Chesham, Bucks, HP5 1UZ
☎(01494) 784541, Fax 785506
Course is off the A41 on the B4504 to
Ley Hill.
Parkland course.
Founded 1900
9 holes, 5296 yards, S.S.S. 66
♦ Welcome Mon and Thurs all day;
afternoon Wed and after 4pm Fri.
⌁ WD £12.
⌁ Welcome on Thurs by prior
arrangement; full catering facilities
and 36 holes of golf; various menus;
from £39.
⦿ Facilities.
⌐ Crown, Old Amersham.

2B 28 **Chesterton**
Chesterton, Nr Bicester, Oxon, OX6
8TE
☎(01869) 241204, Pro 242023
1 mile from M40 exit 9 by A41
towards Bicester, 2nd left, left again
at Red Cow, 150 yards on right.
Meadowland course.
Pro Jack Wilkshire; Founded 1973
Designed by R.R. Stagg
18 holes, 6229 yards, S.S.S. 70
♦ Welcome.
⌁ WD £7.50-15; WE £12-18.
⦿ Bar and bar snacks.

Welcome WD by arrangement; min 16 persons; full facilities. Practice ground.
Littlebury (Bicester).

2B 29 **Chiltern Forest**
Aston Hill, Halton, Aylesbury, Bucks, HP22 5NQ
☎ (01296) 631267, Fax 631267, Pro 631817, Bar/Rest 630899
Between Aylesbury, Tring and Wendover.
Wooded hilly course.
Pro Andy Lavers; Founded 1920
18 holes, 5760 yards, S.S.S. 70
† Welcome WD; with member at WE.
☐ WD £20.
Welcome Mon, Wed and Thurs; full day of golf, lunch and dinner; £45.
Full facilities.
Red Lion, Wendover; Forte, Aylesbury.

2B 30 **Chipping Norton**
Southcombe, Chipping Norton, Oxon, OX7 5QH
☎ (01608) 641150, Fax 645422, Pro 643356, Sec 642383, Bar/Rest 644321
Follow A44 to Evesham from Oxford and turn left at Chipping Norton sign; club 50 yards.
Downland course.
Pro Derek Craik Jnr; Founded 1890
18 holes, 6241 yards, S.S.S. 70
† Welcome WD; with members at WE.
☐ WD £25; WE £12.
Welcome WD by prior arrangement; morning coffee, buffet lunch and evening meal with full day of golf (27 or 36 holes); £45.
Full facilities.
Crown & Cushion; White Hart; Fox, all Chipping Norton.

2B 31 **Datchet**
Buccleuch Rd, Datchet, Slough, Berks, SL3 9BP
☎ (01753) 5438872
Close to Slough and Windsor, easy access from M4.
Parkland course.
Pro to be appointed; Founded 1890
9 holes, 6087 yards, S.S.S. 70
† Welcome WD, 9am-3pm.
☐ WD £16; WE £16.
Small societies welcome by prior arrangement; full facilities.
Bar snacks and lunches available.
The Manor.

2B 32 **Deanwood Park**
Stockcross, Newbury, Berks, RG20 8JS
☎ (01635) 48772, Fax 48772
From the A4 take the B4000 towards Stockcross; the course lies 500 yards on the right.
Parkland course.
Pro James Purton; Founded 1995
Designed by Dion Beard
9 holes, 4228 yards, S.S.S. 61
† Welcome with prior booking.
☐ WD £13.50; WE £15.50.
Welcome by prior arrangement; full practice, clubhouse facilities; packages available; terms on application.
Bar and restaurant facilities available.
Elcot Park; Folley Lodge.

2B 33 **Denham**
Tilehouse Lane, Denham, Bucks, UB9 5DE
☎ (01895) 832022, Fax 835340, Pro 832801
From M40 take Uxbridge/Gerrards Cross turn off on to A40 towards Gerrards Cross; right on to A412 towards Watford; 2nd turning left.
Parkland course.
Pro Stuart Campbell; Founded 1910
Designed by H.S. Colt
18 holes, 6462 yards, S.S.S. 71
† Welcome Mon-Thurs by prior arrangement.
☐ WD £40.
Welcome Tues, Wed, Thurs by prior arrangement; from £80 for full day's package and £40 for half a day.
Full facilities; lunches served daily.
Bull, Gerrards Cross.

2B 34 **Donnington Grove Country Club**
Grove Road, Donnington, Newbury, Berks, RG14 2LA
☎ (01635) 581000, Fax 552259, Pro 551975
Follow signs to Donnington Castle off A34; after 2.5 miles, Grove Road is on the right.
Moorland/parkland course.
Pro Gareth Williams; Founded 1993
Designed by Dave Thomas
18 holes, 7045 yards, S.S.S. 74
† Must become day member.
☐ WD £30; WE £35.
Welcome; full facilities, tennis courts, lake fishing; from £36.
Japanese and English restaurant.
On site.

2B 35 **Donnington Valley Hotel**
Oxford Road, Donnington, Newbury, Berks, RG16 9AG
☎ (01635) 551199
Off the old Oxford road N of Newbury.
Parkland course.
Pro Edward Lainchbury; Founded 1985
18 holes, 6358 yards, S.S.S. 71
† Welcome.
☐ WD £20; WE £30.
Welcome by prior arrangement; packages on request.
Full facilities.
Hotel on site.

2B 36 **Downshire**
Easthampstead Park, Wokingham, Berks, RG11 3DH
☎ (01344) 302030, Fax 301020
Between Bracknell and Wokingham off Nine Mile Ride.
Municipal parkland course.
Pro Wayne Owers/Will Alsop; Founded 1973
Designed by F. Hawtree
18 holes, 6416 yards, S.S.S. 71
† Welcome.
☐ WD £13.50; WE £17.50.
Welcome by arrangement.
Full bar and restaurant.
Practice range, 30 bays covered.
Ladbroke Mercury; St Annes Manor.

2B 37 **Drayton Park**
Steventon Rd, Drayton, Oxon, OX14 2RR
☎ (01235) 528989, Fax 525731, Pro 550607
2 miles S of Abingdon off A34.
Parkland course.
Pro Dinah Masey; Founded 1992
Designed by Hawtree & Co
18 holes, 5503 yards, S.S.S. 67
Also: 9 holes, 776 yards, par 3
† Welcome.
☐ WD from £12; WE from £15.
Welcome; packages available.
Full bar and dining facilities.
Practice range, 21 bays; floodlit.

2B 38 **East Berkshire**
Ravenswood Ave, Crowthorne, Berks, RG45 6BD
☎ (01344) 772041, Fax 777378, Pro 774112
M3 Junction 3 towards Bracknell and follow Crowthorne signs.
Heathland course.
Pro Arthur Roe; Founded 1903

FRILFORD HEATH GOLF CLUB

Visitors and Societies are warmly welcomed to Frilford Heath Golf Club one of a select group of complexes able to boast 54 holes of championship golf. Founded in 1908 on traditional heathland it offers a true test of golf on three distinctive course layouts. The recently enlarged and refurbished clubhouse also provides a warm and attractive atmosphere for refreshment and dining. For details please contact – **Frilford Heath Golf Club, Abingdon, Oxon OX13 5NW. Tel: 01865 390864**

Designed by P. Paxton
18 holes, 6344 yards, S.S.S. 70
♦ Welcome WD.
▏ WD £37.
⌐ Welcome Thurs and Fri only; golf, lunch and dinner; £60.
◉ Clubhouse facilities.
↝ Waterloo.

2B 39 Ellesborough
Butlers Cross, Aylesbury, Bucks, HP17 0TZ
☎ (01296) 622114
On B4010 1 mile W of Wendover.
Undulating downland course.
Pro Mark Squire; Founded 1906
Designed by James Braid
18 holes, 6283 yards, S.S.S. 71
♦ Welcome WD except Tues.
▏ Terms on application.
⌐ Welcome by prior arrangement; packages available for full day's golf and catering; from £55.
◉ Full clubhouse facilities available.
↝ Red Lion, Wendover.

2B 40 Farnham Park (Bucks)
Park Rd, Stoke Poges, Bucks, SL2 4PJ
☎ (01753) 647065, Pro 643332, Bar/Rest 643335
M4 Junction 5 take A355 to Farnham Pump; at 2nd roundabout turn right into Park Road.
Parkland course.
Pro Paul Warner; Founded 1977
Designed by Hawtree & Sons
18 holes, 6172 yards, S.S.S. 69
♦ Public pay and play.
▏ WD £10; WE £13.50.
⌐ Welcome Tues and Thurs; terms on application.
◉ Full clubhouse facilities available.
↝ Burnham Beeches.

2B 41 Flackwell Heath
Treadaway Rd, Flackwell Heath, Bucks, HP10 9PE
☎ (01628) 520027, Fax 530040, Sec 520929
Off A40 High Wycombe-Beaconsfield road at Loudwater roundabout; 1.5 miles from M40 Junction 3 or 4.

Undulating heathland course.
Pro Paul Watson; Founded 1905
18 holes, 6211 yards, S.S.S. 70
♦ Welcome WD with handicap certs.
▏ WD £24.
⌐ Welcome Wed & Thurs only.
◉ Full facilities Tues-Sun; limited Mon.
Practice facilities are available
↝ Bellhouse; Crest.

2B 42 Frilford Heath
Frilford Heath, Abingdon, Oxon, OX13 5NW
☎ (01865) 390864, Fax 390823, Pro 390887, Sec 390866
3 miles W of Abingdon on A338.
Parkland/heathland course.
Pro Derek Craik; Founded 1908
Designed by J.H. Taylor, C.K. Cotton and S. Gidman
Red: 18 holes, 6884 yards, S.S.S. 73; Green: 18 holes, 6006 yards, S.S.S. 69; Blue: 18 holes, 6728 yards, S.S.S. 72
♦ Welcome with handicap certs.
▏ WD £45; WE £60.
⌐ Welcome WD; packages using 3 golf courses available; £70-£80.
◉ Full clubhouse facilities available.
↝ Four Pillars; Upper Reaches, both Abingdon.

2B 43 Gerrards Cross
Chalfont Park, Gerrards Cross, Bucks, SL9 0QA
☎ (01753) 883263, Fax 883593, Pro 885300, Bar 278513
Off A413 at Gerrards Cross.
Wooded parkland course.
Pro Matthew Barr; Founded 1922
Designed by Bill Pedlar
18 holes, 6212 yards, S.S.S. 70
♦ Welcome WD with handicap certs
▏ WD £33.
⌐ Welcome on Thurs and Fri with handicap certs; terms on application.
◉ Full facilities.
↝ Bull; Bellhouse Gerrards Cross.

2B 44 Goring & Streatley
Rectory Rd, Streatley-on-Thames, Berks, RG8 9QA

☎ (01491) 873229, Fax 875224, Pro 873715
On A417 Wantage road 0.25 miles from the Streatley crossroads.
Parkland course.
Pro Jason Hadland; Founded 1895
18 holes, 6320 yards, S.S.S. 70
♦ Welcome WD; WE with member.
▏ WD £35.
⌐ Welcome by prior arrangement; packages available; from £55.
◉ Full restaurant facilities.
↝ Swan Diplomat, Streatley; Miller at Mansfield, Goring.

2B 45 Hadden Hill
Wallingford Rd, Didcot, Oxon, OX11 9BJ
☎ (01235) 510656, Fax 510410, Sec 510410
On A4130 E of Didcot.
Parkland course.
Pro Adrian Waters; Founded 1990
Designed by Michael V. Morley
18 holes, 6563 yards, S.S.S. 71
♦ Welcome; start times are bookable.
▏ WD £14; WE £18.50.
⌐ Welcome WD by arrangement; packages available.
◉ Full bar and restaurant.
Practice range, 20 bays; floodlit.
↝ George; Springs, both Wallingford; George; White Hart, both Dorchester.

2B 46 Harewood Downs
Cokes Lane, Chalfont St Giles, Bucks, HP8 4TA
☎ (01494) 762308, Fax 766869, Pro 764102, Sec 762184
Course lies 2 miles E of Amersham on the A413.
Rolling tree-lined parkland course.
Pro G C Morris; Founded 1903
18 holes, 5958 yards, S.S.S. 69
♦ Welcome with advance application.
▏ WD £25; WE £33.
⌐ Welcome; 2 rounds of golf and full day's catering with refreshment hut; from £56.
◉ Full clubhouse facilities are available.

2B 47 Harleyford Golf

Henley Road, Marlow, Bucks, SL7 2SP
☎ (01628), Fax 487434, Pro 402300
Courseis on the A4155 Marlow-Henley road two miles from Marlow town centre
Downland course.
Pro Alistair Barr; Founded 1996
Designed by Donald Steel
18 holes, 6604 yards, S.S.S. 72
† Welcome by arrangement.
⌊ Terms on application.
⌁ Welcome by prior arrangement; minimum 12 maximum 60; winter and summer packages available; terms on application.
⍟ Full clubhouse facilities.
Practice range.
⌐ Danesfield House.

2B 48 Hazlemere Golf & Country Club

Penn Rd, Hazlemere, Bucks, HP15 7LR
☎ (01494) 714722, Fax 713914, Pro 718298
4 miles N of M40 Junction 4 on A404.
Parkland course.
Pro A McKay/P Harrison; Founded 1982
Designed by Terry Murray
18 holes, 5807 yards, S.S.S. 69
† Welcome.
⌊ WD £26; WE £40.
⌁ Welcome; packages available; from £45.
⍟ Full restaurant and bar facilities.
⌐ White Harte, Beaconsfield; Bellhouse; Bull, Gerrards Cross; Crown, Amersham.

2B 49 Heathpark GC

Stockley Rd, West Drayton, Middlesex, UB7 8BQ
☎ (01895) 444232, Fax 445122
In carpark of Crowne Plaza Hotel at M4 Junction 4.
Undulating heath/parkland course.
0 holes, 3050 yards, S.S.S. 62
† Welcome.
⌊ Pay and play; £7.
⌁ Limited facilities.
⍟ Tea and snacks only; hotel close by with full bar and restaurant facilities.

2B 50 Henley Golf Club

Harpsden, Henley-on-Thames, Oxon, RG9 4HG
☎ (01491) 575742, Fax 412179, Pro 575710, Bar/Rest 575781

1 mile SW of Henley; off A4155 Henley-Reading road.
Parkland course.
Pro Mark Howell; Founded 1907
Designed by James Braid
18 holes, 6329 yards, S.S.S. 70
† Welcome WD with handicap certs and prior arrangement; WE with member.
⌊ WD £30.
⌁ Wed and Thurs only; packages available; £57.50.
⍟ Full clubhouse facilities.

2B 51 Hennerton

Crazies Hill Rd, Wargrave, Reading, Berks, RG10 8LT
☎ (0118) 9401000, Fax 9401042, Pro 9404778
Off A321 into Wargrave village; club signposted.
Parkland course.
Pro William Farron; Founded 1992
Designed by Col. Dion Beard
9 holes, 5460 yards, S.S.S. 67
† Welcome with prior booking.
⌊ WD £15; WE £18.
⌁ Welcome; terms on application.
⍟ Full bar and restaurant facilities.
Practice range, 7 bays.

2B 52 Hinksey Heights

South Hinksey, Oxford, OX1 5AB
☎ (01865) 327 775
Off the A34 at Oxford between the Botley and Hinksey Hill interchanges.
Heathland and links type course with water coming into play.
Founded 1996
Designed by David Heads
18 holes, 7023 yards, S.S.S. 74
† Welcome any time.
⌊ WD £15; WE and BH £20.
⌁ Welcome any time by prior arrangement.
⍟ Fully licensed bar providing home cooked meals and snacks.
⌐ Oxford Spires Four Pillars Hotel.

2B 53 Huntercombe

Nuffield, Henley-on-Thames, Oxon, RG9 5SL
☎ (01491) 641207, Fax 642060, Pro 641241
On A4130 6 miles from Henley towards Oxford.
Woodland/heathland course.
Pro J Draycott; Founded 1902
Designed by Willie Park Jnr
18 holes, 6311 yards, S.S.S. 70
† Welcome WD; no 3 or 4 balls.
⌊ WD £27.

⌁ Welcome Tues and Thurs only.
⍟ Restaurant and bar facilities.
⌐ White Hart, Nettlebed.

2B 54 Huntswood

Taplow Common Rd, Burnham, Bucks, SL1 8LS
☎ (01628) 667144
Off M4 Junction 7; turn left at roundabout and then right at next mini-roundabout; straight on for 1.5 miles and course is just past Grovefield Hotel.
Wooded valley course.
Pro Alan Lithins; Founded 1996
9 holes, 5138 yards, S.S.S. 64
† Welcome.
⌊ WD £11; WE £14.
⌁ Welcome by prior arrangement with club manager Mark Collard; packages available; terms on application.
⍟ Full bar and catering; Sun lunches.
⌐ Grovefield.

2B 55 Hurst

Sandford Lane, Hurst, Berks, RG10 0SQ
Sec (0118) 9344355
Between Reading and Twyford signposted from Hurst village.
Parkland course.
Founded 1977
9 holes, 6308 yards, S.S.S. 70
† Welcome.
⌊ WD £6.50; WE £8.
⌁ Welcome by prior arrangement.
⍟ Bar facilities.

2B 56 Iver

Hollow Hill Lane, Langley Park Rd, Iver, Bucks, SL0 0JJ
☎ (01753) 655615, Fax 654225
Near Langley station.
Parkland course.
Pro Karl Teschner; Founded 1984
Designed by David Morgan
9 holes a further 9 holes will be completed in Spring 2001
† Welcome.
⌊ WD £11; WE £14.50.
⌁ Welcome; packages available; terms on application.
⍟ Full facilities.
Practice range, 18 bays, 9 covered.
⌐ Marriott.

2B 57 Kirtlington

Kirtlington, Oxon, OX5 3JY
☎ (01869) 351133, Fax 351143

On A34 to Kirtlington off M40
Junction 9.
Parkland course.
Founded 1995
Designed by Graham Webster
18 holes, 6084 yards, S.S.S. 69
� Welcome.
🖫 WD £15; WE £20.
☝Welcome; packages available;
terms on application.
🍽 Full facilities.
Practice range, 12 bays.

2B 58 **Lambourne**

Dropmore Rd, Burnham, Bucks SL1
8NF
☎(01628) 666755, Fax 663301, Pro
662936, Bar/Rest 669984
From M4 Junction 7 to Slough and
Burnham; M40 Junction 2 to
Burnham.
Parkland course.
Pro David Hart; Founded 1991
Designed by Donald Steel
18 holes, 6771 yards, S.S.S. 72
� Welcome WD with handicap certs.
🖫 Terms upon application.
☝Not welcome.
🍽 Full clubhouse facilities available.
Practice range, grass.
↜ Burnham Beeches.

2B 59 **Lavender Park**

Swinley Rd, Ascot, Berks, SL5 8BD
☎(01344) 893344
On A329 opposite the Royal
Foresters Hotel.
Parkland course.
Pro David Johnson; Founded 1974
9 holes, 2248 yards, S.S.S. 56
� Welcome any time.
🖫 WD from £5; WE from £8.
☝Welcome by prior arrangement.
🍽 Full bar and catering facilities
available.
Practice range, 30 bays; floodlit.
↜ Royal Foresters.

2B 60 **Little Chalfont**

Lodge Lane, Little Chalfont, Bucks,
HP8 4AJ
☎(01494) 764877, Fax 762860, Pro
762942
From M25 Junction 18 take A404
towards Amersham; course first left
after garden centre.
Parkland course.
Pro: Mike Dunne; Founded 1982
Designed by James Dunne
9 holes, 5852 yards, S.S.S. 70
� Welcome by prior arrangement.
🖫 WD £11.50; WE £13.50

☝Welcome by arrangement;
package includes day's golf and full
catering; £30.
🍽 Bar and clubhouse.
↜ White Hart.

2B 61 **Lyneham**   ℭ

Lyneham, Chipping Norton, Oxon,
OX7 6QQ
☎(01993) 831841, Fax 831775
1 mile off A361 Chipping Norton to
Burford road.
Parkland course with water hazards.
Pro R Jefferies; Founded 1992
Designed by D. Carpenter, A. Smith
18 holes, 6669 yards, S.S.S. 72
� Welcome.
🖫 WD £20; WE £24.
☝Welcome; full day's golf and
catering; scorecard and scoreboard
administration available; from £30.
🍽 Full facilities.
↜ Mill, Kingham; Crown & Cushion;
Kings Arms, both Chipping Norton.

2B 62 **Maidenhead Golf Club**

Shoppenhangers Road, Maidenhead,
Berkshire, SL6 2PZ
☎(01628) 624693, Fax 624693
Off A404 signposted Henley.
Parkland course.
Pro S Geary; Founded 1896
18 holes, 6364 yards, S.S.S. 70
� Welcome WD; not afternoons on
Fri. WE by prior arrangement.
🖫 WD £27; WE £35.
☝ Welcome Wed and Thurs; terms
on application; winter society
packages are £25 for food and golf
on Mon-Thurs.
🍽 Full catering and bar facilities.
↜ Fredericks; Holiday Inn.

2B 63 **Mapledurham**

Chazey Heath, Mapledurham,
Reading, Berks, RG4 7UD
☎(0118) 9463353, Fax 9463363
Off A4074 NW of Reading 1.5 miles
from Mapledurham village.
Undulating parkland course.
Pro Simon O'Keefe; Founded 1992
Designed by MRM Sandow
18 holes, 5621 yards, S.S.S. 67
� Welcome.
🖫 WD £15; WE £18.
☝Welcome by prior arrangement;
packages available; terms on
application.
🍽 Bar and restaurant facilities
available.
Practice range.
↜ Holiday Inn, Caversham.

2B 64 **Mill Ride**

Mill Ride Estate, Mill Ride, North
Ascot, Berkshire, SL5 8LT
☎(01344) 891494, Fax 886820, Pro
886777
From Ascot take A329 until lights,
then right into Fernbank Road, which
leads to Mill Ride.
Blend of parkland and links course.
Pro: to be appointed
Founded 1991
Designed by Donald Steel
18 holes, 6762 yards, S.S.S. 72
� Welcome by prior arrangement
only.
🖫 WD £35; WE £50.
☝Welcome; terms on application.
🍽 Full catering and club facilities.
↜ Royal Berkshire, Ascot;
Berystede, Sunningdale.

2B 65 **Newbury &**   ℭ
Crookham

Bury's Bank Rd, Greenham, Newbury,
Berks, RG19 8BZ
☎(01635) 40035, Fax 40045, Pro
31201
2 miles SE of Newbury.
Wooded parkland course.
Pro David Harris; Founded 1873
Designed by J.H. Turner
18 holes, 5940 yards, S.S.S. 68
� Welcome WD.
🖫 WD £20.
☝ Welcome by prior arrangement;
terms on application.
🍽 Full clubhouse facilities.
↜ Hilton, Newbury.

2B 66 **Newbury Golf Centre**

The Racecourse, Newbury, Berks,
RG14 7NZ
☎(01635) 551464
Signposted off the A34 for
racecourse/conference centre.
Parkland course.
Pro Nick Mitchell; Founded 1994
18 holes, 6500 yards, S.S.S. 70
� Welcome.
🖫 WD £13; WE £17.
☝Welcome by prior arrangement.
🍽 Full catering facilities available.
Practice range, 20 floodlit bays.
↜ Hilton National.

2B 67 **North Oxford**

Banbury Rd, Oxford, Oxfordshire,
OX2 8EZ
☎(01865) 554924, Fax 515921, Pro
553977
Between Kidlington and N Oxford 2.5
miles N of the city centre.

Parkland course.
Pro Robert Harris; Founded 1907
18 holes, 5456 yards, S.S.S. 67
✝ Welcome WD.
⌷ WD £25.
⌗ Welcome by prior arrangement;
packages available; terms on
application.
◉ Full facilities.
⌐ Moat House; Linton Lodge;
Randolph.

2B 68 The Oxfordshire

Rycote Lane, Milton Common,
Thame, Oxon, OX9 2PU
☎ (01844) 278300, Fax 278003, Pro
278505
M40 Junction 7 turn on to A329; club
is 1.5 miles on right.
Championship parkland course; hosts
B&H Masters.
Pro Neil Pike; Founded 1993
Designed by Rees Jones
18 holes, 7187 yards, S.S.S. 76
✝ Members guests' only.
⌷ WD £35; WE £55.
⌗ None.
◉ Outstanding clubhouse bar and
catering facilities.
⌐ Manoir aux Quat Saisons, Great
Milton; Oxford Belfry, Milton
Common.

2B 69 Princes Risborough ☏

Lee Rd, Saunderton Lee, Princes
Risborough, Bucks, HP27 9NX
☎ (01844) 346989, Pro 274567
7 miles NW of High Wycombe on
A4010.
Parkland course.
Founded 1990
Designed by Guy Hunt
Pro Simon Lowry
9 holes, 5440 yards, S.S.S. 66
✝ Welcome.
⌷ WD £14; WE £18.
⌗ Welcome by prior arrangement;
packages available; terms on
application.
◉ Full clubhouse facilities available.
Practice ground, tuition with Pro
available by prior arrangement.
⌐ Rose and Crown, Saunderton.

2B 70 Reading

Kidmore End Rd, Emmer Green,
Reading, Berks, RG4 8SG
☎ (0118) 9472169, Pro 9476115,
Sec 9472909, Bar/Rest 9472909
2 miles N of Reading off Peppard
Road.
Parkland course.

Pro to be appointed; Founded 1910
18 holes, 6212 yards, S.S.S. 70
✝ Welcome Mon-Thurs.
⌷ WD £30.
⌗ Welcome Tues-Thurs; catering
packages available; terms on
application.
◉ Full catering and bar facilities
available.
⌐ Holiday Inn.

2B 71 Rectory Park

Huxley Close, Northolt, Middlesex
UB5 5UL
☎ (020) 8841 5550
Course is off the Target roundabout
on the M40, then the fourth turning
on the left.
9 holes, 3000 yards, S.S.S. 52
Parkland course
✝ Welcome.
⌷ Pay and play; £5.
⌗ No facilities.
◉ Snack bar.

2B 72 Richings Park

North Park, Iver, Bucks, SL0 9DL
☎ (01753) 655370, Pro 655352, Sec
655370
From M4 Junction 5 head towards
Colnbrook; turn left at the lights to
Iver.
Parkland course.
Pro Sean Kelly; Founded 1995
Designed by Alan Higgins
18 holes, 6094 yards, S.S.S. 69
✝ Welcome WD.
⌷ WD £20.
⌗ Welcome WD by arrangement;
packages available; terms on
application.
◉ Restaurant and function room
available.
Practice range, 12 bays; academy
course, tuition available.
⌐ Marriott.

2B 73 Royal Ascot

Winkfield Rd, Ascot, Berks, SL5 7LJ
☎ (01344) 625175, Fax 872330, Pro
624656
Inside Ascot racecourse.
Heathland course.
Pro Alastair White; Founded 1887
Designed by J.H. Taylor
18 holes, 5716 yards, S.S.S. 68
✝ Members' guests only.
⌗ Welcome Wed and Thurs by prior
arrangement; 36 holes, lunch and
dinner; £47.
◉ Restaurant.
⌐ Royal Berkshire; Berystede.

2B 74 Rye Hill ☏

Milcombe, Banbury, Oxon, OX15
4RU
☎ (01295) 721818, Fax 720089
Off A361 between Banbury and
Chipping Norton, take road
signposted Bloxham.
Links style course, 2 holes
redesigned in late 1998.
Pro Tony Pennock; Founded 1993
18 holes, 6692 yards, S.S.S. 73
✝ Welcome.
⌷ WD £14; WE £17.
⌗ Welcome by prior arrangement;
packages available; terms on
application.
◉ Full facilities.
⌐ White Horse.

2B 75 Sandmartins ☏

Finchhampstead Rd, Wokingham,
Berks, RG40 3RQ
☎ (0118) 9792711, Fax 9770282,
Pro 9770265
1 mile S of Wokingham & 4 miles
from Reading on B3016.
Parkland first 9; links style back 9.
Pro Andrew Hall; Founded 1993
Designed by E.T. Fox
18 holes, 6204 yards, S.S.S. 70
✝ Welcome WD.
⌷ WD £22.
⌗ Welcome; minimum 12 in summer;
various packages available with
dining facilities in the Georgian style
clubhouse; terrace; video analysis;
terms on application.
◉ Full clubhouse catering and bar
facilities.
⌐ Stakis St Annes Manor.

2B 76 Silverstone

Silverstone Rd, Stowe, Buckingham,
MK18 5LH
☎ (01280) 850005, Fax 850156
1.5 miles beyond race track on
Silverstone road from Buckingham
and Stowe.
Farmland course.
Pro Rodney Holt; Founded 1992
Designed by David Snell
18 holes, 6213 yards, S.S.S. 71
✝ Welcome.
⌷ WD £14; WE £18.
⌗ Welcome WD by prior
arrangement; private dining room; 9-
hole pitching course; swing analysis;
terms on application.
◉ Full bar and restaurant facilities.
Practice range, 11 bays; floodlit.
⌐ White Hart, Buckingham; Green
Man, Syresham; Travelodge,
Towcester.

2B 77 **Sonning**

Duffield Rd, Sonning-on-Thames, Berks, RG4 6GJ
☎ (0118) 9693332, Fax 9448409
S of A4 between Reading and Maidenhead.
Parkland course.
Pro Richard MacDougall; Founded 1914
18 holes, 6366 yards, S.S.S. 70
† Welcome WD if carrying handicap certs.
↳ WD £25-£35.
☞ Welcome Wed; terms on application.
🍽 Full clubhouse catering facilities available.

2B 78 **Southfield**

Hill Top Rd, Oxford, Oxon, OX4 1PF
☎ (01865) 242158
1.5 miles SE of Oxford city centre off B480.
Undulating parkland course.
Pro Tony Rees; Founded 1875
Designed by James Braid (1875), Redesigned H. Colt (1923)
18 holes, 6328 yards, S.S.S. 70
† Welcome WD; with a member only at WE.
↳ Terms on application.
☞ Welcome but must make prior application in writing; the home of Oxford University GC, Oxford City and Oxford Ladies; terms available on application.
🍽 Full catering facilities are available in Southfield restaurant and 19th bar.
↳ Randolph Hotel; Eastgate Hotel, both Oxford; Travel Inn, Cowley.

2B 79 **Stoke Poges**

Stoke Park, Park Rd, Stoke Poges, Bucks, SL2 4PG
☎ (01753) 717171, Fax 717181, Pro 717172, Sec 717162
Take the exits from the M4 or A4 into Slough, head for Stoke Poges Lane, then into Park Road.
Parkland course.
Pro David Woodward; Founded 1909
Designed by H.S. Colt
27 holes, 6721 yards, S.S.S. 71
† Welcome.
↳ WD £110; WE £180 (18 holes).
☞ Society and corporate days welcomed; various packages and prices available on application to the events organiser; terms on application.
🍽 Full facilities.
Practice range, grass.

Bellhouse; Bull Gerrards Cross; Copthorne, Slough; Chequers Inn, Wooburn Common.

2B 80 **Stowe**

Stowe, Buckingham, Bucks, MK18 5EH
☎ (01280) 816264 Sec 813650
At Stowe school.
Parkland course.
Founded 1974
9 holes, 4573 yards, S.S.S. 63
† Private; members only.
↳ WD £10; WE £10.

2B 81 **Studley Wood** ℭ

The Straight Mile, Horton-cum-Studley, Oxon, OX33 1BF
☎ (01865) 351144, Fax 351166, Pro 351122
From M40 Junction 6 take A40 to Headington roundabout; follow signs to Headly-cum-Studley.
Woodland course.
Pro Tony Williams; Founded 1996
Designed by Simon Gidman
18 holes, 6315 yards, S.S.S. 71
† Welcome.
↳ WD £24; WE £33.
☞ Welcome only by prior arrangement.
🍽 Restaurant and function room.
Practice range, 15 bays; floodlit range.
↳ Studley Priory.

2B 82 **Swinley Forest**

Bodens Ride, Coronation Rd, South Ascot, Berks, SL5 9LE
☎ (01344) 620197, Fax 874733, Pro 874811, Sec 620197
2 miles S of Ascot.
Heathland course.
Pro R C Parker; Founded 1909
Designed by H.S. Colt
18 holes, 5952 yards, S.S.S. 69
† Members' guests only.
↳ WD £65; WE £65.
☞ By introduction of a member only; packages £120.
🍽 Clubhouse bar and catering.
↳ Royal Berkshire; Highclere; Berystede.

2B 83 **Tadmarton Heath**

Wigginton, Banbury, Oxon, OX15 5HL
☎ (01608) 737278, Fax 730548, Pro 730047
Off A361 at Banbury Castle on B4035 for 5 miles to Tadmarton.
Heathland course.

Pro Tom Jones; Founded 1922
Designed by Major C.K. Hutchison
18 holes, 5917 yards, S.S.S. 69
† Welcome WD by prior arrangement.
↳ WD £30.
☞ Welcome WD except Thurs by arrangement; 36 max; full day's golf, coffee, lunch and dinner; £50.
🍽 Full facilities.
↳ Banbury Manor; Wheatley Hall; Cromwell Lodge.

2B 84 **Temple**

Henley Rd, Hurley, Maidenhead, Berks, SL6 5LH
☎ (01628) 824795, Fax 828119, Pro 824254, Bar/Rest 824248
Off A4130 Maidenhead to Henley Road or A404.
Parkland course.
Pro James Whiteley; Founded 1908
Designed by Willie Park Jnr
18 holes, 6207 yards, S.S.S. 70
† By appointment only.
↳ WD £30; WE £35.
☞ By prior appointment; packages available on request; coffee, lunch and dinner all available; from £69.
🍽 Full clubhouse catering facilities.
↳ Compleat Angler, Marlow; Bell Inn, Hurley.

2B 85 **Thorney Park**

Thorney Mill Lane, Iver, Bucks, SL0 9AL
☎ (01895) 422095
Off A4 at Langley into Parlaunt Road.
Parkland course.
Pro Andrew Killing; Founded 1993
Designed by Grundon Leisure Ltd
9 holes, 5668 yards, S.S.S. 67 (a further 9 holes planned for 2001)
† Welcome.
↳ WD £12; WE £15 (18 holes).
☞ Welcome; terms on application.
🍽 Restaurant.
↳ Any Heathrow hotel.

2B 86 **Three Locks**

Great Brickhill, Milton Keynes, Bucks, MK17 9BH
☎ (01525) 270470, Fax 270470, Pro 270050
3 miles from Leighton Buzzard on A4146.
Parkland course with several water hazards.
Founded 1992
Designed by MRM Sandow/ P Critchley
18 holes, 6025 yards, S.S.S. 68

Welcome; booking strongly recommended.

WD £13.50; WE £16.

Welcome with prior booking; various packages available to cover day's golf and catering; terms on application.

Full catering facilities available.

Limited accommodation on site.

2B 87 Waterstock

Thame Rd, Waterstock, Oxford, OX33 1HT

01844) 338093, Fax 338036

Direct access from M40 Junction 8 on to A418 Thame road.

Parkland course; further 9 holes due 1999.

Pro Julian Goodman; Founded 1994

18 holes, 6535 yards, S.S.S. 71

Welcome.

WD £14.50; WE £17.50.

Welcome by prior arrangement; packages available for groups of 70; terms on application.

Bar and grill facilities.

Practice range, 24 bays; floodlit.

Belfry, Milton; County Inn; Travelodge, both Wheatley.

2B 88 Wavendon Golf Centre

Lower End Road, Wavendon, Bucks, MK17 8DA

(01908) 281811, Fax 281257, Sec 281297

M1 Junction 13 to A421, 1st left at roundabout; take first left into Lower End Road.

Parkland course.

Founded 1989

Designed by John Drake/Nick Elmer

18 holes, 5460 yards, S.S.S. 67

Public pay and play.

WD £12; WE £17.50.

Welcome WD and after 10 AM at WE; packages available; from £24.99.

Facilities; carvery, bar and bar snacks.

Driving range, 9 hole par 3 course

The Bell, Woburn.

2B 89 West Berks

Chaddleworth, Newbury, Berks, RG20 7DU

(01488) 638574, Fax 638781, Pro 638851

M4 Junction 14 follow signs to RAF Welford.

Downland course.

Pro Paul Simpson; Founded 1975

Designed by R Stagg

18 holes, 7059 yards, S.S.S. 74

Welcome; afternoons only at WE.

WD £25; WE £35.

Welcome by prior arrangement; packages available; terms on application.

Full facilities.

Queens, E Gaston; Blue Boar, Chiveley; Littlecote House, Hungerford.

2B 90 Weston Turville

New Rd, Weston Turville, Aylesbury, Bucks, HP22 5QT

(01296) 424084, Pro 425949

2 miles from Aylesbury between Aston Clinton and Wendover.

Parkland course.

Pro Gary George; Founded 1975

18 holes, 6008 yards, S.S.S. 69

Welcome except Sun am.

Terms on application.

Welcome WD, some WE, by prior appointment; terms available on application.

Lunches and evening snacks.

Post House.

2B 91 Wexham Park

Wexham St, Wexham, Slough, Berks, SL3 6ND

(01753) 663271, Fax 663318

2 miles from Slough towards Gerrards Cross; follow signs to Wexham Park Hospital; course 0.5 mile further on.

Parkland course.

Founded 1976

Designed by Emil Lawrence and David Morgan

18 holes, 5251 yards, S.S.S. 66; 9 holes, 2727 yards, S.S.S. 34; 9 holes, 2219 yards, S.S.S. 32

Welcome.

Terms on application.

Welcome; full catering facilities; terms on application.

Bar and catering facilities.

Wexham Park Hall

2B 92 Whiteleaf

Upper Icknield Way, Whiteleaf, Bucks, HP27 0LY

(01844) 343097, Pro 345472, Sec 274058

From Monks Risborough turn right into Cadsden road and 100 yards on turn right into Whiteleaf village; course 0.25 miles on left.

Hilly Chilterns course.

Pro Ken Ward; Founded 1904

9 holes, 5391 yards, S.S.S. 66

Welcome WD and with member at WE.

WD £18; WE £18.

Welcome on Thurs by prior arrangement; special packages available

Full facilities.

Red Lion, Whiteleaf; Rose & Crown, Saunderton.

2B 93 Windmill Hill

Tattenhoe Lane, Bletchley, Milton Keynes, Bucks, MK3 7RB

(01908) 631113, Fax 630034

Off A421 through Milton Keynes towards Buckingham.

Parkland course.

Pro Colin Clinghan; Founded 1972

Designed by Henry Cotton

18 holes, 6720 yards, S.S.S. 72

Welcome.

WD £10.75; WE £14.50

Welcome WD and after 11am at WE; packages available for catering and golf; from £19.50.

Full clubhouse facilities available.

Practice range: 23 indoor, 6 outdoor bays.

Forte Crest, Milton Keynes; Shenley, Bletchley.

2B 94 Winter Hill

Grange Lane, Cookham, Maidenhead, Berks, SL6 9RP

(01628) 527613, Pro 527610

M4 Junction 8/9 through Maidenhead to Cookham; club signposted.

Parkland course.

Pro Roger Frost; Founded 1976

Designed by Charles Lawrie

18 holes, 6408 yards, S.S.S. 71

Welcome WD; with member at WE.

Terms on application.

Welcome Wed and Fri; packages can be arranged; terms on application.

Full facilities.

Spencers, Cookham

2B 95 Witney Lakes

Downs Road, Witney, Oxon, OX8 5SY

(01993) 779000

Course is west of Witney on the B4047 Burford road, 1.5 miles from town centre.

Lakeland style course.

Pro Paul Hunt; Founded 1994

Designed by Simon Gidman

18 holes, 6675 yards, S.S.S. 71

Welcome.

WD £16; WE £22.

Welcome; various packages available; £17-£44.
Full clubhouse facilities. Practice range, 24 bays; floodlit.
Four Pillars, Witney.

2B 96 **Woburn**

Bow Brickhill, Milton Keynes, MK17 9LJ
(01908) 370756, Fax 378436, Pro 647987
Course is four miles W of M1 Junction 13; one mile E of Little Brickhill junction.
Woodland course
Pro Luther Blacklock; Founded 1976
Designed by Charles Lawrie
Duchess course: 18 holes, 6651 yards, S.S.S. 72; Dukes course: 18 holes, 6961 yards, S.S.S. 74
Welcome WD by prior arrangement.
Terms on application.

Welcome WD by prior arrangement; terms on application.
Full clubhouse catering, restaurant and bar facilities.
Practice range.

2B 97 **Wokefield Park** ℭ

Mortimer, Reading, Berkshire, RG7 3AG
(01189) 334 072
Exit from the M4 at Junction 11 and take the A33 towards Basingstoke. At first roundabout, take first exit, golf course is 2.5 miles down this road on the right.
Mature parkland course built in an American style.
Founded March 1998
Designed by Jonathan Gaunt
18 holes, 7000 yards, S.S.S. 73
Welcome any time.
WE £36; WD £19.50+.
Welcome by prior arrangement.

3 restaurants.
Own accommodation: 300 rooms and full leisure facilities for residents.

2B 98 **Wycombe Heights** ℭ **Golf Centre**

Rayners Ave, Loudwater, High Wycombe, Bucks, HP10 9SW
(01494) 816686, Sec 813185, Fax 816728
Off A40 from M40 Junction 3.
Parkland course.
Pro Joseph Awuku; Founded 1991
Designed by John Jacobs
18 holes, 6253 yards, S.S.S. 72
Pay and play.
Terms on application.
Welcome WD by prior arrangement; packages available.
Bar, restaurant, family room.
Practice range, 24 floodlit bays.
Post House Forte; Cressex; Alexandria.

3

THE SOUTH WEST

It was one of the goals of the now retired secretary of the Royal and Ancient Golf Club of St Andrews, Sir Michael Bonallack, to bring the Open Championship to the South West of England. The course he had in mind was glorious Saunton, the one venue in the region that could accommodate the excess baggage that comes with the world's most prestigious golf event.

Sadly, Bonallack never succeeded in that ambition but it is to be hoped that one day, whatever problems that do exist are overcome and that the Open does head down to a sublime corner of Devon.

Certainly, the East Course at Saunton would be a worthy test, as has been proven on the many occasions when amateur events have been held there. Mention needs to be made, too, of the West Course, which was greatly improved a dozen years ago.

Royal North Devon at Westward Ho! is another pilgrimage that links enthusiasts need to make. This is the oldest links course in England, the club where Horace Hutchinson and JH Taylor spent many happy days, and you will too.

Similarly, two jewels gleam brightly in Cornwall – Trevose and St Enodoc. From the start you know you are in for a magical day at the latter, the opening tee shot calling for a cracking drive to a fairway that sits snugly between two dunes. Trevose, meanwhile, has a well-deserved reputation for offering excellent value for money.

Such is the power of television, St Mellion, home for several years to the Benson and Hedges International, may be Cornwall's best-known venue, where Jack Nicklaus carved out 18 holes from the most unpromising of locations.

La Moye achieved similar fame owing to its hosting of the Jersey Open on the European Tour, but Royal Jersey and Royal Guernsey are two more fine venues that help make the Channel Islands a popular spot for golfers.

Along the coastline of Somerset, at the entrance to the Bristol Channel, we come to Burnham and Berrow, a championship links course in anyone's book, and where the aforementioned Taylor, five times an Open champion lest we forget, was given his first professional post. On a day of brisk breezes this is golf of the most demanding nature, as the holes wind their way through a succession of towering sandhills.

Two courses in Dorset stand out: Ferndown, which has a reputation for being one of the best-conditioned courses in England, and the Isle of Purbeck, once owned by Enid Blyton, with views so grand that even a gifted storyteller would struggle to do them justice.

In Wiltshire, Bowood Golf Club only opened in 1992 but looks a lot older. Situated in the grounds of one of the great country estates, the gifted architect Dave Thomas has done justice to the sumptuous surroundings. Visitors are made very welcome too. — **DL**

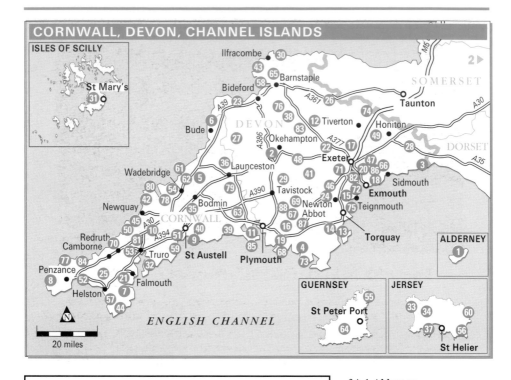

CORNWALL, DEVON, CHANNEL ISLANDS

	KEY				
1	Alderney	29	Hurdwick	58	Royal North Devon
2	Ashbury	30	Ilfracombe	59	St Austell
3	Axe Cliff	31	Isles of Scilly	60	St Clements
4	Bigbury	32	Killiow Park	61	St Enodoc
5	Bowood	33	La Grande Mare	62	St Kew
6	Bude and N Cornwall	34	La Moye	63	St Mellion International
7	Budock Vean Hotel	35	Lanhydrock	64	St Pierre Park Hotel
8	Cape Cornwall Golf &	36	Launceston	65	Saunton
	Country Club	37	Les Ormes Golf and	66	Sidmouth
9	Carlyon Bay Hotel		Leisure	67	Sparkwell
10	Carvynick	38	Libbaton	68	Staddon Heights
11	China Fleet Country Club	39	Looe	69	Tavistock
12	Chulmleigh	40	Lostwithiel Hotel G & CC	70	Tehidy Park
13	Churston	41	Manor House Hotel &	71	Teign Valley
14	Dainton Park		Golf Course	72	Teignmouth
15	Dartmouth Golf &	42	Merlin	73	Thurlestone
	Country Club	43	Mortehoe & Woolacombe	74	Tiverton
16	Dinnaton	44	Mullion	75	Torquay
17	Downes Crediton	45	Newquay	76	Torrington
18	East Devon	46	Newton Abbot (Stover)	77	Tregenna Castle Hotel
19	Elfordleigh Hotel Golf &	47	Northbrook	78	Treloy
	Country Club	48	Okehampton	79	Trethorne
20	Exeter Golf & CC	49	Padbrook Park	80	Trevose Country Club
21	Falmouth		(Cullompton)	81	Truro
22	Fingle Glen	50	Perranporth	82	Warren
23	Hartland Forest Golf &	51	Porthpean	83	Waterbridge
	Leisure Park	52	Praa Sands	84	West Cornwall
24	Hele Park	53	Radnor Golf Centre	85	Whitsand Bay Hotel Golf
25	Helston Golf and Leisure	54	Roserrow		and Country Club
26	Highbullen Hotel	55	Royal Guernsey	86	Woodbury Park Golf &
27	Holsworthy	56	Royal Jersey		Country Club
28	Honiton	57	Royal Naval Air Station	87	Wrangaton
			Culdrose	88	Yelverton

3A 1 Alderney

Routes des Carriers, Longis Rd,
Alderney, Channel Islands, GY9 3YD
☎ (01481) 822835
1 mile E of St Annes.
Undulating seaside course.
Designed by Frank Pennink
9 holes, 4952 yards, S.S.S. 65
† Welcome at all times; except
competition days.
⌐ WD from £12.50; WE from £17.50.
⌐ Welcome by arrangement WD and
WE for special events; catering
available.
⌐ By arrangement.
⌐ Bellevue; Seaview.

3A 2 Ashbury

Higher Maddaford, Southcott,
Okehampton, Devon, EX20 4NL
☎ (01837) 55453, Fax 55468
Leaving Okehampton, take
Holsworthy Road and turn right to
Ashbury; course half mile on right.
Hilly parkland course.
Pro Reg Cade; Founded 1991
Designed by D.J. Fensom
Ashbury course: 27 holes,
4300/5880/5300 yards, S.S.S. 68;
Oakwood course: 18 holes, 5207
yards, S.S.S. 68

A beautiful 18-hole course overlooking the sea in South Devon

BIGBURY GOLF CLUB LIMITED

Bigbury, Kingsbridge, South Devon TQ7 4BB; Club Pro (01548) 810412, Secretary (01548) 810557

No golfer visiting the South Hams should miss the opportunity of playing at Bigbury. It's an ideal holiday course – challenging enough for low handicappers but not too daunting for the average golfer. There are outstanding views from almost everywhere on the course – with Dartmoor to the North, the river Avon running near a number of holes and breathtaking scenes of Bantham Beach and Burgh Island.

---

† Welcome; normal dress codes apply; half-price if playing with a member; booking essential.
⌞ WD £14; WE £18.
⌐ Essential to book at least 2 weeks in advance; no societies March, April, May, June, September and October; packages available; terms on application.
⌐ Manor House Hotel, Okehampton; golf free to hotel guests.

3A 3 Axe Cliff
Squires Lane, Axmouth, Seaton, Devon, EX12 4AB
☎ (01297) 24371, Pro 21754, Bar/Rest 20499
Off A3052 Axmouth-Seaton road.
Coastal/parkland course.
Pro Mark Dack; Founded 1984
18 holes, 6040 yards, S.S.S. 70
† Welcome.
⌞ WD £20; WE £22.
⌐ Welcome by prior arrangement; packages available; terms on application.
⌐ Bar and restaurant facilities available.

3A 4 **Bigbury**
Bigbury-on-Sea, Kingsbridge, Devon, TQ7 4BB
☎ (01548) 810207, Pro 810412, Sec 810557
Turn off the A379 Kingsbridge/Plymouth road near Modbury, on to the B3392; follow signs to Bigbury-on-Sea which lead to the course.
Clifftop course.
Pro Simon Lloyd; Founded 1926
Designed by J.H. Taylor
18 holes, 6048 yards, S.S.S. 69
† Welcome, but essential to belong to a golf club and have current handicap certs.
⌞ WD £25; WE £27.
⌐ Bookings taken in advance for Wed and Thurs; all players must have handicap certs; prices from £25.
⌐ Full facilities.
⌐ Cottage Hotel, Hope Cove; Thurlestone Hotel, Thurlestone; Pickwick Inn, St Ann's Chapel.

3A 5 **Bowood**
Lanteglos, Camelford, Cornwall, PL32 9RF
☎ (01840) 213017, Fax 212622
3A39 through Camelford to Valley Truckle, then right on to B3266 Boscastle-Tintagel road, 1st left after garage towards Lanteglos; entrance 0.5 mile on left.
Parkland course with woodland and lakes.
Pro Alan Johnston; Founded 1992
18 holes, 6692 yards, S.S.S. 72
† Welcome with handicap certs.
⌞ WD £25; WE £25.
⌐ Welcome anytime by arrangement; full facilities available; day ticket £35; terms on application.
⌐ Full facilities.
Practice range available.
⌐ Lanteglos Country House Hotel; Bowood Park Hotel.

3A 6 **Bude and North Cornwall**
Burn View, Bude, Cornwall, EX23 8DA
☎ (01288) 352006, Fax 356855, Pro 353635, Bar/Rest 353176
Through the Bude one-way system on A39 and turn right and right again to the Golf Club; 1 minute from town centre.
Seaside links course.
Pro John Yeo; Founded 1892
Designed by Tom Dunn
18 holes, 6057 yards, S.S.S. 70
† Welcome.
⌞ WD £20; WE £25.
⌐ Some societies are welcome but not at WE; available depending on numbers; terms on application.
⌐ Wide selection of meals available throughout the day.
⌐ Many in local area.

3A 7 **Budock Vean Hotel**
Nr Mawnan Smith, Falmouth, Cornwall, TR11 5LG
☎ (01326) 250288 Pro 252102
On main road between Falmouth and Helston; head for Mabe then go through Mawnan Smith; golf course approx 1.5 miles on right.

Undulating parkland course.
Founded 1932
Designed by James Braid, D. Cook and P.H. Whiteside
9 holes, 5222 yards, S.S.S. 65
† Welcome with handicap certs; phone for start time am only.
Day Ticket: Mon-Sat £18; Sun £20.
⌐ Welcome; full facilities available.
⌐ Full facilities available.
⌐ Budock Vean.

3A 8 **Cape Cornwall Golf & Country Club**
Cape Cornwall, St Just, Penzance, Cornwall, TR19 7NL
☎ (01736) 788611, Fax 788611
3A3071 to St Just-in-Penwith, turn left at memorial clock, 1 mile down road on left.
Coastal parkland course.
Founded 1990
18 holes, 5650 yards, S.S.S. 68
† Welcome except Sat and Sun between 8am and 11.30am.
⌞ WD £20; WE £20.
⌐ Welcome by arrangement; full bar all weekend, lunch 12am- 2pm, dinner 7-10pm.
⌐ Full facilities in summer.

3A 9 **Carlyon Bay Hotel**
Carlyon Bay, St Austell, Cornwall, PL25 3RD
☎ (01726) 812304, Fax 814250, Sec 814250
Main Plymouth-Truro road 1 mile W of St Blazey.
Clifftop/parkland course.
Pro Mark Rowe; Founded 1926
Designed by J. Hamilton Stutt
18 holes, 6578 yards, S.S.S. 71
† Handicap certs required; phone for start times.
⌞ Varies from £24-£35 depending on season.
⌐ Welcome by arrangement.
⌐ Full facilities available.
⌐ Carlyon Bay.

3A 10 **Carvynick Golf & CC**
Summercourt, Newquay, Cornwall, TR8 5AF

☎(01872) 510716
Off A30 at Summercourt exit on the road towards Newquay.
9 holes, 2492 yards, par 66
♦ Welcome at all times.
⌐ 9 holes £5; 18 holes £8; reduced rates for players staying in the cottages.
⌐ Welcome.
⊙I Evenings only after 6.30 pm.

3A 11 China Fleet Country Club
Saltash, Cornwall, PL12 6LJ
☎(01752) 848668, Fax 848456
1 mile from Tamar Bridge, leave A38 before tunnel and follow signs.
Parkland course.
Founded 1991
Designed by Martin Hawtree
18 holes, 6551 yards, S.S.S. 72
♦ Welcome by prior arrangement only.
⌐ WD £25; WE £30.
⌐By arrangement with Sec; full facilities available.
⊙I Full facilities.
⌐ Accommodation available, telephone for details.

3A 12 Chulmleigh   ℭ
Leigh Rd, Chulmleigh, Devon, EX18 7BL
☎(01769) 580519
From Barnstaple follow Tourist Route Exeter signs; from Exeter follow A377 Crediton road, continue through Crediton, after approx 12 miles turn right into Chulmleigh.
Meadowland course.
Founded 1976
Designed by J.W.D. Goodban OBE
9/18 holes, 1450/2310 yards, S.S.S. 54
♦ Welcome.
⌐ WD £6.50; WE £6.50.
⌐Welcome by arrangement; bar and light snacks available.
⊙I Bar and light snacks.
⌐ Cottage for rent, phone for details; Thelbridge Cross Inn.

3A 13 Churston
The Club House, Churston, Nr Brixham, Devon, TQ5 0LA
☎(01803) 842218, Fax 845738, Pro 843442, Sec 842751
5 miles south of Torquay along the main road towards Brixham.
Parkland course.
Pro Neil Holman; Founded 1890
Designed by H.S. Colt

18 holes, 6208 yards, S.S.S. 70
♦ Welcome with handicap certs.
⌐ WD £26; WE £30; concessions apply.
⌐Mon, Thurs and Fri only; minimum 12; reductions for 50+; bar, restaurant, pro shop, function and conference room; terms on application.
⌐ Grand Hotel, Torquay; Imperial Hotel, Torquay; Redcliffe Hotel, Paignton; Berry Head Hotel, Brixham.

3A 14 Dainton Park
Ipplepen, Newton Abbot, Devon, TQ12 5TN
☎(01803) 813812
2 miles south of Newton Abbot on the A381.
Parkland course.
Pro Martin Tyson; Founded 1993
Designed by Adrian Stiff
18 holes, 6207 yards, S.S.S. 70
♦ Unrestricted access.
⌐ WD £15; WE £18.
⌐Groups of 15 or more welcome; bar and catering available as well as practice ground; £15.
⊙I Full bar and catering service.
Practice range, 12 bays; floodlit.
⌐ Passagehouse, Kingsteignton; Coppa Dolla, Broadhempston; Sea Trout Inn, Totnes.

3A 15 Dartmouth Golf &   ℭ Country Club
Blackawton, Totnes, Devon, TQ9 7DE
☎(01803) 712686, Fax 712628, Pro 712650
Off A3122 between Totnes and Dartmouth, 5 miles W of Dartmouth.
Moorland/parkland course.
Pro Steve Dougan; Founded 1992
Designed by Jeremy Pern
18 holes, 6663 yards, S.S.S. 74
♦ Welcome; phone for starting times.
⌐ WD £27, WE £30.
⌐Welcome by arrangement; full facilities available.
Also a 9-hole course; terms on application.
⊙I Bar meals, restaurant, function room.
⌐ Fingals (Dittisham).

3A 16 Dinnaton   ℭ
Dinnaton Sporting and Country Club, Blachford Road, Ivybridge, Devon, PL21 9HU
☎01752) 892512, Pro 690020

Leave A38 at Ivybridge and head to town centre; follow signs to club from roundabout.
Parkland course.
Pro David Ridyard; Founded 1987
Designed by Cotton & Pink
9 holes, 4089 yards, S.S.S. 59
♦ Welcome.
⌐ WD £7.50; WE £7.50 (9 holes).
⌐Welcome.
⊙I Snacks available.
⌐ Accommodation on site.

3A 17 Downes Crediton
The Clubhouse, Hookway, Crediton, Devon, EX17 3PT
☎(01363) 773991, Pro 774464, Sec 773025
Leave A377 Exeter to Crediton road, 8 miles NW of Exeter at Crediton station; turn left at crossroads to Hookway.
Parkland course with water.
Pro Howard Finch; Founded 1976
18 holes, 5884 yards, S.S.S. 68
♦ By arrangement and with handicap certs.
⌐ WD £20; WE £25.
⌐Welcome by arrangement; catering facilities available; terms on application; day tickets available from £27.50.
⊙I Meals and snacks with coffee available.

3A 18 East Devon
North View Rd, Budleigh Salterton, Devon, EX9 6DQ
☎(01395) 443370, Pro 445195, Bar/Rest 442018
M5 junction 30; follow signs to Exmouth and the course is on the right as you enter Budleigh Salterton.
Clifftop, heathland course.
Pro Trevor Underwood; Founded 1902
18 holes, 6239 yards, S.S.S. 70
♦ Welcome by prior arrangement and with handicap certs.
⌐ WD £27; WE £35.
⌐Welcome on Thurs only; bar and restaurant as well as practice facilities; £27 per round, £35 per WD.
⌐ Recommendations available from secretary.

3A 19 Elfordleigh Hotel   ℭ Golf & Country Club
Colebrook, Plympton, Plymouth, Devon, PL7 5EB
☎(01752) 336428, Fax 344581, Pro 348425

Off A38 5 miles NE of Plymouth 2 miles from Marsh Mills roundabout.
Parkland course.
Pro Ross Troake; Founded 1932
Designed by J.H. Taylor
9 holes, 5664 yards, S.S.S. 67
🏌 Welcome with handicap certs.
⌐ WD £15; WE £20.
⌐ Terms on application.
🍴 Full facilities available.
⌐ Elfordleigh Hotel.

3A 20 Exeter Golf & CC ☎

Countess Wear, Exeter, Devon, EX2 7AE
☎ (01392) 874139, Pro 875028, Sec 874639, Booking 876303
Exit 30 off M5; follow road marked Topsham; course is 4 miles south east of Exeter.
Parkland course.
Pro Mike Rowett; Founded 1895
Designed by James Braid
18 holes, 6008 yards, S.S.S. 69
🏌 Welcome with handicap certs; not on Tues mornings, Sats; booking advisable
⌐ WD £28; WE £28.
⌐ Welcome on Thurs only; function room, four bars and spike bars; players' guests welcome; terms on application.
⌐ Buckerell Lodge; Countess Wear Lodge; Devon Motel.

3A 21 Falmouth

Swanpool Road, Falmouth, Cornwall, TR11 5BQ
☎ (01326) 314296, Fax 317783, Pro 311262
Half a mile west of Swanpool beach on the road to Maenporth.
Seaside parkland course.
Pro Bryan Patterson; Founded 1894
18 holes, 6061 yards, S.S.S. 70
🏌 Welcome.
⌐ WD £20; WE £20.
⌐ Welcome by prior arrangement; bar, lunch and tea facilities; terms on application.
🍴 Available.
Practice range; driving range.
⌐ Royal Duchy; Meudon Vean; Park Grove.

3A 22 Fingle Glen

Fingle Glen Family Golf Centre, Nr Exeter, Devon, EX6 6AF
☎ (01647) 61817, Fax 61135
4 miles from Exeter on the A30 to Okehampton, 400 yards from Fingle Glen Junction.

Parkland course.
Founded 1989
Designed by W. Pile
9 holes, 2483 yards, S.S.S. 63
🏌 Welcome.
⌐ WD £8; WE £10 (9 holes).
WD £11; WE £15 (18 holes).
⌐ Welcome; golfing packages can be arranged; terms on application.
🍴 Bar, lounge and restaurant.
Practice range.
⌐ Own accommodation on site.

3A 23 Hartland Forest ☎ Golf & Leisure Park

Woolsery, Bideford, Devon, EX39 5RA
☎ (01237) 431442, Fax 431734
6 miles S of Clovelly off A39.
Parkland course.
Founded 1987
Designed by John Hepplewhite
18 holes, 6015 yards, S.S.S. 69
🏌 No restrictions except acceptable standard of golf; dress code applies.
⌐ WD £20; WE £20; booking advisable.
⌐ Welcome by arrangement; full facilities available.
🍴 Full facilities.
⌐ 34 units of accommodation available on site sleeping 130.

3A 24 Hele Park

Ashburton Road, Newton Abbot, Devon, TQ12 6JN
☎ (01626) 336060, Fax 332661
On edge of Newton Abbot on the A383 Newton Abbot-Ashburton road.
Parkland course.
Pro J Langmead; Founded 1992
Designed by M Craig/N Stanbury
9 holes, 5168 yards, S.S.S. 65
🏌 Welcome.
⌐ WD from £7; WE from £10.
⌐ Welcome on application to the secretary; terms on application.
🍴 Full facilities.
Practice range, floodlit driving range and outdoor grass tees.
⌐ Passage House, kingsteignton, Newton Abbot.

3A 25 Helston Golf and Leisure

Wendron, Helston, Cornwall, TR13 0LX
☎ (01326) 565103
1 mile N of Helston on B3297 Redruth road.
Short park and downland course.
Founded 1988

18 holes, 2100 yards, S.S.S. 54
🏌 Welcome anytime.
⌐ WD £5; WE £5.
⌐ Welcome by prior arrangement.
🍴 Full facilities available at Whealdream Bar.

3A 26 Highbullen Hotel

Chittlehamholt, Umberleigh, Devon, EX37 9HD
☎ (01769) 540561, Fax 540492
10 mins west on A361 from South Molton.
Parkland course; fishing also available.
Pro Paul Weston; Founded 1960
Designed by Hugh Neil. New Extension by M Neil & H. Stutt Desi
18 holes, 5455 yards, S.S.S. 66
🏌 Welcome; free for hotel guests.
⌐ WD £14; WE £16.
⌐ Highbullen Hotel.

3A 27 Holsworthy ☎

Killatree, Holsworthy, N Devon, EX22 6LP
☎ (01409) 253177
1.5 miles out of Holsworthy on the A3072 Bude road.
Parkland course.
Pro Grasham Webb; Founded 1937
18 holes, 6062 yards, S.S.S. 69
🏌 Very welcome.
⌐ WD up to £15; WE up to £20.
⌐ By arrangement; packages available; terms on application.
🍴 Clubhouse facilities.
⌐ Court Barn, Clawton.

3A 28 Honiton

Middlehills, Honiton, Devon, EX14 9TR
☎ (01404) 44422, Fax 46383, Pro 42943, Bar/Rest 47167
1 mile S of Honiton.
Parkland course.
Pro A Cave; Founded 1896
18 holes, 5902 yards, S.S.S. 68
🏌 Welcome by arrangement.
⌐ WD £22; WE £27.
⌐ Welcome on Thurs; terms on application.
🍴 Bar facilities available.
⌐ Space for 10 touring caravans available.

3A 29 Hurdwick

Tavistock Hamlets, Tavistock, Devon, PL19 8PZ
☎ (01822) 612746
Signposted from centre of Tavistock;

La Moye

Once a venue on the European PGA Tour, La Moye has now the honour of staging the Seniors Tour each year. But 2002 will be a really special year for the club celebrating its centenary.

Standing out as the major course in the Channel Islands, La Moye has been a haven for keen golfers and holiday-makers alike.

Nearby Guernsey has Royal Guernsey at L'Ancresse Vale and Ian Botham and at one time John Arlott used to be found on the undulating seaside course of Alderney. But Jersey is especially proud of the wonderful links course at La Moye. To celebrate the centenary of the year James Braid, the famous designer, laid down the course in 1902 there are a series of events planned.

Among them are a Festival of Golf, the Seniors Open and an exhibition match which is to be staged by one of the clubs most public and famous members, Ian Woosnam.

It has more trees for shelter than most links courses as the course meanders away on both sides of the magnificent clubhouse offering spectacular views across St Quen's Bay.

The debate around the most difficult hole rages among the members. There are those who insist that it is the fourth that will strike fear into the hearts of any timid golfer. It is a 424-yard dog-leg par four with out of bounds to the right into the trees and out of bounds left into the clubhouse. It needs accuracy and no shortage of courage.

The professionals, though, have a special regard for the seventh. Although the hole plays away from the sea, the drive is down into the valley and from there the elevated green looks an intimidating place.

The impression is further created by the mounds and sand-hills that guard the elevated green and make accuracy not just helpful but a necessity.

The fact that the course is only two miles away from Jersey's airport which is served by regular flights from all over Britain means that the course has become very popular with visiting golfers who are welcome by prior arrangement with the club secretary.

There are others who will combine the course visit with an island-hoping golfing experience in the Channel Islands which has its own unique flavour.

The fact that La Moye comes with the recommendation of both the European Tour, who return between June 2-4 this year, and Woosnam, a former Masters winner, would be good enough for most golfers. — **CG**

MULLION GOLF CLUB

CURY, HELSTON, CORNWALL TR12 7BP. TEL: SECRETARY (01326) 240685
THE MOST SOUTHERLY GOLF COURSE IN ENGLAND • 18 HOLES • 6037 YDS • PAR 70
SOCIETIES & VISITORS WELCOME • FULL BAR AND CATERING FACILITIES.
"The most unorthodox and sporting club where golf is played in the most beautiful scenery"
TURLY SMITH - writer and critic 1905. *His wish was granted - so come to Mullion*

Course is one mile N of Tavistock on Brentor road.
Parkland course.
Founded 1988
Designed by Hawtree
18 holes, 5217 yards, S.S.S. 67
🏳 Welcome at any time; dress code applies.
Ⓛ WD £14; WE £14.
✎ Welcome; packages available; 36 holes of golf and lunch available from £18.
🍴 Lunch and snacks.
🛏 Bedford Hotel, Tavistock; Castle Inn, Lydford.

3A 30 **Ilfracombe**   ℭ
Hele Bay, Ilfracombe, N Devon, EX34 9RT
☎(01271) 862050, Fax 867731, Pro 863328, Sec 862176, Bar/Rest 862675
Course is one mile from Ilfracombe towards Combe Martin on the A399 coast road.
Undulating heathland course with spectacular views of sea.
Pro Mark Davis; Founded 1892
Designed by T.K. Weir
18 holes, 5893 yards, S.S.S. 69
🏳 Welcome by prior arrangement, particularly in the summer.
Ⓛ WD £19; WE £22.
✎ Welcome by prior arrangement with the secretary; terms on application.
🍴 Full clubhouse facilities.
🛏 Club can recommend in local area.

3A 31 **Isles of Scilly**
St Mary's, Isles of Scilly, TR21 0NF
☎(01720) 422692
1.5 miles from Hugh Town in St Mary's.
Heathland/seaside course.
Founded 1904
Designed by Horace Hutchinson
9 holes, 6001 yards, S.S.S. 69
🏳 Welcome Mon-Sat; phone one hour before.
Ⓛ WD £17; WE £17.
🍴 Available.
🛏 Star Castle Hotel.

3A 32 **Killiow Park**
Killiow, Kea, Nr Truro, Cornwall, TR3 6AG
☎(01872) 270246, Sec 240915
Leave Truro on A39 Truro/Falmouth road, turn right at first roundabout 3 miles from Truro, clearly signposted thereafter.
Picturesque parkland course.
Founded 1987
18 holes, 4029 yards, S.S.S. 60
🏳 Welcome after 8:30am; advisable to book in high season.
Ⓛ WD £13.50; WE £13.50.
🍴 Lounge bar.
🛏 Hospitality Hotel (St Agnes).

3A 33 **La Grande Mare**
Vazon Bay, Castel, Guernsey, CI, GY5 7LL
☎(01481) 53544, Fax 55194, Pro 53432, Bar/Rest 56576
On the west coast of Guernsey at Vazon Bay.
Parkland course.
Pro Matt Groves; Founded 1994
Designed by Hawtree
18 holes, 5112 yards, S.S.S. 66.
🏳 Welcome.
Ⓛ WD £25; WE £28.
✎ Book in advance; restaurant and bar; hotel has 5 crowns; terms on application.
🍴 Bar, restaurant and hotel.
🛏 La Grande Mare Hotel.

3A 34 **La Moye**
La Moye, St Brelade, Jersey, Channel Islands, JE3 8GQ, JE3 8GQ
☎(01534) 743401, Pro 743130, Bar/Rest 742701
2 miles W of airport off Route des Orange.
Links course.
Pro Mike Deeley; Founded 1902
Designed by James Braid
18 holes, 6664 yards, S.S.S. 72
🏳 Welcome by prior arrangement.
Ⓛ WD £40; WE £45.
✎ Welcome by prior arrangement WD between 9.30am-11am; 2.30pm-4pm; £5 booking fee; meals can be organised through the head steward; £40.

3A 35 **Lanhydrock**   ℭ
Lostwithiel Rd, Bodmin, Cornwall, PL30 5AQ
☎(01208) 73600, Fax 77325
1 mile south of Bodmin.
Parkland course.
Pro Jason Broadway; Founded 1992
Designed by J. Hamilton Stutt
18 holes, 6100 yards, S.S.S. 70
🏳 Welcome.
Ⓛ WD £28; WE £28.
✎ Welcome; packages available for groups of 16 and above players; private suite available with own bar facility.
🍴 Full facilities.
🛏 Lanhydrock Golfing Lodge adjacent to first tee.

3A 36 **Launceston**
St Stephens, Launceston, Cornwall, PL15 8HF
☎(01566) 773442, Pro 775359
1 mile N of Launceston on Bude road (B3254).
Parkland course.
Pro John Tozer; Founded 1927
Designed by J. Hamilton Stutt
18 holes, 6407 yards, S.S.S. 71
🏳 Welcome by arrangement.
Ⓛ WD £20; WE £20.
✎ Welcome WD by arrangement; full facilities available; terms on applicationt.
🍴 Available by prior arrangement.
🛏 White Hart.

3A 37 **Les Ormes Golf and Leisure**
Mont à la Brune, St Brelade, Jersey, Channel Islands, JE3 8FL
☎(01534) 744464, Fax 7499122
Course is five minutes from Jersey Airport following the signs for St Brelade.
Parkland course.
Pro Andrew Chamberlain; Founded 1996

🍴 Full clubhouse restaurant and bar facilities.
🛏 Atlantic; L'Horizon, both St Brelade.

Lower Polscoe, Lostwithiel, Cornwall, PL22 0HQ.

AA ★★★ RAC ★★★ ETB ★★★

LOSTWITHIEL *Hotel*
GOLF & COUNTRY CLUB

Tel: 01208 873550
Fax: 01208 873479
E-mail:
reception@golf-hotel.co.uk

With magnificent views and in a peaceful setting, Lostwithiel's 18-hole undulating parkland course in richly wooded hill country is a joy to play. It's situated alongside the river Fowey and overlooked by Restormel Castle in the heart of the beautiful Cornish countryside.

Plus we've got a superb golf and leisure hotel boasting 18 charming bedrooms, tennis, indoor swimming pool, gym, bar and restaurant, with the stunning Cornish coast just a short drive away.

---

9 holes, 5018 yards, S.S.S. 65
† Welcome.
Ḻ WD £12; WE £14.
⌁ Welcome by prior arrangement.
⫯⊚⫯ Full catering facilities.
Practice range, 17 bays, 4 very modern indoor tennis courts.
⌐ Many in Jersey; contact local tourist board.

3A 38 Libbaton
High Bickington, Umberleigh, N Devon, EX37 9BS
☎ (01769) 560269, Pro 560167
A377 to Atherington and then B3217 to High Bickington.
Parkland course.
Founded 1988
Designed by Col P Badham
18 holes, 6494 yards, S.S.S. 72
† Welcome.
Ḻ WD £15; WE £18.
⌁ Welcome Mon, Wed, Fri; golf, coffee, snack lunch, evening meal; £25.
⫯⊚⫯ Facilities available.
Practice range.
⌐ Northcote Manor, Umberleigh; Exeter Inn, Chittlehamholt.

3A 39 Looe
Bin Down, Looe, Cornwall, PL13 1PX
☎ (01503) 240239, Fax 240864
Course is three miles W of Looe just off the B3253.
Parkland/downland course.
Pro A MacDonald; Founded 1933
Designed by Harry Vardon
18 holes, 5940 yards, S.S.S. 68
† Welcome.
Ḻ WD £24; WE £27.
⌁ Welcome but minimum of 8 players; catering packages available; from £18, special society weekend rates available; details on application.
⫯⊚⫯ Facilities available.
⌐ St Mellion.

3A 40 Lostwithiel Hotel ☏
Golf & Country Club
Lower Polscoe, Lostwithiel, Cornwall, PL22 0HQ
☎ (01208) 873550, Fax 873479, Pro 873822
On the A390 from Plymouth to Lostwithiel.
Parkland course.
Pro Tony Nash; Founded 1991
Designed by Stewart Wood R.I.B.a
18 holes, 5984 yards, par 72
† Welcome.
Ḻ WD £21; WE £25.
⌁ Welcome; golf only £15; coffee and lunch, evening meal and day's golf £28; terms on application.
⫯⊚⫯ Full facilities.
Practice range, 6 undercover bays; floodlit.
⌐ 18 country-style bedrooms on site with tennis courts, swimming pool.

3A 41 Manor House Hotel &
Golf Course
Moretonhampstead, Newton Abbot, Devon, TQ13 8RE
☎ (01647) 440998, Fax 440961, Bar/Rest 440355
On B3212 towards Mortonhampstead.
Parkland built around 2 rivers
Pro Richard Lewis; Founded 1921
Designed by J.F. Abercrombie
18 holes, 6016 yards, S.S.S. 69
† Welcome but must book start time.
Ḻ WD £25; WE £32.
⌁ Welcome by prior arrangement; packages can be arranged; terms on application.
⫯⊚⫯ Hotel facilities.
⌐ Manor House Hotel.

3A 42 Merlin ☏
Mawgan Porth, Newquay, Cornwall, TR8 4AD
☎ (01841) 540222, Fax 541031

On coast road between Newquay and Padstow. After Mawgan Porth take St Eval Road.
Heathland course.
Founded 1991
Designed by Ross Oliver
18 holes, 5305 yards, S.S.S. 67
† No restrictions.
Ḻ WD £12; WE £12.
⌁ Welcome by prior arrangement; includes unlimited golf only; lunch and dinner are available at special rates; £10.
⫯⊚⫯ Bar and restaurant.
Practice range, 6 covered bays.
⌐ Bedruthan Steps; Merrymoor Inn; Whitelodge; Sea Vista, all Mawgan Porth; Falcon, St Mawgan.

3A 43 Mortehoe &
Woolacombe
Easewell, Mortehoe, N Devon, EX34 7EH
☎ (01271) 870225, Fax 870745
1 mile before Mortehoe on the Ilfracombe road.
Parkland with superb sea views.
Founded 1992
Designed by Hans Ellis/David Hoare
9 holes, 4638 yards, S.S.S. 63
† Welcome.
Ḻ WD £7; WE £7; £12 for 18 holes.
⌁ Welcome with pre-booking; terms on application.
⌐ Woolacombe Bay; Watersmeet; Lundy House; Rockham Bay.

3A 44 Mullion ☏
Cury, Helston, Cornwall, TR12 7BP
☎ (01326) 240276, Fax 240685, Pro 241176, Sec 240685, Bar/Rest 241231
S of Helston on A3083 towards The Lizard past Culdrose Naval Air station.
Parkland/links course.
Pro P Blundell; Founded 1895

Designed by W Sich
18 holes, 6037 yards, S.S.S. 70
† Welcome with handicap certs.
⌐ WD £20; WE £20.
⌐ Welcome with prior arrangement;
packages available; terms on
application.
◎ Full catering and bar available.
⌐ Polurrian; Mullion Cove; Angel.

3A 45 Newquay
Tower Rd, Newquay, Cornwall, TR7
1LT
☎ (01637) 872091, Fax 874066, Pro
874830, Sec 874354
Adjacent to Fistral Beach.
Seaside links course.
Pro Mark Bevan; Founded 1890
Designed by H.S. Colt
18 holes, 6136 yards, S.S.S. 69
† Welcome; handicap certificates
required.
⌐ WD £25; WE £25.
⌐ By arrangement only; full facilities;
terms on application.
◎ Bar and restaurant.
⌐ Bristol; Esplanade, Narrowcliff.

3A 46 Newton Abbot (Stover)
Bovey Rd, Newton Abbot, Devon,
TQ12 6QQ
☎ (01626) 352460 Pro 362078, Sec
352460, Bar/Rest 356798
Off A 38 at Drumbridges and turn
towards Newton Abbot on the A382;
course is 500 yards on right.
Wooded parkland course.
Pro Malcolm Craig; Founded 1931
Designed by James Braid
18 holes, 5862 yards, S.S.S. 68
† Welcome with handicap certs
unless with a member.
⌐ WD £24; WE £24.
⌐ Thurs only; minimum 24; full
catering facilities to order; £450 for
first 24 players plus £17 thereafter.
◎ Bar and restaurant.
⌐ Dolphin; Edgemoor, both Bovey
Tracey.

3A 47 Northbrook
Topsham Rd, Exeter, Devon, EX2 6EU
☎ (01392) 667010
From M5 Junction 30 take A379 then
on to B3182 Topsham road.
Wooded parkland.
Founded 1968
Par 3 course,18 holes, 1078 yards
† Welcome; pay as you play.
⌐ WD £2.75; WE £2.75.
◎ Vending machines and
confectionery.

3A 48 Okehampton
Okehampton, Devon, EX20 1EF
☎ (01837) 52113, Fax 52734, Pro
53541, Sec 52113
Enter town centre from A30 and
follow signs from the main lights.
Parkland course.
Pro Simon Jefferies; Founded 1913
Designed by J H Taylor
18 holes, 5252 yards, S.S.S. 67
† Welcome but only by prior
arrangement; booking essential.
⌐ WD £20; WE £20
⌐ Welcome by prior arrangement;
Group discounts available; terms on
application.
◎ Available.
⌐ Fox and Hounds, Bridestowe;
White Hart, Okehampton.

3A 49 Padbrook Park ℂ
(Cullompton)
Padbrook Park, Cullompton, Devon,
EX15 1RU
☎ (01884) 38286, Fax 34359
Exit 28 of the M5; follow signs
through Okehampton; across
roundabout and then first on right.
Parkland course.
Pro Stewart Adwick/Robert Thorpe;
Founded 1991
Designed by Bob Sandow
9 holes, 6108 yards, S.S.S. 69
† Welcome but must pre-book tee
time.
⌐ WD £12; WE £16.
⌐ Welcome with prior arrangements;
full catering for society and corporate
packages; terms on application.
◎ Bar and restaurant.
⌐ Exeter Inn, Brampton.

3A 50 Perranporth
Budnic Hill, Perranporth, Cornwall,
TR6 0AB
☎ (01872) 573701, Fax 573701, Pro
572317, Sec 573701
Take Perranporth road off the A30;
course is on the right when entering
town.
Links course with panoramic sea
views.
Pro Derek Michell; Founded 1929
Designed by James Braid
18 holes, 6286 yards, S.S.S. 72
† Welcome with prior booking.
Day ticket: WD £25; WE £30.
⌐ Welcome with booking; packages
can be arranged; terms on
application.
◎ Bar and restaurant.
⌐ Ponsmere, Perranporth; White
Lodge, Mawgan Porth.

3A 51 Porthpean
Porthpean, St Austell, Cornwall, PL26
6AY
☎ (01726) 64613
Off A390 2 miles from St Austell.
Parkland course.
Founded 1992
Designed by R Oliver/ A Leather
18 holes, 5184 yards, S.S.S. 67
† Welcome.
⌐ WD £12; WE £12.
⌐ Welcome by prior arrangement;
packages available; terms on
application.
◎ Clubhouse facilities.
Practice range, 9 bays; floodlit range.
⌐ Cliff Head; Pier House; Porth
Avallen.

3A 52 Praa Sands ℂ
Germoe Crossroads, Praa Sands,
Penzance, Cornwall, TR20 9TQ
☎ (01736) 763445, Fax 763399
7 miles east of Penzance on A394 to
Helston
Seaside parkland course.
Founded 1971
9 by 2 holes, 4122 yards, S.S.S. 60
† Welcome except Sun mornings.
⌐ 9 holes £10; 18 holes £15; day
ticket £20.
⌐ By arrangement; packages
available; terms on application.
◎ Meals and snacks.
⌐ Praa Sands Hotel; Queens,
Penzance.

3A 53 Radnor Golf Centre
Radnor Road, Redruth, TR16 5EL
☎ (01209) 211059
Take A30 from Redruth to
Porthtowan; after 200 yards turn
right; golf centre on left after 1 mile.
Heathland course with gorse.
Pro Gordon Wallbank; Founded 1988
Designed by Gordon Wallbank
9 holes, 1312 yards
† Pay and play.
⌐ WD £7.50; WE £7.50 (18 holes).
⌐ None.
◎ None.

3A 54 Roserrow Golf & ℂ
CC
Roserrow, St Minver, Wadebridge,
Cornwall, PL27 6QT
☎ (01208) 863000, Fax 863002
From Wadebridge take the B3314
towards Polzeath.
Parkland course.
Founded 1997
18 holes, 6951 yards, S.S.S. 72

† Welcome anytime.
⌐ £25 any time.
✎ Welcome by prior arrangement.
🍽 Full bar meals and brasserie.
↙ Own accommodation.

3A 55 **Royal Guernsey**
L'Ancresse Vale, Guernsey, Channel
Islands, GY3 5BY
☎(01481) 47022, Fax 43960, Pro
45070, Sec 46523
3 miles north of St Peter Port.
Seaside links course.
Pro Norman Wood; Founded 1890
Designed by MacKenzie Ross
18 holes, 6206 yards, S.S.S. 70
† Welcome; restricted times on
Thurs and Sat morning; no visitors on
Sun.
⌐ WD £36; WE £36.
✎ Not welcome.
🍽 Coffee, afternoon teas and meals
available.
↙ Pembroke Bay; L' Ancresse
Hotel.

3A 56 **Royal Jersey**
Grouville, Jersey, Channel Islands,
JE3 9BD
☎(01534) 854416, Fax 854684, Pro
852234, Bar/Rest 851042.
4 miles east of St Helier on road to
Gorey.
Links course.
Pro David Morgan; Founded 1878
18 holes, 6089 yards, S.S.S. 70
† Welcome between 10am-12 noon
and 2pm-4pm on WD and after
2.30pm at WE.
⌐ WD £35; WE £40.
✎ Apply in writing to Sec; full
catering by prior arrangement with
Steward; 40+ £7 for tee reservation.
🍽 Bar and catering facilities.

3A 57 **Royal Naval Air Station Culdrose**
RNAS Culdrose, Helston, Cornwall,
TR12 8QY
☎(01326) 552413, Sec 573929
3A3083 1 mile from Helston towards
Lizard.
Flat parkland course built around part
of airfield.
Founded 1962
14 holes 6132 yards, S.S.S. 70
† Must be accompanied by club
member.
⌐ Terms on application.
✎ Welcome by arrangement.
🍽 Clubhouse bar and hot/cold
snacks available.

3A 58 **Royal North Devon**
Golf Links Rd, Westward Ho,
Bideford, Devon, EX39 1HD
☎(01237) 473817, Fax 423456, Pro
477598, Bar 473824
Take M5 to A361 and go through
Northam Village to Sandymere road
and then into Golf Links Road.
Links course.
Pro Richard Herring; Founded 1864
Designed by Tom Morris
18 holes, 6653 yards, S.S.S. 72
† Welcome with handicap certs.
⌐ WD £30; WE £36.
✎ Welcome; bar, restaurant, snooker
room; terms on application.
🍽 Full facilities.
↙ Anchorage Hotel; Durrant House,
Northam; Riversford Hotel, Northam.

3A 59 **St Austell**
Tregongeeves Lane, St Austell,
Cornwall, PL26 7DS
☎(01726) 72649, Fax 74756, Pro
68621, Sec 74756
1 mile out of St Austell on the A390
Truro road; signposted.
Heathland/parkland course.
Pro Tony Pitts; Founded 1911
18 holes, 6089 yards, S.S.S. 69
† Must be a member of a golf club
and hold handicap cert.
⌐ WD £20; WE £22.
✎ Welcome by appointment except
on WE; restaurant and lounge bar;
meals to be arranged with the
caterer; £20.
🍽 Full catering facilities.
Practice range, opening 1998.

3A 60 **St Clements**
Jersey Recreation Grounds Co Ltd,
Graeve d'azette, St Clements, Jersey,
JE2 6PN
☎(01534) 721938
Close to St Helier.
Public meadowland course.
Founded 1913
9 holes, 2244 yards
† Welcome every day except before
11.30 Tues and 1pm Sun.
⌐ WD £10; WE £10.
✎ Welcome by arrangement; buffet
bar and restaurant.
🍽 Buffet bar and restaurant.
↙ Hotel de Normandy, Merton.

3A 61 **St Enodoc**
Rock, Wadebridge, Cornwall,
PL276LD
☎(01208) 863216, Fax 862976, Pro
862402, Sec 862200

6 miles NW of Wadebridge.
Links course.
Pro Nick Williams; Founded 1890
Designed by James Braid
18 holes, 6243 yards, S.S.S. 70
† Welcome; max handicap 24 on
Church course.
⌐ WD £35; WE £40.
✎ Welcome by prior arrangement;
meals can be arranged through
restaurant; £35-£40.
Separate 18-hole course available.
🍽 Full restaurant and bar.

3A 62 **St Kew**   ℭ
St Kew Highway, Nr Wadebridge,
Bodmin, Cornwall, PL30 3EF
☎(01208) 841500, Fax 841500
Main A30 Wadebridge to Camelford
road; course two and a half miles
north of Wadebridge.
Parkland course.
Pro Nick Rogers; Founded 1993
Designed by D Derry
9 holes, 4543 yards, S.S.S. 62
† Welcome at all times.
⌐ WD £13; WE £13.
✎ Welcome by arrangement;
discounts on application; catering
available; terms on application.
🍽 Full facilities.
Practice range, covered.
↙ Bodare Hotel, Daymer Bay;
Molesworth Arms, Wadebridge; St
Moritz, Trebetherick.

3A 63 **St Mellion International**   ℭ
St Mellion, Nr Saltash, Cornwall,
PL12 6SD
☎(01579) 351351, Fax 350537, Pro
352002, Sec 352000, Bar/Rest
352005
3 miles south of Callington on A388.
Parkland course; former home of
Benson and Hedges Masters.
Pro D Moon/ C Hodgson; Founded
1986
Designed by Jack Nicklaus, Old
course designed by J Hamilton Stutt
Nicklaus course: 18 holes, 6651
yards, S.S.S. 72; Old course: 18
holes, 5782 yards, S.S.S. 68
† Welcome by prior arrangement;
WE after 1.30pm only.
⌐ Nicklaus WD £25, WE £25; Old
WD £20; WE £20.
✎ Welcome subject to availability;
coffee, 18 holes of golf, 3-course club
meal packages available.
🍽 Full catering; coffee shop, grill
room.
↙ Own hotel and lodges.

Saunton and Royal North Devon

They have a dream in North Devon that one day they will host the Open Championship. It may be a distant hope – especially with the lack of an international airport in the region. But should the situation ever change, and Bristol is a possibility, then the course that started as a nine-holer in a farmer's field will be a real option.

Saunton began at Braunton Burrows and in the 1920s developed into an 18-hole links by Herbert Fowler built among the sandhills, scrubland and rushes. The area around the course is wonderful, with golden sands, wide estuaries of the Taw and the Torridge and those huge dunes which prevent a glimpse of Westward Ho!

There has long been a rivalry between the two courses. Westward Ho! or Royal North Devon as it is more grandly named, is the oldest seaside course in all England.

And of Royal North Devon, the Solheim Cup player Trish Johnson argues that there are few better courses around. It is, of course, her home club but she believes that it is this longevity that generates its appeal.

Coastal erosion is threatening the eighth hole but there has been constant work in the last few years to rescue it. "It is a unique course," she argues.

It is populated as much by the local wildlife of rabbits, sheep and horses as golfers but has "a fabulous feel". In her mind there is no doubt about the best hole – the fifth. It is a par-three 130-yard hole called The Table. It is slightly uphill with a raised green protected by the bunkers. Should the ball ever make the green there is a fantastic view of the ocean. It is something to behold.

Like Saunton, this course oozes charm and much of that is assured because of the few changes that there have been to the course over the years.

The wind plays an important part on both courses and has protected Westward Ho! rather successfully but it is Saunton that still has the Open Championship feel.

It had a chequered history after the early extension. The course closed in 1939 and during the war years and beyond lay dormant until CK Cotton re-opened it in 1950.

And although it prospered there was a time when, in the early 1960s, it appeared again to be floundering, but it was CK Cotton's forward thinking which helped the club prosper. His main contribution was the reconstruction of the first, 17th and 18th of the old course.

The first would test the most accomplished of players. Long at 470 yards, it remains a par four – there is only one par three in the first 12 holes.

There is never any respite. The 16th is widely regarded as the toughest on the course at 430 yards but still requires a staggering drive to carry a high sandhill and then head down the dog-leg.

The second shot then has to climb over the deepest of sandtraps on to a green which is perched between sandhills. Add a sloping putting surface and there is no question of the dangers involved.

The 18th is a curving hole that brings the golfer to the green in front of the clubhouse windows. A charming finish to a charming course.

The old course was joined by the new in 1974 and a new name the East and West, with its remodelled greens. There is, claimed Bernard Darwin, a reverent pilgrimage to be made to North Devon for a truly wonderful golfing experience. — **CG**

3A 64 **St Pierre Park Hotel**
Rohais, St Peter Port, Guernsey,
Channel Islands, GY1 1FD
☎(01481) 727039, Fax 712041,
Bar/Rest 728282
1 mile west of St Peter Port on
Rohais Road.
Hilly course with water hazards.
Pro Roy Corbet; Founded 1982
Designed by Tony Jacklin
9 holes, 2610 yards, S.S.S. 50
♦ Welcome.
↳ WD £12; WE £14 (9 holes).
⌁Welcome; packages available;
terms on application.
⑩ Full facilities at the hotel.
↵ St Pierre Park Hotel.

3A 65 **Saunton** ☏
Saunton, Nr Braunton, N Devon,
EX33 1LG
☎(01271) 812436
On B3231 from Braunton to Croyde,
7 miles from Barnstaple.
Traditional links course.
Pro Albert MacKenzie; Founded 1897
Designed by Herbert Fowler
East: 18 holes, 6373 yards, S.S.S.
73; West: 18 holes, 6138 yards,
S.S.S. 72
♦ Welcome with handicap certs.
↳ (All inclusive of a meal voucher)
WD £40, WE £50 (18 holes); WD
£50, WE £75 (36 holes).
⌁Welcome by arrangement; full
facilities available.
⑩ Full restaurant facilities.
↵ Saunton Sands; Kittiwell House;
Preston House; Croyde Bay House,
Woolacombe Bay.

3A 66 **Sidmouth**
Cotmaton Road, Peak Hill, Sidmouth,
Devon, EX10 8SX
☎(01395) 513451
Take Station Road to Woodlands
Hotel and then turn right into
Cotmaton Road.
Undulating parkland course.
Pro Gaele Tapper; Founded 1889
18 holes, 5068 yards, S.S.S. 65
♦ Welcome by arrangement with the
Pro.
↳ WD £20; WE £20; packages on
request.
⌁Welcome; terms on application.
⑩ Full facilities.

3A 67 **Sparkwell**
Welbeck Manor Hotel, Sparkwell,
Plymouth, Devon, PL7 5DF
☎(01752) 837219, Fax 837219

From Plymouth take A38, turn left at
Plympton and then signposted to
Sparkwell.
Parkland course.
Founded 1993
9 holes, 5772 yards, S.S.S. 68
♦ Welcome; pay as you play course.
↳ WD £6; WE £7.
⌁Welcome; full facilities available.
⑩ Full bar and restaurant facilities.
↵ Welbeck Manor.

3A 68 **Staddon Heights**
Staddon Heights, Plymstock,
Plymouth, Devon, PL9 9SP
☎(01752) 402475
Club is five miles south of the city
near the Royal Navy aerials.
Parkland cliff top course; no par fives.
Pro Ian Marshall; Founded 1904
18 holes, 5845 yards, S.S.S. 68
♦ Welcome if carrying handicap
certs.
↳ WD £18; WE £22.
⌁Welcome with prior arrangement
and handicap certs; catering
available; £25.
⑩ Bar available.

3A 69 **Tavistock**
Down Rd, Tavistock, Devon, PL19
9AQ
☎(01822) 612049, Fax 612344, Pro
612316, Sec 612344
From town centre take Whitchurch
road; turn left at Down Road.
Moorland course.
Pro Dominic Rehaag; Founded 1890
18 holes, 6250 yards, S.S.S. 70
♦ Welcome WD by prior
arrangement; must be accompanied
by member at WE.
↳ WD £22; WE £27.
⌁Welcome WD by prior
arrangement; minimum 20; terms on
application.
⑩ Full clubhouse facilities.
↵ Bedford.

3A 70 **Tehidy Park**
Tehidy, Nr Camborne, Cornwall, TR14
0HH
☎(01209) 842208, Fax 843680, Pro
842914, Bar/Rest 842557
Off A30 at Camborne exit; follow
Portreath signs to club, 2 miles NE of
Camborne.
Parkland course.
Pro James Dumbreck; Founded 1922
18 holes, 6241 yards, S.S.S. 71
♦ Welcome with handicap certs; day
ticket: WD £22.50; WE £27.50.

⌁Welcome with handicap certs;
packages available.
⑩ Full bar snacks and meals
available.

3A 71 **Teign Valley**
Christow, Nr Exeter, Devon, EX6 7PA
☎(01647) 253026, Pro 253127
From M5 to A38 Plymouth road
taking exit marked Teign Valley.
Parkland course.
Pro Richard Stephenson; Founded
1995
Designed by David Nicholson
18 holes, 5913 yards, S.S.S. 68
♦ Welcome.
↳ WD from £15; WE from £18.
⌁Welcome; packages available;
discounts for larger groups; catering
packages arranged; terms on
application.
⑩ Full bar and catering facilities.
↵ Ilsington; Passage House; club
manager can arrange local B&Bs.

3A 72 **Teignmouth**
Exeter Rd, Teignmouth, Devon, TQ14
9NY
☎(01626) 774194, Pro 772894, Sec
777070
2 miles from Teignmouth on Exeter
road B3192.
Heathland course.
Pro Peter Ward; Founded 1924
Designed by Dr Alister MacKenzie
18 holes, 6083 yards, S.S.S. 70
♦ Must be members of a club and
have handicap certs.
↳ WD from £22.50; WE from £25.50.
⌁Welcome Tues/Thurs by
arrangement; full facilities available.
⑩ Full facilities available.
↵ London; The Bay Hotel.

3A 73 **Thurlestone**
Thurlestone, Nr Kingsbridge, Devon,
TQ7 3NZ
☎(01548) 560405, Fax 560405, Pro
560715
Seaward side of A379 Kingsbridge-
Salcombe road.
Downland course; all par fives on
back nine.
Pro Peter Laugher; Founded 1897
18 holes, 6340 yards, S.S.S. 70
♦ Welcome with booking and
handicap certs.
↳ WD £28; WE £28.
⌁None.
⑩ Available.
↵ Thurlestone Hotel; Cottage Hotel,
Hope Cove.

TREVOSE GOLF & COUNTRY CLUB

Constantine Bay, Padstow, Cornwall. Tel: (01841) 520208 Fax: (01841) 521057
E-mail Info@trevose-gc.co.uk http://www.trevose-gc.co.uk.

- Championship Golf Course of 18 holes. S.S.S.71. Fully automatic watering on all greens.
- 2 x 9 hole courses. One 3100 yds, par 35, the other 1369 yds, par 29.
- Excellent appointed Clubhouse with Bar and Restaurant providing full catering facilities. A/C throughout.

- Superior Accom. in 7 Chalets, 6 Bungalows, 11 Luxury Flats & 12 Dormy Suites. Daily Rates available. Mid-week bookings encouraged. **Open all Year.**
- 3 Hard Tennis Courts.
- Heated Swimming Pool open from mid May to mid September.

- In addition to Membership for Golf and Tennis, Social Membership of the Club is also available with full use of the Clubhouse facilities.
- 6 glorious sandy bays within about a mile of the Clubhouse, with pools, open sea and surf bathing.
- 8 miles from Civil Airport.
- Daily flights to and from London Gatwick.
- Societies welcome.

3A 74 Tiverton
Post Hill, Tiverton, Devon, EX14 4NE
☎ (01884) 252187, Fax 251607, Pro
254836, Bar/Rest 252114
5 miles from Junction 27 on M5
towards Tiverton on A373; take first
exit left on dual carriageway through
Samford Peverell to Halberton.
Parkland/meadowland course.
Pro David Sheppard; Founded 1931
Designed by James Braid
18 holes, 6236 yards, S.S.S. 71
♦ Welcome with letter of introduction
or handicap certs; not Wed, WE,
Bank Holidays or competition days.
○ WD £20; WE £30.
◑ By prior arrangement.
◉ Lunch and teas available.
◄ Parkway Hotel; Tiverton; Hartnol.

3A 75 Torquay
Petitor Rd, St Marychurch, Torquay,
Devon, TQ1 4QF
☎ (01803) 314591, Pro 329113
N of Torquay on A379 Teignmouth
road, on outskirts of town.
Parkland course.
Pro Martin Ruth; Founded 1910
18 holes, 6165 yards, S.S.S. 70
♦ Welcome with handicap certs.
○ WD £20; WE £24.
◑ Welcome by prior arrangement.
◉ Full facilities.

3A 76 Torrington
Weare Trees, Torrington, Devon,
EX38 7EZ
☎ (01805) 622229
Between Bideford and Torrington.
Heathland course.
Founded 1895/1932
9 holes, 4429 yards, S.S.S. 62
♦ Welcome.
○ WD £12; WE £12.
◑ Welcome by prior application to
secretary; terms on application.
◉ Facilities available.

3A 77 Tregenna Castle Hotel ♛
St Ives, Cornwall, TR26 2DE
☎ (01736) 795254, Fax 796066, Sec
797381
In grounds of Tregenna Castle Hotel,
signposted to left just before St Ives
on A3074 from Hayle.
Parkland course.
Founded 1982
18 holes, 3478 yards, S.S.S. 58
♦ Welcome.
○ WD £13.50; WE £13.50.
◑ Welcome by arrangement; full
facilities available; terms on
application.
◉ Full bar and restaurant.
◄ Tregenna Castle.

3A 78 Treloy
Newquay, Cornwall, TR7 4JN
☎ (01637) 878554, Fax 871710
On A3059 St Columb Major-Newquay
road 3 miles from Newquay.
Public heathland/parkland course.
Founded 1991
Designed by M.R.M. Sandow
9 holes, 4286 yards, S.S.S. 62
♦ Welcome.
○ WD £12.50; WE £12.50.
◑ Welcome.
◉ Bar, full facilities.
◄ Barrowfield; California Hotel,
Newquay.

3A 79 Trethorne ♛
Kennards House, Launceston,
Cornwall, PL15 8QE
☎ (01566) 86903, Fax 86981
2 miles west of Launceston, 200
yards off the A30 on the A395.
Parkland course.
Founded 1993
Designed by F Frayne
18 holes, 6432 yards, S.S.S. 71
♦ Welcome.
○ WD £22; WE £22.

◑ Welcome £15 for 18 holes.
◉ Available.
Practice range, floodlit driving range
and 11 bays.
◄ Guest house on site.

3A 80 Trevose Country Club
Constantine Bay, Padstow, Cornwall,
PL28 8JB
☎ (01841) 520208, Fax 521057, Pro
520261.
▭ www.trevose-gc.co.uk
◄ info@trevose-gc.co.uk
Course is four miles W of Padstow off
the B3276.
Seaside links course.
Pro Gary Alliss; Founded 1925
Designed by H.S. Colt
18 holes, 6435 yards, S.S.S. 71
♦ Welcome; 3 and 4 ball matches
restricted; phone first.
○ WD £36; WE £36 (summer).
◑ Welcome anytime except July-
Sept; full facilities available.
◉ Full facilities.
◄ Own self-contained
accommodation available; phone for
details.

3A 81 Truro ♛
Treliske, Truro, Cornwall, TR1 3LG
☎ (01872) 272640, Fax 278684, Pro
276595, Sec 278684
On edge of Truro adjacent to Treliske
Hospital on the A390 Truro to
Redruth road.
Undulating parkland overlooking
Truro; no par fives.
Pro Nigel Bicknell; Founded 1937
Designed by Colt, Alison & Morrison
18 holes, 5347 yards, S.S.S. 66
♦ Welcome if carrying handicap
certs.
○ WD £20; WE £25.
◑ Welcome; inclusive price on
application.
◉ Two bars and a restaurant.

3A 82 **Warren**
Dawlish Warren, Dawlish, Devon, EX7 0NF
☎ (01626) 862255, Fax 888005, Pro 864002, Sec 862255, Bar/Rest 862493
12 miles south of Exeter off the A379.
Links course.
Pro Darren Price; Founded 1892
Designed by J Braid & Sir Guy Campbell
18 holes, 5965 yards, S.S.S. 69
† Welcome.
⌾ WD £21.50; WE £24.50.
⌁ Welcome; terms on application.
⍟ Bar and meals available.
⌁ Langstone Cliff; Sea Lawn Lodge.

3A 83 **Waterbridge**
Down St Mary, Nr Crediton, Devon, EX17 5LG
☎ (01363) 85111
Off A377 Barnstaple road 1 mile after Copplestone.
Parkland course.
Founded 1992
Designed by David Taylor
9 holes, 3910 yards
† Welcome.
⌾ WD £6; WE £7 (9 holes).
⌁ Welcome by arrangement; packages available; terms on application.
⌁ New Inn, Crediton.

3A 84 **West Cornwall**
Lelant, St Ives, Cornwall, TR26 3DZ
☎ (01736) 753401, Pro 753177, Bar/Rest 753319
Take A30 to Lelant, turn right at Badger Inn.
Links course.
Pro Paul Atherton; Founded 1889
Designed by Rev Tyack
18 holes, 5884 yards, S.S.S. 69
† Welcome with handicap certificates.
⌾ WD £25.50; WE £30.50.
⌁ Welcome; catering to be negotiated; snooker.
⍟ Restaurant, snack bar and bar.
⌁ Badger Inn, Lelant; Pedn Olna, St Ives.

3A 85 **Whitsand Bay Hotel** ♛ **Golf and Country Club**
Portwrinkle, Torpoint, Cornwall, PL11 3BU
☎ (01503) 230276, Fax 230329, Pro 230788
💻 www.cornish-golf.hotels.co.uk
✉ carlehotels@btconnect.com

On B3247 6 miles off A38 from Plymouth.
Clifftop course.
Pro S Poole; Founded 1905
Designed by William Fernie of Troon
18 holes, 5885 yards, S.S.S. 69
† Handicap certs required except for residents.
⌾ WD £20; WE £22.50.
⌁ Welcome; bar and leisure facilities; terms on application.
⌁ Whitsand Bay.

3A 86 **Woodbury Park** ♛ **Golf & Country Club**
Woodbury Castle, Woodbury, Exeter, Devon, EX5 1JJ
☎ (01395) 233382, Fax 233384
From M5 Junction 30, take A3052 Sidmouth road, turn right on to B3180, after approx 1 mile turn right to Woodbury, then immediately turn right to course.
Parkland/moorland/heathland course.
Founded 1992
Designed by J. Hamilton Stutt
18 holes, 6626 yards, S.S.S. 72
† Welcome with handicap certs.
⌾ WD £35; WE £45.
⌁ Welcome by prior arrangement; catering packages by arrangement; 9-hole Acorn course: 4582 yards, par 65; terms on application.
⍟ Full facilities.
Practice range, available.
⌁ Swiss style lodges on site with leisure complex.

3A 87 **Wrangaton**
Golf Links Road, Wrangaton, South Brent, TQ10 9HJ
☎ (01364) 73229, Pro 72161
Turn off A38 between South Brent and Bittaford at Wrangaton Post Office.
Moorland/parkland course.
Pro Adrian Whitehead; Founded 1895
Designed by Donald Steel
18 holes, 6083 yards, S.S.S. 69
† Welcome with handicap certs or member of recognised club; no beginners.
⌾ WD £18; WE £24.
⌁ Welcome by arrangement.
⍟ Bar and catering (except Mon in winter).
⌁ The Coach House Inn; Glazebrook.

3A 88 **Yelverton**
Golf Links Rd, Yelverton, Devon, PL20 6BN

☎ (01822) 852824, Fax 852824, Pro 853593, Bar/Rest 855658
Off A386 8 miles north of Plymouth.
Moorland course.
Pro Tim McSherry; Founded 1904
Designed by Herbert Fowler
18 holes, 6351 yards, S.S.S. 72
† Welcome with handicap certs.
⌾ WD £30; WE £40.
⌁ Welcome with handicap certs; full bar and restaurant facilities
⍟ Restaurant and bar.
⌁ Moorland Links course; Burrator Inn; Rosemount Guest House.

3B 1 **The Ashley Wood Golf Club**
Wimborne Rd, Blandford, Dorset, DT11 0HN
☎ (01258) 452253, Fax 450590, Pro 450379
Half a mile from Blandford.
Parkland course; two par 5s in first three holes.
Pro Spencer Taylor; Founded 1896
Designed by Patrick Tallack
18 holes, 6276 yards, S.S.S. 70
† Welcome WD.
⌾ WD £20.
⌁ Welcome WD; by prior application to Sec.
⌁ Anvil (Pimperne).

3B 2 **Bath Golf Club**
Sham Castle, North Rd, Bath, Somerset, BA2 6JG
☎ (01225) 425182, Fax 331027, Pro 466953, Sec 463834
1.5 miles SE of Bath off A36 Warminster road.
Downland course.
Pro Peter Hancox; Founded 1880
Designed by H S Colt
18 holes, 6438 yards, S.S.S. 71
† Welcome; handicap certs required.
⌾ WD £25; WE £30.
⌁ Welcome Wed and Fri only; coffee, 18 holes, soup & sandwiches, £25; 18 holes, 3-course dinner, £40.
⌁ Bath; Beaufort, Dukes; Spa.

3B 3 **Blue Circle**
Trowbridge Rd, Westbury, Wilts
☎ (01373) 828489
Part of Blue Circle Works Sports Complex.
Parkland course.
9 holes, 5600 yards, S.S.S. 66
† With member only or on county card system.
⌾ Terms on application.

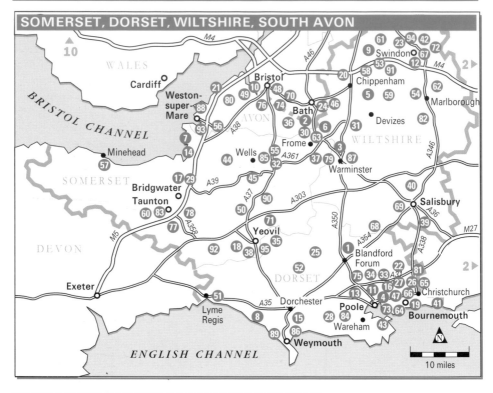

SOMERSET, DORSET, WILTSHIRE, SOUTH AVON

KEY		32	Farrington	65	Parley Golf Centre
1	The Ashley Wood Golf Club	33	Ferndown	66	Queen's Park
2	Bath Golf Club	34	Ferndown Forest		(Bournemouth)
3	Blue Circle	35	Folke	67	RMCS Shrivenham
4	Bournemouth & Meyrick	36	Fosseway Country Club	68	Rushmore Park
	Park	37	Frome	69	Salisbury & South Wiltshire
5	Bowood Golf & Country	38	Halstock	70	Saltford
	Club	39	Hamptworth Golf & Country	71	Sherborne
6	Bradford-on-Avon		Club	72	Shrivenham Park
7	Brean	40	High Post	73	Solent Meads Par 3
8	Bridport & West Dorset	41	Highcliffe Castle	74	Stockwood Vale
9	Brinkworth	42	Highworth Golf Centre	75	Sturminster Marshall
10	Bristol & Clifton	43	Isle of Purbeck	76	Tall Pines
11	Broadstone	44	Isle of Wedmore	77	Taunton & Pickeridge
12	Broome Manor	45	King Weston	78	Taunton Vale
13	Bulbury	46	Kingsdown	79	Thoulstone Park
14	Burnham & Berrow	47	Knighton Heath	80	Tickenham
15	Came Down	48	Knowle	81	Two Riversmeet
16	Canford Magna	49	Long Ashton	82	Upavon (RAF)
17	Cannington	50	Long Sutton	83	Vivary
18	Chedington Court	51	Lyme Regis	84	Wareham
19	Chichester	52	Lyons Gate	85	Wells (Somerset)
20	Chippenham	53	Manor House Golf Club	86	Wessex Golf Centre
21	Clevedon		(at Castle Combe)	87	West Wilts
22	Crane Valley	54	Marlborough	88	Weston-super-Mare
23	Cricklade Hotel & Country	55	Mendip	89	Weymouth
	Club	56	Mendip Spring	90	Wheathill
24	Cumberwell Park	57	Minehead & West Somerset	91	The Wiltshire Golf Club
25	Dorset Heights	58	Monkton Park Par 3	92	Windwhistle
26	Dudmoor Farm	59	North Wilts	93	Worlebury
27	Dudsbury	60	Oake Manor	94	Wrag Barn Golf & Country
28	East Dorset	61	Oaksey Park		Club
29	Enmore Park	62	Ogbourne Downs	95	Yeovil
30	Entry Hill	63	Orchardleigh		
31	Erlestoke Sands	64	Parkstone		

🖊 Welcome by prior arrangement; terms on application.
🍴 By prior arrangement.

3B 4 Bournemouth & Meyrick Park
Central Drive, Meyrick Park, Bournemouth, BH2 6LH
☎ (01202) 292425, Fax 290233
In centre of Bournemouth. Picturesque parkland course (Meyrick Park).
Founded 1890
18 holes, 5461 yards, S.S.S. 69
🚶 Welcome any time; advisable to book up to 7 days in advance.
📏 WD £13.40; WE £14.60.
🖊 Welcome by prior arrangement; packages available; full facilities.
🍴 Bars and restaurant.

3B 5 Bowood Golf & Country Club   🍵
Derby Hill, Calne, Wilts, SN11 9PQ
☎ (01249) 822228, Fax 822218
Off the A4 between Chippenham and Calne.

Parkland course.
Pro Nigel Blenkarne; Founded 1992
Designed by Dave Thomas
18 holes, 7317 yards SSS 72
♠ Welcome on WD and after 12
noon WE.
 WD £34; WE £34.
🌙Welcome by prior arrangement;
special rates on Mon (£20 for 18
holes); coffee & bacon roll, 9 holes,
Ploughman's lunch, 18 holes, 3-
course dinner; £51.
🍴 Full facilities.
Practice range, 10 bays; floodlit
range.
🛏 Queenwood Golf Lodge, Dowood
Golf & CC; Lucknam Park Hotel,
Colerne.

3B 6 Bradford-on-Avon

Avon Close, Trowbridge Rd,
Bradford-on-Avon
☎(01225) 868268
From Bradford towards Trowbridge
on left near Police station.
Picturesque parkland course next to
River Avon.
Founded 1991
9 holes, 2109 yards, S.S.S. 61
♠ Welcome anytime; pay and play
course.
 £6 for 9 holes; £10 for 18 holes.
🌙Welcome by prior arrangement.
🍴 None.

3B 7 Brean ♌

Coast Rd, Brean, Burnham-on-Sea,
Somerset, TA8 2QY
☎(01278) 751595, Fax 751595, Pro
752111, Sec 751570
Follow tourist signs for Brean Lesiure
Park from Junction 22 of M5.
Meadowland course.
Pro David Hanes; Founded 1973
Designed by Brean Leisure Park
18 holes, 5715 yards, S.S.S. 68
♠ Welcome at all times except
competition days.
 WD £15; WE £18.
🌙Welcome WD and after 1pm at
WE; packages available; from £14-
£16.
🍴 Facilities available.
🛏 Accommodation available on the
Brean Leisure Park.

3B 8 Bridport & West Dorset ♌

East Cliff, West Bay, Bridport, Dorset,
DT6 4EP
☎(01308) 421095, Fax 421095, Pro
421491, Bar/Rest 422597

1.5 miles south of Bridport at West
Bay.
Clifftop links course.
Pro David Parsons; Founded 1891
Designed by G.S.P. Salmon / 1996
modified by F Hawtree
18 holes, 6028 yards, S.S.S. 69
♠ Welcome; dress codes apply.
 WD £22; WE £22.
🌙Welcome; bookings must be made
in advance; packages can be
arranged to meet individual
requirements; terms on application.
🍴 Full facilities.
🛏 Haddon House, West Bay.

3B 9 Brinkworth

Longmans Farm, Brinkworth,
Chippenham, Wilts, SN15 5DG
☎(01666) 510277
Between Swindon and Malmesbury
on B4042.
Meadowland course.
Founded 1984
18 holes, 6000 yards, S.S.S. 70
♠ Welcome anytime.
 WD £8; WE £10.
🌙Welcome by arrangement.
🍴 Full facilities.

3B 10 Bristol & Clifton

Beggar Bush Lane, Failand, Nr
Clifton, Bristol, BS8 3TH
☎(01275) 393474, Fax 394611, Pro
393031
Junction 19 off M5, 4 miles along
A369 to Bristol turn right at traffic
lights, then further 1.5 miles.
Parkland course.
Founded 1891
18 holes, 6316 yards, S.S.S. 70
♠ Welcome WD with handicap certs;
restrictions at WE.
 WD £32; WE £35.
🌙Welcome by arrangement on
Thurs only; full facilities available.
🍴 Full facilities.
🛏 Redwood Lodge.

3B 11 Broadstone

Wentworth Drive, Broadstone, BH 18
8DQ
☎(01202) 692595, Fax 692595, Pro
692835, Bar/Rest 693363
Take the A349 from Poole to the
village; the club is signposted off the
main roundabout.
Heathland course.
Pro Nigel Tokley; Founded 1898
Designed by George Dunn (1898) &
H.S. Colt (1925)
18 holes, 6315 yards, S.S.S. 70

♠ Members may introduce one guest
per round.
 WD £25; WE £40.
🌙Welcome but there are restricted
times available so it is essential to
phone in advance.
🍴 Full bar and restaurant facilities.

3B 12 Broome Manor

Piper's Way, Swindon, Wilts, SN3
1RG
☎(01793) 495761, Fax 433255, Pro
532403, Bar/Rest 490939
Take Junction 15 off M4 and follow
signs; course 2 miles off motorway.
Parkland course.
Pro Barry Sandry; Founded 1976
Designed by Hawtree & Son
18 holes, 6283 yards, S.S.S. 70; 9
holes, 2690 yards, S.S.S. 33
♠ Pay and play course.
 9 holes £7.20; 18 holes £12.
🌙Welcome Mon-Fri; 27 holes,
driving range and most packages
include first tee video analysis; £15-
£40.
🍴 Full facilities.
Practice range, 34 bays.

3B 13 Bulbury ♌

Halls Rd, Lytchett Matravers, Nr
Poole, Dorset, BH16 6EP
☎(01929) 459574/459100, Fax
459000
On main A35 3 miles from Poole.
Parkland course set in ancient
woodlands.
Pro Vance Waters; Founded 1989
Designed by J. Sharkey
18 holes, 6313 yards, S.S.S. 70
♠ Welcome.
 WD £20; WE £22.
🌙Welcome; full catering packages
available on application; terms on
application.
🍴 Full à la carte and bistro menu.
🛏 On-site accommodation.

3B 14 Burnham & Berrow

St Christopher's Way, Burnham-on-
Sea, Somerset, TA8 2PE
☎(01278) 783137, Fax 795440, Pro
784545, Sec 785760
M5 Junction 32; 1 mile N of Burnham.
Seaside links; also has a 9-hole
course.
Pro Mark Crowther-Smith; Founded
1890
18 holes, 6393 yards, S.S.S. 71
♠ Must be members of golf clubs
with handicaps of 22 and under.
 WD £38; WE £50.

Terms on application.
Full facilities.
Batch Farm, Lympsham; Lulworth GH; Warren GH, both Burnham-on-Sea.

3B 15 **Came Down**
Came Down, Dorchester, Dorset, DT2 8NR
☎ (01305) 812531, Fax 813494, Pro 812670
2 miles S of Dorchester off A354. Undulating downland course.
Pro David Holmes; Founded 1896
Designed by J.H. Taylor
18 holes, 6244 yards, S.S.S. 71
† Welcome by arrangement with handicap certs; midweek after 9am; Sun after 11am.
Terms on application.
Welcome by arrangement on Wed; packages available, approx £32; full facilities.
Bar and restaurant.
Rembrandt (Weymouth); Junction Hotel (Dorchester).

3B 16 **Canford Magna**
Knighton Lane, Wimborne, Dorset BH21 3AS
☎ (01202) 592552, Fax 592550, Sec 503902
Off the A341 Magna road, near the Bearcross roundabout on the main A348 Ringwood road.
Parkland course.
Designed by Howard Swan & Trevor Smith
Pro Martin Thompson; Founded 1994
(3 courses) Parkland: 18 holes, 6495 yards, Combination par 3, 415 yards. Riverside: 18 holes, 6231 yards, S.S.S. 70. Knighton: 9 holes, 2754 yards.
† Welcome.
Parkland WD 18, WE £21; Riverside WD £13, WE £16; Knighton: WD £18, WE £21 (18 holes).
Welcome by prior arrangement; Cygnet Suite available for corporate hire.
Two bars and a restaurant.
6-hole Academy course and driving range.
Contact local tourist board.

3B 17 **Cannington**
Cannington College, nr Bridgwater, Somerset, TA5 2LS
☎ (01278) 655050
Leave the M5 at Junction 23. Take the A38 to Bridgwater; course is 4 miles from Bridgwater on the A39 road to Minehead.
Links/parkland course.
Pro Ron Macrow; Founded 1993
Designed by Martin Hawtree
9 holes, 5858 yards, S.S.S. 68
† Welcome.
Terms on application.
Apply to Pro; 25% off for groups of 12+; terms on application.
Bar and restaurant.
New driving range, 10 floodlit bays, two piece balls

3B 18 **Chedington Court**
South Perrott, Beaminster, Dorset, DT8 3HU
☎ (01935) 891413
0.5 mile E of South Perrott on A356 Crewkerne-Dorchester road.
Parkland course.
Pro Stephen Richie; Founded 1991
Designed by D. Hemstock, P. & H. Chapman
18 holes, 5924 yards, S.S.S. 70
† Welcome; properly dressed.
WD £16; WE £20.
Welcome by arrangement; terms on application.
Refreshments available.
Practice range, basic pitch and putt course; driving and practice area.
Chedington Court.

3B 19 **Chichester**
Iford Bridge Sports Centre, Barrack Rd, Christchurch, Dorset, BH23 2BA
☎ (01202) 473817
Off the A35 between Bournemouth and Christchurch.
Parkland course.
Pro Laurence Moxon; Founded 1977
9 holes, 4360 yards, S.S.S. 61
† Welcome.
WD £6.40; WE £7.25.
Welcome by prior arrangement; also tennis, bowling.
Full bar facilities.
Practice range.
Contact local tourist board.

3B 20 **Chippenham**
Malmesbury Rd, Chippenham, Wilts, SN15 5LT
☎ (01249) 652040, Fax 446681, Pro 655519, Bar/Rest 443481
From M4 Junction 17 take A350 towards Chippenham; course on right before town.
Parkland course.
Pro Bill Creamer; Founded 1896
18 holes, 5600 yards, S.S.S. 67
† Welcome.
WD £20; WE £25.
Welcome Tues, Thurs, Fri by prior arrangement; full day golf and catering packages available.
Clubhouse facilities.

3B 21 **Clevedon**
Castle Rd, Clevedon, North Somerset, BS21 7AA
☎ (01275) 874057, Fax 341228, Pro 874704, Bar/Rest 873140
Leave the M5 at Junction 20 and follow the signs to Portishead; turn right into Walton Road, then Holly Lane.
Hilltop course overlooking Bristol Channel.
Pro Robert Scanlan; Founded 1908
Designed by J H Taylor
18 holes, 6117 yards, S.S.S. 69
† Welcome with handicap certs.
WD £25; WE £40.
Welcome except Fri, must book in advance and minimum of 12; terms on application.
Facilities and bar.
Walton Park; Highcliffe House.

3B 22 **Crane Valley**
West Farm, Romford, Verwood, Dorset, BH31 7LE
☎ (01202) 814088, Fax 813407
On B3081 0.5 miles after Verwood.
Parkland course.
Pro Paul Cannings; Founded 1992
Designed by Donald Steel
Valley Course: 18 holes, 6424 yards, S.S.S. 71
Woodland Course: 9 holes, 2060 yards, S.S.S 33
† Welcome with handicap certs.
Terms on application.
Welcome WD; packages available.
Clubhouse facilities.
Practice range, 12 bays; floodlit.
West Farm SC; St Leonards Hotel.

3B 23 **Cricklade Hotel & Country Club**
Common Hill, Cricklade, Wilts, SN6 6HA
☎ (01793) 750751, Fax 751767
B4040 Cricklade-Malmesbury road, 15 mins from M4 Junctions 15/16.
Parkland course.
Pro Ian Bolt; Founded 1990
Designed by Ian Bolt/C Smith
9 holes, 3660 yards, S.S.S. 57

⚑ Welcome Mon-Fri; WE must be accompanied by a member.
🏌 WD £10; WE £10.
↻ Welcome; terms available on application.
🍽 Full bar and restaurant facilities.
⌂ Cricklade.

3B 24 Cumberwell Park

Bradford on Avon, Wiltshire, BA15 2PQ
☎ (01225) 863322, Fax 868160
🖥 www.cumberwellpark.co.uk
M4 Junction 18; take A46 to Bath and then A363 to Bradford-on-Avon.
Parkland course.
Pro John Jacobs; Founded 1994
Designed by Adrian Stiff
27 holes, 315 acres, S.S.S. 73
⚑ Welcome.
🏌 WD £20; WE £25.
↻ Welcome Mon-Fri; 27 holes of golf plus 3-course private dinner and coffee on arrival; prices on application.
🍽 Bar and restaurant.
⌂ Bath Spa Hotel; Homewood Park; Swan Hotel, Bradford-on-Avon.

3B 25 Dorset Heights

Belchalwell, Blandford Forum, Dorset, DT11 0EG
☎ (01258) 861386
On A357 Sturminster Newton-Blandford road.
Woodland course.
Founded 1991
Designed by Project Golf (D.W. Asthill)
18 holes, 6138 yards, S.S.S. 70
⚑ Welcome with prior arrangement.
🏌 Terms on application.
↻ Welcome by prior arrangement; packages available; restaurant; terms on application.
🍽 Restaurant, bar.
⌂ Crown Hotel, Blandford.

3B 26 Dudmoor Farm

Dudmoor Farm Rd, Christchurch, Dorset, BH23 6AQ
☎ (01202) 483980
Off A35 W of Christchurch.
Woodland course.
Founded 1974
9 holes, 1428 yards
⚑ Welcome anytime.
🏌 Terms on application.
↻ Welcome by arrangement.
🍽 Snacks and soft drinks.
⌂ Avon Causeway; B&B available on site.

3B 27 Dudsbury ☎

64 Christchurch Rd, Ferndown, Dorset, BH22 8ST
☎ (01202) 593499, Fax 594555, Pro 594488
On B3073 off A348 from Ferndown.
Parkland course.
Pro Mark Thomas; Founded 1992
Designed by Donald Steel
18 holes, 6765 yards, S.S.S. 72
⚑ Welcome with prior booking.
🏌 WD £30; WE £35.
↻ Welcome; packages available from secretary; restaurant, lounge bar, 6-hole par 3 course; terms on application.
🍽 Spikes and lounge bar, function room and restaurant.
⌂ Dormy Hotel, Bridge House.

3B 28 East Dorset ☎

Bere Regis, Wareham, Dorset, BH20 7NT
☎ (01929) 472244, Fax 471294, Pro 471294
A35 or A31 50 Bere Regis, take Wool road and signs to the club.
Parkland course.
Pro Derwyn Honan; Founded 1978
Designed by Martin Hawtree
18 holes, 6580 yards, S.S.S. 73
⚑ Welcome with prior reservation.
🏌 Lakeland: WD £29, WE £34; Woodland: WD £20, WE £22.
↻ Welcome any day with reservation; combination of courses and catering on application; from £30.
🍽 Full facilities.
Practice range; floodlit and covered.
⌂ Own accommodation, the Dorsetshire Golf Lodge, includes free golf.

3B 29 Enmore Park

Enmore, Bridgewater, Somerset, TA5 2AN
☎ (01278) 671481, Fax 671481, Pro 671519, Bar/Rest 671244
M5 to Junction 23 or 24; follow A39/A9 to Bridgwater, A39 to Minehead, then left to Spaxton/Durleigh, left at reservoir and course is 2 miles on right.
Parkland course.
Pro Nigel Wixon; Founded 1906
Designed by Hawtree and Son
18 holes, 6406 yards, S.S.S. 71
⚑ Welcome but handicap certs required at WE.
🏌 WD £18; WE £25.
↻ Mon, Thurs or Fri with advance booking; 27-hole packages available; from £22.

🍽 Full facilities.
Practice range.

3B 30 Entry Hill

Entry Hill, Bath, Somerset, BA2 5NA
☎ (01225) 834248
Take A367 Wells road from city centre, fork left into Entry Hill Road after 1 mile; course is 0.5 mile on right.
Compact, hilly parkland course.
Pro Tim Tapley; Founded 1984
9 holes, 2103 yards, S.S.S. 61
⚑ Welcome; book up to 7 days in advance for WE, Bank Holidays and peak periods.
🏌 WD before 4pm and WE before 2pm: 9 holes £5, 18 holes £8; WD after 4pm and WE after 2pm: 9 holes £0, 18 holes £9.50; concessions for juniors.
↻ Welcome.
⌂ Sienna; Hautecombe.

3B 31 Erlestoke Sands

Erlestoke, Devizes, Wiltshire, SN10 5UB
☎ (01380) 831069, Fax 831069, Pro 831027, Bar/Rest 830507
On B3098 off A350 at Westbury signposted Bratton, course 6 miles on left before village of Erlestoke (3 miles) on right after Erlestoke village.
Parkland course.
Pro Adrian Marsh; Founded 1992
Designed by Adrian Stiff
18 holes, 6406 yards, S.S.S. 71
⚑ Welcome.
🏌 WD £18; WE £25.
↻ Preferably WD by prior arrangement; full facilities.
🍽 Full facilities.

3B 32 Farrington ☎

Marsh Lane, Farrington Gurney, Bristol, BS18 5TS
☎ (01761) 241274, Fax 4510021, Pro 241787, Sec 241274
Course is 12 miles south of Bristol on the A37.
Parkland course with lakes.
Pro Peter Thompson; Founded 1993
Designed by Peter Thompson
18 holes, 6693 yards, S.S.S. 72
⚑ Welcome; advisable to phone in advance for weekends.
🏌 WD £20; WE £25.
↻ Welcome WD only; 2 courses, driving range, spikes bar, restaurant and private suite seating 150; BBQ area; terms on application.
🍽 Bar and restaurant.

Practice range, 16 bays covered; floodlit.

Hunstrete House, Hunstrete; Hamham House, Paulton; Stow Easton Park, Stow Easton.

3B 33 Ferndown

119 Golf Links Rd, Ferndown, Dorset, BH22 8BU
☎(01202) 874602, Fax 873926, Pro 873825
A31 to Trickett's Cross and A348 to Ferndown.
Heathland course.
Pro Ian Parker; Founded 1913
Designed by Harold Hilton (Old course)
Championship course: 18 holes, 6452 yards, S.S.S. 71
President Course: 9 holes, 2797 yards, S.S.S. 68
♦ With prior permission, handicap certs required; limited WE.
[WD £42; WE £50.
Tues and Fri only; full facilities; 9-hole course: 5604 yards.
Full facilities all week.
Coach House Motel; Dormy; Bridge House.

3B 34 Ferndown Forest

Forest Links Road, Ferndown, Dorset, BH22 9QE
☎(01202) 876096, Fax 894095, Sec 894096, Rest 896107
Midway between Ringwood and Wimborne directly off the Ferndown by-pass A31.
Parkland course
Pro Kevin Spurgeon; Founded 1993
Designed by G Hunt & R Grafham
18 holes, 4450 yards, S.S.S. 63
♦ Welcome.
[WD £10; WE £12.
Welcome; catering facilities; £8-£10.
Full bar and restaurant facilities. Practice range, floodlit bays with targets.
Dormy House on course; Coach House Motel, Ferndown.

3B 35 Folke

Folke Golf Centre, Alweston, Sherborne, Dorset, DT9 5HR
☎(01963) 23330
From Sherborne head towards Sturminster Newton, 2 miles from Sherborne turn off towards Alweston; course is 200 yards away.
Parkland course.
Founded 1993

9 holes, 2847 yards, S.S.S. 66
♦ Welcome.
[WD £9; WE £11.
Welcome by prior arrangement; terms on application.
Sandwiches, snacks, bar.
Practice range, 10 covered bays; floodlit.

3B 36 Fosseway Country Club ☎

Charlton Lane, Midsomer Norton, Bath, Somerset, BA3 4BD
☎(01761) 412214, Fax 418357
10 miles south of Bath on the A367.
Parkland course.
Founded 1971
Designed by C K Cotton/F Pennink
9 holes, 4278 yards, S.S.S. 65
♦ By prior arrangement.
[WD £10; WE £12.
Terms on application.
Facilities.
Centurion Hotel (on site).

3B 37 Frome

Critchill Manor, Frome, Somerset, BA 11 4LJ
☎(01373) 453410, Fax 453410
Take A361 from Frome towards Shepton Mallett; at Nunney Catch roundabout follow signs to course.
Parkland course.
Founded 1994
18 holes, 4890 yards, S.S.S. 64
♦ Welcome.
[WD £10.50; WE £12.50.
Welcome; contact club for details.
Available.

3B 38 Halstock

Halstock Golf Enterprises, Common Lane, Nr Yeovil, Somerset, BA22 9SF
☎(01935) 891689, Fax 891839
300 yards from centre of Halstock village, turn right at green, from Quiet Woman pub, 50 yards on left past village shop/P.O. signposted.
Parkland course.
Founded 1988
18 holes, 4351 yards, S.S.S. 63
♦ Welcome.
[WD £10; WE £12.
Welcome by arrangement; terms on application.
Light refreshments available.

3B 39 Hamptworth Golf & Country Club ☎

Hamptworth Rd, Hamptworth, Wilts, SP5 2DU

☎(01794) 390155, Fax 390022
6 miles from M27 Junctions 1 and 2, off A36 to Salisbury, follow Landford and then Downton road signs.
Parkland course among ancient woodlands, lakes and river.
Founded 1994
18 holes, 6512 yards, S.S.S. 71
♦ Welcome by arrangement; handicap certs required.
[WD £25; WE £25.
Welcome by arrangement, handicap certs required for entire group; full facilities.
Full facilities.
Devore Grand Harbour.

3B 40 High Post

Great Durnford, Salisbury, Wilts, SP4 6AT
☎01722) 782356, Fax 782356, Pro 782219
Halfway between Salisbury and Amesbury on the A345, opposite the Inn at High Post.
Downland course.
Pro Ian Welding; Founded 1922
18 holes, 6305 yards, S.S.S. 70
♦ Welcome WD without restriction; handicap certs required at WE.
[WD £25; WE £30.
Welcome WD by arrangement; full facilities available.
Full facilities.
The Inn; High Post; Milford Hall (Salisbury).

3B 41 Highcliffe Castle

107 Lymington Rd, Highcliffe on Sea, Dorset, BH23 4LA
☎(01425) 272953, Sec 272210
1 mile W of Highcliffe on A337.
Parkland course.
Founded 1913
18 holes, 4776 yards, S.S.S. 63
♦ Welcome if member of recognised golf club.
[WD £15.50; WE £20.50.
By prior arrangement with the secretary; terms on application.
Clubhouse facilities.

3B 42 Highworth Golf Centre

Highworth Community Golf Centre, Swindon Road, Highworth, Wilts, SN6 7SJ
☎(01793) 766014
Take A361 from Swindon.
Parkland course.
Pro Mark Toombs; Founded 1990
Designed by Swindon Council
9 holes, 3120 yards

☏ Pay as you play.
⏰ WD £7.20; WE £7.20
🗓 Pay as you play.

3B 43 Isle Of Purbeck
Studland, Swanage, Dorset, BH19 3AB
☎ (01929) 450361, Fax 450501, Pro 450354
3 miles north of Swanage on the B3351 Corfe Castle road.
Heathland, set in a nature reserve.
Pro Ian Brake; Founded 1892
Designed by H.S. Colt
18 holes, 6295 yards, S.S.S. 71
☏ Welcome.
⏰ WD £30; WE £35.
🗓 Welcome; morning coffee, Ploughman's lunch, 2 rounds of golf, two course dinner; £47.50-£50
🍽 Bar, snooks and restaurant.

3B 44 Isle of Wedmore ℭ
Lineage, Lascots Hill, Wedmore, Somerset, BS28 4QT
☎ (01934) 713649, Fax 713696, Pro 712452
Junction 22 off M5; take A38 north to Bristol, after 5 miles turn right in Lower Weare; follow signposts to Wedmore.
Parkland course.
Founded 1992
Designed by Terry Murray
18 holes, 6009 yards, S.S.S. 68
☏ Welcome but after 9.30am at WE.
⏰ WD £18; WE £22.
🗓 Welcome; packages available; private function room and professional lessons; £24-£32.
🍽 Bar and restaurant

3B 45 King Weston
Millfield Enterprises Sports & Recreation, Nr Glastonbury, BA16 0YD
☎ (01458) 448300
1 mile SE of Butleigh.
Parkland course.
Founded 1970
9 holes, 4434 yards, S.S.S. 62
☏ Welcome with member when not required by school.
⏰ Terms on application
🗓 Limited.

3B 46 Kingsdown
Kingsdown, Corsham, Wilts, SN13 8BS
☎ (01225) 742530, Fax 743472, Pro 742634, Sec 743472

5 miles E of Bath on A365.
Downland course.
Pro Andrew Butler; Founded 1880
18 holes, 6445 yards, S.S.S. 71
☏ Welcome Mon-Fri; handicap certs required.
⏰ WD £23.
🗓 Welcome Mon-Fri; full bar and catering facilities; £23.
🍽 Bar and catering facilities.

3B 47 Knighton Heath
Francis Ave, Bournemouth, Dorset, B11 8NX
☎ (01202) 572633, Fax 590774, Pro 578275
Course is signposted from the junction of the A348/A3049 (at Mountbatten Arms).
Heathland course
Pro Jane Miles; Founded 1976
18 holes, 6084 yards, S.S.S. 69
☏ Welcome after 9.30 WD; members guests at WE.
⏰ WD £25; WE £25.
🗓 Welcome by arrangement; minimum 12 players; packages available; from £35.
🍽 Full catering facilities.

3B 48 Knowle ℭ
Fairway, West Town Lane, Brislington, Bristol, BS4 5DF
☎ (0117) 9776341, Fax 9720615, Pro 9779193, Sec 9770660
3 miles S of City Centre on A4 to Bath or A37 to Shepton Mallett.
Parkland course.
Pro Gordon Brand; Founded 1905
Designed by Hawtree & J.H. Taylor
18 holes, 6016 yards, S.S.S. 69
☏ Welcome with handicap certs.
⏰ WD £22; WE £27.
🗓 Welcome on Thurs; coffee, lunch, evening meal available.
🍽 Full facilities.

3B 49 Long Ashton
Clarken Combe, Long Ashton, Bristol, BS18 9DW
☎ (01275) 392316, Fax 394395, Pro 392265
Leave M5 at Junction 19, take A369 to Bristol, turn right into B3129 at traffic lights and then left on to B3128;
club is 0.5 mile on right
Undulating moorland/downland course.
Pro Denis Scanlan; Founded 1893
Designed by Hawtree & Taylor
18 holes, 6177 yards, S.S.S. 70

☏ Welcome with official club handicap certs.
⏰ WD £30; WE £35.
🗓 Welcome by arrangement; full facilities available.
🍽 Full facilities daily until 6pm; evening meals by arrangement.
🛏 Redwood Lodge.

3B 50 Long Sutton
Long Load, Nr Langport, Somerset, TA10 9JU
☎ (01458) 241017, Fax 241022
Course after Long Sutton village.
Parkland course.
Pro Michael Blackwell; Founded 1990
Designed by Patrick Dawson
18 holes, 6368 yards, S.S.S. 70
☏ Welcome with advance tee reservation.
⏰ WD £16; WE £20.
🗓 Welcome by prior arrangement; full facilities; terms on application.
🍽 Bar, restaurant and function rooms.
🛏 List can be provided.

3B 51 Lyme Regis ℭ
Timber Hill, Lyme Regis, Dorset, DT7 3HQ
☎ (01297) 442963, Pro 443822, Bar/Rest 442043
Off A3052 Charmouth road 1 mile E of town.
Clifftop course.
Pro Andrew Black; Founded 1893
18 holes, 6283 yards, S.S.S. 70
☏ Welcome with handicap certs or proof of membership of recognised club; restrictions Thurs and Sun am.
⏰ WD £23; WE £23.
🗓 Welcome by arrangement, not Thurs or Sun am; full facilities available.
🍽 Hot and cold snacks all day; full restaurant.
🛏 Alexander; Bay; Buena Vista; Devon; Fairwater Head; Tudor House.

3B 52 Lyons Gate
Lyons Gate Farm, Lyons Gate, Dorchester, DT2 7AZ
☎ (01300) 345239
3 miles N of Cerne Abbas on A352 Sherborne-Dorchester road.
Wooded farmland/parkland course.
Founded 1991
Designed by Ken Abel
9 holes, 2000 yards, S.S.S. 30
☏ Welcome; no restrictions.
⏰ WD £5.00; WE £5.00.

✐ Welcome by arrangement.
🍽 Light refreshments available.
🍸 Kings Arms.

3B 53 **Manor House Golf** ☂ **Club**
Castle Combe, Wilts, SN14 7PL
☎ (01249) 782982, Fax 782992, Pro 783101
On B4039 to N of Castle Combe village.
Ancient woodland/parkland course.
Pro Chris Smith; Founded 1992
Designed by Peter Alliss and Clive Clark
18 holes, 6340 yards, S.S.S. 71
🏌 Welcome anytime with handicap certs and by making prior tee reservation.
⌊ WD £37.50; WE £60.
✐ Welcome by arrangement; full facilities.
🍽 Two bars, restaurant, private dining facilities, bar snacks available all day.
🍸 Manor House.

3B 54 **Marlborough**
The Common, Marlborough, Wilts, SN8 1DU
☎ (01672) 512147, Fax 513164
On the A346 1 miles north of Marlborough; 7 miles south of M4 exit 15.
Downland course.
Pro Simon Amor; Founded 1888
Designed by T Simpson / upgraded 1920 by H Fowler
18 holes, 6491 yards, S.S.S. 72
🏌 Welcome with prior arrangement.
⌊ WD £22; WE £30.
✐ Welcomed midweek, particularly Tues and Thurs; packages available; day's golf, coffee, light lunch and dinner from £25.
🍽 Full facilities.
🍸 Castle and Ball Hotel; Ivy House Hotel, both Marlborough.

3B 55 **Mendip**
Gurney Slade, Bath, Somerset, BA3 4UT
☎ (01749) 840570, Fax 841439, Pro 840793
3 miles N of Shepton Mallett off A37.
Undulating downland course.
Pro Ron Lee; Founded 1908
Designed by H. Vardon with extension by F. Pennink
18 holes, 6381 yards, S.S.S. 70
🏌 Welcome.
⌊ WD £21; WE £31.

✐ Welcome by arrangement Mon & Thurs; full facilities.
🍽 Full facilities.
🍸 Stone Easton Park Hotel.

3B 56 **Mendip Spring**
Honeyhall Lane, Congresbury, North Somerset, BS19 5JT
☎ (01934) 852322, Fax 853021, Bar/Rest 852322
Take A370 from M5 Junction 21 to Congresbury.
Parkland/water features; also 9-hole Lakeside course.
Pro John Blackburn/ Robert Moss; Founded 1991
Designed by Terry Murray
18 holes, 6334 yards, S.S.S. 70
🏌 Welcome by prior arrangement.
⌊ WD £22; WE £25.
✐ Welcome; full catering facilities; halfway house facilities for refreshments, buggies; terms on application.
🍽 Full facilities.
Practice range, 10 bays.

3B 57 **Minehead & West Somerset**
The Warren, Minehead, Somerset, TA24 5SJ
☎ (01643) 702057, Fax 705095, Pro 704378
Course at end of seafront.
Links course.
Pro Ian Read; Founded 1882
Designed by Johnny Alan
18 holes, 6228 yards, S.S.S. 71
🏌 Welcome.
⌊ WD £22; WE £25.
✐ Welcome on written application; full facilities.
🍽 By prior arrangement with caterer; snacks always available.
🍸 York; Northfield; Marshfield.

3B 58 **Monkton Park Par 3**
Monkton Park, Chippenham, Wilts, SN15 3PE
☎ (01249) 653928, Fax 653928
Into Chippenham, past railway station, turn right.
Parkland course.
Founded 1960
Designed by M. Dawson
9 holes, 990 yards, S.S.S. 27
🏌 Welcome.
⌊ WD £3.85; WE £3.85; concessions apply
✐ Welcome.
🍽 Refreshments available.
Pool table.

3B 59 **North Wilts**
Bishops Cannings, Devizes, Wilts, SN10 2LP
☎ (01380) 860257, Fax 860877, Pro 860330, Sec 860627
Take A361 Devizes to Swindon road and after 3 miles turn to Calne.
Downland course.
Pro Graham Laing; Founded 1890/1972
Designed by K Cotton
18 holes, 6333 yards, S.S.S. 70
🏌 Welcome by prior arrangement.
⌊ WD £21; WE £24.
✐ Welcome WD by prior arrangement; brochure and price list available; terms on application.
🍽 Clubhouse facilities.
🍸 Bear, Devizes; Landsdown, Calne.

3B 60 **Oake Manor** ☂
Oake, Taunton, Somerset, TA4 1BA
☎ (01823) 461993, Fax 461995, Bar/Rest 461992
5 minutes from Junction 26 off M5.
Gently undulating parkland course with water.
Pro Russell Gardner; Founded 1993
Designed by Adrian Stiff
18 holes, 6109 yards, S.S.S. 69
🏌 Welcome by prior arrangement.
⌊ WD £16.50; WE £20.
✐ Welcome; contact golf manager Russell Gardner; from £20.
🍽 Function rooms, bar and restaurant.
Practice range, 11 bays.
🍸 Rumwell Manor.

3B 61 **Oaksey Park**
Oaksey, Nr Malmesbury, Wilts, SN16 9SB
☎ (01666) 577995, Fax 577174
Off A419 between Swindon and Cirencester, W of Cotswold Water Park.
Public parkland course.
Founded 1991
Designed by Chapman & Warren
9 holes, 2904 yards, S.S.S. 69
🏌 Welcome.
⌊ WD £7; WE £9.
✐ Welcome; full facilities; terms on application.
🍽 Full facilities.
🍸 Oaksey Park Country Cottages Hotel (10 farm cottages).

3B 62 **Ogbourne Downs**
Ogbourne St George, Marlborough, Wilts, SN8 1TB

☎ (01672) 841327, Fax 841327, Pro 841287, Sec 841327,
Junction 15 off M4; course on A345.
Downland course.
Pro Colin Harraway; Founded 1907
Designed by Taylor, Hawtree and Cotton
18 holes, 6353 yards, S.S.S. 70
† Welcome with handicap certs.
⌐ WD £25; WE £35.
☞ Terms on application from secretary; bar, dining room, ball hire, buggy hire.
⦿ Full bar and restaurant facilities.
↗ Parklands Hotel, Ogbourne St George.

3B 63 Orchardleigh
Frome, Somerset, BA11 2PH
☎ (01373) 454200, Fax 454202, Pro 454206
On A363 between Frome and Radstock.
Parkland course.
Pro Peter Green; Founded 1995
Designed by Brian Huggett
18 holes, 6810 yards, S.S.S. 73
† Welcome.
⌐ WD £17.50; WE £25.
☞ Welcome; terms on application.
↗ Stone Easton House; Bishopstrow House; Homewood Park.

3B 64 Parkstone ☖
49a Links Rd, Parkstone, Poole, Dorset, BH14 9JU
☎ (01202) 708025, Fax 706027, Pro 708092, Sec 707138, Bar/Rest 708025
On A35 between Bournemouth and Poole; signposted left off Bournemouth road.
Links course.
Pro Andy Peach; Founded 1910
Designed by Willie Park and James Braid
18 holes, 6250 yards, S.S.S. 70
† Welcome with handicap certs.
⌐ Terms on application.
☞ Welcome but booking is essential.
⦿ Full catering.

3B 65 Parley Golf Centre
Parley Green Lane, Hurn, Christchurch, Dorset, BH23 6BB
☎ (01202) 591600
Opposite Bournemouth International Airport.
Parkland course.
Founded 1992
Designed by Paul Goodfellow
9 holes, 4584 yards

† Welcome.
⌐ WD £7; WE £8 (18 holes).
☞ Welcome by arrangement; full facilities.
⦿ Full catering facilities.
Practice range, 23 bays floodlit, 2 teaching bays.

3B 66 Queen's Park (Bournemouth)
Queen's Park West Drive, Bournemouth, Dorset, BH8 9BY
☎ (01202) 396198, Fax 396817, Pro 396817, Sec 302611, Bar/Rest 394466
Off Wessex Way in Bournemouth.
Parkland course.
Pro R Hill; Founded 1906
18 holes, 6319 yards, S.S.S. 70
† Welcome.
⌐ WD £10; WE £10; concessions apply.
☞ Welcome but prior booking essential.
⦿ Full catering.
↗ Embassy; Wessex; Marsham Court.

3B 67 RMCS Shrivenham
RMCS Shrivenham, Swindon, Wilts, SN6 8LA
☎ (01793) 785725
In the grounds of Royal Military College of Science on A420, 1 mile NE of Shrivenham.
Parkland course.
Founded 1953
18 holes, 5684 yards, S.S.S. 69
† Restricted access; welcome with member.
⌐ WD £8; WE £10.
☞ Welcome WD subject to availability.
⦿ Coffee and soft drinks.

3B 68 Rushmore Park ☖
Tollard Royal, Salisbury, Wiltshire, SP5 5QB
☎ (01725) 516326, Fax 516466
12 miles from Salisbury off the A354 Blandford road through Sixpenny Handley; course is just before Tollard Royal.
Parkland course; 9-hole extension opening summer 1998.
Pro Sean McDonagh; Founded 1994
18 holes, 5585 yards, S.S.S. 67
† Welcome.
⌐ WD £13; WE £16.
☞ Welcome by prior arrangement.
⦿ Full menu available.
Practice range, 6 bays.

3B 69 Salisbury & South Wiltshire
Netherhampton, Salisbury, Wilts, SP2 8PR
☎ (01722) 742645, Pro 742929
On A3094 2 miles from Salisbury and from Wilton.
Downland course.
Founded 1888
Designed by J.H. Taylor; extra 9 holes by S Gidman 1991
27 holes, 6200 yards, S.S.S. /1
† Welcome.
⌐ WD £25; WE £40.
☞ Welcome by arrangement; full facilities.
⦿ Full facilities.
↗ Rose & Crown, Kings Arms, both Salisbury; Pembroke Arms, Wilton.

3B 70 Saltford ☖
Golf Club Lane, Saltford, Bristol, BS31 3AA
☎ (01225) 873513, Fax 873525, Pro 872043
Off A4 between Bath and Bristol.
Meadowland course.
Pro Dudley Millensted; Founded 1904
18 holes, 6046 yards, S.S.S. 70
† Welcome with handicap certs.
⌐ WD £24; WE £32.
☞ Welcome Mon and Thurs by arrangement; full facilities.
⦿ Full facilities.
↗ Grange (Keynsham); Crown; Tunnel House.

3B 71 Sherborne
Higher Clatcombe, Sherborne, Dorset, DT9 4RN
☎ (01935) 814431, Fax 814218, Sec 814431, Pro 812274
1 miles north of Sherborne off B3145.
Parkland course.
Pro Stewart Wright; Founded 1894
Designed by James Braid
18 holes, 5882 yards, S.S.S. 68
† Welcome with handicap certs.
⌐ WD £26; WE £30.
☞ Welcome Tues and Wed only; full playing, practice and dining facilities; terms on application.
⦿ Full facilities.
↗ Sherborne Hotel; Eastbury; Antelope.

3B 72 Shrivenham Park
Pennyhooks, Shrivenham, Swindon, Wilts, SN6 8EX
☎ (01793) 783853, Fax 782999
Off A420 between Swindon and Oxford.

Parkland course.
Pro Barry Randall; Founded 1969
Designed by Glen Johnson
18 holes, 5769 yards, S.S.S. 69
♦ Welcome.
▯ WD £15; WE £17.
⌁Welcome anytime with prior booking; packages available.
⬥ Facilities available.
⌐ Blunsdown House.

3B 73 **Solent Meads Par 3**
Rolls Drive, Nr Hengistbury Head, Bournemouth, Dorset
☎(01202) 420795
Off Broadway at Hengistbury Head.
Seaside course.
18 holes, 2182 yards
♦ Welcome; pay and play.
▯ WD £7; WE £7 (includes club hire); concessions apply.
⌁Limited.
⬥ Light refreshments and snacks.
Practice range, 10 bays floodlit.

3B 74 **Stockwood Vale**
Stockwood Lane, Keynsham, Bristol, BS18 2ER
☎(0117) 9866505, Fax 9860509, Sec 9860509
In Stockwood Lane off A4.
Undulating parkland course.
Pro John Richards; Founded 1991
Designed by J Wade & M Ramsay
18 holes, 5794/6031 yards, S.S.S. 71
♦ Welcome with prior reservation.
▯ WD £14; WE £16.
⌁Welcome by prior arrangement; terms on application.
⬥ Available.

3B 75 **Sturminster Marshall**
Moor Lane, Sturminster Marshall, Dorset, BH21 4AH
☎(01258) 858444, Fax 858262
In village centre on the A350 midway between Blandford and Poole.
Parkland course.
Pro Graham Howell; Founded 1992
Designed by John Sharkey
9 holes, 4882 yards, S.S.S. 65
♦ Welcome.
▯ WD £11; WE £11 (18 holes).
⌁Welcome with prior bookings accepted 7 days in advance; terms on application.
⬥ Full facilities.

3B 76 **Tall Pines**   ℭ
Cooks Bridle Path, Downside, Backwell, Bristol, BS48 3DS

☎(01275) 474869, Fax 474869, Pro 472076, Bar/Rest 474889
Take A38 or A370 from Bristol and course is next to Bristol International Airport.
Public parkland course.
Pro Alex Murray; Founded 1990
Designed by Terry Murray
18 holes, 6049 yards, S.S.S. 68
♦ Welcome; no restrictions.
▯ WD £14; WE £16.
⌁Welcome; full facilities; terms on application.
⬥ Bar and restaurant.

3B 77 **Taunton & Pickeridge**
Corfe, Taunton, Somerset, TA3 7BY
☎(01823) 421537, Fax 421742, Pro 421790
B3170, 4 miles S of Taunton, through Corfe village, then first left.
Undulating course.
Pro Gary Milne; Founded 1892
Designed by Hawtree
18 holes, 5926 yards, S.S.S. 68
♦ Welcome WD; handicap certs required.
▯ WD £20; WE £28.
⌁Welcome by arrangement; full facilities.
⬥ Full facilities.
⌐ Castle.

3B 78 **Taunton Vale**
Creech Heathfield, Taunton, Somerset, TA3 5EY
☎(01823) 412220, Fax 413583, Pro 412880
Just off A361 junction with A38, exits 24 or 25 from M5.
Parkland course.
Pro Martin Keitch; Founded 1991
Designed by John Pyne
18 holes, 6142 yards, S.S.S. 69
♦ Welcome; dress code applies.
▯ WD £16; WE £24.
⌁Welcome WD; terms on application.
⬥ Full facilities.
⌐ Walnut Tree (North Petherton); Castle (Taunton); Falcon (Henlade); Tudor (Bridgwater).

3B 79 **Thoulstone Park**
Chapmanslade, Nr Westbury, Wilts, BA13 4AQ
☎(01373) 832825, Fax 832821, Pro 832808
3 miles NW of Warminster on the A36.
Parkland course.
Pro Tony Isaacs; Founded 1991

Designed by M.R.M. Sandow
18 holes, 6312 yards, S.S.S. 70
♦ Welcome.
▯ WD £18; WE £24.
⌁Welcome; terms on application.
⬥ Full facilities.

3B 80 **Tickenham**
Clevedon Rd, Tickenham, N Somerset, BS21 6SB
☎(01275) 856626
Take M5 Junction 20 and follow signs for Nailsea; course on left after Tickenham.
Parkland course.
Pro Andrew Sutcliffe; Founded 1994
Designed by A Sutcliffe
9 holes, 3776 yards, S.S.S. 58
♦ Welcome.
▯ WD £5; WE and after 4pm £7 (9 holes).
⌁Welcome by arrangement; catering and bar facilities; driving range; teaching academy; terms on application.
⬥ Bar, club room and breakfast catering.
Practice range, 24 bays floodlit.
⌐ Redwood Lodge.

3B 81 **Two Riversmeet**
Two Riversmeet Leisure Centre, Stony Lane South, Christchurch, Dorset, BH23 1HW
☎(01202) 477987, Fax 470853
Signposted from the centre of Christchurch.
Public seaside course.
Founded 1986
Designed by local authority
18 holes, 1591 yards, 3 par
♦ Pay and play.
▯ WD £4.75; WE £4.75.
⌁Welcome; terms on application.
⬥ Bar and restaurant.
⌐ Many by the seaside; list available from the club.

3B 82 **Upavon (RAF)**
Andover Rd, Upavon, Nr Pewsey, Wilts, SN9 6BQ
☎(01980) 630787, Fax 630787, Pro 630281
On the A342 1.5 miles SE of Upavon village.
Undulating chalk downland course.
Pro Richard Blake; Founded 1918/1997
18 holes, 6407 yards, S.S.S. 71
♦ Welcome on WD and afternoon at WE.
▯ WD £18; WE £20.

◞ Welcome WD; from £18 per head.
🍽 Bar and restaurant.
Practice range.

3B 83 Vivary
Vivary Park, Taunton, Somerset, TA1
3JW
☎ (01823) 289274, Pro 333875, Sec
289274
Centre of Taunton in Vivary Park.
Parkland course.
Pro Mike Steadman; Founded 1928
Designed by Herbert Fowler
18 holes, 4620 yards, S.S.S. 63
⚑ Welcome.
⌞ WD £8.10, WE £8.10.
◞ Welcome on WD only; contact
Pro; terms on application.
🍽 Full restaurant and bar facilities.
⌐ Corner House; Castle.

3B 84 Wareham
Sandford Rd, Wareham, Dorset,
BH20 4DH
☎ (01929) 554147, Fax 554147, Sec
554147
N of Wareham off A351 between
Sandford and Wareham.
Mixture of parkland and heathland
course; fine views.
Pro Richard Emery; Founded 1908
Designed by C. Whitcome
18 holes, 5603 yards, S.S.S. 67
⚑ Welcome WD 9.30am-5pm; WE
after 1pm.
⌞ WD £20; WE £20.
◞ Welcome WD; packages
available; group prices negotiable; full
facilities for dining.
🍽 Full bar and catering.
⌐ Worgret Manor; Springfield;
Priory; Kemps.

3B 85 Wells (Somerset) ℂ
East Horrington Rd, Wells, Somerset,
BA5 3DS
☎ (01749) 675005, Fax 675005, Pro
679059, Sec 675005
E of Wells off B3139.
Parkland course
Pro Adrian Bishop; Founded 1893
Redesigned by Adrian Stiff
18 holes, 6015 yards, S.S.S. 69
⚑ Welcome.
⌞ WD £22; WE £25.
◞ Welcome on Tues and Thurs by
prior arrangement; packages
available; from £33.
🍽 Full facilities.
Practice range, 12 bays floodlit.
⌐ Swan; White Hart both Wells;
Charlton House, Shepton Mallett.

3B 86 Wessex Golf Centre
Radipole Lane, Weymouth, Dorset,
DT4 9HX
☎ (01305) 784737
Off Weymouth bypass behind the
football club.
Parkland course.
Pro N Statham;
9 holes, 1432 yards, par 3
⚑ Public pay and play.
⌞ WD £4; WE £4.
Practice range, available.
🍽 None at all.

3B 87 West Wilts
Elm Hill, Warminster, Wilts, BA12
0AU
☎ (01985) 213133, Fax 219809, Pro
212110, Bar/Rest 212702
Course is in Warminster off the
Westbury road.
Downland course.
Pro Andy Lamb; Founded 1891
Designed by J.H. Taylor
18 holes, 5709 yards, S.S.S. 68
⚑ Welcome with handicap certs or
as members' guests.
⌞ WD £20; WE £36.
◞ Welcome but advance booking
essential.
🍽 Full facilities.
⌐ Bishopstrow; Old Bell.

3B 88 Weston-super-Mare
Uphill Rd North, Weston-super-Mare,
N Somerset, BS23 4NQ
☎ (01934) 621360, Fax 621360, Pro
633360, Sec 626968, Bar/Rest
641826
M5 to Junction 21 and then follow
road to seafront.
Links course.
Pro M Laband; Founded 1892
Designed by T. Dunn
18 holes, 6208 yards, S.S.S. 70
⚑ Welcome; handicap certs required
at WE.
⌞ WD £24; WE £36.
◞ Welcome; terms on application
🍽 Full bar and restaurant facilities.
⌐ Beachlands; Commodore; Rozel;
Timbertops.

3B 89 Weymouth
Links Rd, Weymouth, Dorset, DT4
0PF
☎ (01305) 784994, Fax 788029, Pro
773997, Sec 773981, Rest 773558
1 mile from Weymouth town centre.
Parkland course.
Pro Des Lochrie; Founded 1909
Designed originally by James Braid;

Redesigned by J. Hamilt
18 holes, 5976 yards, S.S.S. 69
⚑ Welcome if carrying handicap
certs.
⌞ WD £24; WE £30.
◞ Welcome WD; catering by
arrangement.
🍽 Full facilities.

3B 90 Wheathill
Wheathill, Somerton, Somerset, TA11
7HG
☎ (01963) 240667, Fax 240230
Take A37 towards Yeovil; at village of
Lydford Cross turn left; course 1 mile
on right.
Parkland course.
Founded 1993
Designed by J Payne
18 holes, 5351 yards, S.S.S. 66
⚑ Welcome.
⌞ WD £10; WE £15.
◞ Welcome by arrangement; full
facilities.
🍽 Full facilities.
⌐ George (Castle Cary).

3B 91 The Wiltshire Golf ℂ
Club
Vastern, Wootton Basset, Swindon,
Wilts, SN4 7PB
☎ (01793) 849999, Fax 849988, Pro
851360
📧 wiltsgc@btinternet.com
Course is on the A3102 one mile S of
Wootton Bassett, close to the M4
Junction 16.
Parkland with water on 8 holes;
rolling downs.
Pro Andy Gray; Founded 1992
Designed by Peter Alliss/ Clive Clark
18 holes, 6522 yards, S.S.S. 72
⚑ Welcome by prior arrangement.
⌞ WD £30; WE £30.
◞ Welcome by arrangement; golf
and catering packages can be
arranged; terms on application.
🍽 Full clubhouse facilities.
Practice range, practice ground.
⌐ Hilton; De Vere, both Swindon.

3B 92 Windwhistle ℂ
Windwhistle, Cricket St Thomas, Nr
Chard, Somerset, TA20 4DG
☎ (01460) 30231, Fax 30055
Course is on the north side of the
A30 five miles from Crewkerne, three
miles from Chard, opposite a wildlife
park; follow signs from the M5
Junction 25.
Downland/parkland course.
Founded 1932

Designed by J.H. Taylor (1932), Leonard Fisher (1992)
18 holes, 6470 yards, S.S.S. 71
† Welcome but best to phone first.
⌇ WD £15; WE £18.
⌇ Welcome by arrangement; full facilities.
⦿ Full facilities.

3B 93 **Worlebury**
Monks Hill, Worlebury, Weston-super-Mare, Avon, BS22 9SX
☎ (01934) 623214, Fax 621935, Pro 418473, Sec 625789
From M5 Junction 21 follow old road to Weston-super-Mare; turn right at Milton Church.
Hilltop parkland course.
Pro Gary Marks; Founded 1908
Designed by W. Hawtree & Son
18 holes, 5936 yards, S.S.S. 69
† Welcome.
⌇ WD £20; WE £30.
⌇ Welcome by prior arrangement; terms on application.

⦿ Bar and restaurant facilities.
↝ Commodore; Beachlands.

3B 94 **Wrag Barn Golf** ☏ **& Country Club**
Shrivenham Rd, Highworth, Wilts, SN6 7QQ
☎ (01793) 861327, Fax 861325, Pro 766027
10 miles from M4 Junction 15; take A419 towards Cirencester, left turn to Highworth, follow A316 to Highworth, then 3rd exit at roundabout on to B4000 to Shrivenham; course is 0.5 miles on right.
Undulating scenic parkland course.
Pro Barry Loughrey; Founded 1990
Designed by Hawtree & Sons
18 holes, 6348 yards, S.S.S. 71/72/73
† Welcome; restrictions apply in afternoon at WE so it is advisable to phone first.
⌇ WD £25; WE £30.
⌇ Welcome WD by arrangement.

⦿ Full bar and restaurant, catering for companies, parties, receptions.
↝ Blunsden House Hotel; Jesmond House (Highworth).

3B 95 **Yeovil** ☏
Sherborne Rd, Yeovil, Somerset, BA21 5BW
☎ (01935) 475949, Fax 411283, Pro 473763, Sec 422965, catering 431130
1 mile from town centre towards Sherborne on A30.
Parkland course; also 9-hole course available.
Pro Geoff Kite; Founded 1919
Designed by Fowler & Alison (18 holes); Sports Turf Rese (9 holes)
18 holes, 6144 yards, S.S.S. 70
† Welcome but ring for tee times.
⌇ WD £25; WE £30.
⌇ Welcome on Mon, Wed, Thurs, Fri; packages can be arranged.
⦿ Full facilities.
↝ Ludgate House, Ilchester.

EAST ANGLIA

Royal West Norfolk, or Brancaster to give it its less formal title, is one of those links courses that once seen is never forgotten. This is golf in its purest form and, on days when the elements are less kind, its rawest. The scorecard shows that the back nine is 300 yards shorter than the front, but naturally it is with good reason; when the prevailing wind blows it feels like the other way round.

Brancaster is squeezed between dunes and tidal marshland, so much so that coastal erosion is a constant source of anxiety for both the membership and golf lovers everywhere. The clubhouse, meanwhile, is among the most convivial spots in England.

Just as good in the opinion of many people is the links at Hunstanton, a verdict offered by a number of golfers who have played in the numerous amateur events that have been staged there over the years.

Certainly a gifted player by the name of Robert Taylor would concur. He once achieved the extraordinary feat of an ace on the 16th hole, which measures 189 yards, for three days in a row; twice in competition and once in practice,

Travelling further along the clifftop we come to Sheringham, which has a number of classic links holes, most notably the fifth with its panoramic view of the north Norfolk coastline, and then the attractive Royal Cromer, with its famous 'lighthouse' hole. The oldest course in Norfolk, however, is to be found at Great Yarmouth, which dates

back to 1882, and which is another fine links. Students of racing will have identified Great Yarmouth and Caister from the stands, the first and last holes hurdling the rails and several others enclosed by the track.

After such golf the journey inland is bound to be a reluctant one but the courses at Kings Lynn, Royal Norwich, Thetford and Barnham Broom all have their appeal.

In Suffolk the heather and gorse venues of Thorpeness and Aldeburgh represent perfect holiday golf. Although by the sea, neither can be classed as seaside. Thorpeness was another James Braid design and is beautifully scenic, and comes complete with an 18th hole that offers a unique backdrop; the 'House in the Clouds', as the unusual water tower is affectionately known, and a restored windmill.

Gourmet golf in every sense is offered at Hintlesham Hall, which dates back to the 16th century. Here the 18 holes on offer serve as a tasty appetiser for the delights to come in the hotel's famed restaurant.

One course in Suffolk, however, rises above all others in terms of status, and it is the incomparable Royal Worlington and Newmarket. Quite simply, it is the best nine-hole golf course in the world. "The Sacred Nine" was Bernard Darwin's beautifully apt description; Donald Steel, meanwhile, came up with an equally evocative metaphor when he described it as "a triumph in fitting a quart into a pint pot". — **DL**

4 1 Aldeburgh

Saxmundham Rd, Aldeburgh, Suffolk, IP15 5PE
☎ (01728) 452408, Fax 452937, Pro 453309, Sec 452890
From the A12 north of Ipswich take the A1094 to Aldeburgh; course is six miles E of the A12.
Open heathland course; no par 5s.
Pro Keith Preston; Founded 1884
Designed by John Thompson/ Willie Fernie
18 holes, 6330 yards, S.S.S. 71
† Welcome by prior arrangement.
↳ WD £40; WE £50.
↳ Welcome by arrangement; terms on application.
Also a 2114-yard, 9-hole course with S.S.S. 62.
🍽 Clubhouse facilities.
↳ Wentworth; White Lion; Brudewell; Uplands.

4 2 Alnesbourne Priory

Priory Park, Nacton Road, Ipswich, Suffolk, IP10 0JT
☎ (01473) 727393, Fax 278372
From A14 take Ransomes Europark exit and follow signs to Priory Park.
Parkland course.
Founded 1987
9 holes, 1760 yards, S.S.S. 58
† Public pay and play (course closed Tues).
↳ WD £10; Sat £11; Sun £12.
↳ Course available for hire every Tues; packages available, adventure playground; terms aailable on application.
🍽 Bar, restaurant.
↳ Lodge cabins on site.

4 3 Barnham Broom ☏

Honingham Rd, Barnham Broom, Norwich, Norfolk, NR9 4DD
☎ (01603) 759393, Fax 758224
9 miles SW of Norwich.
River valley setting.
Pro P Ballingall; Founded 1977
Designed by Frank Pennink (Valley), Donald Steel (Hill)
Hill course: 18 holes, 6628 yards, S.S.S. 72; Valley course: 18 holes, 6470 yards, S.S.S. 71
† Welcome by prior arrangement.
↳ WD £30; WE £30.
↳ Many golfing breaks and corporate packages available; complete hotel, conference and golfing leisure breaks available at the hotel.
🍽 Full club and hotel facilities available.
↳ Barnham Broom Hotel.

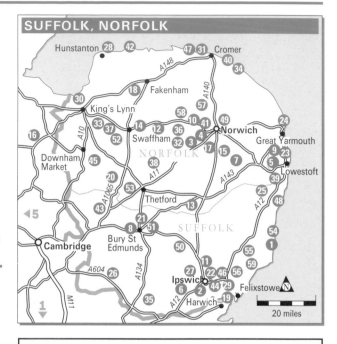

SUFFOLK, NORFOLK

4 4 Bawburgh

Glen Lodge, Marlingford Road, Bawburgh, Norfolk, NR9 3LU
☎ (01603) 740404, Fax 740403, Pro 742323
Off the Norwich southern by-pass (A47) at the Royal Norfolk Showground junction; follow road to Bawburgh.
Parkland/heathland course.
Pro Chris Potter; Founded 1978
Designed by S. Manser
18 holes, 6224 yards, S.S.S. 70
† Welcome.
↳ WD £18; WE £20.
↳ Welcome by prior arrangement; normal packages involve 18-36 holes; lunch and evening meal; terms on application.
🍽 Full clubhouse facilities.
Practice range, 14 bays; floodlit.
↳ Park Farm, Hethersett.

4 5 Beccles

The Common, Beccles, Suffolk, NR34 9BX
☎ (01502) 712244, Sec 714616
Leave A146 Norwich-Lowestoft road at Sainsbury's roundabout.

Parkland course; formerly Wood Valley (Beccles).
Founded 1899
9 holes, 5562 yards, S.S.S. 67
† Welcome; with a member on Sun am.
 WD £8; WE £10.
Welcome with prior notice; terms on application.
Clubhouse facilities.
King's Head; Waveney House, both Beccles.

4 6 Brett Vale
Noaks Rd, Raydon, Ipswich, Suffolk IP7 5LR
☎ (01473) 310718, Fax 824482
Founded 1993
Course is 8 miles from Ipswich off the A12.
18 holes, 5847 yards, S.S.S. 70
† Welcome by prior arrangement.
 WD £15; WE £20.
Welcome by prior arrangement; terms on application.
Full clubhouse facilities.

4 7 Bungay & Waveney Valley
Outney Common, Bungay, Suffolk, NR35 1DS

☎ (01986) 892337, Fax 892222
Signposted from Bungay by-pass.
Heathland course.
Pro N Whyte; Founded 1889
Designed by James Braid
18 holes, 6044 yards, S.S.S. 69
† Welcome by arrangement.
 Terms on application.
Welcome by prior arrangement; discounted day rates and green fees for groups of more than 20.
Clubhouse facilities.
Practice range.

4 8 Bury St Edmunds
Tuthill, Bury St Edmunds, Suffolk, IP28 6LG
☎ (01284) 755979
1st exit off A14 for Bury St Edmunds; 0.25 miles down B1106 to Brandon.
Parkland course.
Pro Mark Jillings; Founded 1924
Designed by Hawtree (9 holes), Ray (18 holes)
18 holes, 6678 yards, S.S.S. 72
18 hole course visitors: Welcome WD; WE with a member.
 WD £24.
Welcome WD by arrangement; also a pay and play 9-hole course; terms on application.

Full clubhouse facilities.
Butterfly.

4 9 Caldecott Hall
Caldecott Hall, Beccles Road, Fritton, Norfolk, NR31 9EY
☎ (01493) 488488, Fax 488561
5 miles SW of Great Yarmouth on A143 Beccles Road.
Parkland course.
Pro Syer Shulver; Founded 1994
18 holes, 6318 yards, S.S.S. 70
† Welcome by prior arrangement.
 WD £20; WE £25.
Welcome by prior arrangement; discounts available for groups of 10 or more; terms available on application.
Also a 9-hole par 3 course.
Full clubhouse facilities.
Practice range, 20 bays; floodlit.
The Cliff, Gorleston-on-Sea; The Star, Great Yarmouth.

4 10 Costessey Park
Old Costessy, Norwich, Norfolk, NR8 5AL
☎ (01603) 746333, Pro 747085
Course is off the A1074 at the Round Well public house three miles W of Norwich.

Parkland/river valley course.
Pro Simon Cook; Founded 1983
Designed by Frank MacDonald
18 holes, 6104 yards, S.S.S. 69
† Welcome; only after 11am at WE.
⌐ WD £20; WE £25.
⌐ Welcome by prior arrangement;
terms on application.
⊙ Full catering and bar facilities
available.
Practice range.

4 11 **Cretingham**

Cretingham, Woodbridge, Suffolk,
IP13 7BA
☎ (01728) 685275, Fax 685037
2 miles from the A1120 at Earl Soham;
10 miles N of Ipswich.
Parkland course.
Pro Neil Jackson; Founded 1984
9 holes, 4380 yards, S.S.S. 64
† Welcome.
⌐ WD £7; WE £9.
⌐ Welcome by arrangement; catering
packages available; snooker; pitch &
putt; swimming pool; tennis; caravan
park.
⊙ Full restaurant and licensed bar
available.
Practice range.

4 12 **Dereham**

Quebec Rd, Dereham, Norfolk, NR19
2DS
☎ (01362) 695900, Fax 695904, Pro
695631, Sec 695900
0.5 miles W of Dereham on B1110.
Parkland course.
Pro R Curtis; Founded 1934
9 holes, 6225 yards, S.S.S. 70
† Welcome by prior arrangement.
⌐ Terms on application.
⌐ Welcome by arrangement;
packages available; terms on
application.
⊙ Clubhouse facilities.
⌐⊓ Phoenix; Kings Head; George.

4 13 **Diss**

Stuston Common, Diss, Norfolk, IP22
3JB
☎ (01379) 642847, Pro 644399, Sec
641025
Course is two miles W of the A140 at
Scole, half-way between Norwich and
Ipswich.
Commonland course.
Pro Nigel Taylor; Founded 1903
18 holes, 6262 yards, S.S.S. 70
† Welcome; WE only as the guest of
a member.
⌐ WD £20.

⌐ Welcome WD by prior
arrangement.
⊙ Full facilities available.

4 14 **Dunham Golf Club (Granary)**

Little Dunham, Nr Swaffham, King's
Lynn, Norfolk, PE32 2DF
☎ (01328) 701718
On A47 at Necton/Dunham
crossroads.
Parkland with lakes.
Founded 1987
9 holes, 4812 yards, S.S.S. 67
† Welcome.
⌐ Terms on application.
⌐ Welcome by prior arrangement.
⊙ Full bar and snack facilities
available.

4 15 **Dunston Hall**

Dunston Hall, Ipswich Road, Norwich,
Norfolk, NR14 8PQ
☎ (01508) 470178
On the main A140 Ipswich road; 10
minutes drive from Norwich city
centre.
Meadowland course.
Pro Peter Briggs; Founded 1994
Designed by M Shaw (1998 extension)
18 holes, 6319 yards, S.S.S. 70
† Welcome but booking essential;
priority to members and hotel guests.
⌐ WD £20; WE £25.
⌐ Welcome by prior arrangement;
catering packages; conference
facilities; leisure and health centre.
⊙ Full clubhouse facilities.
Practice range, 22 covered, floodlit
bays.
⌐⊓ Dunston Hall on site.

4 16 **Eagles**

28 School Road, Tilney All-Saints,
King's Lynn, Norfolk, PE34 4RS
☎ (01553) 827147, Fax 829777, Sec
829777
Off A47 between King's Lynn and
Wisbech.
Parkland course.
Pro Nigel Pickerell; Founded 1992
Designed by David Horn
9 holes, 4284 yards, S.S.S. 61
† Welcome.
⌐ WD £6.75; WE £7.75.
⌐ Welcome by arrangement; catering
facilities available by negotiation;
terms on application.
⊙ Facilities available.
Practice range.
⌐⊓ Bufferfly; Park View, both King's
Lynn.

4 17 **Eaton**

Newmarket Rd, Norwich, Norfolk, NR4
6SF
☎ (01603) 451686, Fax 451686, Pro
452478, Bar/Rest 452881
Off A11 1 mile S of Norwich.
Predominantly parkland course.
Pro Mark Allen; Founded 1910
18 holes, 6114 yards, S.S.S. 69
† Welcome WD; only after 11.30 on
WE.
⌐ WD £30; WE £40.
⌐ Welcome by arrangement; terms
on application.
⊙ Bar and catering facilities.
⌐⊓ Norwich; Nelson and Post House.

4 18 **Fakenham**

Sports Centre, The Race Course,
Fakenham, Norfolk, NR21 7NY
☎ (01328) 862867, Pro 863534, Sec
855665
Course is on the B1146 from Dereham
or the A1067 from Norwich.
Parkland course.
Pro Colin Williams; Founded 1981
Designed by Charles Lawrie
9 holes, 6174 yards, S.S.S. 69
† Welcome; restrictions Sat and Sun
morning.
⌐ WD £18; WE £24.
⌐ Welcome by arrangement.
⊙ Bar and restaurant in Sports
Centre.
⌐⊓ Wensum Lodge; Crown; Limes.

4 19 **Felixstowe Ferry**

Ferry Rd, Felixstowe, Suffolk, IP11
9RY
☎ (01394) 286834, Fax 283975
3A14 to Felixstowe following signs for
the yacht centre.
Links course.
Pro Ian MacPherson; Founded 1880
Designed by Henry Cotton & Sir Guy
Campbell
18 holes, 6272 yards, S.S.S. 70
† Welcome WD.
⌐ Terms on application.
⌐ Welcome Tues, Wed and Fri by
arrangement; catering packages; also
9-hole Kingsfleet course opened in
April 1997: 5980 yards, par 70.
⊙ Full catering facilities.
Practice range.
⌐⊓ Orwell House; self-catering flats
above the clubhouse for rent.

4 20 **Feltwell**

Thor Ave, Feltwell, Thetford, Norfolk,
IP26 4AY
☎ (01842) 827644, Pro 827666

Off B1112 Lakenheath-Feltwell road just before Feltwell village.
Inland links course.
Pro Peter Field; Founded 1972
9 holes, 6256 yards, S.S.S. 70
Welcome.
WD £15; WE £24.
Welcome WD; by arrangement; terms on application.
Bar and catering except Mon.
Brandon House, Brandon.

4 21 Flempton
Flempton, Bury St Edmunds, Suffolk, IP28 6EQ
(01284) 728291.
4 miles NE of Bury St Edmunds on A1101 to Mildenhall.
Breckland course.
Pro Mark Gillings; Founded 1895
Designed by J. H. Taylor
9 holes, 6240 yards, S.S.S. 70
Welcome WD with handicap certs; with member at weekend.
WD £25.
Limited availability.
By arrangement.
Priory & Angel; The Riverside.

4 22 Fynn Valley
Witnesham, Ipswich, Suffolk, IP6 9JA
(01473) 785267, Fax 785632, Pro 785463, Bar/Rest 785202
From A14 or A12 take A1214 and then B1077 to N of Ipswich.
Parkland course.
Pro P Wilby/ K Vince/ J Bevan; Founded 1991
Designed by Tony Tyrrell
18 holes, 5873 yards, S.S.S. 70
Welcome except before 10.30am Sun; Ladies day Wed.
WD £18; WE £21.
Welcome WD; catering and golf packages available; also 9-hole par 3 course; from £18.
Excellent restaurant.
Novotel, Ipswich; Travel Lodge, Claydon; Marlborough Hotel, Ipswich.

4 23 Gorleston
Warren Rd, Gorleston, Great Yarmouth, Norfolk, NR32 6JT
(01493) 661911, Fax 611911, Pro 662103, Bar/Rest 441922
Off A12 between Great Yarmouth and Lowestoft.
Clifftop course.
Pro N Brown; Founded 1906
Designed by J R Taylor
18 holes, 6391 yards, S.S.S. 71
Welcome with handicap certs.
WD £21; WE £25.
Welcome by prior arrangement; Full golf and catering package; terms on application.
Full clubhouse catering facilities.
Cliffs, Gorleston; Potters HH, Hopton.

4 24 Great Yarmouth & Caister
Beach House, Caister-on-Sea, Great Yarmouth, Norfolk, NR30 5TD
(01493) 728699, Fax 728699, Pro 720421, Bar/Rest 720214
From Yarmouth N to Caister-on-Sea.
Pro: James Hill
Links course.
Founded 1882
Designed by T Dunn/ H S Colt
18 holes, 6330 yards, S.S.S. 70
Welcome; handicap certs preferred.
WD £27; WE £30.
Welcome by prior arrangement; packages available; dining room, TV lounge, snooker; terms available on application.
Full catering and bar facilities available.
Imperial; Burlington; Caister Old Hall.

4 25 Halesworth
Bramfield Rd, Halesworth, Suffolk, IP19 9XA
(01986) 875567, Fax 874565, Pro 875697
On A144 off the A12 1 mile N of Darsham.
Parkland course; was St Helena GC
Pro R Whyte; Founded 1990
Designed by J.W. Johnson
27 holes, 6580 yards, S.S.S. 72
Welcome.
WD £12, WE 12.
Welcome by prior arrangement; Full day packages available; company days organised; also 9-hole par 33 course available; terms on application.
Full clubhouse facilities.

4 26 Haverhill
Coupals Rd, Haverhill, Suffolk, CB9 7UW
(01440) 761951, Fax 761951, Pro 712628
Leave Haverhill on A604 towards Colchester and turn second left after railway viaduct; first right into Coupals Road.
Parkland course; new 18 opened April 1998.
Pro Simon Mayfield; Founded 1973
Designed by Charles Lawrie
18 holes, 5898 yards, S.S.S. 68
Welcome.
WD £18; WE £22.
Welcome by prior arrangement.
Bar facilities and catering available.
Woodlands.

4 27 Hintlesham Hall
Hintlesham, Ipswich, Suffolk, IP8 3NS
(01473) 652761, Fax 652750
4 miles W of Ipswich; 10 mins from A12 or A14.
Parkland course.
Pro Alistair Spink; Founded 1991
Designed by Hawtree & Sons
18 holes, 6638 yards, S.S.S. 72
Welcome with handicap certificates.
WD £28; WE £35.
Welcome WD by prior arrangement with the secretary; packages available; spa; sauna; steam room.
Full bar and restaurant service.
Hintlesham Hall.

4 28 Hunstanton
Golf Course Rd, Old Hunstanton, Norfolk, PE36 6JQ
(01485) 532811, Fax 532319, Pro 532751, Bar/Rest 533932
On the North Norfolk coast; take the A149 Cromer Road through Old Hunstanton and follow signs to club.

Links course; 2 ball play only.
Pro John Carter; Founded 1891
Designed by George Fernie; updated
by J Braid
18 holes, 6735 yards, S.S.S. 72
♦ Welcome from 9.30am to 11.30am
and after 2pm on WD in summer; 10-
30am-11am and after 2pm at WE.
Ⅼ WD £50; WE £60.
♪ Welcome by prior arrangement but
2 ball play only; packages available;
Full facilities; terms on application.
◉ Full catering facilities.
↵ The Lodge; Le Strange Arms,
Hunstanton; Lifeboat Inn, Thornham.

4 29 Ipswich
Bucklesham Rd, Purdis Heath,
Ipswich, Suffolk, IP3 8UQ
☎ (01473) 728941, Fax 715236, Pro
724017, Bar/Rest 713030
3 miles E of Ipswich off A14.
Heathland course with pine trees;
present site since 1927.
Pro S Whymark; Founded 1895/ 1927
Designed by James Braid, Hawtree &
Taylor
27 holes, 6435 yards, S.S.S. 71
♦ Welcome WD by arrangement; WE
as member's guest only.
Ⅼ WD £25; WE £28.
♪ Welcome by prior arrangement;
packages including breakfast, lunch
and dinner available.
◉ Full catering facilities.
↵ Marriott Courtyard.

4 30 King's Lynn
Castle Rising, King's Lynn, Norfolk,
PE31 6QH
☎ (01553) 631654, Fax 631036, Pro
631655, Bar/Rest 631656
On A149 King's Lynn to Hunstanton,
turn at Castle Rising.
Parkland course.
Pro John Reynolds; Founded
1923/1975
Designed by Alliss & Thomas
18 holes, 6609 yards, S.S.S. 72
♦ Welcome with handicap certificate
by prior arrangement.
Ⅼ WD £40; WE £50.
♪ Welcome Thurs and Fri only;
catering available from society menu;
minimum 16.
◉ Full facilities.

4 31 Links Country Park ☎
Sandy Lane, West Runton, Cromer,
Norfolk, NR27 9QH
☎ (01263) 838383, Fax 838264, Pro
838215, Bar/Rest 838383

Off the A149 road.
Coastal course with heath; 300 yards
from sea.
Pro L Patterson; Founded 1899/1903
Designed by J H Taylor (1903 when
18 holes)
9 holes, 4842 yards, S.S.S. 64
♦ Welcome.
Ⅼ WD £22.50; WE £27.50.
♪ Welcome with prior arrangement;
Full catering and golf packages; hotel
on site with pool, sauna, sun bed and
tennis court; terms on application.
◉ Full catering facilities.
↵ ETB 4 crown Links Country Park
Hotel.

4 32 Mattishall
South Green, Mattishall, Dereham,
Norfolk
☎ (01362) 850111
B1063 to Mattishall; right at church;
course 1 mile on left.
Parkland course.
Founded 1990
9 holes, 6218 yards, S.S.S. 68
♦ Welcome.
Ⅼ Terms on application
♪ Limited availability.
◉ Limited.
↵ Phoenix, E Dereham.

4 33 Middleton Hall
Hall Orchards, Middleton, Nr King's
Lynn, Norfolk, PE32 1RH
☎ (01553) 841800, Pro 841801
On A47 between King's Lynn and
Swaffham.
Parkland course.
Pro D Edwards; Founded 1989
Designed by D Scott
18 holes, 6007 yards, S.S.S. 69
♦ Welcome.
Ⅼ WD £20; WE £25.
♪ Welcome by prior arrangement;
golfing and catering packages
available; carvery available for 30 or
more players.
◉ Full catering and bar facilities
available.
↵ Butterfly; Knight's Hill, both King's
Lynn.

4 34 Mundesley
Links Rd, Mundesley, Norwich,
Norfolk, NR11 8ES
☎ (01263) 720279, Fax 720279, Sec
720095
Turn off Mundesley-Cromer road at
Mundesley church.
Undulating parkland with fine views.
Pro Terry Symmons; Founded 1903

Designed by Harry Vardon (in part)
9 holes, 5377 yards, S.S.S. 66
♦ Welcome WD except Weds; after
11.30am at WE.
Ⅼ WD £12; WE £25.
♪ Welcome as with guests; catering
by prior arrangement; terms on
application.
◉ Clubhouse bar and catering
facilities.
↵ Manor House, Mundersley.

4 35 Newton Green
Newton Green, Sudbury, Suffolk,
CO10 0QN
☎ (01787) 377217, Pro 313215
Course is on the A134 three miles E
of Sudbury.
Moorland course.
Pro Tim Cooper; Founded 1907
18 holes, 5893 yards, S.S.S. 68
♦ Welcome WD; WE by prior
arrangement.
Ⅼ Terms on application.
♪ Welcome by prior arrangement;
packages available; from £15.
◉ Bar and restaurant facilities.
↵ Mill, Sudbury.

4 36 Norfolk Golf & CC ☎
Hingham Rd, Reymerston, Norwich,
Norfolk, NR9 4QQ
☎ (01362) 850297, Fax 850614
Signposted from B1135.
Parkland course; was Reymerston
GC.
Pro T Varney; Founded 1993
Designed by Adas
18 holes, 6609 yards, S.S.S. 72
♦ Welcome with prior arrangement.
Ⅼ WD £19; WE £23.
♪ Welcome WD; Full golf, catering
and leisure packages; terms on
application.
◉ Full facilities; function room.
Practice range, golf academy.
↵ White Hare, Hingham; Mill,
Yaxham.

4 37 RAF Marham
King's Lynn, Norfolk PE33 9NP
☎ (01760) 337261
7 miles SE of King's Lynn near
Narborough.
9 holes, 5244 yards, S.S.S. 66
♦ Restricted as property is MoD
land; apply on ext 7262.

4 38 Richmond Park ☎
Saham Road, Watton, Thetford,
Norfolk, IP25 6EA

Royal Worlington and Newmarket

Miss this course at your peril. A real jewel in the golfing world. It is rare to find a nine-hole course talked of in such reverent terms but praise for this masterpiece is universal.

Suffolk cannot count the same number of truly memorable courses as its northerly neighbour. There was not the same enthusiastic development of the county as in Norfolk.

But in Royal Worlington those golfing architects of more than a century ago found something that will bring joy to every visitor.

The accolades are many and varied. The sum total is a course that "is unmissable", or "a real gem" or "simply the greatest nine-hole course ever created".

No less a judge than Bernard Darwin, who schooled his golf at Felixstowe Ferry, described Royal Worlington as "the sacred nine". Rare praise indeed.

Its origins are simple. It was created in 1890 by a local golfer, Captain AM Ross. He decided that the light sandy soil of Suffolk was the perfect site for a golf course.

It is the quality of the soil that has made the greens quick but, just as importantly, allows play almost every day of the year. Avoid Mondays though, when the course is closed.

As far as Donald Steel is concerned, there is no better place than Royal Worlington in the winter. "It is," he writes, "a veritable haven that offers the ideal of a day of foursomes with the lure of characteristic refreshment to re-fuel the system.

"I have," he said "throughout the world never enjoyed anything better." Royal Worlington has that sort of effect on people.

The fifth is a stunning, bunkerless short hole which dances to the tune of the wind. There are those who swear that they have used every iron in their bag on the 157-yard hole. The wrong selection, though, brings trouble. It is guarded to the back by trees which offer little chance of recovery if the drive is too long.

It is the short holes that are the signatures of Royal Worlington. The second is a long and testing 224 yards while the seventh, with its saucer green, leaves the golfer with little more than the top of the pin as a mark.

But every second of the day at the club is one to savour and the effort to play is well rewarded. — **CG**

☎(01953) 886100, Fax 881817, Pro 881803, Bar/Rest 881803
Course is at bottom of Watton High Street.
Parkland course.
Founded 1990
Pro Alan Himfley
Designed by R. Jessup, R. Scott
18 holes, 6289 yards, S.S.S. 70
† Welcome.
॒ WD £18; WE £18.
⌁Welcome WD by prior arrangement; coffee on arrival, light lunch and 3-course dinner; other packages available.
🍽 Full facilities.
⌁ Accommodation on site.

4 39 **Rookery Park**
Carlton Colville, Lowestoft, Suffolk, NR33 8HJ
☎(01502) 560380, Pro 515103
Course is two miles W of Lowestoft on the A146.
Parkland course.
Pro Martin Elsworthy
Founded 1975
Designed by Charles Lawrie
18 holes, 6729 yards, S.S.S. 72
† Welcome.
॒ WD £30; WE £35.
⌁Welcome by prior arrangement except Tues; packages by arrangement; also 9-hole par 3 course; snooker.
🍽 Full facilities.
⌁ Hedley House; Broadlands.

4 40 **Royal Cromer**
145 Overstrand Rd, Cromer, Norfolk, NR27 0JH
☎(01263) 512884, Fax 512884, Pro 512267
1 mile E of Cromer on the B1159 coast road close to the Cromer lighthouse.
Undulating seaside course.
Founded 1888
Designed by James Braid
18 holes, 6508 yards, S.S.S. 71
† Welcome WD and after 11am most WE.
॒ Terms available upon application.
⌁Welcome WD by prior arrangement.
🍽 Daily facilities.
⌁ Cliftonville; Cliff House; Roman Camp Inn; Anglia Court; Red Lion.

4 41 **Royal Norwich**
Drayton High Rd, Hellesdon, Norwich, NR6 5AH

☎(01603) 425712, Fax 429928, Pro 408459, Sec 429928
On A1067 3 miles from Norwich on Fakenham road.
Mature undulating parkland course.
Pro Dean Futter; Founded 1893
Designed by J J W Deuchar 1893; J Braid 1924
18 holes, 6603 yards, S.S.S. 72
† Welcome; bookings necessary at WE.
॒ Available upon request.
⌁Welcome; book through general manager; packages available; catering and golf facilities; from £40.
🍽 Bar and restaurant facilities availabe.
⌁ Norwich Sports Village; Hotel Norwich; Stakis Hotel.

4 42 **Royal West Norfolk**
Brancaster, King's Lynn, Norfolk, PE31 8AX
☎(01485) 210223, Fax 210087, Pro 210616, Sec 210087
Course is seven miles E of Hunstanton; in Brancaster village turn at the Beach/Broad Lane junction with the A149; course one mile.
Historic links course.
Pro S Rayner; Founded 1892
Designed by Holcombe Ingleby
18 holes, 6428 yards, S.S.S. 71
† Welcome at secretary's discretion; deposit needed to confirm booking; not last week of July.
or August or first week of September.
॒ WD £50; WE £60.
⌁Welcome but prior booking essential.
🍽 Full facilities.
Practice range.
⌁ Hoste Arms, Burnham Market; Titchwell Manor, Titchwell.

4 43 **Royal Worlington & Newmarket**
Golf Links Rd, Worlington, Bury St Edmunds, Suffolk, IP28 8SD
☎(01638) 712216, Pro 712224, Sec 717787
6 miles NE of Newmarket on A14 then A11 towards Thetford; follow signs to Worlington.
Inland links course.
Pro Malcolm Hawkins; Founded 1893
Designed by H.S. Colt
9 holes, 6210 yards, S.S.S. 70
† WD only.
॒ WD £35; WE £35.
⌁Welcome Tues and Thurs by arrangement; catering packages; limit 24 players; from £50.

🍽 Full clubhouse facilities.
⌁ Worlington Hall; Riverside, Mildenhall.

4 44 **Rushmere**
Rushmere Heath, Ipswich, Suffolk, IP4 5QQ
☎(01473) 727109, Fax 725648, Pro 728076, Sec 725648 Bar/Rest 719034
3 miles E of Ipswich off A1214 Woodbridge road.
Heath and commonland course.
Pro N T J McNeill
Founded 1927
18 holes, 6262 yards, S.S.S. 70
† Welcome WD and after 2.30pm WE; handicap certs required and proof of membership of another club.
॒ WD £25; WE £25.
⌁Welcome by arrangement; packages available; terms on application.
⌁ Full clubhouse facilities.

4 45 **Ryston Park**
Ely Rd, Denver, Downham Market, Norfolk, PE38 0HH
☎(01366) 382133, Sec 383834
On A10 1 mile S of Downham Market.
Parkland course.
Founded 1933
Designed by J Braid
9 holes, 6310 yards, S.S.S. 70
† Welcome WD; with members at WE.
॒ Terms on application.
⌁Welcome; maximum 45; catering packages available from the steward; terms on application.
🍽 Full facilities.
⌁ Castle Hotel, Downham Market.

4 46 **Seckford**
Seckford Hall Rd, Great Bealings, Woodbridge, Suffolk, IP13 6NT
☎(01394) 388000, Fax 382818, Bar/Rest 384588
Off A12 at Woodbridge Junction.
Parkland course; Mizuno golf academy.
Pro Simon Jay; Founded 1991
Designed by Johnny Johnson
18 holes, 5303 yards, S.S.S. 66
† Welcome with prior arrangement.
॒ WD £16; WE £18.50.
⌁Welcome by prior arrangement; special leisure and golf breaks can be arranged in old Manor House hotel with 34 rooms; spa pool, swimming pool; packages available; terms on application.

🍽 Bar, bistro, terrace and hotel restaurant.
Practice range.
🛏 Seckford Hall.

4 47 Sheringham
Weybourne Rd, Sheringham, Norfolk, NR26 8HG
☎ (01263) 823488, Fax 825189, Pro 822980, Bar/Rest 822038
From the A148 follow the signs into Sheringham; left at roundabout; club 0.5 miles.
Clifftop course.
Pro M W Jubb; Founded 1891
Designed by Tom Dunn
18 holes, 6464 yards, S.S.S. 71
† Welcome with prior booking.
┇ WD £37; WE £42.
🗘 Welcome with prior arrangement; terms on application.
🍽 Clubhouse facilities.
Practice range.

4 48 Southwold
The Common, Southwold, Suffolk, IP18 6TB
☎ (01502) 723234, Pro 723790, Sec 723248
From A12 Henham to Blythborough; take A1095 to Southwold.
Links course.
Pro Brian Allen; Founded 1884
Designed by J Braid
9 holes, 6052 yards, S.S.S. 69
† Welcome.
┇ WD £18; WE £20.
🗘 Welcome by arrangement; packages available; terms on application.
🍽 Clubhouse facilities.
Practice range.
🛏 Swan; Crown; Cricketers; Pier Avenue Hotel.

4 49 Sprowston Park
Wroxham Rd, Sprowston, Norwich, Norfolk, NR7 8RP
☎ (01603) 410657, Fax 788884, Pro 417104
On A1551 Norwich to Wroxham road; 10 minutes from city centre.
Parkland course.
Pro G Ireson; I Rollett; Founded 1980
18 holes, 5763 yards, S.S.S. 68
† Welcome.
┇ WD £19; WE £25.
🗘 Welcome by prior arrangement; Full package of golf and catering, including morning coffee, lunch and dinner.
🍽 Full catering facilities.

Practice range, 27 bays; floodlit covered range.
🛏 Sprowston Manor (adjoining course); Maid Head; Norwich; Catton Old Hall.

4 50 Stowmarket
Lower Rd, Onehouse, Stowmarket, Suffolk, IP14 3DA
☎ (01449) 736733, Pro 736392, Sec 736473, Bar/Rest 736473
Course is 2.5 miles south-west of Stowmarket off the B1115 Stowmarket-Bildestone road.
Parkland course.
Pro Duncan Burl; Founded 1962
18 holes, 6107 yards, S.S.S. 69
† Welcome after 9.15 am with handicap certs, except Wed.
┇ WD £23; WE £29
🗘 Welcome Thurs and Fri.
🍽 Full facilities.
Practice range, with 12 bays; four outdoor, eight indoor; two practice grounds.
🛏 Cedars.

4 51 Suffolk Golf & CC ☕
St John's Hill Plantation, Fornham All Saints, Bury St Edmunds, Suffolk, IP28 6JQ
☎ (01284) 706777, Fax 706721
From A14 take B1106 to Fornham.
Parkland course; was Fornham Park; rebuilt course in 1998.
Pro Steven Hall; Founded 1969
18 holes, 6077 yards, S.S.S. 70
† Welcome by prior arrangement.
┇ WD £20; WE £25.
🗘 Welcome WD; packages with golf, catering and leisure on request; terms on application.
🍽 Full clubhouse catering facilities available.
Practice range.

4 52 Swaffham
Cley Rd, Swaffham, Norfolk, PE37 0AF
☎ (01760) 721611
1 mile out of town on Cockley Cley road; signposted in market place.
Heathland course.
Pro Peter Field; Founded 1922
9 holes, 6252 yards, S.S.S. 70
† Welcome WD; with member at WE.
┇ WD £20.
🗘 Welcome WD by arrangement.
🍽 Full catering except Mon and Tues; snacks.
Practice range.
🛏 George.

4 53 Thetford
Brandon Rd, Thetford, Norfolk, IP24 3NE
☎ (01842) 752258, Pro 752662, Sec 752169
Wooded heathland course.
Pro Gary Kitley
Founded 1912
Designed by C.H. Mayo, Donald Steel
18 holes, 6879 yards, S.S.S. 73
† Welcome WD with handicap certs; weekend with member only.
┇ Terms on application.
🗘 Welcome Wed, Thurs, Fri only; packages available; terms on application.
🍽 Full facilities.
🛏 Bell; Thomas Paine; Wereham House.

4 54 Thorpeness
Thorpeness, Nr Aldeburgh, Suffolk, IP16 4NH
☎ (01728) 452176, Fax 453868, Pro 454926
25 miles N of Ipswich on A12; then B1094 to Aldeburgh and then B1069 to Thorpeness.
Heathland course.
Founded 1923
Designed by James Braid
18 holes, 6271 yards, S.S.S. 71
† Welcome if carrying handicap certs.
┇ WD £25; WE £30.
🗘 Welcome; packages available; catering facilities, snooker; lounge, function room; tennis courts; terms on application.
🍽 Restaurant, patio bar, lounge.
Practice range.
🛏 30-room hotel on site; guests have priority tee-times.

4 55 Ufford Park Hotel ☕
Yarmouth Road, Ufford, Woodbridge, Suffolk, IP12 1QW
☎ (01394) 382836, Fax 383582, Pro 382836
Course is two miles N of Woodbridge on the B1438.
Parkland with ponds
Pro S Robertson; Founded 1991
Designed by Phil Pilgrim
18 holes, 6300 yards, S.S.S. 70
† Welcome by arrangement.
┇ WD £20; WE £30.
🗘 Welcome on WD; packages available; leisure facilities inc pool, spa, sauna, gym; terms on application.
🍽 Full facilities.
Practice range, driving nets.
🛏 Ufford Park Hotel on site.

4 56 Waldringfield Heath

Newbourne Road, Waldringfield,
Woodbridge, Suffolk, IP12 4PT
☎(01473) 736426, Pro 736417, Sec
736768
3 miles NE of Ipswich.
Heathland course.
Pro Robin Mann; Founded 1983
Designed by P. Pilgrem
18 holes, 6225 yards, S.S.S. 70
♦ Welcome WD; after 11am WE.
⌞ WD £15; WE £18.
⌁Welcome WD by prior
arrangement; day tickets are available
from £22.50 and £25 on WE.
🍽 Full facilities.
⌁⌐ Marlborough, Ipswich.

4 57 Wensum Valley

Beech Avenue, Taverham, Norwich,
Norfolk, NR8 6HP
☎(01603) 261012, Fax 261664
Take the A1067 Fakenham to
Taverham road.
Parkland course; golf school.
Founded 1989
Designed by B.C. Todd
Valley course: 18 holes, 6172 yards,
S.S.S. 69; 9 holes, 6470 yards, S.S.S.
71
♦ Welcome.
⌞ WD £18; WE £18 (day ticket that
includes a bar meal of up to £5).
⌁Welcome; packages on request;
TV lounge, pool table; bowling green.
Other leisure facilities can be
organised; conference facilities; golfing
breaks available; terms on application.
🍽 Clubhouse facilities; Morton
restaurant; Wensum suite; bars.
Practice range, 8 bays; floodlit.
⌁⌐ Hotel on site.

4 58 Weston Park

Weston Longville, Norwich, Norfolk,
NR9 5JW
☎(01603) 872363, Fax 873040, Pro
872998, Bar/Rest 871842
9 miles NW of Norwich off A1067
Norwich-Fakenham road.
Parkland course.
Pro Michael Few; Founded 1993
Designed by Golf Technology
18 holes, 6603 yards, S.S.S. 72
♦ Welcome.
⌞ WD £25; WE £30.
⌁Welcome with a minimum of 12
players; packages available £25-£45;
group lessons; snooker room;
conference room.
🍽 Full restaurant facilities.
⌁⌐ Lenwade House.

4 59 Woodbridge

Bromeswell Heath, Woodbridge,
Suffolk, IP12 2PF
☎(01394) 382038, Fax 382392, Pro
383213, Bar/Rest 383212
2 miles E of Woodbridge on A1152.
Heathland course.
Pro A Hubert; Founded 1893
Designed by F. Hawtree
27 holes, 6299 yards, S.S.S. 70
♦ Welcome WD with handicap certs;
9-hole course open all week to
visitors.
⌞ WD £32.
⌁Welcome WD by prior
arrangement; maximum 36; packages
available; from £32.
🍽 Restaurant and bar facilities
11am-10pm.
⌁⌐ Crown & Castle, Orford; Melton
Grange, Woodbridge.

5

SOUTH MIDLANDS

Mark James once declared that it was "not fit to hold a Lincolnshire Ladies monthly medal". Yet 15 years on, the Brabazon course at The Belfry is preparing to host its fourth Ryder Cup and has become one of the most famous courses in Britain.

To be fair to James, the Brabazon hardly compares to the venue that so upset him during its early years, when it rather resembled the disused potato field it once was. Now, following an overhaul by designer Dave Thomas, it has evolved into one of the best modern golf courses in Britain. Neighbouring it is another Thomas creation, PGA National, which is also worth playing, and particularly if you are staying at The Belfry on a corporate jolly, and someone else is picking up the stiff green fee.

Golf in Warwickshire has become well-known because of The Belfry but its suitability as a destination to play is certainly not confined to the place. Sutton Coldfield, Moor Hall, Edgbaston, Copt Heath, and Finham Park are all fine destinations. Edgbaston lies just one mile from Birmingham city centre, but don't let that put you off; it is a lovely tree-lined golf course.

Across the border into Worcestershire, Blackwell stands head and shoulders above all other courses in the county, and is one of the finest tests of golf to be found in the Midlands. Moseley is also worthy of note.

Cotswold Hills and the charmingly named Lilley Brook are the most famous courses in Gloucestershire, located to the north and south of Cheltenham respectively, and offering commanding views of the countryside.

Belmont in Herefordshire is a new course that has already acquired a good reputation. It is certainly situated in a beautifully tranquil spot, just south of Hereford, with good use made of a stream that meanders through the attractive grounds.

Bedfordshire is where Henry Longhurst learned to play golf, or more specifically the Bedfordshire GC. John O'Gaunt, however, is perhaps the county's best-known course, possessing 36 excellent holes.

Luffenham Heath is one of England's hidden gems, a resplendent heathland course situated close to the Leicestershire border with Lincolnshire.

For a while Collingtree Park gave golf in Northamptonshire a bad name, which was patently unfair. Remember the debacle over the greens during one British Masters there, when Paul Broadhurst described them as so bad he would not park his car on them?

The underlying problem the pros had, though, was that Collingtree was never designed to be a tournament venue and, seen in its proper guise as a club golfer's retreat, it is perfectly acceptable. The best golf in the county, however, is probably to be found at Church Brampton, or Northamptonshire County as it is more formally known.

Gog Magog holds a similar place in the affections of those who play their golf in Cambridgeshire but Ramsey, St Ives and St Neots will not disappoint. Nor will the Cambridgeshire Moat House Golf Club and Ely City, which meet local needs more than adequately. — **DL**

BEDFORDSHIRE, NORTHAMPTONSHIRE, CAMBRIDGESHIRE, LEICESTERSHIRE

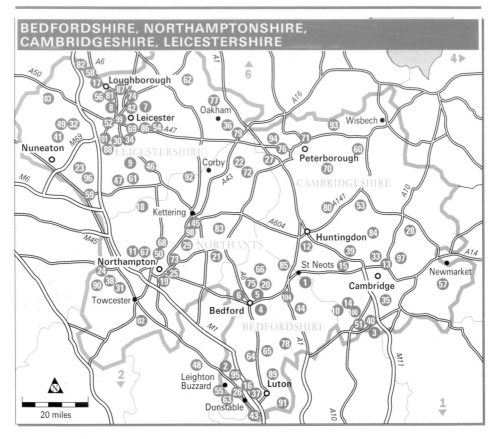

KEY

1	Abbotsley	25	Delapre Park	53	Lakeside Lodge	79	RAF North Luffenham
2	Aspley Guise & Woburn Sands	26	Dunstable Downs	54	Leicestershire	80	Ramsey
3	Barkway Park	27	Elton Furze	55	Leighton Buzzard	81	Rothley Park
4	Beadlow Manor Hotel	28	Ely City	56	Lingdale	82	Rushcliffe
5	Bedford & County	29	Embankment	57	Links	83	Rushden
6	Bedfordshire	30	Enderby	58	Longcliffe	84	St Ives
7	Beedles Lake	31	Farthingstone Hotel G & LC	59	Lutterworth	85	St Neots
8	Birstall	32	Forest Hill	60	March	86	Scraptoft
9	Blaby	33	Girton	61	Market Harborough	87	Shelthorpe
10	Bourn	34	Glen Gorse	62	Melton Mowbray	88	Six Hills
11	Brampton Heath	35	Gog Magog	63	Mentmore	89	South Bedfordshire
12	Brampton Park	36	Greetham Valley	64	Millbrook	90	Staverton Park
13	Cambridge	37	Griffin	65	Mount Pleasant	91	Stockwood Park
14	Cambridge Meridian	38	Hellidon Lakes Hotel and CC	66	Mowsbury	92	Stoke Albany
15	Cambridgeshire Moat House Hotel	39	Hemingford Abbots	67	Northampton	93	Thorney Golf Centre
16	Chalgrave Manor Golf Club	40	Heydon Grange G & CC	68	Northamptonshire County	94	Thorpe Wood
17	Charnwood Forest	41	Hinckley	69	Oadby	95	Tilsworth
18	Cold Ashby	42	Humberstone Heights	70	Old Nene Golf & Country Club	96	Ullesthorpe
19	Collingtree Park	43	Ivinghoe	71	Orton Meadows	97	Waterbeach Barracks
20	Colmworth & N Beds	44	John O'Gaunt	72	Oundle	98	Wellingborough
21	Colworth	45	Kettering	73	Overstone Park	99	Western Park
22	Corby	46	Kibworth	74	Park Hill	100	Whaddon Golf Centre
23	Cosby	47	Kilworth Springs	75	Pavenham Park	101	Whetstone
24	Daventry & District	48	Kingfisher CC	76	Peterborough Milton	102	Whittlebury Park Golf & Country Club
		49	Kingstand	77	RAF Cottesmore	103	Willesley Park
		50	Kingsthorpe	78	RAF Henlow	104	Wyboston Lakes
		51	Kingsway				
		52	Kirby Muxloe				

5A 1 Abbotsley Golf Hotel and CC

Eynesbury Hardwicke, St Neots, Cambs, PE19 4XN
Operated by American Golf UK Ltd
☎ (01480) 474000, Abbotsley Pro 477669, Cromwell Pro 215153
2 miles SE of St Neots leaving A428 at Tesco roundabout.
Parkland course.
Golf Operations manager Tim Hudson; Founded 1976 (Abbotsley), Founded 1989 (Cromwell)
Designed by Derek Young, Vivien Saunders, Jenny Wisson
Abbotsley: 18 holes, 6311 yards, S.S.S. 72; Cromwell: 18 holes, 6087 yards, S.S.S. 69
♦ Welcome; restrictions at WE (Abbotsley); 7-day bookings availability for tee times.
⌊ Terms on application.
⌐♢ Welcome by prior arrangement; packages available; tailored to suit individual needs, prices on request; residential packages; residential golf schools: Denise Hastings and Vivian Saunders.
⦿ The Garden restaurant and choice of bars.
21-bay floodlit driving range; 300-yard grass driving range; 9-hole par 3 course; health club; 4 squash courts.
⌐ Hotel on site; 40 well-appointed, en suite bedrooms.

5A 2 Aspley Guise & Woburn Sands

West Hill, Aspley Guise, MK17 8DX
☎ (01908) 583596, Fax 583596, Pro 582974, Sec 583596
2 miles W of M1 Junction 13 between Aspley Guise and Woburn Sands.
Undulating parkland course.
Pro David Marsden; Founded 1914
Designed by Sandy Herd
18 holes, 6079 yards, S.S.S. 70
♦ Welcome WD; WE as member's guest.
⌊ WD £35.
⌐♢ Welcome Wed and Fri; April to October; catering and golf packages available; from £49.50 for an all day package.
⦿ Full catering facilities; limited Mons.

5A 3 Barkway Park

Nuthampstead Rd, Barkway, Nr Royston, Herts, SG8 8EN
☎ (01763) 848215 Pro 849070
On B1368 5 miles S of Royston.
Gently undulating links course.

Founded 1992
Pro Jamie Bates; Designed by Vivien Saunders
18 holes, 6997 yards, S.S.S. 74
♦ Welcome; WE tee times cannot be booked until Fri pm.
⌊ WD £10; WE £15.
⌐♢ Welcome by prior arrangement; packages available; function room; pool table and darts; terms on application.
⦿ Full facilities
Practice area.
⌐ Vintage Puckeridge; Flintcroft Motel.

5A 4 Beadlow Manor Hotel

Beadlow, Nr Shefford, Beds, SG17 5PH
☎ (01525) 860800, Fax 861345, Pro 861202
✉ beadlow@kbnet.co.uk
On the A507 between Ampthill and Shefford; 1.5 miles W of Shefford.
Parkland course.
Pro G Dixon; Adrienne Engelmann; Founded 1973
Baron Manhattan: 18 holes, 6619 yards, S.S.S. 72; Baroness Manhattan: 18 holes, 6072 yards, S.S.S. 69
♦ Welcome.
⌊ Terms on application.
⌐♢ Welcome by prior arrangement; several golf and catering packages available; health club; conference rooms; terms on application.
⦿ Bar, restaurants.
Practice range, 25 bays floodlit; buggies and clubs for hire.
⌐ 33-room hotel on site.

5A 5 Bedford & County

Green Lane, Clapham, Beds, MK41 6ET
☎ (01234) 352617, Fax 357195, Pro 359189, Sec 352617, Bar 354010
Off the A6 N of Bedford before Clapham village.
Parkland course.
Pro Roger Tattersall; Founded 1912
18 holes, 6399 yards, S.S.S. 70
♦ Welcome WD; with a member at WE.
⌊ WD £24.
⌐♢ Welcome WD except Wed; all day golf packages available; from £50.
⦿ Full facilities.
⌐ Woodlands Manor.

5A 6 Bedfordshire

Bromham Rd, Biddenham, Bedford, MK40 4AF

☎ (01234) 261669, Fax 261669, Pro 353653, Bar/Rest 353241
1.5 miles W of Bedford on A428 Northampton road.
Flattish parkland course.
Pro Peter Sanders; Founded 1891
Designed by Tom Dunn
18 holes, 6305 yards, S.S.S. 70
♦ Welcome WD; as members' guests at WE.
⌊ WD £24-£28.
⌐♢ Welcome WD; full clubhouse facilities; green fee plus catering. Moving Sept 2000, upgraded facilities.
⦿ Full clubhouse facilities.
⌐ Shakespeare; Swan; Moat House.

5A 7 Beedles Lake

Broome Lane, East Goscote, Leics, LE7 3NQ
☎ (0116) 2606759, Bar/Rest 2607086
Between A46 Leicester-Newark road and A607 Leicester-Melton Mowbray.
Parkland course.
Pro Sean Bryne; Founded 1993
Designed by D Tucker
18 holes, 6625 yards, S.S.S. 71
♦ Welcome at all times.
⌊ WD £9; WE £12.
⌐♢ Welcome any time; terms on application.
⦿ Clubhouse facilities.
Practice range, 17 bays.

5A 8 Birstall

Station Rd, Birstall, Leicester, LE4 3BB
☎ (0116) 2674322, Fax 2674322 Pro 2675245
Off A6 3 miles N of town.
Parkland course.
Pro David Clarke; Founded 1901
18 holes, 6222 yards, S.S.S. 70
♦ Welcome except WE.
⌊ WD £25-£30.
⌐♢ Welcome Wed and Fri by prior arrangement; reductions for groups of more than 20; snooker; billiards; prices on application.
⦿ Full facilities except Mon.
⌐ The Stakis Hotel; The Grand.

5A 9 Blaby

Lutterworth Rd, Blaby, Leics, LE8 3DP
☎ (0116) 2784804
From Leicester through Blaby village; course on the left-hand side.
Parkland course.

Founded 1991
9 holes, 5312 yards, par 68, S.S.S. 68
♦ Welcome; pay and play.
⌊ WD and WE 9 holes £4, 18 holes £6.
⤳Welcome; special company days available; terms on application.
🍽 Bar and bar meals.
Practice range, 27 floodlit bays; crazy golf course.

5A 10 **Bourn**
Toft Rd, Bourn, Cambridge, CB3 7TT
☎(01954) 718057, Fax 718908, Pro 718958, Sec 718088
6 miles W of Cambridge off A14 through Bourn village.
Parkland course.
Pro Craig Watson; Founded 1991
Designed by J. Hull and S. Bonham
18 holes, 6417 yards, S.S.S. 71
♦ Welcome.
⌊ WD £16; WE £22.
⤳Welcome; full clubhouse facilities; terms on application.
Practice area, bring own balls; buggies for hire.
🍽 Clubhouse facilities.
⤳ Many in Cambridge.

5A 11 **Brampton Heath**
Sandy Lane, Church Brampton, Northants, NN6 8AX
☎(01604) 843939, Fax 843885
⤳_slawrence@bhgc.co.uk_
3 miles N of Northampton just off A5119.
Undulating heathland course.
Pro R Hudson; Founded 1995
Designed by D Snell
18 holes, 6366 yards, S.S.S. 70
♦ Welcome at all times.
⌊ WD £12; WE £16.
⤳Welcome WD and WE; packages from only £14 arranged to suit.
PGA-approved short course; driving range.
🍽 Full facilities.

5A 12 **Brampton Park** ℭ
Buckden Rd, Brampton, Huntingdon, Cambs, PE18 8NF
☎(01480) 434700, Fax 411145, Pro 434705
Take A1 or A14 to RAF Brampton; club is opposite airbase.
Meadowland course.
Pro A Currie; Founded 1991
Designed by Simon Gidman (Hawtree & Sons)
18 holes, 6403 yards, S.S.S. 73

♦ Welcome.
⌊ Winter: WD £15, WE £35; Summer: WD £25, WE £35.
⤳Welcome WD; function room; practice area; trolleys for hire; full facilities; from £29.75.
🍽 Clubhouse facilities.
⤳ Limited accommodation on site.

5A 13 **Cambridge**
Station Road, Longstanton, Cambs, CB4 5DR
☎(01954) 789388, 01223 207325
10 mins N of Cambridge on B1050 off A14.
Parkland course.
Pro G Huggett; Founded 1992
Designed by G Huggett
18 holes, 6736 yards, S.S.S. 74
♦ Welcome.
⌊ WD £9; WE £12.
⤳Welcome at all times; various packages and reductions available; terms on application.
🍽 Full clubhouse facilities.

5A 14 **Cambridge Meridian** ℭ
Comberton Road, Toft, Cambs, CB3 7RY
☎(01223) 264700, Fax 264701, Pro 264702
On B1046 at Toft 3 miles W of M11 Junction 12.
Parkland course.
Pro Michael Clemons; Founded 1994
Designed by P Alliss/C Clark
18 holes, 6651 yards, S.S.S. 72
♦ Welcome with telephone booking.
⌊ WD before 9am £25 after 9 £14; WE before 9 £30, after £18.
⤳Welcome WD and after 1pm WE; max 24; range of packages available; £19-£49.
🍽 Full clubhouse catering facilities.
Practice range, large practice facilities.
⤳ University Arms Hotel; Abbotsley Golf Hotel.

5A 15 **Cambridgeshire** ℭ **Moat House Hotel**
Bar Hill, Cambridge, Cambs, CB3 8EU
☎(01954) 780098, Fax 780010, Sec 249971, Bar/Rest 249988,
🖥 _www.cambridgeshiregolf.co.uk_
On A14 5 miles N of Cambridge.
Parkland course.
Pro Paul Simpson; Founded 1974
Designed by F Middleton
18 holes, 6734 yards, S.S.S. 72
♦ Welcome.

⌊ WD £20; WE £30.
⤳Welcome; day packages can be organised; terms on application.
🍽 Full hotel and clubhouse facilities. Practice area, buggies and clubs for hire; group tuition available.
⤳ Cambridgeshire Moat House, 134 en suite rooms; just undergone a four million pound refurbishment.

5A 16 **Chalgrave Manor**
Dunstable Road, Chalgrave, Toddington, Bedfordshire, LU5 6JN
☎(01525) 876556, Fax 876556, Pro 876554
2 miles W of M1 Junction 12 on A5120 between Toddington and Houghton.
Undulating parkland course.
Pro Terry Bunyan; Founded 1994
18 holes, 6022 yards, S.S.S. 72
♦ Welcome.
⌊ WD £15; WE £30.
⤳Welcome midweek; full golf and catering packages can be arranged; £21-£37.
🍽 Full catering facilities.

5A 17 **Charnwood Forest**
Breakback Rd, Woodhouse Eaves, Loughborough, Leics, LE12 8TA
☎(01509) 890259, Fax 890925
Close to M1 Junctions 22/23.
Heathland course with heather, gorse and bracken.
Founded 1890
Designed by James Braid
9 holes, 5960 yards, S.S.S. 69
♦ Welcome.
⌊ WD £15; WE £25.
⤳Welcome Wed, Thurs and Fri; full catering package plus 27 holes of golf £33.50.
🍽 Full catering facilities; limited catering Mon.
⤳ Friendly Hotel.

5A 18 **Cold Ashby**
Stanford Road, Cold Ashby, Northampton, NN6 6EP
☎(01604) 740548, Fax 740548, Pro 740099,
⤳ _coldashby.golfclub@virgin.net_
11 miles N of Northampton near A5199/A14 junction 1.
Undulating parkland course with spectacular views.
Pro Shane Rose; Founded 1974
Designed by John Day; Extension by D Croxton 1995
27 holes, 6308 yards, S.S.S. 70
♦ Welcome; some WE restrictions.

WD £14; WE £16.

☞ Welcome any day by prior arrangement; full day's golf and catering packages available; 27-hole course; 3 loops of 9; Winwick/Ashby par 70; Ashby/ Elkington par 72; Elkington/Winwick par 70; dining room facilities; £37.

🍽 Full clubhouse facilities. Extensive practice area, buggies and clubs for hire.

🛏 Pytchley, W Haddon; Post House, Crick; Broomhill, Spratton.

5A 19 **Collingtree Park** ☏

Windingbrook Lane, Northampton, Northamptonshire, NN4 0XN
☎ (01604) 700000, Fax 702600, Pro 701202
M1 Junction 15 just past Stakis Hotel. Championship course; owned by European PGA.
Pro Henry Bareham; Geoff Pook; Founded 1990
Designed by Johnny Miller
18 holes, 6908 yards, S.S.S. 73
† Welcome with 7-day advance booking; handicap certs required.
☐ WD £30; WE £40.
☞ Welcome with prior arrangement; full clubhouse facilities and driving range and practice ground; terms on application.
🍽 Full facilities in clubhouse.
🛏 Stakis Hotel; Swallow Hotel; Midway Hotel.

5A 20 **Colmworth & N Beds**

Mill Cottage, New Rd, Colmworth, Beds, MK44 2NU
☎ (01234) 378181, Fax 376235, Pro 378822, Sec 378181, Bar/Rest 378181
From Bedford just off B660.
Links style course.
Founded 1991
Designed by John Glasgow
18 holes, 6435 yards, S.S.S. 71
† Welcome after 9.30am WD and with booking at WE.
☐ WD £10; WE £17.
☞ Welcome every day; packages can be arranged; restaurant facilities all day; terms on application.
🍽 Full restaurant and bar. Driving range, putting green.

5A 21 **Colworth**

Unilever Research, Colworth House, Sharnbrook, Bedford, MK44 1LQ
☎ (01234) 781781
10 miles N of Bedford off A6 through village of Shambrook.
Parkland course.
Founded 1985
9 holes, 5000 yards, S.S.S. 64
† Private members only.
☐ Terms on application.

5A 22 **Corby**

Stamford Rd, Weldon
☎ (01536) 260756, Fax 260756
A43 Corby to Stamford road 2 miles E of Weldon.
Parkland course.
Pro Jeff Bradbrook; Founded 1965
18 holes, 6677 yards, S.S.S. 72
† Welcome.
☐ WD £9.35; WE £12.00.
☞ Welcome anytime; large golf shop; packages for golf and catering available; from £9.35.
🍽 Snacks and meals available.
🛏 Stakis.

5A 23 **Cosby** ☏

Chapel Lane, off Broughton Rd, Cosby, Leics, LE9 1RG
☎ (0116) 2864759, Fax 2864484, Pro 2848275
From M1 Junction 21 take B4114 for 3 miles until Cosby turning.
Parkland course.
Pro Martin Wing; Founded 1895
Designed by C Sinclair
18 holes, 6410 yards, S.S.S. 71
† Welcome midweek; members guest only at WE.
☐ WD £18.
☞ Welcome, maximum 80 with prior arrangement; various packages available; £34-£37.
🍽 Full clubhouse bar and catering facilities.
Practice range, practice ground.
🛏 Stakis, Leicester; Mill on the Soar, Broughton Astley.

5A 24 **Daventry & District**

Norton Rd, Daventry, Northants, NN11 5LS
☎ (01327) 702829
1 mile N of the town next to the BBC station.
Undulating meadowland course.
Founded 1922
9 holes, 5812 yards, S.S.S. 68
† Welcome; except before 11am Sun.
☐ WD £10; WE £15.
☞ Welcome by prior arrangement with the Sec; packages by arrangement; discounts for more than 16 players; terms on application.

🍽 Bar and restaurant.
🛏 Britannia; Hanover.

5A 25 **Delapre Park**

Eagle Drive, None Valley Way, Northampton, NN4 7DU
☎ (01604) 764036, Fax 706378 , Sec 763957
M1 Junction 15 then 4 miles on A45.
Parkland course course; also has 9 hole Hardingstone course.
Pro J Corby/J Cuddihy; Founded 1976
Designed by J. Jacobs/ J. Corby
The Delapre: 18 holes, 6299 yards, S.S.S. 70; The Hardingstone: 9 holes, 2109 yards, par 32.
† Welcome at all times.
☐ WD 9 holes £6.50, 18 holes £9.50; WE 9 holes £8, 18 holes £13.
☞ Welcome one per day but also welcome WE; packages can be arranged; terms on application.
🍽 Full clubhouse catering and bar facilities.
Practice range, 40-bays floodlit range; also grass tees; two par 3 courses; pitch and putt course; senior PGA professional tutor; three teaching professionals; club hire available.
🛏 Swallow; Stakis; Northampton Moat House; Courtyard by Marriott.

5A 26 **Dunstable Downs**

Whipsnade Rd, Dunstable, Beds, LU6 2NB
☎ (01582) 604472, Fax 478700, Pro 662806
2 miles from Dunstable on Whipsnade road B4541.
Downland course.
Pro M Weldon; Founded 1907
Designed by James Braid
18 holes, 6251 yards, S.S.S. 70
† Welcome WD; members guests at WE.
☐ WD £23.50.
☞ Welcome WD except Wed, full golf and catering package including lunch and dinner; half-day packages also available; £40-£55.
🍽 Full clubhouse facilities.
🛏 Old Palace Lodge; Hertfordshire Moat House.

5A 27 **Elton Furze** ☏

Bullock Rd, Haddon, Peterborough, Cambs, PE7 3TT
☎ (01832) 280189, Fax 280299, Pro 280614
4 miles W of Peterborough on old

A606; leaving A1 at the Alwalton/Showground exit.
Parkland course.
Pro Frank Kiddie; Founded 1993
Designed by Roger Fitton
18 holes, 6279 yards, S.S.S. 71
♣ Welcome by prior arrangement; handicap certs preferred; dress codes apply.
⌊ WD £22; WE £32.
⌃Welcome by prior arrangement with the secretary WD; golf and catering packages available; terms on application.
◉ Full facilities.
Practice range, practice ground; 4 bays; buggies for hire; tuition available.
↵ Swallow, Peterborough.

5A 28 Ely City ♘
Cambridge Rd, Ely, Cambs, CB7 4HX
☎(01353) 662751, Fax 668636, Pro 663317, Bar/Rest 661966,
≞ elygolf@line.net
1 mile S of City Centre on old A10.
Parkland course.
Pro Andrew George; Founded 1961
Designed by Henry Cotton
18 holes, 6627 yards, S.S.S. 72
♣ Welcome with handicap certs.
⌊ WD £28; WE £34.
⌃Welcome Tues-Fri in official organised groups; full packages available; also practice area; snooker; terms on application.
Practice area; tuition available.
◉ Full bar and restaurant facilities.
↵ Nyton Hotel; Lamb Hotel.

5A 29 Embankment
The Embankment, Wellingborough, Northants, NN8 1LD
☎(01933) 228465
In the Embankment area of the city alongside the river.
Parkland course.
Founded 1977
9 holes, 3562 yards, S.S.S. 57
♣ Welcome with members only.
⌊ WD and WE £4.
⌃None.
◉ Bar and limited food.

5A 30 Enderby
Mill Lane, Enderby, Leics, LE9 5LH
☎(0116) 2849388, Fax 284388
From M1 Junction 21 to Enderby and then follow the signs to Leisure Centre.
Municipal heathland course.
Pro Richard Allen; Founded 1986

9 holes, 4212 yards, S.S.S. 61
♣ Welcome.
⌊ WD 9 holes £4.95, 18 holes £5.95; WE 9 holes £5.95, 18 holes £7.95.
⌃Welcome by arrangement.
◉ Bar and bar snacks.
↵ The Stakis

5A 31 Farthingstone Hotel Golf & LC
Farthingstone, Towcester, Northants, NN12 8HA
☎(01327) 361291, Fax 361645, Pro 361533, Bar/Rest 361560
M1 Junction 16; take signs to Weedon, then Everdon and Farthingstone.
Parkland course.
Founded 1972
Designed by M. Gallagher
18 holes, 6299 yards, S.S.S. 70
♣ Welcome at all times.
⌊ WD £16; WE £20.
⌃Welcome any time by prior arrangement; packages available; also pool and snooker tables; squash court; hotel facilities; terms on application.
◉ Full bar, restaurant and hotel facilities.
Practice range and nets; buggies and buggies for hire.
↵ Farthingstone 16 en-suite twin-bedded rooms.

5A 32 Forest Hill
Markfield Lane, Botcheston, Leics, LE9 9FJ
☎(01455) 824800, Fax 828522
2 miles from Botcheston; 3 miles SW of the A50.
Well-wooded parkland course.
Pro Philip Harness; Founded 1991/1995
18 holes, 6039 yards, S.S.S. 69
♣ Welcome.
⌊ WD £15; WE £20.
⌃Welcome WD by arrangement; packages for golf and catering available; terms on application.
◉ Bar; restaurant and function room.
Practice range, 20 bays floodlit; electric trolleys and clubs for hire; tuition available.
↵ Forest Lodge.

5A 33 Girton
Dodford Lane, Girton, Cambs, CB3 0QE
☎(01223) 276169, Fax 277150, Pro 276991

Course is three miles N of Cambridge on the A604.
Flat open course.
Pro Scott Thomson; Founded 1936
18 holes, 6080 yards, S.S.S. 69
♣ Welcome WD; with member at WE.
⌊ WD £16.
⌃Welcome Tues-Fri by prior arrangement; packages available; terms on application.
◉ Lunches and dinners served except Mon.
↵ Post House, Impington.

5A 34 Glen Gorse
Glen Rd, Oadby, Leicester, LE2 4RF
☎(0116) 2712226, Fax 2714159, Pro 2713748, Sec 2714159, Bar/Rest 2718875
On A6 Leicester- Market Harborough road between Oadby and Great Glen, 5 miles S of Leicester.
Parkland course.
Pro Dominic Fitzpatrick; Founded 1933
18 holes, 6648 yards, S.S.S. 72
♣ Welcome WD by arrangement; WE with member.
⌊ WD £24; WE £8.50 with member.
⌃Tues-Fri by arrangement with secretary; full golf and catering facilities; terms on application.
Practice area; tuition available.
◉ Full catering facilities.
↵ Hermitage, Oadby.

5A 35 Gog Magog
Shelford Bottom, Cambridge, Cambs, CB2 4AB
☎(01223) 247626, Fax 414990, Pro 246058
On A1307 5 miles from Cambridge.
Chalkdownland course.
Pro Ian Bamborough; Founded 1901
Designed by Hawtree
Old course: 18 holes, 6398 yards, S.S.S. 70; Wandlebury course:18 holes, 6754 yards, S.S.S. 72
♣ Welcome WD; booking required Wed.
⌊ WD £35; WE £35.
⌃Welcome WD Tues and Thurs; full day's golf and catering package; prices on application.
◉ Full clubhouse facilities available.
↵ Duxford Lodge, Duxford; many in Cambridge.

5A 36 Greetham Valley ♘
Wood Lane, Greetham, Oakham, Leics, LE15 7NP

☎(01780) 460004, Fax 460623, Pro 460666, Bar/Rest 460444
✉ gvgc@rutnet.co.uk
1 mile from A1 off the B668, signposted Greetham.
Parkland courses with water.
Two 18-hole courses: 'Lakes' Course: 6779 yards, par 72; 'Valley' Course: 5595 yards, par 68
Pro John Pengelly; Founded 1991
Designed by Ben Stevens Course Design
† Welcome.
▌ 18 holes: WD £24, WE £28; 36 holes: WD £32, WE £35.
♢Welcome WD in groups of 10 or more.
🍽 Full restaurant and bar facilities.
Driving range, Par 3 and golf video academy; 20 EZGO buggies available only £12 per round.
↙ Barnsdale Lodge; Barnsdale CC; Hambleton Hall; Stapleford Park.

5A 37 Griffin
Chaul End Rd, Caddington, Luton, Beds, LU1 4AX
☎(01582) 415573, Fax 415314
10 mins from M1 Junction 9 or 11 via A5 or A5056.
Parkland course.
Founded 1982
18 holes, 6240 yards, S.S.S. 70
† Welcome WD after 9am; by arrangement at WE.
▌ WD £12; Fri £14; WE £17.
♢Welcome WD; packages can be arranged for full day's catering and golf; from £29.
🍽 Full catering facilities.

5A 38 Hellidon Lakes Hotel and Country Club ☎
Hellidon, Nr Daventry, Northants, NN11 6LN
☎(01327) 262550, Fax 262559, Pro 262551.
▤ www.hellidon.demon.co.uk
✉ stay@hellidon.demon.co.uk
15 miles from M1 Junction 16 by A45 and A361 Banbury road; turn right before village of Charwelton.
Undulating parkland course.
Pro Gary Wills; Founded 1991
Designed by David Snell
Two courses: 18 holes, 6587 yards, S.S.S. 72; 9 hole course, 2791 yards, par 35.
† Welcome; handicap certs needed WE.
▌ WD £15; WE £25.
♢Welcome by arrangement; packages available through the hotel;

conference facilities can be arranged; fly fishing; tennis; health studio; swimming pool; 4-lane tenpin bowling alley; smart golf simulator; terms on application.
🍽 Full bar and restaurant facilities:
The Lakes Restaurant, The Four Seasons open Fri-Sat evenings; fine dine; The Brunswick Bar.
Practice range, 14 bays; buggies and clubs for hire; tuition available with prior arrangement.
↙ 4-star hotel on site.

5A 39 Hemingford Abbots ☎
Cambridge Rd, Hemingford Abbots, Cambs, PE18 9HQ
☎(01480) 495000, Fax 496000,
▤ astroman8.co.uk
✉ ray/george@astroman8.freeserve.co.uk
Alongside A604 between Huntingdon and St Ives.
Public parkland.
Founded 1991
Designed by Advanced Golf Services
18 holes, 5414 yards, S.S.S. 68
† Welcome.
▌ WD £12.50; WE £17.
♢Small groups welcome by prior arrangement.
🍽 Full catering facilities; bar and restaurant.
Practice range; clubs for hire; tuition available.
↙ St Ives; The Bridge.

5A 40 Heydon Grange Golf & Country Club
Heydon, Royston, Herts, SG8 7NS
☎(01763) 208988, Fax 208926,
✉ heydon-grange@compuserve.com
Leave the M11 at Junction 10 on to the A505 towards Royston; take third left to Heydon.
Downland/parkland courses with lakes.
Pro Stuart Smith; Founded 1994
Designed by Alan Walker
Cambs/Essex: 18 holes, 6336 yards, S.S.S. 71; Cambs/Herts:18 holes, 6503 yards, S.S.S. 72; Herts/Essex:18 holes, 6193 yards, S.S.S. 71
† Welcome; book in advance.
▌ Winter: 18 holes + food WD £12.50; WE £17.50. Summer: 18 holes WD £15; WE £20.
♢Welcome by prior arrangement; company days arranged; packages available; conferences and functions available; terms on application.

🍽 Lounge, cocktail and wine bar; restaurants; carvery on Sun; full Indian menu.
Practice range and practice ground; Buggies and clubs for hire; tuition available .

5A 41 Hinckley⬦ ☎
Leicester Rd, Hinckley, Leics, LE10 3DR
☎(01455) 615124, Fax 890841, Pro 615014,
▤ hinckleygolfclub.com
✉ proshop@hinckleygolfclub
From Hinckley Town Centre follow signs for Earl Shilton.
Lakeside parkland course; (Burbage Green until 1983).
Pro Richard Jones; Founded 1894/1993
Designed by Southeren Golf
18 holes, 6517 yards, S.S.S. 71
† Welcome WD; members of guests WE.
▌ WD £25; WE £30.
♢Welcome WD with handicap certs; packages available; terms on application.
🍽 Full catering facilities.
↙ Sketchley Grange.

5A 42 Humberstone Heights
Gipsy Lane, Leicester, Leics, LE5 0TB
☎(0116) 27619805, Fax 299569, Pro 2995570, Bar/Rest 2761905
Off Uppingham Road opposite Towers Hospital.
Parkland course.
Pro Philip Highfield; Founded 1978
Designed by Hawtree & Son
18 holes, 6343 yards, S.S.S. 70
† Pay and play.
▌ Winter WD £7.99; WE £9.99; Summer WD £8.99 WE £10.99.
♢Terms on application.
🍽 Clubhouse facilities.
Practice range, 30 bays; buggies and clubs for hire; tuition available; 9-hole par 3 course.
↙ City-centre hotels in Leicester.

5A 43 Ivinghoe
Wellcroft, Ivinghoe, Leighton Buzzard, Beds, LU7 9EF
☎(01296) 668696, Fax 662755, Bar/Rest 661186
4 miles from Tring and 6 miles from Dunstable behind the Kings Head in Ivinghoe village.
Meadowland course.
Pro Bill Garrad; Founded 1967

Designed by R. Garrad & Sons
9 holes, 4508 yards, S.S.S. 62
♦ Welcome after 9am WD; after 8am WE.
⌣ WD £8; WE £9.
⌣ Welcome WD by prior arrangement; includes 36 holes of golf; coffee; light lunch and evening meal; from £22.
◉ Full facilities except Mon.
Tuition available.
⌐ Rose & Crown, Tring; Stocks, Aldbury.

5A 44 John O'Gaunt

Sutton Park, Sandy, Beds, SG19 2LY
☎(01767) 260360, Fax 262834, Pro 260094, Sec 260360, Bar/Rest 261469
Between Biggleswade and Potten on B1040.
Parkland course.
Pro Peter Round; Founded 1948
Designed by Hawtree
Carthagena: 18 holes, 5869 yards, S.S.S. 69; The John O'Gaunt: 18 holes, 6513 yards, S.S.S. 71
♦ Welcome with handicap certs and by prior arrangement.
⌣ WD £45; WE £50.
⌣ Welcome WD by prior arrangement through administrators office; packages for catering and green fees on application; terms on application.
◉ Full clubhouse catering.
Tuition available through pro; buggies for hire.
⌐ Holiday Inn; Stratton House, Biggleswade; Rose & Crown, Potten.

5A 45 Kettering

Headlands, Kettering, Northants, NN15 6XA
☎(01536) 511104, Fax 511104, Pro 481014, Bar/Rest 512074
S of Kettering, adjacent to A14.
Parkland course.
Pro K Theobald; Founded 1891
Designed by Tom Morris
18 holes, 6081 yards, S.S.S. 69
♦ Welcome WD; with member at WE.
⌣ WD £15-£22.
⌣ Welcome Wed and Fri; full catering and golf packages; from £40.
◉ Full clubhouse facilities.
⌐ Kettering Park; George; Royal.

5A 46 Kibworth

Weir Rd, Kibworth, Beauchamp, Leics, LE8 0LP

☎(0116) 2796172, Fax 2792301, Pro 2792283, Sec 2792301, Bar/Rest 2796172
Course is 10 miles south of Leicester off the A6.
Flat woodland/parkland course.
Pro Bob Larratt; Founded 1904/62
18 holes, 6338 yards, S.S.S. 70
♦ Welcome WD; WE with a member.
⌣ WD £22-£30.
⌣ Welcome by arrangement; golf and catering available; from £20.
◉ Full catering facilities.
Practice grass range; trolleys for hire; tuition available from PGA qualified professsional.
⌐ Angel, Market Harborough.

5A 47 Kilworth Springs

North Kilworth, Lutterworth, Leics, LE17 6HJ
☎(01858) 575974, Fax 575078, Sec 575082
Course is five miles from the M1 Junction 20.
Front 9: Inland links; back 9: Parkland.
Pro Anders Mankert; Founded 1993
Designed by Ray Baldwin
18 holes, 6718 yards, S.S.S. 72
♦ Welcome.
⌣ WD £17; WE £21.
⌣ Welcome WD and after 12 at WE; catering and golf packages; bar, spike bar, private 36-seat boardroom, restaurant, driving range; prices on application.
◉ Full clubhouse bar, spikes bar and restaurant facilities.
Practice range, sunken range with specialised short game areas; buggies and clubs for hire; tuition available.
⌐ Club can supply list.

5A 48 Kingfisher CC

Buckingham Rd, Deanshanger, Northants, MK19 6DG
☎(01908) 562332, Fax 260557, Sec 560354
Course is on the A422 Buckingham road seven miles from Milton Keynes opposite the village of Deanshanger.
Parkland course with lake features.
Pro Brian Mudge; Founded 1994
9 holes, 5066 yards, S.S.S. 65
♦ Welcome; pay and play.
⌣ WD 9 holes £6.50, 18 holes £10; WE 9 holes £9, 18 holes £13.
⌣ Welcome by prior arrangement; corporate days organised; fishing; model steam railway; function room; terms on application.

◉ Full facilities; 2 restaurants and 2 bars.
Practice range, 10 bays.
⌐ Shires.

5A 49 Kingstand

Beggars Lane, Leicester Forest East, Leicester, LE3 3NQ
☎(0116) 2387908, Fax 2388087
Off main A47 Hinckley road; 5 mins from M1 Junction 21.
Parkland course.
Pro Simon Sherrit; Founded 1991
Designed by S. Chenia
9 holes, 5380 yards, S.S.S. 66
♦ Welcome.
⌣ WD £9; WE £10.
⌣ Welcome by prior arrangement with the professional; packages and discounts available; gymnasium.
◉ Indian restaurant on site.
Practice range, 16 bays floodlit.
⌐ Red Cow.

5A 50 Kingsthorpe

Kingsley Rd, Kingsley, Northampton, NN2 7BU
☎(01604) 719602, Fax 719602, Sec 710610, Bar/Rest 711173
Off A508 2 miles N of Northampton town centre.
Parkland course.
Pro Paul Armstrong; Founded 1908
Designed by Charles Alison
18 holes, 5918 yards, S.S.S. 69
♦ Welcome with handicap certs.
⌣ WD £25; WE £25.
⌣ Welcome; catering facilities and golf packages available; from £20.
◉ Clubhouse catering facilities available.
⌐ Westone Hotel; Broom Hill.

5A 51 Kingsway

Cambridge Rd, Melbourne, Royston, Herts, SG8 6EY
☎(01763) 262727, Fax 263298, Pro 262727
On A10 N of Royston.
Landscaped farmland course.
Pro Mark Sturgess; Founded 1991
9 holes, 4910 yards, S.S.S. 64
♦ Welcome.
⌣ WD £8 (18 holes); WE £11 (18 holes).
⌣ Welcome by prior arrangement; corporate days arranged; 9-hole pitch and putt; terms on application.
◉ Bar and restaurant facilities.
Practice range, 36 bays floodlit; crazy golf.
⌐ Sheene Mill Hotel.

5A 52 Kirby Muxloe
Station Rd, Kirby Muxloe, Leicester,
LE9 9EN
☎ (0116) 2393457, Fax 2393457,
Pro 2392813, Bar/Rest 2396577
From M1 Junction 21a follow signs to
Kirby Muxloe.
Parkland course.
Pro Bruce Whipham, Founded 1893
18 holes, 6279 yards, S.S.S. 70
† Welcome Mon, Wed and Fri.
⌣ £25.
⌣ Welcome with handicap certs only;
all day and individual round packages
available; from £37.
🍽 Full clubhouse catering facilities.
↝ Travel Inn; Red Cow.

5A 53 Lakeside Lodge
Fen Road, Pidley, Huntingdon,
Cambs, PE17 3DD
☎ (01487) 740540, Fax 740852, Pro
741541, Bar/Rest 740968
From A14 Cambridge-St Ives road
take B1040 to Pidley.
Open parkland with 8 lakes and
15,000 trees.
Pro Scott Waterman; Founded 1991
Designed by Alister Headley
The Lodge course: 18 holes, 6865
yards, S.S.S 73; The Manor course: 9
holes, 2601 yards, S.S.S. 33.
† Welcome any time.
⌣ The Lodge course: WD £11, WE
£17; The Manor course: WD £6, WE
£8.
⌣ Welcome any time; golf, catering
and other corporate activities can be
arranged (ten pin bowling); terms on
application.
🍽 Full catering facilities.
Floodlit covered driving range,
buggies for hire, 9-hole pitch and putt
course; tuition available.
↝ On-site accomodation, 5 en suite
twin rooms.

5A 54 Leicestershire
Evington Lane, Leicester, Leicester,
LE5 6DJ
☎ (0116) 2738825, Fax 2738825,
Pro 2736730, Bar/Rest 2731307
2 miles E of Leicester.
Parkland course course; no par 5s.
Pro Darren Jones; Founded 1890
Designed by James Braid
18 holes, 6326 yards, S.S.S. 70
† Welcome with handicap certs and
prior arrangement.
⌣ WD £24; WE £30.
⌣ Welcome with handicap certs;
packages can be arranged; terms on
application.

🍽 Full clubhouse facilities.
↝ Gables Hotel.

5A 55 Leighton Buzzard
Plantation Rd, Leighton Buzzard,
Beds, LU7 7JF
☎ (01525) 244800, Fax 244801, Pro
244815, Bar 244805, Rest 244810
1 miles N of Leighton Buzzard.
Parkland/woodland course.
Pro Lee Scarbrow; Founded 1925
18 holes, 6101 yards, S.S.S. 70
† Welcome WD with handicap certs;
WE with member.
⌣ WD £24.
⌣ Welcome WD except Tues (ladies
day); day's golf and catering from
morning coffee to evening meals;
from £45.
🍽 Full clubhouse catering facilities.
↝ Cock Horse Hotel.

5A 56 Lingdale
Joe Moore's Lane, Woodhouse Eave,
Loughborough, Leics, LE12 8TF
☎ (01509) 890703, Pro 890684, Sec
890703, Bar/Rest 890035
2 miles off M1 Junction 22 towards
Woodhouse Eaves.
Parkland course.
Pro P Sellears; Founded 1967
Designed by D.W. Tucker & G. Austin
18 holes, 6545 yards, S.S.S. 71
† Welcome.
⌣ WD £22; WE £32.
⌣ Welcome with prior arrangement
with secretary; minimum 12;
day's golf and catering packaging
available; prices on application.
🍽 Full clubhouse facilities.
Practice range, practice ground;
tuition available.

5A 57 Links Course
Cambridge Rd, Newmarket, Suffolk,
CB8 0TG
☎ (01638) 663000, Fax 661476, Pro
662395, Bar/Rest 662708
On A1304 1 mile S of Newmarket
midway between racecourse
entrances.
Parkland course.
Pro John Sharkey; Founded 1902
Designed by Col Hotchkin
18 holes, 6574 yards, S.S.S. 71
† Welcome with handicap certs; not
before 11.30am Sun.
⌣ WD £28; WE £32.
⌣ Welcome by prior arrangement;
booking fee of £35; catering
packages; maximum 60; prices on
application.

🍽 Full restaurant and bar.
↝ Bedford Lodge.

5A 58 Longcliffe
Snell's Nook Lane, Nanpantan,
Loughborough, Leics, LE11 3YA
☎ (01509) 239129, Pro 231450,
Rest/Bar 216321
1 mile from M1 Junction 23 off A512
towards Loughborough.
Heathland course.
Pro Ian Bailey; Founded 1904
18 holes, 6611 yards, S.S.S. 72
† Welcome WD 9am-4.30pm except
Tues; WE with a member.
⌣ WD £27.
⌣ Welcome WD except Tues (ladies
day); packages available for groups
of 20 or more; from £27.
🍽 Bar, restaurant and snacks.
↝ Friendly Hotel.

5A 59 Lutterworth
Rugby Rd, Lutterworth, Leics, LE17
4HN
☎ (01455) 552532, Fax 553586, Pro
557199, Sec 552532
On A426 0.5 mile from M1 Junction
20.
Parkland course.
Pro Roland Tisdall; Founded 1904
Designed by D. Snell
18 holes, 6226 yards, S.S.S. 70
† Welcome WD; guests of members
only at WE.
⌣ WD £20-£26.
⌣ Welcome Mon, Wed and Thurs all
day and Tues pm and Fri am; indoor
academy; terms on application.
🍽 Clubhouse facilities.
Practice range.
↝ The Denby Arms; The
Greyhound, both Lutterworth.

5A 60 Lyshott Heath GC ☎
Millbrook, Bedford, Beds, MK45 2JB
☎ (01525) 840252, Fax 406249, Pro
402269, Bar/Rest 041222
In Millbrook Village off A507 road just
before Ampthill.
Inland links course.
Pro David Armor; Founded 1980
Designed by W. Sutherland
18 holes, 7021 yards, S.S.S. 73
† Restricted; phone club manager
Derek Cook for details.
⌣ WD £19.00; WE £28.
⌣ Welcome by prior arrangement
WD except Thurs; golf and catering
packages can be arranged; from £15.
🍽 Clubhouse facilities; restaurant
and conference facilities.

↗ White Hart, Ampthill; Flitwyck Manor, Flitwyck.

5A 61 March
Frogs Abbey, Grange Rd, March, Cambs, PE15 0YH
☎ (01354) 652364, Fax 652364
Course is on the A141 west of the March bypass.
Parkland course.
Founded 1920
9 holes, 6204 yards, S.S.S. 70
† Welcome WD; guests of members only at weekends.
↳ WD £16.50.
↷ Welcome WD by prior booking.
🍽 Bar facilities; meals by prior booking.
↗ Griffin.

5A 62 Market Harborough
Great Oxendon Rd, Market Harborough, Leics, LE16 8NB
☎ (01858) 463684, Fax 432906
Course is one mile south of Market Harborough on the A508 towards Northampton.
Parkland course.
Pro F Baxter; Founded 1898
Updated by H Swan
18 holes, 6022 yards, S.S.S. 69
† Welcome WD; WE guests of members only.
↳ WD £20.
↷ Welcome WD by arrangement; inclusive packages available; from £35.
🍽 Clubhouse facilities.
↗ Three Swans, Market Harborough; George, Oxendon.

5A 63 Melton Mowbray ☎
Waltham Rd, Thorpe Arnold, Melton Mowbray, Leics, LE14 4SD
☎ (01664) 562118, Fax 562118, Pro 569629
2 miles NE of Melton Mowbray on A607.
Undulating parkland course.
Pro James Hetherington; Founded 1925
18 holes, 6222 yards, S.S.S. 70
† Welcome before 3pm.
↳ WD £20; WE and BH £23.
↷ Welcome WD by prior arrangement; golf and lunch, dinner packages can be organised; from £21.
🍽 Full catering, bar and dining facilities.
↗ Sysonsby Knoll; George; Harborough; Stapleford Park.

5A 64 Mentmore ☎
Mentmore, Leighton Buzzard, Beds, LU7 0QN
☎ (01296) 662020, Fax 662592
1 mile from Cheddington, E of A41 to Aylesbury.
Parkland course.
Pro Pip Elson; Founded 1992
Designed by Bob Sandow
Rosebury: 18 holes, 6855 yards, S.S.S. 73; Rothschild: 18 holes, 6791 yards, S.S.S. 72.
† Welcome WD; after 11am WE.
↳ WD £30; WE £30.
↷ Welcome WD; max 120; facilities; also pool, sauna, 2 tennis courts, sports bar, fitness room, jacuzzi; £55-£75.
🍽 Full bar, restaurant facilities.
↗ Pendley Manor; Rose and Crown, both Tring.

5A 65 Mount Pleasant ☎
Station Rd, Lower Stondon, Henlow, Beds, SG16 6JL
☎ (01462) 850999, Fax 850257
0.75 miles W of Stondon-Henlow Camp roundabout off A600 Hitchin to Bedford road; 4 miles N of Hitchin.
Undulating meadowland course.
Pro Mike Roberts; Founded 1992
Designed by Derek Young
9 greens/18 tees, 6003 yards, S.S.S. 69
† Welcome at all times; booking advisable; can be made up to 2 days in advance.
↳ WD 9 holes £7, 18 holes £12; WE 9 holes £9, 18 holes £16; OAPs: discounts of £1.50 for 9 holes; Juniors: discounts of £2.
↷ Welcome WD; packages available; 24 maximum for full catering, 36 for buffet; terms on application.
🍽 Clubhouse bar facilities.
Practice facilities available, buggies, shoes and clubs for hire; P.G.A tuition available.
↗ Sun, Hitchin.

5A 66 Mowsbury Golf and Squash Complex
Cleat Hill, Kimbolton Rd, Ravensden, Bedford, MK41 8DQ
☎ (01234) 771493, Pro 216374, Sec 771041, Bar/Rest 771493
On B660 at northern limit of city boundary.
Parkland course.
Pro M Summers; Founded 1975
Designed by Hawtree
18 holes, 6514 yards, S.S.S. 71

† Welcome.
↳ WD £7.50; WE £9.90.
↷ Welcome anytime; golf and catering packages; driving range, squash court; terms on application.
🍽 Full facilities.

5A 67 Northampton
Harlestone, Northampton, Northants, NN7 4EF
☎ (01604) 845155, Fax 820262, Pro 845167, Bar/Rest 845102
On A428 Rugby road 4 miles from Northampton.
Parkland course.
Pro Kevin Dickins; Founded 1893
Designed by Donald Steel
18 holes, 6615 yards, S.S.S. 72
† Welcome WD; members and members guests at WE.
↳ WD £30.
↷ Welcome by prior arrangement WD except Wed; packages for golf and catering available; snooker; banqueting; terms on application.
🍽 Full facilities.
↗ Northampton Moat House; Heyford Manor.

5A 68 Northamptonshire County
Golf Lane, Church Brampton, Northampton, NN6 8AZ
☎ (01604) 843025, Fax 843025, Pro 842226, Sec 843025, Bar/Rest 842170
5 miles NW of Northampton in village of Church Brampton.
Heathland course with woods, gorse and streams.
Pro Tim Rouse; Founded 1909
Designed by H.S. Colt
18 holes, 6503 yards, S.S.S. 71
† Welcome by arrangement with handicap certs.
↳ WD £40; WE £40.
↷ Large groups on Wed; smaller groups Thurs; terms on application.
🍽 Full catering facilities.
↗ Broomshill; Limetrees.

5A 69 Oadby
Leicester Rd, Oadby, Leicester, LE2 4AB
☎ (0116) 2709052, Sec 2703828, Bar/Rest 2700215
On A6 from Leicester inside Leicester racecourse.
Meadowland municipal course; 9 holes inside adjacent Leicester Racecourse.
Pro Allan Kershaw, Assistant Pro

OVERSTONE PARK
HOTEL, GOLF & LEISURE RESORT

• Superb 18-hole, Par 72, 6602 yards, Championship Golf Course • Set in beautiful Victorian parkland with interesting water features • Practice area, putting green • Corporate golf days & societies welcome • All-day bar and restaurant facilities • 28-bedroom hotel with luxury pool complex • Special prices for Sunday to Thursday golfing breaks • Minutes from Junction 15, M1

To discover more: Pro Shop: 01604 643555. Main reception: 01604 647666.
E-mail: sales@overstonepark.co.uk. Billing Lane, Overstone, Northamptonshire NN6 0AP

Fred Fearn; Founded 1975
18 holes, 6311 yards, S.S.S. 70
♦ Welcome.
⌴ Prices on application.
☞Welcome by prior application to the professional; welcome WD and after 12 noon WE; terms on application.
🍽 Bar meals and snacks; meals on request.
↪ The Chase Hotel: adjacent hotel and leisure complex.

5A 70 Old Nene Golf & Country Club
Muchwood Lane, Bodsey, Ramsey, Cambs, PE17 1XQ
☎(01487) 813519, Pro 710122, Bar/Rest 815622
1 mile N of Ramsey.
Parkland course course with water hazards.
Pro Roland Tinsdale; Founded 1992
Designed by Richard Edrich
9 holes, 5675 yards, S.S.S. 68
♦ Pay and play.
⌴ WD: 9 holes £7, 18 holes £10; WE: 9 holes £9, 18 holes £15.
☞Welcome; reductions for 10 or more players WD; packages available; terms available on application.
🍽 Bar and bar snacks available.
Practice range, floodlit; 2 piece balls; tuition available.
↪ Several in area.

5A 71 Orton Meadows
Ham Lane, Orton Waterville, Peterborough, Cambs, PE2 5UU
☎(01733) 237478
On the A605 Peterborough-Oundle road 2 miles W of Peterborough.
Parkland course.
Pro Jason Mitchell; Founded 1987
Designed by Dennis & Roger Fitton
18 holes, 5664 yards, S.S.S. 68

♦ Welcome; advance bookings available.
⌴ WD £10.20; WE £13.
☞Welcome WD except Tues and before 11am Sun; terms on application.
🍽 In adjoining steakhouse The Granary.
↪ Travelodge.

5A 72 Oundle
Benefield Rd, Oundle, Northants, PE8 4EZ
☎(01832) 273267, Fax 273267, Pro 272273, Bar/Rest 274882
On A427 Oundle-Corby road, 1.5 miles from Oundle.
Parkland course.
Pro Richard Keys; Founded 1893
18 holes, 6235 yards, S.S.S. 70
♦ Welcome WD and after 10.30am WE.
⌴ WD £25.50; WE £35.50.
☞Welcome WD except Tues; golf and catering packages available; from £35.
🍽 Full clubhouse facilities.
Practice range, 2 practice areas; trolleys for hire; contact pro about tuition.
↪ Talbot, Oundle; Travel Lodge, Thrapston.

5A 73 Overstone Park
Billing Lane, Northampton, Northants, NN6 0AP
☎(01604) 647666, Pro 643555,
🖥 www.overstonepark.co.uk
✉ steph@overstonepark
Take A45 Northampton road to Billing Lane.
Parkland course in walled Victorian estate.
Pro Brian Mudge
Founded 1993
Designed by Donald Steel
18 holes, 6602 yards, S.S.S. 72

♦ Welcome WD and from 11am WE; only after 2pm at WE.
⌴ Summer WD £26, WE £31; Winter WD £20, WE £25.
☞Welcome by prior arrangement; packages; health and leisure club.
🍽 Bar and brasserie.
Practice range, practice area.
↪ Hotel on site; 24 en suite bedrooms.

5A 74 Park Hill
Park Hill, Seagrave, Leics, LE12 7NG
☎(01509) 815454, Fax 816062, Pro 815775, Bar/Rest 815885
Off A46 from Leicester; turn left at Seagrave.
Parkland course; five par 5s more than 500 yards
Pro David Mee; Founded 1895
18 holes, 7219 yards, S.S.S. 74
♦ Welcome.
⌴ WD £20; WE and BH £24.
☞Welcome; terms on application; from £20.
🍽 Clubhouse catering facilities.
↪ Rothley Court; Willoughby.

5A 75 Pavenham Park
Pavenham Park, Pavenham, Beds, MK43 7PE
☎(01234) 822202, Fax 826602
Course is on the A6 six miles N of Bedford.
Parkland course.
Pro Zac Thompson; Founded 1994
Designed by Derek Young/ Z Thompson
18 holes, 6353 yards, S.S.S. 71
♦ Welcome WD; guests of members only at WE.
⌴ WD £20.
☞Welcome WD; full catering and golf packages; from £16.
🍽 Clubhouse facilities.
Practice range, practice area; buggies and clubs for hire.

5A 76 Peterborough Milton
Golf Club, Milton Ferry, PE6 7AG
☎ (01733) 380489, Fax 380489, Pro 380793, Sec 380489, Bar/Rest 380204
Course is two miles W of Peterborough on the A47.
Parkland course.
Pro Mike Gallagher; Founded 1938
Designed by James Braid
18 holes, 6463 yards, S.S.S. 72
† Welcome with handicap certs.
ℹ WD £25; WE £35.
♻ Welcome Tues-Fri; full catering facilities and golf packages; prices on application.
🍴 Full facilities.
Practice range, large practice area.
🛏 Haycock, Wansford; Swallow; Butterfly, both Peterborough.

5A 77 RAF Cottesmore
Oakham, Leicester, Leics, LE15 7BL
☎ (01572) 812241 ex.6706
Course is seven miles N of Oakham off the B668.
Parkland course.
Founded 1980
9 holes, 5622 yards, S.S.S. 67
† With member only.
ℹ Terms on application.

5A 78 RAF Henlow
Henlow Camp, Beds, SG16 6DN
☎ (01462) 851515 ex 7083
3 miles SE of Shefford on A505, follow signs to RAF Henlow.
Meadowland course.
Founded 1985
9 holes, 5618 yards, S.S.S. 67
† Only with a member.
ℹ Terms on application.
♻ Can be arranged through Sec.
🍴 Light refreshments available.
🛏 Bird in Hand.

5A 79 RAF North Luffenham
North Luffenham, Oakham, Leics, LE15 8RL
☎ (01780) 720041 ex. 7523
Follow signposts for RAF North Luffenham from A606, station is close to Rutland Water.
Meadowland course.
Founded 1975
9 holes, 6010 yards, S.S.S. 70
† With member or by appointment through Sec.
ℹ Terms on application.
♻ Can be arranged through Sec.
🍴 Bar and restaurant facilities.
🛏 George; Crown.

5A 80 Ramsey
4 Abbey Terrace, Ramsey, Huntingdon, Cambs, PE17 1DD
☎ (01487) 812600, Fax 815746, Pro 813022, Bar/Rest 813573
Off B660 Ramsey road from the A1 between Huntingdon and Peterborough.
Parkland course.
Pro Stuart Scott; Founded 1964
Designed by J. Hamilton Stutt
18 holes, 6163 yards, S.S.S. 70
† Welcome WD; WE as member's guest.
ℹ WD £25.
♻ Welcome WD only; minimum 20; 18 holes of golf and catering packages available; from £25; large well stocked pro shop, offering society prizes.
🍴 Clubhouse facilities.
Practice range, 4 large practice areas; PGA tuition available; bowling green.
🛏 George, Huntingdon; Bell, Stilton; Dolphin, St Ives.

5A 81 Rothley Park
Westfield Lane, Rothley, Leicester, LE7 7LH
☎ (0116) 2302809, Fax 2302809, Pro 2303023, Sec 2302809, Bar/Rest 2302019
Off A6 N of Leicester.
Parkland course.
Pro Andrew Collins; Founded 1912
18 holes, 6476 yards, S.S.S. 71
† Welcome WD except Tues; handicap certs required.
ℹ WD £25.
♻ Welcome Mon, Wed, Thurs, Fri; 10 per cent discount for more than 40 players; full catering available; terms on application.
🍴 Full clubhouse facilities.
Practice ground, tuition available.
🛏 Rothley Court; Quorn Country Hotel; Quorn Grange.

5A 82 Rushcliffe
Stocking Lane, East Leake, Loughborough, Leics, LE12 5RL
☎ (01509) 852959, Pro 852701, Bar/Rest 852209
From M1 Junction 24 take A453 towards West Bridgford; turn at Gotham, East Leake signs.
Parkland course.
Pro Chris Hall
Founded 1910
18 holes, 6013 yards, S.S.S. 69
† Welcome.
ℹ WD £25; WE £29.

♻ Welcome WD; packages available; prices available on application; enquire with Sec for details.
🍴 Clubhouse facilities.

5A 83 Rushden
Kimbolton Rd, Chelveston, Wellingborough, Northants, NN9 6AN
☎ (01933) 312581, Sec 418511, Greenkeeper 413554
Course is on the A45 two miles E of Higham Ferrers.
Undulating meadowland course.
Founded 1919
10 holes, 6350 yards, S.S.S. 70
† Welcome WD except Wed pm; WE with member.
ℹ WD £18.
♻ Welcome WD except Wed pm by prior arrangement.
🍴 Full facilities except Mon.

5A 84 St Ives
Westwood Rd, St Ives, Cambs, PE17 4RS
☎ (01480) 468392, Fax 468392, Pro 466067, Bar 464459
Course is on the B1040 off the A45 in St Ives.
Parkland course.
Pro Darren Glasby; Founded 1923
9 holes, 6100 yards, S.S.S. 69
† Welcome WD; with member WE.
ℹ WD £20; WE £20.
♻ Welcome Wed and Fri by prior arrangement; packages available; from £20.
🍴 Full clubhouse facilities.
Practice ground; tuition available.
🛏 Slepe Hall.

5A 85 St Neots   ♟
Crosshall Rd, St Neots, Huntingdon, Cambs, PE19 4AE
☎ (01480) 474311, Fax 472363, Pro 476513, Sec 472363
On B1048 off the A1.
Parkland course with water hazards.
Pro Graham Bithrey; Founded 1890
Designed by Harry Vardon (original 9)
18 holes, 6026 yards, S.S.S. 69
† Welcome WD; WE with member; handicap certs preferred.
ℹ WD £25.
♻ Welcome Tues, Wed, Thurs by prior arrangement; packages available; snooker; function room; terms on application.
🍴 Full clubhouse facilities.
Practice area available.
🛏 Eaton Oak; Kings Head.

5A 86 Scraptoft

Beeby Rd, Scraptoft, Leicester, LE7 9SJ
☎(0116) 2418863, Fax 2418863, Pro 2419138, Bar/Rest 2419000
Turn off A47 main Peterborough-Leicester road at Scraptoft at Thurnby.
Meadowland course.
Pro Simon Wood; Founded 1928
18 holes, 6235 yards, S.S.S. 70
† Welcome; dress code applies after 7pm.
WD £20; WE £25.
Welcome WD by prior arrangement; packages available; terms on application.
Full facilities.
White House.

5A 87 Shelthorpe

Poplar Road, Loughborough, Club
☎(01509) 267766
From Leicester on A6 turn left at first traffic lights, over island and then 2nd left.
Municipal parkland course.
18 holes, 2054 yards, S.S.S. 54
† Welcome.
WD £3.20; WE £3.20.

5A 88 Six Hills

Six Hills, Melton Mowbray, Leics, LE14 3PR
☎(01509) 881225
From M1 take A46 N; course 0.5 mile from A46.
Parkland course.
Founded 1986
18 holes, 5758 yards, S.S.S. 69
† Welcome; pay and play.
WD £9; WE £12.
Welcome but no advance booking system.
Limited to coffee, tea and light refreshments.
Ragdale Hall.

5A 89 South Bedfordshire

Warden Hill Rd, Luton, Beds, LU2 7AA
☎(01582) 591500, Fax 495381, Pro 591209, Rest 596486
3 miles N of Luton on A6 signposted into Warden Hill Rd.
Undulating course with trees and hawthorn hedges.
Pro Eddie Cogle; Founded 1892
18 holes, 6389 yards, S.S.S. 71
† Welcome WD; WE by prior arrangement.
Prices on application.
Welcome mainly Wed and Thurs by prior arrangement; packages available; snooker; also Warden course: 9 holes, 4914 yards, par 64; prices on application.
Restaurant and bar facilities available.
Practice area; tuition available.
Chiltern; Strathmore.

5A 90 Staverton Park �‍

Staverton, Daventry, Northants, NN11 6JT
☎(01327) 302000, Fax 311428, Pro 705506
Course is on the A425 Daventry to Leamington road; one mile S of Daventry.
Undulating meadowland course.
Pro Richard Mudge; Founded 1978
Designed by Comm. John Harris
18 holes, 6100 yards, S.S.S. 72
† Welcome.
WD £25; WE £30.
Welcome WD by prior arrangement; snooker; solarium; sauna; banqueting suites; terms on application.
Full facilities at all times.
Practice range, 11 bays floodlit; tuition available; buggy hire £20; club hire individually £1, set £7.50.
Staverton Park offers golfing weekends.

5A 91 Stockwood Park

Stockwood Park, London Rd, Luton, Beds, LU1 4LX
☎(01582) 413704, Fax 481001, Bar 731421
Leave the M1 at Junction 10; head towards town centre and then left at the first traffic lights.
Meadowland course.
Pro Glyn McCarthy; Founded 1973
Designed by Charles Lawrie
18 holes, 6049 yards, S.S.S. 69
† Welcome.
WD £8.15; WE £11.
Welcome Mon, Tues and Thurs by prior arrangement with Pro; packages for catering and golf by arrangement; 9-hole pitch & putt; terms on application.
Full facilities.
Practice range, 24 bays floodlit; 9-hole pitch and putt; clubs and trolleys.
Strathmore; The Hertfordshire Moathouse (full leisure facilities).

5A 92 Stoke Albany

Ashley Rd, Stoke Albany, Market Harborough, Leics, LE16 8PL
☎(01858) 535208, Fax 535505
Course is off the A427 Market Harborough-Corby road just through Stoke Albany.
Parkland course.
Pro Adrian Clifford; Founded 1995
18 holes, 6132 yards, S.S.S. 69
† Welcome.
WD £13; WE £17.
Welcome by prior arrangement; packages for golf and catering available; terms on application.
Fairways Bar and Restaurant; spike bar.
Practice ground and bunker, chipping green and putting green; trolleys for hire
Three Swans, Market Harborough; Rockingham Forest, Corby.

5A 93 Thorney Golf Centre

English Drove, Thorney,
Peterborough, Cambs, PE6 0TJ
☎ (01733) 270570, Fax 270842
On A47 E of Peterborough.
Thorney Lakes is parkland members
course.
Pro Mark Templeman; Founded
1991/1995
Designed by A Dow.
The Lakes course: 18 holes, 6402
yards, par 71, S.S.S. 71; The Fen
course: 18 holes, 6104 yards, par
70, S.S.S. 69; 9 hole, par 3 course.
✝ Welcome.
Ⅼ The Lakes Course: WD £11, WE
£17.50; The Fens course: WD £6.75,
WE £8.75; Par 3 course: £2.75 all
week.
⚲ Welcome WD; anytime on Fen;
packages available; terms on
application.
🍽 Bar and restaurant.
Practice range, 12 bays floodlit;
lessons available; buggies, trolleys
and clubs for hire.

5A 94 Thorpe Wood

Nene Parkway, Peterborough, PE3
6SE
☎ (01733) 267701, Fax 332774, Bar
267601
On A47 to Leicester 2 miles W of
Peterborough.
Parkland course.
Pro Gary Casey; Founded 1975
Designed by Peter Alliss and Dave
Thomas
18 holes, 7086 yards, S.S.S. 74
✝ Welcome.
Ⅼ WD £10.50; WE £13.50.
⚲ Welcome by arrangement up to a
year in advance.
🍽 The Woodman PH (next door).
Tuition available.
꜠ Moat House.

5A 95 Tilsworth

Dunstable Rd, Tilsworth, Leighton
Buzzard, Beds, LU7 9PU
☎ (01525) 210721, Fax 210465 ,
Bar/Rest 210722
2 miles N of Dunstable on A5; take
Tilsworth/Stanbridge turning.
Parkland course; 13th is 97 yards.
Pro Nick Webb; Founded 1977
18 holes, 5306 yards, S.S.S. 67
✝ Welcome except before 10am Sun
morning.
Ⅼ WD £10; WE £12.
⚲ Welcome WD; terms on
application.
🍽 Full facilities.

Practice range, open all week; tuition
available; buggy and club hire.
꜠ Travel Lodge.

5A 96 Ullesthorpe

Frolesworth Rd, Ullesthorpe,
Lutterworth, Leics, LE17 5BZ
☎ (01455) 209023, Fax 202537, Pro
209150
Close to the M1 and M69, just off the
A5.
Parkland course.
Pro David Bowring; Founded 1976
18 holes, 6650 yards, S.S.S. 72
✝ Welcome WD; with members at
WE.
Ⅼ WD £20.
⚲ Golf day packages and overnight
accommodation can be organised
through the hotel; full clubhouse and
hotel facilities for both corporate and
society golf days; from £28.
🍽 Full hotel and clubhouse facilities
available.
꜠ On-site hotel Ullesthorpe Court.

5A 97 Waterbeach Barracks

39th Engineering Regiment,
Waterbeach, Cambs, CB5 9PA
☎ (01223) 860681, Clubhouse
440007, Fax 440007
Fenland course.
Founded 1972
9 holes, 6237 yards, S.S.S. 70
✝ HM Forces welcome; civilians
must be introduced by and play with
a member.
Ⅼ Terms on application.
🍽 Limited bar available.

5A 98 Wellingborough

Harroween Hall, Great Harroween,
Wellingborough, Northants, NN9 5AD
☎ (01933) 677234, Fax 679379, Pro
678752, Sec 677234, Bar/Rest
402612
Course is two miles north of
Wellingborough on the A509.
Undulating parkland course.
Pro David Clifford; Founded
1893/1975
Designed by Hawtree & Sons
18 holes, 6617 yards, S.S.S. 72
(course under reconstruction; ready
May 2000)
✝ Welcome WD.
Ⅼ WD £35.
⚲ Welcome WD except Tues; full
day's golf, bar, restaurant, snooker;
from £35.
Tuition available.
🍽 Full clubhouse facilities available.

꜠ Foxford; Tudor Gate, Finedon;
Kettering Park; Oak House and Hind,
both Wellingborough.

5A 99 Western Park

Scudamore Rd, Braunstone Frith,
Leicester, LE3 1UQ
☎ (0116) 2995566, Fax 2995568,
Bar/Rest 876158
Off A47 2 mile W of city centre.
Parkland course.
Pro David Butler; Founded 1920
Designed by F.W. Hawtree
18 holes, 6518 yards, S.S.S. 70
✝ Welcome; must book at WE.
Ⅼ Winter: WD £7.99, WE £9.99;
Summer: WD £8.99, WE £10.99;
discounted rate for juniors and OAPs.
⚲ Welcome by prior arrangement;
catering and golf packages available;
terms on application.
🍽 Full clubhouse facilities.
꜠ Stakis Hotel.

5A 100 Whaddon Golf Centre

Church St, Whaddon, Nr Royston,
Herts, SG8 5RX
☎ (01223) 207325, Fax 207325
4 miles N of Royston off A1198.
Parkland course.
Pro G Huggett; Founded 1990
Designed by Richard Green
9 holes, 905 yards, par 3
✝ Public pay and play.
Ⅼ WD £3; WE £3.50.
⚲ Welcome; terms on application.
🍽 Bar snacks.

5A 101 Whetstone

Cambridge Rd, Cosby, Leics, LE9
5SH
☎ (0116) 2861424, Fax 2861424
4 miles from M1 Junction 21 SE of
Leicester; take A46 to Narborough
then signposts for Whetstone.
Wooded parkland course with water
features.
Pro David Raitt; Founded 1963
Designed by Nick Leatherland
18 holes, 5795 yards, S.S.S. 68
✝ Welcome.
Ⅼ WD £14; WE £16.
⚲ Welcome by arrangement.
🍽 Full bar and catering facilities.
Practice range, 20 bays.
꜠ Time Out, Blaby.

5A 102 Whittlebury Park Golf & Country Club

Whittlebury, Nr Towcester, Northants,
NN12 8XW

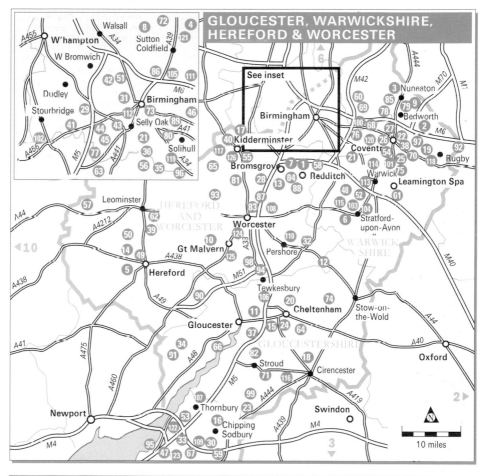

GLOUCESTER, WARWICKSHIRE, HEREFORD & WORCESTER

KEY								
1	Abbey Hotel G &CC	24	Cotswold Hills	49	Hereford Municipal	75	Newbold Comyn	101	Stoneleigh Deer Park
2	Ansty Golf Centre	25	Coventry	50	Herefordshire	76	North Warwickshire	102	Stourbridge
3	Atherstone	26	Coventry Hearsall	51	Hill Top	77	North Worcestershire	103	Stratford Oaks
4	The Belfry	27	Cromwell Course at	52	Ingon Manor G & CC	78	Nuneaton	104	Stratford-upon-Avon
5	Belmont Lodge and GC		Nailcote Hall	53	The Kendleshire	79	Oakridge	105	Sutton Coldfield
6	Bidford Grange	28	Droitwich G & CC	54	Kenilworth	80	Olton	106	Tewkesbury Park Hotel
7	Blackwell	29	Dudley	55	Kidderminster	81	Ombersley	107	Thornbury Golf Centre
8	Boldmere	30	Dymock Grange	56	Kings Norton	82	Painswick	108	Tolladine
9	Bramcote Waters	31	Edgbaston	57	Kington	83	Perdiswell	109	Tracy Park Country Club
10	Bransford at Bank House	32	Evesham	58	Ladbrook Park	84	Kibbersali	110	Vale Golf & CC
	Hotel	33	Filton	59	Lansdown	85	Purley Chase G & CC	111	Walmley
11	Brickhampton Court	34	Forest Hills	60	Lea Marston Hotel	86	Pype Hayes	112	Warley
12	Broadway	35	Fulford Heath	61	Leamington & County	87	Ravenmeadow	113	Warwick
13	Bromsgrove Golf Centre	36	Gay Hill	62	Leominster	88	Redditch	114	Warwickshire
14	Burghill Valley	37	Gloucester	63	Lickey Hills (Rose Hill)	89	Robin Hood	115	Welcombe Hotel
15	Canons Court	38	Grange (GPT Golf Club)	64	Lilley Brook	90	Ross-on-Wye	116	Westonbirt
16	Chipping Sodbury	39	Grove Golf Centre	65	Little Lakes	91	Royal Forest of Dean	117	Wharton Park
17	Churchill & Blakedown	40	Habberley	66	Lydney	92	Rugby	118	Whitefields
18	Cirencester	41	Hagley Country Club	67	Mangotsfield	93	Sapey	119	Widney Manor
19	City of Coventry	42	Halesowen	68	Marriott Forest of Arden	94	Sherdons	120	Windmill Village Hotel
	(Brandon Wood)	43	Handsworth	69	Maxstoke Park	95	Shirehampton Park	121	Wishaw
20	Cleeve Hill	44	Harborne	70	Memorial Park	96	Shirley	122	Woodlands
21	Cocks Moor Woods	45	Harborne Church Farm	71	Minchinhampton	97	Sphinx	123	Woodspring
22	Copt Heath	46	Hatchford Brook	72	Moor Hall	98	Stakis Puckrup Hl Hotel	124	Worcester G & CC
23	Cotswold Edge	47	Henbury	73	Moseley	99	Stinchcombe Hill	125	Worcestershire
		48	Henley Golf & CC	74	Naunton Downs	100	Stonebridge	126	Wyre Forest

☎(01327) 858092, Fax 858009, Pro 858588
Course is on the A413 15 mins from the M1 Junction 15a, three miles S of Towcester.
Parkland/lakeland course.
Pro Tom Jones; Founded 1992
Designed by Cameron Sinclair
36 holes, 6662 yards, S.S.S. 72
⚑ Welcome.
⚐ Winter: Mon £10, Tues-Fri am £20, WE am £30; 7 days a week pm £10; Summer rates: prices on application.
⚒Welcome at all times by prior arrangement; 4 x 9 loops (1905, Royal Whittlewood, Grand Prix, Wedgewood); indoor course; clay pigeon shooting, archery, cricket ground, croquet lawn, corporate hospitality; function suites; terms on application.
🍽Bars, bistros, restaurant.
🛏 On site Whittlebury Hall Hotel; 124 en-suite rooms.

5A 103 Willesley Park
Tamworth Rd, Ashby-de-la-Zouch, Leics, LE65 2PF
☎(01530) 411532, Fax 414596, Pro 414820, Sec 414596
2 miles S of Ashby-de-la-Zouch on B5006.
Parkland/heathland course.
Pro C J Hancock; Founded 1921
Designed by C.K. Cotton
18 holes, 6304 yards, S.S.S. 70
⚑ Welcome with handicap certs.
⚐ WD £30; WE £35.
⚒Welcome Wed, Thurs, Fri; terms on application; from £30.
🍽Clubhouse facilities.
Tuition available.
🛏 Royal; Fallen Knight.

5A 104 Wyboston Lakes
Wyboston Lakes, Wyboston, Beds, MK44 3AL
☎(01480) 223004, Fax 407330, Hotel Reception 212625
Off A1 at St Neots.
Public parkland with lake features.
Pro Paul Ashwell; Founded 1981
Designed by Neil Oackden
18 holes, 5955 yards, S.S.S. 70
⚑ Welcome; bookings taken 7 days in advance for WE.
⚐ WD £11; WE £15.
⚒Welcome WD by prior arrangement.
🍽Full catering facilities.
Practice range, 12 bays floodlit; lessons available.

🛏 Hotel on site offers golf packages.

5B 1 Abbey Hotel Golf & Country Club
Dagnell End Rd, Redditch, Worcs, B98 7BD
☎(01527) 63918, Fax 584112, Pro 68006
On A441 Redditch to Birmingham road.
Parkland course.
Pro Spencer Edwards
Founded 1985
Designed by Donald Steel
18 holes, 6561 yards, S.S.S. 71
⚑ Welcome subject to course availability.
⚐ WD 18 holes £14; WE 18 holes £19.
⚒Welcome by prior arrangement; special packages available for members of golf club and guests of hotel; snooker; gym; swimming pool; sauna.
🍽The Nineteenth Hole Bar and The Brambling's restaurant.
🛏 Abbey Hotel on site.

5B 2 Ansty Golf Centre
Brinklow Rd, Ansty, Coventry, Warwicks, CV7 9JH
☎(024) 7662 1341, Fax 7660 2568, From M6 Junction 2 take B4065 to Ansty; turning on to B4029 to Brinklow.
Parkland course.
Pro C Phillips; Founded 1990
Designed by D. Morgan
18 holes, 6079 yards, S.S.S. 69
⚑ Pay and play.
⚐ WD £9; WE £13.
⚒Welcome with 24 hours notice.
🍽Full facilities.
Practice range, 18 bays; 9-hole academy course; tuition available 7 days a weeek; buggies and clubs for hire.
🛏 Ansty Hall; Hanover at Hinckley.

5B 3 Atherstone
The Outwoods, Atherstone, Warwicks, CV9 2RL
☎(01827) 713110
On A5 in town centre on Coleshill Road.
Parkland course.
Founded 1894
18 holes, 6006 yards, S.S.S. 70
⚑ Welcome; guests of members at WE.
⚐ WD £20.

⚒Welcome by arrangement; packages available; full catering facilities; terms on application.
🍽Full catering and bar.
🛏 Chapel House; Mancetter Manor, both Atherstone.

5B 4 The Belfry   ☂
Lichfield Rd, Wishaw, N Warwickshire, B76 9PR
☎(01675) 470301, Fax 470301
M42 Junction 9 follow A446 towards Lichfield and course is 1 mile on left.
Parkland course courses; Ryder Cup course; 2001 host.
Pro Peter McGovern; Founded 1977
Designed by Peter Alliss & Dave Thomas
Brabazon: 18 holes, 6393 yards, S.S.S. 71; Derby: 18 holes, 6009 yards, S.S.S. 69; PGA National: 18 holes, 6153 yards, S.S.S. 70
⚑ Welcome
⚐ WD £90, WE £90 (Brabazon); WD £30, WE £30 (Derby); WD £60, WE £60 (PGA National).
⚒Welcome; full championship course, clubhouse and hotel facilities; terms on application.
🍽First-class clubhouse and hotel facilities; choice of three restaurants. Practice ground; buggies and clubs for hire; tuition available, group lessons available; caddies and bag carriers available.
🛏 The Belfry.

5B 5 Belmont Lodge and GC   ☂
Belmont House, Belmont, Hereford, HR2 9SA
☎(01432) 352666, Fax 358090, Pro 352717
🖳 www.belmontlodge.co.uk
📧 info@belmontlodge.co.uk
1.5 miles from centre of Hereford just off A436 Abergavenny road.
Parkland course with back 9 bordering the river.
Pro Mike Welsh; Founded 1983
Designed by R. Sandow
18 holes, 6511 yards, S.S.S. 71
⚑ Welcome.
⚐ Winter: 18 holes WD £14, WE £20; Summer: 18 holes WE £18, WE £25.
⚒Welcome; packages can be organised; terms on application.
🍽Full club and hotel facilities. Practice ground; tuition available; caddy cars for hire £14 per round.
🛏 Belmont Lodge; self-catering accommodation on site.

The Belfry

The Belfry has become one of European golf's most famous courses and the reason has been the rise of the status of the Ryder Cup in the last 20 years.

Pictures of the deeds of great golfers have been beamed across the world and it has become almost inevitably linked with the Ryder Cup.

It has been a staggering rise for a Sutton Coldfield course that was once no more than a potato field. No more than 10 years later it was hosting its first Ryder Cup.

Europe's victory in 1985 sparked great rejoicing and the images of the long drive across the water at the 275-yard 10th or the threat the lake poses on nine and 18 are unforgettable.

Now the Ryder Cup will return in 2001 for its fourth visit – there are those who believe that this is an unwarranted reward for what was, in the main, an ordinary course when water was not in play.

But for the 2001 Cup, where the Americans will defend, there has been much resculpturing of the Brabazon course to amend the mediocre holes that certainly dominated the front nine.

However, during the renovations to the 500-acre site there have been great efforts to ensure that the signature holes at The Belfry remain intact.

History has been made with the stirring finishes at the 18th and it is something that The Belfry have been happy to build on. It is probably the single reason that the Ryder Cup keeps returning to the West Midlands. It has provided the moving images of Christy O'Connor rejoicing as his shot in 1985 clambered over the water that had claimed so many American shots.

There was the sight of Sam Torrance standing arms aloft and of Davis Love leaping for joy in 1993. There were also the tears of Costantino Rocca.

In Ryder Cup golf no less than 25 of the 36 singles matches played out their last dramas on the 18th where the need is to measure the tee shot to perfection.

Try to cut off too much of the water from the tee and the ball will almost certainly disappear into the drink. Play too conservatively and the second shot needs to be of staggering length and accuracy.

Rest assured, the 18th will play its part in Ryder Cup history again and in the year 2000 the Benson and Hedges event moved to the HQ of the European Tour from its previous home at The Oxfordshire.

But The Belfry is more than just a golf course. The resort boasts 267 four-star bedrooms, 20 conference rooms, four restaurants, eight bars, a superb leisure centre with swimming pool, warm water whirlpool, two beauty salons, two solariums, a fully equipped gymnasium, steamroom, two saunas, three squash courts and a snooker room with four full-sized championship tables, an outdoor tennis court and jogging trail.

Yet another £8 million development opened in 1997, with an additional 60 bedrooms and upgraded facilities.— **CG**

5B 6 **Bidford Grange**
Stratford Rd, Bidford on Avon,
Warwicks, B50 4LY
☎ (01789) 490319, Fax 778184
Course is off the A439 Evesham-
Stratford road.
Parkland course with last 4 holes
close to River Avon.
Founded 1992
Designed by Howard Swan and Paul
Tillman
18 holes, 7233 yards, S.S.S. 74
† Welcome.
⌄ WD £12; WE £15.
⌁ Welcome; various packages
available, including golf, catering,
dinner and accommodation; minimum
12; from £20-£50.
◉ New clubhouse with spikes bar,
restaurant and hotel facilities.
Practice range, 20 bays.
⌐ Bidford Grange.

5B 7 **Blackwell**
Blackwell, Bromsgrove, Worcs, B60
1PY
☎ (0121) 4451994, Fax 4454911,
Pro 4453113, Rest 4451781
3 miles E of Bromsgrove close to
Blackwell village centre.
Parkland course.
Pro Nigel Blake; Founded 1893
Designed by H. Fowler and T
Simpson
18 holes, 6230 yards, S.S.S. 71
† Welcome WD; with member at
WE.
⌄ WD £50.
⌁ Welcome Wed, Thurs, Fri by prior
arrangement with Sec.
◉ Full clubhouse facilities.
⌐ Perry Hall; Bromsgrove.

5B 8 **Boldmere**
Monmouth Drive, Sutton Coldfield, W
Midlands, B73 6JL
☎ (0121) 354 3379
Off A452 Chester Road 6 miles NE of
Birmingham.
Parkland course.
Pro Trevor Short; Founded 1936
18 holes, 4493 yards, S.S.S. 62
† Welcome.
⌄ WD £8.50; WE £9.
⌁ Welcome WD only.
◉ Bar and catering.
⌐ Parson & Clerk.

5B 9 **Bramcote Waters**
Bazzard Rd, Bramcote, Nuneaton,
Warwickshire, CV11 6QJ
☎ (01455) 220807

5 miles SE of Nuneaton off the
B4114.
Parkland course.
Pro Nic Gilks; Founded 1995
9 holes, 4982 yards, S.S.S. 64
† Pay and play.
⌄ 18 holes WD £10, WE £11; 9
holes WD £6, WE £7.
⌁ None.
◉ None.
⌐ The Hanover International.

5B 10 **Bransford at Bank** ☏
House Hotel
Bank House Hotel, Bransford,
Worcester, WR6 5JD
☎ (01886) 833545, Fax 832461, Pro
833621, Bar/Rest 833754
Course s three miles W of Worcester
on the A4013 Hereford road in
Bransford village.
Florida-style course with 14 lakes and
2 island greens.
Pro Craig George/Lysa Jones;
Founded 1993
Designed by Bob Sandow
18 holes, 6204 yards, S.S.S. 70
† Welcome.
⌄ Terms on application.
⌁ Welcome; various packages
including 2-night golfing break for
£160; hotel and clubhouse facilities,
outdoor pool, fitness centre; prices on
application.
◉ Bars, restaurants.
Practice range, 20-bay range;
buggies and clubs for hire; tuition and
golf clinics available.
⌐ On site Bank House Hotel.

5B 11 **Brickhampton Court**
Brickhampton Court, Cheltenham
Road, Churchdown, Glos, GL2 9QF
☎ (01452) 859444, Fax 859333
On B4063 between Cheltenham and
Gloucester; 3 miles from Junction 11
of the M5.
Parkland course.
Pro Bruce Wilson; Founded 1995
Designed by S. Gidman
18 holes, 6387 yards, S.S.S. 31
† Welcome.
⌄ WD £16; WE £22.50.
⌁ Welcome WD; golf and catering
packages; also 9-hole Glevum
course; on-course refreshments;
welcome packs and golf clinics; £21-
£37.50.
◉ Clubhouse facilities, bar,
restaurant.
Practice range, 26-bay floodlit range;
Mizuno teaching academy; buggies
for hire.

⌐ Golden Valley; Hatherley Manor;
White House.

5B 12 **Broadway**
Willersey Hill, Broadway, Worcs,
WR12 7LG
☎ (01386) 858997, Fax 858643, Pro
853275, Sec 853683, Bar/Rest
853561
1.5 miles E of Broadway on A44.
Inland links.
Pro M Freeman; Founded 1896
Designed by James Braid
18 holes, 6228 yards, S.S.S. 70
† Welcome with prior arrangement
except before 3pm on Sat in summer.
⌄ WD £28-£33; WE £35.
⌁ Welcome Wed, Thurs, Fri; terms
on application.
◉ Clubhouse facilities.
⌐ Dormy house next door; Lygon
Arms, Broadway.

5B 13 **Bromsgrove Golf**
Centre
Stratford Road, Bromsgrove,
Worcestershire, B60 1LD
☎ (01527) 570505, Fax 570964
1 mile from Bromsgrove at junction of
A38 and A448.
Gently undulating parkland course.
Pro G Long/M Davies; Founded 1992
Designed by Hawtree & Sons
18 holes, 5869 yards, S.S.S. 68
† Pay and play.
⌄ WD £13.50; WE £17.
⌁ Welcome by prior arrangement;
group and society packages
available; terms on application.
◉ Full facilities with bar and lounge.
Practice range, 41-bay covered
floodlit range; large practice bunker;
putting gree; tuition available;
equipment for hire.
⌐ List available on request.

5B 14 **Burghill Valley** ☏
Tillington Road, Burghill, Hereford,
HR4 7RW
☎ (01432) 760456, Fax 761654, Pro
760808,
▭ www.bvgc.co.uk
⌐ golf@bvgc.co.uk
4 miles NW of Hereford.
Built around cider orchards, 2 lakes
and woods.
Pro Nigel Clarke; Founded 1991
18 holes, 6239 yards, S.S.S. 70
† Welcome.
⌄ WD £20; WE £25.
⌁ Welcome; golf and catering
packages available; from £25.

COPT HEATH GOLF

1220 WARWICK ROAD • KNOWLE • SOLIHULL • WEST MIDLANDS • B93 9LN

- Enjoy a game at a well known Midlands venue.
- Within half a mile of Junction 5 on the M42, the course, basically flat and parkland by nature, is a challenging one.
- Bar and catering facilities are available throughout the day.

Telephone: Professional (01564) 776155 • Secretary (01564) 772650

🍽 Clubhouse facilities.
Practice ground; tuition and golf clinics available; buggies and clubs for hire

5B 15 Canons Court
Canons Court Farm, Bradley, Wotton-under-Edge, Glos, GL12 7PN
☎ (01453) 843128, Fax 844151
3 miles from M5 Junction 14 on Wotton-under-Edge to N Nibley road.
Parkland course.
Founded 1982
9 holes, 5323 yards, S.S.S. 68
♦ Public pay and play.
🍸 WD £8; WE £10.
⛳ Welcome WD; terms on application.
🍽 Bar and bar snacks.

5B 16 Chipping Sodbury
Chipping Sodbury, Bristol, Gloucs, BS17 6PU
☎ (01454) 319042, Pro 314087, Bar/Rest 315822,
✉ csgc@breathmail.net
Leave M4 Junction 18 or M5 Junction 14 and from Chipping Sodbury take the Wickwar road; first right turn.
Parkland course; also 9 holes, 1076 yards.
Pro Mike Watts; Founded 1906
Designed by Fred Hawtree
18 holes, 6786 yards, S.S.S. 73
♦ Welcome after 12 noon at WE.
🍸 Terms on application.
⛳ Welcome WD by prior arrangement.
🍽 Full bar and meal service.
Practice ground; tuition available; buggies and clubs for hire.
✈ Moda; Cross Hands.

5B 17 Churchill & Blakedown
Churchill Lane, Blakedown, Kidderminster, Worcester, DY10 3NB

☎ (01562) 700018, Pro 700454
Off A456 3 miles NE of Kidderminster; turn under railway viaduct in village of Blakedown.
Undulating parkland course,
Pro Keith Wheeler; Founded 1926
9 holes, 6472 yards, S.S.S. 71
♦ Welcome WD; WE with a member.
🍸 WD £17.50; WE £10.
⛳ Welcome by prior arrangement; from £15.
🍽 Full facilities except Mon.
✈ Cedars.

5B 18 Cirencester
Cheltenham Rd, Bagendon, Cirencester, Glos, GL7 7BH
☎ (01285) 652465, Fax 650665, Pro 656124, Rest 659987, Bar 653939
Off A435 Cirencester-Cheltenham road 1.5 miles from Cirencester.
Undulating course.
Pro Peter Garratt; Founded 1893
Designed by James Braid
18 holes, 6055 yards, S.S.S. 69
♦ Welcome.
🍸 WD £25; WE £30.
⛳ Welcome by arrangement.
🍽 Full facilities.
Driving range, tuition and golf clinics available, 6-hole short academy course, buggies for hire.
✈ Kings Head.

5B 19 City of Coventry (Brandon Wood)
Brandon Lane, Wolston, Coventry, CV8 3GQ
☎ (024) 7654 3133, Sec 7654 3141
6 miles S of Coventry off A45.
Parkland course.
Pro Chris Gledhill;
Designed by Frank Pennink
18 holes, 6610 yards, S.S.S. 72
♦ Welcome.
🍸 WD £8.45; WE £11.25.
⛳ Welcome on application to

professional; terms on application.
🍽 Clubhouse facilities.
Driving range, practice putting greens, tuition and golf clinics available, buggies and clubs for hire.
✈ Brandon Hall Hotel.

5B 20 Cleeve Hill
Cleeve Hill, Cheltenham, Glos, GL52 3PW
☎ (01242) 672025, Fax 672025, Pro 672592
6 miles N of M5; 4 miles from Cheltenham off A46.
Municipal heathland course.
Pro Dave Finch; Founded 1891
18 holes, 6411 yards, S.S.S. 71
♦ Welcome WD; some restrictions WE.
🍸 WD £11; WE £13.
⛳ Welcome by prior arrangement; catering packages; skittles alley.
🍽 Bar snacks.
✈ Rising Sun.

5B 21 Cocks Moor Woods
Alcester Rd South, Kings Heath, Birmingham, W Midlands, B14 6ER
☎ (0121) 4443584, Fax 4411305
On A435 near city boundary.
Public parkland course.
Pro Steve Ellis; Founded 1924
18 holes, 5769 yards, S.S.S. 68
♦ Welcome.
🍸 WD £9; WE £10.
⛳ Welcome by arrangement.
🍽 Full clubhouse facilities.
Leisure centre on site.

5B 22 Copt Heath
1220 Warwick Rd, Knowle, Solihull, Warwickshire, B93 9LN
☎ (01564) 772650, Fax 771022, Pro 776155, Rest 771504
From M42 Junction 5 take A4141; course 0.5 miles.

Edgbaston

So where do the stars of other sports play their golf? After any Test match – and as far as England are concerned too many of them finish too early in Birmingham – Edgbaston is often the golfing sanctuary.

Around England there are many special courses that the players retreat to either to reflect on outstanding achievements or to lick their wounds.

Edgbaston is one of those chosen courses. Conveniently close to the cricket ground it may be, but the course has much more to commend it.

A mixture of tranquility and history provides the perfect backdrop on a golf course that like so many is a haven from the roar of the city.

Edgbaston is an area of Birmingham that is rich in sporting tradition. It has the tennis courts where the women play their annual pre-Wimbledon tournament. But it is, of course, the cricket ground that has made the leafy suburb most famous. And all the players and commentators have nothing but the highest regard for the course.

Follow the cricket circuit around the Test grounds and you will find some of the better courses. In Manchester many head for courses in Cheshire after the close of play.

It is not unusual to find them wandering the fairways at Mottram Hall on the southern edge of the metropolis close to the expensive town of Wilmslow.

In Nottingham the refuge from Trent Bridge tends to be Radcliffe on Trent and from Headingley Ilkley leads the options but Sand Moor, Moor Town and, for the lucky few, Alwoodley as well.

There are newer and more well known courses in the Midlands like The Belfry and the newly sculptured Forest of Arden where the English Open was resident for several years and is now the host of Senior events on the circuit.

But it is the ageing process that has gracefully given Edgbaston its strongest features so that now, along with older clubs like Handsworth, Harborne, Kidderminster and Moseley, it offers a more rounded golfing day out. — **CG**

Parkland course.
Pro B J Barton; Founded 1910
Designed by H. Vardon
18 holes, 6508 yards, S.S.S. 71
† Welcome WD.
⌤ WD £40 all day.
⌁ Welcome by prior arrangement
with secretary; maximum 36; terms
on application; from £40.
⍟ Clubhouse facilities.
⌐ Greswolde Arms; St Johns.

5B 23 Cotswold Edge
Upper Rushmire, Wotton-under-Edge,
Gloucestershire, GL12 7PT
☎ (01453) 844167, Fax 845120, Pro
844398
On B4058 Wotton-under-Edge/
Tetbury road 8 miles from M5
Junction 14.
Meadowland course.
Pro David Gosling; Founded 1980
18 holes, 6170 yards, S.S.S. 71
† Welcome WD; WE with member.
⌤ WD £15; WE £20.
⌁ Welcome WD by prior
arrangement; packages available;
from £30.
⍟ Full clubhouse facilities.
⌐ Hunters Hall; Calcot Manor.

5B 24 Cotswold Hills
Ullenwood, Cheltenham, Glos, GL53
9QT
☎ (01242) 515264, Fax 515264, Pro
515263, Bar/Rest 573210
3 miles S of Cheltenham.
Parkland course on limestone; 1981
English Ladies Amateur.
Pro Norman Allen; Founded
1902/1976
Designed by M.D. Little
18 holes, 6750 yards, S.S.S. 72
† Welcome by prior arrangement.
⌤ WD £25; WE £30.
⌁ Welcome Wed and Thurs;
packages available; from £25.
⍟ Clubhouse facilities.
⌐ Crest Motel; George Hotel;
Lilleybrook; Golden Valley.

5B 25 Coventry
St Martin's Rd, Finham Park,
Coventry, Warwicks, CV3 6PJ
☎ (024) 7641 1452, Fax 7669 0131,
Pro 7641 1298, Sec 7641 4152,
Bar/Rest 7641 1123
Close to A45/A46 junction; take A45
towards Birmingham and left at island.
Parkland course.
Pro Phil Weaver; Founded 1887
Designed by Tom Vardon

18 holes, 6601 yards, S.S.S. 73
† Welcome WD; with member WE.
⌤ WD £35.
⌁ Welcome Wed and Thurs;
packages available; from £50-£55.
⍟ Clubhouse facilities.
⌐ Chesford Grange; Old Mill.

5B 26 Coventry Hearsall
Beechwood Ave, Earlsdon, Coventry,
CV5 6DF
☎ (024) 7667 2935, Fax 7669 1534,
Pro 7671 3156, Sec 7671 3470,
Bar/Rest 7667 5809
From A45/A429 towards City Centre
turn into Beechwood Avenue.
Parkland course.
Pro Mike Tarn; Founded 1894/1921
18 holes, 6005 yards, S.S.S. 69
† Welcome with member.
⌤ Terms on application.
⌁ Welcome Tues and Thurs.
⍟ Clubhouse facilities.
⌐ Hylands Hotel.

5B 27 Cromwell Course at Nailcote Hall
Nailcote Hall Hotel, Nailcote Lane,
Berkswell, Warwickshire, CV7 7DE
☎ (024) 7646 6174, Fax 7647 0720,
▤ www.nailcotehall.co.uk
⌁ info@nailcotehall.co.uk
Take A452 Balsall Common junction
from B4101 and follow brown signs
towards Tile Hall/ Coventry; hotel 1.5
miles on right.
Parkland course.
Pro Sid Mouland; Founded 1994
Designed by Short Course Golf Ltd
9 holes, 1023 yards, par 27
† Welcome.
⌤ WD £10; WE £10.
⌁ Welcome by prior arrangement;
terms on application.
⍟ Full hotel facilities.
Practice putting green, tuition
available, leisure facilities (swimming
pool, croquet lawn tennis, sauna).
⌐ Nailcote Hall on site.

5B 28 Droitwich Golf & Country Club
Westford House, Ford Lane,
Droitwich, WR9 0BQ
☎ (01905) 774344, Fax 797290, Pro
770207, Rest 796226
Off A38 1 mile N of town.
Undulating meadowland course.
Pro Chris Thompson; Founded 1897
18 holes, 5976 yards, S.S.S. 68
† Welcome WD with handicap certs;
with member at WE.

⌤ WD £26.
⌁ Welcome Wed and Fri.
⍟ Bar, bar meals and restaurant.
⌐ The Chateau Impney; Raven.

5B 29 Dudley
Turners Hill, Rowley Regis, Warley, W
Midlands, B65 9DP
☎ (01384) 254020, Sec 233877, Fax
233877
1 mile S of town centre.
Undulating parkland course.
Pro Paul Taylor; Founded 1893
18 holes, 5714 yards, S.S.S. 68
† Welcome WD.
⌤ WD £18.
⌁ Welcome by prior arrangement;
packages available for 20 or more;
10% reduction; from £25.
⍟ Lunch and evening meals.
⌐ Travelodge.

5B 30 Dymock Grange
The Old Grange, Dymock, Glos,
GL18 2AN
☎ (01531) 890840, Fax 890852
On A4172 off the A449 Ledbury-
Ross-on-Wye Rd.
Parkland course.
Pro Sara Foster (touring pro);
Founded 1995
18 holes, 4600 yards, S.S.S. 65
† Welcome with prior reservation.
⌤ WD £10; WE £14.
⌁ Welcome by prior arrangement.
⍟ Bar, restaurant; fitness centre.

5B 31 Edgbaston
Edgbaston Hall, Church Rd,
Edgbaston, Birmingham, B15 3TB
☎ (0121) 454 1736, Fax 454 2395,
Pro 454 3226, Bar/Rest 454 8014
From city centre take A38 Bristol
road; after 1.5 miles turn right into
Priory Road (B4217); after mini
roundabout, club 100 yards.
Parkland course; woods and lake.
Pro J Cundy; Founded 1090/1935
Designed by H.S. Colt
18 holes, 6106 yards, S.S.S. 69
† Welcome except Sat comp days
before 2pm and Sun before 11.15am.
⌤ WD £37.50; WE £50.
⌁ Welcome WD except Thurs;
packages available including private
function room, changing rooms, golf
and catering; minimum 20, maximum
100.
⍟ Extensive clubhouse facilities;
restaurant, bars and private rooms.
Practice range, practice areas and
nets.

Copperfield House; Portland House; Apollo; Plough & Harrow; Swallow.

5B 32 Evesham
Craycombe Links,Fladbury Cross, Pershore, Worcs, WR10 2QS
☎(01386) 860395, Fax 861356, Pro 861144
3 miles W of Evesham towards Worcester on A4538.
Parkland course by river.
Pro Charles Haynes; Founded 1894
9 holes, 6415 yards, S.S.S. 71
♦ Welcome with prior arrangement WD; WE with a member.
Ⅰ WD non members £20, guests of members £10.
☞Welcome with prior arrangement; terms on application.
⚑ Clubhouse facilities.
One practice ground, two practice greens, PGA tuition available.

5B 33 Filton
Golf Course Lane, Filton, Bristol, BS34 7QS
☎(0117) 9692021, Fax 9314359, Pro 9694158, Sec 9694169
M5 Junction 16 to A38 at Filton roundabout turn right then first right at lights.
Parkland course with views of Brecon Beacons.
Pro Nicky Lums; Founded 1909
Designed by F. Hawtree & Son
18 holes, 6318 yards, S.S.S. 69
♦ Welcome WD only; guests of members at WE.
Ⅰ WD £20.
☞Welcome by prior arrangement; terms on application.
⚑ Full clubhouse facilities.
✒ Aztec; Stakis; Premier.

5B 34 Forest Hills
Mile End Road, Coleford, Gloucestershire, GL16 7QD
☎(01594) 810620, Fax 810823
Course is on the B4028 towards Gloucester 0.5 miles from Coleford town centre.
Meadowland course.
Pro Richard Ballard; Founded 1992
Designed by Adrian Stiff
18 holes, 5674 yards, S.S.S. 67
♦ Welcome.
Ⅰ WD £15; WE £20.
☞Welcome by prior arrangement; terms on application.
Driving range, buggies and clubs for hire, tuition available 7 days a week;

junior academy Sat morning; new juniors always welcome.
⚑ Full clubhouse facilities.

5B 35 Fulford Heath
Tanners Green Lane, Wythall, Birmingham, B47 6BH
☎(01564) 822930, Fax 822629, Pro 822930, Sec 824758, Bar/Rest 822806
8 miles S of Birmingham.
Parkland course.
Pro David Down; Founded 1933
18 holes, 5959 yards, S.S.S. 69
♦ Welcome WD; with member WE.
Ⅰ WD £34.
☞Welcome by arrangement on Tues and Thurs, possibly one other day; golf and catering packages available; prices on application.
⚑ Clubhouse facilities.

5B 36 Gay Hill
Hollywood Lane, Hollywood, Birmingham, W Midlands, B47 5PP
☎(0121) 430 8544, Fax 436 7796, Pro 474 6001, Sec 430 8544, Bar/Rest 430 6523
On A435 7 miles from Birmingham city centre and 3 miles from Junction 3 of the M42.
Meadowland course.
Pro Andrew Potter; Founded 1913
18 holes, 6532 yards, S.S.S. 71
♦ Welcome WD; WE with member but not before 12.30pm Sun.
Ⅰ WD £28.50.
☞Welcome Thurs by arrangement.
⚑ Full facilities.
✒ George.

5B 37 Gloucester
Jarvis Hotel & CC, Robinswood Hill, Matson Lane, Gloucester, Gloucestershire, GL4 9EA
☎(01452) 411331, Fax 307212, Bar/Rest 525653
2 miles S of Gloucester on B4073 to Painswick.
Parkland course.
Pro Peter Darnell; Founded 1976
Designed by Donald Steel
18 holes, 6170 yards, S.S.S. 69
♦ Welcome.
Ⅰ WD £19; WE £25.
☞Welcome; terms on application.
⚑ Full hotel and clubhouse facilities.
✒ Jarvis Gloucester Hotel & CC.

5B 38 Grange (GPT GC)
Copsewood, Coventry, W Midlands, CV3 1HS

☎(024) 7656 2336, Bar/Rest 7645 1465
2.5 miles from Coventry on A428 Binley Rd.
Meadowland course.
Founded 1924
Re-designed by T.J. McAuley
9 holes, 6100 yards, S.S.S. 71
♦ Welcome WD before 2pm; except Wed; not Sat; Sun after 11am.
Ⅰ WD £10; Sun £15.
☞Welcome by arrangement with secretary.
⚑ By arrangement only.
✒ Hilton.

5B 39 Grove Golf Centre
Fordbridge, Leominster, Herefordshire, HR6 0LE
☎(01568) 610602, Fax 615333, Pro 615333
3 miles S of Leominster on A49.
Wooded parkland course.
Pro Phil Brooks; Founded 1994
Designed by J Gaunt/R Sandow
9 holes, 3560 yards, S.S.S. 60
♦ Public pay´and play.
Ⅰ WD £4; WE £5.
☞Welcome any time; terms on application.
⚑ Full bar and restaurant.
Practice range, floodlit bays; putting green.

5B 40 Habberley
Low Habberley, Kidderminster, Worcs, DY11 5RG
☎(01562) 745756
2 miles NW of Kidderminster.
Parkland course.
Founded 1924
9 holes, 5481 yards, S.S.S. 69
♦ Welcome WD if member of recognised club; WE and Bank Holidays with member only.
Ⅰ WD £10; WE £10.
☞Welcome by prior arrangement; terms on application.
⚑ Clubhouse facilities.
✒ Gainsborough; Heath Hotel.

5B 41 Hagley Country Club
Wassell Grove, Hagley, W Midlands, DY9 9JW
☎(01562) 883701, Pro 883852
4 miles S of Birmingham on A456.
Undulating parkland course.
Pro Ian Clark; Founded 1979
18 holes, 6353 yards, S.S.S. 72
♦ Welcome WD; WE with a member after 10am.
Ⅰ WD £22.50.

Welcome WD by prior arrangement through the club manager; packages available; also squash.
Bar and restaurant facilities.

5B 42 Halesowen
The Leasowes, Halesowen, west Midlands, B62 8QF
(0121) 550 1041, Pro 503 0593, Sec 501 3606, Bar/Rest 550 8680
M5 Junction 3; A456 Kidderminster 2 miles.
Parkland course.
Pro J Nicholas; Founded 1907
18 holes, 5754 yards, S.S.S. 68
Welcome; WE with member only; Bank Holidays by arrangement.
WD £18; WE £18.
Welcome by prior arrangement with Sec, packages available for groups of 25 or more; from £18.
Clubhouse facilities except Mon evening.

5B 43 Handsworth
11 Sunningdale Close, Handsworth, Handsworth, Birmingham, W Midlands, B20 1NP
(0121) 554 0599, Fax 554 3387, Pro 523 5594, Sec 554 3387
Course is close to either Junction 1 of the M5 or Junction 7 of the M6 off Hamstead Hill.
Parkland course.
Pro Lee Bashford; Founded 1895
18 holes, 6267 yards, S.S.S. 70
Welcome WD with handicap certs; guests of members at WE.
WD £30.
Welcome WD by arrangement; special packages available.
Full clubhouse facilities except Mon.
Practice range, practice ground; squash; tuition available.
Post House.

5B 44 Harborne
40 Tennal Rd, Birmingham, W Midlands, B32 2JE
(0121) 427 1728, Pro 4273512, Sec 427 3058, Bar 427 1728, Rest 428 3373
2 miles SW of city centre adjacent to M5 Junction 3.
Parkland course.
Pro Alan Quarterman; Founded 1893
Designed by H.S. Colt
18 holes, 6235 yards, S.S.S. 70
Welcome WD.
WD £35; WE £35.

Welcome by prior arrangement; terms on application; £30.
Clubhouse facilities.
Hotels The Strathallan; The Hyatt.

5B 45 Harborne Church Farm
Vicarage Rd, Harborne, Birmingham, B17 0SN
(0121) 427 1204, Fax 428 3126
5 miles SW of Birmingham city centre.
Parkland course.
Pro Paul Johnson; Founded 1926
9 holes, 4882 yards, S.S.S. 64
Welcome with prior booking.
WD £8; WE £8.50.
Welcome by prior arrangement; terms on application.
Full facilities

5B 46 Hatchford Brook
Coventry Rd, Sheldon, Birmingham, B26 3PY
(0121) 743 9821, Fax 743 3420, Sec 779 3780, Bar/Rest 743 9250
On A45 Birmingham to Coventry road close to Birmingham airport.
Parkland course.
Pro Mark Hampton; Founded 1969
18 holes, 6120 yards, S.S.S. 69
Welcome.
WD £9, WE £10.
Welcome by prior arrangement; terms on application.
Full facilities.
Metropole; Arden Motel.

5B 47 Henbury
Henbury Hill, Westbury-on-Trym, Bristol, Gloucs, BS10 7QB
(0117) 9500044, Fax 9591928, Pro 9502121, Bar/Rest 9500660
Leave M5 Junction 17, 2nd exit from roundabout into Crow Lane, course at top of hill.
Parkland course.
Pro Nick Riley; Founded 1891
18 holes, 6007 yards, S.S.S. 70
Welcome WD with handicap certs.
WD and WE: non-members £25, guests of members £15.
Welcome Tues and Fri by arrangement.
Tuition available, club and trolley hire.
Full facilities.
Many in local area.

5B 48 Henley Golf & CC
Crocketts Manor, Birmingham Rd, Henley in Arden, Warwicks B95 5QA

(01564) 793715, Fax 795754
On A3400·4 miles N of Stratford-on-Avon.
Parkland course.
18 holes, 6933 yards, S.S.S. 73
Welcome by prior arrangement.
WD £20; WE £25.
Full packages available via Pro shop.
Full Country Club facilities.
Driving range.

5B 49 Hereford Municipal
The Racecourse, Holmer Road, Hereford, HR4 9UD
(01432) 344376, Pro 344376
A49 towards Leominster in centre of race track.
Public parkland course.
Pro Gary Morgan; Founded 1983
9 holes, 6120 yards, S.S.S. 69
Welcome except race days.
9 holes: WD £4.25, WE £5.25; 18 holes: WE £6.50, WE £8.00; reduced green fees available for juniors and OAPs.
Welcome by prior arrangement; packages include 18 holes, coffee and 2-course meal; please ring for details.
Bar and restaurant facilities.
Practice range, practice ground; club hire £2.50; trolley hire £1.20; tuition available.
Starling Gate; Travel Inn.

5B 50 Herefordshire
Ravens Causeway, Wormsley, Hereford, HR4 8LY
(01432)*830219, Pro 830465, Sec 830817, Bar 830877
Off Roman Road from Hereford in direction of Weobley.
Parkland course.
Pro D Hemming; Founded 1898
Designed by Major Hutchison
18 holes, 6078 yards, S.S.S. 69
Welcome WD; WE by arrangement.
WD £19; WE £22.
Welcome; terms available on application.
Clubhouse facilities.
The Burton Hotel; The Pilgrim Hotel.

5B 51 Hill Top
Park Lane, Handsworth, Birmingham, W Midlands, B21 8LJ
(0121) 554 4463
From M5 Junction 1 follow signs for Handsworth.

Parkland course.
Pro Kevin Highfield; Founded 1980
18 holes, 6208 yards, S.S.S. 69
† Welcome; link card service, book
8 days in advance.
⌐ WD £8.50; WE £9.
⌐Welcome WD by prior
arrangement with the professional;
packages available.
◉ Full clubhouse facilities.
↵ Post House, W Bromwich.

5B 52 **Ingon Manor Golf &
Country Club**
Ingon Lane, Snitterfield, Nr Stratford
Upon Avon, Warwickshire, CV37 0QE
☎(01789) 731857, Fax 731657, Pro
731938
Course is signposted from the M40
Junction 15.
Parkland course.
Pro Rob Greer; Founded 1993
Designed by David Hemstock
Associates & Colin Geddes
18 holes, 6623 yards, S.S.S. 71
† Welcome.
⌐ WD £20; WE £25.
⌐Welcome by prior arrangement;
terms on application; packages
available; terms available on
application.
◉ Full clubhouse and hotel
restaurant and bar facilities.
Driving range, club, buggy, trolley and
shoe hire, tuition for adults and
juniors, group tuition available,
practice putting green.
↵ On site Ingon Manor Hotel.

5B 53 **The Kendleshire**
Henfield Rd, Coalpit Heath, Bristol,
Glos, BS17 2TG
☎(0117) 9567007, Fax 573433, Pro
9567000
1 mile from M32.
Parkland course with soft spikes.
Pro Paul Barrington; Founded 1997
Designed by A Stiff
18 holes, 6507 yards, S.S.S. 71
† Welcome WD; WE by
arrangement.
⌐ WD £18; WE £24.
⌐Welcome by prior arrangement;
packages on request; function room
for 250.
◉ Bar and restaurant facilities
available.
Grass practice range, 6-hole short
course, tuition available, children's
club 'Kendleshire Kubs'; buggies,
shoes and clubs for hire.
↵ Post House; Emerson Green
Beefeater.

5B 54 **Kenilworth**
Crewe Lane, Kenilworth, Warwicks,
CV8 2EA
☎(01926) 854296, Fax 864453, Sec
858517, Pro 512732
6 miles from Coventry.
Undulating parkland course.
Pro Steve Yates; Founded 1889/1936
Designed by Hawtree
18 holes, 6400 yards, S.S.S. 71
† Welcome by arrangement.
⌐ WD £30; WE £37.
⌐Welcome Wed; packages
available; small conference room;
terms on application.
◉ Clubhouse facilities.
6-hole par 3 course, tuition and golf
clinics available, contact Pro for
details.
↵ Chesford Grange; DeMontfort.

5B 55 **Kidderminster**
Russell Rd, Kidderminster, Worcs,
DY10 3HT
☎(01562) 822303, Fax 862041
Course signposted off A449 within 1
mile of town centre.
Parkland course.
Pro Nick Underwood; Founded 1909
18 holes, 6405 yards, S.S.S. 71
† Welcome WD only; WE with
member only.
⌐ WD £30.
⌐Welcome Thurs by prior
arrangement.
◉ Full facilities except Mon.
↵ The Gainsborough; Collingdale;
Stone Manor.

5B 56 **Kings Norton**
Brockhill Lane, Weatheroak,
Alvechurch, Birmingham, B48 7ED
☎(01564) 826706, Fax 826955, Pro
822635, Sec 826789, Bar/Rest
822821
1 miles N of M42 Junction 3 just off
A435.
Parkland course; 3 x 9 combinations.
Pro Kevin Hayward; Founded 1892
Designed by F. Hawtree & Son
18 holes, 7019 yards, S.S.S. 74; 9-
holes, 3256yards, par 36
† Welcome WD.
⌐ WD £30.
⌐Welcome by prior arrangement;
full catering and golf packages;
separate reception room, bar; 100-
seater ball room; use of club starter;
from £30.
◉ Full clubhouse facilities.
Practice range, 12-hole par 3 short
course, PGA tuition available.
↵ Inkford Cottage; Pine Lodge.

5B 57 **Kington**
Bradnor Hill, Kington, Herefordshire,
HR5 3RE
☎(01544) 230340, Fax 340270, Pro
231320, Sec 340270
From A44 take the B4355 Presteigne
road for 100 metres and then left to
Bradnor Hill.
Mountain links: highest 18-hole
course in England.
Pro Dean Oliver; Founded 1925
Designed by C.K. Hutchinson
18 holes, 5228 yards, S.S.S. 68
† Welcome with prior arrangement.
⌐ WD £15; WE £20.
⌐Welcome by prior arrangement
with Pro shop; extensive menu and
facilities available; winter packages
available; prices on application.
◉ Full catering and bar facilities.
↵ Royal George.

5B 58 **Ladbrook Park**
Poolhead Lane, Tamworth-in-Arden,
Warwicks, B94 5ED
☎(01564) 742264, Pro 742581,
Bar/Rest 742220
Take A435 to Tamworth/Portway; left
into Penn Lane; then left into Broad
Lane and left into Poolhead Lane.
Parkland course.
Pro Richard Mountford; Founded
1908
Designed by H.S. Colt
18 holes, 6427 yards, S.S.S. 71
† Welcome WD; except Tues am.
⌐ WD £25.
⌐Welcome by prior arrangement
with the Secretary; full golfing and
catering packages; terms on
application.
◉ Restaurant and bar facilities.
↵ Regency; Plough Inn.

5B 59 **Lansdown**
Lansdown, Bath, Avon, BA1 9BT
☎(01225) 420242, Fax 339252, Pro
420242, Sec 422138, Bar/Rest
425007
From M4 Junction 18 take A46
towards Bath; at roundabout take
A420 towards Bristol; take first left
and club is 2 miles on right by Bath
racecourse.
Elevated parkland course.
Pro Terry Mercer; Founded 1894
Designed by Harry Colt
18 holes, 6316 yards, S.S.S. 70
† Welcome; handicap certs
preferred.
⌐ WD £20; WE £20.
⌐Welcome by prior arrangement;
from £20.

🍽 Clubhouse snacks and meals.
🛏 Hilton.

5B 60 Lea Marston Hotel & Leisure Complex
Haunch Lane, Lea Marston, Warwickshire, B76 0BY
☎ (01675) 470468, Fax 470871, Pro 470707,
💻 www.leamarstonhotel.co.uk
📧 info@leamarstonhotel.co.uk
1 mile from M42 Junction 9 on A4097 Kingsbury road; 1.5 miles from The Belfry.
Parkland course.
Pro Andrew Stokes; Founded 1983
Designed by J.R. Blake
9 holes, 775 yards, par 3
⚑ Welcome.
💰 WD £1.25; WE £5; discounts for juniors and OAPs.
🌿 Welcome by prior arrangement; tennis; pool table; health club; swimming pool.
🍽 Bar and restaurant facilities.
Practice range, 26 bays floodlit; golf simulator; tuition available.
🛏 Lea Marston on site; golf breaks, call reservations for details.

5B 61 Leamington & County
Golf Lane, Whitnash, Leamington Spa, Warwicks, CV31 2QA
☎ (01926) 425961, Fax 425961, Pro 428014, Sec 425961
6 mins from M40 towards Leamington Spa and then take Whitnash signs.
Parkland course.
Pro Iain Grant; Founded 1908
Designed by H.S. Colt
18 holes, 6437 yards, S.S.S. 71
⚑ Welcome with handicap certs.
💰 WD £30; WE £40.
🌿 Welcome Mon, Wed, Thurs; full golf and catering facilities; from £28.
🍽 Clubhouse facilities.
🛏 Marriott Courtyard.

5B 62 Leominster
Ford Bridge, Leominster, Hereford, HR6 0LE
☎ (01568) 610055, Fax 610055, Pro 611402, Sec 610055
3 miles S of Leominster on A49.
Undulating parkland course running alongside River Lugg.
Pro Andrew Ferriday; Founded 1903/67/90
Designed by Bob Sandow
18 holes, 6026 yards, S.S.S. 69
⚑ Welcome by arrangement.
💰 WD £17; WE £23.

🌿 Welcome WD except Mon; 36 holes of golf; coffee, light lunch and 3-course dinner; fishing on river also available; from £31.
🍽 Full bar and bar snacks; restaurant every day except Mon.
Practice range, 18 bays.
🛏 Talbot; Royal Oak.

5B 63 Lickey Hills (Rose Hill)
Lickey Hills, Rednal, Birmingham, W Midlands, B45 8RR
☎ (0121) 453 3159
M5 Junction 4 or M42 Junction 1 signposted to Lickey Hills Park.
Public parkland course.
Pro Joe Kelly; Founded 1927
Designed by Carl Bretherton
18 holes, 5835 yards, S.S.S. 68
⚑ Welcome.
💰 WD £9, WE £10.
🌿 Welcome by arrangement.
🍽 Snacks.
🛏 Westmead.

5B 64 Lilley Brook
Cirencester Rd, Charlton Kings, Cheltenham, Glos, GL53 8EG
☎ (01242) 526785, Fax 256880, Pro 525201, Bar/Rest 580715
2 miles SE of Cheltenham on A435 Cirencester road.
Parkland course.
Pro Forbes Hadden; Founded 1922
Designed by MacKenzie
18 holes, 6212 yards, S.S.S. 70
⚑ Welcome with handicap certs.
💰 WD £25; WE £30.
🌿 Welcome WD by arrangement; packages available; terms on application.
🍽 Full clubhouse facilities.
🛏 Cheltenham Park; Charlton Kings.

5B 65 Little Lakes
Lye Head, Rock, Beweley, Worcs, DY12 2UZ
☎ (01299) 266385, Fax 266398
Course is on the A456 2 miles W of Beweley; turn left at Greenhouse and Garden Centre.
Undulating parkland course.
Pro Mark Laing; Founded 1975
Designed by Michael Cooksey
18 holes, 5644 yards, S.S.S. 68
⚑ Welcome.
💰 WD £14; WE £19.
🌿 Welcome by prior arrangement; packages available; from £28.
🍽 Lunches available.
Practice range, buggies for hire,

tuition and golf clinics available, individually and on a group basis.
🛏 Heath.

5B 66 Lydney
Lakeside Ave, Lydney, Glos GL15 5QA
☎ (01594) 842614
Entering Lydney on A48 from Gloucester, turn left at bottom of Highfield Hill and look for Lakeside Ave on left.
Parkland course.
Founded 1909
9 holes, 5298 yards, S.S.S. 66
⚑ Welcome; WE with member.
💰 WD £10.
🌿 Small societies by arrangement; packages can be arranged.
🍽 Bar, lunch and dinners.
🛏 Speech House.

5B 67 Mangotsfield
Carson's Rd, Mangotsfield, Bristol, Glos, BS16 9LW
☎ (0117) 9565501, Fax 9565501
From M32 leave at junction for Filton/Downend; follow signs for Downend and Mangotsfield.
Hilly meadowland course.
Pro Craig Trewin; Founded 1975
18 holes, 5290 yards, S.S.S. 66
⚑ Welcome.
💰 WD £10; WE £12.
🌿 Welcome by prior arrangement; packages available.
🍽 Full clubhouse facilities.
🛏 Post House.

5B 68 Marriott Forest of Arden
Maxstoke Lane, Meriden, Coventry, Warwicks, CV7 7HR
☎ (01676) 526113, Fax 526125, Pro 0958 632170, Sec 522335, Bar/Rest 522335,
Off A45 close to M42 Junction 6 or M6 South Junction 4.
Championship parkland course; site of English Open 2000.
Pro Kim Thomas; Founded 1970/91
Designed by Donald Steel
Arden: 18 holes, 7134 yards, S.S.S. 71; Aylesford: 18 holes, 6525 yards, S.S.S. 71
⚑ Residents and visitors welcome.
💰 Terms on application.
🌿 Corporate packages can be booked through golf office; 27 holes, coffee, buffet lunch, dinner, strokesaver and driving range tokens; £135.
🍽 Clubhouse and hotel facilities.

Practice range, 6 undercover bays; teaching facility.
↝ Marriott Forest of Arden.

5B 69 Maxstoke Park
Castle Lane, Coleshill, Warwicks, B46 2RD
☎(01675) 466743, Fax 466743, Pro 464915, Bar/Rest 462158
From M6 take Coleshill road and at high street lights turn towards Nuneaton; club 2 miles.
Parkland course.
Pro Neil McEwan; Founded 1898/45
Designed by Tom Marks
18 holes, 6442 yards, S.S.S. 71
† Welcome with handicap certs.
Ⅰ WD £25; WE £27.50.
◌ Welcome Tues and Thurs; packages on application; from £25.
◉ Clubhouse facilities.
Practice range, practice area; lessons available from Pro.
↝ Lea Marston Hotel.

5B 70 Memorial Park
Memorial Park Golf Office, Kenilworth Rd, Coventry, W Midlands
☎(024) 7667 5415
1 mile from the city centre.
Municipal parkland course.
Designed by John Bredemus
18 holes, 2840 yards
† Welcome.
Ⅰ WD £3.45; WE £3.45.
◌ Welcome; tennis courts; playground; bowling greens.
◉ Café in park in summer.

5B 71 Minchinhampton ℭ
Old Course, Minchinhampton Common, Stroud, Glos GL6 9AQ
☎(01453) 832642, Pro 836382, Fax 832642
New course, Minchinhampton, Stroud, Glos, GL6 9BE
☎(01453) 833866, Pro 833860, Fax 835703, Bar/Rest 833858
Old course is on Minchinhampton Common 3 miles SE of Stroud; New course between Avening and Minchinhampton off B4014.
Common land course (Old); Parkland course (New).
Pro C Steele; Founded 1889 (Old); Founded 1975 (New)
Designed by R Wilson (Old); Designed by F.W. Hawtree (New)
Old: 18 holes, 6019 yards, S.S.S. 69; New: Avening 18 holes, 6279 yards, S.S.S. 70; Cherington: 18 holes, 6320 yards, S.S.S. 70

† Welcome (Old); Welcome by prior arrangement (New).
Ⅰ WD £12, WE £15 (Old); WD £26, WE £30 (New).
◌ Welcome by prior arrangement; full range of packages available; terms on application.
◉ Both clubs provide clubhouse bar and catering facilities.
Both have practice grounds; tuition available by contacting Pro.
↝ Amberley Inn; Bear of Rodborough; Burleigh House.

5B 72 Moor Hall
Moor Hall Drive, Sutton Coldfield, W Midlands, B75 6LN
☎(0121) 308 6130, Pro 308 5106, Bar 308 0103
From M42 take A446 to Bassets Pole roundabout; follow Sutton Coldfield road and at first lights; course 200 yards on left.
Parkland course.
Pro Alan Partridge; Founded 1932
18 holes, 6249 yards, S.S.S. 70
† Welcome WD; after 12.30pm Thurs.
Ⅰ WD £30.
◌ Welcome Tues and Wed by prior arrangement.
◉ Full facilities.
↝ Moor Hall.

5B 73 Moseley
Springfield Rd, Kings Heath, Birmingham, B14 7DX
☎(0121) 444 2115, Fax 441 4662, Sec 444 4957
✉ admin@mosgolf.freeserve.co.uk
On Birmingham ring road 0.5 miles E of Alcester road.
Parkland course.
Pro Gary Edge; Founded 1892
18 holes, 6300 yards, S.S.S. 70
† Welcome WD with letter of introduction/handicap certs.
Ⅰ WD £37.
◌ Welcome Wed only by prior arrangement with secretary.
◉ Full facilities.
↝ The Strathallan, Edgbaston; Oxford Hotel, Mosely; St John's Swallow, Solihull.

5B 74 Naunton Downs ℭ
Naunton, Cheltenham, Gloucs, GL54 3AE
☎(01451) 850090, Fax 850091, Pro 850092, Bar/Rest 850093
On B4068 Stow-on-the-Wold to Cheltenham road near Naunton.

Downland course.
Pro Martin Seddon; Founded 1993
Designed by Jacob Pott
18 holes, 6078 yards, S.S.S. 69
† Welcome; WE by prior arrangement.
Ⅰ WD £19.95; WE £25.
◌ Welcome by prior arrangement; new conference room open; 3 astroturf tennis courts; terms on application.
◉ Lounge, spike bars; restaurant facilities; limited Mon.
↝ Washbourne Court; The Manor; local hotels in Stow on the Wold.

5B 75 Newbold Comyn
Newbold Terrace East, Leamington Spa, Warwicks, CV32 4EW
☎(01926) 421157, Sec 887220
Off B4099 Willes road.
Parkland course.
Pro R Carvell; Founded 1972
18 holes, 6259 yards, S.S.S. 70
† Welcome.
Ⅰ WD £8.75; WE £11.75.
◌ Welcome by prior arrangement; packages on request.
◉ At The Newbold Comyn Arms (next door).

5B 76 North Warwickshire
Hampton Lane, Meriden, W Midlands, CV7 7LL
☎(01676) 522259, Fax 522915, Sec 522915
Off A45 between Coventry and Birmingham.
Parkland course.
Pro Andrew Bownes; Founded 1894
9 holes, 6390 yards, S.S.S. 71
† WD only by prior arrangement.
Ⅰ WD £18.
◌ Welcome WD by arrangement; maximum 30 players; meals available in restaurant; terms available on application.
◉ Restaurant and bar facilities available.
↝ Manor Hotel; Strawberry Bank.

5B 77 North Worcestershire
Frankley Beeches Rd, Northfield, Birmingham, B31 5LP
☎(0121) 475 1026, Fax 476 8681, Pro 475 5721, Sec 475 1047
On A38 from Birmingham.
Parkland course.
Pro Finlay Clark; Founded 1907
Designed by James Braid
18 holes, 5950 yards, S.S.S. 68
† Welcome WD.

 WD £18.50.
Welcome Tues and Thurs; terms on application.
Full facilities available.
Norwood, King's Norton.

5B 78 Nuneaton
Golf Drive, Whitestone, Nuneaton, Warwicks, CV11 6QF
☎(024) 7634 7810, Fax 7632 7563, Pro 7634 0201
Leave M6 Junction 3 on A444 2 miles S of Nuneaton.
Wooded undulating meadowland course.
Pro Steve Bainbridge; Founded 1906
18 holes, 6480 yards, S.S.S. 71
Welcome WD; WE only with member.
 WD £25.
Welcome by prior arrangement; terms on application.
Full facilities except Mon.
Long Shoot; Chase.

5B 79 Oakridge
Arley Lane, Ansley Village, Nuneaton, Warwicks, CV10 9PH
☎(01676) 541389, Fax 542709, Pro 540542
Off B4112 3 miles W of Nuneaton.
Parkland course.
Pro Tony Harper; Founded 1993
18 holes, 6242 yards, S.S.S. 70
Welcome WD; WE with member.
 WD £15.
Welcome Mon-Thurs and Fri am.
Full meals and bar except Mon.
Marriott Forest of Arden.

5B 80 Olton
Mirfield Rd, Solihull, W Midlands, B91 1JH
☎(0121) 705 1083, Fax 711 2010, Bar/Rest 704 1936
2 miles from M42 Junction 5 on A41 towards Birmingham.
Parkland course.
Pro Craig Phillips; Founded 1893
18 holes, 6623 yards, S.S.S. 71
Welcome by arrangement.
 WD £30; WE £30.
Welcome WD by prior arrangement; terms on application.
Clubhouse facilities.
Ingon Manor.

5B 81 Ombersley
Bishops Wood Road, Lineholt, Ombersley, Droitwich, Worcs, WR9 0LE

☎(01905) 620747, Fax 620047, Sec 620047, Bar/Rest 620621
Off A449 Kidderminster to Worcester road at A4025.
Rural parkland setting.
Pro Graham Glenister; Founded 1991
Designed by On Course Design (David Morgan)
18 holes, 6139 yards, S.S.S. 69
Welcome; pay and play.
 WD £14.70; WE £19.60.
Welcome; society and corporate packages; prices on application.
Restaurant, bar, terrace.
Practice range, 36 bays (20 covered); chipping green, putting green; tuition available from PGA professionals; custom fit club maker Debbie Hall; open from 5am in summer; buggies and clubs for hire.
Hadley Bowling Green Inn.

5B 82 Painswick
Painswick Beacon, Painswick, Stroud, Glos, GL6 6TL
☎(01452) 812180
On the A46 one mile N of Painswick.
Commonland course.
Founded 1891
18 holes, 4680 yards, S.S.S. 64
Welcome WD and Sat; with member Sun.
 WD £15,Sat £20.
Welcome by prior arrangement with Sec; special packages.
Bar and catering facilities.
Practice range, practice ground.
The Painswick Hotel.

5B 83 Perdiswell
Bilford Road, Worcester, Worcs, WR3 8DX
☎(01905) 457189, Fax 756608, Pro 754668
Off main Droitwich road N of Worcester.
Pro Mark Woodward; Founded 1981
Meadowland course (extended, opened 2000).
18 holes, 5297 yards, par 68, S.S.S. 68
Welcome.
 Prices on application.
Welcome by prior arrangement; catering packages available.
Bar and snacks.
Teaching area, lessons available; leisure centre adjacent to course.

5B 84 Pitcheroak
Plymouth Rd, Redditch, Worcs, B97 4PB

☎(01527) 541054, Pro 541054, Bar/Rest 541043
Signposted from centre of Redditch.
Municipal parkland course.
Pro David Stewart; Founded 1973
9 holes, 18 tees, 4561 yards, S.S.S. 62
Welcome.
 WD £7.85; WE £9.10.
Welcome by prior arrangement.
Licensed clubhouse; bar and restaurant.
Practice range, practice area; putting green; tuition available; hire equipment available.
Mont Ville.

5B 85 Purley Chase G & Country Club
Ridge Lane, Nr Nuneaton, Warwickshire, CV10 0RB
☎(024) 7639 3118, Fax 7639 8015, Pro 7639 5348, Bar/Rest 7639 7468
From A5 Mancetter to Atherstone road; follow signs.
Parkland course.
Pro Gary Carver; Founded 1977
Designed by B. Tomlinson
18 holes, 6772 yards, S.S.S. 72
Welcome WD; WE afternoons only.
 WD £15; WE £25.
Welcome WD; various packages available; terms on application.
Full clubhouse facilities.
Hanover International; Bosworth Hall.

5B 86 Pype Hayes
Eachelhurst Rd, Walmley, Sutton Coldfield, W Midlands, B76 8EP
☎(0121) 351 1014
Off M6 Junction 6 on to Tyburn Rd; 1 mile to Eachelhurst Rd.
Public parkland course.
Pro Jim Bayliss; Founded 1932
18 holes, 5927 yards, S.S.S. 68
Welcome with prior booking.
 WD £8.50; WE £0.
Welcome WD by prior arrangement.
Cafeteria.
Pens Hall.

5B 87 Ravenmeadow
Hindlip Lane, Claines, Worcester, Worcs, WR3 8SA
☎(01905) 757525, Fax 759184, Sec 759183, Rest 458876
4 miles N of Worcester off the A38.
Parkland course.
Pro Dean Davis; Founded 1996

9 holes, 5435 yards, S.S.S. 66
Welcome.
9 holes: WD £7.75, WE and BH £9.75; 18 holes: WD £10.75, WE and BH £14.75 .
Welcome by prior arrangement; packages available; terms on application.
Bar and restaurant facilities.
Practice range, 10 bays floodlit; smart golf simulator; junior academy; adult and junior tuition.
The Founds; Star.

5B 88 **Redditch**
Lower Grinsty Lane, Callow Hill, Redditch, Worcs, B97 5JP
(01527) 543309, Fax 543079, Pro 546372, Sec 543079
2 miles W of Redditch.
Parkland course.
Pro Frank Powell; Founded 1913/72
Designed by F. Pennink
18 holes, 6671 yards, S.S.S. 72
Welcome; WE with members.
WD £20-£27.50.
Welcome by prior arrangement; catering packages and reductions available; terms on application.
Two practice areas; 9-hole putting course; buggies and clubs for hire; tuition available
Full clubhouse facilities.
The Quality Hotel; Mont Ville.

5B 89 **Robin Hood**
St Bernards Rd, Solihull, W Midlands, B92 7DJ
(0121) 706 0061, Fax 706 0061, Pro 706 0806, Sec 706 0061, Bar 706 0159,
robin.hood.golf.club@dial.pipex.com
2 miles S of M42 Junction 4 & 5.
Parkland course.
Pro A J Harvey; Founded 1893
Designed by H.S. Colt
18 holes, 6635 yards, S.S.S. 72
Welcome WD.
WD £29-£35; WE £12 with member.
Welcome Tues, Thurs, Fri with handicap certs; packages available; from £40.
Clubhouse facilities.
Arden Hotel.

5B 90 **Ross-on-Wye**
Two Park, Gorsley, Ross-on-Wye, Hereford, HR9 7UT
(01989) 720267, Fax 720212, Pro 720439, Bar/Rest 720457
5 miles N of Ross-on-Wye; close to M50 Junction 3.
Parkland course.
Pro Nick Catchpole; Founded 1903
Designed by C.K. Cotton
18 holes, 6451 yards, S.S.S. 73
Welcome.
WD £32-42; WE £32-42.
Welcome Wed, Thurs, Fri; packages available for 20+; deposit required; snooker tables; from £28.
Clubhouse facilities; bar and restaurant.
Practice range, practice area; tuition.
Chase Hotel; Royal Hotel.

5B 91 **Royal Forest Of Dean**
Lords Hill, Coleford, Glos, GL16 8BD
(01594) 832583, Fax 832584, Pro 833689
4 miles from Monmouth; 8 miles from Ross and Chepstow.
Parkland/meadowland course.
Pro John Hansel; Founded 1973
Designed by John Day of Alphagreen Ltd
18 holes, 5813 yards, S.S.S. 69
Welcome.
Winter WD and WE £10; Summer WD and WE £18.
Welcome by prior arrangement with the hotel; packages available for golf, catering and hotel; tennis; bowls; prices on application.
Full bar and restaurant service.
Bells, on site.

5B 92 **Rugby**
Clifton Rd, Rugby, Warwicks, CV21 3RD
(01788) 575134, Fax 542306, Pro 575134, Sec 542306, Bar 544637
On Rugby-Market Harborough road on right just past railway bridge.
Parkland course.
Pro Nathanial Summers; Founded 1891
18 holes, 5614 yards, S.S.S. 67
Welcome WD; WE with a member.
WD £20; WE £10 with a member .
Welcome WD by arrangement; packages available; minimum 12.
Full catering except Sun and Tues.
Practice range, practice area; tuition available with two teaching pros; trolleys for hire.
Carlton; Grosvenor.

5B 93 **Sapey Golf** 𝕿
Upper Sapey, Nr Worcester, Worcs, WR6 6XT
(01886) 853288, Fax 853485, Pro 853567/853288, Sec 853506, Bar/Rest 853567
On B4203 between Bromyard and Stourport.
Parkland course.
Pro Chris Knowles; Founded 1990
The Rowan: 18 holes, 5935 yards, S.S.S. 68; The Oaks: 9 holes, 1203 yards, par 27.
Welcome.
Rowan: WD £16; WE £22. Oaks: WD £4; WE £5.
Welcome by prior arrangement; terms on application.
Clubhouse facilities.
Hundred House; The Granary.

5B 94 **Sherdons**
Manor Farm, Tredington, Tewkesbury, Gloucs, GL20 7BP
(01684) 274782, Fax 275358
2 miles out of Tewkesbury on the A38; turn off at the Odessa Inn.
Parkland course.
Pro Philip Clark/John Parker; Founded 1995
9 holes, 2618 yards, S.S.S. 66
Welcome; pay and play.
9 holes: WD £6; WE £7.50; 18 holes: WD £11, WE £14.
Welcome WD; WE by arrangement.
Soft drinks, coffee, snacks.
Practice range, 26 floodlit bays.
Gubshill Manor.

5B 95 **Shirehampton Park** 𝕿
Park Hill, Shirehampton, Bristol, BS11 0UL
(0117) 9823059, Fax 9822083, Pro 9822488, Sec 9822083
2 miles from M5 Junction 18 on B4054 through Shirehampton.
Undulating parkland course.
Pro Brent Ellis; Founded 1907
18 holes, 5430 yards, S.S.S. 67
Welcome.
WD £18; WE £25.
Welcome; snacks, lunch available; dinner by appointment; from £18.
Clubhouse facilities.

5B 96 **Shirley**
Stratford Rd, Monkspath, Shirley, Solihull, W Midlands, B90 4EW
(0121) 744 6001, Fax 745 8220, Pro 745 4979, Clubhouse 744 7024
Towards Birmingham off M42 Junction 4.
Parkland course.
Pro S Botterill; Founded 1956

18 holes, 6507 yards, S.S.S. 71
⚑ Welcome WD; with member at
WE.
⚐ WD £25; WE £25.
⚲ Welcome by arrangement;
packages available; terms on
application.
⌾ Restaurant and bar facilities.
⌁ Regency Hotel.

5B 97 Sphinx Club
Siddeley Ave, Coventry, Warwicks,
CV3 1FZ
☎ (024) 7645 1361
4 miles S of Coventry, close to main
Binley Rd.
Parkland course; Founded 1948
9 holes, 4262 yards, S.S.S. 60
⚑ Welcome WD; with member at
WE.
⚐ Terms on application.
⚲ Welcome by arrangement.
⌾ Bar and bar meals.

5B 98 Stakis Puckrup Hall Hotel
Puckrup, Tewkesbury, Glos, GL20
6EL
☎ (01684) 296200, Fax 850788, Pro
271591
M50 Junction 1 towards Tewkesbury
on the A38.
Parkland course.
Pro Kevin Pickett; Founded 1992
Designed by Simon Gidman
18 holes, 6189 yards, S.S.S. 70
⚑ Welcome.
⚐ WD £25; WE and BH £30.
⚲ Welcome by prior arrangement;
full day and half-day packages can
be arranged; £19.50-£45.
⌾ Full clubhouse facilities;
restaurant for 50, licensed bar.
Practice area; tuition available; full
leisure facilities (gym, pool, jacuzzi,
beauty rooms, etc).
⌁ 112-room hotel on site.

5B 99 Stinchcombe Hill ♛
Stinchcombe Hill, Dursley, Glos,
GL11 6AQ
☎ (01453) 542015, Fax 549545, Pro
543878
From A38 at Dursley; right past Post
Office.
Downland course.
Pro Paul Bushell; Founded 1889
Designed by Arthur Hoare
18 holes, 5734 yards, S.S.S. 68
⚑ Welcome.
⚐ WD £20; WE £25.
⚲ Welcome Mon, Wed and Fri;

catering packages available for 12 or
more players; terms on application.
⌾ Full facilities and bar.
Practice range, putting green and
practice net, Pros available for tuition.
⌁ Club can provide full list.

5B 100 Stonebridge
Somers Rd, Meriden, Warwicks, CV7
7PL
☎ (01676) 522442, Fax 522447
2 miles from M42 Junction 6.
Parkland course.
Pro Steve Harrison; Founded 1995
18 holes, 6240 yards, S.S.S. 70
⚑ Welcome; bookings taken 9 days
in advance.
⚐ Mon-Thur £14, Fri £15; WE £16.
⚲ Welcome Mon to Thurs by prior
arrangement; from £20.
⌾ 2 bars, restaurant and conference
facilities.
Practice range, 21 bays floodlit.
⌁ Strawberry Bank.

5B 101 Stoneleigh Deer Park
The Old Deer Park, Coventry Rd,
Stoneleigh, Warwicks, CV8 3DR
☎ (024) 7663 9991, Fax 7651 1533,
Pro 7663 9912, Bar/Rest 7663 9916
Off A46 or A454 at Stoneleigh village.
Parkland course.
Pro Matt McGuire; Founded 1991
Designed by K. Harrison/Brown
18 holes, 5846 yards, S.S.S. 68
⚑ Welcome.
⚐ WD £14.50; WE £22.50.
⚲ Welcome with prior arrangement;
packages available; catering from
8am-9pm; also 9-hole, 1251-yard, par
3 course; from £14.50.
⌾ Catering and bar facilities.
Practice area.
⌁ Club can recommend.

5B 102 Stourbridge
Worcester Lane, Pedmore,
Stourbridge, Glos, DY8 2RB
☎ (01384) 393129, Fax 444660, Pro
393129, Sec 395566, Bar 393062
Course is one mile S of Stourbridge
on the B4147.
Parkland course.
Pro Mark Male; Founded 1892
18 holes, 6231 yards, S.S.S. 70
⚑ Welcome WD; with member WE.
⚐ WD £28.
⚲ Welcome Tues and Thurs;
packages available; from £25.
⌾ Restaurant and bar facilities.
⌁ Limes, Pedmore; Travelodge,
Hagley.

5B 103 Stratford Oaks
Bearley Road, Snitterfield, Stratford-
upon-Avon, Warwicks, CV37 0EZ
☎ (01789) 731982, Pro 731980
On A34 to Stratford following signs to
Snitterfield.
Parkland course.
Pro Andrew Dunbar; Founded 1989
Designed by Howard Swan
18 holes, 6121 yards, S.S.S. 69
⚑ Welcome with booking.
⚐ WD £20; WE £25.00.
⚲ Welcome WD by arrangement;
catering packages available.
⌾ Bar and restaurant facilities.
Practice range, 22 floodlit covered
bays.
⌁ Arden Valley; Alveston Manor.

5B 104 Stratford-upon-Avon
Tiddington Rd, Stratford-upon-Avon,
Warwicks, CV37 7BA
☎ (01789) 205749, Fax 414909, Pro
205677, Bar 297296, Rest 414546
On B4089 0.5 miles from river bridge.
Parkland course.
Pro David Sutherland; Founded 1894
18 holes, 6303 yards, par 72, S.S.S. 70
⚑ Welcome WD; WE by prior
arrangement.
⚐ WD £29.50; WE £35.
⚲ Welcome Tues and Thurs by
arrangement; catering packages
available.
⌾ Full bar and catering.
Two practice areas; lessons
available.
⌁ Many in Stratford.

5B 105 Sutton Coldfield
110 Thornhill Rd, Streetly, Warwicks,
B74 3ER
☎ (0121) 353 9633, Fax 3535503,
Bar/Rest 353 2014, Sutton Coldfield
Ladies ((0121) 3531682
On B4138 9 miles NE of Birmingham.
Heathland course.
Pro Jerry Hayes; Founded 1889
18 holes, 6541 yards, S.S.S. 71
⚑ Welcome WD; WE with member
only.
⚐ WD £25.
⚲ Welcome WD by arrangement
only.
⌾ Full clubhouse facilities.
Practice area.
⌁ Sutton Court; Post House.

5B 106 Tewkesbury Park ♛ Hotel
Lincoln Green Lane, Tewkesbury,
Glos, GL20 7DN

☎(01684) 295405, Fax 292386, Pro 294892, Sec 299452,
🖥 *www.chorushotels.com*
0.5 miles S of Tewkesbury on A38; 2 miles from M5 Junction 9.
Parkland course.
Pro Robert Taylor; Founded 1976
Designed by Frank Pennink
18 holes, 6533 yards, S.S.S. 72
🏌 Welcome.
🍴 WD £15; WE £25.
☝ Welcome WD; packages available; terms on application.
🍽 Clubhouse & hotel facilities.
🛏 75-bedroom Tewkesbury Park Hotel on site.

5B 107 Thornbury Golf Centre
Bristol Rd, Thornbury, Avon, BS35 3XL
☎(01454) 281144, Fax 281177, Pro 416543, Bar/Rest 281166
Off A38 at Berkeley Vale Motors; 5 miles from M4/M5.
Parkland course.
Pro Simon Hubbard; Founded 1992
Designed by Hawtree
18 holes, 6154 yards, S.S.S. 69
🏌 Welcome; pay and play.
🍴 WD £14.50; WE £17.
☝ Welcome; packages available; conference and function rooms; terms on application.
🍽 Full catering facilities.
Floodlit driving range; 2 piece balls; 18 hole, par 3 course; Europro teaching centre.
🛏 11-bedroom lodge on site.

5B 108 Tolladine
The Fairways, Tolladine Rd, Worcester, WR4 9BA
☎(01905) 21974, Fax 21974
M5 Junction 6 towards Warndon; club towards Worcester city centre.
Parkland course; steep in parts.
Founded 1898
9 holes, 5432 yards, S.S.S. 67
🏌 Welcome WD except after 4pm Wed; with member at WE.
🍴 WD £10; WE £8.
☝ Welcome by prior arrangement; terms on application.
🍽 By prior arrangement.

5B 109 Tracy Park Country Club
Bath Rd, Wick, Bristol, BS15 5RN
☎(0117) 9372251, Fax 9374288, Pro 9373521
From Junction 18 on M4, head S on the A46 towards Bath, then right on the A420 to Bristol, 4 miles.
Parkland course.
Pro Tim Thompson-Green; Founded 1975
Designed by Grant Aitken
18 holes, 6430 yards, S.S.S. 71
🏌 Welcome.
🍴 18 holes WD £24, WE £30; 36 holes WD £30, WE £35.
☝ Welcome; packages available; terms on application.
🍽 Clubhouse facilities; two restaurants.
🛏 On site hotel wth 18 en suite bedrooms.

5B 110 Vale Golf & CC
Hill Furze Rd, Bishampton, Pershore, Worcs, WR10 2LZ
☎(01386) 462781, Fax 462597, Pro 462520,
🖥 *www.gch.co.uk*
📧 *thevale@btinternet.com*
5 miles from Evesham on A4538; take Bishampton turn.
Parkland course.
Pro Caroline Griffiths; Founded 1991
Designed by M R M Sandow
18 holes, 7114 yards, S.S.S. 74
🏌 Welcome.
🍴 WD £20; WE £25.
☝ Welcome WD; terms on application; corporate packages can be arranged; conference and hospitality suites; terms on application.
🍽 Clubhouse and country club.
Practice range, 20 bays floodlit; 9-hole par 35 course; tuition available; equipment hire.
🛏 Club can recommend.

5B 111 Walmley
Brooks Rd, Wylde Green, Sutton Coldfield, Warwickshire, B72 1HR
☎(0121) 373 0029, Fax 377 7272, Pro 373 7103, Sec 377 7272

6 miles N of Birmingham.
Parkland course.
Pro Chris Wicketts; Founded 1902
18 holes, 6559 yards, S.S.S. 72
🏌 Welcome WD; with member WE.
🍴 WD £30.
☝ Welcome WD; discounts available for 30+ players; from £30.
🍽 Clubhouse facilities.
🛏 Penns Hall.

5B 112 Warley
Lightwoods Hill, Smethwick, Warley, W Midlands, B67 5ED
☎(0121) 429 2440, Fax 434 4430,
Off A465 4.5 miles W of Birmingham behind the Cock & Magpie.
Municipal parkland course; part of Link card system.
Pro David Owen; Founded 1921
9 holes, 5370 yards, S.S.S. 66
🏌 Welcome; opportunity to join on site club.
🍴 WD £8; WE £9; with a link card £1.50 off 18 holes, £1 holes; juniors WD £2-£3.25, WE £2.20-£4; discount with passports to leisure.
☝ None.
🍽 Café.

5B 113 Warwick
The Racecourse, Warwick, Warwicks, CV34 6HW
☎(01926) 494316
In centre of Warwick racecourse.
Public meadowland course.
Pro Philip Sharp; Founded 1886
Designed by D.G. Dunkley
9 holes, 5364 yards, S.S.S. 66
🏌 Welcome except on race days.
🍴 WD £4.50; WE £5.
☝ Welcome by arrangement.
🍽 Bar (open from 7pm).
Practice range, 26 floodlit covered bays.
🛏 Tudor House.

5B 114 Warwickshire
Leek Woolton, Warwick, Warwickshire, CV35 7QT
☎(01926) 409409, Fax 408409
🖥 *www.clubhaus.com*
📧 *wwshire@waderider.com.uk*

M49 Junction 15 take A46 towards Coventry; turn at signs for Leek Wootton on B4115.
4 x 9 holes; 637 is 4th North.
Pro Danny Peck; Founded 1993
Designed by K. Litten
18 holes, 7407 yards, S.S.S. 74
♦ Welcome.
⌑ Summer: WD £45, WE £45;
Winter: WD £25, WE £25.
⌕ Welcome; minimum 12; packages available; private function suites; buggies; coaching clinics; terms on application.
⦿ Full restaurant and bar facilities. Practice range, 30 bays, 9 covered; Leisure complex as of summer 2000.
⌐ Chesford Grange; Alveston Hall; Charlecote Pheasant; Walton Hall.

5B 115 Welcombe Hotel
Warwick Rd, Stratford-upon-Avon, Warwicks, CV37 0NR
☎ (01789) 299012, Fax 262665, Sec 262665, Bar/Rest 295252
▤ www.welcombe.co.uk
▱ sales@welcombe
5 miles from M40 Junction 15; 1.5 miles from Stratford on A439.
Parkland course; being upgraded and remeasured.
Pro Carl Mason/Karen Thatcher; Founded 1956/80
Designed by T.J. McCauley
18 holes, 6288 yards, S.S.S. 70
♦ Welcome with prior arrangement.
⌑ Summer WD £40, WE £50; Winter WD £25, WE £25.
⌕ Welcome; packages available; discounts available; golf clinics; floodlit tennis courts; corporate days, snooker, fitness room, solarium, conference facilities; terms on application.
⦿ Full clubhouse and hotel facilities including Trevelyan Restaurant.
⌐ Welcombe Hotel; 63 en-suite rooms.

5B 116 Westonbirt Girls School
Tetbury, Glos, GL8 8QG
☎ (01666) 880242, Fax 880385
From A433 Tetbury to Bath road turn into Westonbirt village; opposite Arboretum.
Parkland course.
Founded 1934
Designed by Monty Hearn
9 holes, 4504 yards, S.S.S. 61
♦ Welcome.
⌑ WD £8; WE £16.
⌕ None.
⌐ Hare and Hounds.

5B 117 Wharton Park ♕
Long Bank, Bewdley, Worcs DY12 2QW
☎ (01299) 405222, Fax 405121, Pro 405163
On A456 at west end of Bewdley by-pass.
Parkland course.
Pro Angus Hoare; Founded 1992
18 holes, 6603 yards, S.S.S. 72
♦ Welcome.
⌑ WD £20; WE £25.
⌕ Welcome by prior arrangement; packages available; terms on application.
⦿ Clubhouse facilities.
⌐ Heath Hotel.

5B 118 Whitefields
Coventry Rd, Thurlaston, Nr Rugby, Warwicks, CV23 9JR
☎ (01788) 815555, Fax 521695, Sec 521800, Pro 815555
Course is on the A45 close to junction with the M45.
Parkland course overlooking Draycote Water.
Founded 1992
Designed by R Mason
18 holes, 6223 yards, S.S.S. 70
♦ Welcome by prior arrangement.

⌑ WD £18; WE £25.
⌕ 3 packages available; terms on application.
⦿ Hotel facilities.
Practice range, 16 bays floodlit; 18-hole putting green; tuition available.
⌐ Whitefields; 50-room hotel on site.

5B 119 Widney Manor
Saintbury Drive, Widney Manor, Solihull, W Midlands, B91 3SZ
☎ (0121) 711 3646, Fax 711 3691
Off M42 Junction 4 take Stratford road and then turn right into Monkshall Path Road; signposted for Widney Manor.
Parkland course.
Pro Tim Atkinson; Founded 1993
Designed by Golf Design Group
18 holes, 5001 yards, S.S.S. 64
♦ Welcome.
⌑ WD £10; WE £13.50.
⌕ Welcome WD but not before 10am at WE; terms on application.
⦿ Full facilities.
Practice range, practice area.

5B 120 Windmill Village Hotel
Birmingham Road, Allesley, Coventry, Warwicks, CV5 9AL
☎ (024) 7640 4041, Fax 7640 7016, Pro 7640 4041
▤ www.windmillvillage.co.uk
▱ windmillvillage@compuserve.com
On A45 westbound Coventry-Birmingham road.
Part flat, part hilly course.
Pro Robert Hunter; Founded 1990
Designed by Robert Hunte & John Harrhy
18 holes, 5169 yards, S.S.S. 68
♦ Welcome.
⌑ WD £9.95; WE £14.95.
⌕ Welcome by arrangement; packages available; swimming pool;

tennis courts; gym; sauna;
conference suites.
🍴 Bar and restaurant facilities.
⌐ Windmill Village on site.

5B 121 **Wishaw**

Bulls Lane, Wishaw, W Midlands, B76
9QW
☎ (0121) 3513221, Pro 3132110
From M42 Junction 9 take second left
at The Belfry to the Cock at Wishaw;
course 0.75 miles.
Parkland course.
Pro Alan Partridge; Founded 1993
18 holes, 5481 yards, S.S.S. 70
⚑ Welcome.
▯ WD £10; WE £15.
⌐ Welcome WD by arrangement;
packages available; terms on
application.
🍴 Restaurant and bar facilities
available.
⌐ Belfry; Moor Hall.

5B 122 **Woodlands**

Woodlands Lane, Almondsbury,
Bristol, BS32 4JZ
☎ (01454) 619319, Fax 619397, Sec
619319, Bar 618121
⌐ woodlands@tracypark.com
Off A38 at the Aztec roundabout
turning left into Woodlands Lane.
Parkland course.
Pro Andy Lowen/Nigel Warburton;
Founded 1989
Designed by C Chapman
18 holes, 6068 yards, S.S.S. 69
⚑ Welcome.
▯ WD £12; WE £14.
⌐ Welcome by prior arrangement;
terms on application.
🍴 Full clubhouse facilities.
Tuition available.
⌐ The Range; Stakis.

5B 123 **Woodspring**

Yanley Lane, Long Ashton, Bristol,
Avon, BS18 9LR
☎ (01275) 394378, Fax 384473
On A38 near Bristol Airport.
Parkland course; 541/136 on Avon 9.
Pro Nigel Beer; Founded 1994
Designed by P Alliss & C Clark/ D
Steel
27 holes, 6587 yards, S.S.S. 70
⚑ Welcome.
▯ WD £20; WE £28.50.
⌐ Welcome; catering packages
available; contact Kevin Pitts; 3 x 9
courses: Avon, Brunel, Severn; terms
on application.
🍴 Full clubhouse facilities.
Practice range, 25 bays floodlit;
sauna, jacuzzi, snooker.
⌐ Swallow Royal; Redwood Lodge;
Town & Country Lodge; Marriott.

5B 124 **Worcester Golf & Country Club**

Boughton Park, Bransford Road,
Worcester, Worcester, WR2 4EZ
☎ (01905) 422555, Fax 749090, Pro
422044, Bar/Rest 421132
From M5 Junction 7 follow signs for
Worcester West.
Parkland course.
Pro Colin Colenso; Founded 1898
Designed by Dr A MacKenzie (1926)
18 holes, 6251 yards, S.S.S. 70
⚑ Welcome WD; guests of members
only at WE.
▯ WD £25.
⌐ Welcome with 12 months prior
booking; catering and golf packages
can be arranged; jacket and tie
required in dining room; tennis;
squash; from £33.
🍴 Full clubhouse restaurant and bar
facilities.
Tuition available.

5B 125 **Worcestershire**

Wood Farm, Malvern Wells, Worcs,
WR14 4PP
☎ (01684) 575992, Fax 575992, Pro
564428, Rest 573905, Sec 575992
Course is two miles south of Great
Malvern; turn off the A449 on to the
B4209.
Parkland course.
Pro Richard Lewis
Founded 1879
Designed by Colt, MacKenzie, Braid;
amended by Jiggins and Hawtree
18 holes, 6470 yards, S.S.S. 71
⚑ Welcome; handicap certs
required; no visitors before 10am WE.
▯ Prices on application.
⌐ Welcome Thurs and Fri; package
includes coffee, light lunch and 3-
course dinner; £45.
🍴 Full catering facilities.
⌐ Abbey; Foley; Cottage in the
Woods.

5B 126 **Wyre Forest**

Zortech Ave, Kidderminster, Worcs,
DY11 7EX
☎ (01299) 822682, Fax 879433, Pro
0500 78989096
Take A451 towards Stourport and
course is signposted.
Parkland course.
Pro Simon Price
Founded 1994
Designed by Golf Design Group
18 holes, 5790 yards, S.S.S. 68
⚑ Welcome.
▯ WD £9.50; WE £13.50.
⌐ Welcome; terms on application;
from £18.
Driving range, buggies and clubs for
hire; tuition available.
🍴 Clubhouse facilities.
⌐ Heath; Gainsborough; Severn
Manor.

NORTH MIDLANDS

When it comes to offering value for money for the visiting golfer, few regions can compete with the counties grouped together here. Collectively they possess some of the finest inland golf England has to offer but far below the amounts charged further south.

The corridor that leads from Chester to Manchester is awash with hidden jewels. Eaton Golf Club, situated in the Duke of Westminster's Estate at Chester, Sandiway, Delamere Forest, Mere, Dunham Forest and a new course, Portal, all represent a memorable day out.

Moving north up the M53 we come to the courses on Wirral peninsula, where the majestic links of Royal Liverpool stands resplendent. In 2000 it will play host to the Amateur Championship, an event one of its members founded in the 19th century. Another member, John Ball, won the event on no less than eight occasions, a record that will never be surpassed.

These days the Amateur needs a second course for qualifying purposes and neighbouring Wallasey is more than suitable. There are a few humdrum holes in the middle but the start and finish is exquisite. Two more Wirral courses, Caldy and Heswall, are also notable.

It was Sandy Lyle who put Hawkstone Park on the map. It was where he learned to play golf, under the tutelage of his father, and it has become a popular destination with excellent hotel facilities complementing the main course and a second layout, much-upgraded by Brian Huggett, that opened for business in 1995.

Bridgnorth and Ludlow are two more fine Shropshire courses, while a personal favourite is Llanymynech, which straddles Offa's Dyke to such an extent that on the fourth hole a player tees off in Wales and holes out in England. Few courses can compete with this one when it comes to panoramic views.

Staffordshire, though, can more than hold its own in this company. Its leading course is Little Aston, which would certainly make my top 10 of the best inland courses in Britain. Here are 18 holes set in mature woodland that offer infinite variety.

There are others which are not far behind, however, including South Staffs, Enville, Beau Desert, Trentham and the wonderful heathland course at Whittington. Once known, somewhat forbiddingly, as Whittington Barracks owing to the army base nearby, it was bought some years ago by the members who changed the name to Whittington Heath, which more accurately reflects its character.

In Nottinghamshire three courses just outside the city form a distinguished trio: Coxmoor, Sherwood Forest and Hollinwell, which quite simply is a national treasure.

The same can also be said of Woodhall Spa, which is just as well given its remote location in deepest Lincolnshire. In 1998 it was ranked the best inland course in England by the US publication *Golf*.

For anyone visiting the Peak District on holiday and placing the golf clubs in the back of the boot, Kedleston Park, just outside Derby, is the course to circle on the map. — **DL**

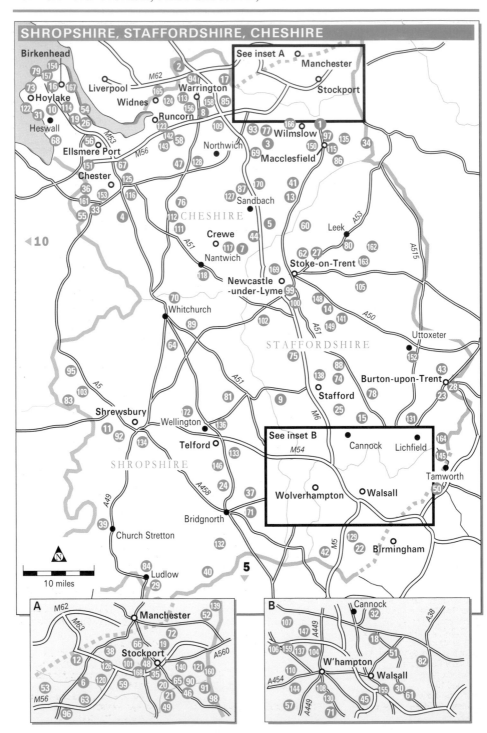

SHROPSHIRE, STAFFORDSHIRE, CHESHIRE

Birkenhead
79 154
157
73 16 167
Liverpool
Hoylake
122 31 10 114 54
19 26
Heswall
68 56
Ellsmere Port 151
67
Chester 125
36 116
161 153
55 33
◄10
95
103
83
Shrewsbury
11
92
134
SHROPSHIRE

M62
2
94
165 Warrington
Widnes 124 113 158 85
156
Runcorn 8
123 109
142 58
143
Northwich
47 128
76
127 Sandbach
112 CHESHIRE
111
Crewe
117 7
Nantwich
118
70
Whitchurch
89
64
72
Wellington
136
Telford
133
146
24
37
71
Bridgnorth
132
39
Church Stretton
84
Ludlow
29
40

See inset A
Manchester
Stockport
17
166
93 77 Wilmslow
3 97 135
150 115
69 Macclesfield 86
170 41
87 13
5
60 Leek
80 162
62 27 163
169 Stoke-on-Trent
Newcastle 105
-under-Lyme 99
100
148
102 14 A50
149 141
STAFFORDSHIRE
75
Uttoxeter
152
88 43
138 74 28
Burton-upon-Trent
81 78 23
9 Stafford
25
15 131
See inset B 164
M54 145
Cannock Lichfield
Wolverhampton Walsall Tamworth
50
129
42 22 Birmingham
5

34
115

N
10 miles

A
M62 139
M63 52
Manchester
66 72
38 19
12 Stockport
126 101 48 A560
120 168 35 140 121 160
59 65 90
53 20 91
M56 63 21 46 98
96 49

B
Cannock
107 32
147 A449 A38
18
106 159 137 104
W'hampton 51
A454 110 82
144 108 Walsall
57 A449 130 45 155 30 61
71

KEY						
		34	Chapel-en-le-Frith	70	Hill Valley Golf & Country	104 Oxley Park	139 Stamford (Stalybridge)
1	Adlington Golf Centre	35	Cheadle		Club	105 Parkhall	140 Stockport
2	Alder Root Golf Club	36	Chester	71	Himley Hall Golf Centre	106 Patshull Park Hotel Golf	141 Stone
3	Alderley Edge	37	Chesterton Valley GC	72	Houldsworth	and Country Club	142 Styal
4	Aldersey Green Golf	38	Chorlton-cum-Hardy	73	Hoylake Municipal	107 Penkridge G & CC	143 Sutton Hall
	Club	39	Church Stretton	74	Ingestre Park	108 Penn	144 Swindon
5	Alsager Golf & Country	40	Cleobury Mortimer GC	75	Izaak Walton	109 Peover	145 Tamworth Municipal
	Club	41	Congleton	76	Knights Grange Sports	110 Perton Park Golf Club	146 Telford Moat House
6	Altrincham	42	Corngreaves		Complex	111 Portal G & Country Club	147 Three Hammers Golf
7	Alvaston Hall Golf Club	43	The Craythorne	77	Knutsford	112 Portal G & Country Club	Complex
8	Antrobus Golf Club	44	Crewe	78	Lakeside (Rugeley)	Premier Course	148 Trentham
9	Aqualate	45	Dartmouth	79	Leasowe	113 Poulton Park	149 Trentham Park
10	Arrowe Park	46	Davenport	80	Leek	114 Prenton	150 The Tytherington
11	Arscott	47	Delamere Forest	81	Lilleshall Hall	115 Prestbury	151 Upton-by-Chester
12	Ashton on Mersey	48	Didsbury	82	Little Aston	116 Pryors Hayes Golf Club	152 Uttoxeter
13	Astbury	49	Disley	83	Llanymynech	117 Queen's Park	153 Vicars Cross
14	Barlaston	50	Drayton Park	84	Ludlow	118 Reaseheath	154 Wallasey
15	Beau Desert	51	Druids Heath	85	Lymm	119 Reddish Vale	155 Walsall
16	Bidston	52	Dukinfield	86	Macclesfield	120 Ringway	156 Walton Hall
17	Birchwood	53	Dunham Forest Golf &	87	Malkins Bank	121 Romiley	157 Warren
18	Bloxwich		Country Club	88	The Manor Golf Club	122 Royal Liverpool	158 Warrington
19	Brackenwood	54	Eastham Lodge		(Kingstone) Ltd	123 Runcorn	159 Wergs
20	Bramall Park	55	Eaton	89	Market Drayton	124 St Michael Jubilee	160 Werneth Low
21	Bramhall	56	Ellesmere Port	90	Marple	125 St Thomas's Priory GC	161 Westminster Park
22	Brand Hall	57	Enville	91	Mellor & Townscliffe	126 Sale	162 Westwood (Leek)
23	Branston Golf & CC	58	Frodsham	92	Meole Brace	127 Sandbach	163 Whiston Hall
24	Bridgnorth	59	Gatley	93	Mere Golf & CC	128 Sandiway	164 Whittington Heath
25	Brocton Hall	60	Goldenhill	94	Mersey Valley	129 Sandwell Park	165 Widnes
26	Bromborough	61	Great Barr	95	Mile End	130 Sedgley Golf Centre	166 Wilmslow
27	Burslem	62	Greenway Hall	96	Mobberley	131 Seedy Mill	167 Wirral Ladies
28	Burton-on-Trent	63	Hale	97	Mottram Hall Hotel	132 Severn Meadows	168 Withington
29	Cadmore Lodge	64	Hawkstone Park Hotel	98	New Mills	133 Shifnal	169 Wolstanton
30	Calderfields	65	Hazel Grove	99	Newcastle Municipal	134 Shrewsbury	170 Woodside
31	Caldy	66	Heaton Moor	100	Newcastle-under-Lyme	135 Shrigley Hall Hotel	171 Worfield
32	Cannock Park	67	Helsby	101	Northenden	136 The Shropshire	172 Wrekin
33	Carden Park Hotel, Golf	68	Heswall	102	Onneley	137 South Staffordshire	
	Resort & Spa	69	Heyrose	103	Oswestry	138 Stafford Castle	

6A 1 Adlington Golf Centre

Sandy Hey Farm, Adlington,
Macclesfield, Cheshire, SK10 4NG
☎(01625) 850660, Fax 850960, Sec
878468
Course is one mile south of Poynton
on the A523 Stockport-Macclesfield
road.
Par 3 course.
Pro David Bathgate; Founded 1995
Designed by Hawtree
9 holes, 635 yards
† Public pay and play.
[WD £3.50; WE £4.50.
⌒ Not available.
†●† Full facilities.
Driving range and golf academy
available.

6A 2 Alder Root Golf Club ☎

Alder Root Lane, Winwick,
Warrington, Cheshire, WA2 8RZ
☎(01925) 291919, Pro 291932
M62 Junction 9 then N on A49, turn
left at first set of lights; then 1st right
into Alder Root Lane.
Parkland course.
Founded 1993
Pro: Chris McKevitt
9 holes with 18 tees, 5834 yards,
S.S.S. 69

† Welcome by arrangement.
[WD £16; WE £18.
⌒ Welcome WD by prior
arrangement; full catering and 27
holes of golf; from £24.
†●† Bar and snacks.
⌐ Winwick Quay.

6A 3 Alderley Edge

Brook Lane, Alderley Edge, Cheshire,
SK9 7RU
☎(01625) 585583
From Alderley Edge turn off A34 to
Mobberley/Knutsford on B5085.
Undulating parkland course.
Pro: Peter Bowring; Founded 1907
Designed by T. G. Renouf
9 holes, 5823 yards, S.S.S. 68
† Welcome with handicap certs;
restrictions Wed and WE.
[WD £18; WE £22.
⌒ Welcome Thurs by prior
arrangement; from £28.
†●† Full catering except Mon.
⌐ De Trafford Arms.

6A 4 Aldersey Green Golf Club

Aldersey, Chester, Cheshire, CH3
9EH

☎(01829) 782453, Pro 782157
On A41 Whitchurch road.
Parkland course.
Pro Stephen Bradbury; Founded
1993
18 holes, 6159 yards, S.S.S. 69
† Welcome.
[WD £12; WE £15.
⌒ Welcome by prior arrangement; 2
packages available WD; 1 at WE;
terms on application.
†●† Bar and bar meals.
⌐ Calverley Arms.

6A 5 Alsager Golf & ☎ Country Club

Audley Rd, Alsager, Stoke-on-Trent,
Staffs, ST7 2UR
☎(01270) 875700, Fax 882207, Pro
877432
Leave M6 Junction 16 taking A500
towards Stoke for 1 mile; first left turn
for Alsager.
Parkland course.
Pro Richard Brown; Founded 1976
18 holes, 6201 yards, S.S.S. 70
† Welcome WD; WE with member.
[WD £24.
⌒ Welcome Mon, Wed and Thurs; 3
packages available for societies;
snooker; bowls; from £27.50.

Clubhouse facilities; banqueting available.
Manor Hotel.

6A 6 Altrincham
Stockport Rd, Timperley, Altrincham, Cheshire, WA15 7LP
☎(0161) 928 0761
On A560 1 mile W of Altrincham.
Undulating parkland course.
Pro Scott Partington; Founded 1935
18 holes, 6162 yards, S.S.S. 69
† Welcome; advance booking at all times.
WD £8.50; WE £11.50.
Welcome.
No catering; facilities at adjacent restaurant.
Cresta Court; Woodlands Park.

6A 7 Alvaston Hall GC
Middlewich Road, Nantwich, Cheshire, CW5 6PD
☎(01270) 624341, Fax 623395
1 mile from Nantwich on A530 to Middlewich.
Meadowland course.
Founded 1989
Designed by A Lindop
9 holes, 3612 yards, S.S.S. 59
† Welcome.
WD £6,50; WE £6.50.
Welcome WD; terms on application.
Full facilities.
Alvaston Hall Hotel.

6A 8 Antrobus Golf Club
Foggs Lane, Antrobus, Northwich, Cheshire, CW9 6JQ
☎(01925) 730890, Fax 730100, Pro 730900
From A559 road off M56 Junction 10 take second left after Birch and Bottle; left into Foggs Lane.
Parkland course with water features.
Pro Paul Farrance; Founded 1993
Designed by Mike Slater
18 holes, 6220 yards, S.S.S. 71
† Welcome.
WD £18; WE £20.
Welcome every day; packages available.
Full clubhouse facilities.
Park Royal, Stretton; Lord Daresbury, Warrington.

6A 9 Aqualate
Stafford Rd, Newport, Shropshire, TF10 9JT
☎(01952) 825343

300 yds E of junction of A41 Newport bypass and A518 Newport to Stafford road.
Heathland course.
Pro K Short; Founded 1995
Designed by M D Simmons/T Juhre
18 holes, 5659 yards, S.S.S. 67
† Welcome.
WD £12; WE £15.
Welcome by arrangement; terms on application.
Coffee shop.
Driving range facilities.
Royal Victoria; Adams House, both Newport.

6A 10 Arrowe Park
Arrowe Park, Woodchurch, Birkenhead, Merseyside, L49 5LW
☎(0151) 677 1527
3 miles from town centre; 1 mile from M53 Junction 3 opposite Landicon Cemetery.
Municipal parkland course.
Pro Colin Disbury; Founded 1932
18 holes, 6377 yards, S.S.S. 70
† Welcome.
WD £7; WE £7.
Welcome by prior arrangement with club Pro.
Restaurant facilities.
Arrowe Park Hotel.

6A 11 Arscott
Arscott, Pontesbury, Shropshire, SY5 0XP
☎(01743) 860114, Fax 860114, Pro 860881
1 miles past Hanwood on the A488 road from Shrewsbury to Bishops Castle; signposted at Lea Cross.
Parkland course.
Pro Ian Doran; Founded 1992
Designed by Martin Hamer
18 holes, 6178 yards, S.S.S. 69
† Welcome by prior arrangement.
WD £16; WE £20.
Welcome WD; packages including golf and catering available; from £20.
Clubhouse facilities.
Prince Rupert; Boars Head.

6A 12 Ashton on Mersey
Church Lane, Sale, Cheshire M33 5QQ
☎(0161) 973 3220, Pro 973 3727
2 miles from Sale station.
Parkland course.
Pro Michael Williams; Founded 1897
9 holes, 6115 yards, S.S.S. 69
† Welcome except Tues after 3pm (Ladies Day).

WD £18; WE £18.
Welcome by arrangement; terms on application.
Bar snacks and evening meals.
Mersey Farm Travelodge.

6A 13 Astbury
Peel Lane, Astbury, Nr Congleton, Cheshire, CW12 4RE
☎(01260) 272 772, Pro 298 663, Sec 279 139
1 mile S of Congleton off A34.
Parkland course.
Pro Ashley Salt; Founded 1922
18 holes, 6296 yards, S.S.S. 70
† Welcome with handicap certs WD; WE with a member.
WD £30 (day ticket).
Thurs only May-October; catering by prior arrangement.
Facilities available.

6A 14 Barlaston
Meaford Rd, Stone, Staffs, ST15 8UX
☎(01782) 372795, Fax 372867, Sec 372867
Between M6 Junction 14-15 just off A34 outside Barlaston village.
Picturesque parkland course with water hazards.
Pro Ian Rogers; Founded 1982
Designed by Peter Alliss
18 holes, 5801 yards, S.S.S. 68
† Welcome midweek; some WE restrictions.
WD £18; WE £22.50.
Welcome WD; packages for golf (maximum 27 holes), catering and prizes available; terms on application.
Bar and restaurant facilities.
Moat House; Stakis Grand both Stoke; Stone House, Stone.

6A 15 Beau Desert
Rugeley Road, Hazel Slade, Cannock, Staffs, WS12 5PJ
☎(01543) 422773, Fax 451137, Pro 422492, Sec 422626
On A460 between Rugeley and Cannock near Hednesford.
Heathland course.
Pro Barrie Stevens; Founded 1921
Designed by H. Fowler
18 holes, 6310 yards, S.S.S. 71
† Welcome by arrangement.
WD £38; WE £48.
Welcome Mon-Thurs by prior arrangement; packages available; from £50.
Facilities available.
Hotels can be recommended by Sec.

6A 16 Bidston
Bidston Link Road, Wallasey,
Merseyside, L46 2HR
☎(0151) 638 3412, Pro 630 6650
Course is close to Junction 1 on the
M53.
Parkland course/links.
Founded 1913
18 holes, 6140 yards, S.S.S. 70
† Welcome WD.
⌞ WD £22.
⟋ Welcome by prior arrangement;
packages available; terms on
application.
🍽 Full clubhouse facilities.
⌐ The Bowler Hat.

6A 17 Birchwood
Kelvin Close, Birchwood, Warrington,
Cheshire, WA3 7PB
☎(01925) 818 819, Fax 822 403,
Pro 816 574
Off M62 at Junction 11 taking A574
road to Leigh and Science Park
North; club entrance just past
Science Park North.
Parkland course with natural water
hazards.
Pro Paul McEwan; Founded 1979
Designed by T. J. MacAuley
18 holes, 6727 yards, S.S.S. 73
† Welcome; restrictions on
competition days.
⌞ WD £26; WE £34.
⟋ Welcome Mon, Wed, Thurs;
packages can be arranged; from £32.
🍽 Full catering facilities.
⌐ Garden Court, Woolston.

6A 18 Bloxwich
136 Stafford Rd, Bloxwich, Walsall, W
Midlands, WS3 3PQ
☎(01922) 476 593, Fax 476 593
1 miles N of Bloxwich on A34 off M6
at Junction 10 or 11.
Parkland course.
Pro R J Dance; Founded 1924
Designed by J. Sixsmith
18 holes, 6288 yards, S.S.S. 71
† Welcome midweek; members
guests at WE only
⌞ WD £25, WE £30.
⟋ Welcome by prior arrangement;
reductions for groups; packages
available.
🍽 Facilities available.
⌐ Many in local area.

6A 19 Brackenwood
Bracken Lane, Bebington, Wirral,
Merseyside, L63 2LY
☎(0151) 608 3093, Sec 608 5394

M53 Junction 4 to Clatterbridge and
Bebington.
Public parkland course.
Pro Ken Lamb; Founded 1933
18 holes, 6045 yards, S.S.S. 70
† Welcome.
⌞ WD £7; WE £7.
⟋ Welcome by arrangement.
⌐ Thornton Hall; Village.

6A 20 Bramall Park
20 Manor Rd, Bramhall, Stockport,
SK7 3LY
☎(0161) 485 3119, Fax 485 7101,
Pro 485 2205, Sec 485 7101
8 miles S of Manchester (club can
provide directions from M56 and
M63).
Parkland course.
Pro M Proffitt; Founded 1894
Designed by J Braid
18 holes, 6214 yards, S.S.S. 70
† Welcome by arrangement.
⌞ Terms on application.
⟋ Welcome Tues and Thurs by prior
arrangement; packages available;
terms on application.
🍽 Clubhouse catering facilities
available.
⌐ County, Bramhall; Belfry,
Handforth.

6A 21 Bramhall
Ladythorn Rd, Bramhall, Stockport,
Cheshire, SK7 2EY
☎(0161) 439 4057, Fax 439 0264,
Pro 439 1171, Sec 439 6092
Off A5102 S of Stockport.
Parkland course.
Pro R Green; Founded 1905
18 holes, 6340 yards, S.S.S. 70
† Welcome; restrictions Thurs.
⌞ WD £24; WE £31.
⟋ Welcome on Wed by prior
arrangement; golf and catering
packages can be arranged; from £24.
🍽 Clubhouse facilities.
⌐ County Hotel, Bramhall.

6A 22 Brand Hall
Heron Road, Oldbury, Warley, W
Midlands, B68 8AQ
☎(0121) 552 2195, Fax 544 5088
6 miles NW of Birmingham, 1.5 miles
from M5 Junction 2.
Public parkland course.
Pro Carl Yates
18 holes, 5734 yards, S.S.S. 68
† Welcome; pay and play.
⌞ Terms on application.
⟋ Welcome by arrangement.
🍽 Cafe, clubhouse bar.

6A 23 Branston Golf & ☏
Country Club
Burton Rd, Branston, Burton-on-
Trent, Staffs, DE14 3DP
☎(01283) 512211, Fax 566984, Sec
543207
On A5121 off A38 at Burton South.
Parkland course on banks of R Trent;
water on 13 holes.
Pro Jacob Sture; Founded 1975
18 holes, 6647 yards, S.S.S. 72
† Welcome WD and afternoons at
WE. April-November soft spikes only
⌞ WD £28; WE £40.
⟋ Welcome by arrangement; terms
on application.
🍽 Full catering facilities.
⌐ Dog and Partridge.

6A 24 Bridgnorth
Stanley Lane, Bridgnorth, Shropshire,
WV16 4SF
☎(01746) 763315, Fax 761381, Pro
762045
On road to Broseley, 0.5 miles from
Bridgnorth.
Parkland course.
Pro Paul Hinton; Founded 1889
18 holes, 6650 yards, S.S.S. 73
† Welcome.
⌞ WD £24; WE £32.
⟋ Welcome Tues, Thurs, Fri;
reserved tee times and packages
available; from £30
🍽 Clubhouse facilities.
⌐ Parlours Hall; Falcon; Croft.

6A 25 Brocton Hall
Sawpit Lane, Brocton, Staffs, ST17
0TH
☎(01785) 662627, Fax 661591, Pro
661485, Sec 661901
4 miles S of Stafford off A34.
Parkland course.
Pro R G Johnson; Founded
1894/1923
Designed by Harry Vardon
18 holes, 6064 yards, S.S.S. 69
† Welcome.
⌞ WD £33; WE £40.
⟋ Welcome Tues and Thurs by prior
arrangement and with handicap
certss; packages for golf and catering
by prior arrangement.
🍽 Full clubhouse bar and restaurant
facilities.
⌐ Tillington Hall; Garth Hotel both
Stafford.

6A 26 Bromborough
Raby Hall Rd, Bromborough, Wirral,
Merseyside, L63 0NW

☎(0151) 334 2155, Fax 334 7300, Pro 334 4499.
Close to M53 Junction 5 0.75 miles from A41 Birkenhead to Chester road; 0.5 miles from Bromborough station.
Parkland course.
Pro Geoff Berry; Founded 1904
18 holes, 6603 yards, S.S.S. 73
♦ Welcome WD; by arrangement WE.
↧ WD £28; WE £30.
⚲Welcome Wed; early booking essential.
📧 Extensive catering and bar facilities.
↴ Thornton Hall; Village.

6A 27 **Burslem**
Wood Farm, High Lane, Tunstall, Stoke-on-Trent, ST6 7JT
☎(01782) 837006
4 miles N of Hanley.
Parkland course.
Founded 1907
11 holes, 5360 yards, S.S.S. 66
♦ Welcome WD only by prior arrangement.
↧ Terms on application.
⚲WD by prior arrangement; catering to be arranged with the steward; terms on application.
📧 By arrangement with the steward.

6A 28 **Burton-on-Trent**
43 Ashby Rd East, Burton-on-Trent, Derbyshire, DE15 0PS
☎(01283) 568 708, Fax 544 551, Pro 562 240, Sec 544 551
On A50 3 miles E of Burton on Trent.
Undulating woodland course.
Pro G Stafford; Founded 1894
Designed by H.S. Colt
18 holes, 6579 yards, S.S.S. 71
♦ Welcome with handicap certs.
↧ WD £28; WE £28.
⚲Welcome WD; catering packages available except Mon; snooker; terms on application.
📧 Full facilities except Mon.
Practice range, practice ground.
↴ Stanhope Arms; Riverside, both Burton-on-Trent; Newton Park, Newton Solney.

6A 29 **Cadmore Lodge**
Berrington Green, Tenbury Wells, Worcester, Worcs, WR15 8TQ
☎(01584) 810044
Off A456 20 miles W of Kidderminster.
Parkland course with lakes.

Founded 1990
Designed by John Weston
9 holes, 5132 yards, S.S.S. 65
♦ Welcome.
↧ WD £10; WE £14.
⚲Welcome by prior arrangement; packages can be arranged; bowls; tennis; fishing.
📧 Full facilities.
↴ Hotel on site.

6A 30 **Calderfields**
Aldridge Rd, Walsall, W Midlands, WS4 2JS
☎(01922) 632243, Fax 638787, Pro 613675, Sec 640540, Bar/Rest 646888
On A454 off M6 Junctions 7 or 10.
Parkland course with lakes.
Pro David Williams; Founded 1981
Designed by Roy Winter
18 holes, 6509 yards, S.S.S. 71
♦ Welcome.
↧ WD £18; WE £18.
⚲Welcome every day; packages available; from £18.
📧 Bar and restaurant facilities.
Practice range, 27 bays floodlit; floodlit bunker and putting green.
↴ Boundary; Fairview; County.

6A 31 **Caldy**
Links Hey Rd, Caldy, Wirral, L48 1NB, Merseyside
☎(0151) 625 5660, Fax 625 7394, Pro 625 1818
A540 from Chester, turn left at Caldy crossroads.
Seaside/parkland course.
Pro Kevin Jones; Founded 1907
Designed by James Braid, John Salvesen
18 holes, 6668 yards, S.S.S. 73
♦ Welcome WD; Tues ladies day; WE with a member.
↧ WD £40.
⚲Welcome Thurs by arrangement; winter packages available.
📧 Bar snacks all day; dinner by arrangement.
↴ Parkgate.

6A 32 **Cannock Park**
Stafford Rd, Cannock, Staffs WS11 2AL
☎(01543) 578850, Fax 578850, Sec 572800
0.5 miles N of Cannock on A34.
Parkland course.
Pro David Dunk; Founded 1990
Designed by John Mainland
18 holes, 5048 yards, S.S.S. 65

♦ Welcome; telephone in advance.
↧ WD £9; WE £10.
⚲Welcome by prior arrangement; packages available; terms on application.
📧 Cafeteria within leisure complex.
↴ Roman Way; Hollies.

6A 33 **Carden Park Hotel, Golf Resort & Spa**
Carden Park, Chester, Cheshire, CH3 9DQ
☎(01829) 731 600, Fax 731 636, Pro 731 600
On A534 E of Wrexham; 1.5 miles from junction with A41.
Parkland course; Nicklaus course, 7010 yards, .
Pro Simon Edwards; Founded 1993
Course redesigned several times
36 holes
♦ Welcome with handicap certs.
↧ WD £40-£60; WE £40-£60.
⚲Welcome with handicap certs and by prior arrangement; packages available for golf and catering; full first-class hotel leisure and catering facilities; terms on application.
📧 Full first-class hotel facilities.
Practice range, also 9-hole course available, par 3, £5; short game practice area.
↴ Carden Park Hotel on site with 192 rooms.

6A 34 **Chapel-en-le-Frith**
Manchester Rd, Chapel-en-le-Frith, Stockport, Cheshire, SK23 9UH
☎(01298) 812118, Fax 813943
On the road between Whaley Bridge and Chapel.
Parkland course with water hazards.
Pro D Cullen; Founded 1905
18 holes, 6054 yards, S.S.S. 69
♦ Welcome by prior arrangement.
↧ Terms on application
⚲Welcome by prior arrangement; 36 holes of golf; coffee and biscuits on arrival, lunch and 5-course meal; from £35.
📧 Full clubhouse facilities.

6A 35 **Cheadle**
Cheadle Road, Cheadle, Cheshire, SK8 1HW
☎(0161) 428 2160, Pro 428 9878, Sec + Bar/Rest 491 3873
1.5 miles from M63 Junction 11 follow signs for Cheadle; 1 mile S of Cheadle village.
Undulating parkland course.
Founded 1885

Designed by R. Renouf
9 holes, 5006 yards, S.S.S. 65
♦ Welcome with handicap certs except Tues and Sat.
⌷ WD £20; WE £25.
⌁Welcome by prior arrangement Mon, Wed, Thurs, Fri; catering packages can be arranged through the steward; no lunchtime catering Thurs; snooker; terms available on application.
⍟ Bar and catering facilities, except Thurs.
⌐ Village, Cheadle.

6A 36 Chester
Curzon Park North, Chester, Cheshire, CH4 8AR
☎(01244) 677760
1 mile from Chester off the A55 behind Chester racecourse.
Parkland course.
Pro George Parton; Founded 1901
18 holes, 6508 yards, S.S.S. 71
♦ Welcome by arrangement.
⌷ WD £25; WE £30.
⌁Welcome by arrangement.
⍟ Full facilities.
⌐ Many in Chester.

6A 37 Chesterton Valley Golf Club
Chesterton, Nr. Worfield, Bridgnorth, Shropshire, WV15 5NX
☎(01746) 783682
On B 44176 Dudley-Telford Road.
Heathland course.
Pro Phil Hinton; Founded 1993
Designed by P Hinton
18 holes, 5671 yards, S.S.S. 67
♦ Pay and play.
⌷ WD £13.60; WE £13.60.
⌁Welcome by prior arrangement; terms on application.

6A 38 Chorlton-cum-Hardy
Barlow Hall Rd, Chorlton-cum-hardy, Manchester, M21 7JJ
☎(0161) 881 3139, Fax 881 4532, Pro 881 9911, Sec 881 5830
4 miles S of Manchester close to A5103/A5145 junction.
Parkland course.
Pro David Valentine; Founded 1902
18 holes, 5980 yards, S.S.S. 69
♦ Welcome by arrangement.
⌷ WD £25; WE £30.
⌁Welcome on Thurs & Fri by prior arrangement; booking form available from Sec; packages available; terms on application.
⍟ Clubhouse facilities.

⌐ Post House; Britannia, both Northenden.

6A 39 Church Stretton ☊
Hunters Moon, Trevor Hill, Church Stretton, Shropshire, SY6 6JH
☎(01694) 722281
From A49 into Church Stretton; right at top of town; first left into Cardinmill Valley; 100 yards to Trevor Hill.
Hillside course.
Pro Peter Seal; Founded 1898
Designed by James Braid
18 holes, 5020 yards, S.S.S. 65
♦ Welcome.
⌷ Terms on application.
⌁Welcome by arrangement; some WE available; golf and catering packages by arrangement; from £12.
⍟ Clubhouse facilities
⌐ Denehurst; Longmynd, both Church Stretton; Stretton Hall, All Stretton.

6A 40 Cleobury Mortimer ☊ Golf Club
Wyre Common, Cleobury Mortimer, Shropshire, DY14 8HQ
☎(01299) 271112, Fax 271468, Pro 271628, Bar/Rest 271320
2 miles E of Cleobury Mortimer just off A4117; halfway between Kidderminster and Ludlow.
Parkland course.
Pro Graham Farr; Founded 1993
Designed by EGU
27 holes, 6438 yards, S.S.S. 71
♦ Welcome by arrangement.
⌷ WD £18.50; WE £21.50.
⌁Welcome by arrangement; packages involving 18, 27 and 36 holes; catering plus private function room for 90; snooker.
⍟ Spike bar, lounge bar and restaurant facilities.
⌐ Redfern Hotel.

6A 41 Congleton
Biddulph Rd, Congleton, Cheshire, CW12 3LZ
☎(01260) 273540
1 mile SE of Congleton station on A527 Congleton-Biddulph road.
Parkland course.
Pro John Colclough; Founded 1898
9 holes, 5119 yards, S.S.S. 65
♦ Welcome; Tues Ladies Day.
⌷ WD £21; WE £31.
⌁Welcome Mon and Thurs by prior booking.
⍟ Full facilities except Mon.
⌐ Lion & Swan; Bulls Head.

6A 42 Corngreaves
Corngreaves Road, Cradley Heath, W Midlands, B64 7NL
☎(01384) 567880
2 miles E of Dudley.
Public parkland course.
Pro Carl Yates; Founded 1985
18 holes, 3979 yards, S.S.S. 61
♦ Welcome.
⌷ Terms on application.
⌁Welcome by arrangement; packages on request.
⍟ Full facilities.

6A 43 The Craythorne ☊
Craythorne Rd, Stretton, Burton-on-Trent, Staffs, DE13 0AZ
☎(01283) 564329, Fax 511908
300 yards from village after leaving A38 at Stretton signs.
Parkland course.
Pro S Hadfield; Founded 1974
Designed by Cyril Johnson/A A Wright
18 holes, 5306 yards, S.S.S. 67
♦ Welcome by prior arrangement; handicap certs required.
⌷ WD £20; WE £25.
⌁Welcome by prior arrangement; packages available; terms on application.
⍟ Full facilities.
⌐ The Willington.

6A 44 Crewe
Fields Rd, Haslington, Crewe, Cheshire, CW1 5TB
☎(01270) 584 227, Fax 584 099, Pro 585 032, Sec 584 099
2 miles NE of Crewe Station off A534.
Parkland course.
Pro Michael Booker; Founded 1911
18 holes, 6424 yards, S.S.S. 71
♦ Welcome WD; WE with a member.
⌷ WD £27.
⌁Welcome Tues; golf and catering packages available.
⍟ Clubhouse facilities.
⌐ Hunter Lodge; Crewe Arms.

6A 45 Dartmouth
Vale St, West Bromwich, W Midlands, B71 4DW
☎(0121) 588 2131
1.5 miles from M5/M6 junction.
Undulating meadowland/parkland course.
Pro Guy Dean; Founded 1910
9 holes, 6036 yards, S.S.S. 71
♦ Welcome WD with handicap certs; with member only at WE.

WD £20 (day ticket).
By arrangement with Pro;
packages available; snooker.
Full facilities.
Moat House; Albion.

6A 46 **Davenport**
Worth Hall, Middlewood Rd, Poynton,
Stockport, Cheshire, SK12 1TS
(01625) 877321, Pro 877319, Sec
876951
From A6 at Hazel Grove take A523
Macclesfield road to Poynton turning
left into Park Lane.
Undulating parkland course.
Pro Gary Norcott; Founded 1913
Designed by Fraser Middleton
18 holes, 6067 yards, S.S.S. 69
Welcome except Sat; ladies only
on Wednesdays.
WD £27; WE £32.
Welcome Tues and Thurs by prior
arrangement.
Full clubhouse facilities except
Mondays.
Belfry; Belgrade.

6A 47 **Delamere Forest**
Station Rd, Delamere, Northwich,
Cheshire, CW8 2JE
(01606) 883 264, Pro 883 307,
Sec 883 800
From A556 take B5152 to Frodsham;
lane to club is 1 mile, next to
Delamere station.
Undulating heathland course.
Pro Ellis Jones; Founded 1910
Designed by Herbert Fowler
18 holes, 6305 yards, S.S.S. 71
Welcome; restrictions at WE and
Bank Holidays.
WD £30; WE £35.
Welcome by arrangement;
packages available.
Bar snacks; restaurant.
Hartford Hall; Swan; Willington
Hall.

6A 48 **Didsbury**
Ford Lane, Northenden, Manchester,
M22 4NQ
(0161) 998 9278, Fax 998 9278,
Pro 998 2811, Bar/Rest 998 2743
6 miles S of Manchester.
Parkland course.
Pro P Barber; Founded 1891
Designed by G Lowe (1891); G
MacKenzie (1921); D Thomas and P
Alliss (1973)
18 holes, 6273 yards, S.S.S. 70
Welcome with handicap certs.
WD £27; WE £31.

Welcome Thurs and Fri; restricted
availability Sun and Mon; catering
and golf packages available;
minimum 12, maximum 80.
Full clubhouse facilities.
Post House; Britannia, both
Northenden.

6A 49 **Disley**
Stanley Hall Lane, Jackson's Edge,
Disley, Cheshire, SK12 2JX
(01663) 762071, Pro 762884
Off A6 in Disley village.
Open hillside/parkland course.
Pro Andrew Esplin; Founded 1889
Designed by James Braid
18 holes, 6015 yards, S.S.S. 69
Welcome WD by prior
arrangement.
WD £25.
Welcome WD by prior
arrangement; catering and golf
packages available; from £35.
Clubhouse facilities except
Mondays.
Stakis Moorside.

6A 50 **Drayton Park**
Drayton Park, Tamworth, Staffs, B78
3TN
(01827) 251139, Fax 284035, Pro
251478, Bar/Rest 287481
On A4091 at Drayton Park leisure
park.
Parkland course.
Pro M W Passmore; Founded 1897
Designed by James Braid
18 holes, 6401 yards, S.S.S. 71
Welcome WD, except Wed.
WD £33.
Welcome Tues and Thurs
between May 1 and Sept 30 by prior
arrangement with Sec, A O Rammell;
minimum of 12 players; catering
packages can be arranged; from £26.
Full facilities available.
Gungate; Beefeater, both
Tamworth.

6A 51 **Druids Heath**
Stonnall Rd, Aldridge, Walsall, W
Midlands, WS9 8JZ
(01922) 455595, Pro 459523
Off A452 6 miles NW of Sutton
Coldfield.
Undulating course.
Pro Glenn Williams; Founded 1973
18 holes, 6659 yards, S.S.S. 73
Welcome WD and after 2pm on
WE.
WD £25; WE £33.
WD by prior arrangement.

By prior arrangement.
Barons Court; Fairlawns.

6A 52 **Dukinfield**
Yew Tree Lane, Dukinfield, Cheshire,
SK10 5DB
(0161) 338 2340
From Ashton Road 1 mile then right
into Yew Tree Lane; club 1 mile on
right on hill behind Senior Service
factory.
Hillside course.
Pro Colin Boyle/Jamie Low; Founded
1913
18 holes, 5303 yards, S.S.S. 66
Welcome WD by prior
arrangement.
WD £18.50.
Welcome by prior arrangement
with Sec.
Full clubhouse facilities except
Mon.
Village, Hyde.

6A 53 **Dunham Forest Golf & Country Club**
Oldfield Lane, Altrincham, Cheshire,
WA14 4TY
(0161) 928 2605, Pro 928 2727
2 miles N of M56 Junction 7 towards
Manchester and course on left.
Woodland course.
Pro Ian Wrigley; Founded 1961
18 holes, 6636 yards, S.S.S. 72
Welcome.
WD £40; WE £45.
Welcome WD except Wed;
discounts for groups of more than 20;
packages available.
Bar and restaurant facilities
available.
Bowdon; Cresta Court.

6A 54 **Eastham Lodge**
117 Ferry Rd, Eastham, Wirral, L62
0AP
(0151) 327 1483, Fax 327 3003,
Pro 327 3008, Sec 327 3003
M53 Junction 5 to A41 follow signs
for Eastham Country Park.
Parkland course; was Port Sunlight
GC from 1932-76.
Pro Bob Boobyer; Founded 1976
Designed by Hawtree & Sons
18 holes, 5706 yards, S.S.S. 68
Welcome WD; with a member only
at WE.
Terms on application.
Welcome Tues by prior
arrangement; some Mon and Fri
dates available also; golf and catering
packages available.

Full clubhouse bar and catering facilities.

Raby House, Willaston.

6A 55 Eaton
Guy Lane, Waverton, Chester, Cheshire, CH3 7PH
☎(01244) 335885, Fax 335782, Pro 335826
3 miles SE of Chester off the A41 through the village of Waverton.
Parkland course.
Pro Neil Dunroe; Founded 1965, altered in 1993
Designed by Donald Steel
18 holes, 6562 yards, S.S.S. 71
† Welcome with handicap certs.
WD £25; WE £30.
Welcome WD except Wed by prior arrangement; full golf and catering packages available; from £25.
Full clubhouse facilities available.
Rowton Hall.

6A 56 Ellesmere Port
Chester Rd, Childer Thornton, S Wirral, Cheshire, L66 1QH
☎(0151) 339 7689
On M53 W to A41 turn S to Chester for 2 miles; club at rear of St Paul's Church, Hooton.
Municipal parkland/meadowland course.
Pro Anthony Roberts; Founded 1971
Designed by Cotton, Pennink, Lawrie & Partners
18 holes, 6432 yards, S.S.S. 71
† Welcome.
WD £6.70; WE £7.40; concessions apply.
Welcome with booking fee of £1.30 per head; winter packages available.
Full bar and restaurant.
Brook Meadow; Chimney; Village.

6A 57 Enville
Highgate Common, Enville, Stourbridge, W Midlands, DY7 5BN
☎(01384) 872074, Fax 873396, Pro 872585
6 miles W of Stourbridge on the A458 to Bridgnorth.
Woodland/heathland course.
Pro Sean Power; Founded 1935
Highgate: 18 holes, 6471 yards, S.S.S. 72; Lodge: 18 holes, 6275 yards, S.S.S. 70
† Welcome WD only.
WD £30 (18 holes).
Welcome by prior arrangement and payment of £10 per player

deposit; minimum 12 players; 10 per cent reduction for 30 or more; terms on application.
Full clubhouse catering.

6A 58 Frodsham ☎
Simons Lane, Frodsham, Cheshire, WA6 6HE
☎(01928) 732159, Pro 739442
Close to M56 Junction 12; turn left at lights in Frodsham centre on to B5152.
Parkland course.
Pro Graham Tonge; Founded 1990
Designed by John Day
18 holes, 6298 yards, S.S.S. 70
† Welcome WD except for competition days; tee times booked through the shop.
WD £30.
Welcome WD by prior arrangement with golf office; packages available; terms on application.
Full bar and catering facilities available.
Forest Hills.

6A 59 Gatley
Waterfall Farm, off Styal Rd, Heald Green, Cheadle, Cheshire, SK8 3TW
☎(0161) 437 2091, Pro 436 2830
Off Yew Tree Grove and Styal Road, 2 miles from Cheadle and 1 mile from Manchester Airport.
Parkland course.
Pro Simon Reeves; Founded 1912
9 holes, 5909 yards, S.S.S. 68
† Welcome except Tues and Wed.
Terms on application.
Welcome by prior arrangement with Sec.
Full facilities except Mon.
Pymgate Lodge.

6A 60 Goldenhill
Mobberley Rd, Goldenhill, Stoke-on-Trent, Staffs, ST6 5SS
☎(01782) 234200, Fax 234303
On A50 between Tunstall and Kidsgrove.
Parkland/meadowland course in old mine basin.
Founded 1983
18 holes, 5957 yards, S.S.S. 69
† Welcome; booking system available.
WD £9; WE £10.
Welcome by arrangement.
Bar and restaurant.
Practice range, practice ground; putting green.

6A 61 Great Barr
Chapel Lane, Great Barr, Birmingham, W Midlands, B43 7BA
☎(0121) 357 1232, Pro 357 5270, Sec 358 4376
Close to M6 Junction 7 6 miles NW Birmingham.
Meadowland course.
Pro Richard Spragg; Founded 1961
Designed by J. Hamilton Stutt
18 holes, 6523 yards, S.S.S. 71
† Welcome WD.
WD £25.
Welcome Tues and Thurs by prior arrangement.
Full clubhouse facilities.
Post House.

6A 62 Greenway Hall
Stanley Road, Stockton Brook, Stoke-on-Trent, Staffs, ST9 9LJ
☎(01782) 503158, Fax 504259
Off A53 Stoke-Leek road at Stockton Brook.
Parkland course/heathland.
Pro Steven Harlock; Founded 1909
18 holes, 5681 yards, S.S.S. 67
† Welcome WD.
WD £14; WE £14.
Welcome by prior arrangement; packages available; terms on application.
Clubhouse facilities.

6A 63 Hale
Rappax Rd, Hale, Altrincham, Cheshire, WA15 0NU
☎(0161) 980 4225, Pro 904 0835
2 miles SE of Altrincham; near Altrincham Priory.
Parkland course.
Pro Alec Bickerdike; Founded 1903
9 holes, 5780 yards, S.S.S. 68
† Welcome WD except Thurs; with member only at WE.
WD £20.
Welcome by prior arrangement; catering available for coffee and lunch; evening meals by prior arrangement with the steward; from £20.
Clubhouse facilities.
Practice ground.
Four Seasons, Manchester Airport.

6A 64 Hawkstone Park ☎
Weston-under-Redcastle, Shrewsbury, Shropshire, SY4 5UY
☎(01939) 200611, Fax 200311
Off A49 12 miles N of Shrewsbury or A442 12 miles N of Telford.

Parkland course.
Pro Paul Wesslingh; Founded 1920
Hawkstone: 18 holes, 6491 yards,
S.S.S. 71; Windmill: 18 holes, 6476
yards, S.S.S. 71
✝ Welcome with prior booking;
handicap certs required.
⌷ WD £30; WE £38.
↷Welcome by prior arrangement
with golf reservation office; terms on
application.
🍽 Full bar and restaurant facilities.
Practice range, 15 bays; also 6-hole
par 3 academy course; putting and
pitching green.
� Hawkstone Park on site; golfing
breaks available.

6A 65 Hazel Grove
Buxton Rd, Hazel Grove, Stockport,
Cheshire, SK7 6LU
☎(0161) 483 3978, Fax 487 4399,
Pro 483 7272, Bar/Rest 483
3217/4399
Off A6 Stockport-Buxton road.
Parkland course.
Pro Mike Hill; Founded 1913
18 holes, 6310 yards, S.S.S. 71
✝ Welcome by prior arrangement.
⌷ WD £30; WE £35.
↷Welcome Thurs and Fri by prior
arrangement; package includes full
day of golf and catering; £38.
🍽 Full clubhouse bar and restaurant
facilities.

6A 66 Heaton Moor
Mauldeth Road, Heaton Mersey,
Stockport, Cheshire, SK4 3NX
☎(0161) 432 2134
From M63 Junction 12 follow
Didsbury signs and Mauldeth Rd is
1.5 miles on right.
Flat, tree-lined parkland course.
Pro Simon Marsh; Founded 1892
18 holes, 5968 yards, S.S.S. 68
✝ Welcome by prior arrangement.
⌷ Terms on application.
↷Welcome by prior arrangement;
Thurs and Fri preferred; golf and
catering packages available; from
£33.
🍽 Full clubhouse facilities.
↷ Rudyard, Heaton Chapel.

6A 67 Helsby
Towers Lane, Helsby, Cheshire, WA6
0JB
☎(01928) 722021
From M56 Junction 14; left to Helsby
and then right and right again for
Towers Lane.

Parkland course.
Pro M Jones; Founded 1901
Designed by James Braid
18 holes, 6229yards, S.S.S. 70
✝ Welcome WD.
⌷ WD £22; WE £22.
↷Welcome Tues and Thurs;
packages include full day's golf and
catering; from £34.50.
🍽 Full clubhouse facilities available.

6A 68 Heswall
Cottage Lane, Gayton, Heswall,
Wirral, Cheshire, L60 8PB
☎(0151) 342 1237, Pro 342 7431
M53 Junction 4; from roundabout,
turn into Well Lane; leads into
Cottage Lane.
Parkland course.
Pro Alan Thompson; Founded 1901
18 holes, 6554 yards, S.S.S. 72
✝ Welcome except Tues.
⌷ WD £35; WE £40.
↷Welcome Wed and Fri only; winter
packages available.
🍽 Full facilities.
↷ Mollington Banastre; Thornton
Hall; Parkgate; Travelodge (Gayton);
Woodhey; Victoria.

6A 69 Heyrose
Budworth Rd, Tabley, Knutsford,
Cheshire, WA16 0HY
☎(01565) 733664, Pro 734267
4 miles W of Knutsford 0.5 miles
along Budworth road off Pickmere
Lane; M6 Junction 19, 1 mile.
Wooded converted farmland course
with water features.
Pro Colin Hiddon; Founded 1990
Designed by E.L.C.N. Bridge
18 holes, 6515 yards, S.S.S. 71
✝ Welcome except before 2pm on
Sat.
⌷ WD £19; WE £24.
↷Welcome WD by prior
arrangement; from £36.
🍽 Clubhouse bar and restaurant.
Practice range, practice ground;
practice bunkers; putting green;
driving net.
↷ Cottons, Knutsford; Swan,
Bucklow Hill; Old Vicarage, Tabley;
Travelodge.

6A 70 Hill Valley Golf ☏
& Country Club
Terrick Rd, Whitchurch, Shropshire,
SY13 4JZ
☎(01948) 663584, Fax 665927, Pro
663032
Off A49/A41 Whitchurch by-pass.

Undulating parkland course.
Pro Tony Minshall; Founded 1975
Designed by P. Alliss & D. Thomas
36 holes
✝ Welcome.
⌷ WD on application.
↷Welcome by prior arrangement;
packages available; also East course,
5280 yards par 66; health and leisure
centre; snooker.
🍽 Full clubhouse facilities.
↷ Motel accommodation at club;
Dodington Lodge; Terrick Hall.

6A 71 Himley Hall Golf
Centre
Log Cabin, Himley Hall Park, Dudley,
W Midlands, DY3 4DF
☎(01902) 895207
From A449 Wolverhampton-
Kidderminster road to Dudley on
B4176; then into Himley Hall Park.
Public parkland course.
Pro Jeremy Nicholls; Founded 1980
Designed by D.A. Baker
9 holes, 6215 yards, S.S.S. 70
✝ Welcome.
⌷ WD £5.80; WE £5.80 (9 holes).
↷Welcome by arrangement.
🍽 Cafe and hot meals.
↷ Himley House; Park Hall.

6A 72 Houldsworth
Houldsworth Park, Reddish,
Stockport, Cheshire, SK5 6BN
☎(0161) 442 9611, Pro 442 1714,
Sec 442 1712
From M63 Junction 13 turn left up to
roundabout then take road to
Reddish; turn left at Houldsworth pub.
Parkland course.
Pro David Naylor; Founded 1911
Designed by T.G. Renouf
18 holes, 6247 yards, S.S.S. 70
✝ Welcome WD (Ladies day Tues).
⌷ WD £20; WE £25.
↷Welcome by prior arrangement.
🍽 Full facilities.

6A 73 Hoylake Municipal
Carr Lane, Hoylake, Merseyside, L47
4BG
☎(0151) 632 2956
Off M53 10 miles SW of Liverpool
following signs for Hoylake; 100 yards
beyond Hoylake station.
Municipal parkland course.
Pro Simon Hooton; Founded 1933
Designed by James Braid
18 holes, 6321 yards, S.S.S. 70
✝ Welcome; book in advance at WE;
Sat from 8.30am.

Little Aston

Another wonderful course set close to the heart of a major city. This time Birmingham is the metropolis that surrounds Little Aston.

Although it is only a few miles from the centre of the city and has the more famous courses of the modern professional game close by, Little Aston offers a real parkland setting.

It was once the setting for the Dunlop Masters in the 1950s and 1960s but many consider that it is too kind to be a real championship test for the professionals.

But while there is more freedom at Little Aston there is no question that this is not a worthy test of golf for anyone. There are still the demands for accurate long iron shots.

Designed by Harry Vardon in 1908, the signature of the course comes early at the sixth, seventh and eighth holes which he created using the fine soil and gravel of the area.

The three peaks are all par fours. They all play between 375 and 430 yards and all demand the greatest of concentration as they cut across the centre of the course.

If any is a classic test of golf it is probably the seventh. It is not the longest – that honour belongs to the sixth – but in its layout it offers the classic par four.

There are no fewer than five fairway bunkers and if these have been avoided there are the sand traps around the green just waiting to snap up any mis-hit shot.

It is the par fives that set the tone for the course but some golfers believe after the zig-zag of six, seven and eight that the 10th at 438 yards is as taxing a hole as there is on the course.

The course also has a long finish with a par-five 15th followed by three par fours. There may be more room to play but the length is there to punish the weak.

The approach to the course is reminiscent in some ways to the long drive up to the Wentworth clubhouse but it all adds to the anticipation of playing the course. — **CG**

Llanymynech

0It is not an easy place to find but for those travelling through the Welsh borders and Midlands counties Llanymynech offers a rare distraction.

Tucked away up a steep drive off the Welshpool drive, Llanymynech is in the unique position where, intentionally, you can drive the ball from one country into another.

On the dog-leg fourth there is a small marker which tells the golfer that his ball has travelled out of England and is now sitting comfortably in Wales.

There are several counties where it is possible to cross the border but to the best of our knowledge there are no other courses which straddle a national border.

For that reason alone there is a constant stream of visitors who leave behind the other border courses such as Hawkstone Park, which was the cradle for Sandy Lyle's great talent and Trentham Park.

Further north into Cheshire there are the delights of Carden Park and Portal, not to mention the more established courses such as Delaware Forest.

Situated on Offa's Dyke the course has an unimposing start with a short par three and an ordinary dog-leg five around a small farm before climbing through the foothills towards the focal point of the course.

But if the trans-national hole is the main attraction for the trivia collectors in golf, the rest of the course should not be ignored.

While for many there are simply too many blind holes for it to be a good test of golf there are some staggering views from the holes on the back nine.

As the ninth crosses the small river and lifts further towards the 10th there are small hints of the challenges ahead. The par-three 10th is played from an elevated tee and only Shropshire air stands between the golfer and the shrubs that surround the green.

But the best vista is from the 12th tee where the land drops suddenly and dramatically to the Shropshire plains in one direction and into Wales in the other.

The raised section of the course falls away at the 18th back to the simple clubhouse where their main pride is not just the staggering sausage sandwiches but also the framed course record collected by a certain I Woosnam.

For those who want to continue on the Woosnam learning curve there is the chance to play what was his home club during his early career – Oswestry, which is just along the A5.

It may not be the grandest golf course in the country but it certainly is unique and when the wind blows it can also be a rare test of golf. — **CG**

WD £6.50; WE £6.50.
Welcome by prior arrangement; after 1.30pm at WE.
Hot snacks, meals and bar.
Green Lodge.

6A 74 Ingestre Park

Ingestre, Stafford, Staffs, ST18 0RE
(01889) 270 845, Fax 270 845, Pro 270 304, Bar/Rest 270 061
Course is six miles east of Stafford off the A51 via Great Haywood and Tixall.
Parkland course in former estate of Earl of Shrewsbury.
Pro D Scullion; Founded 1977
Designed by Hawtree & Son
18 holes, 6251 yards, S.S.S. 70
Welcome WD with handicap certs; with member at WE.
WD £23.
Welcome WD except Wed with prior arrangement; special packages available for 15 or more; snooker room; lounge; from £34.
Bar and restaurant facilities available.
Practice area.
Dower House, Ingestre; Garth, Tillington Hall, both Stafford.

6A 75 Izaak Walton

Eccleshall Rd, Cold Norton, Stone, Staffs, ST15 0NS
(01785) 760900
On B5026 between Stone and Eccleshall.
Parkland course.
Pro Julie Brown; Founded 1992
Designed by Mike Lowe
18 holes, 6281 yards, S.S.S. 72
Welcome.
WD £15; WE £20.
Welcome by prior arrangement; packages for catering and golf available; full facilities; terms on application.
Full clubhouse facilities.
Stone House, Stone.

6A 76 Knights Grange Sports Complex

Grange Lane, Winsford, Cheshire, CW7 2PT
(01606) 552780
Course in centre of Winsford.
Public meadowland course.
Pro Graham Moore; Founded 1983
9 holes, 5438 yards, S.S.S. 66
Welcome.
WD £3.80; WE £5.25; concessions apply.

Welcome by prior arrangement in writing.
Hot drinks and snacks.
Practice area; tennis; bowls.

6A 77 Knutsford

Merchcath Lane, Knutsford, Cheshire, WA16 6HS
(01565) 633355, Pro 755781
2 miles from M6 Junction 19; make for Knutsford entrance to Tatton Park.
Parkland course.
Pro Allan Gillies; Founded 1891
10 holes, 6195 yards, S.S.S. 70
Welcome WD except Wed.
Terms on application.
Welcome Thurs by prior arrangement.
Full facilities.
George; Angel; Cottons; Rose & Crown; Swan.

6A 78 Lakeside (Rugeley)

Rugeley Power Station, Armitage Rd, Rugeley, Staffs, WS15 1PR
(01889) 575667
Between Lichfield and Stafford.
Parkland course.
Founded 1969
18 holes, 5534 yards, S.S.S. 67
Welcome with a member.
WD on application.
Evening service.

6A 79 Leasowe

Leasowe Rd, Moreton, Wirral L46 3RD
(0151) 677 5852, Pro 678 5460
Off M53 1 miles after tunnel; 1 mile W of Wallasey village.
Links course.
Pro Andrew Ayre; Founded 1891
Designed by John Ball Jnr
18 holes, 6263 yards, S.S.S. 70
Welcome WD; WE by prior arrangement.
WD £20.50; WE £25.50.
Welcome by arrangement; minimum 16 players; not Sat.
Restaurant, bar and snacks.
Large practice area.
Leasowe Castle.

6A 80 Leek

Cheddleton Rd, Leek, Staffs ST13 5RE
(01538) 385889, Pro 384767, Sec 384779
On A520 0.75 miles S of Leek.
Parkland course.
Pro P A Stubbs; Founded 1892

18 holes, 6240 yards, S.S.S. 70
Welcome with handicap certs.
WD £24; WE £30.
Welcome Wed; golf and catering packages available.
Full clubhouse facilities.
Bank End Farm; Horse Shoes, Blacksham Moor.

6A 81 Lilleshall Hall

Lilleshall, Newport, Shropshire, TF10 9AS
(01952) 604776, Fax 604776, Pro 604104, Bar/Rest 603840
Between A41 and A5 at Sherrifhales.
Parkland course.
Pro S McKane; Founded 1937
Designed by H.S. Colt
18 holes, 5789 yards, S.S.S. 68
Welcome WD and WE with a member.
WD £20; WE £15.
Welcome WD by prior arrangement; terms on application.
Clubhouse facilities.

6A 82 Little Aston

Roman Road, Streetly, B74 3AN
(0121) 353 2066, Fax 580 8387, Pro 353 0330, Sec 353 2942
www.ne.quik.co.uk/lagolf
4 miles NW of Sutton Coldfield off A454.
Parkland course.
Pro John Anderson; Founded 1908
Designed by Harry Vardon
18 holes, 6670 yards, S.S.S. 73
Welcome by arrangement.
Terms on application.
Welcome Mon, Tues, Wed and Fri by prior arrangement; catering and golf packages available.
Full clubhouse facilities.

6A 83 Llanymynech

Pant, Oswestry, Shropshire, SY10 8LB
(01691) 830542, Pro 830879, Sec 830983
6 miles S of Oswestry on A483; take turning at Cross Guns Inn at Pant Hilltop; 4th hole tee in Wales, green in England.
Pro Andrew Griffiths; Founded 1933
18 holes, 6114 yards, S.S.S. 69
Welcome by arrangement.
WD £18; WE £21.
Welcome WD except Thurs; catering available by prior arrangement.
Bar and restaurant facilities.
Many in Oswestry area.

6A 84 **Ludlow**
Bromfield, Ludlow, Shropshire SY8
2BT
☎ (01584) 856285, Pro 856366
Course is one mile north of Ludlow
off the A49.
Heathland course.
Pro Russell Price; Founded 1889
18 holes, 6277 yards, S.S.S. 70
♦ Welcome.
⌐ WD £18; WE £24.
↻ Welcome by prior arrangement;
terms on application.
🍽 Clubhouse facilities.
↝ Feathers, Ludlow.

6A 85 **Lymm**
Whitbarrow Rd, Lymm, Cheshire,
WA13 9AN
☎ (01925) 755054, Sec 755020,
Clubhouse 752177
5 miles SE of Warrington.
Parkland course.
Pro Steve McCarthy; Founded 1907
18 holes, 6304 yards, S.S.S. 70
♦ Welcome WD; Thurs ladies day,
no visitors before 2.30pm; with
member at WE.
⌐ WD £22.
↻ Welcome, usually on Wed; winter
packages.
🍽 Full meals facilities.
↝ Lymm; Statham Lodge.

6A 86 **Macclesfield**
The Hollins, Macclesfield, Cheshire,
SK11 7EA
☎ (01625) 423227, Fax 260061, Pro
616952, Sec 615845
From the southern end of the A523
(Silk Road), turn into Windmill St.
Parkland/heathland course.
Pro Tony Taylor; Founded 1889
Designed by Hawtree & Son
18 holes, 5769 yards, S.S.S. 68
♦ Welcome.
⌐ WD £20; WE £25.
↻ Welcome by arrangement;
packages available; contact Sec;
terms on application.
🍽 Full clubhouse facilities.
↝ Sutton Hall.

6A 87 **Malkins Bank**
Betchton Rd, Sandbach, Cheshire,
CW11 4XN
☎ (01270) 765931
1.5 miles from M6 Junction 17.
Municipal parkland course course.
Pro David Wheeler; Founded 1980
Designed by Hawtree & Son
18 holes, 5971 yards, S.S.S. 69

♦ Welcome; booking system in
operation.
⌐ WD £7.25; WE £8.25.
↻ Welcome.
🍽 Bar and catering daily.
↝ Old Hall; Saxon Cross Motel.

6A 88 **The Manor Golf Club (Kingstone) Ltd**
Leese Hill, Kingstone,
Uttoxeter, Staffordshire, ST14 8QT
☎ (01889) 563234
On the main Uttoxeter to Stafford
road.
Parkland course.
Founded 1992
Designed by David Gough
18 holes, 5360 yards, S.S.S. 69
♦ Welcome.
⌐ Terms on application.
↻ Welcome by prior arrangement.
🍽 Bar and catering facilities.
Practice range, 5-bay driving range,
putting green.

6A 89 **Market Drayton**
Sutton, Market Drayton, Shropshire,
TF9 2HX
☎ (01630) 652266
1.5 miles S of Market Drayton.
Undulating meadowland.
Pro Russell Clewes; Founded 1911
18 holes, 6290 yards, S.S.S. 71
♦ Welcome WD except Tues which
is ladies day; Sat with a member; Sun
members only.
⌐ WD £24.
↻ Welcome by arrangement.
🍽 Full facilities.
↝ Bungalow at course (sleeps six);
Bear; Corbet Arms.

6A 90 **Marple**
Bransfold Rd, Hawk Green, Marple,
Stockport, Cheshire, SK6 7EL
☎ (0161) 427 2311, Fax 427 1125,
Pro 427 1195, Sec 427 1125
Signposted from Hawk Green.
Parkland course.
Pro David Myers; Founded 1892
18 holes, 5552 yards, S.S.S. 67
♦ Welcome except comp days.
⌐ WD £20; WE £30.
↻ Welcome by prior arrangement;
golf and catering packages available;
from £32.50.
🍽 Clubhouse facilities.

6A 91 **Mellor & Townscliffe**
Tarden, Gibb Lane, Mellor, Stockport,
Cheshire, SK6 5NA

☎ (0161) 427 9700, Pro 427 5759,
Sec 442 2208
Off A626 opposite Devonshire Arms
on Longhurst Lane, Mellor.
Parkland/moorland course.
Pro Gary Broadley; Founded 1894
22 holes, 5925 yards, S.S.S. 69
♦ Welcome except Sat.
⌐ WD £20; WE £27.50.
↻ Welcome by prior arrangement;
winter packages available.
🍽 Full facilities except Tues.
↝ Pack Horse Inn.

6A 92 **Meole Brace**
Meole Brace, Shrewsbury,
Shropshire, SY2 6QQ
☎ (01743) 364050
At junction of A5/A49 S of
Shrewsbury.
Municipal course with water features.
Pro Nigel Bramall; Founded 1976
12 holes, 3400 yards, S.S.S. 43
♦ Welcome; pay as you play.
⌐ WD £4.70; WE £5.70.
↻ Welcome by prior arrangement.
🍽 Drinks and confectionery
machines.
9-hole pitch and putt.

6A 93 **Mere Golf & Country Club** ℭ
Chester Rd, Mere, Knutsford,
Cheshire, WA16 6LJ
☎ (01565) 830155, Fax 830713, Pro
830219
1 mile E of M6 Junction 19 on A556;
2 miles W of M56 Junction 7.
Parkland course.
Pro Peter Eyre; Founded 1934
Designed by George Duncan and
James Braid
18 holes, 6817 yards, S.S.S. 73
♦ Welcome Mon, Tues and Thurs by
prior arrangement.
⌐ WD £70.
↻ Welcome Mon, Tues and Thurs by
arrangement; full range of clubhouse
facilities, golf days and golf
packages; terms on application.
🍽 Bar and restaurant service.
↝ Cottons.

6A 94 **Mersey Valley**
Warrington Rd, Bold Heath, Nr
Widnes, Cheshire, WA8 3XL
☎ (0151) 424 6060, Fax 424 6060
Leave M62 Junction 7; 1.5 miles on
A57 towards Warrington.
Parkland course.
Pro Andy Stevenson; Founded 1995
Designed by Mellion Leisure

18 holes, 6374 yards, S.S.S. 70
⛳ Welcome.
WD £17; WE £20.
Welcome by arrangement; deposit required; packages available for 18 and 27 holes of golf with meals; from £26.
🍴 Bar and bar snacks; function suite available.
Practice area.
Hillcrest, Widnes.

6A 95 Mile End
Mile End, Oswestry, Shropshire, SY11 4JE
☎ (01691) 670580, Pro 671246
1 mile SE of Oswestry; signposted from A5.
Parkland course(converted farmland).
Pro Scott Carponter; Founded 1992
Designed by Michael Price/D Gough
18 holes, 6194 yards, S.S.S. 69
⛳ Welcome.
WD £14; WE £18.
Welcome WD by prior arrangement; terms on application.
🍴 Full clubhouse facilities.
Practice range, 12 bays floodlit.
Wynnstay; Sweeney Hall.

6A 96 Mobberley ☎
Burleyhurst Lane, Mobberley, Knutsford, Cheshire, WA16 7JZ
☎ (01565) 880178, Pro 880188
From M56 Junction 6 head towards Wilmslow and after Moat House turn right.
Parkland course.
Pro Steve Norris; Founded 1995
9 holes, 5542 yards, S.S.S. 67
⛳ Welcome.
WD £12.50; WE £16.
Welcome by prior arrangement.
🍴 Bar and restaurant.
Practice range, practice area; indoor teaching facilities.
Moat House; Boddington Arms.

6A 97 Mottram Hall Hotel
Wilmslow Road, Mottram St Andrew, Prestbury, Cheshire, SK10 4QT
☎ (01625) 820064
From M56 Junction 6 follow A538 through Wilmslow; follow signposts.
Parkland/woodland course.
Pro Tim Rastall; Founded 1991
Designed by David Thomas
18 holes, 7006 yards, S.S.S. 74
⛳ Welcome with handicap certs.
WD £39; WE £44.
Welcome by arrangement; packages available; on-course

drink/food buggy; leisure centre.
🍴 Full clubhouse and hotel facilities.
Mottram Hall on site (133 beds).

6A 98 New Mills
Shaw Marsh, New Mills, High Peak, Cheshire, SK22 3QD
☎ (01663) 743485, Pro 746161
0.75 miles from centre of New Mills on St Mary Rd.
Moorland course.
Pro Stephen James; Founded 1907
9 holes, 5633 yards, S.S.S. 67
⛳ Welcome WD and Sat mornings except on competition days.
WD £18; WE £20.
Welcome WD by prior arrangement; from £26.
🍴 Bar and clubhouse catering.
Pack Horse; Sportsman; Moorside.

6A 99 Newcastle Municipal
Keele Rd, Newcastle under Lyme, Staffs, ST5 5AB
☎ (01782) 617006, Bar 616583
Off M6 Junction 15, on A525 for 2 miles.
Public parkland course.
Pro Colin Smith; Founded 1975
18 holes, 6396 yards, S.S.S. 70
⛳ Welcome; book any time.
Terms on application.
Welcome on application to local council.
🍴 Bar and meals.
Practice range, 26 bays floodlit (01782 717417).
Keele Hospitality Inn.

6A 100 Newcastle-under-Lyme
Whitmore Rd, Newcastle-under-Lyme, Staffs, ST5 2QB
☎ (01782) 618526
1.5 miles SW of Newcastle-under-Lyme on A53.
Parkland course.
Pro Paul Symonds; Founded 1908
18 holes, 6317 yards, S.S.S. 71
⛳ Welcome WD.
WD £26.
Welcome on Mon all day and Thurs pm; packages on application; snooker.
🍴 Bar and restaurant.
Post House; Borough Arms.

6A 101 Northenden
Palatine Rd, Northenden, Manchester, M22 4FR

☎ (0161) 998 4738, Fax 945 5592, Pro 945 3386, Bar/Rest 998 4079
0.5 miles from M56 Junction 9; M63 Junction 9.
Parkland course.
Pro Peter Scott; Founded 1913
Designed by T Renouf
18 holes, 6503 yards, S.S.S. 71
⛳ Welcome by arrangement.
WD £27; WE £30.
Welcome Tues and Fri; packages include 27 holes of golf; coffee and bacon sandwich on arrival; light lunch and dinner; from £41.
🍴 Full clubhouse facilities.
Britannia Country House; Post House, Northenden.

6A 102 Onneley
Onneley, Crewe, Cheshire, CW3 5QF
☎ (01782) 750577
1 mile from Woore on A51 to Newcastle.
Undulating meadowland course.
Founded 1968
9 holes, 5474 yards, S.S.S. 67
⛳ Welcome WD; WE only with a member.
WD on application.
Welcome by prior arrangement with Sec; from £18.
🍴 Clubhouse facilities.
Wheatsheaf.

6A 103 Oswestry
Aston Park, Oswestry, Shropshire, SY11 4JJ
☎ (01691) 610221, Fax 610535, Pro 610448, Sec 610535
3 miles SE of Oswestry on A5.
Parkland course.
Pro David Skelton; Founded 1930
Designed by James Braid
18 holes, 6024 yards, S.S.S. 69
⛳ Welcome with handicap certs.
WD £22; WE £30.
Welcome Wed and Fri; packages available; from £31.
🍴 Full clubhouse facilities.

6A 104 Oxley Park
Bushbury, Wolverhampton, W Midlands, WV10 6DE
☎ (01902) 420506; Pro 425445, Sec 425892
On A449 1 mile N of Wolverhampton.
Parkland course.
Pro Les Burlison; Founded 1913
18 holes, 6222 yards, S.S.S. 70
⛳ Welcome; only with a member at WE in winter.
WD £25; WE £25.

⌁ Welcome Wed by arrangement; snooker.
🍽 Full clubhouse catering.
⌁ Mount; Goldthorn; Park Hall.

6A 105 Parkhall
Hulme Road, Weston Coyney, Stoke-on-Trent, Staffs, ST3 5BH
☎ (01782) 599584
1 mile outside Longton on A50.
Public moorland course.
Founded 1989
18 holes, 4770 yards, S.S.S. 54
♦ Welcome.
⌷ WD £6; WE £7.
⌁ Welcome by arrangement.
🍽 None.

6A 106 Patshull Park Hotel ⊂ Golf and Country Club
Pattingham, Wolverhampton, WV6 7HR
☎ (01902) 700100, Fax 700874, Pro 700342
From A41 Wolverhampton-Whitchurch road follow signs to Pattingham.
Parkland course.
Pro for 2000 Peter Baker; Founded 1972
Designed by John Jacobs
18 holes, 6412 yards, S.S.S. 72
♦ Welcome with handicap certs.
⌷ WD £25; WE £30.
⌁ Welcome by prior arrangement; packages including catering from £29.95 per person.
🍽 Full clubhouse and hotel facilities.
Practice ground.
⌁ Patshull Park Hotel on site.

6A 107 Penkridge G & CC
Pottal Pool Rd, Penkridge, Stafford, Staffs, ST19 5RN
☎ (01785) 716455
📧 www.leadingedgegolfacademy.com
Off A34 at Penkridge/ Rugeley cross roads; turn to Penkridge and course is 0.75 miles on left; from M6 Junction 12, take A5 towards Telford, then A449 followed by B5102 towards Cannock, turning left in Pottal Pool Rd after Wolgarston School.
Parkland course.
Pro Andrew Preston; Founded 1995
Designed by John Reynolds
18 holes, 6613 yards, S.S.S. 72
♦ Welcome.
⌷ WD £14.50; WE £19.50.
⌁ Welcome by arrangement; deposit required; discounts for larger groups; video analysis; from £16.

🍽 Full clubhouse facilities.
Practice range, 20 bay, teaching academy, putting green, chipping green.
⌁ Hatherton Country Hotel.

6A 108 Penn
Penn Common, Penn, Wolverhampton WV4 5JN
☎ (01902) 341142, Pro 330472
On A449 2.5 miles W of Wolverhampton at Penn.
Heathland course.
Pro A Briscoe; Founded 1908
18 holes, 6462 yards, S.S.S. 71
♦ Welcome WD; with member at WE.
⌷ WD £20.
⌁ Welcome Mon, Wed, Fri; reductions for groups of 20+; catering packages available; from £17.
🍽 Full clubhouse facilities.

6A 109 Peover
Plumley Moor Road, Lower Peover, Cheshire, WA16 9SE
☎ (01565) 723337, Fax 723311
Leave M6 Junction 19 to A556; follow signs to Plumley and Lower Peover on Plumley Moor Rd; course 1.5 miles.
Parkland course.
Pro Bobby Young; Founded 1996
Designed by P Naylor
18 holes, 6702 yards, S.S.S. 72
♦ Welcome.
⌷ WD £18; WE £23.
⌁ Welcome WD; packages available on application; from £18.
🍽 Full clubhouse catering available.
⌁ Belle Epoque.

6A 110 Perton Park Golf Club
Wrottesley Park Road, Perton, Wolverhampton, WV6 7HL
☎ (01902) 380103, Fax 326219, Pro 380073, Sec 897031
Just off the A454 Bridgnorth to Wolverhampton road.
Meadowland course.
Pro Jeremy Harrold; Founded 1990
18 holes, 6620 yards, S.S.S. 70
♦ Welcome with tee time from starter.
⌷ WD £12; WE £18.
⌁ Welcome by prior arrangement; golf and catering packages available; from £15.
🍽 Full clubhouse catering facilities available.
Practice range, 18-bay range.

6A 111 Portal Golf & Country Club
Cobblers Cross, Tarporley, Cheshire, CW6 0DJ
☎ (01829) 733933, Fax 733928
11 miles SE of Chester off A49 near Tarporley.
Parkland course; 3rd: Haddington's Ground, 602 yards.
Pro Mike Slater; Founded 1989
Designed by Donald Steel
18 holes, 7037 yards, S.S.S. 74
♦ Welcome by arrangement.
⌷ WD £50; WE £50.
⌁ Welcome by arrangement; packages available; also Arderne course, par 30; from £35.
🍽 Restaurant and bar facilities.
⌁ The Swan, Tarporley; Wild Boar, Beeston; Nunsmere Hotel.

6A 112 Portal Golf & Country Club Premier Course
Forest Rd, Tarporley, Cheshire, CW6 0JA
☎ (01829) 733884, Fax 733666, Pro 733703, Rest 733445
1 mile S of Tarporley between Chester and Northwich.
Parkland course.
Pro Judy Statham; Founded 1990
Designed by T Rouse
18 holes, 6508 yards, S.S.S. 72
♦ Welcome.
⌷ WD £30; WE £35.
⌁ Welcome WD by prior arrangement; on application; from £29.
🍽 Full clubhouse facilities.
⌁ Swan, Tarporley; Wild Boar, Beeston.

6A 113 Poulton Park
Dig Lane, Off Crab Lane, Cinnamon Brow, Cheshire, WA2 0SH
☎ (01925) 812034, Pro 825220, Sec 822802
3 miles from Warrington off A574.
Parkland course.
Pro Andrew Matthews; Founded 1978
9 holes, 4978 yards, S.S.S. 67
♦ Welcome by arrangement.
⌷ WD £17; WE £19.
⌁ Welcome by prior arrangement; packages for golf and catering available; minimum 8; £20-£26.
🍽 Clubhouse facilities.

6A 114 Prenton ⊂
Golf Links Rd, Prenton, Birkenhead, Wirral, L42 8LW

☎ (0151) 608 1461, Fax 609 1580,
Pro 608 1636, Sec 608 1053
From M53 Junction 2 take A552
towards Birkenhead.
Parkland course.
Pro Robin Thompson; Founded 1905
Designed by Colt MacKenzie & Co
18 holes, 6429 yards, S.S.S. 71
⚑ Welcome by arrangement.
⌂ WD £30; WE £35.
☞ Welcome by prior arrangement;
golf and catering packages available;
from £24.
🍽 Full clubhouse bar and catering
facilities.
Practice range, two practice areas.

6A 115 Prestbury

Macclesfield Rd, Prestbury, Cheshire,
SK10 4BJ
☎ (01625) 829388, Fax 828241, Pro
820242, Sec 828241, Bar/Rest
829977
Course is two miles NW of
Macclesfield.
Parkland course.
Pro Nick Summerfield; Founded 1920
Designed by Colt & Morrison
18 holes, 6359 yards, S.S.S. 71
⚑ Welcome by prior arrangement on
WD; with a member at WE.
⌂ WD £38.
☞ Welcome Thurs; minimum 20;
from £34pp.
🍽 Full clubhouse bar and catering
facilities.
☞ Bridge; White House, both
Prestbury.

6A 116 Pryors Hayes Golf ℃ Club

Willington Road, Oscroft, Tarvin, Nr
Chester, Cheshire, CH3 8NL
☎ (01829) 741250, Fax 749077, Pro
740140
5 miles from Chester near Tarvin
between A54 and A51.
Parkland course.
Founded 1993
Designed by John Day
18 holes, 6074 yards, S.S.S. 69
⚑ Welcome by prior booking.
⌂ WD £20; WE £25.
☞ Welcome every day by prior
arrangement; catering and golf
packages available.
🍽 Clubhouse facilities.
☞ Willington Hall.

6A 117 Queen's Park

Queen's Park Drive, Crewe,
Cheshire, CW2 7SB

☎ (01270) 662378, Pro 666724, Sec
628352
1.5 miles from town centre off Victoria
Avenue.
Parkland course.
Pro H Bilton; Founded 1985
9 holes, 4922 yards, S.S.S. 64
⚑ Pay and play; restrictions on Wed,
Sun, Thurs so call in advance.
⌂ WD £5; WE £7 (18 holes).
☞ Welcome.
🍽 Clubhouse facilities.

6A 118 Reaseheath

Reaseheath College, Nantwich,
Cheshire, CW5 6DF
☎ (01270) 625131
1 mile from Nantwich on A51
Chester road.
Research course used for
greenkeeper training.
Founded 1987
Designed by D. Mortram
9 holes, 3729 yards, S.S.S. 54
⚑ Limited availability for non-
members; phone in advance .
⌂ WD £5; WE £5.
☞ Small groups; prior booking
essential
🍽 Restaurant on site WD.

6A 119 Reddish Vale

Southcliffe Rd, Reddish, Stockport,
Cheshire, SK5 7EE
☎ (0161) 480 2359
1.5 miles N of Stockport off B6167
Reddish road.
Undulating course in valley.
Founded 1912
Designed by Dr A. MacKenzie
18 holes, 6086 yards, S.S.S. 69
⚑ Welcome WD (lunchtime
restrictions); with a member at WE.
⌂ Terms on application.
☞ Welcome WD by prior
arrangement; packages available.
🍽 Restaurant and bar service.
☞ Belgrade; Old Rectory; Haughton
Green.

6A 120 Ringway

Hale Rd, Hale Barns, Altrincham,
Cheshire, WA15 8SW
☎ (0161) 980 8432, Pro 980 8432,
Sec 980 2630
8 miles S of Manchester 1 mile from
M56 Junction 6 on the A538 towards
Altrincham through Hale Barns.
Parkland course.
Pro Nick Ryan; Founded 1909
Designed by Harry Colt and James
Braid

18 holes, 6494 yards, S.S.S. 71
⚑ Welcome except Fri; Tues & Sat
are club competition days.
⌂ WD £35; WE £45.
☞ Welcome Thurs in summer by
prior arrangement; packages
available; corporate days organised;
snooker.
🍽 Full facilities.
☞ Cresta Court; Four Seasons;
Unicorn.

6A 121 Romiley

Goosehouse Green, Romiley,
Stockport, Cheshire, SK6 4LJ
☎ (0161) 430 2392
On B6104 off A560 0.75 miles from
Romiley station.
Undulating parkland course.
Pro Robert N Giles; Founded 1897
18 holes, 6454 yards, S.S.S. 71
⚑ Welcome except Thurs (Ladies
day).
⌂ WD £30; WE £40.
☞ Welcome Tues and Wed by prior
arrangement.
🍽 Full clubhouse service.
☞ Almonds, Marple.

6A 122 Royal Liverpool

Meols Drive, Hoylake, Wirral,
Merseyside, L47 4AL
☎ (0151) 632 3101, Fax 632 6737,
Pro 632 5868, Bar/Rest 632 3102
On A540 between Hoylake and West
Kirby, off Junction 2 of M53.
Championship links course.
Pro John Heggarty; Founded 1869
Designed by Robert Chambers &
George Morris
18 holes, 7128 yards, S.S.S. 76
⚑ Welcome by appointment only;
WE very restricted.
⌂ WD £65; WE £100 (for 18 holes
and lunch).
☞ Welcome by prior arrangement
only; from £65, including snack lunch
except July; full facilities.
🍽 Full restaurant and clubhouse
facilities.
Practice ground.
☞ Thornton Hall, Thornton-le-
Hough; Crabwell Manor, Mollington.

6A 123 Runcorn ℃

Clifton Rd, Runcorn, Cheshire, WA7
4SU
☎ (01928) 572093, Pro 564791, Sec
574214
M56 Junction 12; signposted off
A557.
Parkland course.

Pro A Franklyn; Founded 1909
18 holes, 6035 yards, S.S.S. 69
♦ Welcome WD except Tues; WE
with member.
⌐ WD £20.
⌐ Welcome Mon and Fri; includes
coffee, lunch and dinner for groups of
12 or more; from £31.
◉ Clubhouse facilities.
⌐ Lord Daresbury, Warrington.

6A 124 **St Michael Jubilee**
Dundalk Rd, Widnes, Cheshire, WA4
8BS
☎ (0151) 424 5636, Pro 424 6230,
Sec 424 6461
Close to centre of Widnes off the
Runcorn Bridge.
Public parkland course.
Pro Darren Chapman; Founded 1977
18 holes, 5667 yards, S.S.S. 68
♦ Welcome WD; with bookings at
WE.
⌐ Available on request.
⌐ Welcome by arrangement.
◉ Full facilities.
Practice area.
⌐ Hillcrest.

6A 125 **St Thomas's Priory Golf Club**
Armitage Lane, Armitage, Nr.
Rugeley, Staffordshire, WS15 1ED
☎ (01543) 491116, Fax 492244, Pro
492096, Sec 491911
1 mile SE of Rugeley on A513;
opposite Ash Tree Inn.
Parkland course; 14th is 601 yards.
Pro Danny Taylor; Founded 1995
Designed by Paul Mulholland
18 holes, 5969 yards, S.S.S. 70
♦ Welcome.
⌐ WD £20; WE £25.
⌐ Welcome by prior arrangement;
terms on application.
◉ Full clubhouse facilities.
⌐ Riverside Inn; Holiday Inn
Express, both Branston.

6A 126 **Sale**
Sale Lodge, Golf Rd, Sale, Cheshire,
M33 2XU
☎ (0161) 973 1730, Fax 962 4217,
Sec 973 1638
Close to M63 Junction 8.
Parkland course.
Pro Mike Stewart; Founded 1913
18 holes, 6358 yards, S.S.S. 70
♦ Welcome WD.
⌐ WD £28.
⌐ Welcome by arrangement with the
secretary/manager; golf and food

packages available on application;
terms on application.
◉ Clubhouse facilities.
⌐ Dane Lodge, Sale.

6A 127 **Sandbach**
117 Middlewich Rd, Sandbach,
Cheshire, CW11 1FH
☎ (01270) 762117
Course is one mile N of Sandbach on
the A533.
Meadowland course.
Founded 1921
9 holes, 5598 yards, S.S.S. 67
♦ Welcome WD; WE by invitation.
⌐ Terms on application.
⌐ Limited; by prior arrangement;
terms on application.
◉ Full facilities except Mon and
Tues.
⌐ Saxon Cross Motel; Old Hall.

6A 128 **Sandiway**
Chester Rd, Sandiway, Northwich,
Cheshire, CW8 2DJ
☎ (01606) 883247, Fax 888548, Pro
883180
On A556 14 miles E of Chester, 4
miles from Northwich.
Undulating parkland course.
Pro Bill Laird; Founded 1921
Designed by Ted Ray
18 holes, 6404 yards, S.S.S. 72
♦ Welcome WD except Thurs (ladies
day); WE by prior arrangement.
⌐ WD £35; WE £40.
⌐ Welcome Tues by prior
arrangement; packages available;
terms on application.
◉ Full clubhouse facilities.
⌐ Hartford Hall; Oaklands.

6A 129 **Sandwell Park**
Birmingham Rd, West Bromwich, W
Midlands, B71 4JJ
☎ (0121) 553 4637, Fax 525 1651,
Pro 553 4384, Bar/Rest 525 4151
On A41 Birmingham road, 200 yards
from M5 Junction 1.
Heathland course.
Pro Nigel Wylie; Founded 1897
Designed by H S Colt
18 holes, 6470 yards, S.S.S. 72
♦ Welcome WD.
⌐ WD £31.
⌐ Welcome WD by prior
arrangement; reductions for bigger
parties; catering facilities available;
from £26.
◉ Full restaurant facilities and two
bars.
⌐ West Bromwich Moat House.

6A 130 **Sedgley Golf Centre**
Sandyfields Rd, Sedgley, Dudley, W
Midlands, DY3 3DL
☎ (01902) 880503
Off A463 0.5 miles from Sedgley town
centre near Cotwell End Nature
reserve.
Parkland course on the side of a
valley with mature trees.
Pro Garry Mercer; Founded 1989
Designed by W.G. Cox
9 holes, 6294 yards, S.S.S. 70
♦ Pay and play course.
⌐ Terms on application.
⌐ Welcome by arrangement; snacks
available; terms on application.
◉ Snacks.
Practice range, 16 bays covered and
floodlit.

6A 131 **Seedy Mill**
Elm Hurst, Lichfield, Staffs, WS13
8HE
☎ (01543) 417333, Fax 418098
3 miles N of Lichfield off A51.
Parkland course with lakes, ponds
and streams.
Pro Simon Jackson; Founded 1991
Designed by Hawtree & Sons
18 holes, 6305 yards, S.S.S. 70
♦ Welcome.
⌐ WD £20; WE £25.
⌐ Welcome by prior arrangement;
limited WE access; packages
available for food and golf ranging
from £16; corporate days available;
also 9- hole Spires course, par 3;
from £24.
◉ Full clubhouse bar and restaurant.
Practice range, 26 bays floodlit.
⌐ Little Barrow, Lichfield.

6A 132 **Severn Meadows**
Highley, Nr Bridgnorth, Shropshire,
WV16 6HZ
☎ (01746) 862212
10 miles N of Bewdley; 8 miles S of
Bridgenorth.
Hilly parkland course in Severn
valley.
Pro Martin Payne; Founded 1989
9 holes, 5258 yards, S.S.S. 67
♦ Welcome WD; pay and play; must
book WE.
⌐ Terms on application.
⌐ Welcome by arrangement.
◉ Clubhouse facilities.
⌐ Bull, Chelmarsh.

6A 133 **Shifnal**
Decker Hill, Shifnal, Shropshire,
TF11 8QL

☎ (01952) 460467, Fax 460330, Pro 460457, Sec 460330
1 mile N of Shifnal close to M54 Junction 4.
Parkland course.
Pro J Flanagan; Founded 1929/1963
Designed by Frank Pennink
18 holes, 6468 yards, S.S.S. 71
† Welcome WD; members only WE.
Ⅰ WD £25.
⏶ Welcome Tues, Wed and Fri; reductions for groups of 20 or more; terms on application.
⦿ Full clubhouse bar and catering facilities except Mondays.
⌁ Park House.

6A 134 Shrewsbury
Condover, Shrewsbury, Shropshire, SY5 7BL
☎ (01743) 872976, Pro 873751, Sec 872977
S of Shrewsbury off A49.
Parkland course.
Pro Peter Seal; Founded 1890/1972
Designed by C.K. Cotton, Pennink, Lawrie & Partners
18 holes, 6205 yards, S.S.S. 70
† Welcome WD; after 2pm Wed; WE between 10am-12 noon and after 2pm.
Ⅰ WD £19; WE £23.
⏶ Welcome Mon and Fri; limited availability Tues, Thurs and Sun am; packages can be arranged through the professional; terms on application.
⦿ Full clubhouse facilities.
⌁ Shrewsbury Hotel.

6A 135 Shrigley Hall Hotel
Shrigley Park, Pott Shrigley, Macclesfield, Cheshire, SK10 5SB
☎ (01625) 575757
Off A523 Macclesfield road; follow Pott Shrigley from Adlington.
Parkland course.
Pro Tony Stevens; Founded 1989
Designed by Donald Steel
18 holes, 6281 yards, S.S.S. 71
† Welcome by arrangement.
Ⅰ WD £30, Fri £35; WE £35.
⏶ Welcome WD by prior arrangement; packages can be arranged; terms on application.
⦿ Full clubhouse and hotel facilities.
Practice range, 20-bay floodlit range.
⌁ 150-room Shrigley Hall Hotel on site.

6A 136 The Shropshire ☏
Muxton Grange, Muxton, Telford, Shropshire, TF2 8PQ

☎ (01952) 677800, Fax 677622, Pro 677866
From M54/A5 take B5060, turning right at Granville roundabout; course opposite equestrian centre.
Parkland course; 3 loops of 9 holes.
Pro Steve Marr; Founded 1992
Designed by Martin Hawtree
27 holes, 6637 yards, S.S.S. 72
† Welcome.
Ⅰ WD £16; WE £22.
⏶ Welcome everyday; minimum 8; catering and golf packages available; private room; from £20.
⦿ Restaurant and three bars.
Practice range, 30 bays covered floodlit.
⌁ White House, Muxton; Telford Moat House.

6A 137 South Staffordshire
Danescourt Rd, Tettenhall, Wolverhampton, WV6 9BQ
☎ (01902) 751065, Pro 754816
On A41 from Wolverhampton in Tettenhall; clubhouse and course behind cricket club.
Parkland course.
Pro Mark Sparrow; Founded 1892
Designed by Harry Vardon (original); H.S. Colt
18 holes, 6513 yards, S.S.S. 71
† Welcome except Tues am.
Ⅰ WD £34; WE £45.
⏶ Welcome except Tues am and WE.
⦿ Clubhouse catering and bar.
⌁ Mount; Connaught.

6A 138 Stafford Castle
Newport Rd, Stafford, Staffs, ST16 1BP
☎ (01785) 223821
On A518 1 mile from Stafford Castle.
Parkland course.
Founded 1907
9 holes, 6382 yards, S.S.S. 70
† Welcome by arrangement.
Ⅰ Terms on application.
⏶ Welcome Mon and Fri by arrangement; terms on application.
⦿ Clubhouse restaurant and bar facilities.
⌁ Tillington Hall.

6A 139 Stamford (Stalybridge)
Oakfield House, Huddersfield Rd, Stalybridge, Cheshire, SK15 3PY
☎ (01457) 834829
On B6175 NE of Stalybridge.
Parkland/moorland course.

Pro Brian Badger; Founded 1901
18 holes, 5701 yards, S.S.S. 68
† Welcome WD.
Ⅰ WD £20; WE £25.
⏶ Welcome by prior arrangement, minimum 12; packages include 27 holes of golf, lunch and dinner; from £30.
⦿ Clubhouse facilities.

6A 140 Stockport
Offerton Rd, Offerton, Stockport, SK2 5DB
☎ (0161) 427 2001, Fax 449 8293, Pro 427 2421, Sec 427 8369
Take A627 Torkington road from A6; course 1.5 miles on right.
Parkland course.
Pro Mike Peel; Founded 1906
18 holes, 6326 yards, S.S.S. 71
† Welcome by arrangement.
Ⅰ WD £35; WE £45.
⏶ Welcome Wed and Thurs; minimum 20 players; catering and golf packages available.
⦿ Full clubhouse bar and restaurant service.
⌁ Moorside, Disley; Britannia, Offerton; Alma Lodge, Stockport.

6A 141 Stone
The Filleybrooks, Stone, Staffs, ST15 0NB
☎ (01785) 813103, Sec 284875
1 miles NW of Stone on A34.
Parkland course.
Founded 1896
9 holes, 6299 yards, S.S.S. 70
† Welcome WD; WE only with a member.
Ⅰ WD on application.
⏶ Welcome by arrangement; catering packages available; terms on application.
⦿ Clubhouse catering facilities.
⌁ Stone House.

6A 142 Styal
Station Road, Styal, Cheshire, SK9 4JN
☎ (01625) 530063, Fax 530063
Off M56 Junction 5 at Manchester Airport; straight on at roundabout instead of turning to Airport; at end of Ringway road turn right into Styal Road; club 1 mile.
Parkland course.
Pro G Traynor; Founded 1995
Designed by T Holmes
18 holes, 6301 yards, S.S.S. 70
† Welcome.
Ⅰ WD £16; WE £20.

⌁ Welcome by prior arrangement; packages available; from £19.
◉ Clubhouse catering and bar.
Practice range, 24 bays; driving range
⌐ Stanneylands; Hilton at Manchester Airport.

6A 143 Sutton Hall
Sutton Hall, Aston Lane, Sutton Weaver, Cheshire, WA7 3ED
☎ (01928) 715530, Fax 759174, Pro 714872, Sec 790747
M56 Junction 12, following signs to Frodsham; turn left at swingbridge for course.
Parkland course.
Pro Ian Smith; Founded 1995
Designed by S Wundke
18 holes, 6547 yards, S.S.S. 71
† Welcome.
 WD £18; WE £22.
⌁ Welcome WD; some at WE; packages for groups and golf available for groups of more than 10; groups up to 100 can be catered for.
◉ Full catering and bar.
⌐ Forte Crest, Beechwood.

6A 144 Swindon
Bridgnorth Road, Swindon, Dudley, W Midlands, DY3 4PH
☎ (01902) 897031, Fax 326219, Pro 896191
On B4176 Dudley to Bridgnorth road; 3 miles off A449 at Himley.
Wooded parkland course with exceptional views.
Pro Phil Lester; Founded 1974
27 holes, 6091 yards, S.S.S. 69
† Welcome.
 WD £18; WE £27.
⌁ Welcome by arrangement with J Smith; terms on application.
◉ Clubhouse facilities.
Practice range, 27 bays; also 9-hole course, par 3.
⌐ Himley Country Club, Himley.

6A 145 Tamworth Municipal
Eagle Drive, Amington, Tamworth, Staffs, B77 4EG
☎ (01827) 709303
From M42 Junction 10 proceed towards Tamworth; course is signposted off the B5000 Polesworth road.
Municipal parkland course.
Pro to be appointed; Founded 1975
18 holes, 6525 yards, S.S.S. 72
† Welcome.
 WD £10; WE £10.

⌁ Welcome WD by appointment.
◉ Bar and daily catering.
⌐ Canada Lodge.

6A 146 Telford Moat House ♕
Great Hay Drive, Telford, Shropshire, TF7 4DT
☎ (01952) 429977, Fax 586602
Off A442 at Sutton Hill S of Telford.
Parkland course.
Pro Daniel Bateman; Founded 1975
Designed by John Harris
18 holes, 6761 yards, S.S.S. 72
† Welcome.
 WD £25; WE £30.
⌁ Welcome by prior arrangement.
◉ Hotel facilities.
⌐ Telford Moat House on site.

6A 147 Three Hammers Golf Complex
Old Stafford Rd, Coven, Staffordshire, WV10 7PP
☎ (01902) 790428, Pro 790940
From M54 Junction 2 travel N on A449 course 1 mile on right.
Parkland course.
Pro Shaun Ball and Ted Large
Designed by Henry Cotton
18 holes, 1438 yards, S.S.S. 54
† Welcome.
 WD £6; WE £7.
⌁ Welcome Mon-Sat.
◉ Bar, bistro, restaurant and private dining facilities.
Practice range, 23-bay floodlit range.

6A 148 Trentham ♕
14 Barlaston Old Rd, Trentham, Stoke-on-Trent, Staffs, ST4 8HB
☎ (01782) 642347, Fax 644024, Pro 657309, Sec 658109
Off A34 from Stoke to Stone, turn left at Trentham Gardens.
Parkland course.
Pro Sandy Wilson; Founded 1894
18 holes, 6619 yards, S.S.S. 72
† Welcome by prior arrangement.
 WD £30; WE £40.
⌁ Welcome Mon and Fri by prior arrangement; terms available on application.
◉ Clubhouse facilities.
Practice ground.
⌐ Trentham Hotel; Post House Hotel; Tollgate Leisure.

6A 149 Trentham Park
Trentham Park, Trentham, Stoke-on-Trent, ST4 8AE

☎ (01782) 642245, Fax 658800, Pro 642125, Sec 658800, Bar/Rest 644130
Course is on the A34 four miles south of Newcastle; one mile from the M6 Junction 15.
Parkland course.
Founded 1936
18 holes, 6425 yards, S.S.S. 71
† Welcome by prior arrangement.
 WD £22.50; WE £30.
⌁ Welcome Wed and Fri by prior arrangement; packages for golf and catering available; from £22.50.
◉ Clubhouse facilities.

6A 150 The Tytherington
Dorchester Way, Macclesfield, Cheshire, SK10 2JP
☎ (01625) 506000; Fax 506040
2 miles from Macclesfield on the A523 Stockport road.
Parkland course; home of WPGA European Tour.
Pro Gordon McCloud; Founded 1986
Designed by Dave Thomas and Patrick Dawson
18 holes, 6765 yards, S.S.S. 74
† Welcome with handicap certs.
 WD £28; WE £34.
⌁ Welcome WD by prior arrangement; full facilities for golf and catering packages; private rooms; snooker and pool; health club; tennis; terms on application.
◉ Restaurant, bars and full catering facilities.
⌐ Contact club for details.

6A 151 Upton-by-Chester
Upton Lane, Chester, Cheshire, CH2 1EE
☎ (01244) 381183, Pro 381333
Off A41 Chester-Liverpool road near Chester zoo.
Parkland course.
Pro Peter Gardener; Founded 1934
18 holes, 5850 yards, S.S.S. 68
† Welcome except on competition days.
 WD £25; WE £30.
⌁ Welcome Wed, Thurs and Fri by prior arrangement.
◉ Full clubhouse facilities.
⌐ Dene; Euromill; Mollington Banastre.

6A 152 Uttoxeter
Wood Lane, Uttoxeter, Staffs, ST14 8JR
☎ (01889) 564884, Fax 566552, Pro 564884, Sec 566552

Off B5017 Uttoxeter-Marchington road 0.5 miles along Wood Lane just past the race course.
Parkland course with views over Dove valley.
Pro Adam McCandless; Founded 1972
18 holes, 5475 yards, S.S.S. 68
♦ Welcome by arrangement.
⌴ WD £15; WE £25.
♂ Welcome by prior arrangement; packages available for groups of 10; more than 20 free place for organiser; from £15.
⦿ Catering and restaurant facilities.
↵ White Hart; Bank Hotel, both Uttoxeter.

6A 153 Vicars Cross
Tarvin Rd, Great Barrow, Chester, CH3 7HN
☎ (01244) 335174, Pro 335595
On A51 4 miles E of Chester.
Undulating parkland course.
Pro J Forsythe; Founded 1939
Designed by E. Parr
18 holes, 6243 yards, S.S.S. 70
♦ Welcome except on competition days.
⌴ WD £25; WE £25.
♂ Welcome Tues and Thurs April-October except June; full golf and catering packages; from £31.50.
⦿ Full clubhouse facilities.

6A 154 Wallasey
Bayswater Rd, Wallasey, Merseyside, L45 8LA
☎ (0151) 691 1024, Fax 638 8988, Pro 638 3888
Leave the M53 at Junction 1; follow the A554 towards New Brighton, course is 0.25 miles on left.
Links course.
Pro Mike Adams; Founded 1891
Designed by Tom Morris Snr
18 holes, 6607 yards, S.S.S. 73
♦ Welcome by arrangement.
⌴ WD £39; WE £42.
♂ Welcome by prior arrangement; packages for groups of 18 or more, catering available.
⦿ Clubhouse facilities.
↵ Grove House, Wallasey.

6A 155 Walsall
The Broadway, Walsall, WS1 3EY
☎ (01922) 613512
Off A34 1 mile S of Walsall.
Wooded parkland course.
Pro R Lambert; Founded 1907
Designed by Dr MacKenzie

18 holes, 6257 yards, S.S.S. 70
♦ Welcome WD; WE as members guest.
⌴ WD £33; WE £33.
♂ Welcome WD by prior arrangement; catering and golf packages available for minimum 16; from £30.
⦿ Clubhouse facilities.
↵ Boundary; County.

6A 156 Walton Hall
Warrington Rd, Higher Walton, Warrington, Cheshire, WA4 5LU
☎ (01925) 266775, Pro 263061
Course is one mile from the M56 Junction 11.
Scenic parkland course.
Pro John Jackson; Founded 1972
Designed by Dave Thomas
18 holes, 6647 yards, S.S.S. 73
♦ Welcome.
⌴ WD £9; WE £11.
♂ Welcome by prior arrangement with the Pro shop; terms on application.
⦿ Full catering facilities in season; limited in winter.
↵ Lord Daresbury.

6A 157 Warren
The Grange, Grove Rd, Wallasey, Cheshire, L45 0JA
☎ (0151) 639 8323; pro 639 5730
500 yards up Grove Rd by Grove Rd station.
Municipal links.
Pro Stephen Konrad; Founded 1911
9 holes, 5714 yards, S.S.S. 70
♦ Welcome WD; book at WE.
⌴ WD £3.20; WE £3.20.
♂ Welcome by prior arrangement.
↵ Grove House.

6A 158 Warrington
London Rd, Appleton, Warrington, Cheshire, WA4 5HR
☎ (01925) 261620, Fax 265933, Pro 265431, Sec 261775.
On A49 1 mile from M56 Junction 10.
Parkland course.
Pro Reay Mackay; Founded 1902
Designed by James Braid
18 holes, 6210 yards, S.S.S. 70
♦ Welcome by prior arrangement.
⌴ WD £27; WE £30.
♂ Welcome on Wed by prior arrangement; summer and winter packages for golf and catering
⦿ Full clubhouse facilities.
Practice ground.
↵ Birchdale Hotel, Stockton Heath.

6A 159 Wergs
Keepers Lane, Tettenhall, Wolverhampton, W Midlands, WV6 8UA
☎ (01902) 742225, Fax 744748
Off A41 2.5 miles from Wolverhampton.
Open parkland course.
Founded 1990
Designed by C.W. Moseley
18 holes, 6949 yards, S.S.S. 73
♦ Welcome.
⌴ WD £13.50; WE £17.
♂ Welcome WD; after 10am at WE; catering packages available; from £13.50.
⦿ Clubhouse catering facilities available.

6A 160 Werneth Low
Werneth Low Rd, Hyde, Cheshire, SK14 3AF
☎ (0161) 368 2503, Pro 367 9376
Course is two miles from Hyde town centre via Gee Cross and Joel Lane.
Hilltop course.
Pro Tony Bacchus; Founded 1912
Designed by Peter Campbell
11 holes, 6113 yards, S.S.S. 70
♦ Welcome except Sun.
⌴ WD £18; WE £24.
♂ WD by prior arrangement.
⦿ Full catering facilities available.
↵ The Village, Hyde.

6A 161 Westminster Park
Hough Green, Chester, Cheshire, CH4 8JQ
☎ (01244) 680231, Fax 680231
Course is two miles west of Chester city centre.
Parkland course.
Pro ; Founded 1980
9 holes, 1000 yards, S.S.S. 27
♦ Pay and play.
⌴ WD £2.50; WE £2.50.
♂ None.
⦿ Llimited soft drinks.

6A 162 Westwood (Leek)
Wallbridge, Newcastle Rd, Leek, Staffs, ST13 7AA
☎ (01538) 398385, Fax 382485, Pro 398897
On A53 1 mile S of Leek.
Heathland/parkland course.
Pro Neale Hyde; Founded 1923
18 holes, 6214 yards, S.S.S. 69
♦ Welcome by prior arrangement.
⌴ WD £18; WE £20.
♂ Welcome by prior arrangement; packages available including golf and

catering; games/snooker room; from £27.50.
☏ Full clubhouse facilities.
Practice area.
⌁ The Hatcheries; Bank End Farm; Abbey Inn.

6A 163 Whiston Hall
Whiston, Nr Cheadle, Staffs ST10 2HZ
☎(01538) 266260
On A52 midway between Stoke-on-Trent and Ashbourne; 3 miles from Alton Towers.
Parkland/heathland course.
Founded 1971
Designed by Thomas Cooper
18 holes, 5784 yards, S.S.S. 69
† Welcome.
⌇ WD £10; WE £10.
⌁Welcome by prior arrangement; packages available both WD and WE; from £33.95.
☏ Full clubhouse facilities.
⌁ Ashbourne Lodge; Alton Towers.

6A 164 Whittington Heath
Tamworth Rd, Lichfield, Staffs, WS14 9PW
☎(01543) 432317, Fax 432317, Pro 432261
On A51 Lichfield to Tamworth road.
Heathland course.
Pro A Sadler; Founded 1886
Designed by H S Colt
18 holes, 6490 yards, S.S.S. 71
† Welcome WD with handicap certs.
⌇ WD £27.
⌁Welcome Wed and Thurs by arrangement; packages for golf and catering; maximum 50.
☏ Full clubhouse facilities.
⌁ Little Barrow, Lichfield.

6A 165 Widnes
Highfield Rd, Widnes, Cheshire, WA8 7DT
☎(0151) 424 2995
Signposted from the town centre.
Parkland course.
Pro Jason O'Brien; Founded 1924
18 holes, 5729 yards, S.S.S. 68
† Welcome WD except Tues.
⌇ WD £22.
⌁Welcome Thurs by prior arrangement; from £30.
☏ Catering and bar facilities.
⌁ Hillcrest; Everglades.

6A 166 Wilmslow
Great Warford, Mobberley, Knutsford, Cheshire, WA16 7AY

☎(01565) 873620, Fax 872172, Sec 872148
From the A34 Wilmslow-Alderley Edge road take the B5085 signposted for Knutsford; Warford Lane is three miles.
Parkland course.
Pro John Nowicki; Founded 1889
Designed by Alexander Herd
18 holes, 6607 yards, S.S.S. 72
† Welcome by arrangement.
⌇ WD £40; WE £50.
⌁Welcome Tues and Thurs by prior arrangement; packages for golf and catering available; minimum 24; from £30.
☏ Full clubhouse facilities.

6A 167 Wirral Ladies
93 Bidston Rd, Oxton, Birkenhead, Merseyside, L43 6TS
☎(0151) 652 1255, Pro 652 2468
On A41 adjacent to M53 Junction 3.
Moorland course.
Pro Angus Law; Founded 1894
Designed by H. Hilton
18 holes, 5182 yards, S.S.S. 66
† Welcome.
⌇ WD £25.50; WE £25.50.
⌁Welcome by arrangement.
☏ Full facilities.
⌁ Bowler Hat.

6A 168 Withington
243 Palatine Rd, West Didsbury, Manchester, M20 2UE
☎(0161) 445 9544
S of Manchester on B5166.
Parkland course.
Pro Bob Ling; Founded 1892
18 holes, 6364 yards, S.S.S. 71
† Welcome by arrangement.
⌇ Terms on application.
⌁Welcome by prior arrangement; 27-hole packages available; from £42.
☏ Full clubhouse facilities.

6A 169 Wolstanton
Dimsdale Old Hall, Hassam Parade, Newcastle-under-Lyme, Staffs, ST5 9DR
☎(01782) 622413, Pro 622718, Bar/Rest 616995
0.5 miles off A34, 3 miles from Newcastle.
Parkland course.
Pro Simon Arnold; Founded 1904
18 holes, 5807 yards, S.S.S. 68
† Welcome WD; with member at WE.
⌇ WD £20.

⌁Welcome WD except Tues; catering packages can be arranged.
☏ Clubhouse facilities.
⌁ Friendly Hotel on A34 at Newcastle.

6A 170 Woodside
Knutsford Rd, Cranage, Holmes Chapel, Cheshire CW4 8HT
☎(01477) 532 388
Off M6 at Junction 18.
9 holes, 18 tees
† Pay and play.
⌇ £5.
⌁Limited facilities.
☏ Limited.

6A 171 Worfield
Roughton, Nr Bridgnorth, Shropshire, WV15 5HE
☎(01746) 716541, Fax 716302, Sec 716372
3 miles outside Bridgnorth on A454, Wolverhampton road.
Parkland course.
Pro Stephen Russell; Founded 1991
Designed by T. Williams/D Gough
18 holes, 6801 yards, S.S.S. 73
† Welcome WD; after 2pm at WE.
⌇ WD £20; WE £25.
⌁Welcome by arrangement; packages arranged through secretary/manager; terms on application.
☏ Full clubhouse facilities.
Practice area.
⌁ Old Vicarage, Bridgnortrh.

6A 172 Wrekin
Ercall Woods, Wellington, Telford, Shropshire, TF6 5BX
☎(01952) 244032, Pro 223101
Course is off the M54; take the B5061 to Golf Links Lane.
Parkland course.
Pro Keith Housden; Founded 1905
18 holes, 5570 yards, S.S.S. 67
† Welcome WD.
⌇ WD £20; WE £28.
⌁Welcome WD.
☏ Clubhouse facilities.

6B 1 Alfreton
Highfields, Wingfield Rd, Oakthorpe, Alfreton, Derbys, DE5 7DH
☎(01773) 832070, Pro 831901
On Matlock Road 1 mile W of Alfreton.
Parkland course.
Pro Julian Mellor; Founded 1892
11 holes 5393 yards, S.S.S. 66

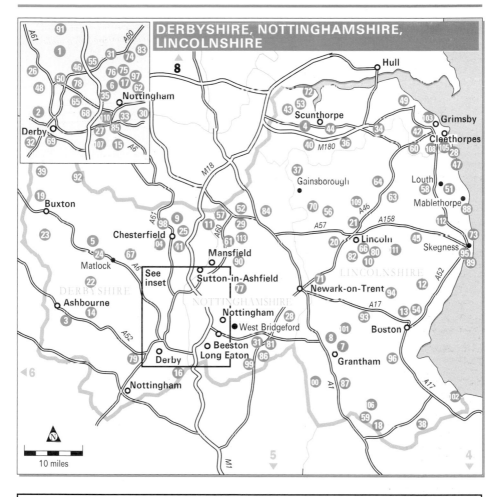

DERBYSHIRE, NOTTINGHAMSHIRE, LINCOLNSHIRE

KEY				
1 Alfreton	23 Cavendish	46 Horsley Lodge	68 Maywood	91 Shirland
2 Allestree Park	24 Chatsworth	47 Humberston Park	69 Mickleover	92 Sickleholme
3 Ashbourne	25 Chesterfield	48 Ilkeston Borough (Pewit)	70 Millfield	93 Sleaford
4 Ashby Decoy	26 Chevin	49 Immingham	71 Newark	94 South Kyme
5 Bakewell	27 Chilwell Manor	50 Kedleston Park	72 Normanby Hall	95 Southview
6 Beeston Fields	28 Cleethorpes	51 Kenwick Park	73 North Shore	96 Spalding
7 Belton Park	29 College Pines	52 Kilton Forest	74 Norwood Park	97 Springwater
8 Belton Woods Hotel	30 Cotgrave Place G & CC	53 Kingsway	75 Nottingham City	98 Stanedge
9 Birch Hall	31 Coxmoor	54 Kirton Holme	76 Notts	99 Stanton-on-the-Wolds
10 Blankney	32 Derby	55 Leen Valley	77 Oakmere Park	100 Stoke Rochford
11 Bondhay Golf & CC	33 Edwalton Municipal	56 Lincoln	78 Ormonde Fields CC	101 Sudbrook Moor
12 Boston	34 Elsham	57 Lindrick	79 Pottergate	102 Sutton Bridge
13 Boston West	35 Erewash Valley	58 Louth Golf Club	80 Pastures	103 Swingtime (Grimsby)
14 Brailsford	36 Forest Pines	59 Luffenham Heath	81 Radcliffe-on-Trent	104 Tapton Park Municipal
15 Bramcote Hills GC	37 Gainsborough	60 The Manor Golf Course	82 RAF Waddington	105 Tetney
16 Breedon Priory	38 Gedney Hill	61 Mansfield Woodhouse	83 Ramsdale Park GC	106 Toft Hotel
17 Bulwell Forest	39 Glossop & District	62 Mapperley	84 Retford	107 Trent Lock Golf Centre
18 Burghley Park	40 Grange Park	63 Market Rasen & District	85 Riverside	108 Waltham Windmill
19 Buxton & High Peak	41 Grassmoor Golf Centre	64 Market Rasen Race Course	86 Ruddington Grange	109 Welton Manor
20 Canwick Park	42 Grimsby	65 Marriott Breadsall Priory	87 Rutland County	110 Wollaton Park
21 Carholme	43 Hirst Priory	66 Martin Moor	88 Sandilands	111 Woodhall Spa
22 Carsington Water	44 Holme Hall	67 Matlock	89 Seacroft	112 Woodthorpe Hall
	45 Horncastle		90 Sherwood Forest	113 Worksop

† Welcome WD; with member at WE.
↕ WD £16; WE £8.
⌁Welcome by prior arrangement; max 36; terms on application.
◉ Clubhouse facilities.
↜ Swallow, South Normanton.

6B 2 **Allestree Park**
Allestree Hall, Allestree Park, Derby, Derbyshire, DE22 2EU
☎(01332) 550616, Fax 541195, Pro 550616, Sec 552971, Bar 552971
4 miles N of Derby; 1 mile N of A38/A6 junction.
Undulating parkland course.
Pro Steven Lamb; Founded 1947
18 holes, 5806 yards, S.S.S. 68
† Welcome.
↕ Terms on application.
⌁Welcome by prior arrangement; various 18, 27, 36-hole packages available; catering; golf clinics; terms on application.
◉ Clubhouse facilities.
↜ International Hotel, Derby.

6B 3 **Ashbourne**
The Clubhouse, Lichfield Rd, Clifton, Nr Ashbourne, Derbys, DE6 2GJ
☎(01335) 342078, Sec 343457, Fax 347937, Pro 347960
On A515 2 miles W of Ashbourne.
Parkland course.
Pro Andrew Smith; Founded 1886/1902
Designed by Frank Pennink
18 holes, 6403 yards, S.S.S. 72
† Welcome WD.
↕ WD £15; WE £25.
⌁Welcome WD; reductions for groups of more than 20; by arrangement with professional; prices on application.
◉ Clubhouse catering and bar.
↜ Green Man; Hanover International, both Ashbourne.

6B 4 **Ashby Decoy**
Burringham Rd, Scunthorpe, Lincs, DN17 2AB
☎(01724) 866561, Fax 271708, Pro 868972, Bar/Rest 842913,
🖥 home.btclick.com/ashby.decoy
⌁ ashby.decoy@btclick.com
From M181, turn right at first three roundabouts; course is 200 yards on right.
Parkland course.
Pro A Miller; Founded 1936
Designed by Members
18 holes, 6281 yards, S.S.S. 71

† Welcome WD except Tues; with a member WE.
↕ Summer WD £18; Winter WD £13.
⌁Welcome WD except Tues by prior arrangement; various packages on application; from £22-£37.
◉ Full clubhouse facilities.
↜ Royal; Wortley, both Scunthorpe.

6B 5 **Bakewell**
Station Rd, Bakewell, Derbys DE451GB
☎(01629) 812307
0.75 miles from Bakewell Square; cross River Wye on A619 Sheffield-Chesterfield Road; up Station Rd, turning right before Industrial estate.
Hilly parkland course.
Founded 1899
Designed by George Low
9 holes, 5240 yards, S.S.S. 66
† Welcome WD; Ladies priority Thurs; WE by prior arrangement.
↕ Prices on application.
⌁Welcome by arrangement.
◉ Meals and bar except Mon.
↜ Rutland Arms.

6B 6 **Beeston Fields**
Old Drive, Beeston Fields, Nottingham, NG9 3DD
☎(0115) 9257062, Fax 9254280, Pro 9220872
1 mile from Beeston, 5 miles W of Nottingham on south side of A52.
Parkland course.
Pro Alun Wardle; Founded 1923
Designed by Tom Williamson
18 holes, 6404 yards, S.S.S. 71
† Welcome WD (after 3pm Tues); some restrictions at WE.
↕ WD £26-£36; WE £31.
⌁Welcome Mon and Wed by prior arrangement; packages available for catering, contact steward; separate dining room; £26-£36.
◉ Clubhouse facilities.
↜ Priory Hotel.

6B 7 **Belton Park** ⏻
Belton Lane, Londonthorpe Rd, Grantham, Lincs, NG31 9SH
☎(01476) 567399, Fax 592078, Bar/Rest 563355, Pro 563911
From A607 Grantham-Sleaford Road; turn right to Londonthorpe; course 1 mile on left.
Parkland course.
Pro Brian McKee; Founded 1890
Designed by T Williamson/Dave Thomas and Peter Alliss
27 holes, 6420 yards, S.S.S. 71

† Welcome with handicap certs except Tues.
↕ WD £24-£30; WE £30-£36.
⌁Welcome WD except Tues; by prior arrangement; terms on application.
◉ Full clubhouse facilities.
Practice range, 2 practice areas.
↜ Angel & Royal/Kings/Swallow.

6B 8 **Belton Woods Hotel** ⏻ **& Country Club**
Belton, Nr Grantham, Lincolnshire, NG32 2LN
☎(01476) 593200, Pro 514332, Fax 574547
2 miles E of A1 via Gonerby Moor services; 2 miles N of Grantham on A607 Lincoln Road.
Parkland course with mature trees and ancient woodland.
Founded 1991
Lakes: 18 holes, 6781 yards, S.S.S. 73; Woodside: 18 holes, 6605 yards, S.S.S. 72
† Welcome; bookings taken 10 days in advance.
↕ WD £27; WE £30.
⌁Welcome WD by prior arrangement; packages available; company days organised; reductions for residents; banqueting facilities for 240; health and sports leisure centres; conference facilities; also Spitfire 9-hole course, 1184 yards, par 3.
◉ Full bar and restaurant facilities.
Practice range, 18 bays floodlit.
↜ Belton Woods on site.

6B 9 **Birch Hall**
Sheffield Rd, Unstone Green, Sheffield, S18 5DH
☎(01246) 291979, Bar/Rest 291087,
Off A61.
Moorland course.
Pro Pete Ball; Founded 1992
Designed by David Tucker
18 holes, 7090 yards, S.S.S. 74
† Welcome.
↕ WD £10; WE £10.
⌁Welcome WD and afternoons at WE; catering on application; from £10.
◉ Clubhouse facilities.
↜ Sandpiper.

6B 10 **Blankney**
Blankney, Lincoln, Lincs, LN4 3AZ
☎(01526) 320263, Fax 322521, Pro 320202

Course is on the B1188 10 miles south of Lincoln.
Parkland course.
Pro Graham Bradley; Founded 1903
Designed by Cameron Sinclair (updated Design)
18 holes, 6638 yards, S.S.S. 73
✝ Welcome by prior arrangement.
⌐ WD £20; WE £30.
↗Welcome by prior arrangement with general manager; from £20.
🍽 Clubhouse facilities available.
↙ Dower House; Golf Hotel, both Woodhall Spa.

6B 11 Bondhay Golf & Country Club
Bondhay Lane, Whitwell, Worksop, Notts, S80 3EH
☎(01909) 723608, Fax 720226, Sec 723608
Just off A619; 5 minutes from M1 Junction 30.
Parkland course.
Pro Tony Tomlinson; Founded 1001
Designed by Donald Steel
18 holes, 6720 yards, S.S.S. 74
✝ Welcome; advance booking.
⌐ Winter WD £12.50, WE £17.50; Summer WD £15; WE £20.
↗Welcome by prior arrangement; catering packages by arrangement; function rooms available; also family course; from £3.
🍽 Full bar and restaurant facilities available.
Practice range, 15-bay floodlit covered range.
↙ Vandykes, Whitwell; Beeches, Rotherham.

6B 12 Boston
Cowbridge, Horncastle Rd, Boston, Lincs, PE22 7EL
☎(01205) 350589, Fax 350589, Pro 362306, Bar/Rest 352533
Course is on the B1183 two miles N of Boston.
Parkland course with water on 8 holes.
Pro Torry Squires, Founded 1962
Designed by B.S. Cooper, Extended by Donald Steel
18 holes, 6490 yards, S.S.S. 71
✝ Welcome by arrangement.
⌐ WD £18; WE £24.
↗Welcome WD except Tues; packages available for 18-36 holes, lunch and dinner; from £27.50-£37.50.
🍽 Clubhouse facilities.
↙ New England; White Hart; Kings Arms, all Boston.

6B 13 Boston West
Hubbert's Bridge, Boston, Lincs, PE20 3QX
☎(01205) 290670, Fax 290725,
🖥 www.boston-westgc.co.uk
At junction of A1121/B1192 2 miles W of Boston.
Parkland course.
Pro Andrew Hare/Alison Johns; Founded 1995
Designed by Michael Zara
9 holes, 6388 yards, S.S.S. 70; will be 18 holes as of Sept 2000
✝ Welcome.
⌐ Terms on application.
↗Welcome at all times; golf and catering packages can be arranged; terms on application.
🍽 Full catering facilities.
↙ Boston Lodge.

6B 14 Brailsford
Pools Head Lane, Brailsford, Ashbourne, Derbys, DE6 3BU
☎(01335) 360096
Signposted off A52 just before Ashbourne.
Parkland course.
Pro David McCarthy; Founded 1994
9 holes, 6292 yards, S.S.S. 70
✝ Welcome.
⌐ WD £12; WE £15.
↗Welcome by prior arrangement; reductions for groups of 16 or more of 20%; terms on application.
🍽 Full catering facilities and bar.
Practice range, 15 bays floodlit; practice bunker and putting green; new clubhouse.

6B 15 Bramcote Hills Golf Course
Thoresby Rd, off Derby Rd, Bramcote, Nottingham, Notts, NG9 3EP
☎(0115) 9281880
Leave M1 Junction 25 take A52 towards Nottingham past Bramcote Leisure Centre; left after 0.25 miles.
Parkland course.
Founded 1981
18 holes, 1501 yards, par 3
✝ Welcome; pay and play.
⌐ WD £6; WE and BH £6.50;
Discounts for juniors, OAP's and students (£5 all week).
↗Welcome.
🍽 None.

6B 16 Breedon Priory
The Clubhouse, Green Lane, Wilson, Nr Derby, DE73 1LG

☎(01332) 863081, Sec 864046, Fax 863081
On A453 3.5 miles W of M1 Junction 23A.
Parkland course.
Pro Ben Hill; Founded 1991
Designed by D Snell
18 holes, 5530 yards, S.S.S. 67
✝ Welcome as members' guest.
⌐ Prices on application.
↗Welcome by prior arrangement; catering and golf packages available; terms on application.
🍽 Full clubhouse facilities.

6B 17 Bulwell Forest
Hucknall Rd, Bulwell, Nottingham, NG6 9LQ
☎(0115) 9770576, Pro 9763172
On A611 close to M1 Junction 26.
Heathland course.
Pro Lee Rawlings; Founded 1870/1902
18 holes, 5501 yards, S.S.S. 67
✝ Welcome; restrictions at WE.
⌐ WD £11; WE £11.
↗Welcome WD; after 11am Tues; 2pm Sat and 12 noon Sun; full day packages available; £25.
🍽 Clubhouse catering facilities.
↙ Moat House; Gateway, both Nottingham.

6B 18 Burghley Park
St Martins Without, Stamford, Lincs, PE9 3JX
☎(01780) 753789, Fax 753789, Pro 762100
On B1081 1 mile S of Stamford.
Parkland course.
Pro Glenn Davies; Founded 1890
Redesigned by Canon J.D. Day in 1936
18 holes, 6236 yards, S.S.S. 70
✝ Welcome WD with handicap certs.
⌐ Prices on application.
↗Welcome WD by prior arrangement; full golf and catering package including insurance; £38.
🍽 Clubhouse facilities.
↙ The George at Stamford; Garden House; Lady Annes; Crown; Royal Oak, Duddington.

6B 19 Buxton & High Peak
Waterswallows Rd, Fairfield, Buxton, Derbyshire, SK17 7EN
☎(01298) 23453, Fax 26333, Pro 23112, Sec 26263
On A6 Manchester -Derby Road just N of Buxton.
Parkland course.

Pro Gary Brown; Founded 1887
Designed by J Morris
18 holes, 5966 yards, S.S.S. 69
† Welcome by prior arrangement.
⌴ WD £25; WE £35.
⌁ Welcome by prior arrangement;
full golf and catering packages
available; £35.
🍽 Full clubhouse facilities.
⌐ Palace Hotel; Hawthorn Farm.

6B 20 Canwick Park
Washingborough Road, Lincoln,
Lincoln, LN4 1EF
☎ (01522) 522166, Fax 536870, Pro
536870, Sec 542912,
📧 www.swingfitgolf.co.uk
⌐ steve@stevejw.demon.co.uk
On B1190 Washingborough Road 2
miles W of Lincoln.
Parkland course.
Pro S J Williamson; Founded
1893/1975
Designed by Hawtree & Partners
18 holes, 6257 yards, S.S.S. 69
† Welcome WD; after 3pm at WE.
⌴ WD £16; WE £20; reduced green
fees at certain times; phone for
details.
⌁ Welcome by prior arrangement;
packages available for catering and
golf; from £18.
🍽 Clubhouse catering facilities.
⌐ Travel Inn; Branston Hall; Grand,
Lincoln.

6B 21 Carholme
Carholme Rd, Lincoln, Lincoln, LN1
1SE
☎ (01522) 523725, Fax 533733, Pro
536811, Sec 533733
On A57 Worksop Road 1 mile from
Lincoln city centre.
Parkland course.
Pro Richard Hunter; Founded 1906
18 holes, 6243 yards, S.S.S. 70
† Welcome by prior arrangement
except Sun.
⌴ WD £13; Sat £16.
⌁ Welcome by prior arrangement;
catering and golf packages available;
terms on application.
🍽 Bar and restaurant (except Mon).
⌐ Delph GH.

6B 22 Carsington Water
Carsington, Wirksworth, Derbys
☎ (01403) 784864
8 miles NE of Ashbourne off B5035.
Parkland course.
9 holes, 3000 yards, S.S.S. 33
† Welcome.

⌴ Pay and play; £9.
⌁ Terms on application.
🍽 Limited.

6B 23 Cavendish
Gadley Lane, Buxton, Derbys, SK17
6XD
☎ (01298) 23494, Fax 79708, Pro
25052, Sec 79708, Bar/Rest 23494
On outskirts of Buxton off the ring
road in direction of A53 Leek.
Moorland/parkland course.
Pro P Hunstone; Founded 1925
Designed by Dr Alister MacKenzie
18 holes, 5721 yards, S.S.S. 68
† Welcome.
⌴ WD/WE £26-£35.
⌁ Welcome by prior arrangement;
minimum 16; 27 holes £25; for
catering contact stewardess.
🍽 Full clubhouse facilities available.
Practice area.
⌐ Leewood; Buckingham; Palace;
Portland all Buxton.

6B 24 Chatsworth
Chatsworth Park, Bakewell,
Derbyshire, DE45 1PJ.
☎ (01246) 582204
On Chatsworth Estate.
Parkland course.
9 holes, 5248 yards, S.S.S. 66
† Private; for estate workers and
members only.
⌴ Terms on application.
🍽 No clubhouse.

6B 25 Chesterfield
Walton, Chesterfield, Derbys, S42
7LA
☎ (01246) 279256, Fax 276622, Pro
276297, Bar/Rest 232035
On A632 Matlock Road 1.5 miles S of
Chesterfield.
Parkland course.
Pro Mike McLean; Founded 1897
Designed by H. Colt
18 holes, 6261 yards, S.S.S. 70
† Welcome WD; with member at
WE.
⌴ WD £25.
⌁ Welcome WD by prior application;
packages available; from £25.
🍽 Full clubhouse facilities.
⌐ Chesterfield Hotel; Swallow, S
Normanton.

6B 26 Chevin
Golf Lane, Duffield, Derbys, DE56
4EE
☎ (01332) 841864, Pro 841112

On A6 5 miles N of Derby outside
Duffield.
Hilly parkland course.
Pro Willie Bird; Founded 1894
18 holes, 6057 yards, S.S.S. 69
† Welcome WD except before
9.30am and between 12.30pm and
2pm; WE with member.
⌴ WD £27.
⌁ Welcome WD by prior
arrangement with Sec.
🍽 Full facilities except Mon.
Small practice area.
⌐ Strutt Arms adjacent.

6B 27 Chilwell Manor
Meadow Lane, Chilwell, Nottingham,
Notts, NG9 5AE
☎ (0115) 9258958, Fax 9257050,
Pro 9258993
4 miles W of Nottingham on A6005
near Beeston.
Parkland course.
Pro Paul Wilson; Founded 1906
18 holes, 6395 yards, S.S.S. 70
† Welcome after 9am WD; after
11am WE.
⌴ WD £18; WE £20.
⌁ Welcome Mon, Wed, Fri.
🍽 Full clubhouse facilities available.
⌐ Post House; Novotel; Village.

6B 28 Cleethorpes
Kings Rd, Cleethorpes, N E Lincs,
DN35 0PN
☎ (01472) 812059, Pro 814060, Sec
816110
On A1301 1 mile S of Cleethorpes.
Meadowland course.
Pro Paul Davies; Founded 1894
Designed by Harry Vardon (now
vastly altered)
18 holes, 6349 yards, S.S.S. 70
† Welcome if member of recognised
club; Ladies only Wed afternoons.
⌴ WD £20; WE £25.
⌁ Welcome by prior arrangement.
🍽 Full facilities.
Practice area.
⌐ Kingsway; Wellow.

6B 29 College Pines
College Drive, Worksop, Notts S80
3AP
☎ (01909) 501431
Half mile S of Worksop on B6034;
just off A57 Worksop by-pass.
Heathland course.
Established 1993
18 holes, 6663 yards, S.S.S. 73
† Welcome by prior arrangement.
⌴ WD £12; WE £18.

⌂ Packages available.
🍴 Bar food.
Driving range.

6B 30 **Cotgrave Place** ♕
Golf & Country Club
Stragglethorpe, Nr Radcliffe on Trent,
Nottingham, NG12 3HB
☎ (0115) 9333344, Fax 9334567
Off A52 5 miles SE of Nottingham.
Parkland course with lake features;
3 x 9 loops.
Pro R Smith; Founded 1992
Designed by P Alliss/J Small
Two course: The Open; 18 holes,
6303 yards, S.S.S. 70; The Masters:
18 holes, 5887 yards, S.S.S. 68.
† Welcome.
Ⅼ WD £15; WE £24 before 10.30am,
£20 after.
⌂ Welcome by prior arrangement;
catering and golf packages available
by prior arrangement; banqueting
facilities available; prices on
application.
🍴 Full clubhouse facilities available.
⌐ Hilton; Moat House; Langar Hall.

6B 31 **Coxmoor**
Coxmoor Rd, Sutton-in-Ashfield,
Notts, NG17 5LF
☎ (01623) 557359, Fax 557359, Pro
559906, Bar/Rest 559878
Course is on the A611 1.5 miles
south of Mansfield.
Heathland course.
Pro D Ridley; Founded 1913
18 holes, 6571 yards, S.S.S. 72
† Welcome WD; with member at
WE.
Ⅼ WD £30-£42.
⌂ Welcome WD except Tues by
prior arrangement; golf and catering
available; from £30.
🍴 Clubhouse catering and bar
facilities.
⌐ Pine Lodge, Mansfield; Cotswold
Hotel, Nottingham; Swallow, Sutton.

6B 32 **Derby**
Wilmore Road, Sinfin, Derby, DE24
9HD
☎ (01332) 766323, Fax 769004, Pro
766462
2 miles from city centre off Wilmore
Road.
Parkland course.
Pro John Siddons; Founded 1923
18 holes, 6163 yards, S.S.S. 69
† Welcome by prior arrangement
Ⅼ Terms on application.
⌂ Welcome by prior arrangement;

packages available; terms on
application.
🍴 Full clubhouse facilities available.
⌐ International, Derby.

6B 33 **Edwalton Municipal**
Edwalton Village, Nottingham, Notts,
NG12 4AS
☎ (0115) 9234775
Off A606 from Nottingham at
Edwalton Hall.
Municipal parkland course; also 9-
hole course, par 3, 1563 yards.
Pro J Staples; Founded 1981
Designed by Frank Pennink
9 holes, 3336 yards, S.S.S. 36
† Welcome.
Ⅼ 9 holes £4.90; 18 holes £9.80;
WD before 5pm concessions for
juniors, unemployed, OAPs, students.
⌂ Welcome WD.
🍴 Lunches and meals available.

6B 34 **Elsham**
Barton Rd, Elsham, Brigg, Lincs,
DN20 0LS
☎ (01652) 680291, Fax 680432, Pro
680432, Bar/Rest 688382
3 miles N of Brigg on B1206 Road.
Parkland course.
Pro Stewart Brewer; Founded 1901
18 holes, 6406 yards, S.S.S. 71
† Welcome WD except Thurs; with
member at WE.
Ⅼ WD £24; WE £18.
⌂ Welcome WD except Thurs; full
packages of golf and catering
available; from £40.
🍴 Full clubhouse catering facilities
available.
⌐ Arties Mill, Castlethorpe; Red
Lion Hotel, Redbourne; Jolly Miller,
Wrawby.

6B 35 **Erewash Valley**
Golf Club Road, Stanton-by-Dale,
Ilkeston, Derbys, DE7 4QR
☎ (0115) 9323258, Fax 9322984,
Pro 9324667, Sec 9322984
Course is tree miles from the M1
Junction 25.
Parkland course; 4th hole (Quarry):
92 yards.
Pro Mike Ronan; Founded 1905
Designed by Hawtree
18 holes, 6557 yards, S.S.S. 71
† Welcome WD and pm at WE.
Ⅼ WD £22.50; WE £27.50.
⌂ Welcome Mon, Wed, Fri by prior
arrangement; catering packages
available; from £22.50.
🍴 Restaurant and bar facilities.

Practice ground; snooker; 9-hole, par
3 course.
⌐ Post House; Novotel.

6B 36 **Forest Pines**
Briggate Lodge Inn, Ermine Street, Nr
Brigg, Lincs, DN20 0AQ
☎ (01652) 650770, Pro 650756, Fax
650495
Take M180 Junction 4 and then A15
towards Scunthorpe; club at first
roundabout.
Forest course.
Pro David Edwards; Founded 1996
Designed by J Morgan
18 holes, 6882 yards, S.S.S. 73
† Welcome by prior arrangement.
Ⅼ WD £30-£35; WE £30-£35.
⌂ Welcome by prior arrangement; 27
holes (club has Forest course, 3291
yards; Pines course, 3591 yards;
Beeches course, 3102 yards), coffee,
lunch and evening meal available;
accommodation packages; golf
schools; from £45.
🍴 Restaurant and bar facilities.
Practice range, 17 bays floodlit
covered; adjoining leisure club with
extensive facilities; free use for hotel
guests; daily membership for visitors.
⌐ Briggate Lodge Inn, 86-bed hotel
on site.

6B 37 **Gainsborough**
The Belt Road, Thonock,
Gainsborough, Lincs, DN21 1PZ
☎ (01427) 613088, Fax 810172
Signposted off A631 Gainsborough-
Grimsby Road.
US-style course with lakes and many
bunkers.
Pro Stephen Cooper; Founded 1997
(Karsten Lakes), Founded 1894/1985
(Thonock Park)
Designed by N Coles (Karsten
Lakes); Designed by B Waites
(Thonock Park, 1985)
Karsten Lakes: 18 holes, 6900 yards,
S.S.S. 70; Thonock Park: 18 holes,
6266 yards, S.S.S. 70
† Welcome; with member at WE
(Thonock Park).
Ⅼ Karsten: £25-£30; Thonock: £18-
£25.
⌂ Welcome (welcome WD for
Thonock Park); packages for golf and
catering can be arranged; snooker
tables; menus available for societies
in restaurant; prices on application.
🍴 Full catering and bar service
including coffee shop and restaurant.
Practice range, 20 bays floodlit.
⌐ Hickman Hill, Gainsborough.

6B 38 **Gedney Hill**
West Drove, Gedney Hill, Nr
Spalding, Lincs, PE12 0NT
☎ (01406) 330922, Fax 330323
On B1166 6 miles from Crowland.
Links style course.
Pro David Hutton; Founded 1988
Designed by C. Britton
18 holes, 5285 yards, S.S.S. 66
♦ Welcome.
⌴ WD £6.25; WE £10.50.
⌁ Welcome by prior arrangement;
catering available; snooker; terms on
application.
🍽 Clubhouse catering.

6B 39 **Glossop & District**
Hurst Lane, off Sheffield Rd, Glossop,
Derbys, SK13 9PU
☎ (01457) 865247, Pro 853117
Off A57 1.5 miles outside Glossop;
turn at Royal Oak pub.
Moorland course.
Pro Daniel Marsh; Founded 1894
11 holes 5800 yards, S.S.S. 68
♦ Welcome; restrictions on Sat.
⌴ Terms on application.
⌁ Welcome by prior arrangement;
terms on application.
🍽 Clubhouse facilities.
⌁ Wind in the Willows, Glossop.

6B 40 **Grange Park**
Butterwick Rd, Messingham,
Scunthorpe, N Lincs, DN17 3PP
☎ (01724) 762945, Fax 762851
⌁ info@grangepark.uk.com
5 miles S of Scunthorpe between
Messingham and E Butterwick; 4
miles S of M180 Junction 3.
Parkland course.
Pro Mark Thornly; Founded 1991
Designed by Ray Price
13 holes 4141 yards, S.S.S. 48
♦ Welcome.
⌴ WD £5.50; WE £7.50.
⌁ Welcome by prior arrangement;
from £5.50.
🍽 By prior arrangement.
Practice range, floodlit; also par 3, 9-
hole course (£3).

6B 41 **Grassmoor Golf Centre**
North Wingfield Rd, Grassmoor,
Chesterfield, Derbys, S42 5EA
☎ (01246) 856044, Fax 853933
2 miles S of Chesterfield close to M1
Junction 29.
Moorland course.
Pro Gary Hagues; Founded 1992
Designed by Michael Shattock
18 holes, 5723 yards, S.S.S. 69
♦ Welcome WE; by prior
arrangement.
⌴ WD £10; WE £12.
⌁ Welcome.
🍽 Full facilities.
Practice range, 25 bays floodlit.
⌁ Chesterfield.

6B 42 **Grimsby**
Littlecoates Rd, Grimsby, NE Lincs,
N34 4LU
☎ (01472) 342823, Fax 342630, Pro
356981, Sec 342630
1 mile W of Grimsby town centre; turn
left off A18 at first roundabout; course
is 0.75 miles on left.
Undulating parkland course.
Pro Richard Smith; Founded 1922
18 holes, 6057 yards, S.S.S. 70
♦ Welcome if member of a golf club;
Ladies Day Tues.
⌴ WD £22-£28; WE £28.
⌁ Welcome Mon and Fri by prior
arrangement.
🍽 Full facilities.
Practice ground.
⌁ Post House.

6B 43 **Hirst Priory**
Hirst Priory Park, Crowle, N E Lincs,
DN17 4BU
☎ (01724) 711621, Pro 711619
Off A1161 Crowle to Goole Road
from M180 Junction 2.
Parkland course.
Founded 1994
18 holes, 6283 yards, S.S.S. 71
♦ Welcome.
⌴ Summer WD £13.75, WE £17.50;
Winter WD/WE £10.
⌁ Welcome WD except Mon and
after 11am at WE.
🍽 Full facilities except Mon.
⌁ Red Lion, Epworth.

6B 44 **Holme Hall**
Holme Lane, Bottesford, Scunthorpe,
DN16 3RF
☎ (01724) 851816, Fax 862078, Sec
862078, Rest 282053, Bar 849185
Close to M180 Junction 4 for
Scunthorpe East.
Heathland course.
Pro R McKiernan; Founded 1908
18 holes, 6404 yards, S.S.S. 71
♦ Welcome WD; only with member
at WE.
⌴ WD £20.
⌁ Welcome WD by arrangement; on
application; from £20.
🍽 Clubhouse facilities.
⌁ Club can provide list.

6B 45 **Horncastle**
West Ashby, Horncastle, Lincs, LN9
5PP
☎ (01507) 526800
Off A158 W of Horncastle.
Parkland course with water hazards.
Pro E C Wright; Founded 1990
Designed by Ernie Wright
18 holes, 5717 yards, S.S.S. 70
♦ Welcome.
⌴ WD £15-£20; WE £15-£20.
⌁ Welcome; packages for golf and
catering available; from £10.
🍽 Clubhouse facilities.
Practice range, 24 bays floodlit.
⌁ Admiral Rodney.

6B 46 **Horsley Lodge**
Horsley Lodge, Smalley Mill Road,
Horsley, Derbys, DE21 5BL
☎ (01332) 780838, Fax 781118, Pro
781400,
🖥 www.horsleylodge.co.uk
⌁ enquiries@horsleylodge.co.uk
Course is off the A38 four miles N of
Derby.
Meadowland course.
Pro Graham Myall; Founded 1990
Designed by Peter McEvoy
18 holes, 6400 yards, S.S.S. 71
♦ Welcome WD, after 2pm WE.
⌴ WD £26; WE £26; half-price for
members, guests, hotel guests and
holders of Derbyshire union card.
⌁ Welcome Tues, Thurs or Fri by
prior arrangement; packages
available; conference facilities; from
£22.
🍽 Clubhouse and à la carte
restaurant available; bars in 1840
clubhouse.
⌁ Horsley Lodge on site.

6B 47 **Humberston Park**
Humberston Ave, Humberston, NE
Lincs, DN36 4SJ
☎ (01472) 210404
⌁ chriscrookes@lineone.net
Off Humberstone Ave behind the
Cherry Garth Scouts Field.
Parkland course; leased by
consortium of 8 members; non profit
making; money put back into course
and facilities; undergoing continuous
redevelopment.
Founded 1970
9 holes, 3672 yards, S.S.S. 58
♦ Welcome.
⌴ WD 18 holes £8, 9 holes £6; WE
18 holes £10, 9 holes £7; discounts
for guests.
⌁ Welcome by arrangement.
🍽 Bar facilities and snacks.

Lincoln Golf Club

TORKSEY · LINCOLN · LN1 2EG

- 6438 yards, SSS 71
- Venue for Lincolnshire Amateur Championship and Lincolnshire County Championships
- Putting green
- Large practice area
- 3-hole pitch and putt
- Golf shop

Founded in 1891, Lincoln is a mature, testing, championship standard course built on sandy subsoil offering a variety of holes from links-style to parkland with mature trees and some water features. We offer golfing packages in summer and winter, including a wide range of excellent snacks and meals.

Manager: Derek B Linton Tel/fax: 01427 718721.
Pro: Ashley Carter Tel/fax: 01427 718273. E-mail: lincolngolfclub@btinternet.com

6B 48 Ilkeston Borough (Pewit)
West End Drive, Ilkeston, Derbyshire, DE7 5GH
☎(0115) 9307704
0.5 miles E of Ilkeston.
Municipal meadowland course.
Founded 1920
9 holes, 4116 yards, S.S.S. 60
♣ Welcome.
⌷ WD 18 holes £6.50, WE £6.50; 9 holes WD £3.75, WE £3.75.
⌁Welcome WD only by prior arrangement.

6B 49 Immingham
Church Lane, Immingham, Grimsby, Lincs, DN40 2EU
☎(01469) 575298, Fax 577636, Pro 575493
2 miles off M180 behind St Andrew's Church.
Flat parkland course.
Pro Nick Harding; Founded 1975
Designed by Hawtree & Son (front 9), F. Pennink (back 9)
18 holes, 6215 yards, S.S.S. 70
♣ Welcome.
⌷ WD £15; WE £22.
⌁Welcome; packages available; special winter packages from £15.99: coffee, round of golf & meal: book in advance/ring for details; company days Welcome; new clubhouse.
🍽 New clubhouse.
Practice area.
☜ Stallingborough Grange.

6B 50 Kedleston Park
Kedleston, Quarndon, Derby, DE22 5JD
☎(01332) 840035, Fax 840035, Pro 841685, Bar/Rest 840634
4 miles N of Derby; from A38 follow signs to Kedleston Hall.
Parkland course.
Pro David J Russell; Founded 1947

Designed by James Braid and Morrison & Co
18 holes, 6675 yards, S.S.S. 72
♣ Welcome by arrangement.
⌷ WD £30; WE £30.
⌁Welcome Mon and Fri; catering packages can be arranged; from £30.
🍽 Full catering facilities.
☜ Kedleston House; Midland Hotel; Mundy Arms.

6B 51 Kenwick Park
Kenwick, Nr Louth, Lincs, LN11 8NY
☎(01507) 605134, Fax 606556, Pro 607161, Bar/Rest 608210
1 mile S of Louth.
Rolling parkland course.
Pro Eric Sharp/Andrew Hoyles;
Founded 1992
Designed by Patrick Tallack
18 holes, 6815 yards, S.S.S. 73
♣ Welcome.
⌷ WD £25; WE £35.
⌁Welcome by prior arrangement; catering and golf packages can be arranged; terms on application.
🍽 Clubhouse facilities.
Practice range, driving range.
☜ Kenwick Park Hotel on site.

6B 52 Kilton Forest
Blyth Rd, Worksop, Notts, S81 0TL
☎(01909) 486563, Sec 479199, Bar 6 (01909)
Course is one mile from Worksop on the Blyth Road.
Parkland course.
Pro Stuart Betteridge; Founded 1977
18 holes, 6424 yards, S.S.S. 71
♣ Welcome; bookings required at WE.
⌷ WD £8.40; WE £11.
⌁Welcome by prior arrangement; catering packages available; terms on application.
🍽 Restaurant and bar facilities.
☜ Regency; Lion, both Worksop.

6B 53 Kingsway
Kingsway, Scunthorpe, N Lincs, DN15 7ER
☎(01724) 840945
Between Berkeley and Queensway roundabouts S of A18.
Undulating parkland course.
Pro Chris Mann; Founded 1971
Designed by R.D. Highfield
9 holes, 1915 yards, S.S.S. 59
♣ Welcome.
⌷ WD £3.60; WE £4.25.
⌁None.

6B 54 Kirton Holme
Holme Rd, Nr Boston, Lincs, PE20 1SY
☎(01205) 290669
Off A52 4 miles W of Boston.
Parkland course.
Pro Alison Johns; Founded 1992
Designed by D.W. Welberry
9 holes, 5778 yards, S.S.S. 68
♣ Pay and play.
⌷ WD £5; WE £5.
⌁Welcome by prior arrangement; maximum 30; meals available; terms on application.
🍽 Full clubhouse facilities.
☜ Poacher Inn.

6B 55 Leen Valley
Wigwam Lane, Hucknall, Notts, NG15 7JA
☎(0115) 9642037, Fax 9642724, Bar/Rest 9680968
On B6011 off A611 from Hucknall.
Parkland course; was Hucknall GC.
Pro John Lines; Founded 1994
Designed by Tom Hodgetts
18 holes, 6233 yards, S.S.S. 72
♣ Welcome.
⌷ WD £9.50; WE £13.50.
⌁Welcome; packages can be arranged; terms on application.
🍽 Full clubhouse facilities.
☜ Premier Lodge, Hucknall.

6B 56 **Lincoln**
Torksey, Lincoln, Lincs, LN1 2EG
☎ (01427) 718721, Fax 718721, Pro 718273, Bar/Rest 718210, Sec 718271
📧 lincolngolfclub@btinternet.com
Course is on the A156 seven miles S of Gainsborough, 10 miles W of Lincoln.
Inland links course.
Pro A Carter; Founded 1891
18 holes, 6438 yards, S.S.S. 71
† Welcome.
⌐ WD £26; WE £26.
⌐ʒWelcome WD by prior arrangement; catering packages available.
†◉† Full clubhouse facilities.
Large practice area, including 3-hole pitch and putt.
⌐ʒ Hume Arms.

6B 57 **Lindrick**
Lindrick Common, Worksop, Notts, S81 8BH
☎ (01909) 485802, Fax 488685, Pro 475820, Sec 475282
On A57 4 miles NW of Worksop.
Heathland course; 1957 Ryder Cup; 1960 Curtis Cup.
Pro John R King; Founded 1891
Designed by Tom Dunn, Willie Park and H. Fowler
18 holes, 6606 yards, S.S.S. 72
† Welcome WD except Tues.
⌐ WD £48; WE £48.
⌐ʒWelcome by prior arrangement; packages available; from £48.
†◉† Full clubhouse facilities.
Practice range, 2 practice areas.
⌐ʒ Red Lion, Todwick.

6B 58 **Louth Golf Club**
Crowtree Lane, Louth, Lincs, LN11 9LJ
☎ (01507) 602554, Fax 603681, Pro 604648, Sec 603681, Bar/Rest 611087
W of Louth close to Hubbards Hills.
Undulating parkland course.
Pro A J Blundell; Founded 1965
Designed by C K Cotton
18 holes, 6424 yards, S.S.S. 71
† Welcome by arrangement.
⌐ WD £16; WE £25.
⌐ʒWelcome by prior arrangement; discounts for groups of more than 25; catering packages available; from £16.
†◉† All day catering and bar facilities.
Practice ground.
⌐ʒ Masons Arms; Beaumont; Priory; Kings Head.

6B 59 **Luffenham Heath**
Ketton, Stamford, Lincs, PE9 3UU
☎ (01780) 720205, Fax 720298, Pro 720298, Sec 720205, Bar/Rest 721095
On A6121 5 miles W of Stamford.
Heathland course.
Pro Ian Burnett; Founded 1911
Designed by James Braid
18 holes, 6273 yards, S.S.S. 70
† Welcome by arrangement.
⌐ WD £35; WE £40.
⌐ʒWelcome by prior arrangement with Sec; packages and catering available on application; terms on application.
†◉† Full clubhouse facilities.
⌐ʒ The George at Stamford; Monkton Arms, Glaston.

6B 60 **The Manor Golf Course** ☏
Laceby Manor, Laceby, Grimsby, Lincolnshire, DN37 7EA
☎ (01472) 873468, Fax 276706, Sec 873469, Bar 873470
On A16 0.5 miles past Oaklands Hotel.
Parkland course.
Pro Paul Rushworth; Founded 1992
Designed by Sir Charles Nicholson and Rushton
18 holes, 6343 yards, S.S.S. 70
† Welcome by arrangement.
⌐ Winter WD £10, WE £10; Summer WD £15, WE £15.
⌐ʒWelcome by prior arrangement; terms on application.
†◉† Full clubhouse facilities.
⌐ʒ Oaklands.

6B 61 **Mansfield Woodhouse**
Leeming Lane North, Mansfield Woodhouse, Notts, NG19 9EU
☎ (01623) 623521
On A60 Mansfield-Worksop road 2 miles N of Mansfield.
Public parkland course.
Pro L Highfield; Founded 1973
9 holes, 4892 yards, S.S.S. 65
† Welcome except before 11am Sat.
⌐ WD £3.20; WE £4.90.
⌐ʒNone.
†◉† Clubhouse bar facilities.

6B 62 **Mapperley**
Central Ave, Plains Rd, Mapperley, Nottingham, NG3 5RH
☎ (0115) 9556672, Pro 9556673, Fax 9556673
Off B684 3 miles NE of Nottingham.
Undulating parkland course.

Pro Malcolm Allen; Founded 1903
18 holes, 6303 yards, S.S.S. 70
† Welcome by prior arrangement.
⌐ WD £15; WE £20.
⌐ʒWelcome by arrangement with secretary; packages available; terms on application.
†◉† Full clubhouse facilities.
⌐ʒ Many in Nottingham.

6B 63 **Market Rasen & District**
Legsby Rd, Market Rasen, Lincs, LN8 3DZ
☎ (01673) 842319, Pro 842416, Bar/Rest 842319
On A361 1 mile E of Market Rasen.
Heathland course.
Pro A M Chester; Founded 1922
18 holes, 6045 yards, S.S.S. 69
† Welcome with handicap certs; with member at WE.
⌐ WD £18-£25.
⌐ʒWelcome Tues and Fri; packages for catering available; from £18.
†◉† Full clubhouse facilities.
⌐ʒ Limes Hotel.

6B 64 **Market Rasen Race Course**
Market Rasen Race Course, Legsby, Market Rasen, Lincs, LN8 3EA
☎ (01673) 843434, Fax 844532
At Market Rasen racecourse; follow signs to golf course from entrance.
In centre of racecourse; sandy.
Founded 1989
Designed by Racecourse/Peter Alliss
9 holes, 2377 yards, S.S.S. 45
† Welcome.
⌐ Terms on application.
⌐ʒWelcome with advance booking.

6B 65 **Marriott Breadsall Priory Golf & CC** ☏
Moor Rd, Morley, Derbys, DE7 6DL
☎ (01332) 832235, Fax 833509, Pro 834425
3 miles NE of Derby off A61 towards Breadsall.
Parkland course.
Pro Darren Steeles/Michael Timpson; Founded 1977
Moorland: 18 holes, 6028 yards, S.S.S. 68; Priory: 18 holes, 6120 yards, S.S.S. 68
† Welcome by prior arrangement.
⌐ Terms on application.
⌐ʒWelcome by prior arrangement; packages available; tennis, swimming pool, gym and leisure facilities; terms on application.

🍽 Full hotel and clubhouse facilities; 5 bars and 2 restaurants.
🛏 On site Marriott Breadsall Priory.

6B 66 **Martin Moor**
Blankney Rd, Martin Moor, Metheringham, Lincs, LN4 3BE
☎ (01526) 378243, Fax 378243
On B1189 2 miles E of Metheringham.
Parkland course.
Pro A Hare; Founded 1992
Designed by S Harrison
9 holes, 6325 yards, S.S.S. 70
♦ Welcome.
⌐ WD £5.50-£7.50; WE £6.50-£9.
♪ Welcome by prior arrangement; packages available; terms on application.
🍽 Clubhouse facilities
🛏 Eagle Lodge; golf Hotel; Petwood Hotel, all Woodhall Spa.

6B 67 **Matlock**
Chesterfield Rd, Matlock, Derbys, DE4 5LZ
☎ (01629) 582191, Pro 584934
On Chesterfield Road 1 mile from Matlock.
Moorland course.
Pro Mark Whithorn; Founded 1907
18 holes, 5996 yards, S.S.S. 69
♦ Welcome WD by prior arrangement.
⌐ WD £25, WE £12.50.
♪ Welcome by prior arrangement; parties of more than 12; catering available; £25.
🍽 Clubhouse facilities.
🛏 New Bath, Matlock Bath; Red House, Darley Dale; East Lodge, Rowsley.

6B 68 **Maywood**
Rushy Lane, Risley, Draycott, Derbys, DE72 3ST
☎ (0115) 9392306, Pro 9490043
Course is off the A52 to Risley from the M1 Junction 25 by the Post House Hotel.
Wooded course with water features.
Pro Simon Sherrat; Founded 1990
18 holes, 6424 yards, S.S.S. 72
♦ Welcome.
⌐ WD £15; WE £20.
♪ Welcome by prior arrangement; full day's golf and coffee, light lunch and 4-course evening meal; from £30.
🍽 Full bar and catering facilities available.
🛏 Post House; Novotel; Risley Park.

6B 69 **Mickleover**
Uttoxeter Rd, Mickleover, Derbyshire, DE3 5AD
☎ (01332) 513339, Fax 512092, Pro 518662, Sec 512092
Course is on the A516/B5020 three miles W of Derby.
Undulating parkland course.
Pro Tim Coxon; Founded 1923
18 holes, 5708 yards, S.S.S. 68
♦ Welcome.
⌐ WD £22; WE £25.
♪ Welcome Tues and Thurs; packages can be arranged; from £22.
🍽 Clubhouse facilities
🛏 Mickleover Court; International, Derby.

6B 70 **Millfield**
Laughterton, Torksey, Nr Lincoln, Lincs, LN1 2LB
☎ (01427) 718473, Fax 718473, Sec 0966 236314
On A113 between A57 and A158 8 miles from Lincoln; 10 miles from Gainsborough.
Inland links course.
Pro Richard Hunter; Founded 1984
18 holes, 6001 yards, S.S.S. 71
♦ Welcome.
⌐ WD £7; WE £7.
♪ Welcome WD by prior arrangement; tennis, bowls; second 18-hole course(4500 yards, par 65) and a 9-hole course (1500 yards, par 3); terms on application.
🍽 Light refreshments; bar meals available.
🛏 Holiday chalets and log cabins on site.

6B 71 **Newark**
Kelwick, Coddington, Newark, Notts, NG24 2QX
☎ (01636) 626241, Fax 626497, Pro 626492, Sec 626282
On A17 between Newark and Sleaford just past Coddington roundabout
Parkland course.
Pro Peter Lockley; Founded 1901
18 holes, 6457 yards, S.S.S. 71
♦ Welcome with handicap certs; Ladies Day Tues.
⌐ WD £22; WE £27.
♪ Welcome WD by prior arrangement; catering packages; snooker; indoor coaching facilities; terms on application.
🍽 Bar and meals.
♪ Practice ground.
🛏 Robin Hood; George Inn, Leadenham; Travelodge.

6B 72 **Normanby Hall**
Normanby Park, Normanby, Scunthorpe, N Lincs, DN15 9HU
☎ (01724) 720226, Bar/Rest 720252
5 miles N of Scunthorpe adjacent to Normanby Hall.
Municipal parkland course.
Pro Chris Mann; Founded 1978
Designed by H.F. Jiggens, Hawtree & Sons
18 holes, 6548 yards, S.S.S. 71
♦ Welcome; telephone for bookings.
⌐ WD £11.85; WE £13.50.
♪ Welcome by prior arrangement with the local council.
🍽 Full facilities including banqueting at Normanby Hall.
Practice range, practice area.
🛏 Royal; Wortley House.

6B 73 **North Shore** ℭ
North Shore Rd, Skegness, Lincs, PE25 1DN
☎ (01754) 763298, Fax 761902
🖳 golf@north-shore.co.uk
Just off A16 main Lincoln Road.
Parkland/links course.
Pro John Cornelius; Founded 1910
Designed by James Braid
18 holes, 6257 yards, S.S.S. 71
♦ Welcome.
⌐ WD £19; WE £29.
♪ Welcome by prior arrangement; minimum 12; packages and hotel rates available; from £29.
🍽 Full clubhouse catering and bar facilities.
🛏 On site North Shore.

6B 74 **Norwood Park** ℭ
Norwood Park, Southwell, Notts, NG25 0DW
☎ (01636) 816 626
Half a mile west of Southwell on the road to Kirklington.
Parkland course, set in the grounds of a stately home.
Founded 1999
Designed by Clyde B Johnston
9 holes, 6666 yards, S.S.S. 71
♦ Welcome at any time
⌐ 9 holes: WD £7.50, WE £9; 18 holes: WD £14, WE £16.
♪ Welcome by prior arrangement
🍽 By arrangement
🛏 The Saracen's Head

6B 75 **Nottingham City**
Lawton Drive, Bulwell, Nottingham, NG6 8BL
☎ (0115) 9276916, Fax 9276916, Pro 9272767, Bar 9278021

2 miles from M1 Junction 26 follow signs to Bulwell.
Municipal parkland course; private club; links with Bulwell Forest gc-arrangements can be made to play both courses on same day and use either or both clubhouses.
Pro Cyril Jepson; Founded 1910
Designed by H Braid
18 holes, 6218 yards, S.S.S. 70
♦ Welcome.
⏣ WD £11; WE £11.
⌒Welcome by prior arrangement; 18 and 36-hole packages with catering available; terms on application.
🍽 Clubhouse facilities.
⌐ The Gateway; Station Hotel, Hucknall; Trusthouse Forte; Moathouse.

6B 76 Notts
Hollinwell, Derby Rd, Kirkby-in-Ashfield, Notts, NG17 7QR
☎ (01623) 753225, Fax 753655, Pro 753087, Bar/Rest 755640
Course is three miles from the M1 Junction 27 off the A611.
Heathland course with gorse/heather; lake at Hollinwell.
Pro Alasdair Thomas; Founded 1887/1900
Designed by Willie Park Jnr
18 holes, 7030 yards, S.S.S. 74
♦ Welcome by prior arrangement; guests of members only at WE and BH.
⏣ WD £45-£65.
⌒Welcome WD except Fri morning by prior arrangement.
🍽 Clubhouse facilities.
⌐ Pine Lodge, Mansfield; Swallow, S Normanton.

6B 77 Oakmere Park ℧
Oaks Lane, Oxton, Notts, NG25 0RH
☎ (0115) 9653545, Fax 9655628
▥ www.ukgolf.net/oakmerepark
⌐ oakmere@ukgolf.net
Course lies between Blidworth and Oxton.
Parkland course; also Commanders course: 9 holes, 6573 yards, par 72.
Pro Daryl St John Jones; Founded 1977
Designed by Frank Pennink
18 holes, 6612 yards, S.S.S. 72
♦ Welcome.
⏣ WD £18; WE £24.
⌒Welcome; restrictions at WE; packages available; terms on application.
🍽 Full clubhouse facilities.
⌐ Moat House, Nottingham.

6B 78 Ormonde Fields Country Club
Nottingham Rd, Codnor, Ripley, Derbys, DE5 9RG
☎ (01773) 742987
On A610 towards Ripley 2 miles from M1 Junction 26.
Undulating course.
Pro Peter Buttifant; Founded 1906
18 holes, 6011 yards, S.S.S. 69
♦ Welcome WD; by prior arrangement WE.
⏣ WD £17.50; WE £22.50.
⌒Welcome by arrangement.
🍽 Full facilities.

6B 79 Pastures
Pastures, Mickleover, Derby, Derbys, DE3 5DQ
☎ (01332) 521074
Course is on the A516 four miles W of Derby.
Undulating meadowland course.
Founded 1969
Designed by Frank Pennink
9 holes, 5095 yards, S.S.S. 64
♦ Welcome with handicap certs.
⏣ Prices on application.
⌒Welcome by prior arrangement; packages include lunch and evening meal; from £22.
🍽 Limited catering.

6B 80 Pottergate
Moor Lane, Branston, Nr Lincoln, Lincs
☎ (01522) 794867
On B1188 in Branston.
Parkland course.
Founded 1992
Designed by W Bailey
9 holes, 5096 yards, S.S.S. 66
♦ Welcome.
⏣ Prices on application.
⌒Welcome.
🍽 Bar and snacks available.

6B 81 Radcliffe-on-Trent
Dewberry Lane, Cropwell Rd, Radcliffe on Trent, Notts, NG12 2JH
☎ (0115) 9333000, Fax 9116991, Pro 9332396, Bar/Rest 9116990
From A52 follow signs to Cropwell Butler.
Wooded parkland course.
Pro Robert Ellis; Founded 1909
Designed by Tom Wilkinson
18 holes, 6381 yards, S.S.S. 71
♦ Welcome by arrangement.
⏣ WD £23; WE £28.
⌒Welcome Wed only; packages available; from £23.

🍽 Full clubhouse catering and bar facilities.
⌐ Westminster Hotel.

6B 82 RAF Waddington
Waddington, Lincoln, Lincs, LN5 9NB
☎ (01522) 720271
Off A15 at Bracebridge Heath 3 miles S of Lincoln.
On RAF airfield.
Founded 1972
9 holes, 5558 yards, S.S.S. 69
♦ Must be accompanied by RAF Waddington member.
⏣ Prices on application.
⌒By arrangement with captain or secretary; terms available on application.
🍽 Terms on application.
⌐ Moor Lodge; Mill Lodge.

6B 83 Ramsdale Park Golf Centre
Oxton Rd, Calverton, Notts, NG14 6NU
☎ (0115) 9655600, Fax 9654105,
▥ www.burhillgolf.net
On B6386 10 miles NE of Nottingham.
Parkland course.
Pro Robert Macey; Founded 1992
Designed by Hawtree & Son
18 holes, 6546 yards, S.S.S. 71
♦ Pay and play.
⏣ WD £14; WE £16.50.
⌒Welcome by prior arrangement; packages and catering available; also par 3 course; prices on application.
🍽 Clubhouse facilities.
⌐ Many in local area.

6B 84 Retford
Ordsall, Retford, Notts, DN22 7UA
☎ (01777) 703733, Sec 860682, Fax 710412
Off A620 midway between Worksop and Gainsborough.
Parkland course.
Pro C Morris; Founded 1920
18 holes, 6409 yards, S.S.S. 72
♦ Welcome by prior arrangement WD; with member only at WE and BH.
⏣ Winter WD and WE £12, £8 with a member; Summer WD £15-20, with a member £10.
⌒Welcome WD by prior arrangement; golf and catering packages available; prices on application.
🍽 New clubhouse facilities.
Practice ground.

THE SHERWOOD FOREST GOLF CLUB LTD

EAKRING ROAD, MANSFIELD, NOTTS NG18 3EW

Secretary:	K. Hall	Tel: 01623 626689
Professional:	K. Hall	Tel: 01623 627403
Catering Manageress	V. Kulec	Tel: 01623 623327
		Fax: 01623 420412

Full catering service available with dining for up to 100 persons at one sitting. Course is heathland, set in the very heart of Robin Hood country, and was designed by James Braid. Yellow markers distance is 6294 yds. S.S.S. 71. White markers distance is 6714 yds. S.S.S. 73.

The Course was the venue for the
Midland region Qualifying Round for the Open Championship 1990 - 1995 and for the British Open Amateur Seniors Championship 1997.
Green Fees on application to the secretary.
Within a few miles of places of interest – such as the Major Oak (Robin Hood's Larder). Newstead Abbey, Thoresby Hall, Clumber Oark, and 14 miles from the centre of Nottingham.

West Retford; The Mill House, both Retford; Ye Olde Bell, Barnby Moor.

6B 85 Riverside
Trentside, Lenton Lane, Notts NG7 2SA
☎ (0115) 986 2220
2 miles from city centre off A52 Ruddington road.
9 holes, 2001 yards, S.S.S. 31
† Welcome.
⌣ WD £6; WE £8.
⌣ Packages available.
🍴 Full bar and restaurant facilities. 24-bay driving range.

6B 86 Ruddington Grange ☏
Wilford Road, Ruddington, Nottingham, Notts, NG11 6NB
☎ (0115) 9846141, Pro 9211951, Sec 9214139,
🖥 www.xaracon.com/ruddingtongrange
📧 info@ruddingtongrange. demon.co.uk
Off A52 Grantham Road S of Nottingham.
Parkland course.
Pro Robert Simpson; Founded 1988

Designed by Eddie McCausland, David Johnson
18 holes, 6543 yards, S.S.S. 72
† Welcome with handicap certs.
⌣ WD £16; WE £23.50.
⌣ Welcome WD by arrangement.
🍴 Full facilities and function room. Practice ground; 24-bay floodlit range at Riverside 2 miles away; also 9-hole pay and play course.
⌐ Cottage, Ruddington.

6B 87 Rutland County
Great Casterton, Stamford, Lincs PE9 4AQ
☎ (01780) 460239, Fax 460437, Sec 460330
4 miles N of Stamford on A1.
Founded 1992
Parkland course.
18 holes, 6401 yards, S.S.S. 71
† Welcome with prior arrangement.
⌣ WD £20; WE £25.
⌣ Packages available.
🍴 Bar and restaurant.
Also Par 3 course; driving range.

6B 88 Sandilands ☏
Roman Bank, Sandilands, Sutton-on-Sea, Mablethorpe, Lincs, LN12 2RJ

☎ (01507) 441432, Fax 441617
Course is on the A52 three miles S of Mablethorpe.
Links course.
Founded 1901
18 holes, 5995 yards, S.S.S. 69
† Welcome; some WE restrictions.
⌣ Winter WD £12-£15, WE £15;
Summer WD £15-£20, WE £18-£25.
⌣ Welcome by prior arrangement.
🍴 Clubhouse facilities.
⌐ Grange and Links.

6B 89 Seacroft
Drummond Rd, Skegness, Lincs, PE25 3AU
☎ (01754) 763020, Fax 763020, Pro 769624
S of Skegness towards Seacroft and Gibraltar Point nature reserve.
Links course.
Pro Robin Lawie; Founded 1895
Designed by Tom Dunn
18 holes, 6479 yards, S.S.S. 71
† Welcome with handicap certs.
⌣ WD £25; WE £30.
⌣ Welcome by prior arrangement; deposit required; catering and golf days can be arranged; from £25.
🍴 Full clubhouse facilities.
⌐ Crown; Vine; Links.

6B 90 Sherwood Forest
Eakring Rd, Mansfield, Notts, NG18 3EW
☎ (01623) 623327, Fax 420412, Pro 627403, Sec 626689
⌨ sherwood@forest43.freeserve. co.uk
Off A617 at Oak Tree Lane to roundabout, second exit, 1 mile to junction, right, club is 500 yards.
Heathland course.
Pro Ken Hall; Founded 1895
Designed by H.S. Colt, Redesigned by James Braid
18 holes, 6715 yards, S.S.S. 73
† Welcome by prior arrangement with Sec; guests of members only at WE.
⌿ WD £40-£55.
⌗ Terms on application.
⍟ Full clubhouse facilities.
⌁ Pine Lodge; Swallow; Fringe

6B 91 Shirland
Lower Delves, Shirland, Nr Alfreton, Derbys, DE55 6AU
☎ (01773) 834935, Sec 832515, Bar/Rest 834969, Fax 832515
Course is off the A61 Chesterfield Road; turn opposite the church in Shirland village.
Parkland course with views over Derbyshire countryside.
Pro Neville Hallam; Founded 1977
18 holes, 6072 yards, S.S.S. 69
† Welcome WD; by prior arrangement at WE.
⌿ WD £15; WE £20.
⌗ By prior arrangement with professional; golf and catering packages can be arranged; terms on application.
⍟ Full clubhouse facilities.
⌁ Riber Hall; Swallow Hotel; Higham Farm.

6B 92 Sickleholme
Saltergate Lane, Bamford, Sheffield, S33 0BN
☎ (01433) 651306, Bar/Rest 651252, Fax 659498
On A625 14 miles W of Sheffield.
Undulating parkland course.
Pro Patrick Taylor; Founded 1898
18 holes, 6064 yards, S.S.S. 69
† Welcome by prior arrangement; except Wed am.
⌿ WD £27; WE £32.
⌗ Welcome by prior arrangement; golf and catering packages can be arranged; from £27.
⍟ Restaurant and bar facilities available.

⌁ George; Plough, both Hathersage; Yorkshire Bridge, Bamford.

6B 93 Sleaford ☂
Willoughby Rd, South Rauceby, Sleaford, Lincs, NG34 8PL
☎ (01529) 488273, Fax 488326/488644, Pro 488644
⌨ sleafordgolfclub@btinternet.com
2 miles W of Sleaford at South Rauceby S of the A153 Sleaford to Grantham Road.
Inland links with trees and scrubland.
Pro James Wilson; Founded 1905
Designed by Tom Williamson
18 holes, 6443 yards, S.S.S. 71
† Welcome by prior arrangement.
⌿ WD £16-£22; WE £36.
⌗ Welcome WD by prior arrangement; packages can be arranged; terms on application.
⍟ Restaurant and bar facilities.
⌁ Carre Arms; Lincolnshire Oak; Tally Ho Motel.

6B 94 South Kyme ☂
Skinners Lane, South Kyme, Lincoln, LN4 4AE
☎ (01526) 861113, Fax 861080
Course is on the B1395 four miles off the A17 midway between Boston and Sleaford.
Fenland course.
Pro Peter Chamberlain; Founded 1990
Designed by Graham Bradley
18 holes, 6597 yards, S.S.S. 71
† Welcome.
⌿ WD £14; WE £16.
⌗ Terms on application.
⍟ Clubhouse facilities.
Practice ground and 6-hole course.

6B 95 Southview
Burgh Rd, Skegness, Lincs, PE25 2LA
☎ (01754) 760589
On the A158 on the outskirts of Skegness signposted to Southview Leisure park.
Parkland course.
Pro Peter Cole; Founded 1990
9 holes, 4816 yards, S.S.S. 64
† Welcome.
⌿ WD £6 per day; WE £6 per round.
⌗ Welcome at all times; tuition; swimming pool; sauna; sunbeds; snooker.
⍟ Full bar and catering in leisure park.
⌁ North Shore; Crown; Links.

6B 96 Spalding
Surfleet, Spalding, Lincs, PE11 4EA
☎ (01775) 680474, Sec 680386, Bar/Rest 680234, Fax 680988
⌨ spence.golfshop@spalding2000. freeserve.co.uk
Off A16 Spalding to Boston Road 4 miles N of Spalding.
Parkland course.
Pro John Spencer; Founded 1908
Designed by Spencer/Price/Ward extension 1993
18 holes, 6478 yards, S.S.S. 71
† Welcome by prior arrangement.
⌿ WD £20; WE £30.
⌗ Welcome Tues pm and Thurs; catering packages can be arranged; from £18.
⍟ Full catering and bar facilities except Tues.
Practice ground.

6B 97 Springwater
Moor Lane, Calverton, Notts NG14 6FZ
☎ (0115) 965 2129, Pro 965 3634
Off A6097 between Lowdham and Oxton.
Extended 1998
9 holes, 3203 yards, S.S.S. 71
† Welcome.
⌿ Pay and play; WD £10; WE £15.
⌗ Packages available.
⍟ Full clubhouse facilities.

6B 98 Stanedge
Walton Hay Farm, Stanedge, Chesterfield, Derbys, S45 0LW
☎ (01246) 566156, Sec 276568
Off B5057 Darley Dale Road from the A632 Chesterfield-Matlock Road.
Moorland course; being extended 1998.
Founded 1934
9 holes, 5786 yards, S.S.S. 69
† Welcome WD (Fri before 2pm); WE with a member.
⌿ WD £15.
⌗ Welcome by arrangement with Sec; catering packages can be arranged; terms on application.
⍟ Full clubhouse facilities.
Practice area.
⌁ Chesterfield Hotel; Olde House, both Chesterfield.

6B 99 Stanton-on-the-Wolds
Stanton-on-the-Wolds, Keyworth, Notts, NG12 5BH
☎ (0115) 9372044, Pro 9372390, Bar/Rest 9372264, Fax 9372390

Off A606 8 miles SE of Nottingham.
Meadowland course.
Pro Nick Hernon; Founded 1906
Designed by Tom Williamson
18 holes, 6437 yards, S.S.S. 71
☂ Welcome WD; WE with a member.
☂ WD £20.
☞ Welcome by prior arrangement
with Sec.
☺ Full bar and catering facilities.
Practice range, practice area;
chipping green.
☞ Edwalton, Nottingham.

6B 100 Stoke Rochford
Stoke Rochford, Grantham, Lincs,
NG33 5EW
☎ (01476) 530275, Pro 530218, Fax
530237, Sec (01572) 756305
6 miles S of Grantham off
Northbound A1.
Parkland course.
Pro Angus Dow; Founded 1926/1936
Designed by Major Hotchkin/ C.
Turner
18 holes, 6252 yards, S.S.S. 70
☂ Welcome by prior arrangement.
☂ WD £22-£30, £12 with a member;
WE £28-£40, £14 with a member.
☞ Welcome by prior arrangement;
catering packages available; snooker;
terms on application.
☺ Full clubhouse bar and restaurant
facilities.
☞ Many in Grantham.

6B 101 Sudbrook Moor
Charity Street, Carlton Scroop, Nr
Grantham, Lincs, NG32 3AT
☎ (01400) 250796, Fax 250796,
Clubhouse 250876
☞ tim0hutton@aol.co.uk
On A607 6 miles NE of Grantham.
Meadowland course in picturesque
valley.
Pro Tim Hutton; Founded 1986
Designed by Tim Hutton
9 holes, 4800 yards, S.S.S. 64
☂ Pay and play.
☂ Winter WD £5, WE £7; Summer
WD £6, WE £9.
☞ None.
☺ Coffee shop only.

6B 102 Sutton Bridge
New Rd, Sutton Bridge, Spalding,
Lincs, PE 12 9RG
☎ (01406) 350323, Pro 351422
☞ kevin.beardsley@tesco.net
Off A17 Long Sutton to King's Lynn
Road at Sutton Bridge.
Parkland course.

Pro Peter Fields; Founded 1914
9 holes, 5770 yards, S S.S. 68
☂ Welcome WD by prior
arrangement; members only at WE.
☂ WD £18.
☞ Welcome WD by prior
arrangement; catering can be
arranged, from £17.
☺ Bar and restaurant facilities.
☞ The Anchor Inn; numerous other
small inns in area.

6B 103 Swingtime (Grimsby)
Cromwell Rd, Grimsby
☎ (01472) 250555, Fax 267447
From A180 follow signs for
Auditorium and Leisure centre.
Parkland course.
Pro Stephen Bennett/Danil Burchell;
Founded 1995
9 holes, 4652 yards, Par 32
☂ Public pay and play.
☂ WD £9; WE £11.
☞ None.
☺ Limited.
Practice ground.

6B 104 Tapton Park Municipal
Murray House, Crow Lane,
Chesterfield, Derbys, S41 0EQ
☎ (01246) 273887, Fax 558024, Pro
239500
Signposted in Chesterfield centre.
Municipal parkland course.
Pro Andrew Carnall; Founded 1934
18 holes, 6025 yards, S.S.S. 69
☂ Welcome; can book 6 days in
advance.
☂ WD £6.25; WE £7.75.
☞ Welcome by prior arrangement;
packages available; terms on
application.
☺ Bar and restaurant facilities
available.
9-hole par 3 course, pitch and putt
course.

6B 105 Tetney
Station Rd, Tetney, Grimsby, Lincs,
DN36 5HY
☎ (01472) 211644, Fax 211644,
Bar/Rest 811344
Off A16 at Tetney; 1.5 miles down
Station Rd.
Parkland course.
Pro Jason Abrams; Founded 1994
18 holes, 6100 yards, S.S.S. 69
☂ Welcome.
☂ WD £10; WE £12.50.
☞ Welcome with some restrictions at
WE; packages available for all-day

catering and golf; from £25.
☺ Bar and restaurant facilities
available.
Practice ground.

6B 106 Toft Hotel
Toft, Nr Bourne, Lincs, PE10 0XX
☎ (01778) 590616, Hotel 590614
6 miles E of Stamford on A6121.
Undulating parkland course with
water features.
Pro Mark Jackson; Founded 1988
Designed by Derek and Roger Fitton
18 holes, 6486 yards, S.S.S. 71
☂ Welcome; tees bookable 14 days
ahead.
☂ WD £20; WE £25.
☞ Welcome by arrangement.
☺ Full bar and restaurant facilities
and function room in hotel.
☞ On site Toft Hotel; golfing
packages available.

6B 107 Trent Lock Golf Centre
Lock Lane, Sawley, Long Eaton,
Notts, NG10 2FY
☎ (0115) 9464398, Fax 9461183,
Bar/Rest 9461184
2 miles from M1 Junction 25.
Parkland course.
Pro Mark Taylor; Founded 1991
Designed by E.W. McCausland
18-hole course: 5900 yards, S.S.S.
68; new 9-hole course: 2900 yards,
par 36
☂ Welcome; must book at WE.
☂ WD £10; WE £12.
☞ Welcome by prior arrangement;
from £24.95.
☺ Bar snacks, restaurant, private
function room.
Practice range, 24 bays floodlit.

6B 108 Waltham Windmill
Cheapside, Waltham, Grimsby, N E
Lincs, DN37 0HT
☎ (01472) 824100, Pro 823063, Fax
820391, Rest 820623
In village of Waltham.
Parkland course.
Pro Nigel Burkitt; Founded 1997
Designed by Jim Payne
18 holes, 6333 yards, S.S.S. 70
☂ Welcome.
☂ WD £18; WE £25.
☞ Welcome WD by prior
arrangement; restrictions at WE;
packages available.
☺ Catering, bar and function room.
Practice ground.
☞ Brackenborough Arms.

6B 109 **Welton Manor**
Hackthorn Rd, Welton, Lincs, LN2 3PD
☎ (01673) 862827,
Off A46 Lincoln-Grimsby road.
Undulating parkland course.
Pro Gary Leslie; Founded 1995
18 holes, 6310 yards, S.S.S. 66
♦ Welcome; pay and play.
⌐ WD £9; WE £12.
⌐⁄ Welcome any time by prior arrangement.
⦿ Construction of new restaurant/bar; completion Sept 2000. Practice range, 10 bays fllodlit.
⌐ Four Seasons.

6B 110 **Wollaton Park**
Lime Tree Avenue, Wollaton Park, Nottingham, NG8 1BT
☎ (0115) 9784834, Fax 9787574, Sec 9787574, Bar/Rest 9787341
Off slip road from A52 at junction with Nottingham ring road.
Parkland course.
Pro John Lower; Founded 1927
Designed by T. Williamson
18 holes, 6445 yards, S.S.S. 71
♦ Welcome.
⌐ WD £26; WE £31.
⌐⁄ Welcome by prior arrangement on Tues and Fri; golf and catering packages available on application to secretary; from £27.

⦿ Clubhouse catering facilities available.
⌐ Toby Lodge, Nottingham.

6B 111 **Woodhall Spa**
The Broadway, Woodhall Spa, Lincs, LN10 6PU
☎ (01526) 352511, Fax 352778, Pro 351803
Course is on the B1191 19 miles SE of Lincoln.
Heathland course.
Pro Campbell C Elliott; Founded 1905
Designed by Col S.V. Hotchkin
The Hotchkin: 18 holes, 6921 yards, S.S.S. 75; The Bracken: 18 hole, 6735 yards, S.S.S. 74
♦ Welcome by prior arrangement; discount for EGU members.
⌐ WD £40; WE £40.
⌐⁄ Welcome by prior arrangement; golf and catering by arrangement; from £30.
⦿ Full clubhouse facilities. Driving range, teaching academy, pitch and putt.
⌐ Golf; Petwood House; Eagle Lodge.

6B 112 **Woodthorpe Hall**
Woodthorpe, Alford, Lincs, LN13 0DD
☎ (01507) 450000, Fax 450000
▦ www.woodthorpehall.co.uk
⌐ info@woodthorpehall.co.uk
Course is off the B1371 three miles N of Alford.
Parkland course.
Founded 1986
18 holes, 5140 yards, S.S.S. 65
♦ Welcome WD; by arrangement WE.
⌐ WD £10; WE £10.
⌐⁄ Welcome WD by prior arrangement; four weeks' notice needed; packages can be arranged for a minimum of 8; from £20.
⦿ Inn on site.

6B 113 **Worksop**
Windmill Lane, Worksop, Notts, S80 2SQ
☎ (01909) 472696, Fax 477731, Pro 477732, Sec 477731, Bar/Rest 472513
Off the B6034 road to Edwinstowe off the A57.
Heathland course with woods and gorse.
Pro C Weatherhead; Founded 1914
18 holes, 6660 yards, S.S.S. 73
♦ Welcome by prior arrangement.
⌐ WD £26; WE £35.
⌐⁄ Welcome WD by prior arrangement; catering packages can be arranged; terms available on application.
⦿ Full clubhouse facilities.

THE NORTH WEST

Lancashire not only boasts the best course in England in Royal Birkdale but another half a dozen that are, with good reason, eminently regarded.

In 1991 Birkdale had fallen from its lofty perch owing to the terrible state of its greens, but they were rebuilt for the 1998 Open, with spectacular results.

What makes the course so good? Its towering dunes, which line virtually every hole, and its innate fairness; if it had views of the sea as well it would be the complete golf course.

In many people's eyes, though not this writer, neighbouring Hillside is even better. It is, however, unquestionably a classic links, from the opening holes that straddle the railway to the stern finish.

The railway links Liverpool to Southport and those who travel along it pass great golf course after great golf course. Next on the line is Formby, and then West Lancs. Southport and Ainsdale is also situated in this glittering sandbelt, and then there is Hesketh, just north of Southport's town centre.

Between them these courses have held every professional and amateur tournament worth shaking a stick at, including 17 Open Championships and five Ryder Cups (back in the days when it was not possible for a course owner to buy the event). Perhaps one has to travel to the Monterey Peninsula in California to find another area where so many great links courses are situated so closely together.

Further along the Lancashire coastline we reach Royal Lytham and St Annes, scene of so many great Open Championships, and where every player seeking a good score has to do well over the first nine holes, for assuredly the difficult closing quintet will tug at the gains.

Situated almost exactly midway between Great Britain and Ireland and easily accessible from Liverpool is the Isle of Man, which has one golf course of deserved repute.

Castletown Golf Links is known in some circles as the "poor man's Turnberry", which is meant as a compliment. Although it is not quite as testing a challenge as the Ailsa, it does possess the same enchanting views for which that course is justifiably famous throughout the world.

And so to Cumbria, sandwiched between the great links of Lancashire and those of Scotland's Ayrshire coast, and so often neglected by golfers. It does not deserve to be. Indeed, in Silloth, it has its own links course that rubs shoulders with the best.

Then there is Ulverston Golf Club, in South Lakeland. Standing on the 18th tee, one is confronted by a downhill par four finishing alongside the clubhouse. To the left and ahead you have the mountains of the Lake District, snowcapped in winter, dappled bright in summer. On the right and lying hundreds of feet below is Morecambe Bay, a tidal estuary alive with bird life and a thriving shrimp industry.

Cumbria may not be fashionable for golf but it would be surprising for anyone to give it a try and then register disappointment. — **DL**

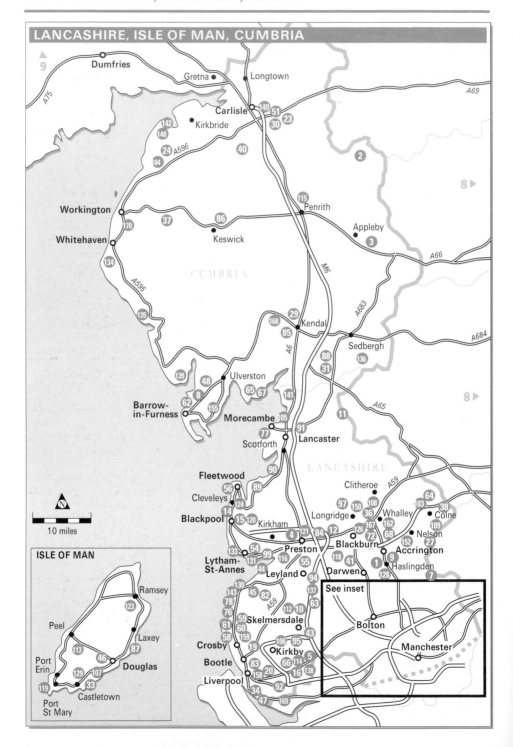

LANCASHIRE, ISLE OF MAN, CUMBRIA

9

Dumfries

Gretna
Longtown

A75

Carlisle
149
51
30
23

Kirkbride
142
140

24 A596
104

40

A69

2

8 ▶

115 Penrith

Workington
170
37
86
Keswick

Appleby
3

Whitehaven
134
A66

A595

CUMBRIA

M6

A683

135

29
168
Kendal

85

Sedbergh
136

A684

88
31

139
48
8
Ulverston

65 67

141

11

A65

8 ▶

62
155

Barrow-
in-Furness

Morecambe
105

77
91 Lancaster

Scotforth

90

LANCASHIRE

Fleetwood
56
89
124

Cleveleys

Clitheroe
A59

64

97
108
150
36
Whalley
103
38
Colne

Longridge
167
162
109
Nelson

14
Blackpool
15 120
Kirkham
121
84
12
126
72
68
152
27
Accrington

4
Preston
Blackburn
118
41
1
9
Haslingden

133
54
99
116
55
94
128
7

Lytham-
St-Annes
131
144
Leyland
Darwen

10 miles

ISLE OF MAN

Ramsey
123

Peel
Laxey
113
87
129
107
Douglas
119
33
Castletown

Port
Erin
46

Port
St Mary

See inset

Bolton

Manchester

130
143
45
82
A59
78
76
137
63

61
59
Skelmersdale
60
58
159
112 10
106 95
43

Crosby
19
Kirkby
5
Bootle
83
66 114
138
158 20 16
Liverpool
34
92
47 169

KEY		36	Clitheroe	71	Greenmount	104	Maryport	138	Gherdley Park
1	Accrington & District	37	Cockermouth	72	Haigh Hall	105	Morecambe	139	Silecroft
2	Alston Moor	38	Colne	73	Harwood	106	Mossack Hall	140	Silloth on Solway
3	Appleby	39	Crompton & Royton	74	Haydock Park	107	Mount Murray	141	Silverdale
4	Ashton & Lea	40	Dalston Hall	75	Heaton Park	108	Mytton Fold	142	Solway Village
5	Ashton-in-Makerfield	41	Darwen	76	Hesketh	109	Nelson	143	Southport & Ainsdale
6	Ashton-under-Lyne	42	Davyhulme Park	77	The Heysham	110	North Manchester	144	Southport Municipal
7	Bacup	43	Dean Wood	78	Hillside Golf Club	111	Oldham	145	Southport Old Links
8	Barrow	44	Deane	79	Hindley Hall	112	Ormskirk	146	Springfield Park
9	Baxenden & District	45	Denton	80	Horwich	113	Peel	147	Stand
10	Beacon Park	46	Douglas	81	Houghwood	114	Pennington	148	Standish Court Golf Club
11	Bentham	47	Dudley	82	Hurlston Hall	115	Penrith	149	Stonyholme Municipal
12	Blackburn	48	Dunnerholme	83	Huyton & Prescot	116	Penwortham	150	Stonyhurst Park
13	Blackley	49	Dunscar	84	Ingol Golf & Squash	117	Pike Fold	151	Swinton Park
14	Blackpool North Shore	50	Duxbury Park		Club	118	Pleasington	152	Towneley
15	Blackpool Park	51	Eden	85	Kendal	119	Port St Mary Golf	153	Tunshill
16	Blundells Hill	52	Ellesmere	86	Keswick		Pavilion	154	Turton
17	Bolton	53	Fairfield Golf & Sailing	87	King Edward Bay	120	Poulton-le-Fylde	155	Ulverston
18	Bolton Old Links		Club		(Howstrake)	121	Preston	156	Walmersley
19	Bootle	54	Fairhaven	88	Kirkby Lonsdale	122	Prestwich	157	Werneth (Oldham)
20	Bowring	55	Fishwick Hall	89	Knott End	123	Ramsey	158	West Derby
21	Boysnope Park	56	Fleetwood	90	Lancaster	124	Reach	159	West Lancashire
22	Brackley	57	Flixton	91	Lansil	125	Regent Park (Bolton)	160	Westhoughton
23	Brampton	58	Formby	92	Lee Park	126	Rishton	161	Westhoughton Golf
24	Brayton Park	59	Formby Golf Centre	93	Leigh	127	Rochdale		Centre
25	Breightmet	60	Formby Hall	94	Leyland	128	Rossendale	162	Whalley
26	Brookdale	61	Formby Ladies	95	Liverpool Municipal	129	Rowany	163	Whitefield
27	Burnley	62	Furness		(Kirkby)	130	Royal Birkdale	164	Whittaker
28	Bury	63	Gathurst	96	Lobden	131	Royal Lytham & St	165	Wigan
29	Caras Green	64	Ghyll	97	Longridge		Annes	166	William Wroe
30	Carlisle	65	Grange Fell	98	Lowes Park	132	Saddleworth	167	Wilpshire
31	Casterton	66	Grange Park	99	Lytham Green Drive	133	St Annes Old Links	168	Windermere
32	Castle Hawk	67	Grange-over-Sands	100	Manchester	134	St Bees	169	Woolton
33	Castletown Golf Links	68	Great Harwood	101	Manor (Bolton)	135	Seascale	170	Workington
34	Childwall	69	Great Lever & Farnworth	102	Marriott Worsley Park	136	Sedbergh	171	Worsley
35	Chorley	70	Green Haworth	103	Marsden Park	137	Shaw Hill Hotel G & CC		

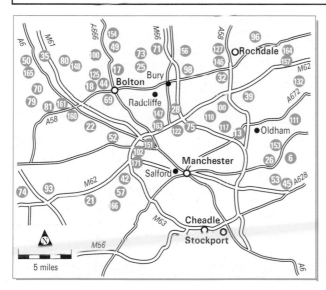

🐾 Welcome by arrangement.
🍽 Full facilities except Mon.
Practice ground.
⛳ County; Kendal; Duncan House.

7 2 **Alston Moor**
The Hermitage, Alston, Cumbria, CA9 3DB
☎ (01434) 381675
Course is on the B6277 1.5 miles south of Alston; signposted from the top of the town.
Parkland and fell course.
Founded 1906/1969
Designed by Members
10 holes, 5518 yards, S.S.S. 67
🚶 Welcome.
⛳ WD £9; WE £11.
🐾 Welcome by prior arrangement; packages for golf and catering can be provided; prices on application.
🍽 Bar and catering facilities from May to October.
⛳ Secretary can provide details.

7 1 **Accrington & District**
New Barn Farm, Devon Ave, West End, Oswaldtwistle, Accrington, Lancs BB5 4LS
☎ (01254) 232734, Fax 233423, Pro 231091, Sec 381614
📧 acgolf@globalnel.co.uk

On A679 5 miles from Blackburn.
Moorland course.
Pro Bill Harling; Founded 1893
Designed by James Braid
18 holes, 6044 yards, S.S.S. 69
🚶 Welcome.
⛳ WD £20; WE £25.

7 3 **Appleby**
Brackenber Moor, Appleby-in-Westmorland, Cumbria, CA16 6LP
☎ (017683) 51432
Course is on the A66 two miles E of Appleby.

Moorland course.
Pro Paul Jenkinson; Founded 1903
Designed by Willie Fernie of Troon
18 holes, 5901 yards, S.S.S. 68
♠ Welcome.
⌐ WD £16; WE £20.
☞Welcome by prior arrangement.
🍽 Full catering and bar except
Tues.
Practice ground.
⌐⌐ Tufton Arms; Royal Oak; Appleby
Manor; The Gate.

7 4 Ashton & Lea
Tudor Ave, off Blackpool Rd, Lea,
Preston PR4 0XA
☎(01772) 726480, Fax 735762, Pro
720374, Sec 735282
Course is on the A5085 three miles
W of Preston.
Parkland course with water features.
Pro M Greenough; Founded 1913
Designed by J. Steer
18 holes, 6370 yards, S.S.S. 70
♠ Welcome by prior arrangement.
⌐ WD £23; WE £25.
☞Welcome by prior arrangement;
Training/conference rooms available;
packages include golf and catering;
from £33.
🍽 Full clubhouse facilities available.
⌐⌐ Travel Inn, Lea; Marriott,
Broughton.

7 5 Ashton-in-Makerfield
Garswood Park, Liverpool Rd,
Ashton-in-Makerfield, Lancs WN4
0YT
☎(01942) 727267, Sec 719330
Off A58 from M6 0.5 miles to course.
Parkland course.
Pro Peter Alan Founded 1902
Designed by F.W. Hawtree
18 holes, 6205 yards, S.S.S. 70
♠ Welcome WD except Wed; WE
only with a member.
⌐ WD £28.
☞Welcome Mon, Tues and Thurs by
prior arrangement.
🍽 Full facilities except Mon (not
applicable for societies).
⌐⌐ Thistle, Haydock.

7 6 Ashton-under-Lyne   ℭ
Gorsey Way, Ashton-under-Lyne,
Lancs OL6 9HT
☎(0161) 330 1537, Fax 330 1537,
Pro 308 2095
3 miles from town centre.
Semi-parkland course.
Pro Colin Boyle; Founded 1913
18 holes, 6209 yards, S.S.S. 70

♠ Welcome by prior arrangement;
guests of members only at WE.
⌐ WD £27.
☞Welcome Tues, Thurs and Fri;
packages for golf and catering
available; terms on application.
🍽 Clubhouse facilities.
⌐⌐ Broadoak Hotel.

7 7 Bacup
Maden Rd, Bacup, Lancs OL13 8HY
☎(01706) 873170
Off A671 7 miles N of Rochdale, 0.5
miles from Bacup centre.
Meadowland course.
Founded 1911
9 holes, 6008 yards, S.S.S. 67
♠ Welcome Wed, Thurs and Fri, and
after competitions at WE.
⌐ Prices on application.
☞Welcome Wed, Thurs and Fri by
prior arrangement.
🍽 Full clubhouse facilities available.
⌐⌐ Royal, Waterfoot.

7 8 Barrow
Rakesmoor Lane, Hawcoat, Barrow-
in-Furness, Cumbria LA14 4QB
☎(01229) 825444, Pro 832121
From M6 Junction 36 take A590 to
Barrow; 3 miles before town follow
Industrial route turning left into Bank
Lane.
Parkland course.
Pro J McLeod; Founded 1922
18 holes, 6200 yards, S.S.S. 70
♠ Welcome with handicap certs and
by prior arrangement.
⌐ WD £20; WE £20.
☞Welcome by prior arrangement
with the professional; packages
include a full day's golf and catering;
snooker table; from £26.
🍽 Full clubhouse facilities.
⌐⌐ Club can recommend local
hotels.

7 9 Baxenden & District
Top-o'-the Meadow, Wooley Lane, Nr
Accrington, Lancs BB5 2EA
☎(01254) 234555
Take M65 Accrington exit and follow
the signs for Baxenden; course
signposted in village.
Moorland course.
Founded 1913
9 holes, 5717 yards, S.S.S. 68
♠ Welcome WD; with member only
WE.
⌐ Prices on application.
☞Welcome WD by prior
arrangement with the Secretary;

packages include coffee, light lunch,
3-course meal and 27 holes of golf;
from £22.
🍽 Bar and snacks available; meals
to order.
⌐⌐ Syke Side House, Haslingden.

7 10 Beacon Park
Beacon Lane, Dalton, Up Holland,
Wigan, Lancs WN8 7RU
☎(01695) 622700, Fax 633066, Sec
726298, Bar/Rest 625551
Off A577 in Up Holland.
Parkland course.
Pro Ray Peters; Founded 1982
Designed by Donald Steel
18 holes, 5931 yards, S.S.S. 69
♠ Pay and play.
⌐ Terms on application.
☞Welcome by prior arrangement;
payment required 10 days in
advance; terms on application.
🍽 Clubhouse facilities.
Practice range, 24 bays floodlit.
⌐⌐ Lancashire Lodge.

7 11 Bentham
Robin Lane, Bentham, Lancaster,
Lancs LA2 7AG
☎(015242) 62455, Bar/Rest 61018
Between Lancaster and Settle on
B6480 13 miles E of M6 Junction 34.
Undulating meadowland course.
Founded 1922
9 holes, 5820 yards, S.S.S. 69
♠ Welcome.
⌐ WD £15; WE £15.
☞Welcome by arrangement.
🍽 Bar snacks and meals.
⌐⌐ Bridge, Ingleton; Post House,
Lancaster.

7 12 Blackburn
Beardwood Brow, Blackburn, Lancs
BB2 7AX
☎(01254) 51122, Sec 51122, Fax
665578, Pro 55942
Odd A677 at W end of Blackburn.
Parkland course.
Pro A Rodwell; Founded 1894
18 holes, 6144 yards, S.S.S. 70
♠ Welcome by prior arrangement.
⌐ WD £24; WE £28; guests of
members £7.70 all week; juniors WD
£5-£9, WE £7.50-£9.
☞Welcome WD except Tues;
catering and golf packages can be
arranged; terms on application.
🍽 Clubhouse facilities except Mon .
Practice ground, putting green, indoor
practice area.
⌐⌐ The County Hotel.

7 13 Blackley

Victoria Ave East, Blackley,
Manchester, M9 7HW
☎(0161) 643 2980, Pro 643 3912,
Sec 654 7770, Bar/Rest 653 5707
5 miles N of City centre.
Parkland course.
Pro Craig Gould; Founded 1907
18 holes, 6217 yards, S.S.S. 70
† Welcome WD; with member at
weekend.
▯ WD £12; WE £12.
✈Welcome WD except Thurs; golf
and catering packages available;
from £20.
🍽 Full clubhouse catering facilities
available.
↴ Bower Hotel, Chadderton.

7 14 Blackpool North Shore

Devonshire Rd, Blackpool,
Lancashire, FY2 0RD
☎(01253) 352054, Fax 591240, Pro
354640, Bar/Rest 351017
From M55 Junction 4 take Preston
New Road to Whitegate Drive and
Devonshire Road.
Seaside links course.
Pro Brendan Ward; Founded 1904
18 holes, 6431 yards, S.S.S. 71
† Welcome by prior arrangement;
tees reserved for members until
9.30am & 12.30-1pm; not before 2pm
Thurs and 4pm Sat.
▯ WD £27.50; WE and BH £32.50.
✈Welcome WD except Thurs; golf
and catering packages available;
terms on application.
🍽 Catering and bar facilities
available daily.
↴ Many in Blackpool.

7 15 Blackpool Park

North Park Drive;Blackpool, Lancs
FY3 8LS
☎(01253) 393960, Fax 397916, Pro
391004, Sec 397916, Bar/Rest
396683
2 miles E of Blackpool signposted off
M55.
Parkland course.
Pro B Purdie
Founded 1926
Designed by Dr MacKenzie
18 holes, 6192 yards, S.S.S. 69
† Welcome; tee reservations
through Blackpool Borough Council.
▯ WD £11; WE £12.
✈Welcome by prior arrangement
with Blackpool Borough Council;
terms on application.
🍽 Clubhouse facilities.
↴ Many in Blackpool.

7 16 Blundells Hill

Blundells Lane, Rainhill, Liverpool,
Merseyside, L35 6NA
☎(0151) 4300100, Fax 4265256,
Sec 4309551, Bar/Rest 4269040
↴info@blundellshill.demon.co.uk
From M62 Junction 7 take A57
towards Prescot; turn left after
garage; then left into Blundells Lane.
Parkland course.
Pro R Burbidge; Founded 1994
Designed by S Marnoch
18 holes, 6256 yards, S.S.S. 70
† Welcome by arrangement.
▯ WD £25, WE £30.
✈Welcome Mon to Thurs, catering
and golf packages for a minimum of
12; £33-£42.
🍽 Full clubhouse facilities.
↴ Ship Inn, Rainhill; Stakis, St
Helens; The Village, Whiston;
Hillcrest, Cronton.

7 17 Bolton

Lostock Park, Chorley New Rd,
Bolton, Lancs BL6 4AJ
☎(01204) 843278, Fax 843067, Pro
843073, Sec 843067
3 miles W of Bolton.
Hilly course.
Pro Robert Longworth; Founded
1891/1912
18 holes, 6237 yards, S.S.S. 70
† Welcome between 10am-12noon
and after 2pm.
▯ WD £30-£36; WE £33-£40.
✈Welcome Mon, Thurs and some
Fris; discounts available for larger
groups; packages for golf and
catering available; terms on
application.
🍽 Clubhouse facilities.

7 18 Bolton Old Links

Chorley Old Rd, Bolton, Lancs BL1
5SU
☎(01204) 842307, Fax 842307, Pro
843089, Bar/Rest 840050
On B6226 N of A58 from Junction 5
on M61.
Moorland course.
Pro Paul Horridge; Founded 1891
Designed by Dr A. MacKenzie
18 holes, 6406 yards, S.S.S. 72
† Welcome except on competition
days; phone in advance to make
booking.
▯ WD £30; WE £40.
✈Welcome WD by prior
arrangement.
🍽 Full clubhouse facilities available
except Mon (possible by prior
arrangement).

Practice ground; indoor practice
facilities.
↴ Crest; Pack Horse; Last Drop;
Moat House.

7 19 Bootle

Dunnings Bridge Rd, Bootle,
Merseyside L30 2PP
☎(0151) 928 1371, Fax 949 1815,
Bar/Rest 928 6196
On A565 5 miles from Liverpool.
Municipal seaside links course.
Pro Alan Bradshaw; Founded 1934
Designed by F Stephens
18 holes, 6242 yards, S.S.S. 70
† Welcome.
▯ WD £5.75; WE £7.50.
✈Welcome by prior arrangement.
🍽 Full clubhouse facilities available.
↴ Park.

7 20 Bowring

Bowring Park Golf Course, Roby Rd,
Huyton, Liverpool, Merseyside, L36
4HD
☎(0151) 489 1901l
6 miles N of Liverpool.
Municipal parkland course; about to
have a million-pound refurbishment of
facilities.
Founded 1913
18 holes, 6147 yards, S.S.S. 70
† Welcome.
▯ Adults WD £6, WE £6.80; OAP
WD £3.25, WE £3.75; juniors WD £3,
WE £3.25.
✈Welcome by prior arrangement.
🍽 Snacks; bar for members only.

7 21 Boysnope Park

Liverpool Rd, Barton Moss, Eccles
M30 7RF
☎(0161) 707 6125
Off M60 at Junction 11 on A57
towards Irlam.
Parkland course.
9 holes, 2975 yards, par 34
Founded 1998
† Welcome.
▯ WD £6; WE £7.
✈Welcome by prior notice.
🍽 Limited to snacks.

7 22 Brackley

Bullows Rd, Little Hulton, Worsley,
Manchester, M38 9TR
☎(0161) 790 6076
9 miles from Manchester on A6; turn
right at White Lion Hotel into Highfield
Rd; left into Captain Fold Rd; left into
Bullows Rd.

Parkland course.
Founded 1976
9 holes, 6006 yards, S.S.S. 69
† Welcome; book at WE.
⌐ WD £4; WE and BH 9 holes £4, 18 holes £7; OAP WD £3; juniors WD £2.50.
⌐ Welcome by prior arrangement; from £7.
⍁ None.

7 23 Brampton
Brampton, Cumbria, CA8 1HN
☎ (016977) 2255, Fax 41487, Pro 2000
1.75 miles from Brampton on B6413 Castle Carrock Road.
Moorland course.
Pro Stewart Wilkinson; Founded 1907
Designed by James Braid
18 holes, 6407 yards, S.S.S. 71
† Welcome; tee booked 9.30am-10.30am Mon, Wed, Thurs.
⌐ WD £22; WE £28.
⌐ Welcome by prior arrangement WD; limited at WE.
⍁ Full facilities in refurbished clubhouse.
Practice ground.
⌐ Details of local guest houses and hotels offering reduced fees from club or pro.

7 24 Brayton Park Golf Course
Brayton, Aspatria, Carlisle, Cumbria, CA5 3TD
☎ (016973) 20840, Fax 20854
Off A596 W of Carlisle.
Parkland course.
Pro Graham Batey; Founded 1978
9 holes, 5042 yards, S.S.S. 64
† Welcome.
⌐ WD £7; WE £8.
⌐ Welcome by prior arrangement; terms on application.
⍁ Full clubhouse facilities.
⌐ Kelsey; Wheyrigg; Green Hill.

7 25 Breightmet
Red Lane, Red Bridge, Bolton, Lancs BL2 5PA
☎ (01204) 527381
Off Bury Road in Bolton.
Moorland/parkland course.
Founded 1911
9 holes, 6416 yards, S.S.S. 72
† Welcome by prior arrangement; some restrictions Sat and Wed.
⌐ WD £15; WE £18.
⌐ Welcome WD; some Suns; packages include full day's golf and

catering; snooker; £25-£30.
⍁ Full clubhouse facilities.
⌐ In Bolton town centre.

7 26 Brookdale
Midlock Rd, Woodhouses, Failsworth, Manchester, Manchester, M35 9WQ
☎ (0161) 681 4534, Fax 688 6872, Pro 681 2655
From Manchester take A62 turning right at Ashton Rd East; 1 mile turn right into Failsworth Rd; 0.25 miles into Midlock Road.
Parkland course.
Pro Tony Cupello
Founded 1960
Designed by available
18 holes, 5874 yards, S.S.S. 68
† Welcome WD only.
⌐ WD £20.
⌐ Welcome Wed, Thurs, Fri; packages include golf and catering from £33.
⍁ Clubhouse facilities.
⌐ Smokies Park; Bower Hotel.

7 27 Burnley
Glen View, Burnley, Lancs BB11 3RW
☎ (01282) 421045, Pro 455266, Sec 451281
🖳 www.burnley-golf.co.uk
🖳 burnleygolf@currantbun.com
Glen View road is off Manchester Road.
Moorland course.
Pro W P Tye; Founded 1905
18 holes, 5911 yards, S.S.S. 69
† Welcome with handicap certs.
⌐ WD £20; WE £25.
⌐ Welcome everyday except Sat; handicap certs required; 36 holes of golf plus meals; £30.
⍁ Full facilities.
⌐ Rosehill House Hotel.

7 28 Bury
Unsworth Hall, Blackford Bridge, Bury, BL9 9TJ
☎ (0161) 766 4897, Fax 796 3480, Pro 766 2213
On A57 1.5 miles from M62 Junction 17.
Undulating moorland course.
Pro S Crake; Founded 1890
Designed by Dr A Mackenzie
18 holes, 5927 yards, S.S.S. 69
† Welcome except on club competition days.
⌐ WD £26; WE £30.
⌐ Welcome Wed-Fri; packages include full day's golf and catering £35.

⍁ Full clubhouse facilities.
⌐ Red Hall; Rostrevor.

7 29 Caras Green
Burnside Road, Kendal LA9 6EB
☎ (01539) 72107, Fax 72107
From roundabout at N end of Kendal follow A591 to Burnside.
18 holes, 5961 yards, S.S.S. 68
Designed by W Adamson
† Welcome; some weekend restrictions.
⌐ Terms on application.
⌐ Contact secretary for packages.
⍁ Full clubhouse catering.

7 30 Carlisle
Aglionby, Carlisle, Cumbria, CA4 8AG
☎ (01228) 513029, Fax 513303, Pro 513241, Sec 513303
Course is on the A69 0.25 miles E of M6 Junction 43.
Parkland course (Open Championship qualifying course).
Pro Martin Heggie; Founded 1909/1940
Designed by T Simpson, MacKenzie Ross/ Frank Pennink
18 holes, 6223 yards, S.S.S. 70
† Welcome except Tues and Sat.
⌐ WD £25-£40; Sun £40.
⌐ Welcome Mon, Wed, Fri by prior arrangement; packages available; club can administer competitions; private dining facilities; terms on application.
⍁ Full clubhouse facilities.
Practice area.
⌐ Cumbrain Hotel, Carlisle; Crown Hotel, Wetherall.

7 31 Casterton
Sedburgh Rd, Casterton, Carnforth, Lancs LA6 2LA
☎ (01524) 271592, Fax 274387
🖳 castertongc@hotmail.com
On A683 Sebergh Road.
Picturesque undulating parkland course.
Pro Roy Williamson; Founded 1946/1993
Designed by W Adamson
9 holes, 5726 yards, S.S.S. 68
† Welcome by prior arrangement; weekend reservations essential.
⌐ WD £9; WE £12.
⌐ Welcome by arrangement; maximum 20; terms available on application.
⍁ Light refreshments only.
⌐ Pheasant, Casterton; Royal, Kirkby Lonsdale.

7 32 Castle Hawk

Chadwick Lane, Heywood Rd,
Castleton, OL11 3BY
☎(01706) 640841, Fax 860587, Pro
633855, Rest 710020,
Leave Rochdale on the Manchester
Road towards Castleton; turn right for
the course directly before Castleton
station.
Undulating parkland/meadowland
course.
Pro Frank Accleton; Founded 1965
Designed by T. Wilson
9-hole course: 3036 yards, S.S.S.
55; 18 hole course 5398 yards,
S.S.S. 68.
† Welcome.
⌑ WD £7; WE £9.
⌒Welcome by prior arrangement.
⦿ Restaurant and bar facilities.
⌐ Royal Toby.

7 33 Castletown Golf Links

Fort Island, Derbyhaven, Castletown,
Isle of Man, IM9 1UA
☎(01624) 822201, Fax 824633
1 mile from airport.
Links course.
Pro Murray Crowe; Founded 1892
Designed by MacKenzie Ross
18 holes, 6711 yards, S.S.S. 72
† Welcome; residents have priority
at WE.
⌑ WD £25; WE £30.
⌒Welcome by prior arrangement;
discounts for residents; catering
packages available; snooker, sauna,
indoor pool; from £25.
⦿ Full club and hotel catering
restaurant and bar facilities.
Practice ground.
⌐ On site hotel.

7 34 Childwall

Naylor's Rd, Liverpool, Merseyside,
L27 2YB
☎(0151) 487 0654, Fax 487 0882,
Pro 487 9871
5 miles from Liverpool, 2 miles from
M62 Junction 6.
Parkland course.
Pro Nigel Parr; Founded 1922
Designed by James Braid
18 holes, 6470 yards, S.S.S. 71
† Welcome WD except Tues
between 9.45 am and 2pm.
⌑ WD £26; WE £35.
⌒Welcome WD except Tues by
prior arrangement.
⦿ Bar and restaurant facilities
available.
Practice ground.
⌐ Village; Derby Lodge.

7 35 Chorley

Hall o' th' Hill, Heath Charnock, Lancs
PR6 9HX
☎(01257) 480263, Fax 480722, Pro
481245
Course is on the A673 100 yds south
of the A6 junction at Skew Bridge
traffic lights.
Heathland course.
Pro Gavin Mutch; Founded 1898
Designed by J.A. Steer
18 holes, 6307 yards, S.S.S. 70
† Welcome WD except Mon by prior
arrangement.
⌑ WD £27.
⌒Welcome Tues to Fri by prior
arrangement.
⦿ Full bar and restaurant facilities
available.
⌐ Yarrow Bridge; Parkville;
Hartwood Hall; Gladmar.

7 36 Clitheroe

Whalley Rd, Pendleton, Clitheroe,
Lancs BB7 1PP
☎(01200) 422618, Fax 422282, Pro
424242, Sec 422292
2 miles S of Clitheroe on the
Clitheroe-Whalley Road.
Parkland course.
Pro J E Twissell; Founded 1891/1932
Designed by James Braid
18 holes, 6326 yards, S.S.S. 71
† Welcome by prior arrangement.
⌑ WD £33; WE £39.
⌒Welcome by prior arrangement;
packages can be arranged for golf
and catering from £33.
⦿ Full clubhouse facilities.

7 37 Cockermouth

Embleton, Cockermouth, Cumbria,
CA13 9SG
☎(017687) 76223, Fax 76941, Sec
76941
3 miles E of Cockermouth.
Fell land course.
Founded 1896
Designed by James Braid
18 holes, 5496 yards, S.S.S. 67
† Welcome by prior arrangement.
⌑ Summer WD £15, WE £20; Winter
WD £10, WE £15.
⌒Welcome; terms on application;
from £15.
⦿ Clubhouse facilities.
⌐ Trout, Derwent Lodge, both
Cockermouth.

7 38 Colne

Law Farm, Skipton Old Rd, Colne,
Lancs BB8 7EB

☎(01282) 863391
From the end of M65 E travel one
mile to roundabout, then take first exit
left for course.
Moorland course with trees.
Founded 1901
Designed by Club members
9 holes, 5961 yards, S.S.S. 69
† Welcome except comp days; 2
balls only on Thurs.
⌑ WD £16; WE £20.
⌒Welcome WD; snooker; function
room; terms on application; from £16.
⦿ Full clubhouse facilities.
Practice ground, practice green,
putting green.
⌐ The Oaks, Burnley; The Old
Stone Trough, Colne.

7 39 Crompton & Royton

High Barn, Royton, Oldham, Lancs
OL2 6RW
☎(0161) 624 0986, Fax 624 0986,
Pro 624 2154, Bar/Rest 624 9867
Off A627 at Royton centre.
Moorland course.
Pro David Melling; Founded 1908
18 holes, 6214 yards, S.S.S. 70
† Welcome; restrictions at WE and
on Tues and Wed.
⌑ WD £24; WE £30; reductions for
guests of members.
⌒Welcome Mon, Thurs and Fri;
terms on application.
⦿ Clubhouse facilities.
⌐ Peraquito, Oldham.

7 40 Dalston Hall

Dalston, Nr Carlisle, Cumbria, CA5
7JX
☎(01228) 710165
From M6 Junction 42 to Dalston
village; course 0.5 miles on right.
Parkland course.
Founded 1990
Designed by David Pearson
9 holes, 5103 yards, S.S.S. 65
† Welcome; tee booking required at
WE and after 4pm WD.
⌑ WD 9 holes £5.50, 18 holes £9;
WE 9 holes £6.50 18 holes £12.
⌒Welcome by arrangement;
packages on application.
⦿ Bar and restaurant.
⌐ Dalston Hall caravan park on site;
Dalston Hall Hotel adjacent.

7 41 Darwen

Winter Hill, Darwen, Lancs BB3 0LB
☎(01254) 701287, Pro 776370, Sec
704367
1.5 miles from Darwen centre.

Moorland/parkland course.
Pro W Lennon; Founded 1893
18 holes, 5863 yards, S.S.S. 68
♣ Welcome.
⌐ Prices on application.
♪ Welcome by prior arrangement;
terms on application.
🍽 Clubhouse facilities.
⌐ Whitehall Hotel & CC.

7 42 Davyhulme Park
Gleneagles Rd, Davyhulme, Urmston,
Manchester, M41 8SA
☎ (0161) 748 2260, Pro 748 3931
Course is eight miles S of
Manchester adjacent to Trafford
Hospital in Davyhulme.
Parkland course.
Pro Dean Butler; Founded 1910
18 holes, 6237 yards, S.S.S. 70
♣ Welcome WD; guests of members
only at WE, by prior arrangement.
⌐ WD £24-£30.
♪ Welcome Mon, Tues, Thurs by
arrangement.
🍽 Full facilities.
Two practice putting greens, practice
area with green and bunker, two
indoor practice nets, tuition available,
group and individual; pro shop caters
for society prizes (giftware/glassware,
etc).
⌐ The Manor Hey Hotel.

7 43 Dean Wood
Lafford Lane, Up Holland,
Skelmersdale, Lancs WN8 0QZ
☎ (01695) 622219, Fax 622245, Pro
622980, Bar/Rest 622980
✉ helen@deanwoodgc.12.freeserve
1.5 miles from M6 Junction 26
following Up Holland signs.
Hilly parkland course.
Pro A B Coup; Founded 1922
Designed by James Braid
18 holes, 6137 yards, S.S.S. 70
♣ Welcome by prior arrangement.
⌐ WD £30; WE £35.
♪ Welcome Mon, Thurs and Fri;
terms on application.
🍽 Clubhouse facilities.
Practice area; practice nets.
⌐ Holland Hall; Travel Inn.

7 44 Deane
Broadford Rd, Bolton, Lancs BL3
4NS
☎ (01204) 61944, Fax 651808, Sec
651808
Course is one mile from Junction 5
on the M61.
Undulating parkland course.

Pro David Martindale; Founded 1908
18 holes, 5652 yards, S.S.S. 67
♣ Welcome by arrangement.
⌐ WD £20; WE £25.
♪ Welcome Tues, Thurs, Fri by prior
arrangement; full day package of golf
and catering; £31.
🍽 Clubhouse facilities.
⌐ Beaumont Hotel.

7 45 Denton
Manchester Rd, Denton, Manchester;
Gtr Manchester; M34 2NU
☎ (0161) 336 3218, Fax 336 4751,
Pro 336 2070
5 miles SE of Manchester off the
A57; also close to the M66 Denton
roundabout.
Parkland course.
Pro Michael Hollingworth; Founded
1909
18 holes, 6541 yards, S.S.S. 71
♣ Welcome WD; WE only with a
member.
⌐ WD £25; WE £30.
♪ Welcome Wed to Fri.
🍽 New clubhouse facilities.
⌐ Stable Gate Travelodge.

7 46 Douglas
Pulrose Rd, Douglas, Isle of Man,
IM2 1AE
☎ (01624) 675952, Pro 661558
1 mile from Douglas town centre,
clubhouse near Power Station cooling
tower.
Municipal parkland course.
Pro Kevin Parry; Founded 1927
Designed by Dr A MacKenzie
18 holes, 5922 yards, S.S.S. 68
♣ Welcome; advisable to phone in
advance.
⌐ WD £7; WE £10.
♪ Welcome by prior arrangement.
🍽 Full meals and bar snacks
throughout season.
⌐ Contact local tourist board.

7 47 Dudley
Allerton Road, Liverpool, Merseyside
L18 3JT
☎ (0151) 428 7490, Fax 428 7490,
Pro 428 1046, Bar/Rest 428 8510
From end of M62 S on to Queens
Drive, on to the ring road to Yewtree
Road, signposted on Allerton Road.
Parkland course; also 9 holes, 1841
yards, SSS 34.
Pro B Large; Founded 1923
18 holes, 5494 yards, S.S.S. 66
♣ Welcome.
⌐ Terms on application.

♪ Welcome WD and WE pm by
arrangement with the professional;
terms on application.
🍽 No facilities; light refreshments
available.
Beginners 9-hole course.
⌐ Redbourne; Grange.

7 48 Dunnerholme
Duddon Rd, Askam-in-Furness,
Cumbria, LA16 7AW
☎ (01229) 462675
Take A590 to Askam, turn left over
railway into Duddin Rd, continue
down towards the seashore over the
cattle grid.
Links course.
Founded 1905
10 holes, 6154 yards, S.S.S. 70
♣ Welcome except before 4.30pm
Sun.
⌐ Prices on application.
♪ Welcome by prior arrangement;
few restrictions.
🍽 Bar and catering facilities.
⌐ Railway; White Water; Clarence;
Wellington; Abbey House.

7 49 Dunscar
Longworth Lane; Bromley Cross,
Bolton, Lancs BL7 9QY
☎ (01204) 598228, Pro 592992, Sec
303321
Off A666 3 miles N of Bolton.
Moorland course.
Pro Gary Treadbold; Founded 1908
Designed by George Lowe
18 holes, 6085 yards, S.S.S. 69
♣ Welcome by prior arrangement.
⌐ WD £20; WE £30.
♪ Welcome by prior arrangement;
terms on application.
🍽 Clubhouse facilities.
⌐ Egerton House; Last Drop.

7 50 Duxbury Park
Duxbury Park; Chorley, Lancs PR7
4AS
☎ (01257) 265380, Fax 241378,
Rest 277049, Sec 241634
1.5 miles S of Chorley on A5106 from
A6.
Municipal parkland course.
Pro Simon Middleham; Founded 1970
18 holes, 6390 yards, S.S.S. 71
♣ Welcome; booking system.
⌐ Terms on application.
♪ Welcome WD by prior
arrangement.
🍽 Limited at club; facilities available
close by.
⌐ Hartwood Hall; Kilhey Court.

7 51 Eden ☏
Crosby-on-Eden, Carlisle, Cumbria
CA6 4RA
☎ (01228) 573003, Fax 818435,
Bar/Rest 573013
🖥 www.edengolf.co.uk
From M6 Junction 44 take A689 to
Low Crosby and Crosby-on-Eden.
Parkland course.
Pro Steve Harrison; Founded 1991
Designed by E. MacCauslin
18 holes, 6368 yards, S.S.S. 72
♦ Welcome; prior booking is
advisable.
˻ Winter WD £15; WE £20; Summer
WD £20; WE £25.
˘ Welcome by prior arrangement;
discounts are available for larger
groups; practice area; driving range;
catering packages; terms available on
application.
🍽 Full clubhouse bar and restaurant
facilities.
˻⌐ Wall Foot Hotel; Crosby Lodge;
Crown Hotel.

7 52 Ellesmere
Old Clough Lane, Worsley,
Manchester; M28 5HZ
☎ (0161) 790 8591, Fax 790 8591,
Sec 799 0554, Bar/Rest 790 2122
Off A580 adjacent to M62.
Parkland course.
Pro Terry Morley; Founded 1913
18 holes, 6247 yards, S.S.S. 70
♦ Welcome except on comp days
and Bank Holidays.
˻ WD £20; WE £25.
˘ Welcome Mon, Tues and Fri; Wed
also in winter; 27 holes of golf plus
catering; from £30.
🍽 Full clubhouse facilities available.
˻⌐ Novotel, Worsley.

7 53 Fairfield Golf & Sailing Club
"Boothdale", Booth Rd; Audenshaw;
Manchester; M34 5GA
☎ (0161) 370 2292, Sec 370 1279,
Fax 370 2292, Bar/Rest 370 1641
On A635 5 miles E of Manchester.
Parkland course around reservoir.
Pro S A Pownell; Founded 1892
18 holes, 5664 yards, S.S.S. 68
♦ Welcome WD; Thurs ladies day;
some weekend restrictions; telephone
in advance.
˻ WD £17; WE £23.
˘ Welcome by prior arrangement
with the secretary; terms on
application.
🍽 Full facilities by prior
arrangement.

˻⌐ Village, Hyde; York, Ashton-
under-Lyne.

7 54 Fairhaven
Lytham Hall Park, Ansdell, Lytham-St-
Annes, Lancs FY8 4JU
☎ (01253) 736976, Sec 736741, Bar
734787
Course is on the B5261 two miles
from Lytham.
Semi links; Open Championship
qualifying course.
Pro Brian Plucknett; Founded 1895
Designed by James Braid
18 holes, 6883 yards, S.S.S. 73
♦ Welcome by arrangement;
restrictions at WE.
˻ WD £33; WE £40.
˘ Welcome by arrangement.
🍽 Full facilities except Mon;
banqueting room.
Practice area.
˻⌐ Clifton Arms; Grand; Dalmeney;
Fearnlea.

7 55 Fishwick Hall
Glenluce Drive, Farringdon Park,
Preston, Lancs PR1 5TD
☎ (01772) 798300, Pro 795870, Fax
704600
From M6 Junction 31 take A59 past
Tickled Trout; Glenluce Drive is first
left at top of the hill.
Undulating meadowland/parkland
course.
Pro Mike Hadfield; Founded 1912
18 holes, 6045 yards, S.S.S. 69
♦ Welcome
˻ WD £26; WE £31.
˘ Welcome WD by prior
arrangement.
🍽 Full catering facilities.
˻⌐ Tickled Trout.

7 56 Fleetwood
Golf House, Princes Way; Fleetwood,
Lancs FY7 8AF
☎ (01253) 873114, Fax 773573, Pro
873661, Sec 773573, Rest 872727,
Bar 873114
Off A587 0.5 miles from Fleetwood.
Links course.
Pro S McLaughlin; Founded 1932
Designed by Edwin Steer
18 holes, 6557 yards, S.S.S. 71
♦ Welcome WD; some restrictions
WE.
˻ WD £30; WE £40.
˘ Welcome by prior arrangement;
discounts available for larger groups;
from £24.
🍽 Full clubhouse facilities.

˻⌐ North Euston; New Boston;
Briardene.

7 57 Flixton
Church Rd, Flixton, Urmston,
Manchester; M41 6EP
☎ (0161) 748 2116, Pro 746 7160,
Sec 748 3456, Rest 749 8834
Course is on the B5213 five miles
SW of Manchester.
Parkland course.
Pro Danny Proctor; Founded 1893
9 holes, 6410 yards, S.S.S. 71
♦ Welcome by prior arrangement;
WE only with a member.
˻ WD £16; WE £16.
˘ Welcome WD by prior
arrangement; packages available;
terms on application.
🍽 Clubhouse facilities.

7 58 Formby
Golf Rd, Formby, Liverpool, Lancs
L37 1LQ
☎ (01704) 872164, Fax 833028
🖥 www.golflinks.co.uk/formby
˻⌐ info@formbygolfclub.co.uk
1 mile W of A565 adjacent to
Freshfield station.
Championship links course.
Pro Gary Butler; Founded 1884
Designed by Willie Park
18 holes, 6993 yards, S.S.S. 72
♦ By prior arrangement only.
˻ WD terms on application.
˘ By prior arrangement only; terms
on application.
🍽 Full clubhouse facilities.
Practice area.
˻⌐ Tree Tops.

7 59 Formby Golf Centre
Moss Side, Formby, Lancs L37 0AF
☎ (01704) 875952
On the Formby by-pass.
Parkland course.
Pro Robert Dunbar; Founded 1985
18 holes, 1510 yards, S.S.S. 54
♦ Welcome; pay and play.
˻ WD £3; WE £3.
🍽 Coffee, tea and light
refreshments.
Practice range, 24 bays floodlit,
putting green and practice bunker.
˻⌐ Club can provide list of local
hotels.

7 60 Formby Hall
Southport Old Road; Formby, Lancs
L37 0AB
☎ (01704) 875699, Fax 832134

Formby

The South Lancashire coastline is littered with outstanding courses including two that are on the present Open Championship rota – Royal Lytham and Royal Birkdale – and three others that are regulars on the championships rota.

In many ways, while not having the tartan tint, and some of the more spectacular views of the Scottish west coast, the Lancashire coast, particularly in the south, can offer golf which is just as intriguing.

Formby is in that category. Golf started on the course back in 1884 and the club was so exclusive that the membership was limited to just 25 players.

For their membership fee of a guinea a year they had the privilege of playing the original nine holes of the course that were carved from the dunes of the coastline. That close proximity was to cause a problem later in the course's history.

There are some rare features on the course such as the numerous pine trees which are seldom found on such classic links courses. They offer a shield from the worst ravages of the wind and a solitude that is also unusual.

The course remains mainly unchanged over the 116 years since its birth apart from the addition of another nine holes on a sandy stretch of land between the railway and the beach.

Most of the better holes at Formby come early in the round although some will find that the first, like that at Prestwick and the closer Hillside, is a worrying challenge.

Just as with Prestwick and Hillside, the railway is the menace as the fairway hugs the track. Anything but total accuracy and steely nerves will lead to an early black mark on the card.

The second and third take the players out from the clubhouse and the third, in particular, is a very tough rugged par five which is beyond the reach of most players in two other than at the height of a long dry summer.

It is at this stage that the course begins its meander. There are no fewer than a dozen changes of direction during a round that takes the golfer towards the part of the course that nature altered.

In 1978 the seventh, eighth and ninth were all victims of coastal erosion and there are those who argue that the replacement holes are not of the same quality.

But while there have obviously been some significant changes, others will insist that it is just an indication of how big a part nature plays at Formby.

And there are some famous names who have discovered its delights over the years. In 1984 a young Spaniard called Jose-Maria Olazabal won a memorable amateur final against Scotland's Colin Montgomerie.

Further back in history Sam Snead also took a Formby trophy – the World Senior title in 1965 when he beat Charly Ward in a play-off in the final. — **CG**

Off Formby by-pass opposite Woodvale Aerodrome.
Parkland course with 11 lakes.
Pro David Lloyd; Founded 1996
Designed by PSA/Alex Higgins
18 holes, 6892 yards, S.S.S. 73
♣ Welcome WD; restrictions at WE.
⌐ WD £35.
⌐ Welcome by prior arrangement; corporate days available; from £40.
⌐ 5 bars and 2 restaurants open from 7.30am-11pm.
Practice range, 31 bays floodlit; academy.
⌐ Treetops; many B&Bs can be recommended.

7 61 Formby Ladies
Golf Rd, Formby, Liverpool, Merseyside L37 1YH
☎ (01704) 873493, Fax 073493, Pro 873090, Bar/Rest 874127
Course is off the A565 five miles S of Southport.
Seaside links course.
Pro Gary Butler; Founded 1896
18 holes, 5374 yards, S.S.S. 71
♣ Welcome by arrangement.
⌐ WD £30; WE £35.
⌐ Welcome by arrangement; full golf and catering available; terms on application.
⌐ Bar snacks available.
⌐ Treetops; selection in Southport.

7 62 Furness
Central Drive, Walney Island, Barrow-in-Furness, Cumbria LA14 3LN
☎ (01229) 471232
Off A590 to Walney Island; 0.5 miles after end of bridge.
Seaside links course.
Pro Alan Cook; Founded 1872
18 holes, 6363 yards, S.S.S. 71
♣ Welcome by prior arrangement; some restrictions apply on Wed and WE.
⌐ WD £17; WE £20.
⌐ Welcome by prior arrangement; must be members of recognised golf clubs; discounts for groups of more than 10; from £17.
⌐ Clubhouse facilities.
⌐ White House; Infield GH.

7 63 Gathurst
Miles Lane; Shevington, Wigan, Lancs WN6 8EW
☎ (01257) 255235, Pro 255882, Clubhouse 252861
1 miles S of M6 Junction 27.
Parkland course.

Pro Robert Eastwood; Founded 1913
Designed by N Pearson
18 holes, 6089 yards, S.S.S. 69
♣ Welcome WD except Wed; WE with member.
⌐ WD £24.
⌐ Welcome WD except Wed; 27 holes, full day's catering; from £33.
⌐ Bar and restaurant facilities available.
⌐ Almond Brook Moathouse (offers reductions for club visitors).

7 64 Ghyll
Ghyll Brow, Barnoldswick, Colne, Lancs BB8 6JQ
☎ (01282) 842466
A56 to Thornton-in-Craven turn left on B6252; 1 mile on left opposite Rolls Royce factory.
Scenic parkland course.
Founded 1907
9 holes, 5770 yards, S.S.S. 67
♣ Welcome except Tues am; Fri after 4.30 or Sun.
⌐ Prices on application.
⌐ Welcome as with visitors; reductions for parties of more than 8; from £14.
⌐ Bar catering by arrangement.
⌐ Stirk House, Gisburn; Tempest, Elslack.

7 65 Grange Fell
Fell Rd, Grange-over-Sands, Cumbria LA11 6HB
☎ (01539) 532536, Sec 532021
From Junction 36 of the M6 follow the signs to Barrow until Grange turn-off; through the town in direction of Cartmel Hillside.
Founded 1952
9 holes, 5312 yards, S.S.S. 66
♣ Welcome.
⌐ WD £12; WE £17.
⌐ None.
⌐ Netherwood; Grange, both in Grange-over-Sands; Aynsome, Cartmel.

7 66 Grange Park
Prescot Rd, St Helens, Merseyside WA10 3AD
☎ (01744) 26318, Fax 26318, Pro 28785, Bar/Rest 22980
M62 Junction 7.
Heathland course.
Pro Paul Roberts; Founded 1891
18 holes, 6422 yards, S.S.S. 71
♣ Welcome WD except Tues; restrictions at WE.
⌐ WD £25; WE £37.50.

⌐ Welcome WD except Tues; packages including all-day food and up to 36 holes of golf available; from £37.50.
⌐ Full clubhouse facilities.
⌐ Stakis; Haydock Thistle; Haydock Moathouse; St.Helens.

7 67 Grange-over-Sands
Meathop Rd, Grange-over-Sands, Cumbria LA11 6QX
☎ (015395) 33180, Fax 33754, Pro 35937, Sec 33754
Off A590 course is located just before entering town
Parkland course.
Pro S Sumner-Roberts; Founded 1919
18 holes, 5958 yards, S.S.S. 69
♣ Welcome with handicap certs.
⌐ WD £18; WE £24.
⌐ Welcome by appointment; packages available; from £18.
⌐ Full clubhouse facilities.
⌐ Grange Hotel; Graythwaite Manor; Clare House.

7 68 Great Harwood
Harwood Bar, Great Harwood, Lancs BB6 7TE
☎ (01254) 884391
Easy access from Clitheroe by-pass.
Parkland course.
Founded 1896
9 holes, 6422 yards, S.S.S. 71
♣ Welcome WD; restrictions at WE.
⌐ WD £16; WE £22.
⌐ Welcome by prior arrangement, catering packages can be arranged; snooker; prices on application.
⌐ Clubhouse facilities.
⌐ Dunkenhalgh, Clayton-le-Moors.

7 69 Great Lever & Farnworth
Off Plodder Lane, Great Lever, Bolton, BL4 0LQ
☎ (01204) 656137, Fax 652780, Pro 656650, Bar/Rest 656493
From M61 Junction 4 take Watergate Lane to Plodder Lane.
Parkland course.
Pro Tony Howarth; Founded 1917
18 holes, 6064 yards, S.S.S. 69
♣ Welcome WD with handicap certs; restrictions at WE.
⌐ WD £16.50; WE £27.
⌐ Welcome WD by arrangement; full day packages available for golf and catering except Mon; £29.50.
⌐ Full facilities except Mon.
Practice area.

7 70 Green Haworth

Green Haworth, Accrington, Lancs
BB5 3SL
☎ (01254) 237580, Sec 382510
From Accrington town centre take
main road to Blackburn; turn left on
Willows Lane; follow road for 2-3
miles; signposted after Red Lion
Hotel.
Moorland course.
Founded 1914
9 holes, 5556 yards, S.S.S. 68
✝ Welcome WD; some restrictions
apply on Wed; Sat by prior
arrangement.
☐ Prices on application.
🍽 Full facilities; restaurant can be
pre-booked.

7 71 Greenmount

Greenhalgh Fold Farm, Greenmount,
Bury, Lancs BL8 4LH
☎ (01204) 883712, Pro 888616
Leave M66 at Bury follow signs to
Ramsbottom until Holcombe village.
Undulating parkland course.
Pro Jason Seed; Founded 1920
9 holes, 4980 yards, S.S.S. 64
✝ Welcome WD; with member at
WE.
☐ Prices on application.
⚘ Welcome WD except Tues by
prior arrangement.
🍽 Full service except Mon; function
suite available.
⌐ Red Hall; Old Mill; Red Lion.

7 72 Haigh Hall

Haigh Country Park, Aspull, Wigan,
Lancs WN2 1PE
☎ (01942) 833337, Pro 831107
Take Junction 27 off the M6 and the
B5239 to Standish; corse is six miles
NE of Wigan.
Municipal parkland course..
Pro I Lee; Founded 1973
18 holes, 6423 yards, S.S.S. 71
✝ Welcome any time by
arrangement; telephone bookings via
professional.
☐ Prices on application.
⚘ Welcome with prior arrangement
with the professional.
🍽 Full restaurant and café service.
⌐ Brocket; Oak; Almond Brook;
Moathouse.

7 73 Harwood

Springfield, Roading Brook Rd;
Harwood, Bolton BL2 4JD
☎ (01204) 522878, Sec 524233, Pro
362834

4 miles NE of Bolton.
Parkland course extended to 18
holes.
Pro Mark Dance; Founded 1926/1998
Designed by Whole New Concept
18 holes, 5851 yards, S.S.S. 69
✝ Welcome WD; with member at
WE.
☐ WD/WE £20.
⚘ Welcome by arrangement; terms
on application.
🍽 Clubhouse facilities.
⌐ Last Drop, Bromley Cross.

7 74 Haydock Park

Golborne Park, Newton Lane,
Newton-le-Willows, Merseyside WA12
0HX
☎ (01925) 228525, Fax 228525, Bar
224389, Rest 291480, Pro 226944
1 mile E of the M6 on A580.
Parkland course.
Pro Peter Kenwright; Founded 1877
18 holes, 6043 yards, S.S.S. 69
✝ Welcome WD except Tues.
☐ WD £27.
⚘ Welcome WD except Mon and
Tues; from £40.
🍽 Full clubhouse facilities.
Practice area, putting green.
⌐ Kirkfield; Post House; Thistle.

7 75 Heaton Park

Middleton Rd, Prestwich, Manchester,
M25 2SW
☎ (0161) 654 9899, Fax 6532003
On A576 close to M62 Junction 19.
Undulating parkland course.
Pro Dennis Durnian/Karl Morris;
Founded 1912
Designed by J.H. Taylor
18 holes, 5815 yards, S.S.S. 68
✝ Welcome; advance booking at
WE.
☐ WD £10; WE £12.50; special
twilight rate.
⚘ Welcome by prior arrangement.
🍽 Bar and catering in café.
Driving range, par 3 course, golf
academy.
⌐ Heaton Park Hotel; Travelodge at
Birch Services.

7 76 Hesketh ☏

Cockle Dick's Lane, off Cambridge
Rd, Southport, Merseyside PR9 9QQ
☎ (01704) 536897, Fax 539250, Pro
530050, Bar 530226, Rest 531055
🖳 secretary@heskethgolf.freeserve.
co.uk
Course is on the A565 one mile N of
Southport.

Seaside links course with some
parkland.
Pro John Donoghue; Founded 1885
Designed by J.O.F. Morris
18 holes, 6522 yards, S.S.S. 72
✝ Welcome by prior arrangement.
☐ WD £38-£50; WE £50.
⚘ Welcome by prior arrangement;
inclusive packages for catering and
golf available for groups of 12 or
more; from £50.
🍽 Bar and dining facilities.
⌐ Prince of Wales; Scarisbrick.

7 77 The Heysham ☏

Trumacar Park, Middleton Rd,
Heysham, Lancs LA3 3JH
☎ (01524) 852000 Fax 853030, Sec
851011, Bar/Rest 859154
Off A683 5 miles from M6 Junction
34.
Parkland course with some wooded
areas.
Pro Ryan Done; Founded 1929
Designed by Alec Herd
18 holes, 6258 yards, S.S.S. 70
✝ Welcome with handicap certs.
☐ WD £20; WE £30.
⚘ Welcome by arrangement with
Sec; discounts for groups of 12 or
more; from £22.
🍽 Full clubhouse facilities.
⌐ Strathmore, Morecambe

7 78 Hillside Golf Club

Hastings Road, Hillside, Southport
PR8 2LU
☎ (01704) 567169, Fax 563192, Pro
568360, Bar/Rest 568682
Course is on the A565 three miles S
of Southport.
Outstanding championship links
course.
Pro B Seddon; Founded 1911/1923
Designed by Fred Hawtree
18 holes, 6850 yards, S.S.S. 74
✝ Restricted WD, no visitors Sat or
BH; contact Sec.
☐ WD £45-£60; Sun £60 (one round
only).
⚘ Restricted; contact Sec; special
approval needed for groups of more
than 24; terms on application.
🍽 Full bar and restaurant seating
100.
Practice ground.
⌐ Scarisbrick; Prince of Wales;
Metropole.

7 79 Hindley Hall

Hall Lane, Hindley, Wigan, Lancs
WN2 2SQ

☎ (01942) 255131, Fax 253871, Pro 255991
Off A6 from M61 Junction 6 then take Dicconson Lane; after 1 mile into Hall Lane; club just after lake.
Moorland course.
Pro Nigel Brazell; Founded 1895
18 holes, 5913 yards, S.S.S. 68
⚑ Welcome if member of a club; check with Sec in advance.
⚖ WD £20; WE £27.
⚘ Welcome by prior arrangement; terms on application.
🍴 Clubhouse facilities.
Practice area.
⌁ Georgian House.

7 80 Horwich
Victoria Rd, Horwich, Bolton, Lancs BL6 5PH
☎ (01204) 696980
Close to M61 Junction 6.
Parkland course.
Founded 1895
9 holes, 5404 yards, S.S.S. 67
⚑ Welcome with member or by prior arrangement with Sec.
⚖ Terms on application.
⚘ Welcome WD and occasional Sun by prior arrangement.
🍴 Full bar and catering facilities.
⌁ Swallowfield; Holiday Inn Express.

7 81 Houghwood
Billinge Hill, Crank Rd, Crank, St Helens, Merseyside WA11 8RL
☎ (01744) Office and Fax 894754, Pro 894444
From M6 Junction 26 follow signs to Billinge; course 1 mile from Billinge Hospital.
Parkland course with USGA standard greens.
Pro Paul Dickenson; Founded 1996
Designed by N Pearson
18 holes, 6202 yards, S.S.S. 70
⚑ Welcome.
⚖ WD £14.50; WE £17.50.
⚘ Welcome by arrangement; from £17-£30.
🍴 Bar and restaurant facilities.
Practice area; new snooker room; indoor golf simulator for all-year use.
⌁ Post House, Haydock; Stakis, St Helens.

7 82 Hurlston Hall ⚉
Hurlston Lane, Scarisbrick, Lancashire L40 8JD
☎ (01704) 840400, Fax 841404, Pro 841120

On A570 8 miles from M58 6 miles from Southport and 2 miles from Ormskirk.
Parkland course with two brooks.
Pro John Esclapez; Founded 1994
Designed by Donald Steel
18 holes, 6746 yards, S.S.S. 72
⚑ Welcome by prior arrangement; handicap certs may be required.
⚖ Summer WD £27.50, WE £33; Winter WD £21, WE £26.
⚘ Registered golf societies welcome by prior arrangement with club office; packages including 36 holes, catering and gourmet dinner can be arranged; satellite TV; golf academy; terms on application.
🍴 Full catering facilities available with 70-seat restaurant; balcony and patio.
Practice range, 10 bays floodlit, 2 teaching bays.
⌁ Beaufort Hotel; Scarisbrick; Prince of Wales.

7 83 Huyton & Prescot
Hurst Park, Huyton Lane; Huyton, Liverpool; Merseyside L36 1UA
☎ (0151) 489 3948, Pro 489 2022
Course is 10 miles from Liverpool just off the M57.
Parkland course.
Pro Gerry Bond; Founded 1905
18 holes, 5839 yards, S.S.S. 68
⚑ Welcome WD; WE with member.
⚖ WD £24.
⚘ By arrangement WD.
🍴 Full facilities.
Practice Bay.
⌁ Derby Lodge; Hillcrest; Bell Tower.

7 84 Ingol Golf & Squash ⚉ Club
Tanterton Hall Rd, Ingol, Preston, Lancs PR2 7BY
☎ (01772) 734556, Fax 729815, Pro 769646
🖥 www.golfers.net
📧 ingolgolfclub@btconnect.com
Leave M6 Junction 32 and turn towards Preston; follow signs for Ingol.
Parkland course.
Pro Mark Richardson; Founded 1980
Designed by Cotton, Pennink, Lawrie & Partners
18 holes, 6294 yards, S.S.S. 70
⚑ Welcome.
⚖ Winter WD £15; WE £20; Summer WD £20, WE £25.
⚘ Welcome by arrangement but not before 2.30pm at WE (summer);

maximum 16 at WE, no max on WD; from £18-£35.
🍴 Full facilities; bar and function rooms.
⌁ Marriott Broughton Park; Barton Grange.

7 85 Kendal ⚉
The Heights, Kendal, Cumbria LA9 4PQ
☎ (01539) 723499, Sec 733708, Fax 723499, Bar/Rest 736466
To Kendal on A6 signposted in town.
Moorland course; redesigned in late 1998.
Pro David Turner; Founded 1891
18 holes, 5800 yards, S.S.S. 68
⚑ Welcome any time except Sat competition days; by prior arrangement WE.
⚖ WD £20; WE £25.
⚘ Welcome anytime subject to availability and by prior arrangement; from £27.
🍴 Full facilities except Mon.
⌁ County; Woolpack.

7 86 Keswick
Threlkeld Hall, Threlkeld, Keswick, Cumbria, CA12 4SX
☎ (017687) 79010, Sec 79324, Clubhouse 79013
Course is off the A66 four miles E of Keswick.
Moorland/parkland course.
Pro Craig Hamilton; Founded 1975
Designed by Eric Brown
18 holes, 6225 yards, S.S.S. 72
⚑ Welcome, even most WE.
⚖ WD £17; WE £22.
⚘ Welcome by prior arrangement with Sec; some WE available; packages for 12 or more; prices on application.
🍴 Bar and dining facilities.
⌁ The Horse and Farrier; Lodore Swiss; Keswick; Borrowdale; Wordsworth; Middle Ruddings.

7 87 King Edward Bay (Howstrake)
Howstrake, Groudle Rd, Onchan, Isle of Man IM3 2JR
☎ (01624) 620430, Pro 672709
5 mins from Douglas.
Moorland/seaside course.
Pro Donald Jones; Founded 1893
Designed by T Morris
18 holes, 5485 yards, S.S.S. 65
⚑ Welcome Mon-Sat; after 10am Sun.
⚖ Prices on application.

☞ Welcome; minimum 10; catering packages available; from £10.
🍽 Full facilities available, restrictions on Mon.
☛ Imperial; Stakis, both Douglas.

7 88 Kirkby Lonsdale ☎
Scalebar Lane, Barbon, Carnforth, Cumbria, LA6 2LE
☎ (015242) 76365, Pro 76366, Fax 76365, Bar/Rest 76367
🖥 www.klgolf.dial.pipex.com
☞ kl.golf@dial.pipex.com
On A683 Sedbergh Road 3 miles from Kirkby Lonsdale.
Parkland course.
Pro Chris Barrett; Founded 1991
Designed by Bill Squires
18 holes, 6481 yards, S.S.S. 71
† Welcome.
_ WD £22; WE £28.
☞ Welcome by arrangement; terms on application.
🍽 Clubhouse facilities.
Practice ground
☛ Whoop Hall, Cowan Bridge; Pheasant, Casterton.

7 89 Knott End
Wyreside, Knott End on Sea, Poulton, Lancs, FY6 0AA
☎ (01253) 810576, Fax 813446
Take A585 Fleetwood road off M55 and then B2588 to Knott End.
Meadowland course.
Pro Paul Walker; Founded 1911
Designed by James Braid
18 holes, 5832 yards, S.S.S. 68
† Welcome WD not before 9.30am or between 12.30pm-1.30pm.
_ WD £21; WE £23.
☞ Welcome by prior arrangement; terms on application.
🍽 Full facilities.
☛ Bourne Arms; Springfield House Hotel.

7 90 Lancaster
Ashton Hall, Ashton-with-Stodday, Lancaster, Lancs, LA2 0AJ
☎ (01524) 751247, Fax 752742, Pro 751802, Bar/Rest 751105
On A588 2 miles S of Lancaster.
Parkland course.
Pro David Sutcliffe; Founded 1933
Designed by James Braid
18 holes, 6500 yards, S.S.S. 71
† Welcome by prior arrangement with handicap certs.
_ WD £32; WE £32.
☞ Welcome by prior arrangement on WD; handicap certs required; catering

and golf packages available; from £32.
🍽 Full clubhouse facilities.
☛ Dormy House with accommodation for 18 on site.

7 91 Lansil
Caton Rd, Lancaster, Lancs, LA1 3PE
☎ (01524) 39269
2 miles E of Lancaster on A683 close to Post House Hotel.
Parkland/meadowland course.
Founded 1947
9 holes, 5608 yards, S.S.S. 67
† Welcome but not before 1pm Sun.
_ WD £12; WE £12.
☞ Welcome WD by arrangement; catering packages organised with steward.
🍽 Meals and bar snacks available.
☛ Post House; Farmers Arms.

7 92 Lee Park
Childwall Valley Rd, Gateacre, Liverpool, Merseyside, L27 3YA
☎ (0151) 487 3882, Pro 488 0800, Bar/Rest 487 9861
On B5171 off A562 next to Lee Manor High School.
Parkland course.
Founded 1950
Designed by Frank Pennink
18 holes, 6095 yards, S.S.S. 69
† Welcome.
_ Prices on application.
☞ Welcome Mon, Thurs and Fri by prior arrangement with Sec; terms on application.
🍽 Bar snacks and meals.
☛ Gateacre Hall.

7 93 Leigh
Kenyon Hall, Broseley Lane, Culcheth, Warrington, Cheshire, WA3 4BG
☎ (01925) 763130, Fax 765097, Pro 762013, Sec 762943
Off B5217 in Culcheth village.
Parkland course.
Pro Andrew Baguley; Founded 1906
Designed by James Braid
18 holes, 5884 yards, SS.S. 68
† Welcome with handicap certs or letter of introduction.
_ WD £23; WE £33.
☞ Welcome Mon, except BH, and Tues; catering packages available; snooker room; from £23.
🍽 Full clubhouse facilities.
Practice range: 3 practice areas; 2 putting greens.

☛ Greyhound, Leigh; Thistle, Haydock.

7 94 Leyland
Wigan Rd, Leyland, Lancs, PR5 2UD
☎ (01772) 436457, Pro 423425
On A49 0.25 miles from M6 Junction 28.
Meadowland course.
Pro Colin Burgess; Founded 1923
18 holes, 6123 yards, S.S.S. 69
† Welcome WD; WE only with a member.
_ WD £25; WE £25.
☞ Welcome by prior arrangement with Sec; packages available on request.
🍽 Full facilities.
Practice area adjacent to first tee.
☛ Jarvis.

7 95 Liverpool Municipal (Kirkby)
Ingoe Lane, Kirkby, Liverpool, Merseyside, L32 4SS
☎ (0151) 546 5435
M57 Junction 6, 300 yards on right of B5192.
Municipal meadowland course.
Pro David Weston; Founded 1966
18 holes, 6706 yards, S.S.S. 72
† Welcome.
_ WD £6.90; WE £7.90.
☞ Welcome every day; tee booking required 1 week in advance.
🍽 Bar and cafeteria.
Practice ground.
☛ Golden Eagle.

7 96 Lobden
Lobden Moor, Whitworth, Lancashire, OL12 8XJ
☎ (01706) 343228, Fax 643241, Sec 643241
Take A671 from Rochdale to Whitworth.
Moorland course.
Founded 1888
9 holes, 5697 yards, S.S.S. 68
† Welcome except Sat.
_ WD £10; WE £15.
☞ Welcome by prior arrangement; terms on application.
🍽 By arrangement with steward.

7 97 Longridge
Fell Barn, Jeffery Hill, Longridge, Preston, Lancs, PR3 2TU
☎ (01772) 783291, Fax 783022
From M6 Junction 31a follow signs to Longridge.

Moorland course with panoramic views.
Pro Stephen Taylor; Founded 1877
18 holes, 5969 yards, S.S.S. 69
† Welcome.
_ WD £15; WE £25.
⌕ Welcome by written prior arrangement with Sec; summer and winter packages available; from £15-30.
◉ Full facilities available except Mon.
↴ Shireburn Arms; Gibbon Bridge; Black Moss GH.

7 98 Lowes Park
Hill Top, Lowes Rd, Bury, Lancs, BL9 6SU
☎ (0161) 764 1231, Fax 763 9503, Sec 763 9503, Bar/Rest 764 1231
On A56 1 mile N of Bury; turn at Bury General Hospital into Lowes Road.
Moorland course.
Founded 1930
9 holes, 6014 yards, S.S.S. 69
† Welcome by prior arrangement.
_ WD £15; WE £25.
⌕ Welcome by prior arrangement; package deals available; ladies only on Wed; terms available on application.
◉ Full clubhouse facilities except Mon.
Practice range, small practice area.
↴ Red Hall.

7 99 Lytham Green Drive
Ballam Rd, Lytham, Lancs, FY8 4LE
☎ (01253) 737390, Fax 731350, Pro 737379, Bar/Rest 736087
1 mile from Lytham centre.
Parkland course.
Pro Andrew Lancaster; Founded 1904
Designed by A Herd
18 holes, 6163 yards, S.S.S. 69
† Welcome WD by prior arrangement.
_ WD £25-£35.
⌕ Welcome WD except Wed; coffee on arrival, soup and sandwiches, 3-course meal, 27 holes of golf; £34-£38.
◉ Full clubhouse facilities available.
↴ Clifton Arms, Lytham; Fernlea, St Anne's.

7 100 Manchester
Hopwood Cottage, Rochdale Rd, Middleton, Manchester, M24 2QP
☎ (0161) 643 2638, Fax 643 2472,

Sec 643 3202, Bar 643 2718, Rest 655 3073
From A627 (M) take the A664 for Middleton.
Parkland/moorland course.
Pro Brian Connor; Founded 1882
Designed by H.S. Colt
18 holes, 6519 yards, S.S.S. 72
† Welcome by arrangement.
_ WD £30; WE £45.
⌕ Welcome by prior arrangement; packages of golf and catering available on application; £40-£47.
◉ Full clubhouse facilities.
Practice area and driving range available to members, guests and visitors only.
↴ Midway; Norton Grange, Royal Toby.

7 101 Manor (Bolton)
Moors Lane, Kearsley, Bolton, Lancs, BL4 8SF
☎ (01204) 701027, Fax 796914
↗ manorsports@netscapeonline.co.uk
1 mile from M62 Junction 17.
Parkland course.
Founded 1995
18 holes, 4914 yards, S.S.S. 66
† Welcome; pay and play.
_ WD £5; WE £8.50.
⌕ Welcome by arrangement.
◉ Bar and restaurant; function suites.
Driving range next door.
↴ Clifton Park Country House.

7 102 Marriott Worsley Park ☎
Worsley Park, Worsley, Manchester, M28 2QT
☎ (0161) 975 2043
Course is just off Junction 13 of the M60.
Set in 200 acres of mature parkland.
Founded May 1999
Designed by European Golf Design
18 holes, 6611 yards, S.S.S. 72
† Welcome WD and restricted at WE.
_ £40 WD; £50 WE.
⌕ Welcome Mon - Fri.
◉ Restaurant and café bar.
↴ Marriott Worsley Park

7 103 Marsden Park
Downhouse Rd, Nelson, Lancs, BB9 8DG
☎ (01282) 661912, Bar/Rest 661915
From M65 Junction 13 and take B5446 on to Leeds Road and right at second roundabout.

Parkland course.
Pro Martin Ross; Founded 1968/1976
Designed by C.K. Cotton & Partners
18 holes, 5681 yards, S.S.S. 68, par 70.
† Pay and play.
_ WD Adults £8.50, OAPs £4.50, juniors £2; WE peak (7.30am-2pm) £11.50; off-peak (2pm-dusk) £9.50, special 9-hole WE ticket (twilight hours only) £6.50.
⌕ Welcome by prior arrangement; golf and catering packages available on application; from £13.
◉ Catering facilities.
↴ The Oaks, Burnley; Great Marsden, Nelson.

7 104 Maryport
Bank End, Maryport, Cumbria, CA15 6PA
☎ (01900) 812605, Sec 815626
N of Maryport turn left off A596 on to the B5300 (Silloth Road).
Seaside links course.
Founded 1905
18 holes, 6088 yards, S.S.S. 69
† Welcome.
_ WD £15; WE £20.
⌕ Welcome by prior arrangement; discounts available for groups of nine or more.
◉ Full clubhouse facilities.
↴ Ellenbank; Skimberness Hotel.

7 105 Morecambe
Marine Rd East, Bare, Morecambe, Lancs, LA4 6AJ
☎ (01524) 412841, Fax 412841, Pro 415596,
Sec 412841, Bar/Rest 418050
On road to Morecambe from A6.
Parkland/links course; superb views over Morcambe Bay; no par fives.
Pro Simon Fletcher; Founded 1922
Designed by Dr Clegg
18 holes, 5770 yards, S.S.S. 68
† Welcome by arrangement.
_ Prices on application.
⌕ Welcome by prior arrangement; terms on application.
◉ Full clubhouse facilities.
↴ The Strathmore; The Elm.

7 106 Mossack Hall
Liverpool Rd, Bickerstaffe, Lancs, L39 0EE
☎ (01695) 421717, Fax 424961, Pro 424969
From M58 Junction 3 take first left to Stanley Gate Pub; turn left and follow road for 2 miles; club on right.

Meadowland course.
Pro Liam Kelly; Founded 1996
Designed by Steve Marnoch
18 holes, 6375 yards, S.S.S. 70
♪ Welcome by prior arrangement
with professional.
L WD £25; WE £30.
⌁ Welcome by prior arrangement
with golf course manager.
🍴 Full catering facilities including
restaurant; catering for private
functions.

7 107 **Mount Murray** ♛
Hotel and CC
Santon, Isle of Man, IM4 2HT
☎ (01624) 661111
On the Castletown road 2 miles from
Douglas.
Parkland course.
Pro Andrew Dyson; Founded 1994
18 holes, 6664 yards, S.S.S. 73
♪ Welcome.
L WD £18; WE £24.
⌁ Welcome by prior arrangement;
hotel's facilities (gym, etc) tennis
courts and squash courts available
for use.
🍴 Bistro and restaurant facilities
available.
Practice range, 20 bays floodlit,
putting green.
⌁ On site Mount Murray Hotel (golf
packages available).

7 108 **Mytton Fold** ♛
Langho, Lancashire BB6 8AB
☎ (01254) 245392, Fax 248119
9 miles N of Blackburn off A59.
18 holes, 6217 yards, S.S.S. 70
♪ Welcome by prior arrangement.
L WD £14; WE £16.
⌁ Welcome by prior arrangement.
🍴 Full hotel facilities.
⌁ Mytton Fold.

7 109 **Nelson**
King's Causeway, Brierfield, Nelson,
Lancs, BB9 0EU
☎ (01282) 614583, Fax 606226, Pro
617000, Sec 611834
On B6248 off A682 at Brierfield from
M65 Junction 12.
Moorland course.
Pro Nigel Sumner; Founded 1902
Designed by Dr A MacKenzie
18 holes, 5977 yards, S.S.S. 69
♪ Welcome.
L WD £25; WE £30.
⌁ Welcome by prior arrangement;
catering and golf packages available;
from £25.

🍴 Full clubhouse facilities available.
⌁ Higher Trapp Country House.

7 110 **North Manchester**
Rhodes House, Manchester Old Rd,
Middleton, Manchester, M24 4PE
☎ (0161) 643 2941, Pro 643 7094,
Sec 643 9033
5 miles N of Manchester off M62
Junction 18.
Moorland/parkland course.
Founded 1894
18 holes, 6498 yards, S.S.S. 72
♪ Welcome WD; by arrangement
WE.
L WD £25; WE £30.
⌁ Welcome WD except Thurs; terms
on application.
🍴 Full catering and bar service.
⌁ Bower, Oldham; Birch, Heywood.

7 111 **Oldham**
Lees New Rd, Oldham, Lancs, OL4
5PN
☎ (0161) 624 4986, Pro 626 8346
Off A669 turning right at Lees.
Moorland/parkland course.
Pro Jason Peel; Founded 1891
18 holes, 5122 yards, S.S.S. 65
♪ Welcome by prior arrangement.
L WD £16; WE £22.
⌁ Welcome by arrangement;
packages for all day golf and
catering; from £22.
🍴 Full facilities.
⌁ Many hotels in 2-mile radius.

7 112 **Ormskirk**
Cranes Lane, Lathom, Ormskirk,
Lancs, L40 5UJ
☎ (01695) 572112, Fax 572227, Pro
572074, Sec 572227, Bar 572112,
Rest 5722781
2 miles E of Ormskirk.
Parkland course.
Pro Jack Hammond; Founded 1899
18 holes, 6480 yards, S.S.S. 71
♪ Welcome.
L WD £35; WE & Wed £40.
⌁ Welcome by prior arrangement;
terms on application.
🍴 Full facilities.
⌁ Briars Hall.

7 113 **Peel**
Rheast Lane, Peel, Isle of Man IM5
1BG
☎ (01624) 843456, Bar/Rest
842227, Pro 844232, Fax 843456
On A1 signposted on outskirts of Peel
Moorland.

Pro Murray Crowe; Founded 1895
Designed by A. Herd
18 holes, 5850 yards, S.S.S. 69
♪ Welcome WD; WE by
arrangement.
L Prices on application.
⌁ Welcome on application to Sec;
packages on request.
🍴 Meals and snacks to order; bar.
⌁ Stakis; Ascot.

7 114 **Pennington**
Pennington Country Park, St Helen,
Leigh, Lancs, WN7 3PA
☎ (01942) 682852, Pro 682852, Fax
682852
Off A572 to S of Leigh.
Parkland course with ponds and
streams.
Pro Tim Kershaw; Founded 1975.
9 holes, 5790 yards, S.S.S. 68
♪ Welcome.
L WD £3.25; WE £4.30.
⌁ Welcome WD by prior
arrangement.
🍴 Snack bar.
⌁ Thistle, Haydock.

7 115 **Penrith**
Salkeld Rd, Penrith, Cumbria, CA11
8SG
☎ (01768) 891919, Fax 891919,
Bar/Rest 865429
From Junction 41 on the M6 follow
the signs for Penrith and turn left
when entering town.
Parkland course.
Pro Garry Key; Founded 1890
18 holes, 6047 yards, S.S.S. 69
♪ Welcome by arrangement.
L WD £20; WE £25.
⌁ Welcome by prior arrangement
with Sec; golf and catering packages
available; terms on application.
🍴 Clubhouse facilities.
Practice ground.
⌁ George, Penrith.

7 116 **Penwortham**
Blundell Lane, Penwortham, Preston,
Lancs, PR1 0AX
☎ (01772) 744630, Fax 744630, Pro
742345, Rest/Bar 743207
Off A59 1.5 miles W of Preston.
Parkland course.
Founded 1908
18 holes, 6056 yards, S.S.S. 69
♪ Welcome WD except Tues and
WE.
L WD £24.
⌁ Welcome WD except Tues by
prior arrangement; tee available

Royal Lytham

Royal Lytham is always going to have a place in the hearts of English golf fans. After all, it was here that Tony Jacklin won the Open Championship in 1969. When it returned in 1974 the young Seve Ballesteros delighted the crowds with his mixture of talent and bravery.

He was to return 12 years later to complete the second of his fantastic triumphs. The Lancashire course held the Open again in 1996, when the American Tom Lehmann was a very popular winner.

Lytham would never argue that it was the most elegant of Open venues but it has always provided a variety of history, including the 1926 championship when the great Bobby Jones took the first of his three titles.

Hidden away alongside the railway line and in the midst of houses, it has a unique start for an Open course. It is the only one commencing with a par three but if the opening holds few terrors the closing holes have claimed some famous victims.

In 1963 Jack Nicklaus stood on the 17th tee knowing that a couple of pars would clinch victory. Instead he found himself in the rough on 17 and then in one of the seven bunkers that guard 18. The Open disappeared.

Drama followed Gary Player at 18 as well when, cushioned by a six-shot lead, he endured a foray into the rough and then ended up in front of the clubhouse windows before playing a bold left-handed shot to clinch the most remarkable of victories.

Playing the 18th depends almost entirely on the positioning of the tee shot. The fairway is littered with treacherous bunkers ready to snap up any wayward drive, particularly to the left.

Of the short holes, the ninth, tucked into the corner of the course under the church, is as tricky as they get with eight bunkers, some extremely deep, guarding the hole. But while the course offers the chance to follow in the footsteps of the greats the one place no one wants to revisit on any round is the patch of ground that Ballesteros found in his first victorious visit.

In 1979 he stood on the 15th tee and lashed his drive to the right. It came to rest in the temporary car park. Unlike mere mortal golfers who would never have recovered, Ballesteros cleared the three giant bunkers and collected a birdie three. A legend was born on a course that brings tradition rather than beauty to the Open circuit.

If the weather is kind Royal Lytham, like so many of the links courses, holds few worries and it was in these conditions on parched fairways that Lehmann collected his trophy in 1996.

With its dormy house and the giant Victorian clubhouse it has a feel of history as well. En route try to persuade Royal Liverpool at Hoylake, which last held the Open Championship before the days of corporate villages and massive television coverage.

Like Royal Lytham, Royal Liverpool, where Roberto di Vicenzo won on his last visit in 1967, has the same feel of history lurking in every corner of the golf club. Great courses in a county with a great sporting tradition. — **CG**

between 10am-12.30pm and after 2pm; golf and catering packages available; from £36.
○ Full clubhouse facilities.
⌐ Carleton; Forte Posthouse, both Preston.

7 117 **Pike Fold**
Hills Lane, Unsworth, Bury, Manchester, BL9 8QP
☎(0161) 766 3561
4 miles N of Manchester off Rochdale road.
Undulating meadowland course.
Pro Mike Vipond; Founded 1909
9 holes, 6312 yards, S.S.S. 72
♦ Welcome Mon-Sat; members only Sun.
_ Mon-Sat £20.
⌐ Welcome by appointment; catering packages by arrangement with manager.
○ Full facilities by prior arrangement.

7 118 **Pleasington**
Pleasington, Blackburn, Lancs, BB2 5JF
☎(01254) 202177, Fax 201028, Pro 201630, Rest 207346
3 miles SW of Blackburn; from A674 turn north on to road signposted Pleasington Station.
Undulating heathland/parkland course.
Pro G J Furey; Founded 1891
18 holes, 6423 yards, S.S.S. 71
♦ Welcome by prior arrangement Mon, Wed, Fri and WE.
_ WD £35; WE £40.
⌐ Welcome Mon, Wed, Fri; some discounts and packages available; £40.
○ Full clubhouse facilities.
⌐ The Millstone Hotel, Mellor, Blackburn.

7 119 **Port St Mary Golf Pavilion**
Port St Mary, Isle of Man, IM9 5EJ
☎(01624) 834932
Just outside Port St Mary; course signposted.
Public seaside links course.
Pro Murray Crowe; Founded 1936
Designed by George Duncan
9 holes, 5418 yards, S.S.S. 66
♦ Welcome but not before 10.30am at WE.
_ WD £11; WE £14.
⌐ Welcome by arrangement; discounts for 10 or more players.

○ Bar, café and restaurant.
⌐ Port Erin; Bay View.

7 120 **Poulton-le-Fylde**
Myrtle Farm, Breck Rd, Poulton-le-Fylde, Lancs, FY6 7HJ
☎(01253) 892444, Fax 892444, Sec 893150
0.5 miles N of Poulton town centre.
Municipal meadowland course.
Pro Lewis Ware; Founded 1974
9 holes, 6056 yards, S.S.S. 70
♦ Welcome.
_ WD £11; WE £13.
⌐ Welcome by prior arrangement; packages available.
○ Bar and catering facilities.
Practice range, indoor two-bay range; tuition available.
⌐ Singleton Lodge.

7 121 **Preston**
Fulwood Hall Lane, Fulwood, Preston, Lancs, PR2 8DD
☎(01772) 700011, Fax 794234, Pro 700022, Bar/Rest 700436
From M6 Junction 32 turn towards Preston and after 1.5 miles into Watling St Rd and then into Fulwood Hall Road.
Parkland course.
Pro Andrew Greenbank; Founded 1892
Designed by James Braid
18 holes, 6312 yards, S.S.S. 71
♦ Welcome WD; some restrictions Tues but only as a guest of member at WE.
_ WD £27-£32.
⌐ Welcome WD except Tues; golf and catering packages can be arranged; parties of more than 48 by special arrangement only; from £27.
○ Bar and restaurant facilities.
⌐ Broughton Marriott; Barton Grange.

7 122 **Prestwich**
Hilton Lane, Prestwich, Manchester, M25 9XB
☎(0161) 773 2544, Fax 773 1404, Pro 773 1404, Bar/Rest 798 8401
On A6044 1 mile from junction with A56.
Parkland course.
Pro Simon Wakefield; Founded 1908
18 holes, 4806 yards, S.S.S. 63
♦ Welcome WD if carrying handicap certs.
_ WD £16.
⌐ Welcome on WD by prior arrangement with professional; 27-

hole golf and catering packages available; from £27.50.
○ Full clubhouse facilities.

7 123 **Ramsey**
Brookfield, Ramsey, Isle of Man, IM8 2AH
☎(01624) 812244, Fax 815833, Pro 814736, Bar/Rest 813365
12 miles N of Douglas; 5 mins from town centre.
Parkland course.
Pro Calum Wilson; Founded 1890
Designed by James Braid
18 holes, 5960 yards, S.S.S. 69
♦ Welcome; please telephone in advance.
_ WD £18; WE £22.
⌐ Welcome by arrangement.
○ Lunches and full facilities available.
⌐ Grand Island.

7 124 **Reach**
De Vere Hotels, East Park Drive, Blackpool, FY3 8LL
☎(01253) 838866, Fax 798800, Pro 766156
From M55 Junction 4, follow signs for Blackpool on A583; at fourth set of lights turn right into South Park Drive; follow signs for zoo.
Parkland course with links characteristics.
Pro Dominik Naughton; Founded 1993
Designed by Peter Alliss and Clive Clark
18 holes, 6406 yards, S.S.S. 72
♦ Welcome; after 10am Fri.
_ WD £35; WE £40.
⌐ Welcome all year round by prior arrangement; packages available; leisure club; swimming pool; tennis; squash courts.
○ Full facilities; spikes bar; 3 restaurants.
Practice range, 18 bays floodlit.
⌐ De Vere Blackpool on site.

7 125 **Regent Park (Bolton)**
Links Rd, Lostock, Bolton, Lancs, BL6 4AF
☎(01204) 844170, Pro 842336, Sec 495421
1 mile from M61 Junction 6.
Municipal parkland course.
Pro Bob Longworth
Founded 1932
18 holes, 6130 yards, S.S.S. 69
♦ Welcome; restrictions on Sat.
_ WD £9; WE £10.50.

METROPOLE HOTEL, SOUTHPORT

Portland Street, Southport PR8 1LL   Tel: (01704) 536836   Fax: (01704) 549041
Web: *www.btinternet.com/~metropole.southport*   Email: *metropole.southport@btinternet.com*
RAC/AA 2-star hotel. Centrally situated and close to Royal Birkdale and 5 other championship courses.
Fully licensed with late bar facilities for residents. Full sized snooker table. Proprietors will assist with tee reservations.

Welcome WD by arrangement.
Bar, restaurant, take away.
Forte Crest; Swallowfield.

7 126 Rishton
Eachill Links, Hawthorne Drive,
Blackburn, Lancs, BB1 4HG
(01254) 884442
3 miles E of Blackburn signposted
from church in village.
Meadowland course.
Founded 1928
0 holes, 6097 yards, S.S.S. 69
Welcome WD; WE with a member.
WD £12.
Welcome with prior arrangement
with Sec.
Bar and catering available except
Mon.
Dunkenhalgh.

7 127 Rochdale
Edenfield Rd, Bagslate, Rochdale,
Lancs, OL11 5YR
(01706) 646024, Fax 643818, Pro
522104, Sec 643818
On A680 3 miles from M62 Junction
20.
Parkland course.
Pro Andrew Laverty; Founded 1888
18 holes, 6050 yards, S.S.S. 69
Welcome by arrangement.
WD £23; WE £27.
Welcome by prior arrangement;
terms on application.
Full clubhouse facilities.

7 128 Rossendale
Ewood Lane Head, Haslingden,
Rossendale, Lancs, BB4 6LH
(01706) 831339, Fax 228669, Pro
213616
16 miles from Manchester off the
M66.
Meadowland course.
Pro Stephen Nicholls; Founded 1903
18 holes, 6293 yards, S.S.S. 70
Welcome except Sat.
WD £23; members only Sat; Sun
£28.
Welcome by prior arrangement.
Full facilities; banqueting
facilities; brand new clubhouse.

Red Hall; Sykeside, both
Haslingden.

7 129 Rowany
Rowany Drive, Port Erin, Isle of Man,
IM9 6I N
(01624) 834072, Bar/Rest 834108
4 miles W of Castletown; located at
end of Port Erin promenade.
Parkland/seaside course.
Founded 1895
10 holes, 5803 yards, S.S.S. 68
Welcome.
WD £12; WE £16.
Welcome by arrangement with the
manager.
Full bar, snacks and restaurant
facilities.
Outdoor practice area; pitch and putt
course.
Cherry Orchard; The Ocean
Castle.

7 130 Royal Birkdale
Waterloo Rd, Birkdale, Southport,
Merseyside, PR8 2LX
(01704) 567920, Fax 562327
www.royalbirkdale.com
royalbirkdalegc@dial.pipex.com
Course is 1.5 miles south of
Southport on the A565.
Open Championship venue 1998;
links course.
Pro Richard Bradbeer; Founded 1889
Designed by Hawtree & Taylor
18 holes, 6690 yards, S.S.S. 73
Handicap certs required; not Sat;
limited Fri and Sun am.
WD £98; WE £125.
Welcome Mon, Wed and Thurs by
prior arrangement, from £98.
Full catering facilities.
Local tourist board can provide
detailed list.

7 131 Royal Lytham & St
Annes
Links Gate, St Annes on Sea, Lancs
FY8 3LQ
(01253) 724206, Fax 780946
1 mile from centre of Lytham.
Links course; Open Championship
venue 2001.

Pro Eddie Birchenough; Founded
1886
18 holes, 6685 yards, S.S.S. 74
Welcome Mon and Thurs only;
WE dormy house guests only.
WD £90 (including lunch).
Welcome by prior arrangement.
Full catering and bar facilities
available.
Dormy house on site: 9 single, 4
twin-bedded rooms (no en suite
facilities) .

7 132 Saddleworth
Mountain Ash, Ladcastle Rd,
Uppermill, Oldham, Lancs, OL3 6LT
(01457) 873653, Bar/Rest
872059, Pro 810412
5 miles from Oldham, signposted off
the A670 Ashton-Huddersfield Road
at the bend where road crosses
railway.
Scenic moorland course.
Pro Robert Johnson; Founded 1904
Designed by Dr A. MacKenzie
18 holes, 5976 yards, S.S.S. 69
Welcome.
WD £23; WE £30.
Welcome WD by prior
arrangement; from £35.
Full facilities.
La Pergola.

7 133 St Annes Old Links
Highbury Rd, St Annes, Lytham St
Annes, Lancs, FY8 2LD
(01253) 723597, Fax 781506,
Course is off the A584 coast road at
St Anne's.
Championship course.
Pro G Hardman; Founded 1901
Designed by James Herd
18 holes, 6616 yards, S.S.S. 72
Welcome except before 9.30am or
between 12 noon-1.30pm WD.
WD £38; WE £48.
Welcome by prior arrangement
WD only; packages available; menus
on request; separate changing
rooms; snooker; from £38.
Full clubhouse dining and bar
facilities.
Practice ground.
Contact local tourist board.

7 134 St Bees

Station Rd, St Bees, Cumbria, CA27 0EJ
☎(01946) 824300
Course is on the B5345 four miles S of Whitehaven
Seaside course.
Founded 1942
9 holes, 5122 yards, S.S.S. 65
♦ Welcome except on competition days.
⌐ Prices on application.
⌐Welcome by arrangement with the school.
⦿ No facilities.
⌐ Queens.

7 135 Seascale

The Banks, Seascale, Cumbria, CA20 1QL
☎(01946) 728202, Fax 728202, Pro 721779
Course is off the A595 at NW edge of Seascale.
Links course.
Pro Craig Hamilton; Founded 1893
Designed by Willie Campbell
18 holes, 6416 yards, S.S.S. 71
♦ Welcome by prior arrangement.
⌐ WD £21-£26; WE £26-£31.
⌐Welcome by prior arrangement; discounts of 10 per cent for 12 or more and 15 per cent for 20 or more; from £20.
⦿ Clubhouse facilities.
Practice area for members and green fee paying visitors only.
⌐ Lutwidge Arms, Holmnook; Calder House, Seascale; Horse & Groom, Gosforth.

7 136 Sedbergh

Catholes-Abbot Holme, Dent Rd, Sedbergh, Cumbria, LA10 5SS
☎(01539) 621551, Sec 729289, Bar/Rest 621551
1 mile from Sedbergh on road to Dent and 5 miles E of M6 Junction 37.
New parkland course in Yorkshire Dales National Park.
Founded 1896/1993
Designed by W.G. Squires
9 holes, 5624 yards, S.S.S. 68
♦ Welcome; by prior arrangement at WE.
⌐ WD £10; WE £12.
⌐Welcome by prior arrangement; various packages can be arranged; from £20.
⦿ Full catering facilities.
⌐ George & Dragon, Dent; Bull, Sedbergh; Sec can assist with stay and play breaks.

7 137 Shaw Hill Hotel ☏ Golf & Country Club

Preston Rd, Whittle-le-Woods, Nr Chorley, Lancs, PR6 7PP
☎(01257) 269221, Fax 261223, Pro 279222, Sec 791164, Conference and Banqueting 226825
Course is one mile north of M61 Junction 8 and two miles from M6 Junction 28.
Parkland course with water hazards.
Pro David Clarke; Founded 1925
Designed by T. McCauley
18 holes, 6239 yards, S.S.S. 73
♦ Welcome WD only with handicap certs; residents of hotel only at WE.
⌐ Prices available on application; subject to weather condition and time of year.
⌐Welcome WD with handicap certs; golf and catering packages can be arranged; terms available on application.
⦿ Bar, restaurant and à la carte menus available.
⌐ Club has 30 rooms; leisure centre with extensive facilities (available for guests of hotel).

7 138 Sherdley Park

Sherdley Park, St Helens, Merseyside, WA9 5DE
☎(01744) 813149/817967, Clubhouse 815518, Fax 817967
2 miles S of St Helens on Warrington Road.
Public undulating parkland course.
Founded 1973
Designed by P.R. Parkinson
18 holes, 5974 yards, S.S.S. 69
♦ Welcome.
⌐ Prices on application; concessions for pensioners and juniors.
⌐Welcome by prior arrangement; terms on application.
⦿ Bar and cafeteria.
Practice range, 12 bays floodlit.
⌐ Stakis, St Helens.

7 139 Silecroft

Silecroft, Cumbria, LA18 4NX
☎(01229) 77434, Clubhouse 774250
On A5093 three miles north of Millom through Silecroft village towards shore.
Seaside course.
Founded 1903
9 holes, 5877 yards, S.S.S. 68
♦ Welcome WD; restricted access WE and BH.
⌐ WD £15; WE £15.
⌐Welcome by arrangement.

⦿ Limited; Miners Arms provides food.
⌐ Bankfield; Miners Arms.

7 140 Silloth on Solway ☏

Silloth on Solway, Carlisle, Cumbria, CA5 4BL
☎(016973) 31304, Fax 31782, Pro 32404, Bar/Rest 32442
🖱www.sillothgolfclub.co.uk
⌐silloth.g.c@btinternet.com
From Wigton follow B5302 to Silloth.
Championship links course; 1997 British women's strokeplay.
Pro Johnathan Graham; Founded 1892
Designed by Willie Park Jnr
18 holes, 6614 yards, S.S.S. 72
♦ Welcome by prior arrangement.
⌐ WD £25 per day; WE £32 per round.
⌐Welcome by prior arrangement; full day packages of golf and catering available; Mon catering only by prior arrangement; from £35.
⦿ Full bar and catering facilities, except Mon.
⌐ Wheyrigg Hall, Wigton; Golf Hotel; Queens; Skinburness, all Silloth-on-Solway.

7 141 Silverdale

Redbridge Lane, Silverdale, Carnforth, Lancs, LA5 0SP
☎(01524) 701300, Sec 702074, Bar/Rest 701300, Fax 702074
3 miles NW of Carnforth by Silverdale station.
Heathland/parkland course.
Founded 1906
12 holes, 5559 yards, S.S.S. 67
♦ Welcome by prior arrangement; some Sun summer restrictions.
⌐ WD £15; WE £18.
⌐Welcome by prior arrangement with Sec, WD and WE packages available; from £22.
⦿ Clubhouse facilities.
⌐ Silverdale Hotel.

7 142 Solway Village Golf Centre

Solway Village, Silloth-on-Solway, Cumbria, CA5 4QQ
☎(016973) 31236, Fax 32553
Easy to locate in village of Silloth.
Scenic parkland course.
Founded 1988
9 holes, 4001 yards, par 3
♦ Welcome.
⌐ WD and WE £5 for daily pass.
⌐Welcome by arrangement.

🍽️ Bar and restaurant.
🛏️ Self-catering log cabins and caravans.

7 143 Southport & Ainsdale
Bradshaws Lane, Ainsdale,
Southport, Merseyside, PR8 3LG
☎(01704) 578000, Fax 570896, Pro
577316, Bar/Rest 579422
Course is on the A565 three miles
south of Southport, 0.5 miles from
Ainsdale station.
Links course.
Pro Mike Houghton; Founded 1907
Designed by James Braid
18 holes, 6583 yards, S.S.S. 73
🏌️ Welcome WD between 10am-12
noon and 2.30pm-4.00pm.
⚐ WD £45-£50; WE £50 for a round.
🕐 Welcome WD; terms on
application; from £45.
🍽️ Full clubhouse facilities.
🛏️ Scarisbrick, Southport.

7 144 Southport Municipal
Park Rd West, Southport,
Merseyside, PR9 0JS
☎(01704) 530133, Pro 535286
N end of Promenade.
Public seaside course.
Pro Bill Fletcher; Founded 1914
18 holes, 6139 yards, S.S.S. 69
🏌️ Welcome.
⚐ WD £6; WE £8.
🕐 Welcome by prior booking at least
six days in advance.
🍽️ Meals and bar facilities.
🛏️ Scarisbrick; Prince of Wales.

7 145 Southport Old Links
Moss Lane, Southport, Merseyside,
PR9 7QS
☎(01704) 228207, Fax 505353
Off Manchester Rd into Roe Lane
and then into Moss Lane; close to
town centre.
Seaside course.
Founded 1920
9 holes, 6244 yards, S.S.S. 71
🏌️ Welcome except Wed and
restrictions at WE.
⚐ WD £18; WE £25.
🕐 Welcome by prior arrangement if
party is more than 12; terms on
application.
🍽️ Full facilities except Mon.
🛏️ Richmond House.

7 146 Springfield Park
Springfield Park, Bolton Rd,
Rochdale, Lancs, OL11 4RE

☎(01706) 656401, Pro 649801
3 miles from M62.
Parkland course.
Pro David Mills; Founded 1927
18 holes, 5237 yards, S.S.S. 66
🏌️ Welcome.
⚐ WD £6; WE £10.
🕐 Welcome by prior arrangement
with the Professional; terms on
application.
🍽️ None.
🛏️ Midway, Rochdale.

7 147 Stand   ♋
The Dales, Ashbourne Grove,
Whitefield, Manchester, M45 7NL
☎(0161) 766 2214, Sec 766 3197,
Bar 766 2388, Fax 796 3234
1 mile N of M62 Junction 17.
Undulating parkland course.
Pro Mark Dance; Founded 1904
Designed by Alex Herd
18 holes, 6426 yards, S.S.S. 71
🏌️ Welcome WD; restricted WE.
⚐ WD £25; WE £30.
🕐 Welcome Wed and Fri; winter
packages.
🍽️ Full facilities except Mon.
🛏️ Hawthorn; Travel Inn.

7 148 Standish Court   ♋ Golf Club
Rectory Lane, Standish, Wigan, WN6
0XD
☎(01257) 425777, Fax 425888
5 mins off M6 Junction 27 following
signs for Standish village.
Parkland course.
Pro Tim Kershaw; Founded 1995
Designed by Patrick Dawson
18 holes, 5750 yards, S.S.S. 66
🏌️ Welcome by arrangement.
⚐ WD £11; WE £16.
🕐 Welcome by prior arrangement;
full day packages available from
£17.50-£36.
🍽️ Full clubhouse facilities
available.
🛏️ Kilbey Court; Wigan Moat House

7 149 Stonyholme Municipal
St Aidans Rd, Carlisle, Cumbria, CA1
1LF
☎(01228) 625511, Bar/Rest 625512,
Fax 625511
Course is off the A69 one mile W of
M6 Junction 43.
Flat meadowland course.
Pro Stephen Ling; Founded 1974
Designed by Frank Pennink
18 holes, 5787 yards, S.S.S. 69
🏌️ Welcome.

⚐ WD £7.80; WE £9.50, day tickets
available all week.
🕐 Welcome by prior arrangement.
🍽️ Clubhouse facilities.
Practice area; practice range, 16
bays floodlit and 9-hole short course
adjacent.
🛏️ Post House; numerous B & B's in
the area.

7 150 Stonyhurst Park
c/o The Bayley Arms, Hurst Green,
Blackburn, Lancs, BB7 9QB
☎(01254) 826470, Fax 826797
On B6243 Clitheroe-Longridge road.
Parkland course.
Founded 1979
9 holes, 5529 yards, S.S.S. 66
🏌️ Welcome except WE; contact The
Bayley Arms.
⚐ WD £15.
🕐 Limited; by prior arrangement
only.
🍽️ None.
🛏️ The Bayley Arms.

7 151 Swinton Park
East Lancashire Rd, Swinton,
Manchester, M27 5LX
☎(0161) 794 0861, Fax 281 0698,
Pro 793 8077
📧 golfer@swintongolf.freeserve.co.uk
On A580 5 miles from Manchester on
Liverpool road.
Parkland course.
Pro Jim Wilson; Founded 1926
Designed by Braid & Taylor
18 holes, 6726 yards, S.S.S. 72
🏌️ Welcome WD except Thurs.
⚐ WD £25.
🕐 Welcome by arrangement Mon,
Tues, Wed and Fri.
🍽️ Bar and restaurant facilities;
function and conference rooms.
🛏️ Large selection in Manchester
city centre.

7 152 Towneley
Towneley Park, Todmorden Rd,
Burnley, Lancs BB11 3ED
☎(01282) 438473 (Towneley),
421517 (Brunshaw), Sec 414555, Bar
451636
From M65 follow signs to Towneley
Hall.
Parkland course.
Founded 1932
Designed by Burnley Council
The Towneley course: 18 holes, 5811
yards, S.S.S. 69; The Brunshaw
course: 9 holes, par 3.
🏌️ Welcome.

WD 9 holes £4.80, 18 holes £8.50; WE 9 holes £5.50, 18 holes £9.75.
🏌 Welcome by prior arrangement; catering can be arranged with steward; from £8.
🍴 Bar and restaurant facilities available.
Small practice ground, two tennis courts, two bowling greens, 18-hole pitch and putt.
🛏 Alexander.

7 153 Tunshill
Kiln Lane, Milnrow; Lancs, OL16 3TS
☎ (01706) 759320
From M62 Junction 21 take road to Milnrow and follow Kiln Lane out of the town to narrow lane for clubhouse.
Moorland course.
Founded 1943
9 holes, 5743 yards, S.S.S. 68
🏌 Welcome WD except Tues evening; by prior arrangement WE.
Terms on application.
🏌 Welcome WD by prior arrangement; terms available on application.
🍴 Restaurant and bar facilities.
🛏 John Milne, Milnrow.

7 154 Turton
Wood End Farm, Chapeltown Rd, Bromley Cross, Bolton, Lancs BL7 9QH
☎ (01204) 852235
4 miles NW of Bolton near Last Drop Hotel.
Moorland course.
Founded 1908
Designed by James Braid
18 holes, 6159 yards, S.S.S. 68
🏌 Welcome except Wed 11.30am-3pm and WE only by prior arrangement.
WD £18; WE £22.
🏌 Welcome by arrangement.
🍴 Full catering facilities.
🛏 Last Drop; Egerton House.

7 155 Ulverston
The Clubhouse, Bardsea Park, Ulverston, Cumbria, LA12 9QJ
☎ (01229) 582824, Pro 582806, Fax 580911
📧 ulverstongolf@bardseapark. freeserve.co.uk
From M6 Junction 36 follow signs for Barrow on A590 and take A5087 to Bardsea.
Parkland course.

Pro M R Smith; Founded 1895/1909
Designed by A Herd
18 holes, 6201 yards, S.S.S. 71
🏌 Welcome by prior arrangement.
WD £25; WE £30.
🏌 Welcome by prior arrangement; packages for golf and catering can be arranged; terms on application.
🍴 Full clubhouse catering and bar facilities.
Practice chipping green, practice grounds adjacent to course.
🛏 The Fisherman's Arms; The Swan; Lonsdale House.

7 156 Walmersley
Garretts Close, Walmersley, Bury, Lancs, BL9 6TE
☎ (0161) 764 7770, Fax 01706 827618, Pro 763 9050, Bar 764 1429
Off A56 3 miles N of Bury.
Moorland course.
Pro P Thorpe; Founded 1906
18 holes, 5341 yards, S.S.S. 67
🏌 Welcome.
WD £20; WE £20.
🏌 Welcome Wed-Fri; 27 holes golf, coffee, light lunch and 4-course meal; from £26.
🍴 Full clubhouse facilities.
🛏 Red Hall, Bury.

7 157 Werneth (Oldham)
Green Lane, Garden Suburb, Oldham, Lancs, OL8 3AZ
☎ (0161) 628 7136, Fax 628 7136, Bar 624 1190
📧 roypenney@wernethgc.freeserve. co.uk
Course is five miles from Manchester, take the A62 to Hollinwood and then the A6104.
Moorland course.
Pro Roy Penney; Founded 1908
18 holes, 5364 yards, S.S.S. 66
🏌 Welcome WD; guests of members only at WE.
WD £18.50 .
🏌 Welcome Mon, Wed and Fri by arrangement.
🍴 Lunch and meals served except Mon.
🛏 Periquito; Smokeys, both Oldham.

7 158 West Derby
Yew Tree Lane, Liverpool, Merseyside, L12 9HQ
☎ (0151) 228 1540, Fax 259 0505, Pro 220 5478, Sec 254 1034
📧 pmilne@westderbygc.freeserve. co.uk

Follow signs for Knotty Ash to roundabout and then into Blackmoor Drive, right into Yew Tree Lane.
Flat parkland course with trees.
Pro Andrew Witherup; Founded 1896
18 holes, 6277 yards, S.S.S. 70
🏌 Welcome WD; except Tues.
WD £26; WE £36.
🏌 Welcome WD except Tues; full golf and catering packages available; from £26.
🍴 Bar and restaurant.
🛏 Derby Lodge, Huyton; Bell Tower, Knowsley.

7 159 West Lancashire
Hall Rd West, Blundellsands, Liverpool, L23 8SZ
☎ (0151) 924 1076, Fax 931 4448, Pro 924 5662, Bar 924 4115
🌐 www.merseyworld.com/wlgc/
📧 golf@wlgc.lancastrian.co.uk
M57 to Aintree then A5036 to Seaforth and A565 to Crosby; signposted close to Hall Rd station.
Links course.
Pro Tim Hastings; Founded 1873
Designed by C.K. Cotton/ D Steel
18 holes, 6767 yards, S.S.S. 73
🏌 Welcome by arrangement.
WD (not Tues) £45-£55; WE £60 per round.
🏌 Welcome WD except Tues; packages available; green fees for groups of 12 or more include soup and sandwich lunch and 3-course meal; £45-£55.
🍴 Full clubhouse facilities.
Practice ground; tuition available; equipment for hire.
🛏 Blundellsands Hotel.

7 160 Westhoughton
Long Island, Westhoughton, Bolton, Lancs, BL5 2BR
☎ (01942) 811085, Fax 608958, Pro 840545, Sec 608958
Course is off School Lane, adjacent to the Parish Church in Westhoughton.
Parkland course.
Pro Jason Seed; Founded 1929
9 holes, 5772 yards, S.S.S. 68
🏌 Welcome.
WD £16; WE £16; £8 with a member.
🏌 Welcome; packages of 18 holes, available with catering; from £25.
🍴 Full clubhouse facilities available.
Practice area.
🛏 Large selection available in Bolton.

7 161 Westhoughton Golf Centre

Wigan Rd, Westhoughton, Nr Bolton, Lancs, BL8 2BX
☎ (01942) 813195
M61 Junction 5; travel through Westhoughton towards Hindley.
Parkland course; home to Hart Common GC.
Pro Gareth Benson
Founded 1996
18 holes, 6101 yards, S.S.S. 73
† Welcome.
Prices on application.
☞ Welcome by prior arrangement; terms on application.
🍽 Clubhouse facilities.
Practice range, 26 bays floodlit covered; also 9-hole par 3 course under construction.

7 162 Whalley

Portfield Lane, Whalley, Blackburn, Lancs, BB7 9DR
☎ (01254) 822236, Pro 824766
Course is off the A671 one mile SE of Whalley following the signs for Sabden.
Parkland course.
Pro H Smith; Founded 1912
9 holes, 6258 yards, S.S.S. 70
† Welcome except Thurs pm and Sat in summer.
WD £16; WE £20.
☞ Welcome by arrangement with secretary; catering and packages on application; from £15.
🍽 Clubhouse facilities.
☞ Higher Trapp, Simonstone; Old Stone Manor, Mytton.

7 163 Whitefield ℭ

81/83 Higher Lane, Whitefield, Manchester, M45 7EZ
☎ (0161) 351 2700, Fax 351 2712, Pro 351 2709, Bar 351 2710
On A665 near Whitefield exit from M62.
Parkland course.
Pro Paul Reeves; Founded 1932
10 holes, 6045 yards, O.S.S. 69
† Welcome by arrangement.
WD £25; WE £35.
☞ Welcome WD except Tues; also some Sat afternoons; groups of less than 12 players £25; 12 or more players £23; groups of 60 or more players should contact the club for rates.
🍽 Full clubhouse facilities.
Practice putting green and practice nets; snooker table.
☞ The Village; Travel Lodge.

7 164 Whittaker

Whittaker Lane, Littleborough, Lancs, OL15 0LH
☎ (01706) 378310
On Blackstone Edge Old Road, 1.5 miles out of Littleborough; turn right at High Peak Hamlet.
Moorland course.
Pro P Lunt; Founded 1906
Designed by N P Stott
9 holes, 5606 yards, S.S.S. 67
† Welcome except Tues pm and Sun.
Prices on application.
☞ Welcome by prior arrangement with Sec; limited catering on application; prices on application.
🍽 Bar can be arranged.

7 165 Wigan

Arley Hall, Arley lane, Haigh, Wigan, Lancs, WN1 2UH
☎ (01257) 421360
From M6 Junction 27 through Standish on B5239; turn left at Canal Bridge lights and course is opposite Crawford Arms.
Parkland course.
Founded 1898
9 holes, 6036 yards, S.S.S. 69; to be extended to an 18-hole course in 2000.
† Welcome any day except Tues, Wed and Sat.
Prices on application.
☞ Welcome by prior arrangement; special packages available; terms on application.
🍽 Full catering.
☞ Bellingham; Brockett Arms; Kilhey Court.

7 166 William Wroe

Pennybridge Lane, Flixton, Manchester, M41 5DX
☎ (0161) 748 8680
Leave M63 Junction 4 and take B5124 then B5158 to Flixton; 12 miles SW of Manchester.
Municipal parkland course.
Pro Scott Partington; Founded 1974.
18 holes, 4264 yards, S.S.S. 62
† Welcome: bookings taken 7 days in advance.
WD £7.90; WE £10.50.
☞ Welcome with booking.
🍽 Clubhouse facilities.
☞ Manor Hey.

7 167 Wilpshire

72 Whalley Rd, Wilpshire, Blackburn, Lancs, BB1 9LF
☎ (01254) 248260, Pro 249558, Fax 246745
Course is on the A666 four miles N of Blackburn.
Moorland course.
Pro Walter Slaven; Founded 1890
18 holes, 5802 yards, S.S.S. 69
† Welcome WD; by arrangement at WE.
WD £25.50; WE £30.50.
☞ Welcome WD by prior appointment.
🍽 Full facilities.
☞ County; Swallow, Salmesbury.

7 168 Windermere

Cleabarrow, Windermere, Cumbria, LA23 3NB
☎ (01539) 43123, Pro 43550, Sec 43123, Bar/Rest 43123
On B5284 1.5 miles from Bowness towards Kendal.
Undulating parkland course.
Pro Stephen Rook; Founded 1891
Designed by George Low
18 holes, 5132 yards, S.S.S. 65
† Welcome by arrangement.
WD £24; WE £28.
☞ Welcome by arrangement; packages can be arranged; from £25.
🍽 Bar and snacks.
☞ The Wild Boar Hotel (golf discounts available).

7 169 Woolton

Doe Park, Speke Rd, Woolton, Liverpool, L25 7TZ
☎ (0151) 486 2298, Fax 486 1664, Pro 486 1298, Bar/Rest 486 1601
6 miles from city centre on road to Liverpool Airport.
Parkland course.
Pro Alan Gibson; Founded 1901
18 holes, 5724 yards, S.S.S. 68
† Welcome.
WD £20; WE £30.
☞ Welcome; packages can be arranged; terms available on application.
🍽 Clubhouse facilities.
☞ Redbourne.

7 170 Workington

Branthwaite Rd, Workington, Cumbria, CA14 4SS
☎ (01900) 603460, Fax 607122, Pro 67828
Off A595 2 miles SE of Workington.
Undulating meadowland.
Pro Adrian Drabble; Founded 1893
Designed by James Braid
18 holes, 6247 yards, S.S.S. 70

♦ Welcome if carrying handicap certs.
⌙ Summer WD £20, WE and BH £25; Winter WD £15, WE and BH £20.
☞ Welcome by prior arrangement with Pro.
🍽 Full facilities, 7 days a week if prior booked.
Practice ground.

◞ Washington Central; Westlands (adjacent to course).

---

7 171 **Worsley**
Stableford Ave, Monton, Eccles, Manchester, M30 8AP
☎(0161) 789 4202, Fax 789 3200
Follow signs to Monton Green, Eccles from M62 then to Stableford Ave.

Parkland course.
Pro C Cousins; Founded 1894
Designed by James Braid
18 holes, 6252 yards, S.S.S. 70
♦ Welcome by prior arrangement.
⌙ WD £20-£25; WE £30.
☞ Welcome Wed and Thurs; tees available 10.15am and 1.35pm.
🍽 Clubhouse facilities.
◞ Wendover, Monton.

THE NORTH EAST

One of the highlights of covering golf on the European Tour used to be the visit each August to Fulford for the Benson and Hedges International. Situated just outside York, here was a venue with greens so good the professionals must have felt like taking off their shoes before treading on them, for fear of causing any damage.

Sadly, Fulford has not hosted the tournament for some years now, and I am not alone in thinking the B&H has lost something too. Out of sight, however, should not mean out of mind: this is an essential visit for any keen golfer.

Indeed, Yorkshire and the North East have quite a few courses in this category and topping them all is glorious Ganton, the venue for this year's Curtis Cup. The setting, on the edge of the Vale of Pickering and the Yorkshire Moors, is so tranquil that every player will leave his troubles behind for three and a half hours or so.

Ganton played host to the Ryder Cup in 1949, a fine match but not so famous as the one held down the road at Lindrick in 1957 where Great Britain and Ireland managed a rare victory.

At 6,600 yards Lindrick will not trouble a player in terms of length but woe betide the one who tries to bludgeon his way to a good score. A strategist's delight therefore, and the clubhouse, behind the 18th green, is a beauty.

Yorkshire's reputation as a haven for those who love inland golf is cemented by the cluster of courses to be found near the fair city of Leeds. Sand Moor, Moortown, and Alwoodley are a distinguished trio indeed, while in West Yorkshire, Ilkley and Otley are both delightful.

I first stumbled across Bamburgh Castle by accident, for it rarely gets highlighted in many golfing guide books. Quite why this is so is probably because it only measures 5,621 yards, but only a fool would let the lack of length put him off. Here lies the perfect holiday course, with the castle itself sitting majestically in the distance. On to the golf; a par of 68 but it is a mighty fine player who can match it.

Staying in Northumberland, and Slaley Hall is earning a good reputation for itself, albeit in a different price range to the exquisite Bamburgh. The region's best-known course, however, is another James Braid classic, Berwick-upon-Tweed, a course that divides neatly into two, the best and most enchanting being the few holes that nestle between the dunes and open up views of the hallowed, ancient ground of Holy Island. For those who prefer hidden gems, meanwhile, Dunstanburgh is another 'castle' course worth investigating.

On to Durham, where two courses stand head and shoulders above all others: Seaton Carew, a fine links course just outside Hartlepool that was revised by Alister Mackenzie in the 1920s, and Brancepeth Castle, designed by the master Harry Colt, and of which Leonard Crawley was inordinately fond. — **DL**

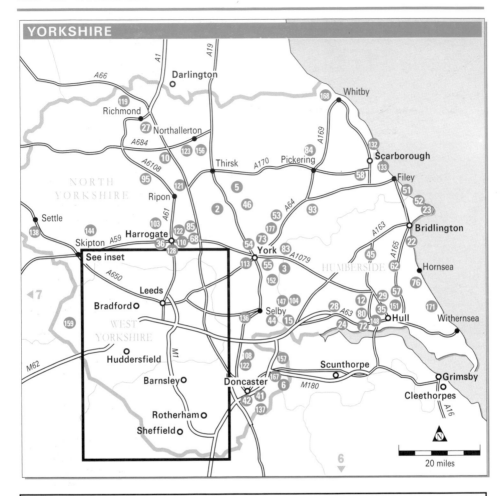

YORKSHIRE

KEY

1	Abbeydale	22	Bridlington	45	Driffield
2	Aldwark Manor	23	Bridlington Links	46	Easingwold
3	Allerthorpe Park	24	Brough	47	East Bierley
4	Alwoodley	25	Calverley	48	Elland
5	Ampleforth College	26	Castle Fields	49	Fardew
6	Austerfield Park Country Club	27	Catterick	50	Ferrybridge 'C'
7	Baildon	28	Cave Castle Hotel	51	Filey
8	Barnsley	29	Cherry Burton	52	Flamborough Head
9	Beauchief	30	City of Wakefield	53	Forest of Galtres
10	Bedale	31	Clayton	54	Forest Park
11	Ben Rhydding	32	Cleckheaton & District	55	Fulford
12	Beverley & East Riding	33	Cocksford	56	Fulneck
13	Bingley St Ives	34	Concord Park	57	Ganstead Park
14	Birley Wood	35	Cottingham	58	Ganton
15	Boothferry Park	36	Crimple Valley	59	Garforth
16	Bracken Ghyll	37	Crookhill Park	60	Gott's Park
17	Bradford	38	Crosland Heath	61	Grange Park
18	Bradford Moor	39	Crows Nest Park	62	Hainsworth Park
19	Bradley Park	40	Dewsbury District	63	Halifax
20	Brandon	41	Doncaster	64	Halifax Bradley Hall
21	Branshaw	42	Doncaster Town Moor	65	Hallamshire
		43	Dore & Totley	66	Hallowes
		44	Drax	67	Hanging Heaton

68	Harrogate	91	Longley Park
69	Headingley	92	Low Laithes
70	Headley	93	Malton & Norton
71	Hebden Bridge	94	Marsden
72	Hessle	95	Masham
73	Heworth	96	Meltham
74	Hickleton	97	Mid Yorkshire
75	Hillsborough	98	Middleton Park
76	Hornsea	99	Moor Allerton
77	Horsforth	100	Moortown
78	Howley Hall	101	Normanton
79	Huddersfield (Fixby)	102	Northcliffe
80	Hull	103	Oakdale
81	Ilkley	104	The Oaks
82	Keighley	105	Otley
83	Kilnwick Percy	106	Oulton Park
84	Kirkbymoorside	107	Outlane
85	Knaresborough	108	Owston Park
86	Leeds (Cobble Hall)	109	Painthorpe House Golf & Country Club
87	Leeds Golf Centre	110	Pannal
88	Lees Hall	111	Phoenix
89	Lightcliffe	112	Phoenix Park
90	Lofthouse Hill		

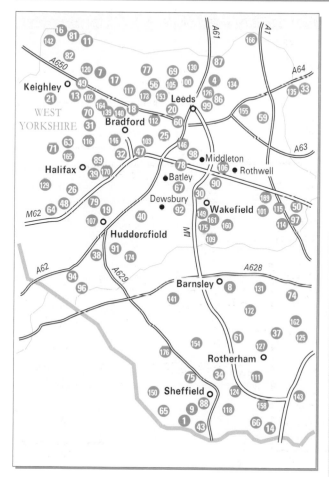

8A 1 **Abbeydale** ☎
Twentywell Lane, Dore, Sheffield, S
Yorks, S17 4QA
☎ (0114) 2360763, Pro 2365633
Course is off the A621 five miles S of
Sheffield.
Parkland course.
Founded 1895
Designed by Nathan Perry
18 holes, 6407 yards, S.S.S. 71
♦ Welcome by arrangement but not
before 9.30am or between 12 noon
and 1.30pm.
⌷ WD £35; WE £40.
⌁ Welcome by prior arrangement;
terms on application.
⏴ By prior arrangement; bar and
restaurant facilities.
⌐ Beauchief; Sheffield Moat House.

8A 2 **Aldwark Manor**
Aldwark, Alne, York, YO61 1UF
☎ (01347) 838353, Fax 830007,
Bar/Rest 838353
Course is off the A1 five miles SE of
Boroughbridge; 13 miles NW of York
off the A19.
Easy walking parkland course built
around the River Ure.
Founded 1978
18 holes 6171 yards, S.S.S. 70
♦ Welcome WD; some WE
restrictions.
⌷ WD £25; WE £30.
⌁ Welcome WD; some WE
restrictions; various packages
available from £27.50.
⏴ Full catering in the Victorian
Manor House built in 1856; minimum
12; private dining rooms available; full
restaurant and bar facilities.
⌐ Aldwark Manor (28 bedrooms).

8A 3 **Allerthorpe Park**
Allerthorpe Park, Allerthorpe, York,
Yorks, YO4 RL
☎ (01759) 306686, Fax 304308.
Off the A1079 York-Hull road 2 miles
W of Pocklington.
Parkland course.
Founded 1994
Designed by J G Hatcliffe & Partners
13 holes, 5514 yards, S.S.S. 67
♦ Welcome.
⌷ WD £16; WE £16.
⌁ Welcome by prior arrangement;
terms on application.
⏴ Clubhouse facilities.

8A 4 **Alwoodley**
Wigton Lane, Alwoodley, Leeds, W
Yorks, LS17 8SA

113	Pike Hills	136	Selby	158	Tinsley Park
114	Pontefract & District	137	Serlby Park	159	Todmorden
115	Pontefract Park	138	Settle	160	Wakefield
116	Queensbury	139	The Shay Grange Golf	161	Waterton Park
117	Rawdon		Centre	162	Wath
118	Renishaw Park	140	Shipley	163	West Bowling
119	Richmond	141	Silkstone	164	West Bradford
120	Riddlesden	142	Silsden	165	West End (Halifax)
121	Ripon City	143	Sitwell Park	166	Wetherby
122	Robin Hood	144	Skipton	167	Wheatley
123	Romanby	145	South Bradford	168	Whitby
124	Rother Valley	146	South Leeds	169	Whitwood
125	Rotherham	147	Spaldington	170	Willow Valley Golf &
126	Roundhay	148	Springhead Park		Country Club
127	Roundwood	149	Springmill	171	Withernsea
128	Rudding Park	150	Stocksbridge & District	172	Wombwell (Hillies)
129	Ryburn	151	Sutton Park	173	Woodhall Hills
130	Sand Moor	152	Swallow Hall	174	Woodsome Hall
131	Sandhill	153	Swingtime (Leeds)	175	Woolley Park
132	Scarborough North Cliff	154	Tankersley Park	176	Wortley
133	Scarborough South Cliff	155	Temple Newsam	177	York
134	Scarcroft	156	Thirsk & Northallerton		
135	Scathingwell	157	Thorne		

☎ (0113) 2681680, Fax 2939458, Pro 2689603.
On A61 5 miles N of Leeds.
Heathland/moorland course.
Pro John Green; Founded 1907
Designed by Dr A. MacKenzie and H. Colt
18 holes, 6686 yards, S.S.S. 73
♣ Welcome by arrangement.
⌐ WD £50; WE £60.
⌐ Welcome by prior arrangement; terms on application.
⌐ Bar and restaurant facilities; catering packages available by prior arrangement.
⌐ Harewood Arms.

8A 5 Ampleforth College
Gilling East, York, York, YO6 5AE
☎ (01653) 628555
Entrance opposite church in the centre of Gilling East.
Parkland course.
Founded 1972
Designed by Ampleforth College
9 holes, 5567 yards, S.S.S. 69
♣ Welcome but restrictions between 2pm-4pm for pupils on WD.
⌐ WD £9; WE £12.
⌐ Club will consider applications.
⌐ None; public house next door.
⌐ Worsley Arms, Hovingham.

8A 6 Austerfield Park Country Club
Cross Lane, Austerfield, Doncaster, Yorkshire, DN10 6RF
☎ (01302) 710841, Fax 710841, Sec 710850
Take A614 towards Finningley; Cross Lane is on right at first roundabout.
Parkland course.
Pro Peter Rothery; Founded 1974
Designed by E.& M. Baker Ltd
18 holes, 6900 yards, S.S.S. 73
♣ Welcome.
⌐ Terms on application.
⌐ Welcome by prior arrangement; terms on application.
⌐ Clubhouse facilities.
⌐ Crown, Bawtry.

8A 7 Baildon
Moorgate, Baildon, Shipley, Yorkshire, BD17 5PP
☎ (01274) 584266, Fax 530551, Pro 595162, Sec 530551
3 miles N of Bradford off the Bradford-Ilkley road.
Moorland course laid out as a links course.
Pro Richard Masters; Founded 1896

Designed by T Morris; modified by J Braid
18 holes, 6231 yards, S.S.S. 70
♣ Welcome by prior arrangement.
⌐ WD £16; WE £20.
⌐ Welcome by prior arrangement; discounts for larger groups; terms on application.
⌐ Clubhouse facilities, catering packages available.
⌐ Many in local area.

8A 8 Barnsley
Wakefield Rd, Staincross, Nr Barnsley, S Yorkshire S75 6JZ
☎ (01226) 382856, Pro 380358
Course is on A61 three miles from Barnsley.
Undulating meadowland course.
Founded 1928
18 holes, 5951 yards, S.S.S. 69
♣ Welcome.
⌐ WD £8; WE £9.
⌐ Welcome by prior arrangement; terms on application.
⌐ Bar meals.
Practice range, 50 yards from club.
⌐ Queens; Ardley Moat House.

8A 9 Beauchief
Abbey Lane, Sheffield, S Yorks, S8 0DB
☎ (0114) 2620040, Pro 2367274
From M1 Junction 33 towards city centre and follow signs A612 to Bakewell for 4 miles, turning left into Abbeydale Road at lights.
Parkland course.
Pro Louis Horsman; Founded 1925
18 holes, 5452 yards, S.S.S. 66
♣ Municipal pay and play.
⌐ WD £8.50; WE £10.
⌐ Welcome by prior written agreement from Sheffield City Council; Recreation Dept, Town Hall, Sheffield 1; terms available on application.
⌐ Meals served daily.
⌐ Beauchief adjacent to course.

8A 10 Bedale
Leyburn Rd, Bedale, N Yorks, DL8 1EZ
☎ (01677) 422568, Fax 422451, Pro 422443, Sec 422451
From A1 take A684 through Bedale; course 400 yards from town centre.
Parkland course.
Pro Tony Johnson; Founded 1894
18 holes, 6565 yards, S.S.S. 71
♣ Welcome with handicap certs.
⌐ WD £20; WE £30.

⌐ Welcome by prior arrangement; catering and golfing packages available; terms available on application.
⌐ Clubhouse facilities.
⌐ Nags Head, Pickhill; White Rose, Leeming Bar.

8A 11 Ben Rhydding
High Wood, Ben Rhydding, Ilkley, W Yorkshire, LS29 8SB
☎ (01943) 608759
From A65 to Ilkley turn up Wheatley Lane and then into Wheatley Grove, left on to High Wood, club signposted.
Moorland course with mix of light parkland and links.
Founded 1890/1947
Designed by W Dell
9 holes, 4711 yards, S.S.S. 64
♣ Welcome WD; limited access with member at WE.
⌐ WD £12; WE £15.
⌐ Very limited access to small parties; terms on application.
⌐ Very limited.
⌐ Local tourist office can supply details.

8A 12 Beverley & East Riding
Anti Mill, Westwood, Beverley, E Yorks, HU17 8PJ
☎ (01482) 867190, Fax 868757, Pro 869519, Sec 868757
On B1230 Walkington road 0.5 miles W of town centre
Common pastureland.
Pro Ian Mackie; Founded 1889
Designed by Dr J.J. Fraser
18 holes, 5972 yards, S.S.S. 69
♣ Welcome.
⌐ WD £13; WE £17.
⌐ Welcome WD; catering packages can be arranged; from £13.
⌐ Clubhouse facilities.
⌐ Lairgate, Beverley.

8A 13 Bingley St Ives
The Golf Clubhouse, Harden, Bingley, BD16 1AT
☎ (01274) 562436, Fax 511788, Pro 562506, Sec 511788
Course is close to A650 Keighley to Bradford road and A629 Bingley to Denholme.
Parkland/moorland/woodland course.
Pro Ray Firth; Founded 1932
Designed by A MacKenzie
18 holes, 6485 yards, S.S.S. 71
♣ Welcome by arrangement.
⌐ WD £24; WE £28.

Alwoodley

A real find. Sitting opposite the more famous Sand Moor and Moortown is a real delight of a golf course. Alwoodley is close to the urban hustle and bustle of Leeds but it is hard to imagine that a huge city rumbles away outside its gates.

On part of Lord Harewood's Estate, Alwoodley is a very private and sedate club that looks as though it belongs to a more gentle era.

A round on the course is, indeed, a privilege. It ranks as one of the finest inland courses in British golf and is as challenging as any around.

It has a moorland feel with gorse and heather to punish the wayward but it also has the most magnificent lush carpet of turf that eases a golfer's long struggle.

Natural as it may seem, the course was lovingly sculptured by Mackenzie and so well has the course been designed that it is hard to persuade anyone that these were not natural features.

The clubhouse is another of those turn-of-the-century buildings that ooze history and style but for many players emerging from the dark-wood luxury of the locker room the first tee is in too much of a public gaze.

It is only a straightforward par four but the burning glare of the club members and the starter in his little hut is enough to test the nerve of any player.

A pull to the left and the ball disappears into a field. Relief follows any half-decent drive and don't be afraid to clip a longish iron safely down the middle.

The second provides little of a test but the third, fourth, fifth and sixth are all real tests of golf where bogeys are not unfamiliar and in many cases not a disgrace.

The short seventh, with its canopy of trees, is followed by the magnificent eighth which tests any golfer's accuracy on the second shot on a narrow elbow of a dog-leg.

Indeed the dog-leg is one of Alwoodley's traits and the classic examples are the 10th and the 15th but that is not to say that great challenges do not lurk on other parts of the finishing nine. — **CG**

Welcome by prior arrangement; all day golf and catering packages available; from £36.
Clubhouse facilities.
Bankfield; Five Flags; Three Sisters.

8A 14 Birley Wood

Birley Lane, Sheffield, S Yorks, S12 3BP
(0114) 264 7262
Course is off the A616 four miles S of Sheffield.
Public open course.
Pro Peter Ball; Founded 1974
18 holes, 5008 yards, S.S.S. 65
Welcome.
WD £8.50; WE £8.90.
Welcome by prior arrangement with the Sheffield Recreation Department.
Catering at Fairways Inn adjacent to course.

8A 15 Boothferry Park

Spaldington Lane, Howden, Goole, E Yorkshire, DN14 7NG
(01430) 430364, Bar/Rest 430371
On B1228 between Howden and Bubwith off M62 Junction 37.
Meadowland with ponds and ditches.
Pro N Bundy; Founded 1981
Designed by Donald Steel
18 holes, 6651 yards, S.S.S. 72
Welcome at all times.
WD £10; WE £15.
Welcome by prior arrangement with the professional; packages can be arranged; terms available on application.
Clubhouse facilities.
Cave Castle.

8A 16 Bracken Ghyll

Skipton Rd, Addingham, Yorks, LS29 0SL
(01943) 831207
Off A65 Skipton-Leeds road in Addingham.
Undulating parkland course.
Founded 1993
Designed by OCM Associates
9 holes, 6560 yards, S.S.S. 72
Welcome by prior arrangement.
WD £10; WE £14.
Welcome; catering and golf packages available; video tuition; indoor practice area; terms on application.
Full clubhouse facilities.
Craiglands; Devonshire Country House; Randells.

8A 17 Bradford

Hawksworth Lane, Guiseley, Leeds, W Yorks, LS20 8LD
(01943) 875570, Fax 875570, Pro 873719, Bar/Rest 873817
Course is off the A6038 3.5 miles NE of Shipley.
Moorland/parkland course.
Pro Sydney Welden; Founded 1862
18 holes, 6303 yards, S.S.S. 71
Welcome WD by prior arrangement; not Sat; limited Sun.
WD £25; SUN £35.
Welcome WD by prior arrangement; catering packages available; terms available on application.
Full clubhouse facilities.
Marriott Hollins Hall; Chevin Lodge.

8A 18 Bradford Moor

Scarr Hall, Pollard Lane, Bradford, W Yorks, BD2 4RW
(01274) 771716
2 miles from Bradford town centre on Harrogate Rd.
Moorland course.
Founded 1907
9 holes, 5900 yards, S.S.S. 68
Welcome WD; discount before 1.30pm.
WD £12.
Welcome WD by prior arrangement; catering and golf packages available; from £16.
Clubhouse facilities.

8A 19 Bradley Park

Bradley Rd, Huddersfield, HD2 2PZ
(01484), Fax 451613, Pro 223772
M62 Junction 26 in direction of Huddersfield; right at first lights.
Parkland course.
Pro Parnell Reilly; Founded 1973
Designed by Donald Steel
18 holes, 6284 yards, S.S.S. 70
Welcome by prior arrangement.
WD £12; WE £14.
Welcome WD; catering packages can be arranged; from £10.
Clubhouse facilities.
Practice range, 18 bays floodlit; also 9-hole par 3 course.

8A 20 Brandon

Holywell Lane, Shadwell, Leeds, W Yorks, LS17 8EZ
(0113) 2737471
1 mile from N Leeds ring road at Roundhay Park.
Parkland course.

Founded 1967
Designed by George Eric Allamby
18 holes, 4800 yards, S.S.S. 62
Welcome.
WD £6; WE £7.
Welcome WD by prior arrangement; 10 days' notice required; from £6.
Clubhouse snack facilities available.
White House; Rydal Bank.

8A 21 Branshaw

Branshaw Moor, Oakworth, Keighley, W Yorks, BD22 7ES
(01535) 643235, Pro 647441, Bar/Rest 643235
Course is on the B6143 two miles SW of Keighley.
Moorland course.
Pro Mark Tyler; Founded 1912
Designed by James Braid, A MacKenzie
18 holes, 5870 yards, S.S.S. 69
Welcome WD; restrictions at WE.
WD £20; WE £30.
Welcome WD by prior arrangement.
Clubhouse catering facilities available.
Three Sisters, Haworth; Newsholme Manor, Oakworth.

8A 22 Bridlington

Belvedere Rd, Bridlington, E Yorks, YO15 3NA
(01262) 672092, Fax 606367, Pro 674721, Sec 606367
Off A165 S of town on Bridlington-Hull road.
Open parkland course.
Pro A R A Howarth; Founded 1905
Designed by James Braid
18 holes, 6577 yards, S.S.S. 71
Welcome by prior arrangement.
WD £15; WE £25.
Welcome by prior arrangement; golf and catering packages available; terms on application.
Full clubhouse facilities available.
Club can provide list on request.

8A 23 Bridlington Links

Flamborough Road, Marton, Bridlington, E Yorks, YO15 1DW
(01262) 401584, Fax 401702
Course is on the B1255 just N of Bridlington towards Flamborough Head.
Clifftop links.
Pro Steve Raybould; Founded 1993
Designed by Howard Swan

18 holes, 6719 yards, S.S.S. 72
† Welcome.
⌐ WD £12; WE £15 (This includes lunch in winter months).
↗ Welcome; summer and winter packages available; driving range; short course; terms available on application.
◉ Full clubhouse facilities.
Practice range, 24 bays covered floodlit.
↗ Rags Hotel; Manor Court; Sewerby Grange; North Star, Flamborough.

8A 24 Brough
Cave Rd, Brough, E Yorks, HU15 1HB
☎ (01482) 667374, Fax 669823, Pro 667483, Sec 667291
Off A63, 10 miles W of Hull.
Parkland course.
Pro G W Townhill; Founded 1893
18 holes, 6134 yards, S.S.S. 69
† Welcome WD except Wed; WE by prior arrangement.
↗ Welcome by prior arrangement; full golf and catering packages available; terms available on application.
◉ Full clubhouse facilities.
↗ Beverley Arms; Walkington Manor.

8A 25 Calverley
Woodhall Lane, Pudsey, Yorks, LS28 5QY
☎ (0113) , Fax 2564362, Pro 2569244, Sec 2569244
Close to M1 & M62 motorways 4 miles for Bradford, 7 miles from Leeds.
Parkland course.
Pro Derek Johnson; Founded 1983
18 holes, 5590 yards, S.S.S. 67
† Welcome; restrictions Sat and Sun am.
⌐ WD £12; WE £17.
↗ Welcome by arrangement; catering packages available for groups up to 30; terms available on application.
◉ Full clubhouse facilities.
Large practice ground, also 9-hole course.
↗ Marriott.

8A 26 Castle Fields
Rastrick Common, Rastrick, Brighouse, W Yorks, HD6 3HL
☎ (01484) 712108

On A643 1 mile out of Brighouse.
Parkland course.
Founded 1903
6 holes, 4812 yards, S.S.S. 50
† Welcome only as a guest of a member.
⌐ WD £5; WE £7.
↗ Welcome only by prior arrangement with Sec.
◉ Facilities at local Inns within 0.25 miles.

8A 27 Catterick
Leyburn Rd, Catterick Garrison, N Yorks, DL9 3QE
☎ (01748) 833401, Fax 833268, Pro 833671, Sec 833208
On B6136 6 miles SW of Scotch Corner.
Parkland/moorland course.
Pro Andy Marshall; Founded 1930
Designed by Arthur day (1938)
18 holes, 6329 yards, S.S.S. 70
† Welcome by prior arrangement.
⌐ Terms on application.
↗ Welcome by prior arrangement; packages can be arranged; 2 practice areas; billiards room; satellite TV.
◉ Lounge bar, restaurant, bar snacks.
Practice range, 2 practice grounds.

8A 28 Cave Castle Hotel
South Cave, Brough, E Yorks, HU15 2EU
☎ (01430) 421286, Bar/Rest 422245
10 miles from Kingston upon Hull.
Parkland course.
Pro Stephen MacKinder; Founded 1989
18 holes, 6524 yards, S.S.S. 71
† Welcome.
⌐ WD £12.50; WE £18.
↗ Welcome WD and after 10.30am at WE; special packages available; conference facilities for 250; à la carte restaurant; practice facilities; terms on application.
◉ Full hotel facilities.
↗ Cave Castle.

8A 29 Cherry Burton
Leconfield Road, Cherry Burton, Beverley, Yorks, HU17 7RB
☎ (01964) 550924
On the B1248 close to Beverley.
Parkland course.
Pro to be appointed; Founded 1993
Designed by W Adamson
9 holes, 6480 yards, S.S.S. 71
† Welcome.
⌐ WD £9; WE £10.

↗ Welcome by prior arrangement.
◉ Bar and catering facilities available.
Practice area.
↗ Beverley; Lairgate.

8A 30 City of Wakefield
Lupset Park, Horbury Rd, Wakefield, W Yorkshire, WF2 8QS
☎ (01924) 367442, Pro 360282
Course is on the A642 two miles W of Wakefield.
Parkland course.
Pro Roger Holland; Founded 1936
Designed by J S F Morrison
18 holes, 6319 yards, S.S.S. 70
† Welcome.
⌐ Terms on application.
↗ Welcome on WD by prior arrangement; packages can be arranged through the stewardess; terms on application.
◉ Clubhouse facilities.
↗ Cedar Court, Wakefield; Forte Post House.

8A 31 Clayton
Thornton View Rd, Clayton, Bradford, W Yorks, BD14 6JX
☎ (01274) 880047
On A647 from Bradford following signs for Clayton.
Moorland course.
Founded 1906
9 holes, 5467 yards, S.S.S. 67
† Welcome WD and Sat unless comps.
⌐ WD £10; WE £12.
↗ Welcome by arrangement with Sec; catering packages by arrangement; snooker; terms on application.
◉ Bar and bar snacks.
↗ Pennine Hilton.

8A 32 Cleckheaton & District
Bradford Rd, Cleckheaton, W Yorks, BD19 6NU
☎ (01274) 851267, Sec 851266
On A638 from M62 Junction 26 towards Bradford.
Parkland course.
Pro Mike Ingham; Founded 1900
18 holes, 5860 yards, S.S.S. 68
† Welcome.
⌐ WD £25; WE £30.
↗ Welcome WD by arrangement; catering packages by arrangement; terms on application.
◉ Clubhouse catering and bar facilities.
↗ Novotel.

8A 33 Cocksford ☏
Stutton, Tadcaster, N Yorks, LS24 9NG
☎ (01937) 834253, Fax 834253, Bar/Rest 530346
Course is in village of Strutton close to the A64.
Parkland course with Cock Beck running through it.
Pro Graham Thompson; Founded 1991
Designed by Townend/ Brodigan
27 holes, 5632 yards, S.S.S. 69
† Welcome by arrangement.
▌ WD £17; WE £23.
⌁ Welcome by prior arrangement; 27 holes golf; all-day catering high season only; 3rd nine added in 1995 to form Plews and Quarry High courses; £29.
▐ Clubhouse facilities, including bistro and Sparrows restaurant all year round.
⌐ Club have cottages to rent.

8A 34 Concord Park
Shiregreen Lane, Sheffield, S Yorks, S5 6AE
☎ (0114) 2577378, Sec 2349802
Course is off the A6135 3.5 miles N of Sheffield.
Parkland course.
Pro Warren Allcroft; Founded 1952
18 holes, 4872 yards, S.S.S. 64
† Welcome by prior arrangement.
▌ WD £7; WE £7.50.
⌁ Welcome; from £7.
▐ Full clubhouse facilities
Driving range.

8A 35 Cottingham
Woodhill Way, Cottingham, E Yorks, HU16 5RZ
☎ (01482) 842394, Fax 8459332, Sec 846030, Bar/Rest 846032
Off A164 4 miles off the M62/A63.
Parkland course.
Pro Chris Gray; Founded 1994
Designed by J Wiles/T Litten
18 holes, 6230 yards, S.S.S. 69
† Welcome by prior arrangement.
▌ WD £14; WE £20.
⌁ Welcome by prior arrangement; WD and WE packages available; from £30.
▐ Fully licensed bar and restaurant.
⌐ Willerby Manor; Jarvis Grange.

8A 36 Crimple Valley
Hookstone Wood Rd, Harrogate, Yorks, HG2 8PN
☎ (01423) 883485, Fax 881018

Course is off the A61 one mile S of town centre.
Parkland course.
Founded 1976
Designed by R Lumb
9 holes, 5000 yards
† Public pay and play.
▌ WD £5; WE £6 (9 holes).
⌁ Welcome by arrangement; from £7.50.
▐ Bar and catering facilities.

8A 37 Crookhill Park
Carr Lane, Conisbrough, Nr Doncaster, S Yorks, DN12 2AH
☎ (01709) 862979, Sec 863566, Bar/Rest 862974
Off A630 Doncaster to Rotherham road.
Parkland course.
Pro R Swaine; Founded 1976
18 holes, 5849 yards, S.S.S. 68
† Welcome by prior arrangement.
▌ WD £9.25; WE £10.50.
⌁ Welcome by prior arrangement with the professional; discounts available depending on group size; terms on application.
▐ Clubhouse facilities.

8A 38 Crosland Heath
Felk Stile Rd, Crosland Heath, Huddersfield, HD4 7AF
☎ (01484) 653216, Pro 653877, Sec 653262
Take A62 Huddersfield-Oldham road and follow signs for Countryside Leisure.
Moorland course.
Pro Chris Gaunt; Founded 1913
18 holes, 6004 yards, S.S.S. 70
† By prior arrangement only; handicap certs required.
▌ Terms on application.
⌁ Welcome except Sat by prior arrangement; catering packages by arrangement; terms on application.
▐ Full facilities available except Mon.
Practice ground.
⌐ Dryclough, Crosland Moor; Durker Roods, Meltham.

8A 39 Crows Nest Park
Coach Road, Hove Edge, Brighouse, W Yorks, HD6 2LN
Pro (01484) 401121, Bar/Rest 401152
Off M62 at Brighouse follow signs for Bradford; turn left at Ritz.
Parkland course.
Pro Bob Parry; Founded 1985

Designed by W Adamson
9 holes, 6020 yards, S.S.S. 72
† Welcome.
▌ WD £10; WE £10.
⌁ Welcome; golf and catering packages available; terms on application.
▐ Clubhouse facilities available.
Practice range, 8 bays floodlit.
⌐ Lane Head.

8A 40 Dewsbury District
The Pinnacle, Sands Lane, Mirfield, W Yorks, WF14 8HJ
☎ (01924) 492399, Fax 492399, Pro 496030, Bar/Rest 491928
Course is two miles W of Dewsbury off the A644; three miles from the M62 Junction 25.
Parkland/moorland course.
Pro N Hirst; Founded 1891
Designed by T Morris / P Alliss
18 holes, 6360 yards, S.S.S. 71
† Welcome WD and after 2.30pm WE.
▌ WD £17.50; WE £12.50.
⌁ Welcome WD and Sun after 2.30pm; full packages of 27 holes of golf and catering available; from £32.
▐ Full clubhouse facilities.
Practice ground.
⌐ Five Arches, Mirfield; Woolpack, Whitley.

8A 41 Doncaster
278 Bawtry Rd, Bessacarr, Doncaster, S Yorks, DN4 7PD
☎ (01302) 865632, Fax 865994, Pro 868404
On A638 between Doncaster and Bawtry.
Undulating heathland course.
Pro Graham Bailey; Founded 1894
18 holes, 6220 yards, S.S.S. 70
† Welcome.
▌ WD £22.50; WE £27.50.
⌁ Welcome WD by prior arrangement with Sec; packages by arrangement; terms available on application.
▐ Full clubhouse facilities.
⌐ Punches; Danum.

8A 42 Doncaster Town Moor
Bawtry Rd, Belle Vue, Doncaster, S Yorks
☎ (01302) 533778, Pro 535286, Bar/Rest 533167
Next to Doncaster Rovers FC and close to racecourse.
Moorland course.
Pro Steve Shaw; Founded 1895

18 holes, 6001 yards, S.S.S. 69
† Welcome; restrictions Sun.
⌐ WD £16; WE £17.
⟲ Welcome by arrangement; full days golf and catering by arrangement; £25.
|●| Clubhouse facilities.
⌐⊐ Royal St Leger; Earl of Doncaster.

8A 43 Dore & Totley
Bradway Rd, Sheffield, S Yorks, S17 4QR
☎ (0114) 2360492, Fax 2353436, Pro 2366844, Sec 2369872
6 miles S of Sheffield on the B6054 for Bradway.
Parkland course.
Pro Greg Roberts; Founded 1913
18 holes, 6256 yards, S.S.S. 70
† Welcome by prior arrangement except Sat; restrictions apply on Sun and Wed.
⌐ WD £26; WE £26.
⟲ Welcome except Wed and Sat; summer and winter packages can be arranged through Pro; terms on application.
|●| Full clubhouse facilities.

8A 44 Drax
Drax, Nr Selby, N Yorks, YO8 8PQ
☎ (01405) 860533
Course is off the A1041 six miles south of Selby opposite the Drax power station.
Tree-lined parkland course.
Founded 1989
9 holes, 5510 yards, S.S.S. 67
† Only with a member.
⌐ Not available.
|●| At Drax Sports and Social Club.

8A 45 Driffield
Sunderlandwick, Beverley Rd, Driffield, E Yorks, YO25 7AD
☎ (01377) 253116, Fax 240599, Pro 256663
Off A164 Beverley to Driffield road off the first main roundabout.
Mature parkland course.
Founded 1934
18 holes, 6215 yards, S.S.S. 70
† Welcome with club or society handicap certs WD 9.30am-12noon & 1.30pm-3pm; WE between 10am-11am.
⌐ WD £20; WE £30.
⟲ Welcome by prior arrangement with handicap certs; catering packages available; practice area; terms on application.

|●| Clubhouse facilities.
⌐⊐ Bell, Driffield.

8A 46 Easingwold
Stillington Rd, Easingwold, N Yorkshire, YO6 3ET
☎ (01347) 821486, Fax 822474, Pro 821964, Sec 822474
On A19 12 miles N of York; 1 miles down Stillington road at S end of Easingwold.
Parkland course.
Pro J Hughes; Founded 1930
Designed by Hawtree
18 holes, 6285 yards, S.S.S. 72
† Welcome by prior arrangement.
⌐ WD £25; WE £30.
⟲ Welcome by prior arrangement; golf and full catering packages; £38.
|●| Clubhouse facilities.
⌐⊐ Garth Hotel; The George.

8A 47 East Bierley
South View Rd, Bierley, Bradford, W Yorkshire, BD4 6PP
☎ (01274) 681023, Sec 683666, Bar/Rest 680450
4 miles S of Bradford.
Parkland course; started as Toftshaw GC in 1904.
Founded 1904/28
9 holes, 4692 yards, S.S.S. 63
† Welcome.
⌐ WD £12; WE £15.
⟲ Welcome by prior arrangement; terms on application.
|●| Full catering facilities.
⌐⊐ Tong Village Hotel, Tong; Cedar Court, Bradford.

8A 48 Elland
Hammerstones, Leach Lane, Elland, W Yorks, HX5 0TA
☎ (01422) 372505, Pro 374886
From M62 Junction 24 in direction of Blackley.
Parkland course.
Pro N Kryzwicki; Founded 1910
9 holes, 5630 yards, S.S.S. 66
† Welcome.
⌐ Terms on application.
⟲ Welcome Tues, Wed, Fri; catering packages available; from £14.
|●| Clubhouse facilities.
⌐⊐ Rock Hotel, Holywell Green.

8A 49 Fardew
Nursery Farm, Carr Lane, East Morton, Keighley, W Yorks, BD20 5RY
☎ (01274) 561229, Fax 561229

1.25 miles from Bingley, then to E Morton.
Parkland course.
Pro Ian Bottomley; Founded 1993
Designed by W Adamson
9 holes, 6208 yards, S.S.S. 70
† Pay and play.
⌐ WD £14; WE £16 (18 holes).
⟲ Welcome by prior arrangement; terms on application.
|●| Café.
Open practice ground.
⌐⊐ Beeches, Keighley.

8A 50 Ferrybridge 'C'
Ferrybridge 'C' P.S. Golf Club, Knottingley, WF11 8SQ
☎ (01977) 674188
On Castleford-Knottingley road 200 yards from A1.
Founded 1976
Designed by N.E. Pugh
9 holes, 5138 yards, S.S.S. 65
† Welcome as the guest of a member.
⌐ Terms on application.
⟲ Welcome by arrangement.

8A 51 Filey
West Ave, Filey, N Yorks, YO14 9BQ
☎ (01723) 513116, Fax 514952, Pro 513134, Sec 513293, Bar/Rest 513293
1 mile S of Filey.
Links/parkland course.
Pro Gary Hutchinson; Founded 1897
Designed by J Braid
18 holes, 6112 yards, S.S.S. 69
† Welcome by arrangement.
⌐ WD £21; WE £30.
⟲ Welcome with prior arrangement; catering packages available; from £21.
|●| Clubhouse facilities.
⌐⊐ White Lodge; Hallam.

8A 52 Flamborough Head
Lighthouse Rd, Flamborough, Bridlington, E Yorkshire, YO15 1AR
☎ (01262) 850417, Fax 850279, Sec 850683
5 miles NE of Bridlington situated on Flamborough headland.
Links course.
Founded 1931
18 holes, 5976 yards, S.S.S. 69
† Welcome.
⌐ WD £15; WE £20.
⟲ Welcome by arrangement; full day golf and catering available; from £17.
|●| Clubhouse facilities.
⌐⊐ North Star; Flaneburg.

8A 53 Forest of Galtres
Moorlands Rd, Skelton, York, Yorks,
YO3 3RF
☎(01904) 766198, Fax 766198,
Bar/Rest 750287
Just of A19 Thirsk road through
Skelton; 1.5 miles from B1237 York
ring road.
Parkland in ancient Forest of Galtres.
Pro Phil Bradley; Founded 1993
Designed by S Gidman
18 holes, 6312 yards, S.S.S. 70
⚑ Welcome.
▯ WD £18; WE £22.
⌁Welcome by prior arrangement
only; discounts for groups of 12 or
more; from £20.
▢ Full clubhouse facilities.
⌐ Beechwood Close; Jacobean
Lodge; Fairfield Manor.

8A 54 Forest Park
Stockton on Forest, York, YO3 9UW
☎(01904) 400425
Course is 2.5 miles from east end of
York by-pass.
Flat parkland course.
Founded 1991
18 holes, 6660 yards, S.S.S. 72
⚑ Welcome.
▯ WD £16; WE £22.
⌁Welcome; all-day golf and catering
packages available; also 9-hole West
Course: 6372 yards, par 70; from
£33.
▢ Full clubhouse facilities.
⌐ B&B in Stockton-on-Forest.

8A 55 Fulford
Heslington Lane, Heslington, York,
Yorks, YO1 5DY
☎(01904) 413212, Fax 416918, Pro
412882, Sec 413579, Bar/Rest
411503
Off A19 1 mile S of York following
sings to University.
Heathland course.
Pro Bryan Hessay; Founded 1909
Designed by Major C. MacKenzie
18 holes, 6775 yards, S.S.S. 72
⚑ Welcome by arrangement.
▯ WD £35; WE £45.
⌁Welcome by prior arrangement;
not Tues am; packages can be
arranged through manager; terms on
application.
▢ Full clubhouse facilities.
⌐ Stakis; Forte Crest; Almeda GH.

8A 56 Fulneck
The Clubhouse, Fulneck, Pudsey, W
Yorks, LS28 8NT

☎(0113) 2565191
Between Leeds and Bradford; at
Pudsey cenotaph turn right, then first
left into Bankhouse Lane and follow
signs.
Undulating wooded parkland course.
Founded 1892
9 holes, 5456 yards, S.S.S. 67
⚑ Welcome WD; with member at
WE.
▯ Terms on application.
⌁Welcome by prior arrangement
with Sec; catering packages by
arrangement; terms available on
application.
▢ By arrangement.

8A 57 Ganstead Park
Longdales Lane, Coniston, Hull, E
Yorks, HU11 4LB
☎(01482) 874754, Fax 817754, Pro
811121, Bar/Rest 811280
On A165 Hull-Bridlington road at
Ganstead.
Parkland course with water.
Pro Mike Smee; Founded 1976
Designed by Peter Green
18 holes, 6801 yards, S.S.S. 73
⚑ Welcome by prior arrangement.
▯ Terms on application.
⌁Welcome by prior arrangement;
special packages can be arranged;
terms on application.
▢ Full clubhouse facilities.
⌐ Kingstown, Hedon; Tickton
Grange, Beverley.

8A 58 Ganton
Ganton, Scarborough, N Yorks, Y012
4PA
☎(01944) 710329, Fax 710922, Pro
710260
On A64 11 miles SW of Scarborough.
Heathland/links course.
Pro Gary Brown; Founded 1891
Designed by Dunn, Vardon, Colt, C.K.
Cotton
18 holes, 6734 yards, S.S.S. 74
⚑ Welcome by prior arrangement.
▯ WD £52; WE £60.
⌁Welcome by prior agreement;
packages can be organised; terms on
application.
▢ Full clubhouse facilities.
⌐ Crescent, Scarborough; Ganton
Greyhound.

8A 59 Garforth
Long Lane, Garforth, Leeds, LS25
2DS
☎(0113) 2862021, Pro 2862063,
Sec 2863308

6.5 miles E of Leeds off A642 1 miles
from Wass Garage.
Parkland course.
Pro Ken Findlater; Founded 1913
18 holes, 6304 yards, S.S.S. 70
⚑ Welcome WD.
▯ WD on application.
⌁Welcome WD by prior
arrangement; terms available on
application.
▢ Full facilities.
⌐ Hilton.

8A 60 Gott's Park
Armley Ridge Rd, Leeds, W Yorks,
LS12 2QX
☎(0113) 2311896, Bar/Rest
2310492
3 miles W of the city centre.
Parkland course.
Founded 1933
18 holes, 4978 yards, S.S.S. 65
⚑ Welcome.
▯ WD £7.25; WE £8.75
⌁Welcome by arrangement.
▢ Café facilities; bar in evenings
and WE.

8A 61 Grange Park
Upper Wortley Rd, Rotherham, S
Yorks, S61 2SJ
☎(01709) 558884, Pro 559497
On A629 2 miles W of Rotherham
municipal parkland course; private
clubhouse.
Pro Eric Clark; Founded 1971
18 holes, 6421 yards, S.S.S. 71
⚑ Welcome.
▯ WD £9; WE £11.
⌁Welcome by prior arrangement
with Sec; special catering and golf
packages available; terms on
application.
▢ Full bar and catering facilities
Tues-Sun; limited Mon.
Practice range, 36 bays, two-tier
floodlit covered.
⌐ Swallow.

8A 62 Hainsworth Park
Brandesburton, Driffield, E Yorks,
YO25 8RT
☎(01964) 542362
Just off A165 8 miles N of Beverley.
Parkland course.
Founded 1983
18 holes, 6027 yards, S.S.S. 69
⚑ Welcome by prior arrangement.
▯ Terms on application.
⌁Welcome by prior arrangement;
day tickets available (WD £18, WE
£22); from £14.

Full catering and restaurant facilities.

Burton Lodge on course.

8A 63 Halifax

Union Lane, Ogden, Halifax, W Yorks, HX2 8XR

(01422) 244171, Fax 241459

Course is on the A629 four miles from Halifax.

Moorland course.

Pro Michael Allison, Founded 1895

Designed by W.H. Fowler, James Braid

18 holes, 6037 yards, S.S.S. 70

Welcome WD; limited at WE.

WD £15; WE £20.

Welcome WD by prior arrangement with Sec; packages available with catering; £24-£32.

Full clubhouse facilities.

Driving range 2 miles away.

Windmill Court; Holdsworth House; Moorlands.

8A 64 Halifax Bradley Hall

Stainland Rd, Holywell Green, Halifax, W Yorks, HX4 9AN

(01422) 374108, Pro 370231

On B6112 off A629 Halifax-Huddersfield road.

Moorland/parkland course.

Pro Peter Wood; Founded 1905/24

18 holes, 6213 yards, S.S.S. 70

Welcome with handicap certs.

WD £18; WE £28.

Welcome with handicap certs and by prior arrangement; golf and catering packages; £33.

Full clubhouse facilities.

Rock Inn, Holywell Green.

8A 65 Hallamshire

The Clubhouse, Sandygate, Sheffield, S Yorks, S10 4LA

(0114) 2301007, Fax 2302153, Pro 2305222, Sec 2302153

3 miles W of Sheffield off A57 at Crosspool.

Moorland course.

Pro Geoff Tickell; Founded 1897

Designed by various, including Dr A MacKenzie.

18 holes, 6359 yards, S.S.S. 71

Welcome; some restrictions at WE.

Terms on application.

Welcome by arrangement with Sec; packages available; terms on application.

Full clubhouse facilities.

Beauchef; Trust House Forte.

8A 66 Hallowes

Hallowes Lane, Dronfield, Sheffield, S Yorks, S18 1UA

(01246) 413734, Fax 411196, Pro 411196

Take A61 Sheffield-Chesterfield road into Dronfield and turn sharp right under railway bridge.

Undulating moorland course.

Pro Philip Dunn; Founded 1892

18 holes, 6342 yards, S.S.S. 71

Welcome WD.

WD £30.

Welcome WD by arrangement; day ticket WD £35; catering by arrangement; terms on application.

Full clubhouse facilities.

Practice ground.

Chantry.

8A 67 Hanging Heaton

White Cross Rd, Bennett Lane, Dewsbury, W Yorks, WF12 7DT

(01924) 461606, Fax 430100, Pro 467077, Sec 430100

On A653 Dewbury-Leeds road 0.75 miles from town centre.

Parkland course.

Pro G Moore; Founded 1922

9 holes, 5902 yards, S.S.S. 69

Welcome WD; with member at WE.

WD £12.

Welcome by arrangement with Sec; full day packages available; terms on application.

Full clubhouse facilities.

8A 68 Harrogate

Forest Lane Head, Harrogate, N Yorks, HG2 7TF

(01423) 863158, Fax 860073, Pro 862547, Sec 862999

On A59 between Knaresborough and Harrogate.

Parkland course.

Pro Paul Johnson; Founded 1892

Designed by Sandy Herd; revised by Dr A McKenzie

19 holes, 6241 yards, S.S.S. 70

Welcome by arrangement.

WD £30; WE £40.

Welcome by prior arrangement; packages can be arranged; min 12.

Bar and restaurant.

Practice area.

Local tourist board can provide brochures.

8A 69 Headingley

Back Church Lane, Adel, Leeds, LS16 8DW

(0113) 2679573, Fax 281/334, Pro 2675100, Sec 2679573

Course is off the A660 Leeds to Otley road.

Undulating parkland course.

Pro Steve Foster; Founded 1892

18 holes, 6298 yards, S.S.S. 70

Welcome by prior arrangement.

WD £30; WE £40.

Welcome by arrangement with the manager; day ticket WD £35; snooker; terms available on application.

Full facilities.

Village Hotel.

8A 70 Headley

Headley Lane, Thornton, Bradford, W Yorks, BD13 3LX

(01274) 833481, Fax 833481

4 miles W of Bradford on B6145 in Thornton village.

Moorland course.

Founded 1907

9 holes, 4920 yards, S.S.S. 64

Welcome WD.

WD £15.

Welcome by arrangement with Sec; special golf and catering packages available.

Dining room and bar.

Guide Post.

8A 71 Hebden Bridge

Wadsworth, Hebden Bridge, HX7 8PH

(01422) 842896, Sec 842732

In Hebden Bridge, cross Keighley road until Mount Skip Inn.

Upland course on edge of moor.

Founded 1930

9 holes, 5242 yards, S.S.S. 65

Welcome by prior arrangement.

WD £12; WE £15.

Welcome, preferably on WD; from £12.

Clubhouse facilities.

Carlton; White Lion.

8A 72 Hessle

Westfield Rd, Cottingham, Hull, E Yorks, HU16 5YL

(01482) 650171, Fax 652679, Pro 650190

Course is 3 miles SW of Cottingham off the A164.

Undulating meadowland; new course opened 1975.

Pro Graeme Fieldsend; Founded 1906

Designed by Peter Alliss & Dave Thomas

Ganton

Tranquility is the key word for Ganton, set as it is in the peaceful surrounds of the Vale of Pickering in what was Yorkshire's North Riding.

For many years it has stood out as the gem of the courses in that area and was rewarded with the British Amateur Championships.

Set in open heathland within striking distance of the seaside town of Scarborough, Ganton has been described as the jewel in the crown of North Yorkshire golf.

Only Catterick Garrison in the army town and Bedale offer any semblance of competition. But the debate is decided once the player walks on to the fantastic inland course.

In many cases courses suffer because of a committee of designers but Ganton is a real exception and the natural contours of the Vale give it character.

If it was the designers who gave the course its style it was Harry Vardon, one of the club's resident professionals, who brought it to national attention.

Vardon won the first of his six Open Championships when he was in charge at Ganton and the course suddenly started to attract prestigious tournaments.

The most significant was probably the Ryder Cup in 1949 when Ben Hogan's side beat Great Britain and Ireland 7-5 in the days when the match was a foursomes and singles contest.

In recent times the professional game has tended to ignore Ganton's charms except for the Senior Tour while the Amateurs have been regular visitors.

If there is a trademark to Ganton it is the stiff finish which begins at 15. The course is littered with steep, almost bottomless, bunkers and it is these that gather to protect the 15th green.

At 440 yards the 15th is a long par four and this is followed by an even more challenging 16th and a 17th which at 250 yards offers the opportunity of a single drive. The reality, though, is much less appealing.

Finishing with a dog-leg through the pines, the course offers a really demanding test of golf. — **CG**

18 holes, 6604 yards, S.S.S. 72
♦ Welcome except Tues 9.15am-1pm or before 11am at WE.
⬙ WD £20; WE £28.
⤳Welcome by prior arrangement with Sec; catering packages by arrangement except Mon; terms on application.
⬤ Catering except Mon.
Practice ground.
⤳ Grange Park; Willoughby Manor.

8A 73 Heworth
Muncaster House, Muncastergate, York, Yorks, YO3 9JX
☎(01904) 424618, Fax 422389, Pro 422389, Sec 426156
On 1036 Scarborough Malton road 1.5 miles NE of City centre.
Parkland course.
Pro G Roberts; Founded 1911
11 holes 6141 yards, S.S.S. 69
♦ Welcome by prior arrangement.
⬙ Terms on application.
⤳Welcome by prior arrangement; full catering packages available except Mon; terms available on application.
⬤ Full clubhouse bar and catering except Mon.

8A 74 Hickleton
Lidget Lane, Hickleton, Nr Doncaster, S Yorks, DN5 7BE
☎(01709) 896081, Fax 896081, Pro 888436
On B6411 Thurnscoe road off the A635 Barnsley road; 4.5 miles from A1 (M) Junction 37.
Parkland course.
Pro to be appointed; Founded 1909
Designed by Huggett, Coles & Dyer
18 holes, 6434 yards, S.S.S. 71
♦ Welcome by prior arrangement.
⬙ WD £17; WE £26.
⤳Welcome by prior arrangement; summer packages available; terms on application.
⬤ Bar, with cask beers, and restaurant available.
⤳ Ardsley House, Barnsley; Doncaster Moat House.

8A 75 Hillsborough ℭ
Worrall Rd, Sheffield, S Yorks, S6 4BE
☎(0114) 2343608, Fax 2349151, Pro 2332666, Sec 2349151
Off A6102 Sheffield to Manchester road NW of the city just past Sheffield Wed's football ground, turning right at Horse and Jockey pub.

Undulating wooded parkland and heathland course.
Pro Louis Horsman; Founded 1920
Designed by T Williamson
18 holes, 6216 yards, S.S.S. 70
♦ Welcome WD and after 2pm at WE.
⬙ WD £28; WE £35.
⤳Welcome by prior arrangement with Sec; larger groups can negotiate rates; snooker; catering packages; driving range; terms on application.
⬤ Full restaurant and bar service.
⤳ Queens Ground, Hillsborough; Grosvenor, Sheffield; Tankersley Manor.

8A 76 Hornsea
Rolston Rd, Hornsea, E Yorks, HU11 5DX
☎(01964) 535488, Fax 532020, Pro 534989, Sec 532020
Follow signs to Hornsea Free Port club, 300 yards past port.
Parkland course.
Pro Brian Thompson; Founded 1898
Designed by Harry Vardon/Dr McKenzie/J Braid
18 holes, 6475 yards, S.S.S. 71
♦ Welcome WD and after 3pm at WE.
⬙ WD £19; WE £19.
⤳Welcome by prior arrangement; packages available; from £26.
⬤ Full clubhouse facilities.
⤳ Burton Lodge, Brandesburton; Merlstead, Hornsea.

8A 77 Horsforth
Layton Rise, Horsforth, Leeds, W Yorkshire, LS18 5EX
☎(0113) 2581017, Fax 2586819, Pro 2585200, Sec 2586819, Bar/Rest 2581703
Off A65 towards Ilkley 6 miles from city centre.
Upland/parkland course.
Pro Neil Bell; Founded 1907
18 holes, 6205 yards, S.S.S. 70
♦ Welcome WD; WE by prior arrangement.
⬙ WD £24; WE £35.
⤳Welcome WD by prior arrangement; full packages of golf and catering available.
⬤ Full clubhouse facilities.

8A 78 Howley Hall
Scotchman Lane, Morley, Leeds, W Yorks, LS27 0NX
☎(01924) 472432, Fax 478417, Pro 473852, Sec 478417

Course is on the B6123 0.75 miles from junction with the A650 at Halfway House pub.
Parkland course.
Pro Gary Watkinson; Founded 1900
18 holes, 6346 yards, S.S.S. 71
♦ Welcome.
⬙ WD £24; WE £35.
⤳Welcome by prior arrangement; catering packages available on application; from £25.
⬤ Full clubhouse facilities.

8A 79 Huddersfield (Fixby)
Fixby Hall, Lightridge Rd, Huddersfield, W Yorks, HD2 2EP
☎(01484) 420110, Fax 424623, Pro 426463, Sec 426203
From M62 Junction 24 follow signs to Brighouse; turn right at traffic lights.
Parkland course.
Pro Paul Carman; Founded 1891
Designed by Herbert Fowler, Amendments by Hawtree
18 holes, 6467 yards, S.S.S. 71
♦ Welcome; handicap certs required.
⬙ WD £35; WE £42.
⤳Welcome WD except Tues; catering can be organised; from £45.
⬤ Full clubhouse bar and restaurant facilities.
⤳ Pennine Hilton.

8A 80 Hull
The Hall, 27 Packman Lane, Kirkella, Hull, E Yorks, HU10 7TJ
☎(01482) 653026, Fax 658919, Pro 653074, Sec 658919
5 miles W of Hull.
Parkland course.
Pro David Jagger; Founded 1904/21
Designed by James Braid
18 holes, 6246 yards, S.S.S. 70
♦ Welcome by prior arrangement; with member at WE.
⬙ WD £26.50.
⤳Welcome Tues and Thurs by prior arrangement; terms available on application.
⬤ Full clubhouse facilities.
⤳ Willerby Manor; Grange Park.

8A 81 Ilkley
Nesfield Rd, Myddleton, Ilkley, W Yorks, LS29 8BL
☎(01943) 607277, Fax 816130, Sec 600214
15 miles N of Bradford.
Parkland course.
Pro John Hammond; Founded 1890
18 holes, 6262 yards, S.S.S. 70

✝ Welcome by arrangement; handicap certs required.
Ⓛ WD £37; WE £40.
⌐Welcome WD by arrangement; catering packages can be arranged; £35.
🍽 Full clubhouse facilities.

8A 82 Keighley
Howden Park, Utley, Keighley, W Yorks, BD20 6DH
☎(01535) 603179, Pro 665370, Sec 604778
1 mile W of Keighley on the old Keighley-Skipton road.
Parkland course.
Pro Mike Bradley; Founded 1904
18 holes, 6141 yards, S.S.S. 70
✝ Welcome except before 9am and between 12.30pm-1.30pm WD; Ladies day Tues; not Sat; by prior arrangement Sun.
Ⓛ WD £28; WE £22.
⌐Welcome by prior arrangement with the manager; day rates available; catering by arrangement; terms on application.
🍽 Full bar and catering facilities available 12 noon-2pm & 4.30pm-10.30pm every day except Mon; à la carte menu.
⌐ Dales Gate.

8A 83 Kilnwick Percy ☎
Pocklington, East Yorkshire, YO42 1UF
☎(01759) 303 090
1 mile east of Pocklington off the B1246.
Parkland course.
Founded 1994
Designed by John Day
18 holes, 6214 yards, S.S.S. 70
✝ Welcome any time
Ⓛ WD £12; WE £15; Full day: WD £18, WE £20.
⌐Welcome by prior arrangement; terms on application.
🍽 Snack menu, full catering service available for societies by prior arrangement.
⌐ Yorkway Motel.

8A 84 Kirkbymoorside ☎
Manor Vale, Kirkbymoorside, York, YO6 6EG
☎(01751) 431525
Course is on the A170 N of Kirkbymoorside.
Oakland course; club moved to present site in 1953.
Founded 1905/53

Designed by T K Cotton
18 holes, 6101 yards, S.S.S. 69
✝ Welcome after 9.30am and not between 12.30pm-1.30pm.
Ⓛ WD £20; WE £27.
⌐Welcome by prior arrangement; packages available for golf and catering; £29.50.
🍽 Full clubhouse facilities available.
⌐ George & Dragon; Kings Head, both Kirkbymoorside.

8A 85 Knaresborough
Butterhills, Boroughbridge Rd, Knaresborough, N Yorks, HG5 0QQ
☎(01423) 863219, Fax 869345, Pro 864865, Sec 862690, Bar/Rest 860173
On A6055 Boroughbridge Road 2 miles outside Knaresborough.
Parkland course with extensive trees; 17th is 627 yards.
Pro Gary J Vickers; Founded 1920
Designed by Hawtree & Son
18 holes, 6507 yards, S.S.S. 71
✝ Welcome after 9.30am WD and 10am WE; during winter season visitors must be accompanied by a member on WE
Ⓛ WD £25; WE £30.
⌐Welcome by prior arrangement between April 1 and Oct 31; parties of 12 or more welcome; full day golf and catering packages available for £42.
🍽 Full restaurant and bar facilities. Large practice area.
⌐ Nidd Hall, Harrogate; Dower House, Knaresborough; Crown Hotel, Boroughbridge.

8A 86 Leeds (Cobble Hall)
Elmete Lane, Leeds, W Yorks, LS8 2LJ
☎(0113) 2658775, Fax 2323369, Pro 2658786, Sec 2659203
On A58 Leeds-Wetherby road.
Parkland course with impressive views of Roundhay Park.
Pro Simon Longster; Founded 1896
18 holes, 6025 yards, S.S.S. 69
✝ Welcome WD by prior arrangement.
Ⓛ WD £27.
⌐Welcome by prior arrangement; packages available; terms on application.
🍽 Limited.
⌐ Weetwood Hall.

8A 87 Leeds Golf Centre
Wike Ridge Lane, Shadwell, Leeds, W Yorks, LS17 9JW

☎(0113) 2886000, Fax 2886185, Bar/Rest 2886160
Just off A61 Harrogate Road, 5 miles N of Leeds.
Open heathland course.
Pro N Harvey, M Pinkett; Founded 1993
Designed by Donald Steel
18 holes, 6482 yards, S.S.S. 71
✝ Welcome.
Ⓛ WD £13.50; WE £15.
⌐Welcome; restricted numbers at WE; golf and catering packages are available; also the 12-hole Oaks course.
🍽 Full facilities.
Practice range, 20 bays covered floodlit.
⌐ Harewood Arms; Weetwood Hall, both Leeds.

8A 88 Lees Hall
Hemsworth Rd, Norton, Sheffield, S8 8LL
☎(0114) 2554402, Pro 2507868, Sec 2552900, Bar/Rest 2551526
3 miles S of Sheffield.
Parkland course.
Founded 1907
18 holes, 6171 yards, S.S.S. 69
✝ Welcome.
Ⓛ WD £20; WE £30.
⌐Welcome WD by prior arrangement; catering packages by arrangement; snooker; terms on application.
🍽 Full facilities except Tues.
⌐ Grosvenor; Hallam Towers; Sheffield Moat House.

8A 89 Lightcliffe
Knowle Top Rd, Lightcliffe, Halifax, W Yorks, HX3 8RG
☎(01422) 202459
Course is just off the A58 Leeds-Halifax road.
Parkland course.
Pro Robert Kershaw; Founded 1907
9 holes, 5826 yards, S.S.S. 68
✝ Welcome except on Wed and comp days.
Ⓛ WD £15; WE £15.
⌐Welcome by prior arrangement; terms on application.
🍽 Full clubhouse facilities.
⌐ Trust House, Brighouse.

8A 90 Lofthouse Hill
Leeds Road, Lofthouse, Wakefield, WF3 3LR
☎(01924) 823703, Fax 823703, Pro 823703

Course is off the A61 four miles from Wakefield.
Founded 1994
Designed by B J Design
18 holes, 5933 yards, S.S.S. 70
† Welcome
  WD £15; WE £17.50.
  Welcome.
  Bar and catering facilities available.
Practice range, new driving range, 8 bays floodlit.

8A 91 Longley Park

Maple St, off Somerset Rd, Huddersfield, W Yorks, HD5 9AX
☎ 01484) 426932, Pro 422304
0.5 miles from Town centre.
Parkland course.
Pro Nick Leeming; Founded 1911
0 holes, 5209 yards, S.S.S. 66
† Welcome WD; restricted WE.
  WD £13; WE £16.
  Welcome by arrangement except Thurs and Sat; catering by arrangement; terms available on application.
  Full facilities except Mon.
  George, Huddersfield.

8A 92 Low Laithes

Parkmill Lane, Flushdyke, Ossett, W Yorks, WF5 9AP
☎ (01924) 273275, Fax 266067, Pro 274667, Sec 266067, Bar/Rest 267517
Close to M1 Junction 40 off A638 towards Dewsbury; turn right at end of slip road.
Parkland course.
Pro Paul Browning; Founded 1925
Designed by MacKenzie
18 holes, 6463 yards, S.S.S. 71
† Welcome WD after 9.30am and not between 12.30pm-1.30pm; WE by prior arrangement with the club Professional.
  WD £19; WE £32.
  Welcome WD by prior arrangement; package includes 27 holes and full catering; £32.
  Full clubhouse facilities.
  Post House; Mews House, both Ossett.

8A 93 Malton & Norton

Welham Park, Malton, N Yorks, YO17 9QE
☎ (01653) 692959, Fax 697912, Pro 693882, Sec 697912
From York take the A64 to the centre of Malton, right at traffic lights and

right at rail crossing; club is 0.75 miles.
Parkland course.
Pro S I Robinson; Founded 1910
Designed by Hawtree & Son
27 holes (3 loops of 9); Welham: 6456 yards, S.S.S. 71; Park: 6242 yards, S.S.S. 70; Derwent: 6286 yards, S.S.S. 70
† Welcome.
  WD £23; WE £30.
  Welcome by prior arrangement; full catering packages available; from £23.
  Full clubhouse facilities.
  Many in local area.

8A 94 Marsden

Mount Rd, Hemplow, Marsden, W Yorks, HD7 6NN
☎ (01484) 844253
Course is off the A62 eight miles from Huddersfield.
Moorland course.
Pro Nick Kryswicki; Founded 1920
Designed by Dr A. MacKenzie
9 holes, 5702 yards, S.S.S. 68
† Welcome WD.
  WD £10.
  Welcome WD by arrangement; packages available; terms on application.
  Clubhouse facilities except Tues.
  Durker Roods, Meltham.

8A 95 Masham

Burnholme, Swinton Rd, Masham, Ripon, N Yorkshire, HG4 4HT
☎ (01765) 689379
Off A6108 10 miles N of Ripon.
Meadowland course.
Founded 1895
9 holes, 6068 yards, S.S.S. 69
† Welcome WD; with a member at WE.
  WD £15 (18 holes).
  Welcome by arrangement with Sec; catering packages available; from £15.
  Full clubhouse facilities.
  Kings Head; Bay Horse; White Bear; Bruce Arms all in Marsham.

8A 96 Meltham

Thick Hollins Hall, Meltham, Huddersfield, W Yorks, HD7 3DQ
☎ (01484) 850227, Pro 851521
On B6107 6 miles SW of Huddersfield.
Parkland course.
Pro P F Davies; Founded 1908
21 holes, 6305 yards, S.S.S. 70

† Welcome except Wed and Sat.
  WD £20; WE £25.
  Welcome by prior arrangement; full catering packages available; terms on application.
  Full clubhouse facilities.
  Durker Roods Hall.

8A 97 Mid Yorkshire

Havercroft Lane, Darrington, Nr Pontefract, Yorks, WF8 3BP
☎ (01977) 704522, Fax 600823, Pro 600844
400 yards on A1 S from the M62/A1 intersection.
Parkland course.
Pro Alistair Cobbett; Founded 1993
Designed by Steve Marnoch
18 holes, 6466 yards, S.S.S 71
† Welcome WD; restrictions on WE mornings.
  WD £12-£18; WE £25.
  Welcome WD; WE between 1pm-4.30pm by prior arrangement; conference facilities; catering packages by arrangement; golf clinic; terms on application.
  Bar and restaurant facilities available.
Practice range, 22 bays floodlit.
  Darrington.

8A 98 Middleton Park

Ring Rd, Beeston, Leeds, W Yorks, LS10 3TN
☎ (0113) 2700449, Pro 2709506
3 miles S of city centre
Public parkland course.
Pro Adrian Newboult; Founded 1932
Designed by Leeds City Council
18 holes, 4947 yards, S.S.S. 69
† Welcome WD; book at WE.
  WD £7.75; WE £9.25.
  Welcome by arrangement.
  Limited.

8A 99 Moor Allerton

Coal Rd, Wike, Leeds, W Yorks, LS17 9NH
☎ (0113) 2661154, Fax 2371124, Pro 2665209, Bar/Rest 2682225
5 miles from Leeds off A61 Harrogate road.
Parkland course.
Pro Richard Lane; Founded 1923
Designed by Robert Trent Jones, Sr.
27 holes (3 x 9 loops forming three different courses): High: 6841 yards, S.S.S. 74; Lakes: 6470 yards, S.S.S. 72; Blackmoor: 6673 yards, S.S.S. 73
† Welcome by prior arrangement.
  WD £43; WE £67.

Welcome by prior arrangement; tee times reserved for groups of 12 or more; reductions Nov-March
Full clubhouse facilities.
Practice range.
Club can provide list of recommended hotels.

8A 100 Moortown

Harrogate Rd, Leeds, W Yorks, LS17 7DB
☎ (0113) 2681682, Fax 2680986, Pro 2683636, Sec 2686521, Bar/Rest 2688746
On A61 Harrogate road 1 miles past outer ring road.
Parkland course.
Pro Bryon Hutchinson; Founded 1909
Designed by Dr A. MacKenzie
18 holes, 7020 yards, S.S.S. 73
Welcome by prior arrangement.
WD £45; WE £50.
Welcome by prior arrangement; day rates also available; terms on application.
Full clubhouse restaurant and bar facilities.
Harewood Arms and others in Leeds area.

8A 101 Normanton

Snydale Rd, Normanton, Wakefield, WF6 1PA
☎ (01924) 200900
Off M62 Junction 31; 0.5 miles from Normanton centre.
Flat meadowland course.
Founded 1903
18 holes, 6991 yards, S.S.S. 69
Welcome except Sun.
WD £22; Sat £22.
Welcome WD by prior arrangement.
Full facilities.

8A 102 Northcliffe

High Bank Lane, Shipley, W Yorks, BD18 4RZ
☎ (01274) 584085, Fax 596731, Pro 587193, Sec 596731
On A650 W of Bradford to Saltaire roundabout.
Undulating parkland course.
Pro M Hillas; Founded 1920
Designed by James Braid/ Harry Vardon
18 holes, 6113 yards, S.S.S. 70
Welcome by prior arrangement.
WD £20; WE £25.
Welcome by prior arrangement; full day's catering and golf package; £35.

Full clubhouse facilities.
Bankfield Hotel, Bingley.

8A 103 Oakdale

Oakdale, Harrogate, Yorkshire, HG1 2LN
☎ (01423) 567162, Fax 536030, Pro 560510
Turn into Kent Road from Ripon Road in Harrogate.
Undulating parkland course with panoramic views.
Pro Clive Dell; Founded 1914
Designed by Dr A. MacKenzie
18 holes, 6456 yards, S.S.S. 71
Welcome.
Terms on application.
Welcome WD by prior arrangement; catering packages by arrangement; terms available on application.
Full facilities except Mon lunchtime.
Crown; Fern; Majestic; Studley; Old Swan; Balmoral.

8A 104 The Oaks

Aughton Common, Aughton, York, Yorks, YO4 4PW
☎ (01757) 288577, Fax 289029, Pro 288007, Bar/Rest 288001
On the B1228 1 mile N of Bubwith.
Wooded parkland course with 4 lakes.
Pro Jo Townshill; Founded 1996
Designed by J Covey
18 holes, 6743 yards, S.S.S. 72
Welcome WD.
WD £20.
Welcome WD by arrangement; packages of golf and catering available; from £28.
Full bar and catering service; à la carte restaurant.
Practice area.
Loftsome Bridge; Ye Olde Red Lion.

8A 105 Otley

West Busk Lane, Otley, W Yorks, LS21 3NG
☎ (01943) 465329, Fax 850387
Off A6038 on the outskirts of the market town of Otley between Leeds and Bradford.
Parkland course.
Founded 1906
18 holes, 6225 yards, S.S.S. 70
Welcome except Sat.
WD £26; WE £33.
Welcome WD by prior arrangement with Sec; packages by

arrangement with Sec; terms on application.
Full clubhouse bar and catering facilities.
Practice ground.
Chevin Lodge, Otley; Jarvis Parkway, Leeds; The Grove, Ilkley.

8A 106 Oulton Park

Pennington Lane, Rothwell, Leeds, LS26 8EX
☎ (0113) 2823152, Fax 2826290
Off M62 Junction 30, take A642 to Rothwell, left at 2nd roundabout.
Parkland course.
Host to the Leeds PGA cup
Pro Steve Gromett; Founded 1990
Designed by Peter Alliss & Dave Thomas
18 holes, 6470 yards, S.S.S. 71
Welcome by prior arrangement.
WD £10; WE £13.
Welcome WD by arrangement; full golf and catering packages available; also a 3169 yards par 35 9-hole course; terms on application.
Full clubhouse restaurant and bar facilities.
Practice range, 22 bays, 2- tier putting green to open in summer 2000.
5-star Oulton Hall on site.

8A 107 Outlane

Slack Lane, Outlane, Huddersfield, W Yorks, HD3 3YL
☎ (01422) 374762, Sec 311789
From M62 take A640 to Rochdale, left under the motorway through Outlane village.
Moorland/parkland course.
Pro D M Chapman; Founded 1906
18 holes, 6015 yards, S.S.S. 70
Welcome by prior arrangement.
WD £18; WE £28.
Welcome by prior arrangement; package details available from Mrs Caroline Hirst; terms available on application.
Full clubhouse facilities.
Old Golf House, Outlane.

8A 108 Owston Park

Owston Hall, Doncaster, S Yorks DN6 9JF
☎ (01302) 330821
5 miles off A19 near Doncaster.
9 holes, 6148 yards, S.S.S. 71
Welcome; pay and play.
WD £4.25; WE £4.50.
No facilities.
Very limited.

8A 109 Painthorpe House Golf & Country Club

Painthorpe Lane, Crigglestone, Wakefield, WF4 5AZ
☎ (01924) 255083, Fax 252022
Close to M1 Junction 39.
Undulating parkland course.
Founded 1961
9 holes, 4548 yards, S.S.S. 62
† Welcome; restrictions on Sun.
⌐ WD £5; WE £6.
⌐ Welcome by arrangement; terms on application.
⌐ Extensive facilities including four bars, 2 ballrooms and a function room.

8A 110 Pannal

Follifoot Rd, Pannal, Harrogate, Yorkshire, HG3 1ES
☎ (01423) 871641, Fax 870043, Pro 872620, Sec 872628, Catering 872629
⌐ pannalgolfclub@btconnect.com
Off A61 Leeds-Harrogate road 3 miles S of Harrogate.
Moorland/parkland course.
Pro David Padgett; Founded 1906
Designed by Sandy Herd
18 holes, 6622 yards, S.S.S. 72
† Welcome by prior arrangement only.
⌐ WD £40; WE £50.
⌐ Welcome by prior arrangement; catering can be arranged; terms on application.
⌐ Full clubhouse bar and catering facilities.
⌐ Majestic, Harrogate.

8A 111 Phoenix

Pavilion Lane, Brinsworth, Rotherham, S Yorks, S60 5PB
☎ (01709) 838182, Fax 383788
Voure is one mile along the Bawtry road turning from the Tinsley roundabout on the M1.
Undulating meadowland course.
Pro M Roberts; Founded 1932
18 holes, 6182 yards, S.S.S. 69
† Welcome.
⌐ Terms on application.
⌐ Welcome WD by prior arrangement; packages for golf and catering available; from £24.
⌐ Full catering facilities.
Practice range, 20 bays covered.

8A 112 Phoenix Park

Phoenix Park, Dick Lane, Thornbury, Bradford, W Yorks, BD3 7AT
☎ 01274) 615546

Off A647 Bradford to Leeds road at Thornbury roundabout.
Undulating parkland course.
9 holes, 4646 yards, S.S.S. 66
† Welcome WD only.
⌐ Terms on application.
⌐ Welcome by prior arrangement; terms on aplication.
⌐ Catering available by prior arrangement.

8A 113 Pike Hills

Tadcaster Rd, Askham Bryan, York, Yorks, YO2 3UW
☎ (01904) 706566, Fax 700797, Pro 708756, Sec 700797, Bar/Rest 704416
On A64 4 miles W of York.
Parkland course; formed 1920 as Hob Moor GC, moved 1946.
Pro I Gradwell; Founded 1920/46
18 holes, 6146 yards, S.S.S. 69
† Welcome WD; only with member at WE.
⌐ WD £18; WE £18.
⌐ Welcome by prior arrangement; packages include full catering and 36 holes of golf; £35.
⌐ Full clubhouse facilities.

8A 114 Pontefract & District

Park Lane, Pontefract, W Yorks, WF8 4QS
☎ (01977) 798886, Pro 706806, Sec 792241
Course is on the B6134 off the M62 Junction 32.
Parkland course.
Pro Nicholas Newman; Founded 1900
18 holes, 6232 yards, S.S.S. 70
† Welcome WD; by prior arrangement WE.
⌐ WD £25; WE £32.
⌐ Welcome WD except Wed; packages available; terms on application.
⌐ Full facilities.
⌐ Rod Lion; Wentbridge House; Park Side Inn.

8A 115 Pontefract Park

Park Road, Pontefract, W Yorkshire,
☎ 01977) 723490
Close to Pontefract racecourse 0.5 miles from M62.
Public parkland course.
9 holes, 4068 yards, S.S.S. 62
† Welcome.
⌐ WD £3; WE £3 (9 holes).
⌐ None.
⌐ None.

8A 116 Queensbury

Brighouse Rd, Queensbury, Bradford, W Yorks, BD13 1QF
☎ (01274) 882155, Pro 816864
From the M62 Junction 26 take the A58 towards Halifax for 3.5 miles then turn to Keighley for three miles; also via the A647, 4 miles from Bradford.
Undulating parkland course.
Pro John Ambler; Founded 1923
9 holes, 5024 yards, S.S.S. 65
† Welcome.
⌐ WD £15; WE £30.
⌐ Welcome by prior arrangement; packages available; function facilities; terms on application.
⌐ Full bar and à la carte restaurant service.
⌐ Novotel.

8A 117 Rawdon

Buckstone Drive, Rawdon, Leeds, W Yorks, LS19 6BD
☎ (0113) 2506040, Pro 2505017, Sec 2506044
On A65 6 miles from Leeds turning left at Rawdon traffic lights.
Undulating parkland course.
Pro Simon Poot; Founded 1896
9 holes, 5982 yards, S.S.S. 69
† Welcome WD.
⌐ Terms on application.
⌐ Welcome WD by prior arrangement; golf and catering packages available; 3 all-weather and 4 grass tennis courts.
⌐ Full facilities except Mon.
⌐ Peas Hill; Robin Hood.

8A 118 Renishaw Park

Golf House, Mill Lane, Renishaw, Sheffield, S Yorks, S21 3UZ
☎ (01246) 432044, Pro 435484
1.5 miles W of the M1 Junction 30 on the A6135.
Parkland course.
Pro J Oates; Founded 1911
Designed by Sir G. Sitwoll
18 holes, 6262 yards, S.S.S. 70
† Welcome by arrangement.
⌐ WD £23.50; WE £32.50.
⌐ Welcome by arrangement; packages on application; WD day ticket £32; WE day ticket £36; terms on application.
⌐ Full clubhouse facilities.
⌐ Sitwell Arms.

8A 119 Richmond

Bend Hagg, Richmond, N Yorks, DL10 5EX

☎ (01748) 825319, Pro 822457, Sec 823231
From A1 Scotch Corner follow the Richmond road to lights in town; turn right.
Parkland course; extended to 18 holes in 1970.
Pro Paul Jackson; Founded 1892
Designed by Frank Pennink
18 holes, 5779 yards, S.S.S. 68
† Welcome, except before 3pm on Sun.
ℓ WD £20; WE £25.
⌁ Welcome by prior arrangement; reduced rates for groups of more than 16; packages available; from £18.
◉ Full bar and restaurant facilities everyday.
⌐ Turf Hotel; Black Lion; Kings Head.

8A 120 Riddlesden ☞
Howden Rough, Riddlesden, Keighley, W Yorks, BD20 5QN
☎ (01535) 602148, Sec 607646
From A650 Bradford road turn into Scott Lane.
Moorland course.
Founded 1927
18 holes, 4295 yards, S.S.S. 61
† Welcome.
ℓ WD £10; WE £15.
⌁ Welcome on WD by prior arrangement; terms available on application.
◉ Clubhouse facilities.
⌐ Dalesgate Hotel.

8A 121 Ripon City
Palace Rd, Ripon, N Yorks, HG4 3HH
☎ (01765) 601987, Pro 600411, Sec 603640, Bar/Rest 603640
Course is on the A6108 one mile N of Ripon.
Undulating parkland course.
Pro Tim Davis; Founded 1908
New 9 holes designed by ADAS
18 holes, 6120 yards, S.S.S. 69
† Welcome with handicap certs preferred.
ℓ WD £20; WE £30.
⌁ Welcome by arrangement; packages available for groups of more than 20.
◉ Full clubhouse facilities.
⌐ Nags Head; Kirkgate House both Thirsk.

8A 122 Robin Hood
Owston Hall, Owston, Nr Carcroft, Doncaster, S Yorks, DN6 9JF

☎ (01302) 722800, Fax 728885
6 miles N of Doncaster on B1220 off the A19.
Parkland course; formerly Owston Park Golf Course.
Founded 1988/1996
Designed by W Adamson
18 holes, 6937 yards, S.S.S. 72
† Welcome.
ℓ WD £12; WE £14.
⌁ Welcome by prior arrangement; full catering packages available for 12 or more players; free golf cart available for groups of more than 20; function room with facilities for 60-100 people; £15-£36.
◉ Full restaurant and bar facilities in 18th century clubhouse.
⌐ Accommodation and health suite on site.

8A 123 Romanby
Yafforth Road, Northallerton, N Yorks, DL7 0PE
☎ (01609) 779988, Fax 779084, Sec 778855, Bar/Rest 777824
Course is on the B6271 Northallerton-Richmond road one mile NW of Northallerton.
Parkland course.
Pro Tim Jenkins; Founded 1993
Designed by W Adamson
18 holes, 6663 yards, S.S.S. 72
† Welcome.
ℓ WD £18; WE £25.
⌁ Welcome 7 days; Premier Tee and Silver Tee packages available; from £26.50.
◉ Full clubhouse bar and restaurant facilities.
⌐ Golden Lion.

8A 124 Rother Valley
Mansfield Rd, Wales Bar, Sheffield, Yorks, S31 8PE
☎ (0114) 2473000, Fax 2476000
Course is between Sheffield and Rotherham off the M1 Junction 31; follow the signs for Rother Valley country park.
Parkland with water features.
Pro Jason Ripley; Founded 1996
Designed by M Roe/M Shattock
18 holes, 6602 yards, S.S.S. 72
† Welcome.
ℓ WD £11 (£7.50 Mon); WE £16.
⌁ Welcome at all times; packages include catering, golf and use of driving range; par 3 course; £10-£30.
◉ Restaurant and bar facilities available.
Practice range, 27 bays floodlit.
⌐ Aston Hall, Sheffield.

8A 125 Rotherham
Thrybergh Park, Doncaster Road, Thrybergh, Rotherham, S Yorks, S65 4NU
☎ (01709) 850466, Fax 855288, Pro 850480, Sec 850812
On A630 Doncaster to Rotherham rd.
Parkland course.
Pro Simon Thornhill; Founded 1903
18 holes, 6324 yards, S.S.S. 70
† Welcome by arrangement with Pro or Sec.
ℓ Terms on application.
⌁ Welcome except Wed by prior arrangement with Sec; minimum 16; discounts for groups of 40 or more; snooker; terms on application.
◉ Full facilities.
Practice area.
⌐ Swallow; Moat House; Limes; Brecon.

8A 126 Roundhay
Park Lane, Leeds, Yorks, LS8 2EJ
☎ (0113) 2662695, Pro 2661686
4.5 miles from city centre on A58 to Wetherby.
Parkland with mature trees.
Pro Jim Pape; Founded 1922
9 holes, 5322 yards, S.S.S. 65
† Municipal pay and play.
ℓ WD £8.50; WE £8.50.
⌁ Welcome by arrangement with Pro; packages available on application; from £8.50.
◉ Catering available in restaurant in evenings Tues-Sat; bar.
⌐ Beechwood.

8A 127 Roundwood
Off Green Lane, Rawmarsh, Rotherham, S Yorks, S62 6LA
☎ (01709) 523471
Course is off the A633 2.5 miles N of Rotherham.
Parkland course.
Founded 1977
9 holes, 5713 yards, S.S.S. 67
† Welcome except WE mornings.
ℓ WD £12; WE £15.
⌁ Welcome WD by prior arrangement; packages available; terms on application.
◉ Bar facilities; catering Wed to Sat.

8A 128 Rudding Park
Follifoot, Harrogate, N Yorks, HG3 1DJ
☎ (01423) 872100, Fax 873011, Pro 873400
Off A658 Harrogate by-pass 2 miles S of Harrogate.

Parkland course.
Pro Simon Hotham; Founded 1995
Designed by Hawtree
18 holes, 6871 yards, S.S.S. 73
🚩 Welcome with handicap certs.
🍴 Terms on application.
🏌 Welcome with prior arrangement;
packages available; terms on
application.
🏆 Full clubhouse facilities.
Practice range, 18 covered bays.
🛏 Rudding Park.

8A 129 **Ryburn**
The Shaw, Norland, Sowerby Bridge,
W Yorks, HX6 3QP
☎ (01422) 831355
3 miles S of Halifax.
Hilly moorland course.
Founded 1910
9 holes, 4907 yards, S.S.S 65
🚩 Welcome WD; WE by
arrangement.
🍴 WD £14; WE £20.
🏌 Welcome by prior arrangement;
terms on application.
🏆 Catering and bar facilities.
🛏 The Hobbit Inn.

8A 130 **Sand Moor**
Alwoodley Lane, Leeds, W Yorks,
LS17 7DJ
☎ (0113) 2685180, Fax 2685180,
Pro 2683925
6 miles from centre of Leeds on the
A61 N.
Undulating parkland/moorland
course.
Pro Peter Tupling; Founded 1926
Designed by A MacKenzie
18 holes, 6429 yards, S.S.S. 71
🚩 Welcome WD, except 12 noon-
1.30pm, Tues 9.30am-10.30am and
Thurs 8.30am-12 noon.
🍴 WD £32.
🏌 Welcome WD by prior
arrangement; catering packages by
arrangement; terms available on
application.
🏆 Full facilities.
🛏 Harewood Arms; Parkway, Forte
Crest.

8A 131 **Sandhill**
Middlecliffe Lane, Little Houghton,
Barnsley, S72 0HW
☎ (01226) 753444, Fax 717420,
Bar/Rest 755079
Off A635 Barnsley-Doncaster road
near Darfield.
Parkland course.
Founded 1993

Designed by John Royston
18 holes, 6250 yards, S.S.S. 70
🚩 Welcome.
🍴 WD £8.50; WE £11.
🏌 Welcome WD; not before 10am
Sat or 12 noon Sun; packages
available; terms available on
application.
🏆 Full clubhouse facilities available.
Practice range, 18 bays floodlit.
🛏 Ardsley Moat House.

8A 132 **Scarborough North Cliff**
North Cliff Ave, Burniston Rd,
Scarborough, YO12 6PP
☎ (01723) 360786, Fax 362134, Pro
365920
2 miles N of town centre on coast
road.
Seaside/parkland course.
Pro Simon Dellor
Founded 1928
Designed by James Braid
18 holes, 6425 yards, S.S.S. 71
🚩 Welcome except before 10am
Sun.
🍴 WD £18; WE £22.
🏌 Welcome by prior arrangement
with Sec; packages for groups
between 8 and 40; catering packages
by arrangement; terms available on
application.
🏆 Full facilities.
Practice area.
🛏 Park Manor; Headlands.

8A 133 **Scarborough South Cliff** ☎
Deepdale Ave, Scarborough, YO11
2UE
☎ (01723) 360522, Fax 376969, Pro
365150, Sec 374737
1 mile S of Scarborough on the main
Filey road.
Parkland/seaside course.
Pro Tony Skingle; Founded 1903
Designed by Dr A. MacKenzie
18 holes, 6039 yards, S.S.S. 69
🚩 Welcome.
🍴 WD £20; WE £25.
🏌 Welcome WD and WE by prior
arrangement; packages available;
terms on application.
🏆 Full facilities.
Practice ground.
🛏 Crown; St Nicholas; Southlands;
Mount House.

8A 134 **Scarcroft**
Syke Lane, Scarcroft, Leeds, W
Yorks, LS14 3BQ

☎ (0113) 2892263, Pro 2892780,
Sec 2892311, Bar/Rest 2892883
Off A58 Leeds to Wetherby road
turning left at Bracken Fox public
house.
Parkland course.
Pro Darren Tear; Founded 1937
Designed by Robert Blackburn
18 holes, 6426 yards, S.S.S. 71
🚩 Welcome; some WE restrictions.
🍴 WD £28; WE £40.
🏌 Welcome by prior arrangement;
packages available for all-day golf
and catering for groups of 20 or
more; £40.
🏆 Full clubhouse facilities.
🛏 Jarvis, Wetherby; Harewood
Arms, Harewood.

8A 135 **Scathingwell**
Scathingwell Centre, Scathingwell,
Tadcaster, Yorks, LS24 9PF
☎ (01937) 557878, Fax 557909, Pro
557864
Course is on the A162 three miles
from the A1 between Tadcaster and
Ferrybridge.
Parkland course.
Pro Steve Footman; Founded 1993
Designed by I Webster
18 holes, 6771 yards, S.S.S. 72
🚩 Welcome but prior booking
essential.
🍴 WD £16; WE £18.
🏌 Welcome by prior arrangement;
individual packages can be arranged;
summer and winter packages
available; terms on application.
🏆 Full clubhouse facilities.
🛏 Hilton, Garforth; Selby Fork Hotel.

8A 136 **Selby**
Mill Lane, Brayton, Selby, N Yorks,
YO8 9LD
☎ (01757) 228622, Pro 228785
3 miles SW of Selby; 1 mile E of A19
at Brayton village
Links style course.
Pro Andrew Smith; Founded 1907
Designed by J.H. Taylor & Hawtree
Ltd
18 holes, 6249 yards, S.S.S. 70
🚩 Welcome WD with handicap certs;
WE with member.
🍴 WD £24.
🏌 Welcome Wed, Thurs and Fri by
prior arrangement; catering packages
by arrangement; snooker; terms on
application.
🏆 Full facilities.
Practice ground.
🛏 Londesbro; Selby Fork Motel; The
Owl.

8A 137 Serlby Park
Serlby, Doncaster, S Yorks, DN10 6BA
☎ (01777) 818268
3 miles S of Bawtry.
Parkland course.
Founded 1895
Designed by Viscount Galway
9 holes, 5376 yards, S.S.S. 66
† Welcome only with member.
⌐ Not available.
♢ Welcome only by prior arrangement with Sec; terms on application.
🍽 Clubhouse facilities.
⌐ Crown, Bawtry; Mount Pleasant; Olde Bell, both Barnaby Moor.

8A 138 Settle
Buckhaw Brow, Settle, Yorks, BD24 0DH
☎ (01729) 825288
Course is on Kendal Road one mile beyond town.
Parkland course.
Founded 1895
Designed by Tom Vardon
9 holes, 5414 yards, S.S.S. 66
† Welcome except Sun.
⌐ WD £12; WE £12.
♢ Welcome by prior arrangement; terms on application.
🍽 Clubhouse facilities available.
⌐ Falcon Hotel, Settle; Royal Oak, Settle.

8A 139 The Shay Grange Golf Centre
Long Lane, Off Bingley Road, Bradford, W Yorks, BD9 6RX
☎ (01274) 491945, Pro 491547
Course is off the A650 Bradford road at Cottingley.
Parkland course.
Pro Neil Reeves, David Delaney, John Clapham; Founded 1996
Designed by Tim Colclough
9 holes, 3380 yards, S.S.S. 58
† Pay and play.
⌐ WD £5; WE £5.
♢ Welcome by prior arrangement; discounts available including golf and meals at nearby restaurant; from £10.
🍽 Limited.
Practice range, 32 bays.
⌐ Jarvis Bankfield.

8A 140 Shipley
Beckfoot Lane, Cottingley Bridge, Bingley, W Yorks, BD16 1LX
☎ (01274) 563212, Fax 568652, Pro 563674, Sec 568652

On A650 6 miles N of Bradford.
Parkland course.
Pro J R Parry; Founded 1896/22
Designed by Colt, Alison and Dr MacKenzie assisted by James Braid
18 holes, 6215 yards, S.S.S. 70
† Welcome except Tues before 3pm and Sat after 3:30pm.
⌐ WD £27; WE £32.
♢ Welcome Wed, Thurs, Fri; packages available; terms on application.
🍽 Full clubhouse facilities available.

8A 141 Silkstone
Field Head, Silkstone, Barnsley, S Yorks, S75 4LD
☎ (01226) 790328, Pro 790128
On A628 1 mile from M1.
Undulating meadowland.
Pro Kevin Guy; Founded 1893
18 holes, 6069 yards, S.S.S. 70
† Welcome WD.
⌐ Terms on application.
♢ Welcome WD by prior arrangement; packages available; terms on application.
🍽 Full facilities except Mon.
Practice area.
⌐ Ardsley Moat House; Brooklands Motel.

8A 142 Silsden
High Brunthwaite, Silsden, Keighley, W Yorks, BD20 0NH
☎ (01535) 652998
4 miles from Keighley on A6034 to Silsden, turn E at canal.
Moorland/meadowland course.
Founded 1913
14 holes 4870 yards, S.S.S. 64
† Welcome; WE restrictions.
⌐ Terms on application.
♢ Terms on application.
🍽 Clubhouse facilities.
⌐ Steeton Hall.

8A 143 Sitwell Park
Shrogswood Rd, Rotherham, Yorkshire, S60 4BY
☎ (01709) 700799, Fax 703637, Pro 540961, Sec 541046
From M1 Junction 33; take 2nd exit at roundabout until signposted; also from M18 Junction 1.
Parkland course.
Pro Nick Taylor; Founded 1913
Designed by Dr A. MacKenzie
18 holes, 6209 yards, S.S.S. 70
† Welcome.
⌐ WD £24; WE £28.
♢ Welcome by prior arrangement

with the Secretary; discounts for parties of 30; terms available on application.
Snooker and billiard tables.
🍽 Clubhouse facilities.
⌐ Campanile; Beefeater The Brecks.

8A 144 Skipton
North-West By-Pass, Skipton, N Yorks, BD23 1LL
☎ (01756) 795657, Fax 796665, Pro 793922
Course is on the A65 one mile N of Skipton.
Undulating parkland course with panoramic views and water.
Pro Peter Robinson; Founded 1896
18 holes, 6049 yards, S.S.S. 69
† Welcome; some restrictions Tues and WE.
⌐ Terms on application.
♢ Welcome WD by prior arrangement with Sec; packages available; snooker and reading rooms; £22.
🍽 Dining, banqueting and bar.
Practice range, 0.5 miles away.
⌐ Hanover, Skipton; Devonshire Arms, Bolton Abbey; Stirk House, Gisburn.

8A 145 South Bradford
Pearson Rd, Odsal, Bradford, BD6 1BJ
☎ (01274) 679195, Pro 673346
From Odsal roundabout take Stadium Road and then Pearson Road.
Undulating meadowland course.
Founded 1906
9 holes, 6068 yards, S.S.S. 69
† Welcome WD.
⌐ WD £15.
♢ Welcome Tues-Fri by prior arrangement; terms available on application.
🍽 Full facilities except Mon.
⌐ Guide Post.

8A 146 South Leeds
Gypsy Lane, off Middleton Ring Rd, Leeds, W Yorks, LS11 5TU
☎ (0113) 2700479, Pro 2702598, Sec 2771676
Close to M1 Junction 45 and M62 Junction 28.
Undulating parkland course.
Pro Mike Lewis; Founded 1914
Designed by Dr A MacKenzie
18 holes, 5769 yards, S.S.S. 68
† Welcome WD; WE only with member.

WD £18; WE £9.
Welcome by prior arrangement; packages can be arranged depending on numbers; terms on application.
Clubhouse facilities.
Practice ground.
Oulton Hall; Leeds International Hilton.

8A 147 Spaldington
Spaldington Lane, Howden, E Yorks, DN12 7NP
☎ (01757) 288262
Take B1288 out of Howden towards Bubwith and then head for Spaldington.
Parkland course.
Founded 1995
Designed by PMS Golf
9 holes, 3482 yards
Welcome.
WD £4; WE £4.
Welcome.
Practice range, 18 bays floodlit.

8A 148 Springhead Park
Willerby Rd, Hull, Yorks, HU5 5JE
☎ (01482) 656309/614968
From A63 follow signs from Humber Bridge to Beverley to major roundabout and then signs to Willerby.
Parkland course.
Pro B Herrington; Founded 1930
18 holes, 6402 yards, S.S.S. 71
Municipal course; clubhouse access with a member only.
WD £7; WE £8.
Welcome by prior arrangement with Sec; terms on application.
Clubhouse facilities.

8A 149 Springmill
Queens Drive, Osset, W Yorks,
☎ (01924) 272515
1 mile from Osset towards Wakefield
Public parkland course.
9 holes, 2330 yards
Welcome.
Terms on application.

8A 150 Stocksbridge & District
30 Royd Lane, Townend, Deepcar, Sheffield, Yorks, S36 2RZ
☎ (0114) 2882003, Pro 2882779
Close to M1 Junction 36.
Moorland course.
Pro Tim Brookes; Founded 1924
Designed by Peter Alliss, Dave Thomas (extension)

18 holes, 5097 yards, S.S.S. 65
Welcome WD.
WD £26; WE £27.
Welcome WD by prior arrangement; packages include 36 holes of golf and all day catering; £25.
Full clubhouse facilities available.
Tankersley Manor; The Wentworth; Ardsley House; Hallam Towers; Grosvenor.

8A 151 Sutton Park
Salthouse Rd, Hull, Yorks, HU8 9HF
☎ (01482) 374242, Fax 701428
A165 E to Salthouse Road.
Parkland course.
Pro Paul Rushworth; Founded 1935
18 holes, 6251 yards, S.S.S. 70
Welcome by prior arrangement.
Terms on application.
Welcome by prior arrangement; terms on application.
Bar facilities.

8A 152 Swallow Hall
Swallow Hall, Crockey Hill, York, YO1 4SG
☎ (01904) 448219
Off A19 S of York; after 1.5 miles turn left to Wheldrake.
Public parkland course.
Founded 1991
9 holes, 3092 yards
Welcome.
WD £7; WE £8.
Welcome by arrangement.
Limited.
Practice range.

8A 153 Swingtime (Leeds)
Redcote Lane, Leeds, W Yorks, LS4 2AW
☎ (0113) 2633030, Fax 2633044
1.5 miles W of Leeds town centre off Kirkstall Road.
Course re-opening in 1998.
Pro Paul Groonomith; Founded 1996
9 holes, 1800 yards, par 30
Welcome.
WD £5; WE £5.
Full facilities.
Welcome with prior booking
Practice range, 30 bays floodlit, putting green.

8A 154 Tankersley Park
High Green, Sheffield, S Yorks, S35 4LG
☎ (0114) 2468247, Fax 2455586, Pro 2455586

From M1 Junction 35A entrance 400 yards.
Parkland course.
Pro Ian Kirk; Founded 1907
Designed by Hawtree
18 holes, 6212 yards, S.S.S. 70
Welcome, booking at WE essential.
WD £25.
Welcome by prior arrangement on WD; catering packages available; terms on application.
Full catering facilities available; bar.
Tankersley Manor; Norfolk Arms.

8A 155 Temple Newsam
Temple Newsam Rd, Leeds, W Yorks, LS15 0LN
☎ (0113) 2645624, Pro 2647362
On A64 York road 5 miles from Leeds.
Undulating parkland course.
Pro Allan Swaine; Founded 1923
Lady Dorothy: 18 holes, 6094 yards, S.S.S. 69; Lord Erwin: 18 holes, 6153 yards, S.S.S. 69
Welcome.
Terms on application.
Welcome by arrangement; packages available; terms on application.
Full facilities; carvery WE.
Windmill; Mercury.

8A 156 Thirsk & Northallerton
Thornton-le-Street, Thirsk, N Yorks, YO7 4AB
☎ (01845) 522170, Pro 526216, Sec 525115
Near A19 and A168 2 miles N of Thirsk.
Parkland course.
Pro Robert Garner; Founded 1914/1997
Designed by W Adamson
18 holes, 6495 yards, S.S.S. 70
Welcome WD; only with member at WE.
WD £20; WE £20.
Welcome WD by prior arrangement; catering packages available; from £20.
Full clubhouse facilities.
Golden Fleece; Three Tuns.

8A 157 Thorne
Kirton Lane, Thorne, Doncaster, S Yorks, DN8 5RJ
☎ (01405) 815173, Fax 741899, Pro 812084, Sec 812084

From M18 Junction 6 to Thorne;
signposted.
Parkland course.
Pro Richard Highfield; Founded 1980
Designed by Richard Highfield
18 holes, 5366 yards, S.S.S. 65
† Welcome.
⌣ WD £9; WE £10.
⌣ Welcome by prior arrangement;
£50 deposit required which is
refunded on the day; terms on
application.
◉ Clubhouse facilities.
Small practice area.
⌐ Belmont.

8A 158 **Tinsley Park**
High Hazel Park, Darnall, Sheffield, S
Yorks, S9 4PE
☎ (0114) 2037435
Course is on the A57 from Junction
33 on the M1.
Parkland course.
Pro R Highfield; Founded 1921
18 holes, 6084 yards, S.S.S. 69
† Welcome.
⌣ WD £8.50; WE £8.90.
⌣ Welcome by arrangement with the
local council.
◉ Full facilities.
⌐ Royal Victoria.

8A 159 **Todmorden**
Rive Rocks, Cross Stone Rd,
Todmorden, OL14 7RD
☎ (01706) 812986
1.5 miles along Halifax road.
Moorland course.
Founded 1895
9 holes, 5878 yards, S.S.S. 68
† Welcome WD; WE by
arrangement.
⌣ WD £15; WE £20.
⌣ Welcome WD by prior
arrangement.
◉ Clubhouse facilities.
⌐ Scaite Cliffe Hall; Brandschatter
Berghoff.

8A 160 **Wakefield**
Woodthorpe Lane, Sandal, Wakefield,
WF2 6JH
☎ (01924) 255104, Fax 242752, Pro
255380, Sec 258778
Course is on the A61 three miles S of
Wakefield.
Parkland course.
Pro Ian Wright; Founded 1891
Designed by Alex Herd
18 holes, 6613 yards, S.S.S. 72
† Welcome by prior arrangement.
⌣ WD £22; WE £30.

⌣ Welcome by application to Sec;
catering packages by arrangement;
snooker; terms on application.
◉ Full facilities.
⌐ Cedar Court; Swallow.

8A 161 **Waterton Park**
The Balk, Walton, Wakefield, WF2
6QL
☎ (01924) 259525, Fax 256969, Pro
255557, Bar/Rest 255855
Course is close to M1 Junction 39
following signs for Barnsley and A61;
left to Wakefield and then to Shay
Lane.
Parkland on Waterton Hall with trees,
26-acre lake.
Pro Patrick Hall; Founded 1995
Designed by S Gidman
18 holes, 6843 yards, S.S.S. 73
† Welcome as members' guests
only.
⌣ Not available.
⌣ None.
◉ Bars and dining room in the
exclusive club house.
⌐ Waterton Park.

8A 162 **Wath**
Abdy, Blackamoor, Rotherham, S
Yorks, S62 7SJ
☎ (01709) 872149, Pro 878677
Off A633 in Wath, 7 miles N of
Rotherham.
Meadowland course.
Pro Chris Bassett; Founded 1904
18 holes, 5801 yards, S.S.S. 68
† Welcome WD; only with a member
WE.
⌣ WD £20; WE n/a.
⌣ Welcome by prior arrangement;
special packages available for golf
and catering; terms on application.
◉ Full facilities.
⌐ Moat House, Rotherham.

8A 163 **West Bowling**
Newall Hall, Rooley Lane, Bradford,
W Yorks, BD5 8LB
☎ (01274) 724449, Pro 728036, Sec
393207
At Junction of M606 and Bradford
ring road.
Parkland course.
Pro Ian Marshall; Founded 1898
18 holes, 5769 yards, S.S.S. 68
† Welcome WD; restrictions at WE.
⌣ WD £22; WE £30.
⌣ Welcome Wed, Thurs, Fri by
arrangement with the manager;
catering by arrangement; snooker;
terms on application.

◉ Full facilities.
⌐ Novotel; Norfolk Gardens; Guide
Post; Tong Village; Victoria.

8A 164 **West Bradford**
Chellow Grange, Haworth Rd,
Bradford, W Yorks, BD9 6NP
☎ (01274) 542767, Pro 542102
Course is off the B6144 three miles
W of Bradford.
Parkland course.
Pro Nigel Barber; Founded 1900
18 holes, 5723 yards, S.S.S. 68
† Welcome except before 9.30am
and between 12 noon-1.30pm.
⌣ WD £18; WE £18.
⌣ Welcome by arrangement;
packages including catering and golf
with reduced green fees available;
terms on application.
◉ Full clubhouse facilities.

8A 165 **West End (Halifax)**
Paddock Lane, Highroad Well,
Halifax, W Yorks, HX2 0NT
☎ (01422) 353608, Fax 341878, Pro
363293, Sec 341878, Steward
369844
2 miles W of Halifax off Burnley-
Rochdale road.
Parkland course.
Pro David Rishworth; Founded 1906
Designed by Members
18 holes, 5937 yards, S.S.S. 69
† Welcome by prior arrangement.
⌣ WD £21; WE £28.
⌣ Welcome by prior arrangement
with Sec; packages available; from
£21.
◉ Clubhouse facilities.
⌐ Windmill Court, Halifax.

8A 166 **Wetherby**
Linton Lane, Wetherby, Yorks, LS22
4JF
☎ (01937) 583375, Fax 531915, Sec
580089, Bar/Rest 582527
Course is one mile west of A1 south
of Linton village.
Parkland course.
Pro David Padgett; Founded 1910
18 holes, 6235 yards, S.S.S. 70
† Welcome Mon and Tues
afternoons; all day Wed, Thurs, Fri.
⌣ WD £25.
⌣ Welcome by prior arrangement;
packages available; discounts for
groups of 40; terms available on
application.
◉ Full clubhouse facilities.
⌐ Linton Springs; Jarvis Resort;
Wood Hall.

8A 167 Wheatley

Armthorpe Rd, Doncaster, S Yorks, DN2 5QB
☎ (01302) 831655, Pro 834085
Close to Doncaster racecourse following the ring road S; opposite large water tower.
Undulating parkland; relocated 1933.
Pro Steve Fox
Founded 1913/1933
Designed by George Duncan
18 holes, 6405 yards, S.S.S. 71
† Welcome.
⌣ WD £20; WE £30.
⌣ Welcome WD by prior arrangement; day ticket (WD £25); catering by prior arrangement; from £20.
◉ Full facilities.
⌐ Balmoral; Earl of Doncaster; Punches.

8A 168 Whitby

Sandsend Rd, Low Straggleton, Whitby, N Yorks, YO21 3SR
☎ (01947) 602768, Fax 600660, Pro 602719, Sec 600660
On A174 coast road between Whitby and Sandsend.
Seaside course.
Pro Richard Wood
Founded 1892
18 holes, 6134 yards, S.S.S. 69
† Welcome by prior arrangement.
⌣ WD £20; WE £25.
⌣ Welcome by prior arrangement; winter and summer packages available for groups of 8 or more; from £19.50.
◉ Full facilities.
Practice area.
⌐ Larpool; Seacliff; White House.

8A 169 Whitwood

Altofts Lane, Whitwood, Castleford, W Yorks, WF10 5PZ
☎ (01977) 604215, Pro 512835, Bar/Rest 512835
Course is 0.5 miles towards Castleford off M62 Junction 31.
Parkland course.
Pro Richard Golding
Founded 1986
Designed by Steve Wells (Wakefield Council)
9 holes, 6282 yards, S.S.S. 70
† Welcome; booking system available.
⌣ WD £5.90; WE £8.
⌣ Welcome by arrangement with the Pro; terms on application.
◉ Available at local inn.
⌐ Bridge Inn.

8A 170 Willow Valley Golf & Country Club

Highmoor Lane, Clifton, Brighouse, W Yorks, HD6 4JB
☎ (01274) 878624, Fax 852805
From M62 Junction 25 take A644 to Brighouse; turn right at first roundabout.
American parkland style course.
Pro Julian Howarth; Founded 1993
Designed by J Gaunt
18 holes, 7021 yards, S.S.S. 74
† Welcome.
⌣ WD £20; WE £24.
⌣ Welcome WD; packages available for groups of 12 or more; from £27.50.
◉ Full clubhouse facilities.
Practice range, 24 bays floodlit.
⌐ Forte Crest; Black Horse Inn; Hartshead Moor.

8A 171 Withernsea

Chestnut Ave, Withernsea, E Yorks, HU19 2PG
☎ (01964) 612258, Sec 612078
25 miles E of Hull on main road to Withernsea.
Seaside links course.
Pro G Harrison; Founded 1907
9 holes, 6191 yards, S.S.S. 64
† Welcome; after 2pm Sun.
⌣ WD £10; WE £10.
⌣ Welcome by prior arrangement; catering packages can be arranged; from £10.
◉ Clubhouse facilities.

8A 172 Wombwell (Hillies)

Wentworth View, Wombwell, Barnsley, S Yorks, S73 0LA
☎ (01226) 754433, Sec 758635
4 miles SE of Barnsley.
Meadowland course.
Founded 1981
9 holes, 4190 yards
† Welcome.
⌣ WD £6.30; WE £7.80.
⌣ Welcome by prior arrangement; limited catering is available; from £6.30.
◉ Bar service only.

8A 173 Woodhall Hills

Woodhall Rd, Calverley, Pudsey, W Yorks, LS28 5UN
☎ (0113) 2564771, Pro 255462857, Sec 2554594
Take A647 Leeds-Bradford road to Pudsey roundabout; follow signs to Calverley; 0.25 miles past Calverley Golf Club.
Parkland course.
Pro Warren Lockett; Founded 1905
18 holes, 6001 yards, S.S.S. 69
† Welcome.
⌣ WD £20.50; WE £25.50.
⌣ Welcome by arrangement with secretary/manager; golf and catering packages available for groups of 20 or more; from £27.
◉ Full clubhouse facilities available.
⌐ Cedar Court, Bradford.

8A 174 Woodsome Hall

Fenay Bridge, Huddersfield, W Yorks, HD8 0LG
☎ (01484) 602739, Fax 608260, Pro 602034, Bar/Rest 602971
From either M62 Junction 23 or 25 towards Huddersfield then A629 towards Sheffield turning right at Farnley Tyas/Honley signs.
Parkland course.
Pro Mike Higginbottom; Founded 1922
Designed by J Braid
18 holes, 6096 yards, S.S.S. 69
† Welcome except Tues.
⌣ WD £27.50; WE £35.
⌣ Welcome by prior arrangement except Tues and Sat; handicap certs required; menus for catering packages available from club; TV lounge; halfway bar available; deposit required; terms available on application.
◉ Full catering and bar facilities; jacket and tie required.
Practice areas available.
⌐ Hanover International; Huddersfield Hotel.

8A 175 Woolley Park

Woolley Park, New Rd, Woolley, Wakefield, W Yorks, WF4 2JS
☎ (01226) 380144, Fax 390295, Sec 382209
From Junction 38 on the M1 follow the signs for Woolley Hall; from the A61 Wakefield to Barnsley road take the Woolley signs from the crossroads.
Parkland course.
Pro Jon Baldwin; Founded 1995
Designed by M Shattock
18 holes, 6471 yards, S.S.S. 71
† Welcome.
⌣ Terms on application.
⌣ Welcome by prior arrangement; packages available; terms on application.
◉ Clubhouse catering facilities available.
Practice range; practice area.

8A 176 Wortley

Hermit Hill Lane, Wortley, Sheffield, S35 7DF
☎ (0114) 2885294, Pro 2886490, Sec 2888469, Bar/Rest 2882139
Course is off the A629 through Wortley village.
Undulating wooded parkland course.
Pro Ian Kirk; Founded 1894
18 holes, 6035 yards, S.S.S. 69
♦ Welcome by prior arrangement.
↳ WD £25; WE £30.
↷ Welcome Mon, Wed and Fri by prior arrangement; catering by arrangement except Mon; terms on application.
🍽 Clubhouse facilities available except Mon.
↪ Ardsley Moat House; Brooklands, both Barnsley; Tankersley Manor.

8A 177 York

Lords Moor Lane, Strensall, York, Yorks, YO3 5XF
☎ (01904) 490304, Fax 491852, Sec 491840
3 miles N of A1237 York ring road from Earswick/Strensall roundabout
Tree-lined heathland course.
Pro T Mason; Founded 1890
Designed by J.H. Taylor (1904)
18 holes, 6302 yards, S.S.S. 70
♦ Welcome by prior arrangement; with member at WE only.
↳ WD £25.
↷ Welcome except Tues am and Sat; packages can include 27 or 36 holes of golf; some Sun available; catering available; from £32.
🍽 Bar and catering facilities.
Practice ground.

8B 1 Allendale

High Studdon, Allenheads Rd, Allendale, Hexham, Northumberland, N47 9DH
☎ (01434) 683926
On B6295 1.5 miles S of Allendale in the direction of Allenheads.
Hilly parkland course; 7 new tees 1998; new site 1992.
Founded 1907/1992
Designed by members with advice from English Golf Union and Sports Council
9 holes, 5044 yards, S.S.S. 65
♦ Welcome except August Bank Holiday Mon.
↳ Prices on application.
↷ Welcome by arrangement; corporate days welcome; catering by arrangement; terms available on application.

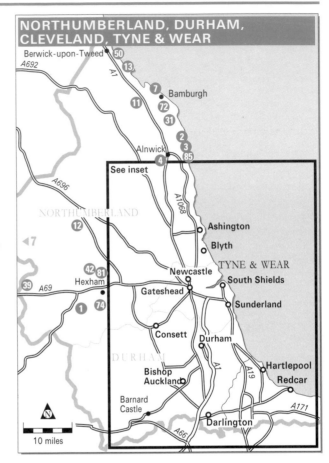

NORTHUMBERLAND, DURHAM, CLEVELAND, TYNE & WEAR

KEY			
1	Allendale	16 Bishop Auckland	33 Eaglescliffe
2	Alnmouth	17 Blackwell Grange	34 Elemore
3	Alnmouth Village	18 Blyth	35 Garesfield
4	Alnwick	19 Boldon	36 George Washington County Hotel & GC
5	Arcot Hall	20 Brancepeth Castle	37 Gosforth
6	Backworth	21 Burgham Park	38 Hall Garth Golf & Country Club
7	Bamburgh Castle	22 Castle Eden & Peterlee	39 Haltwhistle
8	Barnard Castle	23 Chester-le-Street	40 Hartlepool
9	Beamish Park	24 City of Newcastle	41 Heworth
10	Bedlingtonshire	25 Cleveland	42 Hexham
11	Belford	26 Close House	43 High Throston
12	Bellingham	27 Consett & District	44 Hobson Municipal
13	Berwick-upon-Tweed (Goswick)	28 Crook	45 Houghton-le-Spring
14	Billingham	29 Darlington	46 Hunley Hall
15	Birtley	30 Dinsdale Spa	47 Knotty Hill Golf Centre
		31 Dunstanburgh Castle	
		32 Durham City	

🍽 Clubhouse facilities available.
↪ Kings Head; Hare & Hounds; Allenheads.

8B 2 Alnmouth

Foxton Hall, Lesbury, Alnmouth, Northumberland, NE66 3BE
☎ (01665) 830231, Fax 830992, Pro 830043
5 miles SE of Alnwick.
Seaside links course with parkland turf.
Founded 1869

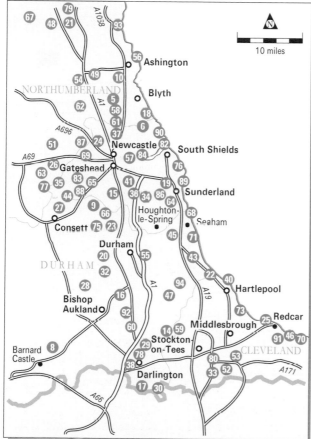

10 miles

48	Linden Hall	64	Ramside	80	Teesside
49	Longhirst Hall	65	Ravensworth	81	Tynedale
50	Magdalene Fields	66	Roseberry Grange	82	Tynemouth
51	Matfen Hall	67	Rothbury	83	Tyneside
52	Middlesbrough	68	Ryhope	84	Wallsend
53	Middlesbrough Municipal	69	Ryton	85	Warkworth
54	Morpeth	70	Saltburn-by-the-Sea	86	Wearside
55	Mount Oswald	71	Seaham	87	Westerhope
56	Newbiggin-by-the-Sea	72	Seahouses	88	Whickham
57	Newcastle United	73	Seaton Carew	89	Whitburn
58	Northumberland	74	Slaley Hall International	90	Whitley Bay
59	Norton Golf Course		Golf Resort	91	Wilton
60	Oak Leaf Golf Complex	75	South Moor	92	Woodham Golf & Country
	(Aycliffe)	76	South Shields		Club
61	Parklands Golf Club	77	Stocksfield	93	Wooler
62	Ponteland	78	Stressholme Golf Centre	94	Wynyard (The Wellington)
63	Prudhoe	79	Swarland Hall		

Designed by H S Colt
18 holes, 6429 yards, S.S.S. 71
♦ Welcome Mon, Tues and Thurs; Dormy House guests welcome at all times.
▸ WD £22-£28.
♦ Welcome Mon, Tues, Thurs; day

packages available; maximum groups of 30; from £20.
🍴 Clubhouse catering facilities available.
💬 Foxton Hall has its own Dormy House and self-catering flat available for letting.

8B 3 Alnmouth Village

Marine Rd, Alnmouth, Northumberland NE66 2RZ
☎ (01665) 830370, Fax 602096
On A1068 from Alnmouth.
Undulating seaside course.
Founded 1869
9 holes, 6078 yards, S.S.S. 70
♦ Welcome; restrictions on comp. days.
▸ Summer WD £15, WE £20; Winter WD £10, WE £15; juniors £7.50.
♦ Welcome with handicap certs; catering packages by arrangement; from £15.
🍴 Catering available by prior arrangement.

8B 4 Alnwick

Swansfield Park, Alnwick, Northumberland NE66 1AT
☎ (01665) 602632, Sec 602499
From A1 S signposted to Willowburn Ave and then into Swansfield Park Road.
7 holes mature parkland; 4 gorse; 7 open parkland.
Founded 1907/1993
Designed by G Rochester/A Rae
18 holes, 6250 yards, S.S.S. 70
♦ Welcome by prior arrangement with the starter.
▸ WD £15-£20; WE and BH £20-£25.
♦ Welcome between April 1 and Oct 1 by prior arrangement; packages available in season of unlimited golf and full day's catering; minimum 4; £23.
🍴 Full clubhouse facilities available.
💬 White Swans; Royal Oak; Plough; Hotspur.

8B 5 Arcot Hall

Dudley, Cramlington, Northumberland, NE23 7QP
☎ (0191) 2362794, Fax 2170070
Course is 1.5 miles off the A1 near Cramlington.
Parkland course; formerly at Benton; moved to present site in 1948.
Pro Graham Cant; Founded 1909/48
Designed by James Braid
18 holes, 6389 yards, S.S.S. 70
♦ Welcome WD; restrictions WE.
▸ WD £26; WE £30.
♦ Welcome by prior arrangement on WD; packages available; from £26.
🍴 Lounge bar and restaurant facilities.
💬 Holiday Inn; Swallow, Gosforth Park.

8B 6 Backworth
Backworth Welfare, The Hall,
Backworth, Shiremoor, NE27 0AH
☎(0191) 2681048, Sec 2581291
Course s on the B1322 one mile from
the A19/A191 junction at Shiremoor
crossroads.
Parkland course.
Founded 1937
9 holes, 5930 yards, S.S.S. 69
† Welcome WD except Tues 11am-
3pm; restrictions at WE.
_ WD £14; WE £18.
⌁Welcome by prior arrangement
with Sec; packages can be
negotiated depending on numbers;
terms on application.
⦿ Full bar and restaurant facilities
available.
↝ Rex; Park; Stakis Wallsend;
Grand.

8B 7 Bamburgh Castle
The Wynding, Bamburgh,
Northumberland, NE69 7DE
☎(01668) 214378, Sec 214321
Course is five miles E of the A1 via
the B1341 or the B1342 into
Bamburgh village.
Seaside course.
Founded 1896/04
Designed by George Rochester
18 holes, 5621 yards, S.S.S. 66
† Welcome by prior arrangement
except on competition days and BH.
_ Prices on application.
⌁Welcome by prior written
arrangement with Sec; full catering
packages available, except Tues;
from £30.
⦿ Full catering available except
Tues.
↝ Victoria; Mizen; Sunningdale;
Lord Crewe.

8B 8 Barnard Castle
Harmire Rd, Barnard Castle, DL12
8QN
☎(01833) 638355, Pro 631980, Bar
637237
Course is on the B6278 one mile N of
town signposted Middleton in
Teesdale.
Parkland course.
Pro Darren Pearce; Founded
1898/1907
Designed by A S Watson
18 holes, 6406 yards, S.S.S. 71
† Welcome by prior arrangement.
_ WD £18; WE £25.
⌁Welcome WD by prior
arrangement; catering packages
available; from £18.

⦿ Restaurant and bar facilities.
Practice range, practice area.
↝ Jersey Farm Hotel; Morris Arms.

8B 9 Beamish Park
The Clubhouse, Beamish, Stanley,
Co Durham, DH9 0RH
☎(0191) 3701382, Fax 3702937,
Pro 3701984
From A1 take A693 towards Stanley
and follow the signs for Beamish
museum.
Tree-lined parkland course.
Pro Chris Cole; Founded 1907/50
Designed by Henry Cotton (part)/ W
Woodend
18 holes, 6218 yards, S.S.S. 70
† Welcome by arrangement.
_ WD £16; WE £20.
⌁Welcome by arrangement; on
application.
⦿ Full clubhouse facilities.
↝ Coppy Lodge GH.

8B 10 Bedlingtonshire
Acorn Bank, Bedlington,
Northumberland, NE22 5SY
☎(01670) 822457, Pro 822087, Fax
822087
Off A189 Ashington road 5 miles N of
Newcastle.
Parkland course.
Pro Marcus Webb; Founded 1972
Designed by Frank Pennink
18 holes, 6813 yards, S.S.S. 73
† Welcome by arrangement.
_ WD £15; WE £20.
⌁Welcome by prior arrangement
with professional; packages can be
arranged; terms available on
application.
⦿ Full clubhouse facilities.
↝ Swan Inn, Choppington; Half
Moon Inn, Stakeford; Holiday Inn,
Seaton Born.

8B 11 Belford   ℭ
South Rd, Belford, Northumberland,
NE70 7DP
☎(01668) 213433, Fax 213919
Just off A1 midway between Alnwick
and Berwick on Tweed.
Parkland course.
Founded 1993
Designed by Nigel W. Williams
9 holes, 6304 yards, S.S.S. 70
† Welcome.
_ WD £13; WE £16.
⌁Welcome by prior arrangement;
some WE available; packages include
27 holes plus all-day catering; from
£23.

⦿ Full clubhouse facilities.
6 indoor, 4 outdoor practice bays.
↝ Blue Bell; Purdy Travel Lodge.

8B 12 Bellingham
Boggle Hole, Bellingham, Hexham,
Northumberland, NE48 2DT
☎(01434) 220152, Sec 220530
Off the B6320 16 miles north-east of
Hexham and the A69, on the outskirts
of Bellingham.
Rolling parkland course with
abundance of natural hazards.
Founded 1893/1996
Designed by E Johnson/I Wilson (96)
18 holes, 6077 yards, S.S.S. 70
† Welcome; prior booking is
advisable.
_ WD £17.50; WE £22.50.
⌁Welcome every day by prior
arrangement; catering and golfing
packages available; from £17.50.
⦿ Full catering and bar facilities
available.
Practice range, 6 bays floodlit.
↝ George; Riverdale; Beaumont.

8B 13 Berwick-upon-Tweed (Goswick)
Goswick, Berwick-upon-Tweed,
Northumberland, TD15 2RW
☎(01289) 387256, Fax 387256, Pro
387380
3.5 miles from A1; 5 miles S of
Berwick-upon-Tweed.
Links course.
Pro Paul Terras; Founded 1890/64
Designed by James Braid/ F Pennick
18 holes, 6462 yards, S.S.S. 71
† Welcome; restrictions before
9.30am, and between 12 noon-2pm
at WE.
_ WD £21; WE £26.
⌁Welcome WD & WE; packages
include full day's golf and catering for
minimum 10; from £30 WD and £36
WE.
⦿ Full clubhouse catering and bar
facilities.
Practice ground.
↝ Blue Bell, Belford; Mizen Head,
Bamburgh; Haggerston Castle
Holiday Park.

8B 14 Billingham
Sandy Lane, Billingham, Cleveland,
TS22 5NA
☎(01642) 533816, Fax 533816, Pro
557060, Bar/Rest 554494
E of A19 near Billingham Town
Centre.
Parkland course.

Pro Mike Ure; Founded 1967
Designed by Frank Pennink
18 holes, 6460 yards, S.S.S. 71
† Welcome.
⌐ WD £20; WE £33.
☺ Welcome by prior arrangement
with Sec; terms available on
application.
◉ Full clubhouse facilities.

8B 15 Birtley

Birtley Lane, Birtley, Co Durham, DH3
2LR
☎ (0191) 4102207
Course is six miles S of Newcastle off
the A6127.
Parkland course.
Founded 1921
9 holes, 5660 yards, S.S.S. 67
† Welcome WD; with member at
WE.
⌐ WD £12.
☺ Welcome WD by prior
arrangement; terms available on
application.
◉ Bar facilities.
↵ George Washington County; local
B&Bs can be recommended.

8B 16 Bishop Auckland

High Plains, Durham Rd, Bishop
Auckland, Co Durham, DL14 8DL
☎ (01388) 602198, Pro 661618, Sec
663648
0.5 miles N of town on Durham road.
Parkland course.
Pro David Skiffington; Founded 1894
Designed by James Kay
18 holes, 6399 yards, S.S.S. 71
† Welcome WD except Tues.
⌐ Prices on application.
☺ Welcome by prior arrangement;
special packages for 20+ including 27
holes golf and all-day catering; prices
on application.
◉ Full clubhouse facilities.
Practice area.
↵ Queens; Park Head, both Bishop
Auckland; Old Manor, W Auckland.

8B 17 Blackwell Grange

Briar Close, Blackwell, Darlington,
DL3 8QX
☎ (01325) 464464, Fax 464458, Pro
462088, Sec 464458
1 mile S of Darlington on A66.
Parkland course.
Pro Ralph Givens; Founded 1930
Designed by Frank Pennink
18 holes, 5621 yards, S.S.S. 67
† Welcome.
⌐ WD £20; WE £30.

☺ Welcome WD except Wed;
catering packages available; from
£20.
◉ Full clubhouse facilities.
↵ Blackwell Grange, Darlington.

8B 18 Blyth

New Delaval, Blyth, Northumberland,
NE24 4DB
☎ (01670) 367728, Pro 356514, Sec
540110
At W end of Plessey Road.
Parkland course.
Pro Andrew Brown; Founded
1905/1976
Designed by Hamilton Stutt & Co
18 holes, 6430 yards, S.S.S. 72
† Welcome WD.
⌐ WD £18; WE £18.
☺ Welcome WD by prior
arrangement; 3 packages available
for society and company days;
minimum 10; from £21.
◉ Full clubhouse catering and bar
facilities.
↵ Large number in Whitley Bay.

8B 19 Boldon

Dipe Lane, East Boldon, Tyne &
Wear, NE36 0PQ
☎ (0191) 5365835, Sec 5365360,
Fax 5190157
Course is on the A184 one mile E of
the A19/A1 junction.
Parkland course.
Pro Sean Richardson/Phillip Carlaw;
Founded 1912
18 holes, 6338 yards, S.S.S. 70
† Welcome WD with some
restrictions; after 3.30pm only at WE.
⌐ WD £18; WE £22.
☺ Welcome by arrangement;
catering packages available; snooker;
from £18.
◉ Bar snacks and restaurant
facilities.
Practice area.
↵ Friendly.

8B 20 Brancepeth Castle

Brancepeth Village, Durham, Co
Durham, DH7 8EA
☎ (0191) 3780075, Fax 3783835,
Pro 3780183, Bar/Rest 3783393
On A690 4 miles W of Durham; left at
the crossroads before Brancepeth.
Parkland course.
Pro D Howson; Founded 1924
Designed by H.S. Colt
18 holes, 6375 yards, S.S.S. 71
† Welcome by prior arrangement.
⌐ WD £29; WE £34.

☺ Welcome WD by prior
arrangement; special rates for groups
of more than 12 and 30; banqueting
facilities available; formal dinners can
be arranged; starter available; video
service for lessons; prices on
application.
◉ Full clubhouse catering and bar
facilities; formal dinner and banquets
can be arranged.
Large practice area.
↵ The Whitworth Hall Hotel;
Waterside GH, Royal Hotel, Durham.

8B 21 Burgham Park

Near Felton, Morpeth,
Northumberland NE65 8QP
☎ (01670) 787898, Fax 787164,
Bar/Rest 787501, Pro 787978
6 miles N of Morpeth off the A1 at
Longhorsley road (C137).
Parkland course.
Pro S McNally; Founded 1994
Designed by A Mair
18 holes, 6751 yards, S.S.S. 72
† Welcome.
⌐ Terms on application.
☺ Welcome except on competition
days; catering packages available;
terms on application.
◉ Full catering and bar facilities.
Practice area.
↵ Sun Inn, Warkworth; Blue Bell,
Belford.

8B 22 Castle Eden & Peterlee

Castle Eden, Hartlepool, Cleveland,
TS27 4SS
☎ (01429) 836220, Fax 836510, Pro
836689, Sec 836510
10 miles S of Sunderland; take slip
road off A19 towards Blackhall; 0.25
miles.
Parkland course.
Pro G Laidlaw; Founded 1927
Designed by Henry Cotton (back 9)
18 holes, 6282 yards, S.S.S. 70
† Welcome by prior arrangement.
⌐ WD £20; WE £30.
◉ Full clubhouse facilities.
↵ Castle Eden Inn.

8B 23 Chester-le-Street

Lumley Park, Chester-le-Street, Co
Durham, DH3 4NS
☎ (0191) 3883218, Fax 3881220,
Pro 3890157
Close to A167 0.5 miles E of Chester-
le-Street close to Lumley Castle and
Durham CCC ground.
Parkland course.
Pro David Fletcher; Founded 1908

Designed by J.H. Taylor (original 9)/ T Ray
18 holes, 6437 yards, S.S.S. 69
† Welcome by prior arrangement.
▯ WD £20; WE £25.
⚲ Welcome by prior arrangement; coffee and catering available depending on numbers; terms on application.
🍽 Full clubhouse facilities.
⌐ Lumley Castle.

8B 24 City of Newcastle
Three Mile Bridge, Gosforth, NE3 2DR
☎ (0191) 2851775, Fax 2840700, Pro 2855481
Course is on the B1318 three miles N of Newcastle.
Parkland course.
Pro Steve McKenna; Founded 1892
Designed by Harry Vardon
18 holes, 6528 yards, S.S.S. 71
† Welcome.
▯ WD £24; WE £28.
⚲ Welcome by prior arrangement most days; packages on application; from £24.
🍽 Full clubhouse facilities.
⌐ Swallow, Gosforth Park.

8B 25 Cleveland
Queen St, Redcar, Cleveland, TS10 1BT
☎ (01642) 471798, Fax 471798, Bar 483693, Rest 481757
Off A174 following signs for Teesside and Redcar.
Links course.
Pro Stephen Wynn; Founded 1897
18 holes, 6707 yards, S.S.S. 72
† Welcome.
▯ WD £20; WE £22.
⚲ Welcome; packages can be arranged depending on numbers; terms on application.
🍽 Clubhouse bar and catering facilities.
⌐ Regency; Park.

8B 26 Close House
Close House, Heddon-on-the-Wall, Northumberland, NE15 0BH
☎ (01661) 852953, Bar/Rest 852255
Course is off the A69 nine miles W of Newcastle.
Parkland/woodland course.
Founded 1965
Designed by Hawtree
18 holes, 5606 yards, S.S.S. 67
† Members' guests only.
▯ WD £6; WE £10.

⚲ Welcome WD by prior arrangement; packages available to include all-day catering; corporate days by arrangement; from £18.
🍽 Catering and bar facilities in the Mansion House.
⌐ Copthorne; Novotel, both Newcastle; Holiday Inn, Seaton Burn.

8B 27 Consett & District
Elmfield Rd, Consett, Co Durham, DH8 5NN
☎ (01207) 502186, Fax 505060, Pro 580210, Sec.505060
Corse is on the A691 14 miles N of Durham.
Parkland course.
Pro Craig Dilley; Founded 1911
Designed by Harry Vardon
18 holes, 6023 yards, S.S.S. 69
† Welcome by prior arrangement with Pro.
▯ WD £17; WE £25.
⚲ Welcome by prior arrangement with Sec; all-day menu available for £9; from £17.
🍽 Full clubhouse facilities.
⌐ Royal Derwent; Raven.

8B 28 Crook
Low Job's Hill, Crook, Co Durham, DL15 9AA
☎ (01388) 762429, Sec 767926
Bar/Rest 767926
On A690 9 miles W of Durham.
Parkland course, hilly in parts.
Founded 1919
18 holes, 6102 yards, S.S.S. 69
† Welcome by prior arrangement.
▯ Prices on application.
⚲ Welcome WD by prior arrangement; packages on application; from £14.
🍽 Clubhouse facilities.
⌐ Helme Park.

8B 29 Darlington
Haughton Grange, Darlington, Co Durham, DL1 3JD
☎ (01325) 355324, Fax 488126, Pro 484198, Bar/Rest 355324
Between A1 and A66 at N end of Darlington.
Parkland course.
Pro Mark Rogers; Founded 1912
Designed by MacKenzie
18 holes, 6270 yards, S.S.S. 70
† Welcome WD.
▯ WD £20.
⚲ Welcome by prior arrangement; packages and special rates for larger groups; from £15.

🍽 Full clubhouse facilities.
9-acre practice ground.
⌐ White Horse; Kings Head, both Darlington; Eden Arms, Rushyford.

8B 30 Dinsdale Spa
Neasham Rd, Middleton-St-George, Darlington, Co Durham, DL2 1DW
☎ (01325) 332222, Fax 332297, Pro 332515, Sec 332297
Off the A67 near Teesside Airport midway between Middleton St George and Neasham.
Parkland course.
Pro Neil Metcalfe; Founded 1910
18 holes, 6090 yards, S.S.S. 69
† Welcome when tee times allow.
▯ WD £20; WE £20.
⚲ Welcome by prior arrangement with Sec; catering packages available; from £20.
🍽 Full clubhouse bar and catering facilities.
⌐ Croft Spa; Devenport.

8B 31 Dunstanburgh Castle ℸ

Embleton, Alnwick, Northumberland, NE66 3XQ
☎ (01665) 576562, Fax 576562
7 miles NE of Alnwick off the A1; follow signs to Embleton.
Seaside links course.
Founded 1900
Designed by James Braid
18 holes, 6298 yards, S.S.S. 70
† Welcome.
▯ WD £16; WE £20-£26.
⚲ Welcome by prior arrangement; packages available; separate dining facilities; from £16.
🍽 Full clubhouse facilities.
⌐ Sportsmans Inn; Dunstanburgh Castle, both Embleton.

8B 32 Durham City ℸ
Littleburn Farm, Langley Moor, Durham, DH7 8HL
☎ (0191) 3780069, Pro 3780029, Sec 3860200
Course is off the A690 two miles SW of Durham.
Meadowland course.
Pro Steve Corbally; Founded 1887
Designed by C.C. Stanton
18 holes, 6279 yards, S.S.S. 70
† Welcome by prior arrangement.
▯ WD £22; WE £30.
⚲ Welcome WD; packages available; terms on application.
🍽 Full catering; limited service Mon.
⌐ Royal County; Three Tuns; Duke of Wellington; Kensington Hall.

8B 33 Eaglescliffe
Yarm Rd, Eaglescliffe, Stockton-on-Tees, Cleveland, TS16 0DQ
☎ (01642) 780098, Fax 780238, Pro 790122, Sec 780238
On A135 Stockton to Yarm.
Undulating parkland course.
Pro Paul Bradley; Founded 1914
Designed by James Braid, Modification By H. Cotton
18 holes, 6275 yards, S.S.S. 69
† Welcome.
↳ WD £25-£30; WE £35-£50.
⌇ Welcome WD by prior arrangement; packages include 18 holes of golf and 3-course meal; prices on application.
†◎! Full clubhouse facilities.
↵ Parkmore; Sunnyside; Clareville.

8B 34 Elemore
Easington Lane, Haughton le Spring, Tyne and Wear,
☎ (0191) 5173057, Fax 5173054
5 miles E of Durham City; W of Easington Lane.
Parkland course.
Founded 1994
18 holes, 5947 yards, S.S.S. 69
† Pay and play.
↳ WD £9; WE £12.
⌇ Welcome by prior arrangement; terms on application.
†◎! Bar and function room.
Practice area.
↵ Fox and Hounds, Hetton-le-Hole.

8B 35 Garesfield
Chopwell, Tyne and Wear, NE17 7AP
☎ (01207) 561309, Fax 561309, Pro 563082, Bar/Rest 561278
On B6315 to High Spen off A694 from A1 at Rowlands Gill.
Undulating wooded parkland course.
Pro David Race; Founded 1922
Designed by William Woodend
18 holes, 6603 yards, S.S.S. 72
† Welcome except before 4.30pm at WE.
↳ Terms on application.
⌇ Welcome by prior arrangement except Mon and Sat; catering packages can be arranged with the steward; terms on application.
†◎! Full clubhouse facilities except Mon.
↵ Towneley Arms, Rowlands Gill.

8B 36 George Washington County Hotel & GC
Stonecellar Rd, Washington, Tyne & Wear, NE37 1PH

☎ (0191) 4029988, Fax 4151166, Pro 4178346, Sec 4168341
Course is signposted from the A1(M) and the A194.
Parkland course.
Pro Warren Marshall; Founded 1990
18 holes, 6604 yards, S.S.S. 72
† Welcome by prior arrangement; special rates for hotel guests.
↳ WD £20; WE £20.
⌇ Welcome by prior arrangement; special rates for groups of more than 15; hotel packages; leisure club; pool; spa; terms on application.
†◎! Full clubhouse and hotel facilities.
Driving range, 21 bays floodlit; 9-hole pitch and putt.
↵ 105-bedroom George Washington County Hotel on site.

8B 37 Gosforth
Broadway East, Gosforth, NE3 5ER
☎ (0191) 2853495, Pro 2850553, Bar/Rest 2856710
Off A6125 3 miles N of Newcastle.
Parkland course with stream feature.
Pro Graeme Garland; Founded 1906
18 holes, 6024 yards, S.S.S. 69
† Welcome by prior arrangement.
↳ WD £20; WE £20.
⌇ Welcome WD by prior arrangement; catering packages available; discounts for groups of more than 12; from £20.
†◎! Full clubhouse facilities.
↵ Swallow Gosforth Park; Novotel.

8B 38 Hall Garth Golf & Country Club
Coatham Mundeville, Nr Darlington, Co Durham, DL1 3LU
☎ (01325) 320246, Fax 310083, Pro 300400, Sec 300400, Bar/Rest 300400
From A1(M) Junction 59 take A167 towards Darlington; top of hill.
Parkland course.
Founded 1995
Designed by D Moore
9 holes, 6621 yards, S.S.S. 72
† Welcome.
↳ WD £10; WE £12.50.
⌇ Welcome; packages available; terms on application.
†◎! Bar and restaurant facilities on site; hotel on site.
↵ Hall Garth, 16th century country house with leisure facilities.

8B 39 Haltwhistle
Banktop, Greenhead, Via Carlisle, Cumbria, CA6 7HN

☎ (016977) 47367, Fax 01434 344311, Sec 01434 344000
Off A69 N of Haltwhistle turn right at Greenhead.
Parkland course.
Founded 1967
Designed by members
18 holes, 5660 yards, S.S.S. 69
† Welcome except after 5pm Wed and Fri and before 3pm on Sun.
↳ WD £12; WE £12.
⌇ Welcome by prior arrangement; packages include 27 holes of golf and all-day catering; from £20.
†◎! Bar and catering facilities available.
↵ Greenhead Hotel.

8B 40 Hartlepool
Hart Warren, Hartlepool, Cleveland, TS24 9QF
☎ (01429) 274398, Fax 274129, Pro 267473
Course is off the A1086 at N edge of Hartlepool.
Seaside links course.
Pro Malcolm Cole; Founded 1906
Designed by James Braid (in part)
18 holes, 6215 yards, S.S.S. 70
† Welcome; restricted to members guests Sun.
↳ WD £20; WE £30.
⌇ Welcome WD by prior arrangement; catering packages available from the steward; snooker; terms on application.
†◎! Full clubhouse facilities, except Mon.
↵ Staincliffe; Marine; Travelodge.

8B 41 Heworth
Gingling Gate, Heworth, Tyne and Wear, NE10 8XY
☎ (0191) 4962137, Sec 4699832
Course is close to the A1 (M) SE of Gateshead.
Parkland course with woods.
Founded 1912
18 holes, 6404 yards, S.S.S. 71
† Welcome but not before 10am at WE.
↳ WD £15; WE £15.
⌇ Welcome by prior arrangement; catering packages by arrangement; dining room; from £15.
†◎! Bar and restaurant.
Practice range, practice area.
↵ George Washington.

8B 42 Hexham
Spital Park, Hexham, Northumberland, NF46 3RZ

LONGHIRST HALL GOLF COURSE

Superb 6572-yard, Par 72 course. USGA spec greens with extensive water features. Opening in May 2001: new 'Hebron' course, 6925 yards, Par 71.

LONGHIRST HALL HOTEL – 75 EN-SUITE BEDROOMS, ETB 4 STAR.
Tel: 01670 791505 or fax: 01670 791385. Website: www.longhirst.co.uk

---

☎(01434) 603072, Fax 601865, Pro 604904, Sec 603072
Course is on the A69 one mile W of Hexham.
Undulating parkland course.
Pro Martin Foster; Founded 1907
Designed by Harry Vardon
18 holes, 6301 yards, S.S.S. 68
☥ Welcome by arrangement.
▨ WD £25; WE £35.
⌁Welcome except WE by arrangement; packages available; from £28.
▧ Clubhouse catering and bar.
⌐ Beaumont.

8B 43 High Throston
Hart Lane, Hartlepool, Co Durham, TS26 0UG
☎(01429) 275325
From A19N take A179 to Hartlepool.
Parkland course with USGA standard greens.
Founded 1996
Designed by J Gaunt
18 holes, 6247 yards, S.S.S. 71
☥ Welcome.
▨ WD £16; WE and BH £19.
⌁Welcome by prior arrangement.
▧ Sandwiches, teas, coffee.
⌐ Raby Arms.

8B 44 Hobson Municipal
Burnopfield, Newcastle-upon-Tyne, NE16 6BZ
☎(01207) 271605, Sec 570189, Bar/Rest 270941
On main Newcastle-Consett road opposite Hobson Industrial estate.
Parkland course.
Pro J W Ord; Founded 1980
18 holes, 6403 yards, S.S.S. 71
☥ Pay and play.
▨ WD £12; WE £16.
⌁Welcome by arrangement with the Pro; packages available; terms on application.
▧ Catering and bar facilities.
⌐ Towneley Arms.

8B 45 Houghton-le-Spring
Copt Hill, Houghton-le-Spring, Tyne and Wear, DH5 8LU

☎(0191) 5847421, Sec 5840048, Bar 58411098, Fax 5840048
On A1085 Houghton-le-Spring to Seaham Harbour road 0.5 miles from Houghton-le-Spring.
Undulating hillside course.
Pro Kevin Gow; Founded 1908
18 holes, 6443 yards, S.S.S 71
☥ Welcome after 9am; WE restrictions.
▨ WD £20-£30; WE £28-£33.
⌁Welcome by prior arrangement; golf and catering packages available; from £30.
▧ Catering and bar facilities available.
⌐ White Lion; Ramside Hall; Rainton Lodge.

8B 46 Hunley Hall ☏
Brotton, Saltburn-by-the-Sea, N Yorks, TS12 2QQ
☎(01287) 676216, Fax 678250, Pro 677444
▤ www.hunleyhall.com
⌐ enquiries@hunleyhall.co.uk
Off A174 from Teesside to Brotton into St Margaret's Way.
Meadowland course; a further 9 holes planned for 1998.
Pro Andrew Brook; Founded 1993
Designed by J Morgan
18 holes, 6918 yards, S.S.S. 73
☥ Welcome.
▨ WD £20; WE £30.
⌁Welcome Mon to Sat; packages for 18 and 27 holes of golf and for catering available; terms on application.
▧ Restaurant and bars; members bar; spike bar; all-day catering available.
Practice range, 12 bays floodlit.
⌐ Accommodation on site; 3 crowns.

8B 47 Knotty Hill Golf Centre
Sedgefield, Stockton-on-Tees, Cleveland, TS21 2BB
☎(01740) 620320, Fax 622227
Course is on the A177 one mile from Sedgefield, and two miles from the A1 (M) Junction 60.

Naturally undulating parkland course.
Pro Nick Walton; Founded 1991
Designed by C. Stanton
18-hole course: 6577 yards, S.S.S. 71; 9-hole course
☥ Welcome.
▨ WD £12; WE £12.
⌁Welcome WD; terms on application.
▧ Full clubhouse facilities available.
Floodlit practice range; grass tees; chipping and putting areas.
⌐ Hardwick Hall.

500011

8B 48 Linden Hall
Linden Hall Hotel, Longhorsley, Morpeth, Northumberland, NE65 8XF
☎(01670) 788050, Fax 788544, Hotel 516611
From A1 take A697 to Coldstream until reaching Longhorsley; course half mile on right.
Parkland course.
Pro David Curry; Founded 1997
Designed by J Gaunt
18 holes, 6846 yards, S.S.S 73
☥ Welcome with handicap certs.
▨ WD £25; WE £28.
⌁Welcome by prior arrangement; packages for golf and catering available; corporate days arranged; leisure club, gym in hotel; prices on application .
▧ Grill room, conservatory and 2 bars.
Practice range, 12 bays.
⌐ Linden Hall on site.

8B 49 Longhirst Hall
Longhirst Hall, Longhirst, Northumberland, NE61 3LL
☎(01670) 791505
From A1 take signs to Hebron Cockle Park; after 2 miles at T junction turn left and follow signs for Longhirst Hall; 2 miles N of Morpeth.
Parkland course.
Founded 1997
18 holes, 6572 yards, S.S.S. 72
☥ Welcome.
▨ WD £14; WE £17.
⌁Welcome by prior arrangement; packages include golf, catering and, if required, hotel and self-catering

accommodation; group and corporate days can be arranged for any size.
🍽 Full facilities in clubhouse and The Hall.
Practice range.
⌁ Longhirst Hall 75-room hotel on site and self-catering at Micklewood Village on site.

8B 50 Magdalene Fields 🏌 ℭ
Berwick-upon-Tweed, Northumberland TD15 1NE
☎(01289) 306384, Fax 306384, Sec 306130
5 miles from centre of town in direction of coast.
Seaside course with parkland fairways
18 holes, 6407 yards, S.S.S. 71
♦ Welcome by prior arrangement.
▯ WD £16; WE £18.
⌁Welcome WD; restrictions Sat and Sun; catering packages available; from £16.
🍽 Bar and restaurant.
⌁ Queen's Head, Berwick.

8B 51 Matfen Hall
Matfen Hall, Matfen, Northumberland, NE20 0RQ
☎(01661) 886500, Fax 886055, Pro 886400
Just off B6318 Military road 15 miles W of Newcastle.
Parkland course; 3rd hole is 663 yards.
Pro John Harrison; Founded 1994
Designed by M James/A Mair
18 holes, 6609 yards, S.S.S. 72
♦ Welcome.
▯ Winter WD £14, WE £19; Summer WD £25, WE £30.
⌁Welcome by prior arrangement; golf and catering packages available; par 3 course; practice range; terms on application.
🍽 Full bar and restaurant facilities available.
Practice range; leisure facilities available end of 2000.
⌁ Matsen Country House Hotel.

8B 52 Middlesbrough
Brass Castle Lane, Marton, Middlesbrough, TS8 9EE
☎(01642) 311515, Fax 319607, Pro 311766, Sec 316430
1 mile W of A172 5 miles S of Middlesbrough.
Parkland course.
Pro Don Jones; Founded 1908
Designed by James Braid

18 holes, 6215 yards, S.S.S. 69
♦ Welcome except Tues and Sat.
▯ Prices on application.
⌁Welcome by prior arrangement; packages of golf and catering available; terms available on application.
🍽 Full facilities; restaurant service available at 24 hours notice.
⌁ Marton Hotel & CC.

8B 53 Middlesbrough Municipal
Ladgate Lane, Middlesbrough, TS5 7YZ
☎(01642) 315533, Fax 300726
Access to the course from the A19 via the A174 to Acklam.
Undulating parkland course.
Pro Alan Hope; Founded 1977
Designed by Middlesbrough Borough Council
18 holes, 6333 yards, S.S.S. 70
♦ Welcome but must arrange starting time.
▯ WD £10.50; WE £13.
⌁Welcome by prior arrangement; terms on application.
🍽 Catering available; lunches.
Driving range.
⌁ Blue Bell.

8B 54 Morpeth
The Common, Morpeth, NE61 2BT
☎(01670) 519980, Pro 515675, Sec 504942, Bar/Rest 504942
On A197 1 mile S of Morpeth.
Parkland course.
Pro Martin Jackson; Founded 1906
Designed by Harry Vardon (1922)
18 holes, 6104 yards, S.S.S. 70
♦ Welcome by prior arrangement after 9.30am.
▯ WD £20; WE £25.
⌁Welcome WD by prior arrangement with Sec; packages for golf and catering available; terms on application.
🍽 Snooker, bar lunches, dinner available.
⌁ Waterford Lodge; Queens Head; Linden Hall.

8B 55 Mount Oswald
Mount Oswald Manor, South Rd, Durham, Co Durham, DH1 3TQ
☎(0191) 3867527, Fax 3860975, Bar 3869791
On A1050 SW of Durham.
Partly wooded parkland course.
Founded 1924
18 holes, 6101 yards, S.S.S. 69

♦ Welcome; after 10am Sun.
▯ Mon-Thurs £11; Fri-Sun and BH £12.50.
⌁Welcome by prior arrangement; special rates for 12 or more; some WE available; function room for 80; other smaller private rooms; packages for golf and catering; from £17.
🍽 Full clubhouse catering.
⌁ Three Tuns.

8B 56 Newbiggin-by-the-Sea
Clubhouse, Newbiggin-by-the-Sea, Northumberland, NE64 6DW
☎(01670) 817344, Fax 520236, Pro 817833
Off A197 following signs for Newbiggin by the Sea from A189 from Newcastle.
Seaside links course.
Pro Marcus Webb; Founded 1884
18 holes, 6452 yards, S.S.S. 71
♦ Welcome after 10am except on comp days.
▯ WD £16; WE £20.
⌁Welcome by prior arrangement with Sec; catering packages available; from £14.
🍽 Full clubhouse facilities.
⌁ Beachcomber.

8B 57 Newcastle United
Ponteland Rd, Cowgate, Newcastle-upon-Tyne, Northumberland, NE5 3JW
☎(0191) 286 4693, Pro 286 9998
1 mile W of the city centre.
Moorland course.
Founded 1892
18 holes, 6612 yards, S.S.S. 71
♦ Welcome WD; not on WE comp days.
▯ Prices on application.
⌁Welcome by arrangement; catering packages by arrangement; snooker; terms available on application.
🍽 Bar and snacks.
Practice ground.
⌁ Gosforth Park.

8B 58 Northumberland
High Gosforth Park, Newcastle-upon-Tyne, Tyne and Wear, NE3 5HT
☎(0191) 2362498, Fax 2362498
Off A1 5 miles N of Newcastle.
Parkland course.
Founded 1898
Designed by Members
18 holes, 6629 yards, S.S.S. 72
♦ Welcome by arrangement.

⌐ WD £35; WE £35.
↩ Very limited availability; terms on application.
🍴 Full clubhouse catering.
↪ Swallow Gosforth Park.

8B 59 Norton Golf Course

Junction Rd, Stockton-on-Tees, Cleveland, TS20 1SU
☎ (01642) 676385, Fax 608467, Sec 674636, Bar/Rest 612452
From A177 2miles N of Stockton roundabout.
Parkland course.
Founded 1989
Designed by T Harper
18 holes, 5855 yards, S.S.S. 71
� Public pay and play.
⌐ WD £9; WE £10.
↩ Welcome by prior arrangement; packages available both for WD; bookings must be made more than 7 days in advance; from £16.
🍴 Full catering facilities.
↪ Swallow, Stockton.

8B 60 Oak Leaf Golf Complex (Aycliffe)

School Aycliffe Lane, Newton Aycliffe, Co Durham, DL 5 6QZ
☎ (01325) 310820, Fax 310820
Take A1 (M) to A68 and then turn into Newton Aycliffe; course on left.
Parkland course.
Pro Andrews Waites
18 holes, 6000 yards, S.S.S. 67
♭ Welcome; no restrictions.
⌐ WD £7.80; WE £8.85; concessions for under-18s and over-60s.
↩ Welcome at off-peak times; minimum of 9 players; deposit required; sports and leisure complex; terms on application.
🍴 Bar and restaurant facilities available.
Driving range.
↪ Redworth Arms, Redworth; Eden Arms; Gretna Hotel.

8B 61 Parklands Golf Club

High Gosforth Park, Newcastle-upon-Tyne, NE3 5HQ
☎ (0191) 2364867, Pro 2364480, Sec 2364480, Bar/Rest 2364480
Course is off the A1 three miles N of Newcastle.
Parkland course.
Pro Brian Rumney; Founded 1971
18 holes, 6060 yards, S.S.S. 69
♭ Welcome.
⌐ WD £15; WE £18.

↩ Welcome by prior arrangement; catering packages available; terms on application.
🍴 Bar and restaurant facilities available.
Practice range, 45 bays floodlit open till 10.30pm; also 9-hole pitch and putt.
↪ Swallow Gosforth Park.

8B 62 Ponteland

53 Bell Villas, Ponteland, Newcastle-upon-Tyne, Tyne and Wear, NE20 9BD
☎ (01661) 822689, Fax 860077
On A696 2 miles N of Newcastle Airport.
Parkland course.
Pro Alan Robson-Crosby; Founded 1927
Designed by Harry Ferney
18 holes, 6524 yards, S.S.S. 71
♭ Welcome Mon-Thurs; Fri, Sat, Sun as members' guest.
⌐ WD £22.50.
↩ Welcome on Tues and Thurs; catering packages can be arranged; from £22.50.
🍴 Full clubhouse facilities.

8B 63 Prudhoe ☏

Eastwood Park, Prudhoe, Northumberland, NE42 5DX
☎ (01661) 832466, Pro 836188
Course is on the A695 12 miles W of Newcastle.
Parkland course.
Pro John Crawford; Founded 1930
18 holes, 5862 yards, S.S.S. 68
♭ Welcome except on competition days.
⌐ Prices on application.
↩ Welcome WD by arrangement; terms on application.
🍴 Bar snacks and meals available.
↪ Beaumont, Hexham.

8B 64 Ramside

Ramside Hall, Carrville, Durham, DH1 1TD
☎ (0191) 3865282, Fax 3860399, Sec 3869514
On A690 Sunderland road 400m from A1(M) Junction 62.
Parkland course; 3 x 9 loops.
Pro Richard Lister; Founded 1996
Bishops Cathedral: 18 holes, 6183 yards, S.S.S. 69; Cathedral Princess: 18 holes, 6133 yards, S.S.S. 69; Prince Bishops: 18 holes, 6520 yards, S.S.S. 73
♭ Welcome by prior arrangement.

⌐ WD £27; WE £33.
↩ Welcome by prior arrangement; full society and corporate packages available; terms available on application.
🍴 Full bar and restaurant facilities; hotel restaurant and bar also.
Practice range, 16-bay driving range; golf academy; sauna, steam room; snooker .
↪ On site Ramside Hall.

8B 65 Ravensworth

Moss Heaps, Wrekenton, Gateshead, Tyne & Wear, NE9 7UU
☎ (0191) 4876014, Pro 4913475, Sec 4887549
Course is off the A1 two miles S of Gateshead.
Moorland/parkland course.
Pro Shaun Cowell; Founded 1906
18 holes, 5966 yards, S.S.S. 68
♭ Welcome.
⌐ Prices on application.
↩ Welcome WD by prior arrangement; catering packages available except Mon; terms on application.
🍴 Full clubhouse facilities except Tues.
↪ Springfield.

8B 66 Roseberry Grange

Grange Villa, Chester-le-Street, Durham, DH2 3NF
☎ (0191) 3700670, Pro 3700660, Sec 3702047
3 miles W of Chester-le-Street close to A1 (M) Junction.
Parkland course.
Pro Alan Hartley; Founded 1987
18 holes, 6023 yards, S.S.S. 69
♭ Welcome WD; by prior arrangement WE.
⌐ WD £11.50; WE £15; telephone booking essential.
↩ Welcome; terms available on application.
🍴 Full clubhouse facilities.
↪ Lumley Castle; Beamish Park.

8B 67 Rothbury

Old Race Course, Rothbury, Morpeth, Northumberland, NE65 7TR
☎ (01669) 621271, Sec 620718
Off A697 at Weldon Bridge following the signs for Rothbury; 15 miles N of Morpeth.
Flat course alongside river.
Founded 1891
Designed by J B Radcliffe
9 holes, 5681 yards, S.S.S. 67

⚑ Welcome WD; restrictions apply at WE.

🏌 WD £11; WE £16.

⛳ Welcome WD by arrangement; catering packages available during the day; by arrangement for evening meals; bar closed between 3pm-7.30pm; reductions for larger groups; from £11.

🍽 Clubhouse facilities.

🛏 Queens Head; Newcastle Hotel, both Rothbury.

8B 68 Ryhope
Leechmore Way, Ryhope, Sunderland, Durham, SR2 0DH
☎ (0191) 523 7333, Sec 553 6373
Turn off the A19 at Ryhope village towards Hollycarrside.
Course being re-designed.
Pro Brian and Roger Janes; Founded 1991
Designed by Sunderland Borough Council
16 holes, 6001 yards, S.S.S. 69

⚑ Welcome.

🏌 WD £6, WE £7; £1 discount for over-60s; £2 discount for cheaper; £1 discount for ladies.

8B 69 Ryton
Dr Stanners, Clara Vale, Ryton, Tyne and Wear, NE40 3TD
☎ (0191) 4133253, Fax 4131642, Sec 4133737, Bar/Rest 4133737
Course is off the A695 signposted Crawcrook.
Parkland course.
Founded 1891
18 holes, 5950 yards, S.S.S. 69

⚑ Welcome WD; by prior arrangement WE.

🏌 Prices on application.

⛳ Welcome; discounts for groups of more than 16; WE available; catering packages; prices available on application.

🍽 Clubhouse facilities.

🛏 Ryton County Club; Hedgefield; Marriott Gateshead.

8B 70 Saltburn-by-the-Sea
Hob Hill, Saltburn-by-Sea, Cleveland, TS12 1NJ
☎ (01287) 622812, Pro 624653
On A1268 1 mile from Saltburn.
Parkland course.
Pro Mike Nutter; Founded 1894
18 holes, 5897 yards, S.S.S. 68

⚑ Welcome; restrictions Sun and Thurs; limited Sat.

🏌 WD £20; WE £25.

⛳ Welcome by prior arrangement; catering available except Mon; terms on application.

🍽 Full clubhouse facilities; limited Mon catering.

🛏 Royal York.

8B 71 Seaham
Dawdon, Seaham, Co Durham, SR7 7RD
☎ (0191) 5812345, Pro 5130837, Sec 5811268
2 miles NE of the A19.
Heathland course.
Pro Glyn Jones; Founded 1911
Designed by Dr A. MacKenzie
18 holes, 6017 yards, S.S.S. 69

⚑ Welcome.

🏌 Prices on application.

⛳ Welcome; terms available on application.

🍽 Full clubhouse facilities.

8B 72 Seahouses
Beadnell Rd, Seahouses, Northumberland, NE68 7XT
☎ (01665) 720794
On the B1340 S of Seahouses village.
Links course; upgraded to 18 holes in 1976.
Founded 1913/1976
18 holes, 5462 yards, S.S.S. 67

⚑ Welcome; groups of more than four must book in advance.

🏌 Prices on application.

⛳ Welcome by prior arrangement everyday except Sun; packages for catering, golf and local hotels available; prices available on application.

🍽 Full catering service except Tues when limited food is available; full bar in summer.

🛏 Sunningdale; Beadnell Towers; Sportsman; Blue Bell, Belford.

8B 73 Seaton Carew
Tees Rd, Seaton Carew, Hartlepool, TS25 1DE
☎ (01429) 266249, Fax 261040, Pro 890660, Sec 261040
Course is off the A178 three miles S of Hartlepool.
Championship links course.
Pro Bill Hector; Founded 1874
Designed by Duncan McCuaig
Old: 18 holes, 6613 yards, S.S.S. 72;
Brabazon: 18 holes, 6855 yards, S.S.S. 73

⚑ Welcome WD; WE restricted.

🏌 WD £30; WE £40.

⛳ Welcome by prior arrangement; catering by arrangement; snooker; from £30.

🍽 Full facilities.
Large practice ground.

🛏 Seaton; Staincliffe Marine.

8B 74 Slaley Hall International Golf Resort
Slaley, Hexham, Northumberland, NE47 0BY
☎ (01434) 673350, Fax 673152, Pro 673154
Off A69; 23 miles from Newcastle.
Wooded, heath and parkland course; European Tour venue.
Pro Mark Stancer; Founded 1989
Designed by Dave Thomas
18 holes, 7021 yards, S.S.S. 74

⚑ Welcome WD by arrangement; hotel residents only at WE.

🏌 WD £50; WE £50.

⛳ Welcome WD for groups of 9+ by arrangement with the golf office; residential groups may play WE; golf packages available through golf office; residential golf breaks from £110; customised golf days available; video analysis; corporate days; hotel has leisure facilities and spa; from £45.

🍽 Full clubhouse and hotel facilities; cocktail bar; Fairways Brasserie; Imperial Restaurant.
Practice range, 8 covered bays.

🛏 On site Slaley Hall.

8B 75 South Moor
The Middles, Craghead, Stanley, Co Durham, DH9 6AG
☎ (01207) 232848, Fax 284616, Pro 283525, Sec 232848 x 101
Off the A693 6 miles W of Chester-le-Street on B6532 1 mile S of Stanley.
Moorland course.
Pro Shaun Cowell; Founded 1923
Designed by Dr A. MacKenzie
18 holes, 6445 yards, S.S.S. 71

⚑ Welcome with handicap certs.

🏌 WD £20; WE £26.

⛳ Welcome WD between 9.30am-11am and 2pm-3.30pm; WE between 10am-11am and 2pm-3.30pm; catering packages available; snooker table; from £15.

🍽 Full clubhouse facilities.

🛏 Lambton Arms; Lumley Castle; South Causey; Harperley Hotel

8B 76 South Shields
Cleadon Hills, South Shields, Tyne and Wear, NE34 8EG

☎(0191) 4560475, Pro 4560110,
Sec 4568942
Close to A19 and A1(M) near
Cleadon Chimney.
Heathland links course.
Pro Gary Parsons; Founded 1893
Designed by McKenzie/Baird
18 holes, 6264 yards, S.S.S. 70
† Welcome.
⌷ WD £25; WE £30.
⌁Welcome by prior arrangement;
terms on application.
◉ Clubhouse catering and bar
facilities available.
⌐ Sea Hotel.

8B 77 Stocksfield
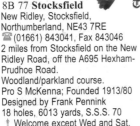
New Ridley, Stocksfield,
Northumberland, NE43 7RE
☎(01661) 843041, Fax 843046
2 miles from Stocksfield on the New
Ridley Road, off the A695 Hexham-
Prudhoe Road.
Woodland/parkland course.
Pro S McKenna; Founded 1913/80
Designed by Frank Pennink
18 holes, 6013 yards, S.S.S. 70
† Welcome except Wed and Sat.
⌷ WD £18; WE £24.
⌁Welcome by arrangement; special
packages with or without catering for
18/27/36 holes available; some
reductions for larger groups; from
£18.
◉ Full clubhouse facilities.
⌐ Beaumont, Hexham; Royal
Derwent, Allensford.

8B 78 Stressholme Golf Centre
Snipe Lane, Darlington
☎(01325) 461002
2 mile N of Darlington.
Parkland course.
Pro Mark Watkins/David Patterson;
Founded 1976
18 holes, 6229 yards, S.S.S. 69
† Welcome.
⌷ WD £9.50; WE £11.50
⌁Welcome by arrangement with
professional; terms available on
application.
◉ Clubhouse facilities.
Practice range, 14 bays floodlit.
⌐ Blackwell Grange.

8B 79 Swarland Hall
Coast View, Swarland, Morpeth,
Northumberland, NE65 9JG
☎(01670) 787010, Bar/Rest 787940
Course is one mile W of the A1 eight
miles S of Alnwick.

Parkland course.
Pro David & Linzi Fletcher; Founded
1993
18 holes, 6628 yards, S.S.S. 68
† Welcome.
⌷ WD £15; WE £20.
⌁Welcome; packages available for
golf and catering; 10 per cent
discount for parties of more than 12;
from £20.
◉ Full dining and bar facilities
available.
Practice area.

8B 80 Teesside
Acklam Rd, Thornaby, Stockton,
Cleveland, TS17 7JS
☎(01642) 676249, Fax 676252, Pro
673822, Sec 616516
Off A1130 Thornaby-Acklam Road.
Parkland course.
Pro Ken Hall; Founded 1901
18 holes, 6535 yards, S.S.S. 71
† Welcome by arrangement; before
4.30pm WD after 11.30am WE.
⌷ WD £26; WE £26.
⌁Welcome WD by prior
arrangement; minimum group 10,
max 35; from £20.
◉ Full clubhouse facilities.
⌐ Swallow, Stockton; Golden Eagle,
Thornaby.

8B 81 Tynedale
Tyne Green, Hexham,
Northumberland, NE46 3HQ
☎(01434) 608154
From A69 Hexham road turn into
Countryside Park; course 0.5 miles
on S of river Tyne.
Parkland course.
Pro Ian Waugh; Founded 1907
9 holes, 5403 yards, S.S.S. 67
† Welcome; except before 11am
Sun.
⌷ Prices on application.
⌁Welcome by prior arrangement;
discounts for groups of more than 10;
prices on application.
◉ Full clubhouse facilities.
⌐ Beaumont; County; Royal.

8B 82 Tynemouth
Spital Dene, Tynemouth, North
Shields, Tyne & Wear, NE30 2ER
☎(0191) 2574578, Sec 2573381,
Fax 2595193
On A695.
Parkland course.
Pro John McKenna; Founded 1913
Designed by Willie Park
18 holes, 6332 yards, S.S.S. 71

† Welcome WD after 9.30am; after
12.30pm Sun; limited Sat.
⌷ WD £16; WE £16.
⌁Welcome WD by prior
arrangement; catering packages
available; terms available on
application..
◉ Lunches, teas and snacks
available.
⌐ Park.

8B 83 Tyneside
Westfield Lane, Ryton, Tyne & Wear,
NE40 3QE
☎(0191) 4132177, Fax 4132742,
Pro 4131600, Sec 4132742, Bar/Rest
4138357
7 miles W of Newcastle off A695 S of
river.
Parkland course.
Pro Malcolm Gunn; Founded 1879
Designed by H.S. Colt (1910)
18 holes, 6033 yards, S.S.S. 69
† Welcome.
⌷ Prices on application.
⌁Welcome by prior arrangement;
reductions for groups of 18 or more;
catering packages available; prices
on application.
◉ Full clubhouse catering and bar
facilities.
Large practice area.
⌐ Ryton Park; Hedgefield Inn;
Copthorne, Newcastle; Marriott,
Gateshead; Ravensdene, Gateshead.

8B 84 Wallsend
Bigges Main, Wallsend-on-Tyne,
Northumberland, NE28 8SU
☎(0191) 2621973, Pro 2624231
E of Newcastle on coast road to
Whitley Bay.
Parkland course.
Pro Ken Phillips; Founded 1905
18 holes, 6606 yards, S.S.S. 72
† Welcome except before 12.30pm
WE.
⌷ WD £13; WE £15.
⌁Welcome by prior written
arrangement; WD only; terms on
application.
◉ Hot and cold snacks available.
⌐ Stakis.

8B 85 Warkworth
The Links, Warkworth, Morpeth,
Northumberland, NE65 0SW
☎(01665) 711596, Sec 711556
Off A1068 at Warkworth; 10 miles N
of Morpeth.
Seaside links course.
Founded 1891

Designed by Tom Morris
9 holes, 5870 yards, S.S.S. 68
☀ Welcome except Tues and Sat.
⌣ WD £12; WE £20.
�⌣ Welcome by prior arrangement
with the secretary, J A Gray; catering
packages are available by
arrangement with the stewardess;
from £12.
🍽 Bar and catering facilities in
season; by arrangement in winter.
Practice area.
↶ Warkworth House; Sun.

8B 86 **Wearside**
Coxgreen, Sunderland, Tyne & Wear,
SR4 9JT
☎ (0191) 5342518, Fax 5342518,
Pro 5344269
Course is off the A183 towards
Chester-le-Street; turn right
signposted Coxgreen to a T junction;
then turn left.
Meadowland/parkland course.
Pro Doug Brolls; Founded 1892
18 holes, 6373 yards, S.S.S. 70
☀ Welcome except on competition
days.
⌣ WD £25; WE £32.
�⌣ Welcome on application to Sec;
catering packages available; from
£25.
🍽 Full clubhouse facilities.
Practice range, also 4-hole par 3
practice course.
↶ Seaburn.

8B 87 **Westerhope**
Whorlton Grange, Westerhope,
Newcastle-upon-Tyne, NE5 1PP
☎ (0191) 2867636, Pro 2860594,
Bar/Rest 2869125
On the B6324 5 miles W of
Newcastle; close to the Jingling Gate
public house.
Wooded parkland course.
Pro N Brown; Founded 1941
Designed by Alexander Sandy Herd
18 holes, 6444 yards, S.S.S. 71
☀ Welcome.
⌣ Terms on application.
☟ Welcome by prior arrangement;
catering packages available; prices
on application.
🍽 Full clubhouse facilities.
↶ Airport Moat House; Holiday Inn;
Novotel, all Newcastle.

8B 88 **Whickham**
Hollinside Park, Whickham,
Newcastle-upon-Tyne, Tyne & Wear,
NE16 5BA

☎ (0191) 4887309, Fax 4881576,
Pro 4888591, Sec 4881576
Off the A1 at Whickham; follow signs
for Burnopfield, club 1.3 miles.
Parkland course.
Pro Graeme Lisle; Founded 1911
18 holes, 5878 yards, S.S.S. 68
☀ Welcome.
⌣ WD £20; WE £25.
☟ Welcome WD by arrangement
with Sec; discounts for larger groups;
catering packages; from £15.
🍽 Full catering facilities.
↶ Gibside Arms, Whickham;
Beamish Park; County; Copthorne;
Derwent Crossing, all Newcastle.

8B 89 **Whitburn**
Lizard Lane, South Shields, Tyne &
Wear, NE34 7AF
☎ (0191) 5292144, Pro 5294210,
Sec 5294944
Off coast road mid-way between
Sunderland and South Shields.
Parkland course.
Pro David Stephenson; Founded
1932
18 holes, 5900 yards, S.S.S. 69
☀ Welcome WD; by prior
arrangement WE.
⌣ WD £20; WE £25.
☟ Welcome WD by prior
arrangement; restrictions Tues;
limited availability WE; discounts for
groups of 11 or more; catering
packages available by prior
arrangement; from £20.
🍽 Full clubhouse facilities.
↶ Seaburn; Roker.

8B 90 **Whitley Bay**
Claremont Rd, Whitley Bay, Tyne &
Wear, NE26 3UF
☎ (0191) 2520180, Fax 2970030
N of Town centre.
Simulated links course.
Pro Gary Shipley; Founded 1890
18 holes, 6529 yards, S.S.S. 71
☀ Welcome WD
⌣ WD £20.
☟ Welcome by prior arrangement;
discounts available for larger groups;
catering packages available; from
£30.
🍽 Clubhouse catering facilities.
↶ The Grand, Tynemouth; Park;
Windsor, both Whitley Bay; Stakis
Wallsend.

8B 91 **Wilton**
Wilton, Redcar, Cleveland, TS10 4QY
☎ (01642) 465265, Pro 452730

Off A174 Whitby-Redcar road through
Lazenby following signs for Wilton
Castle.
Parkland course.
Pro Pat Smillie; Founded 1954/66
18 holes, 6145 yards, S.S.S. 69
☀ Welcome if carrying handicap
certs.
⌣ WD £18; WE £24.
☟ Welcome WD except Tues; some
Sun by prior arrangement; discounts
of £2 for groups of more than 20; Sun
£24; catering packages available by
arrangement from £7.95-£11.95; from
£18.
🍽 Full clubhouse facilities.
↶ Post House, Thornaby; Marton
Way; Blue Bell, both Middlesbrough.

8B 92 **Woodham Golf & Country Club**
Burnhill Way, Newton Aycliffe,
Durham, DL5 4PN
☎ (01325) 320574, Fax 315254, Pro
315257, Bar/Rest 301551
Off the A167 to Woodham village in
Newton Aycliffe.
Parkland course.
Pro Ernie Wilson; Founded 1983
Designed by J. Hamilton Stutt
18 holes, 6771 yards, S.S.S. 72
☀ Welcome by prior arrangement.
⌣ WD £20; WE £24.
☟ Welcome by prior arrangement;
some WE available; minimum 12
players; catering packages by
arrangement; buggy hire available;
practice area; from £15.
🍽 Full bar and restaurant facilities
available.
Practice ground.
↶ Eden Arms, Rushyford.

8B 93 **Wooler**
Dod Law, Doddington, Wooler,
Northumberland, NE71 6EA
☎ (01668) 281791
Course is east of the B6525 Wooler-
Berwick road; signposted from
Doddington village.
Moorland course.
Founded 1976
Designed by Club Members
9 holes, 6372 yards, S.S.S. 70
☀ Welcome.
⌣ Terms on application.
☟ Welcome by prior arrangement
with Sec; catering can be arranged;
terms on application.
🍽 Bar and catering facilities
available.
↶ Wheatsheaf; Black Bull; Ryecroft;
Tankerville Arms.

8B 94 **Wynyard**
(The Wellington)
Wynyard Park, Billingham, TS22 5NQ
☎ (01740) 644399, Fax 644592
On A689 at Wynyard Park between
A1 and A19.
Parkland course with mature woodlands; extension in 1998.
Pro Andrew Oliphant; Founded 1996
Designed by Hawtree & Son
18 holes, 7100 yards, S.S.S. 73
♦ Members' guests only.
⌞ Terms on application.
⌁ Corporate days only; full corporate golf day organisation and packages available; terms on application.
🍽 Full restaurant and bar facilities. Floodlit driving range; practice ground; short game academy areas.
⌐ Club can supply a list of local hotels.

9

SCOTLAND

For all the wonderful courses to be found in all corners of England, there is still nothing quite like stepping over the border into the Home of Golf. From Southerness in the south-west to Royal Dornoch in the far north-east, here is a land where golf is not so much an optional extra in the curriculum of life but a compulsory subject.

From Southerness one travels upwards to Ayrshire, a county so laden with fabulous golf courses it is almost unfair. Only Lancashire can compare when it comes to marrying quality links golf with quantity.

Best of all is Turnberry, which is now an even more desirable place to visit following the substantial upgrading of the Arran course which neighbours the more famous Ailsa. Nowhere in the United Kingdom is there a stretch of holes to compare with the fourth through to the 10th, which run alongside the craggy shore.

Stepping on to Prestwick is like walking through a museum. This is where the Open began and but for the intrusive Prestwick airport which can be seen from some of the outlying holes, you could almost be back in 1860.

Troon is the other member of Ayrshire's triumvirate of Open Championship courses, and an unsung member perhaps of those venues on the modern Open rota. It is, none the less, every inch a classic links, with its forbidding finish and the classic short eighth, the textbook hole that conclusively demonstrates that a par three need not be 200 yards long to be difficult.

These may be the most famous links courses but do not for a minute underestimate the charms of Western Gailes, Glasgow Gailes, Irvine and Barrassie.

All these courses look out towards the Mull of Kintyre, where perhaps the most geographically remote of all the great courses in the British Isles is to be found: mystical Machrihanish, which may well possess the finest opening hole in all golf.

On the west coast the best courses are to be found in the southern half of the country; on the east they stretch virtually to the tip. Most of the names will be familiar: Gullane, Muirfield, St Andrews, Carnoustie and Dornoch.

There are plenty of other, slightly less well-known courses that are anything but second division golf. In particular it was good to see Nairn, just outside Inverness, bask in the limelight last year as it hosted the Walker Cup, for this is a course worth travelling a long way to play. Then there is Royal Aberdeen and Cruden Bay, the former, with its valleyed fairways between dunes, the latter with its resplendent views worthy of Turnberry. Royal Aberdeen, incidentally, was formed in 1780, which makes it one of the oldest clubs in the world.

And that's just the links courses! A personal favourite among those inland is Blairgowrie at Rosemount, which is almost as spectacular as the more celebrated Gleneagles, and a fraction of the price. Meanwhile, for those visiting Carnoustie, or the nearby links of Monifieth or Panmure, Downfield represents a delightful contrast. — **DL**

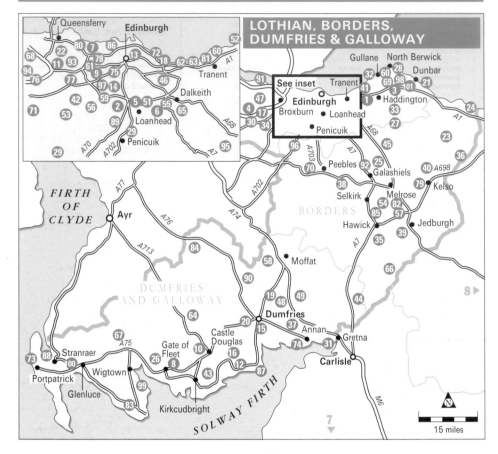

LOTHIAN, BORDERS, DUMFRIES & GALLOWAY

15 miles

9A 1 Aberlady
Aberlady, Lothian EH32 0QD
☎ (01875) 7374
Club plays at Kilspindie.

9A 2 Baberton
Baberton Ave, Juniper Green,
Edinburgh, EH14 5DU
☎ (0131) 4534911, Pro 4533555,
Bar/Rest 4533361
On A70 5 miles W of central
Edinburgh.
Parkland course.
Pro Ken Kelly; Founded 1893
Designed by Willie Park
18 holes, 6123 yards, S.S.S. 70
† Welcome by prior arrangement
with the secretary.
⌐ Terms available on application to
the club.
⌐ Welcome by prior arrangement;
catering packages available; from
£18.50.

🍽 Full clubhouse facilities.
⌐ Braid Hills, Edinburgh.

9A 3 Bass Rock
6 Harperdean Cottages, Harperdean,
Haddington, E Lothian EH41 3SQ
☎ (01620) 822082
Club plays at North Berwick.

9A 4 Bathgate
Edinburgh Rd, Bathgate, W Lothian
EH48 1BA
☎ (01506) 630505, Fax 636775, Pro
630553, Bar/Rest 652232
Club lies five mins E of town centre
and station.
Parkland course.
Pro S Strachan; Founded 1892
Designed by Willie Park
18 holes, 6250 yards, S.S.S. 70
† Welcome.
⌐ WD £16; WE £32.

⌐ Welcome by prior arrangement;
full day's catering package £8.50.
🍽 Full clubhouse facilities.
⌐ Hillcroft; Dreadnought; Kaim
Park; Hilton, Livingston.

9A 5 Braid Hills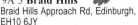
Braid Hills Approach Rd, Edinburgh,
EH10 6JY
☎ (0131) 4529408, Pro 447 6666
Course is on the A702 S from City
centre.
Hillside course with panoramic views.
Founded 1897
18 holes, 5731 yards, S.S.S. 68
† Welcome.
⌐ WD £8; WE £8.
⌐ Welcome by prior arrangement; in
summer two courses (second course:
4832 yards, S.S.S. 64); in winter
they amalgamate as one; from £8.
🍽 Clubhouse facilities.
⌐ Braid Hills.

KEY

1	Aberlady	34	Harburn	68	Niddry Castle
2	Baberton	35	Howick	69	North Berwick
3	Bass Rock	36	Hirsel	70	Peebles
4	Bathgate	37	Hoddom Castle	71	Polkemmet Country Park
5	Braid Hills	38	Innerleithen	72	Portobello
6	Broomieknowe	39	Jedburgh	73	Portpatrick (Dunskey)
7	Bruntsfield Links	40	Kelso	74	Powfoot
8	Cally Palace Hotel	41	Kilspindie	75	Prestonfield
9	Carrickknowe	42	Kingsknowe	76	Pumpherston
10	Castle Douglas	43	Kirkcudbright	77	Ratho Park
11	Cogarburn	44	Langholm	78	Ravelston
12	Colvend	45	Lauder	79	The Roxburghe
13	Craigentinny	46	Liberton	80	Royal Burgess Golfing
14	Craigmillar Park	47	Linlithgow		Society of Edinburgh
15	Crichton Royal	48	Lochmaben	81	Royal Musselburgh
16	Dalbeattie	49	Lockerbie	82	St Boswells
17	Deer Park Golf &	50	Longniddry	83	St Medan
	Country Club	51	Lothianburn	84	Sanquhar
18	Duddingston	52	Luffness New	85	Selkirk
19	Dumfries & County	53	Marriott Dalmahoy	86	Silverknowes
20	Dumfries & Galloway	54	Melrose	87	Southerness
21	Dunbar	55	Melville	88	Stranraer
22	Dundas Park	56	Merchants of Edinburgh	89	Swanston
23	Duns	57	Minto	90	Thornhill
24	Eyemouth	58	Moffat	91	Torphin Hill
25	Galashiels	59	Mortonhall	92	Torwoodlee
26	Gatehouse-of-Fleet	60	Muirfield – Honourable	93	Turnhouse
27	Gifford Golf Club		Co of Edinburgh Golfers	94	Uphall
28	Glen	61	Murrayfield	95	Vogrie
29	Glencorse	62	Musselburgh	96	West Linton
30	Greenburn	63	Musselburgh Old Course	97	West Lothian
31	Gretna	64	New Galloway	98	Whitekirk
32	Gullane	65	Newbattle	99	Wigtown & Bladnoch
33	Haddington	66	Newcastleton	100	Wigtownshire County
		67	Newton Stewart	101	Winterfield

9A 6 Broomieknowe

36 Golf Course Rd, Bonnyrigg,
Midlothian EH19 2HZ
☎(0131) 6639317, Fax 6632152,
Pro 6602035, Bar/Rest 6637844
Clus is off the A7 at the Eskbank
Road roundabout 0.5 miles from
Bonnyrigg.
Parkland course.
Pro Mark Patchett; Founded 1906
Designed by James Braid; Alterations
by Hawtree/Ben Sayer
18 holes, 6150 yards, S.S.S. 70
♦ Welcome.
⌐ WD £17.50; WE £20.50.
⌐Welcome WD by prior
arrangement; day tickets available for
£25.50; catering available; group
discounts available.
◉ Clubhouse facilities.
⌐ Dalhousie Castle.

9A 7 Bruntsfield Links

32 Barnton Ave, Davidsons Mains,
Edinburgh EH4 6JH
☎(0131) 3362006, Fax 3365538,
Pro 3364050, Sec 3361479
Off A90 Forth Bridge road 3 miles
NW of Edinburgh city centre; 6 miles
from the airport.
Mature parkland with stunning views
of the Firth of Forth.

Pro Brian Mackenzie; Founded
1761/1898
Designed by Willie Park/ Mackenzie
(22)/ Hawtree (74)
18 holes, 6407 yards, S.S.S. 71
♦ Welcome by prior arrangement
with Secretary or Pro.
⌐ WD £50; WE £60.
⌐Welcome by prior written
arrangement; packages available for
lunch, high tea and dinner in the
club's magnificent dining room; jacket
and tie required in clubhouse; from
£36.
◉ Full catering and bar facilities
available.
⌐ Many available in the Edinburgh
area.

9A 8 Cally Palace Hotel

Gatehouse of Fleet, Dumfries and
Galloway DG7 2DL
33 miles W of Dumfries on A75;
signposted from Gatehouse.
☎(01557) 814341, Fax 814522
Inland course.
18 holes, 5531 yards, par 70
♦ Hotel guests only.
⌐ Packages available from £70 per
day.
◉ Full hotel facilities.
⌐ On site Cally Palace.

9A 9 Carrickknowe

Glendevon Park, Edinburgh, EH12
5VZ
☎(0131) 3371096
Opposite the Post House Hotel on
Balgreen Road.
Parkland course.
Founded 1933
18 holes, 6166 yards, S.S.S. 70
♦ Welcome.
⌐ WD £7.95; WE £7.95.
⌐Welcome; golf only; £7.95.
◉ No catering facilities.

9A 10 Castle Douglas

Abercromby Rd, Castle Douglas,
Dumfries & Galloway, DG7 1BA
☎(01556) 502801, Sec 502099
On A713 towards Ayr 400 yards from
the town clock.
Parkland course.
Founded 1905
9 holes, 5408 yards, S.S.S. 66
♦ Welcome.
⌐ WD £12; WE £12.
⌐Welcome; bar meals can be
arranged; from £12.
◉ Bar meals available.
⌐ Kings Arms; Imperial; Douglas
Arms.

9A 11 Cogarburn

Hanley Lodge, Newbridge, Midlothian
EH28 8NN
☎(0131) 333 4110, Sec 333 4110,
Bar/Rest 3334110
Close to Edinburgh Airport sliproad
off A8 Glasgow Road.
Parkland course.
Founded 1975
12 holes, 5070 yards, S.S.S. 65
♦ Welcome by prior arrangement
with Sec.
⌐ WD £10; WE £15.
⌐Welcome by prior arrangement
with Sec; catering can be arranged in
new clubhouse; from £10.
◉ Full catering and bar facilities
available.
⌐ Barnton; Royal Scot.

9A 12 Colvend

Sandyhills, by Dalbeattie, Dumfries &
Galloway DG5 4PY
☎(01556) 630398, Sec 610878
On A710 Solway coast road 6 miles
from Dalbeattie.
Parkland course.
Founded 1905
Designed by Willie Fernie 1905; D
Thomas (1985); J Soutar extension to
18 (1997)

18 holes, 5220 yards, S.S.S. 67
♦ Welcome.
⚑ WD £18; WE £18.
⚐ Welcome by prior arrangement;
tee reservations require £5 per head
deposit; concession of £2 for groups
of 10 or more; catering packages
available; from £15.
🍽 Full catering and bar facilities
available.
⌁ Cairngill; Clonyard; Baron's Craig;
Pheasant.

9A 13 **Craigentinny**
143 Craigentinny Ave, Edinburgh
☎ (0131) 554 7501, Sec 657 4815
Clus is one mile from Meadowbank
Stadium.
Links course.
Founded 1891
18 holes, 5413 yards, S.S.S. 66
♦ Public links course.
⚑ WD £8.80; WE £9.65.
⚐ Welcome by prior arrangement
with Council; details available on
application.
🍽 By prior arrangement.

9A 14 **Craigmillar Park**
1 Observatory Rd, Edinburgh EH9
3HG
☎ (0131) 6672499, Pro 6672850,
Sec 6670047, Bar/Rest 6672837
From A68 Princes Street turn right at
Cameron Toll; course 100 yards on
right.
Parkland course.
Pro Brian McGhee; Founded 1895
Designed by James Braid
18 holes, 5851 yards, S.S.S. 69
♦ Welcome WD and Sun. after 2pm.
⚑ WD £7.50, WE £9.50.
⚐ Welcome WD by prior
arrangement with Sec; separate
facilities; catering packages available;
from £17.50.
🍽 Full catering facilities.
⌁ Iona Hotel, Edinburgh.

9A 15 **Crichton Royal**
Bankend Rd, Dumfries DG1 4TH
Tel/Fax 01387 247894
1 mile from Dumfries near Crichton
Royal Hospital.
Wooded parkland course.
9 holes, 3084 yards
♦ Welcome by prior arrangement,
but must avoid competition days.
⚑ £12.
⚐ Welcome by advance notice;
terms on application.
🍽 Clubhouse facilities.

9A 16 **Dalbeattie**
off Maxwell Park, Dalbeattie,
Kirkcudbrightshire DG5 4JR
☎ (01556) 611421, Sec 610682
Course is 1 mile from Dalbeattie on
the B794 (Haugh of Urr road), 10
miles south-west of Dumfries.
Parkland hilly course.
9 holes, 5710 yards, S.S.S. 68
♦ Restrictions Mon, Wed, Thurs
after 5pm.
⚑ £12 (day ticket £15).
⚐ Welcome outside restricted times.
🍽 Clubhouse facilities.

9A 17 **Deer Park Golf** 🏌 ⚑
& Country Club
Golf Course Rd, Knightsbridge,
Livingston, West Lothian EH54
8PG
☎ (01506) 431037, Fax 435608
Leave M8 at Junction 3 and follow
signs to Knightsbridge; club is
signposted.
Parkland course.
Founded 1978
Designed by Charles Lawrie
18 holes, 6192 yards, S.S.S. 72
♦ Welcome.
⚑ WD £20; WE £30.
⚐ Welcome by prior arrangement
both WD and WE; catering
packages available; from £20.
🍽 Full clubhouse and country club
facilities.
⌁ Deer Park; Houston House;
Hilton.

9A 18 **Duddingston**
Duddingston Rd West, Edinburgh
EH15 3QD
☎ (0131) 6611005, Fax 6614301,
Pro 6614301, Sec 6617688
2 miles from city centre near A1
turning right at Duddingston
crossroads.
Parkland course.
Pro Alastair McLean; Founded 1895
Designed by Willie Park Jnr
18 holes, 6420 yards, S.S.S. 72
♦ Welcome WD.
⚑ WD £29.
⚐ Welcome Tues and Thurs by prior
arrangement; catering packages can
be arranged; from £23.
🍽 Full clubhouse facilities.
⌁ Many in Edinburgh.

9A 19 **Dumfries & County**
Edinburgh Rd, Dumfries, Dumfries &
Galloway, DG1 1JX
☎ (01387) 253585, Pro 268918

On A701 Moffat to Edinburgh road 1
mile NE of town centre.
Parkland course; The Wee Yin: 90
yards, 14th.
Pro Stuart Syme; Founded 1912
Designed by James Braid
18 holes, 5928 yards, S.S.S. 68
♦ Welcome WD between 9.30am-
11am; 2pm-3.30pm; WE not
Saturday; Sunday after 10am.
⚑ WD £25; WE £25.
⚐ Welcome by prior arrangement
with Sec; separate facilities; catering
packages available; from £23.
🍽 Club bar and dining room.
⌁ Cairndale; Station; Moreig;
Balmoral; Edenbank.

9A 20 **Dumfries & Galloway**
Laurieston Ave, Dumfries, Dumfries &
Galloway DG2 7NY
☎ (01387) 253582, Fax 270297, Pro
256902, Sec 263848
On A75 W of Dumfries.
Parkland course.
Pro Joe Fergusson; Founded 1880
18 holes, 5803 yards, S.S.S. 68
♦ Welcome except comp days; prior
booking essential in summer.
⚑ WD £25; WE £30.
⚐ Welcome by prior arrangement;
catering packages available except
Mon; from £25.
🍽 Full facilities available; except
Mon.
⌁ Cairndale; Station.

9A 21 **Dunbar**
East Links, Dunbar, E Lothian EH42
1LT
☎ (01368) 862317, Fax 865202, Pro
862086
0.5 miles E of Dunbar; 30 miles E of
Edinburgh off A1.
Links course.
Pro Derek Small; Founded 1794/1856
Designed by Tom Morris
18 holes, 6426 yards, S.S.S. 71
♦ Welcome WD by prior
arrangement 9.30am-12.30pm & 2pm
onwards except Thurs; WE 10am-12
noon and after 2pm.
⚑ Terms upon application.
⚐ Welcome by prior arrangement
WD; catering packages available;
from £30.
🍽 Full clubhouse facilities.
⌁ Cruachan GH; Royal Mackintosh.

9A 22 **Dundas Park**
Dundas Estate, South Queensferry,
W Lothian EH30 9SP

☎0131) 331 5603
Course is one mile south of S
Queensferry on the A8000.
Parkland course.
Founded 1957
9 holes, 6024 yards, S.S.S. 69
† Welcome by arrangement.
⌐ Terms on application.
↷Welcome by prior arrangement;
terms on application.
◉ Snacks in clubhouse.
Practice range.

9A 23 Duns
Hardens Rd, Duns, Berwickshire
TD11 3HN
☎(01361) 882194, Sec 882717
Course is one mile W of Duns off the
A6105 Greenlaw-Duns road, taking
the junction signposted
Longformacus.
Parkland/upland course.
Founded 1894/1921
Designed by A H Scott
18 holes, 6209 yards, S.S.S. 70
† Welcome.
⌐ WD £14; WE £17.
↷Welcome by prior arrangement
with Sec; some WE tee-times
available; all day golf; limited
clubhouse facilities but snack meals
can be arranged April-October; from
£15.
◉ Full facilities.
⌐ Barniken House.

9A 24 Eyemouth
The Clubhouse, Gunsgreenhill,
Eyemouth TD14 5SF
☎(01890) 750551, Pro 750004
One mile off the A1 on the A1107
east of Burmouth.
Seaside parkland course.
Pro Paul Terras; Founded 1884/1996
18 holes, 6472 yards, par 72, S.S.S.
71
† Welcome any day.
⌐ WD £18; WE £22.
↷Welcome by prior arrangement;
special catering packages available.
◉ Full clubhouse facilities.
⌐ Press Castle; Cul-Na-Sithe;
Dunlaverock House; Ship; Dolphin.

9A 25 Galashiels
Ladhope Recreation Ground,
Galashiels, Selkirkshire TD1 2NJ
☎(01896) 753724
On A7 to Edinburgh 0.5 miles N of
town centre.
Hilly parkland course.
Founded 1883

Designed by James Braid
18 holes, 5185 yards, S.S.S. 67
† Welcome.
⌐ WD £15; WE £17.
↷Welcome by prior arrangement
with Secretary; package deals
available; terms available on
application.
◉ Full clubhouse facilities.
⌐ Abbotsford Arms; Kingsknowes;
Kings.

9A 26 Gatehouse-of-Fleet
Laurieston Rd, Gatehouse-of-Fleet
☎(01557) 814766, Sec 450260,
Bar/Rest 814459
From A75 into Gatehouse-of-Fleet
follow signs for Laurieston; course
0.5 miles.
Parkland course with stunning views.
Founded 1921
9 holes, 5042 yards, S.S.S. 64
† Welcome.
⌐ WD £10; WE £10.
↷Welcome by prior arrangement;
local hotels can provide catering
arrangements; terms on application.
◉ None at course.
⌐ Masonic Arms; Murray Arms.

9A 27 Gifford Golf Club
Edinburgh Road, Gifford, E Lothian
EH41 4QN
☎(01620) 810267, Fax 810267
On A1 4 miles from the market town
of Haddington.
Undulating parkland course in
Lammermuir foothills.
Founded 1904
Designed by Willie Watt
9 holes, 6255 yards, S.S.S. 70
† Welcome.
⌐ WD £12; WE £12.
↷Welcome; discounts for larger
groups; from £10.
◉ Full facilities at village hotels;
clubhouse.
⌐ Goblin Ha'; Tweeddale Arms.

9A 28 Glen
East Links, Tantallon Terrace, North
Berwick, E Lothian EH39 4LE
☎(01620) 892726, Fax 895288, Pro
894596, Sec 895288, Bar/Rest
892221
Signposted from A198 1 mile E of
town centre.
Seaside links course.
Founded 1906
Designed by MacKenzie Ross
18 holes, 6043 yards, S.S.S. 69
† Welcome.

⌐ WD £17; WE £23.
↷Welcome by prior arrangement;
catering packages available; from
£17.
◉ Full clubhouse facilities.
⌐ Marine; Belhaven; Golf.

9A 29 Glencorse
Milton Bridge, Pencuik, Midlothian
EH26 0RD
☎(01968) 677189, Fax 674399, Pro
676481, Bar/Rest 677177
On A701 Peebles road 9 miles S of
Edinburgh.
Parkland course with stream on 10
holes.
Pro C Jones; Founded 1890
Designed by Willie Park Jnr
18 holes, 5217 yards, S.S.S. 66
† Welcome; restrictions on comp
days.
⌐ WD £18.50; WE £24.50.
↷Welcome Mon-Thurs and Sun
afternoon by prior arrangement;
packages for golf and catering also
available for parties of 10 or more;
from £18.
◉ Full clubhouse catering and bar
packages.
Practice range: Glencorse range 0.5
miles from course; 30 floodlit bays.
⌐ Royal Hotel, Pencuik.

9A 30 Greenburn
6 Greenburn Rd, Fauldhouse EH47
9AY
☎(01501) 771187.
4 miles S of M8 Junction 4 and 5.
Parkland/moorland course.
Pro M Leighton; Founded 1953
18 holes, 6046 yards, S.S.S. 70
† Welcome by prior arrangements;
WE 9am-10am and 2pm-3pm.
⌐ WD £17; WE £20.
↷Welcome WD by prior
arrangement; catering packages
available; terms on application.
◉ Full clubhouse facilities.
Practice area.
⌐ Hillcroft.

9A 31 Gretna
"Kirtle View", Gretna, Dumfriesshire
DG16 5HD
☎(01461) 338464
Course is 0.5 miles W of Gretna on S
side of the A75; 1 mile from the
M74/A75 junction.
Parkland course.
Founded 1991
Designed by Nigel Williams/ Bothwell
9 holes, 6430 yards, S.S.S. 71

⚓ Welcome except on competition days.
🏌 WD £8; WE £10.
🍽 Welcome by prior arrangement; catering packages by arrangement; terms on application.
🍴 Catering available by prior arrangement.
Practice range.
🛏 Many hotels in local area.

9A 32 **Gullane** ♙

West Links Rd, Gullane, E Lothian EH31 2BB
☎ (01620) 842255, Fax 842327, Pro 843111
Leave the A1 S to the A198.
300-year-old seaside links course; Open qualifying course.
Pro Jimmy Hume; Founded 1882 (Course 1), Founded 1898 (Course 2), Founded 1910 (Course 3)
Course 1: 18 holes, 6466 yards, S.S.S. 71
Course 2: 18 holes, 6244 yards, S.S.S. 71
Course 3: 18 holes, 5252 yards, S.S.S. 68
⚓ Welcome with handicap certs by prior arrangement.
🏌 WD £56, WE £69 (Course 1); WD £25, WE £31 (Course 2); WD £15, WE £20 (Course 3).
🍽 Welcome by prior arrangement; corporate days can be arranged; also conference day packages with exclusive use of the first-class accommodation in the Members' clubhouse for seminars and conferences for groups of 12-24; Heritage of Golf Museum; coaching clinics; terms available on application.
🍴 Full clubhouse catering facilities in the Members' clubhouse.
🛏 Club can provide a list in Gullane, North Berwick and Aberlady.

9A 33 **Haddington**

Amisfield Park, Whittinghame Dr, Haddington EH41 4PT
☎ (01620) 826058, Fax 826580, Pro 822727, Sec 823627
0.75 miles E of Haddington just off the A1; 17 miles E of Edinburgh.
Parkland course.
Pro John Sandilands; Founded 1865
18 holes, 6317 yards, S.S.S. 70
⚓ Welcome WE pre-booking essential.
🏌 WD £18; WE £23.
🍽 Welcome; full day's golf; catering packages available in the season by arrangement Oct-March; from £25.

🍴 Full catering and bar facilities April-Sept.
🛏 Plough; Maitlandfield.

9A 34 **Harburn**

West Calder, W Lothian, EH55 8RS
☎ (01506) 871582, Fax 871131, Sec 871131, Bar/Rest 871256
Course is on the B7008 off the A705 from M8 Junction 4.
Parkland course.
Pro Stephen Mills; Founded 1933
18 holes, 5921 yards, S.S.S. 68
⚓ Welcome except on comp days.
🏌 WD £18; Friday £21; WE £23.
🍽 Welcome except on comp days; packages for Mon-Thurs; Fri, Sat and Sun available including day's golf, lunch and high tea; separate changing facilities; from £30.
🍴 Full clubhouse facilities.
🛏 Bankton House; Livingston Hilton.

9A 35 **Hawick** ♙

Vertish Hill, Hawick, Roxburgh TD9 0NY
☎ (01450) 372293, Sec 374947
Just S of Hawick on A7.
Parkland course.
Founded 1877
18 holes, 5933 yards, S.S.S. 69
⚓ Welcome; restrictions until after 3.30pm on some Sats; not before 10.30am Sun.
🏌 WD £20; WE £20.
🍽 Welcome by arrangement; catering packages in season; separate facilities; terms on application.
🍴 Full clubhouse facilities in summer.
🛏 Kirkland; Mansfield House; Elmsfield.

9A 36 **Hirsel**

Kelso Rd, Coldstream, Berwickshire, TS12 4NJ
☎ (01890) 882678, Fax 882233, Sec 882233
On A697 through Coldstream; golf club is signposted.
Parkland course.
Founded 1948
18 holes, 6111 yards, S.S.S. 70
⚓ Welcome.
🏌 WD £20; WE £27.
🍽 Welcome by prior arrangement; catering and golf packages available; more than 10 players must book in advance; 2-10 must book up to 10 days in advance; no starts before 10am; terms on application.

🍴 Full clubhouse facilities.
🛏 Tillmouth park; Collingwood Arms; Cross Keys.

9A 37 **Hoddom Castle**

Hoddom, Lockerbie, Dumfries and Galloway DG11 1AS
☎ (01576) 300251
Course is three miles from the A74 and 2 miles SW of Ecclefechan on the B725; M74 junction 6.
Pay and play inland course.
9 holes, 2274 yards, S.S.S. 33
⚓ Welcome.
🏌 £9.
🍽 Limited.
🍴 Snacks.

9A 38 **Innerleithen**

Leithen Water, Leithen Road, Innerleithen, Peebleshire EH44 6NL
☎ (01896) 830951, Sec 830071
0.75 miles from town centre down Leithen Road.
Heathland/parkland course.
Founded 1886
Designed by Willie Park
9 holes, 6056 yards, S.S.S. 69
⚓ Welcome.
🏌 WD £11; WE £13.
🍽 Welcome but groups of more than six should book; maximum 42; from £11.
🍴 Dacilities available by prior arrangement.
🛏 Corner House; Traquar Arms.

9A 39 **Jedburgh**

Dunion Rd, Jedburgh, Roxburghshire, TD8 6LA
☎ (01835) 863587
0.75 mile W of Jedburgh on Hawick road.
Undulating parkland course.
Founded 1892
9 holes, 5555 yards, S.S.S. 67
⚓ Welcome except on competition days; WE booking advisable.
🏌 Terms on application.
🍽 Welcome with at least 2 weeks' notice; catering and bar facilities available between May and September; from £12.
🍴 Available in season.
🛏 Royal; Jedforest.

9A 40 **Kelso**

Racecourse Rd, Kelso, Roxburgh, TD5 7SL
☎ (01573) 223009, Sec 223259

Liberton Golf Club was founded in 1920 and is situated on the A7, south east of Edinburgh City Centre. This city course is 18 holes of rolling parkland; the 5306 yards of tight fairways and small greens make this par 67 a good test of golf for anyone. Guests are welcome to make use of the bar and catering facilities. Green fees: £20 per round. Golf packages available.

Liberton Golf Club, Kingston Grange, 297 Gilmerton Road, Edinburgh EH16 5UJ. Tel: 0131-664 3009. Fax: 0131-666 0853

1 mile N of Kelso inside National Hunt racecourse.
Flat parkland course.
Founded 1887
Designed by James Braid
18 holes, 6046 yards, S.S.S. 70
♠ Welcome.
⌐ WD £16; WE £20.
⌐ Welcome by prior arrangement; includes all day golf; catering packages available; notice needed for Mon or Tues; from £20.
⌐ Clubhouse facilities; closed Mon-Wed in winter.
⌐ Cross Keys; Queen's Head.

9A 41 Kilspindie
The Clubhouse, Aberlady, EH32 0QD
☎ (01875) 870216, Pro 870695, Sec, P. B. Casely 870358
Off A198 North Berwick Road immediately E of Aberlady; private road leads to the club.
Seaside course.
Pro Graham Sked; Founded 1867
Designed by Ross & Sayers;
Extended by Willie Park
18 holes, 5480 yards, S.S.S. 66
Expecting 2nd course May 2000: 18 holes, 6,600 yards, S.S.S. 72
♠ Welcome by prior arrangement with the club.
⌐ WD £25; WE £30.
⌐ Welcome by prior arrangement; catering packages available; terms on application.
⌐ Full catering facilities with bar and dining room.
⌐ Kilspindie House.

9A 42 Kingsknowe
326 Lanark Rd, Edinburgh EH14 2JD
☎ (0131) 441 1144, Fax 441 2079, Pro 441 4030, Sec 441 1145
On A70 on the SW outskirts of Edinburgh.
Undulating parkland
Pro Andrew Marshall; Founded 1908
Designed by Alex Herd, James Braid, J.C. Stutt
18 holes, 5979 yards, S.S.S. 69
♠ Welcome by prior arrangement with Pro.
⌐ WD £21; WE £30.

⌐ Welcome by prior application to Sec; full day's golf and catering available; separate changing; from £18.
⌐ Full clubhouse catering and bar facilities.
⌐ Orwell Lodge; Edinburgh Post House.

9A 43 Kirkcudbright
Stirling Crescent, Kirkcudbright, DG6 4EZ
☎ (01557) 330314
Off A711 road from the A75 Dumfries-Stranraer Road.
Parkland course.
Founded 1893
18 holes, 5739 yards, S.S.S. 69
♠ Welcome; some restrictions Tues/Wed.
⌐ WD £18; WE £18.
⌐ Welcome by prior arrangement; full day £23; from £18.
⌐ Clubhouse facilities.
⌐ Royal; Selkirk; Commercial.

9A 44 Langholm
Whitaside, Langholm, Dumfriesshire DG13 0JR
☎ (013873) 81247, Sec 80673
Off the A7 Edinburgh-Carlisle road in centre of Langholm; follow signs to the course.
Hillside course.
Founded 1892
9 holes, 5744 yards, S.S.S. 68
♠ Welcome.
⌐ WD £10; WE £10.
⌐ Welcome by prior arrangement; catering available by prior arrangement; £10.
⌐ Clubhouse facilities.
⌐ Eskdale; Buck; Crown.

9A 45 Lauder
Galashiels Rd, Lauder, TD2 6QD
☎ (01578) 722526, Fax 722526
On A68 30 miles S of Edinburgh; 0.5 miles outside Lauder.
Parkland course.
Founded 1896
Designed by W. Park of Musselburgh
9 holes, 6002 yards, S.S.S. 70

♠ Welcome except before noon Sun and 5.30pm-7.30pm Wed.
⌐ WD £10; WE £10.
⌐ Welcome by prior arrangement; golf only available; from £10.
⌐ Catering can be arranged with local hotels.
⌐ Lauderdale; Eagle; Black Bull.

9A 46 Liberton
297 Gilmerton Rd, Edinburgh EH16 5UJ
☎ (0131) 664 3009, Fax 666 0853, Pro 664 1056, Bar/Rest 664 8580
Exit Edinburgh city by-pass at Gilmerton A7 junction; course 3 miles towards city.
Parkland course.
Pro Iain Seith; Founded 1920
18 holes, 5306 yards, S.S.S. 66
♠ Welcome.
⌐ WD £17; WE £25.
⌐ Welcome WD by prior written arrangement; 36 holes of golf, coffee, lunch, high tea; max 40; £33.
⌐ Full clubhouse facilities.

9A 47 Linlithgow
Braehead, Golf Course Rd, Linlithgow, W Lothian, EH49 6QF
☎ (01506) 671044, Fax 842764, Pro 844356, Sec 842585
Approx 10 miles from Edinburgh on M9.
Undulating parkland course.
Pro Steve Rosie; Founded 1913
Designed by Robert Simpson of Carnoustie
18 holes, 5729 yards, S.S.S. 68
♠ Welcome except Sat and comp days.
⌐ WD £17 (£10 winter); WE £25 (£10 winter).
⌐ Welcome by arrangement with Sec; catering packages available except Tues; from £17.
⌐ Full clubhouse facilities.
⌐ Star & Garter; West Port.

9A 48 Lochmaben
Castlehill Gate, Lochmaben, Lockerbie, Dumfries & Galloway DG11 1NT

☎(01387) 810552
Course is four miles from the A74 at Lockerbie on the A709 road to Dumfries.
Parkland course; extended in 1993.
Founded 1926
Designed by James Braid
18 holes, 5377 yards, S.S.S. 66
† Welcome; on competition days by prior arrangement.
⌞ WD £18; WE £22.
⌐Welcome by prior arrangement; catering packages available; caddie car hire; from £16.
⊙ Full clubhouse facilities.
Practice area.
↙ Balcastle; Queens; Somerton House.

9A 49 Lockerbie
Corrie Rd, Lockerbie, Dumfriesshire DG11 2ND
☎(01576) 203363, Fax 203363
Leave M74 at Lockerbie and course is signposted.
Tree-lined parkland course with pond in play on 3 holes.
Founded 1889
Designed by James Braid (original 9)
18 holes, 5463 yards, S.S.S. 67
† Welcome; prior booking is advisable.
⌞ WD £15; WE £18.
⌐Welcome by prior arrangement; 36 holes of golf; morning coffee, light lunch; evening meal (£30 Sat); from £27.
⊙ Full clubhouse facilities.
↙ Queens; Kings; Ravenshill; Dryfesdale.

9A 50 Longniddry
Links Rd, Longniddry, E Lothian EH32 0NL
☎(01875) 852141, Fax 853371, Pro 852228, Bar/Rest 852623
On B6363 in Longniddry village from the A1.
Parkland and links course.
Pro John Gray; Founded 1921
Designed by Harry Colt
18 holes, 6186 yards, S.S.S. 70
† Welcome WD; WE by arrangement.
⌞ WD £30; WE £40.
⌐Welcome by prior arrangement and with handicap certs; catering packages can be arranged with the clubmaster; tee times between 9.30am and 4pm; deposit of £10 per person required; credit cards accepted; max 40; from £42.
⊙ Full clubhouse facilities.

↙ Kilspindie House; Maitlandfield; Greencraigs.

9A 51 Lothianburn
106 Biggar Rd, Edinburgh, EH10 7DU
☎(0131) 445 5067, Pro 445 2288, Bar/Rest 445 2206
On A702 Biggar to Carlisle road, 200 yards from City by-pass at Lothianburn exit.
Hilly course.
Pro Kurt Mungall; Founded 1893/1928
Designed by James Braid (1928)
18 holes, 5662 yards, S.S.S. 68
† Welcome WD up to 4.30pm; WE with member.
⌞ WD £16.
⌐Welcome WD by prior arrangement with Sec; discounts available for more than 16 in a party; catering packages by prior arrangement; from £13.
⊙ Clubhouse facilities.
↙ Braid Hills.

9A 52 Luffness New
Aberlady, E Lothian, E32 0QA
☎(01620) 843114, Fax 842933, Sec 843336, Bar/Rest 843376
1 mile outside Aberlady on the A198 Gullane road.
Links course.
Founded 1894
Designed by Tom Morris (1894)
18 holes, 6122 yards, S.S.S. 70
† Welcome WD only;
⌞ WD £37.50.
⌐Welcome WD by prior arrangement; full day's golf £55; catering by prior arrangement; from £35.
⊙ Smoke room; dining room; lunch daily except Mon; high tea/dinner by arrangement (min 10).
Practice range: 5-hole course.
↙ Marine, N Berwick; Golf, Greywalls (Gullane).

9A 53 Marriott Dalmahoy
Kirknewton, Midlothian, EH27 8EB
☎(0131) 3358010, Fax 3353203, Sec 3334105
Course is on the A71 seven miles W of Edinburgh.
Rolling parkland course.
Pro Stuart Callan; Founded 1927
Designed by James Braid
East: 18 holes, 6677 yards, S.S.S. 72; West: 18 holes, 5185 yards, S.S.S. 66

† Welcome WD and WE by prior arrangement and with handicap certs.
⌞ WD £55 (East), £35 (West); WE £75 (East), £45 (West).
⌐Welcome WD by prior arrangement; corporate days can be organised; catering and residential packages available; leisure facilities, including indoor heated pool, spa, sauna, tennis, gym, health & beauty salon; terms on application.
⊙ Facilities in the Long Weekend Restaurant.
Practice range, 12 bays all-weather floodlit.
↙ Marriott Dalmahoy.

9A 54 Melrose
Dingleton, Melrose, Roxburghshire
☎(01896) 822855, Sec 822758
2 miles N of St Boswell off the A68 Newcastle-Edinburgh Road; 0.5 miles S of Melrose.
Undulating wooded parkland course.
Founded 1880
9 holes, 5562 yards, S.S.S. 68
† Welcome WD; Sat very limited; most Sun available.
⌞ WD £16; WE £16.
⌐Welcome by arrangement; catering can be arranged; from £16.
⊙ Available by prior arrangement.

9A 55 Melville
South Melville, Lasswade, EH18 1AN
☎(0131) 663 8038, Fax 654 0814, Sec 654 0224
Off the Edinburgh city by-pass on the Galashiels A7 road.
Parkland course.
Founded 1995
Designed by P Campbell/G Webster
9 holes, 4310 yards, S.S.S. 62
† Welcome.
⌞ WD £12; WE £16.
⌐Welcome by prior arrangement Mon-Thurs; minimum 10, maximum 20; from £12.
⊙ Snacks available.
Practice range: 34 bays; 22 covered, 12 outdoor.
↙ Eskbank; Dalhousie Castle.

9A 56 Merchants of Edinburgh
10 Craighill Gardens, Edinburgh, EH10 5PY
☎01506) 871 933, Pro 447 8709
Course is off the A701 S of Edinburgh.
Hilly parkland course
Pro N E M Colquhoun; Founded 1907

18 holes, 4889 yards, S.S.S. 64
♦ Welcome WD before 4pm.
ℒ WD £15.
⤵Welcome WD before 4pm by prior arrangement; catering packages can be arranged; from £15.
🍽 Available except Thurs; full bar facilities.
⤵ Braid Hills.

9A 57 Minto
Minto Village, by Denholm, Hawick, Roxburghshire TD9 8SH
☎(01450) 870220, Sec 375841, Fax 870126
5 miles NE of Hawick leaving A698 at Denholm.
Parkland course.
New course for season 2000.
Founded 1928
18 holes, 5453 yards, S.S.S. 67
♦ Welcome by arrangement.
ℒ WD £17; WE £22.
⤵Welcome by prior arrangement; packages available; from £17.
🍽 Full clubhouse facilities.
Practice range.
⤵ Contact the Scottish Tourist Board.

9A 58 Moffat
Coatshill, Moffat, Dumfriesshire DG10 9SB
☎(01683) 220020
Leave A74 (M74) at Beattock; take A701 to Moffat for 1 mile; club is signposted.
Moorland course with tree plantations, spectacular views.
Founded 1884
Designed by Ben Sayers
18 holes, 5263 yards, S.S.S. 67
♦ Welcome except Wed pm.
ℒ WD £18.50; WE £28.50.
⤵Welcome by prior arrangement except Wed; includes 2 rounds of golf, morning coffee; snack lunch; evening dinner; from £30.
🍽 Full clubhouse facilities.
⤵ Booohwood Country, Moffat House; Annandale Arms; Balmoral; Buchanan; Star.

9A 59 Mortonhall
231 Braid Rd, Edinburgh, EH10 6PB
☎(0131) 447 6974, Fax 447 8712, Pro 4475185
On A702 2 miles S of the city.
Moorland course.
Pro Douglas Horn; Founded 1892
Designed by James Braid & Fred Hawtree

18 holes, 6557 yards, S.S.S. 71
♦ Welcome by prior arrangement.
ℒ WD £30; WE £30.
⤵Welcome WD by arrangement; catering packages available; terms on application.
🍽 Bar and catering facilities available.
⤵ Braid Hills.

9A 60 Muirfield (Honourable Company of Edinburgh Golfers)
Muirfield, Gullane, E Lothian EH31 2EG
☎(01620) 842123
Course is on the A198 to the NE of Gullane.
Links course; staged 14 Open Championships since 1892.
Founded 1744
Designed by Tom Morris
18 holes, 6970 yards, S.S.S. 73
♦ Welcome only Tues and Thurs.
ℒ WD £80.
⤵Welcome on Tues and Thurs only by prior arrangement; no more than 12 golfers allowed; must have handicap certs; 18 handicap maximum for men; terms available on application.
🍽 Full catering and bar service available (ladies may not lunch in clubhouse).
⤵ Greywalls; Kilspindie House.

9A 61 Murrayfield
Murrayfield Rd, Edinburgh EH12 6EU
☎(0131) 337 3478
2 miles W of city centre.
Parkland course.
Founded 1896
18 holes, 5725 yards, S.S.S. 68
♦ Welcome only with member.
ℒ Terms on application.
⤵Limited.
🍽 Bar snacks; dining room; meals served daily except Mon.
⤵ Ellersly House; Murrayfield

9A 62 Musselburgh
Monktonhall, Musselburgh, E Lothian EH21 6SA
☎(0131) 665 2005, Pro 665 7055
On B6415 to Musselburgh from the end of the A1 Edinburgh by-pass.
Parkland course.
Pro Fraser Mann; Founded 1938
Designed by James Braid
18 holes, 6614 yards, S.S.S. 73
♦ Welcome by prior arrangement.
ℒ WD £18; WE £22.

⤵Welcome by prior arrangement; catering packages available; terms on application.
🍽 Bar and restaurant facilities available.
⤵ Kings; Manor; Woodside.

9A 63 Musselburgh Old Course
10 Balcarres Rd, Musselburgh, E Lothian EH21 7RG
☎(0131) 665 6981
Course is seven miles east of Edinburgh on the A199 at Musselburgh racecourse.
Seaside links course.
9 holes, 5380 yards, S.S.S. 67
♦ Welcome WD, prior booking essential.
ℒ Terms on application.
⤵Welcome by prior arrangement; terms on application.
🍽 Catering facilities.

9A 64 New Galloway
New Galloway, Castle Douglas, Kirkcudbrightshire DG7 3RN
☎(01644) 420737, Sec 450685
Course is on the A713 to New Galloway.
Moorland course.
Founded 1902
Designed by G Baillie
9 holes, 5006 yards, S.S.S. 67
♦ Welcome.
ℒ WD £12.50; WE £12.50.
⤵Welcome by prior arrangement with Sec; catering packages can be organised; from £10.
🍽 Bar and snack facilities available.
⤵ Kenmure Arms; Cross Keys; Kalmar.

9A 65 Newbattle
Abbey Rd, Dalkeith, Midlothian EH22 3AD
☎(0131) 663 2123, Pro 660 1631, Sec 663 1810, Bar/Rest 0032123
On A7 7 miles SW of Edinburgh; taking Newbattle exit at Eskbank roundabout.
Undulating parkland course.
Pro Scott McDonald; Founded 1935
18 holes, 6025 yards, S.S.S. 70
♦ Welcome WD up to 4pm.
ℒ WD £17; WE £17.
⤵Welcome Mon-Fri by prior arrangement between 9:30am and 4pm; catering packages available; terms on application.
🍽 Full clubhouse facilities.
⤵ Lugton; Eskbank.

9A 66 **Newcastleton**
Holm Hill, Newcastleton,
Roxburghshire TD9 0QD
☎(013873) 75257
On A7 25 miles N of Carlisle; 10
miles from Canonbie/Newcastleton
junction.
Hilly course.
Founded 1894
Designed by J. Shade (74)
9 holes, 5748 yards, S.S.S. 68
♦ Welcome.
▯ WD £7; WE £8.
☞Welcome by prior arrangement;
packages can be arranged with local
hotel; from £7.
🍽 Facilities at Liddlesdale Hotel.
☞ Liddlesdale; Grapes.

9A 67 **Newton Stewart** ℭ
Kirroughtree Ave, Minnigaff, Newton
Stewart DG8 6PF
☎(01671) 402172
Course is close to the A75 Carlisle-
Stranraer road; one mile from the
town centre.
Parkland/hill course.
Founded 1896/1992
18 holes, 5887 yards, S.S.S. 69
♦ Welcome.
▯ WD £20 (winter £10); WE £23
(winter £10).
☞Welcome by prior arrangement;
catering by prior arrangement with
the steward; terms available on
application.
🍽 Full clubhouse facilities available.
☞ Glencalm; Crown.

9A 68 **Niddry Castle**
Castle Rd, Winchburgh, W Lothian,
EH52 6RQ
☎(01506) 891097
Course is on the B9080 in centre of
village; five miles from the Newbridge
interchange.
Parkland course.
Founded 1982
Designed by Derek Smith
9 holes, 5518 yards, S.S.S. 67
♦ Welcome WD; by arrangement at
WE.
▯ WD £13; WE £19.
☞Welcome WD by prior
arrangement; full catering packages
by arrangement; £12.
🍽 Full clubhouse facilities.
☞ Tally-ho, Winchburgh.

9A 69 **North Berwick**
New Club House, Beach Rd, North
Berwick, E Lothian, EH39 4BB
☎(01620) 894766, Fax 893274, Pro
893233, Sec 892135 or 895050
In North Berwick take the last left turn
before the town centre.
Links course.
Pro D Huish; Founded 1832
Designed by MacKenzie Ross
18 holes, 6420 yards, S.S.S. 71
♦ Welcome by prior arrangement.
▯ WD £36; WE £56.
☞Welcome by prior arrangement;
catering packages can be arranged;
terms on application.
🍽 Full clubhouse catering facilities
available.
☞ Marine Hotel; many B&Bs in the
area.

9A 70 **Peebles**
Kirkland St, Peebles, EH45 8EU
☎(01721) 72(0197, Sec 720099
Located on NW side of Peebles off
A72; signposted; 23 miles S of
Edinburgh.
Undulating parkland course.
Founded 1892
Designed by James Braid; Alterations
by H.S. Colt
18 holes, 6160 yards, S.S.S. 70
♦ Welcome by prior arrangement
with the club.
▯ WD £18; WE £25.
☞Welcome by prior arrangement
except on Sat; new clubhouse
opened in 1997; catering packages
available by arrangement; terms on
application.
🍽 Full clubhouse facilities available.
☞ Peebles Hotel Hydro; Park;
Kingsmuir; Greentree.

9A 71 **Polkemmet Country
Park**
Park Centre, Polkemmet Country
Park, Bathgate, W Lothian, EH47
0AD
☎(01501) 743905, Bar/Rest
744441
Park is on the N side of the B7066
midway between Harthill and
Whitburn.
Parkland course.
Founded 1981
Designed by W Lothian District
Council
9 holes, 6531 yards
♦ Welcome; no restrictions.
▯ WD £4.50; WE £5.25.
☞Welcome.
🍽 Bar and restaurant facilities
available.
☞ Eillcroft, Whitburn; Holiday Inn;
Dreadnought, both Bathgate.

9A 72 **Portobello**
Stanley St, Portobello, Edinburgh,
EH15 1JJ
☎(0131) 669 4361
On A1 E of Edinburgh, off Milton
Road.
Parkland course.
Founded 1826
9 holes, 4504 yards, S.S.S. 64
♦ Welcome.
▯ WD £4.35; WE £4.85.
☞Welcome by prior arrangement;
catering packages available by prior
application; from £4.
🍽 By prior arrangement.
☞ Kings Manor.

9A 73 **Portpatrick (Dunskey)**
Golf Course Rd, Portpatrick,
Stranraer, Wigtownshire DG9 8TB
☎(01776) 810273, Fax 810811
Follow A77 or A75 to Stranraer and
then follow signs for Portpatrick; on
entering village turn right at the War
Memorial.
Links style cliff-top course.
Founded 1903
Designed by Dunskey Estate/W M
Hunter of Prestwick
18 holes, 5908 yards, S.S.S. 68
♦ Welcome with handicap certs.
▯ WD £19; WE £22.
☞Welcome by prior arrangement;
handicap certs required; catering
packages available; weekly tickets
£100; day rates; also Dinvin course:
1504 yards, par 3; from £8.
🍽 Full clubhouse facilities; meals
until 9pm daily.
Practice range.
☞ Fernhill; Portpatrick; Downshire;
Harbour House; Mount Stewart.

9A 74 **Powfoot**
Cummertrees, Annan, Dumfriesshire,
DG12 5QE
☎(01461) 700276, Fax 700276, Pro
700327, Sec 700276
Course is off the A75 road to
Annan/Dumfries taking the second
turning for Annan until signs for
Cummertrees and Powfoot on the
B724; 3 miles later sharp left after
railway bridge.
Links course.
Pro Gareth Dick; Founded 1903
Designed by James Braid
18 holes, 6266 Yards, S.S.S. 71
♦ Welcome except Sat and after
2pm on Sun.
▯ WD £23; WE £23.
☞Welcome by prior arrangement;
terms on application.

Full clubhouse facilities.
Cairndale, Dumfries; Carrutherstown.

9A 75 Prestonfield
6 Priestfield Rd N, Edinburgh EH16 5HS
☎(0131) 667 9665, Pro 667 8597, Sec 667 9665
Close to Commonwealth Games pool.
Parkland course.
Pro John MacFarlane; Founded 1920
Designed by Peter Robertson.
Redesigned by James Braid.
18 holes, 6214 yards, S.S.S. 70
Welcome by arrangement.
WD £20; WE £30.
Welcome WD starting from 9.30am and 2pm; catering packages available; terms on application.
Full catering except Mon.
Prestonfield House; March Hall; Rosehall.

9A 76 Pumpherston
Drumshoreland Rd, Pumpherston, W Lothian, EH53 0LH
☎(01506) 432869
400 yards, E of the Village cross.
Undulating parkland course.
Founded 1895
9 holes, 5434 yards, S.S.S. 66
Welcome with a member.
£4 with a member.
Welcome WD by prior arrangement; max party 24; bar snacks and meals to order; terms on application.
Clubhouse facilities.

9A 77 Ratho Park
Ratho, Newbridge, Midlothian EH28 8NX
☎(0131) 333 1752, Fax 333 1752, Pro 333 1406, Sec 333 1752, Bar/Rest 333 2566

Adjacent to Edinburgh Airport 8 miles W of Edinburgh.
Parkland course.
Pro Alan Pate; Founded 1928
Designed by James Braid
18 holes, 5900 yards, S.S.S. 68
Welcome by prior arrangement with the Pro.
WD £25; WE £35.
Welcome Tues, Wed, Thurs by prior arrangement; packages for golf and catering available for groups of 12 or more; terms available on application.
Full clubhouse bar and restaurant facilities.

9A 78 Ravelston
24 Ravelston Dykes Rd, Blackhall, Edinburgh, EH4 5NZ
☎(0131) 3152486
From city centre turn left at Blackhall junction then across the crossroad and turn right 100 yards further on.
Parkland course.
Founded 1912
Designed by James Braid
9 holes, 5200 yards, S.S.S. 65
Welcome WD.
WD £7.50.
Small groups welcome by prior arrangement; from £15.
Snacks and bar facilities available.
Garden Court Holiday Inn.

9A 79 The Roxburghe
Heiton, Kelso, Roxburghshire TD5 8JZ
☎(01573) 450333, Judith for bookings, Fax 450611
On A698 between Jedburgh and Kelso.
Woodland/parkland course.
Pro Gordon Niven; Founded 1997
Designed by Dave Thomas
18 holes, 7111 yards, S.S.S. 75

Welcome by prior arrangement.
WD £40; WE £40.
Welcome by prior arrangement; catering packages by prior arrangement.
Spikes bar; full facilities available in hotel.
Practice range and short game area.
The Roxburghe Hotel (on site).

9A 80 Royal Burgess Golfing Society Of Edinburgh
181 Whitehouse Rd, Edinburgh EH4 6BY
☎(0131) 339 2075, Pro 339 6474, Bar/Rest 339 2012
Course is on the west side of Edinburgh on the Queensferry road, 100 yards from the Barnton roundabout.
Parkland course.
Pro George Yuille; Founded 1735
Designed by Tom Morris
18 holes, 6494 yards, S.S.S. 71
Welcome by prior arrangement; no lady members.
By prior arrangement.
Welcome WD by prior arrangement; catering by arrangement; terms available on application.
Clubhouse lunches and bar snacks.
Barnton, Royal Scot.

9A 81 Royal Musselburgh
Prestongrange House, Prestonpans, E Lothian EH32 9RP
☎(01875) 810276, Fax 810276, Pro 810139, Bar/Rest 813671
Course is on the B1361 North Berwick Road.
Parkland course.
Pro John Henderson; Founded 1774/1926
Designed by James Braid
18 holes, 6237 yards, S.S.S. 70

† Welcome by prior arrangement.
⌐ WD £20; WE £35.
⌐ Welcome WD except Fri afternoons by prior arrangement; catering can be arranged; £35 per day for golf; from £20.
🍽 Full catering facilities available.
⌐ Marine Hotel; Golf Inn.

9A 82 St Boswells

Braeheads, St Boswells, Melrose, Roxburghshire TD6 0DE
☎(01835) 823527
Off the A68 in St Boswells.
Parkland course.
Founded 1899
Designed by William Park, Altered by John Shade (1956)
9 holes, 5250 yards, S.S.S. 66
† Welcome by prior arrangement.
⌐ WD £15; WE £15.
⌐ Welcome by prior arrangement if more than six in party; catering can be arranged for groups in advance; from £15.
🍽 Bar and light snacks available at WE; other times by prior arrangement.
⌐ Buccleuch Arms.

9A 83 St Medan

Monreith, Port William, Newton Stewart, Wigtownshire, DG8 8NJ
☎(01988) 700358
Off the A747 3 miles S of Port William following the A714 from Newton Stewart.
Links course.
Founded 1905
9 holes, 4454 yards, S.S.S. 63
† Welcome.
⌐ WD £12; WE £12.
⌐ Welcome by prior arrangement; terms on application.
🍽 Clubhouse facilities.

9A 84 Sanquhar

Old Barr Rd, Sanquhar, Dumfries, DG4 6JZ
☎(01659) 50577, Sec 58181
Course is off the A76, 0.5 miles from Sanquhar.
Parkland course.
Founded 1894
9 holes, 5594 yards, S.S.S. 68
† Welcome.
⌐ WD £10; WE £12.
⌐ Welcome by arrangement; catering by arrangement; snooker; bowls; darts; from £10.
🍽 Clubhouse facilities.
⌐ Blackaddie; Glendyne; Nithsdale.

9A 85 Selkirk

The Hill, Selkirk, TD7 4NW
☎01750) 20621
Course is 0.5 miles south of Selkirk on the A7.
Heathland course.
Founded 1883
Designed by Willie Park
9 holes, 5620 yards, S.S.S. 67
† Welcome WD by prior arrangement except Mon pm; WE by prior arrangement.
⌐ WD £15; WE £15.
⌐ Welcome WD; some WE; catering packages by prior arrangement; from £15.
🍽 Bar open evenings and WE during the summer; at other times by arrangement.
⌐ Heatherlie; Woodburn; Glen all Selkirk.

9A 86 Silverknowes

Silverknowes, Parkway, Edinburgh, EH4 5ET
☎(0131) 336 3843.
W end of Edinburgh off Cramond Foreshore.
Municipal links course.
Founded 1958
18 holes, 6202 yards, S.S.S. 70
† Welcome by prior arrangement.
⌐ WD £8.80; WE £9.65.
⌐ Welcome by prior arrangement; terms on application.
🍽 Clubhouse facilities.
⌐ Commodore, adjacent.

9A 87 Southerness

Southerness, Kirkbean, Dumfries, Dumfries, DG2 8AZ
☎(01387) 880677, Fax 880644
Course is on the A710 15 miles south of Dumfries.
Links course on Solway Firth.
Founded 1947
Designed by MacKenzie Ross
18 holes, 6566 yards, S.S.S. 72
† Welcome by prior arrangement; handicap certs required.
⌐ WD £28; WE £40.
⌐ Welcome by prior arrangement; packages available; from £28.
🍽 Full catering facilities.
⌐ Cairndale; Clonyard; Cavens House; Paul Jones Hotel.

9A 88 Stranraer

Creachmore, Leswalt, Stranraer DG9 0LF
☎(01776) 870245, Fax 870445, Sec 870445

On A718 to Kirkcolm 3 miles from Stranraer.
Parkland/seaside course; on present site since 1953.
Founded 1905/1953
Designed by James Braid
18 holes, 6308 yards, S.S.S. 72
† Welcome except at members' times; not before 9.15am or between 12.30pm-1.30pm and 5pm-6pm.
⌐ WD £20; WE £25.
⌐ Welcome by prior arrangement; same restrictions apply as to visitors; catering can be arranged; separate locker rooms; terms on application.
🍽 Full catering and bar service available.
⌐ North West Castle; Kelvin House; Fernhill.

9A 89 Swanston

111 Swanston Rd, Edinburgh EH10 7DS
☎(0131) 445 2239; Pro 445 4002
S side of the city on the lower slopes of Pentland Hills.
Hillside course
Pro Ian Taylor; Founded 1927
Designed by Herbert More
18 holes, 5004 yards, S.S.S. 65
† Welcome WD; some WE restrictions.
⌐ WD £15; WE £20.
⌐ Welcome by prior arrangement; catering and golf packages available; from £15.
🍽 Full facilities.
⌐ Braid Hills; Newland Inn.

9A 90 Thornhill

Blacknest, Thornhill, Dumfriesshire, DG3 5DW
☎(01848) 330546, Pro (01848) 331779
Off A76 at Thornhill 14 miles N of Dumfries.
Moorland/parkland course.
Founded 1893
Pro: James Davidson
18 holes, 6085 yards, S.S.S. 70
† Welcome by prior arrangement.
⌐ WD £22; WE £28.
⌐ Welcome by prior arrangement; catering packages can be arranged through the steward; terms on application.
🍽 Full clubhouse facilities.
⌐ George; Gillbank.

9A 91 Torphin Hill

Torphin Rd, Colinton, Edinburgh EH13 0PG

WHITEKIRK GOLF COURSE

HOST TO MASTERCARD TOUR EAST LOTHIAN CLASSIC 1998, 1999 AND 2000.
QUALITY CHAMPIONSHIP COURSE IN NATURAL SURROUNDINGS WITH STUNNING PANORAMIC VIEWS
Green fees: £18/£30 wkday, £25/£40 wkend • Society packages £25/£50 (special weekday offers)
• Golf cart hire: £15 per round, £25 per day • Club hire: £10 • Range balls: £1 for 25/£2 for 50

Near North Berwick, East Lothian, EH39 5PR. Tel: 01620 870300. Fax: 01620 870330. E-mail: golf@whitekirk.u-net.com

☎ (0131) 441 1100, Pro 441 4061, Sec 441 4061
SW of Colinton village.
Hilly course.
Pro Jamie Browne; Founded 1895
18 holes, 4580 yards, S.S.S. 67
† Welcome except before 2pm at WE.
WD £12; WE £20.
Welcome WD by prior arrangement; terms available on application.
Clubhouse facilities.
Braid Hills.

9A 92 Torwoodlee
Edinburgh Road, Galashiels, TD1 2NE
☎ (01896) 752660
2 miles outside Galashiels on the main Edinburgh road.
Parkland course.
Pro R Elliot; Founded 1895
Designed by Willie Park (new layout, John Gurner)
18 holes, 6087 yards, S.S.S. 68
† Welcome by prior arrangement.
Terms on application.
Welcome by prior arrangement; packages for golf and catering available; from £20.
Full clubhouse facilities.
Kingsknowe, Galashiels; Burts, Melrose.

9A 93 Turnhouse
154 Turnhouse Rd, Edinburgh EH12 0AD
☎ (0131) 339 1014, Pro 339 7701
Course is on the A9080 west of city near the airport.
Parkland/heathland course.
Pro John Murray; Founded 1909
18 holes, 6153 yards, S.S.S. 69
† Welcome by arrangement WD only.
WD £18.
Welcome by prior arrangement WD only; catering packages available everyday for 12 or more; terms on application.
Full facilities Mon-Sat, prior arrangement for Sunday.
Royal Scot; Posthouse; Stakis.

9A 94 Uphall
Houston Mains, Uphall, W Lothian, EH52 6JT
☎ (01506) 856404, Fax 855358, Pro 855553
On A899 200 yards W of Uphall; 0.5 miles from M8 Junction 3; 15 miles W of Edinburgh.
Tree-lined parkland course.
Pro Gordon Law; Founded 1895
18 holes, 5592 yards, S.S.S. 67
† Welcome by prior arrangement except on competition days.
WD £14; WE £18.
Welcome by prior arrangement; catering packages available; snooker; disabled facilities; from £14.
Full bar and catering facilities available.
Houston House.

9A 95 Vogrie
Vogrie Estate Country Park, Gorebridge, Lothian, EH23 4NN
☎ (01875) 821716, Sec 8217986
Off A68 Jedburgh Road.
Parkland course.
Founded 1989
9 holes, 5060 yards, S.S.S. 66
† Public pay and play.
Terms on application.
Welcome; some restrictions; terms on application.
Tea room in park.

9A 96 West Linton
Medwyn Road, West Linton, Peebleshire EH46 7HN
☎ (01968) 660463, Pro 660256, Sec 660970, Bar/Rest 660580
Course is off the A702 at West Linton.
Moorland course.
Pro I Wright; Founded 1890
Designed by Braid/Millar/Fraser
18 holes, 6132 yards, S.S.S. 69
† Welcome WD and after 1pm on non-comp WE.
Terms on application.
Welcome WD by prior arrangement with Sec; catering packages available; from £18.
Full clubhouse facilities.
Gordon Arms.

9A 97 West Lothian
Airngath Hill, Linlithgow, W Lothian EH49 7RH
☎ (01506) 826030, Fax 826030, Pro 825060
Take A706 from Linlithgow to Bo'ness for 2.5 miles, and then turn right to the Golf Club.
Parkland course.
Founded 1892
Designed by W Park (1892); J Adams (1923); F Middleton (1975)
18 holes, 6046 yards, S.S.S. 71
† Welcome WD; WE by prior arrangement.
WD £17; WE £22.
Welcome WD and non-competition WE by prior arrangement; catering packages available by prior arrangement; terms available on application.
Full clubhouse facilities available.
Richmond Park; Earl o'Moray.

9A 98 Whitekirk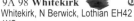
Whitekirk, N Berwick, Lothian EH42 1XS
☎ (01620) 870300, Fax 870330
Course is seven miles SE of N Berwick on the A198.
Links course.
18 holes, 6470 yards, S.S.S. 71
† Welcome.
WD £18; WE £22.
Full clubhouse meals available.
Golf Academy.

9A 99 Wigtown & Bladnoch
Lightlands Terrace, Wigtown, Dumfries & Galloway DG8 9EF
☎ (01988) 403354
On A746 0.25 miles from town centre.
Parkland course.
Founded 1960
9 holes, 5462 yards, S.S.S. 67
† Welcome.
WD £10; WE £10.
Welcome by prior arrangement; packages with local hotels; terms on application.
Clubhouse facilities.
Conifers Leisure Park.

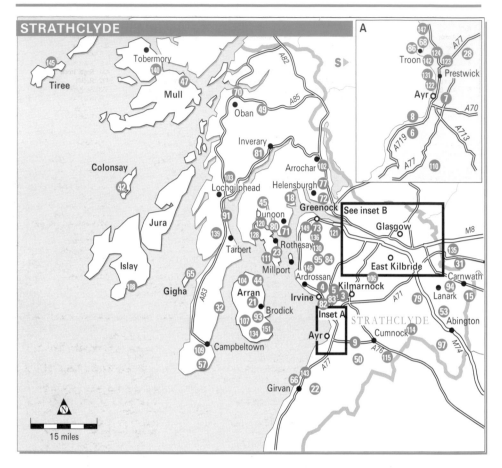

STRATHCLYDE

Tiree
145
Tobermory
140
Mull
47
Colonsay
42
Jura
Islay
108
Gigha
65
Oban
70
49
Inverary
81
Lochgilphead
103
91
139
128
Tarbert
Dunoon
45
120 80
71
111
23
Millport
104 44
Arran
21
Brodick
32
107 93
134 151
Campbeltown
109
57
Helensburgh
77
72
18
Greenock
95 84
146
Ardrossan
4 5
83 3
82
Girvan
66 143
22

S ▶

A
147
86 68
Troon
142 124
123
131
122
Ayr
7
8
6
110
28
Prestwick
A70
A713
A719
A77

See inset B
Glasgow
East Kilbride
Kilmarnock
106
Irvine
Inset A
Ayr
9
50
Cumnock 114
STRATHCLYDE
M8
135
31
Carnwath
79
Lanark 15
53
Abington
97
115

15 miles

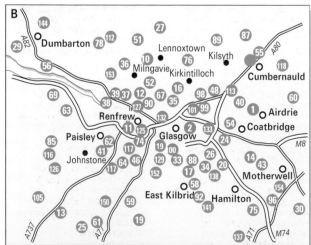

B
144
29
Dumbarton
78 112
51
27
56
10
Milngavie
153 36
69
39 37 12
63
38
127 90
Renfrew
11
125
Paisley
85
62
74
116
41
126
Johnstone
64 46
117
105
13
25 61
19
Lennoxtown
Kilsyth
76
Kirkintilloch
52
67 16
35
101 99
132
89 87
55
118
Cumbernauld
98 48 113
40
1
Airdrie
60
54
Coatbridge
2 133
24
Glasgow
19 00
129 33 88
152
17
58
East Kilbride
92
Hamilton
150 59
137
14
43
Motherwell
154
96
75
30
M8
M74

9A 100 Wigtownshire County
Mains of Park, Glenluce, Newton
Stewart, Wigtownshire, DG8 0NN
☎ (01581) 300420
On the A75 8 miles east of Stranraer.
Links course.
Founded 1894
Designed by G Cunningham/C Hunter
18 holes, 5847 yards, S.S.S. 68
♦ Welcome.
☷ WD £18.50; WE £20.50.
♨ Welcome by prior arrangement;
discounts for groups of 10 or more;
catering packages available; from
£18.50.
🍽 Clubhouse facilities.
🛏 Glenbay; Kelvin, both Glenluce;
North West Castle, Stranraer.

9A 101 Winterfield
North Rd, Dunbar, E Lothian EH42
1AU

☎ (01368) 862280, Pro 863562, Sec 865119
Off A1 to Dunbar; club 0.5 miles from High Street.
Links course.
Pro Kevin Phillips; Founded 1935
18 holes, 5155 yards, S.S.S. 64
⚑ Welcome; WE by prior arrangement.
⚐ WD £14.50; WE £17.75.
⚐ Welcome by prior arrangement with Pro; packages available for 18 or 36 holes of golf plus catering; from £14.50.
🍽 Full clubhouse facilities.
⚑ Bayswell; Hillside; Goldenstones; Craigengelt; Royal Mackintosh.

9B 1 Airdrie

Rochsoles, Airdrie, ML6 0PQ
☎ (01236) 762195, Pro 754360
Course is north of Airdrie on Glenmavis road.
Parkland course.
Pro Gregor Monks; Founded 1877
Designed by James Braid
18 holes, 6004 yards, S.S.S. 69
⚑ Welcome by letter of introduction.
⚐ WD £15; WE £15.
⚐ Welcome WD by prior arrangement with Sec; catering packages can be arranged; snooker; from £15.
🍽 Full clubhouse facilities.
⚑ Tudor; Kenilworth.

9B 2 Alexandra Park

Alexandra Park, Sannox Gdns, Glasgow, G31 8SE
☎ (0141) 556 1294, Pro 770 0519
Course is off the M8 before Blochairn.
Wooded parkland course.
Pro Alistair Baker; Founded 1818
Designed by Graham McArthur
9 holes, 4016 yards
⚑ Welcome.
⚐ Terms on application.
⚐ None.
⚑ Copthorne; Kelvin Park; Stakis Ingram Hotel; Central; Courtyard.

9B 3 Annanhill

Irvine Rd, Kilmarnock, Ayrshire, KA1 4RT
☎ (01563) 521644, Sec 525557
1 mile N of Kilmarnock on the A71 Irvine road.
Parkland course.
Founded 1957
Designed by J. McLean
18 holes, 6269 yards, S.S.S. 70
⚑ Welcome by prior arrangement.
⚐ WD £12; WE £17.
⚐ Welcome by prior arrangement; catering packages can be arranged in advance; terms available on application.
🍽 Full clubhouse facilities available.
⚑ Howard Park; Portman.

9B 4 Ardeer

Greenhead, Stevenston, Ayrshire, KA20 4JX
☎ (01294) 464542, Pro 601327, Sec 465316
Follow A78 signs for Largs and Greenock on High road by-passing Stevenston; turn right in Kerelaw Road for course.
Parkland course; Founded 1880
18 holes, 6409 yards, S.S.S. 71
⚑ Welcome except Sat.
⚐ WD £18; WE £30.
⚐ Welcome Sun-Fri; full day's golf (£40 on Sun); discounted packages available for groups of 12 or more; from £32.
🍽 Full clubhouse catering facilities available.

9B 5 Auchenharvie Golf Complex

Moor Park Rd West, Brewery Park, Stevenston, Ayrshire, KA20 3HU
☎ (01294) 603103
Links/parkland course.
Founded 1981
Designed by Michael Struthers
9 holes, 5203 yards, S.S.S. 66
⚑ Welcome.
⚐ WD £5.00; WE £6.80.
⚐ Welcome by prior arrangement; from £5.00.
🍽 Clubhouse bar.
Driving range.

9B 6 **Ayr Belleisle**
Belleisle Park, Doonfoot Rd,
Doonfoot, Ayr, Ayrshire, KA7 4DU
☎ (01292) 441314, Fax 442632, Sec
441258, Bar/Rest 442331
Follow the signs for Burns Cottage
Drive on the A719 1.5 miles south of
Ayr.
Parkland course/on same site as Ayr
Seafield.
Pro David Gemmel; Founded 1927
Designed by James Braid & Stutt
18 holes, 6431 yards, S.S.S. 71
† Public pay and play.
⌶ WD £19; WE £21.
⌁ Welcome; 7-day advance booking
system; catering by prior
arrangement in local hotels; separate
locker room; from £19.
⍟ Limited facilities.
Practice area.
⌁ Belleisle.

9B 7 **Ayr Dalmilling**
Westwood Ave, Ayr, Strathclyde, KA8
0QY
☎ (01292) 263893, Fax 610543
On A77 1 mile N of Ayr near
racecourse.
Parkland course/meadowland
Pro Philip Cheyney; Founded 1960
18 holes, 5724 yards, S.S.S. 67
† Welcome by prior arrangement.
⌶ WD £13.50; WE £14.
⌁ Welcome by at least seven days'
prior arrangement; catering packages
involving snacks/lunches/high tea
available; terms available on
application.
⍟ Full clubhouse facilities
available.

9B 8 **Ayr Seafield**
Belleisle Park, Doonfoot Rd, Ayrshire,
KA7 4DU
☎ (01292) 441258, Fax 442632
Course is 1.5 miles south of Ayr on
the A719 following signs for Burns
Cottage Drive.
Parkland/seaside course; on same
site as Ayr Belleisle.
Pro David Gemmel; Foundd 1927
Designed by J Braid
18 holes, 5481 yards, S.S.S. 68
† Welcome
⌶ WD £11; WE £11.
⌁ Welcome by prior arrangement;
seven-day booking system in
operation; catering can be arranged
in the local hotels; from £11.
⍟ Limited.
Practice range.
⌁ Belleisle

9B 9 **Ballochmyle**
Ballochmyle, Mauchline, Ayrshire,
KA5 6LE
☎ (01290) 550469, Fax 553150
On B705 off A76 1 mile S of
Mauchline; following signs for
Ballochmyle Hospital.
Inland/parkland course.
Founded 1937
18 holes, 5972 yards, S.S.S. 69
† Welcome except Sat.
⌶ Terms on application.
⌁ Welcome Mon, Tues, Thurs, Fri
and Sun; tee times available between
9am-10am and 2pm-3pm WD; Sun
10am-10.45am and 2.30pm-3.15pm;
catering packages available; terms on
application.
⍟ Full clubhouse facilities.
⌁ Royal; Dumfries Arms.

9B 10 **Balmore**
Balmore, Torrance, Stirlingshire, G64
4AW
☎ (01360) 620240, Sec 620284
2 miles N of Glasgow on A807 off
A803.
Parkland course.
Founded 1906
Designed by James Braid
18 holes, 5542 yards, S.S.S. 67
† Welcome by introduction of a
member.
⌶ Terms on application.
⌁ None.
⍟ Full clubhouse facilities.

9B 11 **Barshaw**
Barshaw Park, Glasgow Rd, Paisley,
Renfrewshire
☎ (0141) 889 2908
1 mile before Paisley Cross off the
A737.
Meadowland course.
Founded 1920
18 holes, 5703 yards, S.S.S. 67
† Welcome.
⌶ WD £7.70; WE £7.70;
concessions apply.
⌁ Limited.
⍟ Limited.
⌁ Water Mill; Brablock.

9B 12 **Bearsden**
Thorn Rd, Bearsden, Glasgow, G61
4BP
☎ (0141) 942 2351, Sec 942 2381
1 mile N of Bearsden Cross on Thorn
Road.
Parkland course.
Founded 1891
9 holes, 6014 yards, S.S.S. 69

† Welcome only as the guest of a
member.
⌶ Terms on application.
⌁ Welcome only by prior
arrangement; terms available on
application.
⍟ Full facilities.
⌁ Black Bull; Burnbrae.

9B 13 **Beith**
Threepwood Rd, Beith, Ayrshire,
KA15 2JR
☎ (01505) 503166
2 miles S of Linwood about 1 mile E
of Beith.
Hilly parkland course.
Founded 1896
18 holes, 5641 yards, S.S.S. 68
† Welcome.
⌶ WD £15; WE £20.
⌁ Welcome by written prior
arrangement; catering packages by
arrangement; from £15.
⍟ Full catering facilities.

9B 14 **Bellshill**
Community Rd, Orbiston, Bellshill,
Lanarkshire, ML4 2RZ
☎ (01698) 745124
Between Bellshill and Strathclyde
Country Park close to M74 Junction 5
for the A725 or the A725 junction on
the A8.
Parkland course.
Founded 1905
18 holes, 6315 yards, S.S.S. 70
† Welcome by prior arrangement;
restricted Sat.
⌶ March-October WD £18; WE £25.
November-February WD £10; WE
£18.
⌁ Welcome by prior written
arrangement; tee off after 1.30pm
Sun; all inclusive packages available
for 18 and 36 holes of golf; from £18.
⍟ Full catering facilities.
⌁ Bothwell Bridge; Moorings House;
Silvertrees.

9B 15 **Biggar**
The Park, Broughton Rd, Biggar,
Lanarkshire, ML12 6QX
☎ (01899) 220618, Pro 220319, Sec
220566
Off the A702 0.5 miles from the town
centre.
Parkland course.
Founded 1895
Designed by Willie Park
18 holes, 5537 yards, S.S.S. 67
† Welcome by prior arrangement.
⌶ WD £8; WE £14.

Welcome by prior arrangement; packages for golf and catering may be available in 1998; terms on application.
￭ Full clubhouse facilities available.
￭ Elphinstone; Clydesdale; Tinto.

9B 16 Bishopbriggs
Brackenbrae Rd, Bishopbriggs, Glasgow, G64 2DX
☎ (0141) 772 1810, Fax 762 2532, Sec 772 8938, Bar/Rest 772 1810
On A803 4 miles north of Glasgow turning 200 yards short of the Bishopbriggs cross.
Parkland course.
Founded 1906
Designed by James Braid
18 holes, 6041 yards, S.S.S. 69
† Welcome by prior arrangement with the club.
￭ Terms on application.
Welcome WD; apply to Sec at least 1 month in advance; terms on application.
￭ Catering facilities.

9B 17 Blairbeth
Fernbrae Ave, Rutherglen, G73 4SF
☎ (0141) 634 3355, Sec 569 7266
1 mile S of Rutherglen off Stonelaw Rd.
Parkland course.
Founded 1910/57
18 holes, 5518 yards, S.S.S. 68
† Welcome either as member's guest or by prior arrangement with te club.
￭ Terms on application.
Terms on application.
￭ Clubhouse facilities.
￭ Kings Park.

9B 18 Blairmore & Strone
Strone, By Dunoon, Argyll, PA23 8TJ
☎ (01369) 840676
On A880 0.75 miles N of Strone and 5 miles N of Dunoon.
Undulating moorland and parkland course with panoramic views of the Clyde.
Founded 1896
Designed by J Braid
9 holes, 4224 yards, S.S.S. 62
† Welcome; some restrictions Sat and Mon evening.
￭ WD £8; WE £10.
Welcome by prior arrangement with Sec; from £8.
￭ Bar facilities available in the summer.

9B 19 Bonnyton
Kirtonmoor Road, Eaglesham, Glasgow, G76 0QA
☎ (01355) 302781, Fax 303151, Pro 302256
1 mile S of Eaglesham; 10 miles S of Glasgow.
Moorland course.
Pro Kendal McWade; Founded 1957
18 holes, 6255 yards, S.S.S. 71
† Welcome by arrangement.
￭ Terms on application.
Welcome Mon and Thurs by prior arrangement; catering packages can be arranged; terms available on application.
￭ Full clubhouse facilities.
￭ Stakis West Point, E Kilbride.

9B 20 Bothwell Castle
Blantyre Rd, Bothwell, Glasgow, G71 8PJ
☎ (01698) 853177, Fax 854052, Pro 852052, Sec 854052
3 miles N of Hamilton on the A9071 from the M74 Junction 5.
Parkland course.
Pro Adam McCloskey; Founded 1922
18 holes, 6243 yards, S.S.S. 70
† Welcome WD 9.30am-3.30pm.
￭ WD £22.
Welcome WD by written prior arrangement; catering packages by arrangement; from £22.
￭ Full clubhouse facilities.
￭ Silvertrees; Bothwell Bridge.

9B 21 Brodick
Brodick, Isle of Arran, KA27 8DL
☎ (01770) 302349, Pro 302513
1 mile N of Pier.
Parkland/links course.
Founded 1897
18 holes, 4736 yards, S.S.S. 64
† Welcome by prior arrangement.
￭ WD £14; WE £17.
Welcome by prior written arrangement; catering packages available; from £14
￭ Full clubhouse facilities.

9B 22 Brunston Castle
Bargany, Dailly, By Girvan, Ayrshire, KA26 9RH
☎ (01465) 811471, Fax 811545
Off the A77 at Girvan then on to B741 to Dailly.
Parkland course.
Pro Stephan Forbes; Founded 1992
Designed by Donald Steel
18 holes, 6681 yards, S.S.S. 73
† Welcome.

￭ WD £26; WE £30.
Welcome by prior arrangement with the club Professional; package includes a full day's golf; company days; pro-ams also catered for; golf clinics; catering packages; 10 per cent discount for larger groups; £5 per person deposit required; from £40.
￭ Full clubhouse facilities with restaurant.
￭ Brunston Castle Holiday Resort; Kings Arms, Girvan; Malin Court, Turnberry.

9B 23 Bute
Kingarth, Isle of Bute, Strathclyde
☎ (01700), Sec 504369
In Stravanan Bay off A845 Rothesay-Kilchattan Bay road.
Links course.
Founded 1888
9 holes, 4994 yards, S.S.S. 64
† Welcome, but not before 12.30pm on Sat.
￭ From £6; details available on application.
￭ Kingarth, St Blanes.

9B 24 Calderbraes
57 Roundknowe Rd, Uddingston, G71 7TS
☎ (01698) 813425
Close to start of M74; 4 miles from Glasgow.
Hilly parkland course.
Founded 1891
9 holes, 5186 yards, S.S.S. 67
† Welcome on WD.
￭ WD £18.
Welcome WD by prior arrangement; maximum 20; catering packages available; from £12.
￭ Full bar and catering facilities available.
￭ Redstones.

9B 25 Caldwell
Uplawmoor, Renfrewshire, G78 4AU
☎ (01505) 850329, Fax 850604, Pro 850616, Sec 850366
Off A736 5 miles SW of Barrhead; 12 miles NE of Irvine.
Moorland course.
Pro Stephen Forbes; Founded 1903
18 holes, 6228 yards, S.S.S. 70
† Welcome WD but advisable to check in advance.
￭ Terms on application.
Welcome WD except Thurs by prior arrangement; catering by arrangement; terms on application.

Clubhouse facilities.
Uplawmoor; Dalmeny Park.

9B 26 **Cambuslang**
30 Westburn Drive, Cambuslang,
Glasgow, G72 7NA
☎ (0141) 641 3130, Sec 6413130,
Bar/Rest 6413130
Off main Glasgow to Hamilton road at
Cambuslang.
Parkland course.
Founded 1891
9 holes, 6072 yards, S.S.S. 69
† Welcome by written application to
secretary.
Terms on application.
Apply in writing to secretary;
catering by arrangement; terms on
application.
Full clubhouse facilities.
Cambus Court.

9B 27 **Campsie**
Crow Rd, Lennoxtown, Glasgow, G65
7HX
☎ (01360) 310244, Pro 310920
Course is on the B822 to north of
Lennoxtown.
Hillside/parkland course.
Pro Mark Brennan; Founded 1897
Designed by W Auchterlonie
18 holes, 5509 yards, S.S.S. 67
† Welcome WD; WE by prior
arrangement after 4pm.
WD £12; WE £15.
Welcome by prior arrangement
with Sec; full day's golf; catering: by
arrangement; from £20.
Clubhouse facilities.
Glazert Country House Hotel,
Lennoxtown.

9B 28 **Caprington**
Ayr Rd, Kilmarnock, Ayrshire, KA1
4UW
☎ (01563) 523702
Course is on the Ayr road south of
Kilmarnock.
Parkland course.
18 holes, 5781 yards, S.S.S. 68
† Welcome.
Terms on application.
Apply to Sec; terms on
application.
Clubhouse facilities.

9B 29 **Cardross**
Main Rd, Cardross, Dumbarton, G82
5LB
☎ (01389) 841213, Fax 841754, Pro
841350, Sec 841754

On A814 to Helensburgh 18 miles
from Glasgow.
Parkland course.
Pro Robert Farrell; Founded 1895
Designed by James Braid
18 holes, 6469 yards, S.S.S. 71
† Welcome WD.
WD £25.
None.
Full clubhouse facilities.
Cameron House; Kirkton House.

9B 30 **Carluke**
Mauldslie Rd, Hallcraig, Carluke, ML8
5HG
☎ (01555) 770574, Pro 751053,
Bar/Rest 771070
Easy access from both the M74 and
the M8; from the M74 leave at
Junction 7 and take the Lanark turn
until the lights at Garron Bridge; then
left on to the A71 and then on to the
B7011; club is 2.5 miles.
Parkland course.
Pro Ricky Forrest; Founded 1894
18 holes, 5853 yards, S.S.S. 68
† Welcome WD 9am-4pm.
WD £18 but variable in the
summer months.
Welcome by prior arrangement;
maximum 24; from £18-£25.
Full clubhouse facilities.
Popinjay; Cartland Bridge.

9B 31 **Carnwath**
1 Main St, Carnwath, Strathclyde,
ML11 8JX
☎ (01555) 840251
5 miles NE of Lanark.
Undulating parkland course.
Founded 1907
18 holes, 5953 yards, S.S.S. 69
† Welcome except Sat or after 4pm
WD.
WD £22; WE £30.
Welcome WD except Tues and
Thurs. by prior arrangement; catering
by arrangement; from £20.
Every day except Tues and
Thurs.
Tinto, Symington.

9B 32 **Carradale**
Carradale, Campbeltown, Argyll,
PA28 6SA
Off B842 from Campbeltown in
Kintyre.
Difficult scenic course with sea views.
Founded 1906
9 holes, 4784 yards, S.S.S. 63
† Welcome.
WD £8; WE £8.

Welcome by prior arrangement;
catering available in local hotels; from
£8.
Catering in local hotels.
Carradale; Ashbank.

9B 33 **Cathcart Castle**
Mearns Rd, Clarkston, Glasgow, G76
7YL
☎ (0141) 638 9449, Pro 638 3436
Course is on the B767 one mile from
Clarkston.
Undulating parkland course.
Founded 1895
18 holes, 5832 yards, S.S.S. 68
† Tourists welcome by prior
arrangement.
WD £30; WE £30.
Welcome Tues and Thurs by
arrangement with Sec; day ticket £35;
catering by prior arrangement; from
£25.
Clubhouse facilities.
Redhurst; Macdonald; Busby.

9B 34 **Cathkin Braes**
Cathkin Rd, Rutherglen, Glasgow,
G73 4SE
☎ (0141) 634 4007, Pro 634 0650,
Sec 634 6605
On B759 SE of Glasgow between
A749 and B766.
Moorland course.
Pro Stephen Bree; Founded 1888
Designed by James Braid
18 holes, 6208 yards, S.S.S. 71
† Welcome WD.
WD £25.
Welcome WD by prior
arrangement; packages available;
from £25.
Full catering facilities.
Stuart; Bruce; Burnside; Busby.

9B 35 **Cawder**
Cadder Rd, Bishopbriggs, Glasgow,
G64 3QD
☎ (0141) 772 7101, Pro 772 7102,
Sec 772 5167
Course is off the A803 Glasgow-
Kirkintilloch road 0.5 miles E of
Bishopbriggs.
Parkland course.
Pro Ken Stevely; Founded 1933
Designed by Donald Steel (Cawder);
Designed by James Braid (Keir)
Cawder: 18 holes, 6295 yards, S.S.S.
71; Keir: 18 holes, 5870 yards, S.S.S.
68
† Welcome WD by arrangement
with Sec.
WD £26.

↗ Welcome WD by prior arrangement with Sec; day ticket £33; catering packages by arrangement; from £26.
🍽 Full catering facilities.
↘ Black Bull; Glazert Country House; Crow Wood House.

9B 36 Clober
Craigton Rd, Milngavie, G62 7HP
☎ (0141) 956 1685, Pro 956 6963, Bar/Rest 956 1685
7 miles NW of Glasgow.
Parkland course.
Pro Alan Tait; Founded 1952
Designed by Lyle Family
18 holes, 4963 yards, S.S.S. 65
⚑ Welcome WD until 4pm.
⌞ WD £15.
↗ Welcome WD by prior arrangement; catering packages available; terms available on application.
🍽 Full clubhouse facilities.
↘ Black Bull; Crosskeys; Burnbrae.

9B 37 Clydebank & District
Glasgow Rd, Hardgate, Clydebank, Dumbartonshire, G81 5QY
☎ (01389) 383832
Off A82 turning right at Hardgate; 10 miles W of Glasgow.
Parkland course.
Pro D Pirie; Founded 1905
Designed by committee members
18 holes, 5825 yards, S.S.S. 68
⚑ Welcome WD.
⌞ WD £15.
↗ Welcome WD by prior arrangement; terms available on application.
🍽 Full clubhouse facilities.
Small practice area.
↘ West Hills; Boulevard; Radnor; Duntugher; West Highways.

9B 38 Clydebank Municipal
Overtoun Rd, Dalmuir, Clydebank, G81 3RE
☎ (0141) 952 8698, Bar/Rest 9528698
8 miles W of Glasgow.
Municipal parkland course.
18 holes, 5349 yards, S.S.S. 67
⚑ Welcome except between 11am-2pm at WE.
⌞ Terms on application.
↗ Contact local district council; terms on application.
🍽 Snack and café facilities available.
↘ Radnor.

9B 39 Clydebank Overtoun
Overtoun Rd, Clydebank, Dumbartonshire, G81 3RE
☎ (0141) 952 6372
Course is five minutes from Dalmuir station.
Municipal parkland course.
Pro Ian Toy; Founded 1928
18 holes, 5349 yards, S.S.S. 66
⚑ Welcome.
⌞ WD £6.55; WE £7.
↗ Welcome by arrangement; limited facilities.
🍽 Café only.

9B 40 Coatbridge
Townhead Rd, Coatbridge, Lanark, ML5 2HX
☎ (01236) 421492
In Coatbridge town.
Public parkland course.
Pro George Weir; Founded 1971
18 holes, 6026 yards, S.S.S. 69
⚑ Welcome.
⌞ WD £5.10; £7.60.
↗ Welcome by prior arrangement.
🍽 Full facilities.
Practice range, 18 bays floodlit.

9B 41 Cochrane Castle
Scott Ave, Craigston, Johnstone, PA5 0HF
☎ (01505) 320146, Fax 325338, Pro 328465
0.5 miles off Beith Road in Johnstone.
Parkland course.
Pro Jason Boyd
Founded 1895
Designed by Charles Hunter of Prestwick; Altered by James Braid
18 holes, 6226 yards, S.S.S. 71
⚑ Welcome WD; with member at WE.
⌞ WD £17.
↗ None.
🍽 Full clubhouse facilities available.
↘ Bird in Hand; Lynnhurst, both Johnstone.

9B 42 Colonsay
Isle of Colonsay, Argyll, PA61 7YP
☎ (01951) 200316 Fax 200353
2 miles W of Scalascraig pier; car ferry two-and-a-half-hour journey from mainland.
Natural machair course.
Founded 1880
18 holes, 4775 yards, S.S.S. 72
⚑ Welcome.
⌞ WD £10; WE £10.

🍽 All facilities at Colonsay Hotel; courtesy car provided to course.
↘ The Colonsay Hotel.

9B 43 Colville Park
New Jerviston House, Merry St, Motherwell, Lanarkshire, ML1 4UG
☎ (01698) 263017, Fax 230418, Pro 265779, Sec 265378
1 mile NE of Motherwell railway station.
Parkland course.
Pro Alan Forrest; Founded 1923
Designed by James Braid
18 holes, 6265 yards, S.S.S. 70
⚑ Welcome only as the guest of a member.
⌞ WD £3; WE £3.
↗ Welcome by written prior arrangement; catering packages can be arranged; maximum 36; £20.
🍽 Full clubhouse facilities available.
↘ Old Mill; Moorings; Silvertrees.

9B 44 Corrie
Sannox, Isle of Arran, KA27 8JD
☎ (01770) 810223
7 miles N of Brodick on A84 coast road.
Picturesque undulating course.
Founded 1892
9 holes, 3896 yards, S.S.S. 61
⚑ Welcome except for some Thurs and Sat afternoons.
⌞ Terms on application.
↗ Welcome by prior arrangement; catering by arrangement; maximum normally 12.
🍽 Catering available in season April-Oct.

9B 45 Cowal
Ardenslate Rd, Dunoon, Argyll, PA23 8NN
☎ (01369) 705673, Fax 705673, Pro 702395, Sec 705673, Bar/Rest 702426
From the Shore road turn up Kirn Brae.
Heath/parkland course.
Pro Russell Weir; Founded 1891
Designed by James Braid
18 holes, 6063 yards, S.S.S. 70
⚑ Welcome.
⌞ WD £22; WE £32.
↗ Welcome; packages include transport, catering, and 18 holes of golf; from £38.
🍽 Full clubhouse catering available.
↘ Local tourist office can provide details.

9B 46 Cowglen
301 Barrhead Rd, Glasgow, G43 1EU
☎ (0141) 632 0556, Pro 649 9401
S side of Glasgow following signs for
Burrell Collection.
Undulating parkland course.
Pro John McTear; Founded 1906
18 holes, 5976 yards, S.S.S. 69
† Welcome on WD if introduced by
a member.
⌊ WD £25.50.
⌁ Welcome by prior arrangement
with Sec; catering packages
available; from £22.
🍽 Clubhouse facilities.
↙ Tinto.

9B 47 Craignure
Scallastle, Craignure, Isle of Mull,
PA65 6AY
☎ (01680) 812487;
Course is one mile from Oban/Mill
ferry terminal.
Links course built on estuary of
Scallastle River; Founded 1895/1979
9 holes, 5072 yards, S.S.S. 65
† Welcome except on comp days.
⌊ Terms on application.
⌁ Welcome by arrangement; weekly
ticket (from £45) available.
🍽 Limited clubhouse facilities.
↙ Isle of Mull; Craignure Inn.

9B 48 Crow Wood
Garnkirk House, Cumbernauld Rd,
Muirhead, Glasgow, G69 9JF
☎ (0141) 779 2011, Fax 779 9148,
Pro 779 1943, Sec 779 4954
Off A80 Stirling road midway between
Stepps and Muirhead 5 miles N of
Glasgow.
Parkland course.
Pro Brian Moffat; Founded 1925
Designed by James Braid
18 holes, 6261 yards, S.S.S. 71
† Welcome WD.
⌊ WD £22.
⌁ Welcome WD only by prior
arrangement; catering can be
arranged; from £10.
🍽 Full clubhouse facilities.
Practice range available.
↙ Garfield House, Stepps; Crow
Wood House, Muirhead.

9B 49 Dalmally
'Orchy Bank', Dalmally, Argyll, PA33
1AS
☎ (01838) 200370
2 miles W of Dalmally Village on A85.
Parkland course.
Founded 1987

Designed by C MacFarlane Barrow
9 holes, 4514 yards, S.S.S. 63
† Welcome.
⌊ WD £10; WE £10.
⌁ Welcome by prior arrangement;
bar snacks and meals can be
arranged; £8.
🍽 By prior arrangement; bar
facilities.
↙ Glen Orchy Lodge.

9B 50 Doon Valley
Hillside Park, Patna, Ayrshire, KA6
7JT
☎ (01292) 531607, Sec 550411
On A713 Ayr to Castle Douglas road
10 miles S of Ayr.
Undulating parkland course.
Founded 1927
Course redesigned by E Ayrshire
Council
9 holes, 5856 yards, S.S.S. 69
† Welcome WD; WE by
arrangement.
⌊ WD £6.50; WE £6.50;
concessions apply.
⌁ Welcome WD; WE by prior
arrangement; day ticket for golf;
catering available by arrangement;
£15.
🍽 Bar open evenings WD; all day
WE.
New practice range.
↙ Smithson Farm B&B; Bellsbank
House; Parsons Lodge.

9B 51 Dougalston
Strathblane Rd, Milngavie, Glasgow,
G62 8HJ
On A81 NW of Glasgow out of
Milngavie going to Aberfoyle.
400-acre parkland course.
Founded 1978
Designed by John Harris
18 holes, 6354 yards, S.S.S. 72
† Welcome WD.
⌊ Terms available upon application.
⌁ Welcome WD by prior
arrangement; packages available for
18 or 36 holes; full day or part-day
catering; 10 per cent deposit
required; from £15.
🍽 Full clubhouse catering.
↙ Black Bull; Burnbrae, both
Milngavie.

9B 52 Douglas Park
Hillfoot, Bearsden, Glasgow, G61 2TJ
☎ (0141) 942 2220, Pro 942 1482
Course is six miles N of Glasgow
adjacent to Hillfoot station off
Milngavie road.

Undulating parkland course.
Pro D B Scott; Founded 1897
18 holes, 5962 yards, S.S.S. 69
† Welcome only as members'
guests; occasional overseas visitors if
course is quiet.
⌊ WD £22.
⌁ Welcome Wed and Thurs only; full
day's golf £30; catering can be
arranged.
🍽 Full catering and licensed bar
available.
↙ Burnbrae; Black Bull.

9B 53 Douglas Water
Ayr Rd, Rigside, Lanark, ML11 9NY
☎ (01555) 880361
Course is on the A70 seven miles
SW of Lanark.
Undulating parkland course.
Founded 1922
Designed by Striking Coal Miners
1921
9 holes, 5890 yards, S.S.S. 69
† Welcome except on competition
days.
⌊ Terms on application.
⌁ Welcome by prior arrangement
with Sec; terms available on
application.
🍽 Very limited.

9B 54 Drumpellier
Drumpellier Ave, Coatbridge, ML5
1RX
☎ (01236) 424139, Pro 432971, Sec
428723
Course is on the A89 eight miles east
of Glasgow.
Parkland course.
Pro David Ross; Founded 1894
Designed by W. Fernie
18 holes, 6227 yards, S.S.S. 70
† Welcome WD.
⌊ Day ticket costs £30.
⌁ Welcome WD by prior
arrangement; catering packages
available.
🍽 Full clubhouse catering facilities.
↙ Georgian.

9B 55 Dullatur
Glen Douglas Drive, Dullatur,
Glasgow, G68 0AR
☎ (012367) 23230, Fax 27271
1.5 miles from Cumbernauld village.
Parkland course.
Pro Duncan Sinclair; Founded 1896
Designed by J Braid
Antonine: 18 holes, 5940 yards,
S.S.S. 69; Carrickstone: 18 holes,
6204 yards, S.S.S. 70

✝ Welcome except on competition days.
⌐ Available upon application.
☞ Welcome except on competition days; catering packages available from £12.50; from £15.
🍴 Full clubhouse facilities available.
⌐ Castlecary House.

9B 56 Dumbarton
Broadmeadows, Dumbarton, Dumbartonshire, G82 2BQ
☎(01389) 732830, Sec 765995
Course is off the A82 15 miles NW of Glasgow.
Meadowland course.
Founded 1888
18 holes, 6017 yards, S.S.S. 69
✝ Welcome WD.
⌐ WD £22.
☞ Welcome by arrangement; catering by arrangement; terms on application.
🍴 Full clubhouse facilities available.

9B 57 Dunaverty
Southend by Campbeltown, Argyll, PA28 6RW
☎(01586) 830677
Course is on the B842 10 miles south of Campbeltown.
Undulating seaside course.
Founded 1889
18 holes, 4799 yards, S.S.S. 63
✝ Welcome.
⌐ From £13.
☞ Limited availability; strictly by prior arrangement; day tickets start at £20.
🍴 Snacks available.
⌐ Argyll.

9B 58 East Kilbride
Chapelside Rd, Nerston, G74 4PF
☎(013552) 20913, Pro 22192, Sec 47728
Course is in Nerston 10 miles SE of Glasgow.
Parkland course.
Pro Willie Walker; Founded 1900/67
Designed by Fred Hawtree
18 holes, 6419 yards, S.S.S. 71
✝ Welcome WD by prior arrangement with Sec.
⌐ WD £20.
☞ Welcome WD by prior written arrangement; catering packages available; pool room; from £20.
🍴 Full clubhouse facilities available.
⌐ Stakis Westpoint; Bruce; Stuart; Crutherland House.

9B 59 East Renfrewshire
Loganswell, Pilmuir, Newton Mearns, Glasgow, G77 6RT
☎(01355) 500256, Pro 500206, Bar/Rest 500256, Sec (0141) 333 9989
Course Is on the A77 Glasgow to Kilmarnock road two miles south of Newton Mearns.
Moorland course.
Pro Gordon D Clarke; Founded 1922
Designed by James Braid
18 holes, 6097 yards, S.S.S. 70
✝ Welcome by prior arrangement with Pro.
⌐ WD £35 or £40 for a day ticket.
☞ Welcome Tues and Thurs by arrangement with Sec; catering and bar facilities by prior arrangement with the clubhouse manager; from £30.
🍴 Full clubhouse facilities available.
Free practice area.

9B 60 Easter Moffat
Mansion House, Plains, by Airdrie, Lanarkshire, ML6 8NP
☎(01236) 842289, Pro 843015, Sec 842878
2 miles E of Airdrie on the old Edinburgh-Glasgow road.
Moorland/parkland course.
Pro Graham King; Founded 1922
18 holes, 6240 yards, S.S.S. 70
✝ Welcome.
⌐ WD £15; WE £15.
☞ Welcome WD by prior arrangement; day tickets £20; catering by prior arrangement; from £15.
🍴 Clubhouse facilities.
⌐ Tudor Hotel, Airdrie.

9B 61 Eastwood
Loganswell, Newton Mearns, Glasgow, G77 6RX
☎(01355) 500261, Pro 500285, Sec 500280
On A77 from Glasgow; 3 miles S of Newton Mearns.
Moorland/parkland course.
Pro Alan McGinness
Founded 1893
Designed by J. Moon
18 holes, 5864 yards, S.S.S. 69
✝ Welcome WD.
⌐ WD £24.
☞ Welcome WD by prior arrangement; catering packages by arrangement; from £24.
🍴 Clubhouse facilities.
⌐ Redhurst; Macdonald.

9B 62 Elderslie
63 Main Rd, Elderslie, Renfrewshire, PA5 9AZ
☎(01505) 323956, Bar/Rest 322835
On A737 between Paisley and Johnstone.
Undulating parkland course.
Founded 1909
18 holes, 6175 yards, S.S.S. 70
✝ Welcome WD.
⌐ WD £21.
☞ Welcome Mon, Wed and Fri by prior arrangement; day ticket £32; catering by arrangement; snooker; from £20.
🍴 Full clubhouse facilities.
⌐ Glasgow Airport hotels.

9B 63 Erskine
Bishopton, Renfrewshire, PA7 5PH
☎(01505) 862302, Pro 862108
Off Erskine Toll Bridge and turn left along B815 for 1.5 miles.
Parkland course.
Pro Peter Thomson; Founded 1904
18 holes, 6241 yards, S.S.S. 70
✝ Welcome if introduced by or playing with a member.
⌐ Terms on application.
☞ Welcome by prior arrangement; catering by prior arrangement only; terms on application.
🍴 Meals served to members or their guests only.
⌐ Erskine; Crest.

9B 64 Fereneze
Fereneze Ave, Barrhead, Glasgow, G78 1HJ
☎(0141) 881 1519, Pro 881 7058, Sec 887 4141
9 miles SW of Glasgow near Barrhead station.
Moorland course.
Pro Stuart Kerr; Founded 1904
18 holes, 5962 yards, S.S.S. 71
✝ Welcome by prior arrangement or with member.
⌐ Terms on application.
☞ Welcome WD only by prior arrangement; catering by arrangement; terms available on application.
🍴 Full clubhouse facilities available; WD evening meals by prior arrangement.
⌐ Dalmeny Park.

9B 65 Gigha
Isle of Gigha, Kintyre, Argyll PA41 7AA
☎(01583) 505254

Ferry from Tayinloan takes 20 mins; course is 0.5 miles north from Gigha Post Office.
Parkland course
Founded 1988
Designed by Members
9 holes, 5042 yards, S.S.S. 65
† Welcome.
˪ WD £10; WE £10.
⌣Welcome; day ticket £10; meals and bar at Gigha Hotel; from £10.
🍴 Meals and bar available at the Gigha Hotel.
↝ Gigha; Tayinloan.

9B 66 Girvan
Girvan, Ayrshire, KA26 9HW
☎(01465) 714346, Bar/Rest 714272.
Course is off the A77 Stranraer to Ayr road.
Seaside links/parkland course.
Founded pre-1877.
Designed by James Braid
18 holes, 5064 yards, S.S.S. 64
† Welcome by prior arrangement.
˪ WD £13, WE £14.50; day tickets: WD £20, WE £26.
⌣Welcome by prior arrangement; catering by arrangement; from £12.
🍴 Catering by arrangement.
↝ Turnberry Hotel; Kings Arms.

9B 67 Glasgow
Killermont, Bearsden, Glasgow, G61 2TW
☎(0141) 942 1713, Fax 942 0770, Pro 942 8507, Sec 942 2011.
6 miles NW of Glasgow near Killermont Bridge taking the A81 or A806.
Parkland course.
Pro Jack Steven; Founded 1787/1905
Designed by Tom Morris Snr
18 holes, 5968 yards, S.S.S. 69
† Welcome by prior arrangement.
˪ WD £42; WE £42.
⌣None.
🍴 Lunches and high teas by application.
↝ Grosvenor; Burnbrae; Black Bull; Pond.

9B 68 Glasgow (Gailes)
Gailes, by Irvine, Ayrshire, KA11 5AE
☎(01294) 311258, Fax 0141 942, Pro 311561, Sec (0141) 942 2011, Bar/Rest 311258
2 miles S of Irvine on A78.
Championship seaside links
Pro Jack Steven; Founded 1787/1892
Designed by Willie Park, Jr.

18 holes, 6513 yards, S.S.S. 72
† Welcome by prior arrangement with Sec or if introduced by a member.
˪ WD £42; WE £47.
⌣Welcome by prior arrangement with Sec only; WD day tickets £52; catering by prior arrangement; from £42.
🍴 Full clubhouse facilities.
↝ Hospitality Inn, Irvine; Marine, Troon.

9B 69 Gleddoch Country Club
Langbank, Renfrewshire, PA14 6YE
☎(01475) 540304 Fax 540459 Pro 540704
M8 to Greenock; first turning to Langbank Houston on B789.
Parkland/moorland course.
Pro Keith Campbell; Founded 1975
Designed by Hamilton Stutt
18 holes, 6357 yards, S.S.S. 71
† Welcome by prior arrangement with Pro.
˪ WD £30, WE £40; day tickets start at £40.
⌣Welcome; catering packages by arrangement; terms on application.
🍴 Clubhouse facilities.
↝ Glenddoch House.

9B 70 Glencruitten
Glencruitten Rd, Oban, Argyll, PA34 4PU
☎(01631) 562868, Pro 564115, Sec 564604
1 mile from the Town Centre.
Parkland course.
Pro Graham Clark; Founded 1900
Designed by James Braid
18 holes, 4250 yards, S.S.S. 63
† Welcome.
˪ WD £16; WE £16.
⌣Welcome by prior arrangement; discounts available; full catering packages by arrangement; from £13.50.
🍴 Full clubhouse facilities.
↝ Kilchrenan House; Barriemore, both Oban.

9B 71 Gourock
Cowal View, Gourock, Renfrewshire, PA19 1HD
☎(01475) 631001, Pro 636834
2 miles uphill from Gourock station.
Moorland course.
Pro Gavin Coyle; Founded 1896
Designed by Henry Cotton
18 holes, 6512 yards, S.S.S. 73

† Welcome by prior arrangement with Pro shop.
˪ WD £20; WE £24.
⌣Welcome by prior arrangement; day tickets available WD £27; WE £29; catering by prior arrangement.
🍴 Bar lunches and high teas; dinners by arrangement.
↝ Gantock.

9B 72 Greenock
Forsyth St, Greenock, Renfrewshire, PA16 8RE
☎(01475) 791912
1 mile SW of the town on the main road to Gourock.
Moorland course.
Pro Stewart Russell; Founded 1890
Designed by James Braid
27 holes, 5838 yards, S.S.S. 69
† Welcome by prior arrangement with Sec.
˪ Terms on application.
🍴 Full clubhouse facilities.
↝ Tontine.

9B 73 Greenock Whinhill
Beith Rd, Greenock, Renfrewshire, PA16 9LN
☎(01475) 724694, Pro 721064
Off Largs Road.
Parkland course.
Founded 1911
Designed by W Fernie
18 holes, 5504 yards, S.S.S. 68
† Welcome.
˪ WD £6.50; WE £6.50.
⌣None welcome.
🍴 By prior arrangement.
↝ Stakis Gantock.

9B 74 Haggs Castle
70 Dumbreck Rd, Glasgow, G41 4SN
☎(0141) 427 0480, Fax 427 1157, Pro 427 3355, Sec 427 1157
Course is close to Junction 1 of the M77.
Parkland course.
Pro J McAlister; Founded 1910
Designed by Peter Alliss & Dave Thomas
18 holes, 6464 yards, S.S.S. 71
† Welcome on WD by prior arrangement.
˪ WD £30.
⌣Welcome WD only by arrangement with Sec; catering by arrangement; terms available on application.
🍴 Full clubhouse facilities.
↝ Shenbrooke Castle, Pollockshields.

9B 75 **Hamilton**

Riccarton, Ferniegair, Hamilton, Lanarkshire, ML3 7UE
☎(01698) 282872, Pro 282324, Sec 459537
Off A74 between Larkhill and Hamilton.
Parkland course.
Pro Maurice Moir; Founded 1892
Designed by James Braid
18 holes, 6264 yards, S.S.S. 71
† Welcome on WD by prior arrangement.
˙ WD £25.
˙By arrangement with Sec; catering packages by arrangement; terms on application.
▯ Clubhouse facilities.

9B 76 **Hayston**

Campsie Rd, Kirkintilloch, Glasgow, G66 1RN
☎(0141) 776 1244, Fax 775 0723, Pro 775 0882, Sec 775 0723
7 miles N of Glasgow.
Parkland course.
Pro Steve Barnett; Founded 1926
Designed by James Braid
18 holes, 6042 yards, S.S.S. 70
† Welcome by prior arrangement on WD only.
˙ Available upon application.
˙Welcome Tues and Thurs by prior arrangement; day tickets from £30; maximum 24; catering by arrangement; from £20.
▯ Full clubhouse facilities.
˙˙ Kincaid House.

9B 77 **Helensburgh**

25 East Abercromby St, Helensburgh, Argyll, G84 9JD
☎(01436) 674173, Fax 671170, Pro 675505
Follow A82 to Helensburgh; signposted in town.
Moorland course.
Pro David Fotheringham; Founded 1893
Designed by James Braid
18 holes, 6104 yards, S.S.S. 70
† Welcome WD.
˙ WD £20.
˙Welcome by prior arrangement; includes food and golf; from £35.
▯ Full clubhouse dining facilities.
˙˙ Commodore, Helensburgh; Camerous House, Balloch.

9B 78 **Hilton Park**

Stockiemuir Rd, Milngavie, Glasgow, G62 7HB
☎(0141) 956 5124, Pro 956 5125, Sec 956 4657
On A809 8 miles N of Glasgow.
Meadowland course; also Allander course: 5374 yards, S.S.S. 66
Pro Billy McCondichie; Founded 1927
Designed by James Braid
36 holes, 6054/5497 yards, S.S.S. 70/73
† Welcome WD by prior arrangement.
˙ WD £24.
˙Welcome WD; day rate of approx £30; catering by arrangement; from £20.
▯ Full catering facilities available.
˙˙ Kirkhouse; Black Bull; County Club.

9B 79 **Hollandbush**

Acretophead, Lesmahagow, S Lanarkshire, ML11 0JS
☎(01555) 893484, Pro 893646, Sec 893484, Bar/Rest 893516
Off M74 at Lesmahagow; course between Lesmahagow and Coalburn.
Parkland course on edge of moorland.
Founded 1954
Designed by K Pate/ J Lawson
18 holes, 6218 yards, S.S.S. 70
† Public municipal course.
˙ WD £8.20; WE £9.30.
˙None.
▯ Full clubhouse facilities but not on Mondays.
Practice range available.
˙˙ Shawlands; Popinjay.

9B 80 **Innellan**

Knockamillie Rd, Innellan, Argyll
☎(01369) 830242
4 miles S of Dunoon.
Parkland course.
Founded 1891
9 holes, 4878 yards, S.S.S. 63
† Welcome anytime except Mon evening.
˙ Terms on application.
˙Welcome by prior arrangement; catering by arrangement; terms on application.
▯ By prior arrangement.
˙˙ Esplanade; Slatefield; Rosscalm.

9B 81 **Inverary**

Inverary, Argyll, Argyll
☎(01499) 302508
SW corner of town on Lochgilphead Road.
Parkland course.
Founded 1993

Designed by Wall Landscaping
9 holes, 5700 yards, S.S.S. 68
† Welcome except competition days.
˙ WD £10; WE £10.
˙Welcome by prior arrangement; golf only; catering available by special arrangement with local hotels; from £10.
▯ None.
˙˙ Loch Fynn; George; Great Inn.

9B 82 **Irvine**

Bogside, Irvine, N Ayrshire, KA12 8SN
☎(01294) 275979, Pro 275626
On the road from Irvine to Kilwinning, turn left after Ravespark academy and carry straight on for 0.5 miles over the railway bridge.
Links course.
Pro Keith Erskine; Founded 1887
Designed by James Braid
18 holes, 6408 yards, S.S.S. 73
† Welcome; but not before 3pm at WE.
˙ WD £30; WE £45.
˙Welcome by prior arrangement with Sec; catering packages by prior arrangement; from £30.
▯ Full clubhouse facilities.
˙˙ Hospitality Inn; Golf Hotel.

9B 83 **Irvine Ravenspark**

13 Kidsneuk Lane, Irvine, Ayrshire, KA12 8SR
☎(01294) 271293, Pro 276467
On A78 midway between Irvine and Kilwinning.
Municipal parkland course.
Pro Peter Bond; Founded 1907
18 holes, 6429 yards, S.S.S. 71
† Welcome; not before 2.30pm on Sat.
˙ WD £9; WE £13.
˙Welcome WD; by prior arrangement with Sec for Sun; catering packages by arrangement; from £15.50.
▯ Full clubhouse facilities.
˙˙ Hospitality Inn; Annfield; Redburn; Golf Inn.

9B 84 **Kilbirnie Place**

Largs Rd, Kilbirnie, Ayrshire, KA25 7AJ
☎(01505) 683398, Sec 684444
On the main Largs road on the outskirts of Kilbirnie.
Parkland course.
Founded 1922
18 holes, 5517 yards, S.S.S. 69

Loch Lomond

It has a magical name and those who have been privileged enough to walk its magnificent fairways and take in the fantastic views believe that Loch Lomond has its own magical qualities.

Only 45 minutes drive from Glasgow Airport, the course has fast become a favourite on the European golf scene and in 2000 will attract the women's professional circuit for the first time when the tournament stages the Solheim Cup.

There are those who argue that Loch Lomond is the best golf course that has been built in the last 25 years, taking into its layout, the wonderful Loch and its dramatic setting.

It has also bucked the trend of multi-million-pound golf courses rapidly becoming white elephants, with the hopes of the developers and owners turning to nightmares. For a time it looked as though Loch Lomond was to suffer a similar fate.

Tom Weiskopf, the American Ryder Cup player turned architect, began the course but with spiralling costs and delays it seemed that it was destined to remain half-finished. In rode Lyle Anderson, the millionaire American.

Golf courses are no different from paintings in giving rise to likes and dislikes. There are those who rave about the extravagance of multi-million-pound ventures although they may be far beyond their financial reach; and there are others who believe that the soundly designed and sensibly built creations highlighting the natural look, represent far better value for money.

The last few years in Britain and Ireland have seen examples but rescue packages have come to the aid of several afflicted courses which undoubtedly deserved a reprieve – and none more so than Loch Lomond, on whose bonny, bonny banks Weiskopf, one of the best professional golfers turned architect, has produced an eye-catching 18 holes to test and dazzle the best.

Admittedly, his canvas is flanked by a frame of gold, though wise heads warn of midges in summer. A stunning setting anywhere in the world is a great asset for a new course, a fact that raises the thought as to what opinion would have made of the actual courses at Pebble Beach, Gleneagles or Killarney if they had been created in Hackney Marshes instead.

Be that as it may, Loch Lomond will stand comparison in any contest, the first golfing requirement being definite control from the tee to hit largely well-guarded fairways. Since the hardest part of the game is to aim straight and hit straight, those finding the fairways should always have a decided advantage over those who do not. Weiskopf, in his time, was as handsome a player as there was and, not surprisingly, his design at Loch Lomond owes nothing to gimmickry.

It would be hard to find a challenge to Loch Lomond in terms of beauty but the Carnegia Links (or Skibo) on the Dornoch Firth in Sutherland manages it easily. It is the first links course to be built in Scotland or England for half a century and, considering the demands of ecologists and environmentalists, could well be one of the last. — **CG**

† Welcome WD.
Ŧ WD £10.
⟲ Welcome by prior arrangement; from £18.
◉ Full facilities.
↴ Ryan.

9B 85 Kilmacolm
Porterfield Rd, Kilmacolm, Renfrewshire, PA13 4PD
☎(01505) 872139, Fax 874007, Pro 872695
From M8 Glasgow Airport follow the main signs to Irvine; turn off 2nd junction and follow A761 to Kilmacolm.
Moorland course.
Pro Iain nicholson; Founded 1890
Designed by James Braid
18 holes, 5961 yards, S.S.S. 69
† Welcome; prior booking essential for WE.
Ŧ WD £20.50; WE £20.50.
⟲ Welcome WD by prior arrangement; packages and prices depend on numbers; terms on application.
◉ Full clubhouse facilities.
↴ Many in Glasgow, Renfrew and Paisley.

9B 86 Kilmarnock (Barassie)
Hillhouse Rd, Barassie, Troon, Ayrshire, KA10 6SY
☎(01292) 313920, Fax 313920, Pro 311322, Bar/Rest 311077
Course is two miles north of Troon directly opposite Barassie railway station.
Championship links course.
Pro Gregor Howie; Founded 1887
Designed by Matthew M. Monie
27 holes, 6484 yards, S.S.S. 74
† Welcome WD except Wed; not before 8.30am or between 12.30pm-1.30pm.
Ŧ WD start at £40.
⟲ Welcome WD except Wed by arrangement; catering can be arranged in advance with club caterer; dining room; television lounge; also 9-hole course available, 2888 yards, par 34.
◉ Full clubhouse dining and bar; jacket and tie must be worn in dining room.
↴ South Beach; Prestland House, both Troon.

9B 87 Kilsyth Lennox
Tak-Ma-Doon Rd, Kilsyth, Glasgow, G65 0HX

☎(01236) 824115, Sec 823213
Course is on the A80 12 miles from Glasgow.
Moorland/parkland course.
Founded 1907
18 holes, 5912 yards, S.S.S. 70
† Welcome by prior arrangement with Sec or starter.
Ŧ WD £14; WE £16.
⟲ Welcome by arrangement with Sec; from £16.
◉ Clubhouse facilities.

9B 88 Kirkhill
Greenlees Rd, Cambuslang, Glasgow, G72 8YN
☎(0141) 641 3083, Pro 641 7972, Sec 641 8499, Bar/Rest 641 3083
Follow East Kilbride road from Burnside, take first turning on left past Cathkin by-pass roundabout.
Meadowland course.
Pro Duncan Williamson; Founded 1910
Designed by James Braid
18 holes, 5900 yards, S.S.S. 70
† Welcome by arrangement.
Ŧ WD £20; WE £20.
⟲ Welcome by prior arrangement; catering by prior arrangement with caterer; from £15.
◉ Full facilities by prior arrangement; snacks and bar meals available.
↴ Kings Park; Burnside; Stuart; Bruce.

9B 89 Kirkintilloch
Todhill, Campsie Rd, Kirkintilloch, Glasgow, G66 1RN
☎(0141) 776 1256, Sec 775 2387
1 miles from Kirkintilloch on road to Lennoxtown.
Parkland course.
Founded 1895
Designed by James Braid
18 holes, 5269 yards, S.S.S. 66
† Welcome with letter of introduction.
Ŧ WD £18; WE £18.
⟲ Welcome by prior arrangement; day ticket from £28; catering by arrangement; from £18.
◉ Clubhouse facilities; restrictions Mon and Tues.
↴ Garfield, Stepps.

9B 90 Knightswood
Lincoln Ave, Knightswood, G13
☎(0141) 959 6358
From City Centre go west along Great Western Road through

Knightswood past the cross and then left into Lincoln Avenue.
Flat parkland course.
Founded 1920
9 holes, 5584 yards, S.S.S. 64
† Welcome, except Wed and Fri from 7.45am-8.45am and 10am-11am.
Ŧ WD £3.20; WE £3.20.
⟲ Welcome with same restrictions as visitors; from £6.50.
◉ Limited.
↴ Charing Cross Tower Hotel.

9B 91 Kyles of Bute
The Moss, Kames, Tighnabruaich, Argyll, PA21 2EE
☎(01700) 811603
Course is on the B3836 on the road from Dunoon to Tighnabruaich, B8000 to Millhouse.
Undulating moorland course.
Founded 1907
9 holes, 4748 yards, S.S.S. 64
† Welcome all times except Wed evenings and Sun 9.30am-1pm.
Ŧ Terms on application.
⟲ Welcome by arrangement with Sec; from £8.
◉ Snacks when available.
↴ Royal; Kames; Kilfenan.

9B 92 Laglands
Auldhouse Rd, E Kilbride, Lanarkshire G75 9DW
☎(01352) 48172, Sec (0141) 644 2623
Course is three miles south-east of E Kilbride.
18 holes, 6202 yards, S.S.S. 70
† Welcome.
Ŧ Terms on application.
⟲ Terms on application.

9B 93 Lamlash
Lamlash, Brodick, Isle of Arran, KA27 8JU
☎(01770) 600296, Fax 600296, Sec 600272
Course is three miles south of pier terminal at Brodick.
Undulating heathland course.
Founded 1889
Designed by W Auchterlonie/W Fernie
18 holes, 4640 yards, S.S.S. 64
† Welcome.
Ŧ £12 but this is only available after 4pm.
⟲ Welcome; day tickets WD £16, WE £20; catering by arrangement; from £10.

🍴 Full clubhouse facilities.
🏌 Glenisle; Lilybank; Marine.

9B 94 **Lanark**
The Moor, Whitelees Rd, Lanark, S
Lanarkshire, ML11 7RX
☎(01555) 663219, Fax 663219, Pro
661456, Bar/Rest 665261
Take A73 or A72 to Lanark; turn left
in town for Whitelees road.
Moorland course.
Pro Alan White; Founded 1851
Designed by T Morris
18 holes, 6423 yards, S.S.S. 71
† Welcome WD; with member at
WE.
⌊ WD £25.
🖉Welcome by prior arrangement on
WD; larger groups welcome Mon-
Wed; maximum of 12 people Thurs &
Fri; catering by arrangement; from
£24.
🍴 Full clubhouse facilities.
🏌 Cartland Bridge; Popinjay; Tinto.

9B 95 **Largs**
Irvine Rd, Largs, Ayrshire, KA30 8EU
☎(01475) 673594, Fax 673594, Pro
686192, Sec 673594, Bar/Rest
674681
Course is on the A78 one mile south
of Largs.
Parkland/woodland course.
Pro Kenneth Docherty; Founded 1891
18 holes, 6115 yards, S.S.S. 71
† Welcome by arrangement.
⌊ WD £25; WE £35.
🖉Welcome Tues and Thurs by prior
arrangement; packages available for
18 and 36 holes of golf plus catering;
from £30.
🍴 Full clubhouse facilities.
🏌 Priory House; Haylie; Queens.

9B 96 **Larkhall**
Burnhead Rd, Larkhall, Lanarkshire
☎(01698) 881113
Take M8 to Larkhall exit then head
SW on B7019.
Municipal parkland course.
9 holes, 6423 yards, S.S.S. 71
† Welcome.
⌊ WD £3.50; WE £3.80.
🖉Welcome by prior arrangement;
limited catering is available; from
£3.50.
🍴 Bar.

9B 97 **Leadhills**
Leadhills, Biggar, Lanarkshire, ML12
6XR

☎(01659) 74324
On B797 in Leadhills village 6 miles
from A74 at Abington.
Moorland course; highest course in
Scotland.
Founded 1935
9 holes, 4100 yards, S.S.S. 62
† Welcome.
⌊ Details available on request.
🖉Welcome; catering organised in
local hotel; from £5.
🍴 Local hotel.
🏌 Hopetoun Arms.

9B 98 **Lenzie**
19 Crosshill Rd, Lenzie, Glasgow,
G66 5DA
☎(0141) 776 1535, Pro 777 7748,
Sec 776 6020
10 miles NE of Glasgow; leave M8 at
Stirling junction then head for
Kirkintilloch.
Parkland course.
Pro J McCallum
Founded 1889
18 holes, 5984 yards, S.S.S. 69
† Welcome by prior arrangement.
⌊ WD £18; WE £18.
🖉Welcome by prior arrangement
with the club Secretary; catering
packages available by prior
arrangement; professional can assist
on society days with golf clinic, etc;
from £28.
🍴 Full clubhouse facilities
available.
🏌 Moodiesburn, Moddiesburn;
Garfield, Stepps.

9B 99 **Lethamhill**
Cumbernauld Rd, Glasgow, G33 1AH
☎(0141) 770 6220
On A80 adjacent to Hogganfield
Loch.
Municipal parkland course.
18 holes, 5836 yards, S.S.S. 70
† Welcome.
⌊ WD £6.50; WE £6.50.

9B 100 **Linn Park**
Simshill Rd, Glasgow, G44 5EP
☎(0141) 637 5871
Off M74 S of Glasgow.
Public parkland course.
Founded 1925
Designed by Glasgow Parks
18 holes, 5005 yards, S.S.S. 65
† Welcome.
⌊ Details upon application.
🖉Welcome by prior application;
from £5.50.
🍴 Clubhouse facilities available.

9B 101 **Littlehill**
Auchinairn Rd, Bishopbriggs,
Glasgow, G74 1UT
☎(0141) 772 1916
3 miles N of city centre.
Public parkland course.
Founded 1924
Designed by James Braid
18 holes, 6228 yards, S.S.S. 70
† Welcome.
⌊ WD £6; WE £6; concessions
apply.
🖉Apply to Council for full details.
🍴 Clubhouse facilities available;
except Mon; no catering on summer
WE.

9B 102 **Loch Lomond**
Rossdhu House, Luss by Alexandria,
Dunbartonshire, G83 8NT
☎(01436) 655555, Pro 655540
On the A82 on the W bank of Loch
Lomond.
Championship parkland course; host
of Loch Lomond Classic.
Pro Colin Campbell; Founded 1995
Designed by Tom Weiskopf and Jay
Morrish
18 holes, 7060 yards, S.S.S. 72
† Private; as the guest of a member
only.
⌊ WD £150; WE £150.
🖉None.
🍴 First-class clubhouse facilities
available.
🏌 Cameron House.

9B 103 **Lochgilphead**
Blarbuie Road, Lochgilphead, Argyll,
PA31 8LE
☎(01546) 602340
Follow signs for Argyll & Bute
Hospital from the centre of
Lochgilphead.
Hilly parkland course.
Founded 1891/1963
Designed by Dr Ian MacCammond
9 holes, 4484 yards, S.S.S. 63
† Welcome.
⌊ WD £10; WE £10.
🖉Welcome; weekly ticket of £30;
reductions for groups registered with
the club; from £10.
🍴 Bar facilities; catering by
arrangement.
🏌 Stag; Argyll Lochgair.

9B 104 **Lochranza**
Lochranza, Isle of Arran, KA27 8HL
☎(01770) 830273, Fax 830600
Course is in Lochranza opposite the
distillery.

Grassland course with rivers/trees: 3 holes on seashore.
Founded 1991
Designed by Iain M. Robertson
18 holes, 5654 yards, S.S.S. 70
♦ Welcome between April and late October.
⌣ WD £12; WE £12; concessions apply.
⌣Welcome by prior arrangement; day ticket £15; available packages can include accommodation, meals, ferry, distillery visit and golf; from £10.
🍽 Snacks available.
↴ Hotel/guest house packages available.

9B 105 Lochwinnoch
Burnfoot Rd, Lochwinnoch, Renfrewshire, PA12 4AN
☎(01505) 842153, Fax 843668, Pro 843029
On A760 10 miles S of Paisley.
Parkland course.
Pro Gerry Reilly; Founded 1897
18 holes, 6025 yards, S.S.S. 71
♦ Welcome WD before 4pm.
⌣ WD £17.
⌣Welcome by prior arrangement WD; catering packages; from £17.
🍽 Clubhouse facilities.
↴ Lindhurst.

9B 106 Loudoun Gowf Club
Galston, Ayrshire, KA4 8PA
☎(01563) 820551, Sec 821993
On A71 5 miles E of Kilmarnock.
Parkland course; Founded 1909
18 holes, 6016 yards, S.S.S. 68
♦ Welcome WD by prior arrangement.
⌣ WD £18.
⌣Welcome WD by prior arrangement; catering packages can be arranged; from £11.
🍽 Full catering facilities.
↴ Loudoun Mains, Newmilns; Fox Bar, Kilmarnock.

9B 107 Machrie Bay
Sheeans, Pirnmill, Brodick, Isle of Arran, KA27 8HM
☎(01770) 850232, Sec 850247, Bar/Rest 840213
9 miles W of Brodick.
Links course.
Founded 1900
Designed by William Fernie
9 holes, 2200 yards, S.S.S. 62
♦ Welcome; day ticket: WD £8; WE £8.

⌣Welcome by prior arrangement; only limited catering available; from £8.
🍽 Tea room.
↴ Lochranza; Kinloch; Catacoc Bay.

9B 108 Machrie Hotel & Golf Links ☎
The Machrie Hotel & Golf Course, Port Ellen, Isle of Islay, Argyll, PA42 7AN
☎(01496) 302310 Fax 302404, Sec 302409
Ferry from Kennacraig (2hrs) or plane from Glasgow (30 mins).
Traditional links course.
Founded 1891
Designed by Willie Campbell/ Donald Steel
18 holes, 6226 yards, S.S.S. 70
♦ Welcome; residents receive discounts.
⌣ WD £25; WE £25.
⌣Welcome by prior arrangement; day rates available; also accommodation and golf packages can be arranged; hotel can also advise on air packages from Glasgow; conference facilities; own beach; salmon & trout fishing; snooker; from £20.
🍽 Full clubhouse and hotel catering and bar facilities with à la carte restaurant.
↴ Machrie Bay Hotel.

9B 109 Machrihanish
Machrihanish, Campbeltown, Argyll, PA28 6PT
☎(01586) 810213, Fax 810221, Pro 810277
Course is five miles W of Campbeltown on the B843.
Natural links course.
Pro Ken Campbell; Founded 1876
18 holes, 6228 yards, S.S.S. 71
♦ Welcome by prior arrangement.
⌣ WD £28; WE £35.
⌣Welcome by prior arrangement with club Pro; some WE available; catering by prior arrangement; some air packages available; accommodation packages also on offer.
🍽 Full clubhouse facilities.

9B 110 Maybole
Memorial Park, Maybole, Ayrshire, KA19
☎(01292) 612000
Course is nine miles S of Ayr on main Stranraer road.

Hillside course with splendid views.
Founded 1905
9 holes, 5304 yards, S.S.S. 65
♦ Welcome.
⌣ Available upon application.
⌣Welcome; book through S Ayrshire District Council; day ticket from £11; from £7.
↴ Many available in local area; Abbotsford.

9B 111 Millport
Golf Rd, Millport, Isle of Cumbrae, KA28 0HB
☎(01475) 530311, Fax 530306, Pro 530305, Sec 530300
10 mins ferry crossing from Largs In Ayrshire; 4 miles from the Ferry Terminal.
Heathland course.
Pro Ken Docherty; Founded 1888
Designed by James Braid
18 holes, 5828 yards, S.S.S. 69
♦ Welcome.
⌣ WD £14.50, WE £24.50.
⌣Welcome by prior arrangement; catering packages by arrangement; from £14.50.
🍽 Full facilities.
Large practice area.

9B 112 Milngavie
Laighpark, Milngavie, Glasgow, G62 8EP
☎(0141) 956 1619; Fax 956 4252
Off A809 NW of Glasgow; club can provide detailed directions.
Moorland course.
Founded 1895
Designed by J Braid
18 holes, 5818 yards, S.S.S. 68
♦ Welcome on WD by prior arrangement.
⌣ WD £22.
⌣Welcome by prior arrangement; packages ranging from £9 can be arranged including 4-course dinner; from £20.
🍽 Full clubhouse facilities available.
↴ Black Bull; Burnbrae, both Milngavie.

9B 113 Mount Ellen
Johnstone Rd, Johnstone House, Gartcosh, Glasgow, G69 8EY
☎(01236) 872277, Fax 872249, Pro 872632
From M8 N and A89 take B752 N to Gastosh on to B804 in direction of Glenboig.
Parkland course.

Pro Iain Bilsborough; Founded 1905
18 holes, 5525 yards, S.S.S. 67
♪ Welcome WD only.
⌐ WD £16.
🝧 Welcome by prior arrangement;
terms on application.
🍴 Full clubhouse facilities.
⌐ Garsfield House, Stepps;
Moodiesburn House, Moodiesburn.

9B 114 **Muirkirk**
Cairn View, Muirkirk, Strathclyde
KA18 3QW
☎(01290) 661556, Fax 661556
13 miles W of Junction 12 on M74 on
A70.
Pay and play.
9 holes, 5366 yards, S.S.S. 67
♪ Welcome at all times.
⌐ £6.
🍴 Limited.

9B 115 **New Cumnock**
Lochill, Cumnock Rd, New Cumnock,
Ayrshire, KA18 4BQ
☎01290) 338848, Sec 423659
On the A76 1 mile to the NW of New
Cumnock.
Parkland course.
Founded 1901
Designed by W Fernie
9 holes, 5176 yards, S.S.S. 66
♪ Welcome; tickets available from
the Lochside Hotel next to course.
⌐ From £6.
🝧None.
🍴 Limited; Lochside Hotel next
door.
⌐ Lochside Hotel.

9B 116 **Old Course Ranfurly**
Ranfurly Place, Bridge of Weir,
Renfrewshire, PA11 3DE
☎(01505) 613612, Fax 613214, Sec
613214
Course is five miles west of Glasgow
Airport.
Heathland course.
Founded 1905
Designed by W Park Jnr
18 holes, 6061 yards, S.S.S. 70
♪ Welcome by prior arrangement
WD; as the guest of a member only
at WE.
⌐ WD £20.
🝧Welcome by written prior
arrangement WD; day ticket of £30
available; from £20.
🍴 Full clubhouse facilities
available.
⌐ Normandy, Renfrew; Glyn Hill,
Paisley.

9B 117 **Paisley**
Braehead, Paisley, PA2 8TZ
☎(0141) 884 2292, Fax 884 3903,
Pro 884 4114, Sec 884 3903
Leave M8 Junction 27 follow B778 to
Braehead.
Moorland course.
Pro Gordon Stewart; Founded
1895/1951
18 holes, 6466 yards, S.S.S. 72
♪ Welcome WD before 4pm.
⌐ WD £20.
🝧Welcome by prior arrangement
WD; day ticket £28; catering can be
provided by prior arrangement;
snooker; from £20.
🍴 Full clubhouse facilities
available.
Two practice grounds.
⌐ Watermill.

9B 118 **Palacerigg**
Palacerigg Country Park,
Cumbernauld, G67 3HU
☎(01236) 734969, Fax 721461, Pro
721461
Take A80 to Cumbernauld and follow
signs for Country Park.
Wooded parkland course.
Pro/Starter John Murphy; Founded
1974
Designed by Henry Cotton
18 holes, 6444 yards, S.S.S. 71
♪ Welcome.
⌐ WD £5.10; WE £7.40.
🝧Welcome WD by prior
arrangement; range of packages
available; full day's golf and catering;
from £25.
🍴 Full clubhouse facilities abaible;
restrictions Mon/Tues.
⌐ Castlecarry; Moodiesburn;
Cumbernauld Travel Inn.

9B 119 **Pollok**
90 Barrhead Rd, Glasgow, G43 1BG
☎(0141) 632 1080, Fax 649 1398,
Sec 632 4351
Course lies four miles south of the
city of Glasgow off M77 Junction 2 on
B736.
Wooded parkland course.
Founded 1892
18 holes, 6257 yards, S.S.S. 70
♪ Welcome WD; gentlemen only.
⌐ WD £30.
🝧Welcome by prior arrangement
with the Secretary; day rate £40; from
£30.
🍴 Full clubhouse catering facilities
available.
⌐ Albany; Macdonald;
Marriott.

9B 120 **Port Bannatyne**
Bannatyne Mains Rd, Port
Bannatyne, Isle of Bute, PA20 0PH
☎(01700) 504544, Sec 502009
Course is two miles north of
Rothesay on the Isle of Bute above
the village of Port Bannatyne.
Hilly seaside course.
Founded 1912
Designed by James Braid
13 holes, 5085 yards, S.S.S. 65
♪ Welcome.
⌐ WD £8; WE £10.
🝧Welcome by prior arrangement;
reductions for groups of 30-39 to £10;
for more than 40, £8.
🍴 New clubhouse.
⌐ Ardmory House; Royal; Ardbeg.

9B 121 **Port Glasgow**
Devol Farm Industrial Estate, Port
Glasgow, Renfrewshire, PA14 5XE
☎(01475) 704181
On M8 towards Greenock SW of
Glasgow in the town of Port Glasgow.
Undulating course.
Founded 1895
18 holes, 5712 yards, S.S.S. 68
♪ WD until 3.55pm; WE by
introduction.
⌐ WD £15.
🝧Welcome by prior arrangement on
non-competition days; catering by
prior arrangement; terms on
application.
🍴 Clubhouse facilities.
⌐ Clune Brae; Star.

9B 122 **Prestwick**
2 Links Rd, Prestwick, Ayrshire, KA9
1QG
☎(01292) 477404, Fax 477255, Pro
479483
1 mile from Prestwick Airport adjacent
to Prestwick station.
Links course; hosted first Open
Championship in 1860.
Founded 1851
Designed by Tom Morris
18 holes, 6544 yards, S.S.S. 73
♪ Welcome by arrangement.
⌐ WD £75; day ticket £100.
🝧Welcome by prior arrangement;
terms on application.
🍴 Full clubhouse facilities; dining
room men only; Cardinal room.
⌐ Parkstone; Fairways; Golf View;
North Beach.

9B 123 **Prestwick St Cuthbert**
East Rd, Prestwick, Ayrshire, KA9
2SX

☎ (01292) 477101, Fax 671730
Take A77 to Whitletts roundabout and
then follow signs for Heathfield
Estate.
Parkland course.
Founded 1899
Designed by Stutt & Co
18 holes, 6470 yards, S.S.S. 71
† Welcome WD but booking
essential; only with member at WE.
▯ WD £22.
⌁ Welcome by prior arrangement,
day ticket £30; meal packages can be
arranged with prior notice from
£10.50; from £22
⬤ Full clubhouse facilities.
⌁ St Nicholas; Golf.

9B 124 Prestwick St Nicholas
Grangemuir Rd, Prestwick, Ayrshire,
KA9 1SN
☎ (01292) 477608, Fax 678570
From Prestwick town centre take the
road to Ayr; turn right at Grangemuir
road junction; proceed under railway
bridge to course.
Links course.
Founded 1851/1892
Designed by C. Hunter & J Allan
18 holes, 5952 yards, S.S.S. 69
† Welcome WD and Sun afternoon;
prior booking essential.
▯ WD £30; WE £35.
⌁ Welcome WD and some Sun
afternoons by prior arrangement;
catering by prior arrangement; from
£30.
⬤ Full clubhouse refurbishment
completed spring 1998.
⌁ Parkstone.

9B 125 Ralston
Strathmore Ave, Ralston, Paisley,
Renfrewshire, PA1 3DT
☎ (0141) 882 1349, Sec 882 1503
Course is off the main Paisley to
Glasgow road.
Parkland course.
Founded 1904
18 holes, 6029 yards, S.S.S. 69
† With members only on WD.
▯ WD £18.
⌁ Welcome by prior arrangement;
catering by arrangement; terms on
application.
⬤ Full clubhouse facilities.
⌁ Abbey.

9B 126 Ranfurly Castle
Golf Rd, Bridge of Weir,
Renfrewshire, PA11 3HN
☎ (01505) 612609, Pro 614795

From the M8 take the Irvine road to
Bridge of Weir; turn left at Prieston
road and at top of the rise the
clubhouse is on right.
Spacious heathland course.
Pro Tom Eckford; Founded
1889/1904
Designed by Andrew Kirkaldy & Willie
Auchterlonie
18 holes, 6284 yards, S.S.S. 71
† Welcome WD.
▯ WD £20.
⌁ Welcome Tues by prior
arrangement; clubhouse catering by
arrangement; from £20.
⬤ Full clubhouse bar and restaurant
service
⌁ Glynhill, Renfrew; Stakis,
Glasgow Airport.

9B 127 Renfrew
Blythswood Estate, Inchinnan Rd,
Renfrew, RA4 9EG
☎ (0141) 886 6692, Fax 886 1808,
Pro 885 1754
Leave the M8 at Junction 26, then
take the A8 to Renfrew, turning to the
club at the Stakis Glasgow Airport
Hotel.
Parkland course.
Qualifer for the British Open
Pro Steven Dundas; Founded 1894
Designed by John Harris
18 holes, 6818 yards, S.S.S. 73
† Welcome if introduced by a
member.
▯ WD £25.
⌁ Welcome Mon, Tues and Thurs by
arrangement; catering by
arrangement; day ticket £35.
⬤ Full clubhouse bar and catering
facilities.
⌁ Dean Park; Glynhill; Stakis
Glasgow Airport.

9B 128 Rothesay
Canada Hill, Rothesay, Isle of Bute,
PA20 9HN
☎ (01700) 502244, Fax 503554, Pro
503554, Sec 503554
30 minutes by steamer from Wemyss
Bay.
Undulating parkland course.
Pro Jim Dougal; Founded 1892
Designed by James Braid
18 holes, 5395 yards, S.S.S. 66
† Public.
▯ Terms on application.
⌁ Welcome by prior arrangement;
catering by prior arrangement, from
£15.
⬤ Full clubhouse facilities in the
season April-October.

⌁ Club will supply comprehensive
list of local hotels.

9B 129 Rouken Glen
Stewarton Rd, Thornliebank,
Glasgow, G46 7UZ
☎ (0141) 638 7044
5 miles S of Glasgow.
Parkland course.
Pro Kendal McReid; Founded 1922
18 holes, 4800 yards, S.S.S. 64
† Welcome.
▯ Terms on application.
⌁ Welcome by prior arrangement;
terms on application.
⬤ Full facilities.
Practice range, 18 bays floodlit.
⌁ The MacDonalds.

9B 130 Routenburn
Largs, Ayrshire, KA30 8SQ
☎ (01475) 673230, Pro 687240
1 mile north of Largs turning left at
first major turning on the Greenock
road.
Seaside hill course.
Pro Greig McQueen; Founded 1914
Designed by James Braid
18 holes, 5680 yards, S.S.S. 68
† Welcome WD by prior
arrangement.
▯ WD £10; WE £13.
⌁ Welcome WD by prior
arrangement; catering packages by
prior arrangement; terms on
application.
⬤ Full facilities except Thurs.

9B 131 Royal Troon
Craigend Rd, Troon, Ayrshire, KA10
6EP
☎ (01292) 311555, Fax 318204, Pro
313261, Bar/Rest 317578
3 miles from A77 and Prestwick
Airport.
Championship links course; host of
1997 Open.
Pro Brian Anderson
Founded 1878
Designed by local members
18 hole courses, 7079 yards, S.S.S.
73
† Mon, Tues and Thurs only;
maximum handicap 20.
▯ WD £125.
⌁ Welcome by prior arrangement;
price includes lunch and coffee; also
Portland course: 18 holes, 6274
yards, par 71; £85 for two rounds.
⬤ Full bar and restaurant service
available.
⌁ Marine; Piersland House.

9B 132 Ruchill
Brassey Street, Maryhill, Glasgow, G20
☎(0141) 770 0519
2.5 miles NW of Glasgow off Bearsden road.
Municipal parkland course.
Founded 1928
18 holes, 4480 yards, S.S.S. 61
♠ Public.
⌐ Terms on application.
⌐ Contact city council.

9B 133 Sandyhills
223 Sandyhills Rd, Glasgow, G32 9NA
☎(0141) 763 1099, Sec 778 0787, Bar/Rest 778 1179
E side of Glasgow from Tollcross road, turn left at Killin St and right into Sandyhills Road.
Parkland course.
Founded 1905
18 holes, 6237 yards, S.S.S. 70
♠ Welcome by prior arrangement.
⌐ Terms on application.
⌐ Welcome by prior arrangement; catering packages available; terms on application.
⌐ Full clubhouse catering facilities available.
⌐ Hilton; Moat House; Marriott, all in Glasgow.

9B 134 Shiskine
Blackwaterfoot, Isle of Arran, KA27 8HA
☎(01770) 860226, Fax 860205, Pro 860226, Sec 860226
Course is 300 yards off the B880 in Blackwaterfoot.
Seaside course with magnificent views.
Founded 1896
Original 9 designed by W Fernie; upgraded to 12 by W Park
12 holes, 2990 yards, S.S.S. 42
♠ Welcome; handicap certs required in July and August period.
⌐ WD £12; WE £15.
⌐ Welcome by prior arrangement with club manager; packages available with Kinloch Hotel travel, accommodation and golf; day tickets available (WD £18, WE £20); also weekly and fortnightly tickets; tennis and bowls; maximum parties of 24 unless by prior agreement; from £12.
⌐ Tea room, lunches, high teas fron April-October; bar at Kinloch Hotel 500 yards.away.
⌐ Kinloch Hotel.

9B 135 Shotts
Blairhead, Shotts, N Lanarkshire, ML7 5BJ
☎(01501) 820431, Pro 822658
Take M8 to Junction 5; then A7057 to Shotts; 1.5 miles to course.
Heathland/parkland course.
Pro John Strachan; Founded 1895
Designed by James Braid
18 holes, 6125 yards, S.S.S. 70
♠ Welcome WD; Sat after 4.30pm and Sun by prior arrangement.
⌐ WD £20; WE £20.
⌐ Welcome WD; full day's golf and catering included in packages; visitors' locker room; £30.
⌐ Full clubhouse facilities.
Practice range available.
⌐ Golden Circle, Bathgate; Travelodge, Newhouse; Hillcroft, Whitburn.

9B 136 Skelmorlie
Skelmorlie, Ayrshire, PA17 5ES
☎(01475) 520152
1 mile from Wemyss station.
Parkland/moorland course.
Founded 1891
Designed by James Braid
18 holes, 5104 yards, S.S.S. 65
♠ Welcome except Sat during season.
⌐ Terms on application.
⌐ Welcome by prior arrangement except Sat; catering by prior arrangement; terms available on application.
⌐ Full clubhouse facilities.
⌐ Haywood.

9B 137 Strathaven
Overton Ave, Glasgow Rd, Strathaven, ML10 6NL
☎(01357) 520421, Fax 520539, Pro 521812, Sec 520421, Bar/Rest 520422
On A723 East Kilbride road on outskirts of the town.
Tree-lined undulating parkland course.
Pro Matt McCrorie
Founded 1908
Designed by William Fernie of Troon, Extended to 18 holes by JR Stutt
18 holes, 6250 yards, S.S.S. 71
♠ Welcome WD until 4pm.
⌐ WD £25.
⌐ Welcome Tues by prior arrangement with Sec; catering by prior arrangement; club can organise morning coffee, hot and cold snacks, lunches, high teas and dinners; from £20.

⌐ Full clubhouse facilities available.
⌐ Strathaven; Springvale.

9B 138 Strathclyde Park
Mote Hill, Hamilton, Lanarkshire, ML3 6BY
☎(01698) 429350
1.5 miles from M74 close to Hamilton Ice rink.
Public parkland course.
9 holes, 6350 yards, S.S.S. 70
♠ Welcome.
⌐ WD £3.10; WE £3.65.
⌐ Welcome; catering by prior arrangement; from £3.
⌐ Catering by prior arrangement.
Practice range available.
⌐ Travelodge.

9B 139 Tarbert
Kilberry Rd, Tarbert, Argyll, PA29 6XX
☎(01880) 820565
1 mile from A83 to Campbeltown from Tarbert, on B8024.
Hilly seaside course.
9 holes, 4460 yards, S.S.S. 63
♠ Welcome by prior arrangement.
⌐ From £8.
⌐ Welcome WD; day ticket for £15; from £10.
⌐ Full clubhouse facilities available.
⌐ Stonefield Castle; West Loch.

9B 140 Tobermory
Erray Rd, Tobermory, Isle of Mull, PA75 6PR
☎(01688) 302338, Fax 302140
Signposted in Tobermory.
Clifftop heathland course with views over Sound of Mull.
Founded 1896
Designed by David Adams (1935)
9 holes, 4890 yards, S.S.S. 64
♠ Welcome; day ticket: WD £13; WE £13.
⌐ Welcome; catering on application to Sec; from £13.
⌐ Clubhouse facilities.
Practice range.
⌐ Western Isles; Fairways (on course).

9B 141 Torrance House
Strathaven Rd, East Kilbride, Glasgow, G75 0QZ
☎(01355) 249720, Sec 248638
Course is on the A726 on the outskirts of East Kilbride travelling south to Strathaven.
Municipal parkland course.
Founded 1969

Designed by Hawtree & Sons
18 holes, 6476 yards, S.S.S. 71
✝ Welcome; advance booking
system.
⌐ Terms on application.
⌁ Welcome by prior arrangement by
calling (01355) 806271; catering
packages by prior arrangement; from
£16.
⦿ Full clubhouse facilities available.
Practice range 1 mile from club.

9B 142 Troon Municipal
Harling Drive, Troon, Ayrshire, KA10
6NE
☎ (01292) 312464
100 yards from the railway station.
Links course.
Founded 1905
Darley: 18 holes, 6360 yards, S.S.S.
71; Lochgreen: 18 holes, 6822 yards,
S.S.S. 72; Fullerton: 18 holes, 4869
yards, S.S.S. 63
✝ Welcome.
⌐ Terms on application.
⌁ Welcome by prior arrangement;
catering by arrangement; terms on
application.
⦿ Full clubhouse facilities.

9B 143 Turnberry Hotel
Turnberry Hotel, Turnberry, Ayrshire,
KA26 9LT
☎ (01655) 331000, Fax 331706
On A77 15 miles SW of Ayr.
Championship seaside links; Open
venue.
Pro Brian Gunson; Founded 1897
Designed by MacKenzie Ross (Ailsa)
Ailsa: 18 holes, 6976 yards, S.S.S.
72; Arran: 18 holes, 6014 yards,
S.S.S. 69
✝ Booking essential.
⌐ WD £80; WE £80.
⌁ Only welcome if society is resident
in the hotel.
⦿ Full clubhouse restaurant and
bar; first-class hotel facilities.
⌐⌐ Turnberry Hotel Golf Courses &
Spa.

9B 144 Vale of Leven
Northfield Rd, Bonhill, Alexandria,
Dumbartonshire, G83 9ET
☎ (01389) 752351, Pro 755012
Off A82 Glasgow to Dumbarton road
at signs marked Bonhill & Alexandria.
Moorland course with views of Loch
and Ben Lomond.
Pro Gordon Brown; Founded 1907
18 holes, 5162 yards, S.S.S. 66
✝ Welcome except Sat.

⌐ WD £17; WE £21.
⌁ Welcome by prior arrangement;
catering packages by prior
arrangement with club caterers.
⦿ Full clubhouse and bar facilities
available.
⌐⌐ Balloch; Duck Bay Marina;
Lomond Park; Tullichewan.

9B 145 Vaul
Scarinish, Isle of Tiree, Argyll, PA77
6XH
☎ (01879) 220334
On the E end of the Island 3 miles
from the pier and 5 miles from the
airport; 40-minute flight from Glasgow;
50 miles W of Oban by ferry.
Links course.
Founded 1920
9 holes, 5674 yards, S.S.S. 68
✝ Welcome.
⌐ WD £5; WE £5.
⌁ Welcome by prior arrangement;
weekly and fortnightly tickets
available; from £5.
⦿ Catering at Lodge Hotel.
⌐⌐ Lodge; Glassary GH; Kirkapol
GH.

9B 146 West Kilbride
33-35 Fullerton Drive, Seamill, W
Kilbride, Ayrshire, KA23 9HT
☎ (01294) 823911, Fax 823911, Pro
823042, Bar/Rest 823128.
On A78 Androssan to Largs road at
Seamill.
Flat seaside links course alongside
Firth of Clyde.
Pro Graham Ross; Founded 1893
Designed by Tom Morris
18 holes, 6452 yards, S.S.S. 70
✝ Welcome WD after 9.30am.
⌐ WD £38.
⌁ Welcome Tues and Thurs only by
prior arrangement; catering to be
arranged in advance with the caterer;
from £38.
⦿ Full clubhouse facilities.
⌐⌐ Seamill Hydro.

9B 147 Western Gailes
Gailes, Irvine, Ayrshire, KA11 5AE
☎ (01294) 311357, Sec 311649
Course is on the A78 five miles north
of Troon.
Championship links; Open qualifying
course.
Founded 1897
18 holes, 6714 yards, S.S.S. 72
✝ Welcome WD except Thurs and
Tues.
⌐ WD £70.

⌁ Welcome by prior arrangement
WD except Thurs and Tuesdays; day
tickets from £95; catering by
arrangement.
⦿ Clubhouse catering and bar.

9B 148 Westerwood Hotel ⦿ Golf & Country Club
St Andrews Drive, Cumbernauld, G68
0EW
☎ (01236) 457171, Fax 738478, Pro
725281
Signposted off the A80 13 miles from
Glasgow.
Parkland course.
Pro Steve Killin; Founded 1989
Designed by Seve Ballesteros and
Dave Thomas
18 holes, 6616 yards, S.S.S. 72
✝ Welcome.
⌐ WD £22.50; WE £27.50.
⌁ Welcome by prior arrangement;
packages available; hotel leisure
facilities; residents discounts; from
£22.50.
⦿ Full clubhouse catering facilities
available.
Practice range available.
⌐⌐ Westerwood Hotel on site.

9B 149 Whinhill
B1eith Road, Greenock, Renfrewshire
☎ (01475) 721064
Just outside Greenock on old Largs
road.
Parkland course.
18 holes, 5434 yards, S.S.S. 68
✝ Welcome.
⌐ Terms on application.
⌁ None.
⦿ Small clubhouse for members
only.

9B 150 Whitecraigs
72 Ayr Rd, Giffnock, G46 6SW
☎ (0141) 639 4530, Pro 639 2140,
Bar/Rest 693 4530
Course is on the A77 seven miles
south of Glasgow.
Parkland course.
Pro Alistair Forrow; Founded 1905
18 holes, 6013 yards, S.S.S. 70
✝ Welcome on WD but booking is
essential.
⌐ WD £37, including coffee, high tea
and light snacks.
⌁ Welcome Wed only; catering by
arrangement; day tickets from £50;
from £35.
⦿ Full clubhouse facilities
available.
⌐⌐ Macdonald.

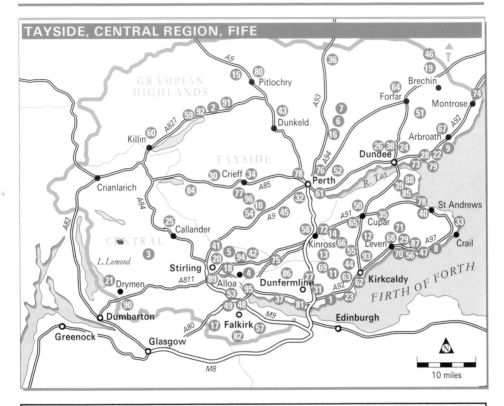

TAYSIDE, CENTRAL REGION, FIFE

KEY							
1	Aberdour	20	Bridge of Allan	39	Drumoig Hotel and	57	Grangemouth	77	Muthill

KEY
1 Aberdour
2 Aberfeldy
3 Aberfoyle
4 Alloa
5 Alva
6 Alyth
7 Alyth Strathmore
8 Anstruther
9 Arbroath
10 Auchterarder
11 Auchterderran
12 Balbirnie Park
13 Ballingry
14 Bishopshire
15 Blair Atholl
16 Blairgowrie
17 Bonnybridge
18 Braehead
19 Brechin

20 Bridge of Allan
21 Buchanan Castle
22 Buddon Links
23 Burntisland
24 Caird Park
25 Callander
26 Camperdown (Municipal)
27 Canmore
28 Carnoustie Golf Links
29 Charleton
30 Comrie
31 Cowdenbeath
32 Craigie Hill
33 Crail Golfing Society
34 Crieff
35 Cupar
36 Dalmunzie
37 Dollar
38 Downfield

39 Drumoig Hotel and Golf Course
40 Duke's Course (St Andrews)
41 Dunblane New
42 Dunfermline
43 Dunkeld & Birnam
44 Dunnikier Park
45 Dunning
46 Edzell
47 Elie Sports Club
48 Falkirk
49 Falkirk Tryst
50 Falkland
51 Forfar
52 Glenalmond
53 Glenbervie
54 Gleneagles Hotel
55 Glenrothes
56 Golf House

57 Grangemouth
58 Green Hotel
59 Kenmore Golf Course
60 Killin
61 King James VI
62 Kinghorn
63 Kirkcaldy
64 Kirriemuir
65 Ladybank
66 Leslie
67 Letham Grange
68 Leven
69 Lochgelly
70 Lundin
71 Lundin Ladies
72 Milnathort
73 Monifieth
74 Montrose Links Trust
75 Muckhart
76 Murrayshall

77 Muthill
78 North Inch
79 Panmure
80 Pitlochry
81 Pitreavie (Dunfermline)
82 Polmont
83 St Andrews
84 St Fillans
85 St Michaels
86 Saline
87 Scoonie
88 Scotscraig
89 Stirling
90 Strathendrick
91 Strathtay
92 Taymouth Castle
93 Thornton
94 Tillicoultry
95 Tulliallan
96 Whitemoss

9B 151 **Whiting Bay**
Golf Course Rd, Whiting Bay, Isle of
Arran, KA27 8QT
☎ (01770) 700487
8 miles S of Brodick.
Undulating heathland course.
Founded 1895
18 holes, 4405 yards, S.S.S. 63
♦ Welcome.

⌙ WD £13; WE £17; after 4pm all
rounds are £10.
⌐ Welcome by prior arrangement
with Sec; discounts available for
groups of 10 or more; from £13.
⌾ Clubhouse catering and bar
facilities.
⌐ Cameronia; Grange House;
Kiscadale; Royal.

9B 152 **Williamwood**
Clarkston Rd, Netherlee, Glasgow,
G44 3YR
☎ (0141) 637 1783, Fax 637 6688,
Pro 637 2715
5 miles S of Glasgow.
Wooded parkland course.
Founded 1906
Designed by James Braid

18 holes, 5878 yards, S.S.S. 69
† Welcome by introduction only.
℄ WD on application.
⌁ Welcome WD by arrangement; catering by arrangement; terms on application.
⦿ Full clubhouse facilities available.
⌐ Macdonald, Giffnock, Redhurst, Clarkston.

9B 153 Windyhill
Baljaffray Rd, Bearsden, Glasgow, G61 4QQ
☎ (0141) Bar 942 2349, Fax 942 5874, Pro 942 7157, Sec 942 2349
⬛ www.windyhill.co.uk
1 mile N of Bearsden.
Parkland course.
Pro Gary Collinson; Founded 1908
Designed by James Braid
18 holes, 6254 yards, S.S.S. 70
† Welcome WD.
℄ WD £20.
⌁ Welcome by prior arrangement; discounts available for larger groups; catering available by arrangement; £20.
⦿ Full bar and restaurant facilities. Practice range available.
⌐ Black Bull, Milngavie; Jury's Pond Hotel, Glasgow.

9B 154 Wishaw
Lower Main Street, Wishaw, Lanarkshire, ML2 7PL
☎ (01698) 372869, Pro 358247
Course is 15 miles SE of Glasgow; five miles from the M74 Motherwell junction.
Parkland course.
Pro Stuard Adair; Founded 1897
Designed by James Braid
18 holes, 6100 yards, S.S.S. 69
† Welcome WD until 4pm; not Sat and by prior arrangement Sun.
℄ WD £13; WE £26.
⌁ Welcome WD; Sun only by special arrangement; day's golf; catering packages by prior arrangement; from £21.
⦿ Full clubhouse facilities available.
⌐ Wishaw Town Hotel.

9C 1 Aberdour
Seaside Place, Aberdour, Fife, KY3 0TX
☎ (01383) 860688, Fax 860050, Pro 860256, Sec 860080, Bar /Rest 860256
In Aberdour village on coast route to Burntisland.

Parkland/seaside course with views of River Forth.
Pro Gordon McCallum; Founded 1896
Designed by Peter Robertson & Joe Anderson
18 holes, 5460 yards, S.S.S. 66
† Welcome by prior arrangement.
℄ Mon-Sat: £17; Sun: £24.
⌁ Welcome except Sat by prior arrangement; day ticket from £28; catering by arrangement with the clubmaster; maximum parties of 24 on Sun; from £17.
⦿ Full clubhouse catering.
⌐ Woodside.

9C 2 Aberfeldy
Taybridge Rd, Aberfeldy, Perthshire, PH15 2BH
☎ (01887) 820535, Sec 820422
Follow signs from A9 at Ballinluig through the centre of Aberfeldy for Weem and first right at Wades Bridge.
Parkland course.
Founded 1895
Designed by Souters
18 holes, 5283 yards, S.S.S. 66
† Welcome.
℄ WD £14; WE £14.
⌁ Welcome by prior arrangement; catering by arrangement; terms on application.
⦿ Full facilities.
⌐ Palace; Crown, both Aberfeldy.

9C 3 Aberfoyle
Braeval, Aberfoyle, Stirlingshire, FK8 3UY
☎ (01877) 382493, Sec 382638, Bar/Rest 382809
1.5 miles from Aberfoyle on the main Stirling road.
Parkland course.
Founded 1890
Designed by James Braid
18 holes, 5218 yards, S.S.S. 66
† Welcome; some restrictions at WE.
℄ Terms on application.
⌁ Welcome by prior arrangement; restrictions on numbers; from £12.
⦿ Full clubhouse facilities.
⌐ Rob Roy Motor Inn; Forth Inn.

9C 4 Alloa
Schawpark, Sauchie, Clackmannanshire FK10 3AX
☎ (01259) 722745, Pro 724476
On the A908 1 mile N of Alloa; 8 miles E of Stirling.

Undulating parkland course.
Pro Bill Bennett; Founded 1891
Designed by James Braid
18 holes, 6229 yards, S.S.S. 71
† Welcome.
℄ WD £23; WE £32.
⌁ Welcome WD by arrangement; catering available by prior arrangement; snooker room; from £23.
⦿ Full clubhouse facilities.
⌐ Harviestoun; Royal Oak; Dunmar House; Claremont Lodge.

9C 5 Alva
Beauclerc St, Alva, Clackmannanshire FK12 5LH
☎ (01259) 760431
Course is on the A91 Stirling to St Andrews road; follow signs for Alva Glen as the club car park is at entrance to Glen Hillside.
Sloping fairways/plateau greens.
Founded 1901
9 holes, 4846 yards, S.S.S. 64
† Welcome.
℄ Terms on application.
⌁ Welcome by prior arrangement; facilities limited; no pro shop, no equipment for hire; terms on application.
⦿ Bar snacks only; clubhouse open for 7pm each night and from noon at WE.
⌐ Alva Glen.

9C 6 Alyth
Pitcrocknie, Alyth, Perthshire, PH11 8HF
☎ (01828) 632668, Fax 633491, Pro 632411, Sec 632268, Bar /Rest 633490
Course is one mile SE of Alyth on the B954.
Parkland course with views over Angus & Perthshire.
Pro Tom Melville; Founded 1894
Part designed by James Braid
18 holes, 6205 yards, S.S.S. 71
† Welcome by prior arrangement.
℄ WD £22; WE £33.
⌁ Welcome by prior arrangement; catering available by prior arrangement; Pro can assist with golf clinics; day and weekly tickets; from £22.
⦿ Full clubhouse facilities.
⌐ Lands of Loyal; Alyth; Lossett.

9C 7 Alyth Strathmore
Leroch, Alyth, Perthshire PH11 8NZ
☎ (01828) 633322, Fax 633533

Carnoustie

The 18th at Carnoustie will be etched on people's minds for a very long time. Every inch of the 444-yard par four Home hole was studied in extraordinary detail this year as Jean van de Velde's attempts to become the Open champion faltered and finally disappeared. And the images beamed around the world of the Frenchman ankle-deep in the Barry Burn short of the 18th green have established Carnoustie's repu-tation as one of the toughest courses on the championship rota.

Even before Van de Velde played a remarkable and many would insist irresponsible final hole at the 1999 Open Championship, the course already carried the memories of many earlier tournaments.

The 18th itself has Johnny Miller's Bunker where, in the tense final rounds of the 1975 Open, the famous American put his ball in the bunker while Tom Watson made a birdie to beat both Miller and Nicklaus and set up a play-off with Newton.

While Watson may have fond memories of the Angus course, many of his countrymen vowed that they would never return to that corner of Scotland. It was, they claim-ed, an unfair test of golf.

But it is a test that has been posed close to the Firth of Tay since the game of 'gowff' was recorded as early as 1520. With a sandy sub-soil and open, rolling terrain it was an obvious place for golf to be played as the sport developed in the 19th century. The east coast of Scotland was a boom area, with St Andrews close by.

Allan Robertson laid out the first 10 holes in 1842, and 25 years later Old Tom Morris added a further eight. Then, in 1926, James Braid added new greens, tees and bunkers, and further changes were made before the 1999 Open.

At that time each area in Scotland developed its own golfing style and the 'Carnoustie Swing' became recognisable throughout the world. A lineage of fine golfers, both amateur and professional, arose in the town and their techniques of play became one of Scotland's greatest exports. These young golfers emigrated to many parts, especially America and the 'Carnoustie Swing' became something of a phenomenon. One of the greatest golfing geniuses, Bobby Jones, remarked: "The best luck that ever I had in golf was when Stewart Maiden came from Carnoustie to be Pro at the East Lake Club."

With a further adjustment to the closing holes forming Carnoustie's famous 'sting-in-the-tail', the Open first came to the course in 1931. With the players battling a strong easterly wind, Tommy Armour triumphed. Six years later, in 1937, Henry Cotton achieved his second championship.

In 1953, the legendary Ben Hogan's victory did much to enhance the course's pre-eminence. The wind blew and blew and Hogan, on his only visit to the Open Championship, found himself being tested to the limits. But he fought back and in particular destroyed the sixth on the final day with two huge drives.

When the inimitable Gary Player took the trophy in 1968 it was the 14th that provided the key moment. He struck a great four-wood over the bunkers and to within three feet of the hole. An eagle followed and soon afterwards the Claret Jug.

The first three days of the 1975 Open saw the links, now with a reputation for ferocity, as mild as a kitten until the final day, when the wind got up and the then unknown Tom Watson battled against the course and its elements to win the trophy in a play-off.

In recent years, the Carnoustie Championship course, often rated among the top three golf courses in the world, has returned to world prominence as the host of the Scottish Open in 1995 and 1996 and the venue for the 1999 Open Championship. It was a championship that was to have its own dramas. — **CG**

Course is five miles east of Blairgowie on the A926.
Founded 1996
Rannaleroch course: 18 holes, 6454 yards, par 72; Leroch course: 9 holes, 1666 yards, S.S.S. 29
♦ Welcome; pay and play.
⌐ Terms on application.
⌐ Welcome; corporate days available.
|◉| Full clubhouse facilities.
10-bay floodlit range.
⌐ Lands of Loyal; Alyth; Lossett.

9C 8 Anstruther
Marsfield, Shore Rd, Anstruther, Fife, KY10 3DZ
☎ (01333) 310956, Fax 312283, Sec 312283
Turn off main road at Craw's Nest Hotel.
Seaside course.
Founded 1890
9 holes, 4588 yards, S.S.S. 63
♦ Welcome.
⌐ WD £12; WE £15.
⌐ None.
|◉| Snacks and lunches.
⌐ Craw's Nest.

9C 9 Arbroath
Elliot, Arbroath, Angus, DD11 2PE
☎ (01241) 872069, Pro 875837
Take A92 from Dundee N and turn right 2 miles before Arbroath.
Seaside links course.
Pro Lindsay Ewart; Founded 1903
Designed by James Braid
18 holes, 6185 yards, S.S.S. 69
♦ Welcome; not before 9.30am WE.
⌐ WD £16; WE £22.
⌐ Welcome by prior arrangement; catering by arrangement; terms on application.
|◉| Full clubhouse facilities.
⌐ Seaforth; Cliffburn; Viewfield.

9C 10 Auchterarder
Orohil Rd, Auchterarder, Perthshire, PH3 1LS
☎ (01764) 662804, Fax 662804, Pro 663711
Course is off the A9 next to Gleneagles Hotel.
Wooded heathland course.
Pro Gavin Baxter
Founded 1892
Designed by Bernard Sayers
18 holes, 5775 yards, S.S.S. 68
♦ Welcome by prior arrangement or with a member.
⌐ WD £20; WE £25.

⌐ Welcome by prior arrangement with Sec; catering and golf packages by arrangement.
|◉| Full catering and bar facilities available.
⌐ Cairn Lodge; Colliearn House; Duchally.

9C 11 Auchterderran
Woodend Rd, Cardenden, Fife, KY5 0NH
☎ (01592) 721579
Course is on the main Lochgelly to Glenrothes road at the north end of Cardenden.
Parkland course.
Founded 1904
9 holes, 5250 yards, S.S.S. 66
♦ Welcome.but prior booking advisable.
⌐ From £9.
⌐ Welcome by arrangement; catering by prior arrangement; from £9.
|◉| Bar and snacks facilities available; meals cooked to order.
⌐ Bowhill; Central.

9C 12 Balbirnie Park
Markinch, Glenrothes, Fife, KY7 6NR
☎ (01592) 612095, Fax 612383, Pro 752006, Sec 752006, Bar /Rest 752006
2 miles E of Glenrothes off A92 on A911.
Scenic parkland course.
Pro David Scott; Founded 1983
18 holes, 6210 yards, S.S.S. 70
♦ Welcome by arrangement.
⌐ WD £25; WE £30.
⌐ Welcome by prior arrangement; catering packages by arrangement; terms on application.
|◉| Full clubhouse facilities; all-day catering.
⌐ Balbirnie House.

9C 13 Ballingry
Lochore Meadows Country Park, Crosshill, By Lochgelly, Ballingry, Fife, KY5 8BA
☎ (01592) 414300, Fax 414345
W of M90 between Lochgelly and Ballingry.
Parkland course.
Founded 1981
9 holes, 6484 yards, S.S.S. 71
♦ Welcome.
⌐ WD £8.50; WE £10.50.
⌐ Welcome by prior arrangement; angling, wind-surfing; terms on application.

|◉| Catering in café in park centre.
⌐ Navitie House.

9C 14 Bishopshire
Kinnesswood by Kinross, Tayside, Tayside
☎ (01592) 780203
Course is three miles east of Kinross off the M90.
Upland course.
Founded 1903
Designed by W. Park
10 holes, 4784 yards, S.S.S. 64
♦ Welcome; restrictions after 5pm Fri.
⌐ Terms on application.
⌐ Limited by arrangement; catering by arrangement or at local hotels; from £6.
|◉| Available at the Lomond Hotel 400 yards away.
⌐ Lomond; Scotlandwell Inn.

✗ 9C 15 Blair Atholl
Blair Atholl, Perthshire, PH18 5TG
☎ (01796) 481407
Course is on the A9 five miles north of Pitlochry.
Parkland course.
Founded 1896
9 holes, 5710 yards, S.S.S. 68
♦ Welcome except comp days.
⌐ WD £13; WE £16.
⌐ Welcome by prior arrangement only; catering by arrangement; from £13.
|◉| Clubhouse facilities.
⌐ Atholl Arms; Tilt.

9C 16 Blairgowrie
Rosemount, Blairgowrie, Perthshire, PH10 6LG
☎ (01250) 872383, Fax 875451, Pro 873116, Sec 872622, Bar/Rest 875527
1 mile S of Blairgowrie off the A93; 15 miles N of Perth.
Heathland course with pine, heather, silver birch, broom.
Pro Charles Dernie; Founded 1974 (Lansdowne), 1889 (Rosemount)
Designed by Thomas/Alliss
Lansdowne: 18 holes, 6913 yards, S.S.S. 72;
Rosemount: 18 holes, 6590 yards, S.S.S. 72
♦ Welcome by prior arrangement; some restrictions apply Wed, Fri and WE.
⌐ WD from £40; WE from £45.
⌐ Welcome with same restrictions as visitors; catering packages by

arrangement; also 9-hole Wee course, 2327 yards, par 32, designed by Old Tom Morris in 1889; terms on application.
🏴 Full clubhouse facilities.
🗬 Kinloch House; Moorfield House; Altamount House; Angus; Royal.

9C 17 **Bonnybridge**
Larbert Rd, Bonnybridge, Stirlingshire, FK4 1NY
☎ (01324) 812822
Course is on the B816 three miles west of Falkirk.
Undulating moorland course.
Founded 1925
9 holes, 6128 yards, S.S.S. 69
† Welcome with a member or by letter of introduction.
⌁ WD £10; WE £10.
⤳ None.
🏴 Meals at WE; bar facilities; limited in winter.
🗬 Royal.

9C 18 **Braehead**
Cambus, by Alloa
☎ (01259) 725766, Pro 722078
On A907 Stirling-Alloa Road about 1.5 miles W of Alloa.
Parkland course.
Pro Paul Brookes; Founded 1891
18 holes, 6086 yards, S.S.S. 69
† Welcome.
⌁ WD £18; WE £24.
⤳ Welcome all week by prior arrangement; catering packages by arrangement; from £24 per day.
🏴 Full catering facilities.
Practice range.
🗬 Royal Oak; Dunmar House.

9C 19 **Brechin**   ☎
Trinity, by Brechin, Angus, DD9 7PD
☎ (01356) 622383, Pro 625270, Sec 622383
1 mile outside Brechin on the A90 road to Aberdeen.
Rolling parkland course.
Pro Stephen Rennie; Founded 1893
Part designed by James Braid
18 holes, 6096 yards, S.S.S. 70
† Welcome; restrictions Sat and Sun 10am-12 noon & 2.30pm-4.30pm.
⌁ WD £15; WE £20.
⤳ Welcome WD by prior arrangement; packages for eight or more include all catering and 2 rounds of golf; £26.
🏴 Full clubhouse facilities.
Practice range.
🗬 Northern Hotel.

9C 20 **Bridge of Allan**
Sunnlaw, Bridge of Allan, Stirlingshire
☎ (01786) 832332
3 miles N of Stirling.
Undulating course; one of toughest par 3s in Scotland.
Founded 1895
Designed by Old Tom Morris
9 holes, 5120 yards, S.S.S. 65
† Welcome WD and Sun.
⌁ WD on application.
⤳ By prior arrangement; terms on application.
🏴 Bar facilities.
🗬 Royal.

9C 21 **Buchanan Castle**
Drymen, Glasgow, G63 0HY
☎ (01360) 660307, Fax 870382, Pro 660330, Bar/Rest 660369
Course is on the A811 Glasgow to Aberfoyle road; entrance just before Drymen.
Secluded parkland course with stunning views.
Pro Keith Baxter; Founded 1936
Designed by James Braid
18 holes, 6059 yards, S.S.S. 69
† Welcome by arrangement.
⌁ WD £30; WE £30.
⤳ Welcome Thurs and Fri by prior arrangement; full day's golf £40; catering by arrangement with Clubmaster; from £30.
🏴 Full clubhouse facilities.
🗬 Buchanan Arms; Winnock Hotel.

9C 22 **Buddon Links**
Links Parade, Carnoustie, Tayside DD7 7JE
☎ (01241) 853249; Fax 852720
10 miles E of Dundee on A92.
Links; 18 holes, 5420 yards, S.S.S. 66
† Welcome; some weekend restrictions.
⌁ £16.
⤳ By arrangement.

9C 23 **Burntisland**
Dodhead, Burntisland, Fife, KY3 9EY
☎ (01592) 873247, Pro 872116
Course is on the B923 0.5 miles east of Burntisland.
Parkland course.
Pro J Montgomery ; Founded 1897
Designed and re-worked by J Braid
18 holes, 5965 yards, S.S.S. 70
† Welcome except competition days.
⌁ WD £17; WE £25; concessions apply for juniors.

⤳ Welcome except on competition days; contact manager for starting times; £5 per head deposit; catering packages by arrangement; terms on application.
🏴 Full clubhouse bar and catering: facilities 8am-8pm.
🗬 Inchview; Kingswood.

9C 24 **Caird Park**
Mains Loan, Dundee, Tayside, DD4 9BX
☎ (01382) 453606, Sec 438871, Office 438868
Course is reached via Kingsway to the NE of the town.
Parkland course.
Pro Jack Black; Founded 1926
18 holes, 6352 yards, S.S.S. 70
† Public.
⌁ Available on request.
⤳ Book through Dundee City Council leisure and parks dept; terms on application.
🏴 By prior arrangement; bar and lounge facilities.
🗬 Swallow; Kingsway.

9C 25 **Callander**
Aveland Rd, Callander, Perthshire, FK17 8EN
☎ (01877) 330090, Fax 330062, Pro 330975, Bar/Rest 331718
Course is off the A84 at the east end of Callander.
Parkland course.
Pro Allen Martin; Founded 1890
Designed by Tom Morris (1890); Redesigned by W Fernie
18 holes, 5151 yards, S.S.S. 66/63
† Welcome by prior arrangement.
⌁ WD £18; WE £26.
⤳ Welcome by prior arrangement; catering packages by arrangement; from £26 for a day ticket.
🏴 Full catering facilities.
🗬 Abbotsford Lodge; Myrtle Inn; Dreadnought.

9C 26 **Camperdown (Municipal)**
Camperdown Park, Dundee, Tayside, DD2 4TF
☎ (01382) 623398
At Kingsway junction of the Coupar-Angus Road.
Parkland/ wooded course.
Pro Roddy Brown; Founded 1959
Designed by Eric Brown
18 holes, 6561 yards, S.S.S. 72
† Welcome; pay and play.
⌁ WD £15; WE £15.

⤳Welcome by prior arrangement; on application; from £15.
🍽 Clubhouse facilities.
⤴ The Swallow.

9C 27 Canmore
Venturefair Ave, Dunfermline, Fife, KY12 0PE
☎(01383) 724969
Course is on the A823 one mile north of Dunfermline.
Undulating parkland course.
Founded 1897
18 holes, 5432 yards, S.S.S. 66
† Welcome WD; Sat after 4pm; not on comp days.
⌊ WD £12; WE £18.
⤳Welcome by prior arrangement; catering and day rates by arrangement; from £12.
🍽 Full clubhouse facilities.
⤴ Several in Dunfermline.

9C 28 Carnoustie Golf Links
Links Parade, Carnoustie, Angus, DD7 7PH
☎01241) 853789, Fax 852720, Sec 853789
Course is on the A930 12 miles east of Dundee.
Open Championship links.
Pro Lee Vannet; Founded 1842
Designed by A Robertson; Tom Morris; James Braid
Three 18-hole courses, 6941 yards, S.S.S. 75
† Welcome by prior arrangement; WE restrictions.
⌊ WD up to £70; WE up to £70.
⤳Welcome by prior arrangement; catering by arrangement; also Burnside course: 18 holes, 6020 yards; Buddon Links: 18 holes, 5420 yards; from £52.
🍽 Full clubhouse facilities.

9C 29 Charleton
Colinsburgh, Fife KY9 1HG
☎(01333) 340505, Fax 340583
0.5 miles W of Colinsburgh on B942.
18 holes, 6152 yards, S.S.S. 70
† Welcome; pay and play course.
⌊ WD £18; WE £22.
⤳Rates for groups of 15 or more.
🍽 Restaurant; bar.
Pitch and putt course.

9C 30 Comrie
Laggan Braes, Comrie, Perthshire, PH6 2LR
☎(01764) 670055, Sec 670941

On A85 7 miles W of Crieff; course signposted from village.
Slightly undulating parkland course.
Founded 1891
9 holes, 6040 yards, S.S.S. 70
† Welcome; restrictions after 4.30pm Mon and Tues.
⌊ WD details on application.
⤳Welcome by arrangement; catering by arrangement; from £10.
🍽 Light refreshments, coffee, teas available.
⤴ Royal; Comrie; Mossgiel GH; Langower GH.

9C 31 Cowdenbeath
Seco Place, Cowdenbeath, Nr Dunfermline, Fife, KY4 8PD
☎(01383) 511918
6 miles E of Dunfermline.
Parkland course.
Founded 1990/1998
18 holes, S.S.S. 71
† Welcome.
⌊ WD £7; WE £8.
⤳Welcome by arrangement; catering by prior arrangement; from £7.
🍽 Bar and snacks available.
Practice range.
⤴ Halfway House; Kingseat.

9C 32 Craigie Hill
Cherrybank, Perth, Perthshire, PH2 0NE
☎(01738) 624377, Pro 622644, Sec 620829
1 mile W of Perth with easy access from A9 and M90.
Hilly course.
Founded 1909
Designed by W. Ferne and J. Anderson
18 holes, 5386 yards, S.S.S. 67
† Welcome; bookings required on Sun.
⌊ WD £15; WE £25.
⤳Welcome WD and some Sun by prior arrangement; catering by arrangement; from £15.
🍽 Full facilities.
⤴ Lovat.

9C 33 Crail Golfing Society
Balcomie Clubhouse, Fifeness, Crail, KY10 3XN
☎(01333) 450686, Fax 450416, Pro 450960, Bar/Rest 450278
Course is 11 miles SE of St Andrews on the A917.
Seventh oldest club in world; moved from Sauchope in 1895.

Pro Graeme Lennie; Founded 1786/1895
Designed by Tom Morris
36 holes, 5922 yards, S.S.S. 69
† Welcome.
⌊ WD £22; WE £27.
⤳Welcome; catering by arrangement; new 18-hole course called Craighead available for limited play in 1998; terms available on application.
🍽 Full service with views over course and N Sea.
⤴ Club can supply detailed list.

9C 34 Crieff
Perth Rd, Crieff, Perthshire, PH7 3LR
☎(01764) 652397, Fax 655096, Pro 652909
Course is on the A85 on the east edge of Crieff.
Parkland ferntower course.
Pro David Murchie; Founded 1891
Designed by Old Tom Morris / R Simpson (1914) / J Braid (1924) / J Stark & J Freeman (1980)
27 holes, 6450 yards, S.S.S. 71
† Welcome.
⌊ WD from £19; WE from £25.
⤳Welcome; catering by arrangement; from £20.
🍽 Full clubhouse facilities.
⤴ Crieff Hydro; Murray Park; Foulford Inn.

9C 35 Cupar
Hilltarvit, Cupar, KY15 5JT
☎(01334) 653549, Fax 653549, Sec 654101
25 miles on Ceres Rd; SE outskirts of Cupar; 9 miles from St Andrews.
National Trust parkland course; oldest 9-hole course in country.
Founded 1855
Designed by Alan Robertson
9 holes, 5074 yards, S.S.S. 65
† Welcome except Sat.
⌊ WD £12; WE £16.
⤳Welcome; discounts available; private room; catering by arrangement; from £12.
🍽 Snacks and meals.
⤴ Eden House.

9C 36 Dalmunzie
Spittal of Glenshee, Blairgowrie, Perthshire, PH10 7QG
☎(01250) 885226
On A93 Blairgowrie to Braemar Rd; 18 miles N of Blairgowrie.
Hilly upland course.
Founded 1922

Designed by Alister MacKenzie
9 holes, 4070 yards, S.S.S. 60
✝ Welcome.
⌐ WD £7; WE £7.
↷ Welcome by arrangement;
discounts of 10 per cent for more
than 10 on WD; terms available on
application.
⦿ Facilities in hotel.
↰ Dalmunzie House.

9C 37 **Dollar**
Brewlands House, Dollar,
Stirlingshire, FK14 7EA
☎ (01259) 742400, Sec 743581
In Dollar signposted 0.5 miles off
A91.
Hillside course; 2nd, Brae, is 97
yards.
Founded 1890
Designed by Ben Sayers
18 holes, 5242 yards, S.S.S. 66
✝ Welcome except comp days.
⌐ WD £12; WE £20.
↷ Welcome by prior arrangement;
packages (WD £30, WE £35) include
36 holes of golf and full day's
catering; maximum 36.
⦿ Full clubhouse facilities.
↰ Castle Campbell Hotel.

9C 38 **Downfield**
Turnberry Ave, Dundee, Tayside, DD2
3QP
☎ (01382) 825595, Fax 813111, Pro
889246, Bar/Rest 811055
Follow Kingsway to A923; right into
Faraday St then first left to Harrison
Road; left at Dalmahoy Drive and
sharp left to club.
Championship parkland course;
Qualifying course for 1999 Open.
Pro Kenny Hutton; Founded 1932
Designed by C.K. Cotton
18 holes, 6822 yards, S.S.S. 73
✝ Welcome WD; restrictions at WE.
⌐ Terms on application.
↷ Welcome by arrangement; special
packages available for golf and
catering; terms on application.
⦿ Full clubhouse facilities.
↰ Gourdie; Swallow, both Dundee;
Invercarse, Inchture.

9C 39 **Drumoig Hotel and Golf Course**
Leuchars, St Andrews, Fife ,KY16 0BE
☎ (01382) 541800, Fax 542211
⊠ drumoig@sol.co.uk
7 miles from St Andrews and 5 miles
from Dundee on the A914 road.
Founded 1996

18 holes, 6376 yards, S.S.S. 70
✝ Any day.
⌐ WD £25; WE £30.
↷ Special rates for 9 or more.
⦿ Full facilities.

9C 40 **The Duke's Course** ☂ **(St Andrews)**
St Andrews, Fife, Scotland, KY16
9SP
☎ (01334) 474 371
Five minutes drive from the centre of
St Andrews.
Classic Scottish parkland course.
Founded 1995
Designed by Peter Thomson
18 holes, 7271 yards, S.S.S. 75
✝ Welcome at any time.
⌐ £50 - £55.
↷ Welcome any time.
⦿ Clubhouse facilities include bar,
restaurant and Boardroom for private
dining and meetings.
↰ Old Course Hotel, Golf Resort &
Spa.

9C 41 **Dunblane New**
Perth Rd, Dunblane, Stirlingshire,
FK15 0LJ
☎ (01786) 823711, Fax 825946
Course is six miles north of Stirling
on the old A9 at the Fourways
roundabout.
Parkland course.
Pro Bob Jamieson; Founded 1923
18 holes, 5957 yards, S.S.S. 69
✝ Welcome WD; restrictions at WE.
⌐ Terms on application.
↷ Welcome Mon, Thurs and Fri by
prior arrangement; catering packages
by arrangement; tennis and squash
adjacent; terms available on
application.
⦿ Full clubhouse facilities.
↰ Dunblane Hydro; Stirling Arms.

9C 42 **Dunfermline**
Pitfirrane, Crossford, Dunfermline,
Fife, KY12 8QW
☎ (01383) 723534, Pro 729061
On S of A994 2 miles W of
Dunfermline on the road to the
Kincardine Bridge.
Parkland course.
Pro Steven Craig; Founded 1887
Designed by J.R. Stutt & Sons
18 holes, 6126 yards, S.S.S. 70
✝ Welcome WD between 10am-
12noon and 2pm-4pm; Sun but not
Sat.
⌐ WD from £20; WE from £25.
↷ Welcome WD by arrangement;

day ticket WD from £30; Sun from
£35; catering by arrangement;
snooker; from £20.
⦿ Bar and restaurant facilities.
↰ Keavil; Pitfirran Arms; The
Maltings.

9C 43 **Dunkeld & Birnam**
Fungarth, Dunkeld, Perthshire, PH8
0HU
☎ (01350) 727524, Fax 728660, Sec
727524
Course is on the A923 one mile norh
of Dunkeld.
Heathland course with panoramic
views.
Founded 1892
9 holes, 5322 yards, S.S.S. 67
✝ Welcome.
⌐ WD £11; WE £16.
↷ Welcome by prior arrangement;
catering packages by prior
arrangement; from £11.
⦿ Full bar and catering facilities.
↰ Royal Dunkeld; Stakis Dunkeld
House Resort.

9C 44 **Dunnikier Park**
Dunnikier Way, Kirkcaldy, Fife, KY1
3LP
☎ 01592) 261599, Pro 642121
Leave A92 at Kirkcaldy West
roundabout and join B981 for 1 mile.
Parkland course.
Pro Gregor Whyte; Founded 1963
Designed by R Stutt
18 holes, 6601 yards, S.S.S. 72
✝ Welcome; invitation needed for
clubhouse.
⌐ Terms on application.
↷ Welcome by prior arrangement
with Sec; catering packages by
arrangement; changing facilities
limited (council owned); minimum 12,
maximum 30; terms on application.
⦿ Full catering facilities.
↰ Dunnikier House; Dean Park.

9C 45 **Dunning**
Rollo Park, Dunning, Perth, PH2 0RG
☎ (01764) 684747, Sec 684237
Off A9 9 miles SW of Perth.
Parkland course.
9 holes, 4836 yards, S.S.S. 63
✝ Welcome except on WE.
⌐ WD £6.
↷ Welcome WD and most Sun; WD
price £14; from £10.
⦿ Soft and hot drinks in clubhouse;
meals by prior application; also in
village hotels.
Small practice area.

9C 46 **Edzell** 🍵
High St, Edzell, by Brechin, Angus,
DD9 7HT
☎(01356) 648235, Fax 648094, Pro
648462, Sec 647283, Bar/Rest
647241
Take B996 off the A90 at the North
end of the Brechin by-pass.
Parkland course.
Pro Alastair Webster; Founded 1895
Designed by Bob Simpson
18 holes, 6348 yards, S.S.S. 71
🏴 Welcome.
⌣ WD £21; WE £27.
⌣Welcome; some restrictions; by
prior arrangement with Secretary;
catering by prior arrangement;
driving range; terms available on
application.
🍽 Full clubhouse bar and restaurant
facilities.
Practice range, opened 1997.
⌐ Glenesk; Central, both Edzell.

9C 47 **Elie Sports Club**
Elie, Fife, KY9 1AS
☎(01333) 330955
Course is on the A917 10 miles south
of St Andrews.
Seaside course.
Pro Robin Wilson
9 holes, 4354 yards, par 31
🏴 Welcome.
⌣ Day ticket WD £9; WE £9.
⌣Welcome by prior arrangement;
packages available; terms on
application.
🍽 Clubhouse facilities.
⌐ Golf; Old Manor; Lundin Links.

9C 48 **Falkirk**
136 Stirling Rd, Camelon, FK2 7YP
☎(01324) 611061, Fax 639573, Sec
634118
On A9 1.5 miles N of Falkirk.
Parkland course.
Founded 1922
Designed by James Braid
18 holes, 6230 yards, S.S.S. 70
🏴 Welcome WD; not Sat.
⌣ WD £15.
⌣Welcome WD and Sun by prior
arrangement; catering by
arrangement; £30.
🍽 Full clubhouse facilities.
⌐ Stakis Park Hotel.

9C 49 **Falkirk Tryst**
86 Burnhead Rd, Larbert, FK5 4BD
☎(01324) 562415, Fax 562091, Pro
562091, Sec 562054, Bar /Rest
570436

On A88 5 miles N of Falkirk close to
the A9 Falkirk-Stirling road.
Links course.
Founded 1885
18 holes, 6053 yards, S.S.S. 69
🏴 Welcome WD by prior
arrangement.
⌣ WD £16.
⌣Welcome WD by prior
arrangement; catering packages by
arrangement; from £16.
🍽 Full facilities.
⌐ Stakis Park; Airth Castle, Airth;
Plough, Stenhousemuir; Commercial,
Larbert.

9C 50 **Falkland**
The Myre, Falkland, Cupar, Fife,
KY15 7AA
☎(01337) 857404
In the Howe of Fife near to Freuchie
and Auchtermuchty.
Parkland course.
Founded 1976
9 holes, 5140 yards, S.S.S. 65
🏴 Welcome except on competition
days.
⌣ WD £5; WE £8.
⌣Welcome by prior arrangement;
packages available; terms on
application.
🍽 Full facilities during summer;
restricted in winter.
⌐ Hunting Lodge.

9C 51 **Forfar**
Cunninghill, Arbroath Rd, Forfar,
Angus, DD8 2RL
☎(01307) 462120, Fax 468495, Pro
465683, Sec 463773
From A90 to Forfar centre; course is
one mile east of town on the A932
Arbroath road.
Heathland course with tree-lined
fairways.
Pro Peter McNiven; Founded 1871
Designed by James Braid
18 holes, 6052 yards, S.S.S. 69
🏴 Welcome by prior appointment.
⌣ Terms on application.
⌣Welcome between 10am-11.30am
and 2.30pm-4pm except Sat morning;
day tickets available; catering by
arrangement; from £16.
🍽 Full clubhouse facilities
available.
⌐ Chakelbank, Forfar; James
House, Letham.

9C 52 **Glenalmond**
Glenalmond, Perthshire, Tayside
☎(01738) 880270

Moorland course; part of Glenalmond
Trinity College.
Founded 1923
9 holes, 4801 yards, S.S.S. 68
🏴 Members only.
⌣ Terms on application.

9C 53 **Glenbervie**
Stirling Rd, Larbert, Stirlingshire, FK5
4SJ
☎(01324) 562983, Fax 551504, Pro
562725, Sec 562605
M876 Junction 2 left on to A9; club
300 yards.
Parkland course.
Pro John Chilles; Founded 1932
Designed by James Braid
18 holes, 6423 yards, S.S.S. 71
🏴 Welcome WD.
⌣ WD £32.
⌣Welcome Tues and Thurs by prior
arrangement; packages for 18/36
holes of golf and catering; from £44.
🍽 Full clubhouse facilities.

9C 54 **Gleneagles Hotel**
Gleneagles Hotel, Auchterarder,
Perthshire, PH3 1NF
☎(01764) 662231, Fax 662134
Halfway between Perth and Stirling
on the A9.
Inland links/moorland course.
Pro Greg Schofield; Founded 1919
(Kings), 1917 (Queens), 1993
(Monarchs)
Designed by James Braid (Kings,
Queens); Designed by Jack Nicklaus
(Monarchs)
Kings: 18 holes, 6471 yards, S.S.S.
69; Monarchs: 18 holes, 7080 yards,
S.S.S. 74; Queens: 18 holes, 5965
yards, S.S.S. 69
🏴 Welcome.
⌣ WD from £75 and up to £100.
Reduced rates for residents
⌣Welcome; catering packages by
arrangement; also 9-hole, par 3
course; country club for residents,
health spa; clay target, shooting
school; equestrian centre; terms on
application.
🍽 Full clubhouse bar and grill
facilities; full hotel restaurant,
conference centre and bars.
Practice range, for members and
residents only.
⌐ Gleneagles Hotel.

9C 55 **Glenrothes**
Golf Course Rd, Glenrothes, Fife,
KY6 2LA
☎(01592) 758686, Sec 754561

Leave M90 at Junction 3; A92 for Glenrothes; follow signs for Whitehill Industrial Estate.
Parkland course.
Founded 1958
Designed by J.R. Stutt
18 holes, 6444 yards, S.S.S. 71
† Welcome.
⌐ Available on request.
⌐ Welcome by prior arrangement; catering available by arrangement with steward; groups of 12-40 only; day tickets available; terms on application.
⍟ Full bar and catering facilities.
⌐ Holiday Inn; Rescobie Hotel.

9C 56 Golf House
Elie, Leven, Fife, KY9 1AS
☎ (01333) 330327, Fax 330895, Pro 330955, Sec 330301
Course is on the A915 12 miles south of St Andrews.
Links course; Ladies club: Elie & Earlsferry GC.
Pro Robin Wilson; Founded 1875
18 holes, 6241 yards, S.S.S. 70
† Welcome after 10am; ballot in July & August; no Sun visitors May-Sept.
⌐ WD £32; WE £40.
⌐ Welcome except in June, July and August; day rates (WD £45, WE £55); catering by arrangement with Steward; from £32.
⍟ Full catering and bar.
⌐ Golf, Elie; Craw's Nest, Anstruther.

9C 57 Grangemouth
Polmonthill, by Falkirk, Stirlingshire, FK2 0YE
☎ (01324) 711500, Pro 503840
M9 Junction 4; follow signs to Polmonthill.
Parkland course.
Pro Stuart Campbell
Founded 1973
Designed by Sportwork
18 holes, 6314 yards, S.S.S. 71
† Welcome.
⌐ WD £12.50; WE £16.
⌐ Welcome by prior arrangement; catering by prior arrangement; from £12.50.
⍟ Clubhouse facilities available.
⌐ Inchrya; Grange; Lea Park.

9C 58 Green Hotel
2 The Muirs, Kinross, KY13 7AS
☎ (01577) 862237, Fax 863180, Pro 865125, Sec 863407, Bar/Rest 862234

Course is opposite Green Hotel.
Parkland course.
Pro Stuart Gerraghy; Founded 1991
Designed by Sir David Montgomery
Blue: 18 holes, 6438 yards, S.S.S. 71; Red: 18 holes, 6256 yards, S.S.S. 71
† Welcome.
⌐ WD £17; WE £27.
⌐ Welcome; catering in hotel or clubhouse by arrangement; swimming pool; squash; tennis; from £17.
⍟ Full facilities at hotel and clubhouse.
⌐ Green Hotel.

9C 59 Kenmore Golf Course
Kenmore, Aberfeldy, Perthshire, PH15 2HN
☎ (01887) 830226, Fax 830211, Bar/Rest 830775
On A827 through Kenmore village.
Slightly undulating parkland course.
Pro Alex Marshall; Founded 1992
Designed by R. Menzies and Partners
9 holes, 6052 yards, S.S.S. 69
† Welcome.
⌐ WD £12; WE £13.
⌐ Welcome by arrangement; catering packages available; £18.
⍟ Full service.
⌐ Kenmore.

9C 60 Killin
Killin, Perthshire, FK21 8TX
☎ (01567) 820312
W end of Loch Tay on A827 Killin to Aberfeldy road.
Parkland course; 5th/14th is The Dyke, 96 yards.
Founded 1913
Designed by John Duncan of Stirling
9 holes, 5016 yards, S.S.S. 65
† Welcome.
⌐ WD £12; WE £12.
⌐ Welcome by prior arrangement; full packages available; minimum 8; from £12.
⍟ Full catering and bar facilities.
⌐ Bridge of Lochay; Killin; Clachaig.

9C 61 King James VI
Moncreiffe Island, Perth, Perthshire, PH2 8NR
☎ (01738) 625170, Fax 445132, Pro 632460, Sec 445132
In the centre of the River Tay; access by footpath from Tay Street or Shore Road.
Parkland course; one of only two courses on river island in the world.

Pro A Coles; Founded 1858/1897
18 holes, 6038 yards, S.S.S. 68
† Welcome by prior arrangement but not Sat.
⌐ Terms on application.
⌐ Welcome by prior arrangement with the Pro; catering by arrangement; from £18.
⍟ Full facilities.
⌐ Salutation; Royal George; Isle of Skye.

9C 62 Kinghorn
Macduff Crescent, Kinghorn, Fife, KY3 9RE
☎ (01592) 890345, Pro 890978
Off A92 3 miles W of Kirkcaldy.
Undulating links course.
Founded 1887
Designed by layout recommended by Tom Morris
18 holes, 5166 yards, S.S.S. 66
† Welcome.
⌐ WD £9; WE £12.
⌐ Welcome by prior written arrangement; groups of 12-30; catering packages by arrangement; from £9.
⍟ Full catering facilities.
⌐ Kingswood; Longboat.

9C 63 Kirkcaldy
Balwearie Rd, Kirkcaldy, Fife, KY2 5LT
☎ (01592) 260370, Fax 203258, Pro 203258, Sec 205240
On A92 at W end of town.
Parkland course.
Pro A Mckay; Founded 1904
Designed by Tom Morris
18 holes, 6038 yards, S.S.S. 69
† Welcome; some restrictions Sat.
⌐ WD £16; WE £22.
⌐ Welcome by prior arrangement; restrictions Sat; day rates and catering packages available; from £16.
⍟ Full clubhouse facilities.
⌐ Parkway Hotel; Dunnikier House.

9C 64 Kirriemuir
Northmuir, Kirriemuir, Angus, DD8 4LN
☎ (01575) 573317, Fax 574608, Sec 572144,
N of Kirriemuir and accessible from A90 Dundee-Aberdeen road.
Parkland course.
Pro Karyn Dalllas; Founded 1908
Designed by James Braid
18 holes, 5510 yards, S.S.S. 67
† Welcome WD.

⌐ WD £18.
☞ Welcome by prior arrangement; day tickets available; catering and hospitality packages available; £5 pp deposit required; from £16.
🍽 Full catering packages.
⌐ Airlie Arms; Thrums: Castleton Park; Chapelbank.

9C 65 Ladybank
Annsmuir, Ladybank, Fife, KY15 7RA
☎(01337) 830320, Fax 831505, Pro 830725, Sec 830814, Bar/Rest 830814
In Ladybank off A914 between Glenrothes and Dundee.
Heathland course.
Pro Martin Gray; Founded 1879
Designed by Tom Morris
18 holes, 6641 yards, S.S.S. 72
⚑ Welcome WD and some Sun by arrangement; handicap certs required.
⌐ WD £30; WE £35.
☞ Welcome WD by prior arrangement with the club Pro; catering packages available; names and handicaps of all players required 7 days before arrival; dining room for 80; from £30.
🍽 Full clubhouse bar and catering facilities.
⌐ Club can provide a list of local hotels, GH and self-catering accommodation.

9C 66 Leslie
Balsillie, Leslie, Fife, KY6 3EZ
☎(01592) 620040
Leave M90 at Junctions 5 or 7; Leslie 11 miles.
Undulating course.
Founded 1898
9 holes, 4940 yards, S.S.S. 64
⚑ Welcome.
⌐ WD £8.50; WE £10.50.
☞ Welcome by arrangement; catering by arrangement; from £8.50.
🍽 Clubhouse facilities.
⌐ Greenside; Rescobie.

9C 67 Letham Grange
Letham Grange, Colliston, by Arbroath, Angus, DD11 4RL
☎(01241) 890377, Fax 890725, Pro 890377, Sec 890377
Follow Letham Grange signs in Arbroath from Dundee-Arbroath road.
Parkland course.
Pro Steven Moir; Founded 1985 (Old), 1988 (Glens)
Designed by Donald Steel & G.K.

Smith (Old); Designed by T MacAuley (Glens)
Old: 18 holes, 6968 yards, S.S.S. 73; Glens: 18 holes, 5528 yards, S.S.S. 68
⚑ Welcome, some restrictions at WE.
⌐ WD £35, WE £40 (Old); WD £18, WE £22.50 (Glens); combination rates available from £40.
☞ Welcome by prior arrangement; catering packages available; contact Ewan Wilson at club; from £25.
🍽 Full clubhouse facilities.
Large practice area.
⌐ 4-star Letham Grange.

9C 68 Leven
PO Box 14609, Links Rd, Leven, Fife, KY8 4HS
☎(01333) 426096, Fax 424229, Sec 424229
Enter Leven on A915 from Kirkcaldy and follow signs to the Beach.
Seaside links course.
Founded 1820
18 holes, 6436 yards, S.S.S. 70
⚑ Welcome; not before 9.30am WD; 10.30am WE.
⌐ WD £26; WE £30.
☞ Welcome by prior arrangement; catering packages by arrangement; snooker table; from £26.
🍽 Full catering facilities.
⌐ Lundin Links Hotel; Old Manor.

9C 69 Lochgelly
Cartmore Rd, Lochgelly, Fife, KY5 9PB
☎(01592) 780174, Sec (01383) 512238
On A910 2 miles NE of Cowdenbeath.
Parkland course.
Founded 1896/1911
18 holes, 5454 yards, S.S.S. 67
⚑ Welcome.
⌐ WD £12; WE £18.
☞ Welcome by prior arrangement; terms on application.
🍽 By arrangement.

9C 70 Lundin
Golf Rd, Lundin Links, Fife, KY8 6BA
☎(01333) 320202, Fax 329743, Pro 320051
On seaward side of the village on East Neuk Coast Road from Kirkcaldy.
Seaside links course.
Pro David Webster; Founded 1868
Designed by James Braid

18 holes, 6394 yards, S.S.S. 71
⚑ Welcome between 9am-3.30pm Mon-Thurs; 9am-3pm Fri; after 2.30pm Sat; not Sun.
⌐ WD £29; WE £37.
☞ Welcome by prior arrangement with Sec; WD ticket of £37; catering packages by arrangement; from £29.
🍽 Full facilities.
⌐ Lundin Links; Old Manor.

9C 71 Lundin Ladies
Woodielea Road, Lundin Links, Fife, KY8 6AR
☎(01333) 320832
Off Leven Road A915 in middle of Loudin Links.
Parkland course.
Founded 1891
Designed by James Braid
9 holes, 4730 yards, S.S.S. 67
⚑ Welcome.
⌐ WD £8; WE £9.50.
☞ Welcome except Wed April-August; from £8.
🍽 Not available.
⌐ Loudin Links; Old Manor.

9C 72 Milnathort
South St, Milnathort, Kinross, KY13 2AW
☎(01577) 864069, Sec 864 294
1 mile N of Kinross leaving M90 at Junction 6/7.
Undulating course with trees.
Founded 1890
9 holes, 5993 yards, S.S.S. 68
⚑ Welcome.
⌐ WD £12; WE £14.
☞ Welcome by prior arrangement; catering by arrangement with clubmaster; from £16.
🍽 Clubhouse facilities.
Practice range.
⌐ Jolly Beggars; Thistle; Royal.

9C 73 Monifieth
Medal Starters Box, Princes St, Monifieth, Angus, DD5 4AW
☎(01382) 532678, Fax 535553, Pro 532945, Sec 535553
5 miles E of Dundee on coast.
Links course.
Pro Ian McLeod; Founded 1850
Medal: 18 holes, 6655 yards, S.S.S. 72
⚑ Welcome.
⌐ WD £30; WE £36.
☞ Welcome; composite tickets available with Ashludie Course (18 holes, 5123 yards, par 68).
🍽 Clubhouse facilities.

St Andrews

Can there be a more fitting home for the first Open Championship of the new Millennium than the course that many regard as the spiritual home of the game? It is the course that will no doubt persuade Jack Nicklaus back across the Atlantic for one final crack at the Claret Jug. The name conjures all sorts of magical images of the most noble of games played on the most noble of courses.

Legend insists that golf has been played on the links of Fife for more than 600 years but it was not until 1873, and the 13th Open championship, that the famous tournament was first played at St Andrews.

Although home to the Royal and Ancient Golf Club, the course itself is owned by the St Andrews Trust and it is possible to play the famous Old Course. However, demand is high and so are the green fees, so many choose to enjoy St Andrews golf on several of the other courses in the area. In all there are five courses in St Andrews.

Until 1912 it was free of charge to all residents, but the ever-increasing interest in the game has pushed prices sky-high and the chances of playing in this Open championship year are remote.

Originally the Old Course had 12 holes and golfers played rounds consisting of 22 holes. In 1764 the first four holes were turned into two and the round cut down to 18, thus setting the standard for the number of holes to be played worldwide.

More than any other great links course, the nature of St Andrews can be altered by the ferocity of the wind blowing off St Andrews Bay. It has been ripped up, most breathtakingly by Curtis Strange in 1987 when he shot a brilliant 62. But there was still a touch of awe in his voice when he told the course designers of the world that St Andrews still set the standards.

The first seven at St Andrews all head out along the coast before looping inland and then completing the journey home. And it is in those closing holes where legends are made and Open Championships are won and lost. The Road Hole is described as one of the most testing in golf championships.

If driving the old railway sheds is not bad enough then the second shot to a tight green protected by treacherous bunkers provides the real hazard with the path and wall so close to the back of the small green. It was here that in 1984 Tom Watson's hold on the Open Championship was broken for good.

In 1995 the play-off for the Open between John Daly and Costantino Rocca was effectively settled by the bunker which guarded the front edge of the green which, according to Bernard Darwin, "eats into the very vitals" of the green. Whatever happens, the 17th is anything but an ordinary golf hole.

It is a course of legends. Few will forget the last time the Open came to St Andrews in 1995 with the emotional farewell as Arnold Palmer wandered across the bridge of the Swilken Burn waving a long and heartfelt thank you to the thousands who had turned up just to see Arnie. Few who were there that day can remember who was leading but they remember saying goodbye to Arnie.

St Andrews is that sort of place but there are other courses in the area that can be enjoyable when you travel north to watch the Open.

It is always worth looking in at the Crail Golfing Society or at Leven and Lundin, who will provide the courses for the 2000 Open qualifying programme. Also worth playing is Monifieth, another classic links course close by. — **CG**

Practice range.
↘ Panmure packages available;
Woodlands.

9C 74 Montrose Links Trust

Traill Drive, Montrose, Angus, DD10
8SW
☎(01674) 672634, Fax 671800, Sec
672932
Turn off Dundee-Aberdeen A90 at
Brechin and take A935 to Montrose.
Links course.
Founded 1562
18 holes, 6470 yards, S.S.S. 71
† Welcome; but not before 2.30pm
Sat or 10am on Sun.
⌐ WD £25; WE £30.
⌐ Welcome by prior arrangement;
same restrictions as for visitors;
facilities available at the 3 clubs
adjacent to courses (Montrose
Caledonia GC (01674) 672313;
Montrose Mercantile GC 672408;
Royal Montrose 672376); also
Broomfield course: 4788 yards, par
66/67.
†⊚! Catering available at member
clubs.
↘ Park Hotel; Links.

9C 75 Muckhart

Drumburn Rd, Muckhart, by Dollar,
Clackmannanshire, FK14 7JH
☎(01259) 781423, Pro 781493
Off A91 6 miles E of Alloa; S of
Muckhart; signposted.
Heathland course on rising ground.
Pro Keith Salmoni; Founded
1908/1971
27 holes, 6034 yards, S.S.S. 69
† Welcome.
⌐ WD £17; WE £25.
⌐ Welcome; catering by
arrangement; £10 addition for playing
9-hole course.
†⊚! Full catering and bar facilities.

9C 76 Murrayshall

Murrayshall Country House Hotel,
Scone, Perthshire, PH2 7PH
☎(01738) 551171, Fax 552595, Pro
552784
On A94 Cupar-Angus road 4 miles
from Perth by Scone.
Parkland course.
Pro Alan Reid; Founded 1981
Designed by J. Hamilton Stutt
18 holes, 6441 yards, S.S.S. 72
† Welcome.
⌐ WD £22; WE £27.
⌐ Welcome; packages by
arrangement; from £22.

†⊚! Full facilities and hotel bar and
restaurants.
↘ Murrayshall on site.

9C 77 Muthill

Peat Rd, Muthill, by Crieff, Perthshire,
PH5 2DA
☎(01764) 681523
From Crieff course is on right before
Muthill at Bowling Green.
Parkland course.
Founded 1935
9 holes, 4700 yards, S.S.S. 63
† Welcome.
⌐ WD £13; WE £16.
⌐ Welcome but booking essential.
†⊚! Meals but no bar.
↘ Drummond Arms.

9C 78 North Inch

Perth & Kinross Council, 3 High
Street, Perth, Perthshire, PH1 5JU
☎(01738) 475000, Pro 636481
N of Perth adjacent to Gannochy
Trust Sports Complex.
Tree-lined course running alongside
river.
18 holes, 5178 yards, S.S.S. 65
† Welcome.
⌐ WD £4.20; WE £5.25.
⌐ Welcome by prior arrangement;
some summer restrictions apply.
†⊚! Catering at Bell's Sports
Complex.

9C 79 Panmure

Burnside Road, Barry, Angus, DD7
7RT
☎(01241) 853120, Fax 859737, Pro
852460, Sec 855120
Off A930 2 miles W of Carnoustie.
Seaside course.
Pro Neil MacKintoch; Founded 1845
18 holes, 6317 yards, S.S.S. 71
† Welcome except for Sat.
⌐ WD £33; WE £33.
⌐ Welcome by arrangement,
catering packages by arrangement;
day ticket £49; from £30.
†⊚! Full facilities.
Practice range.
↘ Carlogie; Panmure; Station;
Woodlands.

9C 80 Pitlochry

Golf Course Rd, Pitlochry, Perthshire,
PH16 5QY
☎(01796) 472792
A9 to Pitlochry then via Atholl Rd,
Larchwood Rd to Golf Course road.
Hill course.

9C 83 St Andrews

St Andrews Links Management
Committee, Pilmour Cottage, St
Andrews, Fife, KY16 9JA
☎(01334) 466666, Fax 477036,
Pro 475757, Sec 475757, Bar/Rest
473107
60 miles north of Edinburgh via
A91 to St Andrews; turning to
course is on the left before the
town; by rail to Leuchars on
Edinburgh-Dundee main line.
⌐ Apply for details
⌐ Welcome; terms on application.
†⊚! Clubhouse facilities and in
local hotels.
↘ Full range in St Andrews from
B&B to international standard.

Old Course

18 holes, 6566 yards, S.S.S. 72
Most famous Championship links
in the world.
Founded 1400
Designed by Nature and Tom
Morris, A. Robertson, A.
MacKenzie
† Welcome with handicap certs;
no play on Sun.

Balgove Course

9 holes, 1530 yards
Founded 1974
† Welcome; children under 16
reduced prices.
⌐ WD £7; WE £7.

Eden Course

18 holes, 6112 yards, S.S.S. 70
Founded 1914
Designed by HS Colt
† Public.

Jubilee Course

18 holes, 6805 yards, S.S.S. 72
Founded 1897/1989
Designed by J Angus/ Donald
Steel (1989)
† Welcome.

New Course

18 holes, 6604 yards, S.S.S. 72
Founded 1895
Designed by Old Tom Morris
† Welcome.

Strathtyrum Course

18 holes, 5094 yards, S.S.S. 65
Founded 1993
Designed by Donald Steel
† Welcome.

Pro George Hampton; Founded 1908
Designed by Willie Fernie of Troon;
Modernised by Major C. Hut
18 holes, 5811 yards, S.S.S. 69
† Welcome by arrangement with the
Pro.
⌶ Terms on application.
⌁Welcome by arrangement;
catering by arrangement with
Steward; terms on application.
⦾ Full clubhouse facilities.

9C 81 **Pitreavie (Dunfermline)**
Queensferry Rd, Dunfermline, Fife,
KY11 5PR
☎(01383) 722591, Fax 722591, Pro
723151
M90 N of Forth Road Bridge; 3rd exit
signposted Dunfermline; club 3 miles.
Parkland course.
Pro Colin Mitchell; Founded 1922
Designed by Dr A. MacKenzie
18 holes, 6032 yards, S.S.S. 69
† Welcome.
⌶ WD £19; WE £26.
⌁Welcome; catering by
arrangement; terms on application.
⦾ Full clubhouse facilities.
⌁ Pitbauchlie House; King Malcolm.

9C 82 **Polmont**　　　　　　ℭ
Manuelrigg Maddiston, by Falkirk,
Stirlingshire, FK2 0LS
☎(01324) 711277
4 miles S of Falkirk, 1st right after
Fire Brigade HQ.
Undulating parkland course.
Founded 1904
9 holes, 6062 yards, S.S.S. 69
† Welcome except on Sat.
⌶ WD £8; WE £14.
⌁Welcome by prior arrangement;
catering by arrangement with Sec;
from £14.
⦾ Clubhouse facilities.
⌁ Inchrya Grange; Polmont.

9C 84 **St Fillans**
South Loch Earn Rd, St Fillans,
Perthshire, PH6 2NJ
☎(01764) 685312
On A85 at E end of the village.
Parkland course; Founded 1903
Designed by W Auchterlonie
9 holes, 5796 yards, S.S.S. 67
† Welcome.
⌶ WD £12; WE £16.
⌁Welcome by arrangement;
maximum 16; catering by
arrangement; from £12.
⦾ Catering facilities; no bar.

⌁ Achray; Four Seasons;
Drummond Arms.

9C 85 **St Michaels**　　　ℭ
Leuchars, Fife, KY16 0DX
☎(01334) 839365, Fax 838666, Sec
838666
5 miles from St Andrews on main
road to Dundee.
Undulating parkland course.
Founded 1903
18 holes, 5802 yards, S.S.S. 68
† Welcome except before 12 noon
on Sun.
⌶ WD £18; WE £20.
⌁Welcome by written prior
arrangement; restrictions apply on
Sun; 36 holes of golf and full
catering.
⦾ Full facilities.
⌁ St Michaels Inn; many in St
Andrews.

9C 86 **Saline**
Kinneddar Hill, Saline, Fife, KY12 9LT
☎(01383) 852591, Sec 852344
Course is five miles north-west of
Dunfermline.
Hillside course.
Founded 1912
9 holes, 5304 yards, S.S.S. 66
† Welcome except Sat.
⌶ WD £9; WE £11.
⌁Welcome WD and Sun only;
maximum 24; catering packages by
prior arrangement; terms on
application.
⦾ Full catering.
⌁ Saline Castle; Campbell;
Pitbauchly.

9C 87 **Scoonie**
North Links, Leven, Fife, KY8 4SP
☎(01333) 307007, Fax 307008, Pro
427437
10 miles SW of St Andrews.
Parkland course.
Founded 1951
18 holes, 4979 yards, S.S.S. 65
† Welcome by arrangement with
Sec except Thurs and Sat.
⌶ WD on application.
⌁Welcome by appointment with
Sec; groups of 12-30; catering by
arrangement; terms on application.
⦾ Full clubhouse facilities.
⌁ Caledonian.

9C 88 **Scotscraig**
Golf Rd, Tayport, Fife, DD6 9DZ
☎(01382) 552515, Pro 552855

On B946 3 miles from S end of Tay
Road Bridge.
Links/seaside course.
Pro Stuart Campbell; Founded 1817
18 holes, 6550 yards, S.S.S. 72
† Welcome WD and by prior
arrangement at WE.
⌶ WD £30; WE £35.
⌁Welcome by prior arrangement;
packages by arrangement; day
tickets WD £40; WE £45; from £30.
⦾ Full catering facilities.
⌁ Seymour; Scores; Rusacks;
Russell.

9C 89 **Stirling**
Queens Rd, Stirling, Stirlingshire,
FK8 3AA
☎(01786) 464098, Pro 471490
On A811 1 mile W of town.
Parkland course.
Pro Ian Collins; Founded 1869
Designed by J Braid/H Cotton
18 holes, 6438 yards, S.S.S. 71
† Welcome WD; some WE
restrictions.
⌶ WD £25; WE £25.
⌁Welcome WD by prior
arrangement; day ticket £35; catering
by arrangement; pool table; from £20.
⦾ Full clubhouse facilities.
⌁ Golden Lion.

9C 90 **Strathendrick**
Glasgow Rd, Drymen, Stirlingshire,
G63 0AA
☎(01360) 660695
Off A811 1 mile S of Drymen; 17
miles N W of Glasgow.
Hilly moorland course.
Founded 1901
9 holes, 5116 yards, S.S.S. 64
† Welcome WD 8.30am-2.30pm
May-Sept.
⌶ WD £12.
⌁Limited access by prior
arrangement; terms on application.
⦾ None.
⌁ Buchanan Arms; Winnock.

9C 91 **Strathtay**
Lyon Cottage, Strathtay, Perthshire
PH9 0PG
☎(01887) 840211
4 miles W of Ballinlug on A827.
Inland course.
9 holes, 4082 yards, S.S.S. 63
† Welcome; restrictions May-Sept
on Sunday afternoons and Monday
evenings.
⌶ £10.
⌁By prior arrangement.

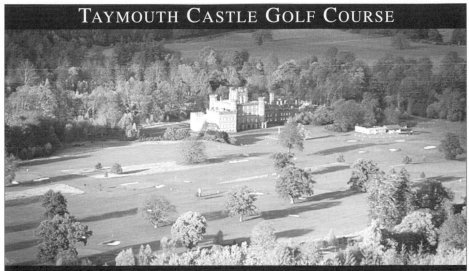

9C 92 Taymouth Castle ☏
Kenmore, by Aberfeldy, Tayside,
PH15 2NT
☎ (01887) 830228, Fax 830228,
Bar/Rest 830397
Course is five miles west of Aberfeldy
on the A827.
Parkland course.
Pro Alex Marshall; Founded 1923
Designed by James Braid
18 holes, 6066 yards, S.S.S. 69
♦ Welcome.
🔟 WD £20; WE £22.
⌁ Welcome by prior arrangement;
packages available; from £20.
🍽 Full clubhouse facilities.
⌐ Kenmore.

9C 93 Thornton
Station Rd, Thornton, Fife, KY1 4DW
☎ (01592) 771111, Fax 774955, Pro
771173, Bar/Rest 771161
1 mile off the A92 road at the
Redhouse roundabout midway
between Kirkcaldy and Glenrothes.
Parkland course.
Founded 1921
Designed by Members
18 holes, 6177 yards, S.S.S. 69
♦ Welcome.
🔟 Terms on application.

⌁ Welcome; catering packages by
arrangement.
🍽 Full clubhouse facilities; new
clubhouse opened in Dec 1997.
⌐ Crown, Thornton; Rescobie;
Albany, both Glenrothes; Royal, Dean
Park, both Kirkcaldy.

9C 94 Tillicoultry
Alva Rd, Tillicoultry, FK13 6BL
☎ (01259) 750124
9 miles E of Stirling on the A91.
Undulating parkland course.
Founded 1899
Designed by Peter Robertson, Braids
Hill G.C. Edinburgh
9 holes, 5358 yards, S.S.S. 66
♦ Welcome by arrangement.
🔟 WD £12; WE £18.
⌁ Welcome by arrangement with
Sec; catering by prior arrangement;
terms on application.
🍽 Restaurant and bar facilities.

9C 95 Tulliallan
Alloa Rd, Kincardine on Forth, FK10
4BB
☎ (01259) 730396, Pro 730798
0.5 miles N of the Kincardine Bridge
on the Alloa road.

Parkland course.
Pro Stephen Kelly; Founded 1902
18 holes, 5965 yards, S.S.S. 69
♦ Welcome by arrangement.
🔟 WD £15; WE £20.
⌁ Welcome by prior arrangement
except Sat; day tickets WD: £27.50;
WE: £35; WD maximum group of 40;
Sun max group of 24; from £15;
catering available with booking in
advance.
🍽 Full clubhouse facilities.
⌐ Powfoulis Manor.

9C 96 Whitemoss
Whitemoss Road, Dunning,
Perthshire, PH2 0QX
☎ (01738) 730300, Fax 730300
1 mile off the A9; 2 miles past the
Gleneagles Hotel.
Parkland course.
Founded 1994
18 holes, 5955 yards, S.S.S. 68
♦ Welcome by arrangement.
🔟 WD £15; WE £15.
⌁ Welcome by prior arrangement;
catering packages available by prior
arrangement; day tickets £20; from
£15.
🍽 Full facilities.
⌐ Gleneagles.

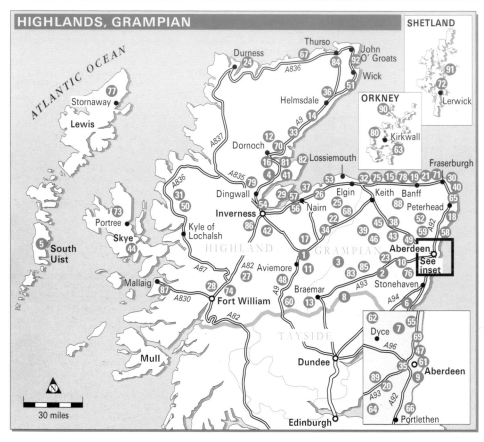

HIGHLANDS, GRAMPIAN

KEY		18	Cruden Bay	36	Helmsdale	55	Murcar	74	Spean Bridge
1	Abernethy	19	Cullen	37	Hopeman	56	Nairn	75	Spey Bay
2	Aboyne	20	Deeside	38	Huntly	57	Nairn Dunbar	76	Stonehaven
3	Alford	21	Duff House Royal	39	Insch	58	Newburgh-on-Ythan	77	Stornoway
4	Alness	22	Dufftown	40	Inverallochy	59	Newmachar	78	Strathlene
5	Askernish	23	Dunecht House	41	Invergordon	60	Newtonmore	79	Strathpeffer Spa
6	Auchenblae	24	Durness	42	Inverness	61	Northern	80	Stromness
7	Auchmill	25	Elgin	43	Inverurie	62	Oldmeldrum	81	Tain
8	Ballater	26	Forres	44	Isle of Skye	63	Orkney	82	Tarbat
9	Balnagask	27	Fort Augustus	45	Keith	64	Peterculter	83	Tarland
10	Banchory	28	Fort William	46	Kemnay	65	Peterhead	84	Thurso
11	Boat of Garten	29	Fortrose and	47	King's Links	66	Portlethen	85	Torphins
12	Bonar Bridge &		Rosemarkie	48	Kingussie	67	Reay	86	Torvean
	Ardgay	30	Fraserburgh	49	Kintore	68	Rothes	87	Traigh Golf Course
13	Braemar	31	Gairloch	50	Lochcarron	69	Royal Aberdeen	88	Turriff
14	Brora	32	Garmouth & Kingston	51	Lybster	70	Royal Dornoch	89	Westhill
15	Buckpool (Buckie)	33	Golspie	52	McDonald	71	Royal Tarlair	90	Westray
16	Carnegie Club	34	Grantown-on-Spey	53	Moray	72	Shetland	91	Whalsay
17	Carrbridge	35	Hazlehead	54	Muir of Ord	73	Skeabost	92	Wick

9D 1 Abernethy
Nethybridge, Inverness-shire, PH25
3DE
☎(01479) 821305; Sec 872479
On B970 Grantown-on-Spey to Boat
of Garten road.

Undulating course with views of Spey
valley.
Founded 1893
9 holes, 4986 yards, S.S.S. 66
♁ Welcome with restrictions applying
on Sun.

⌇ WD £12; WE £16.
⌔ Welcome by arrangement with
Sec; packages available; terms on
application.
⍢ Full clubhouse facilities in
season.

Nethybridge; Mountview; Heatherbrae.

9D 2 Aboyne

Formaston Park, Aboyne, Aberdeenshire, AB34 5HP
☎(013398) 86328, Sec 87078, Pro 86328
Course is off the A93 from Aberdeen; take first turning on right after entering village.
Undulating parkland course.
Pro Ennis Wright; Founded 1883
18 holes, 5975 yards, S.S.S. 69
† Welcome.
☐ WD £18; WE £22.
☞Welcome by prior arrangement except Sun; day tickets available (WD £24, WE £28); catering packages by arrangement between April and October; from £18.
🍽 Full facilities during summer.
☞ Charleston; Birse Lodge; Huntly Arms.

9D 3 Alford

Montgarrie Rd, Alford, AB33 8AE
☎(019755) 62178, Fax 62178
On A944 in the village of Alford 25 miles W of Aberdeen.
Parkland course.
Founded 1982
Designed by David Hurd
18 holes, 5402 yards, S.S.S. 65
† Welcome; some restrictions on club comp days.
☐ WD £13; WE £21.
☞Welcome by prior arrangement; day tickets available (WD £19, WE £27); shotgun starts can be organised for a minimum of 50 players; catering packages by prior arrangement; from £13.
🍽 Full clubhouse facilities available.
☞ Kildrummy Castle; Forbes Arms.

9D 4 Alness

Ardross Rd, Alness, Ross-shire
☎(01349) 883877
Course is on the A9 10 miles north of Dingwall.
Founded 1904
Designed by John Sutherland
18 holes, 500 yards, S.S.S. 64
† Welcome except 4.30pm-7.30pm Mon.
☐ Terms upon application.
☞Welcome by prior arrangement; catering by prior arrangement; terms on application.
🍽 By prior arrangement.
☞ Commercial Hotel.

9D 5 Askernish

Lochboisdale, Askernish, South Uist, Western Isles, HS81 5SY
☎Niel Elliot (01878) 700298
Take the ferry from Oban to Lochboisdale; course is 5 miles N of Lochboisdale.
Links course; most Western course in Scotland; 18 tees.
Founded 1891
Designed by Tom Morris
18 holes, 5042 yards, S.S.S. 67
† Welcome.
☐ WD £10; WE £10.
☞Welcome; terms available on application.
🍽 By prior arrangement.
☞ Lochboisdale Hotel.

9D 6 Auchenblae

Myreside, Auchenblae, Laurencekirk, Kincardineshire, AB30 1BU
☎(01561) 320002
Course is two miles west of Fordoun off the A94.
Parkland course.
9 holes, 4496 yards, S.S.S. 63
† Welcome except Wed and Fri evenings between 5.30pm-9pm.
☐ WD £8; WE £10.
☞Welcome WD by prior arrangement; limited catering; terms on application.
🍽 Village hotels provide catering.
☞ Drumtochty; Thistle.

9D 7 Auchmill

Bonny View, Auchmill, AB16 7FQ
☎(01224) 715214
5 miles N of Aberdeen.
Municipal parkland course.
18 holes, 5560 yards, S.S.S. 69
† Welcome.
☐ WD £6.50; WE £6.50.
☞Only with prior arrangement through Council.
🍽 Limited.

9D 8 Ballater ⚷

Victoria Rd, Ballater, Aberdeenshire, AB35 5QX
☎(013397) 55567, Fax 55057, Pro 55658, Bar/Rest 56241
42 miles W of Aberdeen on the A93.
Heath/parkland course.
Pro Billy Yule; Founded 1891
Designed by James Braid/H Vardon
18 holes, 6112 yards, S.S.S. 69
† Welcome by arrangement.
☐ Terms on application.
☞Welcome by arrangement; catering and day rates; from £18.

🍽 Bar and catering facilities.
☞ Club can provide comprehensive list.

9D 9 Balnagask

St Fitticks Rd, Balnagask, Aberdeen, ☎(01224) 876407
2 miles SE of the city.
Municipal seaside course.
Founded 1955
Designed by Hawtree & Son
18 holes, 5986 yards, S.S.S. 69
† Welcome.
☐ WD £9; WE £11.25.
☞Welcome by prior arrangement with the council.
🍽 By arrangement with the council.
☞ Caledonian.

9D 10 Banchory

Kinneskie Rd, Banchory, Kincardineshire, AB31 3TA
☎(01330) 822365, Fax 822491, Pro 822447, Bar/Rest 822274
Course is 100 yards off the A93, the main Aberdeen to Braemar road.
Parkland course; 16th hole, Doo'cot, is 88 yards.
Pro David Naylor; Founded 1905
18 holes, 5775 yards, S.S.S. 68
† Welcome; booking advisable on Thurs and at WE.
☐ WD £19; WE £21.
☞Welcome; catering packages by prior arrangement; terms on application.
🍽 Full catering, lounge and dining room facilities.
☞ Burnett Arms; Tor-na-coille; Banchory Lodge.

9D 11 Boat of Garten

Boat of Garten, Inverness-shire, PH24 3BQ
☎(01479) 831282, Fax 831523, Bar/Rest 831731
2 miles E of A9 30 miles S of Inverness.
Heathland course.
Pro James Ingram; Founded 1898
Designed by James Braid
18 holes, 5866 yards, S.S.S. 69
† Welcome WD 9.30am-6pm; WE 10am-4pm.
☐ WD £23; WE £28.
☞Welcome by prior arrangement; day tickets available (WD £28, WE £33); catering by arrangement; separate changing rooms available; from £23.
🍽 Full clubhouse facilities.
☞ The Boat; Craigand.

9D 12 **Bonar Bridge & Ardgay**

Market Stance, Migdale Rd, Bonar Bridge, Sutherland, IV24 3EJ
☎ (01863) 766199, Fax 766738, Sec 766375
Off A836 at Bonar Bridge 0.5 miles up Migdale Rd; 12 miles W of Dornoch.
Parkland course.
Founded 1904
9 holes, 5284 yards, S.S.S. 63
♦ Welcome.
Ⅰ WD £12; WE £12.
⚡ Welcome WD by prior arrangement; terms available on application.
🍽 Clubhouse facilities in season.

9D 13 **Braemar** ℃

Cluniebank Rd, Braemar, Aberdeenshire, AB35 5XX
☎ (013397) 41618, Sec (01224) 704471
Signposted from the village centre; turn left opposite Fife Arms Hotel.
Parkland course.
Founded 1902
Designed by Joe Anderson
18 holes, 4935 yards, S.S.S. 64
♦ Welcome.
Ⅰ WD £14; WE £17.
⚡ Welcome; packages include 36 holes of golf and catering; from £20; WE £32.
🍽 Full clubhouse facilities.
⚡ Invercauld Arms; Fife Arms; Moorfield House.

9D 14 **Brora**

43 Golf Rd, Brora, Sutherland, KW9 6QS
☎ (01408) 621417, Fax 622157, Pro 621473
On A9 N of Inverness; turn right over bridge in centre of Brora.
Traditional links course.
Founded 1891
Designed by James Braid
18 holes, 6110 yards, S.S.S. 69
♦ Welcome.
Ⅰ WD £20; WE £20.
⚡ Welcome by prior arrangement; on application; from £20.
🍽 Clubhouse facilities.
Practice range.
⚡ Royal Marine; Links.

9D 15 **Buckpool (Buckie)**

Barhill Rd, Buckie, Banffshire, AB56 1DU
☎ (01542) 832236, Fax 832236

Turn off the A98 at Buckpool.
Links course.
Founded 1933/65
Designed by Hawtree & Taylor
18 holes, 6257 yards, S.S.S. 70
♦ Welcome.
Ⅰ WD £12; WE £15.
⚡ Welcome by prior arrangement; packages include 36 holes of golf with full catering; WE discounts for groups of more than 20; from £22.
🍽 Full clubhouse facilities.
⚡ Marine, Buckie.

9D 16 **Carnegie Club**

Skibo Castle, Dornoch, Sutherland, IV25 3RQ
☎ (01862) 894600, Fax 894601, Pro 881260
Take A9 towards Wick from Inverness; first left after Dornoch Bridge signposted Meikle Ferry North; continue for 1 mile and turn right at Green Sheds.
Links course; new 9-hole parkland course (members course) opens 1998.
Pro David Thompson; Founded 1994
Designed by Donald Steel
18 holes, 6671 yards, S.S.S. 72
♦ WD only teeing off between 11am-12 noon; by arrangement only.
Ⅰ WD £130.
⚡ WD only teeing off between 11am-12 noon; includes soup, sandwiches and house wine; £130.
🍽 Full facilities in the club.
⚡ Morangie House; Mansfield House, both Tain; Royal Golf; Burghfield, both Dornoch.

9D 17 **Carrbridge**

Inverness Rd, Carrbridge, Inverness-shire, PH23 3AU
☎ (01479) 841623, Sec 841506
Off A9 25 miles S of Inverness.
Parkland course/heathland course.
Founded 1980
9 holes, 5402 yards, S.S.S. 68
♦ Welcome.
Ⅰ WD £12; WE £13.
⚡ Limited to small groups.
🍽 Tea, coffee and snacks.from April-October.
⚡ Contact Carrbridge Tourist Association.

9D 18 **Cruden Bay**

Aulton Rd, Cruden Bay, Peterhead, Aberdeenshire, AB42 7NN
☎ (01779) 812285, Fax 812945, Pro 812414

Course is off the A90 10 miles from Peterhead; or from Aberdeen off the A90 and then the A975.
Championship links course.
Pro Robbie Stewart; Founded 1899
Designed by Tom Morris & Archie Simpson
Main course: 18 holes, 6395 yards, S.S.S. 72; St Olaf: 9 holes, 5106 yards, S.S.S. 65
♦ Welcome; restrictions until after 9.30am Mon; after 10.30am Tues and at WE (Main); Welcome (St Olaf).
Ⅰ WD £45, WE £55 (Main); WD £15, WE £20 (St Olaf).
⚡ Welcome WD except Wed by prior arrangement; handicap certs needed; minimum 16 players; catering by prior arrangement; from £25 (Main); Welcome (St Olaf).
🍽 Full clubhouse facilities.
Practice range, covered bays.
⚡ Club can provide list.

9D 19 **Cullen**

The Links, Cullen, Buckie, Banffshire, AB56 2UU
☎ (01542) 840685, Sec 840174
Off the A98 at the western end of the town on the Moray Firth coastline.
Traditional links course with natural rock landscaping.
Founded 1879.
Designed by Tom Morris (original 9 holes); Charles Neaves
18 holes, 4610 yards, S.S.S. 62
♦ Welcome WD; some restrictions on WE and July/August.
Ⅰ Terms on application.
⚡ Welcome by prior arrangement; restrictions on Wed and Sat; day tickets available; catering packages by arrangement; from £10.
🍽 Clubhouse catering and bar.
⚡ Cullen Bay; Royal Oak; Bayview; Three Kings; Grant Arms; Seafield Arms; Waverley.

9D 20 **Deeside**

Golf Rd, Bieldside, Aberdeen, Aberdeenshire, AB15 9DL
☎ (01224) 869457, Pro 861041
Course is on the A93 three miles west of Aberdeen.
Parkland course.
Pro F J Coutts; Founded 1903
18 holes, 5971 yards, S.S.S. 70
♦ Welcome after 9am WD and 4pm Sat; letter of introduction needed.
Ⅰ WD £25; WE £30.
⚡ Welcome Thurs only by arrangement; catering packages by arrangement; terms on application.

◉ Full facilities.
⌐ Cults; Bieldside Inn.

9D 21 Duff House Royal
The Banyards, Banff, Banffshire,
AB45 3SX
☎ (01261) 812062, Pro 812075
On A98.
Parkland course.
Pro R Strachan; Founded 1909
Designed by Dr A. & Major C.A.
MacKenzie
18 holes, 6161 yards, S.S.S. 70
† Welcome except before 11am and
between 12.30pm-3.30pm WE and in
July/August.
⌐ WD £18; WE £24.
⌐ Welcome by prior arrangement;
catering and day packages by
application; terms on application.
◉ Full facilities.
⌐ Banff Springs; County; Fife
Lodge.

9D 22 Dufftown
Tomintoul Road, Dufftown, Keith,
Banffshire, AB55 4BX
☎ (01340) 820325, Fax 820325, Sec
820325
On A9009 1 mile S of Dufftown.
Moor/parkland course; Founded 1896
Designed by A Simpson
18 holes, 5308 yards, S.S.S. 67
† Welcome.
⌐ WD £10; WE £10.
⌐ Welcome by prior arrangement;
discounts for groups of more than 12;
catering by prior arrangement; from
£10.
◉ Full clubhouse facilities.
⌐ Fife Arms; Craigellachie.

9D 23 Dunecht House
Dunecht, Skene, Aberdeenshire, AB3
7AX
☎ (01224)
Course on B994 to Dunecht.
Inland wooded course.
Founded 1925
9 holes, 6270 yards, S.S.S. 70
† Members only.
⌐ Terms on application.

9D 24 Durness
Balnakeil, Durness, Sutherland, IV27
4PN
☎ (01971) 511364
57 miles NW of Lairg on A838; turn
left in village square.
Links/parkland course.
Founded 1988

Designed by F Keith, L Ross,
I Morrison
9 holes, 5555 yards, S.S.S. 69
† Welcome.
⌐ Terms on application.
⌐ Welcome; terms available on
application.
◉ Clubhouse facilities.
⌐ Cape Wrath; Parkhill; Rhiconich.

9D 25 Elgin
Hardhillock, Birnie Rd, Elgin, Moray,
IV30 3SX
☎ (01343) 542338, Fax 542341, Pro
542884
On A941 Birnie road.
Parkland course.
Pro Ian Rodger; Founded 1906
Designed by John MacPherson
18 holes, 6411 yards, S.S.S. 71
† Welcome.
⌐ WD £22; WE £28.
⌐ Welcome by prior arrangement
with Sec David Black; discounts for
larger groups; catering by
arrangement; from £22.
◉ Clubhouse bar and catering.
⌐ Sunninghill; Laichmoray; Eight
Acres; Mansion House; Rothes Glen.

9D 26 Forres
Muiryshade, Forres, IV36 0RD
☎ (01309) 672949, Fax 672250, Pro
672250
On A96 26 miles E of Inverness; 1
mile S of Forres.
Parkland course.
Pro Sandy Aird; Founded 1889
Designed by James Braid
18 holes, 6141 yards, S.S.S. 69
† Welcome by prior arrangement
with the Professional.
⌐ WD £18; WE £18.
⌐ Welcome by prior arrangement;
maximum number 60; terms on
application.
◉ Full clubhouse facilities.
⌐ Ramnee.

9D 27 Fort Augustus
Markethill, Fort Augustus, Inverness-
shire, PH32 4DT
☎ (01320) 366660, Sec 366660
0.75 miles S of Fort Augustus on A82
Moorland course.
Founded 1905
Designed by Dr Lean
9 holes, 5452 yards, S.S.S. 67
† Welcome.
⌐ WD £10; WE £10.
⌐ Welcome by prior arrangement; on
application; from £8.

◉ Limited.
⌐ Lovat Arms; Richmond House.

9D 28 Fort William
North Rd, Torlundy, Inverness-shire,
PH33 6SN
☎ (01397) 704464, Fax 705893, Sec
702404
On A82 2 miles N of Fort William.
Parkland course.
Founded 1975
Designed by J.R. Stutt
18 holes, 6217 yards, S.S.S. 71
† Welcome.
⌐ WD £15; WE £15.
⌐ Welcome by arrangement; golf
packages only; no catering; £15.
◉ Bar snacks available.
⌐ Milton; Moorings.

9D 29 Fortrose & Rosemarkie
Ness Rd East, Fortrose, Ross-shire,
IV10 8SE
☎ (01381) 620529, Fax 620529, Pro
620529
Off A832 to Fortrose off the A9 at
Tope roundabout.
Links course on headland; stunning
views.
Founded 1888
Redesigned by James Braid
18 holes, 5858 yards, S.S.S. 69
† Welcome.
⌐ WD £20; WE £25.
⌐ Welcome by prior arrangement
with Sec; day tickets available (WD
£30, WE £35); from £20.
◉ Clubhouse facilities.
⌐ Royal; Kinkell House.

9D 30 Fraserburgh
Philnorth, Fraserburgh,
Aberdeenshire, AB43 8TL
☎ (01346) 516616, Pro 517898,
Bar/Rest 518287
✉ fburghgolg@aol.com
3 of first roundabout when entering
Fraserburgh and then first right.
Links course.
Founded 1881
Designed by James Braid
27 holes, 6278 yards, S.S.S. 70
† Welcome.
⌐ WD £15; WE £25.
⌐ Welcome by prior arrangement;
catering packages by arrangement;
also 9-hole course, 4800 yards, par
64; from £15.
◉ Bar and dining room facilities
available.
⌐ Royal; Tufted Duck, both
Fraserburgh.

9D 31 **Gairloch**

Gairloch, Ross-shire, IV21 2BE
☎(01445) 712407, Sec 741327
On A832 60 miles W of Inverness.
Seaside course with stunning views;
7th hole, An Dun, is 91 yards.
Founded 1898
Designed by Captain A W Burgess
9 holes, 4514 yards, S.S.S. 64
† Welcome.
ↆ WD £15; WE £15.
⤴Welcome by prior arrangement;
weekly ticket: £49; catering by prior
arrangement; from £15.
🍽 Clubhouse facilities.
⌐ Gairloch; Myrtle Bank Millcroft;
Old Inn; Gairloch Sands.

9D 32 **Garmouth & Kingston** ⓣ

Spey St, Garmouth, Morayshire, IV32
7NJ
☎(01343) 870388, Fax 870388, Sec
870388
3 miles N of A96 at Mosstodloch
cross roads.
Links/parkland course.
Founded 1932
Designed by George Smith
18 holes, 5874 yards, S.S.S. 69
† Welcome by prior arrangement.
ↆ Terms on application.
⤴Welcome by prior arrangement;
catering by arrangement; games
room; terms on application.
🍽 Bar and dining room facilities.
⌐ Garmouth; Gordon Arms,
Fochabers.

9D 33 **Golspie**

Ferry Rd, Golspie, Sutherland, KW10
6ST
☎(01408) 633266, Fax 633393
On A9 to Golspie.
Links course.
Founded 1889
Designed by James Braid
18 holes, 5890 yards, S.S.S. 68
† Welcome.
ↆ WD £20; WE £20.
⤴Welcome by prior arrangement;
day tickets: WD £25; WE £25;
discounts for groups; catering by
arrangement; from £20.
🍽 Bar and catering facilities.
⌐ Stags Head; Golf Links; Ben
Bhraggie; Sutherland Arms.

9D 34 **Grantown-on-Spey**

Golf Course Rd, Grantown-on-Spey,
Morayshire, PH26 3HY
☎(01479) 872079, Fax 873725, Pro
872079

On NE of town, signposted off the
Grantown-Nairn/Forres road.
Parkland/woodland course.
Pro to be appointed; Founded 1890
Designed by Willie Park /James
Braid/AC Brown
18 holes, 5710 yards, S.S.S. 68
† Welcome except before 10am at
WE.
ↆ WD £20; WE £25.
⤴Welcome by prior arrangement
except before 10am at WE; catering
by arrangement; from £20.
🍽 Full bar and catering facilities.
Practice range.
⌐ Culdearn House; Garth;
Muckrach Lodge.

9D 35 **Hazlehead**

Hazlehead Park, Aberdeen, AB15
8BD
☎(01224) 310711, Sec 310711
Course is four miles north-west of the
city centre.
Municipal moorland courses.
Pro Alistair Smith
18 holes, 6304 yards, S.S.S. 68
† Welcome.
ↆ WD £9; WE 25.
⤴Apply to council; two other
courses: 18 holes, 6045 yards, S.S.S.
68; 9 holes, 2770 yards, S.S.S. 34;
terms on application.
🍽 Available nearby.
⌐ Treetops; Belvedere; Queens.

9D 36 **Helmsdale**

Golf Rd, Helmsdale, Sutherland, KW8
6JA
☎(01431) 821650
Off A9 in village of Helmsdale.
Moorland course.
Founded 1895
9 holes, 3720 yards, S.S.S. 60
† Welcome.
ↆ Terms on application.
⤴Welcome by application.
🍽 None.
⌐ Navidale; Bridge; Belgrave.

9D 37 **Hopeman**

Hopeman, Morayshire, IV30 2YA
☎(01343) 830578, Fax 830152
On B9012 7 miles N of Elgin.
Seaside links-type course.
Founded 1923
Designed by J. MacKenzie
18 holes, 5531 yards, S.S.S. 67
† Welcome except some Sat comp
days.
ↆ WD £10; WE £10; concessions
apply.

⤴Welcome by prior arrangement
with Sec; catering packages by
arrangement; pool table; terms on
application.
🍽 Full catering facilities.
⌐ Station.

9D 38 **Huntly**

Cooper Park, Huntly, Aberdeenshire,
AB54 4SH
☎(01466) 792643, Pro 794181
On A96 0.5 miles from the town
centre through school arch.
Parkland course.
Founded 1892
18 holes, 5399 yards, S.S.S. 66
† Welcome but booking advisable;
day ticket: WD £18, WE £24.
⤴Welcome by prior arrangement
with Sec; catering packages by
arrangement in the summer; from
£18.
🍽 Bar meals and snacks.
⌐ Full facilities; some winter
restrictions.

9D 39 **Insch**

Golf Terrace, Insch, Aberdeenshire
☎(01464) 820363
Off A96 28 miles NW of Aberdeen.
Parkland course with water hazards;
extended 1997.
18 holes, 5395 yards, S.S.S. 67
† Welcome.
ↆ WD £15; WE £20.
⤴By arrangement with Sec; catering
by arrangement; snooker; darts;
terms on application.
🍽 Clubhouse facilities.
⌐ Commercial; Station.

9D 40 **Inverallochy**

Inverallochy, Nr Fraserburgh, AB43
8XY
☎(01346) 582000
4 miles SE of Fraserburgh.
Seaside links course.
Founded 1888
18 holes, 5244 yards, S.S.S. 65
† Welcome by prior arrangement
except before 10am at WE.
ↆ WD £10; WE £15.
⤴Welcome by prior arrangement;
catering by arrangement; terms on
application.
🍽 Catering and licensed bar.
⌐ Tufted Duck.

9D 41 **Invergordon**

King George St, Invergordon, Ross-
shire, N17 0BD

☎ (01349) 852715
Course is off the B817 from the A9 to
Invergordon.
Parkland course; extended to 18
holes, 1996.
Founded 1893
Designed by J Urquhart; Extended by
A Rae 1996
18 holes, 6030 yards, S.S.S. 69
⚑ Welcome.
WD £12; WE £12.
⚐ Welcome by prior arrangement
with Sec; day ticket £15; catering by
arrangement; from £12.
🍽 Bar and bar meals service.
🛏 Kincraig; Marine.

9D 42 Inverness
Culcabook Rd, Inverness, IV2 3XQ
☎ (01463) 233422, Pro 231989, Sec
239882
1 mile W of A9 near Raigmore
Hospital.
Parkland course.
Pro Alistair Thomson; Founded 1883
18 holes, 6226 yards, S.S.S. 70
⚑ Welcome; restrictions on Sat
comp days.
WD £28, WE £30; concessioins
apply.
⚐ Welcome by prior arrangement;
limited; terms on application.
🍽 Full resaurant and bar.
🛏 Kingsmills; Craigmonie; Inverness
Thistle.

9D 43 Inverurie
Blackhall Rd, Inverurie, AB51 9WB
☎ (01467) 624080, Pro 620193, Sec
624080, Bar/Rest 620207
17 miles W of Aberdeen off the A96.
Slightly wooded parkland course.
Founded 1923
Designed by G. Smith and J.M. Stutt
18 holes, 5711 yards, S.S.S. 68
⚑ Welcome.
WD £14; WE £18.
⚐ Welcome by prior arrangement;
some discounts for larger groups;
catering packages by arrangement;
from £14.
🍽 Full bar and catering.
🛏 Strathburn; Kintore Arms.

9D 44 Isle of Skye
Sconser, Isle of Skye, IV48 8TD
☎ (01478) 650351, Fax 650351, Sec
650235
On A87 between Skye Bridge and
Portree.
Parkland course.
Founded 1964

Designed by Dr F. Deighton
9 holes, 4677 yards, S.S.S. 64
⚑ Welcome.
Terms on application.
⚐ Welcome by arrangement with
Sec; discounts for groups of 15 or
more; from £10.
🍽 By arrangement.
🛏 Sligachan Hotel; Sconser Lodge.

9D 45 Keith
Fife Park, Keith, Banffshire, AB55
3DF
☎ (01542) 882469
A96 to Keith; course 0.5 miles.
Parkland course.
Founded 1965
18 holes, 5802 yards, S.S.S. 68
⚑ Welcome.
Terms on application.
⚐ Welcome by prior arrangement;
day tickets available; catering
packages by arrangement; pool table;
from £10.
🍽 Clubhouse facilities.
🛏 Fife Arms; Grampian; Royal; Ugie
House, all in Keith.

9D 46 Kemnay
Monymusk Road, Kemnay,
Aberdeenshire, AB51 5RA
☎ (01467) 642225, Sec 643746
On A96 15 miles N of Aberdeen; turn
on to B994.
Parkland course.
Pro Ronnie McDonald; Founded 1908
Designed by Greens of Scotland Ltd
(new Course)
18 holes, 5903 yards, S.S.S. 70
⚑ Welcome except on competition
days.
WD £17; WE £19.
⚐ Welcome by prior arrangement;
day tickets available; catering by
arrangement; from £17.
🍽 Full clubhouse facilities
available.
🛏 Park Hill Lodge; Grant Arms;
Burnett Arms.

9D 47 King's Links
Golf Rd, King's Links, Aberdeen,
AB24 5QB
☎ 01224) 632269
Close to Pittodrie Stadium in the E of
the city.
Municipal seaside course.
18 holes, 6384 yards, S.S.S. 71
⚑ Welcome.
Terms on application.
⚐ Welcome by prior arrangement;
terms on application.

9D 48 Kingussie
Gynack Rd, Kingussie, Inverness-
shire, PH21 1LR
☎ (01540) 661600, Fax 662066,
Bar/Rest 661374
Off A9 and turn in to club at Duke of
Gordon Hotel.
Scenic hilly course.
Founded 1891
Designed by Vardon & Herd
18 holes, 5555 yards, S.S.S. 67
⚑ Welcome.
WD £16; WE £18.
⚐ Welcome by prior arrangement;
day tickets (WD £20, WE £25);
reductions for 20 or more golfers;
from £16.
🍽 Clubhouse facilities.
🛏 Silverfjord; Scot House.

9D 49 Kintore
Balbithan Rd, Kintore, Inverurie,
Aberdeenshire, AB51 0UR
☎ (01467) 632631
Off A96 12 miles N of Aberdeen.
Undulating moorland course.
Founded 1911
18 holes, 6019 yards, S.S.S. 69
⚑ Welcome except Mon & Wed
4.30pm-6pm and after 4.30pm Fri.
Terms on application.
⚐ Welcome by prior arrangement;
catering by arrangement; day tickets
available; terms on application.
🍽 Full clubhouse facilities.
Practice nets.
🛏 Toryburn; Thainstone; Crown.

9D 50 Lochcarron
East End, Lochcarron, IV 54
☎ (01520) 722229
0.5 miles E of Lochcarron.
Parkland/links course.
Founded 1908
9 holes, 3578 yards, S.S.S. 60
⚑ Welcome except Sat 2-5pm.
WD £7.50; WE £7.50.
⚐ Welcome by prior arrangement;
catering by arrangement at village
hotel; weekly ticket £20; from £7.50.
🍽 No clubhouse facilities; catering
at local hotels.
🛏 Rockvilla Hotel.

9D 51 Lybster
Main St, Lybster, Caithness, KW1
6BL
☎ (01593) 721 308
On A9 13 miles S of Wick.
Moorland course; smallest in
Scotland.
Founded 1926

9 holes, 3796 yards, S.S.S. 62
† Welcome; honesty box.
⌣ WD £7; WE £7.
⌣ Welcome except Sat evening (club comp).

9D 52 McDonald
Hospital Rd, Ellon, Aberdeenshire,
AB41 9AW
☎ (01358) 720576, Fax 720001, Pro
722891, Bar/Rest 723741
Course is off the A90 16 miles north of Aberdeen.
Parkland course.
Pro Ronnie Urquhart; Founded 1927
18 holes, 5991 yards, S.S.S. 69
† Welcome by prior arrangement.
⌣ WD £14; Sat £16; Sun £20.
⌣ Welcome by prior arrangement; day tickets available (WD £20, Sat £24, Sun £30); from £14.
◉ Full clubhouse facilities.
⌐ Buchan Hotel; New Inn; Station Hotel.

9D 53 Moray
Stotfield Rd, Lossiemouth, Moray,
IV31 6QS
☎ (01343) 812018, Fax 815102, Pro
813330, Bar/Rest 812338
At Lossiemouth turn off from A96.
Links course.
Pro Alistair Thomson; Founded 1972
New: 18 holes, 6005 yards, S.S.S. 69; Old: 18 holes, 6667 yards, S.S.S. 73
† Welcome after 10am; not between 1pm-2pm and not after 4pm.
⌣ WD £17, WE £25 (New); WD £30, WE £40 (Old).
⌣ Welcome by prior arrangement; some discounts available for larger groups; day tickets WD £22, WE £30 (New); WD £40, WE £50 (Old); from £30.
◉ Full clubhouse facilities.
⌐ Stotfield; Skerry Brae.

9D 54 Muir of Ord
Great North Rd, Muir of Ord, Ross-shire, IV6 7SX
☎ (01463) 870825, Pro 871311
15 miles N of Inverness.
Moorland/parkland course with links-type fairways.
Pro Graham Legate; Founded 1875
Part designed by James Braid
18 holes, 5557 yards, S.S.S. 68
† Welcome but not before 11am at WE and on comp days.
⌣ WD £14; WE £18.
⌣ Welcome by prior arrangement;

discounts available for groups of more than 15; daily and weekly tickets available; snooker and pool tables; from £14.
◉ Bar and catering facilities.
⌐ Ord Arms; Priory.

9D 55 Murcar
Bridge of Don, Aberdeen,
Aberdeenshire, AB23 8BD
☎ (01224) 704354, Fax 704370, Pro
704370
On A92 3 miles from Aberdeen on road to Fraserburgh.
Seaside course.
Pro Gary Forbes; Founded 1909
Designed by Archie Simpson
18 holes, 6241 yards, S.S.S. 71
† Welcome; restrictions Sat until 4pm; Sun & Tues am; Wed pm.
⌣ WD £30; WE £35.
⌣ Welcome WD with prior arrangement with Sec; daily tickets from £40; catering packages by arrangement; from £28.
Also 9-hole course with a par of 35.
◉ Full clubhouse facilities.
⌐ Mill of Mundurno.

9D 56 Nairn
Seabank Rd, Nairn, IV12 4HB
☎ (01667) 453208, Fax 456328, Pro
452787, Bar/Rest 452103
Off A96 at Nairn Old Parish Church.
Championship links; 1990 Walker Cup venue.
Pro Robin Fyfe; Founded 1887
Designed by Tom Morris, James Braid, A Simpson
18 holes, 6745 yards, S.S.S. 72
† Welcome by prior arrangement.
⌣ WD £60; WE £65.
⌣ Welcome by prior arrangement; handicap certs required; catering packages by arrangement; £60.
◉ Full clubhouse facilities.
Practice range.
⌐ Golf View; Newton; Altonburn; Ramleh.

9D 57 Nairn Dunbar
Lochloy Rd, Nairn, IV12 5AE
☎ (01667) 452741, Fax 456897, Pro
453964
0.5 miles E of Nairn on A96.
Links course.
Pro D Torrance; Founded 1899
18 holes, 6712 yards, S.S.S. 73
† Welcome.
⌣ WD £28; WE £33.
⌣ Welcome but booking essential.
Group rates are negotiable.

◉ Full clubhouse facilities available.
⌐ Golf View; Links; Claymore.

9D 58 Newburgh-on-Ythan
The Links, Newburgh, Aberdeenshire,
AB41 6FD
☎ (01358) 789058, Fax 789956, Sec
789084
From A90 12 miles N of Aberdeen to A975 to Newburgh.
Links course; new 9 holes, added 1996.
Founded 1888/1996
Designed by Greens of Scotland (Aberdeen)
18 holes, 6162 yards, S.S.S. 70
† Welcome.
⌣ WD £15; WE £22.
⌣ Welcome by prior arrangement; full day's golf and catering packages available; from £15.
◉ New clubhouse opened in July 1999.
⌐ Udny Arms; Ythan Hotel.

9D 59 Newmachar
Swailend, Newmachar, Aberdeen,
AB21 7UU
☎ (01651) 863002, Fax 863055, Pro
863222, Bar/Rest 863002
12 miles N of Aberdeen off A947 Aberdeen-Banff road.
Parkland course.
Pro Gordon Simpson; Founded 1990
Designed by Dave Thomas
Hawkshill: 18 holes, 6623 yards,
S.S.S. 73; Swailend: 18 holes, 6388 yards, S.S.S. 70
† Welcome but handicap certs are required.
⌣ WD £30, WE £40 (Hawkshill); WD £15, WE £20 (Swailend).
⌣ Welcome by prior arrangement; from £30 (Hawkshill); from £15 (Swailend).
◉ Full clubhouse facilities available.
Practice range, 12 bays.
⌐ Dunavon House; Kirkhill; Marriott, Dyce.

9D 60 Newtonmore
Golf Course Rd, Newtonmore,
Highland, PH20 1AT
☎ (01540) 673328, Pro 673611, Sec
673878
2 miles S of Newtonmore off the A9.
Moorland/parkland course.
Pro Bob Henderson; Founded 1893
Designed by James Braid
18 holes, 6029 yards, S.S.S. 69
† Welcome.
⌣ WD £15; WE £17.

✆ Welcome by prior arrangement with Sec; day tickets available; catering packages by arrangement; pool table; from £15.
🍽 Full clubhouse facilities; some restrictions Tues.
🛏 Glen; Balavil Sports; Lodge; Mains.

9D 61 **Northern**
Golf Rd, Kings Links, Aberdeen, AB24 5QB
☎ (01224) 636440, Sec 622679
East of City
Municipal seaside course.
18 holes, 6270 yards, S.S.S 69
♦ Welcome.
£ WD £7.80; WE £7.80.
✆ Welcome by arrangement; terms on application.
🍽 Full facilities at WE; by arrangement WD.

9D 62 **Oldmeldrum**
Kirk Brae, Oldmeldrum, Aberdeenshire, AB51 0DJ
☎ (01651) 872648, Pro 873555
On A947 from Aberdeen.
Parkland course; extended to 18 holes in 1994.
Founded 1885/1994
Pro: J Carver
18 holes, 5988 yards, S.S.S. 69
♦ Welcome by prior arrangement.
£ WD £14; WE £20.
✆ Welcome by prior arrangement with pro; catering packages by arrangement; from £14.
🍽 Full facilities.
🛏 Meldrum House; Meldrum Arms; Redgarth; Cromlet Hill B&B.

9D 63 **Orkney**
Grainbank, Kirkwall, Orkney, KW15 1RD
☎ (01856) 872457
W boundary of Kirkwall.
Parkland course.
Founded 1889
18 holes, 5411 yards, S.S.S. 67
♦ Welcome.
£ WD £10; WE £10.
✆ Welcome; day's golf; snacks and meals can be arranged at lunchtime during the summer; games room; from £10.
🍽 Full clubhouse facilities.

9D 64 **Peterculter**
Oldtown, Burnside Rd, Peterculter, Aberdeen, AB14 0LN

☎ (01224) 735245, Fax 735580, Pro 734994, Bar/Rest 735245
Take the A93 to Royal Deeside into Peterculter turning left before Rob Roy Bridge.
Undulating scenic parkland course on banks of River Dee.
Pro Dean Vannet; Founded 1989
Designed by E. Lappin/Greens of Scotland
18 holes, 5947 yards, S.S.S. 69
♦ Welcome.
£ WD £12; WE £16.
✆ Welcome WD by prior arrangement; day tickets (WD £18, WE £21); catering by prior arrangement, from £12.
🍽 Full clubhouse facilities.
🛏 Golden Arms.

9D 65 **Peterhead** ☎
Craigewan Links, Peterhead, Aberdeenshire, AB42 1LT
☎ (01779) 472149, Fax 480725, Sec 480725
On A92 and A975, 30 miles N of Aberdeen.
Seaside links course.
Founded 1841
Designed by Willie Park and James Braid
18 holes, 6173 yards, S.S.S. 71
♦ Welcome; some Sat restrictions apply.
£ WD £16; WE £20.
✆ Welcome by arrangement with Sec; restrictions Sat; catering packages by arrangement; also 9-hole course, 2400 yards, S.S.S. 60; from £16.
🍽 Clubhouse with full facilities.
🛏 Palace; Waterside Inn.

9D 66 **Portlethen** ☎
Badentoy Rd, Portlethen, Aberdeenshire, AB12 4YA
☎ (01224) 781090, Fax 781090, Pro 782571, Bar/Rest 782575
Course is on the A90 six miles south of Aberdeen.
Parkland course.
Pro Muriel Thomson
Founded 1986
Designed by Donald Steel
18 holes, 6707 yards, S.S.S. 72
♦ Welcome WD 9.30am-3pm; not Sat; Sun after 1pm.
£ WD £15; WE £22.
✆ Welcome by prior arrangement with admin dept; catering packages available; pool table and buggy hire; from £14.
🍽 Full clubhouse facilities.

9D 67 **Reay**
The Clubhouse, Reay, by Thurso, Caithness, KW14 7RE
☎ (01847) 811288
11 miles W of Thurso.
Seaside links course.
Founded 1893
18 holes, 5884 yards, S.S.S. 68
♦ Welcome except competition days.
£ Available upon application.
✆ Welcome by prior arrangement with Sec; catering by prior arrangement; from £15.
🍽 Full clubhouse facilities.
🛏 Forss House, Forss; Park Hotel, Thurso; Melvich Hotel, Melvich.

9D 68 **Rothes**
Blackhall, Rothes, Aberlour, Banffshire, AB38 7AN
☎ (01340) 831443, Sec 831277
10 miles S of Elgin on A941 at S end of the town.
Parkland course.
Founded 1990
Designed by John Souter
9 holes, 4972 yards, S.S.S. 65
♦ Welcome.
£ WD £11; WE £13.
✆ Welcome by prior arrangement; packages for golf and catering can be arranged; terms available on application.
🍽 Full bar facilities.
🛏 Ben Aigen; Eastbank; Rothes Glen, all Rothes; Craigellachie Hotel, Craigellachie.

9D 69 **Royal Aberdeen**
Balgownie, Bridge of Don, Aberdeen, AB23 8AT
☎ (01224) 702571
2 miles N on the main road from Aberdeen on the A92 to Fraserburgh.
Seaside links course.
Pro R MacAskill; Founded 1780
Designed by Robert Simpson and James Braid
18 holes, 6372 yards, S.S.S. 71
♦ Welcome WD; WE restrictions.
£ WD £55; WE £65.
✆ Welcome by prior arrangement WD; day ticket £75; also Silverburn shorter course for high handicappers, 4066 yards; from £55.
🍽 Dining room; lounge and bar.
🛏 Atholl; Marcliffe; Udny Arms.

9D 70 **Royal Dornoch**
Golf Rd, Dornoch, Sutherland IV25 3LW

☎(01862) 810219, Fax 810792, Pro 810902, Sec 811220, Bar/Rest 810371
🖥 *www.royaldornoch.com*
Course is 45 miles north of Inverness off the A9.
Championship links course.
Pro A Skinner; Founded 1877
Designed by Tom Morris, John Sutherland, George Duncan
36 holes, 6514 yards, S.S.S. 72
⚲ Welcome with handicap certs.
⚑ WD £57; WE £65.
⚲ Welcome by prior arrangement; handicap certs required; catering by prior arrangement; three-day tickets and combination tickets with Struie course also available; from £57.
🍽 Full clubhouse facilities.
⚲ Club can provide a list of local hotels, GH and B&Bs.

9D 71 **Royal Tarlair**
Buchan St, Macduff, Aberdeenshire, AB44 1TA
☎(01261) 832897
Course is on the A98 48 miles from Aberdeen.
Parkland course.
Founded 1923
Designed by George Smith
18 holes, 5866 yards, S.S.S. 68
⚲ Welcome.
⚑ WD £10; WE £13.
⚲ None.
🍽 Full catering and bar.
⚲ Highland Haven; Banff Springs.

9D 72 **Shetland**
Dale, Gott by Lerwick, Shetland Is
☎(01595) 840369
3 miles N of Lerwick.
Undulating moorland course.
Founded 1891
Designed by Fraser Middleton
18 holes, 5776 yards, S.S.S. 69
⚲ Welcome.
⚑ WD from £12; WE from £12.
⚲ Welcome by arrangement; weekly tickets available; from £12.
🍽 Bar and snacks.
⚲ Lerwick; Grand; Queens

9D 73 **Skeabost**
Skeabost Bridge, Isle of Skye, IV51 9NP
☎(01470) 532322, Bar/Rest 532202
40 miles from Kyle of Lochalsh.
Parkland course.
Founded 1984
9 holes, 3224 yards, S.S.S. 60
⚲ Welcome.

⚑ WD £10; WE £10.
🍽 Bar and restaurant in the hotel April-Oct.
⚲ Skeabost (26 beds).

9D 74 **Spean Bridge**
Station Rd, Spean Bridge, Fort William PH34 4EU
☎(01397) 704954
Course is eight miles north of Fort William on the A82.
Inland course.
9 holes, 2203 yards, par 63
⚲ By arrangement only.
⚑ £8.
⚲ By arrangement only.

9D 75 **Spey Bay**
Spey Bay, Fochabers, Moray, IV32 7PJ
☎(01343) 820424
Turn off the A96 near Fochabers Bridge, follow the B9104 Spey Bay road to coast.
Links course.
Founded 1907
Designed by Ben Sayers
18 holes, 6092 yards, S.S.S. 69
⚲ Welcome but booking advisable on Sundays.
⚑ WD £10; WE £13.
⚲ Welcome by application; day packages available; tennis; petanque; putting; terms available on application.
🍽 Full facilities; meals and bar all day; bar lunches in winter.
Practice range.
⚲ Spey Bay.

9D 76 **Stonehaven**   ♔
Cowie, Stonehaven, Kincardineshire, AB39 3RH
☎(01569) 762124, Fax 765973
N of Stonehaven on A92; signposted at the mini roundabout near the Leisure Centre.
Parkland course on cliffs overlooking Stonehaven Bay.
Founded 1888
Designed by A. Simpson
18 holes, 5103 yards, S.S.S. 65
⚲ Welcome except before 4pm Sat and on comp days.
⚑ WD £15; WE £20.
⚲ Welcome WD and Sun; catering available by prior application to Secretary; terms available on application.
🍽 Full facilities.everyday except Mondays.
⚲ Heugh; County; Station; Crown.

9D 77 **Stornoway**
Castle Grounds, Stornoway, Isle of Lewis, HS2 0XP
☎(01851) 702240
0.5 miles outside Stornoway in the grounds of Lews Castle.
Parkland course.
Founded 1890
Designed by J.R. Stutt
18 holes, 5252 yards, S.S.S. 66
⚲ Welcome except on Sun.
⚑ Terms on application.
⚲ Welcome by prior written arrangement with Sec; special rates by application; from £12.
🍽 Bar and bar snacks.
⚲ Caberfeidh; Royal; Seaforth.

9D 78 **Strathlene**
Portessie, Buckie, Banffshire, AB56 2DJ
☎(01542) 831798
Off the Elgin-Banff coast route 2 miles E of Buckie Harbour.
Undulating moorland/seaside course.
Founded 1877
Designed by Alex Smith
18 holes, 5936 yards, S.S.S. 69
⚲ Welcome except before 9.30am and between 12 noon-2pm at WE.
⚑ Terms on application.
⚲ Welcome by prior arrangement; catering by arrangement; day and weekly tickets available; terms on application.
🍽 Full facilities; two bars and meals.
Practice range.
⚲ St Andrews.

9D 79 **Strathpeffer Spa**
Strathpeffer, Ross-shire, IV14 9AS
☎(01997) 421219, Pro 421011
5 miles N of Dingwall.
Upland course.
Founded 1888
Designed by W. Park
18 holes, 4813 yards, S.S.S. 64
⚲ Welcome except before 10am Sun.
⚑ Available on application.
⚲ Welcome by prior arrangement; packages available for golf and catering.
🍽 Full facilities.
⚲ Ben Wyvis; Highland; Holly Lodge.

9D 80 **Stromness**
Ness, Stromness, Orkney, K16 3DU
☎(01856) 850772, Sec 850622
Situated at the S end of town bordering Hoy Sound.

Parkland course.
Founded 1890
18 holes, 4762 yards, S.S.S. 63
† Welcome.
⌐ WD £12; WE £12.
↷Welcome; catering packages by arrangement; tennis, pool table; darts and bowls; terms on application.
🍽 Stromness; Royal.

9D 81 **Tain** ⚮
Chapel Road, Tain, Ross-shire, IV19 1PA
☎(01862) 892314
35 miles N of Inverness on A9; 0.25 miles from Tain.
Links course.
Founded 1890
Designed by Tom Morris
18 holes, 6404 yards, S.S.S. 71
† Welcome.
⌐ WD £27; WE £35.
↷Welcome by prior arrangement; discount of 10% for groups; catering by arrangement; terms on application.
🍽 Full facilities.
↝ Morangie; Mansfield House, both Tain; Royal; Carnegie Lodge, both Tain.

9D 82 **Tarbat**
1 East Tarrel Cottages, Portmahomack, Ross-shire, IV20 1SL
☎(01862) 871486
↷christina@portmahomack.fsnet. co.uk
9 miles east of Tain on the B9165 off the A9.
Seaside links course.
Founded 1909
Designed by J. Sutherland
9 holes, 5082 yards, S.S.S. 65
† Welcome; some restrictions on Sat
⌐ Day ticket: WD £10; WE £10.
↷Welcome by prior arrangement with Sec; catering by arrangement; local hotels provide full meal and bar service; from £10.
🍽 Limited facilities; see local hotels. Practice ground.
↝ Castle; Caledonian; Oyster Catcher.

9D 83 **Tarland**
Aberdeen Rd, Tarland, Aboyne, Aberdeenshire, AB34 4YN
☎(01339) 881413
5 miles NW of Aboyne; 30 miles W of Aberdeen.
Parkland course.
Founded 1908

Designed by Tom Morris
9 holes, 5875 yards, S.S.S. 68
† Welcome.
⌐ WD £12; WE £15.
↷Welcome by prior arrangement; terms on application.
🍽 Full facilities June-Sept; otherwise by arrangement.
↝ Aberdeen Arms; Commercial.

9D 84 **Thurso**
Newlands of Geise, Thurso, Caithness, KW14 7XF
☎(01847) 893807
2 miles SW from centre of Thurso on B870.
Parkland course.
Founded 1893
Designed by W. Stuart
18 holes, 5828 yards, S.S.S. 69
† Welcome.
⌐ Terms on application.
↷Welcome by prior arrangement; terms on application.
🍽 Full facilities.
↝ Park Hotel.

9D 85 **Torphins**
Bog Rd, Torphins, Aberdeenshire, AB31 4JU
☎(01339) 882115, Sec 882402
Signposted in village; 6 miles W of Banchory on A980.
Parkland course with Highland views.
Founded 1896
9 holes, 4738 yards, S.S.S. 63
† Welcome.
⌐ WD £10; WE £12.
↷Welcome by prior arrangement; catering packages at WE; from £10.
🍽 Full facilities at WE.
↝ Learney Arms.

9D 86 **Torvean**
Glenurquhart Rd, Inverness, Inverness-shire, IV3 6JN
☎(01463) 225651, Fax 225651, Starters office T11131, Bar/Rest 236648
On A82 Fort William road approx 1 mile from Inverness Town Centre.
Municipal parkland course.
Founded 1962
Designed by T Hamilton
18 holes, 5784 yards, S.S.S. 68
† Welcome; tee bookings advisable.
⌐ WD £13; WE £15.
↷Welcome by arrangement with Highland Council, Town Hall, Inverness; terms on application.
🍽 Meals by arrangement.
↝ Loch Ness.

9D 87 **Traigh Golf Course**
Traigh, Arisaig, by Mallaig, Arisaig, Inverness-shire, PH39 4NT
☎(01687) 450337, Sec 450645
On the A830 Fort William to Mallaig road.
Links course.
Founded 1995
Designed by John Salvesen
9 holes, 4912 yards, S.S.S. 65
† Welcome.
⌐ Terms on application.
🍽 Clubhouse snacks.
↝ Arisaig Hotel; Arisaig House; Marine; Glas na Cardoch; West Highland.

9D 88 **Turriff**
Rosehall, Turriff, Aberdeenshire, AB53 4HD
☎(01888), Pro 563025, Sec 562982
On B9024 1 mile up Huntly road.
Meadowland/parkland course.
Pro Robin Smith; Founded 1896
18 holes, 6107 yards, S.S.S. 69
† Welcome except before 10am WE; handicap certs required.
⌐ WD £16; WE £21.
↷Welcome by arrangement with Sec; day tickets available (WD £20, WE £27); from £16.
🍽 By prior arrangement.
↝ Union; White Heather.

9D 89 **Westhill** ⚮
Westhill Heights, Skene, Aberdeenshire, AB32 6RY
☎Pro (01224) 740159, Sec 742567
Course is on A944, 6 miles from Aberdeen.
Undulating parkland/moorland course.
Pro George Bruce; Founded 1977
Designed by Charles Lawrie
18 holes, 5849 yards, S.S.S. 69
† Welcome except Sat.
⌐ WD £12; WE £16.
↷Welcome WD and Sun by prior arrangement; catering packages by special arrangement; terms on application.
🍽 Bar facilities.
↝ Broadstreik Inn; Westhill Inn.

9D 90 **Westray**
Tulloch's Shop, Westray, Orkney, KW17 2DH
☎(01857) 677373, Sec 677211
0.5 miles from Pierowall village.
Links course.
Founded 1890
9 holes, 4810 yards

✝ Welcome.
🍺 WD £3; WE £3.
⛳Welcome by prior arrangement; only limited catering available; from £3.
🍽 By prior arrangement.
🛏 Cleaton House.

9D 91 **Whalsay**

Skaw Taing, Island of Whalsay, Shetland, ZE2 9AL
☎ (01806) 566483
At N end of Island.
Moorland course.

Founded 1975
18 holes, 6009 yards, S.S.S. 68
✝ Welcome; restrictions on comp days.
🍺 WD £10; WE £10.
⛳Welcome by prior arrangement; packages available; terms on application.
🍽 Bar and catering facilities available.
🛏 Hotels on Shetland.

9D 92 **Wick**

Reiss, Wick, Caithness, KW1 4RW

☎ (01955) 602726, Sec 602935
Course is on the A9 three miles north of Wick.
Links course.
Founded 1870
Designed by McCulloch
18 holes, 5976 yards, S.S.S. 70
✝ Welcome.
🍺 WD £15; WE £15.
⛳Welcome by prior arrangement; catering by prior arrangement; pool table; terms on application.
🍽 Bar and limited catering facilities available.
🛏 Mackays.

WALES

In 2000 the European Tour will hold the first Wales Open, long overdue recognition of a land that is often unjustly overlooked by golfing pilgrims.

The journalist Peter Corrigan once wrote that exploring Wales in search of golfing experiences, even for a Welshman like himself, was like stumbling upon a row of Rembrandts in the attic. It is a lovely simile and one that is easily justified when one considers the praise lavished upon virtually every other part of the United Kingdom while Wales stands largely ignored.

The Wales Open will be staged at Celtic Manor, a huge complex where the championship course, designed by Robert Trent Jones Snr, is situated amid 1,000 acres of mature woodland in the Wentwood Hills.

The man behind Celtic Manor is a Welsh billionaire called Terry Matthews, of whom much more will be heard. His ambition is for Celtic Manor to stage a Ryder Cup; certainly Wales deserves one.

The best course in the Principality, however, remains Royal Porthcawl, one of the great tests of links golf to be found in the British Isles. There are few spots to compare with the 18th tee on a warm summer's day, looking towards the tranquil waters of Rest Bay, and knowing that whatever the standard of golf a warm welcome awaits in one of the great clubhouses.

Porthcawl is the biggest of the big three of Welsh golf. To the north lies Royal St David's, or Harlech to use its less formal name. Harlech Castle casts an imposing eye over the course, which has been described as the world's hardest par 69. It has its share of fine dune holes and the spectacular backdrop of the Snowdonia mountains completes a majestic picture.

In deep mid-winter many professionals naturally travel to warmer climes abroad to prepare for a new season. When he was based in Oswestry Ian Woosnam never used to bother. He would travel 80 miles instead to the Welsh coast and play Aberdovey, where the greens were as good in January as at many places in July. Aberdovey was close to the heart of the doyen of golf writers, Bernard Darwin, and many others since.

These are the courses that Wales can justly put forward as the equal to more celebrated names found elsewhere. They are hardly the only venues worth investigating. There is Southerndown to the South, Ashburnham in the west, Conway to the north, and Llanymynech to the east that emphasise fine courses lay all over the country.

Then there is St Pierre, once a favoured stop for the pros. It remains a fine weekend destination, with an excellent hotel and a main golf course that has its share of feature holes; none more so than the par-three 18th that appears to go on forever. One can only imagine what it must be like in a competition, standing on this tee in the knowledge that a regulation figure is required for victory. — **DL**

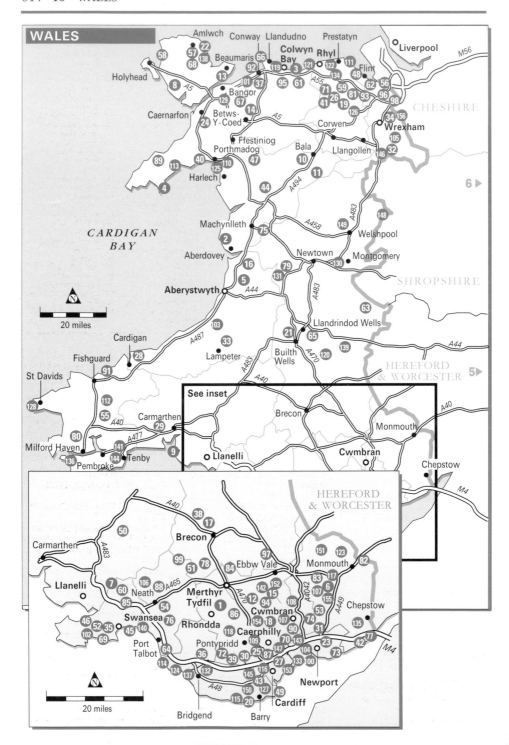

WALES

Liverpool

Amlwch Conway Llandudno Prestatyn

Beaumaris **Colwyn Bay** **Rhyl**

Holyhead

Bangor

Caernarfon Betws-Y-Coed

Ffestiniog Porthmadog Bala

Harlech Llangollen

Corwen

Wrexham

CHESHIRE

CARDIGAN BAY

N
20 miles

Machynlleth

Aberdovey

Newtown Montgomery

Welshpool

Aberystwyth

SHROPSHIRE

Llandrindod Wells

Cardigan

Lampeter

Builth Wells

HEREFORD & WORCESTER

Fishguard

St Davids

Carmarthen

Brecon

Monmouth

See inset

Llanelli

Cwmbran

Chepstow

Milford Haven Tenby

Pembroke

HEREFORD & WORCESTER

Carmarthen

Brecon

Ebbw Vale Monmouth

Llanelli

Neath **Merthyr Tydfil** **Cwmbran**

Chepstow

Swansea

Rhondda

Caerphilly

Port Talbot

Pontypridd

Newport

Cardiff

Bridgend Barry

N
20 miles

KEY							
1	Aberdare	32	Chirk	63	Knighton	95	Old Colwyn	126	Ruthin Pwllglas

10 1 Aberdare

Abernant, Aberdare, Mid-Glam, CF44 0RY
☎(01685) 871188, Fax 872 797, Pro 878735, Sec 872797
0.5 miles E of Aberdare, 12 miles NW of Pontypridd.
Mountain course with parkland features.
Pro A W Palmer; Founded 1921
18 holes, 5875 yards, S.S.S. 69
♦ Welcome.
WD £14; WE £18.
Welcome by prior arrangement with Sec; from £12.
Bar and dining room, snooker available.
Practice area.
Baverstock.

10 2 Aberdovey

Aberdovey, Gwynedd, LL35 0RT
☎(01654) 767493, Fax 767027, Pro 767602, Sec 767493
On A493 W of Aberdovey, adjacent to station.
Pro John Davies; Founded 1892
18 holes, 6445 yards, S.S.S. 71
♦ Welcome with handicap certs.
WD £29; WE £35.
Welcome by prior arrangement; handicap certs needed; terms on application.
Clubhouse facilities.

Practice area.
Trefeddian; Bodfor; Plas Penhelig; Brodawell.

10 3 Abergele & Pensarn

Tan-y-Gopa Rd, Abergele, Denbighshire, LL28 8DS
☎(01745) 824034, Pro 823813, Bar/Rest 826716
A55 at Abergele/Rhuddlan exit; through town; first left past the police station.
Parkland course.
Pro I R Runcie; Founded 1910
Designed by Hawtree & Sons
18 holes, 6520 yards, S.S.S. 71
♦ Welcome by arrangement.
WD £25; WE £30.
Welcome by arrangement; members have priority until 10.15am and until 2pm in afternoon; 27 holes of golf, light lunch, 3-course meal; £35.
Full clubhouse facilites.
Kinmel Manor; Colwyn Bay; Dol Hyfryd.

10 4 Abersoch

Golf Rd, Abersoch, Gwynedd, LL53 7EY
☎(01758) 712622, Fax 712777
6 miles from Pwlheli; first left through the village.

Seaside links course.
Pro Alan Jones; Founded 1910
Designed by Harry Vardon
18 holes, 5671 yards, S.S.S. 68
♦ Welcome with handicap certs.
WD £18; WE £20.
Welcome by prior arrangement.
Full facilities.
Deucoch; Carisbrooke.

10 5 Aberystwyth

Bryn-y-Mor, Aberystwyth, Dyfed, SY23 3QD
☎(01970) 615104, Fax 626622, Pro 625301
N end of the promenade behind the seafront hotels; access road adjacent to cliff railway; 1 mile from the town centre.
Undulating meadowland course.
Pro Mark Newson; Founded 1911
Designed by Harry Vardon
18 holes, 6150 yards, S.S.S. 71
♦ Welcome; some WE restrictions.
WD £18; WE £22.
Welcome by prior arrangement; packages available.
Bar and restaurant facilities.
Practice ground.
Apply to Sec for details.

10 6 Alice Springs

Court Wyndermere, Bettws Newydd,

Abersoch Golf Club

Golf Road, Abersoch, Pwllheli, Gwynedd LL53 7EY.
Tel: 01758 712622 Fax: 01758 712777
www.abersochgolf.co.uk

Abersoch Golf Course is a picturesque Links and Parkland course with far-reaching breathtaking views across Cardigan Bay and the Snowdonian mountains, with mature trees and water hazards, providing a challenge for golfers of all standards. Designed in 1908 by the great Harry Vardon – six time winner of the Open Championship, the course has since been extended to 18 holes. Built on a spacious sixty-acre site adjoining the beach – all the greens are constructed on sand to ensure optimum conditions for golfers in all conditions. With a sheltered position and a mild climate, Abersoch is the ideal course all year round. To make your visit as comfortable as possible, we also have a full catering service, all-day bar facilities and special golfing weekend breaks including accommodation. Enjoy a warm welcome at Abersoch!

Usk, Monmouthshire, NP5 1JY
☎(01873) 880708, Fax 880838, Pro 880914, Sec 880244
3 miles N of Usk and 8 miles N of Abergavenny on B4598.
Parkland course.
Pro Paul Williams; Founded 1986
Designed by Keith R. Morgan
Kings Course: 18 holes, 5996 yards, S.S.S. 72; Queens Course: 5596 yards, S.S.S. 69.
♦ Welcome; book at WE and Bank Holidays.
⌇ WD £13; WE £15.
⌁Welcome by prior arrangement; packages available from Emma Ralph; driving range.
⍟ Full catering and bar facilities; recommended to phone before arrival; terms on application.
⌐ Cwrt Bleddybn; The Three Salmons Hotel, Usk; The Rat Trap.

10 7 Allt-y-Graban

Allt-y-Graban Rd, Pontlliw, Swansea, SA4 1 DT
☎(01792) 885757 or 883279
From M4 Junction 47 take the A48 to Pontlliw.
Parkland course.
Founded 1993
Designed by F.G. Thomas
9 holes, 4453 yards, S.S.S. 63
♦ Welcome.
⌇ 18 holes WD £8.50; WE £9.50.
⌁Welcome; minimum 10; catering by arrangement; from £6.
⍟ Clubhouse facilites.
⌐ Forest Motel; The Fountain Inn.

10 8 Anglesey

Station Rd, Rhosneigr, LL64 5QX
☎(01407) 810219, Fax 811202, Pro 811202, Sec 811202
8 miles SE of Holyhead; on A4080 off A5 between Gwalchmai and Bryngwran.

Links course with dunes and heather.
Pro P Lovell; Founded 1914
18 holes, 6300 yards, S.S.S. 68
♦ Welcome.
⌇ WD £10-15; WE and BH £20.
⌁Welcome by prior arrangement; packages and reductions available for more than 10 players; terms on application.
⍟ Clubhouse bar and catering facilities.
⌐ Treaddur Hotel; Trecastell; Maelog Lake; Gadleys Country House; Eryl Mor.

10 9 Ashburnham

Cliffe Terrace, Burry Port, Camarthenshire, SA16 0HN
☎(01554) 832466, Sec 832269, Pro 833846 Bar 832466
4 miles from Llanelli; 9 miles from M4.
Championship links.
Pro R.A Ryder; Founded 1894
Championship course: 18 holes, 6936 yards, S.S.S. 74; Medal course: 6627 yards, S.S.S 73.
♦ Welcome by prior arrangement.
⌇ WD £27.50; WE £32.50.
⌁Welcome WD by prior arrangement.
⍟ Full facilities except Mondays.
⌐ Ashburnham; Stradey Park Hotel; Diplomat Hotel.

10 10 Bala

Penlan, Bala, Gwynedd, LL23 7YD
☎(01678) 520359, Fax 521361
Off the main Bala-Dolgellau road.
Upland course with Snowdonia views.
Pro Tony Davies; Founded 1973
10 holes, 4791 yards, S.S.S. 64
♦ Welcome; some WE restrictions.
⌇ WD £12; WE £15.
⌁Welcome by prior arrangement; terms on application.
⍟ Bar with snacks available.

⌐ The Plas Coch Hotel, special packages available.

10 11 Bala Lake Hotel

Bala, Gwynned, LL23 7YF
☎(01678) 520344
Off the B4403 1.5 miles from Bala.
Parkland course.
Founded 1960
9 holes, 3818 yards, S.S.S. 61
♦ Welcome.
⌇ Terms on application.
⌁Welcome by arrangement.
⍟ Full facilities.
⌐ Bala Lake Hotel.

10 12 Bargoed

Heolddu, Bargoed, CF8 9GF
☎(01443) 830143, Pro 836411
10 miles from Caerphilly.
Part moorland/mountain course.
Pro Clive Coombes; Founded 1912
18 holes, 6049 yards, S.S.S. 70
♦ Welcome WD; with member only at WE.
⌇ WD £18.
⌁Welcome by prior arrangement.
⍟ Bar facilities and evening meals.
⌐ Maes Manor; Park; Baverstocks.

10 13 Baron Hill

Beaumaris, Anglesey, N Wales, LL58 8YW
☎(01248) 810231
A545 from Menai Bridge to Beaumaris; course just before Beaumaris.
Heathland course.
Founded 1895
9 holes, 5596 yards, S.S.S. 68
♦ Welcome by arrangement with Sec or steward; handicap certs required; restrictions depending on time of year.
⌇ WD £13; WE £13.
⌁Welcome by prior arrangement;

bar and catering packages available; terms on application.
🍽 Clubhouse facilities.
🍺 Bull's Head; Bishop's Gate; Bulkeley.

10 14 Betws-y-Coed
The Clubhouse, Betws-y-Coed, Gwynedd, LL24 0AL
☎ (01690) 710556
Off A470 or A5 opposite Midland Bank in village centre.
Parkland course.
Founded 1971
9 holes, 4998 yards, S.S.S. 63
🏌 Welcome.
⏺ WD £10-15; WE £20.
🏌 Welcome by prior arrangement; catering and bar packages available; terms on application.
🍽 Full clubhouse facilites.
🍺 Glen Aber; Four Oaks; Gwydir; Waterloo.

10 15 Blackwood
Cwmgelli, Blackwood, Gwent, NP2 1EL
☎ (01495) 223152, Sec 222121
Course is 0.25 miles N of Blackwood on the A4048 Blackwood-Tredegar road.
Parkland course.
Founded 1914
9 holes, 5304 yards, S.S.S. 66
🏌 Welcome WD; with a member at WE.
⏺ WD £13; WE £13.
🏌 Welcome by prior arrangement; terms on application.
🍽 Bar and catering facilities.
🍺 Maes Manor.

10 16 Borth & Ynyslas   ☫
Borth, Ceredigion, SY24 5JS
☎ (01970) 871202, Fax 871202, Pro 871557
💻 www.borthgolf.co.uk
📧 secretary@borthgolf.co.uk
8 miles S of Macynlleth; 4 miles N of Aberystwyth on A487.
Links course.
Pro J G Lewis; Founded 1885
18 holes, 6116 yards, S.S.S. 70
🏌 Welcome by arrangement.
⏺ WD £20; WE £27.
🏌 Welcome; minimum 8 in summer, 6 in winter; catering packages available; from £10.
🍽 Bar and catering facilities.
🍺 Black Lion, Talybont; Belle View; Marine Hotel, Aberystwyth; Ynyshir Hall.

10 17 Brecon
Newton Park, Llanfaes, Brecon, Powys, LD3 8PA
☎ (01874) 622004
50 yards, from A40 on W of town.
Parkland course by R Usk and Tarrell.
Founded 1902
Designed by J Braid
9 holes, 5256 yards, S.S.S. 66
🏌 Welcome.
⏺ WD £10; WE £10.
🏌 Welcome by arrangement; catering packages available; terms on application.
🍽 Catering facilities available.
🍺 Peterstone Court.

10 18 Bryn Meadows G & CC
The Bryn, Hengoed, Mid-Glam, CF8 7SM
☎ (01495) 22559, Fax 228272, Pro 221006, Sec 225590
💻 www.brynmeadows.co.uk
Off A469 15 miles from Cardiff.
Parkland course.
Pro Bruce Hunter; Founded 1973
Designed by E. Jefferies & B. Mayo
18 holes, 6156 yards, S.S.S. 70
🏌 Welcome.
⏺ WD £17.50; WE £22.50.
🏌 Welcome WD by arrangement; special golf packages; function rooms; new gym; indoor pool; jacuzzi; pool table.
🍽 Full facilities; bar and à la carte restaurant.
Practice area; buggies available £15 a round.
🍺 On site hotel Bryn Meadows.

10 19 Bryn Morfydd Hotel   ☫
Llanrhaeadr, Denbighshire, LL16 4NP
☎ (01745) 890280, Fax 890488
Off A525 between Denbigh and Ruthin.
Founded 1982/92
Designed by Alliss/Thomas (Duchess course); Muirhead/Henderson (Dukes course)
Dukes course: 18 holes, 5800 yards, S.S.S. 68; Duchess course: 9 holes, 2000 yards, par 27
🏌 Welcome.
⏺ WD £15; WE £20.
🏌 Welcome by arrangement; packages available; from £20.
🍽 Full clubhouse and hotel facilities.
🍺 3-star hotel on site.

10 20 Brynhill
Port Rd, Barry, CF02 0PN

☎ (01446) 735061, Fax 733660, Pro 733660, Sec 720277
M4 Junction 33 take signs for Barry and Cardiff Airport on to the A4050.
Undulating meadowland course.
Pro Peter Fountain; Founded 1921
Designed by G.K. Cotton
Summer: 18 holes, 5884 yards, S.S.S. 70; Winter: 18 holes, 5732 yards, S.S.S. 69
🏌 Welcome except Sun; handicap certs may be required.
⏺ WD £20; WE £25.
🏌 Welcome WD by prior arrangement; from £17.
🍽 Bar and catering facilities; lunches, afternoon teas and dinners.
🍺 Mount Sorrel; International; Copthorne.

10 21 Builth Wells
Golf Club Rd, Builth Wells, Powys, LD2 3NF
☎ (01982) 553296, Fax 551064
On A483 Builth-Llandovery road just after River Irfon bridge on outskirts of Builth.
Parkland course; no par 5s.
Founded 1923
18 holes, 5376 yards, S.S.S. 67
🏌 Welcome with handicap certs.
⏺ WD £15; WE £20.
🏌 Welcome; packages and reductions; terms on application.
🍽 Clubhouse bar and catering.
🍺 Pencerrig House, Caerberis Manor; Greyhound Hotel; Cedars GH.

10 22 Bull Bay   ☫
Bull Bay Rd, Amlwch, Anglesey, LL68 9RY
☎ (01407) 830960, Fax 832612, Pro 831188, Bar/Rest 830213
On A5025 via Benllech and course is 1 mile beyond Amlwch.
Clifftop heathland course, northernmost course in Wales.
Pro John Burns; Founded 1913
Designed by Herbert Fowler and Walton Heath
18 holes, 6217 yards, S.S.S. 70
🏌 Welcome by prior arrangement.
⏺ WD £20; WE £25.
🏌 Welcome; meals can be provided; from £13.
🍽 Clubhouse facilities.
🍺 Trecastell; Bull Bay; Lastra Farm Hotel.

10 23 Caerleon
Broadway, Caerleon, Newport, Gwent, NP6 1AY

Enter a new dimension – 3 Trent Jones championship courses, luxury hotel, 2 health clubs and spa, 4 restaurants, superb Clubhouse and Golf Academy.

THE CELTIC MANOR RESORT

- Home of The Wales Open, PGA European Tour.
- A 1400-acre resort on the beautiful Usk valley. Severn Bridge 5 minutes.

Tel: 01633 413000. *E-mail:* postbox@celtic-manor.com *Web:* www.celtic-manor.com

---

☎ (01633) 420342
3 miles from M4 Junction 25 for Caerleon.
Parkland course.
Pro Chris Jones; Founded 1974
Designed by Donald Steel
9 holes, 5800 yards, S.S.S. 68
† Welcome.
↧ WD: 18 holes £5.60, 9 holes £3.75; WE: 18 holes £7, 9 holes £4.75.
⌁ Welcome by arrangement; terms on application.
⦿ Snacks and bar.
Practice range, 12 bays floodlit.
⌐ Priory.

10 24 **Caernarfon**   ☎

Aberforeshore, Llanfaglan, Gwynedd, LL54 5RP
☎ (01286) 678359/673783, Fax 672535, Pro 673783
A470 from A55 at Caernarfon towards Porthmadog; at new road bridge turn right, club 1.5 miles.
Parkland course.
Pro Aled Owen; Founded 1907/1981
18 holes, 5891 yards, S.S.S. 68
† Welcome.
↧ WD £15; WE £20.
⌁ Welcome; special rates for 10 or more players; full facilities available; terms on application.
⦿ Full catering and bar facilities.
⌐ Celtic Royal; Seiont Manor; Bryn Eisteddfod; Erw Fair, all Caernarfon; Eryl Mor, Bangor.

10 25 **Caerphilly**

Pencapel, Mountain Rd, Caerphilly, Mid-Glam, CF83 1HJ
☎ (029) 2088 3481, Fax 2086 3441, Pro 2086 9104, Sec 2086 3441
On A469 7 miles from Cardiff; 250 yards from rail and bus stations.
Steep wooded mountainside course; 5 new holes by mid-1999.
Pro Richard Barter; Founded 1905
Designed by Fernie (original 9)
18 holes (from spring 2000), 6400 yards, S.S.S. 71
† Welcome WD; WE only with a member.
↧ WD £20.

⌁ Limited numbers by prior arrangement only.
⦿ Bar and dining room.
⌐ Mount; Greenhill; Moat House; Cedar Tree.

10 26 **Caerwys Nine Of Clubs**

Caerwys, Mold, Flintshire, CH7 5AQ
☎ (01352) 720692, Fax (01691) 777793
1.5 miles S of the A55 midway between St Asaph and Holywell.
Undulating parkland course.
Founded 1988
Designed by Eleanor Barlow
9 holes, 3080 yards, S.S.S. 60
† Welcome.
↧ WD £7; WE £8.
⌁ Welcome by prior arrangement.
⦿ Light refreshments.

10 27 **Cardiff**

Sherborne Ave, Cyncoed, Cardiff, CF2 6SJ
☎ (029) 2075 3320, Fax 2068 0011, Pro 2075 4772, Sec 2075 3320, Bar 2075 3067, Rest 2068 9375
⌨ *cardiff.golfclub@virgin.net*
3 miles N of Cardiff, 2 miles W of Pentwyn of A48(M), M4 Junction 29.
Undulating parkland course.
Pro Terry Hanson; Founded 1922
18 holes, 6013 yards, S.S.S. 70
† Welcome.
↧ WD £35; WE £40.
⌁ Welcome by prior arrangement; Thurs only; terms on application; snooker room available.
⦿ New clubhouse facilities.
⌐ Post House, Pentwyn.

10 28 **Cardigan**

Gwbert-on-Sea, Cardigan, Ceredigion, SA43 1PR
☎ (01239) 612035, Fax 621775, Pro 615359, Sec 621775
3 miles N of Cardigan.
Links/parkland course with view of River Teifi.
Pro C Parsons; Founded 1895
Designed by Hawtree
18 holes, 6687 yards, S.S.S. 72
† Welcome.

↧ WD £20; WE and BH £25.
⌁ Welcome by prior arrangement; packages and catering available; satellite TV; pool table; squash courts; discounts available, please contact sec for details.
⦿ Clubhouse facilities.
⌐ Cliff Hotel; Gwbert Hotel.

10 29 **Carmarthen**

Blaenycoed Rd, Carmarthen, Carmarthenshire, SA33 6EH
☎ (01267) 281214, Fax 281493, Pro 281493, Sec 281588
4.5 miles N of town.
Upland course.
Pro Pat Gillis; Founded 1929
Designed by J H Taylor
18 holes, 6245 yards, S.S.S. 71
† Welcome; ladies day Tues.
↧ Winter: WD £15, WE £20; Summer: WD £20, WE £25.
⌁ Welcome WD; packages and discounts available; terms on application.
⦿ Full clubhouse facilities.
⌐ Falcon; Ivy Bush; Forge Motel.

10 30 **Castell Heights**

Blaengwynlais, Caerphilly, Mid-Glamorgan, CF8 1NG
☎ (029) 2088 6666, Fax 2086 3243, Sec 2086 1128, Bar/Rest 2088 6686
4 miles from M4 Junction 32 on the Tongwynlais-Caerphilly road.
Mountainside course.
Pro Sion Bebb; Founded 1982
9 holes, 5376 yards, S.S.S. 66
† Welcome; dress codes apply.
↧ WD £5.50; WE £5.50.
⌁ Welcome by arrangement; advised to phone Sec.
⦿ Bar and bar snacks.
Practice range, 6 bays.
⌐ The Friendly Hotel.

10 31 **The Celtic Manor Resort**

Coldra Woods, Newport, NP18 1HQ
☎ (01633) 413000, Fax 410272, Pro 410311
⌨ *www.celtic-manor.com*
⌨ *postbox@celtic-manor.com*

Celtic Manor

It is called the Gateway to Wales. Well, it certainly is the modern gateway to Welsh golf. Celtic Manor is another new addition to the championship circuits and is bidding hard to become a Ryder Cup venue in the year 2009. To that end, a new course was opened on August 7, 1999 by the former England cricket captain and keen golfer Tony Lewis. It was a memorable moment for the course.

The Wentwood Hills course immediately was pressed into action for the European Amateur Championship in late August. Designed by Robert Trent Jones Jnr, the 7,400-yard course was actually finished in September 1998 but it was decided that it would not be played until the summer of 1999.

Then Ian Woosnam, the Celtic Manor's touring pro, and Mark James, the European Ryder Cup captain, teed off on the first hole as a forerunner to the many great matches to come. It has already been listed as a venue for the PGA match between the professionals of the United States and Great Britain and Ireland for later this year.

Wentwood Hills was the latest course to be added to the Celtic Manor resort. The first course was the aptly named Roman Road, which opened in 1995 and is a 6,700-yard par 69 course built on the old Coldra Hills ridge that was once occupied by the Roman highway called the Via Julia.

It is, itself, a stunning course with golfers across the world captivated by the third hole which has spectacular views across the Usk River Valley. In fact, the entire front nine of the Roman Road course weaves beside the Usk River valley and enjoys great reviews.

Coldra Woods executive course, a par 59 at 4,001 yards, is considered one of the finest short courses in the British Isles. Add to those features a resort and health spa with swimming pools and a 400-bedroom hotel with conference facilities and it is obvious that Celtic Manor means business.

There has also been substantial investment away from the course with a £10 million clubhouse and an Ian Woosnam golf academy that helps with every aspect of the troubled player's game as well as a driving range.

If Wales is going to attract the Ryder Cup and it does not go to one of the classic established courses like Royal Porthcawl or Royal St David's at Harlech then it seems likely that a course like Celtic Manor, with its easy access from the M4 motorway and railway services from London, is certain to be a serious contender. — **CG**

M4 Junction 24, just 5 minutes from the Severn Bridge.

Three championship courses in 1400 acres of panoramic undulating parkland.

Pro Steve Bowen; Founded 1995

Designed by Robert Trent-Jones Jnr (Wentwood Hills 1999) & Robert Trent-Jones Snr (Roman Road 1995; Coldra Woods 1996)

Wentwood Hills: 7403 yards, par 72, S.S.S. 77 (PGA European Tour venue – Wales Open); Roman Road: 18 holes, 6685 yards, par 69, S.S.S. 72; Coldra Woods: 4001 yards, par 59.

† Welcome.

 Wentwood Hills £45; Roman Road £35; Coldra Woods £15 (1999/2000).

 Welcome by prior arrangement; corporate and society packages available. Ian Woosnam Golf Academy; two-tier, floodlit driving range, coaching with video graphics, short play areas, practice range. Superb clubhouse with luxury locker rooms. Resort offers two health clubs and spa, tennis, riding, mountain biking, corporate hospitality.

 Clubhouse lounge bar and dining terrace, Owens and The Olive Tree restaurants, 40 function rooms for private banqueting.

 400-room, 32 suite, 5-star hotel with 1500-delegate Convention Centre.

10 32 Chirk

Chirk, Nr Wrexham, Flintshire, LL14 5AD

☎ (01691) 774407, Fax 773878, Bar/Rest 774243

Course is five miles S of Wrexham just off the A5.

Parkland course; 2 holes greater than 600 yards.

Pro Mark Maddison; Founded 1991

18 holes, 7045 yards, S.S.S. 73

† Welcome.

 Terms on application.

 Welcome; full clubhouse facilities; terrace; buggies; driving range; also 9-hole Mine Rock course, par 3.

 Clubhouse facilities; spike bar, restaurant; snacks and meals. Practice range, 15 undercover floodlit bays; practice bunker.

 Golden Pheasant, Glyn Cieriog; The Royal Hotel, LLangollen.

10 33 Cilgwyn

Llangybi, Lampeter, Ceredigion, SA48 8NN

☎ (01570) 493286

Course is four miles N of Lampeter on the A485.

Parkland course.

Founded 1905/1977

9 holes, 5309 yards, S.S.S. 67

† Welcome.

 WD £10; WE £15.

 Welcome; minimum of 10 players; bar and restaurant packages available; from £8.

 Clubhouse facilities.

 Falcondale; Black Lion, both Lampeter.

10 34 Clay's Farm Golf Centre

Bryn Estyn Road, Wrexham, Wrexham, LL13 9UB

☎ (01978) 661406, Fax 661417, Bar/Rest 661416

From A483 Wrexham-Chester road, take A534 for Nantwich and Wrexham Industrial Estate; 2 miles, turn to golf centre.

Parkland course; new 9-hole pitch and putt course.

Pro D Larvin; Founded 1991

Designed by R D Jones

18 holes, 5794 yards, S.S.S. 68

† Welcome all times.

 WD £13; WE £18.

 Welcome by prior arrangement; minimum 12; deposit required; practice balls, 18-27 holes of golf; light lunch; 3-course dinner; terms on application.

 Catering facilities.

 Cross Lane, Marchweil; Holt Lodge, Wrexham.

10 35 Clyne

118/120 Owls Lodge Lane, Mayals, Swansea, SA3 5DP

☎ (01792) 401989, Fax 401078, Pro 402094, Rest 403534

From the M4 to Swansea; exit for Mumbles at Blackpill, head for Gower and then take first right into Owls Lodge Lane.

Moorland course.

Pro Johnathan Clewett; Founded 1920

Designed by H.S. Colt/Harris

18 holes, 6334 yards, S.S.S. 71

† Welcome with handicap certs.

 WD £25; WE £30.

 Welcome WD except Tues; catering packages and reductions for more than 20 players; from £21.

 Clubhouse facilities.

Practice area.

 Marriott, Swansea; St Anne's, Mumbles.

10 36 Coed-y-Mwstwr Golf Club

The Club House, Coychurch, Nr Bridgend, CF35 6AF

☎ (01656) 862121, Fax 864934, Bar/Rest 862121

From M4 Junction 35 turn towards Bridgend and then into Coychurch.

Parkland course.

Founded 1994

9 holes, 5834 yards, S.S.S. 68 (12-hole course available in summer)

† Welcome with handicap certs; dress codes apply.

 Prices on application.

 Welcome by prior arrangement; packages available; terms on application.

 Clubhouse facilities.

 Coed-y-Mwstwr.

10 37 Conwy (Caernarvonshire)

Beacons Way, Morfa,Conwy, Gwynedd, LL32 8ER

☎ (01492) 593400, Fax 593363, Pro 593225, Sec 592423, Bar 593400

Just off A55 at Conwy.

Links course.

Pro Peter Lees; Founded 1890

18 holes, 6647 yards, S.S.S. 72

† Welcome with handicap certs; standard golf dress code.

 Winter: WD £17, WE £20; Summer: WD £24, WE £30; juniors £8 all year.

 Welcome with prior arrangement through Sec; catering available; winter package; coffee and biscuits, 18 holes of golf and 3-course meal WD £20, WE £25; summer packages also available; snooker room; dartboards; function room; Pro is a commentator and after-dinner speaker.

 Clubhouse facilities.

Practice ground, largest in the area; buggies for hire.

 Royal; Esplanade; The Risborough, all Llandudno; The Castlebank, Conway.

10 38 Cradoc

Penoyre Park, Cradoc, Brecon, Powys, LD3 9LP

☎ (01874) 623658, Fax 611711, Pro 625524, Bar/Rest 624396

Take B 4520 road to Upper Chapel past Brecon Cathedral and turn left to Cradoc village.

Parkland course.

Pro Richard W Davies; Founded 1967

Designed by C.K. Cotton
18 holes, 6301 yards, S.S.S. 72
♦ Welcome by prior arrangement.
⚑ WD £20; WE £25.
♫ Welcome with prior arrangement
through Sec; packages available;
terms on application.
⚇ Clubhouse facilities.
⌐ Peterstone Court; Llangoed Hall;
Castle of Brecon; Lansdown; The
George Hotel.

10 39 Creigiau
Creigiau, Cardiff, CF15 9NN
☎ (029) 2089 0263, Pro 2089 1909,
Bar/Rest 2089 1243, Fax (07070)
601734
4 miles NW of Cardiff towards
Llantrisant.
Parkland course.
Pro Ian Luntz; Founded 1926
18 holes, 6063 yards, S.S.S. 70
♦ Welcome WD except Tues (ladies
day), members only at weekends.
⚑ WD £30.
♫ Welcome by prior arrangement;
min 20 maximum 40.
⚇ Bar and full catering facilities.
Practice area for members only.
⌐ Friendly Hotel; Miskin Manor;
Park; Royal; Angel; Hilton; St Davids;
Celtic Manor.

10 40 Criccieth
Ednyfed Hill, Criccieth, Gwynedd,
LL52
☎ (01766) 522154
On A497 4 miles from Portmadoc;
turn right past Memorial Hall; course
0.5 miles.
Undulating hilltop course.
Founded 1904
18 holes, 5787 yards, S.S.S. 68
♦ Welcome.
⚑ WD £14; WE £18.
♫ Welcome by prior arrangement.
⚇ Full bar and catering facilities.
⌐ George IV; Bron Eifion; Marine;
Lion.

10 41 Denbigh
Henllan Rd, Denbigh, LL16 5AA
☎ (01745) 814159, Fax 814888, Sec
816669, Rest 816664
Course is 0.5 miles from Denbigh on
the B5382.
Parkland course.
Pro Mike Jones; Founded 1922
Designed by John Stockton
18 holes, 5712 yards, S.S.S. 68
♦ Welcome with prior arrangement.
⚑ WD £22; WE £27.

♫ Welcome; packages and catering
available; from £22.
⚇ Clubhouse facilities available.
⌐ Talardy Park; Oriel House, both
St Asaph.

10 42 Dewstow
Caerwent, Newport, Monmouthshire,
NP6 4AH
☎ (01291) 430444, Fax 425816
⚏ www.dewstow-golf-club.co.uk
✉ johnharris@btconnect.com
Off A48 between Newport and
Chepstow.
Parkland course.
Pro Johnathan Skeuse; Founded
1988
Park: 18 holes, 6176 yards, S.S.S.
60; Old: 10 holes, 6091 yards, S.S.S.
70
♦ Welcome.
⚑ WD £14; WE £17.
♫ Welcome WD; some restrictions at
WE; packages available; from £20.
⚇ Full bar and restaurant facilities.
Practice range, 26 bays floodlit
covered.
⌐ Beaufort; Old Course

10 43 Dinas Powis
Golf House, Old Highwalls, Dinas
Powis, CF64 4AJ
☎ (029) 2051 2727, Fax 2051 2727,
Pro 2051 3682, Bar 2051 2157, Rest
2051 4128
Centre of Dinas Powys 5 miles from
Cardiff.
Parkland course; 90 yards 7th.
Pro Gareth Bennett; Founded 1914
18 holes, 5500 yards, par 68, S.S.S.
68
♦ Welcome with handicap certs;
dress codes apply.
⚑ WD £25, WE £30.
♫ Welcome by prior arrangement
and with handicap certs; terms on
application.
⚇ Clubhouse facilities.
⌐ Many in Cardiff.

10 44 Dolgellau
Pencefn, Golf Rd, Dolgellau,
Gwynedd, LL40 2ES
☎ (01341) 422603, Fax 422603
0.5 miles N of Dolgellau.
Parkland course.
Founded 1911
9 holes, 4671 yards, S.S.S. 63
♦ Always welcome.
⚑ WD £15; WE £18; two-for-one
vouchers.
♫ Welcome by prior arrangement;

catering packages available; from
£13.
⚇ Clubhouse facilities.
Practice range; club and trolley hire.
⌐ Royal Ship Hotel, Dolgellau

10 45 Earlswood
Jersey Marine, Neath, W Glamorgan,
SA10 6JP
☎ (01792) 321578, Sec 812198
Signposted off B 4290 road off the
A483 Neath-Swansea road.
Parkland course.
Pro Mike Day; Founded 1993
18 holes, 5174 yards, S.S.S. 68
♦ Welcome.
⚑ WD £8; WE £8.
♫ Welcome by prior arrangement;
packages available.
⚇ By arrangement with Sec.
⌐ The New Tower Hotel.

10 46 Fairwood Park
Blackhills Lane, Upper Killay,
Swansea, SA2 7JN
☎ (01792) 297849, Fax 297849, Pro
299194, Bar/Rest 203648, Sec
297849
Turn into Blackhills Lane opposite
Swansea Airport.
Parkland championship course.
Pro Gary Hughes; Founded 1969
Designed by Hawtree & Co
18 holes, 6741 yards, S.S.S. 72
♦ Welcome by prior arrangement.
⚑ WD £25; WE £30.
♫ Welcome by prior arrangement;
terms on application.
⚇ Clubhouse facilities.
⌐ Winston Hotel, Bishopston;
Langrove Hotel, Parkmill, Hillcrest,
Mumbles.

10 47 Ffestiniog
Clwb Golff Ffestiniog, Y Cefn,
Ffestiniog, Gwynned
☎ (01766) 762637
On the B4391 1 mile from Ffestiniog.
Scenic mountain course.
Founded 1893
9 holes, 5032 yards, S.S.S. 65
♦ Welcome; some WE restrictions.
⚑ WD £10; WE £10.
♫ Welcome by prior arrangement.
⚇ Clubhouse facilities by
arrangement; bar.
⌐ Abbey Arms; The Pengwren.

10 48 Flint
Cornist Park, Flint, Flintshire, CH6
5HJ

☎ (01352) 732327, Fax 811885, Sec 812974
📧 slwflint@aol.com
Course is one mile from the centre of Flint.
Parkland course.
Founded 1965
Designed by H Griffith
9 holes, 5980 yards, S.S.S. 69
† Welcome.
⌷ WD £10; WE £10.
⌖ Welcome WD by arrangement; up to 27 holes of golf, 3-course meal from £12.
🍽 Clubhouse facilities.
⌸ The Mountain Park View Hotel, Flint; Springfield, Halkyn.

10 49 Glamorganshire
Lavernock Rd, Penarth, CF64 5UP
☎ (029) 2070 1185, Fax 2070 1185, Pro 2070 7401, Sec 2070 1185, Bar 2070 7048, Rest 2070 1033
5 miles SW of Cardiff just off M4 Junction 33.
Parkland course.
Pro Andrew Kerr-Smith; Founded 1890
Designed by W East & T Simpson
18 holes, 6056 yards, S.S.S. 70
† Welcome by arrangement; dress codes apply.
⌷ WD £30; WE £35.
⌖ Welcome Thurs and Fri only; catering packages available; reductions for more than 60; from £22.
🍽 Clubhouse facilities.
Practice ground with net, buggies and clubs for hire.
⌸ Walton House Hotel; Raisdale, both Penarth.

10 50 Glynhir
Glynhir Rd, Llandybie, Ammanford, Carmarthenshire, SA18 2TF
☎ (01269) 850472, Fax 851365, Pro 851010, Sec 851365
3.5 miles from Ammanford; off A483 towards Llandello.
Parkland course.
Pro Duncan Prior; Founded 1967
Designed by F.W. Hawtree
18 holes, 6026 yards, S.S.S. 70
† Welcome except Sun with handicap certs.
⌷ WD £16; WE £22.
⌖ Welcome by arrangement; Tues and Fri; terms on application.
🍽 Clubhouse facilities.
⌸ The Mill at Glynhir (next to course); Cawdor Arms; White Hart Inn; Plough Inn, all Llandello.

10 51 Glynneath
Pen-y-craig, Pontneathvaughan, Nr Glynneath, W Glamorgan, SA11 5HH
☎ (01639) 720452, Fax 720452
From A465 road at Glynneath take B4242 for 1.5 miles to Pontneathvaughan.
Parkland and wooded hilltop course.
Founded 1931
Designed by Cotton, Pennink, Lawrie & Partners
18 holes, 5487 yards, S.S.S. 68
† Welcome; no restrictions.
⌷ WD £15; WE £20.
⌖ Welcome; catering and bar snacks available.
🍽 Clubhouse facilities.
⌸ Baverstock; Tynewydd Hotel, Penderyn.

10 52 Gower
Cefn Goleu, Three Crosses, Gowerton, Swansea, SA4 3HS
☎ (01792) 872480, Fax 872480, Pro 879905
Follow the A484 towards Gowerton and then take the B4295 to Penclawdd; after one mile turn to Three Crosses.
Parkland course with lakes.
Pro Alan Williamson; Founded 1995
Designed by Donald Steel
18 holes, 6441 yards, S.S.S. 71
† Welcome.
⌷ Variable.
⌖ Welcome by prior arrangement; maximum 100; from £12.
🍽 Bar and catering facilities available.
⌸ The Mill at Glynhir; Winston, Bishopston.

10 53 Greenmeadow
Treherbert Road, Croesyceiliog, Cwmbran, Gwent, NP44 2BZ
☎ (01633) 869321, Fax 868430, Pro 862626
Off A4042 5 miles N of M4 Junction 26.
Parkland course.
Founded 1978
18 holes, 6078 yards, S.S.S. 70
† Welcome.
⌷ Terms on application.
⌖ Welcome by prior arrangement; packages available; professional clinics; tennis courts; private function rooms.
🍽 Full clubhouse catering facilities available.
Practice range, 26 bays covered and floodlit.
⌸ Parkway; Commodore.

10 54 Grove
South Cornelly, Nr Bridgend, Mid Glamorgan, CF33 4RP
☎ (01656) 788771, Fax 788414, Pro 788300
Off M4 Junction 37 near the Glamorgan Heritage Coast at Porthcawl.
Parkland course with water features.
Founded 1997
18 holes, 6128 yards, S.S.S. 69
† Welcome; bookings essential.
⌷ WD £10; WE £10.
⌖ Welcome by prior arrangement.
🍽 Bar and restaurant; function rooms.

10 55 Haverfordwest   ℭ
Arnolds Down, Haverfordwest, Pembrokeshire, SA61 2XQ
☎ (01437) 763565, Fax 764143, Pro 768409, Sec 764523
1 miles E of Haverfordwest on A40.
Parkland course.
Pro Alex Pile; Founded 1904
18 holes, 6005 yards, S.S.S. 69
† Welcome by prior arrangement.
⌷ WD £18; WE £22.
⌖ Welcome by arrangement; catering packages available; terms on application.
🍽 Bar, bar snacks and dining room.
⌸ Mariners.

10 56 Hawarden
Groomsdale Lane, Hawarden, Deeside, Flintshire, CH5 3EH
☎ (01244) 531447, Fax 536901, Pro 520809
Off A55 at Ewloe towards Hawarden; Groomsdale Lane opposite police station after playing fields.
Undulating parkland course.
Pro Alec Rowlands; Founded 1911/1950
18 holes, 5894 yards, S.S.S. 68
† Welcome; members comp day Saturday.
⌷ WD £16; Sun £20.
⌖ Welcome by prior arrangement with Sec.
🍽 Bar and full catering facilities; meals by arrangement.
⌸ St David's Park, Ewloe.

10 57 Henllys Hall
Beaumaris, Anglesey, Gwynedd, LL58 8HU
☎ (01248) 810412, Fax 811511, Pro 811717
4 miles from A55.
Parkland course with Snowdonia

views and water features.
Pro Peter Maton; Founded 1997
Designed by Roger Jones
18 holes, 6098 yards, S.S.S. 71
† Welcome by prior arrangement.
⌞ Terms on application.
⌁ Welcome by prior arrangement;
catering and hotel packages terms on
application; sun room; fitness centre;
tennis court; swimming pool; leisure
centre (under construction).
◉ Full hotel facilities; bar and
restaurant.
⌐ Henllys Hall on site.

10 58 Holyhead
Trearddur Bay, Holyhead, Anglesey,
LL65 2YG
☎ (01407) 763279, Fax 763279, Pro
762022, Bar 762119, Rest 765113
4 miles off the A5 after turning left at
the Valley traffic lights.
Undulating heathland
Pro Steve Elliott; Founded 1912
Designed by James Braid
18 holes, 6060 yards, S.S.S. 70
† Welcome; advised to book in
advance.
⌞ Terms on application.
⌁ Welcome by arrangement.
◉ Full bar and catering facilities.
Practice range, 0.5 miles away, 10
bays.
⌐ On site dormy house hotel;
Trearddur Bay; Anchorage; Beach.

10 59 Holywell
Brynford, Nr Holywell, Flintshire, CH8
8LQ
☎ (01352) 713937, Fax 713937, Pro
710040
⌐ holywell_golf_club@lineone.net
From A55 at Holywell exit take
A5026, then take Brynford signs.
Natural moorland/links type course
around quarries.
Pro Jim Law/Sean O'Connor;
Founded 1906
18 holes, 6164 yards, S.S.S. 70
† Welcome; dress codes apply.
⌞ WD £15; WE £20.
⌁ Welcome by arrangement with
Sec; catering packages available;
snooker; reduced rates for groups of
20; from £15.
◉ Full catering facilities and bar.
Practice area and buggies for hire.
⌐ Club can recommend hotels.

10 60 Inco
Clydach, Swansea, W Glamorgan,
SA6 5EU

☎ (01792) 844216, Sec 843336
Course is two miles N of the M4
Junction 45.
Parkland course with river and trees
featured.
Founded 1965
18 holes, 6064 yards, S.S.S. 69
† Welcome.
⌞ Terms on application.
⌁ Welcome by prior arrangement.
◉ Catering by arrangement.

10 61 Kinmel Park Golf Complex
Bodelwyddan, Denbighshire, LL18
5SR
☎ (01745) 833548
Just off A55 between St Asaph and
Abergele.
Parkland course.
Pro Peter Stebbings; Founded 1988
Designed by Peter Stebbings
9 holes, 3100 yards, par 58.
† Pay and play.
⌞ WD £4; WE £4.50.
⌁ Welcome; Peter Stebbing's Golf
Academy; snack bar and
refreshments; terms on application.
◉ Bar.

10 62 Kinsale
Llanerchymor, Holywell, Flintshire,
CH8 9DX
☎ (01745) 561080, Fax 561079
Off A548 coast road at turning for
Maes Pennant.
Parkland course.
Pro Alec Backhurst; Founded 1994
Designed by Ken Smith
9 holes, 6005 yards, S.S.S. 70
† Welcome; pay and play.
⌞ WD and WE: 9 holes £6.60; 18
holes £9.90; special price for juniors
every day but Sunday.
⌁ Welcome by arrangement.
◉ Café facilities; Kinsale Hall next
door for bar and restaurant.
Practice range, 12 bays floodlit.
⌐ Kinsale Hall.

10 63 Knighton
The Ffrydd, Knighton, Powys, LD7
1DL
☎ (01547) 528646, Fax 529284, Sec
520297
SW of Knighton off the A488
Shrewsbury-Llandrindod Wells road
at junction with A4113.
Upland course.
Founded 1913
Designed by Harry Vardon
9 holes, 5338 yards, S.S.S. 66

† Welcome; advised to book in
advance for weekends.
⌞ WD £10; WE £12.
⌁ Welcome by prior arrangement;
terms on application.
◉ Clubhouse facilities.
⌐ Red Lion; Knighton Hotel.

10 64 Lakeside
Water St, Margam, Port Talbot, SA13
2PA
☎ (01639) 899959, Rest 883486
0.5 miles from M4 Junction 38 off
A48 to Margam Park.
Parkland course.
Pro M Wootton; Founded 1992
Designed by M Wootton/D.T. Thomas
18 holes, 4480 yards, par 63, S.S.S.
63
† Welcome.
⌞ WD £9.50; WE £9.50.
⌁ Welcome except Sun; golf and
meal; £14.
◉ Catering available.
⌐ Twelve Knights; Seabank;
Esplanade.

10 65 Llandrindod Wells ☎
Llandrindod Wells, Powys, LD1 5NY
☎ (01597) 822010, Fax 823873, Pro
822247, Sec 823873, Bar/Rest
824487
Signposted in the town.
Parkland course.
Pro Phil Davies; Founded 1905
Designed by Harry Vardon
18 holes, 5759 yards, S.S.S. 69
† Welcome.
⌞ Prices on application.
⌁ Welcome by prior arrangement
with Sec; terms on application.
◉ Clubhouse facilities.
⌐ Metropole; Montpellier; Griffin
House; Penybont; Pencerrig.

10 66 Llandudno (Maesdu)
Hospital Rd, Llandudno, Gwynedd,
LL30 1HU
☎ (01492) 876016, Fax 871570, Pro
875195, Sec 876450, Bar 876016,
Rest 878759
A55 to Conwy-Deganwy exit, then
A546 to clubhouse.
Parkland course.
Pro Simon Boulden; Founded 1915
Designed by Tom Jones
18 holes, 6545 yards, S.S.S. 72
† Welcome by arrangement.
⌞ WD £25; WE £30.
⌁ Welcome everyday; maximum 36
at WE; 50 in week; no concessions;
from £25.

🍽 Catering and bar facilities.
Practice range, clubs and buggies for hire.
🛏 Royal; Esplanade; Risboro.

10 67 Llanfairfechan
Llannerch Road, Llanfairfechan, Conwy, LL33 0EB
☎ (01248) 680144, Sec 680524
Course is south of the A55 in Llanfairfechan.
Parkland course.
Founded 1972
9 holes, 3119 yards, S.S.S. 57
🏌 Welcome.
⌊ WD £5; WE £10.
⌒ Welcome by prior arrangement; catering by arrangement; terms on application.
🍽 Some catering and bar facilities.
🛏 Split Willow.

10 68 Llangefni (Public)
Llangefni, Anglesey, LL77 8YQ
☎ (01248) 722193
On the outskirts of Llangefni towards Amlwch.
Parkland course.
Pro Paul Lovell
Founded 1983
Designed by Hawtree & Sons
9 holes, 1467 yards, par 3, S.S.S. 28
🏌 Welcome.
⌊ WD £3; WE £3.30; children and OAPs £1.65.
⌒ Welcome by prior arrangement.
🍽 In local café.

10 69 Llangland Bay
Llangland Bay, Swansea, SA3 4QR
☎ (01792) 366023, Sec 366721
6 miles W of Swansea
Seaside parkland course.
Pro Mark Evans; Founded 1904
18 holes, 5857 yards, S.S.S. 69
🏌 Welcome.
⌊ Terms on application.
⌒ Welcome by prior arrangement; maximum 36; catering packages available by prior arrangement; winter packages available; terms on application.
🍽 Clubhouse facilities except Mondays.
🛏 Llangland Court; Osborne.

10 70 Llanishen
Cwm, Lisvane, Cardiff, CF4 5UD
☎ (029) 2075 5078, Fax 2075 5078, Pro 2075 5076, Sec 2075 5078, Rest 2075 2205

5 miles N of Cardiff, 1 mile N of Llanishen.
Parkland course.
Pro R A Jones; Founded 1905
18 holes, 5296 yards, S.S.S. 66
🏌 Welcome WD; WE only with a member.
⌊ WD £24; WE £12.
⌒ Welcome Thurs afternoons; packages available with catering; from £18.
🍽 Clubhouse facilities.
🛏 Cardiff Bay; Angel; Manor House; New House.

10 71 Llannerch Park
North Wales Golf Range and Course, St Asaph, Denbighshire, LL17 0BD
☎ (01745) 730805
On A525 between St Asaph and Trefnant.
Parkland course.
Pro Michael Jones; Founded 1988
9 holes, 1587 yards, par 3 and 4.
🏌 Public pay and play.
⌊ WD £2.50; WE £2.50.
🍽 Refreshments.

10 72 Llantrisant & Pontyclun
Lanlay Rd, Talbot Green, Mid-Glam, CF72 8HZ
☎ (01443) 222148, Pro 228169, Sec 224601
M4 Junction 34 then A4119 to Talbot Green.
Parkland course.
Pro Mark Phillips; Founded 1927
18 holes, 5950 yards, par 67.
🏌 Welcome WD; with member at WE.
⌊ WD £20; WE £15.
⌒ Welcome; menus available at all times; from £15.
🍽 Bar and restaurant facilities.
🛏 Miskin Manor.

10 73 Llanwern
Tennyson Ave, Llanwern, Newport, NP6 2DY
☎ (01633) 412029, Fax 412029, Pro 413233, Sec 412029, Bar/Rest 413278
1 mile from M4 Junction 24.
Parkland course.
Pro Stephen Price; Founded 1928
18 holes, 6177 yards, S.S.S. 69
🏌 Welcome.
⌊ WD non-members £20, guests of members £10; WE non-members £25, guests of members £15.
⌒ Welcome Wed, Thurs, Fri with

prior arrangement; reduced rates for golf and catering for more than 20; terms on application.
🍽 Catering available.
🛏 Stakis Country Court; Hilton National; Holiday Inn; Travel Inn; Celtic Mabnor.

10 74 Llanyrafon
Llanfrechfa Way, Cwmbran, NP44 8HT
☎ (01633) 874636
N to Pontypool off the M4 Junction 26.
Parkland course.
Pro Dave Woodman; Founded 1981
9 holes, 2566 yards, S.S.S. 54
🏌 Welcome.
⌊ WD £3; WE £3.50; under 16s and over 60s: WD £2.15, WE £2.25.
⌒ Welcome by arrangement.
🍽 Refreshments.

10 75 Machynlleth
Newtown Road, Machynlleth, Powys, SY20 8DU
☎ (01654) 702000
0.5 miles out of town on the A480 Newtown road.
Parkland course.
Founded 1905
Designed by James Braid
9 holes, 5726 yards, S.S.S. 67
🏌 Welcome; Thurs 12-3 ladies; Sun 8-11.30 am.
⌊ WD £12; WE £15.
⌒ Welcome; 10% reduction for groups of 8 or more; terms on application.
🍽 Clubhouse facilities.
Buggies not allowed on course; clubs for hire.
🛏 Wynnstay, Plas Dolguog.

10 76 Maesteg
Mount Pleasant, Neath Rd, Maesteg, Mid-Glam, CF34 9PR
☎ (01656) 732037, Pro 735742, Sec 734106, Fax 734106
Adjacent to B4282 main Maesteg to Port Talbot road 0.5 miles from Maesteg.
Hilltop course with forest views down the valley.
Pro Christopher Riley; Founded 1912
Designed by James Braid (1945)
18 holes, 5939 yards, S.S.S. 69
🏌 Welcome.
⌊ WD £17; WE £20.
⌒ Welcome by prior arrangement.
🍽 Bar meals available.
Practice ground.

↗ Heronstone, Bridgend; Aberavon, Port Talbot; Greenacres GH, Maesteg.

10 77 Marriott St Pierre Hotel Golf & CC

St Pierre Park, Chepstow, Monmouthshire, NP6 6YA
☎ (01291) 625261, Pro 635205, Fax 629975
Course is two miles from Chepstow on the A48.
Parkland course.
Pro Craig Dun; Founded 1962
Designed by Bill Cox
Mathern: 18 holes, 5569 yards, S.S.S. 68; Championship: 18 holes, 6538 yards, S.S.S. 72
† Welcome with handicap certs.
⌐ Terms on application.
⌒ Welcome WD; WE residents only; catering packages available; function rooms available; terms available on application.
🍽 Long Weekend Café Bar; The Orangery restaurant.
↗ On site Marriott hotel.

10 78 Merthyr Tydfil (Cilsanws)

Cloth Hall Lane, Cefn Coed, Merthyr Tydfil, Mid-Glam, CF48 2NU
☎ (01685) 723308
Course is two miles north of Merthyr on Cilsanws Mountain in Cefn Coed.
Mountain top heathland course.
Founded 1908
18 holes, 5622 yards, S.S.S. 69
† Welcome except on Sun competition days.
⌐ WD £10; WE £15.
⌒ Welcome by prior arrangement; meals available; terms available on application.
🍽 Clubhouse facilities.
↗ Mount Dolu Lodge.

10 79 Mid-Wales Golf Centre

Maesmawr, Caersws, Nr Newtown, Powys,
☎ (01686) 688303, Fax 688303
6 miles W of Newtown.
Farmland course.
Founded 1992
Designed by Jim Walters
9 holes, 2554 yards, S.S.S. 54
† Welcome.
⌐ WD £6; WE £8.
⌒ Welcome by prior arrangement.
🍽 Light snacks and bar.
Practice range, 12 bays floodlit.
↗ Maesmawr Hall.

10 80 Milford Haven

Woodbine House, Hubberston, Milford Haven, SA73 3RX
☎ (01646) 692368, Pro 697762
0.75 miles W of town on road to Dale.
Meadowland course.
Founded 1913
Designed by David Snell
18 holes, 6035 yards, S.S.S. 70
† Welcome.
⌐ WD £15; WE £20.
⌒ Welcome at all times; terms on application.
🍽 Restaurant facilities.
Driving and practice area
↗ Lord Nelson; Sir Benfro; Little Haven.

10 81 Mold

Cilcain Rd, Pantymwyn, Mold, Flintshire, CH7 5CH
☎ (01352) 741513, Fax 741517, Pro 740318
3 miles from Mold; leave on Denbigh road; turn left after 100 yards, and follow road for 2.5 miles.
Undulating parkland course.
Pro Richard Hughes; Founded 1909
Designed by Hawtree
18 holes, 5528 yards, S.S.S. 67
† Welcome
⌐ WD £18; WE £20.
⌒ Welcome by prior arrangement; catering packages by arrangement.
🍽 Full facilities.
Practice ground.
↗ Bryn Awel.

10 82 Monmouth ☎

Leasebrook Lane, Monmouth, Monmouthshire, NP5 3SN
☎ (01600) 712212
Signposted from the Monmouth-Ross on Wye (A40) road.
Undulating parkland course.
Pro Brian Gurling; Founded 1896
18 holes, 5698 yards, S.S.S. 69
† Welcome anytime except Sunday morning before 11.30am,
⌐ WD £15, WE £20.
⌒ Welcome with prior arrangement with the secretary Mrs E Edwards; packages available; from £18.
🍽 Clubhouse facilities.

10 83 Monmouthshire

Llanfoist, Abergavenny, Monmouthshire, NP7 9HE
☎ (01873) 852606, Fax 852606, Pro 852532, Bar/Rest 853171
✉ secretary@monmouthshire-g-c.sagehost.co.uk

2 miles SW of Abergavenny.
Parkland course; three successive par 5s: 6, 7, 8
Pro Brian Edwards; Founded 1892
Designed by James Braid
18 holes, 5978 yards, S.S.S. 70
† Welcome by arrangement.
⌐ WD £25; WE £30.
⌒ Welcome Mon and Fri by prior arrangement; 10% reduction if more than 25 in party; terms on application.
🍽 Full clubhouse facilities.
↗ The Bear Hotel, Creek Howell; The Manor, Creek Howell.

10 84 Morlais Castle

Pant, Dowlais, Merthyr Tydfil, Mid-Glam, CF48 2UY
☎ (01685) 722822, Fax 388700, Pro 388700
Follow signs for Brecon Mountain Railway.
Moorland course.
Pro H Jarrett; Founded 1900
18 holes, 6320 yards, S.S.S. 71
† Welcome anytime.
⌐ WD £16; WE £20.
⌒ Welcome WD by prior arrangement with Sec.
🍽 Full catering and bar facilities in new clubhouse.
Practice ground; buggies and clubs for hire.
↗ Tregunna; Travel Lodge.

10 85 Morriston

160 Clasemont Rd, Morriston, Swansea, W Glamorgan, SA6 6AJ
☎ (01792) 771079, Fax 795628, Pro 772335, Sec 796528, Bar 771079
3 miles N of Swansea city centre on A4067.
Parkland course.
Pro Darryl Rees; Founded 1919
18 holes, 5755 yards, S.S.S. 68
† Welcome.
⌐ WD £21; WE £30.
⌒ Welcome by prior arrangement only.
🍽 Lunches and bar facilities available.
↗ Dragon; Dolphin; Forest Motel; Hilton; Holiday Inn.

10 86 Mountain Ash ☎

The Clubhouse, Cefn Pennar, Mountain Ash, Mid-Glam, CF45 4DT
☎ (01443) 472265, Fax 479459, Pro 478770, Sec 479459
Off A470 Cardiff to Abercynon road at Mountain Ash; follow signs to Cefn Pennar.

Marriott St Pierre

In the summer of 1987, St Pierre – now Marriott St Pierre – celebrated its 25th anniversary. In a game which goes back centuries, that might not seem much of a landmark, but St Pierre earned itself pride of place by being the first post-war championship course to be built in Britain.

In the winter of 1961-62, Ken Cotton was invited to design two courses in the border country of England and Wales, one in the old deer park alongside the main road from Chepstow to Newport and the other in unpromising woodland at Ross-on-Wye. He thought a visit to see how it was done would be a good experience for a young writer – and how right he was.

The two courses could not possibly have been more of a contrast. St Pierre was largely ready-made in terms of fairways whereas Ross-on-Wye, a miracle of enterprise by a devoted band, had to be stripped root by root before the holes took shape.

That Cotton succeeded in both instances showed that he was a master of his craft. You can only judge the results if you knew the original terrain, the difficulties encountered and the budgets available. Both St Pierre and Ross-on-Wye were built on the thinnest of shoestrings. Bill Graham, who had dreamed of a course in the lovely park at St Pierre, drove past one day, and discovering that it was on the market, proved himself a man of action by buying it.

The land, the ancient manor house where the Crown Jewels were stored during the Battle of Agincourt, and the cost of construction of the course came to something under £30,000. However absurdly modest that seems nowadays, one or two sacrifices had to be made but Graham's reasons for purchasing had to be commercially based and there he showed how valid his instincts were. Floodlit golf proved to be one of his few ideas to misfire. When St Pierre was built, motorway systems were already well launched, and the opening of the Severn Bridge only a few years away. St Pierre was, and is, wonderfully accessible from London, Birmingham and Bristol, as well as South Wales.

It wasn't given long to settle down before it was much in demand. Dunlop made it a frequent home for their much lamented Masters and in 1980 the Ladies Golf Union paid it the ultimate compliment by holding the Curtis Cup there. Regular calls have been made upon it by organisers of small tournaments and company days, all of whom flock to take advantage of the Marriott Hotel and a host of other sporting facilities.

The addition of the second course brought alteration to Cotton's original design, and more land was purchased on higher ground. However, nothing destroyed Cotton's first impression that, for club golfers at large, it is a delightful place to play.

Stately ancient trees feature strongly. After a mild introduction to them at the first, the second is dominated by them, although there follows a break on the loftier reaches of the third to the sixth. At the sixth, the eye is caught by the distant sights but, with the seventh, the trees return and, from then on, there is no let-up.

Several recent changes and a few new back tees have made the professionals flex their muscles a little more. However, one hole where no change is contemplated, and certainly none required, is the 18th across the lake. One of golf's oldest cliches is that nothing is certain until the last putt is holed; nowhere is it more apt than at Marriott St Pierre.

Mountain heathland course.
Pro Marcus Wills; Founded 1908
18 holes, 5553 yards, S.S.S. 67
♦ Welcome.
⌴ WD £15; WE £18.
◌Welcome; special packages
available from secretary; terms on
application.
◉ Clubhouse facilities.
⌐ Baverstocks, Aberdare.

10 87 Mountain Lakes ₵

Blaengwynlais, Nr Caerphilly, Mid-
Glam, CF83 1NG
☎ (029) 2086 1128, Fax 2086 3243,
Pro 2088 6666, Bar/Rest 2088 6686
4 miles from M4 Junction 32 on
Tongwynlais-Caerphilly road.
Parkland course.
Pro S Bebb; Founded 1989
Designed by R Sandow/ J Page
18 holes, 6343 yards, S.S.S. 73
♦ Welcome.
⌴ WD £18; WE £18.
◌Welcome by prior arrangement;
terms on application; function,
conference facilities.
◉ Restaurant and bar facilities.
Practice range, 15 bays.
⌐ New Country House.

10 88 Neath

Cadoxton, Neath, SA10 8AH
☎ (01639) 643615, Pro 633693, Sec
632759
2 miles from Neath in Cadoxton.
Mountain course.
Pro E M Bennett; Founded 1934
Designed by James Braid
18 holes, 6490 yards, S.S.S. 72
♦ Welcome WD; with member at
WE.
⌴ WD £18; WE £13.
◌Welcome by arrangement with
Sec; terms on application.
◉ Full clubhouse facilities
⌐ Castle, Neath.

10 89 Nefyn & District

Morfa Nefyn, Pwllheli, Gwynedd,
LL53 6DA
☎ (01758) 720966, Fax 720476, Pro
720102, Bar 720218, Rest 721626
⌨ nefyngolf@tesco.net
1 mile W of Nefyn; 18 miles W of
Caernarfon.
Seaside clifftop course on Llyn
peninsula.
Pro John Froom; Founded 1907
New: 18 holes, 6548 yards, S S.S.
71; Old: 18 holes, 6201 yards, S.S.S.
71

♦ Welcome by prior arrangement;
handicap certs preferred; dress code
apply.
⌴ WD £31; WE £36.
◌Welcome by prior arrangement
except for 2 weeks in August; 10 per
cent reduction for groups of 12 or
more; snooker table; terms on
application.
◉ Full clubhouse facilities;
restaurant and bar.
⌐ Nanhoron, Nefyn; The Linksway,
Morfa Nefyn.

10 90 Newport

Great Oak, Rogerstone, Newport,
Gwent, NP1 9FX
☎ (01633) 892683, Fax 896676, Pro
893271, Sec 892643, Rest 894496
3 miles from Newport M4 Junction 27
on B4591.
Parkland course.
Pro Paul Mayo; Founded 1903
18 holes, 6431 yards, S.S.S. 71
♦ Welcome by prior arrangement.
⌴ WD £30; WE £40.
◌Welcome Wed, Thurs, Fri and
some Sun; handicap certs required;
discounts available at off-peak times;
from £30.
◉ Full clubhouse facilities.
⌐ Celtic Manor, Newport.

10 91 Newport (Pembs)

Newport, Pembrokeshire, SA42 0NR
☎ (01239) 820244, Fax 820244
Follow signs for Newport Sands from
Newport.
Seaside course.
Pro Colin Parsons; Founded 1925
Designed by James Braid
9 holes, 5815 yards, S.S.S. 68
♦ Welcome.
⌴ WD £15; WE £15.
◌Welcome by prior arrangement;
terms on application.
◉ Full bar and restaurant facilities.
⌐ Self-catering flats on site.

10 92 North Wales ₵

72 Bryniau Rd, West Shore,
Llandudno, Gwynedd, LL30 2DZ
☎ (01492) 875325, Fax 875325, Pro
876878, Bar/Rest 875342
2 miles from A55 on A546
Llandudno/Deganwy road.
Links course.
Pro Richard Bradbury; Founded 1894
Designed by Tancred Cummins
18 holes, 6247 yards, S.S.S. 71
♦ Welcome.
⌴ WD £25; WE and BH £35.

◌Welcome with handicap certs;
menu, practice area and snooker;
from £23.
◉ Full bar and restaurant facilities.
⌐ Many in Llandudno.

10 93 Northop Country Park ₵

Northop, Nr Chester, Flintshire, CH7
6WA
☎ (01352) 840440, Fax 840445
Off A55 at Northop/Connahs Quay
exit; entrance is on slip road.
Parkland course.
Pro Matthew Pritchard; Founded
1994
Designed by John Jacobs
18 holes, 6735 yards, S.S.S. 73
♦ Welcome by prior arrangement.
⌴ WD £30; WE £35.
◌Welcome by prior arrangement
WD; catering packages available;
corporate days arranged; tennis;
gym; sauna.
◉ Full restaurant facilities; bar;
terrace.
Practice range, 8 bays.
⌐ St Davids Park, Ewloe.

10 94 Oakdale

Llwynon Lane, Oakdale, Gwent, NP2
0NF
☎ (01495) 220044, Driving range
220440
M4 Junction 28 then A467 to Crumlin
and B4251 to Oakdale.
Parkland course.
Founded 1990
Designed by Ian Goodenough
9 holes, 2688 yards, S.S.S. 56
♦ Welcome.
⌴ WD £4.50; WE £4.50 (second 9
£2.75); basket of range balls £1.30.
◌Welcome by prior arrangement.
◉ Snacks in clubhouse.
Practice range, 18 bays floodlit.
⌐ The Old Forge.

10 95 Old Colwyn

Woodland Ave, Old Colwyn, Clwyd,
LL29 9NL
☎ (01492) 515581
Off A55 at Old Colwyn exit towards
Old Colwyn.
Undulating meadowland course.
Founded 1907
Designed by J Braid
9 holes, 5263 yards, S.S.S. 66
♦ Welcome; by prior arrangement at
WE.
⌴ WD £10; WE £15.
◌Welcome by arrangement;
reductions for 10 or more players;

menus by arrangement; terms on application.
🍽 Full clubhouse facilities.
↰ Bodelwyddan Castle has reduced rates for golfers; Lyndale.

10 96 Old Padeswood
Station Rd, Padeswood, Mold, Clwyd, CH7 4JL
☎ (01244) 547701, Pro 547401, Sec 550414
On A5118 between Penyfford and Mold close to A55.
Meadowland course in valley.
Pro Tony Davies; Founded 1933/1978
Designed by Arthur Joseph
18 holes, 6685 yards, S.S.S. 72
🏌 Welcome.
Ⅼ WD £18; WE £20.
↻ Welcome WD; restaurant, bar, also par 3 course; from £18.
🍽 Full clubhouse facilities.
Practice range, par 3 course.
↰ Many in Chester, Wrexham and Mold.

10 97 Old Rectory Hotel
Llangattock, Crickhowell, Powys, NP8 1PH
☎ (01873) 810373, Fax 810373
A40 to Crickhowell.
Parkland course.
Founded 1968
9 holes, 2600 yards, S.S.S. 54
🏌 Welcome.
Ⅼ WD £7.50; WE £7.50.
↻ Terms on application; bars, meals and restaurant available.
🍽 Bar and restaurant.
↰ On site hotel; 20 en suite rooms.

10 98 Padeswood & Buckley
The Caia, Station Lane, Padeswood, Mold, Flintshire, CH7 4JD
☎ (01244) 550537, Fax 541600, Pro 543636, Bar 550537, Rest 556072
↰ padeswoodgc@compuserve.com
Off Penyfford-Mold road A5118 at Old Padeswood turning; club 50 yards further on.
Parkland course alongside River Alyn.
Pro D V Ashton; Founded 1933
Designed by Williams Partnership
18 holes, 5982 yards, S.S.S. 70
🏌 Welcome; members only at weekends; dress codes apply.
Ⅼ WD £20.
↻ Welcome WD; packages include 28 holes of golf; coffee on arrival, light lunch and dinner; prices on application.

🍽 Full clubhouse facilities and restaurant.
↰ St David's Park, Ewloe; Beaufort Park, New Brighton.

10 99 Palleg
Palleg Rd, Lower Cwmtwrch, Swansea, SA9
☎ (01639) 842193
Course is off the Swansea-Brecon road.
Meadowland course.
Pro Sharon Roberts; Founded 1930
Designed by C.K. Cotton
9 holes, 6418 yards, S.S.S. 72
🏌 Welcome with handicap certs WD; with member at WE.
Ⅼ WD £13.
↻ Welcome by prior arrangement; terms on application.
🍽 Clubhouse facilities.
Tuition available.
↰ Y Stycle, Upper Cwmtwrch; Dab-Yr-Ogof Caves, Abercrane; Goufch Arms B and B.

10 100 Parc Golf Academy
Church Lane, Coedkernew, Newport, Gwent, NP1 9TU
☎ (01633) 680933, Fax 681011, Pro 680933, Sec 680933
M4 Junction 28; on to A48 towards Cardiff for 1.5 miles.
Parkland course.
Pro Darren Griffiths; Founded 1989
Designed by B. Thomas & T. Hicks
18 holes, 5619 yards, S.S.S. 68
🏌 Welcome WD; WEs by prior arrangement.
Ⅼ WD £12; WE £15.
↻ Welcome by arrangement.
🍽 Full facilities; bar, restaurant, function room, conference suite.
Extensive tuition by Darren Griffiths, Russell Jones and Barry Thomas.
Practice range, 38 bays floodlit and carpeted; buggies and clubs for hire.
↰ Coach & Horses, Travel lodge, both Castleton.

10 101 Penmaenmawr
Conway Rd, Penmaenmawr, Conwy, LL34 6RD
☎ (01492) 623330
3 miles W of Conwy on A55 to Dwygyfylchi.
Undulating parkland course.
Founded 1910
9 holes, 5350 yards, S.S.S. 66
🏌 Welcome except Sat.
Ⅼ WD £12; Sun £18.
↻ Welcome by prior arrangement;

inclusive package of 27 holes, lunch and dinner; from £25.
🍽 Bar and restaurant.
↰ Caerlyr Hall.

10 102 Pennard
2 Southgate Rd, Southgate, Swansea, W Glamorgan, SA3 2BT
☎ (01792) 233131, Pro 233451
8 miles W of Swansea via A4067 and B4436.
Undulating seaside.
Pro Mike Bennett; Founded 1896
18 holes, 6265 yards, S.S.S. 72
🏌 Welcome; dress codes apply (no jeans or trainers) on course and in clubhouse.
Ⅼ WD £24; WE £30.
↻ Welcome by prior arrangement; minimum group 12; snooker; squash; from £16.
🍽 Bar snacks; lunches and evening meals.
Practice area; no buggies allowed on course; trolleys and clubs for hire.
↰ Osborne; Winston; Nicholaston; Cefn Goleua; Fairy Hill.

10 103 Penrhos Golf & Country Club ℭ
Llanrhystud, Nr Aberystwyth, Cardiganshire, SY23 5AY
☎ (01974) 202999, Fax 202100
9 miles S of Aberystwyth on A487; take Llanrhystud turning on to B4337.
Parkland course.
Pro Paul Diamond; Founded 1991
Designed by Jim Walters
18 holes, 6641 yards, S.S.S. 72
🏌 Welcome except Sun am.
Ⅼ WD £18; WE £25.
↻ Welcome by arrangement; catering packages available; £17-£38.
🍽 Full clubhouse facilities.
↰ On site motel; 15 en suite rooms; Marine; Conrah Country, both Aberystwyth; Plas Morfa, Llanon.

10 104 Peterstone Golf & Country Club
Peterstone Wentloog, Cardiff CF3 8TN
☎ (01633) 680009, Fax 680563, Pro 680072
Take A48 towards Cardiff from M4 Junction 28 turning left to Marshfield; course 2.5 miles.
Parkland/links course.
Founded 1990
Designed by Bob Sandow
18 holes, 6555 yards, S.S.S. 72
🏌 Welcome.

WD £16.50; WE £22.50.
Welcome Mon-Fri; full packages;
corporate days; photographs; starter;
half-way house; on-course
competition; presentation evenings;
terms on application.
Full bar and restaurant facilities;
Fairways restaurant.
Wentloog; Travelodge; Moat
House.

10 105 Plassey
The Plassey Golf Course, Eyton,
Wrexham, Flintshire, LL13 0SP
(01978) 780020
2 miles SW of Wrexham signposted
from A483.
Parkland course.
Founded 1992
Designed by K Williams
9 holes, 2379 yards, par 32.
Pay and play; telephone first.
WD £6; WE £7.
Unlimited access; terms on
application.
Practice area restricted to members
only.
On site caravan site with
swimming pool; visitors can play in
comps.

10 106 Pontardawe
Cefn Llan, Pontardawe, Swansea,
SA8 4SH
(01792) 863118, Fax 830041, Pro
830977
From M4 Junction 45 take A4067 to
Pontardawe.
Moorland course.
Pro Gary Hopkins; Founded 1924
18 holes, 6038 yards, S.S.S. 70
Welcome WD with handicap certs.
WD £22.
Welcome by arrangement; prices
vary depending on numbers; catering
by arrangement.
Full clubhouse facilities.
Pen-yr-Alt.

10 107 Pontnewydd
West Pontnewydd, Cwmbran, Gwent,
NP44 1AB
(01633) 482170
Follow signs for West Pontnewydd or
Upper Cwmbran; W slopes of
Cwmbran.
Meadowland course.
Founded 1875
9 holes, 5353 yards, S.S.S. 67
Welcome WD; WE as guest of a
member.
WD terms on application.

Welcome by prior arrangement;
terms on application.
Limited.
Parkway; Commodore.

10 108 Pontypool
Lasgarn Lane, Trevethin, Pontypool,
Gwent, NP4 8TR
(01495) 763655, Pro 755544
Off A4042 at St Cadoc's Church in
Pontypool.
Mountain course.
Pro James Howard; Founded 1919
18 holes, 5963 yards, S.S.S. 69
Welcome by arrangement.
WD £20; WE £24.
Welcome by prior arrangement;
packages available; terms on
application.
Full catering facilities except Mon.
Three Salmons; Glyn-yr-Avon,
both Usk; Parkway, Cwmbran.

10 109 Pontypridd
Ty-Gwyn, The Common, Pontypridd,
Mid-Glam, CF37 4DJ
(01443) 402359, Fax 491622, Pro
491210, Sec 409904
12 miles NW of Cardiff E of
Pontypridd off A470.
Mountain course.
Pro Wade Walters; Founded 1905
Designed by Bradbeer
18 holes, 5881 yards, S.S.S. 66
Welcome with handicap certs.
Terms on application.
Welcome by arrangement with the
Pro Wade Walters; packages
available; terms on application.
Clubhouse facilities.
Lechwen Hall; The Millfield Hotel.

10 110 Porthmadog
Morfa Bychan, Porthmadog,
Gwynedd, LL49 9UU
(01766) 512037, Fax 514638, Pro
513828, Sec 514124
1 mile W of Porthmadog High Street
after turning towards Black Rock
Sands.
Parkland/links course.
Pro Pete Bright; Founded 1902
Designed by James Braid
18 holes, 6363 yards, S.S.S. 71
Welcome by arrangement.
WD £20; WE £26.
Welcome by prior arrangement;
discounts for groups of more than 16;
catering available; terms on
application.
Clubhouse facilities.
Tydden Llwyn; Sportsmans.

10 111 Prestatyn
Marine Rd East, Prestatyn,
Denbighshire, LL19 7HS
(01745) 854320, Fax 888353, Pro
852083, Sec 888353, Bar/Rest
886172
Off A548 coast road to Prestatyn.
Championship links.
Pro M L Staton; Founded 1905
Designed by S. Collins
18 holes, 6808 yards, S.S.S. 73
Welcome except Sat and Tues
morning.
WD £20; WE £25.
Welcome except Sat and Tues am
by prior arrangement; 27 holes; lunch
and dinner; from £30.
Clubhouse facilities.
Talardy, St Asaph; Traeth Ganol;
Sands, Prestatyn; Craig Park,
Dyserth.

10 112 Priskilly Forest Golf Club
Castlemorris, Haverfordwest,
Pembrokeshire, SA62 5EH
(01348) 840276 Fax 840276
On B4331 towards Mathry off A40 at
Letterstone.
Picturesque mature parkland course.
Founded 1992
Designed by J. Walters
9 holes, 5874 yards, par 70, S.S.S.
69
Welcome.
WD 18 holes £12; WE 18 holes
£12.
Welcome by arrangement; limited
catering facilities.
Licensed bar and tea rooms.
Priskilly Forest GH on site.

10 113 Pwllheli
Golf Rd, Pwllheli, Gwynedd, LL53
5PS
(01758) 612520, Fax 701644, Sec
701644, Bar/Rest 701633
Turn into Cardiff Road in town centre;
bear right at the first fork; course
signposted.
Parkland/links course.
Pro John Pilkington; Founded 1900
Designed by Tom Morris; extended by
James Braid
18 holes, 6200 yards, S.S.S. 69
Welcome.
WD £22; WE £27.
Welcome most days by prior
arrangement.
Full facilities.
Caeau Capel, Nefyn; Bryn
Eisteddfod, Clynnogfawr; Nanhoron,
Morfa.

10 114 Pyle & Kenfig
Waun-y-Mer, Kenfig, S Wales, CF33
4PU
☎(01656) 783093 and 771613, Fax
772822, Pro 772446, Rest 771788
M4 Junction 37 through Porthcawl
and follow signs.
Links/downland.
Pro Robert Evans; Founded 1922
Designed by H. Colt
18 holes, 6688 yards, S.S.S. 73
♦ Welcome;.
_ WD £30; WE £30.
♪Welcome by arrangement; prices
vary according to numbers; terms on
application.
®I Full bar and catering facilities.
⌐ Fairways; Atlantic; Seabank.

10 115 Radyr
Drysgol Rd, Radyr, Cardiff, CF4 8BS
☎(029) 2084 2408, Fax 2084 3914,
Pro 2084 2476, Bar/Rest 2084 2735
4 miles from M4 Junction 32; 8 miles
from Cardiff.
Parkland course.
Pro R Butterworth; Founded 1902
18 holes, 6078 yards, S.S.S. 70
♦ Welcome by prior arrangement.
_ WD £36; WE £36.
♪Welcome with prior arrangement;
catering packages available; separate
facilities for parties of 35-40; dining
room for 125+; terms on application.
®I Full dining and bar facilities
available.
Extensive practice ground.
⌐ Quality Inn.

10 116 RAF St Athan
St Athan, Barry, Vale of Glamorgan,
CF62 4WA
☎(01446) 751043, Sec 797186
first right after St Athan village on
Cowbridge road.
Parkland course.
Founded 1982
9 holes, 6542 yards, S.S.S. 72
♦ Welcome except Sun.
_ WD £10; Sat £15.
♪Welcome by arrangement with
Sec.
®I Full facilities available, except
Mon.

10 117 Raglan Parc ♛
Golf Club
Parc Lodge, Raglan, Monmouthshire,
NP5 2ER
☎(01291) 690077, Fax 690075
0.5 miles from Raglan at junction of
A40 and A449.

Undulating parkland course.
Founded 1994
18 holes, 6604 yards, S.S.S. 72
♦ Welcome; booking advisable.
_ 18 holes WD £15; WE £18.
♪Welcome by prior arrangement;
packages of coffee, light lunch and 3-
course meal; from £25.
®I Bar, snacks and light meals.
⌐ The Beaufort; The Country Court;
Travellodge.

10 118 Rhondda
Golf House, Penrhys, Mid-
Glamorgan, CF43 3PW
☎(01443) 433204, Fax 441384, Pro
441385, Sec 441384
On Penrhys road between Rhondda
Fach and Rhondda Fawr.
Mountain course.
Pro Gareth Bebb; Founded 1910
18 holes, 6205 yards, S.S.S. 70
♦ Welcome WD; restrictions WE.
_ WD £20; WE £25.
♪Welcome by prior arrangement;
function room available; terms on
application.
®I Full clubhouse bar and catering
facilities.
⌐ Heritage Park.

10 119 Rhos-on-Sea
Penrhyn Bay, Llandudno, Conwy,
LL30 3PU
☎(01492) 549100, Pro 548115,
Bar/Rest 549641
From A55 take Old Colwyn exit and
follow coast road to Penrhyn Bay;
course is between Rhos-on-Sea and
Llandudno.
Links course.
Pro Mike Macara; Founded 1899
Designed by J J Simpson
18 holes, 6064 yards, S.S.S. 69
♦ Welcome.
_ WD £10; WE £20.
♪Welcome everyday but only with
prior arrangement; catering terms on
application; from £10.
®I Full clubhouse facilities.
⌐ On site dormy house hotel.

10 120 Rhosgoch
Rhosgoch, Builth Wells, Powys
LD23JY
☎(01497) 851251
Off B4594 at turning to Clyro between
Erwood and Kington.
Parkland course.
Founded 1984
Designed by Herbie Poore
9 holes, 5078 yards, S.S.S. 67

♦ Welcome.
_ WD £7; WE £10.
♪Welcome by prior arrangement;
terms on application.
®I Bar and snacks.
⌐ Clyro Court.

10 121 Rhuddlan
Meliden Rd, Rhuddlan, Denbighshire,
LL18 6LB
☎(01745) 590217, Fax 590472, Pro
590898, Rest 591978
Course is off the A55 three miles N of
St Asaph.
Parkland course.
Pro Andrew Carr; Founded 1930
Designed by Hawtree & Co
18 holes, 6471 yards, S.S.S. 71
♦ Welcome; only with a member
Sun.
_ WD £24; Sat £30.
♪Welcome WD by arrangement.
®I Lunch and dinner daily; bar
facilities.
⌐ Plas Elwy; Kinmel Manor
(packages available for both).

10 122 Rhyl
Coast Rd, Rhyl, Denbighshire, LL18
3RE
☎(01745) 353171, Pro 360007, Sec
334136
1 mile from station on A548 Prestatyn
road.
Seaside links course.
Pro Tim Leah; Founded 1890
Redesigned by James Braid
9 holes, 6220 yards, S.S.S. 70
♦ Welcome.
_ WD £15; WE £20.
♪Welcome by prior arrangement;
discount of 20 per cent for parties of
more than 20 players; full catering
packages available; snooker; from
£12.
®I Full catering facilities.
⌐ Grange; Marina.

10 123 The Rolls of
Monmouth
The Hendre, Monmouth,
Monmouthshire, NP5 4HG
☎(01600) 715353, Fax 713115
4 miles NW of Monmouth on the
B4233.
Parkland course.
Founded 1982
Designed by Urbis Planning
18 holes, 6733 yards, S.S.S. 73
♦ Welcome by arrangement.
_ Prices on application.
♪Welcome by prior arrangement;

Royal Porthcawl

Water, water everywhere. There is not a hole where the sea is not visible at Royal Porthcawl. While many seaside links courses are nestled among the sand dunes with little more than the odd glimpse of the distant roar of the sea, Royal Porthcawl is quite different.

Hugging the beach over the opening holes, the golfer is offered an immediate sighting of the real influence on the course. Many believe that the second hole, certainly the former England cricket captain Tony Lewis among them, is one of the finest tests in all of British golf.

So often the hapless and wayward golfer can be found wandering the shore in search of a ball that has missed the subtle green or been caught by the wind blowing off the Bristol Channel.

After the short fourth the course swings inland through the long fifth with its sculptured green that gives a sharp reminder of how steep the sides were and how simple it was to find a misplaced shot catching the rim and ending up close, if not in, the hole. It is here that the climb to the upper slopes begins, although with the wind often being a help rather than a hindrance, the real test does not really start until the turn for home.

The steep 12th, a shortish par five, is a testing preamble to the long 13th which so often is buffeted by the howling wind off the sea. When the wind doesn't blow the green can look an inviting place from the brow of the fairway but just ask the great Tiger Woods how demanding it can be in the wind and rain.

When the Walker Cup was first played in Wales in 1995, Royal Porthcawl was the obvious choice and it brought the best out of a British and Irish team that had the benefit not only of having played the seaside course several times but also the experience of Bernard Gallacher, the then Ryder Cup captain.

Woods was the biggest amateur name in the world at the time and was on the verge of launching his professional career. However, he struggled to come to terms with the demands of the magnificent and brooding Royal Porthcawl.

Against Englishman Gary Wolstenholme they approached the wonderful 18th level. Although maybe not as famous, or some would say infamous as the 17th, the finishing hole can hold some demons. It falls gently away towards the sea and has a sliding green which falls away quite quickly.

It was a remarkable hole of contrasts that day for Woods and Wolstenholme as they made their differing approaches through the hollows and heather that leads to the shoreline and the 18th green. Wolstenholme needed a wood for his second shot, Woods, showing his power, needed only a short iron.

Wolstenholme judged his perfectly and hit the green. Woods, on the other hand, over-egged his and watched in horror as the ball disappeared out of bounds. With it went the game and the initiative as Great Britain and Ireland recorded yet another victory against the overwhelming odds.

Woods was to exact some revenge later in the weekend against Wolstenholme but by then it was too late. The tale serves as a constant reminder that power alone is not enough at Royal Porthcawl. It calls for subtlety and a large measure of good fortune.

As a golf course it can be tough and demoralising but as a spectacle, when the sun is glinting off the Bristol Channel on a long, warm June afternoon it can be one of the most enchanting golf courses in all of Britain. — **CG**

Royal St David's and Nefyn

There can be few more spectacular nor, at times, more intimidating places to play golf than on the Llyn Peninsula in Northwest Wales. And two of the jewels are, without doubt, Royal St David's and the raw course at Nefyn.

Royal St David's has one of the most magnificent backdrops in golf. The ancient Harlech castle, grey and imposing, sits on the cliffs above the course which has been the host for many top amateur competitions. The castle was once on the cliffs overlooking the sea but now the reclaimed land provides a perfect setting for the championship course.

It is an unrelenting test among sandhills and is renowned for its beauty and test of golf. Few of the holes are played in continuous directions. It is the finish of the course that troubles but still intrigues most of the golfers who have made the long journey to the course.

The par-four 15th is the toughest at 427 yards. The dog-legged fairway means that the drive has to thread its way through the sandhills and on to the narrow fairway which is potted with hollows. Against the prevailing wind only the brave or the experts can normally reach the green, protected by another hollow, in two.

Finishing with a par three is a relief after another testing hole at 17 and then it's a short walk back to a modest but history-filled clubhouse and then across the railway line to the car park.

Royal St David's is much more famous than Nefyn, which lies further north on the coast and while it doesn't possess the same history it can be just as much a test of golf

and offer even more spectacular views across the Irish Sea from the back nine of the seaside course.

There can be few courses where you play blind on to most of the holes around a lifeboat station and a lighthouse. Most of the tee positions are not for the faint-hearted with long drops to sea-lashed rocky coastlines. On a calm day it is still a real test. On a windy day – and that is most of them in that part of the world – it can be as treacherous.

You know the problems you are likely to encounter when you address the 11th, which plays away from the clubhouse towards the greenkeeper sheds. The lay up, wherever you are on the course, means that the green is always blind.

The 12th is even more tricky as it is cut in half by the road leading to the lifeboat station and the beach cottages. Just to add to the hazards are a continual stream of walkers interspersed by a steady stream of visitors to the busy lifeboat station and the lighthouse.

Golfing on the Peninsula is never lonely, let alone dull. Inland courses may be testing, but without drives across wind-blown cliffs they do not have the same dramatic impression as the Peninsula. As both courses hug the sea, there is little chance of them ever being snow-bound or frozen although many of the winding roads around can make sure they are cut off.

On the right day there are few better courses on which to blow away the cobwebs and they are very popular with visiting golfers around the Christmas and New Year period. — **CG**

special offers on Mon; coffee on arrival, lunch, 18 holes; prices on application.
🍽 Full catering facilities available.
🛏 Riverside.

10 124 Royal Porthcawl
Rest Bay, Porthcawl, Mid-Glam, CF36 3UW
☎(01656) 782251, Fax 771687, Pro 773702
M4 Junction 37 and follow signs for Porthcawl/Rest Bay.
Championship links course.
Pro Peter Evans; Founded 1891
Designed by Charles Gibson
18 holes, 6685 yards, S.S.S. 74
⚑ Welcome Mon afternoon, Tues, Thurs, Fri; handicap certs required.
⌣ WD £50; WE £50.
⌣Welcome by arrangement; restaurant and bar facilities; from £50.
🍽 Full restaurant and bar service.
🛏 Club has own dormy house from £25 pp; Atlantic; Fairways.

10 125 Royal St David's
Harlech, Gwynedd, LL46 2UB
☎(01766) 780203, Fax 781110, Pro 780857, Sec 780361, Bar/Rest 780182
On the A496 Lower Harlech road under the Castle.
Championship links course.
Pro John Barnett; Founded 1894
18 holes, 6571 yards, S.S.S. 74
⚑ Welcome; booking essential.
⌣ WD £35; WE £40.
⌣Welcome; booking essential; 10 per cent reduction for more than 40 players; £5 deposit per player 2 months before visit; from £30.
🍽 Full catering facilities.
🛏 Rum Hole; St David's, both Harlech.

10 126 Ruthin Pwllglas
Ruthin Pwllglas, Ruthin, Denbighshire, LL15 7AR
☎(01824) 702296
On A494 2.5 miles S of Ruthin; right fork before Pwllglas village.
Parkland/meadowland course.
Pro Michael Jones; Founded 1906
Designed by David Lloyd Rees
10 holes, 5418 yards, S.S.S. 66
⚑ Welcome.
⌣ WD £12.50; WE £18.
⌣Welcome by prior arrangement.
🍽 Bar and catering facilities; by prior arrangement

🛏 Ruthin Castle; The Whitstay; The Anchor; The Manor House; The Eagles.

10 127 St Andrews Major
Coldbrook Rd East, Nr Cadoxton, Barry, S Glamorgan, CF6 3BB
☎(01446) 722227
From M4 Junction 33 follow signs to Barry and Cardiff Airport; turn left to Sully.
Parkland course.
Founded 1993
Designed by MRM Leisure
18 holes, 5862 yards, S.S.S. 70
⚑ Welcome; pay and play course.
⌣ WD and WE: 9 holes £8, 18 holes £13.
⌣Welcome; packages available; 18 holes and 2-course meal £15.
🍽 Full bar and restaurant facilities; Sun lunches; catering facilities.
🛏 Copthorne; The International; Mount Sorrel; Travel lodge.

10 128 St Davids City
Whitesands, St Davids, Pembrokeshire, SA62 6PT
☎(01437) 721751, Sec 720312
Course is two miles west of St Davids following the signs for Whitesands Bay.
Links course; most westerly Welsh course.
Founded 1902
9 holes, 18 tees, 6117 yards, S.S.S. 70
⚑ Welcome; some restrictions Fri pm.
⌣ Day tickets: WD £13 (winter £10). WE £13 (winter £10).
⌣Welcome by arrangement.
🍽 At the Whitesands Bay Hotel adjacent to course.
🛏 Whitesands Bay; Old Cross; St Nons; Warpool Court.

10 129 St Deiniol
Pen y Bryn, Bangor, Gwynedd, LL57 1PX
☎(01248) 353098, Pro 353728
From A5/A55 intersection follow A5122 for 1 mile to E of Bangor.
Undulating parkland course; views of Menai and Snowdonia.
Founded 1906
Designed by James Braid
18 holes, 5654 yards, S.S.S. 68
⚑ Welcome; phone in advance for weekends.
⌣ WD £14; WE £18.
⌣Welcome by appointment;

packages vary; terms on application; contact Viv Williams.
🍽 Full clubhouse facilities; no catering Mon.
🛏 Eryl Mor.

10 130 St Giles
Pool Rd, Newtown, Powys, SY16 3AJ
☎(01686) 625844, Fax 625044
1 mile E of Newtown on A483.
Riverside/parkland course.
Pro D P Owen; Founded 1895
9 holes, 6012 yards, S.S.S. 70
⚑ Welcome.
⌣ Terms on application.
⌣Welcome by arrangement; packages include refreshments; from £14.
🍽 Clubhouse facilities with bar and restaurant.
🛏 Elephant and Castle.

10 131 St Idloes
Penrallt, Llanidloes, Powys, SY18 6LG
☎01686) 412559, Sec 650712
Off A470 at Llanidloes; 1 mile down B4569.
Undulating course; superb views from hill plateau.
Founded 1906
Designed by Members
9 holes, 5510 yards, S.S.S. 66
⚑ Welcome.
⌣ WD £12.50; WE £15.50.
⌣Welcome; packages available; terms on application.
🍽 Clubhouse facilities.
🛏 Mount Inn; Unicorn; Lloyds.

10 132 St Mary's Hotel
St Mary's Hill, Pencoed, S Glamorgan
☎(01656) 860280, Sec 861100, Pro 861599, Fax 863400
Off Junction 35 of M4.
Parkland courses
18 holes, 5273 yards, par 68
also 9 holes, 2426 yards, par 34
⚑ Welcome by prior arrangement.
⌣ By negotiation.
⌣Welcome; packages available.
Country club; floodlit driving range.

10 133 St Mellons
St Mellons, Cardiff, CF3 8XS
☎(01633) 680401, Fax 681219, Pro 680101, Sec 680408
Close to M4 Junctions 28 (W); 30 (E).
Parkland course.
Pro Barry Thomas; Founded 1964
18 holes, 6275 yards, S.S.S. 70

† Welcome WD; members only at WE.
⌞ WD £32.
⟋ Welcome Tues and Thurs; packages vary according to numbers; terms on application.
◉ Clubhouse facilities.
⌐ St Mellons Hotel; Travel lodge.

10 134 St Melyd

The Paddock, Prestatyn, Denbighshire, LL19 9NB
☎ (01745) 854405
On A547 on the main Prestatyn to Meliden road.
Undulating parkland course.
Pro Andrew Carr; Founded 1922
9 holes, 5839 yards, S.S.S. 68
† Welcome except Thurs (Ladies day) and Sat.
⌞ WD £12; Sun £15.
⟋ Welcome except Thurs and Sat; 18 holes and 3-course meal £16.
◉ Full facilities except Tues.
⌐ Nant Hall; Graig Park.

10 135 Shirenewton Golf Club

Shirenewton, Nr Chepstow, Gwent, NP6 6RL
☎ (01291) 641642
Off M4 take A48 towards Newport on reaching Chirk take road to Shirenewton (2.5 miles).
Parkland course.
Pro Remton Doig; Founded 1995
Designed by M. Weeks/Tony Davies
18 holes, 6650 yards, S.S.S. 72
† Welcome.
⌞ WD £12; WE £15.
⟋ Welcome by prior arrangement.
◉ Full facilities.
Practice range.

10 136 South Pembrokeshire

Defensible Barracks, Military Rd, Pembroke Dock, Pembrokeshire, SA72 6SE
☎ (01646) 621453
Main A477 road from Carmarthen to Pembroke dock; 100 yards, after town boundary sign turn right to Pembroke.
Parkland course.
Founded 1970
18 holes, 6100 yards, S.S.S. 70
† Welcome.
⌞ WD £16; WE £20.
⟋ Welcome by prior arrangement; catering packages available; some discounts for larger groups; from £16.
◉ Clubhouse facilities.

⌐ Coach House; Cleddau Bridge; Kings Arms.

10 137 Southerndown

Ewenny, Bridgend, Mid-Glam, CF32 0QP
☎ (01656) 880476, Fax 880317, Pro 880326
4 miles from Bridgend on the coast road to Ogmore-by-Sea.
Links/downland course.
Pro Denis McMonagle; Founded 1906
Designed by W. Herbert Fowler, Willie Park, H.S. Colt
18 holes, 6417 yards, S.S.S. 72
† Welcome; WE only with a member.
⌞ WD £25; WE £35.
⟋ Welcome WD by prior arrangement; handicap certs required.
◉ Full facilities.
⌐ Sea Lawns; Sea Bank; Heronston; Great House.

10 138 Storws Wen

Brynteg, Yns Mon, Anglesey, LL78 8JY
☎ (01248) 852673, Fax 852673
Bar/Rest 853892
Follow the A5025 to Amlwch and then the B5108 to Llangefni; course is 1.5 miles on right before the California Hotel.
Parkland course.
Pro; Founded 1996
Designed by K Jones
9 holes, 5002 yards, S.S.S. 65
† Welcome.
⌞ WD: 9 holes £10, 18 holes £15; WE: 9 holes £13, 18 holes £18.
⟋ Welcome by arrangement; packages available.
◉ Clubhouse facilities.
Buggies for hire; practice range; tuition available.
⌐ Fully furnished, self-catering accommodation on site; Bryntiyon; Glanrafon; Bay Court; California.

10 139 Summerhill Golf Club

Hereford Road, Clifford, Hay-on-Wye, HR3 5EW
☎ (01497) 820451, Fax 820451
On B4352 from Hay towards toll bridge.
Parkland course.
Pro Graham Priday; Founded 1994
9 holes, 5858 yards, S.S.S. 68
† Welcome.
⌞ Terms on application.
⟋ Welcome by prior arrangement;

private function room; catering packages.
◉ Full facilities.
⌐ Kilvert; Swan.

10 140 Swansea Bay

Jersey Marine, Neath, W Glamorgan, SA10 6JP
☎ (01792) 812198, Pro 816159, Sec 814153, Bar 812198
From A483 take B4290 to Jersey Marine.
Links course.
Pro Mike Day; Founded 1892
18 holes, 6605 yards, S.S.S. 72
† Welcome with handicap certs; dress code applies.
⌞ WD £16; WE £22.
⟋ Welcome by arrangement; packages by arrangement; terms on application.
◉ Full clubhouse facilities.
⌐ Many in Swansea area.

10 141 Tenby

The Burrows, Tenby, Pembrokeshire, SA70 7NP
☎ (01834) 842978, Fax 842978, Pro 844447, Bar/Rest 845122
On A477 to Tenby W of town.
Championship links; oldest in Wales.
Pro Mark Hawkey; Founded 1888
18 holes, 6224 yards, S.S.S. 71
† Welcome with handicap certs.
⌞ WD £26; WE £30.
⟋ Welcome by arrangement; catering packages by arrangement.
◉ Full facilities.

10 142 Tredegar & Rhymney

Cwmtysswg, Rhymney, NP2 3BQ
☎ (01685) 840743, Fax 843440
On B4256 1.5 miles from Rhymney.
Undulating mountain course.
Founded 1921
12 holes, 6120 yards, S.S.S. 67
† Welcome.
⌞ WD £12; WE £15.
⟋ Welcome except Sun am.
◉ Bar and snacks; meals by prior arrangement.
⌐ Red Lion, Tredegar.

10 143 Tredegar Park

Parc-y-brain road, Rogerstone, Newport, NP10 9TG
☎ (01633) 895219, Fax 897152, Pro 894517, Sec 894433
⌐ secretary.tpgc@breathemail.net
Leave M4 Junction 27 to Newport; first right at Western Ave and right at

end of Western Ave.
Parkland alongside River Ebbw.
Pro M Morgan; Founded 1923
Designed by James Braid
18 holes, 6600 yards, S.S.S. 72
↑ Welcome with handicap certs and member of golf club.
⌞ WD £25; WE £35.
↷ Welcome by prior arrangement; minimum group 16; from £35.
🍽 Restaurant and bar facilities.
Practice ground; clubs for hire
↰ Celtic Manor.

10 144 Trefloyne
Trefloyne Park, Penally, Tenby, Pembrokeshire SA70 7RG
☎(01834) 842165, Fax 842165
🖳 www.walesholidays.co.uk/trefloyne
Off A4139 Tenby to Pembroke road at Penally.
Parkland course.
Pro S Laidler; Founded 1996
18 holes, 6635 yards, S.S.S. 71
↑ Welcome.
⌞ WD £18; WE £22.
↷ Welcome by prior arrangement; clubhouse facilities; minimum 8.
🍽 Catering by arrangement; light refreshments; licensed bar.
Practice ground; buggies and clubs for hire.

10 145 Vale of Glamorgan Golf and Country Club
Hensol Park, Hensol, S Glamorgan, CF7 8JY
☎(01443) 665899, Fax 665890
From M4 Junction 34 follow signs to Pendoylan.
Parkland course.
Pro Peter Johnson; Founded 1993
Designed by P. Johnson
18 holes, 6401 yards, S.S.S. 71
↑ Welcome WD; with member at WE; standard dress.
⌞ WD £30.
↷ Welcome by arrangement with Adrian Davies; full society packages; function room; Vale of Glamorgan health and racket club; computer analysis; £25-£39.
🍽 Full clubhouse facilities and bar; Hotel restaurant 'Lakes Brasserie' and 'Hogan's Bar'.
Practice range, 20 floodlit bays; buggies and clubs for hire; tuition.
↰ On site hotel 143 rooms.

10 146 Vale of Llangollen
The Club House, Holyhead Rd, Llangollen, Denbighshire, LL20 7PR

☎(01978) 860613, Fax 860906, Pro 860040, Sec 860906
1.5 miles E of Llangollen on the A5.
Parkland course set in valley floor.
Pro David Vaughan; Founded 1908
18 holes, 6656 yards, par 72, S.S.S. 73
↑ Welcome with handicap certs.
⌞ WD £25; WE £30.
↷ Welcome WD; 30 holes of golf with club catering; from £25.
🍽 Clubhouse facilities.
↰ Bryn Howel; Tyn-y-Wew; Wild Pheasant, all Llangollen.

10 147 Virginia Park
Virginia Park, Caerphilly, Mid-Glam, CF8 3SW
☎(029) 2086 3919, Fax 2089 0132
In centre of town next to Caerphilly recreation centre.
Parkland course.
Pro Peter Clark; Founded 1992
9 holes, 4661 yards, S.S.S. 66
↑ Welcome.
⌞ WD: 9 holes £7.50, 18 holes £14; WE: 9 holes £7.50, 18 holes £14.
↷ Welcome by arrangement.
🍽 Full bar and refreshments.
Practice range, 22 bays floodlit.

10 148 Welsh Border Golf Complex
Bulthy Farm, Bulthy, Middletown, Nr Welshpool, Powys, SY21 8ER
☎(01743) 884247
Via A458 Shrewsbury/Welshpool road following sign from Middletown.
Parkland course.
Pro Andy Griffiths; Founded 1991
Designed by Andrew Griffiths
Long course: 9 holes, 6012 yards, S.S.S. 69; Short course 2: 9 holes, 3228 yards, S.S.S. 59.
↑ Welcome; dress codes apply for Long course.
⌞ Long: WD £10, WE £10; Short: £6.
↷ Welcome by prior arrangement.
🍽 Bar and restaurant facilities.
Practice range, 10 bays floodlit; clubs and trolleys for hire.
↰ Rowton Castle; Bulthy Farm.

10 149 Welshpool
Golfa Hill, Welshpool, Powys SY21 9AQ
☎(01938) 850249
On the A458 out of Welshpool towards Dolgellau.
Hilly course.
Founded 1931

Designed by James Braid
18 holes, 5708 yards, S.S.S. 70
↑ Welcome.
⌞ Terms on application.
↷ Welcome by prior arrangement; WD packages available from £18.
🍽 Clubhouse facilities.
↰ Gorfa; Royal Oak, both Welshpool.

10 150 Wenvoe Castle
Wenvoe, Cardiff, CF5 6BE
☎(029) 2059 1094, Fax 2059 4371, Pro 2059 3649, Sec 2059 4371, Bar/Rest 2059 1094
Follow signs for Cardiff Airport from M4 Junction 33.
Parkland course.
Pro J Harris; Founded 1936
Designed by J Braid
18 holes, 6422 yards, S.S.S. 71
↑ Welcome WD only.
⌞ WD £24.
↷ Welcome WD; minimum 16; catering packages; from £18.
🍽 Clubhouse facilities.
Two practice facilities, putting green, trolleys for hire.
↰ The Copthorn.

10 151 Wernddu Golf Centre
Old Ross Rd, Abergavenny, Monmouthshire, NP7 8NG
☎(01873) 856223, Fax 852177
1.5 miles NE of Abergavenny on B4521 off A465.
Parkland course; 18th is 615 yards.
Pro Alan Ashmead; Founded 1992
Designed by G. Watkins/A Ashmead
18 holes, 5413 yards, S.S.S. 67
↑ Welcome.
⌞ WD £15; WE £15.
↷ Welcome; maximum 24; terms on application; from £15.
🍽 Bar snacks.
Practice range, 26 bays floodlit.
↰ Great George.

10 152 West Monmouthshire
Golf Road, Nantyglo, Gwent, NP3 4QT
☎(01495) 310233, Fax 311361, Pro 313052, Sec 310126
A465 Heads of Valley road, western valley A467 to Semtex roundabout; follow Winchestown signs.
Mountain heathland course; highest in England and Wales.
Founded 1906
18 holes, 6300 yards, S.S.S. 69
↑ Welcome; with member Sun.
⌞ WD £15; Sat £15.

↗Welcome WD by prior arrangement; package includes meals; from £20.
⚬ Full clubhouse facilities available.
⌐ Nearby GH's available.

10 153 Whitchurch (Cardiff)
Pantmawr Rd, Whitchurch, Cardiff, CF4 6XD
☎(029) 2062 0958, Fax 2052 9860, Pro 2061 4660, Sec 2062 0985, Bar 2062 0125, Rest 2061 8287
400 yards, along A470 towards Cardiff from M4 Junction 32.
Parkland course.
Pro Eddie Clark; Founded 1915
Redesigned by James Braid/F Johns
18 holes, 6321 yards, S.S.S. 71
⚑ Welcome; guests of members only at WE, welcome if no major competitions.
⌐ WD £35; WE £40.
↗Welcome Thurs; reductions for groups over 60 and between 24-40; minimum 24; 24-40 £26, 41-60 £22, 61+ £18.
⚬ Full clubhouse facilities available.
⌐ Quality Inn; Friendly Hotel; Masons Arms.

10 154 Whitehall
The Pavilion, Nelson, Treharris, Mid-Glam, CF46 6ST
☎(01443) 740245
Off A470 at Treharris and Nelson exit.
Mountain course.
Founded 1922
9 holes, 5666 yards, S.S.S. 68
⚑ Welcome WD; with captain's permission at WE.
⌐ WD £15; WE £20.
↗Welcome by arrangement with Sec; catering packages by arrangement.
⚬ Clubhouse facilities.
⌐ Llechwen Hall, Pontypridd.

10 155 Woodlake Park
Glascoed, Pontypool, Monmouthshire, NP4 0TE
☎(01291) 673933, Fax 673811
3 miles W of Usk overlooking Llandegfedd reservoir.
Undulating parkland course.
Pro Adrian Pritchard; Founded 1993
Designed by M.J. Wood/ H.N. Wood
18 holes, 6284 yards, S.S.S. 72
⚑ Welcome WD; with booking at WE.

⌐ WD £20; WE £25.
↗Welcome by prior arrangement; catering and golf packages available; snooker; pool table; from £20.
⚬ Full clubhouse bar and restaurant facilities.
Practice range, nets available.
⌐ Three Salmons; Rat Trap; New Court and Greyhound Inn, all Usk.

10 156 Wrexham
Holt Rd, Wrexham, Flintshire, LL13 9SB
☎(01978) 261033, Fax 364268, Pro 351476, Sec 364268, Bar 261033, Rest 358705
Course is two miles NE of Wrexham on the A534.
Sandy parkland course.
Pro Roy Young; Founded 1906/1924
Designed by James Braid
18 holes, 6233 yards, S.S.S. 70
⚑ Welcome with handicap certificates.
⌐ WD £25; WE £30.
↗Welcome WD except Tues; 27 holes of golf, coffee on arrival, light lunch, evening meal; £32.
⚬ Full clubhouse catering facilities.

11

NORTHERN IRELAND

It is a question most golf writers get asked from time to time: where do you like to play golf most of all? I think if narrowed down to one destination I would always plump for the plethora of fabulous golf courses to be found on the Monterey Peninsula in California. But I am always as happy as a sandboy to travel across the Irish Sea to play Royal County Down.

Heaven knows what more you could want from a golf course than the pleasures to be found here in Newcastle in the imposing shadow of the mountains of Mourne. Better weather perhaps?

Many professionals would probably like one or two less blind shots as well but for me they are part and parcel of the rough and tumble of links golf.

And over the next 20 years, if the peace process holds, there is no question that more and more people are going to play County Down and realise why it is the favourite golf course of Sir Michael Bonallack and a million others besides.

Why is it so good? Because it really does have it all. A wonderful variety of holes, from the hellish to the straightforward, and all played out in the most breathtaking scenery imaginable.

Does Northern Island possess the two best links courses in the British Isles? They certainly have an argument, for as good as County Down in the south of the province is, there are plenty who believe that Royal Portrush to the north is at least its equal.

If visiting both, make sure you take the slow road along the Antrim coast, which is quite simply one of the most beautiful journeys in Britain. The ruins of Dunluce castle precede the first glimpse of the magnificent Dunluce links itself, with its holes with names like Purgatory and Calamity, which hint at the nature of the challenge to follow.

In recent years Portrush has been back on the map through its staging of both the Amateur Championship and the senior British Open (which this year moves to County Down). It had led to speculation that the Open might be heading back there after an absence of half a century. Alas, the Royal and Ancient have ruled that out for the moment. Hopefully it will happen again one day.

It is only understandable that these two links courses overshadow all the other golf available in Northern Ireland. There are other splendid venues and particularly in the vicinity of Portrush. Links golf lovers, in particular, will also want to play Portstewart and Castlerock.

Belfast itself is also well served, Royal Belfast, with excellent views of the city, and Malone being the pick.

There is also Balmoral, the home club of the late Fred Daly, Hollywood and Shandon Park, which used to stage the Gallaher's Ulster Open at a time when a young Tony Jacklin was taking his first steps on to the world golfing stage. — **DL**

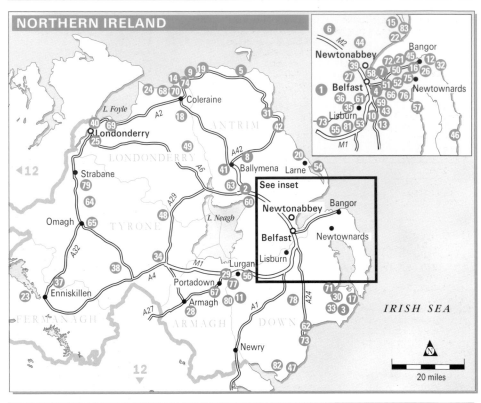

NORTHERN IRELAND

KEY

1	Aberdelghy	16	Blackwood	33	Downpatrick	50	Kirkistown Castle
2	Allen Park	17	Bright Castle	34	Dungannon	51	The Knock
3	Ardglass	18	Brown Trout	35	Dunmurry	52	Knockbracken Golf & CC
4	Ashfield	19	Bushfoot	36	Edenmore Golf Course	53	Lambeg
5	Ballycastle	20	Cairndhu	37	Enniskillen	54	Larne
6	Ballyclare	21	Carnalea	38	Fintona	55	Lisburn
7	Ballyearl Golf and	22	Carrickfergus	39	Fortwilliam	56	Lurgan
	Leisure Centre	23	Castle Hume	40	Foyle	57	Mahee Island
8	Ballymena	24	Castlerock	41	Galgorm Castle	58	Mallusk
9	Ballyreagh	25	City of Derry	42	Garron Tower	59	Malone Golf Club
10	Balmoral	26	Clandeboye	43	Gilnahirk	60	Massereene
11	Banbridge	27	Cliftonville	44	Greenisland	61	Mount Ober
12	Bangor	28	County Armagh	45	Helen's Bay	62	Mourne
13	Belvoir Park	29	Craigavon	46	Holywood	63	Moyola Park
14	Benone Par 3	30	Crossgar	47	Kilkeel	64	Newtownstewart
15	Bentra	31	Cushendall	48	Killymoon	65	Omagh
		32	Donaghadee	49	Kilrea	66	Ormeau

67	Portadown
68	Portstewart
69	Radisson Roe Park Hotel
70	Rathmore
71	Ringdufferin
72	Royal Belfast
73	Royal County Down
74	Royal Portrush
75	Scrabo
76	Shandon Park
77	Silverwood
78	Spa
79	Strabane
80	Tandragee
81	Temple
82	Warrenpoint
83	Whitehead

11 1 Aberdelghy

Bell's Lane, Lambeg, Co Antrim
☎ (028) 9266 2738
Between Dunmurry and Lambeg off
the Belfast-Lisburn road.
Municipal parkland course.
Founded 1986
9 holes, 4139 metres, S.S.S. 62
† Welcome.
⌴ WD £7.20; WE £9.20.
⌁ Welcome; discounts for groups of
15 or more.

11 2 Allen Park

45 Castle Rd, Antrim, Co Antrim
BT41 4NA
☎ (01489) 429001
Inland course.
18 holes, 6683 yards, S.S.S. 70
† Welcome.
⌴ Terms on application.
⌁ Packages available; terms on
application.
🍽 Full bar and restaurant facilities
available.

11 3 Ardglass

Castle Place, Ardglass, Co Down,
BT30 7TP
☎ (028) 4484 1219, Fax 4484 1841,
Pro 4484 1022
On B1 7 miles from Downpatrick; 30
miles S of Belfast.
Seaside course.
Pro Philip Farrell; Founded 1896
18 holes, 6065 yards, S.S.S. 69
† Welcome WD; Sun afternoon.
⌴ WD £18; WE £24.

⌐ Welcome by prior arrangement
WD and Sun am; packages on application; £15.
◉ Full facilities.
⌐ Burrendale; Slieve Danard; Burford Lodge GH.

11 4 Ashfield
Freeduff, Cullyhanna, Co Armagh
☎ (028) 3086 8180, Fax 3086 8111
Parkland course.
Founded 1990
18 holes, 5620 yards, S.S.S. 67
⚑ Welcome.
⌐ WD £10; WE £12.
⌐ Terms on application.
◉ Clubhouse facilities.

11 5 Ballycastle
Cushendall Rd, Ballycastle, Co Antrim, BT54 6QP.
☎ (028) 2076 2536, Fax 2076 9909, Pro 2076 2506
On A2 between Portrush and Cushendall.
Mixture of parkland, links and heath.
Pro Ian McLaughlin; Founded 1890
18 holes, 5757 yards, S.S.S. 70
⚑ Welcome by prior arrangement; some WE restrictions.
⌐ WD £20; WE £28.
⌐ Welcome by arrangement; WE restrictions; terms on application.
◉ Full clubhouse facilities.
⌐ Marine.

11 6 Ballyclare
25 Springvale Rd, Ballycare, BT39 9JW
☎ (028) 9332 2696, Fax 9332 2696, Rest 9332 4542, Bar 9334 2352
1.5 miles N of Ballyclare at Five Corners.
Parkland course.
Founded 1923
Designed by Tom McCauley
18 holes, 5745 yards, S.S.S.71
⚑ Welcome.
⌐ WD £16; WE £22.
⌐ Welcome by prior arrangement; minimum 20 players; catering by arrangement; snooker; from £14-£18.
◉ Bar and restaurant service.
Practice range.
⌐ Country House; Dunadry Inn; Chimney Corner; Five Corners B&B; Fairways B&B.

11 7 Ballyearl Golf and Leisure Centre
585 Doagh Rd, Newtownabbey, Belfast, BT36 8RZ

☎ (028) 9084 8287, Fax 9084 2896
1 mile N of Mossley off B59.
Public parkland course.
9 holes, 2306 metres
⚑ Welcome.
⌐ WD £4.90 (non-members), £4.70 (members); WE £5.70 (non-members), £5.50 (members).
◉ No facilities.
Practice range.

11 8 Ballymena
128 Raceview Rd, Ballymena
☎ (028) 2586 1487, Pro 2586 1652, Bar 2586 1207, Rest 2586 2087
2.5 miles E of the town on the A42 to Brough Shane and Carnlough.
Heathland/parkland course.
Founded 1902
18 holes, 5299 metres, S.S.S. 67
⚑ Welcome except Tues, Sat.
⌐ WD £17; WE £22.
⌐ Welcome by prior arrangement with the Hon Secretary.
◉ Full clubhouse bar and restaurant.
⌐ Adair Arms; Tullyglass House; Hotel One; The Country House

11 9 Ballyreagh
Glen Rd, Portrush, Antrim, BT56 8LX
☎ (01265) 822028
In Portrush.
9 holes, 2800 yards, S.S.S. 33
⚑ Welcome.
⌐ £9.
⌐ Limited.

11 10 Balmoral
518 Lisburn Rd, Belfast, BT9 6GX
☎ (028) 9038 1514, Pro 9038 7747, Bar/9038 8540, Rest 9038 4571
2 miles S of Belfast city centre; immediately beside the King's Hall on the Lisburn road opposite Balmoral Halt station.
Parkland course.
Pro Geoff Blakeley; Founded 1914
18 holes, 0278 yards, S.S.S. 70
⚑ Welcome except Sat and after 3pm Sun.
⌐ WD £20; WE £30.
⌐ Welcome by prior arrangement Mon and Thurs; special packages are available.
◉ Full clubhouse bar and restaurant.
⌐ Forte Crest; Europa; Plaza; York; Balmoral; Beechlawn.

11 11 Banbridge
116 Huntly Rd, Banbridge, Co Down, BT32 3UR

☎ (028) 4066 2211, Fax 4066 9400, Bar 4066 2211, Rest 4066 2342, Pro 4062 6189
1 mile N of Banbridge.
Parkland course.
Founded 1913
Extension by F Ainsworth
18 holes, 5047 yards, S.S.S. 67
⚑ Welcome; dress code.
⌐ WD £15; WE £20.
⌐ Welcome by prior arrangement; must be GUI recognised societies; catering by arrangement; from £12.
◉ Lounge and bar facilities available.
⌐ Belmont; Downshire; Bannview.

11 12 Bangor   Ⓣ
Broadway, Bangor, Co Down, BT20 4RH
☎ (028) 9127 0922, Fax 9145 3394, Pro 9146 2164, Bar/Rest 9127 0483
0.75 miles S of town centre.
Parkland course.
Pro Michael Bannon
Founded 1903
Designed by James Braid
18 holes, 6410 yards, S.S.S. 71
⚑ Welcome except Sat; ladies have priority Tues.
⌐ WD £20; WE £25.
⌐ Welcome by prior arrangement except Tues and Sat; catering by arrangement; from £15.
◉ Full bar and catering facilities.
⌐ Marine Court; Royal.

11 13 Belvoir Park
73 Church Rd, Newtownbreda, Belfast, BT8 4AN
☎ (028) 9049 1693, Fax 9064 6113, Pro 9064 6714, Bar 9064 2817, Rest 9064 1159
4 miles from Belfast off the Ormeau road.
Parkland course.
Pro Maurice Kelly; Founded 1927
Designed by H.S. Colt
18 holes, 6516 yards, S.S.S. 71
⚑ Welcome.
⌐ WD £33; WE £38.
⌐ Only 6 per month permitted by prior arrangement with the club Secretary.
◉ Full facilities supplied by Brian McMillan.
Practice range.
⌐ La Mon House; Stormont.

11 14 Benone Par 3 Course
53 Benone Ave, Benone, Limavady, Derry BT49 0IQ

☎(015047) 50555
10 miles N of Limarvady on A2.
Inland course.
9 holes, 1447 yards
⚲ Pay and play.
⚑ £4.

11 15 Bentra
1 Slaughterford Rd, Whitehead, Co
Antrim, BT38 9TG
☎(028) 9337 8996
5 miles N of Carrickfergus on Larne rd.
Municipal parkland course.
9 holes, 6084 yards, S.S.S. 68
⚲ Pay and play.
⚑ WD £7.50; WE £11.
⚘Welcome; tee times can be
reserved.
◉ Bar, snacks at Bentra roadhouse.
Practice range, 200 yards, 10 bays.
⚓ Magheramorne House; Coast
Road; Dobbins, Carrickfergus.

11 16 Blackwood
150 Crawfordsburn Rd, Clandeboye,
Bangor, BT19 1GB
☎(028) 9185 2706, Fax 9185 3785
On A2 towards Bangor from Belfast
turn to Newtonards; course 1.5 miles.
Heathland/parkland course.
Pro Roy Skillen; Debbie Hanna;
Founded 1994
Designed by Simon Gidman
18 holes, 6337 yards, S.S.S. 70
⚲ Welcome; pay and play.
⚑ WD £15; WE £20.
⚘Welcome by prior arrangement.
◉ Bar, snacks and restaurant.
Practice range, 25 bays floodlit.
⚓ Clandeboye Lodge.

11 17 Bright Castle
14 Coniamstown Rd, Bright, Co
Down, Co Down
☎(028) 4484 1319
5 miles S of Downpatrick.
Parkland course; 16th hole, par 6, is
735 yards.
Founded 1970
Designed by Arnold Ennis
18 holes, 7143 yards, S.S.S. 74
⚲ Welcome.
⚑ WD £10; WE and BH £12.
⚘Welcome by prior arrangement;
catering by arrangement.
◉ Catering facilities.
⚓ Abbey Lodge, Downpatrick.

11 18 Brown Trout
209 Agivy Road, Aghadowey, Nr Coleraine, Co Londonderry, BT51 4AP

☎(028) 7086 8209, Fax 7086 8878
7 miles S of Coleraine on the intersection of A54 & B66.
Parkland course.
Pro Ken Revie; Founded 1973
Designed by Bill O'Hara Snr
9 holes, 5510 yards, S.S.S. 68
⚲ Welcome.
⚑ WD £10; WE £15.
⚘Welcome by prior arrangement;
catering packages by prior
arrangement; private room for meals
and presentations; accommodation
for small groups; society rates from
£7.
◉ Full catering and bar facilities.
⚓ Brown Trout Country Inn on site.

11 19 Bushfoot
50 Bushfoot Rd, Portballintrae, Co
Antrim, BT57 8RR
☎(028) 2073 1317, Fax 203 1852,
Bar/Rest 2073 2588
4 miles E of Portrush on the coast.
Seaside links course.
Founded 1890
9 holes, 5914 yards, S.S.S. 67
⚲ Welcome except on competition
days.
⚑ WD £15; WE £20.
⚘Welcome by prior arrangement.
◉ Bar, restaurant, function room;
snooker room.
⚓ Beech; Bushmills Inn; Causeway.

11 20 Cairndhu
192 Coast Rd, Ballygally, Larne, Co
Antrim, BT40 2QG
☎(028) 2858 3324, Fax 2858 3324
4 miles N of Larne on the Glens of
Antrim coast road.
Parkland course.
Pro Bob Walker; Founded 1928/1958
Designed by John S.F. Morrison
18 holes, 6700 metres, S.S.S. 69
⚲ Welcome.
⚑ WD £15; WE £24.
⚘Welcome by prior arrangement;
discounts for groups of 20 or more;
from £15.
◉ Clubhouse facilities.
⚓ Highways; Londonderry Arms;
Ballygally Holiday Apartments.

11 21 Carnalea
Station Rd, Bangor, Co Down, BT19
1EZ
☎(028) 9127 0368, Fax 9127 3989,
Pro 9127 0122, Sec 9127 0368, Bar
9146 5004, Rest 9146 1901
1.5 miles from Bangor adjacent to
Carnalea station.

Parkland course on shore of Belfast
Lough.
Pro Thomas Loughran; Founded 1927
18 holes, 5574 yards, S.S.S. 67
⚲ Welcome; Sat after 2.30pm.
⚑ WD £15; WE £19.
⚘Welcome except Sat; catering by
arrangement; from £13.
◉ Bar and restaurant facilities.
⚓ Royal; Marine Court; Crawfords-
burn Inn.

11 22 Carrickfergus
35 North Rd, Carrickfergus, Co
Antrim, BT38 8LP
☎(028) 9336 3713, Pro 9336 1803,
Bar/Rest 9336 9200
Odd A2 9 miles NE of Belfast on the
North Rd; 1 mile from Shore Road.
Parkland/meadowland course.
Pro Mark Johnson; Founded 1926
18 holes, 5623 yards, S.S.S. 68
⚲ Welcome except Sat.
⚑ Terms on application.
⚘Welcome WD by arrangement.
◉ Full facilities.
⚓ Coast Road; Dobbins; Glenavna;
Quality Inn.

11 23 Castle Hume
Castle Hume, Enniskillen, Co Fer-
managh, BT93 7ED
☎(028) 6632 7077, Fax 6632 7076
5 miles from Enniskillen on the Done-
gal road.
Parkland course.
Pro Gareth McShea; Founded 1991
18 holes, 6492 yards, S.S.S. 72
⚲ Welcome
⚑ WD £15; WE £20.
⚘Welcome; minimum group of 12;
discounted fees for groups 12 or
more: WD £12, WE £18.
◉ Bar and restaurant.
⚓ Fort Lodge; Killyhevlin.

11 24 Castlerock
65 Circular Rd, Castlerock, Co Lon-
donderry, BT51 4TJ
☎(028) 7084 8215, Fax 7084 9440,
Pro 7084 8314, Sec 7084 8314, Bar
7084 8215, Rest 7084 8314
Off A2 6 miles W of Coleraine.
Links course.
Pro Robert Kelly; Founded 1901
Designed by Ben Sayers
18 holes, 6687 yards, S.S.S. 72
⚲ Welcome; arrange with Pro.
⚑ WD £30; WE £40.
⚘Welcome by prior arrangement;
catering by prior arrangement; from
£25.

🍽 Full catering facilities.
⛳ Golf Hotel.

11 25 City of Derry
49 Victoria Rd, Londonderry, BT47 2PU
☎ (028) 7134 6369, Pro 7131 1496, Bar/Rest 7131 1610
On main Londonderry-Strabane road three miles from Craigavon Bridge.
Parkland course; also 9-hole pay and play Dunhugh course.
Pro Michael Docherty; Founded 1912
18 holes, 6429 yards, S.S.S. 71
♦ Welcome WD before 4.30pm; WE by prior arrangement.
▫ WD £20; WE £25.
⛳ Welcome WD; limited WE availability.
🍽 Full facilities.
Practice range.
⛳ Everglades; Broomhill House; White Horse Inn; Waterfoot.

11 26 Clandeboy Ava
Tower Rd, Conlig, Newtownards, Co Antrim, BT23 3PN
☎ (028) 9127 1767, Fax 9147 3711, Pro 9127 1750, Bar/Rest 9127 0992
In village of Conlig off the Belfast-Bangor road at Newtonards.
Parkland course.
Pro Peter Gregory; Founded 1933
Designed by Baron von Limburger
Ava: 18 holes, 5755 yards, S.S.S. 68; Dufferin: 18 holes, 6559 yards, S.S.S. 71
♦ Welcome; Sat restrictions.
▫ WD £20, WE £25 (Ava); WD £25, WE £30 (Dufferin).
⛳ Welcome WD except Thurs; packages include golf and food; from £20-£35 (Ava); from £30-£40 (Dufferin).
🍽 Full clubhouse dining and bar facilities.
⛳ Clandeboye Lodge; Marine Court; Crawfordsburn Inn.

11 27 Cliftonville
44 Westland Rd, Belfast, BT14 6NH
☎ (028) 9074 4158, Sec 9074 6595
From Belfast take Antrim road for two miles then turn into Cavehill Rd and left again at Fire Station.
Parkland course.
Pro Peter Hanna; Founded 1911
9 holes, 5706 yards, S.S.S. 70
♦ Welcome except Tues afternoon and Sat.
▫ WD £13; WE £16.
⛳ Welcome by arrangement with secretary J M Henderson.

🍽 Bar facilities.
Practice range.
⛳ Lansdowne Court.

11 28 County Armagh
The Demesne, Newry Rd, Armagh, Co Armagh, BT10 1EN
☎ (028) 3752 2501, Pro 3752 5861 Sec/Fax 3752 5861
Off Newry Rd 0.25 miles from the city.
Parkland course.
Pro Alan Rankin; Founded 1893
18 holes, 6212 yards, S.S.S. 69
♦ Welcome except 12 noon-2pm Sat; 12 noon-3pm Sun.
▫ WD £15; WE £20.
⛳ Welcome by arrangement except Sat.
🍽 Full facilities except Mon.
Practice range.
⛳ Charlemont Arms; Drumshill House.

11 29 Craigavon
Turmoyra Lane, Silverwood, Lurgan, Craigavon, Co Armagh, BT66 6NG
☎ (01762) 326606
Off M1 from Belfast at A76 Junction 10; continue for 500 yards on the sliproad; first right into Kiln road and then right again.
Public parkland course.
Pro Des Paul
18 holes, 6118 yards, S.S.S. 72
♦ Welcome; phone at WE.
▫ WD £10.50; WE £13.50.
⛳ Welcome mainly Sun by arrangement; 12-hole pitch and putt; 9-hole putting green; ski centre.
🍽 Full facilities at Silverwood Golf and Ski Centre.
Practice range, 5 bays floodlit.
⛳ Silverwood.

11 30 Crossgar
231 Derryboye Rd, Crossgar, Co. Down, BT30 9DL
☎ (028) 4483 1523, Fax 4483 1523, Pro 4483 1629
From Belfast 5 miles S of Saintfield close to town of Crossgar.
Parkland course.
Founded 1993
Designed by John Cuffey
9 holes, 4580 yards, S.S.S. 63
♦ Welcome.
▫ WD £9; WE £11.
⛳ Welcome by prior arrangement; from £8.
🍽 Small restaurant and bar.
⛳ Millbrook Lodge, Ballynahinch.

11 31 Cushendall
Shore Rd, Cushendall, Ballymena, Co Antrim, BT44 0QG
☎ (028) 2177 1318, Sec 2175 8366
On main Antrim coast road 25 miles N of Larne.
Parkland course.
Founded 1937
Designed by Daniel Delargy
9 holes, 4384 yards, S.S.S. 63
♦ Welcome; start sheet on Thurs, Sat, Sun.
▫ WD £10; WE £15.
⛳ Welcome on application to secretary Mr S McLaughlin; catering packages available in summer; from £10.
🍽 Full catering in summer; bar facilities.
⛳ Thornlea.

11 32 Donaghadee
84 Warren Rd, Donaghadee, Co Down, BT21 0PQ
☎ (028) 9188 8697, Fax 9188 8891, Pro 9188 2392, Sec 9188 3624, Bar 9188 8697, Rest 9188 2519
6 miles S of Bangor on the coast road.
Part links and inland course.
Pro Gordon Drew; Founded 1899
18 holes, 5570 yards, S.S.S. 69
♦ Welcome by prior arrangement.
▫ WD £14; WE £18.
⛳ Welcome Mon, Wed, Fri by prior arrangement; discounts for groups of 24 or more; catering packages available by arrangement; from £14.
🍽 Clubhouse facilities.
⛳ Copeland.

11 33 Downpatrick
43 Saul Rd, Downpatrick, Co Down, BT30 6PA
☎ (028) 4461 5947, Pro 4461 5167, Bar/Rest 4461 5244
23 miles SE of Belfast off A24 and A7.
Parkland course
Founded 1930
Designed by Hawtree & Sons
18 holes, 6299 yards, S.S.S. 69
♦ Welcome; some WE restrictions.
▫ WD £15; WE £20.
⛳ Welcome by prior arrangement.
🍽 Full facilities.
⛳ Denvir; Abbey Lodge.

11 34 Dungannon
34 Springfield Lane, Mullaghmore, Dungannon, Co Tyrone, BT70 1QX
☎ (028) 8772 7338, Fax 8872 7338, Pro 8772 7485, Bar/Rest 8772 2098

0.5 miles from Dungannon on Donaghmore road.
Parkland course.
Founded 1890
18 holes, 6046 yards, S.S.S. 69
† Welcome; restrictions Tuesdays (ladies day).
⌐ WD £16; WE £20.
⌐ Welcome by prior arrangement except Tues and Sat.
⦿ Full facilities.
↗ Glengannon Hotel; Oaklin Hotel.

11 35 Dunmurry
91 Dunmurry Lane, Dunmurry, BT17 9JS
☎ (028) 9061 0834, Fax 9060 2540, Pro 9062 1314, Sec 9062 0834, Bar 9030 1402, Rest 9030 1124
Follow signs for Dunmurry from the M1; turn left at first traffic lights.
Parkland course.
Pro J Dolan; Founded 1905
Designed by T.J. McAuley
18 holes, 5832 yards, S.S.S. 68
† Welcome by prior arrangement.
⌐ WD £17; WE £26.50.
⌐ Welcome WD by written arrangement; packages available; from £16.
⦿ Full clubhouse facilities.
↗ Forte Crest; Beech Lawn.

11 36 Edenmore Golf Course
Edenmore House, 70 Drumnabreeze Rd, Maralin, Co. Armagh, BT67 0RH
☎ (028) 9261 1310, Fax 9261 3310, Rest 9261 9199
↗ edenmoregc@aol.com
M1 from Belfast to Junction 5 for Moira to Maralin.
Parkland course.
Founded 1992
Designed by Frank Ainsworth
18 holes, 6244 yards, S.S.S. 70
† Welcome except Sat am; priority for members before 2pm on Sat.
⌐ WD £12; WE £15.
⌐ Welcome by prior arrangement; packages on request; private dinners for groups of 25-80.
⦿ Full restaurant facilities available.
↗ Seagoe, Portadown; White Gables, Hillsborough; Silverwood, Lurgan.

11 37 Enniskillen
Castlecoole, Enniskillen, Co Fermanagh, BT74 6HZ
☎ (028) 6632 5250
1 mile from Enniskillen off Tempo Rd.
Parkland course.
Founded 1896

Designed by Dr Dixon & George Mawhinney/ T.J. McAuley
18 holes, 6189 yards, S.S.S. 69
† Welcome.
⌐ WD £15; WE and BH £18.
⌐ Welcome by arrangement; catering by arrangement with the steward; snooker.
⦿ Full catering and bar facilities.
↗ Fort Lodge; Ashbury; Killyhevlin; Railway; Belmore Court.

11 38 Fintona
Ecclesville Demesne, Fintona, Co Tyrone, BT78 2BJ
☎ (028) 8284 1480, Fax 8284 1480, Pro 8284 0777, Bar/Rest 8284 1480
9 miles SW of Omagh.
Parkland course.
Founded 1904
9 holes, 5866 yards, S.S.S. 70
† Welcome WD.
⌐ WD £15; guests of members £10.
⌐ Welcome by prior arrangement; packages available; groups of more than 20 £10; under 20 £15.
⦿ Full facilities on request.
↗ Silver Birches.

11 39 Fortwilliam
8A Downview Ave, Belfast, B15 4EZ
☎ (028) 9037 0770, Fax 9037 1891, Pro 9037 0980, Bar 9037 6798, Rest 9037 0072
3 miles from Belfast off Antrim road.
Parkland course.
Pro Peter Hanna; Founded 1891
Designed by Butchart
18 holes, 5973 yards, S.S.S. 69
† Welcome.
⌐ WD £22; WE £29.
⌐ Welcome by prior arrangement; discounts for groups of more than 15; catering packages available by arrangement; from £18.
⦿ Clubhouse facilities.
↗ Lansdowne Court; Chimney Corner.

11 40 Foyle
12 Alder Road, Londonderry, Co Londonderry, BT48 8DB
☎ (028) 7135 2222, Fax 7135 3967
2 miles N of Londonderry off Culmore road.
Parkland course.
Pro Kieran McLoughlin; Founded 1994
Designed by F Ainsworth
18 holes, 6678 yards, S.S.S. 71
† Welcome.
⌐ WD £11; WE £14.

⌐ Welcome; bookings taken 12 months in advance; discount for groups of 14 or more; packages with hotels and catering available; also 9-hole par 3 course; from £12.
⦿ Restaurant and bar facilities.
Practice range, 19 bays covered and floodlit.
↗ Waterfoot Hotel & CC; Whitehorse Inn.

11 41 Galgorm Castle   ⊺
Galgorm Rd, Ballymena, Antrim BT42 1HL
☎ (01266) 46161, Fax 651151
On outskirts of Ballymena off A42.
Parkland course.
18 holes, 6736 yards, par 72
Designed by S Gidman; Founded 1997
† Welcome by prior arrangement.
⌐ WD £19; WE £25.
⌐ Packages; corporate days.
⦿ Full clubhouse facilities.
24-bay driving range.
↗ Galgorm Manor.

11 42 Garron Tower
St Macnissi's College, Carnlough, Co Antrim, BT44 0JS
☎ (028) 2888 5202
Playing facilities at Cushendall and Ballycastle Golf Clubs.
Founded 1968

11 43 Gilnahirk
Manns Corner, Upper Braniel Rd, Gilnahirk, Castlereagh, Belfast, BT5 7TX
☎ (028) 9044 8477
3 miles from Belfast off Ballygowan road.
Public moorland course.
Pro Kenneth Gray; Founded 1983
9 holes, 5924 yards, S.S.S. 68
† Welcome.
⌐ WD: 18 holes £8.50, 9 holes £5; WE: 18 holes £10, 9 holes £6.
⌐ Welcome by prior arrangement.
⦿ No catering facilities.
↗ Stormont; Lamorne House.

11 44 Greenisland
156 Upper Rd, Greenisland, Carrickfergus, Co Antrim, BT38 8RW
☎ (028) 9086 2236
8 miles N of Belfast; 2 miles from Carrickfergus.
Parkland course.
Founded 1894
Designed by C Day

9 holes, 5624 yards, S.S.S. 69
† Welcome.
☷ WD £12; WE £18.
☝ Welcome by prior arrangement; on application; from £12.
🍽 Full clubhouse facilities.
⌐ Coast Road Hotel; Glenavna.

11 45 **Helen's Bay**

Golf Rd, Helen's Bay, Bangor, Co Down, BT19 1TL
☎ (028) 9185 2601, Fax 9185 2815, Sec 9185 2815, Bar/Rest 9185 2816
4 miles W of Bangor off the B20; next to Crawfordsburn Country Park.
Parkland course on shores of Belfast Lough.
Founded 1896
9 holes, 5181 yards, S.S.S. 67
† Welcome except Tues and Sat; restrictions Thurs pm and Fri summer am.
☷ WD £12; WE £17.50.
☝ Welcome by prior arrangement Sun, Mon, Wed, Thurs morning and Fri; minimum 10 maximum 40; private room for dining or presentations; catering packages available; from £12.
🍽 Full bar and restaurant facilities.
⌐ Crawfordsburn Old Inn; Clandeboye Lodge; Marine Court; Culloden.

11 46 **Holywood**

Nuns Walk, Demesne Rd, Holywood, Co Down, BT18 9LE
☎ (028) 9042 3135, Fax 9042 5040, Pro 9042 5503, Bar 9042 138, Rest 9042 6832
On A2 6 miles E of Belfast.
Undulating course.
Pro Paul Gray; Founded 1904
18 holes, 6028 yards, S.S.S. 68
† Welcome except Sat.
☷ WD £15; Sundays £20.
☝ Welcome except Thurs, Sat and BH.
🍽 Bar and catering facilities.
⌐ Culloden.

11 47 **Kilkeel**

Mourne Park, Kilkeel, Co Down, BT34 4LB
☎ (028) 9176 2296, Fax 9176 5095, Sec 9176 3787
3 miles W of Kilkeel; 45 miles S of Belfast.
Parkland course.
Founded 1948/1993
Designed by Lord Justice Babbington, Eddie Hackett
18 holes, 6615 yards, S.S.S. 72

† Welcome by prior arrangement.
☷ WD £16; WE £20.
☝ Welcome by arrangement; catering on application; from £14.
🍽 Full clubhouse facilities.
Practice range, close to course.
⌐ Kilmurey Arms; Cronfield Arms; Slieve Danard; Burrendale.

11 48 **Killymoon**

200 Killymoon Rd, Cookstown, Co Tyrone, BT80 8TW
☎ (028) 8676 3762, Pro 8676 3460, Bar 8676 2254, Rest 8676 6382
Off A29 0.5 miles S of Cookstown.
Parkland course.
Pro Gary Chambers; Founded 1889
Designed by Hugh Adair
18 holes, 5486 yards, S.S.S. 69
† Welcome except Sat after 4pm.
☷ WD £21; WE £25.
☝ Welcome except Thurs and Sat by prior arrangement; rates negotiable.
🍽 Full facilities.
⌐ Glenavon; Greenvale; Royal.

11 49 **Kilrea**

38 Drumagarner Rd, Kilrea, Co Londonderry, Co Londonderry
☎ (028) 7082 1048
0.5 miles from Kilrea Village on Maghera road.
Parkland course.
Founded 1919
9 holes, 4514 yards, S.S.S. 62
† Welcome except after 4.30pm Tues and Wed and Sat pm.
☷ WD £10; WE £12.50.
☝ Welcome by prior arrangement; limited catering; from £10.
🍽 Limited.
⌐ Port Neal Lodge.

11 50 **Kirkistown Castle**

142 Main Rd, Cloughey, Co Down, BT22 1JA
☎ (028) 4277 1233, Fax 4277 1699, Pro 4277 1004
A20 from Belfast to Kircubbin; follow signs to Newtonards and Portaferry; then B173 to Cloughey.
Links course.
Pro John Peden; Founded 1902
Designed by B Polley
18 holes, 6125 yards, S.S.S. 70
† Welcome.
☷ WD £15; WE £20.
☝ Welcome WD by prior arrangement; packages for groups of 16 or more.
🍽 Full facilities.
⌐ Portaferry.

11 51 **The Knock**

Summerfield, Upper Newtownards Rd, Dundonald, BT16 0QX
☎ (028) 9048 2249, Fax 9048 3251, Pro 9048 3825, Sec 9048 3251, Bar/Rest 9048 0915
4 miles E of Belfast off the Upper Newtonards road.
Parkland course.
Pro Gordon Fairweather; Founded 1895
Designed by Colt, MacKenzie & Allison
18 holes, 6435 yards, S.S.S. 71
† Welcome every day except Sat.
☷ WD £20; WE £25.
☝ Welcome Mon and Thurs; discounts for groups of more than 40; catering packages; from £18.
🍽 Full bar and restaurant facilities.
⌐ Stormont; Clandeboye; Strangford.

11 52 **Knockbracken Golf & Country Club**

Ballymaconaghy Rd, Knockbracken, Belfast, BT8 4SB
☎ (028) 9079 2108, Pro 9079 5666
Near Four Winds restaurant on SE outskirts of the city.
Pro Geoff Loughrey
18 holes, 5391 yards, S.S.S. 68
† Welcome
☷ WD £9; WE £13.
☝ Welcome by prior arrangement; packages on request; putting green; ski slopes.
🍽 Full bar and restaurant facilities.
Practice range, 25 bays floodlit.

11 53 **Lambeg**

Aberdelly, Bells Lane, Lambeg, Lisburn, Co. Antrim, BT27 4QH
☎ (028) 9266 2738, Fax 9260 3432
Off the main Lisburn road at Bells Lane in Lambeg.
Parkland course.
Pro Ian Murdoch; Founded 1986
9 holes, 4139 yards, S.S.S. 62
† Welcome except Sat am.
☷ WD £7; WE £9.
☝ Welcome except Sat am.
🍽 Snacks available.
⌐ Forte Post House.

11 54 **Larne**

54 Ferris Bay Rd, Islandmagee, Larne, BT40 3RT
☎ (028) 4372 4234
From Belfast N to Carrickfergus and 6 miles from Whitehead; from Larne S along the coast road to Islandmagee.

Royal County Down

The backdrop to Royal County Down is simply breathtaking. A symphony of mountains and the sea make it the most picturesque course in the British Isles.

Throw in the gorse in its early summer bloom and the rich green of the fairways and the beauty of the course is not a subject for debate.

More often than not the mountains of Mourne, as folklore suggests they must be, are shrouded in cloud to add to the drama of the setting on the edge of Dundrum Bay.

The origins of the course are a part of golf's rich history. The land was turned into this magnificent links course in 1889 by Tom Morris for the princely sum not to exceed 4 pounds.

Within a decade the course was fabled to be the finest in Ireland. It was reconstructed later, again with a sympathy that maintains its original flavour. It was granted a royal title in 1908 by King Edward VII and has lived up to the honour ever since.

In 1999 it welcomed the amateur championship and with it a mass of rave reviews from another generation of enchanted players.

Every course, however, will have its critics and Royal County Down is no exception. The main argument levelled against it is that it simply has too many blind holes and that is one of the reasons that major events have stayed away allied to the social problems in Northern Ireland.

Like most links courses the main contributing factor to the test that the golfer faces but it is not the only hazard awaiting the player who lacks anything other than 100 per cent accuracy.

It can be a cruel day if the massive sand dunes and the thick gorse come into play too often and no where is that more true than on the ninth, the highest point. The ninth is one of the most photographed and described holes in golf. Every guide book, every golf atlas and every reference work mentions it, so why should this book be any different?

The key element, as with much of the course, is the drive. The tee shot flies into the next valley below as the fairway leads to a distant green on a plateau under the menacing Slieve Donard, the highest mountain in the range.

It finished what Tom Watson said was as fine a nine holes of golf that he had played. Quite what he made of the inward nine was not recorded.

But after such a wide variety of challenges the back nine can seem, to some as talented as Watson anyway, a rather less threatening prospect.

After the short 10th, the 11th heads for open country while the 12th adds more photo-opportunities as it sweeps down a valley of its own. A magnificent place to watch which offers a greater knowledge of the hole than the player ever gets.

But the course will be burnt into the memory for ever and the push for major golf to come to the seaside town of Newcastle are growing by the day. There can be few more charming venues. — **CG**

Seaside course.
Founded 1894
Designed by Babington
9 holes, 6288 yards, S.S.S. 69
♦ Welcome except Sat.
⌐ WD £8; WE £15.
☞ Welcome except Sat.
⦿ Full clubhouse facilities available.
↵ Magheramorne House.

11 55 Lisburn
68 Eglantine Rd, Lisburn, Co Antrim,
BT27 5RQ
☎ (028) 9267 7216, Fax 9260 3608,
Pro 9267 7217, Bar 9266 2186, Rest
9267 7218
Take Springfield roundabout exit from
M1 in direction of Hillsborough.
Parkland course.
Pro Blake Campbell; Founded
1905/1973
Designed by Hawtree & Sons
18 holes, 6647 yards, S.S.S. 72
♦ Welcome WD before 3pm; Sat
after 5.30pm; Sundays with member.
⌐ WD: Adult £25, Juvenile £12.50;
WE: Adult £30, Juvenile £15.
☞ Welcome Mon and Thurs before
3pm; discounts for groups of 20 or
more before 12.30; from £25.
⦿ Clubhouse facilities available.
↵ White Gables Hotel.

11 56 Lurgan
The Demesne, Lurgan, Co Armagh,
BT67 9BN
☎ (028) 3832 2087, Fax 3832 5306,
Pro 3832 1068, Bar/Rest 3832 2087
Centre of Lurgan off Windsor Avenue
past park and down road between
Park Lake and Brownlow House.
Parkland course.
Pro Des Paul; Founded 1893
Designed by Frank Pennink
18 holes, 6257 yards, S.S.S. 70
♦ Welcome except Sat; Tues Ladies
day; Wed competition day; visitors
permitted certain times; restrictions
Fri pm; best to ring in advance.
⌐ WD £16, WE £20.
☞ Welcome by prior arrangement as
guest policy; discounts for groups of
50 or more; catering packages avail-
able; from £15.
⦿ Restaurant and lounge bar.
↵ Ashburn; Silverwood; Carngrove;
Seagoe.

11 57 Mahee Island
Comber, Newtownards, Co Down,
BT23 6ET
☎ (028) 1754 1234

Turn left 0.5 miles from Comber off
Comber to Killyleagh road.
Parkland/seaside course.
Club Steward Archie McCracken;
Founded 1929
9 holes, 5590 yards, S.S.S. 68
♦ Welcome; restrictions Sats only.
⌐ WD £10; WE £15.
☞ Welcome WD except Mon; Sun-
days available; catering by prior
arrangement; from £10.
⦿ By prior arrangement; no bar.
↵ Old Schoolhouse; Lisbarnet
House.

11 58 Mallusk
City of Belfast Golf Course, Mal,
Newtownabbey, Co Antrim, BT36 2RF
☎ (028) 9084 3799
From Belfast on A8 to Antrim; course
just before Chimney Corner Hotel.
Parkland course.
Founded 1992.
9 holes, 4686 yards, S.S.S. 64
♦ Welcome except Sat before
11.30am.
⌐ WD £6.50; WE £9.
☞ Welcome by prior arrangement.
⦿ None.
↵ Chimney Corner.

11 59 Malone Golf Club
240 Upper Malone Rd, Dunmurry,
Belfast, BT17 9LB
☎ (028) 9061 2695, Fax 9043 1394,
Pro 9061 4917, Sec 9061 2758,
Bar/Rest 9061 4916
5 miles from Belfast city centre
Parkland course.
Pro Michael McGee; Founded
1895/1962
Designed by Fred Hawtree/ Comdr. J
Harris
18 holes, 6599 yards, S.S.S. 71
♦ Welcome; start sheet operates
Wed pm, Sat, Sun am.
⌐ WD: non-members £33, guests of
members £15; WE: non-members
£38, guests of members £17.
☞ Welcome Mon and Thurs by prior
arrangement; catering packages by
prior arrangement; also Edenderry
course: 9 holes, 3160 yards, par 72;
from £32.
⦿ Full clubhouse catering and bar
facilities.
Two practice grounds.
↵ Wellington Park; Beechlawn.

11 60 Massereene
51 Lough Rd, Antrim, Co Antrim,
BT41 4DQ

☎ (028) 9442 8096 or 9448 7661,
Pro 9446 4074, Bar 9442 9293
1 mile S of town; 3.5 miles from
Aldergrove Airport.
Parkland course.
Pro Jim Smyth; Founded 1895
Designed by F.W. Hawtree
18 holes, 6559 yards, S.S.S. 71
♦ Welcome WD and WE; Fri Ladies
day; Sat restrictions.
⌐ WD £20; WE £25.
☞ Welcome by prior arrangement;
from £15.
⦿ Full facilities.
↵ Dunadry.

11 61 Mount Ober   ⚷
24 Ballymaconaghy, Knockbracken,
Belfast BT8 4SB
☎ (028) 9079 5666, Fax 9070 5862,
Pro 9070 1648, Sec 9040 1811,
Bar/Rest 9079 2100
Off Four Winds roundabout.
Parkland course.
Pro G Loughrey/S Rourke; Founded
1985
18 holes, 5391 yards, S.S.S. 68
♦ Welcome except Sat.
⌐ WD £12.
☞ Welcome except Sat; catering
packages; function rooms; 10% dis-
count in Pro shop; from £11.
⦿ Full clubhouse facilities.
Practice range, floodlit bays.
↵ La Mon House; Stormont Hotel.

11 62 Mourne
36 Golf Links Rd, Newcastle, Co
Down, BT33 0AN
☎ (01396) 723889
Playing facilities at Royal Co Down.

11 63 Moyola Park
Shanemullagh, Castledawson,
Magherafelt, Co Londonderry, BT45
8DG
☎ (028) 7946 8160, Fax 7946 8626,
Pro 7946 8830, Rest 7946 8270
Course is off the M2 Belfast-
Coleraine road at Magherafelt
roundabout.
Mature parkland course.
Pro Vivian Teague; Founded 1976
Designed by Don Patterson
18 holes, 6491 yards, S.S.S. 71
♦ Welcome by arrangement.
⌐ WD £17; WE £25.
☞ Welcome by prior arrangement
only; discounts available; packages
by arrangement; from £17.
⦿ Clubhouse facilities.
↵ Rural College; Glenavon Hotel.

11 64 Newtownstewart

38 Golf Course Rd, Newtownstewart,
Omagh, Co Tyrone, BT78 4HU
☎ (028) 8166 1466, Pro 8166 2242,
Fax 8166 2506
🖳 www.globalgolf.com/
m.newtownstewart
🖅 newtown.stewart@lineone.net.
2 miles SW of Newtownstewart on
B84.
Parkland course.
Founded 1914
Designed by Frank Pennink
18 holes, 5341 metres; White: 5341
metres, par 70, S.S.S 69; Red: 4603
metres, par 71, S.S.S 69.
† Welcome.
⌣ WD £12; WE £17.
🥸 Welcome if affiliated to the GUI;
catering packages by arrangement;
special society packages from £15
WD, £20 WE (meal inclusive).
🍽 Bar and restaurant facilities.
Practice range; buggie hire and club
hire available at the golf shop.
🖙 Hunting Lodge Hotel; Chalets
close to clubhouse; Grange Court.

11 65 Omagh

83a Dublin Rd, Omagh, Co Tyrone,
BT78 1 HQ
☎ (028) 8224 1442/8224 3160, Fax
8224 3160, Bar/Rest 8224 3160
On A5 on outskirts of Omagh.
Parkland course.
Founded 1910
18 holes, 5674 yards, S.S.S. 68
† Welcome WD and WE; Tues
Ladies day.
⌣ WD £10, guests of members £8;
WE £15, guests of members £13.
🥸 Welcome WD and WE by prior
arrangement.
🍽 Clubhouse facilities.
🖙 Silverbirch.

11 66 Ormeau

50 Park Rd, Belfast, BT7 2FX
☎ (028) 9064 1069, Fax 9064 0250,
Pro 9064 0999, Sec 9064 0700,
Bar/Rest 9064 1999
Adjacent to Ormeau road alongside
Ravenhill Rd and Park Rd.
Parkland course.
Pro Bertie Wilson; Founded 1892
9 holes, 4862 yards, S.S.S. 65
† Welcome; Sat members only.
⌣ WD £9; WE £11.
🥸 Welcome mainly Thurs and Sun;
packages available.
🍽 Full bar and catering facilities
available.
🖙 Stormont Hotel.

11 67 Portadown

192 Gilford Rd, Portadown,
Craigavon, Co Armagh, BT63 5LF
☎ (028) 3835 5356, Pro 3833 4655,
Bar 3835 5356, Rest 3835 2214
3 miles from Portadown on Gilford
road.
Parkland course.
Pro Paul Stevenson; Founded 1908
18 holes, 5649 yards, S.S.S. 70
† Welcome by arrangement; members only Tues (ladies) and Sat
(men).
⌣ WD £17; WE £ 22.
🥸 Welcome by prior written arrangement; green fees from £16; catering
packages by prior arrangement;
snooker, squash and indoor bowls
available for members.
🍽 Bar and restaurant facilities
available.
🖙 Seagoe; Bonnview.

11 68 Portstewart

117 Strand Rd, Portstewart, Co Lon-
donderry, BT55 7PG
☎ (028) 7083 2015, Pro 7083 2601,
Fax 7083 4097, Bar 7083 2015
4 miles W of Portrush.
Links course.
Pro Alan Hunter; Founded 1894
3 courses; Strand: 18 holes, par
72,6779 yards, S.S.S. 73; Riverside:
9 holes, par 32, 2662 yards; Old
course: 18 holes, par 64, 4783 yards,
S.S.S 62.
† Welcome WD on application.
⌣ Strand: WD £50, WE £70; River-
side: WD £12, WE £17; Old: WD £10,
WE £14.
🥸 Welcome WD by prior booking.
🍽 Full facilities in season.
🖙 Edgewater.

11 69 Radisson Roe Park Hotel

Roe Park, Limavady, Co Derry, BT49
9LB
☎ (028) 7776 0105
Course is on the A2 Londonderry-
Limavady road 16 miles from
Londonderry.
Parkland course.
Pro Seamus Duffy; Founded 1993
18 holes, 6309 yards, S.S.S. 71
† Welcome.
⌣ WD £20; WE £20.
🥸 Welcome by prior arrangement;
catering packages; from £15.
🍽 Restaurant and bar facilities.
Practice range, 10 covered floodlit
bays.
🖙 Radisson Roe Park Hotel on site.

11 70 Rathmore

Bushmills Rd, Portrush
☎ (028) 7082 2996, Fax 7082 2996,
Bar 7082 2285
Playing facilities at Royal Portrush.
Founded 1947
🖙 Magherabuoy House; Royal Court.

11 71 Ringdufferin

Ringdufferin Rd, Toye, Killeagh, CO
Down, BT30 9PH
☎ (028) 4482 8812, Fax 4482 8812
2 miles N of Killeagh on the Comber
road.
Parkland course.
Founded 1992
Designed by F Ainsworth
18 holes, 5044 yards, par 68, S.S.S.
66.
† Welcome.
⌣ 9 holes: WD £6, WE £7; 18 holes:
WD £9, WE £10.
🥸 Welcome; catering by arrange-
ment; from £6.
🍽 Clubhouse facilities.
🖙 Dufferin Arms.

11 72 Royal Belfast

11 Station Rd, Craigavad, Holywood,
Co Down, BT18 0BP
☎ (028) 9042 8165, Fax 9042 1404,
Pro 9042 8586, Bar/Rest 9042 8307
2 miles E of Holywood on A2.
Parkland course.
Pro Chris Spence; Founded 1881
Designed by H.C. Colt/ Donald Steel
(1988)
18 holes, 6306 yards, S.S.S. 71
† Welcome except Wed or Sat
before 4.30pm.
⌣ WD £35; WE £45.
🥸 Welcome by arrangement.
🍽 Full facilities.
🖙 Culloden.

11 73 Royal County Down

Newcastle, Co Down, BT33 0AN
☎ (028) 4372 3314, Fax 4372 6281,
Pro 4372 2419
On A24 30 miles S of Belfast.
Links course.
Pro Kevan Whitson; Founded 1889
Designed by Tom Morris Senior
Championship course: 7037 yards,
par 71, S.S.S. 74; Annesley Links
course: 4681 yards, par 66, S.S.S.
63.
† Welcome WD except Wed; other
days by prior arrangement.
⌣ Championship: WD £70, WE £80;
Annesley: WD £16, WE £23.
🥸 Welcome by arrangement with Sec.

Royal Portrush

If the pressure is on for Royal County Down to be included on the major British golf rota then the outcry about Royal Portrush's absence is even more vociferous.

Not since 1951 has the Open Championship been to Northern Ireland and although the Senior event visited in 1995 there is little chance of it changing. Although the Northern Ireland troubles have accounted for many of the reasons that this majestic golf course has been overlooked, security is not its only problem.

Like the wonderful Royal Liverpool Royal Portrush has a challenging enough course but little hope of providing the infrastructure that surrounds such an event. While Royal Liverpool misses out because of the lack of access and the problems in housing the tented village, Portrush has a chronic lack of hotel rooms.

This was, for a long time, the concern surrounding Carnoustie but was finally overcome last year. Everyone hopes that a similar solution can be found to bring this great Antrim course back to the world stage.

Just beyond the ruins of Dunluce Castle – Dunluce is the name now given to the main championship course – lies the Royal Portrush Golf Club, estab-

lished by the golf playing lords of County Antrim in 1888.

Harry Colt is mainly responsible for the layout of the course that exists now, although a man named O'Neill seems to take the credit for the original layout.

Ask what the main requirement for negotiating the wonderful links course and the answer is always unanimous. There has to be accuracy and length in tee shots.

No great course should ever ignore wayward driving but there are few more severe punishers of the erratic tee shot than Royal Portrush.

It is a course that has few bunkers, particularly around the greens, but there are many scattered across the fairways and beyond them lies the savage rough.

The signature hole at Portrush comes at 14. A short hole with the famous name of Calamity Corner, it is 210 yards from tee to green but between the two lies little but lurking rough.

When the wind blows club selection can be almost impossible and many players have lingered long before pulling out anything between a long iron and a wood. Miss the green and trouble awaits.

But that is the charm of Royal Portrush. Trouble awaits all but the most steady and steely of players. — **CG**

🍽 Full clubhouse facilities.
⌇ Slieve Donard; Burrendale; Glassdrumman Lodge.

11 74 **Royal Portrush**
Bushmills Rd, Portrush, Co Antrim, BT56 8JR
☎ (028) 7082 2311, Fax 7082 3139, Pro 7082 3335
1 mile from Portrush off A1.
Championship links; 1951 Open course.
Pro Gary McNeil; Founded 1888
Designed by H.S. Colt
18 holes, 6818 yards, S.S.S. 73
† Welcome WD between 9.10am-11.50am; Mon between 9.20am-11.50am, Wed and Fri after 2pm; restrictions at WE.
⌐ WD £70; WE and BH £80.
⌇ None.
🍽 Local hotels can provide meals. Two practice grounds.
⌇ Club can provide list.

11 75 **Scrabo**
233 Scrabo Rd, Newtownards, Co Down, BT23 4SL
☎ (028) 9181 2355, Fax 9182 2919, Pro 9181 7848, Sec 9181 6516, Office 9181 2355, Rest 9181 5048
Off A20 10 miles E of Belfast; near Scrabo Tower.
Hilly parkland course.
Pro Paul McCrystal; Founded 1907
18 holes, 5699 yards, S.S.S. 71
† Welcome WD except Wed.
⌐ WD £15; WE £20.
⌇ Welcome any day except Sat; not in June; from £13.
🍽 Full bar and restaurant.
⌇ Strangford Arms; George; La Mon House.

11 76 **Shandon Park**
73 Shandon Park, Belfast, BT5 6NY
☎ (028) 9079 3730, Fax 9040 2773, Pro 9079 7859, Sec 9040 1856
3 miles from city centre via Knock dual carriageway.
Parkland course.
Pro Barry Wilson; Founded 1926
Designed by Brian Carson
18 holes, 6282 yards, S.S.S. 70
† Welcome WD and Sun.
⌐ WD £22; WE £27.
⌇ Welcome Mon and Fri only by prior arrangement; reductions available for groups of more than 24 and 40.

🍽 Meals and bar snacks.
⌇ Stormont.

11 77 **Silverwood**
Tormoyra Lane, Silverwood, Lurgan, Co Armagh, BT66 6NG
☎ (028) 3832 6606, Fax 3834 7272
Playing facilities at Craigavon.
Founded 1984

11 78 **Spa**
20 Grove Rd, Ballynahinch, Co Down, BT24 8PN
☎ (028) 9756 2365, Fax 9756 4158
0.5 miles from Ballynahinch; 11 miles S of Belfast.
Wooded parkland course.
Founded 1907/1987
Designed by F Ainsworth
18 holes, 6003 yards, S.S.S. 72
† Welcome except Sat.
⌐ WD £15; WE £20.
⌇ Welcome except Sat; discounts for parties of more than 16; 10% reduction for groups of more than 30; catering packages by arrangement.
🍽 Full clubhouse facilities.
⌇ White Horse; Millbrook.

11 79 **Strabane**
Ballycolman, Strabane, Co Tyrone, BT82 9PH
☎ (028) 7138 2007, Fax 7188 6514, Bar/Rest 7138 2271
1 mile from Strabane on Dublin road beside church and schools.
Parkland course.
Founded 1908
Designed by Eddie Hackett
18 holes, 5854 yards, S.S.S. 69
† Welcome WD; WE by arrangement.
⌐ WD £15; WE £17.
⌇ Welcome by arrangement with Sec.
🍽 Full facilities.
⌇ Fir Trees Hotel.

11 80 **Tandragee** ℭ
Market Hill Rd, Tandragee, Co Armagh, BT62 2ER
☎ (028) 3884 0727, Fax 3884 0664, Pro 3884 1761, Sec 3884 1272, Bar 3884 0727, Rest 3884 1763
On B3 in Tandragee.
Parkland course.
Founded 1922
Designed by F. Hawtree
18 holes, 5747 yards, S.S.S. 69
† Welcome WD 10.30am-2pm and WE after 3pm.

⌐ WD £15; WE £20.
⌇ Welcome by prior arrangement; catering by prior arrangement; from £15.
🍽 Full bar and restaurant facilities.
⌇ Carngrove; Seagoe; Bannview.

11 81 **Temple**
60 Church Rd, Boardmills, Lisburn, Co Down, BT27 6UP
☎ (028) 9263 9213, Fax 9263 8637
On main Ballynahinch road out of Belfast.
Parkland course.
Pro Joe McBride; Founded 1994
9 holes, 5451 yards, S.S.S. 66
† Welcome except Sat am in summer.
⌐ WD £10; WE £14.
⌇ Welcome by arrangement; from £16.
🍽 Full facilities.
⌇ Ivanhoe; Millbrook.

11 82 **Warrenpoint**
Lower Dromore Rd, Warrenpoint, Co Down, BT34 3LN
☎ (028) 4175 3695, Fax 4175 2918, Pro 4175 2371, Rest 4175 2273, Bar 4175 2219
5 miles from Newry on Warrenpoint road.
Parkland course.
Pro Nigel Shaw; Founded 1893
18 holes, 6161 yards, S.S.S. 70
† Welcome by prior arrangement.
⌐ WD £20; WE £27.
⌇ Welcome by prior arrangement.
🍽 Full facilities.
⌇ Canal Court, Newry.

11 83 **Whitehead**
McCrae's Brae, Whitehead, Co Antrim, BT38 9NZ
☎ (028) 9337 0822, Pro 9337 0821, Sec 9337 0820
On the Co Antrim coast between Larne and Carrickfergus.
Parkland course.
Pro Colin Farr; Founded 1904/1975
Designed by A B Armstrong
18 holes, 6050 yards, S.S.S. 69
† Welcome WD; WE with a member.
⌐ WD £14; WE £20.
⌇ Welcome WD anytime and Sun 10.30am-12 noon by prior arrangement; catering by prior arrangement with chef.
🍽 Full clubhouse facilities.
⌇ Coast Road; Magheramorne.

REPUBLIC OF IRELAND

In 2005 the Ryder Cup, as you must surely have heard, will be going to Ireland for the first time. It will be played at the K Club, which is a terrible mistake. Nothing against the K Club, which is a decent enough inland venue. But going to Ireland and playing an inland course is like a football lover wanting to sample football on Merseyside and going to Tranmere Rovers.

So forgive me if I overlook the delights of the K Club and Druid's Glen, Mount Juliet, Killarney, Dooks and one or two others. Here we are going to concentrate on a quick tour of the links courses of the Emerald Isle, and when planning your itinerary you are strongly advised to do so as well.

Let's go clockwise shall we, and start at County Louth, which is better known as Baltray. It is a very good place to start, and though it is well known in Irish golfing circles, its fame has mysteriously not spread across the Irish Sea.

Around Dublin there is, of course, Portmarnock, and now Portmarnock Links, which, rather like Turnberry, recovers from a plain start to enchant. Then there is Royal Dublin and the Island Golf Club. Moving south we come to the European, featured in the introduction to this book, and much, much further on, there is the Old Head links in Cork, and a more spectacular course it would be hard to find.

The golf on the west coast of Ireland has now become so popular that the names of the great courses trip off the tongue as readily as those in Scotland.

Ballybunion, Waterville, Killarney and Tralee has become an established foursome for the golfing tourist and one that every player should experience at least once. As Peter Dobereiner once wrote, no player is qualified to talk about golf courses until he has been to Kerry, because he has not experienced the upper range of quality.

The quality does not sag as we move up the west coast either and reach Lahinch in County Clare, two miles from the Cliffs of Moher and once referred to as the "St Andrews of Ireland".

Westport, with its wonderful views of Croagh Patrick, the largest mountain in Ireland, is perhaps the most famous course in Mayo but Belmullet, the most westerly course in Ireland, has gained deserved 'hidden gem' status, as has Enniscrone. Into Sligo and Rosses Point is rightly considered among the top 10 courses in Eire.

And so finally we reach Donegal where Dunfanaghy, North West (Buncrana) and Narin and Portnoo are three links courses to be considered before turning to the county's jewel, Ballyliffin.

I remember visiting about eight years ago, when it was unknown and the two players in front were complaining because it had cost them £8 to play. As you can imagine, my expectations were not high. How wrong can you be? Ballyliffin is so good it is almost worth paying £8 to play each hole. And they have since built a second course of the same stature. — **DL**

REPUBLIC OF IRELAND

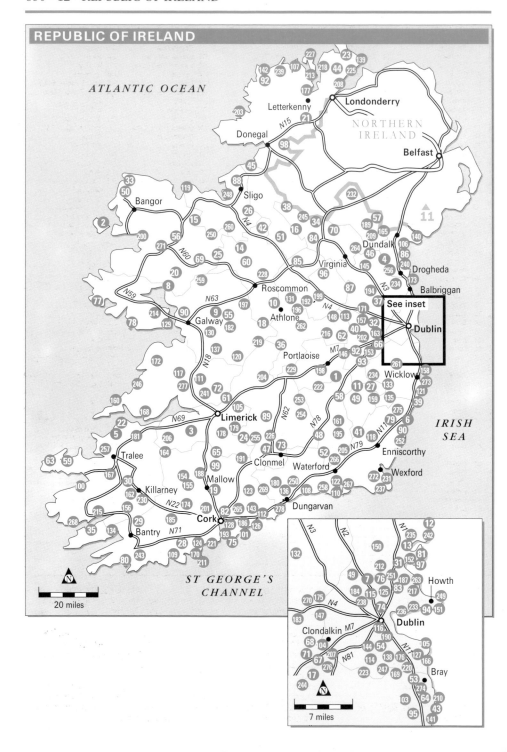

ATLANTIC OCEAN

Letterkenny
Londonderry

NORTHERN IRELAND

Donegal
N15
21
98

Belfast

45
88
248
Sligo
119
26
38
245
34
70
232

33
50
Bangor
2
200
15
250
260
16
51
84
85
11

57
189
209
264
46
4
256
234
173
Dundalk
106
86
240
Drogheda
Balbriggan

271
N60
56
69
25
60
228
Roscommon
131
192
199
196
262
216
62
40
202
66
87
194
N3
171
157
32
163
Dublin
See inset
37

N59
20
8
259
214
90
9
55
182
130
137
219
36
10
197
18
Athlone
148
113
146
92
153
93
261
Wicklow
158

77
78
129
Galway
120
229
198
1
222
253
58
11
49
27
159
234
133
135
275
121
39
273
IRISH
SEA

172
117
277
111
72
61
105
204
48
195
161
41
118
N11
79
90
252
6

160
168
22
5
257
Tralee
181
206
3
178
179
N62
254
N78
52
205
N79
266
118
Enniscorthy

63
59
167
30
Killarney
164
65
191
99
Clonmel
Waterford
272
231
Wexford
237

100
162
230
N22
174
155
154
188
9
180
250
269
136
108
258
110
267
122
Dungarvan

215
156
29
185
201
82
265
143
278
Cork
128
186
126
35
134
Bantry
N71
28
124
221
193
101
75

268
80
243
109
170
211

St GEORGE'S
CHANNEL

N

20 miles

N3
N2
N1
12
235
242
132
150
13
81
97
212
31
152
49
7
76
251
187
83
217
Howth
249
184
115
125
238
74
94
151
236
Dublin
Clondalkin
M7
116
183
147
175
N4
190
105
68
04
144
54
138
127
71
207
N81
114
169
166
Bray
67
276
220
223
247
53
17
274
244
03
64
210
95
43
141

7 miles

KEY

#	Name	#	Name	#	Name	#	Name	#	Name
1	Abbeyleix	59	Castlegregory Golf and Fishing Club	115	Elm Green	171	Knockanally Golf & Country Club	228	Roscommon
2	Achill Island	60	Castlerea	116	Elm Park	172	Lahinch Golf Club	229	Roscrea
3	Adare Golf Club	61	Castletroy	117	Ennis	173	Laytown & Bettystown	230	Ross
4	Ardee	62	Castlewarden Golf & Country Club	118	Enniscorthy	174	Lee Valley	231	Rosslare
5	Ardfert			119	Enniscrone	175	Leixlip	232	Rossmore
6	Arklow	63	Ceann Sibeal (Dingle)	120	Esker Hills Golf & Country Club	176	Leopardstown Golf Centre	233	Royal Dublin Golf Club
7	Ashbourne	64	Charlesland	121	The European Club	177	Letterkenny	234	Royal Tara Golf Club
8	Ashford Castle	65	Charleville	122	Faithlegg	178	Limerick	235	Rush
9	Athenry	66	Cill Dara	123	Fermoy	179	Limerick County Golf & Country Club	236	St Annes
10	Athlone	67	City West Hotel	124	Fernhill	180	Lismore	237	St Helen's Bay
11	Athy	68	Clane	125	Forrest Little	181	Listowel	238	St Margaret's Golf & Country Club
12	Balbriggan	69	Claremorris	126	Fota Island	182	Loughrea	239	St Patricks
13	Balcarrick	70	Clones	127	Foxrock	183	Lucan	240	Seapoint
14	Ballaghaderreen	71	Clongowes	128	Frankfield	184	Luttrellstown Castle	241	Shannon
15	Ballina	72	Clonlara	129	Galway	185	Macroom	242	Skerries
16	Ballinamore	73	Clonmel	130	Galway Bay Golf & Country Club	186	Mahon	243	Skibbereen & West Cabbery
17	Ballinascorney	74	Clontarf	131	Glasson G & CC	187	Malahide	244	Slade Valley
18	Ballinasloe	75	Cobh	132	Glebe	188	Mallow	245	Slieve Russell Golf & Country Club
19	Ballininamona	76	Coldwinters	133	Glencullen	189	Mannan Castle	246	Spanish Point
20	Ballinrobe	77	Connemara	134	Glengarriff	190	Milltown	247	Stackstown
21	Ballybofey & Stranorlar	78	Connemara isles	135	Glenmalure	191	Mitchelstown	248	Strandhill
22	Ballybunion	79	Coollattin	136	Gold Coast Golf and Leisure	192	Moate	249	Sutton
23	Ballyhaunis	80	Coosheen	137	Gort	193	Monkstown	250	Swinford
24	Ballykisteen Golf & Country Club	81	Corballis	138	Grange	194	Moor-Park	251	Swords
25	Ballyliffin	82	Cork	139	Greencastle	195	Mount Juliet	252	Tara Glen
26	Ballymote	83	Corrstown	140	Greenore	196	Mount Temple	253	Templemore
27	Baltinglass	84	County Cavan	141	Greystones	197	Mountbellew	254	Thurles
28	Bandon	85	County Longford	142	Gweedore	198	Mountrath	255	Tipperary
29	Bantry Bay	86	County Louth	143	Harbour Point	199	Mullingar	256	Townley Hall
30	Beaufort	87	County Meath (Trim)	144	Hazel Grove	200	Mulranny	257	Tralee
31	Beaverstown	88	County Sligo	145	Headfort	201	Muskerry	258	Tramore
32	Beech Park	89	County Tipperary Golf & Country Club	146	Heath	202	Naas	259	Tuam
33	Belmullet			147	Hermitage	203	Narin & Portnoo	260	Tubbercurry
34	Belturbet	90	Courtown	148	Highfield	204	Nenagh	261	Tulfarris Hotel & Country Club
35	Berehaven	91	Craddockstown	149	Hollystown	205	New Ross		
36	Birr	92	Cruit Island	150	Hollywood Lakes	206	Newcastle West	262	Tullamore
37	The Black Bush	93	Curragh	151	Howth	207	Newlands	263	Turvey Golf & CC
38	Blacklion	94	Deer Park Hotel	152	The Island Golf Club	208	North West	264	Virginia
39	Blainroe	95	Delgany	153	The K Club	209	Nuremore	265	Water Rock
40	Bodenstown	96	Delvin Castle	154	Kanturk (18 holes)	210	Old Conna	266	Waterford
41	Borris	97	Donabate	155	Kanturk (9 holes)	211	Old Head Links	267	Waterford Castle Golf & Country Club
42	Boyle	98	Donegal	156	Kenmare	212	The Open Golf Centre		
43	Bray	99	Doneraile	157	Kilcock	213	Otway	268	Waterville Golf Links
44	Buncrana	100	Dooks	158	Kilcoole	214	Oughterard	269	West Waterford
45	Bundoran	101	Douglas	159	Kilkea Castle	215	Parknasilla	270	Westmanstown
46	Cabra Castle	102	Dromoland Castle	160	Kilkee	216	Portarlington	271	Westport
47	Cahir Park	103	Druids Glen	161	Kilkenny	217	Portmarnock Golf Club	272	Wexford
48	Callan	104	Dublin Mountain	162	Killarney Golf Club	218	Portsalon	273	Wicklow
49	Carlow	105	Dun Laoghaire	163	Killeen	219	Portumna	274	Woodbrook
50	Carne Golf Links	106	Dundalk	164	Killeline	220	Powerscourt	275	Woodenbridge
51	Carrickmines	107	Dunfanaghy	165	Killin Park	221	Raffeen Creek	276	Woodlands
52	Carrick-on-Shannon	108	Dungarvan	166	Killiney	222	Rathdowney	277	Woodstock
53	Carrick-on-Suir	109	Dunmore	167	Killorglin	223	Rathfarnham	278	Youghal
54	Castle	110	Dunmore East Golf & Country Club	168	Kilrush	224	Rathsallagh House		
55	Castle Barna	111	East Clare	169	Kilternan Golf & Country Club	225	Redcastle		
56	Castlebar	112	East Cork	170	Kinsale	226	Reelwell		
57	Castleblayney	113	Edenderry			227	Rosapenna		
58	Castlecomer	114	Edmondstown						

12 1 Abbeyleix

Stradbally Rd, Abbeyleix, Co Laois, Ireland
☎ (0502) 31450, Sec 31051
Course is situated 0.5 miles off Main Street.
Parkland course; Founded 1895
9 holes, 5626 yards, S.S.S. 68
† Welcome.
⌣ Terms on application.
⌣ Welcome.
↝ Hibernian; Killeshin; Montague; Globe House.

12 2 Achill Island

Keel, Achill, Co Mayo
☎ (098) 43456
Via Castlebar or Westport.
Seaside course.
Founded 1952
Designed by P. Skerrit
9 holes, 5378 yards, S.S.S. 66
† Welcome.
⌣ WD £5; WE £5.
⦿ Full clubhouse facilities available.
↝ Atlantic; McDowalls; Slievemore; Strand, Gray's GH.

12 3 Adare Golf Club

Adare Manor, Adare, Co Limerick
☎ (061) 395044, Fax 396987, Sec 396204
10 miles from Limerick on the Killarney Road.
Parkland course built round castle and friary ruins.
Founded 1995
Designed by Robert Trent Jones, Sr.
18 holes, 7138 yards, S.S.S. 69
† Welcome WE with member or by prior arrangement.

WD £15; WE £20.
Welcome by prior arrangement; catering packages can be arranged; terms on application.
Clubhouse facilities available.
Dunranen Arms; Woodlands.

12 4 **Ardee**
Town Parks, Ardee, Co Louth,
(041) 685 3227, Fax 685 6137, Bar/Rest 685 6283
0.25 miles N of town on Mullinstown Road.
Parkland course.
Founded 1911
Designed by Eddie Hackett
18 holes, 5500 yards, S.S.S. 69
Welcome WD.
WD 17; WE £25.
Welcome Mon-Sat by prior arrangement.
Full facilities available.

12 5 **Ardfert**
Sackville, Ardfert, Tralee
(353) 66 34744
15 miles N of Tralee on R551.
Parkland course.
9 holes
Welcome.
Terms on application.
Limited but welcome.

12 6 **Arklow**
Abbeylands, Arklow, Co Wicklow
(0402) 32492, Fax 91604, Sec 32971
Signposted from town centre after turning at bridge.
Links course.
Founded 1927
Designed by Hawtree & Taylor
18 holes, 5604 yards, S.S.S. 69
Welcome by arrangement.
WD £20; WE £20.
Welcome by prior arrangement; Welcome WD and Sat morning; deposit of £100 required; catering packages; from £18.
Bar and restaurant facilities.
Practice range; practice bunkers and nets.
Arklow Bay.

12 7 **Ashbourne**
Archerstown, Ashbourne, Co Meath
(01) 835 2005, Bar/Rest 835 2005, Fax 835 2562
On N2 12 miles from Dublin.
Parkland course with water features.
Pro John Dwyer; Founded 1994

Designed by Des Smyth
18 holes, 5872 yards, S.S.S. 70
Welcome.
WD £20; WE £25.
Welcome WD; golf and catering packages available; terms on application.
Full bar and restaurant service.
Practice area.
Professional Shop.
Ashbourne House.

12 8 **Ashford Castle**
Cong, Co Mayo
(092) 46003
27 miles N of Galway on shores of Lough Corrib.
Parkland course.
Founded 1972
Designed by Eddie Hackett
9 holes, 4506 yards, S.S.S. 70
Welcome.
WD £40; WE £40.
Welcome by prior arrangement.
Bar facilities.
Ashford Castle; packages available.

12 9 **Athenry**
Palmerstown, Oranmore, Co Galway
(091) 94466, Sec 751405
5 miles from Athenry on N6 Galway-Dublin road.
Parkland course.
Founded 1902
Designed by Eddie Hackett
18 holes, 5552 yards, S.S.S. 69
Welcome except Sun.
WD £15; WE £18.
Welcome by prior arrangement.
Full bar and catering facilities.

12 10 **Athlone**
Hodson Bay, Athlone, Co Roscommon
0902) 92073, Fax 94080, Bar/Rest 92235
3 miles N of Athlone on the Roscommon Road.
Parkland course; All Ireland finals course 1998.
Pro Martin Quinn; Founded 1892
Designed by J McAllister
18 holes, 5935 yards, S.S.S. 71
Welcome; some restrictions Tues and Sun.
WD £18; WE £20.
Welcome by prior arrangement; discount for groups of more than 40; catering packages available; terms on application.
Full clubhouse facilities.

Hodson Bay; Prince of Wales; Shamrock; Royal Hoey.

12 11 **Athy**
Geraldine, Athy, Co Kildare
(0507) 31729
On T6 2 miles N of Athy.
Undulating parkland course.
Founded 1906
18 holes, 5500 yards, S.S.S. 69
Welcome WD.
Terms on application.
Welcome Sat mornings.
By arrangement with the steward.

12 12 **Balbriggan**
Blackhall, Balbriggan, Co Dublin
(01) 841 2173, Fax 841 3927, Sec 841 2229
0.75 miles S of Balbriggan on the N1 Dublin-Belfast Road.
Parkland course.
Founded 1945
Designed by R. Stilwell, J. Paramour
18 holes, 5922 metres, S.S.S. 71
Welcome WD except Tues.
WD £18.
Welcome by prior arrangement with Sec; discounts for more than 30 players; from £18.
Full clubhouse facilities.

12 13 **Balcarrick**
Corballis, Donabate, Co Dublin
(01) 843 6228, Bar/Rest 843 6957, Sec 843 6947
Founded 1972
18 holes, 6362 yards, S.S.S. 73
Welcome.
WD £15; WE £22.

12 14 **Ballaghaderreen**
Aughalista, Ballaghaderreen, Co Roscommon
(0907) 60295, Sec 60573
3 miles from Ballaghaderreen.
Parkland course.
Founded 1937
9 holes, 5363 yards, S.S.S. 67
Welcome.
WD £10; WE £10.
Welcome by prior arrangement.
Bar and snack facilities.

12 15 **Ballina**
Mossgrove, Shanaghy, Ballina, Co Mayo
(096) 21050, Fax 21050
On the outskirts of Ballina on the Bonniconlon Road.

Parkland course.
Founded 1910
Designed by Eddie Hackett
18 holes, 6103 yards, S.S.S. 69
♱ Welcome.
꠵ WD £12; WE £15.
꙼ Welcome; reductions for groups of
12 or more; from £10.
꠵ Full clubhouse facilities.
꙼ Downhill; Bartra House.

12 16 Ballinamore
Creevy, Ballinamore, Co Leitrim
☎ (078) 44346
1.5 miles NW of Ballinamore.
Parkland course.
Founded 1939
Designed by Arthur Spring
9 holes, 4782 yards, S.S.S. 68
♱ Welcome.
꙼ Welcome; special deals
depending on numbers; catering
packages also available; terms on
application.
꠵ Bar and catering facilities.
꙼ Commercial; McAllisters; Slieve-
an-Iaraim.

12 17 Ballinascorney
Bohernabreena, Tallaght, Co Dublin
☎ (01) 4512082
10 miles SW of Dublin.
Parkland course.
Founded 1971
18 holes, 5648 yards, S.S.S. 67
♱ WD welcome; WE phone in
advance.
꠵ WD £15; WE £20; group rates
available.
꠵ Bar facilities.

12 18 Ballinasloe
Rossgloss, Ballinasloe, Co Galway
☎ (0905) 42126, Fax 42538
2 miles off the N6 on the Portumna
Road.
Parkland course.
Founded 1894
Designed by Eddie Connaughton
18 holes, 5865 yards, S.S.S. 70
♱ Welcome Mon-Sat.
꠵ Terms on application.
꙼ Welcome Mon-Sat; catering
packages; terms on application.
꠵ Bar and restaurant facilities.
Practice area.
꙼ Haydens; East County; Gullanes.

12 19 Ballininamona
Mourne Abbey, Mallow, Cork
☎ (353) 29314

Founded 1997
Parkland course.
9 holes, 3110 yards
♱ Welcome.
꠵ Terms on application.

12 20 Ballinrobe
Castlebar Road, Ballinrobe, Co Mayo
☎ (092) 41448
30 miles from Galway.
Parkland course set in beautiful
scenery.
Founded 1895
9 holes, 5540 yards, S.S.S. 68
♱ Welcome; some restrictions Tues
and Sun.
꠵ Terms on application.
꙼ Welcome WD by arrangement;
catering packages by arrangement;
fishing can be organised; terms on
application.
꠵ Bar and restaurant facilities
available.
꙼ Lakeland.

12 21 Ballybofey & Stranorlar
Stranorlar, Ballybofey, Co Donegal
☎ (074) 31093
Course is signposted off the
Strabane-Ballybofey Road; 14 miles
from Strabane.
Parkland course.
Founded 1957
Designed by P.C. Carr
18 holes, 5437 yards, S.S.S. 69
♱ Welcome.
꠵ Terms on application.
꙼ Welcome by prior arrangement;
terms on application.
꠵ Bar facilities; meals by
arrangement.

12 22 Ballybunion
Sandhill Rd, Ballybunion, Co Kerry
☎ (068) 27146, Fax 27387, Bar/Rest
27611
20 miles N of Tralee.
Traditional links course.
Pro Brian O'Callaghan; Founded
1893
Designed by Simpson McKenna
Old: 18 holes, 6593 yards, S.S.S. 72;
Cashen: 18 holes, 6216 yards, S.S.S.
72
♱ Welcome WD; limited at WE.
꠵ WD £65, WE £65 (Old); WD £35,
WE £30 (Cashen).
꙼ WD by arrangement; from £55;
both courses £72.
꠵ Full catering facilities.
꙼ Club can provide detailed list;
some golf packages available.

12 23 Ballyhaunis
Coolnaha, Ballyhaunis, Co Mayo
☎ (0907) 30014, Fax 81829
Course is two miles from Ballyhaunis
on the N83.
Parkland course.
Pro David Carney; Founded 1929
9 holes, 5413 yards, S.S.S. 68
♱ Welcome Mon-Sat; with member
Sun.
꠵ Terms on application.
꙼ Welcome Mon-Sat by prior
arrangement; reductions for groups of
more than 20; from £10.
꠵ Full catering facilities available.
꙼ Cill Aodain; Belmont.

12 24 Ballyklsteen Golf &
Country Club
Ballykisteen, Co Tipperary
☎ (062) 33333
3 miles from Tipperary on the
Limerick Road.
Parkland course.
Founded 1994
Designed by Des Smyth
18 holes, 6765 yards, S.S.S. 73
♱ Welcome.but booking advisable.
꠵ WD £20; WE £25.
꙼ Welcome.
꠵ Bar and restaurant.

12 25 Ballyliffin
Ballyliffin, Carndonagh P.O, Co
Donegal
☎ (077) 76119, Fax 76672
8 miles from Buncrana.
Seaside links course.
Founded 1947
39 holes, 6612 yards, S.S.S. 72
♱ Welcome.
꠵ WD £21; WE £24.
꙼ Welcome by prior arrangement;
terms on application.
꠵ Bar snacks and meals.

12 26 Ballymote
Carrigans, Ballymote, Co Sligo
☎ (071) 89059, Bar/Rest 83089, Sec
83504
Course is off the N4 15 miles S of
Sligo Town.
Parkland course.
Founded 1993
9 holes, 5302 yards, S.S.S. 65
♱ Welcome.
꠵ WD £7; WE £7.
꙼ Welcome; discount for groups of
more than 20.
꠵ At local restaurant.
꙼ Sligo Park; Tower Hotel, Sligo;
Noreen Mullen GH; Eileen Cahill GH.

Ballybunion

It was symbolic that President Bill Clinton should insist that Ballybunnion be on his tour of Ireland in 1998. It is a reflection not only of a golfing president but also the importance that the course holds for the American traveller.

Before the Open Championship was held at Carnoustie in 1999 some of the world's greatest golfers went to the Ring of Kerry to get in some links practice.

They, like President Clinton, were captivated by what they found after playing some of the other Kerry courses like Waterville and Killarney.

There is no question in the minds of most golfers that Ballybunnion's Old Course is the pick of all those available. And some argue that it is by some distance as well. It hugs the Atlantic coast of Kerry and part of its attraction, particularly to the Americans, is its very isolation in an area that can seem charming and desolate in equal measure.

The ocean holes at Ballybunnion are thought to be some of the best that will be found anywhere in the world, although its recently published history reveals that it might never have survived a century ago.

Formed in 1886, the club had financial problems and for eight years staggered towards ruin until an Indian Army officer retired to the area and formed the present club in 1906. Without his initiative and some early design work by a local magazine editor who laid out nine new holes, there is no doubt that it would have struggled to survive.

By 1926 there were another nine holes added to the course and these now form the basis of the course that has persuaded Americans to make it their second golfing choice after St Andrews in Scotland.

The opening holes offer little hint of the treachery that follows, although there is a cemetery close by the first if a golfer strays. And the third is like Troon's wonderful Postage Stamp that is scarred by the site of caravan parks and rubbish tips.

It is not until the sixth that the excitement builds. On the dog-leg par four the Shannon Estuary finally comes into view and of course into play.

By the seventh the sea is not only in view but almost attacking the course. The cliff-top tee is balanced precariously above the beach and any slip would lead to more than a ruined round.

After a triangle formed by the next three holes comes one of the most famous and highly regarded holes in links golf. The 11th is 453 yards of drama.

It runs along the cliff tops past a sentry of dunes that guard the left-hand side of the fairway. If that is not enough the length is a real test for any player short of the highest calibre.

Add that to the 16 and 17th – both punishing dog-legs – and the course's quality is complete. Sadly the 18th is such a disappointment that many writers simply ignore it. The biggest criticism is the placement of a giant stretch of sand in the middle of the fairway. Called Sahara, it has won few friends over the years but it is a minor blemish on an otherwise outstanding course. — **CG**

12 27 Baltinglass
Baltinglass, Co Wicklow
☎ (0508) 81350, Sec 81514
40 miles S of Dublin.
Parkland course.
Founded 1928
Designed by Dr. W.G. Lyons, Hugh
Dark and Col. Mitchell
9 holes, 5554 yards, S.S.S. 69
† Welcome.
▪ WD £10; WE £12
♢ Three welcome per month; terms
on application.
◉ By arrangement.

12 28 Bandon
Castlebernard, Bandon, Co Cork
☎ (023) 41111, Fax 44690, Pro
42224
2 miles W of Bandon.
Parkland course.
Pro Paddy O'Boyle; Founded 1909
18 holes, 5663 yards, S.S.S. 69
† Welcome by prior arrangement.
▪ WD £20; WE £25.
♢ Welcome between March and
October on WD, except Wed and Sat;
catering packages available.
◉ Full bar and catering facilities.

12 29 Bantry Bay ☾
Donemark, Bantry, Co Cork
☎ (027) 50579, Fax 50579
2 km NW of Bantry on the Killarney
Road.
Clifftop parkland course with views of
Bantry Bay/Beara.
Pro Finbar Condon; Founded 1975
Designed by E Hackett & C O'Connor
Jnr
18 holes, 5910 yards, S.S.S. 72
† Welcome WD 8.30am-4.30pm; by
arrangement WE and Bank Holidays.
▪ WD £20; WE £20.
♢ Welcome by prior arrangement;
catering packages available; from
£12.
◉ Full catering facilities.
↝ West Lodge; Bantry Bay;
Reendesert; Ballyliokey Manor;
Seaview.

12 30 Beaufort ☾
Churchtown, Beaufort, Killarney, Co
Kerry
☎ (064) 44440, Fax 44752
7 miles W of Killarney off the N72.
Parkland course.
Pro Hugh Duggan; Founded 1995
Designed by Arthur Spring
18 holes, 6605 yards, S.S.S. 72
† Welcome.

▪ WD £25; WE £30.
♢ Welcome; discounts available for
groups.
◉ Full bar and catering.
↝ Europe; Great Southern; Dunloe
Castle.

12 31 Beaverstown
Beaverstown, Donabate, Co Dublin
☎ (01) 843 6439
15 miles N of Dublin; 3 miles from
Dublin Airport.
Parkland course.
Founded 1984
Designed by Eddie Hackett
18 holes, 5874 yards, S.S.S. 71
† Welcome WD.
▪ WD £20; WE £25.
♢ Welcome by prior arrangement;
terms on application.
◉ Full facilities.

12 32 Beech Park
Johnstown, Rathcoole, Co Dublin
☎ (01) 458 0522, Fax 458 8365,
Bar/Rest 458 0100
3km from Rathcoole village off the
Naas dual carriageway.
Parkland course.
Founded 1974
Designed by Eddie Hackett
18 holes, 5762 yards, S.S.S. 70
† Welcome Mon, Thurs and Fri; only
with a member at weekends.
▪ WD £25.
♢ Welcome Mon, Thurs, Fri; catering
packages available; from £19.
◉ Full bar and catering.
↝ Green Isle; City West; Bewleys;
Ambassador.

12 33 Belmullet
Carne, Belmullet, Co Mayo
☎ (097) 82292, Sec 81136
1.5 miles W of Belmullet.
Seaside links course.
Founded 1925
Designed by Eddie Hackett
18 holes, 6058 yards, S.S.S. 72
† Welcome.
▪ March-October £25; November-
April £15.

12 34 Belturbet
Erne Hill, Belturbet, Co Cavan
☎ (04995) 22287, Sec 22498
0.5 miles on the Cavan Road from
Belturbet.
Parkland course.
Founded 1950
9 holes, 5347 yards, S.S.S. 65

† Welcome.
▪ Terms on application.
♢ Welcome by prior arrangement.
◉ Full facilities.

12 35 Berehaven
Millcove, Castletownbere, Co Cork
☎ (027) 70700
On the main Castletownbere Road 20
miles W of Glengarriff.
Links course.
Founded 1993
9 holes, 4759 yards, S.S.S. 65
† Welcome.
▪ WD £12; WE £12.
♢ Details of special rates available
on application; tennis, fishing,
swimming, sailing available.
◉ Clubhouse facilities.

12 36 Birr
The Glenns, Birr, Co Offaly
☎ (0509) 20082, Pro 21606
2.5 miles W of Birr on the Banagher
Road.
Parkland course.
Founded 1893
18 championship holes, 5748 yards,
S.S.S. 69
† Welcome; must book at WE.
▪ WD £12; WE £14; details of
seasonal offers available on
application.
♢ Welcome by prior arrangement;
discounts available depending on
numbers; catering packages
available; terms on application.
◉ Full catering facilities.
↝ Dooleys; County.

12 37 The Black Bush
Thomastown, Dunshaughlin, Co
Meath
☎ (01) 825 0021, Fax 825 0400
0.5 miles E of Dunshaughlin on
Ratoath Road.
Parkland course.
Founded 1987
Designed by Robert Brown
27 holes, 6434 yards
† Welcome.
▪ WD £20; WE £23.
♢ Welcome WD; catering packages
available; also 9-hole course; terms
on application.
◉ Full catering facilities.
Practice range.

12 38 Blacklion
Toam, Blacklion, Co Cavan
☎ (072) 53024

Off the Sligo-Enniskillen Road at Blacklion.
Parkland course.
Founded 1962
Designed by Eddie Hackett
9 holes, 5605 yards, S.S.S. 69
♦ Welcome.
⌘ WD £8; WE £10.
⚘ Welcome by arrangement.
🍽 Full facilities.

12 39 Blainroe
Blainroe, Co Wicklow
☎ (0404) 68168, Fax 69369, Sec 67022
3 miles S of Wicklow on coast road.
Seaside course.
Founded 1978
Designed by Hawtree & Sons
18 holes, 6171 yards, S.S.S. 72
♦ Welcome by prior arrangement.
⌘ WD £29; WE £40.
⚘ Welcome by prior arrangement; catering packages available.
🍽 Full clubhouse facilities.

12 40 Bodenstown
Bodenstown, Sallins, Co Kildare
☎ (045) 897096
5 miles N of Naas.
Parkland course.
Founded 1973
36 holes, 6321 yards, S.S.S. 73
♦ Welcome; members only on Old course at WE.
⌘ WD £12; WE £12.
⚘ Welcome by prior arrangement.
🍽 Full catering facilities.

12 41 Borris
Deer Park, Borris, Co Carlow
☎ (0503) 73143, Sec 73310
16 miles from Carlow off the Dublin Road.
Parkland course.
Founded 1902
9 holes, 5596 yards, S.S.S. 69
♦ Welcome.
⌘ WD £12; WE £12.
⚘ Welcome; terms on application.
🍽 Bar and catering facilities available.
⛳ Lord Bagenal; Seven Oaks; Newpark.

12 42 Boyle
Knockadoo Brusna, Boyle, Co Roscommon
☎ (079) 62594, Sec 62192
2 miles S of Boyle on the N61 Roscommon Road.

Parkland course.
Founded 1911/1972
Designed by Eddie Hackett
9 holes, 4914 yards, S.S.S. 66
♦ Welcome.
⌘ Available on application.
⚘ Welcome by prior arrangement; discounts and catering packages available; from £8.
🍽 Full bar and catering facilities.
⛳ Forest Park; Royal.

12 43 Bray
Ravenswell Rd, Bray, Co Wicklow
☎ (01) 286 2484, Sec 288 8435
Off the L29 from Dublin.
Parkland course.
Founded 1897
9 holes, 5782 yards, S.S.S. 70
♦ Welcome WD except Mon.
⌘ WD £17.
⚘ Welcome by prior arrangement; must be affiliated to GUI.
🍽 Limited facilities.

12 44 Buncrana
Buncrana, Co Donegal,
☎ (077) 62279
Parkland course.
9 holes, 4250 yards, S.S.S. 62
♦ Welcome.
⌘ Available on application.

12 45 Bundoran
Great Northern Hotel, Bundoran, Co Donegal
☎ (072) 41302, Fax 42014
22 miles N of Sligo.
Links/parkland course.
Pro David Robinson; Founded 1894
Designed by Harry Vardon
18 championship holes, 5599 yards, S.S.S. 70
♦ Welcome by arrangement.
⌘ Details on application.
⚘ Welcome by prior arrangement.
🍽 Limited on course to snacks; hotel on site for meals.
⛳ Great Northern on course; Holyrood; Addingham; Fox's Lair; Marlborough; Atlantic.

12 46 Cabra Castle
Kingscourt, Co Cavan
☎ (04296) 67030
6 miles S of Carrickmacross.
Parkland course.
Founded 1977
9 holes, 5308 yards, S.S.S. 68
♦ Welcome; only with a member on Sun.

⌘ Terms on application.
⚘ Welcome by prior arrangement except Sun.
🍽 Full facilities.

12 47 Cahir Park
Kilcommon, Cahir, Co Tipperary
☎ (052) 41474, Sec 41680
1 mile S of Cahir on Clogheen Road.
Parkland course.
Founded 1965
Designed by Eddie Hackett
18 holes, 5446 yards, S.S.S. 69
♦ Welcome; by prior arrangement at WE.
⌘ WD £15; WE £15.
⚘ Welcome on Sat by prior arrangement; catering packages can be arranged with 72 hours notice; terms on application.
🍽 Bar facilities.

12 48 Callan
Geraldine, Callan, Co Kilkenny
☎ (056) 25136
10 miles S of Kilkenny; 0.5 miles from Callan.
Parkland course.
Founded 1929
Designed by Des Smyth
18 holes, 6400 yards, S.S.S. 70
♦ Welcome.
⌘ WD £15; WE £15.
⚘ Welcome WD and Sat am.
🍽 Full bar facilities, catering also available.

12 49 Carlow
Deerpark, Dublin Rd, Carlow, Co Carlow
☎ (0503) 31695, Fax 40065, Pro 41745
1 mile from Carlow station off Naas to Dublin Road.
Undulating parkland.
Founded 1899
Designed by Tom Simpson
18 holes, 5844 yards, S.S.S. 71
♦ Welcome.
⌘ WD £25; WE £30.
⚘ Welcome WD by prior arrangement.
🍽 Full catering facilities.

12 50 Carne Golf Links
Belmullet, Co Mayo, Ireland
☎ (097) 82292, Fax 81477
Near Belmullet, 95 miles N of Galway.
Links course.
18 holes, 6608 yards, par 72
Designed by E Hackett

Founded 1925
♦ Welcome.
£20.
⌕ Welcome by arrangement.
🍽 Bar and restaurant.
Practice range, greens.

12 51 Carrick-on-Shannon
Woodbrook, Carrick-on-Shannon, Co Roscommon
☎ (079) 67015
3 miles W of Carrick on N4.
Parkland course.
Founded 1910
Designed by Eddie Hackett
9 holes, 5545 yards, S.S.S. 68
♦ Welcome.
Terms on application.
⌕ Welcome by prior arrangement with Sec.
🍽 Full bar and catering facilities.

12 52 Carrick-on-Suir
Garravoone, Carrick-on-Suir, Co Tipperary
☎ (051) 640047, Sec 640558
15 miles from Waterford.
Parkland course.
Founded 1939
Designed by Edward Hackett
18 holes, 6061 yards, S.S.S. 71
♦ Welcome Wed and Sat-Sun but booking advisable.
WD £15; WE £17; reduced rates if with a member; group rates available.
⌕ Welcome; catering packages; private rooms; group discounts; from £12.
🍽 Full catering facilities.
⌖ Carraig.

12 53 Carrickmines
Golf Lane, Carrickmines, Dublin 18
☎ (01) 295 5972
8 miles S of Dublin.
Heath/parkland course.
Founded 1900
18 holes, 6103 yards, S.S.S. 69
♦ Welcome except Wed and Sat.
WD £20; WE £23.
⌕ None.
🍽 Limited.

12 54 Castle
Woodside Drive, Rathfarnham, Dublin
☎ (01) 490 4207, Fax 492 0264
Turn left after Terenure and take second right.
Parkland course.
Founded 1913
Designed by H.S. Colt

18 holes, 6024 yards, S.S.S. 69
♦ Welcome WD but booking advisable.
WD £35.
⌕ Welcome by prior arrangement only.
🍽 Full facilities.

12 55 Castle Barna
Daingean, Co Offaly
☎ (0506) 53384, Fax 53077
7 miles S of N6 at Tyrellspass.
Parkland course.
Founded 1996
Designed by A Duggan
18 holes, 6200 yards, S.S.S. 69
♦ Welcome; restrictions Sun am.
WD £9; WE £12.
⌕ Welcome by arrangement.
🍽 Coffee shop and restaurant

12 56 Castlebar
Rocklands, Castlebar, Co Mayo
☎ (094) 21649
1.25 miles from town centre.
Parkland course.
Founded 1910
18 holes, 5698 yards, S.S.S. 70
♦ Welcome WD.
Terms on application.
⌕ Welcome by prior arrangement.
🍽 By arrangement.

12 57 Castleblayney
Onomy, Castleblayney, Co Monaghan
☎ (042) 974 9485
Almost in Castleblayney town centre.
Parkland course.
Founded 1984
Designed by Bobby Browne
9 holes, 4923 yards, S.S.S. 66
♦ Welcome.
Available upon application.
⌕ Welcome by prior arrangement.
🍽 Full facilities.
⌖ Glencarn; Central.

12 58 Castlecomer
Drumgoole, Castlecomer, Co Kilkenny
☎ (056) 41139
On N7 10 miles N of Kilkenny.
Parkland course.
Founded 1935
Designed by Pat Ruddy
9 holes, 5923 yards, S.S.S. 71
♦ Welcome Mon-Sat by prior arrangement.
WD 12; WE £12.
⌕ Welcome except Sun.
🍽 By prior arrangement.

12 59 Castlegregory Golf and Fishing Club
Stradbelly, Castlegregory, Kerry
☎ (066) 39444
2 miles W of Castlegregory.
Founded 1989
Parkland course.
9 holes 5842 yards, S.S.S. 68
♦ Welcome.
Terms on application.
🍽 Club facilities.

12 60 Castlerea
Clonalis, Castlerea, Co Roscommon
☎ (0907) 20068
On main Dublin-Castlebar Road.
Parkland course.
Founded 1905
9 holes, 4974 yards, S.S.S. 66
♦ Welcome.
Terms on application.
⌕ Welcome by prior arrangement; catering packages by arrangement.

12 61 Castletroy
Castletroy, Co Limerick
☎ (061) 335753, Fax 335373, Pro 330450, Bar/Rest 335261
Course is three miles from Limerick on the N7.
Parkland course.
Pro Kevin Bennis; Founded 1937
18 holes, 5802 metres, S.S.S. 71
♦ Welcome by prior arrangement.
WD £24; WE £30.
⌕ Welcome by prior arrangement; £18.
🍽 Full catering facilities.
⌖ Castletroy Park; Kilmurry Lodge.

12 62 Castlewarden Golf & Country Club
Castlewarden, Straffan, Co Kildare
☎ (01) 458 9254, Pro 458 8219
Between Rathcoole and Kill.
Moorland course.
Founded 1989
Designed by Tommy Halpin; Redesigned By R.J. Browne (1992)
18 holes, 6008 yards, S.S.S. 71
♦ Welcome Mon, Thurs, Fri, WE only with member.
WD £17 in winter, £20 in summer; WE £20.
⌕ Welcome Mon, Thurs, Fri and some Sat mornings.
🍽 Full facilities.
Practice area.

12 63 Ceann Sibeal (Dingle)
Ballyougheragh, Tralee, Co Kerry

☎ (06691) 56225, Fax 56409, Sec 56408
1.5 miles from Ballyferriter.
Traditional links course.
Pro Dermot O'Connor; Founded 1924
Designed by Eddie Hackett (1972)/
Christy O'Connor (1988)
18 holes, 6690 yards, S.S.S. 71
† Welcome.
Ⅼ WD £25; WE £25.
⌁ Welcome; catering packages by arrangement; day ticket £27; from £21.
◉ Full bar and restaurant service available.
⌁ Skellig; Benners.

12 64 **Charlesland**
Charlesland, Greystones, Co Wicklow
☎ (01) 2874350, Fax 2874360,
Bar/Rest 2876764
Off the N11 Dublin-Wexford Road at Delgarny turning.
Parkland course.
Pro Paul Heeney; Founded 1992
Designed by E Hackett
18 holes, 6739 yards, S.S.S. 72
† Welcome.
Ⅼ WD £26; WE £33.
⌁ Welcome by prior arrangement; discounts for group bookings; terms on application.
◉ Full facilities.
⌁ La Touche; Charlesland.

12 65 **Charleville**
Smiths Rd, Ardmore, Charleville, Co Cork
☎ (063) 81257
On main road from Cork to Limerick.
Parkland course.
Founded 1909
27 holes, 6430 yards, S.S.S. 70
† Welcome by prior arrangement.
Ⅼ Terms on application.
⌁ Welcome except Sun by prior arrangement.
◉ Bar and restaurant service available.

12 66 **Cill Dara**
Kildare, Co Kildare
☎ (0455) 21433, Pro shop 521295
1 mile E of Kildaire.
Moorland course.
Founded 1920
9 holes, 5738 yards, S.S.S. 70
† Welcome.
Ⅼ Terms on application.
⌁ Welcome by prior arrangement; catering packages available.
◉ Clubhouse facilities.

12 67 **City West Hotel**
City West Country House Hotel, Saggart, Dublin
☎ (01) 458 8566, Fax 458 8565
Off M50 at M7 for S of Ireland, at City West Business Park.
Designed by Christie O Connor
Parkland course
18 holes, 6691 yards, par 70
† Welcome.
Ⅼ WD £25; WE £30; residents' reductions.
⌁ Welcome, packages available.
Hotel and conference facilities.

12 68 **Clane**
Clane, Co Kildare
☎ (01) 628 6608
Playing facilities at Clongowes.
Founded 1976
9 holes
† Not welcome.

12 69 **Claremorris**
Rushbrook, Castlemagarett, Claremorris, Co Mayo
☎ (094) 71527, Sec 71868
1.5 miles from Claremorris on Galway Road.
Parkland course.
Founded 1917
9 holes, 5600 yards, S.S.S. 69
† Welcome except Sun.
Ⅼ WD £8; WE £8.
⌁ Welcome WD by prior arrangement; catering packages by arrangement.
◉ By arrangement.

12 70 **Clones**
Hilton Park, Clones, Co Monaghan
☎ (047) 56017
3 miles from Clones.
Parkland course.
Founded 1913
9 holes, 5206 yards, S.S.S. 67
† Welcome.
Ⅼ WD £10; WE £12.
⌁ Welcome by prior arrangement with the secretary; catering by arrangement; also 9-hole course: 2608 metres, par 34; from £5.
◉ Clubhouse facilities.
⌁ Lennard Arms; Creighton; Hibernian; Riverdale.

12 71 **Clongowes**
Naas, Co Kildare
☎ (0458) 68202
Parkland course.
Founded 1966

9 holes, 5400 yards, S.S.S. 65
† Welcome by prior arrangement.
Ⅼ Terms on application.
⌁ Terms on application.
◉ Full facilities.

12 72 **Clonlara**
Clonlara Golf and Leisure, Clonlara, Co Clare
☎ (061) 354141, Fax 354143, Bar/Rest 354191
Course is seven miles north-east of Limerick on the Corbally-Killaloe Road.
Woodland/parkland course.
Pro Noel Cassidy; Founded 1993
12 holes, 5187 yards, S.S.S. 69
† Welcome; pay and play.
Ⅼ WD £5; WE £5.
⌁ Welcome by prior arrangement; discounts for groups of 20 or more; tennis; sauna; games room; fishing; terms on application.
◉ Bar facilities; catering by order.
⌁ Self-catering accommodation on site.

12 73 **Clonmel**
Lyreanearla, Mountain Rd, Clonmel, Co Tipperary
☎ (052) 21138, Fax 24050, Pro 24050, Sec 24050
3 miles from Clonmel.
Parkland course.
Pro Robert Hayes; Founded 1911
Designed by Eddie Hackett
18 holes, 5845 yards, S.S.S. 71
† Welcome
Ⅼ WD £18; WE £20; with member £14.
⌁ Welcome from April to October; terms on application.
◉ Full clubhouse facilities available.
⌁ Clonmel Arms; Minella; Hearns; Hanora's Cottage.

12 74 **Clontarf**
Donnycarney House, Malahide Rd, Co Dublin
☎ (01) 833 1892, Fax 883 1933, Pro 833 1877, Bar/Rest 833 0622
2.5 miles NE of city centre off Malahide Road.
Parkland course.
Pro Joe Craddock; Founded 1912
18 holes, 5317 metres, S.S.S. 67
† Welcome.
Ⅼ WD £26; WE £35.
⌁ Welcome Tues or Fri; packages include catering; from £30.
◉ Full clubhouse facilities available.
⌁ Skylon.

County Louth

County Louth, or Baltray as it is known to almost everyone, is among the most stunning but least publicised courses in all of Ireland. Approaching Baltray is as thrilling a prospect as any golf course in the world.

The hour's journey north from Dublin is always filled with great expectation, for golf at Baltray has the feel of magnificent traditionalism. There have been modifications in recent years but none so drastic as to alter the authenticity of the touch brought by Tom Simpson.

The holes have been carefully carved from the Irish countryside and the views, in particular, are simply magnificent. The opening nine have a feeling of tumbling away especially at the third. The drive is not the most taxing on the course but the second could well be.

Over the natural humps lies the narrow path to the green beyond which lies the most difficult of greens to hit. A par for most golfers is a rare triumph on a hole that leads many players beyond temptation and into ruin.

But while the front nine, with its classic short hole at four and its long and testing par five at six, are dramatic, the holes from 10 to16 may in fact be the best signatures of a truly excellent course. The feel is different. There is more space as the course makes its way away from the clubhouse and towards the sea to the trio of 12, 13 and 14 which are nothing other than great par fours. They don't rely on excessive length or gimmicks but provide a proper test of golf.

If there is a disappointment at County Louth, and this must be taken in the context of an otherwise memorable course, it is the last two holes. The par-three 17th possesses none of the challenge of the other three heavily guarded greens on the course. Instead it is rather characterless and the 18th is a par five with little to distinguish it other than its length.

Being so close to Dublin, this is a popular course for day-trippers and also has two distinct feels. It can pose the problems that characterise a real championship course but it is not so daunting as to scare the social golfer. And the approach still captures enough magic to ensure that one visit to County Louth will guarantee that there will always be a longing to return. — **CG**

Corrstown Golf Club

Corrstown Golf Club has achieved in eight short years a success envied by new and old clubs alike. The club boasts two courses: the Championship par 72 'River' course complete with fairway mounds, burns, lakes and river hazards – regarded as amongst the best in Ireland; and the 9-hole 'Orchard' course set amidst thousands of mature trees, offering a peaceful game in a challenging, yet relaxed environment.

With full bar and catering facilities and just 10 minutes north of Dublin Airport, you're guaranteed a warm welcome at Corrstown Golf Club

Corrstown, Kilsallaghan, Co. Dublin. Tel: 003531 864 0533/864 0534 Fax: 003531 864 0537

---

12 75 Cobh
Ballywilliam, Cobh, Co Cork
☎ (021) 812399
1 mile E of Cobh.
Public parkland course.
Founded 1987
Designed by Eddie Hackett
9 holes, 4366 yards, S.S.S. 63
† Welcome WD; by prior arrangement WE.
⌊ WD £12; WE £12.
⌃ Welcome Mon-Sat.
†◎† Bar facilities.

12 76 Coldwinters
Newtown House, St Margaret's, Co Dublin
☎ (01) 864 0324, Fax 834 1400
Parkland course; also 9-hole course, 2163 metres, par 31.
Pro Roger Yates
18 holes, 5973 yards, S.S.S. 69
† Welcome; pay and play.
⌊ Terms on application.
⌃ Welcome by prior arrangement.
†◎† Clubhouse facilities.
↘ Many in Dublin.

12 77 Connemara
Ballyconneely, Clifden, Co Galway

☎ (095) 23502, Fax 23662, Bar/Rest 23502
Signposted from Clifden.
Links course.
Pro Hugh O'Neill; Founded 1973
Designed by Eddie Hackett
27 holes, 6611 yards, S.S.S. 75
† Welcome.
⌊ WD £25; WE £25.
⌃ Welcome; minimum parties of 20; catering packages available; from £13.
†◎† Full bar and restaurant facilities.
↘ Rock Glen; Abbey Glen; Foyles; Alcock & Brown; Ballinahynch.

12 78 Connemara Isles
Annaghuane, Lettermore, Connemara, Galway
☎ (091) 572 498, 572 214
5 miles W of Costello.
Parkland course.
9 holes, 5168 yards, S.S.S. 67
† Welcome.
⌊ Terms on application.
†◎† Full facilities in thatched clubhouse.

12 79 Coollattin
Coollattin, Shillelheh, Co Wicklow

☎ (055) 29125
12 miles SW of Aughrim.
Parkland course.
Founded 1922
18 holes, 6148 yards, S.S.S. 69
† Welcome WD.
⌊ WD £20; WE £25.
⌃ Welcome WD by prior arrangement.
†◎† Bar and snacks; meals by arrangement.

12 80 Coosheen
Coosheen, Schull, Co Cork
☎ (028) 28182
1 mile E of Schull.
Seaside parkland course.
Founded 1989
Designed by Daniel Morgan
9 holes, 4020 yards, S.S.S. 58
† Welcome.
⌊ WD £10; WE £10.
⌃ Welcome; from £10.
†◎† Full bar and restaurant.
↘ East End; West Cork; Westlodge.

12 81 Corballis
Dunabate, Co Dublin
☎ (01) 843 6583
N of Dublin on Belfast Road.

Links course.
Founded 1971
Designed by City Council
18 holes, 4971 yards, S.S.S. 64
† Public pay and play.
↳ WD £9; WE £12.
☞ None.
◉ Snack facilities.
↝ Dunes.

12 82 Cork
Little Island, Cork, Co Cork
☎ (021) 353451, Fax 353410, Pro 353421
5 miles E of Cork City off N25.
Parkland/heathland course.
Pro Peter Hickey; Founded 1888
Designed by Alister MacKenzie
18 holes, 6119 yards, S.S.S. 72
† Welcome.
↳ Available upon request.
☞ Welcome by prior arrangement; minimum 20; catering packages by arrangement; from £24.
◉ Bar and catering facilities.
↝ Ashbourne House; Silver Springs; Jurys.

12 83 Corrstown
Corrstown, Kilsallaghan, Co Dublin
☎ (01) 864 0533, Fax 864 0537
10 minutes from Dublin Airport, access from Swords Road and Ashbourne Road.
Parkland course.
Founded 1993
27 holes, 5584 yards, S.S.S. 72
† Welcome Mon-Fri; after 1pm WE.
↳ WD £20; WE £25.
☞ Welcome by prior arrangement.
◉ Full bar and catering facilities.
↝ Forte Crest; Great Southern, both Dublin Airport; Forte Posthouse, Swords Road.

12 84 County Cavan
Arnmore House, Drumelis, Cavan, Co Cavan
☎ (04943) 31541, Fax 31541, Pro 31388, Bar/Rest 31283
1 mile from Cavan on the Killeshandra Road.
Parkland course.
Pro Ciaran Carroll; Founded 1894
Designed by E Hackett
18 holes, 5634 yards, S.S.S. 70
† Welcome.
↳ Terms on application.
☞ Welcome; restrictions Wed and Sun.
◉ Full catering facilities.
↝ Farnham Arms; Kilmore.

12 85 County Longford
Glack, Longford
☎ (043) 46310, Sec 45556
E of Glack off the Dublin-Sligo N4 Rd.
Undulating parkland course.
Founded 1894
Designed by E. Hackett
18 holes, 5494 yards, S.S.S. men 67, women 72
† Welcome.
↳ Terms on application.
☞ Welcome by prior arrangement.
◉ Clubhouse catering facilities.

12 86 County Louth
Baltray, Drogheda, Co Louth
☎ (04198) 22329, Fax 22969, Pro 22444, Bar/Rest 22442
5 miles NE of Drogheda.
Links course.
Pro Paddy McGuirk; Founded 1892
Designed by Tom Simpson
18 holes, 6783 yards, S.S.S. 72
† Welcome by prior arrangement.
↳ WD £40; WE £50.
☞ Welcome by prior arrangement; catering packages by arrangement; from £40.
◉ Full bar and catering facilities.
↝ Boyn Valley.

12 87 County Meath (Trim)
Newtownmoynagh, Trim, Co Meath
☎ (046) 31463
3 miles from Trim on the Longwood Road.
Parkland course.
Founded 1898
Designed by Eddie Hackett
18 holes, 6503 yards, S.S.S. 72
† Welcome; restrictions Thurs, Sat, Sun.
↳ Terms on application.
☞ Welcome Mon-Sat by prior arrangement.
◉ Full bar and catering facilities.

12 88 County Sligo
Rosses Point, Co Sligo
☎ (071) 77134, Fax 77460, Pro 77171, Sec 77186, Bar/Rest 77186
5 miles N of Sligo.
Links course.
Pro Leslie Robinson; Founded 1894
Designed by Colt & Alison
27 holes, 6043 yards, S.S.S. 72
† Welcome; not before 10.30am at WE.
↳ WD £35; WE £45.
☞ Welcome by prior arrangement; special rates and packages for 20 or more players.

◉ Full clubhouse facilities.
Practice area.
↝ Tower Hotel; Sligo Park; Yeats Country Hotel; Ballincar House.

12 89 County Tipperary Golf & Country Club
Dundrum, Cashel, Co Tipperary
☎ (062) 71717, Fax 71718
6 miles W of Cashel.
Parkland course.
Founded 1993
Designed by Philip Walton
18 holes, 6709 yards, S.S.S. 72 and 71
† Welcome.
↳ WD £25; WE £28.
☞ Welcome; information about group discounts available upon request.
◉ Full catering and bar facilities.
↝ Dundrum House on site.

12 90 Courtown
Kiltennel, Gorey, Co Wexford
☎ (055) 25166, Fax 25553
Leave N11 at Gorey following the Road to Courtown Harbour.
Parkland course.
Pro John Coone; Founded 1936
Designed by Harris & Associates/Henry Cotton
18 holes, 5898 metres, S.S.S. 71
† Welcome; some restrictions Tues and WE.
↳ May-September: WD £20, WE £25; October-April: WD £15, WE £20.
☞ Welcome by prior arrangement with secretary/manager; reductions for groups of more than 20.
◉ Full catering and bar facilities.
↝ Marlfield; Courtown; Bayview.

12 91 Craddockstown
Craddockstown, Naas, Co Kildare
☎ (045) 97610
Parkland course.
Founded 1983
18 holes, 6134 yards, S.S.S. 72
† Welcome.
↳ Available upon application.

12 92 Cruit Island
Kincasslagh, Letterkenny, Co Donegal
☎ (075) 43296, Sec 48151
6 miles from Dungloe opposite the Viking House Hotel.
Links course.
Founded 1986
9 holes, 4860 yards, S.S.S. 64
† Welcome.

⌒ Welcome by prior arrangement; catering packages available by arrangement; from £8.
🍽 Bar and catering facilities.
Practice area.
↗ Viking House; Ostan na Rosann.

12 93 Curragh
Curragh, Co Kildare
☎ (045) 441714, Fax 441714, Sec 441238
2 miles SE of Newbridge.
Parkland course.
Pro Gerry Burke; Founded 1883
Designed by David Ritchie
18 holes, 6035 yards, S.S.S. 71
† Welcome by prior arrangement.
⌐ WD £18; WE £22.
⌒ Welcome by prior arrangement
Mon-Fri & Sat morning; from £16.
🍽 Full clubhouse facilities available.
↗ Standhouse; Keadeen.

12 94 Deer Park Hotel
Deer Park Hotel, Howth, Co Dublin
☎ (00 353 1) 832 2624, Fax 832 6039, Sec 832 6039
9 miles E of the City centre.
Parkland course; 2 x 9-hole courses; 12-hole pitch and putt.
Founded 1973
Designed by Fred Hawtree
18 holes, 6770 yards, S.S.S. 71
† Welcome; restrictions Sun am.
⌐ WD IR£10; WE IR£13.50.
⌒ Welcome WD by prior arrangement; catering packages available by prior arrangement; function rooms.
🍽 Full restaurant and bar facilities.
↗ Deer Park on site.

12 95 Delgany
Delgany, Co Wicklow
☎ (01) 287 4536, Fax 287 3977
Off N11 1 mile past Glenview Hotel.

Parkland course.
Pro Gavin Kavanagh; Founded 1908
Designed by H Vardon
18 holes, 5480 metres, S.S.S. 68
† Welcome.
⌐ WD £23; WE £27.
⌒ Welcome by prior arrangement; from £23.
🍽 Full bar and catering facilities.
↗ Glenview; Delgany Inn.

12 96 Delvin Castle
Delvin Castle, Delvin, Westmeath
☎ (044) 64315
On N52 in the village of Delvin.
Mature parkland with lakes.
Founded 1995
Designed by J Day
18 holes
† Welcome; restrictions Wed and Sun.
⌐ Available upon request.
⌒ Welcome by prior arrangement.
🍽 Full bar and catering service available.

12 97 Donabate
Donabate, Balcarrick, Co Dublin
☎ (00 353 1) 843 6346, Sec 843 1264
1 mile N of Swords on the Dublin-Belfast Road.
Parkland course.
Founded 1925
18 holes, 5704 yards, S.S.S. 69
† Welcome WE with a member.
⌐ Available upon request.
⌒ Welcome by prior arrangement.
🍽 Clubhouse catering facilities.

12 98 Donegal
Murvagh, Laghey, Co Donegal
☎ (073) 34054, Fax 34377
8 miles from Donegal on the Ballyshannon Road.
Links course.

Founded 1960/73
Designed by Eddie Hackett
18 holes, 6547 yards, S.S.S. 75
† Welcome.
⌐ WD £20; WE £27.
⌒ Welcome by prior arrangement; discounts for more than 16 golfers; snooker;
🍽 Full bar and restaurant facilities.
Practice range, large practice ground.
↗ Sandhouse.

12 99 Doneraile
Doneraile, Co Cork
☎ (022) 24137
Off T11 28 miles from Cork; 9 miles from Mallow.
Parkland course.
Founded 1927
9 holes, 5055 yards, S.S.S. 67
† Welcome.
⌐ Terms on application.
⌒ Welcome by prior arrangement.
🍽 Full clubhouse facilities available.

12 100 Dooks
Glenbeigh, Co Kerry
☎ (06697) 68205, Fax 68476
On the N70 between Killonglin and Glenbeigh.
Links course.
Founded 1889
Designed by Eddie Hackett/Donald Steel
18 holes, 6010 yards, S.S.S. 68
† Welcome.
⌐ WD £25; WE £25; advisable to book for weekends.
⌒ Welcome by prior arrangement; from £20.
🍽 Full clubhouse facilities.
↗ Towers; And na si; Bianconi.

12 101 Douglas
Douglas, Co Cork
☎ (021) 895297

3 miles from Cork; 0.5 miles past Douglas village.
Parkland course.
Founded 1909
18 holes, 5664 yards, S.S.S. 69
🏌 Welcome; reservations needed at WE.
▢ Terms on application.
🏌 Welcome by prior arrangement before start of the season.
🍽 Catering facilities.

12 102 Dromoland Castle ☏
Newmarket-on-Fergus, Co Clare
☎ (061) 368444, Fax 368498
14 miles from Limerick on N18 and 6 miles from Shannon on N19.
Parkland course.
Pro Philip Murphy; Founded 1963
Designed by Wigginton
18 holes, 5719 yards, S.S.S. 71
🏌 Welcome.
▢ WD £25; WE £25.
🏌 Welcome by prior arrangement; catering packages available; leisure, spa and health studios; from £22.
🍽 Full clubhouse facilities.
Practice area.
⌁ Clare Inn; Oakwood Arms; Limerick Inn.

12 103 Druids Glen
Newtonmountkennedy, Co Wicklow
☎ (01) 2873600, Fax 287399
Signposted from N11 from Dublin taking Newtonmountkennedy/ Glengalaugh junction.
Parkland course; European Tour venue.
Pro Eamonn Darcy; Founded 1993
Designed by T Craddock & P Ruddy
18 holes, 7026 yards, S.S.S. 73
🏌 Welcome.
▢ WD £85; WE £85.
🏌 Welcome every day by prior arrangement; minimum 20 players; catering packages by arrangement; from £65.
🍽 Full clubhouse bar and restaurant facilities.
Practice range, practice facilities and 3-hole academy.
⌁ Glenview; Tinakilly.

12 104 Dublin Mountain
Gortlum, Brittas, Co Dublin
☎ (01) 4582622
Undulating parkland course.
Founded 1993
18 holes, 5433 yards, S.S.S. 69
🏌 Welcome.
▢ Terms on application.

🏌 Terms on application.
🍽 Clubhouse facilities.

12 105 Dun Laoghaire
Eglinton Park, Tivoli Rd, Dun Laoghaire, Co Dublin
☎ (01) 280 5116, Fax 280 4868, Pro 280 1694, Sec 280 3916, Bar/Rest 280 1055
7 miles S of Dublin; 0.5 miles from Ferry port.
Parkland course.
Pro Owen Mulhall; Founded 1910
Designed by H S Colt
18 holes, 5298 yards, S.S.S. 68
🏌 Welcome except Thurs and Sat.
▢ WD £30; WE £30.
🏌 Welcome by prior arrangement with the manager; discounts for groups of 30 or more; from £25.
🍽 Full clubhouse facilities.
⌁ Royal Marine; Rochestown; Killiney Castle.

12 106 Dundalk
Blackrock, Dundalk, Co Louth
☎ (04293) 21731, Fax 22022, Pro 22102
2 miles S of Dundalk taking the coast Road to Blackrock.
Parkland course.
Pro James Cassidy; Founded 1904
Designed by Dave Thomas & Peter Alliss
18 holes, 6160 yards, S.S.S. 72
🏌 Welcome.
▢ WD £20; WE £24.
🏌 Welcome by prior arrangement; catering packages by arrangement;
🍽 Bar and restaurant facilities available.
Large practice area.
⌁ Fairway.

12 107 Dunfanaghy
Dunfanaghy, Letterkenny, Co Donegal
☎ (074) 36335, Pro 36488
On N56 from Letterkenny 0.5 miles E of Dunfanaghy.
Seaside links course.
Founded 1904
Designed by H Vardon
18 holes, 5006 yards, S.S.S. 66
🏌 Welcome but notice is essential.
▢ WD £13; WE £17.
🏌 Welcome by prior arrangement; discounts for groups of more than 12 and 20; from £9 and £10 at weekends.
🍽 Full clubhouse facilities available.
⌁ Arnolds; Carrig Rua; Port-n-Blagh; Shandon.

12 108 Dungarvan
Knocknagranagh, Dungarvan, Co Waterford
☎ (058) 43310, Fax 44113, Pro 44707, Bar/Rest 41605
2.5 miles E of Dungarvan on the N25 Waterford to Rosslare Road.
Parkland course.
Pro David Hayes; Founded 1924/1993
Designed by Maurice Fives
18 holes, 6785 yards, S.S.S. 73
🏌 Welcome; booking needed at WE.
▢ WD £20; WE £25.
🏌 Welcome by prior arrangement; catering packages available; from £13.
🍽 Full clubhouse facilities available.
Practice range, 1 mile.
⌁ Clonea Strand; Gold Coast; Lawlors; Park.

12 109 Dunmore
Dunmore House, Muckross, Clonakilty, Co Cork
☎ (023) 33352
Signposted 3 miles from Clonakilty.
Hilly Open course.
Founded 1967
Designed by E. Hackett
9 holes, 4464 yards, S.S.S. 61
🏌 Welcome.
▢ Details upon request.
🏌 Welcome by prior arrangement.
🍽 Bar and restaurant facilities in Dunmore House.

12 110 Dunmore East Golf & Country Club
Dunmore East, Co Waterford
☎ (051) 383151, Fax 383151
10 miles from Waterford in the village of Dunmore East.
Seaside parkland course.
Founded 1993
Designed by Eamon Condon & Assoc
18 holes, 6655 yards, S.S.S. 71
🏌 Welcome.
▢ WD £12; WE £15.
🏌 Welcome by prior arrangement; terms on application.
🍽 Full clubhouse facilities.
⌁ Ivory Lodge; Dunmore Holiday Villas; Haven.

12 111 East Clare
Coolreigh, Bodyke, Co Clare
☎ (061) 921322, Fax 921717, Sec 921388
15 miles E of Ennis.
Parkland course.
Founded 1997

Designed by A Spring
18 holes, 5922 yards, S.S.S. 71
† Welcome.
↳ WD £13; WE £15.
☞ Welcome; discounts for groups of 25 or more; from £13.
◉ Limited.
↬ Smyths Village.

12 112 **East Cork**

Gortacrue, Midleton, Co Cork
☎ (021) 631687, Fax 613695, Pro 633667, Bar/Rest 631273
Leave Cork to Waterford road at Midleton; course is two miles on the Fermou Road.
Parkland course.
Pro Don MacFarlane; Founded 1970
Designed by Edward Hackett
18 holes, 5774 yards, S.S.S. 67
† Welcome with prior booking.
↳ WD £15; WE £15.
☞ Welcome by prior arrangement; minimum 10 players from £15.
◉ Full clubhouse facilities.
↬ Commodore; Middleton Park; Garryvoe.

12 113 **Edenderry**

Kishawanny, Edenderry, Co Offaly
☎ (0405) 31072
Off the R402 to Edenderry from the N4.
Parkland course.
Founded 1947
Designed by E Hackett
18 holes, 6029 yards, S.S.S. 72
† Welcome.
↳ WD £13; WE £15.
☞ Welcome except Thurs and Sun; from £10.
◉ Clubhouse facilities.
↬ Wells; Tullamore Court.

12 114 **Edmondstown**

Edmondstown Rd, Rathfarnham, Co Dublin
☎ Sec (01) 493 1082, Bar/Rest 493 2461, Fax 493 3152, Pro 494 1049
8 miles SW of City centre.
Parkland course.
Pro Andrew Crofton; Founded 1944
Designed by McAlister
18 holes, 5663 yards, S.S.S. 70
† Welcome but it is advisable to make reservations.
↳ WD £30; WE £35.
☞ Welcome; terms available on application.
◉ Full facilities.
Practice ground.
↬ Many in Dublin.

12 115 **Elm Green**

Castlerock, Dublin
☎ (01) 820 0797, Fax 820 8134
15 mins from Dublin Airport.
Public course.
18 holes, 4951 yards, par 71
† Welcome.
↳ WD £12; WE £18.
☞ Welcome.
◉ Limited, local pubs available.

12 116 **Elm Park**

Nutley Lane, Donnybrook
☎ (01) 269 3438, Pro 269 2650
2 miles from City centre.
Parkland course.
Founded 1925
Designed by Fred Davies
18 holes, 5355 metres, S.S.S. 68
† Welcome by prior arrangement.
↳ Terms on application.
☞ Welcome Tues.
◉ Full facilities.

12 117 **Ennis**

Drumbiggle, Ennis, Co Clare
☎ (06568) 29211, Fax 41848, Pro 20690, Sec 24074, Bar/Rest 24074
1 mile from town centre.
Parkland course.
Pro Martin Ward; Founded 1912
18 holes, 5592 metres, S.S.S. 69
† Welcome.
↳ WD £18; WE £18.
☞ Welcome by prior arrangement; minimum group 10.
◉ Full clubhouse facilities.
↬ Auburn Lodge; Old Ground; West County.

12 118 **Enniscorthy**

Knockmarshal, Enniscorthy, Co Wexford
☎ (054) 33191, Fax 37637
1 mile from town on the Newross-Waterford Road.
Parkland course.
Pro Martin Sludds; Founded 1926
Designed by E. Hackett
18 holes, 6115 yards, S.S.S. 72
† Welcome by prior arrangement.
↳ April-Sept: WD £20, WE £22; Oct-March: WD £15, WE £20.
☞ Welcome by prior arrangement with group rates available; terms on application.
◉ Full facilities.
↬ Murphy Floods.

12 119 **Enniscrone**

Enniscrone, Co Sligo

☎ (096) 36297, Fax 36657
7 miles from Ballina.
Championship links course.
Pro Charlie McGoldrick; Founded 1918/31
Designed by E. Hackett
18 holes, 6720 yards, S.S.S. 72
† Welcome by prior arrangement.
↳ WD £25; WE £34.
☞ Welcome by prior arrangement; minimum 12; catering packages by arrangement; from £13.
◉ Full bar and catering.
Practice area.
↬ Downhill, Ballina; Atlantic; Benbulbow; Castle, all Enniscrone.

12 120 **Esker Hills G & CC**

Tullamore, Co Offaly
☎ (0506) 55999, Fax 55021
2.5 miles W of Tullamore.
Undulating parkland course.
Founded 1996
Designed by C O'Connor Jnr
18 holes, 6612 yards, S.S.S. 70
† Welcome.
↳ WD £16; WE £20.
☞ Welcome by arrangement; terms on application.
◉ Coffee shop facilities.

12 121 **The European Club**

Brittas Bay, Co Wicklow
☎ (0404) 47415, Fax 47449
Midway between Wicklow and Arklow S of Dublin.
Links course.
Founded 1993
Designed by Pat Ruddy
18 holes, 7089 yards, S.S.S. 73
† Welcome by prior arrangement.
↳ WD 50; WE £50.
☞ Welcome by prior arrangement; minimum group 24; from £30.
◉ Full clubhouse facilities.
Practice range, practice ground.
↬ Tinakilly House; Grand, Wicklow; Hunters, Ashford.

12 122 **Faithlegg**

Faithlegg House, Co. Waterford
☎ (051) 382241, Fax 382664
6 miles from Waterford city centre on the banks of the Suir.
Parkland course.
Founded 1993
Designed by Patrick Merrigan
18 holes, 6674 yards, S.S.S. 72
† Welcome.
↳ Mon-Thurs £16 before 9am and £22 after; Fri-Sun £27.
☞ Welcome by prior arrangement;

packages available; terms on application.
○ Full bar and restaurant facilities. Practice area.

12 123 Fermoy
Corrin, Fermoy, Co Cork
☎ (025) 31472
2 miles from Fermoy off Cork-Dublin Road.
Undulating parkland course.
Founded 1893
Designed by Commander Harris
18 holes, 5795 yards, S.S.S. 70
† Welcome WD.
⌐ Terms on application.
⌐ Welcome WD and Sat am.
○ By arrangement.

12 124 Fernhill
Carrigaline, Co Cork
☎ (021) 373103, Fax 371011
Parkland course.
Founded 1994
18 holes
† Welcome.
⌐ Terms on application.
⌐ Terms on application.

12 125 Forrest Little
Forest Little, Cloghran, Co Dublin
☎ (01) 840 1763, Fax 840 1000, Pro 840 7670
0.5 miles beyond Dublin Airport on the Dublin-Belfast Road, take first left.
Parkland course.
Founded 1940
Designed by Fred Hawtree
18 holes, 5865 yards, S.S.S. 70
† Welcome WD.
⌐ Terms on application.
⌐ Welcome normally Mon and Thurs afternoon.
○ Full bar, snacks and restaurant.

12 126 Fota Island
Fota Island, Carrigtwohill, Co Cork
☎ (021) Bookings 883700, Fax 883713, Pro 883710, Bar/Rest 883700
Take N25 E from Cork City towards Waterford and Rosslare; after 9 miles take the exit for Cobh/Fota, course 0.5 miles.
Parkland course.
Pro Kevin Morris; Founded 1993
Designed by Peter McEvoy and Christy O'Connor Jnr
18 holes, 6927 yards, S.S.S. 73
† Welcome.

⌐ WD £45; Fri-Sun £55.
⌐ Welcome by prior arrangement; group rates available on application; from £26.
○ Full facilities.
⌐ Midleton Park; Ashbourne House; Jury's Cork.

12 127 Foxrock
Torquay Rd, Dublin, Co Dublin
☎ (01) 289 3992, Fax 289 4943, Pro 289 3414, Bar/Rest 289 5668
About 6 miles from Dublin; turn right off T7 just past Stillergan on the Leopardstown Road then left into Torquay Road.
Parkland course.
Founded 1893
9 holes, 5667 yards, S.S.S. 69
† Welcome Mon-Wed am, Thurs, Fri and Sun with a member.
⌐ WD £30; WE £30.
⌐ Welcome Mon and Thurs.
○ Snacks.

12 128 Frankfield
Frankfield, Douglas, Co Cork
☎ (021) 363124
10 miles S of Cork.
Parkland course.
Founded 1984
9 holes, 4621 yards, S.S.S. 65
† Welcome.
⌐ Terms on application.
○ Lunches.

12 129 Galway
Blackrock, Salthill, Co Galway
☎ (091) 522033, Fax 529783, Pro 523038, Bar/Rest 521827
3 miles W of Galway.
Tight tree-lined parkland course.
Pro Don Wallace; Founded 1895
Designed by A MacKenzie
18 holes, 5832 yards, S.S.S. 71
† Welcome.
⌐ WD £20; WE £25.
⌐ Welcome WD by prior arrangement; catering packages by arrangement.
○ Full catering facilities.
⌐ Salthill; Galway Bay; Jameson's; Spinnaker.

12 130 Galway Bay Golf ☏ & Country Club
Renville, Oranmore, Co Galway
☎ (091) 790500
From Galway take the coast road through Oranmore; course is signposted from there.

Seaside parkland course.
Founded 1993
Designed by Christy O'Connor Jnr
18 holes, 7190 yards, S.S.S. 72
† Welcome if carrying handicap certs.
⌐ WD £38; WE £43.
⌐ Welcome by prior arrangement; group rates available for groups of over 20.
○ Restaurant; spikes bar; bar. Practice range, practice bays.

12 131 Glasson Golf & CC
Glasson, Athlone, Co Westmeath
☎ (0902) 85120, Fax 85444
6 miles N of Athlone on the N55.
Parkland course.
Founded 1994
Designed by C O'Connor
18 holes, 7120 yards, S.S.S. 72
† Welcome.
⌐ Mon-Thurs £30; Fri & Sun £32; Sat £35.
⌐ Welcome by prior arrangement; catering packages by arrangement; from £23.
○ Full clubhouse facilities.

12 132 Glebe
Kildalkey Rd, Trim, Meath
☎ (046) 31926
1 mile from Trim.
Parkland pay-and-play course.
18 holes, 6466 yards, par 73
† Welcome.
⌐ WD £8; WE £10.
⌐ By arrangement.
○ Snacks available.

12 133 Glencullen
Glencullen, Co Wicklow
☎ (01) 294 0898
4 miles from Kilternan; follow signs for Johnny Fox's pub.
9 holes, 5400 yards, par 69
† Welcome.
⌐ £12.
○ Snack facilities.

12 134 Glengarriff
Glengarriff, Co Cork
☎ (027) 63150
On T65 55 miles W of Cork.
Seaside course.
Founded 1936
9 holes, 4094 yards, S.S.S. 66
† Welcome.
⌐ Terms on application.
⌐ Welcome by prior arrangement; special packages available.

12 135 Glenmalure
Greenane, Rathdrum, Co. Wicklow
☎(0404) 46679, Fax 46783, Sec 46783
2 miles W of Rathdrum.
Parkland course.
Founded 1993
Designed by Pat Suttle
18 holes, 5850 yards, S.S.S. 66
✝ Welcome.
∟ WD £18; WE £22.
↷Welcome by prior arrangement; discounts depending on group numbers; from £12.
⦿ Full facilities.
↙ Self-catering lodge accommodation on site.

12 136 Gold Coast Golf ⛳ and Leisure Club
Ballinacourty, Dungarvan, Co Waterford
☎(058) 44055, Fax 43378, Bar/Rest 42249
Located 3 miles from Dungarvan.
Parkland course by the sea.
Founded 1937; Amended 1997
Designed by Capt R Hewson/ Maurice Fives
18 holes, 6171 yards, S.S.S. 70
✝ Welcome by prior arrangement.
∟ WD £16; WE £20.
↷Welcome by prior arrangement; discounts depending on size of group and date of visit.
⦿ Full facilities.
Practice range, driving range near golf course.
↙ Gold Coast Hotel; Gold Coast Holiday homes; Clonea Strand.

12 137 Gort
Castlequarter, Gort, Co Galway
☎(091) 632244
Off Kilmacduagh Road.
Parkland course.
Founded 1924/1996
Designed by C O'Connor Jnr
18 holes, 5939 yards, S.S.S. between 68 and 71
✝ Welcome; some restrictions Sun morning.
∟ WD £15; WE £15.
↷Welcome by prior arrangement; deposit of £Ir100 in advance; catering packages available; from £10.
⦿ Lunches and snacks available.
↙ Sullivans, Gort.

12 138 Grange
Rathfarnham, Dublin
☎(01) 493 2889, Fax 493 9490, Pro
493 2299, Sec 493 9490, Bar/Rest 493 1404
7 miles S from city.
Parkland course.
Founded 1910
Designed by James Braid
18 holes, 5517 yards, S.S.S. 69
✝ Welcome WD except Tues and Wed afternoon.
∟ WD £35.
↷Welcome Mon and Thurs by prior arrangement.
⦿ Full facilities.

12 139 Greencastle
Greencastle, Moville, Co Donegal
☎(077) 81013, Sec 82280
On L85 23 miles NE of Londonderry through Moville.
Public seaside course.
Founded 1892
Designed by Eddie Hackett
18 holes, 5211 yards, S.S.S. 67
✝ Welcome.
∟ WD £12; WE £18.
↷Welcome by prior arrangement.
⦿ Bar and catering facilities.

12 140 Greenore
Greenore, Co Louth
☎(04293) 73678
15 miles out of Dundalk on the Newry Road.
Wooded seaside course.
Founded 1896
Designed by Eddie Hackett
18 holes, 6506 yards, S.S.S. 71
✝ Welcome WD; by prior arrangement at WE.
∟ Terms on application.
↷Welcome by arrangement.
⦿ Full facilities.

12 141 Greystones
Greystones, Co Wicklow
☎(01) 287 4136, Fax 287 3749, Pro 287 5308
N11 out of Dublin towards Wexford.
Parkland course.
Founded 1895
✝ Welcome Mon, Tues and Fri.
∟ WD £25; WE £30.
↷Welcome by arrangement.
⦿ Full facilities.

12 142 Gweedore
Derrybeg, Letterkenny, Co Donegal
☎(075) 31140, Fax 31666
L82 from Letterkenny or T72 from Donegal.

Seaside course; Founded 1926
Designed by Eddie Hackett
9 holes, 6150 yards, S.S.S. 69
✝ Welcome.
∟ Details available upon application.
↷Welcome at WE.
⦿ Lunches at WE.

12 143 Harbour Point
Little Island, Cork, Co Cork
☎(021) 353094, Fax 354408, Pro 353719
6 miles E of Cork.
Parkland course.
Pro Brendan McDaid; Founded 1991
Designed by Paddy Merrigan
18 holes, 6063 yards, S.S.S. 72
✝ Welcome.
∟ WD £23; WE £26.
↷Welcome; minimum nine; reductions for groups of more than 20 and 40; from £17.
⦿ Full facilities.
↙ John Barley Corn; Ashbourne House; Midleton Park; Fitzpatricks Silver Springs.

12 144 Hazel Grove
Mt Seskin Rd, Jobstown, Tallaght, Dublin
☎(01) 452 0911, Sec 452 2931
On the Blessington Road 2.5 miles from Tallaght.
Parkland course.
Founded 1988
Designed by Jim Byrne
11 holes, 5030 yards, S.S.S. 67
✝ Welcome Mon, Wed, Fri; not after 12 Tues, not after 11am Sat.
∟ WD £8; WE £10.
↷Welcome by prior arrangement; maximum 50 players; Sat morning maximum 40; catering packages available.
⦿ Bar, function room.
Large practice ground.

12 145 Headfort
Kells, Co Meath
☎(046) 40146, Fax 49282, Pro 40639
N3 from Dublin on Cavan route.
Parkland course.
Pro Brendan McGovern; Founded 1928
18 holes, 5973 yards, S.S.S. 71
✝ Welcome.
∟ WD £20; WE £25.
↷Welcome by prior arrangement; catering package by arrangement.
⦿ Full facilities.
↙ Headfort Arms.

The K Club

If you are going to establish a new golf course in Ireland and want to make it into one of the finest in Europe then you know that the competition is going to be tough. Last summer Tiger Woods wandered the courses of Southern Ireland and declared that they were as magical as any he had come across.

So when Tom Lehmann, the 1996 Open champion, declares that the K Club is not just one of the best properties but definitely the best property that he has ever visited then you know that Dr Michael Smurfit, the mastermind behind the project, has succeeded in his aim.

The course is already earmarked for the Ryder Cup's return to Ireland in 2005 and that will come 14 short years after a dilapidated country house on the banks of the Liffey was identified as the centrepiece for the greatest jewel in Ireland's golfing crown.

The house, Straffan House, had its origins on the site around 550AD and went through a number of owners before it was sold in 1831 to Hugh Barton, who held numerous vineyards in France before being forced out in the Reign of Terror.

The parkland course was designed by Arnold Palmer and has the Liffey meandering through its grounds and is the main feature of the holes around the turn, particularly the eighth. It is called the "Half Moon" because the fairway forms a crescent shape. It is just one of the many holes on the course that will provide the players of the United States and Europe with the most demanding test in 2005.

The eighth is a short par 4 at only 375 yards but like the seventh it hugs the river and while offering great birdie opportunities it also means that the player must at some stage flirt with danger.

Many, like the resident pro Ernie Jones, a former British Seniors and Irish PGA champion, believe that the seventh, called Inish More, is the signature hole on the course, which has become a regular on the European Tour. At 606 yards it is the longest and again has the Liffey cutting across it.

Like the eighth, it offers the gamblers a chance. A long drive offers half a chance of cutting the corner and making the green in two. However difficult that may seem, it is no easier if the players decide to lay up because the green, surrounded by bunkers and mature trees, is still packed with hazards.

Expect this to be the spectators' hot ticket for the Ryder Cup, with the massive crowds all flooding to the hole that could cause the maximum excitement and, for some of the players, embarrassment.

If seven and eight pose problems at the close of the front nine then the finish, particularly 16 and 18, throw up even more worries for those chasing the big prizes or those trying to salvage a decent round. Michael Smurfit's favourite is the 16th hole and is surrounded by water. With the Liffey to the right, a huge lake to the front and a pond on the right back this is not a hole for the faint-hearted.

Nor is the 18th – the hookers' graveyard. It is reachable in two at 518 yards but any second shot is always tempered by the presence of the lake on the left. Like the entire K Club course, it is a challenge of golf and of nerve. And never will those two characteristics be tested more than in the Ryder Cup. — **CG**

12 146 **Heath**
The Heath, Portlaoise, Co Laois
☎(0502) 46533, Pro 46622
4 miles NE of Portlaoise off the main
Dublin to Cork/Limerick Road.
Heathland course.
Founded 1930
18 holes, 5721 yards, S.S.S. 70
♦ Welcome WD; WE by prior
arrangement.
〓 Terms on application.
☞ Welcome by prior arrangement.
◉ Full facilities.
Practice range, available.

12 147 **Hermitage**
Lucan, Co Dublin
☎(01) 626 8049, Pro 626 8072,
Bar/Rest 626 5396
8 miles from Dublin; 1 mile from
Lucan.
Parkland course.
Pro Simon Byrne; Founded 1905
Designed by Eddie Hackett
18 holes, 6051 yards, S.S.S. 71
♦ Welcome WD.
〓 WD £34; WE £45.
☞ Welcome WD by arrangement;
five golf and meal packages; latest
tee time 1.45pm; from £34.
◉ Full clubhouse catering facilities.
↰ Finnstown; Bewley; Spa; Morans
Red Cow; Green Isle.

12 148 **Highfield**
Carbury, Co Kildare
☎(0405) 31021
In Carbury.
Parkland course.
Founded 1992
18 holes, 5707 yards, S.S.S. 70
♦ Welcome.
〓 WD £10; WE £14.
☞ Welcome; booking is advisable.

12 149 **Hollystown**
Hollystown, Dublin 15, Co Dublin
☎(01) 820 7444, Fax 820 7447
8 miles off N3 Dublin-Cavan road at
Mulhuddart or off the main N2
Dublin-Ashbourne road at Ward.
Parkland course.
18 holes, 6303 yards, par 72
Founded 1993
♦ Welcome.
〓 WD £14; WE £18.
◉ Coffee shop.
Practice ground, driving range.

12 150 **Hollywood Lakes**   ☎
Hollywood, Ballyboughal, Co Dublin

☎(01) 843 3406, Fax 843 3002,
Bar/Rest 843 3407
15 minutes N of Dublin Airport via N1
and R129 to Ballyboughal.
Parkland course.
Founded 1991
Designed by Mel Flanagan
18 holes, 6246 yards, S.S.S. 72
♦ Welcome except Sat and Sun
before 12.30; booking advisable.
〓 WD £18; WE £23.
☞ Welcome by prior arrangement;
reductions for larger groups; catering
packages by arrangement; early bird
rates between 8am and 10am Mon-
Fri; from £17.
◉ Full facilities.
Practice range, practice bar.
↰ Grove; Grand; Airport.

12 151 **Howth**
Carrickbrack Rd, Sutton, Dublin
☎(01) 832 3055, Fax 832 1793, Pro
839 2617
Situated on Howth Head to the NE of
Dublin.
Heathland course.
Pro John McGuirk; Founded 1912
Designed by James Braid
18 holes, 5672 yards, S.S.S. 69
♦ Welcome WD except Wed.
〓 WD £20; Fri £22.
☞ Welcome WD except Wed;
reductions on numbers over 25 and
35; catering packages by
arrangement; from £20.
◉ Bar and restaurant.
Practice ground.
↰ Marine; Sutton Castle; Howth
Lodge; Bailey Court.

12 152 **The Island Golf Club**
Corballis, Donabate, Co Dublin
☎(01) 843 6462, Fax 843 6860, Sec
843 6462, Bar/Rest 843 6205
Leave N1 1 mile beyond Swords at
Donabate signpost, then L91 for 3
miles and turn right at sign.
Seaside course.
Founded 1890
Designed by F. Hawtree & Eddie
Hackett
18 holes, 6053 yards, S.S.S. 72
♦ Welcome by prior arrangement.
〓 WD £50; WE £60.
☞ Welcome Mon, Tues and Fri by
prior arrangement.
◉ Full facilities.

12 153 **The K Club**
Kildaire Hotel & County Club,
Straffan, Co Kildare

☎(01) 601 7300, Fax 601 7399
22 miles from Dublin via N7 Naas
Road.
Parkland course; 7th is 606 yards.
Pro Ernie Jones; Founded 1991
Designed by Arnold Palmer
18 holes, 7159 yards, S.S.S. 74
♦ Welcome by prior arrangement.
〓 WD £120; WE £120.
☞ Welcome groups of 16 or more;
catering packages by arrangement;
from £80.
◉ Full clubhouse catering facilities,
bar, coffee shop.
Practice range, available.
↰ Kildaire Hotel & Country Club, 5-
star, on site.

12 154 **Kanturk (18 holes)**
Fairyhill, Kanturk, Co Cork
☎(029) 50534, Sec 0872 217510
1 mile from Kanturk via Fairyhill
Road.
Parkland course.
Founded 1973
Designed by Richard Barry
18 holes, 5721 metres, S.S.S. 70
♦ Welcome but prior arrangement is
advisable
〓 WD £12; WE £16.
☞ Welcome by prior arrangement
with the secretary; catering packages
by arrangement through the
secretary; group rates available.
◉ Full facilities.
↰ Duhallow Park; Assolas.

12 155 **Kanturk (9 holes)**
Fairy Hill, Kanturk, Cork
☎(029) 47238, Fax 50534
Course is three miles SW of Kanturk
on the R579.
Founded 1974
9 holes, 6026 yards, S.S.S. 69
♦ Welcome.
〓 £12.
◉ Bar and catering facilities.

12 156 **Kenmare**
Killowen Rd, Kenmare, Co Kerry
☎(064) 41291, Fax 42061
Off the N22 Cork to Killarney Road
and then on to the R569.
Parkland course on the mouth of a
river.
Pro Charlie McCarthy; Founded 1903
Designed by Eddie Hackett
18 holes, 6000 yards, S.S.S. 69
♦ Welcome but booking will be
necessary on weekends.
〓 Details available on application.
☞ Welcome by prior arrangement;

minimum 18 players; catering by arrangement;.
◉ Only snacks are available; restaurant next door.
⌁ Park; Kenmare Bay; Sheen Falls.

12 157 **Kilcock**
Gallow, Kilcock, Co Meath
☎ (01) 628 4074
2 miles N of Kilcock.
Parkland course.
Founded 1985
Designed by Eddie Hackett
18 holes, 5801 metres for men, 5178 metres for women, S.S.S. 70
✦ Welcome WD, WE by prior arrangement.
Ⅰ WD £11; WE £13.
⌁ Welcome by prior arrangement.
◉ Bar snacks.

12 158 **Kilcoole**
Kilcoole, Co Wicklow
☎ (01) 287 2066
21 miles S of Dublin on coast.
Parkland course.
Founded 1992
9 holes, 5506 yards, S.S.S. 69
✦ Welcome except Sat and Sun am.
Ⅰ WD: 9 holes £10, 18 holes £15;

WE: 9 holes £12, 18 holes £18.
⌁ Welcome by prior arrangement.
◉ Clubhouse facilities.

12 159 **Kilkea Castle** ♆
Castle Dermot, Co Kildare
☎ (0503) 45555
40 miles from Dublin.
Parkland course.
Founded 1994
Designed by McDadd & Cassidy
18 holes, 6200 yards
✦ Welcome; booking always advisable.
Ⅰ WD £25; WE £30.
⌁ Welcome by prior arrangement; terms on application.
◉ Full facilities.

12 160 **Kilkee**
East End, Kilkee, Co Clare
☎ (06590) 56048, Fax 56977
400 yards from town centre.
Meadowland course.
Founded 1896
Designed by McAlister
18 holes, 5537 yards, S.S.S. 69
✦ Welcome.
Ⅰ WE £20; WD £20.
⌁ Welcome by prior arrangement;

restrictions in July and early August; catering packages by arrangement.
◉ Full facilities.

12 161 **Kilkenny**
Glendine, Kilkenny, Co Kilkenny
☎ (056) 65400, Pro 61730
1 miles NW of Kilkenny off the Castlecomer Road.
Parkland course.
Founded 1896
18 holes, 5857 yards, S.S.S. 70
✦ Welcome.
Ⅰ WD £20; WE £25.
⌁ Welcome but booking is essential.
◉ Clubhouse facilities.

12 162 **Killarney Golf Club**
Mahoney's Point, Killarney, Co Kerry
☎ (064) 31034, Fax 33065, Pro 31615
2 miles W of Killarney on the N70.
Parkland and lakeside course.
Pro Tony Covemy; Founded 1939
Designed by Sir Guy Campbell & Henry Longhurst
Killeen: 54 holes, 6474 metres, S.S.S. 73
✦ Welcome by prior arrangement.
Ⅰ WD £40; WE £40.

Welcome with prior arrangement and handicap certificates essential; discounts for groups of 20 or more; from £40.
Full clubhouse facilities.
Club can provide a detailed list.

12 163 Killeen
Kill, Co Kildare
(0458) 66003
N7 to Kill village then head to Straffan.
Parkland course.
Founded 1991
18 holes, 4989 yards, S.S.S. 70
Welcome.
WD £17; WE £20.
Welcome.
Full bar and catering.

12 164 Killeline
Newcastle West, Co Limerick
(069) 61600
On the edge of Newcastle West.
Parkland course.
Founded 1993
Designed by E Hackett
18 holes, 6720 yards, S.S.S. 72
Welcome.
WD £12; WE £12.
Welcome at all times by arrangement; catering packages by arrangement; from £10.
Full facilities.
Courtney Lodge; Rathkeale House; Devon Inn.

12 165 Killin Park
Killin Park, Dundalk
(042) 39303
3 miles NW of Dundalk on Castledown Rd.
12 holes, 3322 yards, S.S.S. 69
Welcome.
Terms on application.
Welcome by prior arrangement.
Snacks and bar.

12 166 Killiney
Ballinclea Rd, Killiney, Co Dublin
(01) 285 2823, Bar/Rest 285 1983
3 miles from Dun Laoghaire.
Parkland course.
Founded 1903
9 holes, 5655 yards, S.S.S. 70
Welcome but booking is essential.
WD £20; WE £20.
Welcome on most days but prior arrangement is necessary.
Full clubhouse facilities.
Killiney Castle; Killiney Court.

12 167 Killorglin
Steelroe, Killorglin, Co. Kerry
(06697) 61979, Fax 61437
On the N70 Tralee Road 3km from the bridge at Killorglin.
Parkland course.
Pro John Gleeson; Founded 1992
Designed by Eddie Hackett
18 holes, 6467 yards, S.S.S. 71
Welcome.
Terms on application.
Welcome; terms on application.
Full clubhouse facilities.
Bianconi Inn; Riverside House; Grove Lodge; Fairways B&B; Laune Bridge; Fern Rock.

12 168 Kilrush
Parknamoney, Kilrush, Co Clare
(06590) 51138, Fax 52633, Sec 51491
0.5 miles from Kilrush on N68 from Ennis.
Parkland course.
Pro Sean O'Connor; Founded 1934
Designed by Dr A Spring (Extended in 1994)
18 holes, 5986 yards, S.S.S. 70
Welcome.
WD £16; WE £18.
Welcome by prior arrangement; from £10.
Full clubhouse facilities available in summer but these are limited in the winter.
Halpins; Stella Maris; Bellbridge.

12 169 Kilternan Golf & Country Club
Kilternan Hotel, Enniskerry Road, Co Dublin
(01) 295 5559, Fax 295 5670, Pro 295 2986
On N11 S of Dublin.
Hilly parkland course.
Pro Gary Headley; Founded 1988
Designed by E Hackett
18 holes, 4952 yards, S.S.S. 66
Welcome.
WD £16; WE £20.
Welcome by prior arrangement; leisure club; tennis courts; workout studios.
Full facilities in hotel.
Kilternan Hotel on site; golf packages available.

12 170 Kinsale
Farrangalway, Kinsale, Co Cork
(021) 774722, Pro 773258
3 miles N of Kinsale on Cork Road.
Parkland course.

Club founded 1912.
Pro Ger Broderick; Founded 1994
Designed by J Kenneally
18 holes, 6609 yards, S.S.S. 72
Also 9-hole course at: Ringenane, Belgooly, Kinsale, Cork
(021) 772197, 773114
3 miles NE of Kinsale.
Founded 1912
Links course.
9 holes, 5332 yards, S.S.S. 68
Welcome.
18 holes: WD £22; WE £27; 9 holes: £15.
Welcome by prior arrangement; restricted to 11.30am-1.30pm only at WE; catering by arrangement.
Full clubhouse facilities.
Actons; Trident; Blue Haven.

12 171 Knockanally Golf & Country Club
Donadea, North Kildare
(0458) 69322
3 miles off the main Dublin-Galway Road between Kilcock and Enfield.
Parkland course.
Founded 1985
Designed by Noel Lyons
18 holes, 6424 yards, S.S.S. 72
Welcome.
WD £18; WE £25.
Welcome by prior arrangement everyday.
Full clubhouse facilities.

12 172 Lahinch Golf Club
Lahinch, Co Clare
(06570) 81003, Fax 81592
34 miles from Shannon Airport.
Seaside course.
Founded 1892
Castle course designed by JD Harris/Donald Steel (Castle); Old course designed by Tom Morris (1892), redesigned by Dr A MacKenzie
Castle: 18 holes, 5138 yards, S.S.S. 70; Old: 18 holes, 6633 yards, S.S.S. 71
Welcome.
Terms on application.
Welcome but booking is essential, especially for Sundays.
Full facilities.

12 173 Laytown & Bettystown
Bettystown, Co Meath
(041) 27563, Fax 28506, Pro 28793, Sec 27110, Bar/Rest 27534
45 miles N of Dublin Airport.
Links course.

Pro Robert Browne; Founded 1909
18 holes, 5668 yards, S.S.S. 69
† Welcome by prior arrangement.
�'Terms on application.
⌒Welcome WD and some Sat;
terms on application.
◉ Full bar and catering facilities.

12 174 Lee Valley ⓣ
Clashanure, Ovens, Co Cork
☎ (0217) 331721, Fax 331695, Pro
331758
On main Cork-Killarney Road.
Parkland course.
Pro John Savage; Founded 1993
Designed by Christy O'Connor Jnr
18 holes, 6715 yards, S.S.S. 72
† Welcome by prior arrangement.
⌐ April Oct: WD £29, WE £32;
Nov-March: WD £20, WE £25.
⌒Welcome by prior arrangement.
◉ Full clubhouse facilities.
⌐ Blarney Park; Farran House.

12 175 Leixlip
Leixlip, Co Kildare
☎ (01) 6244978, Sec 6246185,
Bar/Rest 6247040
Off N4 past Lucan.
Parkland course.
Founded 1994
Designed by E Hackett
18 holes, 6068 yards, S.S.S. 70
† Welcome.
⌐ Details upon application.
⌒Welcome by prior arrangement;
discounts for large groups.
◉ Clubhouse facilities.
⌐ Becketts; Springfield; Spa.

12 176 Leopardstown Golf Centre
Foxrock, Dublin
☎ (01) 289 5341
5 miles S of Dublin.
Parkland course.
18 holes, 5384 yards, S.S.S. 66
† Welcome.
⌐ Terms on application.
⌒Welcome but booking in advance
will be essential.
◉ Café and restaurant facilities.

12 177 Letterkenny
Barnhill, Letterkenny, Co Donegal
☎ (074) 21150
On T72 2 miles N of Letterkenny.
Parkland course.
Founded 1913
Designed by E Hackett
18 holes, 6239 yards, S.S.S. 71

† Welcome.
⌐ WE £15; WD £12.
⌒Welcome by arrangement.
◉ Bar and snacks available; meals
by prior arrangement.

12 178 Limerick
Ballyclough, Co Limerick
☎ (061) 415146, Pro 412492
Course is south of the city on the
Fedamore Road.
Parkland course.
Founded 1891
18 holes, 5938 yards, S.S.S. 71
† Welcome before 4pm WD except
Tues.
⌐ WD £22.50.
⌒Welcome Mon, Wed, Fri mornings.
◉ Full facilities.

12 179 Limerick County Golf & Country Club
Bellyneety, Co Limerick
☎ (061) 351881, Fax 351384
5 miles S of Limerick towards
Bruff/Kilmallock.
Parkland course.
Founded 1994
Designed by Des Smyth
18 holes, 6191 yards, S.S.S. 72
† Welcome.
⌐ WD £20; WE £25.
⌒Welcome; deposit required; from
£18.
◉ Full facilities.
Practice range, driving range and golf
school.
⌐ Castleray Park; Woodlands;
Jury's.

12 180 Lismore
Lismore, Co Waterford
☎ (058) 54026, Sec 54222
0.5 miles from Lismore on the
Killarney Road.
Parkland course.
Founded 1966
Designed by Eddie Hackett
9 holes, 5291 yards, S.S.S. 67
† Welcome; some Sun reserved.
⌐ Details available upon application.
⌒Welcome by arrangement; terms
on application.
◉ Clubhouse facilities.

12 181 Listowel
Feale View, Listowel, Kerry
☎ (068) 21592
In village of Listowel.
Parkland course.
9 holes, par 70

† Welcome.
⌐ £10.
◉ Snack bar facilities.

12 182 Loughrea
Loughrea, Co Galway
☎ (091) 841049
On L11 1 mile N of Loughrea.
Meadowland course.
Founded 1924
Designed by Eddie Hackett
18 holes, 5176 yards, S.S.S. 68
† Welcome.
⌐ £12 daily.
⌒Welcome by prior arrangement.
◉ Clubhouse facilities.

12 183 Lucan
Celbridge Rd, Lucan, Co Dublin
☎ (01) 628 0246, Fax 628 2929, Sec
628 2106
Take the N4 from Dublin and turn of
at Celbridge.
Parkland course.
Founded 1897
18 holes, 5994 yards, S.S.S. 71
† Welcome.
⌐ WD £25; WE £25.
⌒Welcome by arrangement.
◉ Full bar and restaurant service.

12 184 Luttrellstown Castle ⓣ
Castleknock, Dublin 15
☎ (01) 808 9988
Leave N1 at M50 intersection
following southbound signs, exit M50
at Castleknock.
Parkland course.
Pro Graham Campbell; Founded
1993
Designed by Dr Nick Bielenberg/
Edward Connaughton
18 holes, 6367 yards, S.S.S. 73
† Welcome.
⌐ WD £50; WE £55.
⌒Welcome; special rates negotiable
for groups; terms available on
application.
◉ Full clubhouse facilities.
⌐ Liffey Valley; Kildaire Hotel & CC;
Conrad International; on-site
accommodation in 2 courtyard
apartments.

12 185 Macroom
Lackaduv, Macroom, Co Cork
☎ (026) 41072, Fax 41391
On main Cork/Killaney road on the
outskirts of the town.
Parkland course.
Founded 1924

Designed by J Kennealy (new 9 holes)
18 holes, 5574 yards, S.S.S. 70
⚑ Welcome; some WE restrictions apply.
▯ Details upon application.
◯ Welcome by prior arrangement between March-October.
◉ Full facilities.
↩ Castle.

12 186 Mahon
Clover Hill, Blackrock, Co Cork
☎ (021) 294280
2 miles SE of Cork.
Municipal parkland course.
Founded 1980
18 holes, 4217 metres, S.S.S. 62
⚑ Welcome WD; WE by prior arrangement.
▯ WD £11; WE £12 for a whole day's golf.
◉ Bar, snacks, lunch and dinner by arrangement.

12 187 Malahide   ℭ
Beechwood, The Grange, Malahide, Co Dublin
☎ (01) 846 1611, Fax 846 1270, Pro 846 0002, Bar/Rest 846 1067
8 miles N of Dublin; 1 mile S of Malahide.
Parkland course.
Pro David Barton; Founded 1892/1990
Designed by Eddie Hackett
27 holes, 6066 yards, S.S.S. 72
⚑ Welcome Mon, Thurs, Fri and Sat up to 9.30.
▯ WD £35; WE £50.
◯ Welcome Mon, Thurs, Fri and Sat morning; discounts available; catering by arrangement; from £30.
◉ Full bar and restaurant facilities available.
↩ Grand Hotel; Portmarnock Links.

12 188 Mallow
Ballyellis, Mallow, Co Cork
☎ (022) 21145, Fax 42501, Pro 43424
1.5 km from Mallow on the Killanvullen Road.
Parkland course.
Pro Sean Conway; Founded 1892/1947
Designed by Commander J.D. Harris
18 holes, 5960 yards, S.S.S. 72
⚑ Welcome but booking is advisable for weekends.
▯ WD £20; WE £25.
◯ Welcome WD by prior

arrangement; packages available; from £20.
◉ Full clubhouse facilities.
↩ Longueville House; Hibernian.

12 189 Mannan Castle
Donaghmoyne, Carrickmacross, Co Monaghan
☎ (04296) 63308, Fax 63195, Sec 62531
4 miles NE of Carrickmacross on the Crossmaglen Road.
Parkland course.
Founded 1994
Designed by F Ainsworth
9 holes, 6008 yards, S.S.S. 71
⚑ Welcome.
▯ Details upon application.
◯ Welcome WD and Sat mornings;
◉ Clubhouse facilities.

12 190 Milltown
Lower Churchtown Rd, Milltown, Co Dublin
☎ (01) 497 6090, Fax 497 6008, Pro 497 7072
3 miles S of the city centre via Ranelagh village.
Parkland course.
Founded 1907
Designed by F E Davies
18 holes, 5638 yards, S.S.S. 69
⚑ Welcome except Tues and Sat; with a member on Sun.
▯ WD £35; WE £35.
◯ Welcome by prior arrangement; catering packages by prior arrangement; private function room; from £30 per head.
◉ Bar and restaurant facilities.
↩ Berkeley Court; Jury's; Herbert Park; Montrose.

12 191 Mitchelstown
Mitchelstown, Co Cork
☎ (025) 24072
1 mile from Mitchelstown off the N1 Dublin to Cork Road.
Parkland course.
Founded 1908
Designed by David Jones
18 holes, 5148 yards, S.S.S. 67
⚑ Welcome.
▯ Details available upon application.
◯ Welcome except Sun; catering packages available.
◉ Full facilities.

12 192 Moate
Aghanargit, Moate, Co Westmeath
☎ (0902) 81271, Sec 81270

On Dublin-Galway Road.
Parkland course.
Founded 1900
Designed by B Browne (1993 extension)
18 holes, 5752 yards, S.S.S. 70
⚑ Welcome.
▯ WD £10; WE £13.
◯ Welcome except after 12.30pm at WE; catering packages available; visitors locker room; from £10.
◉ Full bar and catering facilities available.
↩ Grand.

12 193 Monkstown
Parkgariffe, Monkstown, Co Cork
☎ (021) 841376, Sec 841376, Pro 841686, Bar 841225, Steward 841098
11 miles E of Cork; turn right off the Rochestown Road at the Rochestown Inn.
Parkland course.
Pro Matt Murphy; Founded 1908/71
Designed by Peter O'Hare/Tom Carey
18 holes, 5669 yards, S.S.S. 70
⚑ Welcome.
▯ WD £23; WE £26.
◯ Welcome by prior arrangement; from £18.
◉ Restaurant and bar facilities available.
Practice ground.
↩ Rochestown Park.

12 194 Moor-Park
Mooretown, Navan, Co Meath
☎ (046) 27661
Parkland course.
Founded 1993
18 holes, 5600 yards, S.S.S. 69 (also 9-hole course)
⚑ Welcome.
▯ WD £8; WE £10.
◉ Limited, snack bars.

12 195 Mount Juliet
Thomastown, Co Kilkenny
☎ (056) 24455, Fax 24522
Course is signposted in Thomastown off the main Dublin-Waterford Road.
Parkland course; associated with David Leadbetter Academy.
Founded 1992
Designed by Jack Nicklaus
18 holes, 7112 yards, S.S.S. between 69 and 74
⚑ Welcome by prior arrangement.
▯ High season: WD £70; WE £80.
Low season: WD £45; WE £55.
◯ Welcome by prior arrangement;

WE price of £50; minimum 20 players; from £45.
◉ Full facilities.
Practice ground with driving bays and 18-hole putting green.
↬ Mount Juliet.

12 196 **Mount Temple**
Mount Temple Village, Moate, Co Westmeath
☎ (0902) 81545, Fax 81957, Sec 81841
4 miles off the main N6 Dublin-Galway route in Mount Temple Village.
Combination of links and parkland course.
Founded 1991
Designed by Robert J. Brown and Michael Dolan
18 holes, 5872 yards, S.S.S. 71
♦ Welcome; by arrangement at WE.
⌷ Available upon application.
⌁ Welcome by prior arrangement; from £14.
◉ Catering and wine licence; pub 100 yards.
Practice range, 3-hole practice area.
↬ Hudson Bay; Prince of Wales; Royal Hoey; Shamrock Lodge; Bloomfield House.

12 197 **Mountbellew**
Shankhill, Mountbellew, Co Galway
☎ (0905) 79259, Sec 79622
Course is on the T4 28 miles E of Galway.
Undulating meadowland course.
Founded 1929
18 holes, 5143 yards, S.S.S. 66
♦ Welcome.
⌷ Details available upon application.
⌁ Welcome by prior arrangement; terms on application.
◉ Catering by arrangement; snacks.

12 198 **Mountrath**
Knockinina, Mountrath, Co Laois
☎ (0502) 32558, Sec 32421
0.5 miles off the main Dublin-Limerick Road.
Undulating parkland course.
Founded 1929
18 holes, 5493 yards, S.S.S. 69
♦ Welcome; some WE restrictions.
⌷ WD £10; WE £10.
⌁ Welcome WD by prior arrangement; discounts for larger groups; from £10.
◉ Full clubhouse facilities available.
↬ Killeshin; Montague; Leix Co; Grants; Racket Hall.

12 199 **Mullingar**
Belvedere, Mullingar, Co Westmeath
☎ (044) 48366, Fax 41499
3.5 miles from Mullingar on the N52.
Parkland course.
Founded 1894
Designed by James Braid
18 holes, 6468 yards, S.S.S. 70
♦ Welcome.
⌷ WD £20; WE £25.
⌁ Welcome by prior arrangement; packages available; terms on application.
◉ Full clubhouse facilities.

12 200 **Mulranny**
Mulranny, Westport, Co Mayo
☎ (098) 36262, Sec 41568
15 miles from Westport.
Links course.
Founded 1968
9 holes, 6255 yards, S.S.S. 69
♦ Welcome.
⌷ Terms on application.
⌁ Welcome by prior arrangement; from £7.
◉ Full clubhouse facilities available.
↬ Many in Westport.

12 201 **Muskerry**
Carrigrohane, Co Cork
☎ (021) 385297, Pro 381445
7 miles W of Cork near Blarney.
Parkland course.
Founded 1897
18 holes, 5786 yards, S.S.S. 71
♦ Welcome WD except Wed afternoons; Thurs mornings and after 3.30pm Fri.
⌷ WD £24; WE £26.
⌁ Welcome by prior arrangement; from £20.
◉ Full facilities.

12 202 **Naas**
Kerdiffstown, Naas, Co Kildare
☎ (0168) 74044, Sec 79321
Between Johnstown and Sallins.
Parkland course.
Founded 1886
Designed by Arthur Spring
18 holes, 5660 yards, S.S.S. 69
♦ Welcome Mon, Wed, Fri and Sat.
⌷ WD £18; WE £24.
⌁ Welcome Mon, Wed, Fri and Sat morning.
◉ Bar; meals by prior arrangement.

12 203 **Narin & Portnoo**
Portnoo, Co Donegal
☎ (075) 45107, Bar/Rest 45332

From Donegal via Ardara.
Seaside course.
Founded 1930
18 holes, 5322 yards, S.S.S. 68
♦ Welcome; some summer restrictions.
⌷ Terms available on application.
⌁ Welcome by prior arrangement.
◉ Snacks and full bar facilities.

12 204 **Nenagh**
Beechwood, Nenagh, Co Tipperary
☎ (067) 31476
4 miles E of Nenagh.
Parkland course.
Founded 1892
Designed by Alister MacKenzie (original 0), E Hackett (additional 9)
18 holes, 5491 yards, S.S.S. 68
♦ Welcome but by prior arrangement at WE.
⌷ Under review due to construction work; details will be available on application.
⌁ Welcome by prior arrangement.
◉ Full facilities.
Practice range, large practice ground.

12 205 **New Ross**
Tinneranny, New Ross, Co Wexford
☎ (0514) 21433
1 mile from town centre off Waterford Road.
Parkland course.
Founded 1905
18 holes, 5751 metres, S.S.S. 70
♦ Welcome; some Sun restrictions.
⌷ WD £14; WE £16.
⌁ Welcome by arrangement; no group discounts available.
◉ Clubhouse facilities.

12 206 **Newcastle West**
Ardagh, Co Limerick
☎ (069) 76500
Off N21 2 miles beyond Rathkeale.
Parkland course.
Founded 1939/94
Designed by Arthur Spring
18 holes, 6317 yards, S.S.S. 72
♦ Welcome.
⌷ Available on application.
⌁ Welcome with prior arrangement; catering packages by arrangement; from £12.
◉ Bar and restaurant.
↬ Courtenay Lodge; Rathkeale House; Devon Inn.

12 207 **Newlands**
Clondalkin, Dublin

☎ (01) 459 3157, Pro 459 3538, Sec 451 3436
6 miles from city centre.
Parkland course.
Founded 1926
Designed by James Braid
18 holes, 5696 yards, S.S.S. 70
† Welcome.
� WD £35; WE £35.
⌒ Welcome WD.
🍽 Full facilities.

12 208 North West
Lisfannon, Fahan, Co Donegal
☎ (077) 61715, Bar/Rest 61841
2 miles S of Buncrana.
Seaside links course.
Founded 1892
18 holes, 5968 yards, S.S.S. 69
† Welcome.
⌐ Available upon request.
⌒ Welcome by prior arrangement WD and WE in the summer.
🍽 Bar and restaurant.

12 209 Nuremore
Carrickmacross, Co Monaghan
☎ (04296) 61438, Sec 62125
1 mile S of Carrickmacross.
Parkland course.
Founded 1964
Designed by Eddie Hackett
18 holes, 6246 yards, S.S.S. 74
† Welcome.
⌐ WD £20; WE £25.
⌒ Welcome by prior arrangement.
🍽 Clubhouse and hotel facilities.

12 210 Old Conna
Ferndale Road, Bray, Co Dublin
☎ (01) 282 6055, Fax 282 5611, Pro 272 0022, Bar/Rest 282 0038
12 miles from Dublin.
Parkland course.
Founded 1977
18 holes, 5590 yards, S.S.S. 72

† Welcome but booking advisable.
⌐ WD £27.50; WE £40; discounts before 9:30am on WD and for those who accompany members.
🍽 Bar and full meal service.

12 211 Old Head Links
Kinsale, Co Cork
☎ (021) 778444, Fax 778022
20 miles S of Cork.
Clifftop setting on Atlantic promontory.
Founded 1996
Designed by J Carr/R Kirby
18 holes, 7200 yards, S.S.S. 72
† Welcome.
⌐ WD/WE Ir£120.
⌒ Welcome by prior arrangement; from £105.
🍽 Bar and light meals; full restaurant service.

12 212 The Open Golf Centre
Newtown House, St Margaret's, Co Dublin
☎ (01) 864 0324, Fax 834 1400
4 miles from Dublin adjacent to Dublin Airport.
Parkland course.
Pro Robin Machin; Founded 1993
Designed by Martin Hawtree
27 holes, 6570 yards
† Welcome.
⌐ WD £10.50; WE £14.50.
⌒ Welcome by prior arrangement; from £10.50.
🍽 Full facilities.
Practice range, 15 bays.
⌐ Forte Crest.

12 213 Otway
Saltpans, Rathmullan, Co Donegal
☎ (074) 58319, Sec 58365
15 miles NE of Letterkenny by Lough Swilly.
Links course.

Founded 1893
9 holes, 4234 yards, S.S.S. 60
† Welcome.
⌐ £10 on WD and WE.
⌒ Welcome.
⌐ Fort Royal; Rathmullan House; Pier Hotel.

12 214 Oughterard
Gortreevagh, Oughterard, Co Galway
☎ (091) 82131
1 mile from Oughterard on N59.
Mature parkland course with elevated greens.
Founded 1973
Designed by Hawtree/Hackett
18 holes, 6089 yards, S.S.S. 69
† Welcome.
⌐ Terms on application.
⌒ Welcome WD.
🍽 Bar snacks; full à la carte menu.

12 215 Parknasilla
Parknasilla, Sneem, Co Kerry
☎ (064) 45122
2 miles E of Sneem on the Ring of Kerry Road.
Undulating seaside course.
Founded 1974
9 holes, 4652 yards, S.S.S. 65
† Welcome.
⌐ Terms on application.

12 216 Portarlington
Garryhinch, Portarlington, Co Offaly
☎ (0502) 23115, Office 23044
On L116 between Portarlington and Mountmellick.
Parkland course.
Founded 1909
18 holes, 6004 yards, S.S.S. 71
† Welcome.
⌐ WD £14; WE £17.
⌒ Welcome; from £14.
🍽 Bar and restaurant facilities.
⌐ East End Hotel.

12 217 Portmarnock ℭ
Portmarnock, Co Dublin
☎ (01) 846 2968
From Dublin along the coast road to
Baldoyle and on to Portmarnock.
Seaside links course.
Founded 1894
Designed by W.G. Pickeman and
George Ross
27 holes, 6497 yards, S.S.S. 75
♦ Welcome.
↳ WD £40; WE £50.
⌐ Welcome Mon, Tues and Fri by
prior arrangement; terms available on
application.
⌐◉ Full facilities.

12 218 Portsalon
Portsalon, Fanad, Co Donegal
☎ (074) 59459, Fax 59459
Course is 20 miles north of
Letterkenny.
Seaside links course.
Founded 1891
Designed by Mr Thompson of
Portrush
18 holes, 5880 yards, S.S.S. 68
♦ Welcome by prior arrangement.
↳ WD £15; WE £18.
⌐ Welcome by prior arrangement;
from £10.
⌐◉ Full facilities.
⌐ Fort Royal; Rathmullan House;
Pier Hotel.

12 219 Portumna
Ennis Rd, Portumna, Co Galway
☎ (0509) 41059
1.5 miles from Portumna on Ennis
Road.
Parkland course.
Founded 1913
18 holes, 5474 yards, S.S.S. 67
♦ Welcome Sun-Mon.
↳ WD £14; WE £14.
⌐ Welcome by prior arrangement
with Sec; special packages available;
terms on application.
⌐◉ Restaurant and bar.
Practice area.
⌐ Shannon Oaks.

12 220 Powerscourt
Powerscourt Estate, Enniskerry, Co
Wicklow
☎ (01) 204 6033, Fax 276 1303
12 miles south of Dublin just off N11
in Enniskerry.
Parkland course.
18 holes, 7063 yards, par 72
♦ Welcome.
↳ WD £45-£50; WE £55-£60.

⌐ Welcome by arrangement WE and
WD.
⌐◉ Snacks, hotel facilities.
⌐ Powerscourt.

12 221 Raffeen Creek
Ringaskiddy, Co Cork
☎ (021) 378430
1 mile from Ringaskiddy ferry.
Seaside/parkland course with water.
Founded 1988
Designed by Eddie Hackett
9 holes, 5098 yards, S.S.S. 68
♦ Welcome WD; WE afternoon only.
↳ WD £12; WE £14; concessions
apply.
⌐ Welcome by arrangement.
⌐◉ Bar food.

12 222 Rathdowney
Rathdowney, Portlaoise, Co Laois
☎ (0505) 46170
Off the N7 in Rathdowney.
Parkland course.
Founded 1930
Designed by Eddie Hackett
18 holes, 5894 yards, S.S.S. 71
♦ Welcome; some Sun restrictions
apply.
↳ WD £10; WE £10.
⌐ Welcome by prior arrangement
with the secretary; bar and catering
packages by prior arrangement; from
£10.
⌐◉ Clubhouse facilities.
⌐ Leix Co; Woodview GH.

12 223 Rathfarnham
Newtown, Rathfarnham
☎ (01) 493 1201
Course is two miles from
Rathfarnham.
Parkland course.
Founded 1899
Designed by John Jacobs
9 holes, 5833 yards, S.S.S. 70
♦ Welcome WD except Tues.
↳ WD £22.50.
⌐ Welcome by prior arrangement.
⌐◉ Lunch and dinners.

12 224 Rathsallagh House
Dunlavin, Co Wicklow
☎ (045) 403316, Fax 4033295
Course is 32 miles south-west of
Dublin.
Parkland course.
Founded 1994
Designed by Peter McEvoy
18 holes, 6916 yards, S.S.S. 71-74
♦ Welcome.

↳ Mon-Thurs £40; Fri-Sun £50.
⌐ Welcome by arrangement.

12 225 Redcastle
Redcastle, Moville, Co Donegal
☎ (077) 82073
Parkland course.
Founded 1983
9 holes, 6152 yards, S.S.S. 70
♦ Welcome
↳ WD £10; WE £14.
⌐ Welcome but booking essential.
⌐◉ Full bar and restaurant.

12 226 Rockwell
Cashel, Co Tipperary
☎ (062) 61444
Parkland course.
Founded 1964
9 holes, 3782 yards, S.S.S. 60
♦ Welcome by arrangement.
↳ Terms on application.
⌐ Terms on application.
⌐◉ Limited facilities.

12 227 Rosapenna
Rosapenna Hotel, Downings, Co
Donegal
☎ (074) 55301, Fax 55128
25 miles from Letterkenny.
Links course.
Pro Don Patterson; Founded 1893
Designed by Tom Morris (1893),
redesigned by Braid & Vardon
18 holes, 6271 yards, S.S.S. 71
♦ Welcome.
↳ Terms on application.
⌐ Welcome but must have handicap
certificates.
⌐◉ Full hotel bar and restaurant
facilities.
⌐ Rosapenna Hotel (4 star) on site.

12 228 Roscommon
Mote Park, Roscommon, Co
Roscommon
☎ (0903) 26382, Sec 26062
Course is 0.25 miles from
Roscommon Town.
Parkland course.
Founded 1904/1996
Designed by Eddie Connaughton
18 holes, 6040 yards, S.S.S. 70
♦ Welcome except Tues and Sun.
↳ November-March: WD £10, WE
£10; April-October: WD £15, WD £15.
⌐ Welcome by prior arrangement; -
catering by arrangement; from £7.
⌐◉ Full bar and restaurant facilities
available.
⌐ Abbey; Royal; Regans; Gleesons.

12 229 Roscrea
Derryvale, Roscrea, Co Tipperary
☎ (0505) 21130
2 miles E of Roscrea on N7.
Parkland course.
Founded 1892
Designed by A. Spring
18 holes, 5708 yards, S.S.S. 70
† Welcome.
⌙ WD £14; WE £17.
↻ Welcome by prior arrangement;
group discounts available.
🍽 Bar and restaurant facilities.

12 230 Ross
Ross Rd, Killarney, Kerry
☎ (064) 31125, Fax 31860, Pro
(0872) 258786
0.5 miles from Killarney.
Parkland course with water features.
9 holes, 3300 yards, par 72
† Welcome.
⌙ Terms on application.
🍽 Full clubhouse facilities with
spectacular views.

12 231 Rosslare
Rosslare Strand, Co Wexford
☎ (053) 32203, Fax 32263, Pro
32032, Sec 32203, Bar/Rest 32113
6 miles from the Rosslare ferry
terminal; 10 miles S of Wexford.
Seaside links course.
Pro Johnny Young; Founded
1905/1992
Designed by Hawtree & Taylor (Old),
Christy O'Connor Jnr (New)
18 holes, 6577 yards, S.S.S. 72
† Welcome.
⌙ WD £25; WE £35.
↻ Welcome by prior arrangement;
catering packages by arrangement.
🍽 Full clubhouse facilities.
↘ Kelly's Resort.

12 232 Rossmore
Rossmore Park, Cootehill Road,
Monaghan, Co Monaghan
☎ (047) 81316, Sec 81473, Pro
71222
1.5 miles on the Cootehill Road out of
Monaghan town.
Parkland course.
Founded 1916
Designed by Des Smyth
18 holes, 5507 yards, S.S.S. 68
† Welcome.
⌙ WD £20; WE £20.
↻ Welcome; from £20 but discounts
are available for larger groups.
🍽 Full bar and restaurant facilities.
↘ Four Seasons.

12 233 Royal Dublin
North Bull Island, Dollymount,
Dublin 3
☎ (01) 833 7153, Fax 833 6504, Pro
833 6477, Sec 833 6346, Bar/Rest
833 3370
NE from Dublin along the coast Road
to Bull Wall.
Links course.
Pro Leonard Owens; Founded 1885
Designed by H.S. Colt
18 holes, 6330 yards, S.S.S. 73
† Welcome WD except Wed, Sun
10am-12 noon and after 4pm on Sat.
⌙ Mon-Thurs £60; Fri-Sun £70.
↻ Welcome but must book a year in
advance; catering by prior
arrangement.
🍽 Full clubhouse facilities, bar and
restaurant.
↘ Marine; Hollybrook; Howth Lodge.

12 234 Royal Tara
Bellinter, Navan, Co Meath
☎ (046) 25244, Sec 25508, Bar/Rest
25508
Off N3 30 miles N of Dublin.
Parkland course.
Founded 1923
Designed by Des Smyth Golf Design
27 holes, 5917 yards, S.S.S. 71
† Welcome by arrangement.
⌙ WD £18; WE £22.
↻ Welcome Mon, Thurs, Fri and Sat
by arrangement.
🍽 Full bar and catering facilities.

12 235 Rush
Rush, Co Dublin
☎ (01) 843 7548, Sec 843 8177
Off the Dublin-Belfast Road at Blakes
Cross.
Links course.
Founded 1943
9 holes, 5598 yards, S.S.S. 69
† Welcome.
⌙ WD £18; WE £18.
↻ Welcome by prior arrangement.
🍽 Full facilities.

12 236 St Annes
North Bull Island, Dollymount,
Dublin 3
☎ (01) 833 6471, Fax 833 4618, Pro
833 6471, Sec 833 6471, Bar/Rest
853 2797
5 miles N of Dublin City.
Links course.
Pro Paddy Skerritt; Founded 1921
Designed by Eddie Hackett
18 holes, 5713 yards, S.S.S. 69
† Welcome.

⌙ WD £27; WE £36.
↻ Welcome; group rates available.
🍽 Full facilities.
Practice area.
↘ Marine; St Lawrence; Forte
Posthouse; Grand; Sutton Castle.

12 237 St Helen's Bay ☏
St Helen's, Kilrane, Rosslare Harbour,
Co Wexford
☎ (053) 33234, Fax 33803, Pro
33669
5 minutes from the Rosslare ferryport
in the village of Kilrane.
Links/parkland course mixture.
Pro Paul Roche; Founded 1993
Designed by Philip Walton
18 holes, 6091 yards, S.S.S. 72
† Welcome.
⌙ Terms on application.
↻ Welcome by prior arrangement;
packages available; tennis;
accommodation on site; terms on
application.
🍽 Full clubhouse dining and bar
facilities.
↘ Great Southern; Rosslare;
Devereux; Ferrycarrig.

12 238 St Margaret's Golf & Country Club
St Margaret's, Co Dublin
☎ (01) 864 0400, Fax 864 0289
4 miles W of Dublin Airport.
Parkland course.
Founded 1992
Designed by Ruddy & Craddock
18 holes, 6917 yards, S.S.S. 73
† Welcome.
⌙ Mon-Thurs £40; Fri-Sun £45.
↻ Welcome by prior arrangement;
corporate days available; £35 for
parties of more than 30.
🍽 2 bars and 2 restaurants.
↘ Forte Crest; Grand, Malahide.

12 239 St Patricks
Hotel Carrigart, Carrigart, Donegal
☎ (074) 551141, Fax 55250
Opening late 1999
36 holes, seaside course.
↘ Carrigart (full facilities with views
across Sheephaven Bay).

12 240 Seapoint
Termonfeckin, Co Louth
☎ (04198) 22333, Fax 22331
In Termonfeckin off the N1 Dublin to
Drogheda Road.
Championship links course.
Founded 1993

Designed by Des Smyth, Declan Branigan
18 holes, 6339 yards, S.S.S. 73
☩ Welcome.
⌾ Rates vary between £25 and £45.
⌁ Welcome WD by arrangement; discounts for larger groups.
⏣ Bar and restaurant facilities. Driving range.

12 241 Shannon

Shannon Airport, Co Clare
☎ (061) 471849, Fax 471507, Pro 471551
0.5 miles from Shannon Airport.
Woodland/parkland course.
Founded 1966
18 holes, 6186 yards, S.S.S. 72-74
☩ Welcome; booking is advisable for WE.
⌾ WD £25; WE £30.
⌁ Welcome by prior arrangement.
⏣ Bar snacks and meals.

12 242 Skerries

Haccketstown, Skerries, Co Dublin
☎ (01) Pro 849 0925, Sec 849 1567, Bar/Rest 849 3135
N of Dublin Airport off the Belfast Road.
Parkland course.
Pro Jimmy Kinsella; Founded 1906
18 holes, 6081 yards, S.S.S. 72
☩ Welcome.
⌾ WD £30; WE £35.
⌁ Welcome on Mon and Thurs by prior arrangement; terms on application.
⏣ Full facilities.
⌁ Trusthouse Forte, Dublin Airport.

12 243 Skibbereen & West Cabbery

Licknavar, Skibbereen, Co Cork
☎ (028) 21227, Fax 22994
2 miles from Skibbereen on the Baltimore Road.
Parkland course.
Founded 1905
Designed by Eddie Hackett
18 holes, 6069 yards, S.S.S. 68
☩ Welcome with handicap certs.
⌾ Terms on application.
⌁ Welcome by prior arrangement; from £12.
⏣ Full clubhouse facilities.
⌁ West Cork; Eldon; Casey's; Baltimore Harbour; Celtic Ross.

12 244 Slade Valley

Lynch Park, Brittas, Co Dublin

☎ (01) 458 2183, Fax 458 2784
8 miles W of Dublin off M7.
Undulating parkland course.
Founded 1970
Designed by W.D. Sullivan and D. O'Brien
18 holes, 5337 yards, S.S.S. 68
☩ Welcome WD; WE with a member.
⌾ WD £17; WE £25.
⌁ Welcome by prior arrangement with Sec.
⏣ Full WE facilities.
⌁ Green Isle; Downshire House.

12 245 Slieve Russell Golf & Country Club

Ballyconnell, Co Cavan
☎ (049) 26444, Fax 26474, Pro 26458
90 miles NW of Belfast.
Parkland course.
Founded 1992
Designed by Paddy Merrigan
18 holes, 6413 yards, S.S.S. 74
☩ Welcome; book in advance.
⌾ Terms on application.
⌁ Welcome by prior arrangement.
⏣ Full facilities.

12 246 Spanish Point

Spanish Point, Miltown Malbay, Co Clare
☎ (06570) 84198
2 miles from Milton Malbay; 8 miles from Lahinch.
Seaside course.
Founded 1896
9 holes, 3574 yards, S.S.S. 58
☩ Welcome.
⌾ Terms on application.
⌁ Welcome; booking is strongly recommended.
⏣ Light snacks only.

12 247 Stackstown

Kellystown Road, Rathfarnham
☎ (01) 404 1000, Pro 494 4561, Bar/Rest 494 2338
8 miles S of Dublin off the N81 and R115.
Hilly course with panoramic views.
Founded 1976
18 holes, 5789 yards, S.S.S. 71
☩ Welcome WD; WE by prior arrangement.
⌾ WD £10; WE £16.
⌁ Welcome by prior arrangement.
⏣ Full bar and restaurant.

12 248 Strandhill

Strandhill, Co Sligo

☎ (071) 68188, Fax 68811, Pro 68725
5 miles W of Sligo.
Links course.
Founded 1932
18 holes, 5516 yards, S.S.S. 68
☩ Welcome; booking is recommended.
⌾ WD £15; WE £15.
⌁ Welcome by prior arrangement; from £15.
⏣ Full facilities.
⌁ Ocean View; Tower.

12 249 Sutton

Cush Point, Sutton, Dublin 13
☎ (01) 832 2965, Fax 832 1603, Pro 832 1703
7 miles NE of city centre.
Seaside links course.
Founded 1890
9 holes, 5226 yards, S.S.S. 67
☩ Welcome; restrictions Tues and Sat.
⌾ WD £20; WE £25.
⌁ Welcome by prior arrangement.
⏣ Clubhouse facilities.

12 250 Swinford

Brabazon Park, Swinford, Co Mayo
☎ (094) 51378, Sec 51502
1 km S of Swinford on the Kiltimagh Road.
Parkland course.
Founded 1922
9 holes, 5542 yards, S.S.S. 70
☩ Welcome.
⌾ £10 per day.
⌁ Welcome except Sun; special packages available; from £10.
⏣ Full catering; lounge bar.
⌁ Cill Aodain; Breaffy; Welcome Inn.

12 251 Swords

Balheary Ave, Swords, Dublin
☎ (01) 890 9819; 890 1303
5 mins from Swords centre.
Parkland course.
18 holes
☩ Welcome.
⌾ Terms on application; pay and play.
⏣ Snack bar.

12 252 Tara Glen

Ballymoney, Courtown, Co Wexford
☎ (055) 25413
Parkland course.
Founded 1993
9 holes

♦ Welcome by prior arrangement.
⌐ £14.
⌐ Welcome by prior arrangement.
♦ Bar.

12 253 Templemore
Manna South, Templemore, Co
Tipperary
☎ (0504) 31400, Fax 31913, Sec
31720
0.5 miles S of town centre off the
N62.
Parkland course.
Founded 1972
9 holes, yards, S.S.S. 70
♦ Welcome.
⌐ WD £8; WE £12.
⌐ Welcome and catering can be
arranged by prior arrangement; terms
on application.
♦ Limited but available by prior
arrangement.
⌐ Templemore Arms; Grants;
Anner; Hayes; Munster.

12 254 Thurles
Turtulla, Thurles, Co Tipperary
☎ (0504) 21983, Fax 24647, Sec
21983
1 mile from Thurles towards the main
Cork-Dublin road.
Parkland course.
Pro Sean Hunt; Founded 1909/44
Designed by J McAllister
18 holes, 6465 yards, S.S.S. 71
♦ Welcome except Sun.
⌐ WD £18; WE £18.
⌐ Welcome except Sun; from £18.
♦ Full facilities.
Practice range, 200 yards from club.
⌐ Anner; Hayes.

12 255 Tipperary
Rathanny
☎ (062) 51119
1 mile from the town on the Glen of
Aherlow Road.
Parkland course.
Founded 1896
18 holes, 5807 yards, S.S.S. 71
♦ Welcome; some Sun restrictions
apply.
⌐ WD £15; WE £17.
⌐ Welcome by prior arrangement.
♦ Bar and snacks available.

12 256 Townley Hall
Townley Hall, Tullyallen, Drogheda,
Co Louth
☎ (04198) 42229
Parkland course.

Founded 1994
18 holes, 4978 yards
♦ Welcome.
⌐ Details available upon application.

12 257 Tralee
West Barrow, Ardfert, Co Kerry
☎ (06671) 36379, Fax 36008,
Bar/Rest 36074
8 miles from Tralee on the Churchill
Road.
Links course.
Founded 1896/1984
Designed by Arnold Palmer Design
18 holes, 6192 yards, S.S.S. 73
♦ Welcome.
⌐ WD £60; WE £60.
⌐ Welcome by prior arrangement;
discounts available for larger groups;
from £60.
♦ Full restaurant, bar and
clubhouse facilities.
Two practice grounds.
⌐ Mount Brandon; Grand;
Abbeygate.

12 258 Tramore
Newtown Hill, Tramore, Co Waterford
☎ (051) 386170, Fax 390961, Pro
381706, Bar/Rest 381247
Course is seven miles south of
Waterford on coast road.
Parkland course.
Pro Derry Kiely; Founded 1894
Designed by Tibbett (1936/37)
18 holes, 6055 yards, S.S.S. 73
♦ Welcome; prior booking is
advisable.
⌐ WD £25; WE £30.
⌐ Welcome by prior arrangement;
full catering packages available; from
£22.
♦ Catering and bar facilities.
⌐ Grand; Majestic; O'Sheas.

12 259 Tuam
Barnacurragh, Tuam, Co Galway
☎ (093) 28993, Fax 26003, Pro
24091
1 miles outside Tuan on the Athewny
Road.
Parkland course.
Pro Larry Smyth; Founded 1907
Designed by E Hackett
18 holes, 6045 yards, S.S.S. 71
♦ Welcome.
⌐ WD £12; WE £14.
⌐ Welcome by prior arrangement
except on Sat afternoon and Sun;
discounts for groups of more than 20;
deposit of £50 required; catering by
arrangement; from £10.

♦ Full clubhouse bar and restaurant
facilities.
Practice range, practice ground.
⌐ Imperial.

12 260 Tubbercurry
Ougham, Tubbercurry, Co Sligo
☎ (071) 85849, Sec 85331
0.5 miles from town on the Ballymote
Road.
Parkland course.
Founded 1991
Designed by Eddie Hackett
9 holes, 5490 yards, S.S.S. 69
♦ Welcome; Sun by arrangement.
⌐ Details on application.
⌐ Welcome except Sun; discounts
available; catering by arrangement;
from £10.
♦ Full bar and restaurant facilities.
⌐ Conleys.

12 261 Tulfarris Hotel & Country Club
Blessington, Co Wicklow
☎ (045) 64612
6 miles from Blessington off N81.
Parkland course.
Founded 1989
Designed by Eddie Hackett
9 holes, 5612 yards, S.S.S. 69
♦ Welcome; some Sun restrictions.
⌐ Terms on application.
⌐ Welcome by prior arrangement;
terms on application.
♦ Restaurant and bar facilities.

12 262 Tullamore
Brookfield, Tullamore, Co Offaly
☎ (0506) 21439, Pro 51757
3.5 miles S of Tullamore off the R451
to Kinnity from the N52.
Parkland course.
Founded 1886
Designed by James Braid;
redesigned by P Merrigan
18 holes, 6434 yards, S.S.S. 70
♦ Welcome but prior booking is
advisable.
⌐ WD £18; WE £22.
⌐ Welcome by prior arrangement;
terms on application.
♦ Full bar and restaurant facilities.

12 263 Turvey Golf & CC
Turvey Ave, Donabate, Dublin
☎ (01) 843 5179, Sec 843 5169
18 holes
♦ Welcome.
⌐ £15.
♦ Snack bar.

12 264 Virginia
Virginia, Co Cavan
☎(04985) 47235
50 miles N of Dublin on the main
Dublin-Cavan Road.
Meadowland course.
Founded 1946
9 holes, 4900 yards, S.S.S. 62
♦ Welcome.
⌐ WD £8.50; WE £8.50.
⦿ Park Hotel.

12 265 Water Rock
Midleton, Cork
☎(021) 613499, Fax 633150, Sec
613499
5 mins from Midleton.
Parkland course.
18 holes, 6223 yards, S.S.S. 70
♦ Welcome.
⌐ Terms on application.
⦿ Clubhouse facilities.

12 266 Waterford
Newrath, Waterford, Co Waterford
☎(051) 876748, Fax 853405, Pro
856568, Bar/Rest 874182
On N9 from Dublin 1 mile from
Waterford or N25 from Rosslare.
Parkland course.
Founded 1912
Designed by Cecil Barcroft and Willie
Park/ James Braid
18 holes, 5722 yards, S.S.S. 70
♦ Welcome.
⌐ WD £22; WE £25.
⟲ Welcome by arrangement with
secretary/manager; terms on
application.
⦿ Full clubhouse facilities available.
� Jury's; Tower; Granville; Bridge.

12 267 Waterford Castle Golf & Country Club
The Island, Ballinakill, Co Waterford
☎(051) 871633, Fax 871634
2 miles from Waterford on the
Dunmore East Road.
Parkland course on island in River
Suir.
Founded 1993
Designed by Des Smyth and Declan
Brannigan
18 holes, 6303 yards, S.S.S. 73
♦ Welcome by arrangement.
⌐ WD £27; WE £30.
⟲ Welcome by arrangement.
⦿ Clubhouse facilities.

12 268 Waterville Golf Links
Rink of Kerry, Waterville, Co Kerry

☎(066) 74102, Fax 74482
1 mile W of Waterville half-way
through the Ring of Kerry.
Links course.
Pro Liam Higgins; Founded
1901/1972
Designed by E. Hackett
18 holes, 7184 yards, S.S.S. 74
♦ Welcome.
⌐ WD £50; WE £50.
⟲ Welcome by prior arrangement;
discount 10% for 20 or more players;
from £50.
⦿ Full clubhouse facilities.
Practice range, open to green fee
paying players and members.
⟲ Waterville House; Butler Arms;
Bay View.

12 269 West Waterford
Coolcormack, Dungarvan, Co
Waterford
☎(058) 43216, Fax 44343, Sec
41475
3 miles W of Dungarvan off the N25
on the Aglish Road.
Parkland course.
Founded 1993
Designed by Eddie Hackett
18 holes, 6802 yards, S.S.S. 74
♦ Welcome.
⌐ WD £20; WE £25.
⟲ Welcome everyday by prior
arrangement.
⦿ Full clubhouse facilities available
everyday.
⟲ Lawlors; Park; Clonea Strand.

12 270 Westmanstown
Clonsilla, Dublin
☎(01) 820 5817, Fax 820 7891
Course is off the Dublin Road in
Lucan village following the signs for
Clonsilla.
Parkland course.
Founded 1988
Designed by Eddie Hackett
18 holes, 5819 yards, S.S.S. 70
♦ Welcome but booking is essential
at WE.
⌐ WD £20; WE £30.
⟲ Welcome by prior arrangement.
⦿ Full clubhouse facilities available.

12 271 Westport
Carrowholly, Westport, Co Mayo
☎(098) 25113, Fax 27217, Pro
27481
2 miles from Westport.
Parkland course.
Founded 1908
Designed by Hawtree & Son

18 holes, 6959 yards, S.S.S. 73
♦ Welcome.
⌐ Terms on application.
⟲ Welcome by prior arrangement;
special packages available; terms on
application.
⦿ Lounge bar and dining facilities
available.

12 272 Wexford
Mulgannon, Wexford
☎(053) 42238, Pro 46300, Sec
44611
In Wexford town.
Parkland course.
Founded 1960
Designed by J. Hamilton Stutt & Co
(original), Des Smyth (new)
18 holes, 5578 yards, S.S.S. 70
♦ Welcome; restrictions Wed
evening and Thurs.
⌐ WD £14; WE £15.
⟲ Welcome by prior arrangement;
discounts for larger groups; terms on
application.
⦿ Bar and snacks.

12 273 Wicklow
Dunbur Rd, Wicklow, Co Wicklow
☎(0404) 67379, Pro 66122, Sec
69386
On L29 32 miles from Dublin.
Seaside course.
Founded 1904
18 holes, 5695 yards, S.S.S. 70
♦ Welcome but booking for WE is
strongly advisable.
⌐ WD £20; WE £20.
⟲ Welcome by prior arrangement.
⦿ Full clubhouse facilities.

12 274 Woodbrook
Dublin Rd, Bray, Co Wicklow
☎(01) 282 4799
Course is 11 miles south of Dublin on
the N11.
Parkland course.
Founded 1921
18 holes, 5996 yards, S.S.S. 71
♦ Welcome by arrangement;
booking essential for weekends.
⌐ Winter: WD £25, WE £35;
Summer: WD £50, WE £60.
⟲ Welcome Mon, Thurs and Fri by
prior arrangement.
⦿ Full clubhouse facilities.

12 275 Woodenbridge
Woodenbridge, Arklow, Co Wicklow
☎(0402) 35202, Fax 31402, Sec
31571

45 miles S of Dublin on N11 to
Arklow.
Parkland course.
Founded 1884
18 holes, 6316 yards, S.S.S. 70
♦ Welcome except Thurs and Sat.
◖ Terms available upon application.
☺ Welcome WD by prior
arrangement.
◉ Full clubhouse facilities.
Practice ground.

12 276 **Woodlands**
Coill Dubh, Naas, Co Kildare
☎ (045) 860777
On outskirts of Naas.
Parkland course.

Founded 1985
18 holes, 5202 yards, S.S.S. 72
♦ Welcome, but booking is normally
needed for weekends.
◖ WD £9; WE £12.
☺ Welcome with prior arrangement.

12 277 **Woodstock**
Woodstock House, Shanaway Road,
Ennis, Co Clare
☎ (065) 6829463
In Ennis.
Parkland course.
Founded 1993
18 holes, 5879 yards, S.S.S. 71
♦ Welcome.
◖ WD £20; WE £25.

☺ Welcome with prior arrangement;
terms of group rates on application.

12 278 **Youghal**
Knockaverry, Youghal, Co Cork
☎ (024) 92787, Fax 92641, Pro
92590
On N25 between Rosslare and Cork.
Parkland course.
Pro Liam Burns; Founded 1898
Designed by Commander Harris
18 holes, 5646 yards, S.S.S. 70
♦ Welcome.
◖ WD £18; WE £20.
☺ Welcome by prior arrangement.
◉ Full clubhouse facilities available.
↝ Walter Raleigh; Devonshire Arms.

The Sunday Telegraph

Golf Course of the Year 2000 Award

Readers are invited to **submit nominations** for *The Sunday Telegraph* Golf Course of the Year. A finalist will be selected from those nominated in each area of **Britain and Ireland:** South & West, South-East & East Anglia, Midlands, North-West, North-East, Ireland, Scotland and Wales, and the **overall winner** will be decided by a judging panel chaired by *Sunday Telegraph* golf correspondent Derek Lawrenson. The **short-listed and winning courses** will be publicised in *The Sunday Telegraph*, and the person who submits the best nomination for the winning course will **win a year's membership** of Telegraph Golf Network. Courses will be assessed on the quality of the 18 holes, the condition of the course, facilities in the clubhouse, friendliness of staff, and value for money.

Please submit your nominations to: **Golf Course of the Year Award**, Telegraph Books, 1 Canada Square, Canary Wharf, London E14 5DT. Each nomination should give the full **name and address** of the golf course, together with why you think they should win the award in 50 words or less, and your own name, address, and daytime telephone number. Entries should be received by **31 December 2000**.

TERMS AND CONDITIONS

1. This competition is open to residents of the UK, Channel Islands, Isle of Man and Republic of Ireland aged 18 years or over. Employees of Telegraph Group Limited ("The Telegraph"), its subsidiaries, agencies, members of their families, employees of golf courses in the UK, Channel Islands, Isle of Man and Republic of Ireland and members of their families and anyone directly associated with the competition are not eligible to enter.
2. Nominated golf courses will be assessed by the judging panel and the award given based on the number of nominations received together with the quality of the 18 holes, condition of the course, facilities in the clubhouse, friendliness of staff and value for money. The award will be marked by a Telegraph certificate.
3. The reader who submits the most novel nomination relating to the winning golf course chosen by the judging panel shall win the prize, which consists of a year's membership of Telegraph Golf Network.
4. Entries should be received by 31 December 2000 and details of the winners will be available after 31 March 2001.
5. The short-listed and winning golf courses will be published in *The Sunday Telegraph*.
6. Instructions for this competition form part of the terms and conditions.
7. No responsibility can be accepted for any application forms lost, delayed or damaged in the post.
8. Damaged, defaced, illegible or incomplete entries will be considered null and void.
9. Proof of posting is not proof of delivery.
10. If you do not wish to receive mailings of offers or services from The Telegraph or other companies carefully selected by The Telegraph please mark the top left-hand corner of your entry letter with a cross.
11. The decision of the judging panel is final and no correspondence will be entered into.
12. It is a condition of entry that all rules are accepted as final and that the competitor agrees to abide by these rules.
13. The prize as described is available on the dates of publication. Events may occur that render the competition itself or the awarding of prizes impossible due to reasons beyond the control of The Telegraph and accordingly The Telegraph may at its absolute discretion vary or amend the competition and the reader agrees that no liability shall attach to The Telegraph as a result thereof.
14. Promoter: Telegraph Group Limited, 1 Canada Square, Canary Wharf, London E14 5DT

INDEX

C

D

I

M

N

O

Q

R

S

T

Two for one green fees . . .

at nearly 400 courses

Telegraph
T
GOLF
NETWORK

Joining the **Telegraph Golf Network** entitles you to two green fees for the price of one at nearly 400 courses **in Britain and abroad**. And at just **£35 for the first year** (and only £30 in subsequent years) membership often **pays for itself** within one round.

Call now for more information or to join the Telegraph Golf Network on

08701 ~~0541~~ 557 200

(calls are charged at national rate)

Or e-mail your postal address to:
tgn@telegraph.co.uk

It's one card you'll want to keep